SO YOU WANT TO BE A ROCK 'N' ROLL STAR
THE BYRDS DAY-BY-DAY 1965–1973

Christopher Hjort

A Jawbone Book
First Edition 2008
Published in the UK and the USA by Jawbone Press
2a Union Court,
20–22 Union Road,
London SW4 6JP,
England
www.jawbonepress.com

ISBN 978-1-906002-15-2

DESIGN Christopher Hjort
EDITORS Peter Chrisp, Tony Bacon

Printed by Colorprint Offset Ltd (Hong Kong)

1 2 3 4 5 12 11 10 09 08

SO YOU WANT TO BE A ROCK 'N' ROLL STAR

THE BYRDS DAY-BY-DAY 1965–1973

Christopher Hjort

Contents

... Harassed by the South African press, the group returns home as founder member **Chris Hillman leaves** ... With only Roger McGuinn left of the original Byrds, he gathers **Clarence White, Gene Parsons,** and **John York** to keep The Byrds airborne.

1969

Roger McGuinn and director Jacques Levy start work on Broadway project **Gene Tryp** ... The Byrds release *Dr. Byrds & Mr. Hyde*, and night by night slowly re-build their shattered concert reputation ... *Easy Rider* film is a major international success this year, featuring The Byrds and Roger McGuinn providing the **pivotal soundtrack** ... **Skip Battin** replaces John York as bass player in October, just as ninth album *Ballad Of Easy Rider* is released.

1970

The Byrds **record** tracks for a **live album** in March, proving their worth as a first-rate concert attraction ... Album sessions in May and June see the group **reunited** with **former producer Terry Melcher** and **original mentor Jim Dickson** ...

The rejuvenated Byrds play s**ummer festivals** in Europe to great critical acclaim ... One-off single **'Chestnut Mare'** fails in the US, but is a **surprise UK hit** early next year.

1971

The month of January is spent recording a new album in Hollywood, but the **sense of direction** that has previously driven the band **seems to be missing** ... In May, The Byrds return to Europe ... Critics are unanimous in their **praise** of the concerts, but the impression is marred by the **poor reception** the group's eleventh album, *Byrdmaniax,* receives ... To redeem matters, The Byrds fly to London to record a self-produced album during a week in July ... **Novelty single**, 'America's Great National Pastime' is released in the US in November and becomes a **radio hit** in California but fails to chart nationally.

1972

A hastily arranged overseas tour in January coincides with twelfth album *Farther Along* ... January newsflash in England says the original five Byrds will reunite for recording and touring purposes ... Meanwhile, the touring Byrds wind down at the end of May as **Gene Parsons is fired** ... A few scattered recording session by the touring Byrds are finally halted as Gene Clark, Michael Clarke, David Crosby, Chris Hillman, and Roger McGuinn

record an album's worth of material under Crosby's guidance ... While the original Byrds rekindle old flames, the touring Byrds continue to undertake selected concerts.

1973

Two kind of Byrds exist briefly side by side in the first months of the year: The touring kind and the original kind ... The touring Byrds limp to the finish line in February, but further hoped-for appearances with an enlarged Byrds withers ... Meanwhile, **the original Byrds** come **full circle** when the self-titled *Byrds* album in March ... The album's lukewarm reception spells the end of any further plans ... Tragedy hits twice this year as two ex-Byrds meet untimely deaths: first Clarence White in July, then Gram Parsons in September ... As Roger McGuinn embarks on a solo career, The Byrds are laid to rest.

The Byrds in spring 1965. From left: Chris Hillman, Gene Clark, Roger McGuinn, Michael Clarke, David Crosby

Introduction

This is a story of adventure. The Byrds had all the ingredients to constitute a Great American Rock Group. They had the drama and the dynamics, the looks and personality, the grace and style, bitter failure, and sweet success. And, of course, they had the music.

The band descended on Hollywood in 1965 just as the British domination of the US pop charts reached saturation point. Through nine years of upheaval and change – which saw four of the five original Byrds leave one by one and new members come in – the sound of The Byrds was kept alive by Roger McGuinn, even if artistry was replaced by craftsmanship on occasion. By 1972 and '73, the original five reunited to bring the adventure full circle.

Their music was founded on timeless qualities that did not bind The Byrds to any particular decade, yet, peculiarly, perfectly reflected the golden 60s. The Byrds developed their own identity, which has become an indelible part of the rock vocabulary, with jangling 12-string guitars and soaring harmony vocals. In the process they defined folk-rock, raga-rock, country-rock, and many other labels created by fans and music journalists.

From their inception in 1964 to their break-up in 1973, the band and their work ran parallel with great changes in American society. The American war in Vietnam escalated in 1965 and a peace of sorts was reached by 1972, while the nation saw the optimism of the Kennedy era replaced by President Nixon's administration.

In the pop music world, The Byrds sometimes found themselves in the calm eye of the storm, as when they socialised with The Beatles while Fab Four hysteria raged in 1965 and '66. Sometimes The Byrds *were* the storm, like the time they travelled unprepared for the onslaught of the British media in 1965. Or when David Crosby, from the stage of the Monterey International Pop Festival in 1967, advocated the use of LSD and claimed the Kennedy assassination was subject to a government cover-up. And then there was the time they chose to visit apartheid South Africa in 1968. At other points along the Byrds timeline, they were so faceless it would be easy to overlook them.

Their influence was not limited to the music world. As sons of Hollywood, it was not surprising that they would be peripherally involved in the film industry, and they contributed music and role models to the *Easy Rider* movie.

But before we get into this great adventure, a word about the research for this book. What I want to do here is to turn back the clock and bring you back to the beginning of the narrative – The Byrds in January 1965, as a sort of extended electric arm of Bob Dylan, with 'Mr. Tambourine Man' – and proceed as if we do not know what events will follow. The aim is to recreate the history of The Byrds in the most precise details possible.

To capture the spirit of the times, contemporary sources fuel the chronology. Locked within the pages of these old newspapers, magazines, music weeklies, publications, and rags (sometimes frail and yellowing, other times retrieved electronically) lies the true unadorned truth – free from the wisdom of hindsight, written as the words were spoken, typed by reviewers minutes after the music from the stage had stopped, or jotted down as the sound of a new Byrds record filled the room for the very first time. The contemporary sources provide the timeline with all the variety, action, and colour that any author could want. On occasion, the text strays outside the narrow Byrd path to describe concurrent events that affect the course of the story.

Whenever I have quoted memoirs and reminiscences, these fall into two categories. One is the published memoirs and more recent interviews with the main characters in the Byrds tale; the other is the previously unpublished eyewitness accounts of many key events between 1965 and 1973. In the former group I warmly recommend the autobiographies of David Crosby (*Long Time Gone*) and Derek Taylor (*As Time Goes By*).

More than 1,000 live performances, TV & radio appearances, and recording sessions are documented in this book in addition to countless other events. Music historian Joe McMichael's extensive groundwork for the early Byrds years (1965–67) formed the basis upon which I built my work. The reader must bear in mind that the information collected here is not complete nor is it without fault. Despite all efforts, some areas of Byrds history remain elusive. Gene Clark's brief return to the fold in late 1967, for example, is still not fully explained. In such instances, I have made informed guesses based on clues of varying reliability.

The music of The Byrds has been my constant companion for many years now. Let their music be the inspiration for the adventure ahead.

Christopher Hjort
Burø, Norway
August 2008

GUIDE TO SYMBOLS

→ An arrow denotes an estimated or probable date

🔊 Studio recording or mixing session

✎ Live recording for the purpose of making an official recording

🎧 Guest session appearance on a studio recording

🖵 An appearance for the purpose of a television broadcast, either live or recorded for subsequent transmission

🖻 An appearance for the purpose of a radio broadcast, either live or recorded for subsequent transmission

📷 Film or video recording

Jim McGuinn In The Limelight

"Ad lads making it: publicity Man Jim McGuinn's 17-year-old son, Jim III (a zingy banjo–guitar man) was graduated from Latin School and promptly signed by The Limeliters for West Coast dates."
(HERB LYON'S TOWER TICKER COLUMN IN THE CHICAGO TRIBUNE, JUNE 20, 1960)

JAMES JOSEPH MCGUINN III (or just Jim for short), born on July 13, 1942 in Chicago, Illinois, is the son of public-relations couple James and Dorothy McGuinn. Jim junior has nurtured an interest in music from an early age and, spurred by the sounds of Elvis Presley and his 1956 hit 'Heartbreak Hotel', receives an acoustic guitar for his 14th birthday. He attends The Latin School of Chicago, and one day his teacher brings folk-singer and 12-string-guitarist Bob Gibson to class – a life-turning moment for the impressionable youngster.

Inspired by the encounter, McGuinn enrols at the Old Town School of Folk Music in 1957 and learns how to play the guitar and the five-string banjo. Founded by Win Strach and Frank Hamilton, the institution approaches music teaching in a scholarly way, giving a thorough background on the origins of folk music. Soon, Jim is proficient enough to play and sing at Chicago coffeehouses, including a fixed arrangement with the Café Roué on Rush Street.

One night in the spring of 1960, Jim drops by the Gate of Horn, a popular folk club on Chicago's North Side run by Albert Grossman. There The Limeliters hold court, a trio of folk singers: Alex Hassilev, Lou Gottlieb, and Glenn Yarbrough. Eyeing McGuinn and his banjo, they ask him to play. Impressed with his talents, Hassilev asks Jim to audition the next day. Armed with the trio's one and only album, McGuinn comes well prepared the next afternoon and passes the audition. Even if he is offered the job there and then, there is a slight hitch, as McGuinn will recount to journalist Dave Harmon more than 35 years later. "Alex said, 'Great! You got the job. When can you start?' 'I get out of high school in June,' I said sheepishly. 'High school!' Alex [said] in disbelief. 'Didn't we meet you in a bar last night?' I told them how the bartender let me in because I played music and didn't make any trouble."

The Limeliters decide to wait, and on July 3, 1960 Jim boards a plane, destination Los Angeles. The young man is ten days shy of his 18th birthday. "There was about a ten-minute lag between my graduating from high school and being a professional musician," McGuinn tells *The Los Angeles Free Press* in 1969.

He quickly settles in and a few days later makes his debut with The Limeliters at the Ash Grove, a popular folk club on Melrose Avenue in West Hollywood operated by Ed Pearl. Initially, McGuinn is flown westwards to record an album with his employers, and he makes his recording debut on *Tonight: In Person* (RCA LPM/LPS 2272), accompanying The Limeliters on guitar and banjo for a collection of folk songs interspersed with comedy routines and jokes. The album is recorded live at the Ash Grove, with some additional work done in a studio.

There is one more assignment: The Limeliters are asked to appear at Eartha Kitt's July 23 show at the Hollywood Bowl for the 'Songs Of Many Lands' show, with Maurice Levine conducting the Hollywood Bowl Pops Orchestra. For the barely 18-year-old McGuinn it must be a nerve-racking experience – the Bowl is an enormous amphitheatre with its own resident symphony orchestra and a capacity of 16,000 seats. Reviewing the concert, *The Los Angeles Times* (July 25) writes: "The Limeliters, who

are a singing and playing trio plus a voiceless fourth man on guitar and banjo, injected fun and high spirits into the entertainment with quasi-folk songs set off with good natured banter, and they stirred up such a storm of applause that two encores had to be added before the show could proceed."

With that, McGuinn's brief stay with The Limeliters is over. But he has made up his mind to become a musician and has no intention to return to Chicago quite yet. A chance meeting at the Ash Grove will prove fortuitous: David Crosby, a young struggling actor, introduces himself and invites McGuinn to the Crosby household in Santa Barbara for a few days before they go their separate ways. Their paths will cross again soon enough.

McGuinn travels north to San Francisco, where he has to find temporary lodgings as he tries to survive as a musician. He passes time at the 'hungry i', the leading folk club in the Bay Area, and samples his first toke of marijuana. In San Francisco, he connects with a songwriter who sets up an audition with The Kingston Trio – absolutely the biggest commercial folk success in the US.

The Kingston Trio mixes tight harmony vocals, simple instrumentation, and easy-on-the-ear songs, and has scored a US Number One hit with the traditional 'Tom Dooley'. The three are Dave Guard, Bob Shane, and Nick Reynolds, but Guard has decided to leave and the two others are looking for a suitable replacement. McGuinn fails the audition – John Stewart gets the job instead – but he opts to remain in the Bay Area, forming a short-lived folk duo with a fellow folk traveller.

Hanging around at the 'hungry i' one afternoon, McGuinn gets word that Chicago promoter Frank Fried is trying to contact him. The promoter brings happy tidings: McGuinn is wanted for the vacancy in The Chad Mitchell Trio. The trio has recorded a pair of well-received albums and appeared on television many times, displaying their classically-trained voices and intricate vocal arrangements.

Taking up the option, McGuinn flies to New York City at the end of the year to join The Chad Mitchell Trio as accompanist. Unlike other folk groups who usually combine singers and strummers, Mitchell's trio is just three vocalists: Chad himself, Mike Kobluk, and Mike Pugh. However, Pugh has already decided to go back to college, and McGuinn joins the two remaining singers as they hold auditions for Pugh's replacement.

The search brings them to Boston, where McGuinn sees the young Joan Baez mesmerise her audiences with the purest voice and her understated guitar accompaniment. Finally, Joe Frazier (not to be confused with the namesake champion boxer) is hired as

Pugh's replacement – in time for a five-week stand at the Riviera Hotel, Las Vegas, NV. Here The Chad Mitchell Trio appear with Bob Crosby & The Bobcats, The Billy Williams Review, and The Four Dukes. The residence gives McGuinn a taste of a different class and clientele than the folk clubs he so far has frequented: the posh Riviera is a combined gambling casino and hotel and has more than 2,000 rooms.

As 1961 dawns, The Chad Mitchell Trio tours on the West Coast before a February residence at the Polynesian Village, Edgewater Beach Hotel, finally takes Jim home to Chicago. Herb Lyon's gossip column in *The Chicago Daily Tribune* (February 1) posts a note: "Publicists Jim and Dottie McGuinn are proud ones: their talented son, Jim Jr, is a click with The Chad Mitchell Trio at the Edgewater Beach."

A few days later, Will Leonard's regular 'On The Town' feature in the same paper reports: "The Edgewater Beach hotel has a lively, light-hearted show in its Polynesian Village, filled with frenetic dancing, lilting folk song, excitement and comedy and noise. It's about as Polynesian as I am, but it's the best entertainment the room has presented in many months. The Chad Mitchell Trio, who scored a hit [here] last season, have the kind of urbanity that marks the Kingston, Gateway, and Limeliters groups but they have not lost the freshness and youthful vigour they brought with them when they first came out of Spokane in the summer of 1959 with less than $40 apiece in their pockets."

The months of March, April, and May find the Mitchell Trio criss-crossing the US with stand-up comedian Bob Newhart. The actor is a genuine star; strong sales push *The Button-*

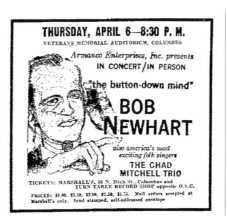

Down Mind Of Bob Newhart to the top of the *Billboard* album charts during May. The tour begins in Iowa (a performance at Iowa State Teachers College, Cedar Falls, IA on March 8 is possibly the premiere) and winds up in Montreal, Canada in early May.

"The Mitchell Trio got off to a slow start with 'Puttin' On The Style'," notes *The Capital Times* (March 14) of yesterday's performance at the Union Theatre in Madison, WI, "but after doing the Temperance Union song ['Rum By Gum'], a Lizzie Borden ditty, the Super Skier lyrics, and an encore about Sig Freud, they put the audience in the mood for Newhart."

On April 16, Newhart and the Trio swing by New York's venerable Carnegie Hall. (Two days earlier, Chad's trio appeared as one of many guests on *The Bell Telephone Hour – The Younger Generation*, an hour-long television special syndicated throughout the US.) Over the summer, the Trio performs as part of the 'Forest Hills Music Festival' with Johnny Mathis at the Forest Hills Tennis Stadium, Queens, New York, NY, which attracts around 10,000 patrons on a warm August evening.

During the first half of 1961, the Mitchell Trio with McGuinn visit the Brooklyn College in New York and record *Mighty Day On Campus* (Kapp KL 1262/KS 3262), an album released later in the year. The record features many of the Trio's popular numbers such as 'Mighty Day', 'Rum By Gum', 'Super Skier', 'Dona Dona Dona', and 'Puttin' On The Style'. Jim is featured on guitars and banjo, is credited as arranger, and poses with the trio on the album jacket.

The successful Bob Newhart excursions are followed by a tour with Miriam Makeba, which takes the Mitchell Trio and McGuinn all over the States again. Born in South Africa, Makeba fled her home country at the same time as her husband, jazz trumpeter Hugh Masekela, in 1960. Makeba and McGuinn strike up a friendship, as she tells him about life and struggle in South Africa.

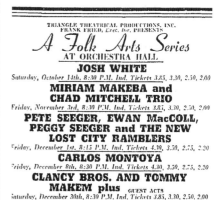

On October 14, the tour visits New York's Orchestra (Town) Hall, and music critic Robert Shelton is there for *The New York Times* (October 16). "The Chad Mitchell Trio, three young men from Spokane, Wash., with the excellent guitar and banjo backing of Jim McGuinn, have in two years established themselves as one of the more credible groups singing popularised folksongs. Their work is polished to a shine. They avoid the smart-aleck patter of many of their fraternity and range intrepidly through many traditions, including some tricky ensembles in Bantu with Miss Makeba.

"The audience was obviously won over by the trio's Irish, American, Scottish, Hebrew, and African songs. American folksong ensembles are generally in such a state of malaise that The Chad Mitchell Trio stands out as one of the most earnest and vocally well equipped. But to tell the truth, it is a further indication of that malaise that one could admire their expertise but still not be very moved by their work."

Another review appears in the *Sheboygan Press* (November 3, following yesterday's appearance at Lakeland College). "It was difficult to keep one's attention from the trio's gifted accompanist, Jim McGuinn, who changed from banjo to guitar for the various numbers, playing each with real authority."

Folk Song Festival, an hour-long TV-show on WBKB (Chicago-area) airs on December 6, displaying the Mitchell Trio, Kathleen O'Grady, The Weavers, and Josh White. Filmed at the Court Theatre on the University of Chicago campus (presumably in early November), the show runs into controversy when director William Friedkin asks for his name to be removed from the list of credits. The director is insulted because producer James McGinn – apparently a misspelling of Jim McGuinn Senior – leaves Josh White's 'Free And Equal Blues' on the cutting room floor.

"The Josh White song, which happens to be an integration song, was the high point by the top soloist of the show," fumes Friedkin,

ORCHESTRA HALL **FRIDAY, NOV. 3, 8:30 P.M.**
From South Africa
MIRIAM MAKEBA &
The Folk Songs of The
CHAD MITCHELL TRIO
Tickets by mail, Triangle Productions, Inc., 11 E. Superior—$2, $2.50, $3.30, $3.85. Tickets for both attractions available at Discount Records, 201 N. LaSalle; Hyde Park, Co-op Credit Union, 55th & Kenwood; Baca Radio, 1741 Sherman, Evanston; All Harmony Hall Record Stores; Grand & Harlem, Scottsdale Shopping Center, Winston Park Shopping Center, Belmont & Central, Lincoln Village.

"the climax of the performance, conviction and communication." The producer replies: "It was my decision. I disapproved of the content." A representative of the show's sponsor, Sara Lee ("Bakers of America's best-loved cake") comments diplomatically: "We felt that Mr. White sang better things on the show."

On January 19, 1962, The Chad Mitchell Trio and Jim McGuinn are stars on the *Bell Telephone Hour – A Measure Of Music,* along with Andres Segovia, Earl Wrightson, Maria Tallchief, Erik Bruhn, and special guest Jane Powell. The Trio sings 'Whup Jamboree' with Jim's machine-gun banjo accompaniment, before he switches to gentle fingerpicked guitar for 'Dona Dona Dona' and 'Hello Susan Brown'. The trio wanted to perform 'Lizzie Borden' – a tale of a female murderer – but the show's producer considers it "too controversial" according to a news item.

DANA ATTRACTIONS 1962 FOLK FESTIVAL
The Sensation of the 1960 Monterey Jazz Festival!
IN PERSON! The Songs of South Africa's
MIRIAM MAKEBA
with the Folksongs of the CHAD MITCHELL TRIO
SAT., FEB. 24 — BERKELEY COMM. THEATRE — 8:30 P.M.
Tickets: $3.75, 3.00 and 2.50. Now on Sale at Sherman-Clay, Oakland (HI 4-8575) and in Berkeley at Breuner's, Record City, and Campus Records.

During February and March 1962, the Trio get together with Miriam Makeba again (February 23 at the Masonic Auditorium, San Francisco, CA; February 24 in the Community Theatre, Berkeley, CA), and make a couple of appearances on *The Bob Newhart Show* (March 7 and then March 14), singing 'Sally Ann' on the latter program.

They record their second live album with Jim during a stay at New York City's premier folk venue in March. Titled *Chad Mitchell Trio At The Bitter End* (Kapp KL 1281/KS 3281) after the club where they appear, the album features their popular song 'The John Birch Society', a light riposte at the right-wing political organisation: "Join the John Birch Society/ There is so much to do."

Outside the Mitchell trio, McGuinn appears with singer, guitarist, and songwriter Hoyt Axton at The Troubadour club in Los Angeles in the winter of 1962. Recording folk singers live is the cheapest way to capture performances on tape, and Axton records *The Balladeer* (Horizon WF 1001) where "Jimmy McQuinn"

plays and sings harmony vocals on 'Brisbane Ladies'.

In the middle of March, The Chad Mitchell Trio and McGuinn embark on a 14-week 'goodwill tour' of South America arranged by the US State Department. It is an exotic adventure, as they perform in 11 countries (including Brazil, the Dominican Republic, Venezuela, and Chile), shadowed by two federal agents wherever they travel. The long time away from home takes its toll on the Trio and their young accompanist ("they treated me like Joe The Butler," McGuinn recalls later to Byrds biographer Johnny Rogan) and Chad and Jim literally come to blows one night.

After being discreetly told to stop performing 'John Birch Society' after an embassy party in Rio De Janeiro, the Trio sticks to their familiar folk repertoire. It is a different world. Chad is quoted in *The Oakland Tribune* (July 13): "We sang at many schools and found that when Latin-American students aren't listening to music, they are talking politics." Mike Kobluk adds: "That's right. After every performance it seemed the students first wanted to know if we were married, then what we thought of their country, and finally they would ask why [infamous robber and rapist] Caryl Chessman was executed."

At last, on June 22, they arrive back on the US mainland. Flying into Miami, FL, they immediately continue to Gatlinburg, TN, for a week of concerts at the Hunter Hills Theatre.

In August 1962, the Mitchell Trio opens for comedian Lenny Bruce at the Crescendo Club on L.A.'s Sunset Strip, which possibly spells the end of McGuinn's time with Mitchell (he may stay around for a week-long appearance at the Du Quoin State Fair, Springfield, IL, on August 27–September 2).

Sensing his time with Mitchell is coming to an end, he seeks out other options. He hangs out with friends at The Troubadour and

graciously rejects then offer of an audition for The New Christy Minstrels, a large ensemble formed by folk entrepreneur Larry Sparks. Fed up with Chad, Jim receives a timely invitation from Bobby Darin to become his accompanist.

Darin is a rock'n'roll singer ('Splish Splash') who has made the transition to all-round entertainer ('Mack The Knife') and then the leap to a successful career in movies (*Come September*). He plans to include a folk-song segment in his act and finds McGuinn to be the man. Offered a dizzying doubling of his Chad Mitchell salary, McGuinn jumps at the chance. On September 14, The Chicago Daily Tribune confirms that McGuinn has teamed with Darin and will make a forthcoming appearance on the season-opening of *The Dinah Shore Show* (slated for October 14, but Darin's appearance seems to be postponed until 1963).

With Bobby Darin, McGuinn begins a new phase of his apprenticeship. Darin performs exclusively on the nightclub circuit in Las Vegas or in other big cities, performing with a big orchestra. McGuinn is required to back Darin for a 15-minute segment.

Speaking to writer Kieron Tyler more than 40 years down the line, Jim will remember his time with Darin. "He wanted me to sing harmony and play 12-string guitar behind him. He represented a pop idol, a waning pop star. I had respect for him, but he wasn't a hero of mine, like Elvis. He really had a passion for folk music and his commitment to it was sincere. I'm not sure what his sources were, but he probably heard a lot of Harry Belafonte. The songs that come to mind are 'Makes A Long Time Man Feel Bad' and 'Alberta'. Bobby's attitude was socially conscious." McGuinn debuts with Darin in Las Vegas, where he meets and befriends a young actor, Peter Fonda.

For the first six months of 1963, McGuinn travels in style with Darin's company, appearing at the Cocoanut Grove, Ambassador Hotel, Los Angeles, CA (February 18–March 3); Harrah's Tahoe, South Shore Room, Lake Tahoe, NV (two weeks in March); followed by two weeks at the Flamingo, Las Vegas, NV, in April. On April 14, Bobby Darin – with McGuinn – appears on *The Dinah Shore Show.*

May is another busy month for Darin as he juggles a residence at the Copacabana in New York City while filming *Captain Newman M.D.* (with Gregory Peck, Tony Curtis, and Angie Dickinson) in California. Darin can command good fees; a one-night stand at the plush Concord Hotel in the Catskills in upstate New York pays $5,000. But the punishing schedule is straining the singer, and when he returns for another engagement in

Las Vegas (now at the Flamingo), he gives notice to his long-serving backing musicians that their contracts are up. It comes to a head in July, when Darin collapses on stage while performing at the Freedomland in the Bronx, New York City, on the 23rd.

Darin imprints an important lesson upon the young McGuinn. "Bobby was a mentor. He was very encouraging, took me under his wing and gave a lot advice," Jim recalls later to Kieron Tyler. "I would ask him questions about how to make it in the business. He was also very tough. We were playing at the Cocoanut Grove. After I finished my set, I sat with my friends in the audience drinking and laughing. Bobby sent his road manager, who dragged me backstage. Bobby said, 'Don't you ever do that again while I'm on-stage, it's distracting and disrespectful.' I've never done that again. It was a good lesson for me." McGuinn contributes to Darin's Golden Folk Hits on Capitol.

Darin withdraws from performances but does not give up music. He moves to New York City and takes along Jim McGuinn, hiring him as a music writer on a fixed salary. He is installed in an office on Broadway at the Brill Building – a veritable factory of hit-writers – where Darin gives McGuinn fairly free rein. Jim plays the folk clubs in Greenwich Village at night and spends the days in the office, listening to the radio and attempting to compose.

Hiding behind the guise of The City Surfers, McGuinn writes and records two singles: 'Beach Ball'/'Sun Tan Baby' (Capitol 5002) and '50 Miles To Go'/'Powder Puff' (Capitol 5052) – the latter in November '63. Despite some airplay, none of them sells. Jim is also involved somehow with Tom & Jerry, an early and unlikely moniker for Paul Simon and Art Garfunkel, but the result of their collaboration never sees the light of day.

New York City in general and Greenwich Village in particular are bustling with folk musicians, and during Jim's months out in the East he meets many like-minded people with whom he will keep in touch over the years: John Sebastian; Texas guitarist Shawn Phillips; record company boss and music connoisseur Jac Holzman; producer Paul Rothschild; Barry McGuire of The New Christy Minstrels; and John Phillips – another expatriate Californian – and his girlfriend Michelle Gilliam.

With time to spare, McGuinn appears on three albums for Holzman's Elektra label. Two of these are released around March 1964. One is *The Patriot Game* by The Irish Ramblers (EKL 249/EKS 7249), where McGuinn is expressly thanked on the album jacket for "preparing these songs for recording". The other is *Folksinger's Choice* (EKL-250/EKS

7250) by Theodore Bikel, where McGuinn is credited with playing banjo.

His most important work is on *Judy Collins No. 3* (EKL 2443), where he is assigned the role of musical director, besides playing guitar and banjo. The album includes three songs that McGuinn will record with The Byrds: 'The Bells Of Rhymney', Woody Gutherie's 'Deportee', and, last but not least, Pete Seeger's 'Turn! Turn! Turn!' – a song Jim will successfully turn into an anthem of hope and peace.

•

While Jim McGuinn gains valuable experience as sideman, arranger, and harmony singer in the years 1960–63, there is another musician who has been cutting hit singles and touring around America for a couple of years. He is **CLYDE 'SKIP' BATTIN** (born February 18, 1934 in Gallipolis, Ohio), who has chosen rock'n'roll over folk music. He forms his first group, The Pledges, with his friend Gary 'Flip' Paxton, before the duo record as just Skip & Flip. In 1959, they have a huge regional hit with 'It Was I' and the follow-up 'Fancy Nancy' the same year, but their biggest hit comes in 1960 when 'Cherry Pie' breaks through nationally to hit 11 on the pop charts. The duo's next singles fail to impress ('Hully Gully Cha Cha Cha' and

'Betty Jean'), even if Paxton finds enormous success with the chart-topper 'Alley Oop' as The Hollywood Argyles in 1960 – produced by Kim Fowley, future songwriting partner to Skip Battin. After their first flurry of success, Skip & Flip part company and Battin plays and records as Skip & The Flips during the next couple of years.

The Year 1962

Nationwide Hootenanny

"Anything called a hootenanny ought to be shot on sight, but the whole country is having one. A hootenanny is to folk singing what a jam session is to jazz, and all over the US there is a great reverberate twang. Guitars and banjos akimbo, folk singers inhabit smoky metropolitan crawl space; they sprawl on the floors of college rooms; near the foot of ski trails they keep time to the wheeze and sputter of burning logs; they sing homely lyrics to the combers of the Pacific.

"The commercial category – also labelled the Impures or the Popularisers – is led by The Kingston Trio. … Competing with the Kingstons for all those filthy gate receipts are other groups like The Limeliters, Peter Paul & Mary, and The Chad Mitchell Trio. … [The] tradition of Broonzy and Guthrie is being carried on by a large number of disciples, most notably a promising young hobo named Bob Dylan. He is 21 and comes from Duluth. He dresses in sheepskin and a black corduroy Huck Finn cap, which covers only a small part of his long, tumbling hair. He makes visits to Woody Guthrie's hospital bed, and he delivers his songs in a studied nasal that has just the right clothespin-on-the-nose honesty to appeal to those who most deeply care. His most celebrated song is 'Talkin' New York' – about his first visit to the city, during the cold winter of 1961, when he discovered 'Green Witch Village'."
(TIME MAGAZINE, NOVEMBER 23, 1962 – JOAN BAEZ COVER STORY)

August 1963

Gene Clark & The New Christy Minstrels

"Randy Sparks, 29, is leader and founder of [The New Christy Minstrels]. He conceived the name from Edwin P. Christy, who, in 1843, formed the famous Christy Minstrels, hailed as the nation's foremost interpreters and popularisers of Stephen Foster songs. ... They were credited with establishing the tradition of minstrel shows, and their billing carried the boast that they were the 'first to harmonise and originate the present type of minstrelsy,' meaning singing in harmony and introducing various acts within the show. Today, without the blackfaces of the 19th century minstrels, the tradition, which Christy fathered, is being given new life by the new organization. All members of The New Christy Minstrels sing together and play folk instruments together. All are accomplished performers in smaller groups and individually. As one member explains: 'We're not just singers and we're not a choir – nor are we a singalong group. We're a new concept of an all-but-forgotten tradition. We're an unbelievable combination of The Norman Luboff Choir, The Kingston Trio, and The Weavers, all in one.'"
(PRESS RELEASE PUBLISHED JULY 7, 1963)

HAROLD EUGENE 'GENE' CLARK (born Tipton, Missouri, November 17, 1944) came from a large family and is encouraged at an early age to play guitar and sing. Influenced at first by Elvis Presley and other rockers, Clark is soon enamoured of the music of The Kingston Trio. Moving to Kansas City following graduation, he is discovered by the entrepreneurial Randy Sparks one night when he performs at the Castaways Lounge. Clark is offered a place in the ensemble and joins literally the day after making a guest appearance with The New Christy Minstrels at the Starlight Theatre, Kansas City, on August 13. It is his ticket out of Kansas.

The New Christy Minstrels enjoy a large following. They've had a couple of Top 40 hits – 'This Land Is Your Land' and 'Green Green' – and the seven-boy-two-girl troupe tours constantly. The personnel fluctuates slightly as singers come and leave, but the present incarnation includes Barry McGuire, Larry Ramos, Nick Wood, Art Podell, Barry Kane, Clarence Treat, and Jackie Miller and Gayle Caldwell – plus Clark on guitar and vocals. Their material is family-friendly and

highlights the singalong factor, and to many folk fans they represent a commercialisation of the form.

Gene blends into the New Christy tapestry, but the ensemble offers the handsome Missourian few if any chances to come forward in a solo spot and certainly no opportunity to display his growing talent as a songwriter. Randy Sparks himself sometimes appears with the group, but by the end of '63 he prefers to stay home and dream up other schemes.

The Associated Press coins the phrase 'Folk Song Tycoon' to describe Sparks and his folk empire, which consists of The New Christy Minstrels, The John Henry Singers ("a Negro group with more animal drive than the Christies," he says in a contemporary review), and The Ledbetters. Then there is the Ledbetter's Store folk club in Westwood and a house in Encino – affectionately called the Folkhaus – which is a California haven for transient folk musicians. Sparks has done well, notes *The Oakland Tribune* (November 29), as he drives off in a chauffeur-driven limousine. "Every man should have his bauble," he quips. "This is mine." Sparks is also a success because he pays fair wages and treats his troops well.

Some of the dates on the New Christy itinerary for fall '63 include West Texas Fair, Abilene, TX (September 9–11); Eastern States Exposition, Coliseum, West Springfield, MA (with Tennessee Ernie Ford, September 18–21); Arkansas Livestock Exposition, Little

Rock, AR (October 1–5); Oklahoma Memorial Union Ballroom, Norman, OK (October 7–8); Municipal Auditorium, Austin, TX (October 9), University of Arizona, Tucson, AZ (October 16, where the troupe is filmed for an appearance on Jack Linkletter's *Hootenanny*, broadcast on October 19); Municipal Auditorium, Lakeland College, Sheboygan, WI (October 17); and The Arena, Winnipeg, Canada (October 19).

The Winnipeg Free Press (October 21) reports from that last Arena gig. "[They] served up a polyglot and rather insipid casserole of popular, folk, humorous, and instrumental music." A couple of days later, on October 25, the Minstrels visit the Hershey Sports Arena, Hershey, PA, with Judy Collins and The Brandywine Singers. *The Hagerstown Morning Herald* (October 28) describes them as "a group of youngsters with verve, vim, and dedication" and lists the repertoire as including 'Waltzing Matilda', 'Saturday Night', 'We Had Some Chickens', 'When The Saints Go Marching In', and 'Michael Row The Boat Ashore'. They round out the month with a sell-out performance at Carnegie Hall in New York on October 27.

Robert Shelton writes about the Carnegie Hall show in *The New York Times*. "Beyond its name, the group's similarity to its [pre-Civil War] namesake ends. This was not a modern minstrel show but a light and generally pleasing program of popular folk songs. The nine singers and instrumentalists make up the equivalent of three pop-folk trios. The voices, heard in small and large ensembles, or as soloists, were uniformly professional. Unfortunately, the singers veered too often toward a skittish, popular-music quality than toward the multi-textured richness of true folk style. When the Christies' arrangements were straightforward affairs, as in 'Hallelujah, I'm A Bum' or 'Railroad Bill', there was an unforced, fresh, we're-having-fun effect. If the group could sustain the traditional sound it often touched on, it could become a first-rate ensemble. As it was, The New Christy Minstrels were entertaining, frothy, and smiling, but rather inconsequential as stylists."

A news item in *The Los Angeles Times* (Octo-

ber 30) says that Randy Sparks will compose the music for MGM's *Company Of Cowards* and record the score with The New Christy Minstrels. Presumably recorded at this time and thus Gene Clark's recording debut, the theme tune appears on *Today* (Columbia CS8959) in March of next year, although it is hard to determine if Gene's contributions are among the many voices and strummers. (The New Christy Minstrels release a Christmas album in November, but that was recorded before Clark joined.)

The pace keeps up during the two remaining months of 1963, where appearances include Orchestra Hall, Chicago, IL (November 1); Ashland High School Gymnasium, Ashland, OH (November 6); ETSU Gym, Johnson City, TN (November 21); Coliseum Auditorium, Greensboro, NC (November 22); and The Twin Coaches, Uniontown, PA (November 25–30).

The New Christy Minstrels are booked for several television shows in this period. On November 5 they appear on *Bell Telephone Hour* in "four fast-singing numbers". They are regular visitors to ABC-TV's popular *Hootenanny*. On November 16 they appear in a pre-recorded insert from Fordham University, New York, NY, among segments by Woody Allen and The Big Three, a trio starring singer Mama Cass Elliot.

On December 14 they are seen in a clip filmed earlier at the University of Arizona, Tucson, AZ, together with The Clancy Brothers & Tommy Makem, Eddy Arnold, plus Woody Allen. On December 10–11, The New Christy Minstrels tape two further editions of *Hootenanny* at the Nathan Goff Armoury, Salem/Clarksburg, WV. The first show is broadcast on January 18, 1964 with Nina Simone and others (the Minstrels perform 'The Cotton

Pickers Song', 'Golden Bells', 'Jamie', and 'Casey Jones'). The second show is aired on March 14 with Ian & Sylvia and bluegrass stars Flatt & Scruggs among the inserts.

Before Christmas, The New Christy Minstrels and Gene Clark record *Land Of Giants* (Columbia CS8987), but again it is hard to discern Clark's roles. (The album is released in July '64.) There seems to be a short lull in the itinerary now, but on Christmas Eve the Christies sign on for a three-week residence at the 7th Floor Fun Room at Harold's Club in Reno, NV, that lasts well into January 1964.

The group breaks from Nevada when they are given the great honour to appear at the White House on the behest of Lady Bird Johnson. The occasion is a formal state dinner for Italy's aging President Antonio Segni on January 14 1964. Since John F. Kennedy's death on November 22, President Lyndon B. Johnson has been under constant pressure, and the Segni dinner is his first such party since his inauguration. Intent to stamp his own mark on the occasion, Johnson invites baseball star Joe DiMaggio, composer Gian Carlo Menotti, and political commentator Walter Lippmann to the festivity. Following opera arias by baritone Robert Merrill, The New Christy Minstrels appear, and if one is to believe *Time Magazine* (January 24) they "flaked the paint from the East Room ceiling with a rousing hootenanny".

Other New Christy appearances in January 1964 include Las Lomas High School, Walnut Creek, CA (19); Southwest Junior High Gym, Albert Lea, MI (26); Winona Senior High School, Winona, MI (29); and Iowa State University Armory, Ames, IA (31).

Around this time, Gene Clark leaves The

New Christy Minstrels. He is tired of the travelling and probably frustrated by the lack of recognition, but also he has not worked out to Randy Sparks's satisfaction. As described later in John Einarson's Gene Clark biography, he jumps just before he is pushed from the group. So, when did Clark leave? A review from the Albert Lea show says specifically that they are nine performers in all (briefly quoting Larry Ramos, Gayle Caldwell, and Nick Woods), while in an article of the Winona show three days later, journalist George McCormick comments in *The Winona Daily News* (January 30) that he counts only eight members on stage – suggesting that Clark may be gone. Still, he is seen on a couple of pre-recorded television shows next month: *A Wild Winters Night* (NBC-TV on February 20). They sing 'Today' and 'Saturday Night' plus a medley of choruses of five different songs, and at the conclusion of each, host Jonathon Winters steps up to the microphone to improvise his own lyrics. On February 22, The New Christy Minstrels and Gene Clark once more guest on Jack Linkletter's *Hootenanny*, pre-recorded at New York's Fordham University.

The New Christy Minstrels carry on with Paul Potash as Gene's replacement and spend most of March '64 entertaining at the swank Venetian Room, Fairmont Hotel, up in San Francisco. Concurrently, Randy Sparks launches yet another ensemble, The Back Porch Majority, designed to duplicate the Christy repertoire so that whenever someone leaves the 'mother group', Sparks can just transfer the required talent. Gene Clark, meanwhile, remains in Los Angeles, working on his song craft and looking for a break.

Autumn 1963

Chris Hillman: Young Mandolin Virtuoso

"[There] was a quintet of bluegrass (hillbilly) singers called The Scottsville Squirrel Barkers, who take their mountain music seriously and whose material probably was as authentic as any on the program. The Squirrel Barkers also presented two capable instrumentalists – Chris Hillman, who performs on a variation of the mandolin, and banjoist Ken Wertz. Their playing in two instrumental numbers – 'Big Sandy River' and 'Three Finger Breakdown' – was about as exciting as anything on last night's show."
(JAMES BORT, JR IN THE FRESNO BEE, SEPTEMBER 23, 1963)

CHRISTOPHER 'CHRIS' HILLMAN (born Los Angeles, California, on December 4 1944) credits an older sister for turning him on to folk and country music. "She went to college in the 50s and she came back with The Weavers and Pete Seeger and stuff, and I started to listen to that," Hillman will reminisce to journalist John Nork about his upbringing in rural San Diego County, south of Los Angeles.

"I bought rock'n'roll records in 1956 and '57, junior high school. You know, 1957: the year of rock'n'roll. So, I bought all that, and then, like a lot of people my age, I drifted into folk music. I didn't really get into The Kingston Trio or The Brothers Four; I lasted maybe a week with that, but I really liked the more traditional stuff."

He comes across records by The New Lost City Ramblers and Flatt & Scruggs and is enthralled by the sound of mandolin – "I thought that it was the most fantastic energy of music I'd ever heard" – and makes expeditions to the Ash Grove in Hollywood to see his favourites.

One of the groups Hillman catches is The Kentucky Colonels, a band of bluegrass brothers. He becomes friends with their guitar player, Clarence White. Hillman arranges to have lessons from the Colonels' stand-in mandolin player Scott Hambly – even if Hambly lives in Berkeley, an arduous 500-mile journey from Hillman's home in Delmar.

By 1962, Hillman is proficient enough to be invited to join San Diego's Scottsville Squirrel Barkers. Besides Hillman, the group lines up as Ed Douglas (double bass), Larry Murray (dobro), Kenny Wertz (banjo), and Gary Carr

(guitar). The group quickly records an album for the low-budget label Crown entitled *Bluegrass Favourites* (Crown CLP 5346/CST 346), made at the label's studio in Los Angeles. The occasion marks Chris Hillman's vinyl debut.

At the end of 1963, Hillman quits as The Scottsville Squirrel Barkers come apart, although they continue in one form or another, and another upstart, 16-year-old Bernie Leadon, plays some gigs on banjo after their mandolin player leaves. Hillman is not out of a job for long, as he is asked to join The Golden State Boys, Southern California's premier bluegrass practitioners. Featuring brothers Vern Gosdin (guitar, banjo) and Rex Gosdin (double bass), plus Don Parmley on banjo, the quartet plays venues such as the Palomino Club, a tough country bar in North Hollywood. In the first month of 1964, The Golden State Boys appear regularly on *Cal's Corral*, a local TV show that goes out on Channel 13 every Sunday at 1:30pm.

•

Bluegrass virtuoso and child prodigy **CLARENCE WHITE** (born Madawaska, Maine, as Clarence Joseph LeBlanc on June 7, 1944) is of French-Canadian ancestry. He and his brothers Roland and Eric (named after their father, Eric Senior) grew up in a house full of music. When Clarence is ten, the family moves to Burbank, California, and the White kids form a trio called Three Little Country Boys – Clarence on guitar, Roland on mandolin, and Eric Jr on banjo.

In 1957, elder brother Roland moves to

Nashville, Billy Ray Lathum comes in on banjo, and LeRoy Mack expands the line-up to four as they shorten the name to The Country Boys. By the turn of the decade, the quartet, who stick to a repertoire of bluegrass classics and gospel tunes, make their first appearances at the Ash Grove – a club that will be a home away from home for Clarence.

In 1961, the quartet appears twice on the sitcom *The Andy Griffith Show*, first on February 15, then on April 21 (although syndication may differ in various regions). The first of these two episodes, 'Mayberry On Record', deals with a record company man who goes looking for talent in the fictitious town of Mayberry.

When Eric White Jr gets married that summer, he quits the group and is replaced by Roger Bush on stand-up bass. During 1961–62, The Country Boys make some singles and in September '62 record their debut album *New Sounds Of Bluegrass America* (Briar International 109). Just before its release, country guitar star Joe Maphis comes up with The Kentucky Colonels as a more suitable name for the quartet.

In a long interview with the British *Melody Maker* (May 15, 1971), Clarence will look back on his chequered career. "People seem to think I'm from the South," he tells Richard Williams. "That's from playing bluegrass when I was a kid, and me and my brothers learned a lot of old-time Canadian jigs and fiddle music from my father, who's Canadian. He got us into music, and [got me] started on guitar when I was six years old. When I was ten, I started travelling with my brothers – we called ourselves The Three Little Country Boys, until in 1963 we became The Kentucky Colonels. Our interest in Canadian music helped us develop into a bluegrass band, because the Canadian thing is a lot like Southern mountain music."

As The Kentucky Colonels, Clarence's group appears at the prestigious Monterey Folk Festival in May 1963 and that same year makes a multitude of appearances around California as well as forays around the States.

Throughout 1964, The Kentucky Colonels perform at countless clubs and concert halls. Places they visit include: the Ash Grove (February, with Buffy St Marie); the '2nd Annual UCLA Folk Festival', Royce Hall, Los Angeles, CA (March 25–29, "picking fiddle and banjo songs and vocalising twangy tunes," says *The Los Angeles Times*); The First Step, Tucson, AZ (April 1964); The Cabal, Berkeley, CA (April 17); Club 47, Cambridge, MA (July 2–4); Newport Folk Festival, Newport, RI (July 23–26); Foghorn Club, Baltimore, MD (August); Fugazi Hall, San Francisco, CA (November 13); and the Comedia Theatre, Palo Alto,

CA (November 15). As they steadfastly perfect their skills, The Kentucky Colonels are considered by 1964 to be one of the country's leading bluegrass combos.

September 1963

David Crosby, Balladeer

"Les Baxter's Balladeers started the show with decent enough music and atrocious jokes. This group should stick to singing."
(WISCONSIN STATE JOURNAL, OCTOBER 22, 1963)

The son of a respected cinematographer, **DAVID VAN CORTLANDT CROSBY** (born Los Angeles, California, on August 14, 1941) attempted a career as an actor before pursuing a life in music. Between 1960 and '63 he roams around the United States, crossing paths with a succession of singers, songwriters, blues musicians, buskers, jazz players, and poets. During these years, his love of music develops from an interest to a career, as he improves his singing skills, dabbles in songwriting, learns to play the guitar, and absorbs an array of impressions.

Tracing his roots to rock journalist Ben Fong-Torres in 1970, he will recall that he started singing "right in the coffeehouses in Santa Barbara. The first one that I ever started in was called Noctambulist. I don't even know where I started listening to music. I started singing when I was a kid with my family. People would pull me into the coffeehouses to see and hear people. Travis Edmondson [of The Gateway Singers and the later duo Bud &

NOW APPEARING
LES BAXTER'S
BALLADEERS
RANDY BOONE
(From TV Show "It's a Man's World")
STEWART CLAY

ICE
HOUSE
THEATRE-RESTAURANT—
24 N. Mentor ● Pasadena ● MU 1-9542

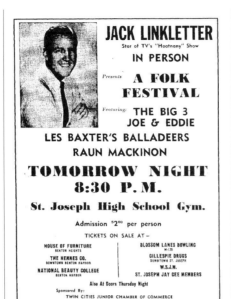

JACK LINKLETTER
Star of TV's "Hootenany" Show
IN PERSON
Presents
A FOLK
FESTIVAL
Featuring THE BIG 3
JOE & EDDIE
LES BAXTER'S BALLADEERS
RAUN MACKINON
TOMORROW NIGHT
8:30 P. M.
St. Joseph High School Gym.
Admission $2.00 per person
TICKETS ON SALE AT –
HOUSE OF FURNITURE   BLOSSOM LANES BOWLING
BENTON HEIGHTS   M-139
THE HENNES CO.   GILLESPIE DRUGS
DOWNTOWN BENTON HARBOR   DOWNTOWN ST. JOSEPH
                                              W.S.J.M.
NATIONAL BEAUTY COLLEGE   ST. JOSEPH JAY CEE MEMBERS
BENTON HARBOR
Also At Doors Thursday Night
Sponsored By:
TWIN CITIES JUNIOR CHAMBER OF COMMERCE

Travis] was the first folk musician that would teach me anything. And it was a good trip."

It is at this time that Crosby meets Jim McGuinn, by chance, after a Limeliters performance at L.A.'s Ash Grove club. A true troubadour and free spirit, Crosby sings his way through Arizona and Colorado, ending up in New York's Greenwich Village. Here he forms a brief alliance with blues singer Terry Collier before detouring to Canada and Chicago on his way to Florida.

In January 1962, David's brother Ethan 'Chip' Crosby joins him, and the two play coffeehouses in Coconut Grove, Fort Lauderdale, and Miami – managing a side trip to Nebraska in between – usually together with friends Bobby Ingram and Mike Clough. Getting itchy again, Crosby backtracks to Denver and winds up in Chicago again – where he hears the power of jazz saxophonist John Coltrane. In his biography, Crosby, high as a kite, will recount the otherworldly experience of seeing Coltrane's mind-blowing quartet at a club on Chicago's South Side.

David ends up back in California again and settles in Sausalito with singer–songwriter Dino Valenti for some time before moving into a commune on Venice Beach outside Los Angeles with some friends. He will list them for *The South California Oracle* (October 67): "Paul Kantner … David Freiberg … and Sheri Snow from Blackburn & Snow. And Ginger Jackson. [We] all lived together in Venice. We kept our money in a bowl. Nobody ever stole it."

In the autumn of 1963, Ethan Crosby entices his brother to come join him in a folk-styled quartet under the aegis of Les Baxter.

Essentially, it is a reunion of the four boys who played coffeehouses in Florida the pervious year: David, Ethan, Bobby Ingram, and Mike Clough, all singing and playing guitars, with Ethan on bass.

Baxter is a musician, composer, and ethno-musicologist with nearly 40 albums to his credit, many in the vacuum between easy listening (*Selections From Rodgers & Hammerstein's South Pacific*) and the plain bizarre (*Perfume Set To Music* or *Festival Of The Gnomes* or *Wild Hi-Fi Drums/Wild Stereo Drums*). Cashing in on the folk boom, Baxter lends his name to The Balladeers, an artificial construction put together in 1962. Starting out as a nine-piece group (seven men and two woman, just like The New Christy Minstrels), they release a self-titled album on Reprise. By May '63, the nine have dwindled to five.

Signed to the William Morris Agency, the reconstructed Balladeers debut at the Ice House, a folk club in Pasadena, CA, and play there straight through September, with Randy Boone and Stewart Clay on the bill (September 3–8, 10–15, 17–22, and finally 24–29). The performance on the 24th is recorded for a live album on Legend Records, TV personality Jack Linkletter's company. The Yachtsmen and Jim & Jean appear on the 24th, too, and the results are collected on the album *Jack Linkletter Presents A Folk Festival* (GNP Crescendo 95), produced by Alex Hassilev of The Limeliters.

Les Baxter's Balladeers perform 'Ride Up', 'Midnight Special', 'Baiion', 'Linin' Track' (the songs are either credited to Les Baxter or as public domain material) and join The Yachtsmen and Jim & Jean for a finale of 'Chloe Marsh'/'Banks Of The Ohio'. (The other songs on the album are by The Yachtsmen and Jim & Jean.) The day following the live recording, Revue Studio video-tapes a pilot for a proposed '64 TV series. The Rooftop Singers, Randy Boone, Jackie De Shannon, Stewart Clay, and The Goodtime Singers are all filmed, but it appears Baxter's Balladeers are not recorded. (They have appeared on Linkletter's *Hootenanny* shows, but that was before David Crosby joined.)

The Balladeers wind up their residence at the Ice House on October 1–6. This is followed by an appearance at the three-day '68th Fresno District Fair' in Fresno, CA (October 11–13) which sees Les Baxter's Balladeers in a cast with The Hardy Family (an acrobatic act) and Peg Leg Bates, "who does incredible things on one good leg and an artificial one" according to *The Fresno Bee*.

Crosby and The Balladeers embark on a month-long tour in October–November as part of a package with popular TV star Jack Linkletter as the main drawing card. Linkletter hosts the weekly *Hootenanny* (ABC-TV) shows every Saturday, but the folk fundamentalists accuse him and his show of whitewashing the culture. The shows are taped at college campuses around the US, and the majority of performers are "popular imitators of the art" according to *The Los Angeles Times* (October 30). The newspaper has spoken to Ed Pearl, respected proprietor of the Ash Grove, who says the only pure music *Hootenanny* has aired is by Flatt & Scruggs, and that is only because the outfit has scored a hit with the theme tune for the *Beverly Hillbillies* TV series. Linkletter brushes the criticism aside in an interview with *The Syracuse Post Standard* (November 16), saying: "American folk music has a much wider background than the bearded minority of ethnics would have you believe."

By pushing Linkletter up front (the tour is being billed as 'Jack Linkletter Presents A Folk Festival', just like the recently recorded live album), the acts are secondary. Besides Baxter's lot, the rest of the bill is Joe & Eddie, female singer Raun MacKinnon, and The Big Three, a reasonably successful folk trio consisting of Cass Elliot, Tim Rose, and James Hendricks. It is David Crosby's first experience of regulated life on the road. "We did 30 one-nighters on a lousy bus; it was a grim trip," Ethan recalls in the Crosby annals.

The complete itinerary is lost to time, but the tour starts at Sioux Falls Arena, Sioux Falls, SD (October 17) and takes in Capitol Theatre, Madison, WI (October 21); Parthenon Theatre, Hammond, IN (October 24); Memorial Auditorium, Cedar Rapids, IA (November 5); St. Joseph High School Gymnasium, Benton Harbor, MI (November 14); War Memorial Auditorium, Syracuse, NY (November 16); a gig in Trenton, NJ (November 22); and RKO Keith's Theatre, Flushing, NY (November 23), which presumably marks the end of the tour.

Back in California, Les Baxter's Balladeers have a residence at the Hootenanny Club, Canoga Park, CA. It starts on November 29 and will run until December 15, but this seems to be the end of the Crosby brothers' involvement with the Balladeers. Advertisements promise that they will appear for a New Year's Party at Waly's Famous Steak House in Eureka, CA, but a last-minute announcement says that The Foremen have been called in as replacements because Les Baxter's Balladeers "are no longer appearing as a group".

Free again, and with 1964 ahead of him, David Crosby is in no hurry to plan his next move.

November 22, 1963

He Was A Friend Of Mine

"His killing had no purpose /
No reason or rhyme /
He was a friend of mine"
(JIM McGUINN)

America comes to a standstill on November 22, 1963 when the news of President John F. Kennedy's assassination in Dallas, Texas, is broadcast to the nation. Jim McGuinn is in New York City and responds by composing new lyrics to the traditional folk tune 'He Was A Friend Of Mine'. Where the original song dealt with the death of a dear friend, McGuinn's lyric sensitively rephrases the message to make Kennedy everyone's close friend – even if the singer "never met him" and the President "never knew my name".

That same night, Chris Hillman does duty on the bluegrass circuit. It will remain a vivid memory many decades later. "We were playing a show in a club called the Harem Lounge to a huge audience of two or three people when we heard the news of President Kennedy's assassination," he tells journalist Chris Kelly. "A drunk woman was yelling to us, 'How can you play when the President has been murdered?'."

Local newspaper headlines, screaming "President Is Dead", greet Gene Clark on tour with The New Christy Minstrels in Greensboro, North Carolina. David Crosby, meanwhile, has arrived in Trenton, New Jersey, with Jack Linkletter's travelling folk circus. "I was in a restaurant when somebody ran in and blurted out the news that someone had shot the President," Crosby will remember in his autobiography. "The rest of the day, everywhere you went, people were grief-stricken, standing around listening to radios and looking at each other with this lost 'What are we gonna do now?' look. It hadn't really occurred to anyone that this could happen. The country wasn't ready for it. We all had a guy in whom we believed – right, wrong, or different. That was the real magic of John Kennedy, that we believed in him."

February 9, 1964

The Beatles Shake America

"'How long will Folk Music Phenomenon last?' enquires an innocent headline in THE WINNIPEG FREE PRESS *on December 14, 1963. Although the subject is the deflation of 'the pure' folk music, an appropriate answer could be '57 days' – the time lapse between the article's publishing date and the arrival of four boys from Liverpool on primetime American television."*

The storm has been rumbling for a couple of weeks already – 'I Want To Hold Your Hand' made Number One on the *Cash Box* charts on January 25, 1964 and in *Billboard* on February 1 – but the real landslide breaks when more than 70 million people in more than 23 million homes across the US sit down at 8:00pm on Sunday February 9 to see The Beatles on *The Ed Sullivan Show*. Like a tidal wave, The Beatles sweep everything aside and change the course of pop culture forever after.

Jim McGuinn has sensed the tremors already. On January 3, at 10:00pm, *The Jack Parr Show* airs BBC footage of The Beatles. "I first saw [them] on television in New York," he later tells journalist Dave Harmon. "It was the clip with all the screaming girls. I loved the music! I got it right away and started playing folk songs with a Beatle beat down in Greenwich Village."

Armed with his guitar and a beatified folk repertoire, Jim is offered an engagement at Joe Stevens' Café Playhouse in the Village. According to legend, Stevens even puts a placard outside, tempting customers with "Beatle Imitations".

The long winter in New York draws to an end when Jim's old friend Bob Hippard in

California calls from out of the blue. Hipp-ard has fixed Jim the opening spot for Roger Miller and Hoyt Axton at L.A.'s Troubadour club. Would he like to come? McGuinn needs little persuasion as he packs his bags and flies westwards in the spring of 1964. ■

Spring 1964

Jet Set Airborne

"I don't remember what month it was, but I think it was early spring [1964]," McGuinn will recall to music historian John Einarson when trying to gauge his arrival in California for the Roger Miller–Hoyt Axton shows at The Troubadour. "It was cold in New York when I left, because I was wearing a black raincoat when I got off the plane in L.A."

As it is, Roger Miller plays The Troubadour on several occasions, and he holds court here in late June – although he played here earlier in the spring too.

Jim's repertoire with a Beatles slant does not go down as well at the Troub as in New York, as he explains to Einarson. "I was really getting a terrible audience reaction. … The folk purists absolutely hated what I was doing. It was blasphemy. They wanted to stone me or burn me at the stake."

Gene Clark is still in town and regularly drops by the club, and his interest is imme-diately piqued when he hears Jim perform. He introduces himself, and the two find they both share a love of The Beatles, a common background in folk music, and an interest in songwriting. Clark and McGuinn start sing-ing and playing together, toying with the idea of performing as a duo – styled after British duo Peter & Gordon. McGuinn will say in hindsight that he and Gene never get beyond informal chirp-and-strum sessions, but the idea makes sense – Peter & Gordon hit jackpot when their debut single 'A World Without Love' first topples The Beatles from the UK charts in April '64 and then repeat the trick when their record also ascends the US charts that June. (It did not hurt sales, either, that Lennon & McCartney wrote the song.)

David Crosby, meanwhile, is performing solo around Hollywood folk clubs when record producer Jim Dickson spots him. Born in 1931 and raised in California, Dickson is a chapter unto himself. He entered the music business when he met comedian Lord Buck-ley and mingled with Hollywood glitterati through his marriage to actress Diane Varsi in 1955. Theirs was a shortlived happiness; by

1957, gossip columns recorded that Varsi mar-ried actor Dennis Hopper as soon as she had divorced Dickson (a hasty announcement, as it turns out).

Splitting his time between earning a living as a cameraman and dabbling in recording engineering and production, Dickson was giv-ing music priority by the turn of the decade. Around 1963, he started recording acts for Elektra Records on the West Coast (The Dil-lards, The Greenbriar Boys) and scored a hit with the instrumental album *12-string Guitar* credited to The Folkswingers and released on World Pacific Records – a label with a long history of jazz albums.

Label-owner Richard Bock controls World Pacific Studios at 8713 West Third Street in Los Angeles but gives Dickson free access to his studio in return for his services. This arrangement allows Dickson to rehearse his acts or to record demo sessions with rough talent. Just recently, Dickson has formed a partnership with Eddie Tickner, primarily to work in music publishing. Tickner is business manager for a number of folk artists includ-ing Odetta.

Dickson finds David Crosby singing one night at the Unicorn, a Hollywood jazz club, in the spring months of 1964. "There was this young guy with a nice, clear pretty voice – and not a soul in the place paying any attention to him at all – just singing his heart out, being totally ignored by a crowd that was too hip," Dickson will say later in Crosby's memoir. "I thought, 'Gee, this guy would be great in a group. He's got the kind of voice that would really harmonise.' So I went over and intro-duced myself to David."

Pursuing his conviction, Dickson at first hires a rhythm section of guitar, bass, and drums to put muscle behind Crosby's lone voice on some recordings, four of which will survive: Hoyt Axton's 'Willie Jean', Ray Charles's 'Come Back Baby', the traditional number 'Jack Of Diamonds', and 'Get Together', the clarion call penned by Crosby's friend Dino Valenti. Reportedly, Crosby is not enamoured with the results, but they typify Dickson's visionary approach: why record the same folk repertoire that everybody else had done? Yet Dickson does not think the test recordings with Crosby are good enough to warrant a recording contract. Something is missing.

Jim McGuinn and Gene Clark sense an anticipatory buzz in the air this spring, and one day David Crosby is there, adding his har-monies to a song they are singing. Although the three have more than a nodding acquaint-ance, they have not performed together. The event is so momentous that, in hindsight, the three will not be able to agree on how exactly

they first sang together. Either it is in the front room of The Troubadour (a place called the Folk Den), or in a stairwell with its natural echo, or perhaps on the stage at the Troub.

Crosby involves Jim Dickson, and this makes all the difference – Clark, McGuinn, and Crosby certainly have talent and they may have a purpose, but it is Dickson who can channel that energy into a recordable sound. The producer opens the doors at World Pacific to the three, where they start rehearsals and record at midnight. A name is needed, and it is McGuinn who comes up with THE JET SET.

Dickson and his business partner Ed Tick-ner arrange to have photos taken of the trio: nattily dressed in white shirts, hair combed neatly back, and McGuinn wearing Clark Kent spectacles, the three still adhere to the folk look. Musically, on the other hand, they have found something unique. A joint McGuinn–Crosby composition called 'The Only Girl I Adore' will be the sole surviving example of The Jet Set. Brisk acoustic guitars accompany Beatle harmonies with a slight British accent. The song bodes well for the future.

The trio enjoy a quick growth thanks to a relentless drive for perfection and quality. The aim is shared by Dickson and World Pacific, who present a unique opportunity: an audio greenhouse where they can record rehearsals and listen to and analyse playbacks right away, a luxury in an age where recording tape is expensive and the idea of a high-quality home studio belongs to a distant future.

"We learned faster than any other garage band you ever saw," Crosby will remember in a conversation with author John Nork, explaining that Dickson "would sit down and make us listen to the tapes, and boy was that cruelty. Aversion therapy! We would look at each other and go, 'Aw, shit! We'll never do this!' But we'd come back and try some more, and eventually we got pretty good at it, and it happened a lot faster than it normally would because of that."

McGuinn agrees, as he tells Nork: "If we hadn't had those tools to work with, it would have taken a lot longer. A lot of bands have to work on the road for years to get the kind of sound we recorded together in about eight or nine months."

At some point in the summer of 1964 – presumably when The Jet Set are still a trio – Jim Dickson works out a one-off deal with Jac Holzman of Elektra Records to bankroll a proper recording session. McGuinn and his buddy Harvey Gerst concoct two Beatles-inflected melodies with 'oh yeah' refrains. The unimaginative lyrics sound like they could be written for the same song: 'Don't Be Long' repeats the title of the other song, 'Please Let

Me Love You', as part of the chorus. McGuinn plays what sounds like an amplified acoustic 12-string rather than an electric guitar, while the two experienced studio stalwarts Ray Pohlman (bass guitar) and Earl Palmer (drums) make up the rhythm section.

The two songs are co-produced by Jac Hozman's right-hand man Paul Rothschild, and Elektra couples them for a single at the end of the year (given the catalogue number EKM-145102). Searching for a name, Holzman credits the record to **THE BEEFEATERS** – a trite name but with a suitable British flavour. It makes no impression when it is finally released – and by then The Jet Set have long since moved on.

•

While grooming The Jet Set in the summer of 1964, Jim Dickson has other irons in the fire. The Golden State Boys have come to his attention earlier in the year, and he applies the same strategy as he does to Clark, McGuinn, and Crosby. Indeed, as Dickson will recall to biographer Johnny Rogan, he has been aware of Chris Hillman since he played with The Scottsville Squirrel Barkers. Collecting satisfactory recordings with the aim to fix The Golden State Boys a deal with Elektra Records, Dickson persuades The Golden State Boys to stray outside the strict bluegrass style.

One of the songs they record is Bob Dylan's 'When The Ship Comes In', from January's The Times They Are A-Changin' album. Documentation of the sessions will not survive, and in the end Elektra passes on the option to release the sides, but everything points to the recordings taking place in the first half of 1964 rather than the previous year. (Eventually, 11 tracks are released in 1969 after Chris Hillman has become famous.)

Jim Dickson and Eddie Tickner sign a man-

agement deal with The Golden State Boys but decide to change the group's name in honour of its mandolin player. The Hillmen is an odd choice as Chris Hillman is neither the group's leader nor its main vocalist.

The Hillmen reputedly pass an audition to appear at the second 'Monterey Folk Festival' on May 30–31. The festival strives to secure the bigger names – Dylan, last year's top draw, does not perform, despite reports to the contrary – and the event is a financial flop. The Hillmen play Disneyland in Anaheim, CA, several times in the summer of 1964: June 22, July 12, August 2, and finally on August 23 and 24. They appear on Hootenanny specials together with artists such as The Ward Singers and The Yachtsmen.

•

The Kentucky Colonels find that 1964 is a year of change for them, too, as they also come under the wing of Jim Dickson. He signs them to World Pacific Records and, adding fiddle player Bobby Slone, the Colonels record Appalachian Swing! (World Pacific 1821), a quintessential album where Clarence White's playing greatly expands the language of bluegrass guitar.

June 9, 1964

Magic Swirling Ship

"In a swirl of chain-lit Camel cigarette smoke, while the whole time, over and over again, Marvin Gaye sang 'Can I Get A Witness', I had my bedroom wired into the hi-fi, too, and I listened to 'Can I Get A Witness' over and over again with Bob through the night, me in my bedroom and Bob out at the breakfast bar, until I shut off my speakers and went to sleep. Bob must have stayed up past dawn, tapping away at the keys in his cigarette fog."

(Bob Dylan writes 'Mr. Tambourine Man' at Al Aronowitz's New Jersey home, spring 1964 – THE NEW YORK SUNDAY NEWS, NOVEMBER 11, 1973)

On the evening of June 9, 1964, Bob Dylan enters Columbia's recording studio in Manhattan for his first session in nine months. He comes well stocked with melodies and lyrics and in an effective session dashes off a dozen brand new songs. When the session nears its end, Dylan is joined in the studio by Ramblin' Jack Elliot, and the two run through 'Mr. Tambourine Man' twice. Ramblin' Jack

harmonises the chorus shakily along with Dylan.

Eleven of the songs are mastered for *Another Side Of Bob Dylan* and released less than two months later, but 'Mr. Tambourine Man' is not included, although Dylan incorporates the new songs into his stage act right away.

He is greeted with fervour at the 1964 'Newport Folk Festival' in Newport, RI, held on the weekend of July 23–26. *The Newport Daily News* (July 27) submits a quaint yet glowing report. "Dylan, appearing better dressed than he did last year or at his brief appearance Friday night, obviously is the voice of the youth of America as well as the oppressed, and is the champion of the little man. His lyrics are very clever and show an absolutely amazing vocabulary. As he sings his songs, or plays them on his harmonica and guitar, he has an almost mesmerising effect on his audience. Despite the long curly hair, his untidy appearance and scrawny frame, there is an aura of greatness about him.

"He started off with 'All I Really Want To Do, Is Be Friends With You' and then sang a song 'To Ramona' which drew the blond Mary Travers of Peter Paul & Mary out to the arena where she draped herself over a stepladder, utterly absorbed in Dylan's performance. After singing 'Hey Mr. Tambourine Man' and 'Signs Of Freedom Flashing', he left the stage, but the fans would not be quieted, so he came back on with Joan Baez to join him in 'With God On Our Side'. Before the fans were subdued he had to come on again to briefly tell them he loved them."

Jim Dickson has seemingly made the journey to Newport together with The Kentucky Colonels, who play later on Sunday evening. Newport's *Daily News:* "[They] played string band music bluegrass style. Their five numbers were chiefly fast and well done."

Dickson sees Dylan's performance and is especially impressed with 'Mr. Tambourine Man'. Through various connections, not least knowing Bob Dylan vaguely, Dickson manages to get his hands on the Dylan–Elliot recording of the song. He later savours the moment to biographer Johnny Rogan: "When I finally got the acetate for 'Mr. Tambourine Man' it was the most magical song I had ever heard in that genre." This moment must be in August 1964 at the earliest.

With the acetate safely in hand, Dickson apparently considers two options for the song. One is to record it by The Jet Set and the other is to let The Kentucky Colonels have a go at it. Clarence White will tell Richard Williams in Britain's *Melody Maker* (May 15, 1971): "The Kentucky Colonels were pretty famous on the bluegrass circuit. There's a couple of clubs for that kind of music in all the major cities throughout America, and we played all of them, plus college gigs and folk festivals.

"I started to do what I've been wanting to do since '64 – I wanted to electrify folk music," White continues. "I'd suggested it in '64, but none of the other guys thought it was a good idea. Vanguard and Elektra had been bidding for me to do a guitar album for them, and I'd started getting material. The first demo I got was of 'Mr. Tambourine Man', sung by Dylan and Ramblin' Jack Elliott. I've still got it – I guess it must be worth a lot now, right? Anyway, I thought, that's folk music, let's do it – but I guess some people are always a little ahead of their time." White draws the shortest straw, and Dickson gives 'Mr. Tambourine Man' to The Jet Set.

August 12 1964

A Hard Day's Night In L.A.

"A Hard Day's Night, starring The Beatles, may well be the surprise film of the year. The surprise is that it is good. … It was [only] natural that a reviewer should approach A Hard Day's Night expecting little more than a tape recording of an orgiastic Beatle concert. But the film shows that the unshorn quartet may be with us for a long

time to come. Not as freaks, but as qualified entertainers. … The movie opens with a mad scramble by the foursome to escape their followers and board a train. It ends with a television performance which pours forth enough of their twangy chantings to satisfy any Beatlemaniac."
(BOB THOMAS, ASSOCIATED PRESS, AUGUST 12, 1964)

The Beatles' first full-length feature film premieres in 500 movie theatres across the US on August 12, 1964 and is a smash hit at the box office – just as a tour of North America begins with The Beatles playing to sold-out stadiums and causing a pandemonium scarcely witnessed before.

Jim McGuinn, Gene Clark, and David Crosby go together to watch *A Hard Day's Night*, and Crosby later describes the unbridling euphoria in his autobiography. "I can remember coming out of that movie so jazzed that I was swinging around stop-sign poles at arm's length. I knew right then what my life was going to be. I wanted to be that. That was It. I loved the attitude and the fun of it; there was sex, there was joy, there was everything I wanted out of life, right there. They were cool and we said, 'Yeah, that's it. We have to be a band. Who can we get to play drums?'"

Autumn 1964

Cardboard Boxes and Tambourines

Jim, Gene, and David make The Jet Set a priority but still have to make a living, so they entertain side projects when time allows. Singer and songwriter Sean Bonniwell will recall to music historian Richie Unterberger that he finds the adaptable Jim McGuinn playing double bass for Jackie & Gayle, two girl singers who have just broken away from The New

Christy Minstrels. The occasion is a county fair up around San Francisco, possibly the Alameda County Fair where Jack Linkletter hosts a daily hootenanny programme between June 28 and July 5. "McGuinn asked me for a ride back to L.A.," Bonniwell recounts, "so when we were coming back … we were singing Beatles songs. … And he told me about The Jet Set."

What The Jet Set miss is a drummer, and in the summer of '64 they find the right boy. **MICHAEL CLARKE** (born Michael James Dick in Spokane, Washington, on June 3, 1946) grew up in an artistic environment, his father a painter and his mother a musician. He left home in 1963 and travelled to California. Here he fell in with a crowd in Sausalito and hung out with Dino Valente, meeting David Crosby very briefly for the first time.

Michael James Dick's entrance into The Jet Set will become a well-worn story, where looks and star appeal matter more than his musical credentials. Jim McGuinn will recall the classic moment to rock journalist Ed Ward. "[He] was walking down Santa Monica Boulevard and he looked right for the part, and we said, 'Hey, you wanna be our drummer?' and he said 'Sure'. And he learned how to play drums – well, he'd played conga drums before. Actually, that's cheating, because we'd met him before in San Francisco up in a North Beach folk club."

Along the way, the tall and handsome drummer has adopted the name Michael Clarke. How the three Jet Setters found a drummer calling himself Clarke may become well known, but when exactly he joins the fledging trio is not clear. Johnny Rogan's later book on these early times explains how an excited Michael returns home to Spokane for his 18th birthday in June before travelling south "to get into a group", while David Crosby's memoir will suggest it could have been after the *Hard Day's Night* premiere in August. Anyway, with limited funds, the frontmen are stuck with their acoustic guitars, while a conga drum, some cardboard boxes, and a tambourine constitute the drum kit.

Of the many tapes Jim Dickson records with The Jet Set, five demo recordings will survive by the transitional unplugged quartet. They are 'Tomorrow Is A Long Ways Away' (a three-way Clark–Crosby–McGuinn partnership on paper but reputedly the sole creation of Gene); 'You Showed Me' (penned by Jim and Gene); two of Gene's songs ('I Knew I'd Want You' and 'You Won't Have to Cry'); and their first attempt at tackling Dylan's 'Mr. Tambourine Man'. As with all their sessions done at World Pacific, no documentation will survive to precisely date the sessions, but September 1964 is a good guess.

19

The five demos reveal that The Jet Set have made a great leap in a short time. Gene Clark is emerging as a genuinely talented songwriter, and the basic arrangement of 'Mr. Tambourine Man' with Jim's vocals is already in place, which later electrification will improve. A key character of their future sound is also there for all to hear – the attractive McGuinn–Clark–Crosby vocal blend, where two voices sing usually in unison while David Crosby is free to add the special ingredient. "I was able to shift between third and fourth and fifth and sixth and seventh easily," Crosby will explain to John Nork. "There wasn't another part above me."

•

A Hard Day's Night is an eye-opener for Jim McGuinn when he sees George Harrison playing an electric 12-string guitar. Harrison received his guitar while visiting New York back in February. It is a Rickenbacker model 360/12 and the second electric 12-string the company ever made. McGuinn is very comfortable with the sound and feel of the acoustic 12-string, after years of playing, and purchases a pickup for his guitar to attain a rockier sound. But quickly he finds out that it does not work.

Inspired by the movie, McGuinn goes looking for a similar guitar to Harrison's. The story goes that he has to watch the movie a second time to see what brand of guitar the Beatle is strumming. It turns out Rickenbacker has made some adjustments to the guitar since George got his one, which was essentially a prototype. The model McGuinn purchases has a rounded body form, rather than the 'sharp-edge' style of Harrison's, and a different finish and bridge/tailpiece.

Besides George Harrison's groundbreaking 12-string work on *A Hard Day's Night*, other isolated examples of electric 12-string pop guitarists are heard in 1964 – primarily Liverpool contemporaries The Searchers. By chance, they infiltrate the California sound by turning two songs performed by Jackie De Shannon into US hits this year: 'Needles And Pins' (Number 13 on the *Billboard* charts) and 'When You Walk in the Room' (which makes the Top 40).

Jim is a hard-working pupil ("I practiced eight hours a day on that Rick," he will tell Andy Ellis in hindsight), but however much he is swayed by the sounds of Harrison and The Searchers, he mainly incorporates his folk techniques as passed down from Leadbelly, Pete Seeger, Frank Hamilton, and Bob Gibson.

To purchase McGuinn's dream instrument, Ed Tickner solicits one of his clients – art collector and artist Naomi Hirshhorn – to invest a hefty $5,000 against a five per cent interest in

the totally unknown pop group. "In retrospect it was a good deal," David Crosby records in his memoir. "At the time, it must've seemed a risky flier, a crapshoot on a band with no name, little experience, dim prospects, and no recording contract. To Naomi Hirshhorn's credit, she went for it."

The cash enables the four poor musicians to purchase high-quality instruments. Michael Clarke discards cardboard boxes in favour of a real Ludwig drum kit; McGuinn gets his Rickenbacker 360/12 (but has to trade his trusted Vega 5-string banjo in the process); while a Gretsch six-string Tennessean and a six-string bass guitar (presumably a Fender) go to Clark and Crosby respectively. Fender amplification is bought to go with the gleaming guitars. (In a couple of months, a management contract is drawn up between the Tickner–Dickson management and the group, and it is also signed by Naomi Hirshhorn as the document refers to her agreement too.)

With new equipment, the Jet Set members settle into the formation of their Beatle role models: David plays bass guitar, Gene rhythm guitar, Jim lead guitar, and Michael drums. Within weeks, it is obvious that the arrangement with David Crosby as bass player and Gene Clark on rhythm guitar is not working out. Crosby is unable to sing and play the bass at the same time, and as Clark is deemed merely a passable guitarist, David persuades him to pass on the Gretsch six-string guitar. That not only leaves Gene without a guitar: it leaves The Jet Set without a bass player.

Jim Dickson has the solution. He asks Chris Hillman if he would be interested in trying out the bass. The Hillmen is still a viable prospect, but Hillman jumps at the chance. He acquires a cheap Japanese bass of unknown origin and joins The Jet Set – making the group a quintet. For Hillman, it is a different challenge compared to the studious bluegrass approach – "In bluegrass, you don't even crack a smile," he quips to Richie Unterberger – but his schooling and experience make it relatively easy to pick up the bass.

Gene Clark's songwriting talent immediately strikes the new bass player. "It wasn't that he was well-read or anything," Hillman will recall to John Nork. "It was just that he had this sixth-sense about things. The rest of us struggled to come up with stuff like that, and he could pull it out of his head."

The exact moment when Chris Hillman joined The Jet Set is guesswork, like so many dates in this eventful year, but he is probably not part of the group before October 1964 at the earliest.

They continue to record at World Pacific whenever opportunities arise, and more than a dozen songs in various states of completion

will later be collected on the *Preflyte Sessions* two-CD set in 2002.

A rough estimate suggests these songs are recorded during the last two–three months of 1964 (and certainly continuing into the first weeks of 1965), and they lay the groundwork for the challenge that awaits The Jet Set next year. They have passed the first test. "We had to learn how to play in rhythm. That was our main concern, really," McGuinn will succinctly sum up to John Nork in hindsight.

The songs of Gene Clark are already way ahead – not only of his band members but also of many of his contemporaries. A remarkable talent, he conjures up unusual lyrical twists and soulful melodies, and by now The Jet Set continually rise to the occasion and do justice to his compositions. There is another factor too, as Chris Hillman emphasises to Richie Unterberger. "Dickson pounded it into our head, literally, to go for a little more depth in the lyric, and really craft the song, and make something you can be proud of 10 to 15 years down the road."

The songs taped in the late winter months of 1964 include four songs that the group already recorded acoustically with conga and cardboard box accompaniment a few months back. These are 'You Won't Have to Cry', 'You Showed Me', 'Tomorrow Is a Long Ways Away', and 'I Knew I'd Want You' – the latter in two alternate versions.

Then there are 'The Reason Why' (two takes), 'She Has A Way' (four different versions), 'Here Without You' (two takes), 'Boston' (three versions with a good dance beat; one an instrumental backing track), 'For Me Again' (two versions), 'It's No Use' (co-written by McGuinn; three different takes), You Movin' (three different takes), and 'The Airport Song' (a McGuinn–Crosby creation sung by David, arranged with jazzy major seventh chords and a wailing harmonica).

Lastly, the reels of tape contain Bob Dylan's 'Mr. Tambourine Man'. Unlike the other tracks in this batch, 'Mr. Tambourine Man' is not an improvement on the acoustic version that The Jet Set did earlier. The marching rhythm sounds stiff, while the vocal arrangement requires further polish.

Dean Webb of The Dillards plays a role here, as he recounts to Richie Unterberger. "I was driving by World Pacific Studios, and I happened to see Dickson's old Volkswagen sitting there. I stopped by to see what was going on. I go in there, and they're working on 'Mr. Tambourine Man', and they couldn't seem to get anything going. ... So Dickson asked me what I would do with it, as far as harmony was concerned. I said, 'OK. Leave the lead singer in there,' which happened to be McGuinn. The other guys go out of the room. I sang the first part of harmony, or the tenor part, and then they played the tape back, and I put the baritone part on the tape, and then they learned the parts from what I did, triad harmonies, the way possibly we would have done it. And it worked for 'em."

(It should be noted that a non-vocal backing track to 'The Times They Are A-Changin', claimed to be from the same sessions and repackaged by Sundazed Records in 2001, is in fact a backing track for a September 1965 television appearance. This inclusion suggests that some of the electrified tracks with all five Byrds said to be from World Pacific in 1964 may cerainly be rehearsal outtakes from 1965.)

•

Armed with demo tapes, Jim Dickson sets his sights higher than the relatively small Elektra label. He wants interest from a big label – and finally succeeds through an unlikely connection. "I was going around to all these shows that were popping up, trying to get The Byrds on them," he writes in Crosby's memoirs.

"Benny [Shapiro, Miles Davis's manager] had this big cathedral-ceiling living room. He didn't know what to make of [the demos]. He never knew unless somebody told him, anyway. … But Michelle, his daughter, who was about 11 at the time, was upstairs. She heard these voices coming up, they sounded like The Beatles to her, so she came running downstairs, all excited.

"The next morning Miles Davis was over for breakfast, and Benny told him: 'I don't know what to do. Dickson's got these kids and my daughter thinks they're hot stuff.' Now, I'd done 15 shows for Miles, live shows with Oscar Brown Jr., so I guess he remembered me. Miles called Irving Townsend at CBS Records. Irving had been kicked upstairs and out to the West Coast, and all he was recording was the Air Force Band and stuff like that in CBS's one big studio. He calls the head of A&R for CBS/Columbia and [says], 'Give these kids a chance.' So they arranged an audition. So, indirectly, you can it was Miles Davis who got The Byrds started."

It sounds deceptively simple. But,

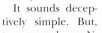
COLUMBIA

true enough, on November 10, McGuinn, Clark, and Crosby sign a recording contract with Columbia. At this stage, the contract is restricted to just two singles (or 'four sides' in record contract parlance) with an option to extend the terms to a five-year contract should The Jet Set succeed. Neither Chris Hillman nor Michael Clarke are part of the contractual obligations.

November 26, 1964

Thanksgiving '64

On November 26, the group has Thanksgiving dinner at Ed Tickner's home. Conversation drifts to the group's name. Nobody seems to be enamoured of The Jet Set, and according to legend it is Gene Clark who sets the ball rolling when he suggests Birdses, as in the song by Dino Valenti.

"I remember you saying, 'How about Birds?' McGuinn says to Tickner in a later interview with music journalist Ed Ward. "I have a very strong audio-visual memory of that. … You said Birds, and I said, 'No, that's English slang for girls, and we don't want them to think we're a bunch of fags, right?' So you said, 'What if we changed the spelling to B-u-r-d-s? And I said, 'Yecchh'. And we got around to **BYRDS**, somehow." The name quickly finds favour with the group, and everybody likes the fact that it begins with the magic 'B', as in Beach Boys and Beatles. The 'y' makes all the difference – with a stroke, the name conjures up visions of aviation and power.

The newly christened group reportedly make a couple of unannounced appearances at L.A.'s Troubadour at the end of 1964, but their energies are in the main spent rehearsing and recording. Jim Dickson persuades some illustrious friends to drop by while The Byrds hone their act. In his book, David Crosby will recall one early visitor. "The arrival of the foremost cosmic mind of our generation had truly awed us. Lenny Bruce came with an entourage and was gracious, kind, and enthusiastic about what he heard. To us scruffy singer types he was like a prince from another land."

Despite the rosy prospects, Chris Hillman still keeps a foot in the folk and hootenanny camp and accepts an invitation to join The Green Grass Group. It is Randy Sparks's latest invention, to follow in the footsteps of The New Christy Minstrels and The Back Porch Majority. Little is known of this group, save that it never matches the success of Sparks's other troupes. McGuinn refers to the group as a "horrible, watered-down, Disneyland kind of version of bluegrass" in an interview with Vincent Flanders, adding: "Chris was just in it for a steady $100 a week and all the beer you could drink at the club or whatever."

Green Grass possibly makes its debut at Ledbetter's in Westwood, CA, on December 3, for a short residence with Randy Sterling and John Denver – both of whom are folk singers in Sparks's stable. "The Green Grass Group will continue with a host of newly researched folk tunes," reports small-town newspaper *The*

Van Nuys News (December 4). Larry Murray is another member of the group, and he will stay behind. But Hillman seems to get out as soon as possible, and by spring next year only Murray remains.

Speaking of his short time with that outfit, Hillman will tell Richie Unterberger: "You know the story of Randy Sparks … where Randy was incensed that Columbia had even signed us, and called up [President of Columbia Records] Goddard Lieberson and was demanding that [The Byrds] be thrown off the label and all of that. … Gene had been in the Christy Minstrels. And I had worked in a sub-band [Sparks] had called The Green Grass Group, which was just awful. I was so poor, I needed to do that. So I did that for a while, but it was just awful."

5-STRING BANJO GREATS
THERE'S A MEETING HERE TONIGHT ♦ GREENBACK DOLLAR
LITTLE BOXES ♦ RED APPLE JUICE ♦ MOVIN' DOWN THE LINE
CRIPPLE CREEK ♦ BANJO WORKOUT ♦ OLD JOE CLARK
HOOKA TOOKA ♦ MILLER'S CAVE ♦ AND SIX OTHERS
Featuring Ten of the Greatest Five-String Banjo Players

(Also at the tail end of 1964, Jim McGuinn is heard as one of eight featured performers on the album *5-String Banjo Greats* (Liberty LST-7357). He plays 'Banjo Cantata', a number where he adopts a Bach motif, to which he will return at a later date.)

As November turns to December, Bob Dylan is on tour in California. He plays up north in San Jose and San Francisco before moving down to the L.A. area, with concerts in San Mateo (December 1), San Diego, Huntingdon, and Los Angeles (December 4–6).

Possibly, it is at this time that Dylan calls at World Pacific to hear The Byrds perform 'Mr. Tambourine Man' (Jim Dickson will suggest later that it takes place earlier in the fall; Jim McGuinn remembers it as January '65). Visiting England next year, McGuinn will recapture the moment for Peter Jones of *Record Mirror* (August 7 1965). "Bob Dylan flew in from New York, got to Los Angeles airport, and rang up our manager [Dickson] to ask what was happening. What was happening was that we were rehearsing 'Mr. Tambourine Man'. And Bob turned up to hear us go through it maybe a dozen times. So Bob eventually said: 'They do it well.' Which is like a million-word work of praise coming from him."

The Byrds record **Bob Dylan's 'Mr. Tambourine Man'** in January. Released as a single in the US in April and in the UK in May it will sound the onset of folk-rock. The group's appearances at Ciro's Le Disc brings a new lease of life to the Hollywood music scene, as 'Mr. Tambourine Man' ascends to the top of first the US charts and then the UK charts. In May, The Byrds open for

1965

The Rolling Stones around California, before they embark on a gruelling tour of Britain – the group's cool California stance does not sit well with the British press, and reviews are pitiful. The Byrds hang out with **The Beatles** in London and then Los Angeles. The group joins a **Dick Clark Caravan of Stars** tour for the whole of November, before they cap the year with a second US chart-topper with the majestic **'Turn! Turn! Turn!'**.

January

As the New Year dawns in Los Angeles, The Byrds – Gene Clark, Michael Clarke, David Crosby, Chris Hillman, and Jim McGuinn – pick up their regular working pattern from before Christmas, preparing for their recording debut and public debut. As the band, newly signed to Columbia Records, stake their future on the unknown Bob Dylan composition 'Mr. Tambourine Man', managers Jim Dickson and Ed Tickner plot their strategy. An image has to be developed, and their ability to perform in front of an audience requires polishing.

The *Billboard* Hot 100 for the first week of January 1965 still reverberates from the sudden arrival last year of British acts in the singles charts. The Beatles are at the top with 'I Feel Fine' – their sixth US Number One. Crowing for attention in the Top Ten are records by Petula Clark ('Downtown'), The Zombies ('She's Not There'), and The Searchers ('Love Potion Number Nine'), while the USA is represented by the Detroit sound of The Supremes, pop crooner Bobby Vinton, and blue-eyed soul duo The Righteous Brothers. The regional pop charts in California largely follow the national trends, although certain singles – such as The Detergents' silly send-up 'Leader Of The Laundromat' and Travis Wammack's guitar instrumental 'Scratchy' – manage to break out locally this month.

The city of Los Angeles is a hub of cultural activity. Movie people, artists, actors, radicals, beatniks, designers, and writers all work in an intensely creative environment. Hollywood enjoys a thriving music scene: many of the US pop television shows are broadcast from here, and some of the largest corporations and best studios in the American recording industry are located here. The Beach Boys may be the biggest group to come out of Los Angeles, but there is an undergrowth of local garage bands, pop singers, guitar combos, teen stars, surf rockers, jazz groups, folkniks, and hootenanny singers. All of them are vying for attention.

When night descends on the city, the many clubs and restaurants dotted around Hollywood and the suburbs of Los Angeles spring to life. The more adult crowd prefer the classy clubs where the patrons are still exhorted to dance the Watusi and the Twist, while the younger generation has a multitude of choices: from Cinnamon Cinder to the New Balladeer, from the Red Velvet to Gazzarri's and the Whisky A Go Go on Sunset Boulevard, to name but a few.

Friday 15
ALSO ...

Over in New York, Bob Dylan and producer Tom Wilson enjoy a particular productive day in the studio. After recording 'On The Road Again' with a full band, Dylan alone tapes three superlative songs in quick succession: 'It's Alright, Ma (I'm Only Bleeding)', 'Gates Of Eden', and a new version of 'Mr. Tambourine Man' – all to be included on the album *Bringing It All Back Home*, which will be released in the USA on March 22 1965. Although Top Ten success has so far eluded Dylan's own records, 'Blowin' In The Wind' was a smash hit for folk trio Peter Paul & Mary in 1963.

Wednesday 20

🔊 **RECORDING** Columbia Recording Studios, Studio A, Sunset and El Centro, Hollywood, CA. 10:00am–1:00pm. Producer Terry Melcher and engineer Ray Gerhardt.

For The Byrds all-important first session for Columbia Records, Terry Melcher is assigned the producer's job. The son of actress and singer Doris Day, 23-year-old Melcher has recently joined Columbia as a staff producer. Together with Bruce Johnston, Melcher has scored a few US hit singles, as Bruce & Terry and as The Rip Chords. The choice of Melcher proves a good one for now. As a young man he connects well with The Byrds, and while his family ties ensure him power, his sympathetic and confident role as a producer is crucial in creating results.

Jim Dickson later tells David Crosby biographer Carl Gottlieb: "Terry had pull because his mother owned a lot of stock in CBS. Hell, she practically owned the company ... And whatever Terry wanted to do at Columbia Records, he got to do. Luckily, he wanted to do The Byrds."

A decision has been reached to call in experienced session musicians to make sure the session runs smoothly. Not only are there doubts about The Byrds' performing abilities, but the initial recording contract with Columbia Records extends only to singers McGuinn, Clark, and Crosby. So, on this January morning, Leon Russell (electric piano), Bill Pittman and Jerry Cole (guitars), Larry Knechtel (bass guitar), and Hal Blaine (drums) assemble at the large Columbia Studio A, with Jim McGuinn the only Byrd allowed in the studio with an instrument.

Although not a seasoned pro behind the console, Melcher guides the session musicians assuredly through 22 takes of 'Mr. Tambourine Man' before he is satisfied. McGuinn sings in what he describes as a voice 'halfway between Dylan and Lennon', while Clark and Crosby add the distinctive harmony arrangement crafted with the help of Dean Webb a few weeks ago. The Byrds have trimmed Dylan's song and tossed out two verses, leaving only a chorus–verse–chorus structure for their single-friendly electric poetry. The studio musicians embellish McGuinn's instrumental arrangement expertly, with Larry Knechtel's introductory swooping bass line providing an instant hook. Above the sparse backing – Russell's piano is eventually mixed out and the supporting guitarists are barely audible – McGuinn's 12-string guitar chimes out like an electronic harpsichord.

Asked many years later about how he conceived the 'jingle jangle sound', McGuinn will explain to Andy Ellis in *Guitar Player*: "The Rick[enbacker 12-string guitar] by itself is kind of thuddy. It doesn't ring. But if you add a compressor, you get that long sustain. To be honest, I found this by accident. The engineer, Ray Gerhardt, would run compressors on everything to protect his precious equipment from loud rock'n'roll. He compressed the heck out of my 12-string ... that's how I got my jingle-jangle tone. It's really squashed down, but it jumps out from the radio." McGuinn will say on another occasion that using an Epiphone amplifier enhanced the special sound on this recording. Another key component is the arrangement of the strings on the Rickenbacker, as McGuinn will tell Ellis. "The pairs are reversed, compared to typical 12-string guitars, [on the Rickenbacker having] the high octave strings come after the low strings [and that] made for a bigger sound."

Also today, Gene Clark's minor-tinged 6/8 shuffle 'I Knew I'd Want You' – one of the many songs they worked on at World Pacific during 1964 – is taped as the proposed B-side to 'Mr. Tambourine Man'.

After today's session, The Byrds will play their own instruments in the studio – when not hiring outside musicians for specific purposes to enhance recordings. But the fact that they do not all perform on this, their initial studio foray will cause doubts and suspicions about the group's musical abilities for many years to come.

•

William Claxton, a highly regarded photographer known for his black-and-white portraits of jazz musicians, by chance portrays the early Byrds. A rare photo of the group, taken at World Pacific with long-limbed models showing off the latest fashions, runs in *Cosmopolitan* (March 1965). Shown the photo years later, McGuinn tells journalist Ed Ward: "That was the first photograph we had taken as a group. It was for *Cosmopolitan*, with [fashion designer] Rudi Gernreich. They'd called up World Pacific looking for a jazz group, but no

February

'Howdy Hop', Ingalls Auditorium, East Los Angeles College (ELAC), Los Angeles, CA

By all accounts, this is the proper live debut of The Byrds. Jim Dickson's aspirations for his protégés are clear: at this early stage in their career, the group are already being touted as the remedy to the British Invasion. "The Byrds, US answer to The Beatles, will play on ELAC's stage tomorrow at 11:00am in Ingalls Auditorium," says the *ELAC Campus News* on the day before the concert. "The first College

jazz groups were available, and so they said, 'How about a rock group?' and it must have been OK."

Hour of the semester, a combination orientation–entertainment hour, will be followed by a dance on the auditorium stage to the music of a mop-haired quintet from the Hollywood Hills called The Byrds. In light of the group's youth, physical and organizational, it is nevertheless made up of a number of veterans from famous rock'n'roll and folk music groups."

The *News* adds that McGuinn is the leader of the group, as well as lead guitarist and lead singer. "The group's first record, to be released in about three weeks, is patterned after the Beatle-beat type of song and is given a folk music touch. The Byrds could not divulge the title of the song yet, but their manager, Jim [Dickson], stated that their performance at tomorrow's College hour will feature sounds similar to their singing." The paper prints what will turn out to be the first published photo of The Byrds, an amateurish group portrait.

A few days later, the same college paper prints the first ever review of a Byrds performance, under the headline 'Birdmania a Hit at Hour'. The reporter writes: "The Byrds received an outstanding reception by the Elac crowd, as did the 'Magic Dolls' [a pantomime act]. ... The 'Beatle-haired' singers played for the Howdy Hop which followed in the Student Center. This dance gave students the chance to get acquainted with each other. An overflow crowd poured onto the dance floor to show approval of the new singing group."

Despite Dickson's reluctance to give away the song title of the group's debut single before the show, the college paper can now reveal it. "Planned in the future for The Byrds is a new recording to be released shortly through Columbia, title 'Mr. Tambourine Man'. As soon as this recording is released the group is scheduled to appear on several television shows, including *Shindig*, *Hullabaloo*, and others."

Jim Dickson writes later in David Crosby's autobiography: "The Byrds' first public gig was booked by Lenny Bruce's mother, Sally Marr. She got them a job at Los Angeles City College, noon assembly, for a half hour, in the yard with nothing but their own equipment – so for a sound system they had to sing through their new guitar amplifiers. It was their first paid job, 50 bucks for all five of them, and happy to get it. Ten bucks a piece: boy! That's a week of cheeseburgers."

•

Following the successful concert at East Los Angeles College, the group attempts a couple of other live performances, with less enthusiasm. Although the exact locations and dates are lost in the mists of time, an appearance at a bowling alley in Los Angeles leaves a lasting impression on McGuinn, as he will recount later to British music journalist Pete Frame. "It was awful. I think there were about 20 people scattered around a room that held a hundred, with their cocktails in their hands, totally apathetic, all looking at the floor. We'd had two sets of suits, which were both stolen, so we started wearing blue jeans, which stayed. Anyway, we played to these mannequins with their martinis, and the bowling pins were going smash as we sang."

David Crosby is booked to play three nights at a folk club in West Los Angeles called The New Balladeer.

Although The Byrds are readying for take off, it is soon apparent that Columbia is hesitant to release 'Mr. Tambourine Man' as quickly as the group hoped. They have no regular cash flow, so Crosby's solo appearances are probably a necessity (he plays further engagements at the New Balladeer on

The Byrds minus Crosby pose for *Cosmopolitan*, March 1965 issue. From left: Gene Clark, Chris Hillman (with Japanese bass guitar), unknown model, Jim McGuinn, and Michael Clarke.

February 12–14, 19–21, and 26–28, and then on March 5–7 and 12–14 and 19–21, although the last trio of dates may be cancelled). Loyalty wavers now as McGuinn briefly entertains an option offered by folk singer Dino Valenti. The temptation seems to be rooted more in McGuinn's interest in technology than a chance to play with the volatile Valenti. "He had this great idea for a group," McGuinn tells *Zigzag*. "He had designed costumes with radio transmitters built into the jackets, a place in your belt buckle to plug into your guitar, and it was a workable idea. … But in the end, I decided not to go along with him."

•

With the group signed to Columbia Records, the doors to World Pacific Studios are probably barred to them, and they have to look elsewhere for a rehearsal facility. Around this time, sculptor Vito Paulekas opens his art studio Clay Vito at 303 North Laurel Avenue in West Hollywood to The Byrds. Here they rehearse – and sometimes sleep – in the early weeks of 1965. Otherwise, the group live in squalid quarters. Music journalist John Trubee later interviews one of Vito's circle, who says: "They were living in a cold-water pad, never had anything to eat. Girls might bring them a package of food or something out of a fast food place, something like that … [The pad] was on the fringe of Beverly Hills and Hollywood, it was right off of Doheny [Drive] somewhere. And they were living over a garage. They didn't have any hot water in that place. McGuinn and David Crosby didn't live there – the other three lived there. So they were poor guys and they didn't have shit."

Friday 19

Publicist and Beatle-friend Derek Taylor takes up the lease on a house on Nichols Canyon Road in West Hollywood today. He has just arrived in Los Angeles from his native Britain and, besides getting his American start with clients such as Paul Revere & The Raiders and San Francisco's The Beau Brummels at Prestige Promotions, Taylor's curiosity is aroused when he comes across The Byrds.

He recounts in the British *Melody Maker* (July 17): "For me, it all started a couple of days after I arrived in Hollywood, when [cameraman Ron Joy, whom] I had met on the [US] Beatle tour, sauntered into my then uncluttered office and dropped a couple of pictures causally on my desk. 'There's a group here you may like to look at,' he said. 'They're called The Byrds. They may be lousy for all I know.' I had come to California to work on salary and percentage as a press agent. I had two clients. All long–haired. So here was a third. Nothing was known about them. They hadn't performed together in public

as a group. They hadn't released a record. They weren't good-looking. And they had no money at all. Very promising.

"However, I called their manager and he came into the office," says Taylor. "His name was Jim Dickson, a roly-poly man, prematurely bald, who had been an A&R man for folk singers. He had a kind smile and gentle eyes and he looked honest. Which is something in Hollywood. He, too, was broke. But, he said, The Byrds were pretty good and Columbia Records had recorded them. … He had a copy of it in an envelope and he played it to me. Bob Dylan, he explained, had written the song and had approved The Byrds' version. I said: 'I think it's a hit.' And he said 'We think so, too.'"

•

Jim Dickson assigns photographer Guy Webster to take some high-quality photos of The Byrds for promotional use. One of the shots is a classic study of the five boys smartly dressed in matching suits, with their hands cleverly arranged against a stark background (resembling Robert Freeman's hip jacket for the US album *Meet The Beatles*). A minor detail of the group's look has been adjusted, as Chris Hillman's natural curly hair has been straggled straight to give him the proper pop-star appearance. The photo will be published for the first time when The Byrds are booked for their initial club engagements next month.

March

Monday 8

🔊 **RECORDING** Columbia Recording Studios, Studio A, Sunset and El Centro, Hollywood, CA. Producer Terry Melcher and probably engineer Ray Gerhardt.

The Byrds spend a day at Columbia, and this time they are on their own, without the support of any session musicians. But as with the January session, the group concentrate on a Bob Dylan composition and a Gene Clark number. They also find time to try out two further songs. Of today's work, only Dylan's 'All I Really Want To Do' will be released this year. Originally heard as the waltz-time opening number on *Another Side Of Bob Dylan* last year (Dylan taped it the same day he recorded the initial attempt of 'Mr. Tambourine Man'), McGuinn now uses his arranging skills to change the tempo of Dylan's take to a more commercial 4/4. Two alternative versions are completed: one in mono will later be released as a single, while the slightly drier stereo version will be reserved for The Byrds' debut album.

The group try out Gene Clark's 'She Has A Way', one of the numbers demoed at World Pacific recently, but it's ultimately rejected – perhaps because the instrumental backing sounds tentative. McGuinn and Clark's Beatle pastiche 'It's No Use' is also recorded, but it will be re-recorded next month. Lastly, the group attempts the hook-laden 'You And Me'. The song, copyrighted by McGuinn, Clark, and Crosby, is missing a vocal track and will languish in the Columbia vaults until released on an expanded CD reissue of the group's debut in the 1990s, an album that also contains the other songs recorded today.

➔ Early March
Jack Tar Motel, San Francisco, CA

Speaking to Ben Fong-Torres in 1970, David Crosby talks about an early out-of-town trip for The Byrds. "The first place we ever played and pleased anybody was [in] San Francisco, at The Jack Tar Motel. There were about 200 little girls who were there for *Teen Screen*, 16; you know, one of those … We played three songs. They loved it. That's cos we got all the way through without dropping the guitars. Actually, we cooked. It was the first time we ever cooked. When we came off stage we nearly thought we would fall down. It was great." Unfortunately, the group's car is robbed of amplifiers and their matching suede suits. The latter may be for the good anyway as, bereft of suits, the group from now on just wear their casual gear on stage.

➔ Saturday 20
Unknown venue, Melrose Avenue, Los Angeles, CA

The United States' presence in Vietnam has slowly escalated since the late 50s, its role changed from military and strategic advisor to full-blown military intruder. Just this year, warfare increases dramatically when President Lyndon B Johnson sanctions a bombing offensive, dubbed Operation Rolling Thunder, in an attempt to force North Vietnam to halt guerrilla warfare in the South. Opposition to the American involvement in Vietnam is scattered and mostly confined to college campuses across the USA, but as warfare steps up so does the opposition.

A local anti-war demonstration is held on Melrose Avenue now, and needing a band to provide some music, Vito Paulekas hires The Byrds. Confusion reigns as to the exact date – the demonstration is not worthy of coverage in the Los Angeles press – but presumably it takes place today. Carl Orestes Franzoni, avant-garde dancer, self-proclaimed freak, and close friend of Paulekas, recalls in an interview with music journalist John Trubee: "What happened was somebody told us that

➔ An arrow denotes an estimated date.

[The Byrds] wanted an audition, so Vito said, 'Yeah, I'll give you an audition. Come over to my place after dinner.' They had gone to San Francisco and had all of their equipment stolen … out of their station wagon, which was parked out in front of the club. Not only did they have their stuff stolen but also they had their tires stolen off the station wagon. They came out and there was nothing there. The thieves had ripped that thing to shreds.

"So [Vito] told them to come, but what happened was the first time they had an audition they didn't show up. So one of the guys in our group had heard them before – we went over to their house and he just ate their asses out. … So the next time they came, and Vito hired them, and he had a place for them to play. He rented this place on Melrose Avenue, upstairs, and it was like a church. … It was a big hall. It would fit 300 people. He sold tickets for $1.50 – packed house. When you walked into this room with The Byrds, there was another band there, the opening band – I don't know who it was, nobody I remember. All over the walls were anti-war Vietnam signs … maybe 25 to 35 signs all over the wall. … The next night, The Byrds' managers asked us, 'Would you come to this place on Sunset Boulevard and do your dancing there?'"

Also today, *Billboard* tells its readers about Columbia Records' new signing, The Byrds, and their imminent single debut, 'Mr. Tambourine Man'.

Sunday 21–Saturday 27
Ciro's Le Disc, Hollywood, CA

The Byrds make their club debut when they are booked for a trial run at this venerable old venue at 8433 Sunset Boulevard in Hollywood – a residence that will give Ciro's its last fling as the most glamorous of all Hollywood clubs while catapulting The Byrds to the forefront of a rejuvenated California music scene. The group are booked at Ciro's as a favour by Frank Sennes Jr, whose father owns the club. The club's Early Bird Delight menu is renamed Early Byrd Delight for the occasion and sells for $4.95. The price covers admission, dinner, and two drinks.

Ciro's has a long and chequered history from when it opened its doors way back in January 1940 with an elegant style and décor inspired by similarly named clubs in London and Paris. It soon became a hot spot for Hollywood movie stars and celebrities – Judy Garland celebrated her 18th birthday here in June 1940 – and lucky patrons could chance upon Marlene Dietrich, Charlie Chaplin, Spencer Tracy, Errol Flynn, or Frank Sinatra during the 40s and 50s. Gossip columnist Lucius Beebe compared the club's swashbuckling atmosphere to "Morocco, the Stork Club, and

Monte Carlo all rolled in one," but proprietor Herman Hover has to follow the latest trends – be it boxing matches or monkey acts – as in tougher times the club struggles to keep afloat.

In August 1958, Hover files for bankruptcy, but he manages to reopen Ciro's on New Year's Eve '58/'59 as a private club. In February 1961, Hover sells the club to impresario Frank Sennes (owner of the nearby Moulin Rouge club), who restyles Ciro's as Le Crazy Horse in an attempt to update its image. Despite staging The World's Twist Championship Contest and other stunts to pull patrons, business falters. So, in the summer of 1962, Sennes resurrects the original name. Then, on May 6 1964, comes the latest change as Ciro's adds Le *Disc* to the name, tempting clubgoers with a combination of entertainment and record spinning. Opening night has San Francisco's George & Teddy & The Condors, two black singers backed by an all-white group.

For the niteries on Sunset Strip, the times are changing. By 1965, traditional nightclubs are losing out to the new in-clubs. Pasadena Star News (February 20) explains the situation. "[It is] the new, casual style of the clubs, where the young – rather than the old-fashioned big-time spenders – set the pattern. Here on the Strip, for instance, while the Crescendo fights for business, the Whisky A Go Go, which gives one the feeling of Dante's Inferno, is jammed night after night. A big beat wailer named Johnny Rivers is the sort of modern star who draws here. … The signs are clear as neon here on the strip. The famous old Ciro's is now called Le *Disc* and features sideburns types in its elegant room. And Frank Sennes Jr, who was looking after the place for his well-known father the other night, did not appear ecstatic over the situation."

March has so far been a lively month at Ciro's. Two weeks of The Ike & Tina Turner Revue plus appearances by The Nooney Rickett IV are followed by a weekend show on March 19–20 by Little Richard – whose backing band hides the unknown Jimi Hendrix – before The Byrds open on March 21. It's a struggle for any act to get noticed in the competing Hollywood nightclubs. Just one of the many craving for attention in the coming week is The Kentucky Colonels, starring fleet-fingered bluegrass guitarist Clarence White, whose band are holding down a residence at the Ash Grove on Melrose Avenue.

The Byrds begin tentatively, as Jim McGuinn recalls to *Record Mirror* (August 7): "Lousy opening … We got no balance, sounded like a gang of roustabouts with no musical sense coming out of it all. We'd never faced an audience and felt like we wanted the floor to open up under us. We didn't even work too well together, cos we were too worried about whether anything else could possibly go wrong."

This view is shared by Derek Taylor in *Melody Maker* (August 7): "The fivesome were due to make their first public appearance for £10 [about $28] at Ciro's, a large, unfashionable club on Sunset Strip. It was the haunt of Errol Flynn and Humphrey Bogart in their brawling prime, and of Van Johnson and Cary Grant and a thousand glamorous ghosts. So I went to see The Byrds. Collectively, they had never faced an audience and they were shy, ill at ease, and not at all a unit. Yet something was happening on stage. It was something over and above normal rock experience. I offered to represent them for a few dollars a week just for the hell of it."

There is some tension because Chris Hillman and Michael Clarke gripe about the fact that they are not under contract, and there are arguments for a change of musical direction. ("Can you imagine The Byrds playing blues?" sighs manager Jim Dickson to author Carl Gottlieb.)

The five have chosen classy musical instruments to go with their stage act. Jim McGuinn plays the Rickenbacker 360/12 model he purchased last year. Chris Hillman picks a Fender Precision bass and Mike Clarke sits behind a Ringo-like Ludwig drum kit. David Crosby fingers the Gretsch Tennessean he has snatched from Gene Clark – while Clark himself hits a tambourine and plays a bit of harmonica. The group uses Fender amplification: Hillman a blonde Bassman amp with separate speaker cabinet, Crosby presumably a Fender Twin Reverb. McGuinn's type of amplifier is not known, though he most likely uses a Fender combo amp as he will later in the year.

With a front line of three extraordinary singers who easily alternate between singing lead and harmony, The Byrds have a vocal blend that can match the best of California Surf and Mersey Beat.

Reviewing the opening show, *The Daily Variety* (March 23) says: "At last, a rock'n'roll group that's considerate of the listener as well as the gyrating, beat-happy terper [*Variety* slang for dancer] who couldn't care less about a lyric! True, it's another long-locked, turtle-necked fivesome physically resembling sundry deportees from Liverpool – but that's where the similarity stops. Recently inked by Columbia Records, the five all-American-type lads [are] four converts from the folk-tunery circuit, where material is all-important. … Guitar breaks are just that: instrumentalising is kept subordinate to vocal work when the group is singing – as it should be. … Though opening night [Sunday] audience was small, biz should perk once word is out that The Byrds, in for a week, are in flight." (Omitting the last paragraph, the review is reprinted in the weekly *Variety* (March 31).)

The review lists many of the songs performed in the group's 40-minute set: Jackie DeShannon's 'When You Walk In The Room' has been a recent Top 40 US hit by UK group The Searchers, while, surprisingly, the group also performs two out-and-out blues numbers: Muddy Waters's 'Got My Mojo Working' plus Jimmy Reed's 'Baby What You Want Me To Do' – a cover that The Byrds will retain in their live act right up to 1973. Then there is Bob Dylan's 'All I Really Want To Do', while the Gene Clark numbers mentioned are given wrong titles: 'Movin' You' (which is 'You Movin") and 'Too Many Things I Don't Know' ('I Knew I'd Want You').

Required to pound out party-friendly music, The Byrds stock their repertoire with several cover songs, of which most will disappear from their act within months and never be performed again. Interviewed by music historian Richie Unterberger many years later, Chris Hillman offers some surprising insight. "It was '65, and a couple months away from 'Mr. Tambourine Man' going out. We were doing all kinds of things in our shows. We were doing a Stones cover here and there, [The Beatles'] 'Things We Said Today', we did [Tamla Motown number] 'Money', just stuff like that. 'Maggie's Farm'. In fact, I think I sang 'Maggie's Farm', which was a real coup, cos I was so shy. I mean, I always just didn't know what the heck this stuff was yet. It took me a year to figure it all out. I just sort of stayed back there and played." Writing for the specialist magazine *Musician* in the early 90s, journalist Jon Young says The Byrds would copy British Invasion material such as 'Tired Of Waiting' (The Kinks) and 'She's Not There' (The Zombies). Another number covered during the early days is 'Sweet Abilene' – presumably Buck Owens' 'Abilene' – which Gene sings. (In addition, The Byrds perform live all of the songs that wind up on their debut album released in June.)

•

Crucial to The Byrds' success at Ciro's is a dance-happy crowd that becomes an attraction in itself. A loosely organised dance troupe with roots in the milieu around Vito Paulekas and led by the magnetic Carl Franzoni ("wild black hair sprouting like corkscrews from his enormous domed head" according to Derek Taylor), the dancers are there right at the beginning.

"The next night [after the anti-war demonstration on Melrose Avenue] was their first night at Ciro's," Franzoni later tells Efram Turchick. "We walk in this place, it's a totally red room, lots of light, the best dance floor in Hollywood; it's about 40 feet by 60 feet, all the stars in Hollywood are there. These guys have never played for them before. We stepped on the dance floor, and from then on it was music and dance for months and months! All right! We were there at the start, maybe 15 of us, coming from this other dance the night before, or maybe a couple nights before. They just pushed us in there, we never paid [to get in]. They said, 'Come in, just come in.' We were famous otherwise for dancing to other groups, like The Gauchos from Fresno. The Gauchos had horns and everything in their band; they were like a Top 40 band and played near Ciro's at another place. We would go back and forth to Ciro's, and sometimes they wouldn't even let us in because the place was so crowded.

"My favourite Byrd was Chris [Hillman]. You know, when you're on the dance floor and you look up and you make contact with whoever it is, I always made contact with the bass player. I could talk to Chris about what was happening. David [Crosby] was cantankerous, but you knew that there was a fine artist there.

"The Byrds were, in my estimation, the best dance band that Hollywood ever saw," says Franzoni. "They made people dance with that kind of music. Those guys were forever fighting with each other, but when they got up there they really cooked. … You never had to do an improvisation for The Byrds, because they were so miraculous: the combination of men, the different factions of what kind of music they came from; it just was such a fantastic blend. I always think of dancing to 'Bells Of Rhymney' and like, it's a church, you know? … They could have started their own church with that kind of music they were playing. That 12-string guitar really worked good."

Writer Trina Robbins recalls: "We caught The Byrds' second ever performance at Ciro's, but Vito and his crew were already there. We stayed to talk and became fast friends – especially with David. We discovered that we all loved science-fiction writer Ted Sturgeon and, in fact, they used the term 'blesh' – a combination of blend and mesh from Sturgeon's *More Than Human* – to describe how they worked together as a group. I think after that we went to Ciro's every night when The Byrds were there. The club itself was dim with two levels, a bar in the back, then tables and chairs, some stairs but not a steep staircase. Then the dance floor, which in the beginning also had tables and chairs, but at a certain point there were too many people dancing, so they removed the tables and chairs. A raised stage, but not too high, for The Byrds or whomever was playing. The club had an 18-year age limit."

Friday 26
Ciro's Le Disc, Hollywood, CA
Bob Dylan – who flew in from Pittsburgh, PA, on Wednesday – meets the Hollywood press today as the first stop of a short West Coast tour due to begin tomorrow night with an appearance in Santa Monica. The Byrds, labelmates of Dylan at Columbia, are invited along. Trina Robbins and her husband, writer Paul Jay Robbins, stand out in the crowd. "It was their PR guy, Billy James, who managed to get us invited into Dylan's press conference," says Trina, "which was filled with guys in suits with short hair, except for me and my husband: him in a shirt I had made him and me in a velvet mini suit. So Dylan came over to me and started a conversation, which led to my husband interviewing him." After the press reception, Dylan and entourage visit Ciro's to hear The Byrds.

1965

April

Trina remembers Dylan at Ciro's. "He simply came there when he was in town, always with Bobby Neuwirth. One outfit I made and wore was a white pantsuit, very prim in front, but open to the waist in back – quite shocking for those days – and I remember Neuwirth dancing with me, arranging it so that my back was to Bob Dylan in order to freak him out."

Dylan steps on stage briefly with The Byrds to blow a bit of harmonica on the Jimmy Reed tune 'Baby, What You Want Me To Do'. Jim Dickson takes what will become a well-known photo of Dylan onstage with The Byrds, with an almost studied feel as if it is arranged and not caught mid-performance. Surprisingly, no contemporary press report of Bob Dylan's night with The Byrds at Ciro's survives.

Paul Jay Robbins interviews Dylan for the weekly radical paper *Los Angeles Free Press*. The interview is not published until September 1965 but marks one of the very few occasions where Dylan chooses to give an opinion of The Byrds. "They're doing something really new now," he says. "It's like a danceable Bach sound. Like 'Bells Of Rhymney'. They're cutting across all kinds of barriers, which most people who sing aren't even hip to. They know it all. If they don't close their minds, they'll come up with something pretty fantastic."

Saturday 27
Ciro's Le Disc, Hollywood, CA
The Byrds end their residence with a Saturday show together with rhythm & blues singer Major Lance. Their success has been overwhelming, and their contract at the club is renewed.

Wednesday 31
Ciro's Le Disc, Hollywood, CA
According to the weekly listings in *Variety*, The Byrds are back at Ciro's.

Thursday 1–Thursday 8
Ciro's Le Disc, Hollywood, CA
The Byrds continue at Ciro's for another week. Tantalisingly, the weekend of April 9–10 stars Little Richard as headliner – again with Jimi Hendrix anonymously blending into the backing band – but The Byrds, although billed, are not there.

Monday 12
The Byrds' first single, 'Mr. Tambourine Man' backed with 'I Knew I'd Want You', is released in the USA.

Surprisingly, considering the efforts Columbia put into promotion, the single is not reviewed by either *Billboard* or *Cash Box*.

The single finds its way to Dylan over in New York, as Bobby Neuwirth recalls in David Crosby's autobiography. "I distinctly remember hearing 'Mr. Tambourine Man' in Albert Grossman's office in New York City. … Bob and I went to the office, cynical as usual, looking forward to reading the fan mail and having great cheeseburgers downstairs on East 55th Street. Somebody said, 'Well, there's this 'Mr. Tambourine Man' record,' and I said, 'Put in on.' It was great, because nobody could figure out how anyone except Peter Paul & Mary could ever cover any of Bob's songs. [The songs] were so unique and forceful that no one could imagine anyone else singing them; they were so dependent on phrasing and inflection. There was this high mountain edge – no one with a commercial sound could get a hold of any of those songs. We heard the record and cracked up, and Bob loved it. Albert wasn't quite that quick to commit, but the upshot was that we thought this was a good idea. We didn't get particularly head-bangingly ecstatic with it, because nobody knew if it has a chance to get on the radio or anything like that, but we were thinking, 'Hey, well, those guys didn't miss the point entirely.'"

Wednesday 14
🔊 **RECORDING** Columbia Recording Studios, Studio A, Sunset and El Centro, Hollywood, CA. Producer Terry Melcher and probably engineer Ray Gerhardt.

The Byrds are back in the studio for the first time in more than a month, and today's recordings show a more confident group, tightened and buoyed by their live performances. 'Spanish Harlem Incident' is the group's third Bob Dylan cover, while 'The Bells Of Rhymney', with Pete Seeger's melody to Welsh poet Idris Davies's ballad, has already proved an unlikely dance floor favourite at

Ciro's – considering its lyric about Welsh miners. Even odder is the group's version of Vera Lynn's World War II anthem 'We'll Meet Again', which they learned from Stanley Kubrick's 1964 movie *Dr. Strangelove*.

Three of the group's original compositions are put on tape, including the Gene Clark/ Jim McGuinn collaborations 'You Won't Have To Cry' (another of the World Pacific demos) and 'It's No Use' (re-recorded after the initial attempt on March 8). The most impressive, however, is Gene Clark's brand new song 'I'll Feel A Whole Lot Better'. It's driven by a guitar riff reminiscent of The Searchers' arrangement of 'Needles And Pins' (a minor US hit by Jackie DeShannon in 1963 and a huge hit for The Searchers in 1964), but the song is proof of Clark's superior songwriting capabilities.

Two other songs are also reputedly recorded today. One is a version of blues composer Willie Dixon's 'I Love The Life I Live (And I Live The Life I Love)'; the other is a group original titled 'Words And Pictures'. Neither survives on tape.

Thursday 15
Not content with the success The Byrds have brought to Ciro's Le Disc, owner Frank Sennes Sr. debuts a dazzling musical revue tonight. Combining new dance fads inspired by TV shows such as *Shindig* and *Hullabaloo*, the show aims to attract the young crowd. Whing-Ding features a cast of 20 dancers led by singer Kelly Garrett, who will perform three times nightly for the next month or so.

→ Friday 16–Sunday 25
Ciro's Le Disc, Hollywood, CA
The Byrds are held over for dancing at Ciro's Le Disc, sharing the bill with the Whing-Ding revue.

The radical music of The Byrds combined with the untamed dancing of Carl Franzo-

---

'Mr. Tambourine Man'

A 'Mr. Tambourine Man'
  (B. DYLAN)
B 'I Knew I'd Want You' (G. CLARK)

US release April 12 1965 (Columbia 43271)
UK release May 15 1965 (CBS 201765)
Chart high US number 1;
UK number 1
Read more … entry for January 20 1965

Bob Dylan and The Byrds in Hollywood, spring 1965.

ni's ensemble continue to blow life into the cobwebbed corners of Ciro's, and the club suddenly finds itself the hip centre of Los Angeles. It is here that The Byrds develop their cool, aloof attitude while playing to a surging dance floor. Stories of The Byrds at Ciro's Le Disc will attain mythic dimensions in hindsight, but few who witness the group during the nights at Ciro's are left unimpressed. Unfortunately, no recordings of The Byrds at Ciro's Le Disc are known to exist.

"Everybody came to Ciro's to see The Byrds," says Trina Robbins, simply. She lists some of the people whom she remembers from the dance floor: "Derek Taylor, Peter Fonda, Kim Fowley, Sonny Bono, Cher, Sue Lyon. Mary of Peter Paul & Mary fame. Barry McGuire, who I danced with. Emerald Thomas, who was then Chris Hillman's girlfriend. I also remember Buffy Sainte-Marie showing up when she was in town, with some gorgeous Native American guy, the two of them looking spectacular on the dance floor in their beaded fringed buckskin."

Jim Dickson tells author Carl Gottlieb: "A whole gang of my contemporaries got on the bandwagon real fast and were wonderfully supportive. Even Lenny Bruce came down to the studio and to Ciro's. There were people we didn't know who helped out, once they saw what was happening. They didn't have to be told … we had them all. We had Jack Nicholson dancing, we had Peter Fonda dancing with Odetta, and we had Vito and his Freakers. … The band had to do five sets a night.

"The first set they'd be like they didn't even remember each other's names, they were so bad. Then they'd get a little warmed up by the second set, but the crowd was with them because everyone would remember they'd been great the night before. About the middle of the third set, there was a Beatles song, and then David would say, 'Me I'm just the lucky kind' [a line in Lennon/McCartney's 'Things We Said Today']. It made you smile, and that was always the kick-off. It was always in the third set that it would start to get good, and by the fourth set David would be out there, grinning like a kid, as if to say, 'Boy, this is such a great party!' And there'd be all these freaks jumping up and down, Vito with his wife nursing her kid on an exposed breast – we made lines in front of Ciro's that hadn't been seen since Peggy Lee played there."

One of David Crosby's other featured numbers at Ciro's is 'Hey Joe', a song that Franzoni favours. "[It was a] favourite of mine because David would sing it with so much gusto and would change the mood. It was just a terrific 'up' tune and great to dance to."

The origins of 'Hey Joe' are complex. Crosby learned the song from Dino Valenti, who may well have got it from Billy Roberts, the song's copyrighted author. Thanks to the excitement that The Byrds create with their live shows, other L.A. groups will quickly pick up on the electrified 'Hey Joe' in the coming months.

Derek Taylor writes in *Melody Maker* (July 17 1965): "The Byrds returned to Ciro's and for the first time in years packed the place. There were queues up and down Sunset Strip of desperate teenagers, clamouring to get in. The dance floor was a madhouse. A hard core of Byrd followers – wayward painters, disinherited sons and heirs, bearded sculptors, misty-eyed nymphs and assorted oddballs – suddenly taught Hollywood to dance again. This was no Shake, Watusi, or Frug session. It was an exercise in Byrdmania. A frenetic expression of the talents of five quite exceptional musicians."

Eddie Tickner will tell Bill Harry in 1967: "The place was packed, and Ciro's holds 400 people! Why the phenomena? Why did an unknown group with no record and no major appearances behind them get such crowds? The Byrds were the catalyst for a new freaky movement that was happening amongst the artists, the poets, and the freaky film people. Some kind of magic happened and for the next ten days of their appearance the streets were lined with people."

Quoted in an article by David Kamp, the group's producer Terry Melcher declares: "The Byrds were the catalyst, they brought all the kids to the Strip. They took the Dylan songs, we electrified 'em and rock'n'rolled 'em, and kids came from everywhere. It just happened. One day you couldn't drive any more. It was, like, overnight, you couldn't drive on the Strip."

Rod McLean Barken, working for Derek Taylor at Prestige Promotions, recaptures the memorable nights many years later. "Ciro's. This faded venue of days long gone to the archives of Hollywood nightlife, a discotheque in its most recent existence, gambled on these five unknowns, gave them a shot. We knew they were good; would the creepy-crawlies of the boulevard, the hirsute and bohemian tribes wandering between San Francisco and the Southland, the jaded groupies that knew the words of every British song and the body parts of every recording artist, accept them?

"By the second week, the crowds came. Standing-room-only, the dancefloor packed with bodies that jumped up and down rather than simply dance. A girl named Brigid and her love-child Godot; Beatle Bob in his raincoat; Vito, the statue maker, and his esoteric band of followers, The Friends of The Hand; Dewey Martin, the drummer from Sir Walter Raleigh & The Coupons, later with Buffalo Springfield; Sonny Bono and his child-bride Cher LaPierre; Tommy Rettig, and a zillion other bit-part actors, believers all."

"It was into this that the Byrds came," CBS publicist Billy James writes later. "Mike Clarke, who was only 17 and everyone knew it but he played in the club anyway, [had] carefully curled-to-straight hair and a Californian coastal grin. Gene Clark with the voice of an angel, wearing sports jacket and Beatle boots; same with McGuinn and Chris Hillman. And David Crosby, with his hair set on his head like a wig hat, and his shirt from deVoss, with sleeves puffed at the shoulder and fitting the body at no point particular. Despite all their attempts on their parts to fit into the mod London/Liverpool look, they were just what we needed – truly American; absurdly Californian, almost painfully Californian." (James's liner notes to the first Byrds album will tip the hat to further names in the Ciro's crowd: folk singer Judy Henske; actor Michael J. Pollard; bikini-movie starlet Mary Hughes.)

To many up and coming musicians, seeing The Byrds creates memories for life. "The night The Byrds opened at Ciro's man, in '65, I knew right away." So says Skip Battin in a 1971 interview. "I wanted to tear off my clothes and grow my hair long. If you're not from L.A. you can't understand what The Byrds did to musicians there. They made everyone crazy." Then there is Arthur Lee in '65, looking for a vision when he chances upon The Byrds. He recalls to *Boston Fusion* (June 3, 1970): "The Byrds made Ciro's … I saw The Byrds and they really flipped me out. Because their music really hit my heart. Up until I heard The Byrds, everything was rhythm & blues. Even the Stones – and The Beatles then, too. Everybody. The Beatles were doing Motown stuff, besides 'I Want To Hold Your Hand' and those trips. They didn't know what they wanted to do, either, it seems. They were doing everybody else's stuff. And The Byrds were the first cats that I saw that were doing their own original material. And it sounded like the music I write on my own, you know what I mean?"

Two years later, Paul Jay Robbins will sum up the times. "In the spring of 1965, The Byrds took to the air. Their launching pad was the Sunset Strip and their hymn sounded from the total collective consciousness of a new breed of people. The Strip, so long a tinsel turkey, had become a flaming phoenix, and the light was seen around the world. … Those days and nights in 1965 were both crucible and catalyst for what followed, and who. We strolled the Strip as though it were the hallway of our common apartment house. We grew, our music grew; our elusive anthem delighted and inspired us."

Saturday 17

ALSO ...

The UK pop blitz on the US charts reaches a new height today as Britain accounts for 30 records in the *Billboard* Hot 100. Freddie & The Dreamers (1), Wayne Fontana (2), Herman's Hermits (3), Petula Clark (5), The Kinks (10), while The Moody Blues, The Beatles, The Rolling Stones, Shirley Bassey, Marianne Faithfull, Gerry & The Pacemakers, The Animals, Sounds Orchestral, Chad & Jeremy, Tom Jones, The Zombies, Sandie Shaw, The Searchers, Peter & Gordon, The Ivy League, Cliff Richard, and others fill up the positions beyond the Top 10.

Thursday 22

◄)) RECORDING Columbia Recording Studios, Studio A, Sunset and El Centro, Hollywood, CA. Producer Terry Melcher and probably engineer Ray Gerhardt.

Today The Byrds wind up sessions for their first album. Gene Clark's ballad 'Here Without You' harks back to the World Pacific demos. Jim Dickson persuades the group to record 'Don't Doubt Yourself Babe' as a thank-you to its composer Jackie DeShannon, an early champion of the band. Switching smoothly between a straight 4/4 beat and a choppy Rolling-Stones-by-way-of-Bo-Diddley rhythm, the song is as rhythm & blues as The Byrds get. Lastly, the group tapes yet another Dylan composition, this time 'Chimes Of Freedom', the third song borrowed from *Another Side Of Bob Dylan*.

Personality clashes are rife in the fledgling Byrds, and David Crosby is often the trigger. Jim Dickson will say in Crosby's autobiography that by the time they finished the last song today, 'Chimes Of Freedom', "... you could have touched me in the middle and I'd have fallen apart in a hundred pieces. I'd had it. I was desperate. And when David balks at playing something he'd just invented, we got into a huge fight, with him ready to walk out and me wrestling him to the floor and getting on top of him. I did everything I could to scare him. I told him, 'You're going to have to go through me. I'll fight you to the fucking death. You're going to finish this fucking tune. Blah blah blah.' That's how the album got done."

The group provide backing for Jackie DeShannon's lightweight vocal number 'Splendour In The Grass' which is probably also recorded today. The track does bear the sonic imprint of the classic Byrds sound. (Released as a single soon after, the song will be collected on the 1998 compilation Byrd Parts.)

In the evening, The Byrds are presumably back at Ciro's with the Whing-Ding revue.

Friday 23

The *Los Angeles Free Press* publishes the first contemporary report of the special atmosphere at Ciro's.

Paul Jay Robbins, who collects his impressions after seeing The Byrds stir up the crowds nightly, puts pen to paper: "Rock'n'roll used to be a phlegmatic blot on the landscape of aural adventuring. Between the lacklustre music, the drivel of lyrics, and the flash-phoney executors of it all, nothing was happening. Enter Beatles. The Beatles brought exploration, competency and freedom into the form. They had many influences but it was their special synthesis which did it. They fomented a school, a new school of music. Those who belong to this school are further delvers into the possibilities, which The Beatles opened up.

"One such group is The Byrds – and there is only one such group as The Byrds ... Their singular method is so unique, in a dynamic and irresistible adventure, the technique and honesty of folk music, the joy and immediacy of r & r, and the virtuosity of jazz. It weds and becomes hypnotically imperative to all who hear – a statement reflected in the brushfire emergence of enthusiastic fans who wildly proselytised an experience which indelibly touched them. In their brief span of professional life, The Byrds have gone through The Beatles and into a totally novel and fascinating place. They successfully united an audience of average teen-agers, Bach, Bartok, and Cage, aesthetics, folkniks, sophisticated middle-agers, r & r devotees, and serious hippies into one joyous commitment. The key words are 'unite' and 'commitment'."

Robbins drives the point home in his fluid and elegant prose. "What The Byrds evoke is an Enlightenment in the full psychedelic sense of the word. And if such paeans sound excessive or extravagant to describe an r & r combo, you just haven't heard The Byrds ... They all crossed over to find freedom and delight – and their discovery of it is ours. The sound is so damned right that you can't deny it. The modes of dancing which The Byrds incite is a thing of open loveliness to behold and a state of ecstasy to involve yourself in. Dancing with The Byrds becomes a mystic loss of ego and tangibility; you become pure energy someplace between sound and motion and the involvement is total. Their first record, released as of this writing, is Dylan's 'Mr. Tambourine Man', backed by a ballad written by Gene Clark. However, hearing a Byrds record is like listening to a record of [Stravinsky's] 'The Rite Of Spring'. The dynamic empathy is rich, but it just doesn't compare to the direct gestalt of music, dancers, aura, and communication."

→ Monday 26

▢ US TV KCOP Television Studios, Hollywood, CA. KCOP Channel 13 Los Angeles *The Lloyd Thaxton Show* (sometimes erroneously referred to as 'KCOP Bash') 5:00pm

Somewhere at the end of April, and possibly today (no documentation exists of either day of performance or songs performed, although 'Mr. Tambourine Man' is certainly done), The Byrds make their television debut on Lloyd Thaxton's TV show in the Los Angeles area between 5:00–6:00pm. Thaxton's show has rapidly become the leading local show in Los Angeles and is syndicated to nearly 100 cities, including New York, Chicago, Philadelphia, San Francisco; in short, all the major markets. It's described as a zany five-a-week, Monday-to-Friday, 60-minute mixture of guest stars from the world of rock'n'roll and off-the-wall content in which kids in the specially invited audience join in lip-sync contests, play instruments, and dance their way through recordings.

The show is recorded and broadcast live and the studio is small, as Thaxton explains in an interview with *The Daily Review* (June 18) out of Hayward, CA. "I can't handle more than 36 [kids] on a show, and the minimum is 20. Since we started three years ago, I guess we have had 20,000 kids appear, and there hasn't been a single serious incident." Thaxton consciously steers clear of the professional dancers used on national TV-shows such as *Hullabaloo* and *Shindig*. "Both of them got their basic idea from my show, but I consider go-go dancers are too much of a contrast to what the average kid is dancing today." Sometimes, the dancing gets a little too wild. "Usually," Thaxton tells the Hayward newspaper, "it's just a case of a girl being uncoordinated. There's nothing wrong with the dance they call the perk if it's done right, which is from the waist up." (Thaxton will comment in hindsight: "There was no dance called the perk. What the writer was referring to was the jerk. Which, by the way, is impossible to do from the waist up only.")

Thaxton hires The Byrds after seeing them at Ciro's, as he recalls many years later. "I remember going to see this new group, The Byrds, at Ciro's nightclub. ... As I was mostly accustomed to the way the dancers danced The Frug, The Mashed Potato, and The Slauson on the show, I was stunned to see the dancers out on the floor at Ciro's. It was a whole new ball game – a whole new ball dance? It reminded me of the movie The Snake Pit. The dancers didn't dance: they jumped – in a constant frenzy – up and down, to the music. ... I was captured by The Byrds' sound and invited them to be on my show."

"My show was produced live in a small studio," Thaxton continues. "We only had room for about 15 couples on the floor and that was it. To make room for guests, we had to crowd the couples off the stage and on to a small bleacher just out of camera range before we could set up for the guest performance. This was particularly difficult for groups like The Byrds that didn't lip-sync but preferred to perform live. We not only had the problem of setting up drums, speakers, microphones, and platforms, [but] we had to do mic checks and all the other requirements for a live performance. And we had to do all this in the two-minute commercial break just before their performance! As soon as the commercial break started, the dancers were ushered out while the stage crew rushed in to set up.

"On this particular set-up we were right on time. As a matter of fact, we were 30 seconds ahead of schedule. However, as we were in the middle of our soundcheck, the audio man in the booth told me that the speakers were too loud for the sound control-panel to handle. The sound was being totally distorted. I ran in and told The Byrds they would have to turn down the speaker volume controls. I explained that we were not in a stadium, that there are only 15 couples sitting in small bleachers just five feet away. The group looked at me like I really didn't understand ('the music has to be loud, man!'), but, to their credit, they did turn down and make the necessary adjustments.

"Just in the nick of time: the commercial was over and we were back on the air. I picked up my mic and said, 'And here they are, The Byrds!' Then, as if someone gave them a cue from off stage, each member of the group reached down and turned their respective speakers back up to full volume. When the first 'hey' of 'Mr. Tambourine Man' hit our mikes, I looked up at the control room window and saw my audio man being literally blown back in his seat. The needles on his control board were spinning like a racetrack-timing clock. But you know what? It was an exciting performance and the kids loved it. I loved it too."

ALSO ...

Tonight at 9:35pm, Bob Dylan flies into London Airport aboard TWA Flight number 702 for a much-anticipated solo tour of Britain. Dylan has visited Britain twice before, but this time is different – he is given a rapturous reception by 200 waiting teenagers at the airport. Dylan is forging ahead at a ferocious tempo this spring and the British public strives to keep pace. *The Freewheelin' Bob Dylan* from May 1963 has suddenly taken off and this week is at Number Three in the UK album charts, with two further albums in the Top

20, while 'The Times They Are A-Changin'' from February 1964 has made the Top Ten in the singles charts. Dylan's latest single, the fully electric 'Subterranean Homesick Blues', has just been unleashed on an unsuspecting public.

Tuesday 27–Thursday 29
The Troubadour, West Hollywood, CA
The Byrds play three nights at Doug Weston's Troubadour. The members of The Byrds are, of course, well acquainted with the club. Earlier, McGuinn, Clark, and Crosby have performed here individually – but the club is not prepared for the onslaught of The Byrds. Music Machine singer Sean Bonniwell tells author Richie Unterberger: "[When] the Byrds were at the Troubadour ... they were the talk of L.A. They were so loud – they were just incredibly loud. It parted your hair right down the middle. So I went backstage to see [McGuinn] ... . Crosby was just absolutely insufferable. He was ego gone mad. I'll never forget that. Of course I forgive him for that, I shouldn't hold it against him. But it was like: how dare I come into his presence unannounced ... I'm sure that he's mellowed and has appreciation for his fellow human beings. He's humbled somewhat. But it was just an experience [and] I remember thinking, I never want to be like that, I just don't want to be like that. In fact, McGuinn said to me, 'Don't pay any attention to him. He's even like that with me.'"

Late April
☐ **US TV** KABC Studios, ABC Television Center, Hollywood, CA. KABC Channel 7 Los Angeles *Shivaree*
At the end of April, The Byrds record an insert on *Shivaree* to be broadcast on May 8, lip-synching both sides of their single, 'Mr. Tambourine Man' and 'I Knew I'd Want You'.

Wednesday 28
The largest newspaper on the West Coast, *The Los Angeles Times*, devotes space in today's edition to describe the Byrds phenomenon. Under the headline 'Natives Quite Restless', staff writer and art critic Art Seidenbaum gives an eloquent description of a recent night at Ciro's, where music, dancing, and fashion clothing all make an impression.

"On first inspection, they looked to be like any other uncut quintet dedicated to the performance of rock'n'roll. They thwacked onto the Ciro's bandstand dressed for a rumble. At least two of the boys' hair-dos were long enough to make nesting places for real birds (not spelled with a why). Their music (hush, hush sweet Ludwig) was the usual mash of drum and strum and can't nobody hum."

Carl Franzoni, although not named, is clearly hiding behind Seidenbaum's description of a dancer. "A man whose chin was thrust behind a large beard stood up and jiggled toward the dance floor. Now, we have all become used to seeing young moderns twitch without touching their partners, but, aside from the Middle East, we have never seen a man writhe on the floor wholly unaccompanied. For one full set, the bewhiskered man performed his solo, occasionally stretching both arms toward the ceiling as if offering personal sacrifice and plucking notice from some pagan deity.

"The third trend hatched by Byrds fans is in fashion. The floor was full of people who looked like they had just straggled out of Sherwood Forest, wearing jerkins and tights and chains and robes and leather aprons. Long-haired, loosely-fitted, who prithee might tell boy from girl? … I remember long ago when Whisky A Go Go opened its doors and proprietor Shelly Davis admitted that he was running a zoo – an establishment prowled by unusual unleashed animals with two human girls in glass cages. Realizing that a creature had to be 21 years old to enter such a veldt, it then appeared adults had gone about as far from type as they could go go (barring a resumption of nuclear testing). Yet The Byrds have brought out the hooded robins who steal from the young and give new mystery to the mature. The Teen-Age Fair, which last year seemed to need sedation, now seems tea-party tame compared to the way adults preen."

Seidenbaum speaks to a befuddled spokesman from Ciro's. "He confirmed the place had become a Nottingham that neither he nor anyone else understood. Forsooth, the man brought flocks of brand new species to Sunset Strip, the likes of which even hardened nightclub operators never met. … [The spokesman] had been taking no chances, staying away from the club until The Byrds' billing was done. Now, he assured me, Ciro's is safe for man and beast, having established a whole new policy called Whing-Ding."

•

In time for The Byrds first proper out-of-town booking (excluding the unannounced visit to the Jack Tar Motel), Jim McGuinn buys three or four pairs of rectangular spectacles [with glass] in different shades, red, grey, or blue, that he takes to wearing everywhere. They become an indelible part of the group's image. (In a later remembrance, McGuinn says it was John Sebastian who pointed out the stylish glasses when the two hung out in New York in the winter of '63/'64.) Described as granted to Ben Franklin, the glass will soon be known simply as McGuinns.

Friday 30

Peppermint Tree, San Francisco, CA

"We drove up to San Francisco to play the Peppermint Tree," begins David Crosby's later biographical recollection of The Byrds' first out-of-town engagement. "We had a black

---

1956 Ford station wagon that we had bought from Odetta for a reasonable sum, like 600 bucks or something, and we took that with all our equipment and all five of us in it and drove to San Francisco. We stayed in some dive, some set of rooms above the club, which was on Broadway in North Beach, just west of the Committee, and awesomely bad.

"Not only was it bad, but when we started there were two go-go dancers, girls in fringed bikinis, one on either side of us, trying to dance, smacking their gum. They'd say things like, 'Don't you guys know anything with a beat?' We're doing our set, with things like Dylan's 'Chimes Of Freedom'. It was a total mismatch. I wish to God I could re-create it. Anybody who saw it now would be in hysterics. It was just funnier than shit and we loved it."

For maximum effect, The Byrds bring Carl Franzoni's crowd with them to bring life to the dance floor. "[The Peppermint] was on Broadway: it was across the street from the old place where I worked, where I was bartender," Franzoni explains to John Trubee. "It was a marathon. We made those guys do six or seven sets. They lived upstairs, and Carol Doda, the famous stripper, was living on the same floor with them, and she didn't have any big bosoms at the time, she was just this fast little waitress chick that could sing." Franzoni indignantly recalls that the dancers had to pay their own way for the San Francisco trip.

May

Saturday 1–Tuesday 4

Peppermint Tree, San Francisco, CA

Ralph J. Gleason, San Francisco's leading pop and jazz critic, writes in *The San Francisco Chronicle* (May 5): "The other night I alternated between Count Basie and his timeless perfection at Basin Street West and The Byrds at the Peppermint Tree, which is to say I went the whole way from Yesterday to Tomorrow. It was fascinating. Nobody dances at a Basie appearance any more and everybody dances to The Byrds. In fact, the dancing is more fun than anything. The Byrds, incidentally, look not like birds, but like The Beatles.

"The wild and exotic Byrd-watchers on the floor at the Peppermint Tree were a gas. They all seem to be part of the president's

---

physical fitness programme doing free style callisthenics. It is by no means a formal thing. Everybody goes out there and wails away in his or her own individual fashion and the dancers generally ignore one another, preferring the fullest flower of individual free enterprise. One male in jeans and a striped shirt had a head of hair that looked like Medusa's snakes and he shook it with abandon. There's a house dancer who performs alongside the band and who is graceless and puzzling unless her presence is to make the other dancers feel good by contrast."

Gleason lists 'Chimes Of Freedom', 'All I Want To Do', and 'Mr. Tambourine Man' as part of the set.

Monday 3

Hollywood gossip reporter Harrison Carroll's notes in one of his syndicated columns how playboy and racing driver "Lance Reventlow finally got that broken leg into a walking cast. He and [actress] Cheryl Holdridge had a date to hear The Byrds. Their pal, Jim Dickson, manages the group. Remember him, he once was wed to Diane Varsi …"

Also, 'Mr. Tambourine Man' enters the *Billboard* single charts (issue dated May 8, but on newsstands today), debuting at a modest Number 114. For next week's edition (cover date May 15), Columbia Records has purchased a whole page to promote 'Mr. Tambourine Man'.

Wednesday 5–Thursday 6

☐ **US TV** NBC Television Studios, Manhattan, New York City, NY. NBC *Hullabaloo*

The Byrds fly from San Francisco to New York City to appear on the musical variety show *Hullabaloo*, instigated in January of this year as an answer to rival channel ABC's *Shindig*. *Hullabaloo* is aired nationally, luxuriously shown in colour, and guarantees an audience many times larger than The Byrds' previous local appearances on essentially California-based TV shows. Although 'Mr. Tambourine Man' has not proved to be a big hit yet, the muscle of Columbia ensures the group a shot on nationwide television. The group probably follow the regular pattern for *Hullabaloo* of one day set aside for rehearsals with recording the following day. The group sing live to backing tracks of 'Mr. Tambourine Man' and 'I'll Feel A Whole Lot Better', to be broadcast on May 11. (The show is reprised on August 10.)

The sight of a genuinely excited McGuinn singing his heart out, shooting for the big time, is mind blowing.

The trend-conscious Crosby rubs manager Jim Dickson the wrong way when he insists on wearing a pilot jacket for the show. "David

had decided that his new image was to wear a pea coat," Dickson tells Carl Gottlieb. "And we're back there, ready to do the show, and they've got these birdhouses around because it's a corny set and a tasteless show anyway. I tell David, 'You look like a butterball with fuzz in that coat.' It made him look fat before he was fat, and everybody was supposed to look young and pretty in those days, so I tried to get him to take off the coat. It was a struggle and it got down to the point where he said, 'If you say one more word, I'm walking out the door.' I let it go and David went on with the pea coat."

There is another incident, according to *KRLA Beat* (May 26). The Byrds refuse to join the programme's showbiz like finale when all the performers come out at the end of the show to sing 'This Diamond Ring', Gary Lewis & The Playboys' recent US Number One.

Following Thursday's filming, The Byrds fly west again to continue their club booking in San Francisco.

Friday 7– Thursday 13
Peppermint Tree, San Francisco, CA
Crosby picks up the story of the Peppermint Tree residence. "San Francisco was a wonderful place, and after we started packing the place … we renegotiated. Then we did three sets a night and the go-go dancers went elsewhere and we filled the joint. To the rafters.

Everybody in San Francisco came. All they'd ever seen up there that was anything like us was The Beau Brummels. It was The Byrds all the way after that. And while we were playing this North Beach go-go palace, 'Mr. Tambourine Man' started to get airplay. Tom 'Big Daddy' Donahue broke us on KYA."

'Mr. Tambourine Man' has been idling briefly following its release in early April, but the sound of The Byrds will soon spread in California thanks to incessant radio play by radio stations KYA (out of San Francisco) and KRLA (Los Angeles). According to legend, Tom Donahue at KYA finds the single languishing on a shelf, demoted and neglected, notices Dylan's writing credit, and starts

The Byrds at the Peppermint Tree, San Francisco, CA, May 1965.

spinning the single. Meanwhile, Dave Hull, a Beatle-maniac disc jockey at KRLA, picks the single as his 'Tip For A Hit'. Derek Taylor, who has close connections to KRLA, goes into print to forecast 'Mr. Tambourine Man' as a nationwide Number One and hands out records to the top disc jockeys on the West Coast.

David Crosby later describes the euphoria in his autobiography. "We knew ['Mr. Tambourine Man'] was a hit when we were back in Los Angeles [from San Francisco], riding down Sunset Boulevard in that funky old station wagon, and KRLA played our 'Mr. Tambourine Man'. We freaked! There is no feeling I'll ever have like that time, hearing our tune on the car radio, without warning, for the very first time ever. And they played it again! It was such a hot item that they played it two or three times in a row. By that time we were so excited we had to pull over. Couldn't drive any more! I mean, we knew at that moment that our lives had changed. Literally. We were going to be able to make a living at playing music."

Saturday 8
Shivaree (show #15) goes on the air at 7:00pm PST on KABC-TV tonight with The Byrds performing 'Mr. Tambourine Man' and 'I Knew I'd Want You' (see late April). The show began syndication nationally on March 13, and tonight's show will later be aired on the East Coast on June 12 and then in the Chicago area on August 8. Presented by the show's regular host Gene Weed surrounded by a bevy of dancers, tonight's *Shivaree* also features Glen Campbell, Carol Crane, James Darren, and The Preachers, plus guests Jerry Naylor and actress Pat Woodell.

Monday 10
The Byrds are signed today to appear on the television show *Shindig* (see June 10).

Tuesday 11
In between sets at San Francisco's Pettermint Tree, the group watch *Hullabaloo* (NBC) at 8:30pm tonight in its final first-run of the season. Hosted by Frankie Avalon, the TV show features The Byrds singing and miming to 'Mr. Tambourine Man' and 'I'll Feel A Whole Lot Better' (see May 5–6). Other guests on the show are The Supremes, British duo Peter & Gordon, Sam The Sham & The Pharaohs, plus Avalon, Barbara McNair, and Joanie Sommers singing a Lennon/McCartney medley. (The clip of 'I'll Feel A Whole Lot Better' is made available on the bonus DVD that comes with the 2006 CD boxed set *There Is A Season*.)

This is the first chance for the wider public to see and hear the impact of The Byrds. Singing live to a pre-recorded instrumental

track, McGuinn, Crosby, and Clark have no problem performing their pristine vocal and harmony blend for the cameras and microphones. The five Byrds are an arresting sight – more longhaired and casual looking than the average pop group of the day, and with McGuinn's Ben Franklin spectacles adding a touch of individuality. While McGuinn and Crosby play their respective Rickenbacker and Gretsch guitars, Chris Hillman at the back mimes the bass part on a Fender VI six-string bass.

Jim Dickson gets a phone call. "[Crosby] sees the show and I get a call from San Francisco. 'Why didn't you rip [the coat] off me? I look terrible in that!' That was the end of the pea coat. Then he got the cape, which I didn't mind."

Thursday 13
The engagement at the Peppermint Tree finishes tonight, but the group stay in San Francisco for a show tomorrow.

Friday 14
New Civic Auditorium, San Francisco, CA
The Rolling Stones are halfway through their third North American tour, which now swings through a week's worth of dates in California, for which The Byrds are signed on as one of the opening acts. The Stones have only cracked the American Top Ten twice, with 'Time Is On My Side' (Number Six) and their latest single 'The Last Time' (which stalls at Nine), but are about to enter a golden era. Just two days ago, the Stones spent a whole day recording at RCA in Hollywood, and one of the songs completed was based on a simple fuzz-boxed three-note riff dreamed up by Keith Richard.

Promoted by radio station KYA ('Boss Of The Bay') with MC Russ 'The Moose' Syracuse, The Rolling Stones are supported by The Beau Brummels, Paul Revere & The Raiders, and The Vejtables, in addition to The Byrds. The crowd is estimated at 5,000. Out front, Carl Franzoni whips up a frenzy in the already delirious crowd. "We danced right in front of The Byrds among the wild and crazy teens. Then, when the Stones came on, we danced in front of them; the teens screaming their lungs out!"

It is around now that the young Bryan McLean ("a cute, freckle-faced kid" according to Trina Robbins), a guitar player in his own right, joins The Byrds as a handyman, carrying amplifiers and setting up microphones.

Saturday 15
Swing Auditorium, San Bernardino, CA
The Rolling Stones plus The Byrds appear

along with three local groups: The Buschmen, The Driftwoods, and The Torquays. The crowd is estimated at 4,500.

'Mr. Tambourine Man' is beginning to move locally in the Bay Area, and *The Oakland Tribune* occasionally publishes a weekly Top Ten chart based on votes by randomly-chosen local high schools. Today, 100 teenagers at Ramon Valley High School present their results. Nesting below Sam The Sham & The Pharaohs' 'Wooly Bully' is The Byrds' debut single (sharing the Number Two position with Herman's Hermits and 'Mrs Brown You've Got A Lovely Daughter'). Below them are Them's 'Gloria' (a huge hit in California) and hits by The Beatles ('Ticket To Ride'), The Beach Boys ('Help Me Rhonda'), and The Rolling Stones ('The Last Time').

Sunday 16
Long Beach Arena, Long Beach, CA
The Rolling Stones with The Byrds, Paul Revere & The Raiders, singer Jerry Naylor, and local groups Don & The Deacons, The Vibrants, and The Dartells. The acts are introduced by KRLA disc jockeys Bob Eubanks and Dave Hull.

The concert is held in the afternoon, and when the Stones finish at 5:30pm several thousand fans storm through the exits and nearly crush the Stones' getaway car. "Jars of cosmetics, shoes, purses, wallets, lipsticks, bottles, and articles of underwear were thrown at the police officers and the [group] as they tried to make their way to the escape car," reports The Independent (May 17) before the Stones arrive at a nearby heliport at 6:15 and are airborne.

Louis Criscione reviews the concert for *KRLA Beat*. "The Byrds were fantastic and the crowd went absolutely wild for them! Flashbulbs flashed and jelly beans flew through their entire performance, especially when the boys started into their hit 'Mr. Tambourine Man'." Criscione gives a snapshot of the chaotic dressing-room scene, where Brian Jones scrutinises the bill for the show and enquires about The Byrds.

Future Moby Grape founder Peter Lewis later tells Jud Cost: "The first time I saw The Byrds, at the Long Beach Arena, I couldn't stop focusing on the harmonies, the Dylan songs, and that sound. I really liked surf music, but when I saw The Byrds, it was just like when Mr. Toad found the motor car!"

Monday 17
Community Concourse, Convention Hall, San Diego, CA
"They are quite nice fellows – very English types, really," Mick Jagger tells Rod Harrod of *Disc* (July 10) when he is asked for an opin-

ion of The Byrds. "They were on our tour for about a week while we were round the West Coast. They used to go on each night before us. One night when we were due to be playing at San Diego, the car we were travelling in to the theatre broke down. This made us half an hour late arriving at the theatre, so The Byrds had to stay on stage to keep the audience entertained. By the time we eventually got there they had run out of all their own numbers and were playing ours. What a gas!"

Allegedly, Mick and company watch with amusement from the side of the stage as The Byrds add 'Not Fade Away' to their act – a Buddy Holly number with which the Stones scored a US Top 50 in the spring of 1964.

•

Presumably now while the group are home in Los Angeles, Michelle Straubing and Susan Wylie interview all five Byrds for a feature in *KRLA Beat* (June 12). Beat is a weekly music paper published under the aegis of various radio stations around the USA. Thus the L.A. version is *KRLA Beat*, San Francisco has KYA Beat, and so on. With offices at 6290 Sunset Boulevard, the paper is right at the nerve centre of the California music scene, bringing its readers the latest news in addition to interviews, features, and concert reports. It should be noted that editions of *KRLA Beat* hit the street a week or two earlier than the issue dates, so the paper marked June 12 in reality is on newsstands around June 1. (There exists also a large selection of glossy magazines aimed at American teenagers, but they are rarely up-to-date and often hopelessly out of sync with actual events.)

The interview itself is not particularly noteworthy, although the lists of their favourite artists make for interesting reading. Chris Hillman names John Lee Hooker and Buck Owens; Jim McGuinn says his early idol was Bob Gibson; and Michael Clarke mentions Joan Baez and Marianne Faithfull. It is David Crosby whose tastes are the most eclectic. He ranks Indian sitar virtuoso Ravi Shankar as his favourite and also mentions jazz musicians John Coltrane and Miles Davis – proving that his deep love for esoteric and Eastern music is not a sudden whim. Additionally, he lists The Rolling Stones and Manfred Mann.

Janey Milstead, then editor and a writer in the burgeoning teen press, has vivid memories of The Byrds. "I first heard Byrd-song when my pal Billy James, an A&R honcho at Columbia Records, called me at my office on Hollywood Boulevard. I was editor of *Teen Screen* magazine at the time, and also writing undercover-freelance for several other mags. Billy said he wanted me to hear a hot new record by a hot new group and he proceeded

to play 'Mr. Tambourine Man'. A Dylan fan to put it mildly, I loved the song and I had to admit, I dug the new version. Billy was right, as he usually was. The Byrds hit hard and hot. All of us press kids interviewed them and they were cool. They worked hard at their craft as the hits kept coming. One of my freelance jobbies was writing for *The Beat*, the first rock music paper. In those early days, there weren't many of us in the rock press and we all wrote for each other's publications. Most of my work there appeared under the name Shirley Poston, which they made up at the Beat one dark deadline night. One of my creations was a fictitious serial called 'The Adventures Of Robin Boyd'. It was the story of a teenager named Robin who could turn herself into a real robin and fly across the Atlantic to terrorise, er, visit her faves. She was blind as six bats, so when she was on the wing, she was forced to wear a tiny pair of, you guessed it!, Byrd glasses."

Friday 21
Civic Auditorium, San Jose, CA
The Rolling Stones with The Byrds plus local groups The Nite Sounds and The Ratts.

Also today, 'Mr. Tambourine Man' is released in Britain. Originally set for the previous week, the release is rescheduled for today, perhaps to avoid conflict with Johnny Cash's version of Bob Dylan's 'It Ain't Me Babe' (also on Columbia Records), which is released on May 14.

'Mr. Tambourine Man' is among a busy rush of releases in the UK. Also out today are singles by Donovan ('Colours'), The Kinks ('Set Me Free'), The Who ('Anyway Anyhow Anywhere'), and The Hollies ('I'm Alive').

Penny Valentine in *Disc* (May 22) writes: "[The Byrds] have really only taken the nucleus of the original fantastic child-like song and they do it rather like The Four Seasons. I love the lead singer and I can't help liking this. It's such a lovely tune I should think it stands a very good chance of getting high in the charts."

The following week (May 29), *Record Mirror* – who credit the single to plain 'Birds' – writes: "A Bob Dylan song of uncommon charm. Group is American, folksy and five-strong. Don't mix them with our Birds. Busy mandolin-guitar backing. Song is the big selling point, for sure." Lastly, *Music Echo*'s Brian Harvey notes (May 22): "The Byrds have a big hit Stateside with their version of [the Dylan number], a folksy, guitar twangy, medium tempo swinger. It's a busy number with lots of echo. Lead voice tells the story and has vocal group backing in the attractive chorus. The melody sticks even after one play."

Jim Dickson explains to Carl Gottlieb: "I went and saw Derek Taylor and said, 'I'll give you two and half per cent: you do what you think it's worth. We won't demand anything from you, but what we want the most is help breaking the record in England.' I'd figured out that everybody was looking at what was happening in England and there were no American groups getting on the charts. If we could break the record in England, then everybody would notice."

Taylor knows well the influence of the pirate radio stations anchored off the English coast that offer a loose daytime programming format aimed at teenagers and housewives. Broadcasting illegally, the ships are outside

The Byrds support The Rolling Stones in San Diego, May 17, 1965.

British jurisdiction. The best known is Radio Caroline, moored off the Suffolk coast in eastern England. Disc jockey Keith Skues writes in his history of the offshore radio phenomenon: "I was sent a tape in April 1965 by Derek Taylor, who was The Beatles' press officer. It was a reel-to-reel tape, and I heard this and played it all week on the ship. Little did I realise people were ringing the office to find out where they could get it. They couldn't – it hadn't been released! Eventually CBS rush-released it and it went to Number One [later in] 1965. What was that record? 'Mr. Tambourine Man' by The Byrds. And it's still my theme tune to this day." Indeed, Skues keeps the Dylan tune as his personal theme tune, although later in a recording by the more sedate Golden Gate Strings rather than The Byrds.

Saturday 22

- **Ratcliffe Stadium, Fresno, CA (10:00am)**
- **Municipal Auditorium, Sacramento, CA (evening)**

For the morning show in Fresno, The Rolling Stones and The Byrds top the bill over three Hollywood groups (The Montclairs, The Ladybirds, The Menn) and three local Fresno bands (The Cindermen, The Road Runners, The Moonstones). The show is promoted by local radio station KMAK, with some of the profits earmarked for the local YMCA Boy Camper Program. However, no more than 4,500 fill the 13,000-capacity stadium, meaning a loss for the promoters after the Stones net their guaranteed fee of $4,000. Despite The Byrds' rising popularity, the local review in *The Fresno Bee* (May 23) lumps them together with the other opening acts as "backup entertainers".

FILMING The Byrds' visit to Fresno is filmed and later sold as a low fidelity 8mm film in black and white and without sound. Advertised in the teen press as *The Byrds Flip Them In Fresno* and sold on mail order basis only, the film comes in three versions: 3 minutes, 6 minutes, or an extended one including similar footage of The Beatles and The Rolling Stones, too.

Following the Fresno show, the Stones and Byrds play two shows in Sacramento, more than 150 miles to the north. Asked about the Stones tour a fortnight later, Jim McGuinn tells Chris Hutchins of *New Musical Express*: "Although we didn't fight, I don't think we really got through to them or them to us."

This week, *The Oakland Tribune* has conducted its weekly Top Ten survey at Encinal High School in Alameda, over the bridge from San Francisco, where the votes from the students place 'Mr. Tambourine Man' at Number Four. By now, the single has made a dent in the lower end of the national charts in *Billboard* and *Cash Box* and is slowly crawling upwards.

Monday 24

'Mr. Tambourine Man' jumps to Number 30 in today's *Cash Box* (May 29 cover date) on sale today, entering from outside the Top 50.

Undated May

At around this time, the managers of The Byrds, under their formalised partnership name Tickner–Dickson Management, move into the eighth floor at 9,000 Sunset Boulevard, an imposing building that houses many music businesses, not least the West Coast offices of the weekly music paper *Billboard*. Derek Taylor, who left employment at KRLA at the turn of April into May, splits the rent with Dickson and Tickner in return for a corner of their office. A Byrds Fan Club is also set up at the address.

Taylor writes in his memoir: "The Byrds took me into their office and, until the man from the tax came for me in spring, 1967, I worked out of there, the eighth floor at 9,000. In the beginning my share of the premises was a small room and my share of the staff was half of the secretary, Jackie. … There was a large room set aside for The Byrds to use for rehearsals. … [Dickson and Tickner] had a publishing company, Tickson Music, and in 1964, with David Crosby, Jim McGuinn, and Gene Clark, they planned The Byrds so completely that it finally happened as planned. They planned to become a big international group without telling any lies, without selling out, without giving up dope, and without dropping any of their bizarre friends to meet the pressures of the music industry.

"Jim and Eddie and I were very pleased with each other. The two and a half per cent was earning me something like $250 a week, and they had 15 per cent between them (plus publishing from Tickson Music); even if none of us had a dime, we would still have been glad to be alive, standing in the wings at Ciro's on the Strip digging The Byrds."

Thus, Derek Taylor makes up one-fifth of a loosely organised back office quintet (Dickson, Tickner, Terry Melcher, and CBS publicist Billy James being the other four-fifths) that perfectly complements The Byrds quintet seen publicly onstage.

Thursday 27

US TV KCOP Television Studios, Hollywood, CA. KCOP-TV Channel 13 Los Angeles *The Lloyd Thaxton Show* 5:00pm

The Byrds make presumably their second appearance on *The Lloyd Thaxton Show* – after the TV debut here at the end on April – and

this time perform Gene Clark's 'I'll Feel A Whole Lot Better' ('Mr. Tambourine Man' and 'Chimes Of Freedom' are taped too, but may be held over for a later transmission). It is probably this performance that is later syndicated in the New York City area on WSYR Channel 3 on July 16.

Friday 28–Saturday 29 –Sunday 30

THE SURFERS FAIR
4 PM 'TIL MIDNIGHT DAILY
- Melinda Marx • The Birds
  Groucho's Daughter   Tambourine Man
- ★ 12 Bands ★ Surf Shop★ Carnival
- ★ Top Names★ The   ★ Displays
- ★ Movies   Fugitives ★ Dancing
FRIDAY, SATURDAY, SUNDAY
MAY 28-29-30
at the SACRAMENTO COUNTY FAIR
Tickets available at the Tower, Coast Radio, College Hi Shops

'The Surfers Fair', Sacramento County Fair, Sacramento, CA

The Byrds – or The 'Birds' as the local advertisement has it – appear daily at the Sacramento County Fair this weekend as one of many distractions: movies, surf shops, displays, a carnival, local bands, and singer Melinda Marx (daughter of Groucho).

Monday 31

'Mr. Tambourine Man' jumps from Number 57 to crack the *Billboard* Top 20 where it lands at Number 17 in the issue on the newsstands today (cover date June 5).

ALSO …
A little-known meeting takes place in London tonight when Brian Jones – freshly back from The Rolling Stones' month-long North American tour this very morning – meets Bob Dylan at London's hip Cromwellian club before ending the night at Dylan's place. Jones says to *Disc* (July 24): "I met Dylan at his hotel while he was in London, and he was playing 'Mr. Tambourine Man' [by The Byrds] all the time. He just loves the sound of them."

Tomorrow, Dylan will film a show in front of a small audience for BBC-1 television, to be broadcast two weeks later. The concert effectively marks his last fully-acoustic performance for a long time. Dylan ends the BBC show with a powerful 'Mr. Tambourine Man'. On Wednesday June 2, he flies back to the States, but his UK visit leaves the door ajar for The Byrds.

Late May

US TV KABC Studios, ABC Television Center, Hollywood, CA. KABC Channel 7 Los Angeles *Shivaree*

The Byrds pre-record a second appearance on *Shivaree* either at the end of May or the first days of June, miming 'I'll Feel A Whole Lot

Better' and 'All I Really Want To Do'. Initially set for broadcast on June 5 on a show that stars The Rolling Stones (performing 'The Last Time' and 'Play With Fire'), the insert is postponed until the following week, June 12.

June

Tuesday 1–Saturday 11
Ciro's Le Disc, Hollywood, CA

The Byrds are back at Ciro's for an almost two-week engagement (possibly starting yesterday, Monday May 31), before the club shuts down for a couple of from Monday June 14. The crowds that came here so faithfully in April are back again, and with them is Carl Franzoni's gaggle of wild dancers. While The Byrds have been away, Ciro's has wound down the Whing-Ding revue as singer Kelly Garrett moves to the Lazy X in North Hollywood. The Nooney Rickett IV have also filled in on several nights in May.

The Los Angeles Times (June 7) is again on hand to report on The Byrds at Ciro's, and Charles Champlin quotes Jim McGuinn. "Jets are the sound of our time," says McGuinn. "It's a high-frequency thing. The kids are ready for it. Rock'n'roll was crisp and fresh when it started with Elvis in 1956. But then it was wilted and the kids got over-exposed to it. They were ready for something else. Kids aren't so stupid as the people who make movies think they are." McGuinn's clever jet-age analogy – a link that Derek Taylor will diligently sell to the press – will be heard time and time again over the coming years.

Champlin, primarily a film critic also associated with *Life,* is overwhelmed by the volume. "The Byrds are currently causing the dark red walls at Ciro's to pulsate. ... Their sound is nothing if not high frequency. The quintet's four guitars feed into as many four-foot high speakers, and the wonder is that an enterprising dentist has not yet left calling cards on the tables to ensnare the trade of customers whose fillings have vibrated loose. The airport is, relatively speaking, a sylvan glade, where you might go to listen to your dashboard clock. ... The big volume, which in a small space makes the music literally breathtaking, is a necessary ingredient of the jet sound, and it's in many ways a pity. It makes it harder to realise that the musicianship is several dozen cuts above the going group average.

"The chord changes are intricate and minor; oftentimes and whenever you can get past the rhythm guitar and the dah-dah-dah triplet drumbeats, you discover some inter-

twining melodic capers whose bite owes a lot to Bach. But what is strictly The Byrds' own is their song choice and the lyrics.

"The group is folk music oriented – 'Mr. Tambourine Man' is a Bob Dylan song, and he digs their big-beat version – and whether the writhing figures on the dance floor hear the words or not, they're being given some very cerebral stuff. One evening last week The Byrds were doing the Pete Seeger setting for a Welsh folk poem about a mining disaster. Billy James, Byrd man of Columbia, was saying: 'When you think about the words in contrast to the dancing, it boggles the mind.' Yes. 'The kids,' says McGuinn, 'were tired of inane lyrics. They were tired of being played down to.'

"Dubious as the elders may remain, the big sound seems to be evolving. What was loud and witless is becoming loud and witty. The first thing you know, it will be completely beyond reach of the guys who can't get beyond three chords and a Yeah."

Champlin compares the group's hairdos to a medieval comics hero. "[The Byrds] adopted Price Valiant haircuts, which make them look as if they were wearing hairy cloche hats for quick identification in smoky clubs."

One guest at Ciro's now is P.J. Proby, an expatriate US singer who makes his living in the UK but is back for a summery visit to Hollywood. He says to *Melody Maker* (July 10): "You know, in America now, The Byrds are really big. ... Herman is really big, but the big sound is Rolling Stones background on Dylan lyrics. I met The Byrds; they are nice guys, and I think they'll go down really big [in Britain]. The Beach Boys can't duplicate their record sound live but The Byrds can."

Friday 4

The Byrds visit a Beach Boys recording session in the afternoon, where Brian Wilson leads an overdub vocal session for his song 'California Girls'.

The Beach Boys usually record at Capitol Studios, but today Wilson has hired the studio at Columbia because it offers the latest in recording technology: an eight-track tape machine. The occasion also marks Bruce Johnston's recording debut with The Beach Boys. Johnston has been an auxiliary Beach Boy on and off since April 8, standing in for hired-hand Glen Campbell.

Saturday 5

Over in Britain, The Byrds get their first press write-ups when *Disc* runs a brief article written by Penny Valentine, complete with the standard short biography and a punch line ("Watch The Byrds! As Mr Hitchcock would say: 'The Byrds Is Coming'!"), while *Melody*

Maker publishes a picture of Dylan and The Byrds, quoting Bob: "They are good musicians – they know what they are doing."

Sunday 6
'Rock, Rock For Sweet Charity', Shrine Auditorium, Hollywood, CA

Jack Good, the British-born TV producer recently relocated to California to lead the popular *Shindig* teen television operation, promotes a grandiose show in support of the Freedom From Hunger Committee of Southern California. A parade of TV and radio personalities (Steve Allen, Bob Newhart, Joey Bishop, Dick Biondi, Bob Eubanks, Dave Hull, Casey Kasem) introduce The Byrds onstage – presumably early on to make time for their Ciro's Le Disc performance at night – as well as Johnny Cash, The Crickets, The Chambers Brothers, Jackie DeShannon, The Everly Brothers, Gary Lewis & The Playboys, The Kingsmen, Sonny & Cher, The Tijuana Brass, and some lesser names. The concert starts at 6:30pm.

Wednesday 9
ALSO ...

The Farmer's Other Daughter, a film starring Judy Pennebaker and Bill Michael, premieres at various movie theatres and drive-ins around California tonight. A highlight of the movie is an appearance by country singer Ernest Ashworth, who sings 'The Ballad Of Farmer Brown' backed by Clarence White and The Kentucky Colonels.

Thursday 10

☐ **US TV** ABC Television Center, Hollywood, CA. ABC network *Shindig*

The ABC Channel's *Shindig* TV venture has proved popular since it first aired in September 1964. The show goes out every Wednesday at primetime and has this year expanded from half an hour to an hour. Hosted by Jimmy O'Neill and produced by Jack Good, the show features on occasion segments filmed in Britain exclusively for the American market. The energetic Good tells *The Press-Courier* (March 6): "I love excitement. That's why I do my own warm-up [of the TV audience]. I love making people respond. I tell them watching *Shindig* is a new spectator sport and that they should jump up and join in. To me, the word 'applause' is a colloquialism for 'bedlam'."

Shindig can also claim a crack house band – The Shindogs – featuring Delaney Bramlett (guitar, bass), Chuck Blackwell (drums), and James Burton (guitar), and with Leon Russell (piano) and Glen Campbell (guitar, bass) as two of their affiliated members. The Byrds lip-synch 'Mr. Tambourine Man' and – surprisingly – 'Not Fade Away', while Crosby and McGuinn are filmed separately harmonising 'Long Tall Sally' as part of an opening medley. 'Not Fade Away' faithfully copies The Rolling Stones' shave-and-a-haircut-two-bits arrangement, and proves that The Byrds could easily tackle rhythm & blues numbers. The song is enhanced by Gene's bluesy harp, Jim's rough vocal, and a nasal guitar solo certainly played by James Burton. The backing track – McGuinn sings live – is likely recorded the day before at L.A.'s Gold Star studios. The Byrds' performance is broadcast on June 23.

Following the TV recording, The Byrds return to Ciro's for the night.

Saturday 12

The Byrds are the main attraction on *Shivaree* (show #20, see entry for late May) at 7:00pm PST on KABC-TV. The group mime to 'I'll Feel A Whole Lot Better' and 'All I Really Want To Do' surrounded by a lively throng of teenagers. Gene Weed is the host, while the other guests are Mel Carter, Chris Crosby (no relation to David), Grady & Brady, and Melinda Marx. (The Byrd insert is syndicated in other areas too.)

West Valley business aides have planned a gala festivity at Ciro's today, the Donner Dinner, but The Byrds probably also perform as usual tonight, for the last time until the end of the month.

Sunday 13

Stockton Civic Auditorium, Stockton, CA

The Byrds, The Kingsmen, and The Emeralds are last-minute added attractions to this concert, headlined by British duo Chad & Jeremy and singer Donna Loren.

Monday 14

The Byrds' second single pairs 'All I Really Want To Do' backed with Gene Clark's 'I'll Feel A Whole Lot Better', for the US market. The A-side is a slightly different mix than the one that will be heard on the group's upcoming debut album.

As 'Mr. Tambourine Man' is steadily climbing the US singles charts, releasing yet another Bob Dylan cover seems from the outside to be a wise move. But there is resentment against the choice in the Byrds camp; they feel that repeating the success could turn the group into Dylan imitators rather than initiators. Columbia Records, however, has overruled any objections. Other artists now have been quick to appreciate the formula of Dylan-plus-Byrds-equals-success. The Turtles, an L.A. group that has also appropriated a suitable name from the world of animals, are readying Dylan's 'It Ain't Me Babe' for launch (it will break into

the *Cash Box* Top 50 on August 14 on its way to Number Eight), and singer Cher, too, is about to release a competing version of 'All I Really Want To Do'. Unkind voices say that Cher has stolen The Byrds' arrangement, but in truth the two are different, and McGuinn's minor-tinged bridge remains unique to The Byrds' version.

However, the chart race between The Byrds and Cher in the USA is won easily by Cher, who sees sales of 'All I Really Want To Do' soar as her single 'I Got You Babe' with partner Sonny hits Number One late in the summer. Cher's version peaks at Number 15 while The Byrds' single falters at a disappointing 40 in the *Billboard* charts. (*Cash Box*, however, lists the single as high as Number 9.) Reportedly, the single is reversed so Clark's 'I'll Feel A Whole Lot Better' is promoted as the topside (but with the same catalogue number), but this does not help.

Billboard (June 26) reviews the single in its usual brief choppy style. "With 'Mr. Tambourine Man' No 1 in the chart, another hot pop, folk-flavoured Bob Dylan tune is offered by the dynamic group." The single makes its debut on the *Billboard* charts on July 3 at Number 83, three positions above Cher's version.

Tuesday 15

ALSO …

Over in New York City, Bob Dylan is back in the studio for the first time since January, raring to go and ready to move *any* goalposts. Backed by a randomly organised yet hand-picked band, Dylan burns through several takes of three brand new songs, of which 'Like A *Rolling Stone*' is re-done and finished tomorrow.

The guitarist on the session, Mike Bloomfield, says later in a radio interview on KSAN-FM: "The producer was a non-producer – Tom Wilson. He didn't know what was happening. I think they wanted rock'n'roll. We did 20 alternate takes of every song, and it got ridiculous … It was never like, 'Here's one of the tunes, and we're gonna learn it and work out an arrangement.' That just wasn't done. The thing just sort of fell together in this haphazard, half-assed way. It was like a jam session.

"The album was astutely mixed," Bloomfield continues. "I believe it was mixed by Dylan. He had a sound in his mind, because he heard records by The Byrds that knocked him out. He wanted me to play like McGuinn. That's what he was shooting for. It was even discussed. He said, 'I don't want any of that B.B. King shit, man.' Dylan would play me Cher's versions of his songs. And different English versions, Animals versions, but the Byrds sound was what he wanted to get in his sessions."

Undated June

During this month, The Byrds also play a '1965 Senior Prom' at Palisades High School, Pacific Palisades, CA (possibly on June 4 or 5), and a graduation-night party at a hotel in Beverly Hills, CA, (possibly on June 18 or 19) together with The Rockin' Roberts and The Gentrys.

Saturday 19

'Mr. Tambourine Man' enters the *Record Mirror/ Record Retailer* chart in the UK at Number 38 this week. The paper also prints a picture of The Byrds with Bob Dylan in today's edition.

Monday 21

The Byrds' debut album, *Mr. Tambourine Man*, is released in the USA. From the fisheye-lens jacket photo to Billy James's fluent liner notes and inside to the music itself, the album radiates quality, care, and consistency. Barry Feinstein's jacket photo will with time become an acknowledged classic, while James's words are hip yet ageless. The album will make a US Number Seven and UK Number Six, which will turn out to make it the group's highest charting album. By October, the album has sold a remarkable quarter of a million copies.

The album collects the four A- and B-sides of the group's two singles plus eight more numbers. Five songs are by Gene Clark, either solo or with Jim McGuinn, and of the seven cover songs, no fewer than four are from Dylan's pen. The album is crafted on time-lessness: strong melodies, interesting lyrics, disciplined musicianship, superior voices, and unique harmony vocals.

McGuinn's philosophy of life – "I trust everything will turn out all right" – is quoted in the liner notes, a pragmatic and optimistic message that will keep him in good stead over the next eight years.

'All I Really Want To Do'

A 'All I Really Want To Do'
  (B. DYLAN)

B 'I'll Feel A Whole Lot Better'
  (G. CLARK)

US release June 14 1965 (Columbia 43332)

UK release August 6 1965 (CBS 201796)

Chart high US number 40; UK number 4

Read more … entries for March 8, April 14 1965

Billboard (June 19) says of the album: "The five Byrds record success started in San Francisco [sic] and rapidly moved across the country prompting this, their debut LP for Columbia. Headed by folk-oriented Jim McGuinn, the group has successfully combined folk material with pop-dance beat arrangements. Pete Seeger's 'The Bells Of Rhymney' is a prime example of the new interpretations of folklore." *Cash Box* (June 19) pens a slightly longer review. "The Byrds who have rocketed into the Top Ten with their initial disking ... promise to do just the same with their first album effort tabbed after the smash single. Their infectious rock ork sound and smooth handlings of folk and folk-like material should score tremendous sales gains though the appeal of the title tune and other highly programmable tracks like 'The Bells Of Rhymney' and 'Don't Doubt Yourself, Babe' as well as four Bob Dylan compositions." By now, the success of The Byrds merits an album review in *Time Magazine* (July 9). "To make folk music the music of today's folk, this quintet has blended Beatle beats with Leadbelly laments, created a halfway school of folk-rock that scores at the *Cash Box* if not with the folk purists. Besides their own quasi-folk creations they blare out four Dylan tunes, including the title song, which they have already popularised as a single."

Wednesday 23

Shindig (show #41) is broadcast on the ABC network at 8:30pm on the West Coast and the East Coast and at 7:30pm in central regions (see June 12). The opening sequence features a rock'n'roll medley with David Crosby and Jim McGuinn miming 'Long Tall Sally' with Willy Nelson, while The Righteous Brothers prance to 'Sticks And Stones' and The Kingsmen and Billy Preston make the best of 'Good Golly Miss Molly'. The Byrds are seen in two spots, doing 'Not Fade Away' and 'Mr. Tambourine Man', while the rest of the hour-long programme features The Kingsmen, Micki Lynn, Jody Miller, The Righteous Brothers, The Stoneman Family, The Everly Brothers, Adam Faith, Melinda Marx, Billy Preston, Jean King, and Willy Nelson – not the country singer but a former mail boy whom producer Jack Good has discovered. Tonight's show also contains a clip of UK singer Dave Berry, filmed in England.

Friday 25

As 'Mr. Tambourine Man' enters England's *New Musical Express* charts today at Number 24, the paper runs a brief article on the group in its weekly instalment 'Newcomers To The Charts'.

The British music press provide details of The Byrds' first visit to England, which is set to commence on July 17 with radio, TV, and personal appearances promoted by Mervyn Conn and impresario Joe Collins. (In fact, the tour will be put back two weeks.)

Ever since the British Invaders started a siege of the American singles charts a year-and-a-half ago, no US pop group has really been able to stem the flow. And no US pop group has toured the UK for a long time, even if a string of pop singers and rock'n'roll and Motown stars have made the trek.

Saturday 26

'Mr. Tambourine Man' tops the US *Billboard* chart for one week, between chart-toppers by The Four Tops with 'I Can't Help Myself (Sugar Pie, Honey Bunch)' and the Rolling Stones juggernaut 'Satisfaction'. The single also tops the charts in *Cash Box*, which assembles its own charts based on different statistics. This sometimes leads to discrepancies between the two tallies, but *Billboard* is – for better or worse – considered the most representative and thus official chart survey. The group's chart-topping success in repeated in the third-largest music industry weekly, *Record World*. (For busy session drummer Hal Blaine, the Byrds hit will join an astonishing year-end tally of 15 Top Ten hits that feature him on drums, of which five make US Number One.)

Disc is again the first of the British pop papers to bring up-to-date news on The Byrds, informing its readers that Dylan's 'All I Really Want To Do' will be the group's UK follow-up single to 'Mr. Tambourine Man'.

Monday 28

◀)) **RECORDING** Columbia Recording Studios, Studio A, Sunset and El Centro, Hollywood, CA. Producer Terry Melcher and probably engineer Ray Gerhardt.

For the first time since April 22, The Byrds are back in the studio, now working on suitable choices for a new single. The group tackles two further Dylan covers: 'The Times They Are A-Changin'' (a fast-paced version of the title cut of Dylan's 1963 album) and 'It's All Over Now, Baby Blue' (like 'Mr. Tambourine Man', another song from the acoustic half of *Bringing It All Back Home*).

Most interesting, however, is Gene Clark's 'She Don't Care About Time'. Clark is a prolific songwriter now and continually growing. With this latest melodic creation he even manages to surpass his impressive batch of songs demoed at World Pacific in 1964–65, with a poetic lyric to match. Terry Melcher adds piano and almost subconsciously injects the three-note riff from '(I Can't Get No) Satisfaction', a song impossible to avoid this summer. A short harmonica solo is overdubbed, blown

---

Mr. Tambourine Man

A1 'Mr. Tambourine Man' (B. DYLAN)
A2 'I'll Feel A Whole Lot Better' (G. CLARK)
A3 'Spanish Harlem Incident' (B. DYLAN)
A4 'You Won't Have To Cry' (G. CLARK/R. McGUINN)
A5 'Here Without You' (G. CLARK)
A6 'The Bells Of Rhymney' (I. DAVIES/P. SEEGER)
B1 'All I Really Want To Do' (B. DYLAN)
B2 'I Knew I'd Want You' (G. CLARK)
B3 'It's No Use' (G. CLARK/R. McGUINN)
B4 'Don't Doubt Yourself Babe' (J. DE SHANNON)
B5 'Chimes Of Freedom' (B. DYLAN)
B6 'We'll Meet Again' (H. PARKER/D. CHARLES)

US release June 21 1965 (Mono LP CL 2372/Stereo LP CS 9172)
UK release August 20 1965 (Mono LP BPG 62571/Stereo LP SBPG 62571)
Chart high US number 6; UK number 7
Read more ... entries for January 20, March 8, April 14 and 22 1965

Bonus CD tracks: 'She Has A Way' (G. Clark), 'I'll Feel A Whole Lot Better' [Alternate Version] (G. Clark); 'It's No Use' [Alternate Version] (G. Clark/J. McGuinn), 'You Won't Have To Cry' [Alternate Version] (G. Clark/J. McGuinn), 'All I Really Want To Do' [Single Version] (B. Dylan), 'You And Me' [Instrumental] (D. Crosby/G. Clark/J. McGuinn)

"To make folk music the music of today's folk, this quintet has blended Beatle beats with Leadbelly laments, created a halfway school of folk-rock that scores at the cash box if not with the folk purists." TIME MAGAZINE, JULY 9, 1965

Dylan-style by Clark, which slightly obscures Jim McGuinn's nimble and ingenious guitar solo – stolen verbatim from part of Johann Sebastian Bach's cantata 'Herz Und Mund Und Tat Und Leben' (and better known as 'Jesu Joy Of Man's Desiring').

A tape box marked "Byrds Convention Tape" is readied for the group's appearance at the Columbia Records Sales Convention in the middle of July. It contains 'It's All Over Now Baby Blue' and 'She Don't Care About Time'. Although obviously considered now as the A- and B-sides of the next single, these and the rest of today's recordings will not be released until the advent of the CD age.

According to the exhaustive discography compiled by Byrds biographer Johnny Rogan, 'The Flower Bomb Song' is also recorded today. The song bears the distinction of

being David Crosby's first original composition recorded by the group, but unfortunately the recording is later lost.

Monday 28–Wednesday 30
Ciro's Le Disc, Hollywood, CA
The Byrds are back at Ciro's Le Disc when the club opens tonight after a fortnight's break. According to *Variety*, proprietor Frank Sennes has a six-week contractual option on The Byrds, of which two weeks were fulfilled in the first half of June.

→ Late June
□ **US TV** KHJ Studios Sunset Boulevard, Hollywood, CA. KHJ-TV *Hollywood A Go Go*
The Byrds pre-tape a performance of 'Mr. Tambourine Man', 'I'll Feel A Whole Lot Better', and 'All I Really Want To Do', broadcast

locally on July 17 and later syndicated nationally (for example on WPIX-TV Channel 11 out of New York City on August 2 and Channel 9 in the Chicago area on September 14).

Hollywood A Go Go springs from *9th Street West* and is hosted by DJ Sam Riddle. Author and music historian Domenic Priore writes later in Riot On Sunset Strip: "What set *Hollywood A Go Go* apart from the rest was the sense that it was being transmitted directly from within the spinning cataclysm of Sunset Strip nightlife. [Programme director] Al Burton recalls intending it to look 'dark and foreboding', the kind of place where, under normal circumstances, teenagers weren't allowed in. … *Hollywood A Go Go* was capped off by a group of non-professional dancers – actual rock'n'roll chicks who would [attend] out of a passion for the records."

Shindig finale, June 23, 1965.

→ Late June

▢ **US TV** Pickwick Gardens, CA. ABC network *Where The Action Is*

Also at some point in June, The Byrds are filmed on location in the Los Angeles area, lip-synching 'Mr. Tambourine Man' and 'I'll Feel A Whole Lot Better' (broadcast on July 7) and 'All I Really Want To Do' and 'Bells Of Rhymney' (August 5).

Masterminded by Dick Clark (the man behind *American Bandstand*), *Where The Action Is* premiered on June 28 and will air on weekday afternoons between 2:00–2:30pm. Where many teenage TV shows are taped at fixed locations, Clark's new show stockpiles footage from various places across the USA. The Byrds segment is apparently filmed at Pickwick Gardens in Burbank, CA, and the filmed snippets find The Byrds waist deep in a swimming pool.

July

Thursday 1– Friday 2
Ciro's Le Disc, Hollywood, CA

The Byrds probably play Ciro's Le Disc on these first two nights of July, but the dates also mark the group's finale here. With a nationwide hit record, managers Dickson and Tickner untangle The Byrds from the Ciro contract and instead send the group out on a tour of the Midwest.

The Byrd migration will sound the death knell for Ciro's Le Disc. Mike Connolly, whose Hollywood gossip columns are published in a series of newspapers across the country, reports on July 30: "Speaking of trends, the old Ciro's sign is gone from the Sunset Strip, at last, after all these years. The saloon is now called It's Boss. That's Beatle-type talk for fab. And it no longer serves hard liquor, only soft drinks, because it's being run strictly for the Junior Jerk Set." This policy is the result of a new law, which will see an increasing influx of teenagers in Hollywood over the next 15 months at the cost of tourists, traffic, and the establishment – finally culminating in an ugly confrontation between youth and police.

Thursday 1

▢ **UK TV** Over in England, The Byrds appear on the BBC institution *Top Of The Pops* (show No.79, at 7:00pm). It is not an actual performance but just the record played against a visual backdrop. A straightforward music-chart television programme, the weekly *Top Of The Pops* has become crucial to promote hit artists in the UK since its inception in January 1964. Where America has a multitude of different television shows, many shown locally, in Britain there are far fewer television channels and, consequently, fewer shows aimed at teenagers. Today's TOTP is presented by DJ Alan Freeman and mirrors the week's chart action with performances by The Dave Clark Five ('Catch Us If You Can'), The Hollies ('I'm Alive'), The Yardbirds ('Heart Full Of Soul'), and others.

•

As 'Mr. Tambourine Man' climbs the UK singles charts, Jim McGuinn takes part in a transatlantic phone interview with *Melody Maker* during the first days of July. It runs on July 10, marking the first exclusive coverage of The Byrds in a UK pop paper. 'America Fights Back – With Groups That Look Just Like Ours!' blasts the headline. "I'm very glad we're getting liked over there in England," says McGuinn. "[Dylan] is a friend of ours. We like him and his music, and his whole attitude to life as a matter of fact. I've been on the same scene as him, singing in coffee-houses in Greenwich Village since 1961. But I don't think I'd like The Byrds to be called a folk group, strictly. Folk is where we came from. We passed through it. I wouldn't put us down as rock'n'roll, either. We're somewhere in between. We are keen on all contemporary music. We don't care for labels. We simply like the music that Bob Dylan writes. Music that is associated with the jet age. All Dylan's material can have that jet age applied to it."

Explaining their recent success, McGuinn offers an analysis. "I think we were lucky with a combination of circumstances. Perhaps there was a gap between pop music that was currently going on, and between the folk and the rock fields, that needed filling. Maybe we filled it. But I don't want to state it categorically. It's all so insignificant. It's part of the natural evolution of music."

Friday 2

New Musical Express's regular 'Life Lines' column in the British pop paper is this week devoted to The Byrds. It has the usual mix of teen trivia (favourite food, favourite drink, favourite clothes), corny facts, and witty asides. Asked of his personal ambition, David Crosby scribbles: "To own and sail a large schooner" – a desire he will, perhaps unintentionally, fulfil two years later. Crosby is also the hippest, listing jazz musicians "Miles [Davis], [Gil or Bill] Evans, [John] Coltrane" as his favourite composers and stating that "jazz, Indian, classical, rock'n'roll, blues" are his preferred listening.

Saturday 3
'The Beach Boys Summer Spectacular', Hollywood Bowl, Los Angeles, CA

KFWB presents one show at 8:15pm with The Beach Boys, Sam The Sham & The Pharaohs, The Byrds, Donna Loren, The Sir Douglas Quintet ('She's About A Mover' is their recent Top 20 hit), Sonny & Cher (a late addition), Dino Desi & Billy, The Kinks ("direct from England!"), Ian Whitcomb, The Righteous Brothers, and The Liverpool Five. The concert grosses $55,135, and attendance is 14,327.

The Kinks are in the middle of an American tour fraught with stress, as they are plagued with problems with the American Federation of Television & Radio Artists. Ian Whitcomb, an oddity in the British Invasion with his novelty hit 'Your Turn Me On', tells *Record Mirror* (August 28): "[The] thing we did at the Hollywood Bowl was really good. Eighteen-thousand kids were there."

Charles Champlin has brought his kids as a sounding board for his review in The *Los Angeles Times* (July 6). "The show wasn't intended as a competition, but the four young reviewers named Champlin who were with me thought it was. They further allowed that the order of finish was: (1) The Beach Boys, (2) The Kinks, (3) The Byrds."

Sunday 4

The Byrds are given the prestigious role as entertainers at an Independence Day party held by actress Jane Fonda at her lavish Malibu home. The group has recently played at a party thrown by wealthy playboy Lance

Reventlow, but today's reception goes one better with its glamorous guest list, and is staged by the Party Planners ("We handle everything, from the time the invitations go out to when the last hors d'oeuvre goes down the disposal unit," boasts chief party planner Stanley J. Weiler in the press).

Among the celebrities are the hostess herself and husband Roger Vadim; Shirlee Adams and Henry Fonda; Peter Fonda and wife Susan Brewer; Arthur Loew Jr.; and British actor David McCallum – star of television series *The Man from U.N.C.L.E.* – with actress wife Jill Ireland. Derek Taylor, writing in *Melody Maker* (July 17), lists a slew of further guests who drop by: Lauren Bacall, Steve McQueen, Tom Tryon, Peggy Lipton, George Cukor, Sidney Poitier, Dianne Carroll, Roddy McDowall (who lives next door), Mia Farrow, Warren Beatty, Peter Finch, Ronald Fraser, James Fox, Ian Bannen, and John Leyton.

Carl Franzoni and Sue and Vito Paulekas are invited to dance about – to the consternation of Taylor, who is afraid that the freaks will clash with the glitterati. Franzoni: "Bryan MacLean and I had set up the equipment early in the day. Bryan knew Jane because his father was a famous architect. That evening, about a dozen of us went to the party in Malibu. The band was in the tent and you could dance in the sand. Then Sue and Vito goosed Jane and things got loose. They loved us!"

Monday 5
Moonlight Gardens, Lakeside Amusement Park, Denver, CO

At 3:16 in the morning following the Jane Fonda party and still in Hollywood, Jim McGuinn is on the line to Chris Hutchins in London for an interview for *New Musical Express* (July 16). "We wanna buy mod clothes in Carnaby Street – then we'll be able to look even more English. And I wanna meet John Lennon: he sounds like a man after my own heart. Who knows, maybe we'll even come home with English accents. Crazy." McGuinn

reveals that The Byrds have plans to make a film later this year, writing and directing the script themselves.

Later in the day, the entourage flies out to Denver for the opening date of The Byrds' first proper tour. In an innovative and daring move, they bring along Carl Franzoni's dancers so that the audiences can see and hear the Byrds multimedia experience first-hand. Besides Franzoni, the troupe consists of Bob Roberts, Karen Odell, and Lizzie Donahue, plus a third girl who is soon fired and flown home. Hiring the dancers is Dickson's idea, reputedly against the wishes of McGuinn, who fears it will upstage the group's act. Also along for the trip is young roadie Bryan McLean, while photographer Barry Feinstein – the man responsible for the jacket photo on the *Mr. Tambourine Man* album – is hired to document the tour. (Apparently, Feinstein does not stay for the whole tour.) Jim Dickson has hired his friend John Barrick to escort the group, while Joe Stevens, a native New Yorker who

Independence Day party 1965 at Jane Fonda's place in Malibu.

43

has followed the tide from Greenwich Village to Hollywood and has fallen in with the Byrds crowd, signs up as driver. The chosen mode of transport is a large bus, and the bus with the equipment leaves ahead of the group and the dancers in order to make the more than 850-mile journey from Los Angeles to Denver.

Local Denver-group The Moonrakers are the opening act. Drummer Bob MacVittie recalls: "The Byrds were getting their feet wet as a touring act from the success of their first album. 'Mr. Tambourine Man' was the big hit. There really wasn't any dressing room that was appropriate. Joel Brandes, our bass player and business brains, was making decisions as the promoter. He had the band come to his parents' house in east Denver. His parents were out of town. We ordered pizza and all hung out there until time to go to the show. There was a group of Sunset Strip club-goers who were following along and dancing in the audience as a group. Similar to what the Dead-heads eventually did. Many people showed up.

"We played and then they did. To us it was a rousing success. Not so much so with The Byrds. When their road manager settled with Joel, he said that in the future they would be more careful about choosing their promoters. That was the beginning of the end of our small town naïveté."

Moonrakers singer Denny Flannigan adds: "We promoted The Byrds at Lakeside Amusement Park. They came with a full troupe of dancers and were quite a show. They were very California-looking at the time and sounded great. There were some very interesting people that came with them and I imagine quite a few drugs of the day."

•

Carl Franzoni, in a later interview with Efram Turchick, recalls the month-long summer journey with The Byrds. "They asked me to pick a good amount of people to go with them [on tour] and we became the Byrds dancers. The tour was really something! The first place we went was Denver. We went into Minnesota; Youngstown, Ohio; Dayton, Ohio – stuff like that. I mean, it was something to see, the way we danced! The kids were dancing in those lines at the time, line dancing, and we came in there and we broke up all that stuff. … I got punched a couple times because they didn't like our style of dance. But after that, the whole United States went into that style. We were trained dancers."

Questioned about the atmosphere on the bus, Franzoni says: "I brought some women, some good looking women that [the group] could relate to. But they didn't really have to worry about that: girls were knocking on their doors as soon as they got in the hotel

rooms. But it was pleasant for them to have a couple of the dancers there – they could talk to them and stuff like that. For the most part, the women were really good dancers. I had to pick the best I could find. There was a guy who was a dancer who came with us – they didn't want any men, they really didn't want any guys. But I convinced them that this guy Bob Roberts should come. Bob Roberts became a saxophonist with Frank Zappa … I was the freak, because I had my own kind of uniform: tights and boots and crazy-looking shirts. There was another guy who was not mentioned: Bryan MacLean. He was their roadie, and I helped him roadie. He and I roomed together on the road."

Tuesday 6
Sioux Falls Coliseum Annex, Sioux Falls, SD
KISD Discotheque presents The Byrds in one show at 8:00pm. A young girl called Linda Lou appears out of nowhere with her chaperone to follow the tour from now until the end. Carl Franzoni: "They were both dancers, and Linda Lou was a special teenybopper. They followed the bus in a separate car."

Wednesday 7
Prom Ballroom, St. Paul, MN
Dance show from 8:30pm until midnight.

The Byrds are seen nationwide this afternoon at 2:00pm on the ABC network's *Where The Action Is* (episode #7, see late June), miming to 'Mr. Tambourine Man' and 'I'll Feel A Whole Lot Better'. Host is Steve Alaimo, while other guests are Jackie DeShannon, house band Paul Revere & The Raiders, and regular dance troupe The Action Kids.

In Britain, The Byrds' coming visit meets unexpected trouble when Musicians Union secretary Harry Francis tells *New Musical Express* today that the union will not allow The Byrds into Britain unless an exchange is made for a British group to go to America for a similar period of time. There is a hair-splitting argument about whether The Byrds are 'an act' (which will easily grant them a working permit) or 'a band of musicians' (which is more troublesome). Francis has backing from the American Federation of Musicians, the equivalent US union, which also supports the exchange system between the USA and the UK. Asked for a comment, impresario Joe Collins tells the paper: "The Government has the final say, not the Union. I give you my word, The Byrds will arrive as scheduled and appear on every one of the dates we have set."

•

The Byrds are subjected to the trouble that affects so many other visiting US musicians this year due to strict visa restrictions on

British artists visiting America. The situation builds resentment on the British side and less willingness to accept US visitors with open arms. Just a few months ago, British singer Wayne Fontana – on the very week in April he sits as Number One in the *Billboard* charts – is only granted an H-2 visa, which entitles him to make only one public performance. Fontana fumes: "It's jealousy. And plain childishness. At first they were not going to grant me a visa at all. We had to get letters of confirmation from *Billboard* and *Cash Box* magazines about my being Number One before they would admit to my being well known in America. … With so many American artists in this country – Screaming Jay Hawkins, The Walker Brothers, and P.J. Proby to name three – [and] all being granted extended work permits, I cannot understand the American attitude."

Editor Derek Johnson makes a sweeping attack on the practice in *New Musical Express* (April 30). "At this very moment, America is striving desperately to seek peaceful solutions to the problems in Vietnam and her own Deep South. Why then is she, at the same time, unashamedly creating another international incident, by being deliberately hostile to British pop business? For, make no mistake, America's attitude to our artists is far more important than a mere squabble within the entertainment industry. It nibbles at the very roots of Anglo-American relations.

"For many decades, during which America has been undisputed top dog in the music business, the steady flow of artists from the States into this country has continued unabated – and we have always welcomed them warmly. … True, there have been intermittent complications with the respective musicians' unions, but these have been ironed out by a system of reciprocal exchange, which until recently was working very smoothly. Suddenly, in the course of a year, the entire picture has changed. For the first time ever, thanks initially to the Beatle boom, Britain has assumed the role of champion of pops. The shoe is on the other foot, and, quite dramatically, our own boys and girls find themselves dominating the American hit parade.

"What happens? Sandie Shaw and Twinkle are banned outright. … The Hollies and Wayne Fontana & The Mindbenders are kept hanging about for days before reluctantly being issued with H-2 visas – which means that they can travel to America but have to obtain renewed permission to work in each individual state or city. … Reasons given by the American Embassy in London for these restrictions are either that 'the artists are insufficiently well-known in America to warrant working there' … or that they have nothing original to add to the American show-business

The Byrds perform for the television cameras. From left: McGuinn, Clark, Clarke, Hillman, and Crosby.

scene. The reason for the Americans' dictatorial attitude is simply – sour grapes. They bitterly resent the success of our artists after themselves being on top for so long. And in true American tradition, they cannot bear to be the underdogs."

→ Thursday 8
[Possibly The Armory], Duluth, MI
The tour swings by Duluth in northern Minnesota on Lake Superior. Carl Franzoni recalls: "Cold as an iceberg, really brrr!! for that time of year."

Friday 9
Although no concerts are accounted for today, the group certainly has a booking as it is a weekend, before the Byrds bus likely travels to Chicago. Franzoni explains to John Trubee that their base was Chicago, from where they'd travel to shows in Ohio, Kentucky, Minnesota, and so on. "When you're out on a tour you have a base place, and you work in Chicago, too – and you work in Indiana [etc] because those are the surrounding states."

It may be right now that David Crosby buys his famed green suede cape, which he purchases at The Leather Shop in Piper's Alley on Chicago's Wells Street. Later, when the cloak becomes his visual trademark, Crosby buys a couple of others in different colours.

Saturday 10
Rockford College Physical Education Building, Rockford, IL
The Byrds play for a dance from 5:15 until 11:30pm. The support is local group The Blackstones, whose guitarist Jerry McGeorge soon joins The Shadows Of Knight.

David Stine is in the audience. "The summer of 1965 I was struggling to get my own little teenage band together when 'Mr. Tambourine Man', the song and the LP, hit the charts. Although we were headed in a Rolling Stones/Yardbirds direction, The Byrds really turned us around. When we learned they would be coming to Rockford, we had to go. As the warm-up band, The Blackstones, played, we noticed a number of people who didn't seem to fit the Midwestern college student mould and guessed they must have come with The Byrds. There were girls with long straight hair, guys with longish hair (which hadn't caught on locally yet), and one guy we were sure was a Byrd in a Russian-looking hat. Turned out this was Bryan McLean.

"Although it was July and hot," Stine continued, "The Byrds took the stage dressed as they looked in the press: turtlenecks, jackets, and jeans. Except David Crosby, who wore his green suede cape, of course. I believe they played a little over an hour. It

was apparent that they didn't have several sets' worth of material yet, but the only song besides 'Mr. Tambourine Man' that I recall is Jackie DeShannon's 'When You Walk In The Room'.

"The Blackstones came back for another set, and then it was announced that The Byrds would play until the close of the concert. As we were underage, we had to leave before the end of the night. We found a way to get up behind them from a floor above and watch them perform below and in front of us, which was pretty cool."

Sunday 11
Terp Ballroom, Austin, MN
Austin is a small town about 75 miles south of Minneapolis, where The Byrds play this dance, which runs from 8:00pm until midnight.

Monday 12
Likely a day off, spent travelling to the next stop on the itinerary.

Tuesday 13
The group are booked to appear at Roof Garden Ballroom, Arnolds Park, in Iowa, but fail to turn up for reasons unknown. The Thunderbolts from nearby Carroll, IA, play the dance instead.

→ Wednesday 14
Inwood Ballroom, Riverside Park, Spillville, IA

Thursday 15
Pla-Mor Ballroom, Rochester, MN
The Byrds play at a "Young People's Dance" from 8:00pm till midnight.
■ **UK TV** Meanwhile in Britain, The Byrds are heard if not seen for a second time on BBC TV's *Top Of The Pops* (episode No.81, at 7:00pm). As with the July 1 show, this is not an actual performance, but rather 'Mr. Tambourine Man' played while show regulars The Go-Jos dance. Tonight's *TOTP* is presented by DJ Pete Murray and features new performances by Billy Fury, Peter Cook & Dudley Moore, The Animals ('We've Gotta Get Out Of This Place'), The Fortunes, and Vikki Carr, plus several repeated performances from earlier shows.

Friday 16
'This Is Where It's At' teen party, Columbia Records International Convention, Americana Hotel Ballroom, Miami Beach, FL

The Byrds fly out to Miami to appear at the Columbia Records Convention, held at one of the city's swankiest hotels. The group almost certainly present the two numbers recorded specifically for the convention (see June 28). They are photographed in swimwear surrounded by local beach beauties, and with Miss Ireland, Elizabeth Neil, one of the participants in the Miss Universe contest to be held next weekend.

Billboard (July 24) writes: "For four weeks prior to the convention, stations WFUN and WQAM had conducted a write-in promotion with kids getting tickets to attend the Columbia teen party. Each station delivered 500 youngsters. The 200 Columbia salesmen and promotion men were seated in the back of the room and exposed to the electric reaction of the 1,000 youngsters as the teen performers put on their show." Other Columbia artists appearing include Paul Revere & The Raiders, The Duprees, and Billy Joe Royal.

Carl Franzoni thinks the Miami detour marks a profound change in the group's attitude, as he tells John Trubee. "We were in there two weeks. We're coming from the west to the east to Chicago … so when we go to Chicago, we're gonna make a southern tour then. OK, so The Byrds get there – and the management says, 'Go to Miami, Florida.' Now, they're not taking us. They told us, 'You sit tight in Chicago in the hotel rooms and just relax, rest yourselves, because the tour is another two weeks.' OK? So for three days they were gone. When they came back, they were different people. They had been swallowed by the capitalist entrepreneurs who were their mentors, who gave them their money."

Far away from Florida, a well-meaning but ultimately damaging headline in today's *New Musical Express* trumpets 'Byrds Biggest Craze Since Beatles!'. Chris Hutchins, who recently interviewed Jim McGuinn (see July 5), writes: "Unless I am very much mistaken, August is going to see Britain gripped by a new phenomenon – Byrdmania. Stand by for the biggest explosion of hysteria since The Beatles first sent love 'from me to you', when The Byrds fly from Hollywood to cash in on the success of this week's haunting chart-topper."

Hutchins even honours Franzoni's role (although he is just plain 'Carl' in the article): "He now superintends coach parties – I'm not joking! – of fans who tag after each Byrds show to follow them to the next city." It is true that

at this point The Byrds are seriously considering bringing Franzoni across the pond for the UK tour.

Saturday 17

Hollywood A Go Go goes out at 8:00pm PST on KHJ-TV with The Byrds performing 'Mr. Tambourine Man', 'I'll Feel A Whole Lot Better', and 'All I Really Want To Do' (see late June). Introduced by Sam Riddle, the guest line-up is completed by Ian Whitcomb, Bobby Vee, Lenny Welch, Jackie Wilson, The Challengers, The Sinners, and the Gazzarri Dancers.

Up north, as the group returns to Chicago, they are barred entry to the O'Hare Inn, a luxury hotel adjacent to Chicago's O'Hare Airport that has earlier served such distinguished guests as presidents John F. Kennedy and Lyndon B. Johnson. Hotel manager John Theodasakis declares that all rock'n'roll musicians will be banned. "During their stay, the longhaired singing unit came to breakfast in the O'Hare Inn Restaurant without shoes," Theodasakis tells *The Oakland Tribune* (July 21) in an Associated Press news feature. "The Byrds dressed more in keeping with a flophouse than a respectable motel, and it is our feeling that we can very well do without their patronage."

(Today was the original date set for the opening of the group's UK visit, with an itinerary including BBC-2 television's Gadzooks (July 19), Granada's Scene At 6.30 (20), BBC-1's *Top Of The Pops* (22), Rediffusion's *Ready Steady Go!* (23), and ABC TV's *Thank Your Lucky Stars* (24), in addition to concerts at Manchester Oasis (24) and White Rock Pavilion, Hastings the following day. The group's arrival has already been postponed two weeks, and many of the bookings have been moved accordingly.)

Disc has acquired an under-the-counter copy of The Byrds' Mr. Tambourine Man album (it will not be released in the UK until August 20). "This is pop-folk at its best. Songs with a message sung in a manner which attracts the younger generations, and gives them something to think about as well as something for dancing," reflects Nigel Hunter. "This LP

enables a bigger and closer assessment to be made, and the boys come triumphantly through. A huge asset is their professionalism. So many parts of the folk scene are marred by amateurism, a futile belief that if you're sincere, that's all that counts, and vocal and instrumental inability don't matter. The Byrds bring a glowing polish to their work while retaining their full quota of sincerity which makes it ring true."

In the same issue of *Disc*, backing-vocalist-to-the-stars Ken Lewis of The Ivy League opines: "The Byrds' 'Mr. Tambourine Man' is a wonderful sound, but technically, it's terrible. It's badly made and edited. Yet the outcome is marvellous."

•

'Mr. Tambourine Man' tops the charts in UK's *Disc*, marking the coveted Double Number One for the group – crowning both UK and US charts. The single will become a worldwide smash, climbing the charts in near and faraway markets such as New Zealand, Norway, Denmark, Sweden, Hong Kong, Holland, West Germany, Italy, South Africa, and Canada. Sometimes the ascent is swift, while at other times in other regions the rise to the top is like a slow wave. At the end of October this year, 'Mr. Tambourine Man' will stand at Number Four in the Hong Kong charts and at Number One in Singapore. A whole year later, in July 1966, the single will be found at Number Four in The Philippines, while 'You Won't Have To Cry' – specially lifted from the debut album for the Asian market – is at Number Ten. By then, the single will have passed the one million mark and still be selling.

Sunday 18
Idora Park Ballroom, Idora Park, Youngstown, OH

Sometimes, Hollywood nonconformity clashes with Midwest attitudes, as Franzoni attests. "I remember in Youngstown, Ohio, somebody slugged me right in the fucking stomach," he says to John Trubee. "They didn't want you to dance other than the way they were dancing. It was that line dance – they had the line dance where the women would line up on one side and the men would line up on the other, and they would come at each other. That was the dance of the day. And here we come in and we're doing this total freak-out dancing."

Monday 19
Stardust Garden Ballroom, LeSourdesville Lake Amusement park, Monroe, OH

Support by Ian & The Sabres.

Monroe is just a few miles north of Cincin-

nati, so Franzoni, Linda Lou the dancer, and a couple of The Byrds drive down to pick up Carl's daughter, who also joins the tour bus.

→ Tuesday 20
Sugar Shack, Chillicothe, OH

The Byrds show up two hours late for their concert in Chillicothe.

Wednesday 21

Cedar Point Ballroom, Sandusky, OH

For $1.50 admission, The Byrds play a dance that runs from 8:00 to 11:30pm.

→ Thursday 22
☐ **US TV** KYW-TV Studios, Cleveland, OH
The Mike Douglas Show

The itinerary allows for a side trip probably today to Cleveland, where the daytime television talk show hosted by Mike Douglas is taped. Douglas has built up a steady audience of several million viewers, as the show is syndicated throughout most of the USA. Uniquely, this is the only occasion where Carl Franzoni's dancing to The Byrds is filmed, as he recalls. "We went to do a TV show with [British actress] Hermione Gingold, and she saw me dancing backstage and brought me out. I danced for The Byrds' encore, as there were no other dancers there." Franzoni bops to 'I'll Feel A Whole Lot Better', one of at least two selections by The Byrds featured on the programme. The show is first broadcast on September 8.

☐ **UK TV** As British chart-toppers, The Byrds are naturally featured for a third time on BBC TV's *Top Of The Pops* (show No.82, at 7:00pm). Lacking a promo clip, presenter Jimmy Savile simply plays the 'Mr. Tambourine Man' Aside. Preparing for The Byrds' visit to British shores, the BBC sends off a letter, dated today, to the Ministry of Labour (Overseas Department) to confirm the group's bookings for the Corporation.

Friday 23
Indiana Beach Ballroom,
Lake Shafer, Monticello,
IN

Pat Rochhio writes an all-to-brief review in the *Kokomo Tribune* (July 31). "Saw The Byrds' recent performance at Indiana Beach. To say the least, this very unusual group with a very unique sound is most entertaining. They were certainly crowd-pleasers and delighted the teen audience."

Happily, *New Musical Express* today declares that last week's work-permit dispute is settled as an agreement has been struck with The Dave Clark Five, who will remain in America for two extra weeks to comply with the exchange for a British group as demanded by the Musicians Union. However, The Byrds' two planned BBC radio appearances (*Saturday Club* and The Joe Loss Show) have to be dropped because of an MU ruling. The logic is that there are no similar programmes in the USA and the Union has therefore barred the bookings. Tomorrow's *Melody Maker* reports: "The Byrds are coming with the full blessing of the Musicians Union, with the proviso that there are no radio shows. The exchange is all fixed."

Saturday 24
McCormick Place,
Arie Crown Theatre,
Chicago, IL

The Byrds play McGuinn's hometown supported by The Shadows Of Knight, house band at the Cellar club over in Arlington Heights. It is probably today that the group sign autographs at four department stores around the city (including a Sears store in Oakbrook), accompanied by WLS radio disc jockey Ron Riley and Columbia promotional chief Fred Salem. The group's in-store appearances cause riots with damages estimated at a hefty $30,000–40,000, according to *KRLA Beat*.

Building anticipation for The Byrds' forthcoming UK trip, the British music weeklies are full of the group. *Disc* has asked "the Jones boys" – *Rolling Stone* Brian and Manfred Mann singer Paul – to share some thoughts in today's issue. "We spent seven nights with The Byrds … so I had plenty of time to get to know them – especially Mike Clarke, who plays drums, and guitarist Dave Crosby," says Brian Jones. "They are very nice fellows. Mike is very much like me, only much taller. We

were always being mistaken for each other and we seemed to be meeting the same girls! I went to dinner with Dave a few times, and we talked about the music scene in Britain. The Byrds seemed very anxious to make it in England, even more so than in America.

"It seems that The Byrds have brought the folk music technique to the electric guitar group sound," Brian continues, "sort of giving folk a rock'n'roll sound. They are great on the Dylan stuff, but off it they tend to sound like second-rate Searchers. But I wish them all the best in Britain. They are very nice fellows." As if warning the British public, Brian concludes: "They don't go in for any showmanship on stage – but I wouldn't like them if they did. They are very static, in fact. But spearheaded by The Who and the Yards [Yardbirds], there seems to be a new rave of groups. Now it's The Byrds."

Paul Jones of Manfred Mann pens his own contribution. "['Mr. Tambourine Man'] is the only record of The Byrds I have heard, but it made an immediate impression on me when I first heard it on [pirate] Radio London. I'm not a purist or anything about folk. In fact, I loathe and detest folk music. … I wouldn't even say 'Mr. Tambourine Man' is folk – or that even Dylan is folk."

Reacting to accusations that The Byrds are merely Beatles copyists, Paul adds: "I can think of 20 groups more like The Beatles than The Byrds. I am looking forward to meeting The Byrds in person. I have seen their photograph, and I think they succeed in looking like what The Pretty Things are trying to look like." (Perhaps inspired by The Byrds, Paul's group Manfred Mann will begin interpreting Bob Dylan numbers too, starting with the EP track 'With God On Our Side' and then 'If You Gotta Go, Go Now', which becomes a big UK hit in October.)

Mick Jagger guests in this week's 'Hit Talk' in *Disc*, where the stars comment on the weekly charts. He says: "The Byrds are Number One again. Fair enough, I suppose, because it's probably one of the best records there is around at the moment." (The following week, Lulu sighs: "I'm sick to death of that Byrds record. I think it's been overexposed on radio stations. I'm looking forward to seeing them, though."

Also today, 'Mr. Tambourine Man' tops the official UK charts in *Record Mirror* and *Record Retailer* for the first of two weeks (before yielding to The Beatles' 'Help!'), with The Yardbirds' single 'Heart Full of Soul' at Number Two. Apparently, some fans confuse the two groups – The Yardbirds are often nicknamed the 'Birds (much to the chagrin of The Byrds, according to *Melody Maker*), and The Yardbirds explain how some devotees ask for 'Mr.

Tambourine Man' to be played at the live appearances.

The Walker Brothers, three California expatriates who have recently established themselves in Britain, occasionally crossed paths with The Byrds in the past. *Melody Maker* has interviewed the trio's drummer, Gary Walker, who makes some interesting claims in today's issue. "They originally copied us," he says of The Byrds. "When they first started out, they used to come to the club where we were working [Gazzarri's]. At that time we were the only group in Hollywood with long hair. They started letting theirs grow and grow and grow. This would be about nine months ago. In those days they were calling themselves The Children – they changed the name to The Byrds later on. They used to watch how we dressed and played. They did our numbers and caught on to just about everything about us. And when they weren't doing us, they were doing a Rolling Stones – with the five guys in the group and everything.

"We weren't really aware of what they were doing at the beginning. They are all very nice guys but kind of quiet: they used to sit in the corner not saying too much. Just listening to us and watching. Now, out of nowhere, here they are at the top. Still, at least we were first with our stuff. And somebody was about due for a break in Hollywood when we left to come to England. The record company found them, I guess, and with Dylan doing the song and everything, that put them right in there."

It turns out that The Walker Brothers have unwittingly helped plug the record: "The song is great," says Gary. "We heard the record and thought it was a nice tune. So when we got back here we plugged the thing on stage. Everybody thought it was our record for a while. Then, about a month ago, it started to climb and we thought, 'What are we doing?' We realised we were helping somebody else's record along so we dropped it from the act."

He continues: "You know, the Dylan thing must have been a big help. He's got so popular, and getting together with him must have helped to take it from there. And, I guess, nobody else could do a cover of the tune without Dylan's permission. … They're all very quiet guys. I heard that Jim McGuinn, the lead guitarist, had done some work with Bobby Darin. That surprised me. As a musician he isn't that good. … Vocally, too, the group is kind of weak to our way of thinking. They swing very softly on 'Mr. Tambourine Man' so it doesn't really give you much idea whether they have improved."

(As for the story of early Byrds supposedly going by the name of The Children, McGuinn denies this when questioned at a press meeting in London on August 2.)

→ Sunday 25

[Possibly Casa-Loma Ballroom], East St. Louis, MO

A couple of students from Washington University, St Louis, interview Jim McGuinn for the teenage magazine *Flip* today. Asked why the group has brought dancers on tour, he says: "They made the whole place livelier, so our manager decided to take them with us everywhere we go."

•

By now, The Byrds are seen regularly in the many teen mags that flourish in the USA, but these are usually tame articles focussing on glossy photographs and mindless trivia – except for the rare occasion when a quick-witted remark or the group's deep musical knowledge brighten the content. Asked what his biggest break in showbiz was, Gene Clark jests: "To my left leg." Asked for his favourite musicians in 16 Magazine (October 1965), Chris Hillman is revealed as a keen blues scholar and lists Muddy Waters, Mose Allison, Sleepy John [Estes], and Robert Johnson. Blues singer and guitarist Johnson – years later to become a household name – is now only known to the most serious devotee.

Derek Taylor, with the benefit of two years hindsight, writes in The *Los Angeles Times* (May 21, 1967): "I discovered the L.A. pop scene had no [James] Boswell, no attentive hack. So I decided to pour written material into the fan magazines, most of which then operated on low budgets with half-trained, underpaid, and overworked staffs, and which were howling for ready-to-print fluent essays which could say anything or nothing as long as you had the colour of the group's eyes right, [and] also their correct birth signs, which, for some reason, seemed to be important."

Hit Parader, published six times a year by Charlton Publications out on the West Coast, represents an exception. The magazine has been in circulation since 1943. It is well informed and well written. Confusingly, the bimonthly editions (the magazine begins publishing monthly in 1966) are on sale months before the date printed on them. Thus, *Hit Parader* of September 1965 is already at the newsstands now, with a brief feature on The Byrds written some time in April. The article focuses on the group's previous credentials and claims boldly that Chris Hillman, an outstanding mandolin player, is equally adept at playing John Coltrane solos or bluegrass.

The edition dated November 1965 has an interview with the five, conducted some time this July. "We're taking something from everywhere to create new music," says an unidentified Byrd. "We want to break the arbitrary delineations between different forms of music. We want to grow as far as we can. Don't call

us a 'Rockfolk' group. It's an awkward word. It dilutes the strength of pure rock. The folk scene is dead today. There's no bread in it except for a few people. The folk boom of two years ago was like a raft that too many people got onto."

ALSO …

"The fifth annual Newport Folk Festival came to an end at 1:00am after a grand finale which delighted everyone," reports Jane Nippert in *Newport Daily News* (July 26), a surprisingly jolly line given the seismic tremor that shakes the stage and will reverberate in years to come. "Bob Dylan seemed to be the attraction of the show. His first three numbers had rock'n'roll accompaniment. He and others played electric guitars, and one musician did nothing to enhance the act by dancing around the stage. When it was announced Dylan would give an encore, there were numerous shouts for him to come back alone and to 'throw away that electric guitar'. He returned alone to sing 'Baby Blue' and 'Mr. Tambourine Man', then left the stage to the disappointment of his fans, who set up a terrific howl for more." Dylan is followed on stage by Peter Paul & Mary, Joan Baez, and Pete Seeger. Nippert adds: "Throughout it all there were cries for Bob Dylan, but those on stage appeared not to hear."

Monday 26

Gypsy Village, Fontaine Ferry Park, Louisville, KY

The Byrds play a dance with The Oxfords and WAKY DJ and MC Gee Williams.

In the UK, an internal memo from the BBC Light Entertainment Booking Manager Patrick Newman to the BBC administration sheds light on the problems the Corporation is up against. "[The Byrds] is at the moment the most successful of this species in America. They sing and accompany themselves – like The Beatles. They were to come to this country and we understood they were anxious to do radio. We offered two engagements [The Joe Loss Show to be recorded on August 6, and *Saturday Club*, to be taped on August 9] and these were accepted by the agent – in addition to which we naturally obtained Ministry of Labour permission. Last week there was a lot of chitchat in the Press which you may have read. It concerned the intervention of the MU who said the group would not be allowed to come into the country because the right exchange or exchanges had not been fixed … A couple of days ago, the agent concerned rang me up to say the MU had been on to him saying that the group would not be allowed to broadcast. I told him that we did not go to the MU for such permission but

to the Ministry of Labour who had already given us a clearance. I then added that the Ministry, if they wished to rescind the permission they had given as a result of anything the MU might say, would no doubt be in touch with the Corporation. With billing for the first programme imminent I rang the Ministry who told me that they had that very day received a four-page letter from the MU However, notwithstanding the contents of the letter, they told me that the permission they had given still stood." When the agent is so told, he says The Byrds are no longer available because he does not want to be at odds with the MU. Instead, the agent suggests to the man from the BBC that the Corporation should fire off a letter to the MU to gently twist the Union's arm. "One knows this sort of reaction to be not of much value," continues the internal BBC memo with understatement, "and indeed possibly a bit immature."

The BBC man adds an exasperating postscript to the formal memo. "True, we had not – as I have said – got a signed contract on this occasion, but even when we do, our contracts seem to be flouted left, right, and centre … It would be nice if one day we could haul someone back and do something drastic like (since hanging is now abolished) clapping them in irons. One sometimes wonders what our contracts are for, and maybe if we are going to be 'computerised' it would be simpler for the computer if we deleted all the written clauses since they do not seem to amount to much anyway."

Tuesday 27–Saturday 31

The Byrds wind up their Midwest tour with dates in Paris, IL (playing the Pavilion in Twin Lakes Amusement Park), and a pair of hastily arranged suburban Chicago school bookings at Morton High School, Berwyn, IL, and Arlington Heights High School, Arlington Heights, IL – the latter with The Shadows Of Knight in support again. Reportedly, the group is also booked for a combined dance and TV show at the Albert Kahn Dance Pavilion, Bob Lo Island Park, an amusement park on the Detroit River, together with Martha & The Vandellas, The Spinners, Barbara Lewis, The Orlons, and Vic Dana. No further documentation will survive of the proposed TV show, called *Teen Town*, or the concert.

Derek Taylor joins the group in Chicago, as he will accompany them on the coming tour of England.

Carl Franzoni is tired of travelling with The Byrds, fatigued by humping gear, frustrated by the lack of female company ("[The Byrds] would have three, four, five teenage girls knock on their doors and they would just gobble them in"), and in the end enforces his own resignation. "The Byrds fired me from their tour. … [On] the last night they said we should assemble at this high school, at a gig, and all through the tour I was tormented about not having any sex," he tells John Trubee. Asking if it is OK to bring a girl with him on the bus, Franzoni is given a curt "no" and decides to leave. "When I got back to L.A. I went to get my last check from the Byrds management, and they said, 'You're no longer a member of this organization,' gave me a check, and that was it." With that, the grand plan to bring Franzoni's dancers to Britain is also dropped.

Looking back, Franzoni sums up: "They were the finest musical group in the white category as far as dancing was concerned. There was no question that when you got on the dance floor with The Byrds, those five guys, that was like heaven. It was like going to church."

Friday 30

Over in the UK, yet more dates are added to the group's itinerary. Originally, promoter Mervyn Conn had planned a fairly relaxed timetable, but as their arrival approaches, the strategy seems to be to milk their presence for all it's worth. Today's front cover of *New Musical Express* has the itinerary in a half-page advertisement placed by Joe Collins & Mervyn Conn International. Business is brisk; rumours circulate that The Byrds command fees in the £200–£300 price range ($550–850), which seems relatively low, and a bargain for a Number One group.

The paper brings the latest news of the difficult USA–UK entertainment exchange, now bordering on revenge. American pop singers are to be barred from visiting Britain for the sole purpose of appearing on television and radio to promote their records. The new ruling will restrict visitors to making one television appearance a month, which would make the transatlantic journey not worthwhile for most. The new rules have been put to the Ministry Of Labour by the *Variety* & Allied Entertainments Council, which is consulted by the Minister on every application by an American artist for a work permit. Essentially, this is retaliation for the trouble that British artists have had trying to enter the American market.

Saturday 31

Preparations for The Byrds' landing in the UK go into overdrive. *Record Mirror* publishes a short biography; the news pages in both *New Musical Express* and *Melody Maker* give the latest updates; *Disc* prints a 'Facts About The Famous Five' rundown which is – for the time – surprisingly correct, although the years of

birth are mixed up. Gene Clark is stated as being born in 1941, making him three years older than he actually is. The piece also says he has no brothers or sisters, which is untrue. Both Mike Clark and Chris Hillman appear two years older than they are – highly uncommon at a time when most pop stars have a few years knocked off their age rather than the opposite. A simple reason may be that the group's youngest members have masqueraded as older to enable them to play in US clubs that operate with age limits.

Also today, Sonny & Cher and their hip management team of Brian Stone and Charlie Greene fly into London. Arriving in the shadow of The Byrds' blaze of publicity, they are quickly compared with the group by the British press. They are here to promote identical Bob Dylan covers – of 'All I Really Want To Do' – although to be accurate it is a Cher solo single rather than a duo recording. Where The Byrds will be unable to live up to the public's expectations, Sonny & Cher wisely chose a different strategy: a relaxed schedule with only radio, TV, and press bookings rather than club and concert dates. (Apparently, the duo plays London's 100 Club on August 5 but it is a brief appearance rather than a concert, probably just to appease MU regulations.) As The Byrds' reputation plummets over the coming three weeks, Sonny & Cher become the darlings of the press and see no fewer than three singles climb the British charts: Sonny's solo single 'Laugh At Me', their joint hit 'I Got You Babe', and Cher's 'All I Really Want To Do'.

In the end, Sonny & Cher's image is also slightly tarnished. When Cher's solo album All I Really Want To Do is released at the end of September – featuring three Bob Dylan covers and even 'The Bells Of Rhymney' – *Record Mirror* rates it a poor two stars. And when the duo returns for British concerts a year later, the novelty has worn off. "They just aren't as good as we have been led to believe," writes *Melody Maker* (September 3, 1966). "Their harmonies were off at times and Sonny's high-pitched voice grates considerably after a while."

August

Sunday 1

The Byrds and Derek Taylor leave Chicago aboard flight TWA 770 bound for London. The band comes straight off their wearisome Midwest tour with no time for a rest back home in Los Angeles. It's unlikely that they are aware of the pressure that awaits them in Britain.

Back in Hollywood, changes are afoot. Gossip journalist Mike Connolly mourns the passing of Ciro's Le Disc in *Pasadena Star-News* (August 2). "Another Hollywood landmark – the world-famous Ciro's – just bit the dust, following the Mocambo, the Biltmore Theatre, and other victims of The TV Age. It has been re-decorated. It is now called It's Boss."

Connolly, who represents the Old Hollywood, does not like what he sees. "Boss is right. You wouldn't recognise the old Ciro's. Gone are the Early Kubla Khan ornamentations and the Late Victorian chandelier from where 20th Century Fox boss Darryl F. Zanuck once swung on an exuberant, hysterical, historic occasion. In their place are a flock of Pop Art paintings by Art Fine, as commissioned by the new owner, Paul Raffles, who also owns [nearby club] P.J.'s. One is a shocking-pink-polka-dot painting of Cartoondom's Dick Tracy nose-to-nose with Beatle Ringo 'Star', who is painted in robin's egg blue. Others are wild, wall-to-wall, Andy Warhol-red blowups of The Supremes, The Rolling Stones, Cilla Black, Jan & Dean, and other Watusi-Wobble bellwethers. Gone too is the spot's old liquor license. You can't get a hard drink of any kind, just soft drinks. It's strictly for teenagers."

Bryan McLean, left behind as The Byrds fly out, returns to Los Angeles and joins singer Arthur Lee in Love – one of the groups that will soon play at It's Boss.

✈ August 2–August 20, 1965: 1ST OVERSEAS TOUR (UK)

Monday 2

The Byrds arrive at London Airport at 8.05am, an hour later than scheduled, but even at this early hour on a grey and rainy day there is a large crowd of fans to meet them at the airport. And not only fans, as it turns out, but also a group from West Drayton, Middlesex, called The Birds, whose manager Leo De Clerck promptly serves The Byrds with writs demanding that the American group change their name.

Claiming damages for loss of work, De Clerck's story is sensational enough to make the rounds in many American newspapers. "The Birds plan to take The Byrds to court and win an injunction preventing The Byrds from appearing here," De Clerck is quoted. "As far as we're concerned they are passing themselves off under our name. We formed The Birds two years ago. We're older Birds than The Byrds."

Promoter Mervyn Conn retorts: "This is just a case of this other group trying to win some publicity. The Byrds play here, but The Birds won't. I'll see to it personally." Asked how he

Byrds in a park, August 1965.

could be so sure, Conn replies mysteriously: "That's for The Byrds. In the meantime, I'm keeping it to myself. But you'll see."

Ronnie Wood, guitarist with the English Birds and just 18 at the time, will recall the incident more than 40 years later in his autobiography – although he gets the story somewhat back to front. "Even though our name wasn't the same as theirs, they didn't see it that way and threatened to get nasty. Leo conned them out of that idea by greeting them at Heathrow Airport with writs that demanded they change their name because they were now infringing on our territory. The Byrds had lawyers, and their lawyers had lawyers, so Leo's writs didn't accomplish anything, except to create a lot of publicity for us."

From the airport, the group drives to the Europa Hotel on Grosvenor Square in central London, designated Byrd headquarters for the British stay. Chris Dunkley from *The Slough Observer* has met the group at the airport and is granted an interview in their hotel suite. Questioned about American attitudes to long hair, Crosby says: "It's like any other country, it depends on where you are. In Greenwich Village nobody bats an eyelid. But I was in a hotel in the Midwest once, and I said to a middle-aged woman beside me, 'I think I'm on the wrong floor.' She said: 'Boy, you're on the wrong world!'"

After a quick nap, The Byrds go on a shopping spree in Carnaby Street, reputedly spending $2,000 (about £725) in a matter of hours – and wiring home for cash to cover the purchases. Then follows a press reception at the fashionable Savoy Hotel on the Strand from 5:30 until 8:00pm. McGuinn – who is singled out as spokesman for the group – charms the press with his eloquence and wit. "How is England?" *Disc* wonders. "Very un-English!" he quips.

"We are going for an international thing. Ours is a sort of broken-down declaration between human beings," McGuinn says to Bob Dawbarn of *Melody Maker* (August 7). "We all have strong folk backgrounds and our influences are widely varied – Pete Seeger, Hank Williams, Muddy Waters, and the blues singers, Dylan, and lots of others. I see The Walker Brothers say they had a big influence on us to start with. Well, in Hollywood we hung out in the different rock clubs and we certainly visited the clubs where The Walker Brothers were working a few times. But I wouldn't say we took anything from them. We weren't the first to grow our hair long in the States. There were others who preceded us, like The Beau Brummels. Then we came along, and The Sir Douglas Quintet came after us. The name? We just picked Byrds out of the air. It seemed to be a good label to start with, and alphabeti-

cally B seems to be a pretty successful letter.

"I've heard a good performer is always nervous before every performance. I suppose fear of the unknown is a prominent thing with us right now. Apart from that, I don't think we really are nervous. I guess everything will work out all right," McGuinn tells *Melody Maker*, quoting himself. "We haven't found out yet how long we will be doing on stage, but it will probably be around 25 minutes or so. We like doing concerts – and dances and TV. But you can get tired in clubs when you work in one place too long. I prefer to move around."

Journalist Peter Jones is at the press conference on behalf of *Record Mirror*, to give his readers a potted history of the group in the paper's August 7 edition. "They are ambitious, amiable, enthusiastic, non-aggressive," he reports. "They want to be liked for themselves, not as a copy of anybody else. And they're very welcome to Britain."

Talking to John Emery from *Beat Instrumental* (published in the September issue), McGuinn returns to his jet-age analogy. "The constant changing of musical tastes lies in the mechanical sounds of our times. The noise of the aeroplane in the 40s was a rrrrooooaaaahhh sound – so Sinatra and other people sang like that with those sorts of overtones. Now we've got the krrrriiiissssshhh jet sound and the kids are signing up there now. It's the mechanical sounds of the era; the sounds are different and the music's different.

"We're very Dylan-influenced. What I'm doing is a continuation of my love for music. Superficially the form may have changed but the essence is the same. The harmonies, the kind of rhythms that are used and the chord changes. The instrumentation is changing somewhat to meet the nuclear expansion and jet age, [but] it's still folk music."

Asked by Emery what he thinks of British groups, McGuinn replies: "We sent something over to your country and you echoed it back with a slightly different flavour because you're different people. Now we can take what the groups gave us and echo it back to them with something else! There's a new package, a new presentation of music, in which music finds a new form. Life is the same thing; it's just going through different manifestations – and music is life."

McGuinn even predicts world music. "There's an international music coming out. It has all these ingredients: Latin and blues and jazz flavours, Anglo-Saxon church music, Negro music. It has a lot of different forms."

Norrie Drummond in *New Musical Express* (August 6) enquires about the slide-rule that McGuinn inexplicably wears stuck in his pocket. "Oh, that. I always carry it, just

in case." (Apparently, McGuinn also carries around an air rifle and 35 pounds of ammunition. "I couldn't kill anything. It's just for target practice," he tells *NME*'s Keith Altham.)

Drummond speaks to David Crosby about the American pop scene. "There are a lot of groups [in the USA] but very few have anything to offer," says Crosby. "There is one, though, which I think will be very big, called The Lovin' Spoonful."

Pop scribe Virginia Ironside reports from the press meeting in the *Daily Mail* (August 7). "We knew there was a scene happening in England, but in Hollywood we could only piece together the fragments through all the nonsense and publicity," Crosby tells her. "Most of the young people in the States are atrophied. They go about in groups, dress alike, think alike."

After the press reception, McGuinn, Crosby, Gene Clark, and Mike Clarke go to the Scotch Of St James, a newly opened nightclub in the heart of London, which is already attracting the VIPs of pop. Late Mondays are time-off for most musicians, so tonight the club is jam-packed with guests including Paul McCartney, Jane Asher, Mick Jagger, Chrissie Shrimpton, Charlie and Shirley Watts, Dave Davies from The Kinks, P.J. Proby, and sundry members of The Dave Clark Five, The Hollies, The Animals, and Georgie Fame's Blue Flames.

A meeting with McCartney gives Gene Clark the inspiration to write the beautiful 'Set You Free This Time'. "When I reached my room," Clark tells *New Musical Express* (February 25, 1966), "I got out my acoustic guitar and started picking out a tune. [In] a couple of hours I was finished, literally! I slept for a full 12 hours after that."

•

Bob Dylan's visit to Britain in the spring has sparked renewed interest about pop using folk music as inspiration, and the dispute about the ethics of this runs long after he has left the country. Controversy follows Mick Jagger's attack on the "folk fakers" in *Melody Maker*. Jagger says: "I shudder to think of the tenth-rate beat groups playing rotten folk music just because it's the in-thing of the moment."

Folk singer Ian Campbell jeers in the following week's issue (June 26): "[Jagger] seems to imagine that folk music is something that comes from America, and that British folk singers must necessarily sing folksy American songs in a nasal whine, accompanying themselves on the uniform acoustic guitar. … It seems comical to hear Mick Jagger talking about folk fakers. Is there nothing fake about an English ex-grammar-school boy trying to sound like a Southern Negro farmhand?"

A few months later, left-wing singer Ewan MacColl lays into Bob Dylan in the pages of *Melody Maker* (September 18), claiming Dylan's anti-everything stance is just commercial prancing. *Ready Steady Go!* programmer Bob Bickford takes MacColl to task the following week, and then a week later readers and pop stars comment on MacColl's sour grapes. Everyone unanimously disagrees with MacColl, but Paul Simon offers a more calculated view. "I think MacColl has a good point – but he is so wrapped up in his own world that he doesn't give Dylan his due. I agree that Dylan is anti-everything – this is something I, myself, have always resented … so many things in it were right, so many wrong. I do agree with the point about Dylan's poetry being punk and old-hat. I think it's just rehashed Ginsberg. Then again, Dylan has written some very good songs."

Simon, who has lived and performed solo in London since May of this year, will see his fortunes change forever when Columbia release 'The Sounds Of Silence'. This was originally conceived as a duo recording last year by Simon and Art Garfunkel, but ex-Bob Dylan producer Tom Wilson artfully overdubs electric instrumentation without asking Simon. By the end of 1965, the single will be heading for Number One in the US charts.

Tuesday 3

Imperial Ballroom, Nelson, Lancashire
☐ **UK TV** The Byrds begin the day with rehearsals and a pre-taping for UK's premier pop show *Ready Steady Go!* at Rediffusion's Wembley Studio 1 in north-west London, which is regularly taped on Tuesdays. Hosted by Cathy McGowan, *Ready Steady Go!* has briefly been a genuinely live show this spring, but now it's back to its earlier format with lip-synched (mimed) performances in front of an invited audience.

The Byrds are allowed to perform two songs, 'Mr. Tambourine Man' and their new single 'All I Really Want To Do', and the show is aired on August 7. Also recording an insert for Friday's show are Sonny & Cher, and in the studio audience sits Donovan and members of The Animals.

Following this, The Byrds travel to the small town of Nelson in north-west England for a ballroom concert at 8:00pm with The Raging Storms and The Invaders. The schedule in the coming weeks is strenuous, even by 60s standards, often with two concerts at different locations during the same night. The strain is palpable. Chris Hillman collapses in the dressing room before tonight's show, suffering from acute asthma and bronchitis. After penicillin injections, he is able to complete the performance. *The Nelson Leader* (August 6) reports: "Panic backstage at the Imperial as a Byrd collapses! It looked as though The

Byrds would have to take to the stage for their first ever appearance in Britain without their bass player Chris Hillman. Those in the crowded ballroom were unaware of the drama as a doctor was called. Chris, a 22-year-old former cowboy, was suffering from bronchitis, which had been irritated by the strain of work in America and the tiresome travelling … Another Byrd who ran into trouble was rhythm guitarist David Crosby. After entering the Golden Room bar in a cloak he was asked to leave by the management for being improperly dressed."

Arriving in Britain with only their guitars, the group have struck a deal with Watkins Electric Music Ltd (WEM) to supply them with sound equipment for the tour. "Be Like The Byrds, Use The Best!" urges the advertisements for WEM's PA-system, as they boast of "the new clean sound which has been missing from the music for too long". Unfortunately for The Byrds, they have problems operating the system and, consequently, the sound often suffers. Mike Clarke drums on a compact Premier 55 drum kit in black pearl (bass drum; snare; two tom-toms; hi-hat; ride and sizzle cymbals), while the group is seen with Marshall amps on occasion. McGuinn has brought with him his trademark Rickenbacker 12-string guitar, but both Hillman and Crosby sport new acquisitions: Hillman plays a hollowbody Guild Starfire bass, while Crosby plays a Gretsch White Falcon – a more luxurious guitar than the Gretsch Tennessean he usually prefers and which he has also brought along.

Derek Taylor travels with the group wherever they go, and Jo Bergman – an American woman who eventually goes to work for The Rolling Stones – is hired to help with publicity for the tour. But it seems the job of road manager is assigned to no one in particular, and indeed it is unclear if the group have a personal roadie for this tour.

"Can they re-produce that sound on stage?" Penny Valentine asks anxiously in *Disc*. Judging by a positive review in the local Nelson paper, they can.

Wednesday 4

Starlight Ballroom, Morecambe, Lancashire
☐ **UK TV** A booking on Granada TV's *Scene At 6.30* today has been the subject of some confusion but is ultimately carried through. The group plugs 'Mr. Tambourine Man' and 'All I Really Want To Do' at Granada's Manchester studio, before they are packed off for a late evening performance at 9:30pm in the seaside town of Morecambe. As Nelson (where the group played yesterday) and Morecambe are almost neighbouring towns, a trip

to Manchester in the afternoon necessitates a 100-mile roundtrip.

Next week, there is a brief write-up in Morecambe newspaper *The Visitor* (August 11). "Birds are usually strictly for the boys but the 'Byrds' we met this week are for anyone who will listen to them. Although it was not raining when we introduced ourselves Dave looked like a walking umbrella in his green suede cape. He told us that he did not care for convention and wears what he likes (a friend designed and made the cape). The group prefer British groups, British cars and British girls to the American counterparts but, sad to say, not the British weather."

Roy Carr, later a long-standing music journalist for *New Musical Express*, plays drums with The Executives, who are booked to open for The Byrds in Morecambe. He jots down a report for *Music Echo* (August 14). "Around 9:30pm they arrived after being waylaid by fans. Their first words were 'we're hungry'; at this an ample supply of sandwiches and cokes were hurriedly sent into the dressing room and quickly devoured. Satisfied, they casually sat around the dressing room … During this time drummer Michael Clarke was making last minute adjustments to his kit. Though extrovert in their modes of dress (David Crosby looked like a refugee from Sherwood Forest), they were shy and withdrawn as personalities. After last minute instructions from publicist Derek Taylor, The Byrds took over the stage for the first of their two half-hour appearances. Amid screams they launched into their opening songs, the titles and lyrics of which were drowned by the crowd … Obviously nervous, they performed with a minimum of stage presentation or movement … Of the five, I found David and Gene the most talkative and showed a keen interest in everything that was happening and were aware of current trends in this country."

With the benefit of 40 years of hindsight, Carr recaptures the story for *Uncut* in 2003. "[The] first thing we wonder is whether any of them has brought a change of clothes with them … In every TV appearance and photo shoot, they appear to be wearing exactly the same clobber. David Crosby, utterly boyish, wears the same vast green suede cape, Roger McGuinn peers over the top of his Mr Pickwick glasses, while Gene Clark, Chris Hillman, and Michael Clarke are jacketed and mute in every TV show and in every picture you see. None of them, you have to say, look especially happy, usually staring glumly from under their moptop helmet of hair at whatever camera is being pointed at them. What also strikes us is how, er, disoriented they are. By which I mean we strongly suspect drugs have been involved. Especially in the case of Michael

Clarke. At one point, I find him slumped in a backstage corridor trying to assemble his drum kit. An hour later, he's still at it. Which is when myself and a stagehand do the job for him. On stage, finally, The Byrds' trademark Rickenbacker guitar sound is accurately replicated, but as a visual spectacle they are a disaster, stiff and distant. They are utterly static during every number. And then after each song, they get together, centre-stage, as if someone's called a band meeting or a group huddle, for a long and usually heated discussion about what they're going to play next." Roy Carr and The Executives, meanwhile, have a guitar player who collapses with flu, and frantically looking for a replacement asks David Crosby in desperation if he could sit in? Against Derek Taylor's protests, Crosby gamely joins The Executives and their repertoire of R&B classics, plugged in and playing a few numbers from the wings.

Thursday 5

- **Fairfield Halls, Croydon, south London**
- **Blaises Club, Kensington, central London**

After two ballroom appearances well outside the capital, The Byrds play their first London-area concerts. The evening commences with two performances (6:45pm and 9:00pm) in Croydon, just to the south of London, supported by The Ivy League, The Quiet Five, Christine Quaife, and The Impacts. The Fairfield Halls seating plan means that the audience is also arranged behind the stage, so the group have to turn to face them for parts of the performance.

Disc gives the concert an in-depth review (August 14). Nigel Hunter sets the scene. "It was the moment of truth. 'Mr. Tambourine Man' has rattled its way to Number One in the charts. The country had been buzzing with news and views of The Byrds. How potent and significant they were. How they were reasserting the American sound in the American chart previously dominated by our boys. How different they were from any who had gone before.

"The Byrds walked on to a hearty wall of welcoming screams. Actually, they didn't walk on. They wandered on, with that unique air of detached vagueness. Each move by The Byrds was calculated. They drifted across the stage in a seemingly aimless fashion, but each went to his allotted place and plugged in or set up. Nothing was hurried, everything was casual and slow-paced, but everyone knew what they were doing and did it on time."

Hunter relays his impressions of the five members: Hillman ("undemonstrative and functional"); Crosby ("a constant showpiece,

moving intelligently to the rhythm and the tune, with that cloak twirling and billowing in audience-winning style"); Clark ("the nonchalant mobile showman of the team with his tambourine … split[ting] his beats between hand and thigh"); McGuinn ("glancing owlishly over and through those small-lensed shades"); and Clarke ("broods over his drums, shoulders hunched and face almost invisible beneath that formidable hair").

The group struggle with a poor sound balance throughout their short set, and on several occasions the words are drowned out. The five perform 'The Times They Are A-Changin'', 'Don't Doubt Yourself Babe', 'All I Really Want To Do', 'Chimes Of Freedom', 'Bells Of Rhymney', and finally 'We'll Meet Again'.

Paul Jones of Manfred Mann is also on hand. "I liked them very much. They're a very good group. I don't think I heard them at their best at Fairfield Halls because they had trouble with the mics. … I think The Byrds are a bit excessive with Dylan material in their stage act. Their stage act is good. I wondered about them when they first came on. They seemed a little too casual in their manner. But it's all well drilled and nice and cool and relaxed, and the way they drift on to the stage is obviously well worked out." Jones singles out 'We'll Meet Again' for praise, and concludes: "That's what I call pop-art. The re-presentation of something already familiar in a way which makes you sit up and take notice. … I wasn't lifted by their act tonight, but I don't think you ever are at a date like that in a venue like that. They were enjoyable, but I didn't get a buzz from it. I think they are obviously much better than we were able to hear, and I think they're going to be a lot better in the future."

Ray Spencer covers the concert for *The Advertiser* (August 13), the local Croydon newspaper. "Distortion was The Byrds' chief problem. Having heard their records, I can now disentangle the hotchpotch of sound that echoed round the hall. The vocals were not clear or easy to hear; I found myself straining to catch the title of the next number. I offer no forecast of the group's success with their second British release, 'All I Really Want To Do', but I am sure it will be better received by the general public than by the Fairfield crowd who heard it 'live' on Thursday. On record their sound is different – attractive, assured and popular. But at this beat show the man responsible for their 'sound' mixed it just a little too much."

Following the Fairfield Halls concert, the group dashes across town to the small Blaises Club. The payment is a meagre £175 (about $500), which later raises questions about

Mervyn Conn's booking policy. Richard Green from *Record Mirror* writes a mini-review in his paper. "Arriving on stage at Kensington Blaises half an hour late, their hair all over the place, The Byrds treated an impatient audience to a good tuning-up session as their first number. One gentleman wore a cloak while the rest presented no stage routine in a miscellany of casual wear. Between numbers, they held impromptu discussions among themselves as to which number should follow. Apart from a solid beat running through all their songs, The Byrds offered little to ensure a big future for them here. After hearing 'All I Really Want To Do', there is little wonder that Cher's version is well ahead of theirs in the USA." Many Byrd fans present do not agree and voice their misgivings in *Record Mirror* (August 28). One says: "That piece of degenerate rubbish about The Byrds at Blaises. I was in the audience and found nothing to complain of. Sure the boys are not going to last long if people like your reporter write such biased drivel."

David Crosby says much later in his autobiography: "I looked out and here were John Lennon … and Brian Jones. That was them out there and God, I was totally terrified. I couldn't believe it. We were so bad that night: Chris Hillman broke a bass string and the stage was so small that McGuinn and I had to play through the same amp, which totally destroyed our guitars. It was a disaster happening right in front of our heroes." Recalling his first impressions of The Byrds, David Crosby's future partner Graham Nash says in the same book: "I saw them down at a club called Blaises and I was astounded because I think I saw either Crosby or McGuinn pull out a joint and start smoking on stage."

Many are curious to hear what The Byrds sound like, and in the audience are John Lennon, George Harrison, Brian Epstein, Bill Wyman, Brian Jones, Pete Townshend, folk-singer Dana Gillespie, Adrienne Posta, club manager Lionel Blake, Perry Ford (vocalist in The Ivy League), The Fairies, The Pretty Things, Denny Laine of The Moody Blues, *Ready Steady Go!* producer Vicki Wickham, dancer Patrick Kerr, and Sue & Sunshine.

The outgoing David Crosby immediately connects with George Harrison, who has just begun to explore Indian music. Harrison says later in *The Beatles – A Diary*: "I remember picking up the sitar [during the *Help!* filming in April] and trying to hold it and thinking, 'This is a funny sound.' It was an incidental thing, but somewhere down the line I began to hear Ravi Shankar's name. The third time I heard it, I thought, 'This is an odd coincidence.' And then I talked with David Crosby of The Byrds and he mentioned the name. I went and bought a Ravi record; I put it on and

The Byrds on *Ready Steady Go!* August 6, 1965.

it hit a certain spot in me that I can't explain, but it seemed very familiar to me." (Harrison uses the sitar for the first time on a Beatles cut when he records 'Norwegian Wood' this October.)

Meanwhile, back home in the USA, The Byrds appear on *Where The Action Is* (show #28, see late June) at 2:00pm, miming to their latest single 'All I Really Want To Do' and (possibly) 'The Bells Of Rhymney'. The show's announcer is Steve Alaimo, while other guests this afternoon are Jewel Akens and Linda Scott.

Friday 6
- **32 Club, Harlesden, west London**
- **All Nighter (Flamingo), central London**

The Byrds are the main attraction on *Ready*

Steady Go! at 6:08–7:00pm (see Tuesday 3), competing for attention among segments by Sonny & Cher ('I Got You Babe'), The Who (without Roger Daltrey, who is sick), Brian Poole & The Tremeloes, The Walker Brothers, The Rockin' Berries, Tom Jones, and The Artwoods.

Their performance does little to win new fans, if one is to believe a pair of letters to *New Musical Express* (August 13). "They were pathetic. The sound was thin, and why was the show built around them? After this performance I shouldn't think there's a Byrds fan left," writes one, while reader Paul Menzies-Reid complains: "On RSG they were just another group – and they're about a year late with their long hair – it's out." In the readers' letters in *Melody Maker*, G. J. Poole writes: "But on *Ready Steady Go!* we were presented with a

pleasant, inoffensive little group who relied heavily on Dylan-type singing and Kink-type guitar distortion. They whipped up about as much hysteria as a plate of cold porridge."

Jim McGuinn and Derek Taylor have dinner at Marianne Faithfull's apartment, where also Paul McCartney and Jane Asher are guests. With McGuinn running short of time for the night's performances, McCartney offers to drive him and Taylor to Harlesden, in northwest London. Derek Taylor's diary-like report in Teen Magazine (November 1965) reports: "Paul volunteered to drive us 15 miles to a rough club on the outskirts of London. The Aston Martin carrying a Beatle and a Byrd was a conspicuous target for fans, and Paul was only able to slow down sufficiently to allow Jim and me to leap out and into the side door of the club."

Backstage somewhere in England, August 1965.

Moving on from the predominantly Irish clientele at the 32 Club, The Byrds finish the long day with a show in Soho. They are totally out of place at the All Nighter (housed in the same building as the Flamingo but operating at different times), a hard-nosed soul and rhythm & blues club that caters for the mod crowd and stays open from midnight until 5:00am. Chris Welch reviews the show for *Melody Maker* (August 14), and shows little mercy. "Flopsville! was London's verdict of the much-publicised Byrds following their weekend club appearances. They left a trail of hot, tired, bored, and disappointed fans who waited hours to see them give a performance described as very, very dull. The Byrds were due at the Flamingo Club All Nighter on Friday, and enough people packed in it for it to take on the appearance of the Black Hole of Calcutta. Apart from being utterly airless, the heat was intense enough to bake bread or fry eggs on the floor, if anybody felt so inclined.

"The Byrds didn't arrive until 2:00am and giving Trojan service in keeping the crowd happy were Geno Washington's Ram Jam Band. A roar of applause greeted The Byrds when they finally arrived and fought their way to the stand. Paul McCartney was among the Byrd diggers, which helped to raise the temperature of several young ladies present even more.

"Eventually The Byrds began their act, lasting only half an hour, during which time they performed about six numbers, mostly in the familiar Dylan-cum-Tambourine Man-cum-Searchers mould. Their reception grew markedly tepid, and the biggest applause came when club proprietor Rik Gunnell announced that gramophone records would be played and the return of Geno Washington & The Ram Jam Band was imminent. 'The Animals are still the top for attendance figures,' said Gunnell later, 'then Georgie Fame and The Byrds, in that order. I think there are a lot of better pop groups in the country than The Byrds. They are definitely a miss!'"

Crosby's autobiography will record: "When we played another place in Soho, things were worse. When we got there, the owner came out to meet us and welcome us to the club, and he was covered in blood. Not his – the club was the kind of place where they had two or three fights an hour, and when we played they didn't care for us. It was primarily a black audience and they didn't like us at all. Paul McCartney was there and he took me and McGuinn home in his Aston Martin. Scared us to pieces, because he was driving drunk, but he was very kind to us.

"The Beatles, obviously, were not impressed with us, but they had a lot of respect for us.

They felt that we were the most original and innovative American band. There wasn't any question about it. They made that very clear, said it over and over again, whenever they were talking about The Byrds.

"George Harrison was the most friendly to me and the nicest," says Crosby. "He and I sort of became friends. I'm not sure if it was me that did it, but there are people that tell me I turned him on to Indian music. I know I was turning everybody I met on to Ravi Shankar, because I thought that Ravi Shankar and John Coltrane were the two greatest melodic creators on the planet, and I think I was probably right."

This busy Friday also marks the UK release date of 'All I Really Want To Do' backed with 'I'll Feel A Whole Lot Better'. Penny Valentine in *Disc* writes (July 31): "I think this is a marvellous song, but, Byrds fan though I have always been, I prefer the Sonny & Cher recording of this particular song." *Record Mirror* (July 31): "More jangly guitar from The Byrds and another Bob Dylan song. Vocal is almost hidden amidst guitar and echo, but basically there is a good tune here. … One of the group penned the flip, which has a 'Needles And Pins' riff running through it. Again, a muzzy sound but a fair tune and unintelligible lyrics. If you like The Byrds, this is good double-sided value." Derek Johnson in *New Musical Express* asks (August 6): "Another Byrds No. 1?" and then adds: "The pattern is much the same as before, with those familiar high-register harmonies – clearly influenced by the West Coast surf sound … coupled with strident twangs throughout, rattling tambourines, and crashing cymbals." He also praises Gene Clark's flipside: "Leader dualtracks with chanting support and a storming, driving shake beat … excellent."

Drummer and bandleader Dave Clark is played the song in *Melody Maker*'s weekly 'Blind Date' column, where a guest is asked to comment on some of the week's new releases. "This is American. I love it and I'm sure I've heard it before. It's The Byrds and they are excellent. 'Mr. Tambourine Man' was one of the best records this year. I'll tip this for the Top Five."

'All I Really Want To Do' performs much better in the UK than in the USA, peaking at Number Four in the *Record Mirror/Record Retailer* chart on September 4 – behind Sonny & Cher's 'I Got You Babe', The Beatles and 'Help!', and the Stones with '(I Can't Get No) Satisfaction'. But The Byrds do have the pleasure of beating Cher's version of 'All I Really Want To Do', which stalls at Number Nine.

Saturday 7
• Adelphi, Slough, Buckinghamshire

• **Pontiac Club, Putney, south-west London**

Another busy day, starting with two houses in Slough (6:00 and 8:30pm) supported by Van Morrison's Them and Kenny Lynch. The Slough show is a late replacement for a proposed booking at the Palais in Peterborough, which in turn replaced a planned concert at the Palace in Douglas on the Isle of Man.

In a letter to *New Musical Express* (August 13), a very dissatisfied Margaret Whitfield writes: "My friend and I went to Slough to see The Byrds and thought they were terrible. The sound was awful, they didn't bother to introduce any of the songs, they tuned-up on stage, and altogether they had no talent or personality."

Following Slough, the group drives back to London for a late-night appearance in Putney at half past midnight, where the crowd has already been warmed up by soul act Herbie Goins & The Night Timers.

Melody Maker's Chris Welch, who saw the Flamingo show two days ago, is back for a second opinion (August 14): "At Putney's Pontiac club at the Saturday all-nighter session The Byrds got a polite reception and played for half an hour. Apart from 'Mr. Tambourine Man' and 'All I Really Want To Do', they played an extraordinary version of Vera Lynn's 'We'll Meet Again'. They managed to dispense with the formalities of announcements and made no attempt to communicate with the audience. It was all a broody scene."

Young fan Denise Hall tells Welch: "I think they are a drag. Absolutely no stage presentation, and they ignore the audience. All their numbers sound like 'Mr. Tambourine Man'. They are completely competent, but they don't go out of their way to do anything. They are not bad, just very, very dull." Welch writes: "It seems a shame to be so hard on our American guests, especially after the receptions British groups have got in The States, but it proves they can't beat The Beatles yet."

Sunday 8
Coventry Theatre, Coventry, Warwickshire

Two houses (5:50 and 8:00pm) in Coventry, about 85 miles north-west of London, supported by Goldie & The Gingerbreads, Van Morrison's Them, The Four Pennies, The Artwoods, Sue Holloway, Tony Rivers & The Castaways, and MC Brian Freeman.

The Byrds attract between 2,500 and 3,000 teenagers in Coventry, and the 25-minute performance registers well with the reviewer from *Coventry Evening Telegraph* (August 9). Despite the large number of Byrd followers, neither house is full. "But so far as the fans were concerned, this merely meant that there was

more space in which to fling one's arms about – even one waving a pair of crutches – and more air to fill with shouts of adoration." On the other hand, *The Coventry Standard* (August 12) complains of the MC's "third-class, even smutty jokes … on a Sunday evening of all times!", and brushes aside the headliners as "very poor on stage. Their act was like that of any second-grade British group – if not worse."

Monday 9

☐ **UK TV** Television Theatre, central London, BBC-2, *Gadzooks!* 7:00–7:30pm.

The frantic schedule is catching up with The Byrds, with both Jim McGuinn and Michael Clarke ailing and missing the afternoon's rehearsals for the *Gadzooks!* television show at 10:30am. The Byrds probably lip-synch 'All I Really Want To Do' on this lightweight programme that today also features Sonny & Cher, Roger Whittaker, and Friday Brown. (The group's fee is £105.) While McGuinn is in bed, Clarke simply disappears for a few hours before the transmission. Derek Taylor slips behind the drum kit as the technicians check the cues and camera angles before Clarke returns with an ailing McGuinn in tow in time for the show. "Mike was not well on the British tour," writes Taylor in his memoir, "and at the BBC one afternoon, rolling over

and over in a simulated agony, ignored by Crosby, rejected by the others, minutes before the final run-through of their act he took a walk and vanished, just like Ringo in *A Hard Day's Night*. He returned – believe it if you will – one second before the live television show started. It was that sort of thing throughout the British trip – all the time [aggravation] and panic."

After the TV show, McGuinn, diagnosed with the flu, returns to bed. As a consequence, today's two appearances (Corn Exchange, Newbury, Berkshire, and St Joseph's Hall, Basingstoke, Hampshire) are cancelled but quickly rescheduled for August 18. Mervyn Conn tells *Disc* the following day: "It was a big disappointment for the fans, I know. There were 1,000 at Newbury and 800 at Basingstoke – but they all took it very well indeed. Especially as The Byrds have agreed to postpone their return to the States next Wednesday in order to appear at these places. But it was impossible for them to be there. Jim had a temperature of 104, owing to a virus infection, and was confined to his London hotel, the Europa."

Newbury Weekly News (August 12) wonders why the group could be seen performing live on television in the early evening, yet fail to turn up for their allotted performance. It is up to Derek Taylor to patiently tell the

newspaper that there is a lot of difference in appearing on television and travelling 60 miles to Newbury.

(Before their arrival in England, The Byrds were booked to appear on two radio shows on the BBC Light Programme, the first of which – the popular *Saturday Club* – was to be recorded this morning. It is cancelled, as was their appearance on *The Joe Loss Show* for August 6.)

Tuesday 10
Whitehall, East Grinstead, Sussex

☐ **UK TV** Television Centre Studio 2, central London, BBC-1. *Top Of The Pops*.

Honouring commitments, McGuinn raises from his bed to tape two inserts with The Byrds in lieu of appearing live on camera for *Top Of The Pops*. Rehearsals and filming commence at 10:30am, and The Byrds lip-synch 'All I Really Want To Do'. The group is video-recorded twice; the first insert is broadcast two days later (August 12), the second is aired August 19.

Following the BBC assignment, The Byrds play a 7:30pm show south of London with "Croydon's fabulous Dagoes". *Melody Maker*'s Chris Welch is again on hand but refrains from publishing a review. Perhaps just as well, as the bad memory of it still lingers three years later when he sees a particularly poor concert by Captain Beefheart. "Until then," he writes, "the worst group I have ever seen had been The Byrds performing at a ballroom in East Grinstead."

The Courier (August 13) is unmerciful. "The five Byrds flew into East Grinstead on Tuesday, gave one of the worst performances ever seen at the Whitehall, and departed with their delicately built 'image' shattered. Their two excellent records … have made The Byrds a top group on both sides of the Atlantic. But, as 800 disappointed fans discovered on Tuesday, discs can lie. The five Americans took to the stage 15 minutes later than planned. They were relaxed almost to the point of disinterest. It wasn't long before the audience felt the same. The appalling racket the group produced for the next 45 minutes was like an incredibly bad copy of a very early rock and roll number. The singers' voices were totally inaudible, drowned by the pounding thump of the drums and the ear-splitting twang and jangle of the 12-string lead guitar … The reaction of the audience throughout the show was mild, to say the least. There were screams at first but the enthusiasm grew less and less with each number. In the end it was just a polite handclap – though their 'Mr. Tambourine Man' drew an understandable roar … Why were the 'fabulous' Byrds so disappointing live? 'Like the vocal amplifiers were too small for the hall. It's kind of like being too near the magician who's performing his tricks – you dig?', said McGuinn. Quite!"

Wednesday 11

Corn Exchange, Bristol, Gloucestershire/Avon

▢ **UK TV** TWW (Television Wales and the West) Television Centre, Bristol. Discs A Go-Go

The Byrds combine an evening concert (9:30pm, with The Fanatics and The Concords) with an in-person appearance on *Discs A Go-Go*, a popular TV show that transmits live-on-air in the western regions of England from 7:00 to 7:30pm. The Byrds probably mime their new single and again share the screen with Sonny & Cher. (A day or two earlier, Cher has sung her take on 'The Bells Of Rhymney' in front of the Albert Memorial in Kensington Gardens for American TV.)

Travelling to Bristol by train, The Byrds sample a whiff of *A Hard Day's Night,* leaving London from Paddington Station, just as in the Beatles film. "It's amazing that there's so much fresh air left in such a small country," Gene Clark says in Teen Magazine (November 1965). "This is the life. Just to jog along at 50 miles an hour with nothing to do but sit and stare at fields and hedges."

Journalist Anne Nightingale has followed the boys since their arrival in London. She befriends McGuinn and fixes them tickets for the recently premiered *Help!* film. "I rate The Byrds best buy, bar The Beatles," she writes in today's *Brighton Evening News.* "Without wishing to sound hysterical I think The Byrds are the most exciting group to happen since The Beatles. I attended their first British concert and felt that same kind of emotional thrill, which up till now only The Beatles have ever evoked for me. Just why one combination of amplifiers, instruments and people can make you react violently and another leave you stone cold is something I don't know. But The Byrds have the former quality."

Columnist Brian K. Jones of the *Western Daily Press* (August 19) says: "[The] verdict on these American chart toppers? Disappointing. At the Corn Exchange their mediocre performance could possibly be excused by the fact that they were telerecording at the TWW studios until 9:30pm. And at the Grand Hotel after the dance they complained of bad tour arrangements, which meant them having to do sometimes three performances a day."

ALSO ...
Over in the States, *The New York Times* today attempts to define the changing pop fashions and the newly coined folk-rock label. Robert Shelton singles out Barry McGuire's

brand new 'Eve Of Destruction' as an example of the new trend, and writes: "There is no clear-cut name for this trend, although 'folk-rock' or 'folk-pop' are frequent." Down in Texas, Renwicke Cary has interviewed the little-known Mike Nesmith for tomorrow's *San Antonio Light.* "We play folk and roll," Nesmith declares. "[It] is a type of music that has evolved from rock'n'roll. It's pretty new, really. It's something that just had to happen. Don Steele, the famous west coast DJ at KHJ, gave it the name 'folk and roll' early this year. ... You must have heard 'Mr. Tambourine Man'? It has been a tremendous record for The Byrds."

Thursday 12

• **Hove Ballroom, Town Hall, Hove, Sussex**
• **Assembly Hall, Worthing, Sussex**

The Byrds make their in-person debut on BBC-1's *Top Of The Pops* (show No.85 at 7:00pm), where they have been featured before (see July 1, 15, and 22) but not in an actual performance. Taped beforehand (see August 10), The Byrds mime to 'All I Really Want To Do'. Clarke and McGuinn wear matching tweeds, Crosby has his cape, and McGuinn peers over his trademark rectangular glasses. Others appearing in person on the show are Horst Jankowski, Jonathan King, Sonny & Cher, and The Walker Brothers (plugging 'Make It Easy On Yourself'), while inserts by The Dave Clark Five, Marianne Faithfull, The Fourmost, The Kinks ('See My Friends'), and The Shadows are repeated from earlier programmes. The show is introduced by DJ Jimmy Savile. (The clip is later made available on the bonus DVD that comes with the *There Is A Season* CD boxed set.)

The tour continues with another double

date, starting with an 8:00pm performance in Hove, near Brighton on the south coast, before travelling to Worthing, about ten miles away. Here, the venue has been moved from the Pier Ballroom to the Assembly Hall.

The Byrds barely fill a half-empty hall in Hove. *Brighton Evening Argus* (August 13) says police on duty were not needed and that the group is voted a flop by their supporting group (The Quiet Five); the sponsors of the show, and the audience. "Only five minutes after they took the stage small groups of people were leaving; the rest looked bored," the newspaper notes. Even John Smith, the promoter of the tour, turns his back on his clients. "When I say that this group haven't got what it takes I know what I'm talking about. They are not even in the same street as British groups." The imperturbable Derek Taylor says in defence of the group: "I am not disappointed by the small audience. I am never disappointed because I never expect anything. But what can you expect from Hove? Who lives here? Only old people. It is August as well, and a great many people are on holiday. You can't expect to fill a house at this time of the year and, in any case, the only people who do that today are The Beatles themselves."

In Worthing attendance is much stronger, but, according to *Worthing Gazette* (August 18), "[the audience] watched in near silence and the applause was rather more polite than enthusiastic." The group plays 'Roll Over Beethoven' and 'We'll Meet Again' among the hit singles.

Friday 13

Gaumont Theatre, Ipswich, Suffolk
Originally scheduled for the Manchester Oasis, today sees the group play two houses (6:35 and 8:45pm) in Ipswich, supported by

Van Morrison's Them and Kenny Lynch plus The Silkie, Sandra Barry, The Deputies, Boz & The Boz People, and Guy Darrell. Compére is Brian Freeman. The group members are interviewed backstage for the *Evening Star* (August 14), lightly conversing on music fashions, clothes trends and hobbies.

Meanwhile, the anti-Byrds backlash in the British press continues. Tony Bromley, readers' letters editor at *New Musical Express*, has set aside space for a few complaints today. "I seem to be knee-deep in anti-Byrds letters," he reports.

ALSO ...
The Beatles fly off to the States for their third North American tour. They leave at 12 noon on TWA flight 703, heading for New York City. The tour will see their popularity scale new heights, with a record-breaking appearance at New York's Shea Stadium on August 15.

Saturday 14
- **Starlight Ballroom, Wembley, north-west London**
- **Finsbury Park Astoria, Finsbury Park, north London**

The day starts at midday as the group sign autographs at the Music Man record shop near Marble Arch in Oxford Street, central London. Before their headlining appearance at the stately Finsbury Park Astoria, The Byrds apparently manage to squeeze in a ballroom dance in Wembley, to the north-west of the capital. The first house at Finsbury Park commences at 6:45pm, the second at 9:10pm, and the bill is completed by Donovan, Van Morrison's Them, Johnnie B. Great, Charles Dickens, Boz, Elkie Brooks, Kenny Lynch, and compère Rod Cameron. (Also today, David Crosby turns 24.)

Keith Altham (in the company of Sonny & Cher) reviews the concert in *New Musical Express* (August 20) and is not amused. "After tuning up for a full five minutes behind the curtain, [The Byrds] were treated to a traditional slow handclap by the impatient audience. Then their first two numbers were completely drowned by over-amplification. … The 'chiming whining' effect which runs through their numbers may be good for a few but not for all seven tunes in their repertoire. Stage presentation is non-existent and so is any communication with the audience, although at one stage Jim McGuinn did say, 'Hello.' … [They] need much more stage know-how to make an impact."

The set includes opening number 'I'll Feel A Whole Lot Better', 'The Chimes of Freedom', 'The Bells Of Rhymney', 'All I Really Want To Do', 'Mr. Tambourine Man', 'The Times They Are A-Changin'", and one other unidentified song, possibly Jackie DeShannon's 'Don't Doubt Yourself Babe'.

Talking to the group backstage after the show, Altham is cold-shouldered by a rude Crosby, who is keener to speak to Donovan than the *NME* journalist. "I thought we were good tonight," Crosby says. "We don't talk much to the audience because we like our music to speak for us. I wonder if people realise how tired we are? We had a month's tour of America before coming here and we're knocked out." Although Altham finds McGuinn an amiable and likeable person, he writes: "The Byrds biggest fault is this 'cool, couldn't-care-less' attitude on stage and off. The audience didn't like it. Neither do I.

"I was with The Byrds all the time while they were here," says Donovan in *Melody Maker* (September 11), "although I didn't go to any of their [bad] jobs. They weren't very happy about some of the places they had to play. Donovan is discussing options for his next single. "[One possibility] is a tribute to The Byrds. I recorded one of my numbers, 'Breezes Of Patchulie', in their style of singing. You could call it returning the compliment as they did a bit for me in 'Chimes Of Freedom'." (In the liner notes to the Mr. Tambourine Man album, there was a reference to McGuinn prefacing the Dylan number at clubs with: "We'd like to dedicate this next song to Donovan.")

•

This weekend, Jim McGuinn talks to David Griffiths for a feature in *Record Mirror* (August 21), answering the many criticisms levelled at the group during the UK stay, including Richard Green's scathing piece in that paper the previous week. "He was quite right," McGuinn says simply, explaining that the group's sound suffered because they could not get two amplifiers and a part of the drum kit onto the already crowded stage. "Yes, the press comment has been harsh. But I was brought up by my parents – who are both in the public relations business – to believe that any publicity is good. And we've had so much, in your national press as well as the music papers. It has been fair. We've been quoted correctly on the whole. We have no complaints. In fact, we're grateful because we've learned a lot about communication with people from reading the reactions to us.

"But we'd like to come back again soon. With a few exceptions we've found British audiences very similar to those in the States. In some cases our reception has been a little ahead of what we've been used to. I think that's because the lyrics of our numbers are poetry and appeal to those who have a cultural heritage a little in advance of some of the isolated agricultural communities we've been playing to back in America.

"We bore in mind some advice from Bobby Darin," says McGuinn. "I'd worked for Darin as an accompanist and he taught me how to follow and understand the trends in pop music. I learned a lot – he'd show me things like how to study the Bobby Vinton approach and then sit down and write a Vinton-type number.

"To some degree we were influenced by The Beatles and other British groups – that's obvious, just as they were influenced by what went before, such as Presley and Ray Charles. It's a leap-frogging process and we set out to add the next thing. First we worked on our own sound and started to assemble material. We began with folksy songs because we were observing the convergence of folk and rock'n'roll. We saw the downfall of folk as a purist thing – the artists were acquiring tricks from The Everly Brothers and Ray Charles, using their chord changes and so on. Folk started as a homemade craft, but with the interest taken in it by college boys, commercial exploration occurred. It became a crowded field so we moved our style to a less crowded frequency. Now it's our aim to get The Byrds internationally known."

Sunday 15
Gaumont Theatre, Bournemouth, Hampshire

Two houses (6:30 and 8:45pm), again with Van Morrison's Them and Kenny Lynch, in addition to Unit Four Plus Two. On a small portable tape recorder, Derek Taylor records the teenage screams that greet The Byrds. This soundbite will later be put to good use on a Byrds single.

Monday 16
Pavilion, Bath, Somerset

In Bath at least, The Byrds are able to whip up some excitement. *The Evening Post* (August 17) writes: "The Byrds came to Bath last night and the girls loved them. They screamed and clawed at the five young Americans on stage at the Pavilion. For a score of them it was just too much. They succumbed to the heat and the hysteria and fainted. Sweating bouncers elbowed through the crush to reach them

and carry them backstage." A second report comes courtesy *Bath & Wilts Evening Chronicle* (August 17). "The Byrds flew into Bath last night, bowled over an enthusiastic audience of screaming girls at the Pavilion, and climbed back into their Austin Princess for London ... In the dressing room before the show these young starlets, who wear Beatle haircuts 'because we like long hair', were showing the signs of a vigorous string of one-night stands."

Brian K. Jones – who also saw The Byrds perform a disappointing show in Bristol a few days ago – is back for a second look. He writes in *Western Daily Press* (August 19): "Their spot [in Bath] was the only booking that day. This, however, made no difference to their time of arrival. Again it was a hurried one – with the result that they were actually tuning their guitars on stage between numbers – most unpro-

fessional! As if this wasn't enough, they played 30 minutes and then left as quickly as they had arrived after playing 10 minutes less than they were contracted to do. Their sound is much of a muchness. Each number sounds like 'Mr. Tambourine Man' except that the words were different. And their performances left much to be desired."

Tuesday 17

More switching around, as an original booking at the Civic Hall in Wolverhampton is replaced by a date at the Guildhall in Portsmouth. Perhaps as a result of the bad press, ticket sales are so poor for the 4,000-seat theatre that it is decided to cancel the show. (The Quiet Five, Christine Quaife, Keith Golden & The Newsboys, Goldie & The Gingerbreads, and The Just Men plus compére Brian Freeman were also set to appear on the show.)

The Byrds in London, August 1965.

The 250 fans who have bought tickets are given their money back.

It's probably on this unexpected day off that McGuinn, Clarke, and Hillman gather in Mike's room at the Europa Hotel to do a 'Blind Date' for this week's *Melody Maker*. Here they comment on new releases by The Rolling Stones ('Satisfaction', already a Number One in the States, is enthusiastically enjoyed by all three); Bob Dylan ('Like A *Rolling Stone*' – Mike: "I love the record"); Johnny Cash ('Ring Of Fire' – Chris: "One of the best records you've played"; Jim: "Johnny Cash is great and we love it. It's one of his best songs"), and The Beach Boys ('California Girls' – Mike: "That lyric is so true"; Jim: "We were in the studio when this was recorded").

Also now, Jim McGuinn is the guest for *Disc*'s weekly 'Hit Talk' column (August 21). His observations are all gently positive as he passes comments on hits by Sonny & Cher, Jonathan King, and The Animals ('We've Got To Get Out Of This Place') – "OK. It's got a coloured sound, like Al Jolson got, I guess." Of Joan Baez, he says: "I feel she was best of all back in Cambridge, Massachusetts, in 1959–60, at the 47 Club." McGuinn speaks warmly of The Searchers: "Always interesting. I liked 'When You Walk In The Room' but my all-time favourite was 'Needles And Pins'. I like that kind of feeling, almost a Bach feeling." Regarding 'Like A *Rolling Stone*', now at Number 12, McGuinn says: "Great. I love the feel of his records." (The Byrds' 'All I Really Want To Do' is at Number Four.)

McGuinn's comment on The Animals does not go unheeded. The group's drummer John Steel says to *Disc* two weeks later: "Jim McGuinn said … that Eric's voice sounds 'like Al Jolson', I guess he meant it sarcastically. Well, he's not exactly in a strong position to say things like that. The Byrds' British appearances certainly weren't the success everyone expected them to be."

Wednesday 18

- Corn Exchange, Newbury, Berkshire
- St Joseph's Hall, Basingstoke, Hampshire

Both concerts have been rescheduled from August 9. In Newbury, The Bunch and The Blues Syndicate are booked as support acts, and the same two groups plus The Proud Walkers open in Basingstoke. (Today was originally scheduled for the group's return to the States.)

Thursday 19

☐ **UK TV** Alpha Television Studios, Aston, Birmingham ABC-TV *Thank Your Lucky Stars*

It is probably today, at the very tail end of their British tour, that The Byrds pre-record an appearance on this popular television show, to be broadcast on August 21. The group mimes 'All I Really Want To Do' on a family friendly bill as part of the show's 'Summer Spin' series.

The Byrds are seen on BBC-1's *Top Of The Pops* today (show No.86, at 7:00pm) in a second video-recording of 'All I Really Want To Do' (see August 10). Appearing in person today are Herman's Hermits, Jonathan King, The Headliners, The Kinks, and The Rolling Stones (miming 'Satisfaction'), while Sonny & Cher, The Shadows, Horst Jankowski, and The Beatles (playing 'Another Girl' and 'Help') are either in repeated performances like The Byrds, or – in the case of The Beatles – seen in specially prepared videos. Jimmy Savile introduces the show. (An initial BBC contract dated August 11 for a return to *Top Of The Pops* today for more filming is cancelled by the BBC.)

An option by The Byrds to visit France, West Germany, and Holland in the wake of the British tour is not taken up.

Friday 20

The Byrds fly back to Los Angeles. Their departure is probably not made together: some of the members possibly left yesterday, and Michael Clarke attends a launch party for Andrew Loog Oldham's new record company today. *Record Mirror* (August 28) says: "Seen chatting at Immediate launching – Eric Clapton and Mick Jagger, Nico and Byrd Mike Clarke." Oldham explains the new label's objectives in the same paper: "We believe that success lies in dispensing with accepted tradition and going against the current trend, which is to deal with pop merchandise in a stiff and unimaginative manner. We want to give an aura of youth. There's no room in the business for an old-club atmosphere. One must adopt streamlined American methods of selling and promotion."

Immediate releases its first batch of singles today, one each by Nico, The McCoys, and an obscure British group called The Fifth Avenue, who do a cover of Pete-Seeger-via-The-Byrds 'The Bells Of Rhymney'. "Good folk song, well sung by duo comprising Denny Gerard and Kenny Rowe. Jimmy Page produced what is basically a protesting folk item but which is coupled with a highly saleable way. Nice arrangement touches," runs the review in *Record Mirror* (September 11).

The Byrds' debut album, with identical track listing and jacket to the US version, is released in the UK today. Allen Evans (*NME*, August 13) writes: "They look like a rock group but are really a fine folk unit. They play their stringed instruments with great skill and invention against the rock-steady drumming.

Their voices merge well. … As the first group to bridge the gap between beat and folk, they deserve to be winners." Equally enthusiastic, *Music Echo* (August 14) concludes: "An album which easily lives up to the promise of their great knock-out singles."

Record Mirror (August 21) is not convinced and deals the album two out of five stars. "We tried to like this. We tried, and in fact we did manage to enthuse over some of the tracks. Like 'Mr. Tambourine Man', 'All I Really Want To Do', and 'I'll Feel A Whole Lot Better'. But in the end we lost. The same nothingy vocals, the same jangly guitar, the same plodding beat on almost every track. Even four Bob Dylan tracks couldn't save this one. The Byrds really must try to get some different sounds. They've flogged this one to death."

Nick Jones in *Melody Maker* (August 14) is pleased. "If you dig The Byrds' style on 'Mr. Tambourine Man', this album is for you. … All the tracks are tremendously singly, but the overall sound is too samey, despite different tempos and composers. They are a very good group and we're going to hear a lot more of The Byrds."

•

The Byrds' attack on Britain has not been a great success and will plague the group for the rest of their career. Chris Hillman, talking to Richard Williams in *Melody Maker* five years later, still has to stand to task for the failure. "We didn't know who we were, or what we were supposed to be doing, and we simply weren't old enough or mature enough to cope with it. So many groups are like this. Sure, the musical ability was good. We were either brilliant or horrible, because there were times when we just did not care. But on the first tour we were messed around, anyway."

Derek Taylor's lovingly written memoir sums it all up. "The British tour had been quite dreadful. We were represented in Britain by a man called Mervyn Conn, whose idea of launching an American group lately translated from folk into rock was to put them in a West Indian blues club and later into an Irish ballroom for something like 11/6 [eleven shillings and sixpence, about 57p, or $1.50] a head (less fines for swearing or pissing in the wash-basin). We flew to Britain economy – Mervyn Conn didn't run to first-class tickets. … George and John came to Blaise's, where The Byrds performed to a room no bigger than the one you're sitting in now. On a stage insufficient to carry all the drum kit. They played louder than anyone else had been known to play.

"I thought they were fantastic and I think John and George did, but some of the British smirkers smirked, and you only need a few English smirkers in a half-lit room to feel pleased you're not proud to be English. Upstairs in Blaises, after the set, John and George sat at a long table and invited us in. Boy, were they big-time then – I'd forgotten. It wasn't them at all; it was the situation. They were absolutely IT. John sat at the end of the table, George at the other end, and they sent for wine for free."

The press must take the blame for the treatment of The Byrds. Immediately following the tour, readers' letters pour into the *Melody Maker* office, which prints seven pro-Byrds replies in its August 28 issue, reflecting the view among the general ticket-buying public. "I saw The Byrds in East Grinstead," writes Valerie Neal, "and they were terrific and obviously good performers." Chris Smith: "At Coventry I found The Byrds refreshingly different and very talented. They reveal a sincerity many British groups have yet to acquire and they came over very well."

Toni Foster: "The British are renowned for making foreign visitors feel at home, but with the reception they gave The Byrds, I begin to doubt this." J. Meenana: "Bravo Byrds! Just because they didn't get up on stage and make fools of themselves by dancing about, they are criticised." Gita, President of British Chapter Of The Official Byrds Fan Club: "It's a shame The Byrds had to learn the hard way. It's too late now, but I wish they will come back to prove how good they really are." George Hurst: "Three cheers for The Byrds!" Ana Joyce: "How could you allow Chris Welch's article to be printed? I would remind him that The Byrds were cramming into a short time as many performances as our groups do in twice the time."

The well-meaning press build-up has ultimately been damaging. Reader B. Price from Darlington comments in *Beat Instrumental* (October 1965): "The Byrds tour was a tremendous flop, but it gave us a chance to see that American artists are, in fact, human. … The Byrds were a classic example of our tendency to accept American artists before they even make an appearance. All the musical papers were busy, in the weeks preceding The Byrds' arrival, building them up saying how fantastic they were. When they came across and made such fools of themselves the papers looked very sick and changed their tune right away."

Still, The Byrds' all during make it easier for some of the American groups and singers who come to Britain in the next few months, including Sam The Sham & The Pharaohs, Sir Douglas Quintet, The McCoys, and Barry McGuire. Expectations never run so high again, and consequently those following in the wake of The Byrds will have an easier time with the British press.

Keith Potger, guitarist with The Seekers, observes in *Record Mirror* (November 29): "[The Byrds'] problem was going on tour on the basis of one hit record. They're good musicians – all first-class session men. But they had no idea of stage presentation, so they had a hard time with our audiences." And Ian Whitcomb, Englishman in exile in the USA, says in The *Los Angeles Times* (January 9, 1966): "[The Byrds' UK tour] was a disaster. The press gave 'em the works because they felt the musicians looked surly and didn't announce the songs."

Mervyn Conn, who held such high hopes for The Byrds' British visit and had even toyed with an extravagant three-and-a-half-week Christmas concert series starring The Byrds, Bob Dylan, Joan Baez, and The Kingston Trio, has a simple message for the British music press as The Byrds flap home. "We have no plans to bring them back. There is no point with so many good British groups around."

Derek Taylor adds in *Melody Maker*: "They will certainly not be returning before next year. No, there is absolutely no question of a Christmas show. The group will return to England when the bill is right, and at the right time and the right place. They have enjoyed the tour immensely; they've learned a tremendous amount how more closely they are scrutinised by the English press and fans than in America, and more about stage presentation and production. It's been hard but invaluable experience."

As a thank you to loyal fans, the group's management takes out a whole page advertisement in *Disc* (August 28) saying: "In Britain we did all we really wanted to do … and now we feel a whole lot better."

And what happened to The Byrds versus The Birds case? *Beat Instrumental* (September 1965) writes scornfully: "Was the issuing of writs to The Byrds really necessary after all? Your American counterparts may be able to beat you on disc, but not, it seems on stage." Then, in October, *Disc* reports that the case has been laid to rest. "Britain's Birds have dropped their writ against the American Byrds about the similarity of their name."

Saturday 21

By now The Byrds are home in Los Angeles for the first time in almost two months, but in the UK they appear on television. They lip-synch 'All I Really Want To Do' on ABC TV's *Thank Your Lucky Stars Summer Spin* (show No.207, broadcast on the ITV network at 5:50pm; see August 17). Introduced by Jim Dale, guests on today's show include The Rockin' Berries, The Walker Brothers, Frank Ifield, Alma Cogan, Barbara Kay, and The Transatlantics.

Monday 23

The Beatles' frenzied North American visit has a few days rest, when John, George, Paul, and Ringo arrive in Los Angeles at 3:00am on this Monday morning and are immediately whisked off to a ranch-styled address in Benedict Canyon. Chris Hutchins, who reports weekly bulletins back to *New Musical Express* in England, writes: "Monday was their first day of rest and they spent it around the swimming pool in the garden, George reading the *NME*, Paul strumming a guitar, John and Ringo inspecting a selection of American causal clothes which had been sent from a Hollywood boutique to the house on their request. The day also presented the first visitor in the form of The Byrds, summoned by The Beatles." Joan Baez is also around, spending time talking with John Lennon.

The Beatles, encapsulated in their own world, have taken to The Byrds right away and do not care about the poor British press reports. David Crosby is the Beatle guide when they are in Los Angeles. "When they came over here and toured America, they called me and I went to see them at the place they were renting in Benedict Canyon," Crosby writes in his later autobiography. "We'd meet and hang out, sometimes for days at a time. I was their connection for getting good weed and, in some cases, acid. We played guitar together. We talked together. We watched movies together. Basically, you could say we had a great time."

Tuesday 24

The Beatles and The Byrds spend another day together, today with actress Eleanor Bron and Peter Fonda.

Dropping acid, John Lennon gets the inspiration to write 'She Said She Said' after Fonda gives him the lyric line "I know what it's like to be dead".

→ Wednesday 25

RECORDING Columbia Recording Studios, Sunset and El Centro, Hollywood, CA. Producer Terry Melcher

Although not dated in any of the surviving session logs, this is by all accounts the occasion when George Harrison and Paul McCartney drop by the studio to hear The Byrds rehearse and record. The Beatles have five days off and no concert appearance until August 28 (and on the 27th they go to a party at Elvis's place in Beverly Hills). Meanwhile, The Byrds will make their first concert tomorrow since their return from England.

Chris Hutchins writes in *New Musical Express* (September 3): "The Beatles rarely slipped out and only did so at night. Early in their stay, George and Paul went to a Byrds recording session and heard the American group wax its new US single 'The Times They Are A-Changin'."

American teen magazine *Flip* gives a detailed account of the meeting (reprinted in Britain in *Music Echo* on September 11 and credited to George Richards). "So The Beatles came down from the hills to listen to The Byrds. In a dusty Simca, The Byrds' publicity officer Derek Taylor brought George Harrison from The Beatles' hilltop hideaway to Columbia Records studios on Sunset Boulevard. … George himself had asked to be present at The Byrds' session, where they were recording their third American single 'The Times They Are A-Changin'."

Terry Melcher breaks proceedings to play Harrison 'She Don't Care About Time', presumably the version taped on June 28. George comments: "Don't they phrase beautifully? Listen to the clever work in the chorus."

Next to arrive is Paul McCartney ("not in an anonymous Simca but in the official long, low, black limousine … [and] screeching, grinding and skidding to a halt behind the official car were dozens of other vehicles, overloaded with sun-bronzed blonde Beatlemaniacs"). He is in time to hear an attempted harmonica overdub on 'The Times They Are A-Changin'. It may well be that this overdub – which is ultimately never used – is done to the first attempt on the Dylan song made on June 28, and so today's work represents no proper recording session, which is why it is not documented in the studio logs.

"Whether or not it was the awe-inspiring presence of two Beatles, little progress was made at the session from that point on," continues the report, "and although a satisfactory harmonica balance was attempted by the three Byrds, it was not achieved. Said Paul: 'Pity John's not here. He would have been glad to help.'" And with that, Harrison and Crosby slip out of the back door for a return to The Beatles' hideaway, soon followed by the other four Byrds.

Thursday 26

'Byrds' Ball', The Hollywood Palladium, Hollywood, CA

John Barrick promotes The Byrds' homecoming party at the gilded Hollywood Palladium, a large dancehall on Sunset Boulevard with a capacity of 5,000. Dyann Starr-King's review in the *Los Angeles Free Press* (September 3) attests to a triumphant return after the dismal British tour. "There was dancing and screaming and a really all-around good time, while The Byrds came on strong with their 'Mr. Tambourine Man', 'I'll Feel A Whole Lot Better', 'The Bells Of Rhymney' and many others. Some of the songs were written by Bob Dylan, some by

members of The Byrds. All came through with the familiar biting, cutting style of The Byrds themselves, driven on by the characteristic sound of the 12-string guitar. It was no longer separately Jim McGuinn, Dave Crosby, Gene Clark, Mike Clarke, and Chris Hillman, but all one unit, one feeling, one taste of excitement – The Byrds!

"The dancing was excited and swinging, and the dancers changed between dancing and simply standing happily and watching the group play. Between sets I was surprised and delighted to see several of The Byrds out wandering in the audience, which added even more to the feeling of closeness than The Byrds seem to hold with their audiences. In all, the whole mood of the evening was one of happiness and excitement. From the wild, colourful clothes worn to the dancing and bouncing around – and to the very feeling of The Byrds' music, which can go right through you and leave a warm sensation – it was an evening of fun, of welcome home Byrds, and the magic feeling of everybody having a good time."

Sharing the bill with The Byrds are local group The Leaves, who soon will borrow Crosby's electrified arrangement of 'Hey Joe' for their own good, releasing it as a single at the end of the year.

🖵 **UK TV** The Byrds make their last appearance on British television for now, when 'All I Really Want To Do' is repeated on today's *Top Of The Pops* on BBC-1 (show No.87, at 7:00pm; see August 12 for original taping). The show is the usual mix of in-person performances (Chubby Checker, The Hollies, The Honeycombs, The Walker Brothers), repeats from earlier shows (Sonny & Cher, The Kinks), plus a specially-made promotional video of Bob Dylan's 'Like A *Rolling Stone*', now racing toward its peak position at Number Four in the UK charts. The show is presented by DJ Alan Freeman.

Late August

A reflective letter penned by Chris Hillman – perhaps ghosted by Derek Taylor – is mailed off to *Melody Maker* and published in the September 4 issue. "We're all glad we came. It was good for us – but we weren't always completely happy. We still feel that there was a slightly negative reaction towards us, as Americans, and as a rock'n'roll group offering what was interpreted as a challenge to the British. This seems to be based particularly on the way we dressed, on the length of our hair and on our music … we certainly didn't receive [that] from The Beatles. They were marvellous from the outset and we certainly hadn't expected them to make a special visit to a club to see us.

"What we wanted to do in England, we did. We wanted to play to British audiences and absorb some of the vitality, which has been around the London scene since The Beatles first became famous. We were heard by many thousands of people and, so far as we could hear from the screaming, most of them seemed to enjoy themselves. The criticism that we were dull on stage may be justified. We are not Jimmy & The Jets. We didn't have any choreography or unified stage movements. We don't laugh and joke with the audience and maybe we were a bit cool. But it wasn't intended to be an affront to the audience. Nor did it mean that we didn't want to communicate. It was simply that we expected our music to do the communicating for us. One of the results of the criticism was that we did examine our stage lightning and we did learn to make announcements on stage.

"The pop scene generally we found tremendously exciting. London seemed alive and vibrant and *Ready Steady Go!* was certainly the best TV show any of us had ever worked on. It seemed much freer than American shows. It didn't have all the routines and the nonsense – the discotheque dancers and the extra clutter and junk of American TV. … The treatment we received from the TV crews was marvellous. British radio we enjoyed tremendously. Radio, too, seemed better in London than in Los Angeles. In Los Angeles they are more concerned with advertisements and gimmicks.

"There was one marked difference as far as we non-conformist, long-haired, young Americans were concerned. Nobody called out after us in the street or queried our right to dress, walk, and look as we please. In fact, the only piece of abuse any of us had during our stay in England was in an elevator in an hotel – and that was from a squat, middle-aged American lady. The problems we experience in Los Angeles are unbelievable. 'Hey Ringo,' they call after us. Or, 'Are you girls or boys?'

Saturday 28

🔊 **RECORDING** Columbia Recording Studios, Studio A, Sunset and El Centro, Hollywood, CA. Producer Terry Melcher and probably engineer Ray Gerhardt.

For the first time since June 28 – not counting the unlogged session on August 25 – The Byrds are back in the studio, concentrating on two Gene Clark numbers. One is a re-recording of 'She Don't Care About Time' from the June session, now re-done without Melcher's piano or the harmonica overdub but with McGuinn's Bach cantata repeated. The other is 'The World Turns All Around Her', one of Clark's catchiest melodies, which will be prepared in two different mixes.

The Byrds on the set for *Hullabaloo*, September 22–23, 1965.

Sunday 29

The Beatles wind up their North American tour this weekend; yesterday they performed in San Diego, and today and tomorrow they play at the Hollywood Bowl. The Byrds attend the concerts in the company of Trina and Paul J Robbins. The Beatles hold a press conference today, and when questioned about which American group they admire the most, John replies: "The Byrds," to which Ringo adds: "The Byrds, yeah. And they admire The Lovin' Spoonful."

September

Wednesday 1

🔊 **RECORDING** Columbia Recording Studios, Studio A, Sunset and El Centro, Hollywood, CA. Producer Terry Melcher and probably engineer Ray Gerhardt.

It has already been announced that 'The Times They Are A-Changin'' will be the next Byrds single, but no one seems impressed with the version recorded earlier (see June 28) so

it is re-recorded again today. The version of the song without vocals to use as a backing track on an upcoming appearance on *Hullabaloo* is probably prepared today too (see mid-to-late September entry)

'The Times They Are A-Changin'' joins a long list of Bob Dylan cover songs recorded and released this year. Everybody seems to be doing Dylan songs now, from the obvious (The Byrds) to the obscure (The Silkie), through country (Johnny Cash) and soul (Solomon Burke), to the odd (jazzmen Duke

Ellington and Gerry Mulligan). Dylan's royalties for the year's first six months is greater than the combined royalties of Rodgers, Hart, Hammerstein, Gershwin, and Porter for the same period.

Friday 3

The Byrds catch Bob Dylan's sold-out appearance at The Hollywood Bowl. He is backed by Al Kooper (organ), Harvey Brooks (bass), Robbie Robertson (guitar), and Levon Helm (drums). Robertson and Helm come from rockabilly singer's Ronnie Hawkins's backing group, and made their Dylan debut barely a week ago at Forest Hills, NY. Bob first does an acoustic show before performing with his group. Speaking to Robert Shelton of *The New York Times* (August 27), Dylan says: "I'll have some electricity and a new song or a couple or three or four new songs. Time goes by very fast up there onstage. I think of what not to do rather than what to do."

Saturday 4

Bob Dylan arrives with David Crosby in tow for a press conference at the Beverly Hills Hotel in Los Angeles.

In England, 'All I Really Want To Do' begins a slow descent down the charts after last week's top marking at Number Four. Donovan says in *Disc*'s weekly 'Hit Talk' feature: "The Byrds' version [is] good but I've heard better. That's Cher, of course! I don't think the public are ready for what The Byrds are trying to do in music." Next week (September 11), Brian Jones says in the same column: "The Byrds I think are great! I like their sound – I prefer The Byrds' version of [the Dylan song] than Cher's," then it is John Walker's turn to contradict (September 25): "I prefer Cher's version of 'All I Really Want To Do' to that of The Byrds." (By then the Byrds single is at Number 27 and on its way out of the charts.)

Early September

☐ **US TV** ABC Television Center, Hollywood, CA. ABC network *Shindig*

The Byrds pre-tape an appearance for the autumn-season premiere of *Shindig*, to be broadcast on September 16. The group performs 'I'll Feel A Whole Lot Better' and 'The Bells Of Rhymney'. They also part-take in the introductory medley with The McCoys, where McGuinn briefly mumbles a line of The Rivieras' hit 'California Sun' while the rest of the group mime to a backing track.

Wednesday 8

The Mike Douglas Show (9:30pm on Channel 7) is broadcast today, featuring The Byrds (see July 22) along with other assorted guests: 67-year-old British actress Hermione Gingold, actor Henry Gibson, comedian Sandy Baron, and Mike Favata. Highlight of the show is described as the dancing of Carl Franzoni, who is joined by Mike Douglas on the dance floor for a rousing finale.

Thursday 9

The Yardbirds are one of the many British groups who have had trouble entering the USA as a result of strict bureaucratic restrictions, but they have finally made it to Los Angeles after a series of delays and with a few concerts and TV appearances booked on the fly.

Kim Fowley – yet another acquaintance from the old Ciro's Le Disc crowd – has been to England with P.J. Proby at the turn of 1964–1965 to check out the British music scene first hand but is now in L.A. He has several irons in the fire. Tonight, Fowley decides to throw a party in honour of The Yardbirds at the home of Bob Markley up in the Hollywood Hills. "Such notables as The Byrds, Peter & Gordon, Jackie DeShannon, Phil Spector, and Danny Hutton dropped in to give The Yardbirds a listen," writes Louise Criscione in *KRLA Beat* (October 9). The Yardbirds' manager calls home to England at 3:00am. "You ought to be here now!" he shouts. "There's The Byrds, Peter & Gordon, and Jackie DeShannon. It's a real loon-up, in the English sense of the word. The Yardbirds played for three quarters of an hour and knocked everyone out!"

Friday 10

◀)) **RECORDING** Columbia Recording Studios, Studio A, Sunset and El Centro, Hollywood, CA. Producer Terry Melcher and probably engineer Ray Gerhardt.

The Byrds assemble at Columbia again to record the song that is destined to be their next single. The song is McGuinn's brilliant adoption of Pete Seeger's 'Turn! Turn! Turn! (To Everything *There Is A Season*)', which takes 70 takes to perfect ("who but me was counting," reports an exhausted Derek Taylor).

McGuinn is already acquainted with the song as he arranged and played guitar on Judy Collins's version two years ago, and it was part of The Limeliters' repertoire. But today's version has the commercial stamp that is needed to push it into the charts. For the poignant lyrics, Seeger has borrowed text from the King James translation of the Book of Ecclesiastes (chapter 3; verses 1–8), almost verbatim: "To every thing there is a season, and a time to every purpose under the heaven," goes the Biblical verse one, while verse eight ends with "a time to love, and a time to hate; a time of war, and a time of peace".

A few years later, McGuinn tells John Cohen about the song's origin. "It was after our first bus tour. Touring around the Midwest, day after day: terrible. I was sitting in the back of the bus with my girl, and she asked me if I knew the song. I said yeah, because I'd arranged it for Judy Collins. It was a standard folk song by that time, but I played it and it came out rock'n'roll, because that's what I was programmed to do, like a computer. I couldn't do it as it had been done traditionally, and it came out with that samba beat. We thought it could make a good single. It had everything: a good message, a good melody, and the beat was there. It fit right into the commercial formula of the time."

Tuesday 14

◀)) **RECORDING** Columbia Recording Studios, Studio A, Sunset and El Centro, Hollywood, CA. Producer Terry Melcher and probably engineer Ray Gerhardt.

The group record Gene Clark's 'The Day Walk', which is destined to remain in the Columbia vaults until it is finally released along with other rare tracks on the remastered Byrds catalogue in the 1990s.

Thursday 16

◀)) **RECORDING** Columbia Recording Studios, Studio A, Sunset and El Centro, Hollywood, CA. Producer Terry Melcher and probably engineer Ray Gerhardt.

'Set You Free This Time', the ballad Gene Clark was inspired to write after meeting Paul McCartney on a late night in London (see August 2), is recorded today. Besides the usual Byrds instrumentation, the fade-out has a harmonica solo added by Clark.

Shindig's second season premieres (show #52) on the ABC network at 7:30pm on the West and East Coasts and at 6:30pm in central regions (see early September). In a programming twist, the hour-long show is split into two 30-minute segments (Thursdays and Saturdays), and the season opening is heavily promoted. The Byrds do 'I'll Feel A Whole Lot Better' and 'The Bells Of Rhymney' and also appear briefly in an opening rock'n'roll medley with The McCoys (miming a few bars of 'California Sun').

Jimmy O'Neill remains the show's host, and the rest of the programme is given over to Jerry Naylor, The Everly Brothers, Chad & Jill (Chad's wife Jill replaces his usual partner Jeremy), Billy Preston, Ketty Lester, The McCoys, and The Rolling Stones – with ABC warbling the line "trying to make some girl" in 'Satisfaction' as a sop to censorship.

Friday 17

◀)) **RECORDING** Columbia Recording Studios, Studio A, Sunset and El Centro, Hollywood, CA. Producer Terry Melcher and probably engineer Ray Gerhardt.

Compiling songs for their next album, Chris Hillman suggests that the group today records a version of country singer Porter Wagoner's '[A] Satisfied Mind' from 1956, although Chris has learned the song off folk singer Hamilton Camp's 1964 album *Paths Of Victory*. McGuinn, Clark, and Crosby sing the whole song in three-part harmony, and a harmonica solo is overdubbed. Although the song is often held up as an example of The Byrds' country roots and is even claimed as the first ever country-rock song to be recorded, it was no more adventurous than The Rolling Stones revving up Hank Snow's 'I'm Movin' On' (a live recording released in the UK in June) or The Beatles' take on Buck Owens's 'Act Naturally' (just this week put out on the B-side of their new US single 'Yesterday'), even if, in the country & western firmament, Owens's Bakersfield sound is far more pop-oriented than the traditional country styling of Wagoner.

Saturday 18
◁) **RECORDING** Columbia Recording Studios, Studio A, Sunset and El Centro, Hollywood, CA. Producer Terry Melcher and probably engineer Ray Gerhardt.

Digging into their backlog of material, the group revives the single they released as The Beefeaters last year and re-records it today as 'It Won't Be Wrong' (the original title was 'Don't Be Long'), a Beatles-inspired song that Jim McGuinn has written with Harvey Gerst.

Also taped today is Crosby's second attempt at recording an original for The Byrds following his 'Flower Bomb Song' (see June 28). Titled 'Stranger In A Strange Land' – the title lifted from Robert A Henlein's science-fiction novel – the song only survives as a backing track, which will finally be released officially in 1996 as part of the remastered Byrds CDs. (Johnny Rogan's all-encompassing session files will mention that a Crosby–Dino Valenti composition called 'I Don't Ever Want To Spoil The Party' is also recorded now – another tape that later goes astray.)

Monday 20
Even the respected magazine *Newsweek* does a feature on the Los Angeles music ... ... this week's edition (dated today), quoting David Crosby: "We put reality in music. It's better than June-Foon-Boon-Spoon."

→ Wednesday 22–Thursday 23
☐ **US TV** NBC Television Studios, Manhattan, New York, NY. NBC *Hullabaloo*

The Byrds fly off to pre-record an insert for *Hullabaloo* in New York City, and as 'The Times They Are A-Changin'' is still the hotly tipped A-side of the next single, that is the song they are singing live to a pre-recorded instrumental track which differs from the version eventually released. (The backing track is later heard on the *Preflyte Sessions* in 2001.)

The group is placed in a bizarre mock landscape with two stock-still girl hunters, complete with rifles and ready to go hunting in a lake of plastic ducks on the studio floor. It is all part of *Hullabaloo*'s overhaul for the new season, which started transmissions on September 13. Producer Gary Smith explains to *The Modesto Bee* (September 12): "Groups like The Kinks, The Byrds and such will be backed by high-fashion models and the 'mod' look. In fact, the only change we'll make will be in the placement of the 'A-Go-Go' segment. It's going to close the show rather than be used at the mid-way mark. Why? Because people of all ages react most strongly to this segment. And why not? It swings."

A close-up of the group shows McGuinn striving to keep his rectangular glasses perched on his nose, while Clark strums an acoustic guitar. The group also appear briefly as part of a 'Top Pop Medley' singing a verse and a chorus of The Lovin' Spoonful's 'Do You Believe In Magic?'. Although the song never formed part of The Byrds' live show, the cameras captures a lovely moment – lanky and lean, McGuinn conducts the voices of all five Byrds as they gloriously come together in the chorus: "Do you believe in magic/In a young girl's heart/How the music can free her/whenever it starts?"

The group's performance is set to be televised on October 4 but is postponed because of Pope Paul IV's peace campaign visit to New York ("No More War – War Never Again"), which attracts an astonishing crowd of 600,000 to the Bronx. The show is rescheduled for November 29.

(Interestingly, the backing track – which is completely different from the officially released version on the group's second album – is heard in its entirety on a 2 CD by Sundazed Records repackage of the World Pacific demos in 2001 and gives listeners a unique chance to hear a pre-recorded track without vocals. Presumably, it is this take that was recorded when The Byrds were visited by George Harrison and Paul McCartney in August.)

Late September
"George Harrison rang Byrds Jim McGuinn and Dave Crosby in Hollywood from his Surrey home for a chat," *Disc* (October 2) reports.

October

Friday 1
The Trip, Hollywood, CA
◁) **RECORDING** Columbia Recording Studios, Studio A, Sunset and El Centro, Hollywood, CA. Producer Terry Melcher and probably engineer Ray Gerhardt.

The Byrds spend the afternoon recording a Jim McGuinn/David Crosby collaboration, 'Wait And See'.

Later they appear for a special showcase at the Trip club, as a preview of their two-week residence to begin on Monday October 4. In the same way that Ciro's Le Disc succumbed to new trends and was reborn as It's Boss, the Trip club is situated in the spot vacated by the jazz club Crescendo.

The Byrds' third single is released in the USA today, coupling 'Turn! Turn! Turn! (To Everything There's A Season)' with Gene Clark's 'She Don't Care About Time'. It will prove a wise move to pick this Pete Seeger song after initially considering 'The Times They Are A-Changin'', which would have been their third Bob Dylan A-side in a row. The single is an almost instant success; within a couple of weeks, Derek Taylor reports that the single sold 30,000 copies in Los Angeles alone in just six days.

Billboard reviews the single in its November 11 issue, suggesting the correct day of release is perhaps at least one or two weeks later than the October 1 date. "Fascinating entry with words from the book of Ecclesiastes and music adapted by Pete Seeger. Performed with respect and taste and a solid dance beat backing. A winner!" *Record World* (October 16) comments: "Set of lyrics from the Old Testament set to music by Pete Seeger and folk-rocked by hit group." *Time Magazine*

'Turn! Turn! Turn!'

A 'Turn! Turn! Turn! (To Everything There Is A Season)'
(BOOK OF ECCLESIASTES/P. SEEGER)
B 'She Don't Care About Time'
(G. CLARK)

US release October 1 1965 (Columbia 43424)
UK release October 29 1965 (CBS 201765)
Chart high US number 1; UK number 26
Read more ... entries for August 28 and September 10 1965

(Friday January 7, 1966): "The Bible, set to rock'n'roll, produced December's biggest hit. The words ('To everything there is a season') are from Ecclesiastes, the music is by Pete Seeger, and the performance is by The Byrds, pioneers of folk-rock."

Billboard's Review Panel later picks the single as recommended for discotheques. The music trade paper regularly assembles such lists, with a helpful column marked 'type of dance' besides title, artist, and record label. 'Turn! Turn! Turn!' is apparently good if you want to do The Frug (*Billboard* December 18).

Saturday 2
'1965 Fall Spectacular', The Cow Palace, San Francisco, CA

The Byrds are one of the many attractions advertised for this concert presented by KYA DJs Bob Mitchell and Tom Donahue, in addition to Sonny & Cher, The Lovin' Spoonful, Charlie Rich, The Strangeloves, The Beau Brummels, local SF group The Tikis, and others. In fact, it's possible that this prestigious Cow Palace spectacular does not take place after all, as the weekend of October 1–3 is reserved at the venue for the 'S.F. Autorama' exhibition.

Sunday 3–Sunday 17
The Trip, Hollywood, CA

The group play the Trip club for two weeks (and possibly not opening until Monday 4). They share the first days of the stay with Barry McGuire, while The Grass Roots are on the bill until the very end of the residence, along with The Skip Battyn Trio. At the end of the second week (October 15–17), The Leaves are added to the bill. Battyn, already a seasoned veteran since his minor charts with Skip & Flip in 1959–60, has recently performed as The Skip Battyn Are Happening (who held a residence at L.A.'s Action club in August). McGuire, an old acquaintance of McGuinn and Clark, has just topped the US charts with P.F. Sloan's bombastic protest song 'Eve Of Destruction'.

Record producer Lou Adler recalls the heady days. "['Eve Of Destruction'] came about because I'd heard the first Dylan album with electrified instruments [*Bringing It All Back Home*]," he remembers in *Melody Maker* (February 5, 1972). "This is strange, but it's really true. I gave P.F. Sloan a pair of boots and a hat and a copy of the Dylan album, and a week later he came back with ten songs, including 'Eve Of Destruction'. It was a natural feel for him – he's a great mimic. Anyway, I was afraid of the song. I didn't know if I could get it played. But the next night I went to Ciro's, where The Byrds were playing. It

was the beginning of the freak period – there was this subculture that no one in L.A. knew about, not even me, and it was growing. The Byrds were the leaders of the cult, and the place was jam-packed, spilling out into the streets. In the middle of it was this guy in furs, with long hair, and dancing. I thought he looked like the leader of a movement. Terry Melcher told me that he was Barry McGuire, and that he'd sung with The New Christy Minstrels. A week later, we cut the record, and it sold about six million." (At it happens, Lou Adler and P.F. Sloan are involved, too, with The Grass Roots – the other opening act at the Trip – who have a minor hit early next year with Bob Dylan's 'Ballad Of A Thin Man' under the title 'Mr. Jones'.)

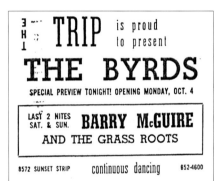

Variety (October 13) reviews the Tuesday show in its usual hep lingo. "The Byrds will be flying about the Trip for the next two frames, playing and singing their brand of music to crowds of 18-plus youths. Quintet has a clean beat, offers a variety of sounds in 40-minute sets, and quits when ahead. Working seven nights a week, they'll draw strong biz. Comparisons to The Beatles are inevitable, and, for commercial reasons, planned that way. Current terpery stint probably restricts The Byrds to patter-less turns, although there's a hint of latent comedy abilities. Musically, they touch all bases, including the Elvis Presley C&W sound of ten years ago. Stephen Foster was recapped by 'Oh Susannah' on show caught, while group is pushing 'Turn! Turn! Turn!' new Columbia platter produced by their A&R man Terry Melcher. Despite howls for encore, The Byrds quit on their own decision, a showmanly bit of aloofness which guarantees repeat biz."

Not everyone is enamoured with The Byrds, as Derek Taylor reports in *Disc* (October 16). "Herman [Peter Noone of the Hermits] is still here and expressing himself freely on this and that. If I were a group, I think I'd stop knocking other groups and take a cool, appraising glance at the top of the British

chart and wonder where I was going wrong. Little Mr Noone was in the Trip, Hollywood's new, hip club, twice this week, gazing in wonderment at the electricity generated by The Byrds and Barry McGuire. On the second visit he and one of his guitarists – the one who wears glasses [Derek 'Lek' Leckenby] – leaned against the bar, sniggered between themselves, attempted a brief impersonation of Byrd-leader Jim McGuinn with the glasses on the end of his nose, and then walked out with an approximation of a swagger. Well … I suppose McGuinn can take it." (Noone recently sneered in *Melody Maker*: "As for The Byrds – we've got five million groups as good as The Byrds. They're just secondhand Rolling Stones.")

Guitar player Gary Rowles watches the first couple of nights and is struck by The Byrds' stage presence. "McGuinn played a Rick 12, Crosby a Gretsch with a Bigsby, and Hillman a Fender Precision bass. The sounds of the 12-string and the voices, plus Hillman's unique approach to his basslines were the main attraction for me. Also, Gene Clark's presence was magnanimous. Couldn't take my eyes off either him or McGuinn. They did 'Mr. Tambourine Man', 'I'll Feel A Whole Lot Better', 'Here Without You', and 'Turn! Turn! Turn!'. I was sorry they did not do 'The Bells Of Rhymney', probably my favourite Byrds song."

Tony Hall reports from Hollywood in *Record Mirror* (October 14). "Despite the heat, this is a groovy town. A few blocks away from each other it's been possible to see Sonny & Cher [at It's Boss], Barry McGuire, The Byrds [at the Trip], and Roy Head [at the Red Velvet Club]. There are discotheques galore. All doing good business. … One observation about the discotheques out here. The records are all early British. Or American versions of our sound. Tastes seem to be much less hip than in London. The music is much more anaemic. 'I hope we sound a little better than we did in England,' David Crosby told me. I must say I thought [The Byrds] were terrific. They get such a big sound. Their musicianship seems infinitely superior to that of many English groups. In fact, I'd say the same applies to a lot of lesser-known American groups, too."

Hilton Valentine of The Animals also drops by, and he tells *New Musical Express*: "Saw The Byrds at the Trip club in Los Angeles. They're greatly improved. At Jim McGuinn's flat later he talked me into buying an LP of Bach organ music!"

Winding down after their nightly appearances at the Trip, The Byrds are reported by gossip columnists to visit other late-night spots on the Sunset Strip such as the Red Velvet Club, hanging out with The Animals, The

Righteous Brothers, Sonny & Cher, and even McGuinn's old boss Bobby Darin and actress Sandra Dee.

•

"The Sunset Strip! It used to be something special, a couple of miles of booming night-clubs and high-class restaurants and happy people. A tourist trap, perhaps, but one of the better ones," reports Hollywood column-ist Dick Kleiner on the 'State Of The Sunset' (*Anniston Star*, October 20).

"That's all changed, and mostly because the whole structure of after-dark entertainment has changed. Nightclubs here, as everywhere else, are dead or dying. In their place have come the go-go spots. Today, the Sunset Strip is the conglomeration of these rock'n'roll (or the newer folk'n'roll) clubs and hamburger stands and parking lots. And the pedestrians these days are mostly kids with long hair and no shoes. [Whisky A Go Go owner and pro-proprietor] Elmer Valentine … is just opening a new place called The Trip. … [The club] will have a new policy – 18-year-olds will be admitted." Valentine tells Kleiner: "You have to face it. The old night club days are dead, stone cold dead."

Monday 4

◁)) **RECORDING** Columbia Recording Stu-dios, Studio A, Sunset and El Centro, Hol-lywood, CA. Producer Terry Melcher and probably engineer Ray Gerhardt.

The group record their almost punkish take on Stephen Foster's classic song 'Oh! Susannah' this afternoon, before playing the Trip club in the evening.

Thursday 7

▭ **US TV** ABC Television Center, Hollywood, CA. ABC network *Shindig*

The Byrds pre-record their third appear-ance on *Shindig* during the afternoon for the edition to be broadcast on October 23. The group perform new single 'Turn! Turn! Turn!' plus 'Chimes Of Freedom'. Jim and Gene sing a couple of lines of John Lennon's 'I'm A Loser' in the opening medley, while David, Chris, and Michael mime to a full orchestral accompaniment. It is not a proper perform-ance as such and the song was not part of the group's repertoire. Following the televi-sion taping, the group returns to the Trip on Sunset.

Sunday 10

▭ **US TV** KABC Studios, ABC Television Center, Hollywood, CA. KABC Channel 7 Los Angeles *Shivaree*

Before continuing the Trip residence in the evening, the group lip-synch 'Turn! Turn! Turn!' and 'I'll Feel A Whole Lot Better' in front of an audience of screaming and danc-ing teenagers. The insert is broadcast this coming Saturday.

Thursday 14

Bonus Auditorium, Fairfax High School, Los Angeles, CA

Still performing nightly at the Trip, The Byrds squeeze in a special afternoon concert today. Aron Kay, one of the students at Fairfax, recalls: "They played the Bonus Auditorium, and the event was sponsored by the Associated Students body. They started with 'Roll Over Beethoven' and finished with 'Turn! Turn! Turn!'. Unfortunately, the acoustics left a lot to be desired since they used their own PA sys-tem in an auditorium that was accustomed to the student choir and other mild-mannered activities."

Another student, Richard Schulman, adds: "For the price of a student-body card, which I think was $3.50, you could attend this show for free. Every semester they brought in at least one band. The acoustics in the audito-rium were pretty poor, as I recall: it was not a music recital hall. The band ran through their first album and some songs from their next album. Crosby wore his typical cape and had to tune his guitar after every song. They pretty much played [each song as it was] on the album – no extended jams, and not much talk between songs. I'm sure in a better venue they might have sounded better. To me, McGuinn always had one of the weaker voices in rock, but the enhancements that are given to it in the recording studio seem to make their songs work."

Saturday 16

As The Byrds play out their last weekend of the residence at the Trip (ending tomorrow, October 17), the group appear on *Shivaree* (show #38, see September 10) at 7:00pm PST on KABC-TV. Introduced by Gene Weed, they mime 'Turn! Turn! Turn!' and 'I'll Feel A Whole Lot Better' before a giddy crowd of dancing teenagers, audibly screaming at the sight of the group. Also on the 30-minute show are The Toys, Dobie Gray, Suzy Clark, and Donovan. (The show is syndicated in other areas.)

ALSO …

At EMI's Abbey Road studio in London, The Beatles record the new George Harrison song 'If I Needed Someone', which the composer graciously acknowledges was inspired by the guitar riff in 'The Bells Of Rhymney'.

The Beatles finish the recording two days later, and the song makes the deadline for *Rubber Soul*, which is in the shops by Christ-mas.

Monday 18

The B5roadway Shopping Mall, Hollywood, CA

The Byrds make in-store appearances at The Broadway (a fashion store) at Del Amo (4:00–5:00pm) and then at Anaheim (6:00–7:00pm).

Wednesday 20

◁)) **RECORDING** Columbia Recording Stu-dios, Studio A, Sunset and El Centro, Hol-lywood, CA. Producer Terry Melcher and probably engineer Ray Gerhardt.

The group record 'If You're Gone', yet another composition from the prolific and consistent pen of Gene Clark, with a choir-like backing vocal.

'Turn! Turn! Turn!' enters the Southern California charts at Number Four this week (published in today's *Los Angeles Times*). The chart mirrors regional chart action – topping the list are The Vogues with 'You're The One' above the Stones ('Get Off Of My Cloud') and The Beatles ('Yesterday').

Friday 22

◁)) **RECORDING** Columbia Recording Stu-dios, Studio A, Sunset and El Centro, Hol-lywood, CA. Producer Terry Melcher and probably engineer Ray Gerhardt.

The Byrds tackle yet another Dylan song in the studio today, choosing to cover the little-known 'Lay Down Your Weary Tune', a song only available through Dylan's publishers as one of the out-takes from Dylan's 1963 album *The Times They Are A-Changin'*. Chris Hillman later suggests that he sings harmony on the recording, and if so, it is his vocal recording debut with The Byrds.

Saturday 23

The group appear on *Shindig* (show #63) on the ABC network at 7:30pm on the West and East Coasts and at 6:30pm in central regions (see October 7). This is their third and last appearance on *Shindig*. The Byrds take part in the mimed opening medley (doing a brief 'I'm A Loser'), which also features Dobie Gray, The Shangri-Las, Bobby Sherman, and Glen Campbell. The group mime to 'Chimes Of Freedom' and a slightly abbreviated ver-sion of 'Turn! Turn! Turn!' (dropping the verse beginning "A time to build up, a time to break down…") but with Clark's tambourine clearly audible above the din of the studio audience. Jimmy O'Neill is the host along with comedian Ed Wynn. The rest of the half-hour show features Dobie Gray, The Shangri-Las, Glen Campbell, Bobby Sherman, plus per-formances by The Shindogs and a *Shindig* Club segment with The Eligibles, The Blos-soms, Joey Cooper, and Delaney Bramlett.

Tuesday 26–Wednesday 27

◁)) **RECORDING** Columbia Recording Studios, Studio A, Sunset and El Centro, Hollywood, CA. Producer Terry Melcher and probably engineer Ray Gerhardt.

Johnny Rogan's notes from the Columbia archives indicate that these two days are logged for further work on 'The Times They Are A-Changin'' and 'Satisfied Mind', and – intriguingly – an otherwise unknown number entitled 'Circle Of Minds', which unfortunately is later lost.

Friday 29

Palos Verdes High School, Palos Verdes Estates, CA

The Byrds and The Baymen play before 1,200 students, in a concert to raise money for the Palo Verdes Pool Fund. Eventually more than $1,000 is donated to the cause.

'Turn! Turn! Turn!'/'She Don't Care About Time' is released in the UK. *New Musical Express* (today) says: "Strident guitar and heavy bass open the side, and maintain throughout, with tambourine and crashing cymbals. It's the familiar harmonic blend, with the all-embracing sound dovetailing with the vocals. Melodically not so catchy as their last two, but the treatment's just as intriguing." Of the B-side, *NME* adds: "Almost exactly the same opening on the flip, and the backing doesn't vary much, either. Still, you expect the same pattern from The Byrds, right?"

"The best record The Byrds have ever made," asserts Penny Valentine in *Disc* (October 30), while *Record Mirror* (October 23) says: "An odd sort of single, but one destined for the charts – no doubt! It's subtitled 'To Everything There's A Season', with the lyrics coming from the Book of Ecclesiastes. All rearranged by Pete Seeger, and The Byrds do a thoroughly competent job on it. Nice and easy beat, very strong instrumentally. Flip is gentler." *Melody Maker* (October 23): "American group The Byrds with their follow-up to the chart-busting 'All I Really Want To Do'. … Performed in identical style to their previous numbers – with the jangling 12-string guitar and falsetto voice. Not outstanding but undoubtedly a hit." *Music Echo* (October 23) thinks the single "will prove they're not just a 'two-hit' group." Pop entrepreneur Jonathan King, regular columnist in *Music Echo*, chips in (October 30): "[In] my opinion the top harmony group around is The Byrds. They got a lot of undeserved bad press over here. For fellow Byrds addicts, their new single, 'Turn! Turn! Turn!', comes out tomorrow. Jangling lead guitar, the high voice of Dave Crosby and Jim McGuinn's tonsillitis are still there, but this disc is original."

However, following The Byrds' two previous UK smash hits, 'Turn! Turn! Turn!' unexpectedly fails and never rises above a disappointing Number 26. Indeed, it will never match the worldwide sales of 'Mr. Tambourine Man', and the poor UK performance seems to translate to other European countries as well.

→ Late October

▢ **US TV** KCOP Television Studios, Hollywood, CA. KCOP-TV Channel 13 Los Angeles *The Lloyd Thaxton Show*

The group make their third appearance on *The Lloyd Thaxton Show*, performing 'Turn! Turn! Turn!' for a November 3 screening. (Supposedly, The Byrds also tape 'The Times They Are A-Changin'' for broadcast on Thaxton's show on November 19.)

November

Monday 1

◁)) **RECORDING** Columbia Recording Studios, Studio A, Sunset and El Centro, Hollywood, CA. Producer Terry Melcher and probably engineer Ray Gerhardt.

For the last session for The Byrds' second album, Jim McGuinn's re-arrangement of the folk song 'He Was A Friend Of Mine' is recorded. McGuinn has altered the lyric about the death of a friend to make President John F. Kennedy the subject of the song. Laying his 12-string Rickenbacker aside for a moment, McGuinn fingerpicks an acoustic guitar for the first time on a Byrds track. The other instrumentation is Hillman's bass, a gently tapping tambourine, and an unobtrusive organ presumably played by Terry Melcher.

This session marks the end of Melcher's reign as producer, although he will work with the group again several years later. The reason for the breakdown of the relationship between Melcher and the Dickson–Tickner–Byrds trinity is not satisfactorily explained, but may have to do with the group's changing musical direction and choice of material. Nevertheless, to the contemporary music press a change of producer is barely noticeable.

The days in the studio have lately been fractious, and *16 Magazine* (April 1966) writes: "David was punched by drummer Mike Clarke at the session for the album Turn! Turn! Turn!. Mike said Dave was off the beat." The magazine hastens to add that "[in] a matter of minutes, however, the boys shook hands and made up".

→ Early November

▢ **US TV** KHJ Studios Sunset Boulevard, Hollywood, CA. KHJ-TV *Hollywood A Go Go*

The Byrds pre-tape a performance of 'Turn! Turn! Turn!', which is broadcast locally on November 6 and syndicated nationally. Lip-synching their new single, this time in its full version, the group look relaxed: McGuinn, resplendent in white jacket and a tie, chimes in with the guitar introduction as Gene Clark casually looks around for his tambourine.

Wednesday 3

The group today appear on Lloyd Thaxton's show – by now broadcast in colour and going out at 4:30pm in the Los Angeles area on KCOP-TV Channel 13 (and at 4:00pm in Chicago on Channel 7). They perform 'Turn! Turn! Turn!' (see late October). Also on are The Spokesmen, a singing trio who have just recorded 'The Dawn Of Correction', their answer to 'The Eve Of Destruction'.

Friday 5

'Dick Clark's Caravan Of Stars', Fairgrounds Coliseum, Louisville, KY

The Byrds enrol for one of Dick Clark's travelling rock'n'roll shows as a replacement for Donovan. Clark has promoted his 'Caravan Of Stars' tours since 1959. The idea is to put together a ready-made package of various recording stars for local consumption, often in out-of-the-way towns. Although the Caravan is Clark's common brand for these tours, the different bills are often given a contemporary slant. For some of the advertisements, this particular tour is dubbed 'Dick Clark's Folk'n'Roll Tour'.

The various Caravans are on the road year-in, year-out, and clock up more than 700 appearances annually. Correctly, it should be A Bus Of Stars as that is the chosen mode of travel – and usually also the nightly accommodation – because the itinerary is often spread across large distances between cities. Reportedly, the pay isn't very good after expenses are deducted. Clark occasionally joins the tour himself to present shows in the bigger cities.

For this autumn's Caravan, The Byrds share top billing with We Five and Paul Revere & The Raiders. We Five have recently scored a US *Billboard* Number Three hit with 'You Were On My Mind', while The Raiders – another of Terry Melcher's productions – have recently become the house band on *Where The Action Is* and have racked up two Top 50 hits this year with 'Steppin' Out' and 'Just Like Me'. (Crosby jokingly calls them Paul Revaid & The Rear Doors.)

Then there are Bo Diddley & The Duchess, while some lesser-known constellations pad out the bottom of the bill: The Results (two female singers from Dick Clark's Cincinnati office), Dale Wright & The Men Of Action, and Soul Inc. In addition, local acts are often added when the Caravan passes through. Tonight, for example, Louisville's own The Indigos and The Rugbys are performing. Soul Inc., also a local group from Louisville, has travelled from Florida on short notice to catch the tour but arrive too late for tonight's show at 8:15pm. They usually play their own spot on the tour and provide backing for The Results.

Saturday 6

TRIANGLE THEATRICAL PRODUCTIONS, FRANKLIN FRIED Executive Director presents

MONTH of the BEAT NOVEMBER, 1965

NOV. 26 & 27 EXTRA PERFORMANCES ADDED DUE TO POPULAR DEMAND

BOB DYLAN

At 8:30 P.M. Tickets: $5.00, 4.00, 3.00, 2.00
Tickets at Box Office and ALL SEARS STORES

NOV. 6 AT 8:30 P.M.
**PAUL REVERE & THE RAIDERS
WE FIVE • THE BYRDS
BO DIDDLEY**
Plus IN PERSON—DICK CLARK

NOV. 14 AT 3:30 P.M.
SONNY & CHER

NOV. 28 2 SHOWS, 3:00 & 7 P.M.
The **ROLLING STONES**

ALL TICKETS $5.50, $4.50, $3.50, $2.50 UNLESS OTHERWISE INDICATED. ALL PERFORMANCES AT ARIE CROWN THEATRE.

 Mail orders for all attractions to Triangle Productions, Inc., Box 10, 156 E. Superior, Chicago, Illinois, 60611. Enclose stamped, self-addressed envelope. Add 25c per order to cover the cost of handling and mailing. Your co-operation in sending separate checks when ordering for more than one show is appreciated. Tickets available AT ALL SEARS STORES.

**'Dick Clark's Caravan Of Stars',
McCormick Place, Chicago, IL**
For tonight's one show at 8:30pm, Clark appears in person to MC the proceedings. The show draws a crowd of 5,000, which means a sell-out. Diane Klecka covers the Chicago concert for *Hit Parader* (June 1966). After the opening acts have finished, she watches the start of the show from the wings with Michael Clarke. First comes Bo Diddley ("There will never be another Bo," Clarke declares. "He's a master, a legend in his own time") followed by The Byrds, then Paul Revere & The Raiders, and finally We Five.

Jerry Burgan, vocalist and guitarist with We Five, recalls: "The bus was a very strange scene. All of the equipment and luggage for all the artists were on one bus. The aisles were

filled and it was pretty scary. I told Jack Nance, the show road manager, that we didn't think it was safe. There was some shuffling and they called Dick Clark, who happened to be at that show.

"Dick took about two steps into the bus, turned around, and told Jack to rent some cars to drive us to the next date in Nashville. When the tour hit the road two days later, there was a full-sized truck filled with equipment. The Byrds had rented one of the original blue Winnebagos, and We Five were back on the bus with everyone else and the luggage. It was still full, but there were two empty seats and there was enough room for a couple of people to lie down in the luggage rack above the seats.

"The tour didn't always go to a hotel after the shows," Burgan explains, "so several of us – including myself and Marc Lindsay [Paul Revere] – would occasionally jockey for those spots to sleep in the rack when we had an all night drive."

Hollywood A Go Go goes out at 7:00pm PST today on KHJ-TV with The Byrds performing 'Turn! Turn! Turn!' and possibly another song (see early November). Introduced by Sam Riddle, the guests include Ian Whitcomb, Bobby Vee, Len Barry, Duane Eddy, Jeannie Smith, and The Bobby Fuller Four.

Sunday 7
**'Dick Clark's Caravan Of Stars',
Municipal Auditorium, Nashville, TN**
Tickets go for $2.50 before the 7:30pm show and cost $3.00 at the door. The Byrds have gamely joined the bus for a few days, but from now on they choose to travel separately from the rest of the touring party.

David Crosby writes in his autobiography: "It worked like this. We were on a tour called the Dick Clark Caravan Of Stars. The Byrds were out there doing 'Mr. Tambourine Man' and 'Turn! Turn! Turn!' Those were our hits, so that's all that we sang. Everybody sang just their hits, on and off, thank you very much, here's the next big act.

"We were all out on the road and we wanted to smoke pot, which we liked to do. We also couldn't handle being locked in a bus with the We Five and Bo Diddley's band and The Raiders, it just wasn't happening. And when I say bus, I'm talking about a Greyhound bus, not one of the air-conditioned custom coaches that we have today … just a big, dirty old bus.

"So, after a while, we broke new ground and started another rock'n'roll trend. We rented an early motor home, some prototype RV, with beds. [McGuinn] rigged a Fender Showman amp in the back to play cassettes, and me and Hillman would do most of the

driving, cos Gene and [McGuinn] were not great drivers.

"This was the time when I was trying to program my partners. I had a tape of John Coltrane's piece *Africa/Brass* and I was trying to program it into McGuinn, along with Ravi Shankar. Those were the two main things I was trying to pour into McGuinn's head. I don't know why I should be so presumptuous as to think I knew how to influence McGuinn, but I was and I did.

"So we're driving along in this motor home," Crosby continues, "and we come up to a railroad crossing, where we had to stop to let a train go by. This, by the way, is the time when we're writing 'Eight Miles High'. We come up to a railroad crossing and we have John Coltrane blasting on this huge Fender amp in this little motor home and we are grooving on it heavily. I look up and I see the train that is passing us is full of coal. It is a 'Coal Train'! It was probably the dope and the time on the road and the song we were writing, but I remember thinking, 'Boy, this is pretty fucking cosmic.'

"It got so I bathed [McGuinn] regularly in Coltrane and Ravi Shankar. Jim Dickson turned me on to Shankar and blew my head out completely. I thought he was and probably still is one of the finest musicians on the planet."

Africa/Brass is an album by John Coltrane from 1961 starring his own quintet (including influential drummer Elvin Jones) backed by a large brass ensemble. The album contains just three pieces: 'Africa', an arrangement of the traditional folk song 'Greensleeves', and 'Blues Minor'.

Where exactly the passengers in The Byrds' Winnebago have their coal-train epiphany is long forgotten, but in a 1966 radio interview McGuinn will say that it was somewhere on Highway 66.

Monday 8
**'Dick Clark's Caravan Of Stars',
Municipal Auditorium, Rome, GA**
Par-Co Enterprises Corp presents two shows, the first at 4:30pm and the second at 8:30pm.

Tuesday 9
**'Dick Clark's Caravan Of Stars',
Memorial Gymnasium, Middle Tennessee State University,
Murfreesboro, TN**

Wednesday 10
**'Dick Clark's Caravan Of Stars',
Unknown venue, Florence, AL**
This scheduled Alabama show may be cancelled.

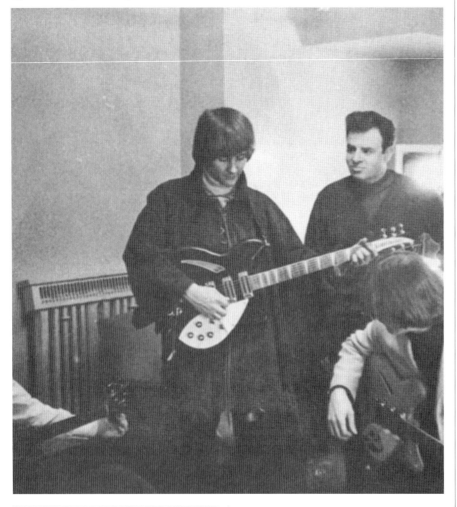

Tuning up backstage in Chicago with radio DJ Art Roberts looking on.

Thursday 11

'Dick Clark's Caravan Of Stars', Atlanta City Auditorium, Atlanta, GA

For the one 8:00pm show, Wayne LoGiudice & The Kommotions are also on the bill.

Friday 12

'Dick Clark's Caravan Of Stars', Municipal Auditorium, Greenville, SC

Saturday 13

'Dick Clark's Caravan Of Stars', [possibly Municipal Auditorium], Ashland, KY

'Turn! Turn! Turn!' flies in at Number 12 from outside the Top 30 in *Billboard*'s Hot 100 this week (for the issue on newsstands on November 8), where The Rolling Stones are presently at the top with 'Get Off Of My Cloud'.

Sunday 14

'Dick Clark's Caravan Of Stars', National Guard Armory, Clarksville, TN

Two shows, the first at 3:30pm and the second at 6:00pm.

Monday 15

'Dick Clark's Caravan Of Stars', University of Tennessee, Martin, TN

Tuesday 16

'Dick Clark's Caravan Of Stars', Fieldhouse, Murray State College, KY

"The concert, in its entirety, was far from being good," writes correspondent D. Ellis Mueller in *Billboard* (December 11), but he says the show draws a strong crowd of 3,500.

Wednesday 17

'Dick Clark's Caravan Of Stars', Madison County Coliseum, Huntsville, AL

Two shows, the first at 4:30pm and the second at 8:00pm.

Thursday 18

'Dick Clark's Caravan Of Stars', Diddle Arena, Bowling Green, KY

Friday 19

'Dick Clark's Caravan Of Stars', Stambaugh Auditorium, Youngstown, OH

Dick Clark appears in person again for today's two shows (7:00 and 8:30pm), for which local DJ Boots Bell joins as guest MC.

Lloyd Thaxton's daily show is rounded up at weekends as *The Best Of Lloyd Thaxton*, and for today's broadcast at 1:30pm on KCOP-TV Channel 13 in the Los Angeles area, The Byrds are reputedly featured miming to 'The Times They Are A-Changin'' (see late October).

Lloyd's main guest is Dionne Warwick.

Saturday 20

'Dick Clark's Caravan Of Stars', Grover Center, Athens, OH

Sunday 21

'Dick Clark's Caravan Of Stars', Gymnasium, Pikeville College, Pikeville, KY

Originally set for Tennessee Tech Gymnasium in Cookeville, TN, this is evidently cancelled or possibly moved to an open day in the itinerary.

Monday 22

'Dick Clark's Caravan Of Stars', Memorial Auditorium, Raleigh, NC

Tuesday 23

'Dick Clark's Caravan Of Stars', Cambria County War Memorial Arena, Johnstown, PA

The 8:00pm show attracts 2,351 patrons and a short review runs in *The Johnstown Tribune Democrat* the following day. "Three excited teenagers, who just couldn't resist the temptation, made it to the stage to touch the stars. One girl practically fainted as she touched the guitarist with The Byrds before a policeman and several ushers led her off the stage." Local radio DJs Larry Ford, John Rubal, and Herb Ruth are ordained as MCs for the occasion, while Wayne McDonald boosts the musical programme.

Wednesday 24

'Dick Clark's Caravan Of Stars', 'KQV Thanksgiving Shower of Stars', Civic Arena, Pittsburgh, PA

Clark's Caravan aligns briefly with The Rolling Stones' fourth North American tour tonight. 'Get Off Of My Cloud' has just topped *Billboard* for two weeks, easily pulling 9,131 for tonight's Thanksgiving show sponsored by radio station KQV. Soul vocal quintet The Vibrations are also on the bill.

We Five's Jerry Burgan: "That was quite a

concert bill. It was the largest venue We Five ever played, with an arena stage that was two flights of steps above the dressing room level. None of the amps or instruments was miked and there were no monitors on stage, so we couldn't hear a thing – but it didn't matter. The screaming started early in the evening and never stopped. We got some shrieks at other dates on the tour – David Crosby could get one any time he wanted by simply lifting his arms to open the green cape – but nothing came remotely close to the deafening sound we got that night in Pittsburgh."

Thursday 25

An appearance possibly booked for Clarksburg, PA, is not confirmed while a proposed visit to the Opera House, Seattle, WA is likely cancelled. In the middle of a string of dates on the East Coast that would necessitate flying out, turn around and fly back the next day – which would have been an expensive side trip.

Friday 26

'Dick Clark's Caravan Of Stars', New Haven Arena, New Haven, CT

Saturday 27

'Dick Clark's Caravan Of Stars', Memorial Auditorium, Worcester, MA

Melody Maker reports today that the group have had an offer to make a film in Europe next year. "The deal has not been finalised yet, but The Byrds have been offered $150,000 to appear in the film, which should be shot in [West] Germany next summer," explains Mervyn Conn. As with so many other pop groups, The Byrds have cinematic ambitions, but this particular project is swiftly forgotten.

Sunday 28

'Dick Clark's Caravan Of Stars', Westchester County Center, White Plains, NY

The Caravan winds down tonight with the tour's only stop in New York State. There is one show at 8:00pm. Bo Diddley & The Duchess and The Byrds immediately fly back to Los Angeles to appear on the set of a new teenage film.

Monday 29

The complete edition of *Hullabaloo* originally scheduled for October 4 but postponed because of Pope Paul IV's American visit is finally screened on NBC TV tonight at 7:30pm (West and East coasts) and an hour earlier in Midwest regions (see entry for mid-to-late September). The full show features Michael Landon, Jackie DeShannon, Chad & Jill, David

Winters, and Paul Revere & The Raiders, plus The Byrds, who are seen singing live to a pre-recorded backing track of 'The Times They Are A-Changin'". They also briefly perform John Sebastian's 'Do You Believe In Magic?' as part of the show's Top Pop Medley.

For TV viewers, it may make little sense that the group promotes a song they have not even released, but at the time the show appearance was videotaped two months ago, 'The Times They Are A Changin'' was considered the next single.

Monday 29–Tuesday 30

FILMING Rushing back from New York, The Byrds appear in the movie *The Big T.N.T. Show*. T.N.T. supposedly means Tune And Talent, although some twist the abbreviation to mean 'This Could Be The Night' after the movie's theme song.

The film features a series of pop performers recorded for two consecutive days at the Moulin Rouge theatre on Sunset Boulevard. Producer Henry G. Saperstein, director Larry Peerce, and musical supervisor Phil Spector aim to repeat last year's very successful *The TAMI Show* (where TAMI could be either 'Teen Age Music International' or 'Teenage Awards Music International').

"Several hundred screaming teenagers and some older long-haired hippies were treated to a free pop-folk-rock bash at Hollywood's Moulin Rouge," writes John L Scott in *The Los Angeles Times* (December 1). "They had queued up for at least an hour, starting at 3:30pm outside the theatre before being admitted. At 6:00 a spokesman announced that refreshments would be served. Cheers!"

David McCallum is the show's host, and introduces – in alphabetic order – Joan Baez (who sings backed by the studio orchestra); The Byrds; Ray Charles; Petula Clark; Donovan; Bo Diddley; The Lovin' Spoonful; Roger Miller; The Modern Folk Quartet (who provide the theme song); The Ronettes; and an explosive performance by Ike and Tina Turner & The Ikettes. The cameras catch both Frank Zappa and Sky Saxon in the audience, and The Byrds perform three songs live: 'Turn! Turn! Turn!', 'The Bells Of Rhymney', and 'Mr. Tambourine Man'.

Using four television cameras and two traditional 35mm film recorders, editing is speedily done during the actual performance. By the end of the second day, producer Saperstein has 140 minutes of action on tape, which is then quickly whittled down to 100-plus minutes and readied for premiere on New Year's Eve, with a general release planned for January 26 next year.

After the filming is wrapped up there is a party at Phil Spector's house. In his autobi-

ography, Derek Taylor will recall an embarrassing moment. "I became a little pissed, a little stoned, and maybe a little pilled, and I went on a word trip about the day when there would be three Byrds, then two, and then one, and what would the group be called then? The Byrd? McGuinn was very uncomfortable; though an egocentric performer in those days – and the better because of it, though not easy to work with, they say – he was shy and withdrawn offstage and was not wanting to be singled out in this way at a party."

December

Friday 3

'Intra-fraternity Council Fall/Winter Dance', William & Mary Hall, College of William & Mary, Williamsburg, VA

The group take a roundtrip to the East Coast for an appearance in Virginia with Sam The Sham & The Pharaohs.

Saturday 4

'Turn! Turn! Turn!' tops the *Billboard* Hot 100 for the first of three consecutive weeks, crowning a great year for The Byrds. (It will also top the *Cash Box* and the Canadian singles charts.)

The failure of the previous single, 'All I Really Want To Do', is a blessing in disguise, as 'Turn! Turn! Turn!' shifts the focus away from Dylan songs and proves the group's ability to interpret and arrange great songs regardless of their source.

Monday 6

The Byrds' second album, *Turn! Turn! Turn!*, is released in the USA, although the actual release date may be postponed by a week (Monday 13). Again the group delivers a package of rich and even quality. It contains a mixture of songs by outside writers and original compositions (weighing six to five in favour of cover songs), and the group's vocals and musicianship are once more of high order. In a pop world crowded by rhythm & blues-influenced guitar players, McGuinn's almost piano-like approach to the electric 12-string guitar unifies the group's special sound.

Guy Webster is responsible for the attractive group portrait – taken at his studio in Beverly Hills – on the jacket and John Berg for the design (the jacket is later nominated for a Grammy), and Derek Taylor has provided the intelligent liner notes. The album will make US Number 17 and UK Number 11.

Robert Shelton in *The New York Times* (January 30 1966) reviews the album as part of a folk-rock round-up. "[By] a West Coast group that took the Dylan sound and put folk-rock on the map on its second LP. The title song is Pete Seeger's melody to a section of Ecclesiastes that was John F. Kennedy's favourite bit of poetry. Otherwise, not so strong as the first Byrds' LP, *Mr. Tambourine Man*, but still an effective program of folk-rock." Two undated reviews – one in *Billboard*, the other in *Variety* – say: "Hot on the heels of their No 1 hit single, 'Turn! Turn! Turn!', the group offers a diversified program of material that is certain to soar up the LP charts. Most of the selections are well written ballads composed by the members of the group. On the familiar side, 'Oh! Susannah' is sparked with pop freshness" (*Billboard*) and "One of the best combos to emerge during the past year in the folk-rock groove, The Byrds have maintained their streak with an excellent selection of material" (*Variety*).

A nice compliment comes courtesy Bob Dylan. "He put ['Lay Down Your Weary Tune'] on and said, 'Hey, this sounds really good. This has some feeling. Before I heard you do this, I thought you were an imitator but this has some soul'," McGuinn recalls to music journalist John Nork.

Wednesday 8

DJ Dave Hull at radio station KRLA has taken over L.A.'s Moulin Rouge theatre – where The Big TNT Show was filmed a week ago – and transformed it into his own club, Dave Hull's Hullabaloo. Although it does not open to the public before tomorrow, the club hosts a lavish show and dinner tonight in honour of the first Pop Music Awards, a joint promotion by KRLA and *The Beat* magazine. The long guest list includes The Beach Boys, Jan & Dean, Chad & Jeremy, Barry McGuire, Sonny & Cher, Dino Desi & Billy, Little Richard, Jackie DeShannon, The Knickerbockers, April & Nino Stevens, Robert Miller, Herb Alpert, Dick & Deidre, Brenda Holloway, Dusty Springfield, P.F. Sloan, The Shangri-Las, The Vogues, The Beau Brummels, Glen Campbell, The Deep Six, Ian Whitcomb, Joey Paige, Jerry Naylor, and – many sources insist – Mick Jagger (the Stones are recording at RCA in Hollywood) and The Byrds (also in town). The Beau Brummels are awarded Best New Vocal Group, probably to the dismay of The Byrds. (Bob Dylan, who is rumoured to be here to accept the Best Male Vocal Performance award, is in fact not in L.A. – he performs a solitary concert tonight at nearby Orange Coast College in Costa Mesa, CA.)

Friday 10

Lake Theatre, Painesville, OH

On their way to New York City again, the group stop for an afternoon performance (4:30pm) in Painesville. MC'd by Cleveland radio DJs Jerry G. and Bill Winters, the opening acts are The Rockers (from nearby Mentor), Joey & The Continentals, Ray Stevens, and, oddly, 'Dolly Pardon' as the ads spell her name, a country songwriter whose record label Monument tries to market her as a pop singer. (Dolly Parton will have to wait until 1967 to gain any widespread recognition, when she turns to country music full time.)

Saturday 11

The Byrds likely play an undocumented concert in the vicinity of New York.

Saturday 11–Sunday 12

☐ **US TV** CBS Studio 50, Manhattan, New York, NY. CBS *The Ed Sullivan Show*

The Byrds are in New York to appear on Ed Sullivan's variety show, a weekly entertainment institution – in its 19th season – that reaches many millions of American TV viewers in its regular 8:00pm Sunday slot. Commonly, rehearsals take place in the couple of days leading up to the performance, and then the show goes live to air. (In the case of The Byrds all rehearsals may take place on the day of broadcast, that is Sunday December 12.) Sullivan's show is variety in its truest sense: this Sunday also includes among the musical acts the Bratislava Slovakian Folkloric Company from Czechoslovakia, a British comedy duo, an animal drill team, and a juggling clown.

Sunday 12

The Byrds appear on *The Ed Sullivan Show* on the CBS network at 8:00pm (episode number 855), performing 'Turn! Turn! Turn!' and 'Mr.

Turn! Turn! Turn!

A1 'Turn! Turn! Turn! (To Everything There Is A Season)' (ECCLESIASTES/P. SEEGER)
A2 'It Won't Be Wrong' (J. McGUINN/H. GERST)
A3 'Set You Free This Time' (G. CLARK)
A4 'Lay Down Your Weary Tune' (B. DYLAN)
A5 'He Was A Friend of Mine' (TRAD. ARR./J. McGUINN)
B1 'The World Turns All Around Her' (G. CLARK)
B2 'Satisfied Mind' (R. HAYES/J. RHODES)
B3 'If You're Gone' (G. CLARK)
B4 'The Times They Are A-Changin'' (B. DYLAN)
B5 'Wait and See' (J. McGUINN/D. CROSBY)
B6 'Oh! Susannah' (S. FOSTER)

US release December 6 1965 (Mono LP CL 2454/Stereo LP CS 9254)
UK release March 22 1966 (Mono CBS BPG 62652/Stereo CBS SBPG 62652)
Chart high US number 17; UK number 11
Read more ... entries for August 28, September 1, 10, 16, 17, 18, October 1, 4, 18, 22, 26, 27, November 1 1965

Bonus CD tracks: 'The Day Walk (Never Before)' (G. Clark), 'She Don't Care About Time' (G. Clark), 'The Times They Are A-Changin'' [First Version] (B. Dylan), 'It's All Over Now, Baby Blue' (B. Dylan), 'She Don't Care About Time' [Version 1] (G. Clark), 'The World Turns All Around Her' [Alternate Mix] (G. Clark), 'Stranger In A Strange Land' [Instrumental] (D. Crosby)

"The title song is Pete Seeger's melody to a section of Ecclesiastes that was John F. Kennedy's favourite bit of poetry. Otherwise, not so strong as the first Byrds' LP, Mr. Tambourine Man, *but still an effective program of folk-rock."*
NEW YORK TIMES , JANUARY 30, 1966

Tambourine Man'. The rest of the hour-long show is made up of trumpeter Al Hirt, singers Wayne Newton and Barbara McNair in separate spots, the Bratislava Slovakian Folkloric Company, comedian Alan King, The Swingle Singers, British comedy duo Tony Hendra and Nick Ullett, and the aforementioned animal and juggling acts.

All does not proceed smoothly, as Chris Hillman recounts later to author John Einarson. "That's the one moment when I regret that nobody had taken Crosby outside and shaken him right up. Gene? He was fine. McGuinn was fine. But David got into an argument with the producer of the show, Ed Sullivan's son-in-law. That's why we only ever did the show once and the sound was so horrible. Crosby was so nervous, so scared, that at the rundown, because it was a live show, he starts yelling at the director and the producer: 'You guys don't know how to record this music. You don't know what you're doing.' On and on. So the producer's thinking, 'You punk little kid,' and he says: 'Your rundown is over. We're going to tape at eight, then you're off the show.' Everybody in the booth started applauding. So, consequently, when we were on we got a bad sound."

The tense moment may be the reason for Ed Sullivan's fumbled introduction: "And now, Mr. Tambourine Man with 'The Byrds'!" Despite Hillman's later misgivings, the transmission presents the original Byrds in fine form, easily duplicating their recorded vocal and instrumental sound even if the sound balance on 'Turn! Turn! Turn!' is way off ('Mr. Tambourine Man', however, is lip-synched to recorded version). They look great, too: Crosby in suede cape, McGuinn with rectangular glasses, Hillman and Clarke bringing up the rear, while Gene Clark and his tambourine command centre stage.

→ Tuesday 14
Auditorium, Mentor, OH
Going back westwards, the group stop by for another one-off appearance in Ohio.

Mid-December
Paul Kantner – David Crosby's old buddy from San Francisco – arrives in Los Angeles with Jefferson Airplane, newly signed to RCA and set for their first Hollywood recording session on December 16. Derek Taylor, holed up in The Byrds' combined office and rehearsal room, writes: "As [The Byrds] never had any rehearsals, they never used it, but David Crosby brought some friends in from San Francisco, and they used it. They were nice young people, poor as can be. They handed out buttons, which said 'Jefferson Airplane

Loves You'. They rehearsed every night. Did it show? Does it ever."

Friday 17
Veterans Memorial Coliseum, Phoenix, AZ
The Byrds appear in a benefit for the Phoenix Jaycees on a show with four local groups. Although unidentified in a short write-up in the local press, one of the groups is reportedly The Spiders, led by vocalist Vincent Furnier, who later adopts the alias Alice Cooper.

Saturday 18(–Sunday 19)
[Possibly Sunset Rollarena], Tucson, AZ
The Byrds with The Spiders, and according to members of The Spiders, the two groups also combine for an Arizona performance tomorrow (Sunday 19).

Wednesday 22
🔊 **RECORDING** RCA Recording Studio, Sunset Boulevard, Hollywood, CA. Producer Jim Dickson and engineer Dave Hassinger.

The Byrds record the two new compositions, 'Eight Miles High' and 'Why', which are the direct result of Crosby force-feeding his bandmates a diet of Ravi Shankar and John Coltrane.

The group has hired RCA's basement studio on Sunset along with in-house technician Dave Hassinger, while Jim Dickson is in the producer's chair in the absence of Terry Melcher. Dickson's previous experience combined with Hassinger's expertise – he has worked on Rolling Stones hits such as 'Satisfaction' and 'Get Off Of My Cloud' – ensure the group's spontaneous energy is captured on tape.

'Eight Miles High' and 'Why' are unlike anything The Byrds have attempted before, and yet they represent the natural evolution of the group's folk, jazz, and blues influences. 'Eight Miles High' will feature an unusually generous composition credit, with Gene Clark, McGuinn, and Crosby all noted. The main body of the lyrics are reputedly the work of Clark, with the theme a brilliant poetic twist on the group's English trip.

David Crosby will explain his autobiography: "Because of the Coltrane influence, the guitar solo in 'Eight Miles High' was shatteringly different, and I have to take credit for that at the same time as I acknowledge that it was [McGuinn] who played it. [He], you know, has brilliance. He synthesized something new on the electric guitar, playing that Indian-flavoured stuff on 'Eight Miles High'. He blew the minds of everyone in the musical world at that time. Nobody had ever heard anything like that in their lives because they

had only listened to guitar players. They hadn't listened to a horn player. They couldn't translate a horn player's feel onto a 12-string guitar. Who's kidding? Nobody could do that, except that McGuinn did it."

Coltrane's *Africa/Brass* had been the group's regular diet on the Dick Clark tour, but McGuinn's four-note introduction also bears a passing resemblance to Coltrane's opening motif on the track 'India' on the saxophonist's 1963 live album *Impressions*.

Eventually, both 'Eight Miles High' and 'Why' have to be re-recorded and will be subject to unforeseen controversy, but for many fans nothing matches the sound and the fury of these original interpretations. (They will be released as part of The Byrds' remastered catalogue in 1996.)

(Johnny Rogan's discography also lists 'The Times They Are A-Changin'' as recorded today, but for what reason is not entirely clear. It is already available on the *Turn! Turn! Turn!* album, and if it is planned as a single, it pales compared to the great leap that the group's original work now represents.)

Saturday 25
▢ **UK TV** Over in England, The Byrds are seen on *Top Of The Pops* (BBC-1 at 10:35pm) in a special end-of-the-year survey of 1965's chart-toppers, along with The Beatles, The Rolling Stones, Ken Dodd, Georgie Fame, The Hollies, Tom Jones, The Kinks, The Moody Blues, Elvis Presley, The Righteous Brothers, The Seekers, Sandie Shaw, Sonny & Cher, Jackie Trent, Unit Four Plus Two, and The Walker Brothers.

TOTP's regular team of four DJs presents this edition together: Jimmy Savile, David Jacobs, Alan Freeman, and Pete Murray. The show is repeated the following day, Boxing Day, at 12:15pm.

The Christmas special features 'Mr. Tambourine Man', but as that was never done as an in-person performance by The Byrds for *Top Of The Pops* the record is probably just played on-air again. (The group performed 'All I Really Want To Do' on *Top Of The Pops*, but 'Tambourine Man' was only played as a disc on the show accompanied by either the Go-Jo dancers or some visual effects.)

Wednesday 29
'K-POI Ball', Honolulu International Center (HIC) Exhibition Hall, Honolulu, HI
The year is rounded off with a visit to Hawaii for a show with local groups The Mop Tops, The Spirits, and The Undertakers.

The Byrds take a few days off to soak up the sun, get high, and ready themselves for the New Year.

The Byrds make groundbreaking **'Eight Miles High'** single for March release in the US and initiate 'raga-rock' fad … **Gene Clark**, plagued by fear of flying, leaves The Byrds on the eve of New York flight in February … Four-man Byrds tour around the US as headlining act, but see 'Eight Miles High' bow out of the US charts after accusations of a drug-related lyric … Group plays

1966

to largest audiences so far at two Beach Boys concerts in California … Group's third album *Fifth Dimension* and accompanying '5D' single see the group's sound evolve and develop … Byrds and **Beatles** meet up again in Hollywood in August … The group plays the Whisky A Go Go and the Fillmore, with Gene Clark making a temporary return … Next, The Byrds become the first pop group to play New York's major jazz club The Village Gate in October … Against a backdrop of riots on Hollywood's Sunset Strip, The Byrds end the year by recording their fourth album *Younger Than Yesterday*.

January

As 1965 gives way to 1966, The Byrds are able to settle down and enjoy the first fruits of their success. *Flip* magazine (March 1966) devotes a spread to the group's domestic life and their Byrd houses dotting the hills above Hollywood – "remote from the multi-coloured glitter of Sunset Strip where they first exploded as a group". (The article appeared earlier in UK's *Music Echo* on November 20, 1965.)

Gene Clark, as the group's principal song-writer, earns a steady income from publishing in addition to performance fees. "Gene is the richest Byrd," notes *16 Magazine* (April 1966) succinctly, a fact that causes slight envy with the other four. He rents a modern little house in the hills and owns an MG, but adds: "Some-day I hope to own a Ferrari or a Porsche." By next month he is reported in *KRLA Beat* as driving around in a new red Porsche with shiny black interior.

David Crosby has found a property a bit farther west, on Lisbon Lane in Beverly Glen Canyon, where he resides in a small and cosy one-bedroom house standing alone on a hill-side. Portrayed in *Flip*, Crosby comes over as ascetic: "David is unlike the rest of the group in that he neither smokes nor drinks alcohol. Also, he never watches television and rarely goes to movies. 'I drink quarts of apple juice every day and my favourite food is fruits and vegetables.'" He lists Ravi Shankar, guitar-ist/composer Sandy Bull, and Miles Davis as musical favourites and science-fiction books as preferred reading. He drives a black Triumph motorcycle but he, too, dreams of a Porsche. Jim Dickson fondly recalls in Crosby's auto-biography: "Somewhere there's a picture of David on a motorcycle with a crash helmet and his cape. I still have that picture. I think it's what prompted someone to call him Law-rence Of Laurel Canyon."

Chris Hillman's spectacular house on Mag-nolia Street is described as a tiny, rustic, two-storied wooden building with a veranda and a panoramic view of the Pacific Ocean and the vast spread of Los Angeles. Seventeen-year-old Pamela Ann Miller (later Pamela Des Barres) from Reseda is smitten: "I latched on to The Byrds as I had The Beatles, only this time they were local and I could obsess in person," she writes in her memoir *I'm With The Band*. "All five of them lived in Laurel Canyon, God's golden backyard. … I had to locate an ancient map to find Magnolia Street; it was at the tip-top of a hill, at the end of a dirt pathway, with only one house overlooking the universe. It belonged to Chris Hillman. I started going over there every day after school, sitting on the ledge, looking out over all of L.A., and

on the clearest days I could see the ocean sparkling. … He lived in this fairy-tale pad right out of Walt Disney's wildest dreams, sur-rounded by eucalyptus trees and wildflowers so fragrant; to breathe was ecstasy." Hillman has a Triumph Bonneville TT Special motor-cycle, but eventually will also become the owner of a Porsche.

Michael Clarke lives with his collection of high fashion clothes and comic books in the basement of Jim Dickson's apartment in the Hollywood Hills, and his choice of transport is a modest Volkswagen.

Jim McGuinn lives in a one-story ranch house with a half-acre garden, situated on Woodrow Wilson Drive at the end of Mulhol-land Drive. McGuinn lives in a house filled with electronic toys, and confides to *Flip*'s Arlene Perlman: "A secret ambition is to plug my Rickenbacker 12-string into the colour TV set and watch the patterns change." For the moment McGuinn drives a rented Chevrolet Impala (soon replaced by a silver-painted Por-sche), spending his spare time playing guitar or banjo. McGuinn also has a way with quot-able thoughts. In *Flip* (May 1966) he para-phrases American novelist Carl Sandburg's saying "Life is like an onion, you peel it off one layer at a time, and sometimes you weep" as "Life is like a piece of butterscotch with a core of uranium. You have to lick away at the candy to get at the precious metal."

Saturday 2

'Turn! Turn! Turn!' drops down the *Record Mirror* charts to Number 44 on its way out of the UK hit parade, despite columnist Tony Hall's pro-Byrds campaign. It hit the top of the US charts, but the single runs out of steam in the UK after barely making the Top 30.

Derek Taylor thanks Hall personally later in a letter to *Record Mirror*: "Guess it was the wrong song at the wrong time. George Har-rison wrote [me] to say British record-buyers didn't realise what they were missing. Still, that's showbiz."

Tuesday 4

Back in Los Angeles in the New Year after a few days of rest in Hawaii, some of The Byrds attend a party in the Hollywood Hills for Brit-ish visitors The Yardbirds. Kim Fowley and Jim De Marco are the hosts, and besides a slew of teenage Hollywood celebrities, Gary Leeds (of The Walker Brothers), Mary Travers, and Derek Taylor are also present.

The Yardbirds are halfway through a North American tour, and right before Christmas they taped the proto-psychedelic master-piece 'Shapes Of Things' in Chicago – the day before The Byrds recorded their first take on the equally daring 'Eight Miles High' at RCA.

Wednesday 5–Sunday 16
The Trip, Hollywood, CA

The Byrds return to this Sunset Strip hot spot for a 12-day residence, this time supported by The Paul Butterfield Blues Band.

Butterfield's group features guitarists Mike Bloomfield and Elvin Bishop, who cross Indian-inspired scales with scorching blues runs on a new tune they for the moment just call 'The Raga'. Over the next months the tune will be further refined before becoming the title-track of Butterfield's epoch-making *East-West*.

New Musical Express's Hollywood corre-spondent Tracy Thomas reports (February 25, 1966): "Currently The Byrds are entertaining SRO-crowds at the Trip, one of the 'in clubs' on the Sunset Strip. Though a few Dylan songs remain in their customarily reserved set, several hard rock and jazz-rock numbers have crept in from behind the 12-string and tam-bourine, displaying a versatility and ability in fields other than folk-rock that is barely hinted at in their albums." In *Record Mirror*, Gary Leeds explains to the uninitiated: "[There's] a place called the Trip in Hollywood that is like the Scotch of St James here [in London]. Any time you walk in there, there's everyone from the Top Hundred sitting around yell-ing!" (Pop star sightings at the Trip this week include The Yardbirds and Peter & Gordon.) British pop personality Jonathan King, on a visit to Los Angeles, writes home to *Music Echo* (January 22): "You might have noticed that my pet hobby-horse recently has been The Byrds. I saw them perform again last week in Los Angeles and they really were unbelievably good. We like to think of ourselves here in

England as able to recognise talent when we see it, but somehow they didn't really click on their first visit. The Byrds must come back here very soon, and then, I trust everything will turn out all right. We all know that the voluble and expressive correspondents are the 'anti' brigade. Let's make an exception. Byrd-fans, put pen to paper and bring them over here by popular demand."

Daily Variety (January 19) notes briefly of the January 14 show: "The Byrds … continue to entice the mixed-age audience with their twangy hutcha of jungle drums beat which has a primitive zing. They manage some interesting masterings of 'She Don't Care About Time', and Bob Dylan's 'The Times They Are A Changing', which is sort of an understatement, musically speaking."

Charles Champlin, one of the first to champion the Byrd sound last year, writes in The *Los Angeles Times* (January 18): "At the Trip … The Byrds are the chief attraction, although the deafening decibel-level at which they pitch their songs makes it even less possible than before to realise that they are doing some interesting things musically and lyrically." Champlin is more impressed with the Butterfield gang: "The stand-out sideman is guitarist Luke [sic] Bloomfield, a very fine instrumentalist, who does most to give the group its driving excitement."

In *Los Angeles Free Press* (January 14), Paul Jay Robbins reports: "January 6, The Byrds returned to the Trip with the Paul Butterfield Blues Band alternating sets. The Byrds now became staggeringly professional and highly adept, incited emotional riot in the heart – their sound sang up the bloodstream and spattered the head with perfected chorales to joy. The audience, a fantastic crush of everybody, dug it all … and I wondered if they really dug it all."

To Chris Hillman, the residence at The Trip is confirmation that The Byrds can cut it live. "We were our own worst enemies as far as presenting a stage show," the bass player recalls to journalist John Nork, "but there were moments when we shined. We had a week-long engagement at this club called The Trip, on Sunset Strip, and Paul Butterfield was the opening act, and let me tell you, the original Paul Butterfield Band was just killer. Amazing. Mike Bloomfield – amazing. And, here's an interesting bill. The Paul Butterfield Band and The Byrds. The Byrds were an established rock-star band and we rose to the occasion. We played good. Just because we had to! And we got up there and we sang good and we played good and we held our own. There wasn't any competition in that sense. So, there were moments – [then] there were other times when it was a disaster."

Friday 7

New Musical Express publishes a survey of the bestselling UK singles of 1965. 'Mr. Tambourine Man' places at Number 16, sharing the same number of points as The Rolling Stones' 'I Can't Get No Satisfaction'. (The best-selling single is Ken Dodd's mawkish 'Tears'.)

Also, this week's *Record Mirror* lists the Top Ten discs spun last year on the BBC Light Programme's Top Ten Game, a weekday show that toured around England in 1965, inviting audiences to vote for their favourite discs of the week, combing results from ten of the week's releases with the ten most popular songs from the previous week. 'We Can Work It Out', The Hollies' 'I'm Alive', and 'Help!' make up the three most popular numbers, with 'Mr. Tambourine Man' at fourth.

Monday 10

To follow the recent American chart-topper 'Turn! Turn! Turn!', Columbia Records chooses to release Gene Clark's 'Set You Free This Time' coupled with 'It Won't Be Wrong' as the new Byrds single. (The day of release may be postponed by a week.) It will prove to be a hasty move, as the ballad-like topside does not have as much of the immediate commercial appeal as the group's recent hits. To rectify slow sales, the single is quickly flipped so that the more poppy 'It Won't Be Wrong' is promoted to a double A-side. This merely seems to confuse the record-buyers, as the single stalls at a poor Number 63 in *Billboard*'s Hot 100. (The single does brisker business in *Cash Box*, where it peaks at Number 39.)

Cash Box labels the single 'Pick Of The Week' (January 29). "The Byrds can easily have their third number one in a row … with this excellent newie tabbed 'It Won't Be Wrong'. This one's a pulsating, fast-moving, blues-tinged romancer about a love-sick fella who begs his girl to give him half-a-chance. 'Set You Free This Time' is a laconic, medium-paced woe-ser essayed in an emotion-charged style by the group."

Billboard (January 29) picks the single as a "Top 20 Pop Spotlight" and describes 'It Won't Be Wrong' as "[a] hard-driving rocker that will fast replace 'Turn! Turn! Turn!' on the Hot 100". The same week as the review runs, 'Set You Free This Time' is registered in the "Bubbling Under" section at Number 110, while the following issue (February 5) it is 'It Won't Be Wrong' that is bubbling at Number 119. Columbia Records has taken out a full-page advertisement in *Billboard* for February 5, promoting both sides of the single, but it is precisely this lack of decision that hinders its chart chances.

In the first edition of *Crawdaddy* (February 7) a journalist writes: "It's a lovely, moving song with Dylan-like 20-syllable lines deckful of well-chosen words … the singer is deliberate and effective; he occasionally under-emotes, but since the group does not rely completely on the vocal to convey feeling, no harm is done. The harmonica at the end is beautiful." Although *Crawdaddy*'s first issue is just an amateur stapled rag, this US magazine will become a pioneering journal of rock'n'roll criticism.

Undated January

Intriguingly, Jim McGuinn and David Crosby encounter beat poet Allen Ginsberg around now, perhaps at one of the gigs during the 12-day Trip club residence. "I ran into Alan Ginzberg [sic] at the club we were working at and he had some tapes," David Crosby will tell a reporter from *Hit Parader* next month. "He's been living in India a long time. Then I saw him again the next day at a party on top of a merry-go-round and he sang me their prayers. These mantras and tantras from India … and I got him to come up to McGuinn's house and we taped it all. Jim's got all kinds of tape equipment. I don't know if we'll make one into a rock'n'roll song, but certainly from listening to them we program ourselves, and an awareness of that comes out in the rest of our music. I'm in the middle of a song now and part of it is coming out like that. I'm not plagiarizing or copying notes, I'm getting the attitude of it and every musician in the country of doing that from Ravi Shankar."

(Allen Ginsberg roamed the world for the past year; he was evicted from Czechoslovakia in May and appeared at a big recital at London's Royal Albert Hall in June before returning to the US.)

'Set You Free This Time'/
'It Won't Be Wrong'
(Double A-side)

A 'Set You Free This Time'
(G. CLARK)
B 'It Won't Be Wrong'
(J. MCGUINN/H. GERST)

US release January 10 1966
(Columbia 43501)
UK release February 11 1966 (CBS 202037)
Chart high US number 63; UK none
Read more … entries for September 16, 18 1965

Wednesday 19

The Big T.N.T. Show premiers in the US after selected previews at Christmas. The movie, made quickly and cheaply at the end of the previous year (see November 29 and 30, 1965) and aimed at the teenage market, does fair business at theatres.

"*The Big T.N.T. Show* isn't any kind of conventional movie," explains *The Hollywood Reporter* (January 19). "It is a straight variety show with some of the biggest names and talents currently operating in the pop, rock and folk music field. … There is not much to say about a film of this sort. The sound might have been more expertly handled. There is a continual din during most of the numbers; that is the way the kids 'listen' today. That's all right. It's part of the program. But for a movie, this audience noise might have been modulated so it does not drown out the artist." *Variety* (January 19) says: "There's a consistent scream track – save for Miss Baez and Donovan – which becomes annoyingly obtrusive; the live crowds, while very enthusiastic, didn't maintain this obviously-phoney background wail." The reporter concludes: "A print of each should be buried in a time capsule." Herb Michelson in *The Oakland Tribune* (January 13) is not so kind: "Roger Miller, the King of the Road, proves he's not a visual performer. Ray Charles is mildly entertaining. Bo Diddley is noisy. The Byrds and Lovin' Spoonful are lousy imitations of The Beatles. Also around are Donovan, Ike & Tina Turner and The Ikettes, The Modern Folk Quartet, a dozen vulgarly choreographed go-go girls, and – Lord help us – those Ronettes."

Friday 21

📺 **US TV** KHJ Television Studios, Hollywood, CA. KHJ Channel 9 Los Angeles *9th Street West* 6:00pm

Jim McGuinn (but none of the other Byrds) is a speaking guest on Sam Riddle's local Los Angeles TV shows *9th Street West*, which today discusses teenage problems. Besides McGuinn, the panel consists of a local DJ, actor Bobby Sherman, and singer Carol Connors. Neil Sedaka winds up proceedings with a musical segment.

Saturday 22

The *Turn! Turn! Turn!* album is given an exclusive preview in the UK's *Music Echo*, even though the album will not be released for another two months in Britain. To Richard Bruce, *Music Echo*'s regular US contributor, it is "so sensationally brilliant that even after [one] hearing, I've no hesitation in saying they are proving they have as big a talent as The Beatles and Stones! A bold, perhaps, dangerous statement. Nevertheless, the lilting beat, fantastic harmonies, and great warmth of the 11 tracks leave one with that outstanding impression."

Monday 24

🔊 **RECORDING** Columbia Recording Studios, Studio A, Sunset and El Centro, Hollywood, CA. 7:00pm. Producer Allen Stanton and (presumably) engineer Ray Gerhardt.

Since The Byrds' brief visit to RCA (see December 22, 1965), some changes have been made that necessitate a return to the recording studio today. In Terry Melcher's place comes Allen Stanton, the man who in part was responsible for signing The Byrds to Columbia Records in the first place. While he has a high and influential administrative rank in the Columbia hierarchy, Stanton has less experience as an actual producer. But by now – fuelled by two Number Ones and intent on developing their sound – Jim Dickson and The Byrds are less dependent on an assertive opinion behind the console.

It is further decided that the group's attempts at RCA cannot be used and need to be re-cut. The reasons may be musical – the tempo wavers slightly, and the drums sound muffled, but perhaps it is also because Columbia demands Columbia staff and Columbia owned studios. Thus The Byrds troop back to Columbia and start today with 'Why'.

Tuesday 25–Wednesday 26

🔊 **RECORDING** Columbia Recording Studios, Studio A, Sunset and El Centro, Hollywood, CA. Producer Allen Stanton and (presumably) engineer Ray Gerhardt.

Picking up from yesterday's session, the group re-records 'Eight Miles High' over two days, with the Wednesday session starting at 7:00pm. Already earmarked as the group's next single, the revitalised 'Eight Miles High' keeps the same arrangement but improves upon the RCA attempt. Everything about the song is unconventional: Hillman's intro, like a thunderball, McGuinn's translation of Coltrane's 'sheets of sound' to the electric guitar, the choir-like vocal melody, and the metaphoric lyrics. Michael Clarke, drummer by default, delivers one of his most inspiring performances.

ALSO …

While The Byrds record at Columbia, Arthur Lee, Bryan MacLean, and Love record the bulk of their debut album over at Sunset Sound. Talking to *Melody Maker* in 1970, Lee recalls: "The first album was definitely influenced by The Byrds and Manfred Mann." One of the songs Love records is 'Hey Joe', inspired by the version that David Crosby sings with The Byrds.

→ January/February

Columbia Records has decided to put some muscle behind the group's new single and bankroll a promotional film to promote 'Set You Free This Time'. Directed by Barry Feinstein and taped at a beach somewhere in the Los Angeles area, the incident will pass into the Byrds ornithology, as mounting frustration and volatile tempers come to the surface.

David Crosby will write later in his autobiography: "I think I'm the only one who ever punched Jim [Dickson], and the only reason I got away with that was because [photographer] Barry Feinstein and Gene Clark grabbed Jim before he could get back at me. It took both of them. Me and Dickson were having a disagreement about how we should make a little bit of film that Barry was shooting of us out on the beach in L.A. Jim was trying to keep it organised and get it done and we were being sullen punks. He just got mad and said, 'You goddamn do it or else!' and I said 'Hey, fuck you.' A day at the beach."

Interviewed by John Einarson years later, Chris Hillman takes up the story: "David [Crosby] didn't want to be there. So David begins to needle Michael, who's gullible. 'Hey, let's leave, we don't want to be here.' So Jim Dickson, being volatile, jumps on David, physically. And Gene saved Crosby. He grabbed Dickson and pulled him off. … He was a strong kid."

Jim McGuinn remembers the event as a promotional film done on assignment for BBC television. He recalls for *New Musical Express* (May 5, 1973): "We were out on the beach filming for the BBC. They wanted a film to go along with one of our songs. I think it was 'Set You Free [This Time]', or one of Gene's songs – doesn't matter. But it was so dumb, because they had arranged that we should walk in front of the camera, just parade in front of the camera. … And we did this five or six times because something was wrong. Someone wasn't looking right, or some dumb thing like that. Then Michael started to get really uptight, you know? He said this is stupid. And Dickson said 'you better stay in' and got everything back in line.

"So then Crosby just hauled off and punched Dickson in the mouth, you know? And Dickson said, 'Wow, you loosened my tooth,' or some number like that, and he had him down in a stranglehold. Dickson was twice as big as Crosby. This is on the beach, and Gene Clark went and grabbed him off of Crosby and we straightened everything out. And it worked out all right. Yeah, that was the first [actual physical rift in the group]. We had a lot of them."

This concurs with Hillman's story to music historian Richie Unterberger: "We had an

➜ An arrow denotes an estimated date.

opportunity to do one of the very first videos, in a sense: 16 millimetre stuff, around Gene's song 'She Don't Care About Time'. And we were going to send it to England. And, of course, it didn't happen, because we got in a big argument with Jim. I don't say we, but David did. And the whole thing was scrapped."

Late January

☐ **US TV** KHJ Studios Sunset Boulevard, Hollywood, CA. KHJ-TV *Hollywood A Go Go*

The Byrds pre-tape segments for the last edition of *Hollywood A Go Go* before the show is taken of the air, set for local broadcast in the Los Angeles area on February 5. The group performs 'Mr. Tambourine Man', 'It Won't Be Wrong', plus 'Turn! Turn! Turn!'.

→ Friday 28
[Unknown venue],
La Jolla, CA

Saturday 29
La Salle High School Auditorium, Pasadena, CA

The Byrds pull 1,700 students to a show where they appear with Jerry Pierce & The Gosdin Brothers. Vernon and Rex Gosdin are entwined in Byrds history as they were once members of The Golden State Boys with Chris Hillman.

The La Salle concert is promoted by the school's Senior Class and makes almost $750. Students line up at 4:30pm and threaten to break down the gym's glass doors when The Byrds soundcheck at 7:00pm. "The enthusi-

astic crowd was visibly pleased as The Byrds performed for an hour, singing their hits and introducing some new songs," notes college paper The Lance. "After the performance, getting The Byrds out was no easy task as The Byrds got into the cars to leave. I noticed many girls dropping letters, rings, and other personal items into The Byrds' cars. The whole thing was very touching."

Sunday 30
Hollywood High School Auditorium, Los Felix Jewish Community Center, Hollywood, CA

Recent students at Hollywood High with musical aspirations include television star and singer Ricky Nelson, guitarist Lowell George, and singer and composer P.F. Sloan.

Five Byrds in early 1966. From left: McGuinn, Hillman, Crosby, Clarke, and Clark.

ALSO ...

Robert Shelton, the staff music critic at *The New York Times*, writes an appraisal of 1965's biggest pop trend in today's edition. "Folk-rock was born when The Byrds, a rock'n'roll group, recorded Bob Dylan's 'Mr. Tambourine Man'," he says. For Shelton, the time has come to ask if this is merely opportunism in the wake of The Beatles. "Did electric instruments cause a power failure or a power success?"

Shelton's article is as much a broadside against the folk music magazine *Sing Out!*, which has questioned the fusion of folk and electricity since Bob Dylan's appearance at the Newport Folk Festival last year, most famously in singer Tom Paxton's diatribe about what he called folk-rot. "What is the function of the secular periodical if not to encourage experimentation, to help shape an avant-garde?" asks Shelton rhetorically. *Sing Out!* editor Irwin Silber replies in The *New York Times* (February 20), which also prints Shelton's reply and additional comments from Nat Hentoff of *Hi-Fi Stereo Review* and critic Paul Nelson. Silber's point is that folk-rock represents just another whitewashing of the American cultural heritage. He sums up: "Its superficial electronic frenzy cannot cover up its fundamental non-involvement with life."

February

Saturday 5

The last edition of *Hollywood A Go Go* goes out at 6:30pm PST on Channel 9 KHJ-TV (see entry for late January). The final show features The Byrds plugging their latest single sides, 'Set You Free This Time' and 'It Won't Be Wrong', in addition to 'Turn! Turn! Turn!'. Host Sam Riddle has also invited The Everly Brothers, Jimmy Darren, Freddy Cannon, Bob Lind, David Watson, Karen Verros, and Brenda Bantam & The Bantams for the show. (While *Hollywood A Go Go* is taken off the air, Riddle still leads *9th Street West* and will return for the autumn season in a brand new show.)

●

In Britain, where the EP format is common (it means Extended Play and is a single-sized record with more playing time), four selections from the group's two albums are combined for an EP this February: 'The Times They Are A Changin'', 'The Bells Of Rhymney', 'It's No Use', and 'We'll Meet Again'.

The French record industry, too, often mixes album tracks and stray single sides for EPs, and has already put out 'Mr. Tambourine Man'/'Here Without You'/'I Knew I'd Want You'/'It's No Use' (CBS EP 6100, 1965) and 'Turn! Turn! Turn!'/'Spanish Harlem Incident'/'Don't Doubt Yourself Babe'/'She Don't Care About Time' (CBS EP 6251, 1965). Now, "Les Byrds" have an EP out with 'It Won't Be Wrong', 'Set You Free This Time', 'The Times They Are A-Changin'', and 'Oh! Susannah' (CBS EP 5668, 1966).

→ Early February

Jim McGuinn and David Crosby talk to *Hit Parader* (June 1966) at the Byrds' 9000 Sunset headquarters. "I spend most of my time trying to borrow Jim Dickson's boat and go sailing," says Crosby, while McGuinn professes a desire to become a jet pilot. "It takes about five years to get a jet pilot's licence, and I just haven't had the time to try yet. So I pretend my Porsche is a jet ... well, not exactly. But all those controls and dials ... you know?"

Friday 11

Today, the single 'Set You Free This Time'/'It Won't Be Wrong' is released in the UK, but the A- and B-sides are soon switched around just as in the US. *Record Mirror* (February 19) rates it four stars and comments "[a] couple of tracks from the boys' new US album. Topside is a bit slow, with dreamy overtones, and though not predictably a hit, it could catch on. Lots of musicianship and interesting vocal touches".

Penny Valentine in *Disc* (February 19) says it "needs listening to. On first play, I didn't like it – but now I do. It's rather unByrd-like and very, very Dylan-like. It's slow and gentle and rather sad about never being a person who had much, and though she laughed at him and has now come for help, he doesn't hold a grudge. Ahh!" The following week, *Melody Maker* explains: "Originally the flipside to 'Set You Free This Time', the disc has been flipped, and 'It Won't Be Wrong' is now the A-side. A blues-infected, lively 12-string guitar intro leads into characteristic falsetto vocals and diving backing. The Byrds have hit an original sound which they stick to, but this disc is different enough to be a big hit for them."

Ringo Starr is the guest in *Melody Maker*'s weekly Blind Date session (February 26), chaperoned by John Lennon who sits in the background during the interview and interjects the odd comment. Listening to Elvis's 'Blue River' (where Ringo shouts: "take it off!" upon hearing a few bars) among an assortment of other recent releases, the Beatle drummer is also played 'Set You Free This Time'. "It's The Byrds," he says, "thank God! I only heard it the other day. They can do no wrong in my book. Great record, man, I love the voices. ... I just like this record; what else can I say? I thought they would be doing better than they are. My regards to Derek Taylor."

Saturday 12
ALSO ...

Previewing the autumn's TV menu, *Long Beach Press-Telegram* announces: "A new type rock'n'roll program is also on the agenda for fall programming. It's a situation comedy called The Monkees and Screen Gems has peddled it to NBC-TV. To quote the publicity release: 'The Monkees are a singing group whose shenanigans with teenage fans and Frug-happy audiences are highlighted in the series.' And you can't get hardly any happier than that."

Sunday 13
Dave Hull's Hullabaloo, Los Angeles, CA
The Byrds play Los Angeles DJ Dave Hull's two-month-old Hullabaloo establishment

on the Sunset. Hull has installed a teenaged house band, The Palace Guard (including drummer Emitt Rhodes and singer David Beaudoin), and the January and February programme sees stars like The Yardbirds, The Everly Brothers, and The Association also visit the club. The Byrds play two shows at 4:00 and 8:00pm. Cass Elliot drops by to see The Byrds backstage. Elliot and Crosby go back a long way, and Cass is now just getting started with The Mamas & The Papas, whose second single 'California Dreamin'' is climbing the charts, aimed for the Top Five.

Kimmi Kobashigawa of *KRLA Beat* does an interview with David Crosby (published March 12), presumably at the *Hullabaloo* as The Byrds play their last Los Angeles concert for some months. Kobashigawa wants to know if there are certain recurring themes in their songs. "Yes, there are several. First – and the biggest one – is freedom; personal freedom, freedom of the thinking, freedom of the being. Then there's love – and that's where it's at. And there's motion, too – there's a lot of motion. Sometimes it's trains, sometimes it's horseback, mostly it's jets, cos that's mostly what we ride, that's where our heads are."

Monday 14
☐ **US TV** KABC Studios, ABC Television Center, Hollywood, CA. KABC Channel 7 Los Angeles *Shivaree*

The Byrds tape two inserts on *Shivaree* to be broadcast on February 19, performing 'Set You Free This Time' and 'It Won't Be Wrong'. For 'Set You Free This Time' the camera zooms in from above, focussing on Gene Clark, who mimes the vocal and the mournful harmonica solo before the song is faded. (Both songs will be made available on the bonus-DVD that comes with the *There Is A Season* CD-box.)

Tuesday 15
☐ **US TV** KCOP Television Studios, Hollywood, CA. KCOP-TV Channel 13 Los Angeles *The Lloyd Thaxton Show* 5:00pm

The Byrds appear on Thaxton's hour-long show out of Los Angeles, now in colour and this time singing 'Mr. Tambourine Man' and 'Set You Free This Time', presumably in person as the programme airs. According to the pre-show blurb, Lloyd himself – through the voice of satirist Allan Sherman – will parody the space age. (Possibly both taping and original broadcast take place a day or two earlier, as today is scheduled for the syndicated broadcast in the Arizona area.)

Today's *Record World* contains Derek Taylor's draft set of liner notes for Turn! Turn! Turn!, reprinted wholesale. Considering the content, it is not surprising Columbia Records

reacted with horror and rejected them. Taylor writes freely of the squabbles in the group ("What [Michael Clarke] did was sulk for a week and ruin every recording session"), and the prose is sometimes humorous (on McGuinn: "boy, has he an ego!"), sometimes flippant ("[Michael's] got a nice smile. So had Hitler"), and sometimes bordering on the cruel: "[Gene Clark] meanders across the stage banging a tambourine; well, he used to play guitar, but McGuinn and Crosby soon fixed that. They nipped at his confidence so that now with a guitar he looks like a spastic carrying an anvil. His answer was to write more songs than Crosby and McGuinn, and they met his bleak challenge by letting time run out on the sessions, so that only three Clark songs made the album. Gene should worry. He's making more bread than all the rest of The Byrds heaped together. And such songs. Oh they're very good. No doubt about that."

→ mid-February
☐ **US TV** [Unknown location], CA. ABC network *Where The Action Is*

The Byrds make pre-recordings for Dick Clark's *Where The Action Is*, lip-synching (miming to) 'Set You Free This Time' (broadcast February 21 and on March 24) and 'It Won't Be Wrong' (broadcast March 24). Clark's productions demand conveyor-belt speed to churn out segments for the daily telecasts (except weekends). The precise location is not known, but it is a rural setting – for 'Set You Free This Time' the four Byrds stand in front of a group of trees while McGuinn is perched on a branch playing guitar; for 'It Won't Be Wrong' the group stands in a corral with some horses.

Saturday 19
Santa Barbara High School Auditorium, Santa Barbara, CA

The Byrds play with The Dillards for one concert, at 8:00pm. According to the review in *Santa Barbara News Press* (January 21), The Byrds open with a medley of 'I'll Feel A Whole Lot Better' and 'Mr. Tambourine Man', then swing by 'It Won't Be Wrong' and 'Set You Free This Time' and some other unspecified numbers, before finishing with the latest hit 'Turn! Turn! Turn!'.

The Dillards are well known to TV viewers throughout the country as their funny alter egos The Darling Family on CBS-TV's *Andy Griffith Show*, although they are just some of the many characters populating the fictional town of Mayberry in the show's plot. The Dillards – named after brothers Doug (banjo) and Rodney (guitar) – are accomplished musicians, share the same manage-

ment as The Byrds, and have three acclaimed bluegrass albums produced by Jim Dickson to their credit. Just recently, the group has added drummer Dewey Martin to the line-up, thereby challenging the bluegrass purists. The rest of the five-man group is Dean Webb (mandolin) and Mitch Jayne (double bass; banjo), and they will provide steadfast support for The Byrds in the coming weeks.

Earlier in the evening, The Byrds are seen on *Shivaree* (show #56, see entry for February 14) at 7:00pm PST on KABC-TV, lip-synching 'Set You Free This Time' and 'It Won't Be Wrong'. Gene Weed is the show's genial host, also introducing Ketty Lester, Chris Montez, Eddie Kallman (star of the sitcom Hank!), and Latin-jazz combo The Eddie Cano Quartet. Music historian Domenic Priore writes: "[One] clear-cut example of [the Latin sound] exists on an episode of *Shivaree* featuring Cano and The Byrds. Each act plays two songs on the show, complementing each other's sound so well that it remains one of the most musically satisfying half-hours in the *Shivaree* archive."

Monday 21
◀)) **RECORDING** Columbia Recording Studios, Studio D, Sunset and El Centro, Hollywood, CA. 7:00–10:00pm. Producer Allen Stanton and (presumably) engineer Ray Gerhardt.

The Byrds are back at Columbia – this time at Studio D – recording a third version of 'Why', which will be held over until the group's fourth album. This will turn out to be Gene Clark's last recording session in the 60s as an official Byrd.

Before that, in the late afternoon at 4:30pm, The Byrds can be seen on Dick

---

'The Times They Are A-Changin'' (EP)

A1 'The Times They Are A-Changin'' (B. DYLAN)
A2 'The Bells Of Rhymney' (I. DAVIES/P. SEEGER)
B1 'It's No Use' (G. CLARK/J. McGUINN)
B2 'We'll Meet Again' (R. PARKER/H. CHARLES)

UK release February 1966 (CBS EP 6069)
Chart high UK none
Read more entries for April 14 and October 26, 1965

Clark's top rated *Where The Action Is* (ABC, episode #168, see entry for mid February), together with show regular Freddy Cannon and guest Steve Alaimo. The Byrds' contributions – 'Turn! Turn! Turn!' and 'Set You Free This Time' – are pre-recorded at a local Los Angeles location.

Later, McGuinn gives journalist John Nork a peek into his customized guitar sound. "I built a little amplifier … . I took a little cigar box and a walkie-talkie two-inch speaker and then I had the guts from an old Philips portable record player in there, with a battery. This thing really sustained, like a sitar-like, ringing type of sound. So, we recorded it through that."

Tuesday 22

Jim Dickson and The Byrds fly to New York City on short notice (possibly taking the red-eye flight the night before) to tape a television special on WNEW-TV. Gene Clark has a fear of flying, and as he boards the plane is suddenly overcome and decides to leave right there. He leaves not only his seat and the plane and the airport but also, in effect, The Byrds.

McGuinn later recounts the scene to journalist Bud Scoppa in 1970. "Gene is on the plane with everyone else. Everybody's there but me, I liked to cut it just under the wire, cos waiting around in airports, long hair [in 1966], was a hassle. So I'd get there just as they were closing the door every time. I think that's what spooked him the most. He was paranoid to the point where he thought I'd put a bomb on the plane or something. He was completely serious. Like vibrating in complete panic.

"I walked on the plane, said hi to everyone. Then I walked up to him and felt this fear for five feet around him. And he said, 'I gotta get off this plane!' And I said, 'Hey, man, it's cool,' and he said, 'I can't make it now.' So I said, 'If you can't fly, you're gonna blow it, man.'"

Quoted in *Hit Parader* (September 1968), McGuinn confesses his unease with the situation. "I got into it and cold sweat came over me, you know? 'Wow! Maybe he's right? Maybe he's psychic and knows something I don't know.'"

"They fixed the engines for half an hour after he left," McGuinn adds in another interview (*New Musical Express* May 5 1973). "They went and checked out the whole plane after he had gotten off, and they found the engines were messed up and they fixed them. He probably saved us all by getting off that plane."

The reasons for Clark's anxiety attack are much more complex, as McGuinn allows in the Scoppa interview. "Maybe the guilt fac-

tor was there, because [Gene] was in Ferraris and things and we were still starving. He was making thousands and we weren't making anything yet. Cos he wrote most of the original songs on the first album." Despite the drama, Gene Clark does not leave right away, and Dickson and the remaining four are at this point still intent on keeping The Byrds a five-piece.

▢ **US TV** Arriving in New York, the four-man Byrds appear on *Murray The K's All-Star Special*, aired locally on Channel 5 at 7:30pm the same night and again on Sunday February 27. (The show is aired in the Los Angeles area on Channel 11 on March 18 at 8:00pm and then repeated on Sunday March 26 at 7:30pm.)

Murray 'The K' Kaufman, self-proclaimed 'fifth Beatle', is an influential New York DJ, and today's grand two-hour television special also features appearances by Jay & The Americans, The Four Tops, Little Anthony & The Imperials, The Ramsey Lewis Trio, The Four Seasons, The Shangri-Las, and Joe Tex.

What The Byrds actually perform on Murray The K's TV special and how they cope as a four-piece is unfortunately not documented. They are a last-minute addition to the show, and the brief blurb that runs in the *Bridgeport Telegram* today is based on the other inserts taped earlier. "Better than the last Murray The K special. The format is simple: Murray The K is at ease and direct as its host, and the music is strictly an album of teenagers' beat, bleat, and sound. For adults, the wail of Frankie Valli's voice in a segment devoted to The Four Seasons may be more than they can take, and the childish cry of The Shangri-Las in another may spell the cry of anguish. But the music of the instrumental Ramsey Lewis Trio and the passionate rhythm of Joe Tex's songs will keep even them entertained, while the teenagers go for the two-hour segment lot."

→ Wednesday 23

Following yesterday's show, The Byrds squeeze in a press meeting at Columbia's Manhattan office, where Derek Taylor is also present. *Hit Parader* runs a seven-page question & answer feature from the conference under the headline "An American Dream Comes True For The Byrds" (although tagged as the July edition it is on the newsstands on April 12). It is the first proper in-depth interview with McGuinn and Crosby.

As an opener, *Hit Parader* quotes Bruce Langhorne (the singer–guitarist that Bob Dylan reportedly used as inspiration for the lyric of 'Mr. Tambourine Man'), who suggests The Byrds' sound is an extension of electrified Chicago rhythm & blues. Crosby: "Some of it, definitely. We've been influenced by it, sure. Chicago rhythm & blues bands. Sure we have.

But, we're much more folk-oriented than that." McGuinn: "We do much more rambling and rolling stuff than R&B: chung chung, that kinda deep hard stuff."

The interview covers several topics, and both McGuinn and Crosby come off as articulate and with interesting viewpoints. *Hit Parader* wants to know if the group arrived at its sound by chance or by strategy. Crosby: "We were both at the same time; we were systematic, though we didn't plan it that way. As it all happened we said, 'Hey, that's groovy, isn't it?' and, 'Hey, look, this is starting to [happen], oh yeah.'" McGuinn: "We knew what the map of things to happen would be, but we didn't plan anything in particular; we just watched them fall into place."

Crosby, in particular, is hip to what is happening on the music scene. Again, he talks enthusiastically about Ravi Shankar and John Coltrane, and he is well acquainted with his contemporaries. "The Lovin' Spoonful are aware of [Indian music]. Neither Zal [Yanovsky] nor John [Sebastian] are raga players. They never get hung up with that. But they're very much aware of the drone qualities of that music. Zal is aware of it from a peculiar point of view. Those scales and sounds are present in an awful lot of places, not just Ravi Shankar's music. For instance, they're present in Arabic prayer calls, which Zal heard first-hand. The Butterfield band is much more aware of it. Mike Bloomfield, their lead guitarist, plays ragas that are really exceptional. We just played with them. It was pretty far out. Beautiful."

Hit Parader wonders if Butterfield could get into the pop charts. "It all depends on what they do and how they handle it," says Crosby. "They could achieve the reputation as the definitive blues group, because they cut everything else that's happening currently, except possibly The Blues Project, but I think they cut them too." Crosby is asked if he has heard of The Miller–Goldberg Blues Band. With Chicagoans Steve Miller and Barry Goldberg, this obscure quartet appeared on *Hullabaloo* in December but otherwise is an unknown quantity to the public at large. He replies: "Sure I have. I think they're a great band. They're beautiful and at least one of them is a very good friend of mine, but I don't think they're as strong as the Butterfield band for one reason – Mike Bloomfield. Bloomfield the incredible. There are a couple of cats, though – Langhorne could give him a run for his money, in blues, but that's about it. There aren't too many around. Bloomfield is just a monster guitar player."

McGuinn says: "Bloomfield's an old friend of mine from Chicago. We met when we were around 15." Then Crosby makes a notable prediction. "There's a tremendous gap, wide open, waiting for the definitive blues band. It hasn't happened yet. Butterfield could be it, maybe Miller–Goldberg, or it could be The Blues Project. There are hundreds of blues groups happening everywhere." McGuinn says that the many young kids getting into rock'n'roll is "some sort of a logarithmic acceleration".

"[Kids in America] don't have to move a long way to hear [different kinds of music]," says Crosby. "The kids are hipper than anybody thinks all the time. Every kid practically in the United States now knows what a sitar is because George Harrison played it on *Rubber Soul*. Most of them are becoming aware of Ravi Shankar, John Coltrane, and a lot of other people too. I'm not trying to justify what we're doing with Indian music. We didn't plan it that way. We went into a room, sat down, and played. And what came out was what we put down later on the record. It'll be our next single! We didn't write it or arrange it. The five of us just played music to each other until it gelled. And that's what it comes out as. I don't want to justify it, either; we don't plan anything we do, and we don't try to scheme trends. We just play music."

"It's mostly just one big guitar," Crosby explains when questioned if his and McGuinn's playing is based on counterpoint. "I usually play the bottom couple of strings [to] Jim's guitar." McGuinn: "The whole thing is one big instrument with the bass and drums. Sounds like an organ or something. We're trying to get churchy."

And what happens if you take away the amplification? McGuinn: "When we play acoustically we sound very folky. Technically we use folk techniques." Crosby: "Except for me. I cheat a lot. I really wasn't suited to folk music. They used to say, 'Hey, you sing like a rock'n'roll singer,' and I used to play with a flat pick on a very loud acoustic 12-string. I used to play rhythm guitar on it. Because I couldn't pick – I don't know how to pick. I played rhythm guitar all along. I made a terrible folk singer. I was very upsetting."

Hit Parader wants to know if the group plans to add other instruments. McGuinn: "Yes, we're doing that all the time. Chris just acquired a mandolin. He's a very, very good mandolin player." Crosby: "We might play with an electric piano, because Mike and Gene both fool with pianos. McGuinn's been fooling with an organ, too, and he also plays banjo. We'll play anything that we ourselves can play. If it fits in a piece of music and it swings and we can play it, we use it."

"Our next single …" begins Crosby, before McGuinn interrupts him with: "We have an electronic device on the guitar that makes it

sound like a sitar." Crosby adds: "It's derivative and new. McGuinn just listened to Shankar and said, 'It's all right.' It's music and it happens here too and it comes out. We let it come into us deliberately."

The magazine inquires about the group's image and, inexplicably, wants to know if any promotion people have thought of posing the group on an iceberg. "Nobody yet. We're hoping nobody will. We're hoping they'll put us in the cockpit of a 707. That would be a beautiful picture. We really like to fly," Crosby replies. But how do The Byrds want to be described? McGuinn: "Aware, free, love-promoting, happiness, put-down negative, high-speed, motion music, fast cars, planes, jets – a vertical shift at 60 miles an hour while you're going that way. 700 miles an hour." Crosby: "We try to avoid boxes and labels and categories as much as we can. We're musicians; we play music. If we were going to use a label, it would have to be folk, bossa nova, jazz, Afro." McGuinn suggests they might take the first letter of each word of all kinds of music and make a word. "Yeah BOFNERGERTZ," says Crosby. "Actually we call it music a lot. But when anybody really insists, we call ourselves a rock'n'roll band."

The evolution from hootenanny to folk-rock is discussed. Crosby: "With Sonny & Cher, The Turtles, and all those they saw a label, Folk Rock, and they said 'Ah ha!'. You see, a label makes people secure. Now that they labelled it, they sat down on it and sold it." The *Hit Parader* journalist confesses they have just put out a magazine called Rock Folk. "So crumbleth it, cookie-wise," mocks Crosby.

It's not only *Hit Parader* and the teen press who are at today's conference. Sylvie Reice, a writer for Hall Syndicate Inc., belatedly reports from the meeting in *The Los Angeles Times* three months later (May 24). Preoccupied with fashion notes, she describes McGuinn as wearing a hounds-tooth jacket and Crosby his perennial green suede cape. "I want to retire in five years and sail off in a big schooner," says Crosby. As 'Eight Miles High' is previewed for the unsuspecting press, he calls out: "Rev it up LOUD!"

Afterwards, The Byrds fly back to Los Angeles. A recording session booked at Columbia's Studio A tonight at 7:00–10:00pm is cancelled.

Thursday 24

🔊 **RECORDING** Columbia Recording Studios, Studio A, Sunset and El Centro, Hollywood, CA. 8:00–11:00pm. No documentation of tonight's pre-booked session has survived. Gene's future in The Byrds is undecided for now, and presumably all five are present today to prepare for tomorrow's concert in Berkeley.

Friday 25

'Byrds' Bash', Berkeley Community Theater, Berkeley, CA

One performance at 8:00pm (with The Dillards as support act) in a benefit concert to raise money for the Board Of Control treasury; eventually, more than $1,000 is brought in. By all accounts, flight-wary Gene Clark is back in the fold again. Berkeley is roughly 350 miles to the north of Los Angeles and easily reached by car.

Tonight's concert is reviewed in *The Oakland Tribune* (February 26). "When The Byrds sing, it's a call to youth to respond with joy, tears, and wails. This was evident at a concert given at Berkeley Community Theater last night under the sponsorship of Berkeley High School students. … Appearing with the group, called America's No. 1 big beat recording group, were The Dillards, called exciting new folksingers who help feather the Byrds' nest. The paper prints photos from the concert, with the following caption: "At left, Dave Crosby, one of The Byrds, in full feather, adds a cherubic smile to his act. The result is shown by the pretty teenager whose expressions mirror her complete delight!"

Campus paper *The Daily Jacket* (March 8) notes: "At one time two girls jumped up on stage to get at The Byrds while doing their rendition of 'Turn! Turn! Turn!' but [the school's principal] was there in a flash and quickly escorted the two backstage. Jellybeans, pens, and everything imaginable were thrown at the group. The audience was made up of people from all over the Bay Area, from college students to Byrd Fan Club members."

Jerry Burgan, who met The Byrds during the Caravan Of Stars tour last year, recalls: "The Byrds were playing in Berkley, and We Five was living on a houseboat on the other side of San Francisco Bay near Sausalito. David Crosby came to see us and brought a rough mix of the still unreleased 'Eight Miles High' that totally blew us away. Pretty cool!"

March

Tuesday 1–Thursday 3

The Byrds commence their first cross-country tour of 1966 with an unspecified concert or two in the first days of March. This tour is a mixture of college and club dates with concerts at larger venues in the bigger cities. Whereas the group's two previous cross-country arrays loosely concentrated on the Midwest (in July 1965), the South, and then the Eastern Seaboard (the 'Caravan Of Stars' tour of November 1965), this time they will touch several states that they have not visited before.

The earthbound Gene Clark decides to remain home while the others go out on the road. Down to a four-piece, The Byrds will adjust the repertoire slightly to accommodate Gene's absence. 'Eight Miles High' is given its first public airings. Clark has at this point not officially left the group, so the explanation given to expectant Gene-fans across the country is that he is sick.

The mode of transport is also updated as the group now flies around in a chartered DC3. "We have tons of equipment. We carry our own amplifier system and our own vocal sound system," David Crosby explains to Associated Press in late March.

Friday 4
Orpheum Theatre, Madison, WI

Two performances at 7:00 and 9:30pm, supported by The Dillards and pop group The New Colony Six from nearby Chicago.

Complaining of excessive volume, Dale Wirsing writes in local paper *The Capital Times* (March 5, 1966): "Time was when the four dimensions of music were melody, timbre, rhythm, and tempo. For a folk-rock concert you have to add a fifth: loudness. The performances that The Byrds, The Dillards, and The New Colony Six put on Friday night at the Orpheum Theater were loud enough to delight a theatre filled with adolescents, mainly girls. And when the management asked the bouncing, swaying, flashbulb-shooting audience to stop showing its affection for the floppy-haired Byrds, they channelled their energy into eardrum-piercing screams. The Byrds, normally a five-member group but playing without one of their members, delighted their fans by singing and strumming some of their top-selling record hits — 'It Won't Be Long', 'All I Really Want to Do', and 'Mr. Tambourine Man.' The blue-jeaned Byrds also included a mournful ballad about the late President Kennedy and a Welsh protest song called 'Bells Of Rimini' [sic] among their numbers."

Robert A. Davis of the *Wisconsin Journal* (March 5, 1966) writes: "The Byrds flew into Madison Friday night to headline a couple of highly-touted 'folk rock' concerts at the Orpheum Theater, and they were OK. Distinguished from the hundreds of other long-haired rock'n'roll groups throughout the country today only by their precise method of choosing good material, the American 'folk rock' group was only four-fifths present at the first session Friday. The absence of the fifth Byrd was explained by the comment that 'He's not feeling well,' four of only a few

words uttered by the members in their brief string of past hits.

"The Byrds have managed to feather their financial nest by providing electronic clanging to accompany well-known folk songs done considerably better by such 'legitimate' folk singers as Pete Seeger, Bob [Dylan], and Dave van Ronk. It is to Dylan that The Byrds owe their greatest debt, having cashed in on 'Mr. Tambourine Man' and 'I Want To Be Friends With You' [sic]. Seeger was represented Friday with another Byrd hit, 'Turn! Turn! Turn!', which is based, believe it or not, on the Book of Ecclesiastes. A disturbing characteristic exhibited by the group was its apparent apathy, and although it's a common practice for rock groups to maintain a surly front on stage, carried to an extreme, apathy breeds apathy."

The Byrds' second album *Turn! Turn! Turn!* is released in the UK today. After the savaging given by the British press last year, the reviews for the new album are very positive, with one exception. Mike Ledgerwood heads his review "Byrds – Poor" in *Disc* (March 26) and concludes: "This is a rather unimpressive LP. The relative sameness of the numbers is a little overpowering. And they've not really improved since their *Mr. Tambourine Man* album." *Record Mirror* (March 5), on the other hand, rates the album four stars: "The worst thing that can be said about this album is that some of the songs have been heard before. Any other comments must be strictly in the raving strata. The Byrds have a sound all their own, which is superbly demonstrated on this excellent LP. 'Set You Free This Time' is beautiful and their treatment of 'Oh! Susannah!' is a delight. Pop folk they may be, but this album shows how original such an outfit can be."

Melody Maker (March 12) writes: "The Byrds have hit on a very pleasant sound – successful too – which they stick to by hook or by crook. Their latest album is no exception. Byrd fans aren't so plentiful nowadays and this probably won't sell as much as the *Mr. Tambourine Man* LP, but they're all typical Byrd numbers with the characteristic 12-string guitar sound. Easy going and immensely enjoyable listening." *New Musical Express* (March 11) chimes in too: "[Whatever] may be said about their poor stage showing here, The Byrds, of California, certainly make dynamic tracks, and here are a dozen more. … They keep up their twangy beat from their own instruments throughout."

Sunday 6
Civic Opera House, Chicago, IL

Playing before an ecstatic 4,000-strong crowd, following a warm-up by six other groups (John

Hammond; Little Boy Blues; The Ricochettes; Spot & The Blotters; The Shadows Of Knight; plus presumably The Dillards), The Byrds see their performance end in a riot. *The Chicago Tribune* (March 7) reports on police arrests, injured fans, and problems with inexperienced ushers. The police demand that the concert be stopped, and as the curtain is lowered Chris Hillman suffers slight injuries in the fracas that ensues between group and stagehands. Despite the Tribune's long report, there is no review of the musical content.

KRLA Beat (April 2): "The Byrds refused to take flight as 300 screaming female fans stormed the stage of the Civic Opera House in one of the wildest rock shows which this city has yet to witness. The Byrds continued performing and absolutely refused to vacate the stage, even when House employees rushed from the wings and attempted to unplug the group's electric guitars. In the end it took a total of 30 policemen to quell the screaming audience as The Byrds calmly sang 'Mr. Tambourine Man'. Ushers were pushed aside like cardboard boxes as about 20 of the girls managed to make it on stage to their heroes. One girl in the audience received a bruised back and two other members of the Byrd audience were arrested – the first for disorderly conduct and the second for simple assault."

Monday 7
Memorial Chapel, Lawrence University, Appleton, WI

Two shows at 7:30 and 9:30pm with support by folk-singer Dave Solberg (The Dillards are not billed and presumably have a night off). David Wagner is not pleased about the volume ("Amplified for Yankee Stadium!") in his review in the local *Post-Crescent* (March 8). The only reprieve comes when Crosby takes off his guitar and Clarke exchanges drumsticks for a tambourine to accompany Jim and David harmonising 'He Was A Friend Of Mine'.

Wagner writes: "Only four members of the quintet were on stage (tambourine man Gene Clark was sick). Attired in a weird assortment of casual dress, The Byrds covered their repertoire of hits including 'Mr. Tambourine Man', 'All I Really Want To Do', 'Turn! Turn! Turn!', and 'It Won't Be Wrong'. The group also previewed its soon-to-be-released Columbia single 'Eight Miles High'. The familiar strains of these songs inspired screaming and cheering, but dominating volume detracted from the potential effectiveness."

Tuesday 8
The Penthouse, Davenport, IA

Two shows at 8:00 and 11:00pm.

Wednesday 9–Thursday 11

The group presumably play concerts in the vicinity of Iowa and Kansas.

Friday 11

Teachers College Student Union, Emporia State University, Emporia, KS

The news of Gene Clark's absence has travelled across the Atlantic, as *New Musical Express* tells its readers today: "Illness has forced Gene Clark to temporarily leave The Byrds." Tomorrow's *Music Echo* prints the same story, bolstered by an exclusive quote by Eddie Tickner: "He's clearly not well enough to cope with the pressures and strains of one-night stands and cross-country travel. Gene, of course, remains a member of the group and will continue to write songs and work with them on their Columbia recordings."

Investigating the matter, journalist and correspondent Maureen Payne talks to both Gene Clark and Chris Hillman, outlining the situation in a press report in the UK's *Record Mirror* (March 19). "[Gene] is suffering from nervous strain and has been advised not to undertake any personal appearances for the time being. He'll continue to write songs while Jim, Dave, Chris, and Mike go off on a six-week tour of the States."

Chris Hillman tells Payne: "I'll be doing more singing now that Gene has left. It was his own decision to leave and we're all sorry to see him go. There were no ill feelings within the group. It was just that Gene found the pace a little too fast and his health was suffering." The official line from Gene himself is: "I feel a lot happier now that I'm not under so much pressure. I'll have time to do everything I never had a chance to do when I was a Byrd! I'll concentrate on writing songs, not only for The Byrds but for other artistes too. The pace was too much for me, I guess, and it just caught up with me."

The pop papers and teen magazines in the US are not quite up to speed; tomorrow's *KRLA Beat* (dated March 12, although already on newsstands) prints two separate articles on The Byrds (one a Crosby interview, the other a joint Jim McGuinn/Gene Clark feature), but with no mention of dissension in the ranks. Nearly three weeks later, *KRLA Beat* (April 2) says: "Gene Clark is in Los Angeles getting over his nervous strain. Byrds' manager states that Gene will return to the group within the next five or six weeks, but a nasty rumour buzzing around the business is that Clark is out for good. *The Beat* is currently checking this rumour and we will, of course, let you know as soon as we find out for sure, but as of right now it is only a rumour."

•

Gene Clark's departure will temporarily stabilise the swerving Byrds, as David Crosby comes to the fore as a creative force and Hillman gets the chance to sing and develops his skills as a bassist. Derek Taylor pens a press release around this time and explains Gene Clark's resignation in his usual eloquent way – at once acknowledging the ex-singer's importance and at the same time giving hope for the future of The Byrds. "They have recently survived a dramatic upheaval – the separation of Gene Clark, tambourine man, most prolific songwriter in the group, physically the strongest – the only one with obvious muscles – vocally the deepest, emotionally the warmest, and a founder member. He left not because of a row, and not because he was fired. He left because he was tired of the multitude of obligations facing successful rock'n'roll groups. Tired of the travel, the hotels, and the food. Tired of the pursuit of the most relentless autograph hunters, weary of the constant screaming. Bothered by the photographs and interviews, and exhausted by the whole punishing scene. Gene was a good friend and a valuable Byrd – and while fans were mourning his absence, The Byrds too were feeling an emptiness which they sublimated by tackling the problems of consolidating their unit into four – four, whom they knew would be expected to equate the impact of five. And, such is the fickleness of fans and of all people, and such is the healing power of time, the foursome made it without Gene."

Saturday 12

Market Hall, Dallas, TX

Down in Texas, The Byrds top a show that also features Mitch Ryder & The Detroit Wheels, Sir Douglas Quintet, The Dillards, The Barbarians, Jim Jones & The Chaunteys, and The Gnats.

Monday 14

The Byrds' fifth single 'Eight Miles High'/ 'Why' is released in the US (although the release is possibly withheld for at least another week). Representing a marked musical departure, the group stakes itsr commercial future on this record after the comparative failure of 'Set You Free This Time'/'It Won't Be Wrong'.

Revolutionary in sound and lyrics, the single ranks with 'Shapes Of Things' (by The Yardbirds) and 'Paint It Black' (by The Rolling Stones) – all three records released this month – as potent examples of the fusion of Indian influences and pop music. The Stones, who take a cue from George Harrison by using a real sitar, also successfully imitate the throb of the tabla drum by way of the Wyman–Watts rhythm section. The Yardbirds, meanwhile, look to Jeff Beck for an Eastern-flavoured guitar solo. But it is The Byrds who raise the bar a notch by putting otherworldly vocal harmonies on top of John Coltrane-styled guitar figures.

Billboard (April 2) cautiously pens a "Top 60 Spotlight" review. "Big beat rhythm rocker with soft lyric ballad vocal and off-beat instrumental backing could be another 'Turn! Turn! Turn!'." The single bypasses the "Bubbling Under" section and enters straight into the Hot 100 at Number 87 on April 9.

"Very Byrd-like sound here," writes *Record World* (March 26). "It's an eerie tune with lyrics bound to hypnotise. Will climb heights." *Cash Box* (March 26) selects the tune as a "Pick Of The Week" (along with The Beach Boys' 'Sloop John B' and The Dave Clark Five's 'Try Too Hard') writing: "The Byrds are a cinch to repeat their recent 'It Won't Be Wrong' coincatcher with this original Columbia offering called 'Eight Miles High'. The side's a rhythmic, shufflin', blues-soaked affair with some real inventive riffs. 'Why' is a pulsating tale concerning lack of personal communication between a couple who are going steady."

Tuesday 15

The 1966 Grammy Awards ceremony is held at the Beverley Hilton in Los Angeles, recognising accomplishments for the year 1965. The Byrds are one of seven nominees in the prestigious category for New Artist but lose out to Tom Jones (the other five are Glenn Yarbrough, Marilyn Maye, Horst Jankowski, Herman's Hermits, and Sonny & Cher). As usual, the awards come under fire for lack of imagination and reactionary tastes. "Raspberries for Grammys!" shouts entertainment weekly *Variety*, and Charles Champlin points out in *The Los Angeles Times* (March 7): "[A] flap is that among the 218 final nominations in the 47 categories, there is nary a single one any place for Bob Dylan. But Dylan, the electric-haired poet-composer-performer of 'Mr. Tambourine Man' and a satchel-full of other

---

'Eight Miles High'

A 'Eight Miles High' (G. CLARK/J. MCGUINN/D. CROSBY)

B 'Why' (J. MCGUINN/D. CROSBY)

US release March 14 1966 (Columbia 43578)

UK release May 29 1966 (CBS 202067)

Chart high US number 14; UK number 24

Read more ... entries for January 24, 25 1966

recording successes, has to be counted one of the most influential as well as one of the biggest money-spinning talents to emerge big in 1965." The policy of who-is-nominated-in-which-category is certainly confusing. Roger Beck sighs in *The Los Angeles Times* (March 27): "Please, let's have no more oranges winning in the Best Apple category."

Wednesday 16
L.L. Culver Gymnasium, Culver-Stockton College, Canton, MO
The Byrds in one show with The Dillards at 8:00pm as the tour swings north to Missouri for two nights.

Thursday 17
Gymnasium, St. Louis University, St. Louis, MO
One show with The Dillards at 8:00pm. The Dillards apparently leave the tour afterwards and return to Los Angeles.

Friday 18
Municipal Auditorium, New Orleans, LA
For The Byrds' first visit to Louisiana, Mitch Ryder & The Detroit Wheels are added to the bill.

ALSO ...
The Los Angeles Times has devoted a quarter page in today's edition to Taj Mahal & The Rising Sons, who this weekend play at the Trip on Sunset Strip. Mahal's four-man group includes guitarist Ry Cooder and Chris Hillman's cousin Kevin Kelley on drums.

Saturday 19
Hirsch Coliseum, Shreveport, LA
Presented by radio station KEEL, with Mitch Ryder & The Detroit Wheels, Sam The Sham & The Pharaohs, Sir Douglas Quintet, and The Barbarians.

Sunday 20
Barton Coliseum, Little Rock, AR
Following the concerts in the South, the group moves north for concerts in New York and New Jersey next weekend.

Wednesday 23
Today's *Los Angeles Times* announces: "The Byrds, formerly a quintet, are now a foursome. Gene Clark has quit, but will continue to write for the group."

Thursday 24
The Byrds can be seen on *Where The Action Is* (ABC, episode #191, see entry for mid February) performing 'It Won't Be Wrong' and 'Set You Free This Time'. Shot on location somewhere in Los Angeles, the insert was recorded

before Gene Clark left. Ketty Lester is the other invited guest, while house band Paul Revere & The Raiders perform 'Poison Ivy'.

Friday 25
Island Garden, West Hempstead, NY
The Young Rascals from New York, presently riding the singles charts with 'Good Lovin'', share the stage with The Byrds for tonight's concert. All of the concerts this weekend are organised by East Coast promoter Charles R. Rothschild.

Saturday 26
Westchester County Center, White Plains, NY
Opening for The Byrds are Thee Strangeurs, featuring a young Steven Tallarico (later Tyler) on vocals.

Sunday 27
• **Symphony Hall, Newark, NJ (1:30pm show)**
• **Convention Hall, Trenton, NJ (evening show)**
Following an afternoon show in Newark, The Byrds continue with an appearance in Trenton. Thee Strangeurs provide support for both occasions.

→ Monday 28
The four Byrds and Derek Taylor hold a press reception in New York City today at the end of their cross-country tour. Jim McGuinn and particularly David Crosby are in a talkative mood, whereas Clarke and Hillman are non-communicative and have their noses buried in magazines for most of the conference. McGuinn is armed with a real sitar and Crosby in cape strums an acoustic guitar while the two of them extol the music of John Coltrane and Ravi Shankar and their influences on 'Eight Miles High' and 'Why'. A brand new term is coined – 'raga rock' – to aptly describe the meeting of Eastern tradition and Western pop culture.

Journalist Sally Kempton of the *Village Voice* (March 31) publishes the first report from the reception. Titled "Raga Rock: It's Not Moonlight On The Ganges", she observes that there is a synthesis of various forms in rock'n'roll at the moment. "Last week the trend reached its peak when Columbia Records called a press

Charles R. Rothschild Presents A Weekend With

The Byrds

In Association with Zeta Beta Tau Queens College

Fri. March 25 / 8:30 P.M.
Plus: The Young Rascals
at Island Garden, West Hempstead
500 Hempstead Turnpike
LONG ISLAND

Sat. March 26 / 8:30 P.M.
at Westchester County Center
WHITE PLAINS

Sun. March 27 / 1:30 P.M.
at Symphony Hall, 1020 Broad St.
NEWARK, N. J.

All Tickets
$4.50   3.75   2.75

Sale: Each Box Office
Mail Orders: Please indicate date for L. I. and White Plains: CONCERTS, 330 E. 48th St., New York, N. Y. 10017
Newark mail orders: Symphony Hall, 1020 Broad St., Newark, N. J. Enc. stamped, self-addressed envelope.

Additional Sales Outlets
Bamberger's, Park Records, Newark
Village Records, So. Orange

conference to announce that The Byrds ... had invented a new form called Raga Rock. Raga Rock, it turned out, was the last word in synthesis; it derived from the sitar music of Ravi Shankar."

"The Byrds innovation burst upon the world with something less than the force which Columbia had intended," she notes, acidly. "For one thing, the press conference was late getting started and the assembled throng, which consisted mostly of girl reporters from teen magazines and music business types in white on white ties, greeted with enthusiasm the news that The Byrds had been delayed because they were having trouble tuning their sitar. When the boys finally walked in, looking innocent and harassed beneath their baroque masses of hair, several reporters eyed the offending instrument as though it were an untrustworthy animal."

In between battling with the tuners on the sitar, McGuinn says: "We're in a new bag now ... It's really a very ancient bag – the Indian raga – but we've kind of adapted it. We play it on the sitar ..." – here McGuinn demonstrates a few runs, according to Kempton – "... and on the guitar." Feeling alone in a room full of pop fans, Kempton sarcastically writes how "one of the girl reporters gasped" when Crosby dashes off a guitar run and announces: "That's a raga scale." The conference ends with McGuinn playing snippets of Shankar and Coltrane on his tape recorder, before the assembled press gets an airing of 'Why' and 'Eight Miles High'. "It sounded pretty good," Kempton has to admit.

Associated Press News editor Mary Campbell rounds up her impressions in a feature that will be syndicated to a multitude of local newspapers across the US from April 23 onwards. "It's rock'n'roll," Crosby explains enthusiastically, "it's neither jazz nor Indian music. But we listen to their music and like it and it influences our minds and our playing. What we play is an abstraction from what we've heard. We don't take their form or their instruments. Our music is done on an electronic 12-string. A much newer and stranger instrument. Most groups accomplish one

thing. They achieve a static form and maintain it for security. In so doing they promptly go straight backwards. Every record we make will differ from every other record, I guarantee." Crosby detects the Indian influence elsewhere. "There are hints of it in some of The Yardbirds' things. In the last Beatles' movie [*Help!*], George played a sitar."

"Rock is going to keep growing," Crosby continues. "It has in it now African, South American, jazz, folk, church, Bach, Indian, Greek, country, bluegrass." He says the group's next album – just in its planning stage; the first session will not be until the end of next month – will have some Dylan songs and it will be called Eight Miles High after the single.

By wrapping his reply on psychedelic music in a harmless joke, Crosby nonetheless speaks truthfully about his interest in drugs. "The only way we could perform [psychedelic music] would be to have all the musicians on LSD! I don't think we've ever managed to play any jobs on LSD." But the innocent remark draws unwanted attention to the lyr-

ics of 'Eight Miles High', as the group will soon find out.

McGuinn, wearing his trademark rectangular glasses, says: "We'll carry the India-influence thing out as far as it goes. It's light – nothing heavy or earth-shaking."

WMCA Go (May 20) also reports from the New York séance and wonders why Hillman and Clark are so quiet. "They're not dumb," explains Derek Taylor helpfully. "Mike and Chris are just as talkative as Dave and Jim."

Hit Parader, whose reporter spoke with The Byrds in New York on February 23, adds further quotes from today's conference for its seven-page feature ("An American Dream Comes True For The Byrds") on sale April 10.

•

The 'Raga Rock' term may not perhaps be the invention of Derek Taylor and The Byrds, but the New York launch is the first time it has been used specifically to promote a single. In *Disc* (March 5) Taylor has his own little wordplay – "Rave Shanka" – but 'Raga Rock' soon catches on in England too: Liverpool's

Music Echo reports "Byrds try raga rock" (April 9) while *New Musical Express* (April 15) unfortunately manages to twist the label somewhat: "Explaining their new '*rage* rock' music, The Byrds say: 'It's an abstraction of things we've been listening to for some time – the music of Shankar, jazzman John Coltrane, and lots of Bach. Shankar is the number-one boss of Indian classical and popular music, and everyone's who's heard him is influenced."

The fusion of Indian music and Western culture goes a little further back. Ravi Shankar, the acknowledged master of the sitar, played concert halls around the US in the late 50s, which in turn led to jazz and folk musicians experimenting with Indian music. But it wasn't until the spring of 1965 in London that the first examples of vaguely Indian-influenced pop singles were recorded – just at the time David Crosby began championing the virtues of Ravi Shankar to his friends and fans. The Yardbirds' Jeff Beck recorded his approximation of a sitar on 'Heart Full Of Soul' (US Number Nine and UK Number Two), while 'See My Friends' by The Kinks

Jim McGuinn, David Crosby, Derek Taylor and a sitar. New York press conference, February 23 1966.

(UK Number 11) was inspired by a visit to Bombay by its composer Ray Davies.

Indian classical music benefits from all the media coverage and booming interest in the sitar. By year's end, Ravi Shankar is able to sell out New York's 3,000-seat Philharmonic Hall three nights in a row, while Ali Akbar Khan – who plays the sitar's sister instrument, the sarod – is met by standing ovations at the city's Carnegie Hall.

Tuesday 29–Wednesday 30

On their way back to Los Angeles, The Byrds reportedly stop over in Kentucky for an undocumented appearance in Louisville.

ALSO ...

The Dillards begin a two-week residence at the Ice House in Glendale on Tuesday March 29 (lasting until April 10) but have decided to go back to their original all-acoustic format, thus leaving their electric equipment in the care of Jim Dickson and Eddie Tickner and dispensing with the services of drummer Dewey Martin.

April

Friday 1

Hamilton High School Old Gym, Los Angeles, CA

→ Saturday 2

The Trip, Hollywood, CA

As a preview to their residence at the Trip next week, The Byrds play a special afternoon concert at 4:00pm with no age limit, while Donovan (with Shawn Phillips), The Jagged Edge (a group that also joins Donovan's act), and The Modern Folk Quartet play out their ten-day engagement at the club in the evening and tomorrow.

→ Sunday 3

[Unknown venue], Pensacola, FL

Jim McGuinn's fascination with science and space travel has led him to John Lear. The son of Bill Lear, who constructed the first commercially successful business jet, Lear junior is a fully qualified pilot. The acquaintance comes in handy today. Derek Taylor writes: "[They] were faced with a one-night stand in Pensacola, on the Florida coast of the Gulf of Mexico, a 4,000-mile round trip from L.A., and rejected the six routine flights available. Instead, they chose their own chartered six-seat Learjet. Cost of the trip: $3,900. For one 30-minute performance!" Asked about such luxury, Taylor quotes McGuinn: "We did it

because it was groovy, man; 530 miles per hour, and it climbs 42,000 feet ... in 15 minutes!"

Monday 4–Sunday 10

The Trip, Hollywood, CA

The Byrds return to the Sunset Strip's own Trip for the third and last time. The Modern Folk Quartet are seemingly held over as opening act from the previous week.

Clem Floyd in the *Los Angeles Free Press* (April 8) writes: "I caught The Byrds at their opening night. In fact, I caught their first set, which I'm sure was not fair and I will ignore what were the obvious faults inherent in that situation. The Byrds are now only four, Gene Clark having left to do independent production. Nothing was lost, however. They still had their fierce amplified groove and, in fact, sounded a little cleaner. Now The Byrds' Super-Jet concept is pure in its sound texture, a thing that Gene was not really into. The Byrds are far and away the best rock outfit in America, which says a lot for them and not much for the scene in general. They have an air of relaxed professionalism that is unique. However, they have not learned to use it the way a British group does. The secret is a form of 'non-game' showmanship and Crosby has the beginning of.

"Michael Clarke must be the happiest, grooviest drummer this side of jazz, and his Elvin Jones-type backing for 'Eight Miles High' shows he has his ears into a lot of other sounds besides backbeat rim-shots. 'Eight Miles High' made it obvious that The Byrds cannot capture the quality of their recorded band tracks on stage. The solo work was dismal. ... McGuinn was, as always, amply filling every requirement – except one. When he is picking in chord patterns it all stays together, but when he goes for a solo line it is nothing but unrelated notes. Perhaps he should listen to [bebop saxophonist] Frank Strozier."

DJ Johnny Mitchell at KHJ writes a belated review in the *Record Beat* (June 21). "As The Byrds took the stage last Monday night [April 4], L.A.'s Byrd cult was anxious to see how they would be without Gene Clark. Their first set was disappointing: it was very short and it seemed that there were four individuals performing instead of a well-integrated group. The second set was different. Gene Clark came on stage first and the roar from the crowd was deafening. He introduced the group and started to step down, but the crowd wouldn't have it. They actually pushed him back onto the stage, and he did the set. It was Gene's show and, after every song, the crowd gave him a thundering ovation. At this writing, I don't know what will happen, but the general opinion was that without Gene Clark, The Byrds didn't make it."

Pamela Miller, besotted by Chris Hillman, sneaks in despite the 18-year age limit to watch the Wednesday show [April 6]. Her book I'm With The Band will reproduce her diary entry for that night. "Chris messed up a song because of me, I know it. He was watching me very avidly and he made a wrong chord." Also around is Reine Stewart, who is there on the Easter weekend (April 8–10) with her sister to see The Byrds and meet David Crosby. Stewart is also a friend of Christine Hinton, the girl who becomes Crosby's soul mate.

Shortly afterward, Derek Taylor gives a status report on The Byrds, addressed to the press. "On a non-musical level, The Byrds have emerged as teen trend leaders and are sought to illuminate the pages of fashion magazines. McGuinn's tinted narrow sunglasses turn up on noses snub and noses short, hooters hooked and long. ... It's clear that The Byrds are no longer the private property of the little hippies on the Strip, for now they belong to too many others. The hippies long for the old days, when The Byrds walked up the Strip to play for 30 dollars per man at Ciro's; the days when they had no homes to call their own; the days when The Byrds were the new thing, and about to make it ... and when The Byrds left the Trip after their nightly stint last week, it was in Porsches equipped with stereo tape players, and it was to the fashionable hills they drove – away from the noise and lights of Sunset Boulevard, past the 15-cent coffee stands of yesterday."

ALSO ...

Meanwhile, as The Byrds play Hollywood's Trip club, the busy traffic on Sunset Boulevard becomes the unlikely birthplace for a new group. Richie Furay and Stephen Stills have been trying for some weeks to put a band together in Los Angeles, when one day while riding in their car – reputedly on April 6 – they chance upon Canadians Neil Young and Bruce Palmer driving down Sunset in the opposite direction. Furay later tells John Einarson: "We were driving in a white van on our way down Sunset Boulevard. I don't remember what we were doing, but we got stuck in traffic and I saw a black hearse with Canadian plates going the other way. I remembered that Stills had told me that Neil drove a black hearse. Stephen was sure that it was Neil. So somehow we pulled up beside the hearse, and, sure enough, there were Neil and Bruce."

Saturday 9

☐ **US TV** ABC Television Center, Hollywood, CA. ABC Network *New American Bandstand* 1:30pm

Chris Hillman (but none of the other

Byrds) is on the 'hot line' on Dick Clark's popular midday show, presumably phoned in live as the programme goes out on the air today. Clark's main guests are The Beau Brummels.

American Bandstand has been up and broadcasting since 1952. As the show gained a larger audience and increased in popularity in the early 60s, the production was moved in February 1964 from Philadelphia in the east to Los Angeles in the west, one of several factors that contributed to Hollywood becoming the Pop Industry Capital of the US. For the autumn season of 1965 the show was given a slight overhaul – the prefix New was added, and its novelty was telephone interviews with recording stars.

Over in England, plans are afoot to bring The Byrds back again. Promoter Roy Tempest says in today's *Melody Maker*: "I will be bringing The Byrds over for two weeks around September and I am lining up the tour at the moment. They will play about 14 venues." Tempest says he may line up a visit to West Germany and France after the British tour, but the plans will fail and The Byrds have to wait until 1967 to return to Europe.

Liverpool's *Music Echo* – a pop paper that seems to be one step ahead of the rest of the music press in many instances – has received an airmailed copy of 'Eight Miles High'. The paper reports: "[By] getting their single out now they've beaten The Beatles to the punch, for Paul admitted recently that the Liverpool foursome are working on a similar sound for their new album and single. The sound The Byrds get is wild and oriental but still beaty. A winner all the way in our ears. Let's hope CBS rush it out here soon."

The throwaway McCartney quote is not dated but cannot be more than a few days old: The Beatles have just entered EMI's Abbey Road studios (on Wednesday April 6) to record for the first time in several months – and they start with a song carrying the unassuming title 'Mark 1', later known as *Revolver*'s 'Tomorrow Never Knows'.

Tuesday 12

Hit Parader's July edition is on sale at newsstands today and contains a bulky seven-page feature on The Byrds. Besides being the most in-depth interview with the group to date (mainly conducted on February 29, with further quotes added from the March 28 press reception), it also offers a graphic description of the group's many influences: Johann Sebastian Bach, John Coltrane, The Beatles, Bob Dylan, Ravi Shankar, Pete Seeger, Odetta, and The Beach Boys. The sitar is described in minute technical detail, and the magazine reveals that an electric sitar is soon going into

production. (An electric sitar will eventually be manufactured by Coral, based on a design by guitarist Vinnie Bell, but not until 1967.)

The Byrds influence The Beach Boys, too, although perhaps without realising. In 1965, The Beach Boys recorded a playful (albeit acoustic) take on Bob Dylan's 'The Times They Are A-Changin'' on the *Beach Boys' Party!* album, while their latest single 'Sloop John B' is a rocked-up version of a traditional folk song originally made popular by The Kingston Trio. Asked to assess his contemporaries, Beach Boy Brian Wilson tells Ron Grevatt in *Melody Maker* (March 19): "The Byrds, well, they represent a certain projected attitude. They've got a place too, no doubt about that."

•

McGuinn and Crosby are asked to recommend their favourite albums in the teenage press. McGuinn lists *Bob Gibson And Hamilton Camp At The Gate Of Horn*, commenting: "I was around [in Chicago] when it was happening. It was a groovy scene. It was one of the first departures from folk music into a rock'n'roll-type folk music. Gibson was doing straight folk music with a kind of Ray Charles, Elvis, Everly Brothers attitude. To me, that was the first attempt at mixing rock'n'roll and folk music." The broad-minded Crosby, besides mentioning Ravi Shankar (the album *Master Musicians Of India* with Ali Akbar Khan) and John Coltrane (specifically pointing to *Africa/Brass* and *Impressions*), ranks the Elektra album *Music Of Bulgaria* by The Ensemble Of Bulgarian Republic as a favourite. "It has the most soulful chorus I've ever heard. Those chicks really sing."

Friday 15

Swing Auditorium Orange County Fairgrounds, San Bernardino, CA
The Byrds embark on a short tour of California – essentially over three consecutive weekends – supported by Buffalo Springfield, the group formed by Richie Furay, Bruce Palmer, Stephen Stills, and Neil Young less than ten days ago. In that short time, the four have added The Dillards' discarded drummer Dewey Martin and even some of the amps and instruments belonging to that group, who have returned to bluegrass purity. The concert is not a sell-out, despite the added attractions of The Dillards and Masten & Brewer.

The show is promoted by local radio station KMEN and compered by John Peel, an Englishman who has temporarily settled in San Bernardino as a radio DJ. Peel meets The Byrds at their rudest: they refuse to speak to him when he introduces himself before the concert. Peel will later be recognised as one of the most influential radio DJs in Britain, but

this first and last meeting with The Byrds will forever taint his feeling for their music.

"Even without Gene, the four remaining feathered friends put on a top notch show," goes the review in the San Bernardino Valley College *Indian War Hoop* (April 22), pointing out that Hillman has taken over as harmony singer in Clark's absence. "The Byrds opened the show with 'Eight Miles High', their newest single release and their finest single recording to date. ... They finished with the million-seller song 'Turn! Turn! Turn!', and between those two numbers they performed eight other vocals in their unique style." One of these is Chuck Berry's 'Roll Over Beethoven' according to the review. There is an altercation with fans after the show, and it takes three National Guardsmen and two policemen to help free Michael Clarke from the clutch of a particularly frenzied girl.

Saturday 16

College of San Mateo (CSM) Gym, San Mateo, CA
One show at 8:30pm with The Dillards, Buffalo Springfield, and Maston & Brewer in San Mateo, a town in the San Francisco Bay Area. Posters promoting the event give prominence to The Dillards, while the as-yet-unknown Buffalo Springfield – who were barely conceived when the posters were printed – are not mentioned.

Sunday 17

David Crosby goes to see Jefferson Airplane and The Paul Butterfield Blues Band, who play a 'Blues-Rock Bash' promoted by Bill Graham at the Fillmore Auditorium in San Francisco. This is one of Graham's first tentative rock'n'roll promotions under his own name. So far, Graham has promoted just a handful of happenings, mainly in his capacity as business manager of the San Francisco Mime Troupe.

While Crosby stays in San Francisco and the group has a week off, Michael Clarke and Chris Hillman reputedly holiday down in Mexico.

Friday 22

Los Angeles Harbor College, Wilmington, CA
The Byrds, The Dillards, and Buffalo Springfield play one concert at 8:00pm in Wilmington, a neighbourhood of Los Angeles.

•

The group is so sure of the new single's commercial potential that Derek Taylor confidently pens a press release. "The Byrds are waiting with the cool, remote aplomb for which they are neither admired nor deplored – for their third Number One single in the

United States. 'Eight Miles High', their fifth US single release, is at Number 24 on the *Cash Box* chart, and no Byrd record has been played so hard coast to coast. The vital element in quick US chart busters is simultaneous nation-wide airplay – ideally, New York should be playing a record at the same time as Chicago and Los Angeles. All three cities picked up on 'Eight Miles High' on the day of release; so, the Byrds are blandly optimistic … 'Eight Miles High' is the decider – this is the one which puts them way, way ahead of the field which is now seething with some tough new sprinters; Mamas & Papas, Spoonful, Revere and The Raiders, Turtles, and the distance runners like The Beach Boys. So here they are in their homes in the Hollywood Hills, smoking cigarettes under the Californian sun, patiently waiting for the charts to rain new glories."

Saturday 23

'Byrd's Bash', Colt Gym, Covina High School, Covina, CA

The Byrds, The Dillards, and Buffalo Spring-field in one two-hour performance starting at 8:00pm.

Thursday 28–Friday 29

🔊 **RECORDING** Columbia Recording Studios, Studio A, Sunset and El Centro, Hollywood, CA. 8:00–11:00pm (both days). Producer Allen Stanton and (presumably) engineer Ray Gerhardt.

The Byrds have not really been in the studio since the end of January (unless you count the re-recording of 'Why' and another fruitless session in February). These two evening sessions mark the first studio visits without Gene Clark in the group. Two songs are recorded: the jaunty 'Mr. Spaceman' (written by Jim McGuinn) and 'What's Happening?!?!'. This is Crosby's first fully realised composition to be recorded by The Byrds after a couple of earlier attempts.

ALSO …

Bob Dylan arrives in Stockholm, Sweden, for the start of a four-week round trip of Europe as the last leg of a 'world tour' that started out in Kentucky in February. On tour in the UK just a year ago, Dylan stretched British politeness to the limit with his acerbic press meetings, but he was adored at his (acoustic) concerts. This year, Dylan splits his shows in two, with an electric section – backed by The Hawks, four Canadians plus Texas drummer Mickey Jones – followed by an acoustic half. The US shows have passed largely unnoticed, but in Europe many are bewildered by Dylan's electrification. Some concertgoers shout of betrayal during the tour as it snakes its way

through Sweden, Denmark, Britain, France, and back to London for two final shows at the Royal Albert Hall on May 27 and 28. These will in fact be Dylan's last concerts for many years.

Friday 29

S/Sgt Barry Sadler's patriotic 'Ballad Of The Green Berets', a tribute to the singer's comrades in the Special Forces fighting in Vietnam, has taken over the Number One position in *Billboard* for the whole of March, finally succumbing in early April to '(You're My) Soul And Inspiration' by The Righteous Brothers. 'Eight Miles High' is at Number 18 in the *Cash Box* charts, its fifth week there, having worked its way steadily upward from 77 to 66, then 33 and 24. The summit ahead is not insurmountable; hovering above The Byrds are singles by The Young Rascals ('Good Lovin'' – the week's Number One), The Mamas & The Papas ('Monday, Monday'), Bob Dylan ('Rainy Day Women Nos. 12 and 35'), while singles by The Yardbirds ('Shapes Of Things') and Cher ('Bang Bang') have had their time and are on the way down. But today the Byrd song is dealt a blow that will probably hurt sales: the *Gavin Report* denounces 'Eight Miles High' as drug-related.

Founded by San Francisco DJ Bill Gavin in 1958 as an aid for radio programmers, *Bill Gavin's Record Report* (its full name) monitors Top 40 hits around the country. It has become a handy tool for radio stations and hundreds of subscribers. Today's issue states: "We have dropped 'Rainy Day Woman' and 'Eight Miles High' for our recommended playlist. In our opinion, these records imply encouragement and/or approval of the use of marijuana or LSD. We cannot conscientiously recommend such records for airplay, despite their acknowledged sales. We reserve the future rights to distinguish between records that simply mention such drugs and those that imply approval of their use." The *Gavin Report* has a reputation, so far, as a reliable source, not prone to irrational judgments or unfair treatment.

It should not come as a surprise that Crosby's careless remark at the New York press conference a month ago – "I don't think we've ever managed to play any jobs on LSD" – may have piqued somebody's curiosity. Student paper *The Tech*, for example, just a week ago (April 22) wrote bluntly that the song is "a description of the condition brought about by drugs and seems particularly appropriate to hallucinogens".

Despite the damning comment in the *Gavin Report*, the effect is not immediate. 'Eight Miles High' continues to advance slowly in the *Cash Box* charts in the coming three weeks: Number 14 (also its top position in the *Bill-*

board Hot 100); then 13; before peaking at 12 in the week ending May 21. But the following Saturday, it falls down to 23, and two weeks later it is gone from the Top 50, while The Rolling Stones have won the Number One spot with 'Paint It Black'.

Coinciding with the storm brewing in the US, 'Eight Miles High'/'Why' is released in the UK today. *New Musical Express* (today) is unsure: "This won't help The Byrds. A compulsive fast-moving rhythm underlines [their] vocal, complete with all the familiar characteristics – strident guitar, crashing cymbals, and a double-time shuffle. A lengthy instrumental intro precedes the vocal. But although the basic idea of the lyric is original, and the title's intriguing, there's virtually no melody. And I thought the backing was far too complex. I rate it the group's most disappointing to date," comments Derek Johnson. Of the flip, he writes: "A jaunty invigorating bounce beat, and a more orthodox treatment. Great stuff for dancing."

Record Mirror (April 30) says: "Odd mixture of musical styles here, with a prolonged instrumental introduction, then some soft-edged vocal work. Song isn't a knockout but the originality of style and the actual performance should see it into the charts – anyway, it's big in the States. Flip is pacier, most routine, but again performed with zest." The Mirror rates the song a Top 50 Tip.

Melody Maker (April 30) writes: "America's highly successful Byrds come up with a new formula! Raga-rock, based on Eastern musical forms (they say!), which sounds like The Who gone haywire. Nevertheless a very interesting, appealing record but maybe a little trying on the ears of the masses." The song, perhaps affected by the disappointing sales in the US, never makes it beyond Number 24 in the *Record Mirror/ Record Retailer* chart in the UK.

Saturday 30

**Harvey Auditorium,
Bakersfield Civic Auditorium,
Bakersfield, CA**

A concert with The Byrds, Buffalo Springfield, and The Dillards. Chris Hillman briefly toys with the idea of managing Buffalo Springfield before having second thoughts ("a fleeting idea that lasted about five minutes," he will recall to John Einarson). Still, he speaks warmly of the group to club manager Elmer Valentine, who on Hillman's recommendation offers to book them at the Whisky A Go Go for a residence beginning May 11. (Stephen Stills, appalled by The Byrds' lack of professionalism, later recalls the short Byrds tour to Ben Fong-Torres with a snigger: "We watched. We laughed a lot.")

May

Sunday 1

Pamela Miller has plucked up the courage to visit Chris Hillman at his house on Magnolia Street but leaves when Hillman has to attend a session – presumably a rehearsal – which Miller notes in her diary he says will be "a drag".

Monday 2

ONE NITE ONLY!

MON. MAY 2 8:30PM
THE BYRDS AND THE DiLLARDS

GET THE HABIT
ORDER YOUR TICKETS BY PHONE ·· 883-9900
Also So. Cal. Music Co., 637 S. Hill St., Mutual Agencies & Wallichs Music City

**Valley Music Theatre,
Woodland Hills, CA**

The Byrds are guaranteed $2,500 against an option on 50 per cent of the gross box office for their one concert at 8:30pm. The fee apparently also covers The Dillards. In a merry moment, the usually reserved Chris Hillman dons David Crosby's cape and puts on Jim McGuinn's rectangular glasses as he takes the stage for the opening number.

The edition of *Hullabaloo* with The Byrds doing 'The Times They Are A-Changin'' from last year is reprised at 7:30pm (PST and EST) on the NBC network (see November 29, 1965).

Tuesday 3

RECORDING Columbia Recording Studios, (presumably) Studio A, Sunset and El Centro, Hollywood, CA. Producer Allen Stanton and (presumably) engineer Ray Gerhardt.

The Byrds record McGuinn's '2-4-2 Fox Trot (The Lear Jet Song)', which mixes sound effects with a rhythm & blues guitar riff, over which the group repeatedly chant the simple lyric line. The title refers to the registration number on John Lear's own jet, which is N242FT.

The Byrds call on their illustrious friends to help create the track, as confirmed by Charles Champlin's lunch date with Jane Fonda, loyally reported in *The Los Angeles Times* (May 6): "As we were lunching, in fact, brother Peter was down at [L.A.] International Airport with The Byrds, recording the sounds of jet take-offs as background for an upcoming Byrds record." McGuinn and Peter Fonda also tape John Lear reading the pre-takeoff checklist that is heard on the finished song.

McGuinn tapes the sounds used in '2-4-2

Fox Trot (The Lear Jet Song)' himself on a portable recorder rather than employing existing recordings available in sound effects libraries. (Coincidentally, on the other side of the Atlantic, The Beatles are working on the album that will become *Revolver*, which also experiments with sound effects and backwards tapes.)

Wednesday 4

RECORDING Columbia Recording Studios, Studio A, Sunset and El Centro, Hollywood, CA. 8:00pm. Producer Allen Stanton and (presumably) engineer Ray Gerhardt.

Today's session yields a jazzy instrumental backing track to 'John Riley', a folk song chord-progression the group will try again a few weeks later (see May 25).

Friday 6

RECORDING Columbia Recording Studios, Studio A, Sunset and El Centro, Hollywood, CA. Producer Allen Stanton and engineer Ray Gerhardt.

A tape box identifying The Byrds' first instrumental recording is dated today (see May 18).

•

One night Gene Clark drops by the studio. Since his informal appearance with The Byrds at the Trip club on April 4 he has been away visiting his family in Kansas before coming back to L.A., but with few plans for the future. He is interviewed by Michelle Straub of *Flip* magazine (belatedly published in November 1966) talking about his departure from The Byrds. "There was never any conflict. I just wanted to be more individual. But I do miss the good time we had together. Last night I showed up at a Byrds' recording session. During the breaks we had jam sessions and it was just like old times. It was groovy."

He reminisces about his brief return at the Trip club. "It was really groovy. It's great to know that your fans want you and appreciate you so much. But I doubt that this will ever happen again. I will continue to write for them and other groups, but my singing days with The Byrds are over. But don't misunderstand: I'm not leaving show business. I'll be back on the scene very soon. The only way I can explain it is that you will understand my leaving in the future when I start singing on my own." (Gene Clark was freed from his contract with The Byrds and Columbia Records on May 2.)

Saturday 7

• Hillside Theatre, Occidental College, Eagle Rock, CA (3:00pm)
• Adolfo Camarillo High School Gym, Camarillo, CA

The Byrds play two colleges around Los Angeles today, starting with a 3:00pm appearance at Eagle Rock. Junior reporter Cindy Lee writes of the evening concert in *The Press-Courier* (May 11). "A long, shiny Cadillac limousine slowly weaved its way to the back of the high school gym. The Byrds emerged with their girlfriends, with flashbulbs lighting the way."

The early concert that day must have been a more formal occasion, as Lee notes. "Being aware of the scandal they were creating by wearing full-dress suits, the four moptop heads dashed into the boys locker room to change into their usual garb of dungarees, beads, and chequered shirts." Lee also interviews Crosby briefly, who reveals that The Byrds hope to tour both Europe and Asia. Besides observing that McGuinn wears Ben Franklin glasses, where "one lens is blue, the other is yellow," Lee sums up the musical content of the show: "For all I know, the excited audience may still be in orbit after hearing The Byrds rock with 'Eight Miles High', their latest single."

Sunday 8

[Unknown venue], Houston, TX

The Byrds fly out for a short tour of Texas. *Disc*, which has recently amalgamated with Liverpool's *Music Echo*, reports on May 21: "The Byrds sustain their mystical image: 250 people turned out to see them near their hometown on Saturday last week; yet in Houston, Texas, 25,000 fans surged into an auditorium to battle with police for 30 minutes of Byrd music." This generous crowd size in Texas is certainly a publicist's exaggeration: the largest audience The Byrds have played to so far was as support to The Beach Boys on July 3 1965.

Monday 9

Memorial Coliseum, Corpus Christi, TX

In the wake of the negative *Gavin Report* comment on 'Eight Miles High', Derek Taylor tries some damage control. "Byrds *Disc* Banned On Drugs Rap," he writes in his weekly instalment in UK's *Disc* (published May 14) after the single has been banned in certain regions, such as Washington, Baltimore, and Houston. "The record was already in the US Top Ten …" – Taylor takes a little poetic licence here – "… when it was labelled a 'drug song' by the *Gavin Report*, a subscription sheet circulated weekly – and widely – to radio stations and other entities in the recording industry. Compiled by record expert Bill Gavin in San Francisco, the report substantially influences a thousand or more radio stations, which, in the US, make or break discs."

Taylor quotes Jim McGuinn: "We could have called the song 'Forty-Two Thousand Two Hundred And Forty Feet' but somehow this didn't seem to be a very commercial song title and it certainly wouldn't have scanned. It seems extraordinary that a very pretty lyric about an intriguing city [London] should be condemned because the phrases are couched in some sort of poetry."

Taylor also secures the front page of *Melody Maker* (May 14) with the same story, which quotes extensively from the *Gavin Report*. The paper wonders if the BBC plans similar action, but the corporation's spokesman merely says that they have already the other record cited by Gavin, Dylan's 'Rainy Day Women Nos. 12 and 35', on the TV show Juke Box Jury. "We don't ban records except in very unusual circumstances," he says.

The single continues to crawl at a snail's pace up the national *Cash Box* and *Billboard* listings and will peak next week at Number 12 before slipping down. In some regional charts, however, it performs slightly better and makes the Top Ten.

Legal action will be taken later in the month, with a letter dispatched to the *Gavin Report* demanding an apology to be printed. It is too little too late: 'Eight Miles High' has already run its course.

Although the *Gavin Report* certainly has an influence on radio programmers, it cannot alone be blamed for the comparative failure of 'Eight Miles High'. Later, the single will rightfully claim its place as a harbinger of the psychedelic era.

•

'Eight Miles High' is quickly covered, rather limply, by guitar instrumental combo The Ventures for their June 1966 album *Go With The Ventures*. At the end of July, Indian sitar virtuoso Harihar Rao releases a version of the song on an album suitably called *Raga Rock* by The Folkswingers. "Hardly ethnomusicology material," writes Pete Johnson in the *The Los Angeles Times* (July 31), "but it all swings and the album is one of those rare records in which material of other groups is treated in an original way."

Tuesday 10–Thursday 12

The group plays undocumented concerts in Texas.

Friday 13

'KFJZ Spring Spectacular', Will Rogers Coliseum, Forth Worth, TX

A second weekend in Texas is sponsored by radio station KFJZ as 'The Byrds Show'. Local Austin group The 13th Floor Elevators fills the opening slot and has just released its debut single, 'You're Gonna Miss Me'.

Monday 16

◁)) **RECORDING** Columbia Recording Studios, (presumably) Studio D, Sunset and

El Centro, Hollywood, CA. Producer Allen Stanton and (presumably) engineer Ray Gerhardt.

'I Come And Stand At Every Door' is recorded today. It is an old folk melody that Pete Seeger has adapted to Turkish poet's Nâzım Hikmet Ran's grisly lyric about a survivor of the Hiroshima bombing.

Tuesday 17

◁)) **RECORDING** Columbia Recording Studios, Studio D, Sunset and El Centro, Hollywood, CA. 8:00–11:00pm. Producer Allen Stanton and (presumably) engineer Ray Gerhardt.

Finally, tonight, The Byrds tape David Crosby's treatment of Billy Roberts's 'Hey Joe (Where You Gonna Go)'. It has been part of the group's live repertoire since the early days at Ciro's. By now, the song is already a minor hit by The Leaves, who have adopted Crosby's version to the extent that a review in *The Oakland Tribune* (April 22) remarks: "Strong dance song that has an instrumental section which is almost identical to the middle of The Byrds' disc 'I'll Feel A Whole Lot Better'."

'Hey Joe' has also been picked up by Chicago group The Shadows Of Knight, who heard The Byrds perform the song during their stint at the Trip club in early April. Arthur Lee and Love have been regularly playing their version of 'Hey Joe' on-stage too and will record it this summer.

Wednesday 18

◁)) **RECORDING** Columbia Recording Studios, Studio A, Sunset and El Centro, Hollywood, CA. Producer Allen Stanton and engineer Ray Gerhardt.

The Byrds tape a jam built around the drum groove of Allen Toussaint's rhythm & blues tune 'Get Out Of My Life Woman', a minor US hit for Lee Dorsey. Perhaps they are inspired by the version that Paul Butterfield's Blues Band churns out as part of its live set this year. The group even overdubs a harmonica, possibly played by McGuinn, but he blows it Brian Jones-style and not like Butterfield's amplified tone. The tape box labels the instrumental as 'Blues?' or 'Thirty Minute Break' before it is given its final title of 'Captain Soul'. The song has the distinction of being The Byrds' first instrumental to be released.

(The tape box identifies the recording date as May 6 and not May 18.)

Thursday 19

◁)) **RECORDING** Columbia Recording Studios, Sunset and El Centro, Hollywood, CA. Producer Allen Stanton and (presumably) engineer Ray Gerhardt.

The group today records 'I See You', an original composition credited to Jim McGuinn and David Crosby.

Friday 20

The Byrds have earlier held an East Coast press meeting (see March 28), but now it is time to meet the West Coast press at a reception, possibly held today.

A pre-booked recording session at 8:00–11:00pm tonight in Columbia's Studio D is cancelled.

Saturday 21

"Bring back The Byrds to Britain!" demands Susan Hogg from Hackney, London, in today's

The Byrds on a swing, spring 1966. From left: McGuinn, Clarke, Crosby, Hillman.

Disc. "I want to show The Byrds someone in Britain does care for them."

Monday 23–Tuesday 24

◄)) **RECORDING** Columbia Recording Studios, Studio A, Sunset and El Centro, Hollywood, CA. 8:00pm (Monday only). Producer Allen Stanton and (presumably) engineer Ray Gerhardt.

The session sheet reveals the clients as being "The Birds" for the Monday date. Although no further documentation exists for either day, it is highly likely that the group works on the three songs that will wrap up sessions for the next album: McGuinn's new composition '5D' and two traditional folk songs, 'John Riley' and 'Wild Mountain Thyme'.

McGuinn later attempts to explain the meaning of '5D' and credits Einstein's theory of relativity as the inspiration, where the fourth dimension is time and the fifth dimension unspecified – "open; channel 5, the next step; I saw it to be timelessness – a sort of void in space, where time has no meaning," he tries to clarify for Michael Ross in *Creem* (November 1970). "'5D' was an ethereal trip into metaphysics, into an almost Moslem submission to an Allah, an almighty spirit, free-floating, the fifth dimension being the 'mesh' which Einstein theorised about. He proved theoretically – but I choose to believe it – that there's an ethereal mesh in the universe, and probably the reason for the speed of light being what it is, is because of the friction going through that mesh. The song was talking about a way of life, a submission to God or whatever you want to call that mesh, that life-force."

Heavy message aside, the song itself is in waltz time with a melody reminiscent of Bob Dylan's work, and Chris Hillman will note it later as one of his Byrds favourites. "[That's] one of the greatest songs McGuinn has ever written ... I love that song. It just swings like a big pendulum," he tells music writer John Nork.

Wednesday 25

◄)) **RECORDING** Columbia Recording Studios, (presumably) Studio A, Sunset and El Centro, Hollywood, CA. 8:00pm. Producer Allen Stanton and (presumably) engineer Ray Gerhardt.

The session sheet has "Sweet" written next to the client name, indicating today as an overdub session for the tracks recorded on Monday and Tuesday. 'Sweetening' is studio jargon for overdubbing additional instruments. Van Dyke Parks, a 23-year-old composer and lyricist, adds keyboards to '5D'. Parks has just released his first solo single, 'Number Nine', on MGM Records and this month has been commissioned by Brian Wilson to collaborate as lyricist on Beach Boys material.

A full string section is scored, apparently by McGuinn, and overdubbed on 'Wild Mountain Thyme' and 'John Riley', two traditional folk songs rearranged by the group. The roots of 'Wild Mountain Thyme' lie in an old Scottish tune (although it is commonly credited to Irishman Francis McPeake) and it has been covered on albums in the US by Judy Collins and Joan Baez. The Byrds credit it to Bob Gibson and Ricky Neff (also noted as its composer on a version that Joan Baez recorded on her debut album). Correctly, however, the song is in the public domain.

Saturday 28

After the features in UK's *Disc* and *Melody Maker* a fortnight ago on the 'Eight Miles High' controversy, both papers follow up the story this Saturday. *Disc* brings news that a 25-year old Birmingham City councillor, one Mr Colin Beardwood, has appealed to Home Secretary Mr Roy Jenkins to have 'Rainy Day Woman Numbers 12 & 35' and 'Eight Miles High' banned by the BBC on the grounds of encouraging drug taking. Beardwood says: "Don't get me wrong – I'm not a fuddy duddy and, in fact, I'm a Dylan fan. But both these songs have a subtle message, encouraging drug taking, and influence of this kind can't be particularly good for young people." The Home Office declines to give any comments, but a BBC spokesman says to *Disc*: "There is no hard and fast rule here. The decision is left to the discretion of producers of programmes."

Melody Maker has their readers voice opinions. "If the Americans believe that The Byrds' 'Eight Miles High' is about drugs they can also class The Lovin' Spoonful's 'Daydream' as a drug song. They'll be saying the National Anthem is a protest song," writes reader Ian M. Hawkins of Enfield, Middlesex. "Perhaps the American authorities think that … 'Eight Miles High' should be rewritten so that the plane takes them to a heroic death in battle. Sung by Barry Sadler, of course," writes Miss S. Lane of Farringdon, who is awarded an LP for her letter.

Melody Maker also prints a long interview with Jim McGuinn and David Crosby under the headline "Byrds Go For Bach, Ragas, Coltrane" as part of a "sitar rock" special. The Byrds feature has no byline, but seems to be the work of Derek Taylor, who nimbly scissors quotes from the New York press reception in early spring (see March 28) and, interestingly, many fresh insights.

David Crosby says: "I have dug [Ravi] Shankar for a long time. I mean, Shankar's sitar sound has always intrigued me. I played some of his records for George Harrison and it turned him on. He bought one, which The Beatles used on 'Norwegian Wood'. We used [the idea] on our new record, 'Eight Miles High', which really means 42,000 feet up in a jet. We like speed, man, and those jets give it to you."

Asked about politics, Crosby says: "We're not a political group. You won't find us on the peace marches. Rather than protesting, which is essentially negativity or a reaction, we're more likely to 'Hey, love somebody' and like that. That's what we are looking for in the way we act, the way we play our music and the way we grow as people. Protest is not a useful tool for us. We prefer the positive, like saying 'UFOs are real'. … The Beatles are the best rock'n'roll singing group in the world – unquestioned, unchallenged, unapproached. The Stones are awfully good too. Why? Because they keep on growing. They never look for a secure place and stay there. They do new things all the time. That's what we are trying to do. 'Eight Miles High' is a lot different from 'Turn! Turn! Turn!' and from 'Mr. Tambourine Man'. The first time you try to play safe with a record, you cease to be creative."

Jim McGuinn says: "The sitar has a beautiful sound. But I don't think that's the real long-term thing. It's not that adaptable. There's going to be a new instrument that will come out of all of this. Maybe a smaller, electrified sitar. But the thing now is an electric 12-string. That's got so many sounds and people just don't seem to know about it. You can do anything on it – Bach organs, harpsichord, jet planes, whining turbine engines, air raid sirens, kittens, a baby crying, anything. You know: the whole thing!"

"You've got to try new things all the time and you make sure you control your own production. And you also get the right engineer. A good engineer is priceless," explains McGuinn, to which Crosby adds: "He rides those controls like an instrument, with the same involvement as us riding our guitars. He's playing that board. He flies it, like by the seat of his pants. The Stones came all the way to Hollywood to record, just because of one engineer there."

As for the future, McGuinn sums up: "I'd like to make an experimental film using electronic colours. But that's my own personal project. We're hoping to all act in a picture which we may even start work on this summer. We've got the script we like already. We're ready to go the straight acting route, with no stand-up guitar playing and singing scenes at all. That would all be in the background track. Now it all hinges on a certain director, who shall remain nameless. This is the guy we want and it's still being talked over and negotiated. When that's settled, we'll be practically ready to go."

→ Late May

☐ **US TV** [Probably ABC Television Center], Hollywood, CA. KABC *Arlene Dahl Beauty Spot* 4:25pm

In Los Angeles between weekends on the road, McGuinn and Crosby are guests on actress Dahl's five-minute weekday spot, which is broadcast on Friday June 17. The extent of their participation is not known.

June

→ Friday 3–Saturday 4

Action House, Island Park, NY

With recording sessions for their third album wrapped up, The Byrds hit the road again, this time flying to the West Coast for four days. Barry Friedman – friend and associate of Buffalo Springfield – has signed up as soundman for The Byrds and will work on and off with the group from now on until next summer.

The group has rented a mobile home and hangs out on Long Island instead of returning to California, preferring to gear up for the summer tour on the East Coast.

Saturday 4

Calling in from sunny Los Angeles, Derek Taylor in his irregular weekly column in *Disc* today takes readers on a trip down Sunset Strip. "The Strip, first of all, is not the official address. It's a term applied with glamorous connotations, real or imaginary, to a length, rather less than a mile long, of Sunset Boulevard, which itself stretches from downtown Los Angeles away in the sunset of the Pacific Ocean at Malibu."

"The girls of Sunset Strip – the little teen-

'5D'

A '5D' (J. MCGUINN)
B 'Captain Soul' (R. MCGUINN/ C. HILLMAN/M. CLARKE/D. CROSBY)

US release June 13 1966 (Columbia 43702)
UK release June 29 1966 (CBS 202259)
Chart high US number 44; UK none
Read more ... entries for May 18 and 25, 1966

---

agers with bronze skin, long blonde hair, tight bell-bottom jeans, worldly eyes in young faces – these are the hippies who flock into the teen nightclubs and into the liquor-serving clubs such as the Trip and the Whisky A Go Go. Those who are really hip wouldn't be seen dead in the teetotal clubs such as It's Boss, and as they have no ID there's not much you can do legally as a young hippy. The 'in' place now is, of course, the Trip, favoured by The Byrds who have their own particular scene. The Byrds and The Lovin' Spoonful are scions of the Strip – lords of all they survey through the afternoon smog of the early twilight when the 15 million lights of Los Angeles flicker into splendid brilliance, or crude squalor, depending on your attitude.

"The Sheriff's Department shows particular interest in these arenas and there have been complaints – how true they are it's impossible to say – of outrageous 'flashlight treatment'. This is when the Sheriff's men haul their clanking leather-and-steel-clad bodies on their motorcycles and march into a coffeehouse brandishing their blazing flashlight in the faces of startled, stone-cold-sober teenagers talking about life, love, music, and liberty to the sound of an acoustic guitar or maybe a mouth-organ."

"The teenage rebellion is complete on the Strip. Here is total deadlock between matriarchal, middle-aged American, youth, and uniformed authority. There is no meeting place between young and old. The young want their folk or rock and freedom; the old want their topless."

"If you're 'in' on the Strip you'll never starve. If there is a fault it's that there's too much talk and not enough action. But it's a benevolent atmosphere and it's from this environment that the new music of America is springing [and] for the time being, at any rate, this is where it's at."

Friday 10

'Sound Blast 66', Yankee Stadium, The Bronx, New York, NY

The Beach Boys headline this New York concert at the enormous Yankee Stadium. The venue has a capacity for 70,000 but has sold only a disappointing 9,000 tickets, despite the varied bill. The concert, promoted by TAJ Enterprises and advertised to begin at 7:30pm, does not get under way for almost an hour and a half after that time. Appearing in chronological order are The Cowsills, The McCoys, The Marvelettes, The Byrds (who are a recent addition), Jerry Butler, Stevie Wonder, and The Jimo Tamos Orchestra. Ray Charles and The Beach Boys are saved until the last. The Gentrys and The Guess Who are billed but presumably do not appear. Jonathan Ran-

dal in *The New York Times* (June 11) reviews the happening but writes mostly about the 66 finalists in a dance contest who ride around the bullpen on bicycles, demonstrating a new dance called The Bike.

Richard Goldstein in *Village Voice* (June 16) terms the occasion worthy of Federico Fellini. "As The Byrds emerged from the home-team dugout, a bell-bottomed body burst from a nearby box and tried to leap a fence. She was stopped by a flying wedge of police. The group raced down the plywood path to the stage, but they had to wait a full ten minutes before their equipment could be assembled. Finally connected to their amplifiers by electric unbiblical cords, they began to play. But the sound wasn't worth the amps. The group seemed incapable of sustaining effective harmony in person, and their ambiguous raga-rhythms lost themselves in a haze of echo and feedback. Priceless details (Jim McGuinn doing a neat two-step as he sang, [Crosby's] phosphorescent buttons, the grin on Mike Clarke's face as he dutifully pounded the drums) were lost on everyone in the audience who had neglected to bring a high power telescope."

Saturday 11

Oakdale Music Theatre, Wallingford, CT

The Byrds kick off the opening of the 15-week summer concert season at the Oakdale Music Theatre, which has a wide variety of upcoming shows, from Broadway musicals to children's shows and from classical orchestras to comedies. For the one performance at 9:30pm, two Connecticut groups support The Byrds: The Young Alley Cats (from Hartford) and The Shags (from New Haven).

**Camden County Music Fair,
Haddonfield, NJ**
The Byrds end the weekend with a 3:00pm concert presented by Hy Lit (of radio station WIBG), supported by The Shadows Of Knight, The Candymen, "plus 3 new groups" (one of these possibly a band called Little Flowers). Afterwards, The Byrds return to Los Angeles.

Today is the official US release date for '5D'/'Captain Soul' from the May sessions, although the actual date may be held back until June 27. However, the group doesn't seem to muster the sort of enthusiasm that came with 'Eight Miles High', and the single is more viewed as a necessary promotional tool for the group's forthcoming album. As a result, the single stalls at Number 44 in the *Billboard* charts (but slightly better in *Cash Box*, where it peaks at Number 39).

Billboard (July 2) picks the song as a "Top 20 Spotlight" and notes: "Hot on the heels of 'Eight Miles High' comes this off-beat lyric rocker with chart-topping potential." First sign of chart movement is the following week, July 9, when the single is found at Number 111 in the Hot 100's "Bubbling Under".

The recent contention over 'Eight Miles High' has alerted radio programmers and other guardians of decency, and even the most innocent lyric is scrutinised for hidden meanings. Tracy Thomas laments in *New Musical Express* (July 8): "The Byrds' 'Eight Miles High' and Dylan's 'Everybody Must Get Stoned' [sic] started it all, and now the latest tune to be banned in the search for hidden references to drugs is, of all things, Gary Lewis & The Playboys' 'Green Grass'. The Lovin' Spoonful have been attacked for the line in 'Daydream' about 'new-mowed lawn'. ... The new Byrds' single '5D' may be taken off radio playlists, too. It's about the expansion of awareness, not specifically through drugs; but then, as the critics put it, it doesn't say how to expand."

•

The debate on drug-related lyrics will flare up on occasion in the US press, and 'Eight Miles High' will, every so often, be pulled out as a prime example of lyrical innocence turned on its head. Indeed, some of The Byrds will later admit that it was consciously written to imply a hidden meaning. In September 1966, Associated Press journalist Mary Campbell writes an essay on the subject ('Drug And Drink Lyrics Rock Record Industry' in *The Los Angeles Times* September 25) that sums up the situation: "There is plenty of disagreement over how much, if any, 'junky words' are being used, since some people hear them and others don't, listening to the same song. There is a concern by some that 'drug songs' might cause youngsters to try drugs, while others say mere lyrics have no effect on behaviour."

Mentioning 'Eight Miles High' and 'Rainy Day Women Numbers 12 & 35' specifically, Campbell continues: "Clive Davis, vice president of CBS Records, which encompasses Columbia and five smaller labels, says the company views the two songs solely as effective entertainment. The Byrds have said 'Eight Miles High' refers to flying in an airplane to

London. Dylan never has said what this, or any, of his songs means. If there is any drug wording involved, Clive Davis concludes, 'Only a small coterie of people might understand. And it doesn't have any influencing factor at all.'"

Friday 17
Civic Center, Baltimore, MD

The Byrds are back on the East Coast for a concert at 8:15pm in Maryland today and Boston tomorrow en route to a brief tour of Canada. Over in the Los Angeles area, viewers can tune in to watch McGuinn and Crosby as unlikely guests on Arlene Dahl Beauty Spot on KABC-TV at 4:25pm.

Saturday 18
'Mayor's Charity Festival', War Memorial Auditorium, Boston, MA

Monday 20
Bingemen Park Arena, Kitchener, Ontario, Canada

The Byrds make their Canadian debut. Attendance is 3,500, and J.B. & The Playboys, The Reefers, and The British Mod Beats provide support.

Don Collins writes in the *Kitchener-Waterloo Record* (June 22): "It was the first Canadian appearance by the mop-haired and beat-garbed foursome since their meteoric rise to fame began two years ago. But the fact they're on top of the heap didn't do much for the teenagers, some of whom came from as far as Peterborough. The youngsters responded more to the supporting Canadian groups. … The Byrds, who were to have taken the stand at 11:00p.m., arrived 15 minutes late, and to even things up at the other end, quit at 11:50, ten minutes ahead of schedule. A handful of the crowd danced to the special sound of their guitars, the continual rattle of the drums and lyrics that were lost in the blare. Some of the others jiggled a bit where they stood, but most moved about listlessly and many headed for home before the act ended.

"An abrupt 'thank you and good night' signalled that the end had come and The Byrds ambled out, protected by several police officers who were conspicuous by the fact that they had no one to move aside. There was no attempt made to mob the group. And no one seemed to care about getting their autographs. Despite this lack of concern, The Byrds had something to chirp about as they headed out of town today. They had the flat rate $2,000 they had been guaranteed for their brief performance and will collect another $3,500 or 60 per cent of the gate tonight at London, Ontario. Things will get even better when they go to Toronto the next

night for $5,000 or 60 per cent of the gate. After that it's on to Winnipeg for an unstated sum and back to the US."

Tuesday 21
'Summer Spectacular', London Arena, London, Ontario, Canada

The Byrds' second Canadian show, set for 8:30pm, is MC'd by radio station CFPL's Dick Williams, and features warm-up acts The Rogues and The London Set.

Wednesday 22
'Rock'n'Soccer Show', Varsity Arena, Toronto, Canada

In a sporty move, football president Joe Peters sandwiches a soccer match between a gaggle of local pop groups and The Byrds. The idea is to draw a younger audience to the soccer games, but only 4,113 pay to see the combined sports and rock show (9,000 is the break-even point, and the stadium can easily hold 20,000). The concert commences at 7:30pm with Jack Hardin & The Silhouettes, Susan Taylor, Five Of A Kind, and Group Therapy, and then breaks for the game, followed by a performance by The Byrds at 10:30pm. The match pits Toronto Italia Falcons versus Hamilton Primos, easily won 3–0 by the Falcons after a hat trick by Janko Daucik.

"Standing on a tiny stage at the Bloor Street end of the playing field, surrounded by (and almost buried under) an ocean of screaming teenagers, [The Byrds] sang about eight numbers in approximately half an hour then quickly left," writes John McFarlane in *The Globe And Mail* (June 23). "It took about 30 policeman and as many attendants to keep the mob from swamping the four Beatle-like performers. Several of their young admirers were carried to the sidelines as they broke through the wall of police and attempted to climb the stage. If The Byrds were concerned about their safety, they certainly didn't show it. And for that they earned my admiration (to say nothing of their share of the gate receipts). As for their performance, no one will ever know whether they were good, bad, or indifferent. At times it was difficult to tell what they were playing above the screams of the crowd."

Jim Kernaghan in *The Toronto Daily Star* (June 23) says: "Then, the magic moment. Referee Ray Morgan's whistle to end the game had the effect of a trumpet to a cavalry group poised to charge. The thundering herd moved in a unit to a portable stage. … They crowded around while a local disc jockey gave directions from the stage: 'C'mon gang, cool it and back up a little, how about sitting down on the grass, gang, or The Byrds will have to split.' No problem arose except for the ejec-

tion of a couple of onlookers. The number of police, security guards, and University police had been tripled over that of a normal soccer game. Finally, about 11:00pm, The Byrds departed and the fans followed slowly."

ALSO …

Gene Clark has formed a sort of supergroup (nonchalantly named The Group) for his return to the public with a residence at the Whisky A Go Go. Besides ex-Byrd Clark himself, the band is made up of drummer Joe Larson (ex-The Grass Roots), bass player Chip Douglas (ex-Modern Folk Quartet), and guitarist Bill Reinhardt (ex-The Leaves). A cautious Gene Clark tells Tracy Thomas in *New Musical Express* (June 17) before tonight's debut: "Of course I'm excited, but plenty scared, too! Everyone's going to be there and they'll all want to say I should have stayed with The Byrds. So we'll have to be very, very good to make it. I hope we will." Clark adds to Thermon Fisk of *KRLA Beat* (July 9): "I cannot describe our sound to you. You will just have to hear it and see for yourself."

Thursday 23
Manitoba Auditorium, Winnipeg, Manitoba, Canada

The Byrds in one show at 8:00pm, promoted by H.G. Bjarnason & Attractions Ticket Office, supported by local groups The Fifth and The Shondels (not to be confused with Tommy James's backing group). The show grosses $4,500 after 1,596 teens pay their way into the 4,100-seat building.

Lesley Foster writes in *The Winnipeg Free Press* the day after the concert: "The lush,

Gene Clark debuting as solo performer at the Whisky A Go Go, June 1966.

full-flavoured sound which distinguishes the long-feathered Byrds from countless fledging groups was lost for want of a cage. Not for them; for their audience. Byrd-watchers, mostly devout copies of Sonny & Cher, turned out in numbers the Audobon Society has never seen. For the most part, they were presentably dressed and well mannered. Screaming, wailing, howling, and gnashing of teeth were regulated to the start and finish of songs. It was a small number of aisle-creepers who could neither sit still nor shut up. They were, however, number enough to keep the stage surrounded by a chorus line of Whipper Billy Watsons, whose job it was to throw bodies back where they belonged." (The promoters have hired professional wrestlers as security for the show.)

"The Byrds certainly didn't lay an egg. Their talent, individually and collectively, is impressive. Their musicianship has everything and then some. They are young, casual, educated, smooth, and they are the In-Crowd's In-Crowd, working as they do with Bob Dylan, Pete Seeger, and Lennon-McCartney's complet .... been surprises, notably the Biblical-inspired 'Turn! Turn! Turn!', more recently an almost-instrumental number called 'Eight Miles High' in which the sounds of space become a magnetic melody. These were included in Thursday's show and met with unqualified appreciation.

"Apart from the well-meaning insults from

their less considerate shrieking fans (who succeeded in calling more attention to themselves than the artists), The Byrds struggled with poor technical work. In those miraculous moments when their audience paid them the ultimate homage of listening, the ears gave out in self-defence and the overall impression was one of electrocution. It is a vicious circle: too much yelling or too much music. Surely there is an alternative answer to just staying home with a cooperative stereo set. The Byrds usually lean on meaningful lyrics, which somehow reached row five sounding like yowyowywyow-rakkety-shankeroop m-m-m-! Not too meaningful, that."

Friday 24
'Beach Boys Summer Spectacular', The Cow Palace, Daly City, CA
The Byrds fly down from Canada to appear for two California concerts headlined by The Beach Boys, the first of which is today. Presented by Irvin Grantz and radio station KFRC, this San Francisco show starts at 8.00pm and the advertised bill is an impressive mix of local talent (Jefferson Airplane), British pop stars (Chad & Jeremy), L.A. groups (The Leaves, The Byrds, The Sunrays), rhythm & blues (Percy Sledge), regional bands (Sir Douglas Quintet from Texas; The Outsiders from Cleveland, Ohio – who fail to appear – and The Lovin' Spoonful from New York). Neil Diamond is a late addition, replacing The Outsiders. The concert is sold out and

draws 16,100 fans and grosses an impressive $62,197.

"The Beach Boys' big show at the Cow Palace Friday night was a mixed bag of performances, some of which were terrible, some interesting, and a couple really first rate," writes Ralph J Gleason in *The San Francisco Chronicle* (June 27). The Byrds may not come in the terrible category, but Gleason is still let down. "The Byrds were something of a disappointment. They never really got started. Their set, which closed the first half, was delayed because of some mechanical problem with the microphones and it seemed to discourage the group." Gleason reserves the accolades for The Lovin' Spoonful, Sir Douglas Quintet, and Jefferson Airplane (praising Signe Anderson's vocals and Jorma Kaukonen's guitar solos), while he finds The Beach Boys "unbearable – they look so cliché surfer".

Jan Silverman writes in *The Oakland Tribune* (June 29): "[After] a concert Friday night that saw the top pop-music groups in the country scuttled by ridiculously loud amplifiers ... our ears were still ringing from the combination of screams and over-amplified guitar (The Byrds must have been singing – we saw their lips moving). And when the Spoonful or Chad & Jeremy came on it was like a thunderstorm, with the roar of the crowd and flashing of light bulbs from hundred of cameras."

Silverman observes the change in fashion and the first inklings of the nascent hippie movement. "Actually, the audience was as entertaining as the show. There were those strange girls in the front row with ponchos and strange markings on their foreheads. And the chubby boy from San Rafael in the brown velvet cape and checked hip-hugger pants. The Mod look seems to be 'in'. And the baby-faced blonde in the dress so short that it nearly hiked up to her belly button as she sat down. She was wearing thongs – not shoes, just rawhide thongs – wrapped around her bare feet. Then there was the girl who walked up to the stage in a trance with a sign proclaiming 'I love The Byrds forever'. And she signed it. But all in all it was a great evening for everyone, thanks to the good sense of our Bay Area younger generation. Class will tell."

Saturday 25
'Beach Boys Summer Spectacular'
Hollywood Bowl, Hollywood, CA
The Summer Spectacular moves south to Los Angeles. Promoted by Irvin Grantz and radio station KRLA, today's show retains The Byrds ("Extra-added attraction!"), The Lovin' Spoonful, Chad & Jeremy, Percy Sledge, The Sunrays, Neil Diamond (again as replacement for The Outsiders), The Leaves, Sir

Jim McGuinn and Chris Hillman tuning up backstage at the Hollywood Bowl, June 25, 1966.

Douglas Quintet – plus of course The Beach Boys – from the San Francisco show, but adds a couple of up and coming Los Angeles groups: Love and Captain Beefheart & The Magic Band. An aggregation called The New Motown Sound also appears. The attendance figure is 12,400 and the box office gross is $51,000. *Variety* (June 29) details the accounting, explaining how The Beach Boys net $32,000 for the two shows, while the rest of the groups split the remaining $26,000 after venue rent, police fees, and Irving Grantz are paid.

Tracy Thomas writes in *New Musical Express* (July 1): "A faulty sound system marred the four-hour Beach Boys Summer Spectacular before 17,000 fans at the Hollywood Bowl Saturday night. Virtually all the acts suffered. … The Byrds, who may have lost Gene Clark but have retained their fanatical and considerable following, are becoming a better four-man group with every performance."

Charles Champlin also complains of the malfunctioning PA system in *The Los Angeles Times* (June 28): "For the most part, it becomes impossible to review such an evening except as a popularity contest. On that basis, The Beach Boys registered loudest on the scream meter, hotly pursued by The Lovin' Spoonful, The Byrds, The Leaves, and The Sunrays (who, it could be guessed, may well be a promising new group). … It must be said that the majority of the audience of around 15,000 were less aggravated by the bad sound than the performers themselves. The peculiar ritual of these evenings is that the faithful come to see, wave, and scream and are content with wisps of sound to evoke the remembered records."

Despite their anglicised name, Sir Douglas Quintet is a Texas-based group that now features bass player John York.

"Oh yes, I remember those Beach Boys concerts, especially the Hollywood Bowl Show. A girl jumped out of the audience and threw her arms around me," says York. "And I was having trouble with my bass, and the Byrds road manager let me borrow one of Chris Hillman's bass guitars." (On this occasion, McGuinn plays a two-pickup Rickenbacker 12-string rather than the three-pickup model he usually favours.)

July

Friday 1
The Surf, Nantasket Beach, Hull, MA
The Byrds strike out on their own as headliners again for a series of dates throughout

July, mainly in the Northeast, beginning tonight in Massachusetts. The bookings are a jumble of nondescript clubs and large arenas. As many of the dates are within travelling distance by car, the promoter provides the group with a Clark Cortez mobile home to get them from city to city. The band carries it own sound system, valued at $12,000.

This tour marks the debut of road manager Jimmi Seiter, who – besides McGuinn – will remain the one permanent fixture through shifts and changes for the next six years. "That tour was my first official one," he recalls, "but I took them to Texas before that for a 12-day tour, where I was just helping out. I officially joined the band for the big East Coast tour that lasted more than 30 days. When I joined I was told to handle the band, period, as the management didn't want to know. I had it all to do, really." A young friend of Chris Hillman is also along to hump gear and drive.

Hampton Beach Casino, Hampton Beach, NH
The Byrds and The Spectras.

Young music fan Rick Hinman is at the ballroom, and recounts: "What I remember is that they were not very impressive musically and they looked like they couldn't care less anyway. When they finished they just laid their guitars down on stage and nonchalantly strolled off stage, with no roadie rushing to pick up the instruments. I was able to reach up and strum McGuinn's 12-string a little. Actually, I had not really seen a proper electric guitar up close before."

ALSO …
Sing Out! editor Irwin Silber writes an astringent report on the folk rock phenomenon in *Melody Maker* today, called "For Sing-in And Sit-in, Read Plug-in".

He says: "More than half the coffee houses that featured folk singers less than two years ago are now strictly rock'n'roll or Folk Rock. The Urban Electrification Program is, for those who want to be where it's at, where it is. Singers who used to 'sing in' and 'sit in' have now plugged in. Electric bills in Greenwich Village, Cambridge, Old Town, and

North Beach are way up – and so are record royalties.

"The development has been in the works for a number of years (even before The Beatles) starting when the hippies began to dig Lightning Hopkins, Muddy Waters, and Chuck Berry. The Paul Butterfield Blues Band bridged the gap to the white kids, and Bob Dylan set it careening off on a new course. Right now, some-time folk-based groups such as The Lovin' Spoonful, The Blues Project, Love, and Simon & Garfunkel have become pop chart-busters. Its value and long-term significance are a source of great controversy among performers and critics. The music seems to be unquestionably part of the 'pop art' upheaval and has won the endorsement of the nouveau 'against interpretation' ('the envelope is the message, baby') critics. A few (count me among them) think the whole thing is a frenzied joke that gives the participant the illusion that his navel is the centre of the universe."

Monday 4
Palace Ballroom, Old Orchard Beach, ME

ALSO …
"The weather did today what their parents couldn't do – sent the mop-haired International Submarine Band rock'n'roll group to the barber shop," says a small notice in the *Chicago Tribune* today. "When the mercury bubbled to 100 degrees, the band leader, Gram Parsons, 19, of Winter Haven, Florida, said, 'I think we've had it.' With that the long hairs took haircuts."

Having been together since the early spring, The International Submarine Band line-up features Gram Parsons (guitar, vocals), John Nuese (guitar), Ian Dunlop (bass), and Mickey Gauvin (drums). The four have spent the spring in New York with little success and are now playing a summer residence at Palisades Amusement Park in Fort Lee, NJ. They have recorded and released a single for the obscure Ascot label in April, whose B-side, 'Truck Drivin' Man', is an early example of the group's rocked-up country hybrid.

Tuesday 5
Commodore Ballroom, Lowell, MA
The Byrds headline, while Commodore regulars Little John & The Sherwoods provide support.

Thursday 7
The Surf, Hyannis Port (Cape Cod), MA
Bob Cianci (author, noted music journalist, and musician) later recalls: "Like a jerk, I blew the only opportunity I ever had to see the

COMMODORE BALLROOM
Lowell, Mass.
TUES. NIGHT "THE BYRDS"
Columbia Recording Stars
Biggest Hits — "Eight Miles High" & "Mr. Tambourine Man"
For Dancing "Little John & The Sherwoods"
Advance tickets $2.00 Commodore Ballroom Office
Daily 1 to 5 pm. Fri., July 1 thru Tues., July 5
At door $2.50
Tonite: Johnny Ambrose   Sat: Little John & the Sherwoods

original Byrds. It was the summer of 1966, and it was one of the last vacations I ever took with my parents. The Byrds, minus Gene, were playing at a local teen club hangout, and for some reason still unbeknownst to me, I didn't go. Instead, I went the next night to see some local New England band. What a blunder!"

Friday 8
Malibu Beach Club, Lido Beach (Long Island), NY

Saturday 9
Convention Hall, Asbury Park, NJ
The Byrds have been constantly on the move for months and they consider it below their dignity to travel around the Northeast in a mobile home. Mutiny is brewing, and around this time the group flies back to Los Angeles for a break, causing a couple of dates to be cancelled around now – although exactly which ones have been lost to time.

Jimmi Seiter recalls: "The band decided that we needed to go back to L.A. The tour sucked and the gigs were terrible. They would not let me call Eddie Tickner, who had told me to deal with the band. He didn't want to know. There were to be two other groups from the UK on the shows but they had not gotten into the US due to visa issues. Eddie was pissed, but since I was new, it was all blamed on the band and Crosby."

Sunday 10
Powder Hill Ski Area, Middletown, CT
(Today and tomorrow's concerts may possibly be cancelled.)

Monday 11
Lakeview Ballroom, Mendon, MA
Columbia Records distributes a memo to all its affiliates, signed Frank Calamita, finally proclaiming the Gene Clark exit of The Byrds as official. The advice is to go about this change with the minimum of fuss, and the memo even dictates a suggested reply to possible enquiries as to why the singer has left: "'Gene Clark for his own personal reasons felt he no longer wanted to perform with the group. He still retains a close friendship with the remaining members."

Tuesday 12
The Fontainbleu Inn, Odessa, NY
Despite some gigs cancelled around this time, for tonight's show in Odessa the group is back on the road. To help Seiter out, Ed 'Chip' Monck is hired as driver for a few dates. (Monck is in charge of sound and light equipment at the Village Gate jazz club in New York.)

Wednesday 13
The Raleigh Hotel, South Fallsburg, NY
The Byrds are but one of many attractions at the summer season at the Raleigh hotel, which also sees performances by Bobby Rydell, Billy Eckstine, Lainie Kazan, and The Young Rascals this month.

Thursday 14
Veterans War Memorial Auditorium, Providence, RI
The Byrds plus three other groups (The Lonely Streets, The Malibus, and The Donuts) perform one show at 8:30pm.

Friday 15
Marine Ballroom, Steel Pier, Atlantic City, NJ
The Byrds play two days at this popular summer funfair, with daily performances at 1:00, 6:30, and 10:00pm. Elsewhere there is a four-times-a-day children's show (Center of Pier); a circus act with a diving horse; The Astro Rocket (on the West Dock); or one can take the Mystery Ride in Crazyville at the ocean end of the pier.

Saturday 16
Marine Ballroom, Steel Pier, Atlantic City, NJ
☐ **US TV** Atlantic City, NJ. KYW-TV *Summertime On The Pier* 5:00pm

Besides performing at the Marine Ballroom again today, The Byrds appear on a two-hour show with highlights from the Steel Pier entertainment.

The other guests are Al Martino, Chad & Jeremy, Monty Rock III, Dean Parrish, Billy & The Essentials, Nina Simone, Steve Perry, The Barons, and The Richie Moore Trio. Ed Hurst is the host.

Sunday 17
Alan B. Shepard Civic Center, Virginia Beach, VA
The Byrds leave Atlantic City too late to make the 200-or-so-miles trip to Virginia Beach in time and arrive three hours late for the first scheduled show there at 4:00pm (the official line is that they are held up because of "faulty brakes") with local group The Swinging Machine. Despite reports to the contrary

in the local press, the 8:00pm performance is also curtailed.

Driving out after the show in Virginia Beach, the group's equipment van is involved in an accident that could have cost lives. Jimmi Seiter: "I was alone with a young guy that Hillman had help me, and he was driving and fell asleep at the wheel and almost killed us all." Seiter is badly bruised although otherwise OK, but the driver and Chip Monck are dismissed. Seiter gets help from unexpected quarters. "I met Antique Sandy at the Virginia Beach gig," he says of the girl who later will be honoured in a Byrds song, "and she helped me finish the tour."

Monday 18
The Byrds' third album, *Fifth Dimension*, is released in the US. This same long summer sees epoch-making albums issued by great contemporaries: The Beach Boys with *Pet Sounds* and Bob Dylan with *Blonde On Blonde* in May; The Rolling Stones with *Aftermath* in June; while The Beatles issue *Revolver* in three weeks time.

The Byrds' album contains 11 tracks, of which three are already available as single sides: 'Eight Miles High', 'Captain Soul', and the title track, which is shortened to '5D' whereas the album title is spelled out as *Fifth Dimension*. The album lacks the harmonious consistency of the group's two previous albums but shows an eagerness to expand and move outside the narrow folk-rock category. The group embraces jazz, Indian music, and rhythm & blues – and reviewers strive to keep up by inventing new and convenient labels: 'Indian rock', 'space rock', and even 'philosorock'.

In the void left by Gene Clark, McGuinn and particularly Crosby are developing as songwriters, and of the 11 tracks, seven are originals, three can loosely be described as reworked traditional material ('Wild Mountain Thyme', 'I Come And Stand At Every Door', 'John Riley'), and there is only one cover ('Hey Joe (Where You Gonna Go)'). Significantly, there are no Bob Dylan songs, although the group will return to his compositions on later occasions.

The album jacket debuts the striking Byrds logo in colourful mosaic. The group portrait is also striking: seated on a fringed rug against a black background, the four Byrds appear as if suspended on a magic carpet. The album peaks in *Billboard* at Number 24 in the US.

Billboard reviews the album in its August 20 edition (suggesting the correct release date is maybe as much as a month later than the official July 18 date; the album first appears in the magazine's charts on August 27). "Chalk up another hit package for The Byrds. With

101

a solid string of top singles and albums, this is certain to be added to the list. Both of their recent hits '5D' and 'Eight Miles High' are included."

"*Fifth Dimension* is the third and best album from The Byrds," says *Hit Parader* (January 1967). "If your friendly neighbourhood radio station banned 'Eight Miles High' and '5D' you can listen to them here and discover that there's nothing suggestive about them. The only danger in this album is that it might addict you to groovy music. The Byrds are playing better than ever and the songs range from some real nice folky tunes … to their own arrangements of the popular 'Hey Joe', to their latest hit, 'Mr. Spaceman', to a unique '2-4-2 Fox Trot (The Lear Jet Song)' which uses sound effects similar to those on The Beatles' 'Yellow Submarine' – but The Byrds did it first."

Nineteen-year-old Jon Landau, just getting his start in music journalism, reviews the album for *Crawdaddy* (September 1966). A sworn Byrds fan, he is not entirely convinced. "Unfortunately, they recently lost vocalist Gene Clark … and the new album suffers greatly from this loss. [Gene] was by far the best writer in the group, and although leader Jim McGuinn usually sang lead, Gene clearly had the best voice."

Tiring of the raga-rock sound, Landau does not find either 'What's Happening!?!?' nor 'I See You' as up to scratch. He finds that 'Mr. Spaceman' lacks a melodic strong point, while 'Captain Soul' should have remained a B-side and '2-4-2 Fox Trot (The Learjet Song)' is described as a throwaway.

"That leaves us with three genuinely unusual cuts on the album. 'John Riley' was a good idea. It is, of course, a really beautiful ballad. However, the vocal lead is simply not strong enough to put it over. Clark is particularly missed here. This same comment pertains to but is less true of another folk ballad, 'Wild Mountain Thyme'. The violins on both cuts are too loud, if they aren't out of place altogether. The best cut on the album for my money is Nâzım Hikmet's 'I Come And Stand At Every Door', a direct protest against the dropping of the Hiroshima bomb, a number which The Byrds do superbly. The harmony on the last chorus is perfect and Clarke's-toned down drumming is in fine taste. … This album, then, cannot be considered up to the standards set by The Byrds' first two and basically demonstrates that they should be thinking in terms of replacing Gene Clark instead of just trying to carry on without him."

The album is given an in-depth analysis by Pete Johnson in *The Los Angeles Times*

(August 14). He says: "Often sounding like a hive full of super-amplified bees, The Byrds have strongly influenced the rock'n'roll trend toward massively overlaid agglomerations of electronic noisemakers. Incoherence occasionally riles this type of sound, but The Byrds generally seem to control it better than their pale followers. The first wave of folk-rock a little more than a year ago swept The Byrds out of the anonymity of a Sunset Strip house group to a position of leadership in the Colonial rebellion against the dominance of the British sound. Since their emergence they have coasted along on a series of good-sized hit records. They have perhaps slipped a bit in popularity as the folk-rock novelty wore off and as their imitators multiplied, but they remain one of the most tuneful and influential American rock groups.

"Their latest album contains songs ranging from the weirdly experimental to the beautiful. The title song and 'Eight Miles High' present the quartet's last two hit records on the LP. 'Gonna ride the Lear Jet, baby,' they sing in their oddest number, '2-4-2 Fox Trot', which blends the repetitive refrain with their heavy electric guitar sound and the chatter between a pilot and a control tower punctuated by whooshing jet sounds. Another side of their ability is shown in 'Wild Mountain Thyme', a folk ballad in which The Byrds sound like a bass-boosted Kingston Trio augmented with some keening violins. 'Mr. Spaceman' blends an inane idea with some Dylan-derivative lyrics for a strangely interesting result. 'Captain Soul' is a foot-stomping rhythm and blues instrumental."

Fifth Dimension

A1 '5D (Fifth Dimension)' (J. MCGUINN)
A2 'Wild Mountain Thyme' (J. MCGUINN/C. HILLMAN/M. CLARKE/D. CROSBY)
A3 'Mr. Spaceman' (J. MCGUINN)
A4 'I See You' (J. MCGUINN/D. CROSBY)
A5 ''What's Happening?!?!' (D. CROSBY)
A6 'I Come and Stand At Every Door' (N. HIKMET)
B1 'Eight Miles High' (G. CLARK/J. MCGUINN/D. CROSBY)
B2 'Hey Joe (Where You Gonna Go)' (B. ROBERTS)
B3 'Captain Soul' (R. MCGUINN/C. HILLMAN/M. CLARKE/D. CROSBY)
B4 'John Riley' (B. GIBSON/R. NEFF)
B5 '2-4-2 Fox Trot (The Lear Jet Song)' (J. MCGUINN)

US release July 18 1966 (Mono LP CL 2549/Stereo LP CS 9349)
UK release September 22 1966 (Mono CBS BPG 62783/CBS SBPG 62783)
Chart high US number 24; UK number 27
Read more … entries for April 28, 29, May 3, 4, 6, 16, 17, 18, 19, 23, 24, 25 1966

Bonus CD tracks: 'Why' [Single Version] (J. McGuinn/D. Crosby), 'I Know My Rider (I Know You Rider)' (J. McGuinn/G. Clark/D. Crosby), 'Psychodrama City' (D. Crosby), 'Eight Miles High' [Alternate RCA Version] (G. Clark/J. McGuinn/D. Crosby), 'Why' [Alternate RCA Version] (J. McGuinn/D. Crosby), 'John Riley' [Instrumental] (B. Gibson/R. Neff)

"Often sounding like a hive full of super-amplified bees, The Byrds have strongly influenced the rock'n'roll trend toward massively overlaid agglomerations of electronic noisemakers. Incoherence occasionally riles this type of sound, but The Byrds generally seem to control it better than their pale followers." THE LOS ANGELES TIMES, AUGUST 14, 1966

Monday 18
[Unknown venue], Sturgeon Bay, WI

Tuesday 19
[Possibly] Riverside Ballroom, Green Bay, WI

Wednesday 20
'Summer Of Stars 66', Arie Crown Theatre, McCormick Place, Chicago, IL
The Byrds join a list of stars performing here in a 7-Up sponsored summer concert series. Since July 10, The Rolling Stones, The Beach Boys, and a "Folk Festival" (including The Chad Mitchell Trio) have played here, and during the next two to three weeks Henry Mancini, Simon & Garfunkel, The Kingston Trio, and The Beatles will appear.

Starting at 7:30pm, The Proper Strangers and The Cryin' Shames play before the intermission. Ticket sales have been disappointing, with only two-thirds of the theatre's lower level sold (the capacity is 4,300 seats), but still the headliner is well received.

"The Byrds' presentation was lost in the din," reports *The Chicago Tribune* (July 29). "So was their first number. After that, only one song title was mentioned. What need was there for introductions? The teens identified with them, right down to the tight levis, long straight hair, and wire-rimmed sunglasses. They chewed gum in time as The Byrds 'moved' for a full hour. When it was all over, one girl exclaimed: 'My ears are just ringing! Isn't it wonderful?'"

Thursday 21

Tippecanoe Ballroom, Lake Tippecanoe, Leesburg, IN
From the modern McCormick Place venue in the Chicago metropolis The Byrds move to a funky old brick ballroom in northern Indiana.

Friday 22

Mesker Amphitheatre, Evansville, IN
The Byrds with The Corvettes, The Casuals, The Idle Few, Sir Winston & The Commons, and The Road Runners. One show at 8:30pm promoted by WJPS Radio.

Saturday 23

Indiana Fairgrounds Coliseum, Indianapolis, IN
The Byrds pull in more than 7,000 fans for the show at the Coliseum, but this still means the large arena is only half full. Four local groups precede The Byrds, including Sir Winston & The Commons and The Idle Few. (The show is originally set for Tyndall Armory in Indianapolis.) The group is tired after weeks on the road and long for the California sun. The performance is interrupted by a cherry bomb thrown from the audience, but no one is hurt.

Sunday 24

The Fabulous Flame, Fort Wayne, IN
A tired group ends the summer tour with an 8:30pm performance in Fort Wayne, presented by Three Star Promotions. (Possibly, tonight's performance is cancelled as The Byrds may already have returned to California after the Indianapolis concert.)

Thursday 28

◁)) **RECORDING** Columbia Recording Studios, Studio D, Sunset and El Centro, Hollywood, CA. 8:00–11:00pm. Producer Allen Stanton and (presumably) engineer Ray Gerhardt.

The Byrds record the traditional folk blues 'I Know My Rider' (also known as 'I Know You Rider'), which is considered as a follow-up single to the ailing '5D'. Although the song is completed, it will remain unissued until

the 1990s, a fate it will share with the other track recorded today, 'Psychodrama City'. Composed by David Crosby and framed by McGuinn's wobbly lead guitar, this tale of claustrophobia includes a verse about Gene Clark's departure. (Both songs will be made available as extra tracks on the revised CD edition of *Fifth Dimension* in 1996.)

Friday 29

◁)) **RECORDING** Columbia Recording Studios, Studio D, Sunset and El Centro, Hollywood, CA. 7:00–10:00pm. Producer Allen Stanton and (presumably) engineer Ray Gerhardt.

Another day in the studio, likely spent finishing the two tracks from yesterday. This also spells the end of Allen Stanton's time as Byrds producer. No one seems to mind. In a conversation with journalist John Nork, McGuinn, Hillman, and Crosby assess the various Byrds producers with the benefit of hindsight. McGuinn: "They assigned us Allen Stanton, who was really just kind of a square, unhip old guy. He was totally out of it. He was like a caretaker – he would keep me after school, asking me what's wrong with Crosby." Hillman: "Allen Stanton was nothing, he was just a fill-in guy. He was sitting there reading the newspapers while we were making the record. We did it ourselves." Crosby, who bluntly claims that their producers were "all idiots and wouldn't know a song if it bit 'em on the nose" adds: "[Stanton] was Columbia's idea of just having someone there to make sure we didn't [hurt] the place."

Today is the official release date of '5D'/'Captain Soul' in the UK (although it may be postponed until next Friday, August 5). Penny Valentine writes in *Disc* (July 30): "Jim McGuinn's composition will undoubtedly have people straining to catch innuendo, drug addiction and that other nonsense in the lyrics. Strain away. Very Byrds-y guitar and a rhythm that is just like a whirligig at a fair – deliberately moving and muzzy. Hard to tell about this if it's more Byrd-like than of late." *Record Mirror* (July 30) tips it a Top 50 entry: "Very clever lyrics, with the sound-balance pretty much as usual. McGuinn-written, there's something of the old Dylan approach to it – almost as compulsive as 'Mr. Tambourine Man'. Should be a sizeable hit, especially for the care taken with the backing sounds. Flip is a rather uninhibited instrumental."

Record Mirror's Tony Hall has already eavesdropped on a US import a couple of weeks ago (July 16) but finds the single "a bit weird. I know it'll grow on me. But it needs a lot of listening to ... so far, the bit that knocks me out is the long instrumental ending". Of 'Captain Soul', Hall notes: "Imagine a white

version of Booker T & The MGs with West Coast–Indian overtones. Plus a hint of John Coltrane-type jazz."

Derek Johnson of *New Musical Express* (August 5) heads his review "Catchy Byrds" and says: "Very reminiscent of 'Mr. Tambourine Man', with a pronounced Dylan quality – particularly noticeable in the enigmatic lyric and the jangling guitar effect. But it was written by McGuinn. This reverts to the original Byrds sound and is certainly quite catchy, though I'd have thought the British fans had now left this phase behind. Flip: a bluesy plodding instrumental, ideal for dancing. But I always think it's a take-on to couple a vocal [side] with a track like this."

Melody Maker (July 30) is not impressed at all. "Another mumbling dirge from The Byrds that could easily crawl into the chart and hang around for endless boring weeks. Usual Byrds backing, consisting of one or possibly two notes on an organ held permanently down, probably with the aid of a brick on the keyboard, [and] some incomprehensible guitar fumbling while the drummer happily slogs away behind them, probably eating his dinner and reading a newspaper at the same time. A heaving drag, by any standard."

The single is barely advertised, failing to make much of an impression, and never threatens the UK Top 50. Sue Horwood, responsible for PR at CBS in the UK, explains the promotional mechanisms to *Melody Maker* (August 13). "We release 200 [singles] a year, about four a week. They all get equal promotion. We spend as much as we can afford. On every single we do a press release, and 250 have to be sent out every week. Fifty review copies are sent to national newspapers, trades, and provincials. We send about 250 pictures as well."

ALSO ...

Bob Dylan survives a motorcycle crash in Woodstock in upstate New York. An Associated Press news bulletin that runs in several American daily papers on August 2 is short and to the point: "Bob Dylan, 25, singer and songwriter, is under a doctor's care for injuries suffered in a motorcycle accident last Friday." Jim Mosby, speaking on behalf of Dylan manager Albert Grossman, says further: "Dylan may be under a doctor's care for a couple of months, and rearrangement of his fall concert schedule might be necessary." Tellingly, the bulletin ends: "Mosby said he had no details on the accident or the injury, or Dylan's present whereabouts."

By the time the news has reached the editorial offices in the UK, Dylan's injuries are described as a broken neck vertebra and concussion (*New Musical Express*, August 5), while Norman Jopling's review in *Record Mirror* (August 13) of Dylan's latest album *Blonde On Blonde*, notes that "now the chances of seeing Dylan in the flesh for UK fans is even more remote". It will take a long time before he is heard of again.

August

→ Monday 1–Tuesday 2

Derek Taylor describes a busy day at the office, as clients, friends, and business associates drop by his office at 9000 Sunset Boulevard: Carl Wilson (just back from a two-week tour with The Beach Boys), Jack Good, Paul Revere, Ian Whitcomb, David Crosby, and Jim McGuinn.

Wednesday 3

Stadium, Waukegan High School, Waukegan, IL

The Byrds have adhered to a rigorous touring schedule since 'Mr. Tambourine Man' topped the charts, but now the group opts for a different policy. Jimmi Seiter explains: "The way we worked was to fly to a big city, do two to three gigs, and fly home to L.A. We did that for years, actually." Besides the announced performance in Waukegan, 40 miles north of Chicago, the group likely play a couple of other dates in the area to make the round trip financially viable.

Thursday 4

☐ **US RADIO** Radio station WFMT, Chicago, IL. Almanac 9:00pm

Jim McGuinn (but none of the other Byrds) is invited to talk about the impact of rock'n'roll music on this radio show out of Chicago. Presumably, the show is recorded today as McGuinn is in the Chicago area. The others may have returned to L.A. already, as Crosby later describes in graphic detail an early acid trip on a visit to the Whisky A Go Go on Sunset Strip, commemorating satirist and comedian Lenny Bruce's death on August 3.

Sunday 7

Pittsfield Boys' Club Auditorium, Pittsfield, MA

The Berkshire Music Barn arranges the '1966 Folk & Jazz Concert Series' for July and August but, as an appearance by The Byrds expects a larger crowd, the venue is moved to the local auditorium for a sell-out concert.

Roger Ballou, then working on the staff of the Boston Symphony Orchestra at Tanglewood in nearby Lenox, recalls vividly this August night. "I was a classically and jazz-trained musician, but in the rock'n'roll vein had adopted the Byrds as 'my band'. I had all their recordings and had memorised every line, chorus, and instrumental part. I felt somewhat badly for the local opening group, because nobody much cared and The Byrds' equipment was set up behind them. What a distraction! I can recall staring at Michael Clarke's drum set and the wall of Fender amps. After a short set, the locals said their goodbyes to the audience, hustled their equipment off the stage, and were gone. The house lights came up. I recall looking around and again realising that the auditorium was packed.

"After a short break as the stage was re-set and checked for The Byrds, I remember that what happened next took me by surprise. The Byrds' concert began like none other I had seen. I recall that the house lights went down, darkness settled over the audience, and the stage was black except for those little red lights on the front of the Fender amps. Everything was quiet. People were staring forward, aware that figures were moving about on the stage in the darkness. Then, I recall the first twang of a Rickenbacker 12-string being tuned. I knew McGuinn was in front of me somewhere. Then the sound of a Gretsch began tuning alongside the Rickenbacker, and a bass guitar joined the tuning chorus. This was followed by someone settling in behind the drum set and hitting drums and cymbals while making adjustments.

"In the darkness, I knew that The Byrds were assembled before me. All of this went on without fanfare, without some skippy DJ shouting 'Ladies and gentlemen, boys and girls …', all out there in front of me on a darkened stage. When it all began, I was initially stunned by excitement. The Byrds suddenly started to play, and the stage was immediately bathed in light. There they were!

"I do not recall The Byrds' first number. What I do remember is that it sizzled. They were loud, with the guitars high-pitched and trebly over a thundering bass and pulsating drums. The vocals came through just fine. I missed Gene Clark mixing with Crosby and McGuinn, but realised quickly that Hillman was up at the mike pouring in the third voice which shored up the classic Byrds' harmonies. The audience was on its feet; it was what they came for. The sound was electrifying.

"Roger McGuinn wore his granny glasses and stood on the right-hand side of the stage as we faced them. He, like each of the other three, wore jeans and was dressed in dark clothing. David Crosby wore a top hat of some kind, and I think he may have been wearing the cape. He stood on the left as we faced the stage, with Chris Hillman moving in the middle.

"Songs I distinctly remember that night, probably because one of The Byrds gave some type of verbal introduction, were 'All I Really Want To Do', 'Hey Joe', and 'Eight Miles High'. I recall that McGuinn introduced 'All I Really Want To Do' by making some remark about the audience having a choice, The Byrds' version or Cher's. And, on 'Hey Joe', I remember Crosby pulling off an amazing vocal, accompanied by McGuinn's lead, which really shot the crowd to its feet. People were in the isles dancing! The Byrds ended with 'Eight Miles High', not giving any indication that it was their final song for the night. Again, like the opening of their set, it was different and put the audience off a bit.

"Most rock bands during that period ended their shows with their biggest hit, like a big encore. Not so The Byrds. I remember they poured through 'Eight Miles High' with all its complexities and haunting vocals, then kept the tune going with a 10–15 minute jam. McGuinn just devoured the song on his Rickenbacker, and I was amazed at the interesting jazz licks that Michael Clarke began adding. Hillman's bass kept pumping throughout, and Crosby maintained a seething guitar chatter to float behind McGuinn.

"The Byrds were creating in front of me, not just playing. At the very end, I remember McGuinn standing in front of Clarke, the two of them looking at each other in a frenzy of music, pulling everything up into a grand crescendo. Then, without comment, they were finished. It seems they walked off stage one by one, Michael Clarke the last to leave. The house lights came up. No encore, no goodbyes, no skippy DJ saying anything. It was so different from the norm in 1966."

Undated August

Following their brief visit to the East Coast, The Byrds have a few weeks off before their next booking at the beginning of September. At this stage, the group is at a crossroads. They can pursue a pop career with hit singles, or they can develop the direction hinted at on *Fifth Dimension*. They sensibly choose the latter.

McGuinn has earlier talked about the merging of music and science (like his dream to plug his Rickenbacker straight into a TV screen), and so The Byrds begin to experiment with stage lighting. McGuinn talks excitedly to Tracy Thomas of *New Musical Express* (August 26) about a completely new stage act that will be "a combination light show and a freak-out, with the music a mixture of jazz and raga!" The group also has several prestigious concerts coming up, including a residence at New York's premier jazz club, the Village

Four Byrds in the fifth dimension: McGuinn, Hillman, Crosby, Clarke.

Gate, plans for which have been in place since July.

Sunday 21–Monday 22

Two appearances on the East Coast are cancelled, at John Terrell's Music Circus, Lambertville, NJ (Sunday) and the Shady Grove Music Fair, Gaithersburg Music Theatre, Gaithersburg, MD (Monday). There is a possibility, however, that that group plays a weekend in Ohio instead – reported appearances at the Holiday Swim Club, Bexley, OH and Powers Auditorium, Youngstown, OH, remain undocumented.

Friday 26(–Saturday 27)

The Beatles arrive in Los Angeles at 5:00 this Friday morning for the last lap of their fourth North American tour. Before their arrival in Chicago on August 12, they have been threatened by boycott and threats after John Lennon's remark about being "more popular than Jesus" is misconstrued in the American press. Autumn is in the air as the trip proceeds as planned, but the happy and carefree mood of earlier Beatles tours is no longer there. (Speaking to Tom Nolan this week as The Beatles descend upon Los Angeles, Derek Taylor is later ominously quoted in *West Magazine* (November 27): "I'm seriously worried about someone with a rifle. After all, there's no Kennedy any more, but you can always shoot John Lennon.")

Barry Tashian, guitarist and singer with The Remains – one of the groups assigned to open for The Beatles – writes in his diary (published in his tour memoir *Ticket To Ride*) on August 26: "The Beatles are staying in a house on Carson Terrace, up in the Hollywood hills. George gave me his phone number there, so I called him from my room at the Hotel Knickerbocker. He sent their limousine to pick me up and take me over there. What a pad! Very spacious. Derek Taylor [and] his wife and children were visiting. I wandered down the hall and found Ringo playing pool with David Crosby from The Byrds. I joined for a short while and sunk two balls in a couple of lucky shots.

"After dinner, George and I hopped into David Crosby's silver Porsche and headed down the hill into the Hollywood night. First stop was a visit with photographer Barry Feinstein and his wife, Mary Travers. We were talking out on the balcony, which has a fantastic view of Los Angeles by night. The lights were really beautiful. It was a brief visit. Next stop was Jim McGuinn's house. He was really nice and showed us a movie that he'd made with flashes of many colours and abstracts of many shapes. The soundtrack was The Beatles' 'Tomorrow Never Knows'.

It worked very well and George really enjoyed it. Then we drove over to Cass Elliot's house. I met Peter Tork of The Monkees there and had a good chat with him. A nice guy. Denny [Doherty] from The Mamas & The Papas and Jim McGuinn were there as well. Had a cup of tea. There was an excited mood in the air. Some of those present were meeting George for the first time. Others knew him already. I felt like George's old friend, having travelled with The Beatles for over two weeks.

"Later, we went on to Derek Taylor's house where John and Paul had already assembled. Brian and Carl Wilson from The Beach Boys were there. At one point, Derek put on a Byrds record, which rubbed Crosby the wrong way. 'Don't play that!' he said, removing the record from the turntable. It was an interesting group of people to observe – Rock Royalty. The Beach Boys and The Beatles! It was funny – they were very friendly and genial, but really shy with each other. The Beach Boys looked so clean-cut in their button-down madras shirts and khakis. I sat quietly and sipped my orange juice. I don't know how John got home, but I squeezed into the Porsche with George, Paul, and David. It wasn't a long drive up the hill to The Beatles' residence. Crosby drove me back to the Hotel Knickerbocker. What a night!"

ALSO …

Gene Clark begins recording his first solo album at Columbia's studios today with producer Larry Marks. Among the musicians joining in are Chris Hillman and Michael Clarke. Further sessions are held on August 29, 30, and 31, and then on September 29.

•

📷 **FILMING** McGuinn steadfastly pursues various film projects at this time. When he talked to *New Musical Express* in July last year he spoke of The Byrds' ambition to star in a film, and indeed an offer was proposed to make a movie in West Germany (see November 27, 1965) although it was later shelved. Discounting The Byrds' appearance in *The Big T.N.T. Show* (which was more like a regular TV show transferred to the big screen), McGuinn has busied himself with making his own experimental films, just as he promised to *Melody Maker* in May. The home movie with the 'Tomorrow Never Knows' soundtrack is an example.

McGuinn purchases a 16 mm Bolex H-16 camera and begins work on a film featuring The Byrds. "We just started and we have already shot about 800 feet," he tells *Hullabaloo* magazine in October, "of which I think 400 feet are useable." One idea is to use films projected on the rear of the stage during performances. "We can have all sorts of great things, like jet planes taking off." The

location for the shooting is not entirely clear, but McGuinn says in the same interview that it is shot indoors.

Saturday 27

The Byrds have been asked to sing 'O Promise Me' at the wedding of actress Stephanie Powers (star of TV series *The Man From U.N.C.L.E.*) to actor Gary Lockwood, who is busy filming in director Stanley Kubrick's magnificent *2001: A Space Odyssey* (which will not premiere until spring 1968). A lavish Polish-Catholic church wedding is set for September 3 somewhere in Hollywood before bride and bridegroom get cold feet, push the event a week forward to this Saturday, and settle for a simple ceremony on Catalina Island south of Los Angeles – without any Byrds.

Sunday 28

David Crosby spends the day playing pool with John and Ringo up at the Carson Terrace hideaway. At 8:00pm The Beatles, Crosby, and Joan Baez pile into a limousine for the ride to the Beatles concert at the Los Angeles Dodger Stadium.

Tomorrow, the Beatles entourage leaves for San Francisco for the final concert at Candlestick Park. Tired of touring, John, Paul, George, and Ringo will choose studio over stage and never officially perform live again.

September

Thursday 1–Sunday 11

Whisky A Go Go, West Hollywood, CA
Monumentally positioned on a corner of West Sunset Boulevard, Elmer Valentine's Whisky A Go Go is the hippest hangout on the Strip. Valentine's club took its name from a 1940s Paris établissement called Whisky à Go-Go. The place, which has been running since January 1964, usually books a big-name headliner along with lesser-known acts, often hometown talent. This summer has seen the rise of L.A.'s latest musical sensation, The Doors.

Finally making their debut at Whiskey A Go Go, The Byrds appear with The Daily Flash (from Seattle) and The Counts Four (at least for some of the nights).

Despite preparations, the opening night is far from successful according to Pete Johnson in *The Los Angeles Times* (September 3). "The Byrds Fly Below Their Capabilities," runs the headline, and Johnson says: "A wall-to-wall deeply piled crowd clapped enthusiastically after a few numbers, but for the most part the applause was spurred more by politeness than appreciation. Especially during the first set, the group was extremely sloppy. They hit wrong notes, played slightly off-time and occasionally sang bad or thin harmony. The quartet's second set was improved, but still far form the capabilities The Byrds have shown in their records and previous appearances.

"Despite the lapses in harmony and timing, The Byrds stirred some excitement from the audience with 'Don't Doubt Yourself Babe', 'Hey Joe', 'It Won't Be Wrong', 'Baby What You Want Me To Do', and 'Chimes Of Freedom'. They botched up 'Mr. Tambourine Man', 'I See You', 'Roll Over Beethoven', 'Eight Miles High', and 'All I Really Want To Do'. Since most of these are in their standard repertoire, they had little excuse. The Byrds were once a conscientious, creative group, and it is a shame that they should put such poor effort into a public appearance."

Johnson suggests two reasons for the downfall. First is the departure of Gene Clark; second is their success, "which may have lulled them into a self-satisfaction which precludes practicing for appearances". Another very real reason is Crosby, who is dogged by a sore throat.

With Crosby's voice in jeopardy, Gene Clark is asked to temporarily rejoin The Byrds. The idea is not so odd. Clark has been in touch with the group since his departure (Hillman and Clarke having recorded with him just a few days ago), he knows the material, and for many fans, seeing the original five back together would be a big thrill.

When exactly Clark rejoins is not entirely clear, but Johnson's poor review in *The Los Angeles Times* has certainly not delayed the decision. Tracy Thomas, *New Musical Express*'s trusted L.A. correspondent, writes (September 23): "Byrds don't know whether they're flying in four or five-man formation these days. Following their opening (which contained some weak spots) at Hollywood's Whisky A Go Go, David Crosby's voice began to fail, leaving them in a serious predicament for a group that has always had two strong lead voices. The solution: ask Gene Clark to return to the flock for the rest of the 12-day engagement. He accepted.

"Hollywood kids were practically dancing in the street with delight. The password around town was, 'Gene's back – isn't it wonderful!' Well, sometimes it was and sometimes it wasn't; it's been a long time since they worked together. Gene did fill in the weak points in harmony with the strength of his beautiful voice when David's fine voice was hushed to a whisper. The quality of performances was influenced also by sometimes-malfunctioning equipment and the individual moods the boys were in. But when they were good, they were very good."

Daily Flash drummer Jon Keliehor recalls: "Excited to play in L.A., we were performing with vitality and confidence. Despite The Byrds' popularity, it was felt that we easily held the stage, performing at a very high level. However, both bands had common roots in folk music and the songs of Bob Dylan, and as 12-string guitars were being used both by us and The Byrds, any conversations between us would revolve around musical influences and general light banter. The Byrds were cohesive and united as far as I could tell, and nothing was mentioned about a split-up or a new line-up at the time."

To give that little bit extra for the last weekend (September 8–10), The Byrds hire lights operator Tony Martin, known for his lightshows at Bill Graham's Fillmore Auditorium presentations up in San Francisco. David Crosby has witnessed first hand the San Francisco scene, where music and stage lighting create an audio-visual experience, and McGuinn has already expressed interest in working with lights.

Martin recalls: "I went down to L.A. from San Francisco specially for that time at the Whisky. I didn't need a rehearsal, knowing their music and feeling confident about what I would be performing, using two overhead projectors. I spent some time setting up that first day, and then David Crosby drove me around in his new Porsche that he was very happy with, telling tales of the group's flights in a Lear Jet. We joined McGuinn at their rehearsal space and I enjoyed conversing with him, a knowledgeable, well-spoken guy.

"Just before the performance, we all set up, just some soundchecks and spotlight-plus-projector and screen area arrangements. I was there for three days. The performances were full of enthusiasm: musically reaching out, exploring. I thoroughly enjoyed what was happening with my projections, sequencing improvisation with a high yellow and orange palette, with times of deep blue, violet, and green, and alternating rapid rhythm work with slower developments of large and small shapes."

Brian Clark of *The Los Angeles Free Press* (September 30) is on hand this weekend and confirms a much improved Byrds. "It was good; with the added attraction of a real flash of a light show by Tony Martin, brought in from San Francisco for the occasion," Clark also involves Gene Clark in a long discussion about the different circumstances in which artists have to perform: studios, clubs, and concerts. Gene prefers the studio to the stage, although he enjoys the stimulus of a live performance. He talks disparagingly of clubs (where the audience "eat, drink, talk, dance, look for their friends, and leave between sets to be

replaced by more of the same") and describes the poor acoustics, trouble with feedback and echo, and the continually changing crowds as specific Whisky A Go Go problems.

Gene is quick to add that this is not an attack on the Whisky. "It was quite clear that [The Byrds] like the Whisky, its management and its patrons," writes Brian Clark. "They pointed out that they owe a good deal, professionally, to the Whisky and to Elmer Valentine, its owner." With its left-wing leanings, The *Los Angeles Free Press* is not overtly welcomed by a cautious Valentine ("is the Free Press going to smear The Byrds, the Whisky, or both?") when they ask him for an opinion on the club scene. The paper writes: "The Whisky accommodates 300 people. Not too many clubs are larger. The commercial nature of the operation, and perhaps the payments on Elmer's Ferrari, demand that there be a high turnover between sets. The prices are steep and the pressure is on to spend big. Whisky A Go Go is not a place to go at nine and relax and dig the entertainment until the morning – unless you're really flush!"

Monday 6

New single 'Mr. Spaceman'/'What's Happening?!?!' is released in the US. Where the previous single '5D' was released to little fanfare and consequently had trouble even entering the Top 50, Columbia Records intend to fully promote the far more commercial 'Mr. Spaceman'.

In order to stir up attention, the Dickson–Tickner management insures The Byrds for one million dollars against their non-return from Outer Space. The management takes out insurance policy at the venerable Lloyd's of London, one of the world's leading insurance firms. They do this because of the message of 'Mr. Spaceman', which is claimed to be an open invitation to the crews of unidentified flying objects to remove The Byrds from earth.

However far-fetched the idea, Columbia follows with a memo to all its affiliates (dated October 7), which quotes Eddie Tickner: "We live in weird times, and it would be foolish not to take seriously the possibility that there may be a response from outer space." In a later interview with Pete Frame for *Zigzag* magazine, McGuinn is asked about the campaign. "To insure me against being taken off by a flying saucer? That would've been a foolish waste of money. Nobody believed it at the time – they wouldn't have done if a policy had really been taken out, either."

Billboard (September 10) comments: "Off-beat rhythm material with clever lyrics from the pen of Jim McGuinn. Novelty has the ingredients of a top-of-the-charts item." *Cash*

Box, same week: "The Byrds will undoubtedly have a hit with this strong follow-up to their [*Fifth Dimension*] click tabbed 'Mr. Spaceman'. The outing is a quick-moving, infectious, happy-go-lucky ditty with the UFO scene as its theme. 'What's Happening?!?!' is a funky, raga-flecked haunter." *Record World* quips: "Group's new effort is literally out of this world. Reaction should be likewise."

'Mr. Spaceman' peaks at Number 36 in the *Billboard* US charts, marginally beating '5D'. (In *Cash Box*, the single fares better and peaks at Number 34.)

→ Monday 11

⬚ **US TV** [Presumably KHJ Television Studios], Hollywood, CA. KHJ-TV Channel 9 *Boss City*

The Byrds tape an insert for the premiere of KHJ-TV's new weekly colour television show, where ex-*Hollywood A Go Go* host Sam Riddle teams up with the station's radio DJs to present highlights from 93/KHJ's own Boss Thirty (the best selling singles). The show goes out live on Saturdays – with the debut on September 17 – mixing studio guests and pre-recorded film inserts. The extent of The Byrds' involvement or which song is performed is not known.

Friday 16–Saturday 17

Fillmore Auditorium, San Francisco, CA
Bill Graham presents The Byrds with The Wildflower over two days at San Francisco's Fillmore Auditorium, a dancehall on Geary Street.

Since February 1966, Graham has promoted a series of shows here – at first alternating concerts presented by Chet Helms and Family Dog Productions – billing nascent San Francisco groups (such as The Great Society, Jefferson Airplane, Grateful Dead, Quicksilver Messenger Service) with out-of-town attractions (The Velvet Underground & Nico, 13th Floor Elevators, The Young Rascals, and

more) and visiting British stars (for example Van Morrison's Them, and The Mindbenders).

For Graham, the key is to create a unique atmosphere. He has installed a proper sound system, employs artists to design elaborate posters, and hires lightshows operated by professionals who soon become attractions in their own right. He has also begun to present concerts with an eclectic mix; for this weekend's shows one can also experience LeRoi Jones's play *The Dutchman* in addition to The Byrds. Graham's organisation may still be in its infancy, but already he is placing San Francisco firmly on the rock'n'roll map.

Gene Clark is still singing with The Byrds, so the group has revised the repertoire to include a couple of Clark's songs, like 'Set You Free This Time'. After the San Francisco shows, however, Clark parts ways with The Byrds again. His two-week stay is never considered permanent, more a reunion for old times' sake.

Saturday 17

The Byrds are among the many stars seen on the premiere of KHJ-TV's *Boss City* at 6:00pm on Channel 9 in the Los Angeles area (see September 11). Presented by Sam Riddle and co-host Robert W. Morgan, tonight's main draw is a filmed insert with The Monkees on a 'Last Train To Clarksville' excursion. The first Monkees episode debuts on the NBC network this week (Monday September 12) and 'Last Train To Clarksville' has just entered the Top 50, but expectations for The Monkees run high thanks to a large-scale promotional

operation. (Others appearing on tonight's *Boss City* are The Four Tops, Lee Dorsey, The Sandpipers, The Count Five, and The Daily Flash.)

Undated September

Jim McGuinn and David Crosby tape a special open-ended interview for use on radio stations, so local commentators can supply prepared questions to their ready-made answers. The interview is done to promote *Fifth Dimension*, and McGuinn and Crosby comment on selected highlights from the album: 'Eight Miles High' (McGuinn: "So fasten your seat belts and no smoking, please, as we'll be up eight miles high"); 'Mr. Spaceman' (McGuinn quotes comedian Lord Buckley: "The entertainers now are the new clergy"); '5D' (McGuinn: "We like to call it philoso-rock"), and more. Talking about how the group came together in the first place, Crosby says with obvious admiration: "Chris we already knew, he was in a bluegrass group here. Playing mandolin. Got to be a fantastic bass player, I never know how he got from one to the other, cos it's from the smallest one to the biggest one, but he did it successfully." (The whole interview will later be tagged on as a bonus cut on the remastered CD version of *Fifth Dimension*.)

Friday 23

The *Fifth Dimension* album is released in the UK. "Where oh where have all the young Byrds gone?" asks *Disc* (October 1). "Here then are those Byrds with the fresh eager exciting music sounding like tired and disillusioned old men looking back on the happy days. This is a sad sound indeed. The tracks that come off best are the ones already released as singles, namely '5D', and 'Eight Miles High' at least retaining a little of the light. Biggest disappointment is their extraordinarily muzzy version of Love's exhilarating 'Hey Joe'. And perhaps the one true beautiful spark of hope for the future of the Byrds sound – 'Wild Mountain Thyme'. A flower amid the weeds." Although interest in The Byrds has dropped since the first flurry of success last year, the album still makes a credible Number 27 in the UK album charts.

Thursday 29

ALSO …
With the brief Byrds reunion already behind him, Gene Clark returns to the studio to continue sessions for his own album, begun in late August. Chris Hillman and Michael Clarke are again there to make up the rhythm section. One of the musicians who joins the sessions as they stretch into October and November is bluegrass guitar virtuoso Clarence White.

'Mr. Spaceman'

A 'Mr. Spaceman' (J. MCGUINN)
B 'What's Happening?!?!'
(D. CROSBY)

US release September 6 1966
(Columbia 43766)
UK release October 14 1966 (CBS 202295)
Chart high number 36; UK none
Read more … entry for April 29

Since the break-up of his Kentucky Colonels in October 1965, White has been working studio sessions and plays tough and stringy leads on electric guitar.

Jim Dickson, involved in Gene Clark sessions from the sidelines, suggests that Gene should join forces with siblings Rex and Vernon Gosdin to complete the sessions for the album that will be released as Gene Clark With The Gosdin Brothers in January 1967.

October

Saturday 1
Stony Brook University, Stony Brook, NY

Concert with The Byrds and Jesse Colin Young & The Youngbloods. A lengthy review in student paper *The Statesman* (October 4) blasts the headliners. "The Byrds can hardly be described as generally good. They created a mood that relied largely upon heavy amplification and force. They drowned out every thought from our consciousness except ones that stood strictly for or against their type of music. The group commanded attention in the crudest and most direct method possible: loud delivery. They saturated our sensibilities with sound; penetrating us like a sonic boom (depriving us of our bodies) until everything was transformed into sound: no-mind."

Listening to a repertoire including 'The Bells Of Rhymney', 'He Was A Friend Of Mine', 'Mr. Tambourine Man', 'All I Really Want To Do', and others, the paper notes: "Maybe it was the first time you saw them in person. Until now, you heard them only on albums. And it's very different, very, very different when they're there; live, in front of you. It is then that you realise how much they believe in their music, how they feel it, how they identify with it. If somehow you too became a part of this identity, it can never be your own in any real sense because it forces itself upon you, driving you out of your body."

Tuesday 4–Sunday 16
The Village Gate, New York City, NY

The Byrds are given the prestige of being the first rock group to appear at Art D'Lugoff's esteemed New York jazz club. The summer and autumn programme puts The Byrds in the honourable company of Lou Rawls, Herbie Mann, Muddy Waters, Art Blakey, Fats Domino, Dizzy Gillespie, Carmen McRae, and Horace Silver. Lothar & The Hand People plus comedian Dave Frye share the bill

with The Byrds, who incorporate a light show to add an extra dimension to the performances.

"Plain enjoyable," chirps *Record World* (October 22), while an undated *Billboard* clipping says: "Opening with a hard-driving 'All I Really Want To Do', The Byrds maintained the frenzied pace throughout. Top number of the evening was their hit version of Bob Dylan's 'Mr. Tambourine Man', the song which thrust them into national prominence. Under the pound-drumbeat of Mike Clark and three rousing guitars, it was difficult to hear the soft voice of Jim McGuinn. But this is their style and the audience wasn't concerned. The Byrds' sound, while in the folk-rock vein, contains a highly complex rhythm line. The group makes use of the Indian sitar raga rock. Included in their act were all of their hit recordings – 'Turn! Turn! Turn!', 'Eight Miles High', and their current 'Mr. Spaceman'."

Pop magazine *Hullabaloo* covers the event. When finally published, several photos taken by Linda Eastman accompany the review. These photographs reveal a new-look Byrds, more attuned to a jazz club than a pop club: Crosby has forsaken the cape and now wears a leather jacket and a characteristic black hat; Michael Clarke is in a raincoat; McGuinn is nattily dressed in a dark jacket and a discreet colourful tie; and Hillman has on a white-chequered shirt. McGuinn also puts away his rectangular glasses for good around this time.

The Byrds are intent on making the Village Gate concerts an occasion by projecting films on a screen behind the stage. Steps are taken to ensure the equipment is in good shape and Hillman has replaced the hollowbody Guild bass with a Fender – presumably the one he used in the early days with the group. McGuinn tells *Hullabaloo*: "Well, the thing is, man, most people know our records and they can sort of sense the words. We didn't want to just duplicate our records. When we do a live show we want people to see and enjoy

something a little different. Otherwise what is the sense of appearing live?"

Many have showed up to see The Byrds on the opening night: rock agitators The Fugs, The Lovin' Spoonful, and Paul & Mary (without Peter). The Byrds seem to draw all kinds of people, as the guest-list for the rest of the week attests: pop groups The Hollies and The Cyrkle; singers Cass Elliot, Phil Ochs, and David Blue; The Velvet Underground, The Blues Project, The Seventh Sons, Peter Asher (one half of Peter & Gordon), actor John Phillip Law, *16 Magazine* editor Gloria Stavers, Dylan's manager Albert Grossman, author Norman Mailer, and psychologist and LSD advocate Timothy Leary. (Speaking of LSD, the drug, which so far has been legal and easily accessible, is prohibited by US law as of October 6.)

British hit makers The Hollies are stopping by New York City as part of a hectic itinerary. Arranging his encounters with David Crosby in an attempted chronological order, Graham Nash recalls in the Crosby memoir: "My first experience with the Crosby vibe was … when I was in America with The Hollies. I was always the one to go down to the jazz clubs, down to the Village Gate, down to the Vanguard, to see all the weird people: Mingus and Miles Davis and Gillespie and Gerry Mulligan. I was walking in the Village one afternoon when I saw The Byrds walking along Bleecker Street, all four of them, and there was Crosby in his leather stuff, with his hat." Crosby has discarded the cape, perhaps because it suddenly looks uncool after someone suggests it resembles Batman's cape in the TV series. *Hit Parader*, however, has made the point that Crosby's garment was introduced before Batman ever came on television (the series premiered on January 12 this year).

Lou Reed and John Cale from The Velvet Underground come and watch The Byrds, and Reed is impressed with McGuinn's extended guitar work on 'Eight Miles High'. He recalls to underground paper *Open City* in 1968: "I think Jim McGuinn is a very good guitar player, really exciting, you know; to this day, no one has done a better solo than 'Eight Miles High'. I mean, people should really support The Byrds; The Byrds are divine."

The metropolitan press has shown up, represented by the tabloid *Village Voice*, the new underground paper *East Village Other* (which The *New York Times* lovingly describes as "a cross between *The Enquirer* and *The Old Farmer's Almanac*"), and The *New York Times*. Robert Shelton in The *New York Times* (October 7) says: "'Man Against The Machine' might be a suitable title of the unconventional electric and eclectic show that was plugged in this week at the Village Gate. In an obvi-

ous bid to its youthful audience and to the electronic fans prevalent across the country, the cabaret show employs enough electrical equipment to make [New York electric service provider] Con Edison light up with ecstasy. … Heading the bill is a West Coast aggregation, The Byrds. This quartet is probably the first group to have fully explored the fusion of folk music with the rock'n'roll generally referred to as folk-rock. Not content with that widely imitated experiment, The Byrds are now soaring into fusions of big-beat music with Indian raga concepts, jazz, and other forms.

"Byrd-watchers who know the group's subtly controlled recordings may be in for a shock hearing their 'jolt music' at the Village Gate. The quartet has let out all stops with its amplifiers, often to the detriment of its fine vocal ensembles. They bring their imaginative, dizzying electric guitar and rhythm interplay to an often ear-shattering set of climaxes. This

may be done purposefully. The chief Byrd, Jim McGuinn, indicated in an interview his great interest in 'the angry barking' of John Coltrane's saxophone. … Beneath the blare, however, The Byrds are four highly gifted musicians. Their translation of the sounds of the Indian sitar into electric-guitar language is only one of their many innovations. They may draw material from the pen of Bob Dylan, Stephen Foster, Chuck Berry, or even 'swing the Bible' with Pete Seeger's setting from Ecclesiastes, 'Turn! Turn! Turn!'."

Richard Goldstein of the *Village Voice* (October 13) writes: "Face it. The Byrds are just one of those groups which sound better on a $450 stereo hook-up than live, onstage. At the Village Gate, with a warehouse of electronic equipment, a Christmas tree of psychedelic lighting, and enough amplification to shatter highball glasses, The Byrds failed to display their considerable talents. The material was

good, the style was fine, but the music was just too damned loud. Such criticism may seem outmoded in these days of supersonic music, when a groaning eardrum is a sign of a good performance. But the essence of The Byrds' sound is its unique blend of soft vocal and complex instrumentation. Songs like 'Mr. Tambourine Man' and 'Eight Miles High' are ruined when they are blasted beyond the point of comprehension. And that's how they came across at the Gate. In 'Mr. Spaceman' the drums were so loud that the words and melody became practically inaudible. The performance of 'Eight Miles High' shows how many takes must have been necessary to capture that song on record. Performed live it falls apart into musical and vocal compartments – ¬there is no blend. The Byrds remain a group to listen to – to listen carefully to. But there was a fifth Byrd present at the Gate, and his spirit hovered perilously over the group's ability to make music. His name is feedback."

Hullabaloo reports a few weeks later: "Needless to say, The Byrds were great. They didn't come on stage and dance, and jiggle, and tell funny stories. They made music. Their music was electrifying and electric. Big sounds boomed out of their amplifiers and headed straight into the audience, engulfing the room, opening the door, running out into the street, telling the whole world that The Byrds were at the Village Gate. Loud music dancing on electric cables, music written in voltage tied everybody up. It was almost impossible to hear the words The Byrds were crooning, but what was important is that you could hear the songs. They would reach into their minds for a special sound and you could be sure that the next day the papers would write about 'their ingenious method of infusing the sitar-sound into today's popular repertoire'. But at the moment the only thing that mattered was the music."

Tracy Thomas, poring over press clippings back on the West Coast, relays to *New Musical Express*'s British readers (October 21): "The Byrds have just become the first rock group to appear at the noted (and therefore exclusively folk-blues-jazz-club) Village Gate in New York, and amazed all the sceptical jazz critics by performing extremely well."

Monday 10

☐ **US TV** [Unknown studio], New York, NY WPIX Channel 11 New York *Clay Cole Diskotek*

The Village Gate is shut on Mondays so today is a day off, and presumably the day when The Byrds prerecord a filmed segment on Clay Cole's hour-long television Saturday dance show to be broadcast on October 15.

David Crosby, Michael Clarke, and Jim McGuinn outside the Village Gate, New York, October 1966.

Earlier plainly *The Clay Cole Show*, the programme has recently shifted to *Diskotek*. What exactly The Byrds perform on Cole's show remains undocumented.

ALSO …

Signed to a one-record deal with Columbia Records, The International Submarine Band tape 'Sum Up Broke' in New York – a number penned by Gram Parsons and guitarist John Nuese. Coupled with Parsons's 'One Day Week' (recorded on September 14), the single is released to little fanfare and even smaller sales.

Friday 14

'Mr. Spaceman'/'What's Happening?!?!' is released in the UK. Byrds fan Penny Valentine says in *Disc* (October 15): "Ah well, something to make me happy! At last a glimmering of hope that The Byrds may be veering back to the dear Byrds we all know and loved instead of that strange muzzy cotton-wool group of the past two singles." *Melody Maker* (October 15): "One of the best performances the American Byrds have beamed to us across the Atlantic so far, with a happy country and western beat and some ear-catching lyrics, including lines like 'I woke up with flies in my beer, and my toothpaste was weird', or something. The Byrds are demanding a trip with a spaceman and promise they won't do anything wrong on the trip. They won't do anything wrong in the chart either."

New Musical Express (October 21): "Not exactly what we expect from The Byrds, this is a novelty story-in-song with a topical lyric about visitors from outer space. It's a catchy tune with a contagious bounce – it if it wasn't for that rasping strident twang which we associate with this group, I'd say the material was reminiscent of the skiffle days." Of the flip, the paper states: "Good beat, but little melody".

Record Mirror (October 15) tips it for the Top 50, and writes: "Should be a sizeable hit, this. It's all very straightforward, with lead voice telling of the tell-tale signs of unearthly visitors, then everybody in on harmony job for the chorus. Very catchy, totally unambitious most of the way … just happy pop. Flip is slower, but very effective." Despite good reviews and *Record Mirror*'s assertive chart tip, the single never makes it past *Record Mirror*'s 'Bubbling Under' spot (on October 29) in the UK Top 50.

Saturday 15

As The Byrds wind down their residence at the Village Gate this weekend, they can be seen in the New York area on Clay Cole Diskotek on Channel 11 at 6:30pm (see October 10).

Also appearing are The Cashmeres (a resident group), The Blues Project, and basketball player George 'Meadowlark' Lemon of the Harlem Globetrotters.

Undated October

The Byrds' second EP (Extended Play seven-inch) is released in the UK, a handy four-track collection of the group's biggest hits: 'Eight Miles High', 'Turn! Turn! Turn!', 'Mr. Tambourine Man', and 'All I Really Want To Do'. *Record Mirror* (October 15) comments: "Four top sides, a best-selling EP obviously for anyone who missed those gems. Actually 'Turn! Turn! Turn!' is probably the best track, even though it didn't hit here."

Friday 21

Rollarena, San Leandro, CA
Promoted by Bill Quarry as part of his Teens And Twenties dances, The Byrds play two shows (7:30pm and 12:30am) with Bay Area groups Peter Wheat & The Breadmen, Jock & The Rippers, and The Baytovens.

Saturday 22

📻 **US RADIO** Cafe Feenjon, New York, NY WKCR-FM Radio Café Feenjon 12:00pm

A radio show from midnight onwards is broadcast live from Café Feenjon on McDougall Street, hosted by Jim Weitzman and featuring an interview with The Byrds at the Village Gate from last week.

→ October–November

🎧 **SESSION** Chris Hillman and David Crosby are invited to work on some demos for South African singer Letta Mbulu under the supervision of trumpeter Hugh Masekela. Also from South Africa, Masekela fled Johannesburg in 1960 and lived in London for some time before moving to the US. Married to singer Miriam Makeba, Masekela has released several albums under his own name, blending jazz with his African musical heritage. Mbulu has released the single 'Walkin' Around' as Letta & The Safaris on Columbia in July, backed by several other exiled African musicians in addition to Masekela.

Besides acknowledging Hillman's ability as bass player, the Mbulu–Masekela session is momentous as it sparks his interest in songwriting. Hillman says later in an interview with journalist Tom Doyle: "Crosby and I had done these sessions for Hugh Masekela. We had the same manager, and we worked with all these South African musicians. I don't know why Hugh even called us in. David played guitar and I played bass, but the rest of them were real good players, jazz players. We couldn't even read a note of music, but we were working for this lady Letta Mbulu, a jazz singer. It

was an epiphany in my life. I went home after these sessions and started writing songs."

November

Saturday 12

A trip for The Byrds to Chicago is presumably postponed until the next weekend (leading to the cancellation of a booking at the Crimson Cougar, Aurora, Chicago, IL, tonight).

ALSO …

The tensions simmering between youths roaming the Hollywood club land on one hand and law and order on the other finally come to a head tonight. The roots of the conflict stretch back to last summer. In June 1965, two types of dance licence were permitted: one in clubs with a no-liquor policy for the 15 to 18 crowd; the other for 18-year-olds-plus in places where liquor can be sold, provided adequate precautions are taken against serving those under 21.

Since then, the Sunset Strip has become a magnet for teenagers, much to the irritation of local businesses along the Boulevard who feel the area is being degraded and thus driving away their honourable clientele. Youths clog the pavements and cars hold up the traffic. Concurrently, businessmen lobby for a renovation at the intersection of Crescent Heights and Sunset Boulevard to raise new office buildings and to ease the traffic flow.

To counteract the influx of teenagers, the police have recently invoked an archaic curfew law, which yesterday meant the arrest of 80 violators who roamed the Strip after 10:00pm. Adding to the complexity of the matter, Sun-

'Eight Miles High' (EP)

A1 'Eight Miles High' (G. CLARK/R. MCGUINN/D. CROSBY)
A2 'Turn! Turn! Turn!' (BOOK OF ECCLESIASTES/P. SEEGER)
B1 'Mr. Tambourine Man' (B. DYLAN)
B2 'All I Really Want To Do' (B. DYLAN)

UK release October 1966 (CBS EP 6077)
Chart high UK none
Read more … entry for October 1966. (Version of 'All I Really Want To Do' is from the single and not the album.)

set Strip is a separate county outside the jurisdiction of Los Angeles, and is thus under the supervision of the local sheriff rather than the tougher Los Angeles Police Department.

Some teenagers decide that a protest must be organised. They print up and hand out fliers with the message "Protest Police Mistreatment of Youth on Sunset Blvd! No More Shackling of 14 and 15 year olds!" and call for demonstrators to meet tonight at 9:00pm at Pandora's Box – a coffeehouse that unfortunately sits right in the path of the planned extension of Sunset Boulevard to the east.

The Los Angeles Times (November 14) reports what happens next. "The demonstration snowballed late Saturday night when an estimated 1,000 persons [3,000 according to *The Los Angeles Free Press*] jammed the street and sidewalks, throwing rocks, damaging buses, and breaking windows. … More than 40 persons were picked up for curfew violations and six others were arrested on charges ranging from assault to arson. Two police officers were treated for injuries at Hollywood Receiving Hospital after a fight with two marines. The rioting broke out after the youths gathered in front of Pandora's Box. … Protesters took to the street at 10:05pm Saturday night when a group of them sat down in the street in front of the nightclub and blocked traffic on Sunset. As [a Rapid Transit District] bus approached, a youth shouted, 'The bus, the bus!' and a score of them boarded it. They broke four windows and squirted the interior with a fire extinguisher. Others climbed on top of it."

Sunday 13
ALSO …
Following yesterday's altercations, crowds of teenagers and curious bystanders gather again tonight. The police come prepared with a large force, armed with batons, bullhorns, and a permit to invoke another archaic legal emergency, the 'unlawful assembly' law.

The Los Angeles Times (November 14) reports: "'You are hereby ordered to leave this arena,' Sgt. Bill Hogue told the crowd. 'You have five minutes to disperse.' The warning was greeted by boos, jeers, and shouts of, 'Gestapo, Gestapo,' but most of the neighborhood was cleared in a matter of minutes … A phalanx of some 100 officers marched toward Sunset, broke into groups of 16, each party under command of a sergeant, and began clearing the street. The street was cleared in less than five minutes."

The night also has its lighter moments, as the *Times* (November 15) reports. "Outside agitators [included] a Sun Valley couple arrested Sunday night while allegedly using walkie-talkies to broadcast anti-police messages at Sunset and Crescent Heights Blvds."

It turns out that the couple, he 59 and she 69, are arrested for suspicion of disturbing the peace after allegedly shouting into a walkie-talkie: "Police brutality! The police are beating up the kids! Are we going to stand for this? Heil Hitler!" The elderly man, freed on bail, explains to the Times that he and his wife simply took walkie-talkie sets to the Strip in case they became separated.

New Musical Express correspondent Tracy Thomas reports breathlessly to UK readers in early December: "War has broken out in Hollywood and this is your at-the-front reporter sending her first despatch. … We youngsters are manning the battle stations and don't intend to let our clubs die without a fight!" She adds in the next instalment of her combat report: "Though the past weeks' battles on the Sunset Strip may seem a bit trivial to the outside world, they are assuming monumental proportions to those of us who make a living here. The idea that a long-haired boy cannot go, at night, to a restaurant of his choice or walk to the all-night market on the corner for a quart of milk, and that a 19-year-old girl cannot dance without her parent or guardian, is abhorrent to all of us."

Writer Tom Nolan has interviewed Frank Zappa, Brian Wilson, and Jim McGuinn for a long exploratory feature on "The Frenzied Frontier Of Pop Music" in *West Magazine*, the glossy Sunday supplement to *The Los Angeles Times*'. Coincidentally, it is published (November 27) as the riots take place. "It's all part of the huge logarithmic explosion of the entire universe, or something like that," says McGuinn. "The Beatles have it now, it's all there: jazz, ragtime, Oriental music, electronic music, even Kurt Weill. Protest songs are dead. I don't see that anything is to be gained by marching around with a sign or anything. I have sympathy for those people, of course. And so the hair is kind of a badge, to show which side I'm on: it comes to that."

•

In the days following the weekend rioting, police and businessmen along the Sunset Strip join forces to effectively kill two birds with one stone: first, by revoking permits to the teenage clubs and thus getting rid of what they consider undesirable elements; second, by forcing through a decision to demolish the plot of land where Pandora's Box is situated to clear the way for new office buildings and to remove a traffic bottleneck.

Captain Charles W. Crumly, Hollywood Division police commander, is quoted in *The Los Angeles Times* (November 15): "There are over a thousand hoodlums living like bums in Hollywood, advocating such things as free love, legalised marijuana, and abortion." This sentiment is seconded by president Allan

Adler of the Sunset Plaza Association, which represents 55 merchants on Sunset Boulevard: "It is now incumbent on the city to close these kid hangouts and to impose restrictions on the unseemly behaviour of the few who cause the trouble." Suddenly, the permits of Sunset Strip clubs the Galaxy, Whisky A Go Go, and Gazzarri's are in jeopardy as police, city officials, and lawyers fight over the future of the clubs.

Friday 18
The Green Gorilla, Chicago, IL
The Byrds leave the turmoil on Sunset Strip and fly out for a weekend of club dates in Chicago. Appearing with them tonight is local group The Squires.

Saturday 19
The Cellar, Arlington Heights, IL
The Cellar is a very popular but small club in suburban Chicago, and this performance by The Byrds is possibly moved to Arlington High School to accommodate the large crowds.

ALSO …
Hollywood is wracked by a second weekend of trouble, starting Friday as 1,000 persons mill about the Sunset Strip before 400 of these march down the street and gather in front of Pandora's Box. On Saturday night, more than 1,000 youngsters peacefully convene on Sunset Boulevard again, but scuffles are few, despite the fact that 250 police are on patrol.

Saturday 26
The media coverage of the Sunset Strip rioting has alerted a variety of sympathisers. *The Los Angeles Times* (November 27 and 28), by now more balanced in its reports as the conflict moves into its third week, writes of clergymen, left-wingers, representatives of militant groups, and adults wearing armbands marked 'Volunteer Parents' mixing with the youths. The crowd is estimated at 2,000 youths and among the many arrests is Peter Fonda, who explains that he is here to make a documentary film on teenagers. He is promptly released. Escaping the arm of the law are David Crosby and actor Brandon de Wilde, both of whom are taking part in Fonda's film.

•

Despite the many protests by city officials and the police, Whisky A Go Go, Gazzarri's, and the Galaxy are given renewed permits by the County Public Welfare Commission in a 4–1 vote. The victory is tainted by the decision by another administrative body, the Board of Supervisors, to ban dancing in youth clubs. "The action does not close the clubs," explains

The Los Angeles Times, "but it denies youths under 21 the right to dance in them, their primary attraction. A county ordinance authorizing such permits, which was adopted less than one and a half years ago, was repealed, effective immediately, by a 5–0 vote."

The riots on Sunset Strip during the last three weeks will scar Hollywood nightlife. Although the main haunts will remain open, Pandora's Box is soon closed down and eventually razed, and by the end of the year other clubs like It's Boss, the London Fog, and the Action will shut their doors. The problem goes much deeper than the closure of a few stray clubs, however, as the incidents shake the vital Los Angeles music scene to the core.

Undated November

✉ **US RADIO** [Unknown studio], Los Angeles, CA KNX-Hollywood *The Young Set*

David Crosby and Roger McGuinn guest on radio DJ Scott O'Neil's show *The Young Set* together with singer Debbie Burton.

Late November

Byrds manager Jim Dickson establishes an organisation to help victims of the recent rioting and raise awareness on police harassment. It is named Community Action For Fact And Freedom (shortened to CAFF). Other prominent board members are: Billy James, now working at Elektra Records; Whisky A Go Go owners Elmer Valentine and Phil Tanzini; Sonny & Cher managers Brian Stone and Charlie Green; and playboy millionaire Lance Reventlow.

Derek Taylor later outlines the organisation's objectives in his memoir. "CAFF was to subsidise, maybe pay for, the defence and (maybe) fines of kids framed by the law enforcement agencies. ... It was the most logical thing in the world that it should have been Dickson who became involved politically, for it was Dickson who had first seen that The Byrds could be ... just a rock'n'roll band but the musical representatives of a whole subculture unrelated to what was passing for the American Way of Life and its many unfulfilled Dreams. [Dickson] brought the whole rotten issue of the Old vs the Young into the open, and eventually curfew enforcement and harassment of the kids grew less and less, at least in Hollywood." One of CAFF's first priorities

is to arrange a fund-raising concert, as *New Musical Express* reports on December 10.

The Byrds, The Beach Boys, The Mamas & The Papas, Lance Reventlow, and actors Bob Denver, Peter Fonda, and Brandon de Wilde make statements pleading for an end to the curfew, and a month-long truce between the police and the teenagers is negotiated in mid-December by chairman Arthur Whizin of the Sunset Strip Fact Finding Committee of The County Crime and Delinquency Commission.

Monday 28

🔊 **RECORDING** Columbia Recording Studios, Sunset and El Centro, Hollywood, CA. Producer Gary Usher and (presumably) engineer Tom May.

The Byrds return to Columbia for the start of an intense two-week period during which they will record a new single and a new album. Columbia has assigned The Byrds a new producer, Gary Usher, who can boast experience as producer, songwriter, and musician. Usher is a Beach Boy associate who has written several songs with Brian Wilson (including 'In My Room'), provided soundtrack to lightweight movies such as *Ski Party*, masterminded The Hondells, a studio surf band creation that scored big with the single 'Little Honda', and has recently produced The Peanut Butter Conspiracy. Usher is assigned the job as Byrds producer on the recommendation of Bill Gallagher, Sales Director at Columbia Records.

The sessions bubble with creative energy and commence with a brand new Jim McGuinn–Chris Hillman composition called 'So You Want To Be A Rock'n'Roll Star'. An up-tempo number with a catchy guitar riff, the song is later boosted by the addition of an overdubbed trumpet line played by Hugh Masekela. A touch of genuine excitement is added when a sea of screaming teenage voices is mixed into the final song, taken from a recording that Derek Taylor made in August last year during The Byrds' visit to Bournemouth, England.

Hillman describes the song's lyric in *Zigzag* (April 1973): "It's not about us at all, in fact: we wrote that when The Monkees came out. We were just being cynical about the way a bunch of people could be contrived into the kind of popularity they got." (The Monkees had their first US Number One three weeks ago with 'Last Train To Clarksville'.)

Referring to the recent studio work with Letta Mbulu and Hugh Masekela, Hillman says in an interview with Tom Doyle: "[It] didn't have anything to do with what I'd been doing in the sessions, but on the second or third day I wrote 'So You Want To Be A Rock'n'Roll

Star' and had McGuinn come over and help me write it. [He] put in the bridge. The first part is something I absorbed from that session. ... That song was just a slight jab at the Monkees. Not at the people, but at the process of taking a contrived thing and making a watered-down version of *A Hard Day's Night* on a weekly sitcom. It cheapened the music. It was never a jab at the four guys; in fact Mike Nesmith was a great songwriter and singer."

McGuinn later told *Zigzag* (April 1973): "Chris and I were working on 'Rock'n'Roll Star' one afternoon at his house. We were looking through a teen magazine, maybe *Hullaballoo*. I don't remember who was on the cover. It was more about the turnover: 'Look who's here this week, and who's not.' And there was a sense of our own ability to maintain the level of success that we'd had."

Tuesday 29

🔊 **RECORDING** Columbia Recording Studios, Sunset and El Centro, Hollywood, CA. Producer Gary Usher and (presumably) engineer Tom May.

'Have You Seen Her Face' is recorded today, a result of Chris Hillman's emergence as a songwriter. Hillman's composition brims with easy-going confidence musically and lyrically. The song marks his lead vocal debut on a Byrds session and features a rare six-string guitar solo by McGuinn. The recent Masekela session is the song's direct inspiration, as Hillman explains to John Nork. "The piano player's name was Cecil [Barnard, also known as Hotep Idris Galeta] and I think Big Black was playing congas. I was on bass, and it was so much fun, and such an easy, free feeling, and they enjoyed what we were doing. ... 'Have You Seen Her Face' really is an outcropping directly from those Masekela sessions. It's those changes and that feel. Cecil played piano, and it [came from that] choppy rhythm and those changes."

Wednesday 30

🔊 **RECORDING** Columbia Recording Studios, Sunset and El Centro, Hollywood, CA. Producer Gary Usher and (presumably) engineer Tom May.

Chris Hillman's 'Time Between' is taped. Faintly resembling something that Paul McCartney might have written, this is Hillman's first ever attempt at songwriting. "I got so excited coming out of [the Masekela] sessions," he exclaims to John Nork, "that I wrote 'Time Between', which had nothing to do, groove-wise, with what I'd been doing all day. ... It's really like a bluegrass tune."

The impressive song also marks another first: Clarence White playing with The Byrds. Hillman will explain to *Zigzag* (April 1973): "I sort of grew up with Clarence; when I was in The Hillmen, we were always bumping into each other, but when I joined The Byrds I lost track of him for a couple of years. Then, around the end of '66, I found him again, living way out of L.A. and playing in country groups in bars and things, playing electric guitar now. So we got him to help us on a couple of tracks. He played real good on them, too." Vernon Gosdin plays acoustic guitar on the track and sings the high tenor part, but Hillman later discloses to John Nork that as soon as Crosby gets wind of this, he replaces Gosdin's vocal with his own.

David Crosby's experimental 'Mind Gardens', also recorded today, represents the opposite of the neat pop structure of 'Time Between'. It's a daring composition beyond rhythm and rhyme that combines Crosby's rippling acoustic guitar and defiant vocal with McGuinn's 12-string taped backwards. "I didn't like it at all, at least, I didn't like the words. I didn't mind the backing track," Chris Hillman says in *Zigzag*. "We fought Crosby on that, but he managed to get it on the album anyway, and it's lousy. What's more, Crosby later admitted that, looking back, he didn't think it was very great either."

The piece is often ridiculed as an example of Crosby's indulgence, but this is unfair at a time when infinite solos on guitars and drums became the mark of true excess – a trend that would afflict so many of The Byrds' contemporaries.

December

Thursday 1

◁) **RECORDING** Columbia Recording Studios, Sunset and El Centro, Hollywood, CA. Producer Gary Usher and (presumably) engineer Tom May.

The group records 'CTA 102', a song Jim McGuinn has written with friend and fellow science-fiction buff Bob Hippard. McGuinn later tells *Zigzag* (April 1973) how he created the song's sound effects. "[This] was a bit more serious than 'Mr. Spaceman' until the end part, where it becomes whimsical. At the time we wrote it I thought it might be possible to make contact with quasars. … We used earphones fed into microphones and talked into them … and then we speeded it up."

As for the gibberish, McGuinn says: "[It] was just nonsense, but we deliberately tried to make it sound like a backwards tape so that people would try to reverse it. We were playing a joke, really, because it was a big fad at the time to play things backwards. … It was

pre-Moog for us; they were in existence then, but we didn't have access to one. We used an oscillator with a telegraph key, and that booming bang that you hear is the sustain pedal of a piano being held down and banged with our fists, sort of a Stockhausen idea."

In January 1968, the highbrow *Astrophysical Journal* (Volume 151) publishes an abstract on "Quasi-Stellar Radio Sources: 88GHz Flux Measurements" which includes an artful reference to the song. "The spectrum of CTA 102 falls off rapidly, giving no indication of an upturn at short wavelengths. As might be expected in this case, we have been unable to detect it; therefore we are unable to comment upon the discussion by McGuinn, Clark, Crosby, Clarke, and Hillman (private communication)." One of the authors, Eugene Epstein, sends the journal to McGuinn, who proudly tells *Zigzag*: "That was the end of the dissertation; he'd put a joke in a very sophisticated journal read by all sorts of crotchety old scientists. He sent it to me with an invitation to come and see him. So we did, and he took us along to this big radio telescope. I really got very elated by it all."

→ Saturday 3

▢ **US TV** Columbia Recording Studios, Sunset and El Centro, Hollywood, CA. ABC Network *The Songmakers*

Producer Stephen Fleischman and a camera team film The Byrds in rehearsal for an hour-long television special to be screened nationwide on February 24 next year. The show will juxtapose traditional composers such as Johnny Mercer and Henry Mancini with modern songwriters such as Burt Bacharach and Paul Simon. Fleischman, quoted in a press bulletin, says: "*The Songmakers* is not just an entertainment show. Rather it is an informational show, in that we are trying to inform the parents of today's teenage generation that these kids have something to say." Reportedly, The Byrds are seen in a brief segment while experimenting with Miles Davis's 'Milestones'.

Monday 5

◁) **RECORDING** Columbia Recording Studios, Sunset and El Centro, Hollywood, CA. Producer Gary Usher and (presumably) engineer Tom May.

For the first time in more than a year, The Byrds return to Dylan's catalogue as they tape 'My Back Pages' today. The song was first recorded by Dylan himself during a marathon session on June 9, 1964 (a day that also yielded four other songs already done by The Byrds: 'Spanish Harlem Incident', 'Chimes Of Freedom', 'All I Really Want To Do', and of course 'Mr. Tambourine Man').

Jim Dickson, sure of the hit potential of 'Back Pages', has persuaded McGuinn to work up an arrangement, but Crosby is incensed. He later recalls to rock journalist Ben Fong-Torres: "It was a formula, it was a cop-out, it was a total backward shot. It was, oh, let's make 'Mr. Tambourine Man' again. It was a formula record, anybody could hear it. It was a piece of shit; [it] had all the commitment of a four-day-old mackerel."

Two different versions are recorded of 'My Back Pages', both featuring an uncredited organ player. The main difference between the two is McGuinn's 12-string guitar solo – one is played straight in his piano-like manner, but for the other he feeds the guitar signal through a Leslie rotating speaker for an organlike effect. The latter is labelled "original single version" but will not be released until the Byrds catalogue is remastered in the 1990s.

Tuesday 6

◁) **RECORDING** Columbia Recording Studios, Studio D, Sunset and El Centro, Hollywood, CA. Producer Gary Usher and (presumably) engineer Tom May.

Two songs are recorded today. 'Thoughts And Words' is another Chris Hillman tune, highlighted by a strong melody, a compelling vocal, and McGuinn's backwards guitar parts. 'Renaissance Fair' is mainly the work of Crosby, although McGuinn receives a composing credit, and it features exemplary instrumental work by all four Byrds. While the guitars weave intricate lines, Hillman's melodious bass effortlessly navigates the song's shifting dynamics. Saxophone player Jay Migliori, a jazzer widely used on sessions by The Beach Boys and others, adds a barely audible part.

The lyric's medieval theme is inspired by Crosby's visit to a real Renaissance Pleasure Faire held at Paramount Ranch in Agoura Hills on April 29–May 1. The event was a fundraiser for radio station KPFK. Judy Sims, correspondent for UK's *Disc*, describes her visit. "[It is a] colourful gathering of stalls and booths with handcrafted merchandise and people in Elizabethan costumes, using Elizabethan speech, vending flowers and jewellery and mead and ale. The faire was spread over a couple of acres of mountain ranch several miles from the city, very pastoral and peaceful. A tiny creek wound through the fairgrounds, and dogs and children splashed in it to combat the intense heat. Three stages were set up (one an ersatz Globe Theatre) where belly dancers, folk-singers, and incredibly costumed actors and actresses entertained constantly. … At one point I was convinced I was experiencing some sort of time warp, that I really was in merry Olde England, and thoughts like that always make me happy."

Wednesday 7

🔊 **RECORDING** Columbia Recording Studios, Sunset and El Centro, Hollywood, CA. Producer Gary Usher and engineer Tom May.

The graceful ballad 'Everybody's Been Burned' is one of David Crosby's strongest songs for The Byrds. The melody is the result of Crosby's experiment with a dropped-D tuning on the guitar and is highlighted by Hillman's outstanding bass playing. Speaking later to Ben Fong-Torres, the composer says: "Chris Hillman isn't exactly a dope, either. He did some things on the bass, man, that nobody up till then had anywhere near enough balls to try. 'Everybody's Been Burned': ever listened to bass on that? It's a running jazz solo, all bass, all the way through the song. Never stops. Nobody else had done that when he did that, man, not from any rock group. No Fender bass player was playing that kind of shit."

Thursday 8

🔊 **RECORDING** Columbia Recording Studios, Sunset and El Centro, Hollywood, CA. Producer Gary Usher and (presumably) engineer Tom May.

A fourth Chris Hillman composition – 'The Girl With No Name' – is recorded today together with Crosby's 'It Happens Each Day'. Hillman's song is about a woman who actually does have a name: she is Julia Dreyer, one of Crosby's friends from his pre-Byrds time in San Francisco, and is married to David Freiberg of Quicksilver Messenger Service. Clarence White plays the guitar solo that gives 'The Girl With No Name' a distinct country flavour. (Like his contribution to 'Time Between', White may overdub his guitar on a separate occasion, and not necessarily today.)

Despite its positive qualities, 'It Happens Each Day' inexplicably will remain in Columbia's care until it is finally released on *The Byrds* in 1990, a boxed set of four CDs. By then the song benefits from a new acoustic guitar overdub by Hillman.

•

📺 **US TV** There is a possibility that The Byrds make a contribution to David Oppenheimer's CBS news special during the November–December sessions at Columbia, where the group is seen performing a version of 'Captain Soul'. An interview with McGuinn is videotaped separately, and the television special is aired next year on April 25.

•

In less than two weeks, The Byrds have quickly and efficiently completed their fourth album. A relieved Derek Taylor delivers two separate reports in *Disc* (December 17 and 24).

"The Byrds have just completed their fourth album," he writes. "It took them 50 hours (spread over ten days) to do 13 tracks. There were two quick rows, no walk-outs, vast inspirational bursts from each of the now-experienced Byrds, and there is no doubt in my partisan, prejudiced mind that it is the finest, by far, Byrd album and probably one of the five best pop LPs of the year.

"[The] Byrds have astounded those of us who wryly love them and offended that ungenerous handful of people who don't – I know 11 who don't; how many do you know? And do any of us know why they don't love them, by completing one song a day in the studios? Voice and music track. This is remarkable for The Byrds. 'Turn! Turn! Turn!', their second US Number One, took 70 takes, or 90.

"One last Byrds story. Involving David Crosby, formerly caped, latterly shorthaired, and always a diplomat. By public-relations-arrangements, a Columbia promotion man came into the control room at the studios the other day, bringing with him Miss Teen Princess Of Oklahoma and her mother. (I leave the personal pleasure of painting your own mind-picture of that curious trio.) Crosby, moving causally across the studio floor like a crazed boar, beat his way into the control room and addressed the three, who were already alarmed. Despite the care and moderation of which Crosby had chosen his words, Miss Teen Princess Of Oklahoma, her mother, and the promotion man thought it would be better if they left. Instantly."

Intriguingly, Derek Taylor specifically mentions 13 tracks, but only 11 will see the light of day, even when the Columbia vaults are later rummaged for outtakes in the 1990s. Hillman talks in an interview with *Melody Maker* (December 19 1970) of a track still laying around. "The old Byrds did quite a few things that were never put out, you know. We recorded a version of 'Milestones', the Miles Davis theme, and a lot of strange things. Columbia still have them in the vaults, and it's a shame that people couldn't hear them."

Saturday 10

'WVOK Shower Of Stars', Temple Theatre, Birmingham, AL

The Byrds head out on the road for a weekend in the South that likely also takes in undocumented appearances on the Friday and the Sunday. Today is hectic anyway, with three performances at 2:00, 6:00, and 9:30pm. The full bill, from bottom up, reads: The Webs, The New Beats, The Rubber Band, Billy Joe Royal, ? & The Mysterians, David Houston, Sandy Posey, Sam The Sham & The Pharoahs, The McCoys, and Roy Orbison – in addition to The Byrds.

Gene Butts writes in *The Birmingham News* following the concert: "The aesthetic Byrds delighted the audience with their music, which they once defined as rambling and rock, but their abrupt departure from the stage caught the audience with its mouth half open and its hands in its lap."

After the rush of recent months – headlining L.A.'s Whisky A Go Go and San Francisco's Fillmore Auditorium, mingling with the New York in-crowd at the Village Gate, and witnessing Sunset Strip riots first-hand – when they come now to play three shows a day with a mishmash of artists in Alabama, it must appear decidedly unhip to The Byrds. True enough; this is the last time they will appear in this type of show.

Saturday 24

In today's *Disc*, Derek Taylor brings the latest news from Sunset Strip in the aftermath of the November riots. "Byrds manager Jim Dickson, president of CAFF, has won permission to hire a 16,000-seat hall for a concert to aid the oppressed on the Strip. So far the line-up for the concert is The Byrds, Chad & Jeremy, Johnny Rivers, Gene Clark, Buffalo Springfield, Ian Whitcomb, Bobby Hart, and others too soon to mention." (The concert is set for February next year.)

Sunday 25

Pandora's Box, the small coffeehouse that has come to the media's attention as the rallying point for the riots, is already doomed after the City Council approved to draft an ordinance condemning the property on November 29. "Without debate, 12 to 0," as *The Los Angeles Times* dryly reports. According to music historian Domenic Priore, the club stays open for one last time tonight in a special acoustic show with Stephen Stills, Michael Clarke, and others. Stills has recently written and recorded 'For What It's Worth' with Buffalo Springfield as a reaction to the police harassment of the Sunset Strip youths. The song will become a US Top Ten hit next year.

The Byrds 1967: Jim McGuinn, David Crosby, Chris Hillman, Michael Clarke.

New single 'So You Want To Be A Rock 'n' Roll Star' peaks at a promising US Number 29 but inexplicably fails in the UK despite promotional tour of England, Sweden, and Italy in February … The group makes exotic flight for one-off appearance in **Puerto Rico** … The Byrds are one of the hoped-for highlights at the **Monterey International Pop Festival** in June, but fail to live up to expectations. David Crosby's free-spoken stage announcements do not endear him to the other Byrds members … Embracing new musical possibilities, The Byrds pioneer **pedal steel guitar** and **Moog synthesizers** on recording sessions for fifth album *The Notorious Byrd Brothers* … Musical and personal differences reach a head when **David Crosby** is unceremoniously fired midway through sessions … In October, Gene Clark briefly rejoins The Byrds in place of Crosby but the arrangement is not set to last – less than a month later, he quietly leaves, followed by **Michael Clarke** who quits just as 1967 draws to a close.

1967

January

Monday 9

The eighth Byrds 45, 'So You Want To Be A Rock'n'Roll Star'/'Everybody's Been Burned', is released in the US today. Taken from the group's two-week creative burst in the studio at the end of 1966, the single makes a decent Number 29 in the *Billboard* charts (Number 28 in *Cash Box*). Surprisingly little is done to promote the single upon release. The Byrds have a clean slate for most of January with neither TV nor press bookings lined up, and alleged live performances in Mexico and in the Northwest on the Canadian border remain unconfirmed but probably do not happen.

The review in *Billboard* (January 14) calls the A-side a "powerful rocker with teen-oriented lyric about becoming a rock star, and the outcome of that stardom could prove a giant".

Although the lyric deals with an outsider's view of the pop business, the message could well be directed at The Byrds themselves. "You're a little insane," they sing, and as if to prove it, the group will break with the loyal Dickson–Tickner management in just a few months. The relationship has been rocky for some time, and it is particularly Jim Dickson's active involvement that causes friction. Simply put, The Byrds and Dickson are growing apart.

Saturday 14

Up in San Francisco, the Golden Gate Park is the site of The Gathering Of The Tribes For A Human Be-In. As thousands assemble peacefully in the park's polo field, the happening binds together the many diverse elements of the burgeoning counterculture: students, artists, Berkeley radicals, hippies from Haight-Ashbury (or 'Hashbury' as a Cali-

---

'So You Want To Be A Rock 'n' Roll Star'

A 'So You Want To Be A Rock 'n' Roll Star' (J. MCGUINN/C. HILLMAN)
B 'Everybody's Been Burned' (D. CROSBY)

US release January 9 1967 (Columbia 43987)
UK release February 17 1967 (CBS 20559)
Chart high US number 29; UK none
Read more ... entries for November 28, December 7 1966

---

fornian newspaper wittily shortens the name), anti-war demonstrators, Hell's Angels, and religious freaks. Grateful Dead, Quicksilver Messenger Service, and Big Brother & The Holding Company provide the music, while jazz trumpeter Dizzy Gillespie wanders about and Allen Ginsberg recites poetry.

"Ginsberg had reason to be tired," reports a UPI press bulletin the following morning. "He had been on stage speaking, dancing, digging blaring rock music, holding up lost babies from the crowd, and finally leading everyone in a Zen Buddhist chant to close the day." Consciously or not, the event marks the start for San Francisco as the musical epicentre of the West Coast.

As the tribes of the counterculture joyously join forces there, Tracy Thomas delivers her latest report on the sorrowful music scene down in Los Angeles in today's *New Musical Express*. "With heavy heart and lagging fingers I type what will most likely be an epitaph for the Sunset Strip scene that began two years ago when the newly formed Byrds added high-voltage and harmony to the gentle tunes of Bob Dylan, while brown leather and green suede-clad teenagers swayed and swirled at their feet. Southern California's surfers combed their long, bleached locks forward, traded their tee shirts and baggies for cords (bell-bottomed) and shirts (flowered).

"But the Strip is going – or is gone. Ciro's, the original rock club, for all practical purposes became It's Boss and then closed when the 'demonstrations' brought about the revocation of its dance permit. The Trip is now the New Crescendo, featuring a Latin band. Pandora's Box will be torn down within three months. The Galaxy was denied a permit to open as a topless club, but is, nevertheless, adult. Next week, the teenagers' last stronghold, the Whisky A Go Go, returns to its over-21 policy. The groups have gone as well. The Byrds have just finished recording what may well be their last album."

Saturday 28

The plans for a European tour by The Byrds are unveiled in the British music weeklies today. At this stage, they hope to play concerts in clubs and ballrooms around England, to be followed by a visit to Scandinavia. Tour opening is set for March 1, and it will be the group's first visit to Britain since the troubled trip in August 1965.

A glance at the British singles charts for this week shows The Monkees at Number One with 'I'm A Believer', while hits by The Move ('Night Of Fear'), The Who ('Happy Jack'), and The Rolling Stones ('Let's Spend The Night Together') sprinkle the Top Ten. At Number Eight and going up is 'Hey Joe',

the debut single by Jimi Hendrix. Although a staple of The Byrds' stage act for two years, Hendrix has based his slower version on an arrangement by folk singer Tim Rose.

•

At the end of the month, Michael Clarke is dispatched to the East Coast for a promotional tour to plug 'So You Want To Be A Rock'n'Roll Star', while the other three Byrds remain in Los Angeles.

While Clarke is away, Chris Hillman's house in Laurel Canyon burns down to the ground and most of his treasured possessions are lost in the fire: his cameras and records, a stereo system, furniture, and even "a poster showing Tijuana in a favourable light" according to a contemporary report. Jim McGuinn, who watches Hillman's house ablaze from his own home, fetches his camera and films the fire, and later sells the video tape to ABC Television for $75. The resourceful Derek Taylor turns the story into a syndicated news bulletin headlined "Filmed friend's burning house". Taylor instructs McGuinn to pass the $75 reward on to Hillman "so it'll look good in the papers".

•

Jim McGuinn was brought up by parents working in public relations and the world of customer surveys and marketing analyses, and it is perhaps this that inspires him to send out an extensive questionnaire to members of the Byrds Fan Club. The teen magazine *Flip*, in an undated article, publishes the results of the survey, noting that 790 members answered the questionnaire within the first week. It turns out that about half the members also belong to other fan clubs, and over half of them call radio stations, asking for Byrds music. About 120 have met The Byrds in person, and of those, 12 did not like them when they met them. Almost 400 have seen them perform live. The average age of the fan club members is just under 16, with two nine-year-old members and two 27-year-old Byrds followers marking the youngest and the oldest. Asked for their top song, 'Mr. Tambourine Man' is the favourite, but 'Eight Miles High' is the one record more fans have bought than any other. The fans are also asked to rate their favourite Byrd, with the results: McGuinn (322 votes), Clarke (251), Crosby (194), and Hillman (192).

February

Friday 3

🔊 **RECORDING** Columbia Recording Studios, Sunset and El Centro, Hollywood, CA.

Producer Gary Usher and (presumably) engineer Tom May.

Johnny Rogan's later Byrds discography identifies today an organ overdub to 'My Back Pages' (see December 5, 1966), which is ultimately rejected.

Monday 6

The Byrds' fourth album, *Younger Than Yesterday*, is released in the US. (This is the stated release date, but it's likely the real issue date is not until the end of February at the earliest.) The title is a subtle rephrasing of the chorus of Dylan's 'My Back Pages', the only non-original song on the album. All songs stem from the recording sessions at the end of last year, with the exception of 'Why'. Originally the B-side of last year's 'Eight Miles High' single, the version of 'Why' here differs from the single and comes from the very last recording session with Gene Clark as an official Byrd (see February 21, 1966).

Unexpectedly, it is Chris Hillman who emerges as the most prolific writer of the band, with four sole composing credits plus one shared with McGuinn. The quality of material is of a very high standard, and so are the playing and singing. *Younger Than Yesterday* will in time be considered a quintessential Byrds album, although it is greeted by a mixed reception upon its release.

In a complex and sometimes rambling analysis of the record, rock critic Sandy Pearlman gets very close to defining the group's unique characteristics (*Crawdaddy* No. 10, July–August 1967). "The Byrds have real formal consistency. From time immemorial they have grounded their music in what are – or what seems to be – obviously regular rhythmic patterns. It is out of this ground that all developments and variations seem to rise – as it were – to the surface. This sound is dense, but not obviously and impressively complicated. That is, it is very coherent; it works because of unity, not out of an accumulation of contrasting effect such as volume changes or syncopation. Here the contrasts inherent in any rhythmic pattern are not at all emphasised. The changes in the basic rhythmic patterns are not necessarily gradual but rather non-dramatic.

"The Byrds' music is not at all progressive. In comparison to, say, Jefferson Airplane, The Doors or The Yardbirds it's awfully calm. It doesn't go anywhere. The resolutions are not dramatic. They don't obviously end anything. Instead they are cyclical. But the cycles aren't closed. It's clear that they could quite probably go on for far too long. It's really nice that The Byrds should stop only when somebody decides to do it. Not when it's necessary. The great Byrds challenge the tradition of the fade-out by making it into a mere decision rather than a matter of pleasure, logic, or endurance. What started out as a folk-rock style on the first album has been turned, via repetition, into a form.

"The formal structure of a constant rhythmic ground can overcome any material," Pearlman continues. "The rhythmic ground is so dependable that once, when lying on a cliff overlooking the Long Island Sound, not so far from where Walt Whitman did it, I thought I heard the earth turning beneath my head and it reminded me of – of all things – The Byrds. That is, The Byrds' music has that sort of dependable self-energising kineticism. It doesn't go anywhere. But it never comes to rest. Turn! Turn! Turn! And that's very strange and also very sad.

"Everybody knows that The Byrds are an odd case. After all, only The Byrds, amongst modern rock stars, have managed to change their status from stardom to cultural heroism – that is, as one 45 after another didn't make it, their quality still kept up. And this maintained the fierce loyalty of the small hard-core of several hundred thousand knowing fans. Not enough to make them traditional rock stars – a category wherein the charisma depends upon the quantity – but enough to keep their name in circulation.

"The Byrds have sounded so bad live that they might as well be in the Stones/Beatles/Herman category. In other words, everybody knows that they could do it well live, if only because lots of folks have seen them do it well. But recently they haven't bothered. The performance quality has become gratuitous. It's as if you couldn't hear them. Because of which, it wasn't worth trying on their party. Except that you can hear them – since nobody screams. And so when an audience refuses to cooperate by screaming, they just ruin everything."

When it comes to actually reviewing the content of the album, Pearlman runs out of steam, after pointing out 'My Back Pages' as a highlight. "The rest of the album continues the mastery over form over an eclectic variety of styles. It is as if The Byrds had developed a modular concept, whereby things could be 'formalised' or plugged into the form."

Richard Goldstein writes in his regular 'Pop Eye' column in The *Village Voice* (March 9): "The most revered cut on the new Byrds album will probably be 'CTA-102', which is a shame. Its mechanised whimsy is overshadowed by an excess of gimmicks, from speeded-up reverbs to banging, scraping notes straight out of a grade-Z horrorflick. It's a fun song the first three times around; after that, you wish the needle would skip onto the real stuff. Which is contained in more ambitious electronic pieces like 'Thoughts And Words', with a finely wrought dissonance and an excellent backup vocal.

"'Mind Gardens' is a David Crosby song with a weak and overblown lyric but a dramatic delivery. The song is built to sound like a chant and the melody is deliberately tuneless, like a child singing to himself. The instrumentation expertly supplements the mood. Both 'Have You Seen Her Face?' and 'Time Between' remind me of *Rubber Soul*-vintage Beatles. 'Why?' is a solid hard-rocker, and 'My Back Pages' is a Dylan song delivered in timeless tambourine-man Byrdesque. It's worth wading through, if only for the refrain.

"There is nothing new or startling on *Younger Than Yesterday*," writes Goldstein. "The Byrds are tighter than ever, and the discipline shows in dozens of musical details, each finely polished so you're not distracted from the music. It's difficult to say where the group's evolution will lead and the album offers no clue. But it's a thoughtful work of consolidation and worth buying on that score alone. Besides, it contains both sides of the new single: 'So You Want To Be A Rock'n'Roll Star' and the haunting 'Everybody's Been Burned', which is, to me, the realest song on the album. One shudders at the thought of Byrds baroque."

While the underground press develops pop critique into full-blown analytical theses, the music-industry papers keep to shorthand summaries. *Billboard* (March 4) writes: "The Byrds will be riding high on the LP charts again with this top rock package. Their current hit single, 'So You Want To Be A Rock'n'Roll Star', is included along with easy folk-rock treatments of 'Time Between' and 'Back Pages'." *Record World* (also March 4) is even briefer: "The latest Byrds single 'So You Want To Be A Rock'n'Roll Star' is the first band on this folk-rock album. 'Have You Seen Her Face' is a pretty rockaballad and there are nine other delectable goodies for the teen fans."

Pete Johnson in The *Los Angeles Times* (April 8) says: "The group is musically adept and the album is a good one, but it would be sad if it served as a monument, marking the end of The Byrds' development. There is little to distinguish it from their previous LPs in terms of creativity." (Johnson reviews the album in tandem with The Mamas & The Papas latest album *Deliver*, which contains the autobiographical song 'Creeque Alley'. Written by John and Michelle Phillips, the lyric namedrops faces and places along the way to the group's formation, with the memorable chorus line: "McGuinn and McGuire just getting higher in L.A./You know where that's at.")

Peter Reilly in *Hi Fi/Stereo Review* (June

1967) makes a point about The Byrds being popularisers (where they are "indeed splen-did") and proselytisers (where they are "moderately effective"), and concludes that it "is an enjoyable and well-made album which, if listened to closely enough, explains a good deal about what is going on around us. I recommend it heartily".

The album also merits a piece in *Time Magazine* (April 14), which says: "The Byrds first took wing as interpreters of Bob Dylan and on their fourth album soar highest with one of Dylan's old songs, 'My Back Pages'. Where Dylan himself sang the disillusioned sermon like a harsh and nasal backwoods evangelist, The Byrds weave it into a more mellifluous and harmonic song. They also chirp sweetly about what seem to be LSDelightful reveries ('Mind Gardens', 'Renaissance Fair')."

Tom Phillips's overdue review in *The New York Times* (August 6) lumps the album together with summer releases by Jefferson Airplane (*Surrealistic Pillow*), The Rolling Stones (*Between The Buttons*), The Blues Project (*Projections*), and The Who (*Happy Jack*). Whereas Jefferson Airplane is described as a breath of fresh air, *Younger Than Yesterday* "is more like a breath of Los Angles air," according to Phillips. "On the whole, it seems to be an uninspired, self-conscious attempt

to do something new. They throw in some avant-garde sound effects on several songs – electronic bleeps and tapes played backwards – but these devices are put to no good use.

"There's also a good deal of intellectual pretentiousness in the lyrics. The sentiments in a song called 'Everybody's Been Burned' are certainly very contemporary, but the words are really nothing more than a string of fashionable pre-packaged notions about alienation, trust, and love. It sounds like a cocktail party

snow-job. Then there's 'Mind Gardens', which is sung free-form with a background of bleeps. And which represents the same notions in the form of a disastrously simple-minded allegory. On the credit side, there is one good original song, 'Renaissance Fair', and a strong version of Bob Dylan's 'My Back Pages'. *Younger Than Yesterday* is a disappointment. The Byrds' *Turn! Turn! Turn!* album of early 1966 was a classic of folk-rock style, but they haven't matched it since."

Saturday 11

The initial idea to undertake a proper concert tour of Britain and Europe is dropped and is instead replaced by a light itinerary with press meetings and radio and TV appearances. The reason for the change is not entirely clear; work permits may pose a problem, or perhaps the group just feels rusty after weeks off the road and with a shaky live reputation. *Disc* today gives details of the forthcoming tour's highlight. "The Byrds come to England later this month to hold a party for members of their fan club and for those who live near London, among 1,700 British supporters who signed a petition demanding the return of The Byrds." The petition is the result of a diligent campaign initiated by Susan Hogg and launched in *Disc*'s readers' letters page last May.

Tuesday 14

In a memo from Derek Taylor to the British press, the latest news from the Byrds camp is relayed. Besides giving minutiae of a "tea party" to be held on February 25 for their many UK fans, Taylor also lets slips that The Byrds have been commissioned by Metro-Goldwyn-Meyer to compose the title song and soundtrack for a full-length movie. Although the title is not yet disclosed, it is *Don't Make Waves*, a comedy starring Tony Curtis, Claudia Cardinale, and Sharon Tate, already filmed on location in Malibu. Based on the novel *Muscle Beach* by Ira Wallach, it is bantamweight in content. The group does not get around to record the title tune until the end of April as post-production on the movie is wrapped up. By then their interest has diminished, so they record no further music for the film.

Taylor's memo also says The Byrds are working on a full-length script for a film to star in themselves and to be shot in Hollywood. Again, it is a lofty idea that never gets beyond the drawing board.

Friday 17

To tie in with the forthcoming UK visit, 'So You Want To Be A Rock'n'Roll Star' (backed with 'Everybody's Been Burned') is released today to very positive reviews. Penny Valentine

Younger Than Yesterday

A1 'So You Want To Be A Rock 'n' Roll Star' (J. McGUINN/C. HILLMAN)
A2 'Have You Seen Her Face' (C. HILLMAN)
A3 'C.T.A. 102' (J. McGUINN/R.J. HIPPARD)
A4 'Renaissance Fair' (D. CROSBY/J. McGUINN)
A5 'Time Between' (C. HILLMAN)
A6 'Everybody's Been Burned' (D. CROSBY)
B1 'Thoughts And Words' (C. HILLMAN)
B2 'Mind Gardens' (D. CROSBY)
B3 'My Back Pages' (B. DYLAN)
B4 'The Girl With No Name' (C. HILLMAN)
B5 'Why' (J. McGUINN/D. CROSBY)

US release February 6 1967 (Mono LP CL 2642/Stereo LP CS 9442)
UK release April 7 1967 (Mono CBS BPG 62988/CBS SBPG 62988)
Chart high US number 24; UK number 37
Read more ... entries for November 28, 29, 30, December 1, 5, 6, 7, 8 1966

Bonus CD tracks: 'It Happens Each Day' (D. Crosby), 'Don't Make Waves' (J. McGuinn/C. Hillman), 'My Back Pages' [Alternate Version] (B. Dylan), 'Mind Gardens' [Alternate Version] (D. Crosby), 'Lady Friend' [Single Version] (D. Crosby), 'Old John Robertson' [Single Version] (C. Hillman/J. McGuinn), 'Mind Gardens' [Instrumental – Hidden Track] (D. Crosby)

"The Byrds have real formal consistency. From time immemorial they have grounded their music in what are – or what seems to be – obviously regular rhythmic patters. It is out of this ground that all developments and variations seem to rise – as it were – to the surface. This sound is dense, but not obviously and impressively complicated." CRAWDADDY, AUGUST–SEPTEMBER 1967

in *Disc* (February 18): "Lovely title. Since they and Terry Melcher split, a certain something has been missing from The Byrds records. This goes some way to getting it back. The sound is still too fuzzy, thank you, but this song has a fascination, especially the jokey part where fans scream terrifyingly near. In an odd way I think this may be why the record is good, because the bad balance and the screaming make it sound as though it was recorded live, and therefore adds excitement."

Melody Maker (February 18) says: "On their last British visit The Byrds were highly criticised – usually with bad reviews. We'll stick to our guns because they're still one of the most original exciting sounds around. Their last few singles have been a bit weak but this is a humorous atmospheric record complete with backing screams and a beaty, sliding fusion of guitars. Good and commercial, and with The Byrds coming over soon it could score heavily." Peter Jones in *Record Mirror* (February 25) awards the single a top score of four stars and writes: "Boys soon tour here which could put this big-beater into the charts. Long intro and bassy, then semi-hidden vocal line – more their old-style sound."

It is only Derek Johnson in *New Musical Express* (February 25) who is a bit apprehensive. "No one can deny that this disc has a sensational dance beat and a stimulating effect, even though it's a bit dated in conception. The Byrds generate a great sound and blend effectively in the vocal – which, by the way, will have considerable appeal for teenagers. But I didn't like the dubbed-in screams, and there's very little melody. Still, their British visit may help. Flip: The era of protest song is not over! Here we have a rippling acoustic guitar backing, folksy quality and a moody depressive feel."

The following week, Paul McCartney spots the song right away when he is a guest in *Melody Maker*'s Blind Date column (February 25): "The Byrds. 'So You Want To Be A Rock'n'Roll Star'. I don't know. I think by now they should be getting off that style of 12-string guitar and that particular brand of harmony. They really should be splitting from that scene because they'll end up finding themselves caught up in it. Dave Crosby knows where they should be going, musically. And so does Jim McGuinn. They know what's happening. They're the only ones who came around to see us in the States. They've done some good stuff on their albums. A funny group, you know? If they go on like this – that's just the same sound speeded up. Dave and Jim know that they've got to put more of themselves into their music. I can't think why it's not happening. They've just got to put more of themselves into it." McCartney, a

keen listener, identifies most of the 12 singles played to him on Blind Date after a few spins, including new releases by Lee Dorsey, Dusty Springfield, The Lovin' Spoonful, Donovan, and Jimi Hendrix ("incredible!").

Disappointingly, particularly in view of The Byrds' coming visit to Britain, the single sells poorly and does not even make the UK Top 50.

Undated February

Phoenix Veterans Memorial Coliseum, Phoenix, AZ

The Byrds visit Arizona for a weekend in February, supported by local group The Spiders – the same group that opened for them in December 1965. Reportedly, the two groups also play the VIP Club in Phoenix.

Tuesday 21

Derek Taylor has arranged for Crosby and McGuinn to speak to Anne Nightingale by transatlantic phone for a feature in *The Daily Sketch*, published February 28. In the end, it is only McGuinn who does the interview, and he is preoccupied by interplanetary life on CTA-102. "We hope to stimulate the star into transmitting further signals by our contribution," he says ("feeling nothing far-fetched about their theory," notes Nightingale dryly). McGuinn adds: "We have reason to believe that any intelligent life form on CTA-102 would probably be smaller than us. We have tried to speak to them by speeding our voices to a higher pitch. This is more likely to simulate the sounds that the CTA people would make."

Wednesday 22

'CAFF Benefit', Valley Music Theatre, Woodland Hills, CA

Since the Sunset Strip riots in November of last year, Jim Dickson has thrown himself wholeheartedly into Community Action For Facts And Freedom (CAFF), the organisation formed by Dickson, Billy James, and others to aid victims of the riots. Dickson's action includes appearing at a public hearing on February 14 called Sunset Strip – What's Happenin' Baby? To raise money for CAFF, promoters Ben Shapiro and Alan Pariser, plus Derek Taylor, organise today's benefit concert with a bill that boasts Peter Paul & Mary, The Byrds, Buffalo Springfield, The Doors, Hugh Masekela, and several speakers: radio personality Elliot Mintz; volunteer attorney Philip Chronis; and director Eason Monroe of American Civil Liberties Union (ACLU).

Peter Paul & Mary's appearance draws the biggest applause, and The Byrds are a little out of practice in their first live performance since the beginning of December 1966. Tracy

Thomas notes in *New Musical Express* (March 4): "The Byrds closed out the first half, playing mostly songs from their new album. Unfortunately, the quartet will do anything for music except rehearse. One felt like introducing them to each other!"

Derek Taylor in *Disc* (March 4): "[The group's] last appearance before flying over the North Pole was in the gala concert to aid the oppressed of Sunset Strip. It was a triumphant affair also starring … Hugh Masekela, a wonderful South African trumpeter. He is tiny and young and full of jazz-beat, and after his own act he and his conga player, rightly splendidly named Mr Big Black [real name Danny Ray], joined The Byrds for 'So You Want To Be A Rock'n'Roll Star'. This six-minute, amplified, Afro-American alliance was one of the great experiences of contemporary music, and it showed an exciting new direction for the better groups who are, everyone knows, bored stiff with their old line-ups."

Chris Hillman unveils a new look in public today: his natural curly coiffure, which has been kept in check for the last two years with a hair straightener.

Although the event is a scaled-down version of Dickson's original plan to hire a 16,000-seat arena (the Valley Music Theatre has a 3,200 capacity), the show is a sell-out. The CAFF benefit whets the organisers' appetite for a grander scheme – an all-day rock music festival to be held in June.

✈ February 23–March 15, 1967: 2ND OVERSEAS TOUR (UK, SWEDEN, ITALY)

Thursday 23

The Byrds leave Los Angeles on Flight PA120 headed for London. Ed Tickner accompanies the group but Jim Dickson opts to stay home. The group travels lightly, without instruments, just bringing pre-recorded backing tapes for television appearances of 'So You Want To Be A Rock'n'Roll Star', 'Mr. Tambourine Man', 'Turn! Turn! Turn!', and 'My Back Pages' (which CBS erroneously and amusingly labels 'Backstage' in an internal memo).

As if to re-enact the story line in 'Eight Miles High', McGuinn films the group's arrival in London with his camera – from the plane's descent and touchdown where a handful of girls await the group, the taxi ride from the airport through the streets of London, and on to the White House Hotel at Regent's Park.

Friday 24

Disc (February 25, but on the newsstands yesterday) dutifully reproduces the highpoints of The Byrds' timetable and serves its readers details of the group's arrival at London

Airport at 6:45am. "They will have flown for 13 hours in the eight-mile-high-air so I cannot presume to anticipate their condition when they come down." The visit is somewhat overshadowed by gale-force Monkees mania: Davy Jones was met at the airport by 800 fans when he arrived earlier in the month, while Mickey Dolenz and Mike Nesmith have sashayed with British pop royalty.

Arriving in London, Crosby meets up with George Harrison, who invites him to the inner sanctum of Abbey Road where The Beatles are putting finishing touches to McCartney's 'Lovely Rita' in a late-evening session that ends past midnight. As one of the privileged few, Crosby is even played the kaleidoscopic 'A Day In The Life' – freshly mixed and completed just the night before.

It will remain a fond memory, as Crosby recalls to writer John Harris in 2007: "I walked in, and they were acting silly and strange and having fun, because I think they were thrilled with what they had done. They knew what they had created. They sat me down in the middle of a room on a stool, and they were laughing about it: they rolled over two of those great big, huge, coffin-sized speakers up on either side of me, and then they played me 'A Day In The Life'. And when they got to the end of the piano chord – man, I was a dishrag. I was floored. It took me several minutes to be able to talk after that."

Crosby is entrusted with an acetate of the song that he will guard closely. "[The Beatles] were way ahead of us," he says to John Harris. "When I was a kid, we'd be standing around in some little burger joint and somebody would put a song like 'Day Tripper' on, and I would get competitive about it. At that stage, I would think, well, gee – we're *almost* there. We could almost do that. I would feel we were almost nipping at their heels. But [they] were so far ahead of everybody. … They had not only stretched the envelope, they had thrown the envelope away. But it was inspiring. All I wanted to do was approach my music with the same freedom."

Meanwhile, in the US, The Byrds are seen on *The Songmakers*, a one-hour TV documentary screened in colour on the ABC network at 10:00pm (see entry for December 8, 1966). Produced by Stephen Fleischman and sponsored by the 3M Company, the documentary focuses on the driving motivation of the song industry and its efforts to tap popular taste to turn out a hit tune. The show examines popular songs from the 1920s right up to brand new material premiered tonight.

Several songwriters of the old guard are interviewed (Henry Mancini, Sammy Fain, Johnny Mercer), while other artists are seen in rehearsal and in actual performances: Dionne Warwick with songwriters Hal David and Burt Bacharach; Judy Collins; Tom Paxton; The Blues Project; The Paul Butterfield Blues Band; The Mamas & The Papas (debuting 'Boys And Girls'); Simon & Garfunkel; blues singer Arvella Gray; blues guitarist Buddy Guy; and Smokey Robinson & The Miracles.

"On several occasions, producer Stephen Fleischman's volatile cameras follow the birth of a song idea to its energetic delivery," claims a preview of the show. "Viewers who imagine today's tunes are the products of rock-brained idiots may be surprised by the intelligent comments of singers Simon and Garfunkel." The Byrds are seen performing 'Turn! Turn! Turn!' as well as trying out Miles Davis's 'Milestones'. (The show will be reprised on July 27, 1967.)

Saturday 25
The Roundhouse, Chalk Farm, north-west London

The rustic Roundhouse, originally built as a winding shed to haul steam trains in the mid 1850s, has been rented by The Byrds to arrange a British-styled tea party for their fan club. Starting at 2:30pm, Jim, David, Chris, and Michael sign autographs, sip tea, drink beer, and chat with the 250 fans in attendance for the two-hour gathering. The Byrds do not perform, but a selection of their records is played.

Music fan Richard Lewis, one of the many who attend the happening, recounts later: "There was an article in one of the UK pop newspapers mentioning the new Byrds album *Younger Than Yesterday*, which was out in the US but not released here yet. The article said that The Byrds were coming over, not to play but to meet their fans at the Roundhouse in north London. It also said they would be bringing copies of the new album with them.

"I went along with two friends who were also huge Byrds fans, but although we saw The Byrds there were no copies of the album. I spotted Ed Tickner and mentioned this and he apologised and took my name and address as well as those of my two friends. Imagine my surprise when, a few weeks later, a promotional copy of *Younger Than Yesterday* arrived by airmail with a letter saying it was from The Office of The Byrds."

Monday 27

David Crosby meets up with Graham Nash at a press reception for American singer Keith, who is visiting London to promote the follow-up to '98.6'. For his next single Keith has chosen to cover Nash's 'Tell Me To My Face'. Nash will recall in Crosby's biography: "The next time Crosby was in England [after the 1965 visit] he was staying at a hotel called the White House, appropriate for David in that it was a good hotel but it was full of blue hair, suits, and tuxedos, so I said to him, 'Listen. My wife and I have an apartment here in town. Why don't you come and stay with us?' He came and stayed with us, and this time I really got to know him."

"So [David and I] got smashed [and] The Hollies were being interviewed. This one guy who is talking to me turns around and asks David, 'Aren't you David Crosby from The Byrds?' David says, 'Fuck off.' I clutched my throat as David proceeded to tell this guy that he was not here as part of The Byrds, he was here as my guest and he didn't want to be asked any questions and the reporter should mind his own fucking business.

"This was a novel approach to doing interviews that I hadn't encountered, you see, because The Hollies would all stand on our heads [in Britain] and do whatever we were asked. We were a good little singles hit-making band and we'd been brainwashed into thinking that this was the thing to do. And here was this guy whom I totally respected who had an entirely different perspective. I decided that this guy Crosby, who was sleeping on my floor, was neat."

Tuesday 28

▢ **RADIO** Sweden Studio 4, Stockholm, Sweden SR *Tonårskväll: The Byrds I Sverige* ["The Byrds In Sweden"]

The Byrds leave London and fly on to Stockholm in Sweden, where they record a live-in-the-studio session for Swedish radio station P3. Using borrowed guitars and drums, the group turns into an admirable albeit ragged performance, running through 'Hey Joe', 'My Back Pages', 'Mr. Tambourine Man', 'He Was A Friend Of Mine', 'So You Want To Be A Rock'n'Roll Star', 'Bells Of Rhymney', and 'Roll Over Beethoven', as well as a snatch of 'We'll Meet Again' sung a cappella. McGuinn, Crosby, and Hillman introduce the songs in turn. Hosted by Ulf Elfving, the show is broadcast on March 29, and repeated in its full length on June 27 as *Popgäster i Stockholm – The Byrds*, now presented by Klas Burling.

The show will turn out to be the earliest surviving example of what The Byrds sound like live in the 60s. 'He Was A Friend Of Mine' will be released officially on the *There Is A Season* boxed set (2006), while the rather shaky take on Chuck Berry's 'Roll Over Beethoven' will be heard on the *Byrds* boxed set (1990).

March

Wednesday 1–Friday 3

Days off in Sweden.

The Byrds arrive in London, February 22, 1967.

Thursday 2

The ninth Grammy Awards ceremony is held at the Beverley Hilton in Los Angeles, recognising achievements for 1966. Photographer Guy Webster and designers Bob Cato and John Berg are awarded the Grammy for the Best Album Cover, Photography, for their work on *Turn! Turn! Turn!*.

Friday 3

MARCH 3, 4, 5, 10, 11, & 12
COLUMBIA RECORDING ARTISTS

Gene Clark
also CLARENCE WHITE

Southside Blues
CURTIS TILLMAN and LITTLE WALTER

Ash Grove
8162 Melrose OL3-2070

ALSO ...

Back home in Los Angeles, Gene Clark returns to the stage for the first time since his appearance at the Whisky A Go Go in June last year. Billed with Clarence White plus The Gosdin Brothers, Clark performs at the Ash Grove to promote the first album under his own name. Tracy Thomas writes in *New Musical Express* (March 18): "The house was full and appreciative of Gene's soft, gently cracking voice and a flock of newly (and well-) written folk-country-Dylan-Donovan-type songs, each more beautiful than the last."

→ Saturday 4

◻ **EURO TV** Sweden Stockholm, Sweden. STV-1 *Drop In*

The Byrds lip-synch (mime) to 'So You Want To Be A Rock'n'Roll Star', 'Mr. Tambourine Man', and 'Eight Miles High' in an empty Stockholm television studio. The group is equipped with borrowed instruments for the performance (likely brought over from London), and while McGuinn and Crosby each strum their preferred Rickenbacker and Gretsch models, Hillman is outfitted with an odd Fender hybrid with a square headstock. Intriguingly, the Swedes have inserted some undated and rare footage from 1965 that has not been screened before. The show is broadcast on Sunday March 5. (The three performances will be made available on the bonus DVD with the 2007 boxed set *There Is A Season*.)

The European itinerary originally includes a three-day visit to Copenhagen and Denmark (set for March 3–5) but this is cancelled as The Byrds fly straight from Stockholm to Italy.

Sunday 5–Wednesday 8

◻ **EURO TV** Italy Studio 3, Corso Sempione, Milan, Italy Radiotelevisione Italiana (RAI) *Diamoci Del Tu*

The Byrds are in Milan, primarily to pre-record an appearance on TV but also to talk to the music press. *Diamoci Del Tu* (translated roughly as "We give ourselves to you") is RAI's grand investment in the teenage market, produced by Romolo Siena and presented by popular pop singers Caterina Caselli and Giorgio Gaber. Besides showing off Italian singers and visiting pop stars, the show intends to offer a critical look at the pop scene and mod culture. The Byrds choose to promote 'Mr. Spaceman' rather than 'So You Want To Be A Rock'n'Roll Star' as this is their most recent single on the Italian market. Their insert is screened in the second instalment of the series on April 3.

Despite the efforts and good intentions to present something new, *Diamoci Del Tu* is given the thumbs-down in the press. *L'Unità* (April 5) calls the second show a "Tribune Of Bad Taste" and writes: "The second nose-dive of *Diamoci Del Tu* has confirmed all the limitations and defects of the debut show. In fact, we could say that the show has become worse and leaves little hope of improvement for the next instalments." Although *L'Unità* is the party organ of the Communist party and inclined to criticise anything to do with a government-run TV station, *Il Giorno* (March 28) is not much kinder, lamenting: "There is nothing new under the sun." The show is taken off the air after the initial six episodes are screened.

Thursday 9

On their way to Britain again, The Byrds stop over in the Netherlands.

Friday 10

The Byrds return to the UK at 9:55pm on flight BE439 from Amsterdam and reside at Regent House, Regent Street, for the rest of their London stay.

Saturday 11

▭ **UK RADIO** Studio B6, Broadcasting House, central London, England BBC Light Programme *Where It's At* 4:00pm

Crosby is a guest on DJ Chris Denning's weekend show, which runs non-stop for 90 minutes and is a mixture of pop records and gossip, news, and interviews, plus inserts by DJ Kenny Everett. Crosby tapes his insert between 3:00–3:25pm.

Sunday 12

A tentative appearance for the group tonight on *The Eamonn Andrews Show*, a popular British talk show with music on ITV, is cancelled.

Monday 13

The Byrds are provisionally booked to guest today on the BBC Light Programme's *Monday*, but the corporation books the group for tomorrow's *Pop Inn* instead.

•

Eddie Tickner seems to have a challenge arranging press interviews on behalf of The Byrds and has to resort to half-threats. *Melody Maker*'s 'The Raver' column chides (March 25): "Loser manager still rings *MM* to ask how much it costs to insert a feature on their group. Subtle PR quote: 'Of course, when we are Number One we won't need you anyway.'"

Nonetheless, McGuinn is invited to fill in the form of *Melody Maker*'s weekly 'Pop Think In' column, published in the paper's March 25 issue. The idea is simple: the week's candidate is asked to reply on a series of subjects, and while many pop stars spend paragraphs to show off their eloquence, McGuinn opts for singular replies. To Folk-rock he replies "Absurdity"; to Harmony, "Bach"; to Philoso-rock, "The coming thing"; to Flying, "Scrambled eggs"; to The Bomb, "Flowers"; and so on.

Tickner manages to arrange a photo-session and an interview with Bill Harry of *Record Mirror* (April 1). It is an interview with Tickner, as the group reluctantly cooperates for the photo shoot but any talking is left to the manager, who confesses: "They're a difficult group to handle." Harry writes: "When they went for a photo-session with Nicky Wright, chaos once again reigned. Chris Hillman kept disappearing during the session whilst Jim McGuinn whiled away his time carving holes in the wall with a flick-knife. Difficult characters? Oddball personalities? Perhaps this is where their charm lies, for despite his aggravations, photographer Nicky admitted to me that he liked the boys. The Byrds session was definitely the most difficult assignment I've ever had – in fact it was almost a waste of time – but I must admit that I like the boys personally."

Tickner lectures Harry on a new phenomenon. "A new trend in America is presenting Allen Ginsberg-type poetry to music and using four-letter words in songs. One group is called The Fugs and their music can't be played on the radio. Perhaps it's curiosity that has led people to buy 10,000 copies of their first album."

Harry's piece does not go unnoticed. "Byrds, Byrds, Byrds," he sighs a few weeks later (*Record Mirror* April 29). "The letters have been pouring in about them following my recent article." One reader describe The Byrds as "a fresh breeze in the might of a storm of bad air" while another says "they are phantasmagorical". A third writes: "They have borne most of the constructive weight of the development of folk-rock, philoso-rock,

→ An arrow denotes an estimated date.

The Byrds at London's Roundhouse, February 25, 1967.

good-time, raga and neo-jazz." These opinions typify the many faithful British Byrds fans who pepper the reader's letter pages in the UK music press during 1967.

Back in the US, the group's ninth single is released today, coupling 'My Back Pages' with 'Renaissance Fair' from *Younger Than Yesterday*. Despite Jim Dickson's diminishing role as manager, he is the one who persuaded The Byrds to use the song in the first place and has campaigned for its release as a single. McGuinn says later to journalist John Nork: "I was driving up Laurel Canyon and [Dickson and I] both had Porsches. He pulled up next to me in his, rolled down the window, and said, 'Hey, Jim! You guys ought to do 'My Back Pages', the right song.' So I went home and got the record and checked it out and learned it and rearranged it." Derek Taylor, always there to champion The Byrds, tells British readers that 'My Back Pages' is the most-requested-record on local radio stations in Los Angeles. The single makes Number 30 on the *Billboard* charts (and 26 in *Cash Box*).

Billboard (March 18) tips the single for the

Top 20. "With a Bob Dylan number, the group returns to the sound of their earlier hits, and this plaintive folk-rocker should match their success by climbing right to the top of the Hot 100." *Record World* (March 18) notes briefly: "The Byrds have chosen another Bob Dylan tune to chant and the kids will fall for it."

Tuesday 14

Speakeasy Club, central London, England

🖅 **UK RADIO** Paris Theatre, central London, England BBC Light Programme *Pop Inn* 1:00–1:55pm

The Byrds appear in person on the BBC's *Pop Inn*, a radio show that is described as a "record mailbag" where visiting guest stars and groups spin records, thus requiring no musical performances. The show is broadcast live as it goes out on the air, and The Byrds earn £10/10s/0d (ten guineas) for their efforts.

When they arrived in Britain two weeks ago, the group decided to arrange a solitary show-case performance in London. The Speakeasy,

situated in the middle of Soho in central London, stays open to 4:00 in the morning and has fast become the preferred in-club for the smart set since opening in December 1966. The Byrds are still able to cause a buzz, and the Speakeasy is jam-packed tonight: Scott Walker, Pete Townshend, Keith Moon, John Entwistle, Marianne Faithfull, The Moody Blues and ex-Moody Denny Laine, Long John

'My Back Pages'

A 'My Back Pages' (B. DYLAN)
B 'Renaissance Fair'
(D. CROSBY/R. MCGUINN)

US release March 13 1967 (Columbia 44504)
UK release May 23 1967 (CBS 2468)
Chart high US number 30; UK none
Read more ... entries for December 5, 6 1966

Baldry, The Pretty Things, songstress Beverly, Gary Farr, The Action, and Roy Orbison's backing group The Candy Man are all there, with Jonathan King hurling unintelligent remarks at The Byrds. *Melody Maker* reports on carloads of visiting American students driving down from Oxford to catch the group. The Beatles have supposedly reserved a table but are busy recording at Abbey Road.

And, as in 1965, The Byrds fail to live up to expectations as a concert attraction. Hugh Nolan writes in *Disc* (March 25): "The Byrds are an exciting, progressive group whose records get better and better and, on the strength of their new album *Younger Than Yesterday*, can be compared favourably with even The Beatles. BUT there seems to be some barrier between the group and British audiences. However good their records are they never rise in the Top 50, and their last visit here two years ago remains the glaring example of a well-thought-of group dying the death after being exposed to critical London audiences.

"Perhaps it was because of their 1965 disaster that this time The Byrds played only one date on their '67 British visit. … And sad to report maybe they should not even have done that. If there was any justice they should have got up on stage and knocked everyone out with the beautiful material they are now doing on record. They should have thought, 'Right, you didn't like us last time so listen to this!' True, they played mostly new material – 'Why', Dylan's 'My Back Pages', Pete Seeger's 'Bells Of Rhymney', and their own 'Renaissance Fair', an LP track they could well release as a single. They did 'Hey Joe' and they did 'So You Want To Be A Rock'n'Roll Star'. But they did not happen.

"Onstage they seemed bored, tired, brought-down and completely out of touch with the packed audience. … Dave Crosby, moustached and wearing a black sombrero, announced the numbers in a vague, take-it-or-leave-it sort of way which couldn't have endeared non-Byrds fanatics. And although they performed the material perfectly adequately – with Chris Hillman in particular doing some nice things on bass – the overall sound lacked the prettiness they reach so well on record. Maybe they should realise what The Beatles are up to and just record, forgetting all about personal appearances. But the sad thing is The Byrds – one of the world's top groups as far as original ideas and making first-class records goes – left Britain for the second time without glory."

Bill Harry of *Record Mirror* (April 1) writes: "They appeared at the Speakeasy Club in London's Margaret Street and chaos reigned. Complete and utter chaos. Capacity crowds of 'faces'; even people like Mick Avory of The Kinks couldn't get in to see them. The Beatles booked a table. The music press turned out in force, and, as far as I'm concerned, it was a damp squib. As a group they are fair, probably less talented than half-a-dozen unknown groups in any major city in the British Isles. An enigma? Yes!"

A somewhat more friendly Nick Jones in *Melody Maker* (March 25) says: "A suspicious audience confronted The Byrds when they played their only gig, an informal affair at London's Speakeasy Club, last Tuesday, no doubt recollecting that rather painful 1965 tour. However, The Byrds have come a long way since all that. Singer Gene Clark has left, and hat-and-cloaked rhythm guitarist David Crosby is up front spearheading that breathy cloudy vocal sound. Lead guitarist Jim McGuinn has developed into a highly original instrumentalist, bending, coaxing, and whining away behind Crosby's forceful rhythm part.

"Admittedly The Byrds didn't really present their act but it was an impromptu gig – and, after all, it's the music that's most important. And musically The Byrds 1967 are too much. They have a pretty, lyrical freedom of thought and form plus a communicative power irresistible to any receptive listener. Dave Crosby's lead vocal stabbed urgently on 'Renaissance Fair' from their forthcoming album; McGuinn's guitar kicked out beautifully on 'What's Happening!?!?' and 'So You Want To Be A Rock'n'Roll Star', while Chris Hillman's bass playing proved devastatingly effective on 'Hey Joe'. The Byrds' sighing vocal sound on 'The Bells of Rhymney' and Dylan's 'My Back Pages' is something unique and, surely, The Byrds are preferable to most of the unimaginative naïve sounds that are inclined to be popular. As Crosby said, rejecting requests for the group to play 'Mr. Tambourine Man': 'Sorry, but that's going too far back.'"

Luckily for readers, it is not *Melody Maker*'s Chris Welch who reviews the concert. He will note sourly more than a year later on the plight of the hapless journalist: "As an example of devotion to duty [I] waited five hours to see The Byrds at the Speakeasy. … It was a case of looking forward to seeing the great group that had made all those great records. And … disappointment."

Wednesday 15

☐ **UK TV** Lime Grove Studios, central London. The Byrds pre-record an insert on BBC-1's *Top Of The Pops*, which is aired tomorrow and then repeated on March 30. For a fee of 100 guineas (£105), the four Byrds mime a performance of 'So You Want To Be A Rock'n'Roll Star'.

Thursday 16

As the group wing their way home to Los Angeles, they can be seen on BBC-1's *Top Of The Pops* (show No 168, at 7:00pm; see yesterday) presented by Alan Freeman. The Byrds are latecomers to the show and are thus unannounced guests on an episode otherwise given over to this week's rather average hit parade: Lee Dorsey, Harry Secombe, Whistling Jack Smith, The Troggs, The Seekers, The Alan Price Set, Engelbert Humperdinck, The Dave Clark Five, and Cliff Richard.

•

Eddie Tickner, fed up after the European tour, resigns and leaves management duties fully in the hands of Jim Dickson for now. Tickner's abdication also marks the end for Rita Rendall's association with The Byrds. Rendall, married to Tickner, has for the two last years been the group's stringent bookkeeper.

With Tickner and Rendall gone and Dickson's paternal care becoming more and more of an irritation, Crosby introduces The Byrds to independent manager Larry Spector. A business-acquaintance-cum-manager of Crosby's actor friends Peter Fonda and Dennis Hopper, Spector has little experience in the music business but wins Crosby's confidence.

Saturday 25

While The Byrds have been away on tour in Europe, Derek Taylor, Ben Shapiro, and Alan Pariser have pursued their plans to stage a full-scale three-day pop music festival in the wake of the CAFF benefit in February. The news of the festival is made public this week with a press release (dated March 22) plus an article in today's *Disc*. The first artists are already in place, and, importantly, the festival site is already chosen. The sleepy town of Monterey, situated less than 100 miles south of San Francisco and overlooking the blue Pacific, is home to the Monterey Jazz Festival, which celebrates its tenth anniversary later this year.

Taylor in *Disc*: "We are holding a large pop festival here in June and we hope you can all come. Tea and cakes will be served and there will be lots of fun in the open air (if wet, in the church hall). Styled 'Monterey International Pop Festival 67', the event starts on June 16 and ends on Sunday night with a concert by Ravi Shankar. … Already booked: The Byrds, The Buffalo Springfield, Jefferson Airplane, and numerous of the tomorrow groups now flourishing on the psychedelic San Francisco scene.

"Monterey on the Pacific is already the beautifully-located arena for international folk and jazz festivals; about 30,000 people can be accommodated over the weekend.

Beach Boys, Stones, Who, Kinks, Donovan are soon to be asked to participate. Fees paid to groups will be moderate-to-high and it should all be great, generally speaking. Specifically, it should be great too because nothing as this has ever been done and if ever pop music was ready, it is now, and there never was a time like the present anyway."

Even if jazz and folk festivals have long traditions in the US, a pop and rock festival is a novel idea and has never been attempted before. So novel, in fact, that when Tracy Thomas conveys the idea in *New Musical Express* next week (April 1), she compares the event to the annual *NME* Poll Concert – which is not a festival at all but a day-long pop cavalcade where pop stars are wheeled in and out to sing their hits.

Sunday 26

Inspired by the Human Be-In held in San Francisco earlier in the year (see January 14), similar happenings are staged in Elysian Park in L.A. and Central Park in New York City today. "Christ is with us here, baby, so is Buddha," declares co-organiser Peter Bergman of the Elysian Park Love-in to *The Fresno Bee* (March 27). "One of the reasons for this is to bring the hippies together. Los Angeles is too spread out; we don't get to meet each other. We want to give California back to the Indians. The Indians are much closer to the land." The day is uneventful, and the only skirmish with the police is when three youths are arrested on suspicion of rolling marijuana joints, which turn out to be innocent banana-peel cigarettes. A local police officer explains to *The Long Beach Independent* (March 27): "What could we do? Book the kids on suspicion of possession of dangerous bananas? They could be picked up on drunk-on-banana charges if they were found banana-intoxicated in a public place."

David Crosby is one of the 4,500 people who wander about Elysian Park, listening to songs, poetry readings, and speeches – and getting the inspiration to write 'Tribal Gathering' about the day.

Thursday 30

Over in Britain, The Byrds are seen on BBC-1's *Top Of The Pops* today (show No.171, at 7:00pm) performing 'So You Want To Be A Rock 'n' Roll Star' in a pre-recorded insert (see March 14 and 15). Reader June Perryman complains in *Record Mirror* (April 29) that "they are a monotonous drag".

Other guests are Cat Stevens, Cliff Richard, Dave Dee Dozy Beaky Mick & Tich, Dusty Springfield, Engelbert Humperdinck, Sandie Shaw, The Alan Price Set, and The Jimi Hendrix Experience (performing their latest single 'Purple Haze'). A promo film with Nancy & Frank Sinatra doing 'Something Stupid' is also shown.

Friday 31(–Saturday April 1)
Winterland, San Francisco, CA

The Byrds, Moby Grape, and Andrew Staples appear for a weekend at Winterland, an old ice-skating rink in San Francisco. With its large capacity of 5,400, the venue is used by promoter Bill Graham as an alternative to the smaller Fillmore Auditorium.

This is the group's first proper concert this year since the CAFF Benefit in February, but they still have trouble adjusting to the demands of a full-blown rock show. They have decided to cut down on the number of live appearances this year, and instead play weekends out of town or the occasional club residence in Los Angeles. Considering this period in the group's career in retrospect, Jim McGuinn explains later to journalist John Nork: "When we first went out on stage, the little girls were screaming because we had a Number One hit, and you didn't have to worry about performing. But when they stopped screaming, they were listening, and that was a problem."

April

Saturday 1
Winterland, San Francisco, CA

Sunday 2
Fillmore Auditorium, San Francisco, CA

The Byrds, Moby Grape, and Andrew Staples switch to Bill Graham's Fillmore Auditorium for an afternoon performance to round out the weekend.

Crosby freely advocates the use of LSD but has the occasional harrowing experience. Writing about one of the occasions on which The Byrds played the Fillmore, he will write in his autobiography: "I was never able to play while that stoned on psychedelics. If I was fully dosed and tried to play, I'd be in another room with a guitar three feet thick, while still onstage with the band I was supposed to be playing with. In one case, that was The Byrds at Fillmore. Guitar strings would turn to rubber, my hands would pass entirely through the instrument, and the audience (if I saw them at all) could be anything from a field of waving buttercups to a pack of howling demons."

Friday 7
Civic Auditorium, San Jose, CA

The Byrds have to stop their performance when the auditorium's PA system breaks down at the end of the night. Gloria Tully writes in *The San Jose Mercury* (April 9): "Luckily, before the breakdown occurred, the important American rock foursome had already performed many of their fans' favourites, such as 'Mr. Tambourine Man', the group's first big hit; 'My Back Pages', another Bob Dylan composition that is the Byrds' current success; 'Turn, Turn! Turn!' based on words from the Bible; and 'Eight Miles High', which unexpectedly closed the show. About 10:00pm, with only one more number to go according to the disc jockey MC, although it has previously been stated the performance would end at 11, the electronic complexities of lead guitarist Jim McGuinn's playing apparently proved too much for the sound equipment and it was 'all over for everybody'." (Opening the show are local groups The People and San Jose's Bogus Thunder.)

ALSO …

Skip Battin, who lately has tried his hand as an actor (appearing in an episode of TV series *Combat!* in February), is back in music again with The Arlyn–Battyn Expedition that starts a spell at Le Red Velour in Van Nuys tonight. Perhaps subtly influenced by The Byrds, both Skip Battin and co-guitarist Bob Arlin (the guy who was responsible for the guitar solo on 'Hey Joe' by The Leaves) change the spelling of their surnames with a 'y'.

Clarence White, meanwhile, has reformed The Kentucky Colonels with his brothers, and they play tonight at the Ash Grove up in Hollywood. Within a couple of weeks, however, they'll disband once more when Roland White accepts an offer to join Bill Monroe's Bluegrass Boys.

•

Younger Than Yesterday is released in the UK to glowing reviews. In *Disc*, Penny Valentine has had access to the album via Derek Taylor since February and was thus the first to review it in the British music press, which publishes her track-by-track analysis on March 4. "It is The Byrds' light from the past darkness of the musical sound. The Byrds' musical progression is an interesting thing to note. First with Terry Melcher they produced a very distinctive, soft, glad, sad sound and did Dylan numbers. Their first LP consequently was a joy and was called *Mr. Tambourine Man*. They had the sound of summer. They changed record producers for a reason best known to themselves and, unfortunately, like many groups who suddenly realise they can write material and are allowed to run wild with their own ideas, ran around with growing pains. The exciting new talent that had been promised was surrounded in a maze of half-crazed recording techniques. Nothing seemed to sell and suddenly their sound developed from delightful harmonies to painful ugliness. Now comes this LP to prove that they are back where they belong with a sound as fresh as cream and sunflowers."

Valentine says of 'Renaissance Fair' that there is "something Hollie-ish about this track, if only that you can hear them doing it, faster". She says of 'Everybody's Been Burned' that Crosby, "he of the cloak and ever-ready smiles, wrote this, a sad vague number that sounds like 'Cry Me A River' at the beginning'. And she finds 'Thoughts And Words' filled with a "weirdly haunting quality … [the] middle break has guitars sounding as though they are being stretched".

Melody Maker (May 13): "If it was possible to hear every note played at a Beatles concert I don't think it would be unfair to say that the sound could or would never be as good as their records. The Byrds usually play before silent audiences, void of screamers, and unfortunately they are all too often condemned for 'sounding bad'. But then it would be a foolish critic who ignored their records just because their live performances were not up to expectation. And if you ignore this album you are not only foolish – but deaf! Naturally it surpasses all other Byrds works, being rich in sparkling ideas, the most incredible feeling, and what's more – beauty.

"The singing and playing of guitarist Jim McGuinn is fantastic, bass man Chris Hillman is positively out of this world, and his enhancement to the lyrics and the feel of 'Everybody's Been Burned', for example, is almost too incredible. The concept of 'Mind Gardens' is just as mind-blowing; the tight, lyrical flow of 'Renaissance Fair' makes one of the most beautiful songs under this sun of sound; 'Rock'n'Roll Star' takes on a dry Mexican sound with the high trumpet of Hugh Masekela; 'My Back Pages' is another delightful Dylan–Byrds amalgamation; and for those of you who dug 'The Lear Jet Song' on the *Fifth Dimension* album, there is another freaky tune about digging Martians, 'CTA-102'. The Byrds are beautiful – there's no other word for it."

Allen Evans in *New Musical Express* (May 20) writes: "This is an exciting album, at times brash and noisy ('So You Want To Be A Rock'n'Roll Star', 'Have You Seen Her Face'), spooky (the science-fiction outer-space sounds on 'CTA-102'); folksy ('Everybody's Been Burned'), weird (the irritating, monotonous backing to 'Mind Gardens'); and pleasant (the soft swinging 'The Girl With No Name'). A lot of thought has gone into this album and it's good because of it."

Record Mirror (May 6): "The Byrds, musically, are one of America's top exports. They may not sell too many records, but there must be many an English group who would like their sort of reputation. Their flowing commercial version of Dylan's very personal 'My Back Pages' is very well performed – but Dylan fans may not – will not, in fact – take to it. The rest of the album is advanced, carefully-produced and recorded pop, with the folk-rock sound brought out again. An LP to listen to." The reviewer awards it four out of five stars.

Tony Hall's regular *Record Mirror* column (April 29) tells readers: "If you have stereo equipment, you must try The Byrds' new album, *Younger Than Yesterday*. I mention stereo because there are things going on in 'So You Want To Be A Rock'n'Roll Star' that I never heard on the single release. What sounded like guitars is actually a very full-throated, melancholy sounding, almost jazzy, trumpet. When you get the LP, try 'CTA-102' at 16 rpm! That gibberishly voice at the end recalls the glorious heydays of the late Lenny Bruce. And if you've never heard Lenny, rectify that omission in your life immediately!" The album makes it to Number 37 in the British album chart.

Sunday 9–Monday 10

Paul McCartney is on a short trip to the States to see his girlfriend Jane Asher and finds room for a 36-hour stopover in Los Angeles. Here he stays at Derek Taylor's place, meets Jim McGuinn, David Crosby, Papa John Phillips and Mama Michelle Phillips, and also attends a Beach Boys session.

McCartney excitedly tells Taylor and the Phillips duo about Jimi Hendrix and suggests adding him to the Monterey Pop Festival. During the two or three weeks since the festival was first announced, some important changes have been made, primarily, during a meeting at John Phillips' place on April 4, the decision to turn the happening into a non-profit event. That night, Phillips and his houseguest Paul Simon tell organisers Ben Shapiro and Alan Pariser that they will only support the festival as a non-commercial enterprise. Either that – or no festival.

According to a press bulletin dated April 10, the Monterey bill still depends heavily on Los Angeles groups and artists: The Mamas & The Papas, Johnny Rivers, The Beach Boys, The Byrds, and Buffalo Springfield have all agreed to appear without fee, and so have Simon & Garfunkel and San Francisco's Jefferson Airplane.

Thanks to Derek Taylor's connections, McCartney, Donovan, Mick Jagger, Andrew Loog Oldham, Smokey Robinson, Johnny Rivers, and Terry Melcher have all agreed to serve on the festival's Board Of Governors.

Saturday 15

▢ **US TV** [Presumably KHJ Television Studios], Hollywood, CA. KHJ-TV Channel 9 *Boss City* 6:00pm

The Byrds and Jefferson Airplane are guests on DJ Sam Riddle's weekly television show. It's possible that both groups appear live on the show as it goes on the air from KHJ's studios in Hollywood, but the exact nature of The Byrds' involvement is not known.

Sunday 16

The Cheetah, Santa Monica, CA

The group plays a special Sunday matinee performance at 2:30pm, open to all age groups, presented by KHJ DJ 'Humble Harve' Miller. The Cheetah is already a fêted New York discotheque, whose owners Olivier Coquelin and Pierre Groleau opened this West Coast version in Santa Monica's Pacific Ocean Park just a few weeks back. Adjacent to the club is a fashion boutique selling its own collection of Cheetah clothes. Despite its role as a sister version of the New York establishment, the California club quickly recognises an opportunity to run a booking policy in line with what is happening up north in San Francisco – a ballroom with a colourful light show that serves local talent. The timing is perfect now that many of the clubs on Sunset Strip are closing down.

The Byrds rise to the occasion, according to Derek Taylor's brief mention in UK's *Disc* (April 29). "I gather The Byrds once again disappointed some of those who saw them either live or on TV in England. A couple of nights ago, The Byrds gave a majestic display at a Los Angeles concert, supplying the battleground with fresh ammunition for argument. It is ceaselessly interesting."

Following the performance, *Guitar Player* (August 1967) interviews Jim McGuinn and Chris Hillman, focusing on their background, their career, and their musical equipment. Asked if he enjoys the Cheetah's light show, McGuinn replies: "Not really, too plastic. Draws attention off musicians; they're getting away from the personalities that originally drew the people. It competes with you. Lightshows should be shown with recorded music. It's a fad, but I think electronic music is in. Electronic music-colour is definitely going to happen."

He adds: "I would like to tell those cats who make amplifiers, they might do well to put in a colour oscilloscope, rigged up so when you play through it, it brings out colours. … I think there would be a big market for it. That way the musicians are actually creating the lights." (Guitar manufacturer Rickenbacker may be listening, as in 1970 they will introduce a 'lightshow guitar' – model 331 – which has a translucent plastic top with coloured lamps responding to different frequencies. McGuinn will eventually play a custom-built species of the guitar, but not until the mid 70s.)

The feature reveals that Hillman plays a Fender Precision bass guitar plugged into a Fender Bassman amplifier with an extension speaker, while McGuinn uses a Rickenbacker 12-string or a Gretsch six-string, run through either Vox or Fender amplification. The group sings through a Macintosh 275 PA system with Altec speakers. As for the unique McGuinn sound, he explains: "I built a treble booster into my Rickenbacker and Gretsch, using the insides of a Vox booster. Occasionally I pick up a local radio station on it."

Monday 17–Tuesday 18

🎧 **SESSION** Jim Dickson is commissioned to produce an album by British actor David Hemmings and calls on the services of both McGuinn and Hillman for two days of sessions. The two Byrds are paired with jazz drummer Ed Thigpen, once of pianist Oscar Peterson's trio, and Gene Clark is also involved peripherally in the sessions. The results are released as *David Hemmings Happens* on MGM in October.

Saturday 22

Marigold Ballroom, Fresno, CA
The Byrds appear for one performance at 8:00pm with The Children, The 5 O'Clock News Hour, and The Family Dog.

Sunday 23

The Pink Panther, Deerfield, Chicago, IL
The Pink Panther is one of several Chicago-area clubs run by Don Manhardt and RHJ DJ Dex Card.

Tuesday 25

📺 **US TV** CBS Network News Special *Inside Pop: The Rock Revolution* 10:00–11:00pm

Although pop music has been an important ingredient of American TV for years, with several shows devoted exclusively to music, it takes time for youth culture to be accepted as anything more than frivolous teenage fun. ABC's recent special *The Songmakers* (see February 24) was an early example of the mainstream news media probing a little deeper into the pop scene, but tonight's one-hour documentary goes one step further by acknowledging the connection between rock music and the blossoming counterculture.

Produced and written by David Oppenheimer, the programme places composer and New York Philharmonic conductor Leonard Bernstein centre stage. He suggests that "perhaps by learning about [pop music and pop

musicians] we can learn something about our own future".

The show features inserts of Herman's Hermits and The Hollies on tour; a snippet of The Beatles; interviews with Jim McGuinn, Frank Zappa, and others; musical performances by Tim Buckley, Janis Ian, The Byrds (riffing on 'Captain Soul'), and Brian Wilson (playing 'Surf's Up' alone at a piano); and news clips from the Sunset Strip riots. In the words of Pete Johnson in *The Los Angeles Times* (April 26): "The program was a smooth compilation of the opinions, language, roots, and ferment currently dominant in pop music, data drawn from a variety of sources. It avoided editorializing and moralizing ('the jury is out on their social ideas'), concentrating instead on the richness and import of the music."

McGuinn airs revolutionary views in his segment. "I think that we're out to break down those barriers that we see to be arbitrary, the big fences that have been built, you know? The walls that will crumble if hit hard enough. And we're out there hitting them. We're cutting them subtly. We're cutting them with laser beams and not dynamite. We're doing other things here. We're cutting them with emotions, which are stronger than fists, and we're getting mass emotions involved. I feel there's some sort of guerrilla warfare going on, some sort of psychological warfare going on. I feel like a guerrilla. I feel good." (The McGuinn interview and the snippet of The Byrds seen in the special were filmed on an earlier, undated occasion – possibly in November or December 1966.)

Wednesday 26

🔊 **RECORDING** Columbia Recording Studios, Sunset and El Centro, Hollywood, CA. Producer Gary Usher and (presumably) engineer Tom May.

The Byrds finally drag themselves back to the studio to record the title song for the MGM movie *Don't Make Waves*. The song lasts barely one and a half minutes, and reportedly this is not much less than the time it took for McGuinn and Hillman to write it. "I think David was involved and we wrote that song in five minutes, literally just whipped it out," Hillman says later to journalist John Nork.

McGuinn in particular has long expressed interest in working with films and projections, but this has a special fascination from his experimental ideas. Although the song marks the group's first venture into the world of movies, the initial idea for the group to provide incidental music is dropped and the job to complete a soundtrack is left to Vic Mizzy. The film premieres in late June and is met with a lukewarm response by critics.

According to session files, the group also

begin work on the new Crosby composition 'Lady Friend' today, work that will pick up again in May and continue in June.

Saturday 29

Rose Hill Gym, Fordham University, New York City, NY
The Byrds are in New York for a concert with Buffy St Marie at 7:30pm.

Sunday 30

Estadio Hiram Bithorn, San Juan, Puerto Rico
From New York, the group flies to appear at this concert in Puerto Rico in the north-eastern corner of the Caribbean. Arriving at the airport and surrounded by a throng of autograph seekers, The Byrds parade in a stylish 1935 Ford convertible model that takes them to the Racquet Hotel Club.

The show is held at a large outdoor baseball stadium. Promoted by Marianito Aratu and sponsored by local radio stations WHOA and WUNO, the concert features support by local group The Soul Robbers interspersed with a dance performance by Elisa & Calin. The Byrds come on stage at 3:30pm for a well-received performance. According to the review in *The San Juan Star* (May 2), it is a mixed audience of Byrd watchers, where an old lady looked "as though she had expected an Audobon Society exhibition" rather than a pop show.

Crosby in his felt hat now sports a Gretsch Country Gentleman guitar decorated with a large red STP sticker. (The innocent-looking logo from the STP motor oil company carries another meaning, as it is an acronym for Serenity, Tranquillity, Peace – the name of a powerful amphetamine mixture.)

Eighteen-year-old Penny Einmo attends the show on behalf of the student paper *Pirate's Pages*. She writes: "The Byrds put on a dynamic performance and thrilled an audience of over 5,000 teenagers. After the show we drove to the hotel. The boys were lounging about in T-shirts and jeans. We had a long talk about music and a variety of subjects. Mike seemed to be sleepy, Chris was shy, Crosby displayed his beard and ran around minus a shirt, while McGuinn was fascinated with looking through his new binoculars toward the airport."

The group flies back to Los Angeles at 11:10pm on Pan Am flight 281 the same night, although Clarke and road manager Jimmi Seiter stay behind in Puerto Rico for another day.

May

Thursday 4
RECORDING Columbia Recording Studios, Sunset and El Centro, Hollywood, CA. Producer Gary Usher and (presumably) engineer Tom May.

According to the discography later assembled by Johnny Rogan, today marks the first of several overdub sessions for Crosby's 'Lady Friend', which will soon become the most complex recording The Byrds have ever made. Over several separate sessions in the coming weeks the arrangement is tweaked, vocal harmonies are fine-tuned, and a full horn section is added.

Saturday 6
The saga of the Monterey Pop festival continues, and while Jimi Hendrix is confirmed today for an appearance, it will take a few more weeks before the bill is stabilised. The Nitty Gritty Dirt Band, for example, is one of several announced acts that for various reasons eventually pull out.

While festival preparations proceed, a nagging conflict of interest between the Los Angeles-based organisers and the San Francisco community is finally resolved. Derek Taylor and Alan Pariser have to go up to San Francisco to get the nod of approval from journalist Ralph J. Gleason, who as co-founder of the Monterey Jazz Festival carries a lot of weight in music circles there.

Taylor will recount in his biography: "The word was that, them being from San Francisco and us being from the land of tinsel, false idols, and broken promises, we were going to have a hard time convincing them we were honest. … [Gleason] was very uptight at first about bringing to Northern California a Los Angeles-oriented pop festival. He was, as he explained, not about to endorse, in *The San Francisco Chronicle*, something crude and exploitative of the burgeoning 'movement'. Like, he didn't want a Flower Power Festival promoted and hyped and skimmed by Victor Vagina Associated of Sunset Boulevard.

"I don't think [Gleason] believed a word of what [Alan and I] said; though we should have been convincing, we weren't. Though we told the truth, we were from L.A. The main objection, as I recall it, was that Alan and Ben stood to make a profit and I was making a nice ($250 a week) salary out of promotion. Gleason said the SF scene was very pure, as pure as reasonably possible given that everyone got some spin-off. But he didn't like all that gold going to Ben Shapiro. … [Shapiro] was finally laid out flat. The festival became a charity trip with artists appearing free, workers (HQ staff excepted) doing it for love and the profits (expected to be half a million bucks) to go to some situation where youth and music coincided, like guitar classes in a ghetto. Ben Shapiro was bought out for five grand and he left with a smile on his face and hate in his heart. Alan Pariser was made co-producer."

With Shapiro gone, John Phillips brings in Mamas & Papas producer Lou Adler as co-director. To raise cash to arrange the festival, Phillips, Adler, Simon & Garfunkel, Terry Melcher, and singer Johnny Rivers all pitch in with loans. The organisers set up headquarters in Stratford On Sunset, a club on the Strip that has been dormant since December 1965. David Crosby regularly drops by the festival office and is often seen there wearing a large furry Cossack hat.

Wednesday 10
RECORDING Columbia Recording Studios, Sunset and El Centro, Hollywood, CA. Producer Gary Usher and (presumably) engineer Tom May.

Second overdub session for Crosby's 'Lady Friend' (see May 4).

Friday 12
The New Place, Algonquin, Chicago, IL
Another Chicago club operated by Don Manhardt and Dex Card, who runs the Pink Panther that The Byrds visited three weeks ago. (Confusingly, there is a Chicago group called The *Bryds* playing Illinois clubs and likely befuddling Byrds fans with their approximated name. It might be that these club appearances are by the Chicago flock and not the L.A. quartet. It should be noted that The Bryds is pronounced 'brides' and that the group later changes the spelling to The Brydes.)

Always a few months behind the American release schedule, the UK record company today issues 'My Back Pages', the ninth single by The Byrds, with 'Renaissance Fair' as the B-side.

Penny Valentine says in *Disc* (May 13): "I really do like this record – mainly, I suspect,

because I have never liked The Byrds as much as when they did Dylan numbers. The Byrds singing Bob Dylan are one of the more comfortable combinations on the pop scene. Ah, I hear the hippies say, but this is a regressive step for the all-progressive Byrds. In fact, they HAVE said it. Well, perhaps, but 'Mr. Tambourine Man' was still one of my favourite records by The Byrds. With the absence of a good Dylan single around at the moment, this should stand a very good chance."

Derek Johnson puts "Dylan song may be hit for Byrds" as the headline for his review in *New Musical Express* (May 13) and writes: "[I] must say The Byrds have considerably moderated their original raucous style. This is a very pretty Dylan song, delightfully harmonised (featuring soloist with chanting), with a fascinating nostalgic lyric. It's really folk-beat, I suppose. Oh, and listen out for the haunting guitar solo. Can't be too optimistic about its chances with all the big-time competition that's around, but it deserves recognition. FLIP: Again, an ear-catching vocal blend – at times like The Four Seasons. Mid-tempo, with an underlying rippling effect, plus a captivating exotic lyric."

The British chart competition Johnson refers to is a mix of American and British hits: The Mamas & The Papas ('Dedicated To The One I Love' at Number Two just below Sandie Shaw's Eurovision hit 'Puppet On A String'), The Tremeloes ('Silence Is Golden', soon at Number One), Jimi Hendrix ('Purple Haze' and 'The Wind Cries Mary'), The Who ('Pictures Of Lily'), The Move ('I Can Hear The Grass Grow'), The Kinks ('Waterloo Sunset'), and The Turtles ('Happy Together'). Also released today is Procol Harum's 'A Whiter Shade Of Pale', which will become the British summer anthem of 1967. In the face of all this, 'My Back Pages' just manages a meagre mention in the 'Bubbling Under' section in *Record Mirror*'s Top 50 on May 20 before fading away.

Tuesday 16–Sunday 21
Whisky A Go Go, West Hollywood, CA
The Byrds, The Doors, and Buffalo Springfield are booked for six solid nights at the Whisky A Go Go. Unfortunately, Jim McGuinn is ill on the first night, forcing The Byrds to cancel the opening and possibly also the Wednesday performance.

Tracy Thomas, who catches one of the nights when The Byrds are back in action, writes in *New Musical Express* (June 3): "Hippie Hollywood turned out in full regalia this week as the Whisky A Go Go booked The Byrds for a six-day stand. They gave one of their most polished performances in months for the wild, packed house. Perhaps they took the many admonitions to rehearse to heart! Supporting Doors group and Buffalo Springfield jammed the old Whisky before The Byrds arrived. Owner Elmer Valentine seemed pleased at the big turn-out for the rock group, but has nevertheless booked The Four Tops and Miracles for upcoming months."

Although Thomas is won over, Derek Taylor reports in near desperation to *Disc* (June 3): "The Byrds, one of the best groups in the world, were again terrible in the Whisky A Go Go here. I cannot work it out. They seem to have a death-wish which is only thwarted by their indomitable heartbeat. They will probably outlive us all. I love them and deplore them."

The Doors have a single, 'Light My Fire', slowly ascending the *Billboard* Hot 100 (it will eventually make Number One in July) and have fast become one of the most popular Los Angeles groups this spring. Their drummer, John Densmore, later recalls in his autobiography: "I dug The Byrds' lyrics, but their arrangements conjured up images of bodies with nothing below the waist. No balls. Their original, 'Eight Miles High', had a nice melody and a hypnotic, electric 12-string sound but the rhythm didn't cut it for me." (The feeling is mutual: speaking to *Mojo* magazine in 2003, Crosby says: "To me The Doors was the band that never swung. Ever.")

Buffalo Springfield, who seemingly play the whole residence even if that means cancelling pre-booked gigs in Illinois at the weekend of May 19–21, are also on a roll. 'For What It's Worth' has been a Top Ten hit earlier in the year, and its composer, Stephen Stills, has become friendly with David Crosby. Spending a lot of time together at Crosby's home in Beverly Glen Canyon, the two work out the chord progression of a song to which Stills later puts words. It will be called 'Rock'n'Roll Woman' as a tribute to Jefferson Airplane's Grace Slick.

Sunday 21

Peter Fonda and members of The Byrds attend a concert by Ravi Shankar at Los Angeles Music Center. Shankar is in Los Angeles to open the Kinnara School Of Indian Music tomorrow on 8718 West Third Street, where he is available for private lessons by special appointment.

Monday 22

The tenth single by the group is released in the US, lifting Chris Hillman's 'Have You Seen Her Face?' from *Younger Than Yesterday* coupled with the *Don't Make Waves* theme tune. Perhaps this is intended to tie in with the movie's forthcoming premiere, but the single performs poorly on the charts (*Billboard*

Number 74; *Cash Box* Number 73) and is the first of the American singles not released in the UK and Europe.

Billboard (May 27) says: "Follow-up to 'My Back Pages', the quartet has a strong commercial entry in this easy-beat folk-rocker with a compelling lyric. Top group vocal workout and arrangement." *Record World* (also May 27) writes telegram-style: "Pretty contemporary love song from the Byrds deserves to hit high chart slots."

Tuesday 23

🔊 **RECORDING** Columbia Recording Studios, Sunset and El Centro, Hollywood, CA. Producer Gary Usher and (presumably) engineer Tom May.

Third overdub session for Crosby's 'Lady Friend' (see May 4 and 10).

Wednesday 24
ALSO ...

Quoted in today's *Oakland Tribune* in an interview by Associated Press's Rob Thomas, director Roger Corman talks excitedly about his newest film, *The Trip*. Starring Peter Fonda, the low-budget movie concerns the real and hallucinatory adventures of a man who has taken LSD. "I'm in the midst of cutting it now; it's the toughest job I ever had," says Corman. Shooting of the film started on March 30 and took 17 days to complete.

One of the trippy sequences is shot in a nightclub and requires a band. Fonda has what he considers perfect candidates for the job: The International Submarine Band. Still captained by Gram Parsons, the group relocated to Los Angeles in March 1967, moving into a house off Laurel Canyon Road. Able to live easily on a family trust fund, Parsons hangs out with his old friend, suave actor Brandon de Wilde, while the Submarine Band lie fallow most of the time.

De Wilde in turn introduces Parsons to Fonda, who gets the Submariners on the set of *The Trip*. (Fonda pursues a sideline as a singer and has signed a deal with the small Chira Records.) Asked to come up with a soundtrack, the group record 'Lazy Days' as a contender for the film. In a twist of interconnected threads, Hugh Masekela – co-owner of the Chira label – produces the session. The driving 'Lazy Days' is more reminiscent of Buck Owens and Chuck Berry than the required psychotropic sounds, and so Michael Bloomfield's new group The Electric Flag is given that assignment. Still, The International Submarine Band get to appear in the film, bizarrely miming to Bloomfield's soundtrack.

(In a couple of months, Parsons and The International Submarine Band will sign a con-

tract with singer–composer Lee Hazlewood's LHI Records. In an interview with *The Lowell Sun* (May 15), Hazlewood describes his label: "We've been in existence for four months of riotous infamy. There's nobody you ever heard of on it: The 98 Per Cent American Mom & Apple Pie 1929 Crash Band, The Kitchen Cinq, The Shacklefords." The addition of The International Submarine Band changes nothing, but Hazelwood's label allows Gram Parsons to record his first long player in the later months of 1967.)

Friday 26
North Lake Ballroom, Federal Way, WA

The Byrds embark on a brief tour of the Pacific Northwest, beginning with an appearance here at North Lake Park.

Saturday 27
Pat O'Day's Dunes, Westport, WA

The Dunes is a small dancehall with a 1,000 capacity built on the sand dunes on the beachfront.

Sunday 28
Portland Memorial Coliseum, Portland, OR

Jefferson Airplane and The Byrds headline, while P.H. Factor and Magic Fern – two groups from the Northwest – play support. Crosby is very fond of the Airplane and envies their communal living style – like Grateful Dead, Jefferson Airplane all live in the same house in Haight-Ashbury – something that is unthinkable in the Byrds regime.

Tuesday 30
'Trips Festival', Seattle Center Arena, Seattle, WA

Manager Sid Clark and promoter Trips Lansing previously held a 'Trips Festival' in Seattle in March, cleverly naming the event after Lansing although it has no association

---

'Have You Seen Her Face' (US only)

A 'Have You Seen Her Face'
(C. HILLMAN)

B 'Don't Make Waves'
(J. MCGUINN/C. HILLMAN)

US release May 22 1967 (Columbia 44157)

Chart high US number 74

Read more ... entries for November 29, 1966 and April 26, 1967

with last year's epoch-making 'Trips Festival' in San Francisco. The two have booked The Byrds, Jefferson Airplane, The Electric Prunes, and Seattle group Don & The Good Times for today's happening (from noon to midnight), topping the day with an enormous lightshow.

June

Friday 2
'Oracle Benefit', Valley Music Theatre, Woodland Hills, CA

The Byrds, Kaleidoscope, Clear Light, and Fraternity Of Man perform in aid of *The Southern California Oracle*, an underground newspaper inspired by its sister publication *The San Francisco Oracle*.

Reportedly, Michael Clarke has digested enough hallucinogens to destroy The Byrds' performance. Whereas his bandmates forge ahead musically and creatively, Clarke seems to be standing still, which causes strife with the other three. Sabotaging the group's live show certainly does little to endear McGuinn, Crosby, and Hillman.

ALSO ...
Sergeant Pepper's Lonely Hearts Club Band is issued in the US today, one day after its UK release.

Early June
David Crosby lends moral support to Buffalo Springfield as they break-in ex-Daily Flash guitarist Doug Hastings as replacement for the departing Neil Young. The rehearsals take place at Stephen Stills and Dewey Martin's beach house on West Malibu Road, and the new guitarist will make his debut in Colorado on June 8. Hastings recalls to author John Einarson: "Crosby was around helping out at those first rehearsals. He didn't go out and do the gigs but he was helping out."

Monday 5
🔊 **RECORDING** Columbia Recording Studios, Sunset and El Centro, Hollywood, CA. Producer Gary Usher and (presumably) engineer Tom May.

Fourth overdub session for Crosby's 'Lady Friend' (see May 4, 10, and 23).

Saturday 10(–Sunday 11)
'KFRC Fantasy Fair and Magic Mountain Music Festival', Tamalpais Mountain Theatre, Marin County, CA

A benefit concert for the Hunter's Point Child Care Center Project, this two-day festival near San Francisco has been postponed for a week because of rain and bad weather (it was originally set for June 3–4). Most of the groups and performers are able to accommodate the switch, although the running order is changed around, and while some lose out (Wilson Pickett and Country Joe & The Fish, for instance),

the festival gains some new acts (The Fifth Dimension, Dionne Warwick, Jim Kweskin Jug Band, and The Lamp Of Childhood).

Among the multitude of performers booked for the weekend are Smokey Robinson & The Miracles, The Seeds, The Doors, Hugh Masekela, Jefferson Airplane, Steve Miller Blues Band, Smokey & His Sister, Moby Grape, The Grass Roots, 13th Floor Elevators, Blackburn & Snow, The Mojo Men, Every Mother's Son, Merry-Go-Round, Blues Magoos, P.F. Sloan, Tim Hardin, Sparrow, Loading Zone, and Tim Buckley.

The Byrds appear on Saturday, and Hugh Masekela joins on trumpet for much of their set. The theatre is situated near the peak of Tamalpais with a spectacular view of the city below, and many of the 15,000-strong crowd make the trek on a specially chartered Trans-Love Busline. A 40-foot-high Buddha is planned to exhale bubbles and incense to greet people as they step off the bus.

Besides continuous music from two stages, artisans and craftsmen have set up stalls, and spectators can enjoy attractions such as The Human Fence, Free Form Water Slide, The Giant Bubble Tub, or The Talking Wind. There are banners and balloons, a lightshow within a large dome, strolling mariachis, and people tinkling finger cymbals or strumming bouzoukis and sitars. Even if Robert Hurwitt writes in the Berkeley Barb that it was "a crowd that had trouble grooving", it is a day to remember. The Magic Mountain Festival will be totally eclipsed by next week's Monterey Pop Festival, but the bill at Tamalpais Mountain is perhaps equally impressive and has an even more diverse mix of artists.

Meanwhile, last-minute preparations for the Monterey festival continue down in Los Angeles. In keeping with the festival's official title – The Monterey International Pop Music Festival – The Who from England have been added to the bill and a grand $400,000 deal has been signed with ABC for the television rights. Zooming in on what makes Monterey so different, Pete Johnson has talked to everyone for a background feature in The *Los Angeles Times* (June 4). Phil Turetsky – an accountant working without salary for the festival – hits the nail on the head. "It gives the audience a sense of participating in something," he tells Johnson, "yet it is socially acceptable. Jazz came out of the saloon into the home. This festival will give pop music community status and acceptability because it is done for a worthwhile purpose."

ALSO ...
Teen pop idol Rick Nelson crosses over to make his country music debut at a KGBS-AM sponsored affair at L.A.'s Shrine Auditorium,

Trips Festival, Seattle, WA, May 30, 1967.

David Crosby at the 'KFRC Fantasy Fair and Magic Mountain Music Festival', June 10, 1967.

topping the bill above George Jones, Glen Campbell, The Dillards, and Charley Greyeagle. Nelson has collected a crack band to back him up, consisting of James Burton and Clarence White on guitars, Glen D. Hardin on piano, Bob Warford on banjo, Lynn Russell on bass, and Junior Nichols on drums. Robert Hilton covers the event for *The Los Angeles Times* (June 13) and says that one of the songs Nelson does is 'Take A City Bride' – a number the singer released as a single in April and that featured White on guitar.

Sunday 11
La Playa Stadium, Santa Barbara, CA
Yet another benefit concert (although for what cause is uncertain), this time with a country & western slant: Eddy Arnold, Don Bowman, The Stoneman Family, Ricky Nelson – plus The Byrds, The Peanut Butter Conspiracy, and The Nitty Gritty Dirt band.

Wednesday 14
🔊 **RECORDING** Columbia Recording Studios, Studio D, Sunset and El Centro, Hollywood, CA. Producer Gary Usher and engineer Tom May.

Today marks the fifth and final overdub session for 'Lady Friend' (see May 4, 10, 23, and June 5), a song of which Crosby has taken full control. He lays down all the vocals himself and takes an active part in the horns that are added to the track.

Journalist John Nork will have a chance to discuss 'Lady Friend' with Crosby, McGuinn, and Hillman when he interviews all three in 1997. Crosby: "I thought that … we did, for that time anyway, some very unusual stuff. Some very pretty stuff." Hillman: "[It] is a great song, but David unfortunately went back into the studio and put all the voices on and took ours off, and he made it this mishmash crazy sounding thing that had no personality. He ripped it of personality and loaded it up with tracks of vocals of his own and it was awful. But it was initially a great song. It's one of his better songs. … The original was simple; it was great; we all sang it. And then, somehow he went back in there and he was hanging out with the Jefferson Airplane and the Springfield and all that." McGuinn: "He kicked us out of the studio because we weren't good enough to be on it, so we said, 'OK, David. Go for it.' So he did."

According to studio sheets, the group also record Hillman and McGuinn's new composition 'Old John Robertson' today, and it is finished on June 21.

Saturday 17
Monterey International Pop Music Festival, Monterey County Fairgrounds, Monterey, CA
"You know, they're shooting this for television. I'm sure they'll edit this out," David Crosby warns the audience from the stage. He is dressed in full hippie insignia with his Cossack fur hat and STP-embossed guitar. The Byrds are halfway through their Monterey performance as night is about to fall. He stops for a quick greeting to Country Joe & The Fish, who played in the afternoon, pauses, and then continues his introduction to 'He Was A Friend Of Mine'.

"I wanna say it anyway, even though they will edit it out. President Kennedy was killed. He was not killed by one man! He was shot from a number of different directions by different guns. The story has been suppressed, witnesses have been killed, and this is your country, ladies and gentlemen."

Hugh Masekela and David Crosby at the 'KFRC Fantasy Fair and Magic Mountain Music Festival', June 10, 1967.

By its second day, the Monterey International Pop Music Festival has already become a huge success. Campers besiege the town, and the total attendance figure for the weekend is reportedly reaching a peak of 200,000, even though the festival grounds are not supposed to accommodate more than 10,000 people. The event has become the multi-cultural cross-pollinating happening that the organisers have hoped for, and more.

The music is outstanding; the weather is perfect, and the large crowds are behaving peacefully and listen attentively to everything – be it acid rock, whispery folk singers, or Indian sitar ragas. A swirling lightshow is projected on a screen behind the performers, while remote television is hooked up to serve the overflowing crowds outside the fairgrounds.

The arrangers have gone to great lengths to make it an event for the musicians, too. The sound system is powerful and crystal clear, and a banquet is laid out backstage with the best foods. Police on duty wander around with little to do. *The Long Beach Independent* (June 27) writes about an officer who points at a screaming jetliner passing overhead and

jokes: "That's the Jefferson Airplane!" The paper adds dryly: "From a policeman in that setting, it was a very good joke."

On Friday night there are performances from The Association, The Paupers, Lou Rawls, British folk singer Beverly, Johnny Rivers, UK act Eric Burdon & The Animals (a last minute stand-in for The Beach Boys, thus boosting the festival's right to be 'International'), and Simon & Garfunkel. The Saturday afternoon programme has Canned Heat, Big Brother & The Holding Company, Country Joe & The Fish, Al Kooper, The Butterfield Blues Band, Quicksilver Messenger Service, Steve Miller Blues Band, plus Michael Bloomfield and Buddy Miles hoisting their Electric Flag in public. A relieved mayor of Monterey, Minnie Coyle, tells the assembled press: "When I was first approached I was reluctant to let the festival happen. But I'm very agreeably surprised that this is being run so well and that everyone is behaving so well."

The Saturday-evening part of the show includes Moby Grape, Hugh Masekela, a return of The Butterfield Blues Band, Laura Nyro, Jefferson Airplane, and the weekend's

only pure soul act, Booker T & The MGs and The Mar-Keys with Otis Redding (hastily booked after accusations of Monterey being 'whitey's festival'). The Byrds are sandwiched between Masekela's band and Butterfield, and perform 'Renaissance Fair', 'Have You Seen Her Face', a flurried 'Hey Joe (Where You Gonna Go)' – which Crosby dedicates to "Love, The Leaves, Tim Rose, Jimi Hendrix" – plus 'I Know My Rider', 'Chimes Of Freedom', 'He Was A Friend Of Mine', 'Lady Friend', and finally 'So You Want To Be A Rock'n'Roll Star' with guests of honour Hugh Masekela (trumpet), Big Black (percussion), and Cecil Barnard (piano).

Crosby's on-stage antics do not go down too well with American reviewers. *Down Beat* (August 10) writes: "Next flew The Byrds. As a recording group it is among America's finest, but it has always been sloppy. A couple of unsubtle spiels between songs – one advocating the use of LSD, the other propounding somebody's guesses about Kennedy's assassination – drew big cheers but certainly did not add to the music." Phillip Elwood of *Billboard* is sorry that The Byrds "felt it necessary for David Crosby to deliver a sophomoric politi-

Hugh Masekela jams with The Byrds at 'Monterey International Pop Music Festival', June 17, 1967.

cal commentary prior to their playing of 'He Was A Friend Of Mine'," and concludes that, anyway, they are not as close-knit as Buffalo Springfield.

The Los Angeles Free Press muddles McGuinn and Crosby, suggesting it is Jim who prefaces the JFK tribute by "announcing in no uncertain terms that the real murderers were still at large and the CIA was in on it". Mike Daley in *Mojo Navigator Rock'n'Roll News* says: "The Byrds I have heard much better before, and David Crosby's comments and little sermons about acid and the fact that Paul McCartney now takes it, and Kennedy's assassination, came off sounding very sophomoric. And the STP sticker on his guitar didn't make it either." Pete Johnson in *The Los Angeles Times* (June 19) notes briefly: "Jazz trumpeter Hugh Masekela, who like Lou Rawls has been adopted by pop music, went over well. So did The Byrds, who were not as good as they should have been."

Members of the British press flown in for the occasion are more positive. David Gooch in *Record Mirror* (July 1): "Hugh Masekela and The Byrds tripped out to the glories of the Jefferson Airplane and Otis Redding." Keith Altham of *New Musical Express* (June 24) is blown away by Big Brother & The Holding Company, whose singer is so little known for now that Altham gives her name as "Janice Joblim". (Just as West Coast sensation Janis Joplin is an unknown quantity to the British public, so are Jimi Hendrix and The Who in America.)

Melody Maker (June 24) has invited American journalist Jann Wenner to submit a report. He writes: "On Saturday night, The Byrds, the first of the post-Beatles–Dylan groups in America, pulled together for a tight and fascinating performance of new material. For the first time in over a year they made an in-person performance equalling their records." Crosby also acts as MC for some of the performers, and Wenner reports that Bloomfield's Electric Flag drummer, Buddy Miles, "who used to be with Wilson Pickett, lived up to David Crosby's introduction as the 'most dangerous drummer alive'."

Sunday 18

The last day of the Monterey International Pop Festival features (in running order): The Blues Project, a reprise performance by Big Brother & The Holding Company, The Group With No Name, Buffalo Springfield, The Who, Grateful Dead, The Jimi Hendrix Experience, and finally Scott McKenzie and The Mamas & The Papas.

After an unspectacular performance by the quickly conceived Group With No Name and a grand introduction by Pete Tork, David

Crosby strolls on stage as a sixth member of Buffalo Springfield, playing guitar and singing harmony for the length of their set. Crosby sees no harm in this, but Hillman and McGuinn are outraged.

"He would have joined [Buffalo Springfield] in a minute if he had been asked," Hillman later tells author John Einarson. "He wasn't happy in The Byrds, and at the time we were working in the studio, he'd take our tapes and run off and play them for the Springfield. So he took the opportunity to jump on stage with them. McGuinn and I were ready to strangle him at that point after he made some stupid comment about Kennedy and the Warren Commission that was totally inappropriate. I don't think we were officially notified that he was going to join them onstage but we heard rumours." Although Crosby sits safely in The Byrds for the time being, his position is lessened and he is not immune any more.

In a lengthy interview with music writer Ben Fong-Torres in 1970, Crosby will tell his side of the story. "It got to be a matter of habit that I would do [other things], and it's hard to break a habit, man. Habit's even harder to break than some kind of deliberate plot, cos it's not maliciousness on anybody's part. There wasn't anybody in that group trying to hold me back. There was no real maliciousness in that group until right near the end, you know. … They used to get uptight that I was playing with Stephen and Buffalo Springfield. They got uptight behind Monterey, me saying that shit about Kennedy and the Warren Report."

Fong-Torres wants to know exactly what

Crosby told the Monterey crowd. Crosby replies that, basically, it was a question of who killed the President. "It was a standard introduction. We used to do it – you saw us do it a hundred times. We used to do it every single time we did 'He Was A Friend of Mine'. The introduction for a year solid was: 'We'd like to do a song about this guy who was a friend of ours. And just by way of mentioning it, he was shot down in the street. And as a matter of strict fact he was shot down in the street by a very professional kind of outfit. Don't it make you sort of wonder? The Warren Report ain't the truth, that's plain to anybody. And it happened in your country. Don't you wonder why? Don't you wonder?' And then we would sing the song.

"Now, admittedly that's a little extreme for an artist to get into those areas at all," Crosby continues. "Got no right talkin' about that. But I was pissed about it, and I'm still pissed about it! I guess I overstepped my bounds as an artist. By rights I shouldn't get into that area at all. I'm sure no political genius. I don't fuckin' know what to do. I sure am sure I was tellin' the truth. But I sure am sure that it didn't fuckin' do no good. I mean he isn't alive, he's dead, and nobody still knows why. Or how or who. And everybody's guessin' and everybody's scared. So I guess it didn't do a hell of a lot of good for me to mouth off."

Keith Altham comments in *New Musical Express* (June 24): "[Buffalo Springfield] has recently mislaid a member and had Dave Crosby of The Byrds deputising on guitar. The Springfields are happy sounding, original and deserve greater recognition – I hope they get it."

David Crosby sits in with The Buffalo Springfield at 'Monterey International Pop Music Festival', June 17, 1967. From left: Crosby, Richie Furay, Stephen Stills.

Whatever Buffalo Springfield are up to at Monterey, it is overshadowed by the following one-two punch of The Who and Jimi Hendrix, who leave the stage literally in smoke and with an adoring crowd zapped of energy. For Scott McKenzie and The Mamas & The Papas, it is the end of the party. Tracy Thomas (*New Musical Express*, July 1): "Their 'medley of hits' were anti-climatic. Musically they were sound, though slightly out of sync with their backing band."

Thomas sums up: "In addition to the musical achievement of the weekend, the entire event was a clear-cut victory for the 'hippies' and pop music lovers in general. Though city officials anticipated the worst, their only complaints afterwards were that the music was so loud it could be heard over 20 miles away!"

Derek Taylor summarises his impressions to *Disc* (June 24). "The Festival spoke for the whole new attitude so well and with such meaning that most of us cried because we couldn't believe it. We bought 200,000 flowers from Hawaii at two cents apiece and we gave them to each other, grown-up and child, policeman and narcotics agents, square and hippie. Incredible. Absolutely incredible. Forty policemen were taken off duty at the Festival ground on the morning of the last day of the three-day event. By that afternoon another forty had been taken away from festival duty. A couple of hours later at the final press conference attended by Eric Burdon, Andrew Oldham, festival director Lou Adler and about 3,000 journalists I took from round my neck a leather necklace bearing a psychedelic spying-glass stone with the words 'this is from us to you and this makes us one'. I placed it around the neck of 59-year-old police chief Frank Marinello, and we shook hands and meant it. 'There are no problems, only dilemmas,' said our first press release when we arrived in Monterey to launch the festival a week ago and tried to persuade Marinello not to arm his men with guns and helmets and sticks on the festival grounds. We told Marinello that we would guarantee not to carry guns, but he was not too impressed then. Now he is. Now the town is. Now the English who came to Monterey know what is happening in California."

American journalist Robert Christgau pens a lengthy story in *Esquire* (January 1968) and writes of the cultural gap between Los Angeles and San Francisco as if it should have been two cities on different continents, much less two cities in the same state. Suddenly the chrome and steel, the surf and sun of Los Angeles are dated, derided as plastic, as its golden skies become grey smog. "The San Franciscans had the cards – the Angelenos needed them badly," jeers Christgau, and he

says that the Friday concert was "dominated by what San Francisco calls plastic" before writing gleefully how Peter Tork tries to curb an enthusiastic Sunday night crowd. "Phil Lesh could no longer resist. Lesh, the Dead's bassist, is 29, classically trained, a Bay Area native, and there, right there, stood Los Angeles, this square, manufactured teen idol, the mouthpiece of safe and sane Adlerism, everything Lesh couldn't stand."

Christgau does not understand Hendrix either. "He was terrible [and], anyway, he can't sing." He calls him "just another Uncle Tom". Christgau later publishes the article with the phrase he originally intended – "psychedelic Uncle Tom" – which was censored at the insistence of *Esquire*'s lawyers.

Despite all the good publicity for the town of Monterey, as soon as the fairground is emptied and the last tent folded up, mayor Minnie Coyle drafts a City Council resolution that will prevent more pop festivals.

•

Contemporary reports estimate the attendance at between 45,000 and 80,000. It is only in hindsight that the number is brought up to a dizzying 200,000. The income from all sources will exceed $500,000 (£210,000 at the time) to the Monterey Foundation that is later given to various charity causes. (At the end of October, the Board of Directors meets up to share out the profits as promised. An initial slice of $165,000 (£70,000) is earmarked for a project to teach New York ghetto kids to play guitar. (Paul Simon administrates the project, and if it proves successful upon review a further $165,000 will be given to the same cause.)

The promised ABC television documentary from Monterey is instead made into a full-length movie by D.A. Pennebaker, *Monterey Pop,* which will be premiered in December 1968. David Crosby's assertion that The Byrds would be edited out comes true: they are nowhere to be seen. It will not be until 2002, when a *Complete Monterey Pop Festival* is released, that The Byrds' performances of 'Chimes Of Freedom', 'He Was A Friend of Mine' (with Crosby's controversial Kennedy comments intact), and 'Hey Joe (Where You Gonna Go)' are available to the general public. The revised version will also feature Crosby and Buffalo Springfield performing 'For What It's Worth'.

In a later interview with *Melody Maker* (June 17, 1972), Pennebaker rewinds to that special summer. "Everybody felt they could've taken the money and just burnt it right in the front of the park. It's funny, [John Phillips and Lou Adler] come right from the centre of Babylon. Yet they managed to get literally everybody there. Monterey was kinda elitist. You just

had a very select in-group, in the sense that they were all Californian who were into everything, and then there were the people from the music industry in the East who were really into the music but in a professional way. And I think they said: 'It really works, man. All you gotta do is have good music.' And everybody sang: '[Fuck] the money'.

"Everyone felt they were at the exact centre for a second of the energy, and that's why when all those people came to hear Ravi Shankar – 40,000 people, you know, drinking and smoking, and anything chemical they could get their hands on – and Shankar said (puts hands together and speaks quietly in sing-song Indian voice), 'Now, please, I don't want any smoking,' they all said, 'Hey! We gotta get rid of that dope!' They were into this fantastic mood where they were ready to do anything to make life more beautiful."

•

Composer, keyboard player, and audio engineer Paul Beaver is at Monterey to demonstrate one of the very first synthesizers. McGuinn is sufficiently impressed to purchase a model, and so is Mickey Dolenz. "I got my first Moog right after Monterey, cos I saw it at the Monterey festival," McGuinn recalls later for John Nork. "Paul Beaver had one up there, and he was selling them, and I bought one. We were using oscillators, which is basically what a Moog is … a tone generator."

Robert Moog's recent invention is not put into regular production yet, and the instrument exists only as a novel prototype. Hillman later tells author Richie Unterberger: "[McGuinn] had that Moog synthesizer, of course; then, it was like owning a computer in 1955. It took up the whole room. It made a lot of noise. It wasn't really musical. It was like a toy, a gadget. But it was interesting."

Wednesday 21

🔊 **RECORDING** Columbia Recording Studios, Sunset and El Centro, Hollywood, CA. Producer Gary Usher and (presumably) engineer Tom May.

McGuinn and Hillman's 'Old John Robertson' is completed at today's session (see June 14). For the recording, the roles are switched around: Hillman plays the guitar while Crosby lays down the basslines. Writing about a neighbouring movie director from his childhood, Hillman later regrets that the song was not done acoustically. He concedes to journalist John Nork that it is "almost a good song" but disowns the middle part with strings. "I don't know what that is. That's trying to be *Sgt Pepper*. That's horrible." It is Gary Usher who suggests the eight-bar baroque interlude, which is scored by McGuinn and performed by an uncredited string quartet. The song is put on the B-side of Crosby's 'Lady Friend' but will be given a little studio treatment when the group prepares the new Byrds album later in the year.

Friday 23

The Byrds are provisionally booked for 'The World Teenage Fair '67' in Chicago that starts today and runs until July 7 but do not appear in the final list of entertainers.

Friday 30

The Byrds–Dickson–Tickner partnership has now run its course, and a contract signed today dissolves their business relationship. "We negotiated a settlement," Tickner will tell Byrds biographer Johnny Rogan in 1979. "I still get a royalty cheque!" Enter Larry Spector at David Crosby's recommendation, who will run the group's business affairs for the next year and a half. This is a mistake, as everyone involved will later unanimously remember.

Where Dickson has been crucial in triggering The Byrds creatively and developing their career, Spector fills only one half of the Tickner–Dickson role, as business accountant. Hillman will recall to John Nork: "[When] we stopped listening to Dickson – [he] wasn't always right, but most of the time he had a pretty good overall view of what we should do – when we stopped listening to him, it sort of fell apart. As it did when Brian Epstein died, it sort of lost the man at the rudder, and that happens." Hillman maintains in an interview with Richie Unterberger: "[Dickson] set this thing on track. And we derailed it ourselves. That's all I can tell you. As things worked out, it was time for maybe us to part company with Jim. But it wasn't long after; we lost a bit of our direction."

The way Crosby will later explain this period, it sounds like The Byrds are adhering to their own warning in 'So You Want To Be A Rock'n'Roll Star' where they sing: "The agent man won't let you down/Sell your soul to the company/Who are waiting there to sell plastic ware." Crosby writes in his biography: "The fact of the matter is that [Dickson] shaped the band and it couldn't have happened without him. No question about it. Even if we had fallen together organically, it would have taken us five or six years of playing together to achieve what we did in less than a year at World Pacific, listening to ourselves on playback. Other bands couldn't do that.

"We just went straight up, and out, and eventually dumped Dickson. We took our whole scene elsewhere. We were finally tired of Eddie and Jim, and our career was not advancing anymore. Gene had left the band and the guy we took it to, as it turned out, turned out to be a total sleazebag, a real rip-off artist. And, to be perfectly frank, I was largely responsible. If I had only known." Talking later to Ben Fong-Torres, he says: "[I] had made a terrible mistake and led everybody to a cat who was taking us to the cleaners. Pure poison. Ruined a lot of people, and I led them all in. The only thing that I can also say is that I tried to lead them all back out again."

Friday 30

Buffalo Springfield are booked for a weekend at Dave Hull's Hullabaloo club on Sunset Strip. The group's singer Richie Furay is laid low with a sore throat, so Crosby offers to help out. At the end of the night Neil Young unexpectedly turns up. As Crosby and guitarist Doug Hastings step down, Young goes on stage to tear through a rendition of 'Mr. Soul' with his old bandmates.

July

Saturday 1

"We may be breaking some rules tonight," Crosby announces from the Hullabaloo stage. "But it's about time someone started experimenting. Besides, music shouldn't have any rules. Rules aren't made for music." Even though Richie Furay is fit again, Crosby plays with Buffalo Springfield again tonight, and drummers Michael Clarke and Buddy Miles also join the onstage frolics as the group's regular percussionist Dewey Martin steps up to the microphone.

"The result was 50 minutes filled with driving improvisations and vocal combinations," writes Tom Paegel in *The Los Angeles Times* (July 6). "The performance as a whole was excellent although there was some lack of unity, which could be expected. Nevertheless the combination shined during numbers such as 'Hey Joe', sung by Crosby in the familiar Byrd style. The Buffalo Springfield hits of 'Nowadays Clancy Can't Even Sing', sung by Richie Furay, and 'For What It's Worth', sung by Steve Stills, were excellent. The Springfield's new release, 'Blue Bird', also was sung by Stills with Furay and Crosby singing background. The product of this performance was refreshing. It is an outgrowth of one of the themes of the Monterey Pop festival: musicians working together for fun and for the betterment of pop music. This theme may be a sign of future pop."

Sunday 2

Crosby is at the Whisky a Go Go to catch The Jimi Hendrix Experience.

Thursday 13

The 11th single by The Byrds is released in the US, matching Crosby's new 'Lady Friend' with Hillman and McGuinn's 'Old John Robertson'. Where the last single ('Have You Seen Her Face') was considered a stopgap release, Columbia Records and the group have great hopes for the commercial 'Lady Friend', with a couple of high-profile television appearances lined up to promote it. Inexplicably, the single fails and stalls at Number 82 in *Billboard* (83 in *Cash Box*), the lowest performance by any Byrds single so far. A *Billboard* review predicts the number will reach the Top 60 and says: "This infectious wild rocker should put The Byrds up the Hot 100 in short order. Good material, performance and strong dance beat in support."

Monday 17
ALSO …

Clarence White signs a recording contract with record producer Gary Paxton and his Bakersfield International Productions. Paxton, once the Flip with Skip Battin in the 50s duo Skip & Flip, has set up a recording studio in a former bank building on Chester Avenue in Bakersfield, 100 miles north of Los Angeles. Here he churns out country records by a wide array of artists, and Clarence White is featured regularly as soloist.

Most of the releases on Paxton's label find only a selected audience, but the company's second single – The Gosdin Brothers with '(Just Enough To Keep Me) Hangin' On', featuring White's guitar, will break out nationally and become a Top 40 single in *Billboard*'s Country chart in October this year.

White finds a kindred spirit in banjoist-turned-drummer Gene Parsons, who is also a regular guest at Paxton's sessions. Parsons has performed with singer Floyd 'Gib' Guilbeau for some time – their single 'Louisiana Rain' was the Bakersfield International label's first release – and in fall 1967 White, Parsons, and Guilbeau will add bass player Wayne Moore to form The Reasons. Working steadily at a club called Nashville West in El Monte, California,

---

'Lady Friend' (US)

A 'Lady Friend' (D. CROSBY)
B 'Old John Robertson' (G. CLARK)

US release July 13 1967 (Columbia 44230)
Chart high US number 82
Read more … entries for April 26, May 4, 10, 23, June 5, 14, 21 1967

they frequently borrow the club's name as their own.

White releases a single under his own name for Bakersfield International's third single, pairing two of Paxton's instrumentals: 'Tuff And Stringy' and 'Tango For A Sad Mood', showcasing his chops on electric guitar.

→ Mid-July

📺 **US TV** ABC Television Center, Hollywood, CA. ABC Network *American Bandstand '67*

The group pre records a segment for Dick Clark's weekend show, now with the added '67' and set to go out on July 29 at 12:30pm, networked throughout the US. The Byrds do their two latest single sides, 'Lady Friend' and 'Eight Miles High' (contrary to reports, 'Have You Seen Her Face' is probably not aired). The four look like they have come straight from the Monterey stage – Crosby complete with Cossack hat – and it is an impressive sight, even if they just lip-synch to the original track.

Clark has run his show for 15 years now and is only surpassed in longevity by Lawrence Welk's maudlin family show. He is one of many showbiz people who have trouble keeping apace with changing trends, as he openly confesses in an interview with UPI's Vernon Scott (syndicated in September). "Until now I've pretty well understood the music and I dig it, but now I'm scared. The hippie scene is more than a fad with long hair, weird clothes, and drugs. It's a deep philosophy embracing religion, politics, manners, and morals. It is a very tiny minority but terribly influential. I've lived through all kinds of fads with teens, but this is the only time it's frightened me – because the influence is so far-reaching. The hippies provide youngsters with arguments to frustrate The Establishment, including the use of marijuana. Another frightening thing about the hippies is that they are against American traditions and institutions, anything that represents authority. It has become fashionable to flaunt the very precepts of our society."

Clark is nonetheless asked to predict coming trends, and sings the praises of an odd new device. "Well, the vogue of the moment is East Indian sounds, but I think the most important thing on the horizon is Ampliphonic instruments. Very soon we'll be hearing brass and reed instruments amplified electronically, just as guitars are now. You almost have to be an electrical engineer to be a musician these days. But Ampliphonic instruments will be used by standard bands and musicians as well as the groups that appeal to teenagers. Herb Alpert, for instance, could use an Ampliphonic trumpet and make it sound like five instruments instead of one. It will mean a whole new era in music." Clark is endorsing a

new product unveiled at the annual National Association of Music Merchants trade show in Chicago in July, where the Vox company displays the 'Ampliphonic stereo multi-voice' unit designed for wind instruments, which splits the signal into octaves.

Tuesday 18–Thursday 20
The Golden Bear, Huntington Beach, CA
Out in Orange County on the Pacific coastline, the Golden Bear club concentrates on folk, blues, and jazz artists. This is the group's first appearance here.

Friday 21

Malibu Shore Club, Lido Beach, Long Island, NY
The Byrds are in New York for a week to tape a couple of television appearances and to play a few concerts, beginning with this outdoor show in Long Island together with two other Los Angeles groups, The Seeds and The Peanut Butter Conspiracy. The Conspiracy is also one of Gary Usher's clients. Originally, The Byrds are billed to appear at the Village Theatre for two days, beginning tonight, but this is cancelled in favour of playing Lido Beach.

Saturday 22
Village Theater, Manhattan, New York, NY
The group headlines, supported by The Seeds and New York group Vanilla Fudge in one of their first concert appearances under their new name (previously they were The Pigeons). The Peanut Butter Conspiracy, who are also billed, cancel in favour of playing New Jersey. Eric Clapton – on a brief holiday to New York City – is in the audience.

Tuesday 25
📺 **US TV** [Presumably] NBC Television Studios, Manhattan, New York, NY. NBC network *The Tonight Show* 11:30pm

Johnny Carson's popular five-day-a-week nationwide show guarantees guests an audience of several million viewers. The Byrds, appearing live on the show, perform 'Renaissance Fair', 'Lady Friend', and 'Have You

See Her Face'. Comedian Bob Newhart is the show's co-host, and the other scheduled participants are child psychologist and author Dr Haim Ginott, actor Paul Ford, and actress Jan Sterling.

There's a story attached to the group's appearance, as journalist Jon Young will re-tell in *Musician* (May 1991). "Back in '67, to promote the single 'Lady Friend', the band appeared on *The Tonight Show*. With obvious disdain, guest host Bob Newhart read The Byrds' stock introduction off cue cards and added, as Roger McGuinn and David Crosby strummed the opening bars of the song, 'I think I hear them tuning up now.' Unfazed, Crosby leaned into the mike and countered, 'We tune because we care.'"

Apparently, at this point Carson fell across his desk laughing. Young continues: "Yours truly was incensed that the button-down comic had dissed my favourite band and immediately fired off a letter, explaining The Byrds' blend of rock, folk, and country, and recommending that Newhart check out *Younger Than Yesterday*. Imagine my surprise to receive a response a few months later. Newhart wrote that while he appreciated my point of view and did in fact like some pop, citing The Supremes, he found The Byrds to be 'cacophonous'."

Friday 28
'The Rheingold Music Festival', Central Park, New York, NY
Rheingold is a New York beer brand that this summer sponsors 42 nights of concerts in Central Park. The Byrds and The Garden State Choir perform twice, at 8:00 and 10:30pm.

Saturday 29
The group appears on *American Bandstand '67* (episode No. 1793, at 12:30pm; see mid-July) performing 'Eight Miles High' and 'Lady Friend'. Also on the show are Sam & Dave (singing 'Soothe Me') and The Forum, a group created by Crosby's old employer Les Baxter, plugging an orchestral version of 'The River Is Wide'.

Billboard prints a release ad for *The Astrology Album* on Columbia Records in today's issue. The brainchild of Gary Usher, this combined spoken-word and music album offers "your horoscope and character analysis in music and narration". Usher has written the music and Phil Austin of comedy troupe The Firesign Theatre is the narrator, while David Crosby (Leo), Chad (Aries) & Jeremy (Sagittarius), and John Merrill (Capricorn) of The Peanut Butter Conspiracy are heard in spoken segments. The record comes packaged with a full-colour zodiac wall chart measuring 22 by 33 inches. The album is presumably not a big seller, as a review in *The Appleton Post Crescent* (August 13) succinctly notes: "It makes for 40 minutes of mild entertainment the first time through, but I would hate to think of paying for the album and then feeling bound to listen to it again."

Sunday 30

The influence of The Byrds is felt in many ways. St Michael And All Angels Episcopal Church in Studio City, CA, uses the music of the group along with that of The Beatles and The Rolling Stones in a special Rock'n'roll Mass today.

Monday 31

◁» **RECORDING** Columbia Recording Studios, Sunset and El Centro, Hollywood, CA. Producer Gary Usher and engineers Tom May and Dave Thompson.

Back in the studio again, the group today begins recording sessions in earnest for their fifth album. Producer Gary Usher has retained the same three-man team of himself, Tom May, and Dave Thompson behind the console. The group tries out the instrumental backing track to a new number, 'Universal Mind Decoder'. Also known as 'Universal Decoding' and 'Changes Now' on the studio sheets, the song is later reworked as 'Change Is Now'. (Today's attempted 'Universal Mind Decoder' will later be released as part of the reissue programme of the Byrds catalogue in the 1990s.) The group also begin work on a new Crosby composition, 'Draft Morning', which they return to tomorrow.

•

Jim McGuinn undergoes a name change this summer. From now on he is to be known as Roger McGuinn. It is McGuinn's connection with the spiritual association of Subud that has inspired him to make the change. Subud helps its members to renew contact with the power of God, but is neither a strictly organised teaching nor a religion. It was founded in Indonesia in the 20s. McGuinn has been a practising member since Ed Tickner's wife introduced him to Subud in January 1965. It will take some time before the new name seeps in, and he is on occasion still referred to as 'Jim' in the press as late as 1970.

McGuinn explains the origin of his adopted first name to Pete Johnson of *The Los Angeles Times* (April 21, 1968). "When we [McGuinn and wife Dolores] had our son, I named him James IV. Then we decided to send to Indonesia to find out what his real name was and it came back Patrick McGuinn. I thought, 'Wow, that's a groovy name'. That's a better name than I would have thought of. So I was curious to see what mine was, and my wife and I both sent for our names. We got them and she was

Ianthe, from Dolores, and I was Roger."

In an interview with Mary Campbell of Associated Press (syndicated in May 1969), McGuinn says: "I changed my name to Roger from Jim because I'm in a group called Subud. It's an Indonesian philosophy, an Eastern mystical thing that offers an optional name change. The theory behind it is that the sound of your name should be appropriate to your essential vibrations. I sent to Indonesia for it. They sent the letter R. I picked ten names and got the reply that my name was Roger. I like the way it feels." (In an early 70s interview, McGuinn will describe Subud as "a westernisation of Islam, really". But by then he has left the association – although the name stays.)

August

Tuesday 1

◁» **RECORDING** Columbia Recording Studios, Sunset and El Centro, Hollywood, CA. Producer Gary Usher and engineers Tom May and Dave Thompson.

Work continues on 'Universal Mind Decoder' and 'Draft Morning' (see July 31).

ALSO ...

George Harrison arrives in Los Angeles to stay for a week. Between visits to Ravi Shankar's Kinnara School of Indian Music, to Derek Taylor and family, and to a Mamas & Papas session, he finds time to welcome David Crosby up at Blue Jay Way, the house he has rented in the Hollywood Hills.

Taylor, who will move back to England early next year, has been a tireless and faithful campaigner for The Byrds, although his patience with the group has at times been stretched to the limit. One of his last Byrds-related assignments is to pen a feature for *Hit Parader* in October (belatedly published in the magazine's March 1968 edition). His place in the history and making of The Byrds looms large, as Crosby will later tell Ben Fong-Torres: "He was an excellent myth-maker. He blew us up, made us bigger than life. Turned our thing not into something else, but I'd say he placed a lens in front of it that blew it up. Huge."

Wednesday 2–Thursday 3

◁» **RECORDING** Columbia Recording Studios, Sunset and El Centro, Hollywood, CA. Producer Gary Usher and engineers Tom May and Dave Thompson.

Work on 'Universal Mind Decoder' again continues. The group will return to it later in August under its other title, 'Change Is Now'. For now, 'Draft Morning' is completed.

Crosby's sensitive lyric about a soldier's last morning before enlistment inspires producer Usher to call on The Firesign Theatre to add sound effects. A comedy group that specialises in audio recordings, the troupe handles the subject of Crosby's lyric seriously enough to come up with an aural recreation of a war battle, added to the track together with an overdubbed trumpet solo. The Firesign Theatre's contribution is supposedly identical to a track already prepared for another of Usher's clients, the English duo Chad & Jeremy, whose soon-to-be-released psyched-out masterpiece *Of Cabbages And Kings* contains the sidelong 'The Progress Suite' that combines vocals, music, and effects.

Despite internal friction, the recent skirmishes with Crosby, and dissatisfaction with Clarke's musicianship, for the moment at least the four-man Byrds seem to pull together to create satisfactory results. However, the story of 'Draft Morning' is not yet closed, and McGuinn and Hillman will later meddle with the finished track.

Saturday 5–Sunday 6
Honolulu International Center Arena, Honolulu, HI
Radio station K-POI presents The Young Rascals and 'special guest stars' The Byrds plus local group The Val Richards V for two nights, at the start of a short Hawaiian tour. The Saturday show pulls a capacity crowd of 8,360, and with a near full house for the Sunday show the expected gross is in the region of $74,000 for both shows.

The Honolulu Star-Bulletin (August 7) reviews the Saturday show and gives a snapshot of a group divided. "And queer Byrds they are too. The group once had a unified image – long, straight hair, combed down Beatle-like, smooth shaven and clean cut. While they're still flocking together, each Byrd has now got his own bag. Drummer Michael Clarke has his hair cut short, and once the group got underway, removed his shirt and played for the reminder of the evening bare-chested. Chris Hillman no longer straightens his hair. It's now plopped atop his head like a giant Russian fur shapka, giving him the appearance of a cross between Dylan, Art Garfunkel, and Dr Zorba. Jim McGuinn has announced he's changing his name to Roger for spiritual reasons, and is sporting a Papa John Phillips-type beard. David Crosby still has that infectious smile, but it's almost hidden behind his downward-twirled moustache. With his T-shirt, jeans, cowboy hat, and long shoulder-length hair, he looked as if he were heading for a costume party dressed as Buffalo Bill."

Reviewer Dave Donnelly continues: "They are expert musicians, sing with a polished

harmony, and re-tune their instruments after each number. The effect on the audience is that The Byrds are not so much performers as excellent musicians who want their songs to sound good and be meaningful. Much of the substance of their material seemed wasted on the audience. Largely teenyboppers who came to scream. In fact, one older woman was heard to remark after surveying the audience, 'Now I know what they mean when they say teenybopper.' The Byrds closed their portion of the program with the satirical 'So You Want To Be A Rock'n'Roll Star', but not before inviting the audience to California to 'sample some of the people, some of the scenes'."

In parting, Donnelly compares the two headlining groups and says: "Put them all together and [The Young Rascals] spell excitement. And this is where The Rascals differ from The Byrds. The Byrds are musicians who perform. The Rascals are performers who play music."

The Honolulu Advertiser (August 7) reviews the Sunday show. "The Byrds have changed their looks, their style, and their music. While 'Turn! Turn! Turn!', 'Mr. Tambou-

rine Man', 'Have You Seen Her Face', and 'Eight Miles High' were obvious clicks, their new tunes seemed to drag. I think it was a case of The Byrds growing up musically and doing what they want to do, rather than that which appeals to the mass public. Leader Jim McGuinn, who now sports a beard, did most of the vocals. David Crosby's 'Hey Joe' was a brightener. Drummer Mike Clarke and [bassist] Chris Hillman – the latter with a shock of hair reminiscent of Dylan and Garfunkel – worked up a sweat. The Byrds, with the exception of Clarke, now look like a hippie combo from Haight-Ashbury. They even had a display of psychedelic lights (reds, blues, yellows) to accompany several of their songs."

Record Mirror today prints an interview with Bruce Johnston of The Beach Boys who is asked about other top groups around the world. "This may sound surprising coming from a Beach Boy, but I always thought The Byrds could be America's equivalent to The Beatles. I dig The Byrds, and although I'm glad that its seems that it's us in America and The Beatles in Britain, The Byrds could have been there. I've seen The Byrds several times

on stage, and they're not consistent. Sometimes they're really great, other times they're not. The other top groups, the ones that will last, are The Lovin' Spoonful, the Stones, and, of course, The Beatles."

Monday 7

Columbia Records releases *The Byrds Greatest Hits* in the US. This first compilation album of the group's work collects 11 of their best known tracks and biggest sellers up to 'My Back Pages'. The record omits this summer's 'Lady Friend', which will not be released on a vinyl album until another Byrds singles compilation in 1982.

Greatest Hits becomes the group's biggest selling album of all time, making Number 6 in the *Billboard* chart to rival the previous peak position held by the *Mr. Tambourine Man* album and certified a platinum-seller by 1986. (The Recording Industry Association of America, RIAA, awards Platinum for sales of 1,000,000 units.)

WCFL Beat (October 7) says in its review of the record: "Remember when the world centred around England and the sounds that were coming out of that small island? America, who for so long had ruled the world as the leading exponent of pop music, suddenly found itself replaced by the Limeys. But during that time, one group did emerge in America to help to revolutionise the pop scene and to pave the way for the so-called psychedelic music of today."

Rock critic Paul Williams, in *Crawdaddy* (September–October 1967), gives the album a flowery appraisal. "Any greatest hits album is insignificant. By definition it contains nothing unfamiliar; and yet this very fact offers great potential beauty, for a well-made greatest hits LP might then unleash the emotion of familiarity in an artistic context. The Byrds have achieved that goal: always masters of the form, they have now taken the concept of a great hits anthology and created from it an essay into rediscovery.

"Greatest Hits are always regarded as suspect. It's part of the American guilt syndrome: packaging is not considered work," Williams writes, "and art without work is invisible. This is crap, of course: the Puritan Ethic; but it is still so strong in this country that it was necessary to invent (and invalidate as art) the concept 'put-on' in order to make Andy Warhol famous and yet be able to ignore his genius at the same time. Confronted with this album (and probably this review) the average Ameri-

can scoffs. 'It's all done with mirrors!' Yes, it is, and look at that cover again.

"Rock criticism is also extremely suspect, as was pointed out to me by none other than David Crosby (he stood on his hind legs in the Tin Angel and proclaimed, me listening, that 'the one thing you absolutely cannot do in this field is intellectualise!'). I think it is understandable and even reasonable for a rock star to want to play God; it was a pretty good *Don't Look Back* parody, and I don't begrudge it. Sandy Pearlman later brought up an interesting point: we write articles about music and art and what's in our minds and stuff, and these performers somehow get the idea we're writing about them!"

Monday 7–Tuesday 8

Following Honolulu, the group has two days off in Hawaii. With all Byrds stuck in the same place, forced together by circumstance rather than design, McGuinn, Crosby, and Hillman work together on a couple of songs. 'Draft Morning', already recorded and apparently completed to everybody's satisfaction before departure for Hawaii, will be a subject of contention in the weeks and months to come, much to its composer's anger. McGuinn and Hillman will wipe out Crosby's contributions and, worse still, rewrite some of the lyrics and claim a shared credit.

Asked if Crosby is on the final recorded version of 'Draft Morning', Hillman later denies it, explaining to Pete Frame in *Zigzag* (May 1973): "No – McGuinn and I did the vocals on that one. ... It was us. [Crosby] had written the basic song, but we had to re-write some of the words because he left right after introducing the song to us, and we could hardly remember the lyrics. We first got that and 'Dolphin's Smile' together in Hawaii, I remember; we were working there and this house on the other side of the island of Oahu – we worked those songs up there, ready to record when we got back."

Whatever the circumstances, it seems that here in Hawaii, Crosby, McGuinn, and Hillman bond creatively.

Wednesday 9
Kauai War Memorial Auditorium, Lihue, HI

From Oahu, the Young Rascals–Byrds tour moves on to Lihue on Kauai, the northernmost island on the Hawaiian archipelago.

Thursday 10
Maui War Memorial Auditorium, Wailuku, HI

The Young Rascals–Byrds island-hopping continues as the tour transfers to Wailuku on Maui, the second-largest of the Hawaiian islands.

Friday 11
Hilo Civic Auditorium, Hilo, Big Island, HI

The Young Rascals–Byrds entourage play Hawaii (Big Island) before The Rascals bow out of the tour.

Saturday 12

Honolulu International Center, Exhibition Hall, Honolulu, HI

K-POI present a 'fly-in' starring The Byrds together with a slew of locals groups: The Val Richards V, Loves Special Delivery, The Intrigues, and Blues Crew. The Byrds fly back to the mainland afterwards.

The Byrds' Greatest Hits

A1 'Mr. Tambourine Man' (B. DYLAN)
A2 'I'll Feel A Whole Lot Better' (G. CLARK)
A3 'The Bells Of Rhymney' (I. DAVIES/P. SEEGER)
A4 'Turn! Turn! Turn! (To Everything There Is A Season)'
    (BOOK OF ECCLESIASTES/P. SEEGER)
A5 'All I Really Want To Do' (B. DYLAN)
A6 'Chimes Of Freedom' (B. DYLAN)
B1 'Eight Miles High' (B. DYLAN)
B2 'Mr. Spaceman' (J. MCGUINN)
B3 '5D' (J. McGUINN)
B4 'So You Want To Be A Rock 'n' Roll Star' (J. MCGUINN/C. HILLMAN)
B5 'My Back Pages' (B. DYLAN)

US release August 7 1967 (Columbia CL 2716)
UK release October 20 1967 (CBS SBPG 63107)
Chart high US number 6; UK none
Read more ... entry for August 7 1967

Bonus CD tracks: 'It Won't Be Wrong' (J. McGuinn/H. Gerst), 'Set You Free This Time' (G. Clark), 'Have You Seen Her Face' (C. Hillman)

> *"Remember when the world centred around England and the sounds that were coming out of that small island? ... But during that time, one group did emerge in America to help to revolutionise the pop scene and to pave the way for the so-called psychedelic music of today." WCLF Beat October 7, 1967*

Monday 14

🔊 **RECORDING** Columbia Recording Studios, Studio D, Sunset and El Centro, Hollywood, CA. Producer Gary Usher and engineers Tom May and Dave Thompson.

The four Byrds reconvene at Columbia to continue work on 'Universal Mind Decoder' (see August 1–3) and to start recording the softly swinging 'Dolphin's Smile', the song mapped out in Hawaii last week. The session soon deteriorates as Crosby, frustrated by Clarke's inability to grasp what the song needs, lays into the drummer. A tape of the ensuing studio conversation exists, and, as author Ric Menck writes, "for those of you who enjoy slowing down at the sight of an automobile accident" one can be a fly on the wall as the group squabbles and Usher tries to retain control.

At first, Crosby tries to help Clarke along. "Can we give you some ideas? Instead of that fast choppy stuff, see, it's supposed to be a kind of long, slow floating thing. Feel like a boat, not like horses clopping or something, you know? It's supposed to be a long, kind of smooth thing."

Attempts follow, and after another take comes to a halt, Crosby tells Clarke: "And the only reason you don't like it, is that you haven't got it. That's always the reason and that's always the reason you do it. Why don't you just try to get something pretty, and then you'll like it?" Usher speaks reassuringly over the intercom: "Michael, that sounded pretty good, let's try it a few times, we got plenty of time." Then Crosby and McGuinn start arguing too. Usher says optimistically, "We're real close to it, it sounded real good; let's try it one more time," before announcing Take 12, which promptly breaks down as Crosby and the hapless drummer engage in a shouting match.

To Crosby's irritated "Try playing right!" Clarke replies: "What do you mean, try playing right? What do you know what the fuck's right or what's wrong, you know? You're not a musician." Crosby comes back: "I've heard you play it before, Michael, I know you, I know you're just fucking up when you're playing. You dig it?"

McGuinn tries to interrupt, but Crosby keeps it up. "You're just fucking up, you know. You're doing your number." Now McGuinn's getting impatient, and an attempted Take 11 also breaks down while Crosby and Clarke swear and curse. "Can't you play the drums? Shall I learn you how to play?"

Clarke is ready to go. "If you don't like me, send me away." Crosby protests: "We love you, man, we want you to play drums right!" But Clarke just repeats: "Send me away." Then comes the final insult: "I don't even like the

song!" With that, his mates just ask, "What are you in the group for?" and suggest bringing in session drummer Hal Blaine.

Tuesday 15

🔊 **RECORDING** Columbia Recording Studios, Sunset and El Centro, Hollywood, CA. Producer Gary Usher and engineers Tom May and Dave Thompson.

Drummer John Keliehor of The Daily Flash – the group that opened for The Byrds at Whisky A Go Go last year – later recalls an interesting incident that may well take place today (or possibly yesterday). "One morning, David Crosby phoned to say that Michael Clarke had left the group," says Keliehor, "and there was a good chance that I could be the drummer they were looking for. He asked if I would like to meet the rest of the group, and would I be free to play at a recording session at CBS studios that morning? 'How do I get my drums there,' I asked. 'I have no cash on me.' He said that he'd meet me in front of the studios in 30 minutes, and pay the taxi fare.

"I arrived and removed my drums from the taxi, and David came out to greet me. As we began to carry the drums into the building, Michael Clarke appeared from around the corner carrying a suitcase in either hand. He looked like he might have just arrived from Hawaii. At that point Crosby set my case on the ground and went to talk to Michael, and in a few minutes came back to me saying, 'Sorry man, but Michael has just returned and I'm going to have to see this through.' He gave me money for a taxi home again. Later he phoned to confirm that Michael was back in the group, and he never contacted me after that."

With Clarke still aboard, the group presumably returns to work today on 'Dolphin's Smile'.

Wednesday 16

🔊 **RECORDING** Columbia Recording Studios, Sunset and El Centro, Hollywood, CA. Producer Gary Usher and engineers Tom May and Dave Thompson.

An effective day in the studio sees two songs are completed: 'Dolphin's Smile' plus a new one, 'Tribal Gathering'. This is yet another Crosby creation, although written in tandem with Hillman, and has a jazzy 5/4 groove. Both songs are washed with lush vocal harmonies.

There will be doubt later about who plays drums on today's session, but aural evidence points to Clarke being the man on both songs. On 'Tribal Gathering' he turns the beat around at about the one-minute break, something that an experienced session drummer would not do.

Thursday 17

🔊 **RECORDING** Columbia Recording Studios, Sunset and El Centro, Hollywood, CA. Producer Gary Usher and engineers Tom May and Dave Thompson.

Songs seem to burst from Crosby's pen at an astonishing rate, and today is devoted to recording a song that will not be released until the CD reissue series in the 90s. The song in question is 'Triad', Crosby's ode to "why we can't go on as three".

The song has a strong melody with a rock steady beat topped by an impassioned vocal, and is an obvious contender for the coming album. However, the lyric is yet another bone of contention, but the reason for leaving the song out of the next album is mundane – after Crosby's eventual departure, a sole Crosby composing credit will be out of the question. (He pitches the song to his friends Grace Slick and Paul Kantner in Jefferson Airplane, who record it on May 29 next year for their *Crown Of Creation* album.)

Today is certainly the debut of Jim Gordon on a Byrds session, the first time The Byrds have used an outside drummer since the recording of 'Mr. Tambourine Man' and 'I'd Knew I'd Want You' back in January 1965. Among his countless credentials, Gordon has toured with The Everly Brothers and played on sessions by The Monkees and The Beach Boys, as well as playing drums on parts of *Gene Clark With The Gosdin Brothers*. He is also in Chad & Jeremy's touring band this fall.

It's possible that a driving instrumental outtake, 'Bound To Fall', is also recorded today. It certainly features McGuinn and Crosby on guitars and it does sound like the assured Gordon is anchoring the song's angular meter. The song is written by (Tom) Maston & (Mike) Brewer, the duo that opened for The Byrds and Buffalo Springfield in May 1966.

Friday 18–Sunday 20

The Cheetah, Chicago, IL

The plush Cheetah has now come to Chicago, establishing itself uptown on Lawrence Avenue. Supported by The Faded Blues and The Holy Om, the pre-show blurb for The Byrds' weekend promises black (really) and stroboscopic lights by Love Unlimited and a nightly Tiger Morse boutique fashion display. Although Michael Clarke did not drum with the group on yesterday's session, he appears with the group tonight on stage.

•

A long, rambling Crosby monologue taped around this time is transcribed in its entirety for the benefit of *South California Oracle* readers and published in the paper's October issue. He talks about 'keeping it loose', 'how I get high', 'enduring trip', and so on, and speaks warmly of up-and-coming groups The Peanut Butter Conspiracy, Clear Light, and The Gentle Soul (Pamela Polland and Rick Stanley), and of musical telepathy. "You get to about 70 per cent level with just sheer technique, but to really play the magic stuff you have to be in rapport with the other cats. You've got to know exactly what is happening on levels that are non-verbal. You've got to be linked with the other people. The Byrds is a perfect example, because if you watch us two nights in a row, you'll see us one night when we're not linked and we're shitty. Come back the next night and we love each other and we cook your brains off, take you right off for a full set!"

Free spirit or dreamer, Crosby's thoughts are reflected in his recent lyrics. "All the rules, all the national rules, all the Federal rules, all the state rules, and all the local rules stop at the three-mile limit. I'm going to buy a boat. I hope a lot of other people do too. Get a bunch of boats together travelling around together, a sea tribe of people that live mostly off what they get from the seas and a little of what they traded in various places, and some of their royalties from the songs they used to write. … No longer a concern to [the establishment], or anybody else, except the dolphins who will watch you pretty closely, and their big brothers, the whales.

"Been saving and figuring, and learning, and hoping, and fucking around, and dreaming and thinking about getting a boat for eight years or so. I'm taking a month off to go look for it in Scandinavia. I got the money in the bank. Sailing is the most joyous and consciousness-expanding experience of my life, next to making love and my music. Sailing is balancing between different kinds of continuum on this multidimensional fulcrum. Part of it is in one whole thing, and another part of it is in another whole thing, and the conditions: water against the air. A boat is graceful as a bird, and a piece of art, and our home. It's a good trip. Very meaningful."

Thursday 24–Sunday 27
Whisky A Go Go, West Hollywood, CA
Since July, the Whisky A Go Go has reverted to its old policy of booking local talent and visiting rock groups of all shades instead of the Motown–soul profile the club cultivated in the first half of this year. The Byrds are supported by The Things To Come, a Long Beach group with the young Russ Kunkel at the back on drums.

The Los Angeles underground paper *Open City* (August 31–September 7) stops by for a chat with Roger (Jim) McGuinn. "For the last year the market has been frustrating," says McGuinn. "Because, like, we proved our point

and it's sort of droning along now. There are so many new groups coming along, the competition's getting to be a drag. A lot of them are fine groups, but very shortlived because of the heavy competition. It's getting very much like the commercial folk music scene was in 1962 and '63. It became plasticised folk music, and they sold it in dime stores, which is what they're doing to rock. It's getting back to where it was before The Beatles came along.

"It's like somebody a few years ago poured a highly concentrated marvellous chemical into a big vat of water. Then they added more water to it. Now there's so much water you can hardly taste the essence anymore. It's time to get a new pool, a new water, to get into a new bag."

Open City journalist John Bryan wonders where that will be. "For me, I think, it will be making films. The underground film thing is just starting off and I think it's a frontier. I went out and bought a Bolex [camera] and projection equipment and tons of film. And I go around shooting stuff, and I'm just nuts on it now."

The Byrds guitarist talks about 'Lady Friend' – "wincing with obvious distaste" as Bryan puts it. "Our latest things are very much in the jazz bag, except one record we've got out now which is sort of our imitation of a commercial record, which is not real. It's sort of an imitation of some commercial group like The Four Seasons. It's sort of we just don't know what to do to make of it now. To make Number One you've got to be a new group and have something fresh, or at least another viewpoint, to catch attention. This seems to be true of everyone but The Beatles." According to McGuinn, 'Lady Friend' has sold 70,000 copies.

He is keen to explore the jazzier side of their music. "We're tending towards jazz now. When we started out we did what they termed folk-rock, which was a hideous name but it was appropriate for the time, I guess. But then we went on. Like 'Eight Miles High' was based on Coltrane. It wasn't technically up to that level, but we wanted to emulate it … trying to get up there."

McGuinn offers some surprisingly radical views. "The revolution will continue. But it will be in many mediums. If we, the revolutionary people, go into films, it will go into films. We'll cop more media as we go along. I'd like to get them all. Politics, too. I don't feel that I want to be a politician, but there's no room for the old style politicians any more. Artists and politicians have always been the same kind of thing in two different areas. Now it's combined. Artists used to pretend they weren't involved in politics. But now it's going the other way around.

"Look at Pete Seeger. It's horrible, man. I mean, we're at a point of extreme tension. We're seeing the beginning of a revolution, whatever you want to call it. It's the young. It happens every generation, but this time there's really a lot of beef about. The only problem is that as a revolution it's really a sloppy one. And if somebody doesn't do something quickly to organise it, it's going to be a drag."

Monday 28–Wednesday 30
ALSO …
Gene Clark is at the Whisky A Go Go with a new group: Clarence White on guitar, ex-Sir Douglas Quintet bass player John York, and itinerant drummer Eddie Hoh. Byrds manager Larry Spector is now also representing Clark. York recalls the gig as a bit of an embarrassment. "I remember the feeling of that band very well. It was exceptional. But at the Whisky, the audience was full of record company people who talked so much that Gene decided it was a waste of time doing his songs. He said 'just jam in E', which we did until he finally just left the stage." (Clark's set includes 'I'm A Loser', 'Hey Joe', 'Black Sheep Boy', 'We Can Work It Out', and 'Roll Over Beethoven', all performed in a medium tempo, "which became deadening despite [Clark's] vocal ability" according to *The Los Angeles Times*.)

Tuesday 29–Wednesday 30
🔊 **RECORDING** Columbia Recording Studios, Sunset and El Centro, Hollywood, CA. Producer Gary Usher and engineers Tom May and Dave Thompson.

Back at Columbia, 'Universal Mind Decoder' (see July 31) is re-recorded as 'Change Is Now' on the Wednesday. The group also tinkers with overdubs for 'Tribal Gathering' (see August 16) on both days.

Although 'Change Is Now' has a perfect Michael Clarke drum groove, the group has called on the reliable services of sessionman Hal Blaine. He is not the only outside musician on the session: besides McGuinn, Crosby, and Hillman, guitarist Clarence White is here, and so is pedal steel player Orville 'Red' Rhodes.

The pedal steel guitar is stigmatised as strictly country & western, and its appearance here on a conventional rock session is a historic one. At nights, Red Rhodes leads The Detours, a group that plays regularly at the Palomino club on Lankershim Boulevard in North Hollywood. Less than ten miles from the Sunset Strip but on the other side of Laurel Canyon, the Palomino is a hardcore country club that might as well have been situated hundreds of miles away in Nashville. As one of the few pedal steel players living in Los Angeles, Rhodes works studio sessions, but it is the Palomino that represents his steady income. Rhodes & The Detours have played the Palomino since January 1966, where they share the ring with the many country stars who ride through town: Merle Haggard, Buck Owens, Connie Smith, Bob Wills, Marty Robbins, George Jones, Tex Williams, Bob Luman, and others.

Crosby may play truant from these sessions, as he certainly adds a harmony vocal to Buffalo Springfield's 'Rock'n'Roll Woman', which is in part recorded at Hollywood's Sunset Sound recording studio on the Wednesday, the same day as he does an interview with radio DJ B. Mitchell Reed for KFWB-AM in Los Angeles. Not only that, another report has Crosby sighted at the Fillmore Auditorium up in San Francisco on Tuesday 29 to see Cream and The Electric Flag.

Thursday 31
Whisky A Go Go, West Hollywood, CA
The Byrds are back at the Whisky for another four-day stretch, once more with The Things To Come booked to play the early part of the evenings. (The Rich Kids may possibly replace them for the weekend.)

Pete Johnson of *The Los Angeles Times* (September 1) reviews the opening night together with Gene Clark's appearance at the club earlier in the week. "Now [The Byrds] are a quartet, Jim has discarded his glasses and changed his name to Roger McGuinn, and their four shaggy hairlines have fluctuated up and down, encroaching on two faces and retracting to surfer length on one pate.

"As in the past, a crowd pressed across the dance floor to the edge of the stage to stare at The Byrds, bob to their rhythm, and chorus requests. The quartet amusedly ignored the requests as they tuned and retuned their instruments and played what they wanted to, which included 'Renaissance Fair', 'He Was A Friend Of Mine', 'Hey Joe', 'The Bells Of Rhymney', 'Turn! Turn! Turn!', 'Chimes Of Freedom', '[I Know My] Rider', and 'So You Want To Be A Rock'n'Roll Star'.

"Crosby, McGuinn, and Hillman blended their voices for most of the selections, though Crosby was a soloist on several numbers, among them 'Everybody's Been Burned'. His timing was loose and his voice, which is strong, was somewhat raw. They altered the arrangement of 'Eight Miles High', introducing it with a snarl of feedback and calming the instrumental backing. Two new numbers were presented: 'The Universal Decoder' ['Change Is Now'], a good song in which Crosby switched to bass guitar to set a compelling tempo through which McGuinn's

guitar made keening organ-like sounds, and 'Why Can't We Go On And Live?' ['Triad'], a ballad in which Crosby's voice slipped into a hackneyed nightclub style."

September

Friday 1–Sunday 3
Whisky A Go Go, West Hollywood, CA
Tracy Thomas reports in *New Musical Express* (September 9): "The Byrds are alive and well in Hollywood! Once again, the Whisky A Go Go opened its doors to folk-rock'n'roll fans, who jammed the club to see this group. The group was the best they've been in a year during their opening show. Their harmonies were good; the songs (mostly from their fourth album and two new numbers) were good. David Crosby is evidently the lead singer now, as Jim McGuinn had only one solo in two sets. David has a lovely tenor folk voice which comes across very well on record, but in person he tries too hard to sound bluesy and loses the sweet quality of this voice. 'He Was A Friend Of Mine', written about the Kennedy Assassination, was the only 'old' song in that set.

"Between times, the stars began to arrive: Davy Jones (looking younger than Springtime), closely followed by Peter Tork (hair shorter than ever, smile broader than ever) hugging everyone in sight. Lou Adler came with Scott McKenzie, who has allowed his hair to grow down to his shoulders, making him look even more like the flower-child he is not. Johnny Rivers and a few local rock stars filled in the few spaces left by the Byrd fans, who were all but climbing on each other's shoulders to see the dear ones. The less said about their second set the better – why they continue to do 'Eight Miles High' without learning the harmony remains a mystery."

For the Whisky shows, Crosby has replaced his favoured Gretsch guitars with a Gibson hollowbody with natural finish and a Bigsby vibrato, and McGuinn switches between his regular Rickenbacker 12-string and a Gretsch six-string. As The Byrds pack up, Eric Clapton and Cream move in at the Whisky for a three-night residence.

Friday 1
'Lady Friend' is released in the UK, but coupled with 'Don't Make Waves' rather than its American counterpart's 'Old John Robertson'. Derek Johnson writes in *New Musical Express*: "An incredible full sound on this disc by The Byrds, obtained by the exaggerated use of echo and excessive 'top'. The familiar

West Coast harmonies are well in evidence, and the arrangement is positively startling. It's described as the sound of tomorrow and that may hamper its chances today! FLIP: The title song from a new Tony Curtis film, and consequently much more orthodox in styling."

Mike Ledgerwood in *Disc* says: "The Byrds are back! With that crashing, full-blooded sound and haunting voice harmony built around Dave Crosby's 'Lady Friend'. A vast improvement on their recent offerings. Deserves to be a hit." *Melody Maker*'s Chris Welch is uncharacteristically positive: "David Crosby wrote this happening Byrds song, which echoes and jangles nicely. There is a resounding middle build-up with brass and the melody and harmonies are warm and exciting. An excellent production that will bring The Byrds back to our attention as a major chart force."

Finally, Peter Jones in *Record Mirror*: "A dubious proposition, currently, but this is good-class Byrd-material, and the rolling harmonies and strong backing punch could help it. Very distinctive sounds, in fact. Good for the discotheque scene. I'd say – and there's something about the song that makes it worth commending – a lot happening. FLIP: Less pungent but another good song." The superior reviews do not help sales, as the single goes nowhere. (All reviews are published on September 2 with the exception of *Record Mirror*, which is published a week later.)

The single is also served up in *Melody Maker*'s 'Blind Date' test (September 9), where pop crooner Engelbert Humperdinck is the week's guest. "I wish there was a bit more separation on this. I must say the arrangements are getting a bit involved lately, aren't they? This certainly isn't easy to listen to. It's a very complex and muddied sound really. I wouldn't like to judge this record because it's slightly mixed-up – oh dear – that's another leave-you-in-the-air chord finish. I don't know who it is. The Byrds. Ummm. Strictly for the birds! I don't think I could ever put that on. Exit Byrds through the window."

'Lady Friend' (UK)

A 'Lady Friend' (D. CROSBY)
B 'Don't Make Waves' (J. MCGUINN/C. HILLMAN)

UK release September 1 1967 (CBS 2924)
Chart high UK none
Read more ... entries for April 26, May 4, 10, 23, June 5, 14 1967

Tuesday 5–Wednesday 6

🔊 **RECORDING** Columbia Recording Studios, Sunset and El Centro, Hollywood, CA. Producer Gary Usher and engineers Tom May and Dave Thompson.

Gary Usher has eagerly pushed for The Byrds to attempt 'Goin' Back', a song written by lyricist Gerry Goffin and composer Carole King, previously a major British hit for Dusty Springfield. The Goffin/King team is a veritable song machine, having written countless hits to order since 1960.

Reportedly, none of The Byrds are keen on the song, and Crosby – who so far in the recording process has been the creative dynamo and supplied the majority of new material – detests it. All the same, McGuinn, Crosby, Hillman, and drummer Jim Gordon complete a version over these two days. An uncredited part played on glockenspiel is added, and although the group will re-record the song a month later, this first attempt will be released much later when it is included as part of the group's revived back catalogue in the 90s.

Usher recalls to chronicler Stephen J. McParland the tense atmosphere in the studio. "Crosby was adamant about not doing ['Goin Back'] and [said:] 'You guys work it up! I don't want to cut the damn thing!' McGuinn looked at him and said, 'Crosby, why don't you just fuck off.' They were his exact words. Then he continued, 'If you don't like it, just get the fuck out of here.' Crosby got up, walked out of the studio, and never came back."

Thursday 7–Saturday 9

Fillmore Auditorium, San Francisco, CA
Supported by Loading Zone and LDM Spiritual Band and with a lightshow by Holy See, the group plays Bill Graham's Fillmore theatre for the third time. Music fan Richard Lewis is in the crowd, snapping photos of the group, and he remembers them as "pretty together".

From the crowd, everything may look all right, but things are not running smoothly on stage. According to road manager Jimmi Seiter, a short-fused Crosby stays at a different hotel than the other three and quarrels with Seiter backstage about the length of the shows.

Friday 15

Don't Make Waves, featuring The Byrds' title song, is premiered in movie theatres in the US to lukewarm reviews.

•

There's a lull in the group's schedule following the Fillmore performances at the beginning of the month, and McGuinn and Hillman decide to take action and kick

Crosby out of The Byrds. It is not an honourable discharge. One morning, they drive up to Crosby's house and give him the news that he is no longer a Byrd. To them, Crosby has become a liability: there's too much rebellion, too much stress, and not enough cooperation. Michael Clarke has already put himself on the sidelines and is not party to the decision, but new manager Larry Spector probably has a hand in the firing.

The precise date of Crosby's dismissal is lost to time, but Jimmi Seiter is certain it was right after the Fillmore shows. The news is not made public for some time, presumably to allow the remaining Byrds to come to a reasonable settlement with Crosby. The first official news of Crosby's departure is announced in the premier issue of *Rolling Stone* (printed October 18 although dated November 9), a magazine founded by Ralph J. Gleason and Jann Wenner.

Next year, in April 1968, McGuinn will speak of the Crosby problem for the first time in some detail to Pete Johnson of *The Los Angeles Times*. "David was always a very acidic character," says McGuinn. "He was always eating into somebody. He was starting to lose interest in the group. It was sort of an underdog group by this time, and his buddies in Buffalo Springfield and Jefferson Airplane were saying, 'Come on, David, you can do better than that.' And he was saying, 'Yeah, man, but I've got to be loyal to McGuinn and Hillman, I can't let them down.' Being noble and everything. And all this time we were wishing he'd split because he was heavy, hard to handle, being a little too outspoken and hip for the wrong reasons. And he started getting very like a tyrant on the material."

Several reasons will be given in hindsight for this dramatic decision. One is the recently

recorded 'Triad'. Another suggests Crosby's lack of interest in 'Goin' Back' is the main argument. Hillman – in an interview in *Zigzag* (May 1973) – denies this. "[His] leaving was the result of a more general dissension between him and us, not based on any one specific incident. We just got to the point where we couldn't work together – he just kept going out on a tangent."

Crosby rants to journalist Ben Fong-Torres in 1970: "I was going on a stage, man, with a band that was a bum. It was like going out and selling parsley on the street and havin' to meet the people the next day. Byrdshit! It wasn't the Byrds; it was the fucking canaries!"

The same interview reveals a lot of affection, too. "We may have been less than sophisticated, man, but we were a goddamned good fucking icebreaker," explains Crosby. "Cos we were unafraid. We made mistakes, but in order to be unafraid, you have to be willing to make mistakes – publicly! At the same time, man, it was a bunch of human cats. And like one of the mistakes they could make was to cop out on the whole thing. And you can be sure, man, that in the course of a long and dreary career you make a lot of the mistakes that there are. That's one thing that got me. Hey, and that's not a slur on those cats, man. Roger McGuinn? Lord knows, that cat has a far-out head and he's certainly one of the farthest out musicians on the scene. Before, then, now, probably always. And Chris Hillman isn't exactly a dope, either."

Crosby will write in his autobiography: "They tossed me out. I was sitting in my house in Beverly Glen Canyon up on Lisbon Lane, when Roger and Christopher came over in two Porsches. Vroom, vroom, screech! Footsteps on the stairs, door opening, they enter and just start right in: 'Hey man, basically we want to get you out of the band.' 'It's not working real well … ' 'We're disagreeing all the time … ' 'You're real difficult to work with … ' 'We don't dig your songs that much and we think we'll do better without you.'

"To this day, I love remembering that last particular phrase, because it was certainly less than a year afterward that we put out [the *Crosby Stills & Nash* album]. I got some cheesy settlement, a total of maybe $10,000 for my part of the name. By that time I was already doing drugs and the ten grand sort of went. I was snorting coke and I had already started doing heroin." To Byrds biographer Johnny Rogan, Crosby will describe his discharge in four words: "It hurt like hell."

Left on his own, Crosby finally has time to realise his long-time dream: he borrows $22,500 from Pete Tork to buy *Mayan*, a 60-foot wooden schooner that he finds in Florida.

David Crosby at the Fillmore Auditorium, San Francisco, September 1967.

October

Monday 9

◁)) **RECORDING** Columbia Recording Studios, Sunset and El Centro, Hollywood, CA. Producer Gary Usher and engineers Tom May and Dave Thompson.

With Crosby kicked out and Michael Clarke dissatisfied and uninterested, the remaining two Byrds, McGuinn and Hillman, take command of the remaining sessions for the new album. Roughly half is in the can, with six songs more or less completed: 'Change Is Now' (or 'Universal Mind Decoder'); 'Draft Morning'; 'Tribal Gathering'; 'Dolphin's Smile'; 'Triad'; and 'Goin' Back'. That's not counting the rough instrumental take of 'Bound To Fall'.

Crosby has been an undisputed creative force so far in the sessions, and, short of material for the moment, McGuinn and Hillman choose to re-record Goffin & King's 'Goin' Back', the very song that Crosby so detested. Jim Gordon is behind the drums again and, as if to make up for Crosby's absence, producer Gary Usher has hired an army of auxiliary musicians to piece together a recording as equally complex as the summer single 'Lady Friend'.

Stephen J. McParland's biography of Gary Usher will list the following participants: Jim Gordon (drums), Red Rhodes (pedal steel guitar), Paul Beaver (Moog synthesizer), Dennis McCarthy (celeste), James Burton (guitar), Terry Trotter (piano), Lester Harris (cello), Victor Sazer (violin), Carl West (violin), Ann Stockton (harp), and Dennis Faust (percussion).

Of particular interest is Paul Beaver's participation, although it is barely audible on the finished result. Even if McGuinn owns a Moog synthesizer, he is not comfortable operating it quite yet, and Beaver is called in because of his expertise with the instrument. It is one of the first instances of a Moog synthesizer being used on a pop recording, although The Monkees beat The Byrds this time around: just a few days earlier, Beaver programmed an overdub on 'Star Collector' – coincidentally, also a Goffin & King composition – for The Monkees. (One of Beaver's earliest assignments was to provide a synthesizer snippet on the track 'Flash, Bam, Pow' for the soundtrack to Roger Corman's movie *The Trip* back in April.)

•

'Goin' Back' is chosen by Columbia Records as the group's next single and, to promote it, The Byrds are booked on a few US television shows this month. To keep up the impression of a four-man group, Gene Clark is called in

to fill the spot vacated by Crosby. Essentially, Clark's role is just as stand-in and, as the shows are lip-synched performances to pre-recorded backing tracks, the demands on Clark are very simple: to look like a Byrd, strum an inaudible guitar, and silently mouth the harmony vocals.

Wednesday 11

◁)) **RECORDING** Columbia Recording Studios, Sunset and El Centro, Hollywood, CA. Producer Gary Usher and engineers Tom May and Dave Thompson.

Further work is done on 'Goin' Back' to prepare it for the television broadcast on Friday, and the recording is mixed and completed. Gene Clark joins The Byrds in the studio, probably today, although it is uncertain if his voice can be heard in the lush harmony choir on 'Goin' Back'.

Friday 13

▭ **US TV** CBS Television Center, Hollywood, CA. CBS Network *The Smothers Brothers Comedy Hour*

The temporarily invigorated Byrds – McGuinn, Hillman, Clark, and Clarke – pre-record 'Mr. Spaceman' and 'Goin' Back' for brothers Tom and Dick Smothers' nationwide television show. Premiered back in February, the brothers' show has already attracted attention and controversy with their overt satire. Also, it has let pop and rock groups such as Jefferson Airplane and The Who loose on the airwaves.

The Byrds' inserts are quite elaborate. For 'Mr. Spaceman' they appear in a simulated merry-go-round orbiting in space. A simpler backdrop with wooden scaffolding is used for 'Goin' Back'. Last year's 'Mr. Spaceman' may seem like an odd choice but is presumably aired to promote *The Byrds' Greatest Hits*. Strumming an acoustic guitar and mouthing the chorus, Clark has dutifully taught himself the chords to 'Goin' Back' for the mimed performance, while he appears with his red Gibson electric guitar for the lip-synched 'Mr. Spaceman'. The show is broadcast on October 22.

Monday 16

◁)) **RECORDING** Columbia Recording Studios, Sunset and El Centro, Hollywood, CA. Producer Gary Usher and engineers Tom May and Dave Thompson.

According to session files, 'Goin' Back' is completed today. (At this point, the chronology of events jars. Last Friday was the documented date for video-recording for *The Smother Brothers Comedy Hour,* so there is a possibility that 'Goin' Back' is filmed at some point this week – thus after today's session

– as the playback track heard on the Smothers show is identical to the released track.)

Wednesday 18

For those who pick up the first issue of *Rolling Stone* published today (although dated November 9), the first official news of David Crosby's departure is there to read. The news is also unveiled in L.A. underground paper *Open City* today.

According to the *Rolling Stone* story, Crosby's one wish is to make it public that he was asked to leave, so the magazine heads the news item "Byrd McGuinn Dumps Crosby". The paper says Crosby and McGuinn have always had a tense and uneasy relationship, citing the incident at the Monterey Pop Festival as an indirect reason for Crosby's dismissal. "[Crosby] sported an STP badge on his guitar," says the item, "and attacked the government over Kennedy's assassination and the War in Vietnam. Crosby has never hidden his opinions about anything. This week, his patience gone, McGuinn decided it would be better for the group's morale if he left." In both *Rolling Stone* and *Open City*, Gene Clark is presented as Crosby's replacement.

→ mid-October

▭ **US TV** The NBC network has hired English actor and singer Noel Harrison – a star of NBC's TV series *The Man From U.N.C.L.E* (the show airs for the last time on January 15 next year) – to host an hour-long special called *Where The Girls Are*. The show starts production now, and The Byrds are among the artists signed to appear.

The segments featuring the group are symptomatic of the chaos in the ranks. They lip-synch 'Mr. Spaceman' taped on two different locations: one is a studio version with Clark, McGuinn, and two non-Byrds (the bass player and the drummer); the other is shot outdoors on a freeway with Clark, McGuinn, and Clarke. They also appear in a rendition of The Beatles' 'Good Day Sunshine' together with Noel Harrison (who sings the first verse), Barbara McNair (who sings the second), while The Byrds – in fact only Clark and McGuinn and the two non-Byrds – sing the third verse. Chris Hillman is nowhere to be seen, and it is road manager Jimmi Seiter who gamely takes his place for this show. The mystery drummer may be the percussionist from The Association, who also appear on the show.

Noel Harrison is interviewed in *The Los Angeles Times* (February 18, 1968) and sighs: "I have terrible trouble with that title [*Where The Girls Are*] anyway; it was in there before I was. I'll have to work the show into that title, rather than the other way around." Harrison suggests his own modification: "Where Are

The Girls?" The show will be broadcast on April 23, 1968.

Undated October

• **Marigold Ballroom, Minneapolis, MI**
• **Imperial Lanes, Mankato, MI**

The group has already been booked to appear on a weekend of dates in Minneapolis, New York, and Pennsylvania, but Chris Hillman is worried about the prospects of a touring trio. A simple equation appears: minus Crosby, The Byrds makes three, but by adding Gene Clark they could be back to four. It so happens that Larry Spector is the manager of both Byrds and Clark, so it is a simple matter: Clark's career has not taken off as expected, so he gamely accepts to rejoin for concert duties. He even promises to curb his fear of flying. But the half-hearted reunion is not set to last.

A rehearsal is duly undertaken by Roger McGuinn, Chris Hillman, Gene Clark, and Michael Clarke, before Clark goes by train to Minneapolis, while McGuinn, Hillman, and Clarke travel by plane. The Minneapolis show is reputedly very shaky. Clark is hit by anxiety again, and for him the plane has literally already left the airport – he takes the train back to Los Angeles, leaving the three others to fly on. Apparently, the other concerts are cancelled. Clark will reappear in a couple of weeks, but only for a few selected TV shows.

Clark's re-enlistment in The Byrds will continue to fascinate and confound fans years later. Shedding light on the incident, Hillman tells journalist John Nork: "He came in and he came out. It's almost like he came in through the door and went right back out again. So quickly! It was like – I can't even remember. It was so brief. It was like a wind hitting you."

Friday 20

The 12th Byrds single is officially issued in the US, consisting of the new recordings 'Goin' Back' and 'Change Is Now'. (The actual release date may be a week or two later.) After the failure of 'Lady Friend', the release seems to be bound to duty rather than a genuine effort to light up the singles charts again. The record makes it to Number 89 in the *Billboard*, but fares better in *Cash Box* with a peak at 58.

'Goin' Back'

A 'Goin' Back' (C. KING/G. GOFFIN)
B 'Change Is Now'
   (C. HILLMAN/R. MCGUINN)

US release October 20 1967 (Columbia 44362)
UK release December 29 1967 (CBS 3093)
Chart high US number 89; UK none
Read more ... entries for August 29, 30, October 9, 11, 16 1967

Gene Clark (left) rejoins The Byrds for a few weeks in October–November 1967.

"Strong Goffin–King material much in the folk-rock bag of the first Byrds' hot ones with the sales potential of those hits," says *Billboard* (November 4), and adds hopefully: "This should prove to be the one to put them back at the top of the charts."

The Byrds Greatest Hits is released in Britain today with identical track listing to its American counterpart. *Record Mirror* (October 28) gives it a top rating of four stars and says: "The Byrds are so underrated here, really ignored. This is a chronological collection of their singles and is really something. Their sound has progressed from the Dylanesque to the sound which is one of the best in the pop world. Clever, controlled, gentle, yet so penetrating. But if you buy this, then you'll have to buy their other albums, so watch it!" *Beat Instrumental* (November 1967): "This is probably the best collection LP to come out of the States this year, and has songs that won't date for years to come."

Sunday 22

The Byrds appear on *The Smothers Brothers Comedy Hour* (second season, episode #108), transmitted on the CBS network at 9:00pm. The group perform 'Mr. Spaceman' and 'Goin' Back' (see October 13 and 16). However, apart from the spectacular effects on 'Mr. Spaceman' there is little enthusiasm in the performance: Michael Clarke plays drums and chews gum, while Gene Clark seems distant and absentminded.

The brothers Smothers are otherwise joined on the show by co-host Pat Paulsen, actor Eddie Albert, and comedienne Jackie 'Moms' Mabley, who all enact a parody of Pinocchio. The two Smothers also sing their send-up of 'The Volga Boat Song' ("Boy, are we vulgar boatmen!").

Monday 23

◁)) **RECORDING** Columbia Recording Studios, Sunset and El Centro, Hollywood, CA. Producer Gary Usher and engineer Roy Halee.

2001: A Space Odyssey is British filmmaker Stanley Kubrick's adaptation of *The Sentinel*, a science fiction novel by Arthur C. Clarke, and has by now been in production for almost two years, although it will not be premiered until April 1968. For McGuinn and his science-fiction friend Bob Hippard, the well-publicised news cannot have passed them by, and together they have come up with the new number 'Space Odyssey'. Juxtaposing a folksy melody with a space-age lyric, McGuinn and producer Usher use McGuinn's Moog synthesizer prominently to fuse the two disparate elements into a compelling whole. Essentially a Roger McGuinn solo perform-

ance, the recording is not completed until next week.

Today also marks the first appearance of engineer Roy Halee, who is in Los Angeles working on tracks by Simon & Garfunkel. Halee's expertise as an engineer has elevated him to co-producer status with Simon & Garfunkel, and he will work closely with Usher, McGuinn, and Hillman to finish the new album.

Wednesday 25

The Byrds are booked to appear on the ABC network's *Joey Bishop Show* tonight, with guests Bing & Kathryn Crosby and actress Dorothy Lamour, but the appearance is postponed until next week (see November 2).

Thursday 26

The Daily Bruin, the newspaper of the University of California, today relays the latest news of musical chairs in The Byrds. Jim Bickhart writes: "In August, rumour had it that Mike Clarke was leaving. This turned out to be false. And there was always the moody David Crosby: the one who stepped in to hold things together when Gene left. But success waned and David's spirit with it. The failure of his 'Lady Friend' was the killer. So he stayed around to record a song which he believed in and then left. With him went a part of every listener who ever appreciated a Byrds performance, live or otherwise. And who could replace David? Only one replacement was appropriate and Gene Clark returned home."

The subject is The Byrds' new single, and Bickhart indicates that 'Change Is Now' has Crosby, while 'Goin' Back' features Clark. "David is gone, maybe to Florida or other places. And no more will he listen to the audience applaud The Byrds in person, and smile his surprised smile at their warmth, then turn to play with new vigour. Vigour that could make The Byrds sound as good as something that valuable was supposed to sound. Gene has returned to take over where he left off. To intensely survey the listeners with his stare. To sing those low parts and write the good music, with Chris and Jim there, as always to play and lead, and Mike's thunder remains."

Saturday 28

And so the news of Crosby's departure makes it across the Atlantic. *Disc*'s US correspondent Nancy Lewis uses the recent *Rolling Stone* news item as its source, and confirms to British readers that Gene Clark has rejoined. But it is Eric Clapton who will break the news to the readers of *Record Mirror* (November 18) when he discusses Cream's 'Dance The Night Away'. "It's a tribute to The Byrds with 12-

string guitars and everything. We admire them tremendously as musicians and they are also friends of ours. We arranged the number to sound like them. David Crosby, who left the Byrds recently, told us he liked it very much – in fact, he was very pleased with [*Disraeli Gears*]."

Monday 30

◁)) **RECORDING** Columbia Recording Studios, Sunset and El Centro, Hollywood, CA. Producer Gary Usher and engineer Roy Halee.

Work on Roger McGuinn's 'Space Odyssey' (see October 23) continues.

November

Wednesday 1

◁)) **RECORDING** Columbia Recording Studios, Studio D, Sunset and El Centro, Hollywood, CA. Producer Gary Usher and engineer Roy Halee.

Work on 'Space Odyssey' is completed, and McGuinn's experimental 'Moog Raga' is recorded (or 'Ragga' as specified on the studio sheet). The number is an Indian-inspired instrumental painstakingly programmed and pieced together by McGuinn, and is not released at this time. It will eventually appear as a bonus track in the 90s.

In a 1970 interview with Vincent Flanders, the composer explains: "Yeah, we did the Moog Raga. It's in the can at Columbia; it's in the library and will never be released because it's out of tune – that's the only reason. You have to stack with the synthesizer. Stacking [is] putting one layer or channel of tape over another: overdubbing. It was a stacked thing. We first put down the tambura sound, and then we put down the melody line.

"The melody line was out of tune with the tambura sound. The 'whaangyang' sound was all right, but when we put the 'dodooya-doooyaa' I was doing it on a linear controller on the Moog. Man, it's really hard. It's like learning to play the violin immediately – you play it across from right to left. Like, it's horizontal and you play it by pushing your finger down on a Teflon strip about a half-inch wide and about a fifth of a millimetre in thickness, and it's about one millimetre off the graphite undercoating. [It's effectively] a big potentiometer. And so I put black grease-pencil marks on the strips to find the notes, but still my ear was a little off that night … . I just wasn't hearing in tune correctly the night that we did it, and we never got to return to it and clean it up."

Thursday 2

☐ **US TV** Joey Bishop Productions Office, Hollywood, CA. ABC Network *The Joey Bishop Show* 10:30pm

Entertainer Joey Bishop, a fifth of the notorious Rat Pack, has successfully led his own talk show since April on the ABC network. The show airs in direct competition with NBC's Johnny Carson Show. Bishop's show is aired live ("ABC didn't say so," notes the press, "but it will probably run a five-second delay to bleep out the naughty words"). His guests tonight are Japanese pop singer Linda Yamamoto, crooner Rudy Vallee, singer-actress Fran Jeffries, Glen Campbell, and The Byrds – with Gene Clark. Unfortunately, in the same way as the group's appearance on *Groovy!* and *Boss City* around this time, no recording of this performance will survive.

Saturday 4

☐ **US TV** [Presumably KHJ Television Studios], Hollywood, CA. KHJ-TV Channel 9 *Boss City* 6:00pm

Sam Riddle has invited The Byrds, Bobby Vee, The Sunshine Company, and The Peanut Butter Conspiracy to his weekly record-based TV show. Presumably, the show is aired live from KHJ's studios in Hollywood, with The Byrds and Gene Clark probably plugging the new single 'Goin' Back'.

Saturday 4–Sunday 5

☐ **US TV** Valley Plaza Park and Recreation Center, North Hollywood, CA. KHJ-TV Channel 9 *Groovy!*

The many teenage television shows that sprang up in 1964 and '65 – Los Angeles shows like *Hollywood A Go Go* and *9th Street West* or nationwide telecasts such as *Shindig!* and *Hullabaloo* – are one by one taken off the air as trends and tastes change. KHJ-TV is an exception and is still going strong with two shows aimed at teenagers: *Groovy!* and Sam Riddle's *Boss City*.

Music historian Domenic Priore will write: "The last of the most far-out show of the go-go era to air on KHJ Channel 9 was *Groovy!*, hosted by another screamer, Michael Blodgett. ... *Groovy!* summed up the previous three years of rock'n'roll television in one daily program. It had the best name since *Hollywood A Go Go*, showed off the cream of L.A.'s early psychedelic graphics, and was broadcast from the beach, usually near Santa Monica Pier, every day at 4:00pm. ... *Groovy!* would broadcast sand-crab races, sack races, and pie fights on the beach."

Blodgett has dabbled in acting, and he even has a small role in Roger Corman's movie *The Trip*. His show debuted on June 26, and this weekend it moves indoors from the beach to Valley Plaza Park & Recreation Center in North Hollywood. Tapings both days begin at 9:30am and go on all day, and musical guests are The Byrds (with Gene Clark), Eric Burdon & The New Animals, and actor and singer Eddie Hodges, while artist Lynne Seemayer – infamous for her 60-feet-tall painting of a nude woman ('The Pink Lady') above a tunnel in Malibu County – exhibits some of her latest works. The insert featuring The Byrds lip-synching (miming) 'Goin' Back' is broadcast on November 14. With their TV commitments honoured, The Byrds and Gene Clark part again.

Monday 13

◀)) **RECORDING** Columbia Recording Studios, Sunset and El Centro, Hollywood, CA. Producer Gary Usher and engineer Roy Halee.

Today's recording of the pretty 'Get To You' is another elaborate arrangement that demands outside help. Stephen J. McParland's later biography of Gary Usher will list the musicians on the session as Hal Blaine (drums), Red Rhodes (pedal steel guitar), plus a string quintet consisting of William Armstrong, Alfred McKibbon, Raymond Kelley, Paul Bergstrom, and Jacqueline Lustgarten. Plus of course McGuinn and Hillman.

McGuinn is believed to be the song's main author, although the final credit reads McGuinn/Hillman. However, in conversation with Gene Clark biographer John Einarson, McGuinn later insists it was Clark who was the song's rightful co-composer. "Gene and I wrote the song. Gene came over to my house. ... It was right after we fired [Crosby]. David had been accusing Chris and me of not being good enough musicians to play with him any more. So I was going to show David: 'Oh yeah? So I was going to write a song in 5/4 time, man, and intersperse it with 6/8 time. I'll show you.' It was kind of my trying to show David that I was a better musician than he thought I was.

"So I was working on the chord progression when Gene came over, and we started working on the song, the actual lyrics, making it about a trip to England like we did in 'Eight Miles High'. So yeah, Gene and I wrote that song, but I don't know how the credit got mixed up. The bureaucrats at Columbia Records got it wrong." Although he contributes as a composer, Clark is not present at the session today.

One person whose contribution is not credited is Curt Boettcher, who has worked with Gary Usher on several other projects and also as producer in his own right (including working with The Association and Tommy Roe). In an interview with music historian McParland,

Boettcher later recalls: "Crosby quit halfway through [the sessions] so Gary called me up and asked me to come over and help him finish up the album. My job was mainly to sing David's parts, which I did, but it was not a real enjoyable time for me. I remember all the time I was working with them, I never felt a part of what was going on. They were always so serious."

Boettcher appears incognito, as his name is not on the album jacket and is not to be found of any AFM (American Federation of Musicians union) files, and the extent of his work is not known. Usher, again speaking to McParland, will say later: "I also played some percussion on the album and sang some background parts, particularly on 'Get To You' with Curt. Normally, I would not get that artistically involved."

Also recorded today is a brief instrumental marked 'Song #2' on the tape box, essentially just a trio performance by McGuinn on electric six-string, Hillman on bass, and Hal Blaine on drums, although McParland's Usher biography will have Red Rhodes and string player William Armstrong also appearing on the demo. (The track will later be known as 'Flight 713' when it is made available on the Never Before anthology in 1989.)

Tuesday 14

The Byrds are guests on Michael Blodgett's *Groovy!* on KHJ Channel 9 at 6:00pm (see November 4–5), promoting 'Goin' Back'.

Thursday 16–Sunday 19

THE GOLDEN BEAR
306 OCEAN AVENUE (HWY 101) HUNTINGTON BEACH

November 16-17-18-19
"THE BYRDS"
SHOW TIMES
Thursday and Sunday
8:00 p.m. and 10:00 p.m.
Friday and Saturday
8:00 p.m., 10:00 p.m. and 11:30 p.m.

Hoyt Axton
November 24 and 25

Reservations PHONE 536-9600
536-9102

The Golden Bear, Huntington Beach, CA

With Gene Clark irrevocably gone, The Byrds are now down to a trio of McGuinn–Hillman–Clarke. This weekend at the Golden Bear is believed to be the three-man group's concert debut. (A newspaper listing for a Chicago show in Algonquin is by Illinois's own The Brydes.)

Joyce Haber's gossip column in *The Los Angeles Times* (November 30) reports on the comings and goings. "The Byrds, who started out as a quintet, dwindled to a quartet and reshuffled into another quartet, are down to trio status with the departure of Gene Clark, who was booted out because he cannot fly. This is Clark's second split from the group. … [David] Crosby, on his part, left a couple of months ago after a spat with Jim McGuinn (now known for metaphysical reasons as Roger McGuinn), and Clark replaced him. But a flightless Byrds restricts tours, so Clark is soloing again and the remainder are trio-ing."

Saturday 25
Swing Auditorium, San Bernardino, CA
The group headlines with support from Fly By Night, Peace & Freedom Movement, and Solid State.

Wednesday 29
◄)) **RECORDING** Columbia Recording Studios, Sunset and El Centro, Hollywood, CA. Producer Gary Usher and engineer Roy Halee.

Hillman, who was so active in making *Younger Than Yesterday* a success with four sole songwriting credits, finally comes forward with a song he has completed on his own. 'Natural Harmony' features Jim Gordon on drums, Red Rhodes on pedal steel guitar, Clarence White on guitar, and Paul Beaver programming a synthesizer for the ethereal sound effects. The tape for 'Tribal Gathering' is taken out of the box again (see August 29 and 30) to add further overdubs. More work will continue on the song tomorrow.

ALSO …
Bob Dylan completes the sessions for his new Columbia album in Nashville with producer Bob Johnston today and tomorrow. Although he has recorded a basement full of demos during his convalescence in Woodstock this spring and summer, these are his first official recordings in more than 18 months and will be readied for *John Wesley Harding*. Working with only a sparse bass and drums backing, he decides to add pedal steel player Pete Drake for 'I'll Be Your Baby Tonight' and 'Down Along The Cove', both of which are recorded today.

Thursday 30
◄)) **RECORDING** Columbia Recording Studios, Sunset and El Centro, Hollywood, CA. Producer Gary Usher and engineer Roy Halee.

The Byrds record 'Wasn't Born To Follow' in today's session. Like 'Goin' Back', it is penned by Gerry Goffin and Carole King, but this is exclusively for The Byrds as it has not

been covered by any other artists yet. Again, it is a number that Gary Usher brings to the table through his connections with Screen Gems. The lightly country-ish melody calls for Red Rhodes (pedal steel guitar) and Clarence White (guitar), while Jim Gordon plays drums. Also, further overdubs are added to 'Tribal Gathering' but apparently not used.

December

Saturday 2
Du Page County Fairgrounds, Wheaton, IL
📻 **US RADIO** The Byrds are interviewed on the WCFL Action Line for *The Jim Stagg Show* (4:00pm) before appearing live in concert for two shows (8:00 and 10:30pm) in Wheaton. DJs Dick Biondi and Jim Stagg MC the evening shows.

Sunday 3
Notre Dame High School, Chicago, IL
One show at 7:30pm with Saturday's Children, introduced by radio personality Ron Riley.

Tuesday 5
◄)) **RECORDING** Columbia Recording Studios, Sunset and El Centro, Hollywood, CA. Producer Gary Usher and engineer Roy Halee.

Further overdubs are added onto 'Tribal Gathering' (see November 29 and 30) but these too are not used, although McGuinn's mind-bending guitar solo is probably recorded as an afterthought. With Crosby gone, McGuinn and Hillman perhaps feel that his vocal and instrumental contributions should be either mixed down or mixed out.

Nearing completion of the sessions for the new album, McGuinn, Hillman, Usher, and Halee work on the final running order. Inspired by The Beatles' groundbreaking idea of running tracks on *Sergeant Pepper's Lonely Heart Club Band* into a seamless flow, they use the same idea to create a unique ambience. 'Old John Robertson', recorded way back in June and already released as a single, is given a sonic overhaul courtesy of Roy Halee's studio wizardry. Presumably around this time, McGuinn and Hillman also tamper with 'Draft Morning' (although the song is in fact completed, see August 2–3 and 7–8). When the track is finally released, Crosby finds to his horror that McGuinn and Hillman have been promoted to co-composers and have taken artistic liberties with his lyrics. "It was one of the sleaziest things they ever did," a furious Crosby will later tell Byrds biographer Johnny

Rogan. Despite Crosby's anger, neither he nor McGuinn nor Hillman can quite pinpoint what the changes to the lyrics were.

Interviewed in 1997 by John Nork, Roy Halee will look back on his work as an engineer with The Byrds. "I was out there in L.A. for a very short time working with Paul [Simon] and Artie [Garfunkel]. We had that rhythm section out there – Hal Blaine [drums], Joe Osborn [bass], Larry Knechtel [keyboard] – they were doing everything. Those guys are the greatest. Hal Blaine is the greatest thing that ever happened to pop records. So anyway, Gary Usher asked me if I would do that twin 8-track thing I'd come up with, for The Byrds, because nobody else was doing that kind of recording."

Halee has experimented with combining two 8-track Ampex tape recorders in an attempt to provide 16 tracks on tape (the sophisticated 16-track machine did not become an industry standard until 1969). He explains that the trick is to make the two 8-tracks run in sync with one another. "Because as it gets hot, they drift. But it worked. It worked on The Byrds stuff too, because I took that to Hollywood to this producer Gary Usher, and he saw it and went out of his mind."

Roger McGuinn will later tell John Nork how the phasing and flanging effects are added to a song such as 'Old John Robertson'. "I like the phasing of the orchestral piece," says McGuinn. "That was Gary Usher's idea, but I said I was into it. I thought the phasing gave it a really interesting quality. I remember we got that by using oscillators with two tape recorders, speeding one up and slowing one down. Usher didn't know how to accomplish that, so he asked [the engineer, Halee] and said that he wanted to get that 'short-wave sound'. The guy said, 'Well, you take the two tape recorders and speed one up and slow it down.' I was into it because of the technology aspect. I really did like the way it sounded."

Wednesday 6
◄)) **RECORDING** Columbia Recording Studios, Sunset and El Centro, Hollywood, CA. Producer Gary Usher and engineer Roy Halee.

For the very last session for the album that will become *The Notorious Byrd Brothers* early next year, Michael Clarke is back on drums. It is he who apparently coins the title of today's ode to amphetamine, 'Artificial Energy', in a Ringo-like moment. Clarke's drumming is at its most powerful as he locks with Hillman to give the impression of two bass drums hammering away. Barry Goldberg adds organ, while a pumping brass section is added consisting of Roy Caron, Virgil Fums, Richard

Hyde (trombone), Jay Migliori (sax), and Gary Weber. The horn track and the vocals are electronically warped to add to the rush, and the song is suitably chosen as the coming album's opening track.

Thursday 7

Fillmore Auditorium, San Francisco, CA
Bill Graham presents The Byrds, The Electric Flag, and B.B. King for one evening show at 9:00pm.

Friday 8–Saturday 9

Winterland, San Francisco, CA
The Byrds–Flag–King package moves to the larger Winterland for the weekend to accomodate bigger crowds.

Thursday 14

A four-day residence at the Whisky A Go Go is cancelled, so Big Brother & The Holding Company pick up the booking instead.

Friday 15

Nevada Southern University Gym, Las Vegas NV
The Byrds, The Sunshine Company, and The Jet Set play a 'Homecoming Concert' at 8:00pm.

Saturday 16–Sunday 17

THE GOLDEN BEAR
306 OCEAN AVENUE (HWY 101) HUNTINGTON BEACH

Presents
December 16-17

The Byrds

December 26 - Jan. 7
(nightly)

Ian and Sylvia

Reservations   PHONE 536-9600
536-9102

The Golden Bear, Huntington Beach, CA
In a return booking to the Golden Bear, The Byrds play three shows a night (8:00pm; 10:30pm; midnight). Also heard: The Things To Come. A quick interview is conducted at the Golden Bear, later syndicated to various newspapers. While Larry Spector hovers around, the group is asked about the change in image ("It's a new year, man. Time for a change") and who their favourite contemporary groups are ("The Beatles. Love The Beatles. They're the tops. And the Stones. And Larry Spector and [actress] Tuesday Weld. But there are those who we used to like but we don't do no more").

Asked whom they do not like any more, someone says: "Like Dylan. He's gone, man. No one's heard from him. Like Chuck Berry. Like Lyndon Johnson. Mao, Fidel, and those boys." The brief reports ends: "Larry Spector interrupted our stimulating and thoroughly high-level intellectual conversation by announcing to the boys that it was time to prepare for their next show. We said goodbye, gave one another the peace sign, and then I watched them fly back to their nests on the stage where several hundred anxious Southern Californians were waiting to hear their trio sock it to them."

Undated December

Dave Hull's Hullabaloo, Los Angeles, CA
Jennifer Starkey offers a timeline of snapshots of The Byrds' rise to Los Angeles fame in *The Happening* (February 1968), mentioning the signposts along the way: Ciro's, The Trip, Whisky A Go Go, and Monterey, before ending with her impressions of the slimmed-down trio. "The scene: the *Hullabaloo*, on the other end of Sunset Boulevard. The time: about 9:30pm in December 1967. This club, which was once the proud and packed Moulin Rouge, has become the haven for those 15 and up. There are few familiar faces in the audience. Most of the kids in attendance are too young to have ever seen the original five Byrds play live, especially back in the good old Ciro's days. They have to rely on the present sound and sights, instead of pleasant memories.

"The curtains open, and the three Byrds play. In the audience, there is silence. They succeed. Only Chris Hillman, Michael Clarke, and newly moustachioed Roger McGuinn are on stage, but they've somewhat captured the spirit of their old music. The vocals need a little work, as Chris's harmonies sometimes overpower McGuinn's melodies, but the magic is still there. Once people get over the initial shock of seeing a trio in place of the familiar quartet or quintet, they'll come to realise this. It just takes a little time. Once you've been as big as a group like this, people demand more; it takes more to satisfy them and their beliefs. The Byrds are aware of this, and are outdoing themselves in order to retain their status in the pop music world."

Friday 22

Anaheim Convention Center, Anaheim, CA
•
Michael Clarke has wavered between dissatisfaction and insecurity during the last few months, and at the very end of 1967 he too leaves The Byrds, reducing the once mighty

flock to just Roger McGuinn and Chris Hillman.

Although many have questioned Clarke's musical abilities, not least the other Byrds, he has been the group's rhythmic heartbeat as well as its heartthrob.

McGuinn will tell Pete Johnson in The *Los Angeles Times* early next year: "[Clarke] began losing interest in the group and decided he wanted to move to Hawaii. He just wanted to take his money and split. He was sick of the pressure and responsibility, although he didn't have much responsibility; he just had to show up on time."

Friday 29

'Goin' Back'/'Change Is Now' is released in the UK today after the initial release date (December 22) has been postponed. Peter Jones says in *Record Mirror* (December 23): "Plaintive vocal on this revival of Dusty Springfield hit – The Byrds' sound is still extremely distinctive and the adventurous guitar work dominates the backing. A sad, moody quality pervades the whole song and this will delight all the Byrds fans, most of who write weekly to James Craig [the readers' letters editor in RM]. A beautiful record, produced by Gary Usher, and could be a smash for the trio. Jim McGuinn and Chris Hillman penned the flip, which is a medium-paced guitar-dominated beater in typical melancholy Byrds style, features a great guitar solo. Hypnotic."

In *New Musical Express* (December 23), Derek Johnson's review is headed "Byrds Make Trio Debut". He writes: "Originally a quintet, The Byrds have now been reduced to a trio, and this is the group's debut in its new streamlined form. Must say their vocal blend and colourful harmonies are just as impressive as ever. The ear-catching sound, which they've always achieved in their backing, mainly a rippling acoustic guitar figure, still adds distinction to their work. We first heard this Goffin–King number as a haunting ballad from Dusty Springfield, and because of this, The Byrds' mid-tempo styling seems a bit out of place. FLIP: A self-penned item, highlighting The Byrds' unmistakable individuality. Fascinating lyric, and a much more subdued approach than in their earlier discs."

Lastly, long-time fan Penny Valentine glows in her *Disc* review (December 30). "This is a record I like, which is good enough for me, and you too I hope. Anyway, it's back to The Byrds of 'Mr. Tambourine Man' and nice too. A soft sand-shifting treatment of the Goffin and King song Dusty loved so and did so splendidly. There's that untouchable Byrds quality about it with their famous guitar work and some nice 'la las'. One to listen to and like."

The Byrds early 1968. From left: Kevin Kelley, Gram Parsons, Roger McGuinn, and Chris Hillman.

The Notorious Byrd Brothers is hailed by critics as a masterpiece and for a time restores the group as a chart act in the UK … McGuinn and Hillman are joined by drummer **Kevin Kelley** and then singer, guitarist, and songwriter **Gram Parsons** … Under Parsons' influence, the group changes course for the countrified sounds of *Sweetheart Of The Rodeo* … Meeting

1968

Nashville head on, The Byrds upset the cart when they break programming rules at the **Grand Ole Opry** … A brief overseas visit to Italy and England is followed by a return to London before the group flies off for **controversial visit** to **South Africa** in July, but without Gram Parsons who decides to quit instead of compromising himself … Harassed by the South African press, the group returns home just to see founder member **Chris Hillman leave** … With only Roger McGuinn left of the original Byrds, he gathers **Clarence White, Gene Parsons, and John York** to keep The Byrds airborne.

January

In 1965, Derek Taylor predicted jokingly that one day the group would be just The Byrd if the members vanished one by one, just like the nursery rhyme. With only Roger McGuinn and Chris Hillman left of the five original Byrds, the two have nevertheless managed to finish the group's fifth album of all-new material – *The Notorious Byrd Brothers* – even in the face of David Crosby's recent discharge.

McGuinn and Hillman do not consider giving up the group, and although New York correspondent Nancy Lewis in *Disc* (January 20) speculates that "maybe they're going to try for a West Coast Simon & Garfunkel type act", the two remaining Byrds decide for the first time to bring in an outside replacement. Drummer Kevin Kelley (born 1945) happens to be free of commitments, plus he is Chris Hillman's cousin, so he is asked to join. It is a case of 'do we know somebody?' rather than long-winded auditions.

Kelley confides to California newspaper *The Daily Review* (May 22) that he wanted to be a composer "since the age of 12. I heard Beethoven's 'Fifth' and thought, 'Hey! Wow! That's what I want to do!'" But it is as a drummer that he is known. He got his start in 1966 with The Rising Sons, a fixture of the Los Angeles music scene as house band at the Ash Grove and Whisky A Go Go. Led by Taj Mahal and featuring guitarist Ry Cooder, the group recorded a solitary single for Columbia Records ('Candy Man' produced by Terry Melcher) before it fell apart last year. McGuinn and Hillman, as the only surviving Byrds, are equal partners, and Kelley is thus hired as a salaried member.

Saturday 6

Rating the three best albums of 1967, Norman Jopling writes a jubilant assessment of *Younger Than Yesterday* in today's *Record Mirror*. A latecomer to the world of The Byrds, he offers some interesting views. "[It is] possibly the most-played LP in my collection to be issued last year. I'd never been a Byrds fan, or even impressed with the group until this album, which really stunned me when I first heard it. Vocals are not their strong point (although their soft voices can and do achieve either harshness or subtlety when required) and consequently the accent is on the instrumentation. And strangely enough, only guitars, drums and bass are used throughout the backing. I've heard that The Byrds' technique used to obtain their hypnotic guitar sound is to play everything very carefully, very slowly and then speed the tape up for the record. The result, as all Byrds fans will know, is overpowering."

"From the first bar of 'Rock'n'Roll Star' to the end of 'Why', that guitar sound, in one form or another, dominates the album. The recording technique on the gimmicky space-age 'CTA 102' is incredible and funny, while Dave Crosby's 'Mind Gardens' can send you reeling with the impact of the harsh compelling backing. [But] certainly the most dramatic track is the reflective ballad 'Everybody's Been Burned', another Dave Crosby song.

"It is hard to imagine how The Byrds will efficiently survive now that Dave has been sacked. He was responsible for some of the best songs on the album. He wrote or co-wrote 'Mind Gardens', 'Why', 'Renaissance Fair' and 'Everybody's Been Burned'. The group cannot be as good without him.

"This is a fantastic, incredible album on which a great deal of care has been lavished and it achieves – with simple instruments, rather ordinary songs, and vocals which could not be called overpowering or ambitious – an effect which most groups could not get. Certainly no group in the world could gain this type of effect without being much more complex and ambitious, as are The Beatles and The Beach Boys." (Jopling's two other picks for 1967 are *Up, Up, And Away* by The Fifth Dimension and *Together Again* by Dion & The Belmonts.)

Monday 8

Manfred Mann release 'Mighty Quinn' in the US (the British release follows at the end of the week), and the single will be a resounding smash hit on both sides of the Atlantic during February and March. 'Mighty Quinn' is an unreleased Bob Dylan song that the Mann group picked up from one of the tapes of seven new numbers that Dylan's manager Albert Grossman brought to London at the tail end of October 1967.

Grossman's visit has a purpose: to get artists and groups to record Dylan's new material. Journalist Nick Jones is allowed an exclusive eavesdropping on the tapes – perhaps at the office of Dylan's British music publisher B. Feldman – and calls them to attention in *Melody Maker* (November 4, 1967). "Dylan has been recording, although the date these tracks were made is not known. The group is still there and sounding good, and Dylan is sounding beautiful. The tapes we heard were rough and unbalanced, although musically good enough to be finished products. Hearing these tracks only once wasn't exactly enough to really get into what was going on, but the main points that stick out in my mind are these: initially there has been quite a lot of change in Dylan's musical outlook. I mean, you hear these tracks and say, 'Wow, they're weird.' They are also too much. They

don't really sound like anything much Bob has done before." *Melody Maker* tries unsuccessfully to pry some information out of Grossman while in London, who reluctantly talks about his client but avoids questions on Dylan's future.

Jones names the seven songs he hears: 'If Your Memory Serves You Well', 'Ride Me High', 'I Shall Be Relieved', 'Waters Of Oblivion', 'Please Mrs. Henry', 'Tears Of Rage', and lastly 'Mighty Quinn'. The first four numbers are later more accurately known as 'This Wheel's On Fire', 'You Ain't Going Nowhere', 'I Shall Be Released', and 'Too Much Of Nothing'.

The identity of Quinn in the lyric remains open to interpretation – actor Anthony Quinn is an obvious candidate – while Byrds fans could be forgiven for thinking it may sneakily refer to Roger McGuinn: "But when Quinn the Eskimo gets here/All the pigeons gonna run to him," where perhaps Quinn is McGuinn and pigeons are Byrds. Perhaps.

The *Melody Maker* tapes are but seven of dozens of fresh songs recorded by Dylan at his rural home in upstate New York in the spring and summer of 1967 with The Hawks: Garth Hudson, Rick Danko, Richard Manuel, and Robbie Robertson (drummer Levon Helm joins in late 1967). A further seven numbers are copyrighted and distributed via Dylan's music publishers – including 'Nothing Was Delivered' – making a total of 14 fresh titles. Dylan's new songs are eagerly picked up by fans and musicians, and copies also wind up in the hands of The Byrds.

Speaking to author and musician Sid Griffin in 2006, Chris Hillman recalls: "I was living in Topanga Canyon and I got sent the tapes – I think a reel tape – around late 1967 sometime. Possibly very early 1968, but I believe late 1967. I don't remember where they came from, but we were no longer managed by Jim Dickson or Eddie Tickner, we were managed by Larry Spector then. Yet Dickson was the one who had the connection to Dylan, so how this material was sent to me I do not know. They did not go to Roger, they were sent to me.

"I remember thinking this was a whole album's worth of good material by Dylan," says Hillman. "All of them were good songs. All of them. But I sort of just passed this material on to Roger, saying: 'Check this out, I don't know what to do with it, but you are our singer so have a listen.'" Griffin will also talk to McGuinn, who suggests maybe Gary Usher as the source for the tapes. "We always had a good relationship with Dylan's publishers … we heard the songs, and we were as thrilled as you might have expected us to have been with this material."

Saturday 13
International Sports Arena, San Diego, CA

Presumably, this marks the debut of Kevin Kelley on drums with Roger McGuinn and Chris Hillman. Also appearing are The Turtles, Buffalo Springfield, and The Stone Poneys – a trio with singer Linda Ronstadt and now a certified chart success with their version of Mike Nesmith's 'Different Drum'.

Monday 15

The fifth Byrds album (not counting last year's greatest hits collection) is released in the US, *The Notorious Byrd Brothers*. A memorable photograph adorns the album jacket. Shot by Guy Webster, who was also responsible for the award-winning *Turn! Turn! Turn!* jacket, the photo has an unintended symbolic message.

During a day on horseback in Topanga Canyon, Webster lined up the group in the windows of a stable for a portrait. During the session, a horse wandered in, and the finished album jacket depicts – from left to right – Hillman, McGuinn, and Clarke plus said horse. Some read this as a jibe at the recently departed Crosby, although the involved parties will deny this.

The Notorious Byrd Brothers is for many fans the most impressive album in the group's entire catalogue. The album uniquely mixes synthesizers and pedal steel guitars, psychedelic guitar solos with passages of baroque beauty. The heady combination of stunning songs, vocals, and musicianship, the sonic innovations, and the many-layered textures add up to produce a masterpiece.

The extent of David Crosby's involvement in the finished album is not entirely explained, but he appears on 'Change Is Now' (harmony vocals and presumably guitar), 'Draft Morning' (vocals and presumably guitar), 'Tribal Gathering' (vocals and guitar), 'Dolphin's Smile' (lead vocals and guitar), and of course the single B-side released while he still was a member of The Byrds, 'Old John Robertson' (bass guitar and harmony vocals). McGuinn, asked by *Hit Parader* in a month's time about Crosby's participation, fails to acknowledge the ex-singer's contribution to 'Draft Morning'.

Pete Johnson writes in *The Los Angeles Times* (January 20): "Ideally a group which decays from a quintet through two quartet permutations then down to a trio, a duo, and another trio has to pay for the process with vitality, retaining only a crippled imitation of the old sound. But Roger McGuinn … guitarist–singer, and Chris Hillman, bassist, the only survivors of what was once the first bright new-wave American group, still have

something to give. 'So catch me if you can, I'm going back,' they sing on the LP, winging their way through 11 good songs spiked with electronic music, strings, brass, natural and supernatural voices, and the familiar thick texture of McGuinn's guitar playing.

"Departed Byrds David Crosby (singer–guitarist) and Mike Clark (drummer) contributed to the album, but much of it was recorded after they left, and McGuinn, Hillman, and producer Gary Usher deserve credit for the totality. Personal favourites include 'Artificial Energy', 'Natural Harmony' (a great song with some elaborate electronic juggling), 'Draft Morning', 'Wasn't Born To Follow', 'Tribal Gathering', and 'Dolphin's Smile', but the album is so good that you strain to select."

Rolling Stone, the new magazine that is steadily increasing in influence and circulation, devotes a whole page to the album (dated April 27, but published March 27). Jon Landau writes: "Lots of people are down on The Byrds. It is very well known that the group is plastic Los Angeles. They haven't been able to perform decently in years. They are essentially a recording act unable to reproduce their music effectively on stage. Like The Beatles, I suppose. What is forgotten in this kind of attitude is that there is a distinction

between performing and making a record, and the two ought to be judged separately. No one has ever seen The Beatles perform *Sgt. Pepper*; but who is exactly complaining? A lot of the West Coast groups and even the Cream have trouble doing things in the studio, and that doesn't keep people from loving them when they are on stage. When The Byrds get it together on record they are consistently brilliant. And it is interesting to speculate about how many of the currently popular groups on the Coast or in England will still be as fresh and inventive as The Byrds are when they get around to recording their fifth album.

"At their best – on records – The Byrds are graceful. No rough edges, no jarring protrusions. Their music is possessed by a never-ending circularity and a rich, child-like quality. It has a timelessness to it, not in the sense that you think their music will always be valid, but in the sense that it is capable of forcing you to suspend consciousness of time altogether.

"*The Notorious Byrd Brothers* is the same old trip, but, at the same time, a brand new one. The lyrics have greater force (the presence of the war is deeply felt) and there is a seriousness to even the lighter pieces. Stylistically, the eclecticism is so marked that one suspects McGuinn of heaving read an article about

The Notorious Byrd Brothers

A1 'Artificial Energy' (R. MCGUINN/C. HILLMAN/M. CLARKE)
A2 'Goin' Back' (C. KING/G. GOFFIN)
A3 'Natural Harmony' (C. HILLMAN)
A4 'Draft Morning' (D. CROSBY/C. HILLMAN/R. MCGUINN)
A5 'Wasn't Born To Follow' (C. KING/G. GOFFIN)
A6 'Get To You' (C. HILLMAN/R. MCGUINN)
B1 'Change Is Now' (C. HILLMAN/R. MCGUINN)
B2 'Old John Robertson' (C. HILLMAN/R. MCGUINN)
B3 'Tribal Gathering' (D. CROSBY/C. HILLMAN)
B4 'Dolphin's Smile' (D. CROSBY/C. HILLMAN/R. MCGUINN)
B5 'Space Odyssey' (R. MCGUINN/R.J. HIPPARD)

US release January 15th 1968 (Mono Columbia CL 2775/Stereo Columbia CS 9575)
UK release April 12th 1968 (Mono CBS 63169/Stereo CBS S 63169)
Chart high US number 47; UK number 12
Read more ... entries for June 14, 21, July 31, August 1, 2, 3, 14, 15, 16, 17, 29, 20, September 5, 6, October 9, 11, 16, 23, 30, November 1, 13, 29, 30, December 5, 6 1967

Bonus CD tracks: 'Moog Raga' [Instrumental] (R. McGuinn), 'Bound To Fal' [Instrumental] (M. Brewer/T. Mastin), 'Triad' (D. Crosby), 'Goin' Back' [Version One] (C. King/G. Goffin), 'Draft Morning' [Alternate End] (D. Crosby/C. Hillman/R. McGuinn), 'Universal Mind Decoder' [Instrumental] (C. Hillman/R. McGuinn)

"At their best – on records – The Byrds are graceful. No rough edges, no jarring protrusions. Their music is possessed by a never-ending circularity and a rich, child-like quality. It has a timelessness to it, not in the sense that you think their music will always be valid, but in the sense that it is capable of forcing you to suspend consciousness of time altogether." ROLLING STONE, APRIL 27, 1968

The Byrds' eclecticism. Yet the pervasive mood, as always, remains a continuous warmth and openness, perhaps for no other reason than McGuinn's inability to sound angry. The Byrds' eclecticism is awesome: C&W, science fiction, light jazz touches, finger-picking rhythms, pop-rock (two fine Goffin–King songs), and touches of strings all play their part on this album. Yet if one doesn't listen closely he may not notice even a fraction of the incongruities which are present. And therein lies a key to The Byrds' ability to assimilate everything that they touch."

Jay Ruby writes in the May issue of *Jazz & Pop*: "The Byrds have the ability to sound the same and yet subtly introduce new ideas in each of their records. I like the view of the world that they project in their music. It is an innocent place where good people do good things and are saddened, even sometimes outraged, by war and other inhuman acts. They are the electronic inheritors of Pete Seeger's world.

"A growing number of people in rock are experimenting with electronic music and there has been much talk about the influence of Cage and Stockhausen. The Byrds are also interested in electronic sounds, but not out of any interest in the serious composers. They are fans of science fiction and UFO phenomena.

"The Byrds have lost their popularity with some people because they appear to be doing the same thing over and over again," says Ruby. "This is not true – their changes are just not as dramatic as some others. And even if they were to remain where they are now, the possibilities of their music have not been exhausted. They still move and involve me in the same way they did in 1965. Rock is becoming more and more cerebral and complex. I hope The Byrds remain unaffected by the pretensions and keep their marvellous lyricism."

Sandy Pearlman (*Crawdaddy* No. 15, May 1968) pens another ornate analysis of the unique Byrds chemistry. "[I'm] trying to tell you how enchantingly beautiful the new Byrds album is and, right away, we gotta turn to their sonic preoccupation. Suffice to say, The Byrds have this unique preoccupation with a constant (although simultaneously evolving) primal sound. Certainly this sound has been some kind of major enchantment. It really puts a spell on you: cos it really puts a spell on its material. And that's a function of The Byrds' form." Here Pearlman adds a large chunk of the review he did of *Younger Than Yesterday* last year as a footnote. A bit further down he starts dissecting the album in detail, writing about the group's "absolute adequacy", their "molecular sound organiza-

tion", and their proof that "only The Byrds can date The Byrds".

Although *Crawdaddy* is exclusively a music magazine, the underground press in the US is booming, and rock music news and reviews are central ingredients. *Open City* (March 1–7) writes: "[*Notorious Byrd Brothers*] approaches the artistic peak reached by their first two LPs. Seldom since the departure of Gene Clark has the group touched upon the sensitivity The Byrds were once known for. [The album's] excursions into mysterious suspensions and jaunty, shifting rhythm changes have imbued folk-rock with even more dimensions and depth. Musically, nonsense was kept to a minimum, and Jim McGuinn's excellent guitar playing fully contemplates the unusually good songs. This is an exceptional album and standouts are difficult to pick, but 'Goin' Back', 'Natural Harmony', 'Draft Morning', and 'Dolphin's Smile' are all excellent."

Kaleidoscope (March 1–14) out of Milwaukee prints a well-formulated review courtesy of Rich Mangelsdorff. "The Byrds are one of the oldest US groups to build and sustain an original style; they were one of the first anywhere to develop an electronic 'wall of sound'. This wall is thinned out somewhat by the loss of a rhythm guitar (although they use electronic sound devices throughout the record), but the ringing, chiming lead guitar is still there, still leaving room for the big and round-toned bass to come through."

Mangelsdorff points out the use of pedal steel guitar ("surprised they didn't think of that before") and detects correctly that 'Tribal Gathering' is comparable to the vocal style of jazz singers Lambert–Hendricks–Ross and vocal group The Four Freshmen. He writes in his last paragraph: "The mysticism of 'Space Odyssey' is serious business, and can only be treated in a cursory manner on a short cut of an LP, but if some of the L.A. heavies are getting them into this kind of thing it would be a mind-blower if they could work some of this out in depth." It's an interesting observation that McGuinn surely takes to heart.

Columbia launches a large advertising campaign this spring, coining the slogan The Columbia Rock Machine. "The Rock Machine never sleeps. Night and day you can hear it. The beat is relentless," runs the hype to promote Bob Dylan (*John Wesley Harding*), The Byrds, The Buckinghams, and The Union Gap, all in one go. Despite this, the new Byrds album halts at a disappointing Number 47 in the *Billboard* album charts.

The Notorious Byrd Brothers will be programmed regularly on the burgeoning FM radio format, where DJs such as Tom Donahue at San Francisco's KMPX will favour album tracks over singles.

Saturday 20
ALSO …
Bob Dylan returns to the stage for the first time since the tense European tour with The Hawks in May 1966 as he performs at a memorial concert for Woody Guthrie in New York's Carnegie Hall. The local Massachusetts newspaper *Lowell Sun* (January 22) notes: "Dylan played an acoustical guitar. A five-piece rock combo, The Crackers, with organ and two guitars amplified, performed along with him. They did 'Grand Coulee Dam', 'I Ain't Got No Home In This World Anymore', and 'This World Was Lucky To See Him Born', Guthrie's tribute to FDR." The Crackers are just The Hawks in another guise, and in six months they will be known to the world as The Band.

Friday 26
'KRLA Radio Promo Show', The Cheetah, Santa Monica, CA
A show with The Byrds (presumably still a trio), The Turtles, and The Lewis & Clarke Expedition is presented by Casey Kasem, well known as the host of the Los Angeles TV show Shebang. One half of the two-man Lewis & Clarke Expedition is singer-songwriter Michael Murphy. They have a single, 'Freedom Bird', out on Colgems, and have nothing to do with Gene Clark's future union with Doug Dillard, which will be named The Dillard & Clark Expedition.

February
Friday 9–Saturday 10
Carousel Theatre, West Covina, CA
A weekend of concerts headlined by The Byrds, plus Things To Come and The Gordian Knot.

•

Sometime in early February, the three Byrds add a fourth member to the group, Gram Parsons (born Ingram Cecil Connor III in Winter Haven, Florida on November 5, 1946). McGuinn and Hillman have realised that the trio format is limiting on stage and in the studio, and McGuinn has a vision to follow the jazzier direction staked out by 'Eight Miles High'. Jazz saxophonist Steve Marcus has just released his version of the Byrds classic as the lead-off track on his album *Tomorrow Never Knows*, reminding McGuinn again how influential the song is. He feels that such a shift requires a piano player, and that is what McGuinn is expecting when Hillman invites Parsons along for an audition.

Although Parsons and McGuinn/Hillman

have a barely nodding acquaintance with each other, the stories of Gram Parsons and The Byrds interweave and can be traced as far back as the fall of 1966. Then on a visit to Los Angeles, Parsons and his actor friend Brandon de Wilde visited David Crosby. Legend has it that the Byrd had flown, so Crosby's then-girlfriend Nancy Ross was alone – and Gram and Nancy promptly fell in love. Nancy followed Gram back to New York, and was with him again when Gram's International Submarine Band had met in Hollywood in search of success in the spring of 1967.

There are other points of contact within the wide Byrds circle. Parsons is a good friend of Peter Fonda (even teaching the actor 'November Nights' – written by Gram – which was released as a Fonda single in '67). Parsons has recorded under the guidance of Hugh Masekela. Parsons is represented by

Larry Spector. And yes, Parsons and Nancy Ross even fleetingly attend Subud meetings. Most important, however, is Parsons's love and understanding of country & western, particularly the harder-edged sounds that are associated with Bakersfield: Buck Owens, Merle Haggard, and Wynn Stewart. Signed to Lee Hazlewood Industries, The International Submarine Band recorded *Safe At Home* at the tail end of 1967, essentially a Gram Parsons project with assistance from Jay Dee Maness (pedal steel), Earl Ball (piano), and others. The album will be released in April.

Parsons is primarily a singer and a promising songwriter. He strums guitar and tinkles a functional keyboard, but he is certainly no jazz pianist. Whatever his shortcomings in that area, he passes the audition when he connects with Chris Hillman. Parsons has fully grasped the vibrancy of country music, and in Hillman

he finds a kindred spirit. But Parsons is not yet ready to throw in his weight fully behind The Byrds as he still considers The International Submarine Band a viable commodity – at least until their album is released.

Like drummer Kelley, Parsons is hired as a salaried member of The Byrds. He is under contract to Lee Hazlewood – and thus cannot technically become a partner of the Byrds Corporation – and it is later suggested that this is one of the reasons McGuinn and Hillman are attracted to him. That will be a shrewd assumption to make in hindsight. It could be argued that getting Parsons is the opposite: an act of courage. The rock music business is in its infancy in 1968 and is still a bewildering composite of clear-headed visions and pure happenstance. Gram Parsons is hired for the wrong reasons, but proves to be just the right man.

Trio Byrds: Roger McGuinn, Kevin Kelley, Chris Hillman.

Wednesday 14

ALSO …

The Hollies are in Los Angeles for a week of television shows and play a special showcase for friends, fans, and the press at the Whisky A Go Go tonight. A couple of days ago, on Saturday February 10, the group's Graham Nash attended a party thrown by Peter Tork following Jimi Hendrix's headlining appearance at the Shrine Auditorium, where he bumps into David Crosby. Tonight, many of the L.A. in-crowd are at the Whisky. "Admirers and friends of The Hollies in the audience," according to Ann Moses's celebrity list in *New Musical Express* (February 24), "were Cass Elliot and her date, Lee Kiefer, Lou Adler, Davy Jones, Mike Nesmith, Mickey Dolenz (who introduced the group), Eric Burdon and Animal Johnny Weider, Marvin Gaye, Jackie de Shannon, Brian Wilson, three of the Buffalo Springfield, and Lee Hazlewood."

Later that night, at a party at Mama Cass Elliot's Laurel Canyon home, David Crosby, Stephen Stills, and Graham Nash find harmony as they share dreams of musical freedom outside The Byrds, Buffalo Springfield, and The Hollies.

Friday 16

AT COLUMBIA MCMILLIN THEATER, B'WAY & 116th ST.
FRIDAY, FEB. 16, 10 P. M. IN CONCERT

THE

BYRDS

AND

Da Da

Tickets: $3.00, 3.50, 4.50   Ferris Booth Box Office
                             B'way & 115th St. 12-3 daily

CALL 280-2417 between 12-3 for information

McMillan Theatre, Columbia University, New York, NY

According to contemporary reviews and reports, The Byrds' concert repertoire at this time includes the obvious hits ('Eight Miles High', 'My Back Pages', 'Turn! Turn! Turn!'), lesser-known classics ('He Was A Friend Of Mine', 'Why'), the occasional surprise (like re-introducing Gene Clark's 'I'll Feel A Whole Lot Better'), and at least a couple of songs from *The Notorious Byrd Brothers* ('Tribal Gathering', 'Old John Robertson'), but no overt country material, at first. McGuinn favours his Gretsch six-string now that he is the only guitar player in the group.

With Gram Parsons aboard – he may have debuted with The Byrds at the West Covina shows on February 9–10 – the group will play selected concerts, primarily at colleges, on the East Coast and in the Midwest this month, which may otherwise mark his debut with the band. This brief transitional period finds Parsons in the role McGuinn originally envisioned, as keyboard player.

Back in New York City for the first time since the summer of 1967, The Byrds – supported by DaDa – play a concert (10:00pm) at Columbia University. Although it is not a high-profile booking, a Byrds concert is still an event and is duly covered by Robert Shelton in *The New York Times* (February 18). "As much as any group, including The Beatles, The Byrds helped formulate the engrossing contemporary mix of rock and lyrical substance," writes Shelton. "Although The Byrds have undergone many personnel changes, Jim McGuinn, the group's shaper and philosopher-in-chief, was still singing his wistful, yearning tenor and still drawing electric charges from his guitar.

"The slick and heavily engineered recordings of The Byrds and their concert appearances cannot be equated, because the eccentricities of electronic bands are too great. Nevertheless, this concert was stimulating and pleasing. Of older hits, the group offered such folkish, rockish and psychedelic hits as 'Turn! Turn! Turn!', 'My Back Pages', 'He Was A friend Of Mine', and 'Eight Miles High'. Here the lyrics came through because of familiarity with recordings, despite some amplification problems. In works recently added to their repertory, one had to strain for comprehension, though the overall effect was good."

Meryl Brodsky of the *Barnard Bulletin* (February 21) says: "The Byrds followed [DaDa], playing a number of their best, starting with 'I'll Feel A Whole Lot Better', interjecting with 'Eight Miles High', and ending with 'Turn! Turn! Turn!'. They didn't talk much but then they didn't really have to. A few words they said rang a bit too true. After a song about the Kennedy assassination, 'I Had A Friend' [sic], Jim McQuinn [sic], the lead guitarist, concluded with, 'and I wish he were here now', which the audience appreciated. As I said, their songs are among the best of folk-rock, with meaningful lyrics, a strong beat, and a total effect that reaches audiences activating their minds as well as their sensibilities. The Byrds don't have to try too hard to succeed, though they didn't hold the audience in the 'palm of their hands', or achieve a kind of mutual 'we-understand-each-other' relationship. They seemed to alienate themselves from the audience. They performed, they did their thing, and you felt free to take it or leave it, listen or drift. It was the combination of this attitude plus some of the best American folk-rock to come out of today's somewhat enigmatic scene, that held some, like me, rapt, involved, and totally turned-on."

Neither the *New York Times* nor the *Barnard Bulletin* reviews note anything extraordinary of the stage set-up and there are no mentions of the number of Byrds nor any new keyboard player on stage.

Saturday 17

Withrow Court, Miami University, Oxford, OH

The University of Cincinnati *News Record* (February 13) does not exactly oversell The Byrds' appearance at Ohio's Miami University, but then the two colleges have long been friendly rivals. "Before you run to see them, however, be forewarned – they are reputed to be very poor concert artists!" The briefest of reviews appears in the University's student paper following the group's appearance, and it is not complimentary. "The Byrds laid an egg, at least according to general consensus after Saturday night's performance. It seems they were less than interested in entertaining at Miami."

Sunday 18

The Grande Ballroom, Detroit, MI

The Byrds play a special no-age-limit show with The Rationals and Wilson Mower Pursuit and a lightshow operated by Trans-Love. This is The Byrds' first appearance in Detroit (not counting an unconfirmed visit in July 1965), where Russ Gibb promotes shows at the Grande Ballroom, clearly inspired by the San Francisco scene.

Author John Nork attends the show and later vividly recalls the event. "Gram Parsons was definitely a background piano accompanist at this concert. He played piano and did not have any lead vocals that I can recall. The group focused on *The Notorious Byrd Brothers–Younger Than Yesterday* material. There were no country songs at all. I remember 'Tribal Gathering', 'Old John Robertson', and 'Why'. McGuinn had his electric 12-string Rickenbacker on a stand on stage but did not play it. Some people in the audience yelled out for McGuinn to use the Rickenbacker, but I don't think he did. Instead, he played a six-string electric. Parsons' electric-piano work added some chime-like arpeggiated elements to the sound. The Byrds arrived very late for the gig, and played only a short set. There was very little commentary from the band between songs. They put on a reasonably good concert, but nothing compared to the live performance ability of the latter-day Byrds ensemble."

Three of four Byrds (Gram Parsons not pictured) in Oxford, OH, February 17, 1968.

ALSO ...

West Magazine, the weekly supplement to *The Los Angeles Times,* is today devoted to the blossoming underground music scene. Derek Taylor pens a tribute to L.A. and Jane Wilson visits Grace Slick (with David Crosby hovering in the background, silently handing Wilson a placard with the message "Acid is a tool. A wrench can break a baby's head or build an iron lung. Same tool. Depends on how you use it."). There is also a long article quoting interviews with Andrew Oldham, Derek Taylor, record company men David Anderle and Andy Wickham, ex-Byrds publicist Billy James, DJ B. Mitchell Reed, and Taj Mahal. Running like a red thread through the feature is the influence of The Byrds on the L.A. scene. Extracting an old McGuinn interview with Tom Nolan in *The Los Angeles Times* from November 1966, the magazine carelessly misquotes the Byrds guitarist on the subject of longhairs. "Maybe it's kind of a badge, so we'll know which side we're on. The old against the young. That's what it's all about, really. Until we do something decisive. Like maybe someday we'll get guns and go out and shoot all the old people."

Friday 23

'Winter Weekend's Wild, Wild, West', Hill Auditorium, University of Michigan, Ann Arbor, MI

The Byrds appear together with Chris Montez, the singer known for his smash '62 hit 'Let's Dance'. *The Michigan Daily* (February 24) writes: "It seems quite strange that these two acts should ever appear within 500 miles of each other, let alone on the same stage. God only knows what the UAC people were thinking when they tucked in this pair of strange bedfellows. It's like serving ketchup with waffles.

"Anyway, The Byrds come out and launch into 'I'll Feel A Whole Lot Better' and it becomes apparent that they will salvage the concert. The group, after an incredible number of personnel changes, now consists of Roger (formerly Jim) McGuinn on lead, Chris Hillman on bass, Kevin Kelley on drums, and some new guy on organ. The organ adds needed depth to the concert performance but seriously detracts from the well-known Byrds style. The Byrds have always depended on crystal clear guitar work, threading the rhythm with the lead, to bring off their songs. But the organ muffles McGuinn's guitar to a great extent and the audience can only hear snatches of his beautiful riffs. The group definitely needs a good rhythm man again."

The "new guy on organ" makes his presence felt in other areas, as the review relates. "The Byrds have started to get into country and western music more and more, and they did two numbers last night that are strictly Nashville: 'Hickory Wind' and 'Satisfied Mind'." The Byrds, of course, did Porter Wagoner's 'Satisfied Mind' on the *Turn! Turn! Turn!* album in '65, but they have probably never performed it live on stage until now, and this weekend may well mark the debut in their set of 'Hickory Wind' by Gram Parsons.

"They also did a jazz-oriented piece in 5/4 time ['Tribal Gathering'] to demonstrate their versatility," continues the *Michigan Daily* review. Although the writer notes hopefully that this "perhaps point[s] out future directions for the group" it is Parsons' country influence that will prevail.

Saturday 24

```
Winter Weekend

Byrds
Strawberry Alarm Clock
Buckinghams

February 23, 24
```

Massachusetts Institute of Technology (MIT), Cambridge, MA

The Byrds, Strawberry Alarm Clock, Ill Wind, and The Buckinghams. "We got a standing ovation at MIT! That never really happened before," McGuinn tells Jerry Hopkins of *Rolling Stone* (May 11).

Steve Grant writes in *The Tech* (February 24): "The Byrds … are one of the half-dozen best groups in rock today. Lead guitarist Jim McGuinn has consistently outdone his previous work throughout the group's history. Unfortunately he also seems to have scared away the other talented people who used to be with The Byrds.

"The Byrds have a reputation for not being able to back up in concert what they put down on record. This is partly true – 'So You Want To Be A Rock'n'Roll Star' loses most of its impact without the dubbed-in screaming of teenybopper fans. More important, however, than the absence of technical effects is the boredom that may have invaded Byrds music. They didn't seem really interested in what they were playing. This came through most clearly in 'Eight Miles High', in which McGuinn seemed merely to be going through the motions of the record. Only on the encores 'Bells Of Rhymney' and 'Chimes Of Freedom' did the group play with any real flair. They had the fortunate insurance that what they were playing was great, but they didn't play up to the music by any means."

Sunday 25

- **Student Union Ballroom, University of Massachusetts, Amherst, MA**
- **New Gymnasium, Salem State College, Salem, MA**

Another disjointed bill starring The Byrds, The Righteous Brothers, and country hotshot Glen Campbell. The review in the university's student paper (February 27) gives a snapshot of backstage activities. "Their offstage manner is cautious as they set themselves apart from the people who surround them in the presence of strangers, but an awareness of the oftentimes lack of sincerity present in fans. Gram Parsons, the newest member of the group, tests the strangers he finds in the dressing room after their performance with a few confusing comments, but soon opens up to speak freely about the group and music in general." The actual performance is "loud and lacking talent. [The] boys didn't communicate with the audience, they didn't joke. The music was loud but there is no doubt about the talent and vast amount of creativity which they displayed in their performance." Apparently, The Byrds manage to squeeze in a second performance today. Salem is about 80 to 90 miles away from Amherst and so within reach.

Late February

For the next Byrds album, McGuinn toys with the idea of recording a musical journey from old age to space age. Following the concerts with the rejuvenated Byrds, journalist Pete Johnson interviews McGuinn at his hilltop home in San Fernando Valley, where he lives with his wife Ianthe and their young son Patrick. The piece first appears in *The Los Angeles Times* (April 21).

"Our next album's going to consist of two whole records," says McGuinn, "22 sides [songs]. The first half, I guess the first six, will be bluegrass with banjo and stuff, and the second half will be modern country. Then we'll move to the synthesizer with voice for the third quarter: lyrics with a synthesizer background. Then pure synthesizer for the last quarter. So it'll be a chronological structure, from old timey to modern to space-age stuff. It'll be the first album that we've ever done that has any planned format or continuity beforehand."

Johnson publishes a fuller interview in *Hit Parader* (September 1968), which takes the McGuinn story from the birth of The Byrds until the present, touching on Gene Clark's defection in 1966 and a track-by-track list of David Crosby's involvement with *The Notori-*

ous Byrd Brothers. McGuinn explains the finer technical points of the synthesizer and mentions another group working specifically in the electronic realm, The United States Of America. (Led by visionary composer Joseph Byrd, they are label-mates of The Byrds and have recently completed their astonishing self-titled cycle of songs for an early March '68 release.)

"It was purely accidental," McGuinn says of the purported musical continuity of *The Notorious Byrd Brothers*. "We didn't plan it that way – it was natural. I think the only continuity occurred in editing, the placement and the lead-in from one song to another. We sort of did it arbitrarily in about 35 seconds."

McGuinn talks about the recent upheavals in the group. "Michael left. We sort of asked him to leave. Not because we don't like him; we like him a lot and we miss him a lot, too. But he was losing interest musically and started to get the Hawaii fever. He just wanted the bread and said he was going to quit after the publishing money came in this time. … He wasn't that good a drummer. He had a certain thing that was groovy, but technically he lacked a lot."

"[Kelley's] a better drummer than Michael," McGuinn adds, but admits it's not the same. "And Gram plays piano and guitar and sings. He's sort of up in the air now between The International Submarine Band and us. It depends on how their record goes." In the *Hit Parader* article, McGuinn confirms that live performances have tightened with the addition of Kelley and Parsons. "We got a standing ovation for the first time at Michigan State [actually University of Michigan] and we got good reviews from Columbia [University] and several other schools. Gram worked with us on this last tour and he was great. The audience loved him. He likes to work with us and we like to tour with him. I never had more fun than we had this last tour." Johnson manages to spell Parsons' forename correctly, but many press reports this spring render his name as Graham.

Before winding down the interview, Johnson wants to know if Hillman is satisfied with the present situation. "Yeah, more or less," replies McGuinn. "He's sort of sick of being a rock'n'roll singer, but if the group developed more of a country sound, he would dig that because that's more his bag."

Thursday 29

The Byrds renew their contract with Columbia Records for a seven-year period, negotiated by Larry Spector on behalf of the group. Johnny Rogan's later Byrds biography will outline the details of the contract, which offers McGuinn and Hillman an advance of $150,000, most of

which is payable upon signing. The contract further stipulates that the group will use a Columbia staff producer. Should they choose to use an outsider, this will be reflected in a 2 per cent cut in their 12 per cent royalty per sold record. This is a slight improvement on their initial Columbia contracts from 1964 and 1965, which specified a 10 per cent royalty per sold record. The main advantage of the new deal with Columbia is a fresh flow of cash to McGuinn and Hillman (not to mention their manager), but the true implications of Spector's action will not be understood until months later. The contract is made effective the following day, March 1, 1968.

March

Saturday 2

Earlier in the year, Britain's NEMS Enterprises formed an alliance with Hollywood's Perenchio Artists, leading The Byrds among others to be represented in England by NEMS. Today, *New Musical Express* reveals that the group is added to this summer's European pop event, a weeklong festival called 'Musica '68' to be held between July 22 and 27 in Majorca in the Mediterranean. The Byrds are booked for the first day with Jimi Hendrix, Eric Burdon & The Animals, Grapefruit, and The Hep Stars from Sweden.

•

With the renewed Columbia contract signed, The Byrds begin preparations for their next album. Neither McGuinn nor Hillman has any particular new material of their own, so the door is open for Parsons to have some of his songs and ideas recorded. He argues for a country-music album – based on the logic that if you can win the country crowds over, you will have a loyal audience forever.

"[Gram] figured that once they dig you, they never let you go," McGuinn will tell Bud Scoppa in 1970. After the elaborate *Notorious Byrd Brothers* project, the shift requires the group to make a complete right-turn. Hillman is all for the project. Speaking to Richard Williams a couple of years later in *Melody Maker* (December 19, 1970), he says: "Well, I'm a country boy by upbringing, and I used to write little songs for the band in that vein, but the rest of the band always shouted me down. Then Gram joined and I had an ally, so we managed to turn Roger's head towards our kind of music." McGuinn is comfortable, too, as the project at this stage is within the bounds of his idea of an album encompassing the evolution from old-timey music to electronic instruments.

To achieve the authentic country sound, The Byrds want to record in Nashville. The plan is feasible because Columbia Records has a popular studio in the city. The group's regular producer Gary Usher, although inexperienced in the field of country music, is game for the venture. Nashville is almost 2,000 miles to the east of Hollywood, geographically as well as culturally, and the group takes the unprecedented step of cutting their hair short for the occasion. Although Bob Dylan recorded in Nashville as early as February 1966, this is the first time a rock group has descended on the town. Just a few days into March, The Byrds with road manager Jimmi Seiter set the course for Nashville. Although their visit to the Music City is brief, it will perhaps be the most momentous week in the group's history.

Saturday 9

🔊 **RECORDING** Columbia Studio A, 34 Music Square East, Music Row, Nashville, TN. Producer Gary Usher and engineer Charlie Briggs.

On the group's first morning in a Nashville studio, Lloyd Green (pedal steel) augments the four Byrds – McGuinn, Hillman, Parsons, and Kelley. Green belongs to a small handful of pedal steel players who can easily work sessions seven days a week in Nashville if he cares.

The first task of the day is to tape Bob Dylan's 'You Ain't Going Nowhere', one of the songs McGuinn and Hillman learned from the tapes of unreleased Dylan songs they were given a couple of months back. Green will tell Alastair McKay on the recording's 40th anniversary: "I wasn't certain how they wanted to do the music. I was sitting on my stool at Columbia A and they walked in. They were all standing there in a line – everything was a little awkward. And then Gram said: 'We're gonna cut "You Ain't Going Nowhere" first.' I said, 'Great, great, how do you want to approach it on steel? Where do you want me to play?' Then, almost in tandem, they said: 'Everywhere'."

Used to regimented Nashville sessions, Green is restrained, despite the chance to fill in everywhere, and it is he who comes up with the song's instantly recognizable introductory hook. McGuinn sings lead vocal and plays acoustic guitar, Kelley adds a distinctive drum lick on the chorus, and the organ track is almost certainly played by Parsons – the only recorded example of his organ playing with The Byrds. Whereas the other songs recorded this week will be subject to further overdubs and enhancements, 'You Ain't Going Nowhere' seems to be completed today, in time for a radio broadcast in a few days.

"Here's what they did that first morning,"

Green will say in the McKay interview. "It was 10:00am on Saturday. They walked in with a case of Lancers Vin Rose – sweet Portuguese wine in a clay jar. I know it caused severe headaches, cos I didn't smoke pot or anything but I did drink a little of that wine. Every day they'd bring a 12-bottle case, and by the end of the day all of it was gone. It tasted good in the moment, but I got the world's worst headaches. They were smoking a lot. That was the first time I saw the studio lit up with marijuana smoke. And I was getting a little heady."

The second song laid down today is 'Hickory Wind', co-written by Parsons with his ex-band mate Bob Buchanan, a yearning waltz-time ode to the South of his childhood. Parsons is the singer and he plays acoustic guitar on the track, his preferred instrument for the rest of the sessions. An outtake is bolstered by Green's velvet-like pedal steel, which suggests overdubs are added later (a fiddle, a piano presumably tinkled by Parsons himself – and the lush, choir-like harmony vocals).

Roland White, the mandolin-playing brother of Clarence, is around to help ease the group in with the Nashville studio crowd. Gary Usher will recall to Stephen J. McParland that McGuinn's old friend Roger Miller is around too, although not participating in the sessions.

While The Byrds are at work in Nashville, the British pop press relay the first news of an ambitious pop festival to be held in Rome between May 4 and 10. Inspired by last year's Monterey International Pop Festival, the organisers name it The First European International Pop Festival and convince Mick Jagger and Lord Harlech (Member of Parliament David Ormsby-Gore) to sign on as official sponsors.

The festival committee is affiliated with Circus Alpha Centauri of London, a charity organisation whose main project is the provision of children's arts centres for orphans and young victims of the Vietnam War. Jagger is appointed 'working sponsor'. Lord Harlech says in a press release: "As for the objectives of the Festival Committee, I find myself in much more general agreement with them than with a number of other enterprises I have supported in the past, and I am therefore happy that you should use my name as a sponsor of the Festival." Lined up at press time are Donovan, Traffic, Blossom Toes, Captain Beefheart, The Brian Auger Trinity & Julie Driscoll, and The Byrds, plus MC John Peel.

Monday 11
◁)) **RECORDING** Columbia Studio A, 34 Music Square East, Music Row, Nashville, TN.

Producer Gary Usher and engineer Charlie Briggs.

After taking Sunday off, the group returns for a second day in the studio to record the rocking 'Lazy Days', the Parsons track that was rejected as a contender for Roger Corman's movie *The Trip*. Two versions are taped: one with Lloyd Green, the other with Parsons' Ringo-like holler atop McGuinn's slightly adjusted 'Roll Over Beethoven' intro on electric 12-string.

Tuesday 12
◁)) **RECORDING** Columbia Studio A, 34 Music Square East, Music Row, Nashville, TN. Producer Gary Usher and engineer Charlie Briggs.

Lloyd Green is not present today, but in the studio now with The Byrds are John Hartford (fiddle, banjo) and Roy M. Husky (double bass). Woody Guthrie's 'Pretty Boy Floyd' is recorded at McGuinn's suggestion. He also sings the song and makes a few passes on banjo before Hartford takes over. Hartford also plays fiddle on the song, and with Husky taking care of the bottom, Hillman is free to play a mandolin solo on what amounts to a completely acoustic track. Kelley is not heard.

The Byrds by spring 1968: Gram Parsons, Kevin Kelley, Chris Hillman, and Roger McGuinn.

163

Wednesday 13

🔊 **RECORDING** Columbia Studio A, 34 Music Square East, Music Row, Nashville, TN. Producer Gary Usher and engineer Charlie Briggs.

'I Am A Pilgrim', a traditional song taught to Hillman by Clarence White, is recorded in a sparse acoustic arrangement with Hillman on lead vocals. Hartford and Husky are held over from yesterday's session; Hartford plays the fiddle, but it sounds as if McGuinn has reclaimed the banjo. They next record 'Pretty Polly', a traditional folk ballad (although later credited to McGuinn–Hillman, as is 'I Am A Pilgrim'), in a near-acoustic setting, with the exception of McGuinn's electric 12-string. Both the lead and overdubbed harmony vocals are courtesy of McGuinn.

📻 **US RADIO** Reportedly, it is later today that The Byrds have a brusque on-air encounter with influential country music DJ Ralph Emery on his radio show on WSM. The group are invited as speaking guests in the hope of getting 'You Ain't Going Nowhere' previewed but are met with distrust and disrespect by Emery. Outside the safe confines of the recording studio, The Byrds sense that the cultural gap between Hollywood and Nashville is an abyss. Session steel guitarist Lloyd Green later recalls how appalled he was by the treatment. "I was with them at that show. I suppose I was a sort of 'security blanket' for them that eventful week in Nashville. Ralph asked me point blank, 'Lloyd, why would you contribute your talents to this album?' I said, 'Ralph, because that's what I do; cut records.' And he was a friend with whom I also recorded a number of times on his recitation singles for various labels. But for the nuances and subtleties of all this stuff to make much sense, one would have to be transported back in time to that divisive era of American history – and have been a part of it." So incensed are McGuinn and Parsons that they will later write an acerbic lyric about the incident, signing it off with "This one's for you, Ralph."

Thursday 14

🔊 **RECORDING** Columbia Studio A, 34 Music Square East, Music Row, Nashville, TN. Producer Gary Usher and engineer Charlie Briggs.

Tim Hardin's 'Reputation' is taped today, a number sung by Parsons with added harmony vocals. Lloyd Green is back again – this time playing Dobro – and so is Kevin Kelley, but apparently no other outside musicians are featured. Gary Usher will recall to Stephen J. McParland: "It was while in Nashville that Parsons really came into his own. He had great charisma and was a very strong person, not strong in the way Crosby was strong, but strong in the sense of what he believed in. He was naturally a great influence during the Nashville sessions. A lot of the times it was just Gram and I working one on one with each other. I always considered the control that he did exert was for the good, because his joining the band at that time was a perfect marriage. It was his laidback simplistic approach that really helped pull the album off."

Friday 15

🔊 **RECORDING** Columbia Studio A, 34 Music Square East, Music Row, Nashville, TN.

The Byrds at the Grand Ole Opry, March 15, 1968.

Producer Gary Usher and engineer Charlie Briggs.

For the last Nashville session, Bob Dylan's 'Nothing Was Delivered' is recorded. It's another of the songs from the batch of Dylan's tapes of unreleased demos, and McGuinn – who also sings it – expertly rearranges the melody from Dylan's triplet feel to a country shuffle. The recording benefits from Lloyd Green's pedal steel guitar, while Parsons presumably plays the unobtrusive piano.

A week in Nashville has yielded eight recordings ('You Ain't Going Nowhere', 'Hickory Wind', 'Lazy Days', 'Pretty Boy Floyd', 'I Am A Pilgrim', 'Pretty Polly', 'Reputation', and 'Nothing Was Delivered'). Intriguingly, three independent reports in the coming weeks claim that nine numbers have been taped, but whatever the ninth title is, it is not disclosed.

▭ **US RADIO** Ryman Auditorium, Nashville, TN *The Grand Ole Opry* Radio WMS

Thanks to Columbia, The Byrds are this evening invited to perform at Ryman Auditorium – the hallowed hall of country music. The occasion is significant: it is the very first time a rock group has been allowed to appear on *The Grand Ole Opry*. The show is broadcast live on radio on Fridays and Saturdays, and in addition a separate television segment is filmed on Friday afternoons for syndicated broadcasts around the US on Saturdays. Tailored to a strict country-music format, the show is efficiently run, family-oriented, and utterly conservative. Steel guitarist Lloyd Green has bravely accepted to appear with the group on stage, and for the occasion they obediently comply with the Opry's unwritten rules regarding instrumentation: McGuinn and Parsons play acoustic guitars; Hillman electric bass; while Kelley just hits a snare drum with a brush and a stick. Green and his steel guitar sit offstage and out of sight.

The night at the Opry does not look promising when the group comes on to an unfriendly reception. "I am sitting stage right, and I looked out of the corner of my eye and they were in the wings waiting," Green recounts later to Alastair MacKay. "And just as the announcer introduced them, they started edging out onto the stage, and the audience glanced up and saw these guys, hair longer than they were used to, and started booing. It was a strange experience. I wasn't frightened. I was angry. I thought: 'What are these idiots doing? These guys just want to come out and sing.'"

In an incident that has grown in magnitude

ever since, Gram Parsons decides to change the running order of the songs they have agreed to perform. The group has discussed with MC Tompall Glaser that they will do a pair of Merle Haggard songs, 'Sing Me Back Home' and 'Life In Prison'. After dutifully doing the opening number as agreed, Parsons seizes the moment and tells the crowd and radio audience that he will be singing 'Hickory Wind' instead of the second Haggard song, before rounding off the performance with the new 'You Ain't Going Nowhere'.

▭ **US RADIO** After completing the *Grand Ole Opry* performance, The Byrds drive over

THE VANDERBILT HUSTLER, MARCH 19, 1968

Soft-Singing Byrds Make Opry Debut Smashing Success Here

By Randy Brooks
The Byrds of "Mr. Tamborine Man," "Turn, Turn, Turn," and "Eight Miles High" fame were ... ration for ...

In its place was the lazy twang of steel guitar and three very pleasant voices, actually audible over the accompaniment. Both ... Ain't ...

untitled, two-record album, which producer Gary Usher describes as "half cou... McGuinn exp... ... one ...

to Vanderbilt University to appear on radio WRVU. In sharp contrast to the stiff Opry show, this is an informal opportunity for the band to act as DJs and be interviewed by Gary Scruggs (son of banjo player Earl Scruggs and a musician in his own right).

The *Vanderbilt Hustler* (March 19), the university's student paper, gives a thorough description of the turbulent night, far more clearly than the reports that will be made in hindsight. "The Byrds of 'Mr. Tambourine Man', 'Turn! Turn! Turn!', and 'Eight Miles High' fame were in last-minute preparation for their *Grand Ole Opry* debut Friday night. Their road manager held a cigarette to the lips of Chris Hillman while he stood and played his electric bass. An unidentified man suggested that, for the sake of public relations, they use the current Number One song, 'Sing Me Back Home', for their encore number. The boys had other ideas, and even after the MC introduced that song, guitarist [Gram] Parsons announced a change of plans and began instead to play 'Hickory Wind', a very pretty and very country tune.

"In performance The Byrds were a far cry from their earlier days. The unbearable volume of amplified instruments, which has impaired the hearing of stalwart Byrds fans in the past, was gone. In its place was the lazy twang of steel guitar and three very pleasant voices, actually audible over the accompaniment. Both 'Hickory Wind' and 'You Ain't Going Nowhere' drew polite but unenthusiastic response from an audience which only

minutes before has cheered heartily for The [Glaser] Brothers and displayed unabashed adoration for Skeeter Davis." In marked contrast to the Opry's old guard, Davis – once unhappily married to Ralph Emery – greets The Byrds warmly as they come off stage.

"Backstage again, Parsons, who is from Florida, was visited by three youngsters, his 'Tennessee kinfolk'. They hovered proudly around their cousin, who has been with the group only a month. Pleasant, soft-spoken [Roger] McGuinn is one of two original Byrds still with the group. He was once the 'fourth member' of the Chad Mitchell trio, accompanying them on banjo and guitar, and has also played with The Limelighters and Bobby Darin. His name has always been Jim McGuinn until last year when he became a follower of the Subud spiritual organization, which revealed to him that his true name is [Roger]. Curly-haired Chris Hillman, the other original Byrd, was fairly reserved. He did say that he got his start playing bluegrass mandolin and that he hates the group's latest single release, 'Goin' Back'. Asked what other performers The Byrds admire, Hillman [said] The Everly Brothers.

"Prior to their Opry performance, The Byrds had been in Nashville for a week of recording at Columbia studios. The results of their efforts are nine new songs to be included on a forthcoming, as yet untitled, two-record album, which producer Gary Usher describes as 'half country, half space'. McGuinn explained further, saying that one disc of the set will be entirely country and western music, the other 'Electronic Music'. This second half of the recording is to be done later in Hollywood.

"Following their appearance at the Opry, the Byrds came to Vanderbilt. The studios of WRVU were crowded with onlookers as each member of the group played disc jockey and answering service during an informal interview conducted by Gary Scruggs and Speed Hopkins. 'We're not gonna work in Washington,' McGuinn said with a grin to Scruggs. 'We refuse to work in a place where there are such terrible things going on.' In reply to a telephoned question, Parsons said that he feels that the next sound in pop music will be an 'exploitation of country music'. One caller who accused The Byrds of being 'dirty Commies' turned out to be Hillman phoning from downstairs."

Saturday 16
University of Virginia, Charlottesville, VA

The Byrds head out on the road again, and presumably play in the vicinity of Virginia tomorrow as well.

•

T. Wilym Grein interviews the four Byrds for *Hit Parader* (which will be belatedly published in its November 1968 issue) right after their return from Nashville. "Our primary goal in singing is to develop ourselves musically," says Parsons. "That includes exposing ourselves to every possible type of music – pop, rock, classical, and country."

Grein asks the group to explain the reasons for recording in Nashville. Kelley: "Actually the group has a strong folk background. We found rock music a good comfortable place for us, but don't forget, our total goal is good music. Country music is another facet of music – probably the biggest and most honest we have. … We don't try to be commercial. We just try to make good music by having everything happen together. Like having the vibrations from each individual finally end up in parallel lines. That's when we get good music."

Hillman: "I'm terribly disillusioned. You walk down the street and on every corner you see a rock group. But they're not really serious musicians. They think just because they have long hair and wear an Indian morning coat that they're saying something, that they're making the scene." Parsons: "That's right, to be really honest about wearing an Indian morning coat you must be an Indian in the morning. It's part of the whole scene. These people don't wear honest clothes and they don't produce honest music. They have absolutely no soul or integrity in their music. What we want to do is to produce honest music." McGuinn: "In Nashville we can forget the business end of the trade and concentrate on the music."

•

Parsons pushes to add a pedal steel guitar player full-time to the group. Jay Dee Maness, who played on the International Submarine Band sessions before Christmas, joins The Byrds for occasional appearances in the Los Angeles area. Maness is a California native and supports himself by a steady gig at a country club in the City Of Industry, CA. The Nashville trip has boosted Parsons' position in the group as he now steps forward to play acoustic guitar and sing lead on several countrified songs, although he will continue to double on keyboards.

Saturday 22
Community Concourse, San Diego, CA
Support by The Brain Police.

•

Jerry Hopkins of *Rolling Stone* gets an update from the Byrds camp in the second half of March. The interview will be printed in the magazine's May 11 edition. "There are fewer hang-ups now," McGuinn reports. "Before, we had some stars to contend with. It's much tighter now. The new group is better in person than the old one. There are fewer errors. There's no grandstanding. Nobody's doing the watch-me-catch-this-one bit. The music's better. We just finished a tour of Eastern schools. Columbia. Amherst. Salem College. MIT. And we started getting encores and standing ovations.

"[Gram] added a whole hunk of country. [His] bag is country and we're going to let him do his thing, and support him and work together on things." Hopkins explains to *Rolling Stone* readers that there is a definite country emphasis in their sound, that the group has recently recorded nine tracks in Nashville and has appeared at the Grand Ole Opry. "Columbia had to pull strings to get us on the bill," explains McGuinn. "They don't fancy rock groups down there, not on Grand Ole Opry."

McGuinn assures Hopkins that the portions of the album to be cut in Los Angeles will have a more contemporary feel, and that electronic sound will be incorporated in their live sound. A synthesizer for this purpose has been ordered. Despite McGuinn's fondness for futuristic sounds, he reveals to Hopkins that the group may expand to five members by adding a pedal steel player. "We don't have a title for the album yet," McGuinn concludes. "That'll come in time. And it probably will have something to say about time – backward, forward, something – because the music we're doing will cover a lot of time."

Friday 28
Ciro's Le Disc, Hollywood, CA
Derek Taylor, now working for A&M Records, has decided to go home to England to assist The Beatles at their Apple Corps. For the occasion, Ciro's Le Disc is re-opened once more as Taylor's many acquaintances, business associates, friends, and followers are invited to say farewell.

Taylor writes in his autobiography: "Captain Beefheart and The Byrds, and also Tiny Tim, were good enough to perform free at a benefit concert I had promoted for myself … on the eve of de-immigrating from California back to Liverpool. I had made quite a lot of money one way or another during our three years in Hollywood, but I didn't seem to have much left when it came to buying an air ticket home to Liverpool, so at the last moment I invited about 500 people to come to Ciro's on the Strip for a farewell party (cost per ticket, $5.50). People responded very well – such is

Hollywood; there is a lot of good among the panic – and 600 came, but I over-ordered on the wine (most of the guests were wiped out on cannabis) and underestimated on the gate-crashing, so there was quite a deficit."

Carl Franzoni and the crowd around Vito Paulekas are here to lend lustre to the festivity, and so are record producer Lou Adler, crooner Andy Williams, and writer and journalist Tom Nolan. Judy Sims reports in *Disc* (April 13): "The Byrds appeared at Derek Taylor's going-away party, which was a sentimental gesture and journey since Derek and The Byrds started out together three years ago. Except that both Derek and The Byrds have changed, so the party wasn't so much an evocation of the past as it was a look into the future. There were five Byrds on stage, although one may not be permanent. The 'temporary' Byrd is called J.D. (that's all, just J.D.) who plays steel guitar." This is, of course, Jay Dee Maness. "Aside from old-guard regulars Roger McGuinn and Chris Hillman there were drummer Kevin Kelley and organist–guitarist–vocalist Gram Parsons. Both J.D. and Gram are very 'country' as was much of The Byrds material. Their next single is also country, complete with sobbing steel guitar and mournful vocal.

"They sounded very good, really together," says Sims, "except on 'Eight Miles High', which was far off. Gene Clark joined them for a couple of old Byrds songs, but the less said about that the better. The Byrds seemed to have settled into a kind of comfortable niche, with a noticeable lack of frenzy and uptightness. Roger, Chris, and Gram are married, which may have some settling effect (Chris married an English ex-publicist, Anya Butler). As for Derek, he is now with the big Apple, and we are left with a large empty space in our hip hierarchy."

Jerry Hopkins is at the party on behalf of *Rolling Stone* (May 11 edition, published April 18). "Today only Hillman, on bass, and McGuinn, on lead guitar, remain, with Kevin Kelley on drums and [Gram] Parsons on keyboard and acoustical guitar, making the group a quartet. To hear them play and to hear the members of the group talk about themselves, the days of war seem past; the 'new' Byrds are a group at last, a combination of musicians and friends, not just a combo of personalities.

"The set performed at Ciro's was, admittedly, an unusual one – created in part of nostalgia. After all, it was here the group started, and many of those present wanted to hear the old hits. So what happened was those in attendance heard two groups, the 'old' and the 'new'. The set was begun with 'You Ain't Going Nowhere', played in country style. In this song and on all other 'country' tunes played that night they were joined by a man known as J.D. sitting in on steel guitar. The second number was equally Nashville in orientation. And then, quite suddenly, came a song from their first album, 'Chimes Of Freedom', and for the rest of the evening they alternated songs from the heady past ('Mr. Tambourine Man', 'Eight Miles High', 'He Was A Friend Of Mine' etc) with something they'd recorded more recently.

"The sounds were distinct and at times it seemed as if two groups were playing, not one. Except, of course, there was Roger's unmistakable voice and Chris's imaginative yet basic basslines throughout. The material was different, surely, but so was the technique and effect. The Byrds, as Roger said, are tighter now. They appear secure in the country milieu. And what vocal force they lack in doing their old material – losing Gene Clark and David Crosby has made its mark – they gained with [Gram] Parsons in the new material. [Gram] sings often and he sings well. Sharing 'lead voice' with Roger. Chris, too, has added dimension to his voice and provides an important part of the vocal sound."

Taylor's autobiography contains a joyful tribute to his favourite American group. "We worshipped The Byrds, [my wife] Joan and I, and there has never been anything to touch us with quite so much magic as the first line-up singing their hits on Sunset Boulevard in the mid 60s. If The Beatles began 'it', then the Byrds too began their 'it', and it is to Roger McGuinn and his four errant, elegant, brilliant friends that we and you, us, and the American nation, and young people should offer a nod of thanks for nudging us, and not so slightly, in a new and better direction. It was the end of the age of innocence in rock. They offered us something very special in those tentative days when, though the peace movement was a baby and LBJ hadn't yet blown it, we knew that there were insufficient options open to the young and free in America. They offered us a maypole around which we could dance.

"Their timing, their eccentric streak, their great love of what was then folk but isn't now, their chemistry as performers, the tensions, the danger that they might bomb (a danger felt by the audience as much as, maybe more than, by the band, which was saying something), their real musical skill, I mean real, and the alternative lifestyle which they were very early to embody, all of these made The Byrds special. And they were The Beatles' favourite group, they really were, in the days when The Beatles were not so free with their endorsements."

April

Tuesday 2

'You Ain't Going Nowhere' is released today as the 13th American single from the group. The most commercial of the batch of songs recorded recently in Nashville, it should stand a chance in the charts. Moreover it is a Bob Dylan number, which should please the group's old fans. Backed with 'Artificial Energy' from *The Notorious Byrd Brothers*, it places at a weak Number 74 in the *Billboard* charts and an even worse 81 in *Cash Box*. Bill Yaryan of *The Independent Star-News* (May 11) out of Pasadena, CA, sums up a view shared by others. "If you think Dylan's *John Wesley Harding* LP was a step forward you'll also think the same of 'You Ain't Going Nowhere'. But if, like me, you think the retreat to country music is a backwards step that compromises some of the great musical progressions made in the last few years, you'll be disappointed. Perhaps The Byrds' new LP, when it is released, will show more promise. It is supposed to contain some new things recorded in Los Angeles as well as the country things which were recorded in Nashville. Let's wait and see."

Thursday 4

🔊 **RECORDING** Columbia Recording Studios, Sunset and El Centro, Hollywood, CA. Producer Gary Usher and engineer Roy Halee.

With not much more than half an album in the can after the Nashville visit in March, The Byrds return to Columbia's Hollywood studio to continue recording. Despite a promise to begin now the 'second half' of the planned part-country, part-electronic rock album, the country line prevails as Parsons sings Merle Haggard's murder ballad 'Life In Prison'. Not only does he persuade the group to tape another out-and-out country number but also he brings in Jay Dee Maness (pedal steel) and Earl P. Ball (piano) who brought the country edge to The International Submarine Band's sessions last year. The inclusion of Ball in particular adds a honky-tonk flavour to the songs that the group will record in Los Angeles over these next two months.

Saturday 6
Terrace Ballroom, Salt Lake City, UT
The Byrds appear in two concerts (7:00 and 10:00pm) with The Sopwith Camel.

Thursday 11
Fieldhouse, University of Pugent Sound, Tacoma, WA

Friday 12
Eagles Auditorium, Seattle, WA
The group appears with support by two neighbouring groups from Washington, Merrilee Rush & The Turnabouts and Magic Fern.

The Notorious Byrd Brothers is released in Britain and will reclaim the group's glory when it peaks at Number 12 on the *Record Mirror/Record Retailer* charts. The album drops out of the Top 40 following a Number 38 placing on July 6. Not since *Turn! Turn! Turn!* have The Byrds done so well on the British album charts.

Record Mirror (April 6) gives the album a rare five-star rating. "Hard though it was for The Byrds to follow-up their near-perfect *Younger Than Yesterday* album, they've done it with this fantastic disc. Like most progressive LPs it runs through a whole unit rather than a collection of tracks, and for the first time

'You Ain't Going Nowhere'

A 'You Ain't Going Nowhere'
(B. DYLAN)
B 'Artificial Energy' (R. MCGUINN/
C. HILLMAN/M. CLARKE)

US release April 2 1968 (Columbia 44499)
UK release May 3 1968 (CBS 3411)
Chart high US number 74;
UK none
Read more ... entries for December 5, 6, 1967 and March 9, 1968

they use strings and brass … and beautifully too. In stereo this is even better – tracks from the drug-warning item 'Artificial Energy', the lovely 'Goin' Back' and the poignant 'Draft Morning', one of the best anti-war songs for a long time. Anyone who buys this LP get their money's worth. Just listen to the guitar break in 'Change Is Now' in stereo!" *Melody Maker* (April 6) saves ink: "Who are they this time? All the faces have changed, and only three are pictured on this satisfying set of brass or guitar-backed vocals. 'Draft Morning' is a standout, and 'Space Odyssey' too." The paper adds another line in their monthly album round-up in May: "A beautiful selection, representing US pop at its finest."

Beat Instrumental (May 1968) concurs. "This really is a superior LP from The Byrds, which, once again, has the McGuinn trademark written all over it. It's very intense and needs a lot of listening for its lyrical content, but the music is immediately beautiful (yes, beautiful!). 'Draft Morning' has one of the best anti-war messages I've heard, 'Space Odyssey' continues the Byrd saga of the future, and 'Change Is Now' has one of the best guitar breaks of the year. It's true to say that The Byrds are one of the two best groups in the world. Nobody can say any different with the proof of this album."

A recent reader's letter to *Disc* declared: "If I were imprisoned for a million years I could never tire of *The Notorious Byrd Brothers*." The paper's review (April 6) is in agreement. "This album is indeed an incredible performance. … Surprisingly but happily several of the songs sound more than somewhat like that excellent group The Association … but always with a strong electronic Byrd flavour, while all the rest of the songs sound like no one more than The Byrds. There is much electric distortion of notes in wave-effects – 'doppling' – some beautiful guitar-work from Jim McGuinn and faultless vocal harmonies throughout. Each track is yet another example of a beautiful Byrd song." The album is accorded four stars by Allan Evans in *New Musical Express* (April 13) who writes: "An easy-on-the-ears set by three of the originally five Byrds [and] for the most part it is just good straightforward listening".

International Times (May 17–30), Britain's premier underground paper, exemplifies the growing trend of in-depth album dissections. Perhaps inspired by American critic Sandy Pearlman's musings, the review reads in part: "This technique of breaking up the form is not new, nor is it the personal property of The Byrds, but the fact that they are so formal makes these breaks in continuity that much more effective. An additional balance is constantly maintained by the warmth and melody of the vocal arrangements, the most outstanding feature of their music. It is the counter-supporting effect attained by the interaction of melody and form, which prevents either becoming oppressive, and gives a sense of wholeness and unity to every song."

→ Saturday 13–Sunday 21

According to a note in *Billboard* (April 6), The Byrds are also booked to appear at unspecified venues in Olympia, WA, and Vancouver BC plus two dates in Iowa.

Sunday 14

Today's *Los Angeles Times* spends several column inches on *Safe At Home*, The International Submarine Band's debut album. Pete Johnson writes: "It is hip to espouse country and western as the current trend in pop music, a rediscovery which has Bob Dylan drawling, Earl Scruggs and Lester Flatt playing to crowds in San Francisco's Fillmore, Elvis Presley twanging downhome hits 'Guitar Man' and 'US Male', and The Byrds trekking westward for steel guitar sounds. The latest example of this root development is The International Submarine Band, a young rock quartet whose name gives no clue to their country leanings. Their initial album, on LHI Records [is] a collection of four originals and six western standards done up purty authentic with a vitality not always found in traditional country performers."

For the first time in a nationally important newspaper, Johnson's review gives Parsons serious recognition. "Gram Parsons is lead singer and chief writer for The International Submarine band. His voice and pen seem meant for the medium, [with] neither sounding artificial in the homey feel of good country music." He concludes: "Parsons has appeared with The Byrds on several recent occasions, bolstering their incursions into country music, a liaison which could cause difficulties for the ISB, but he and his cohorts have produced a successful fusion of modern ideas and C&W sounds in this album."

The album sells poorly, which marks the end for The International Submarine Band. Worse still, it causes difficulties for Parsons' own career when Lee Hazlewood refuses to let him go unless he signs over the rights for future royalties and even the group's name. Parsons agrees (remarkably, without conferring with the other members of the Submarine Band), but the Hazlewood connection will cause further headaches as The Byrds continue sessions for their next album.

Monday 15

🔊 **RECORDING** Columbia Recording Studios, Sunset and El Centro, Hollywood, CA. Producer Gary Usher and engineer Roy Halee.

In a spirited crossing of musical styles, Parsons brings in William Bell's soul jerker 'You Don't Miss Your Water (Till Your Well Runs Dry)', rearranging the song and singing it country style. Jay Dee Maness and Earl P. Ball help on pedal steel guitar and piano respectively.

Wednesday 17

🔊 **RECORDING** Columbia Recording Studios, Sunset and El Centro, Hollywood, CA. Producer Gary Usher and engineer Roy Halee.

The Byrds, Jay Dee Maness, and Earl P. Ball spend a day perfecting 'You're Still On My Mind', written by country–rockabilly singer Luke McDaniels, which reputedly requires 60 takes. They still do not get it right, as Parsons later complains in an interview for Dutch radio in 1972. He claims that the released versions of 'Life In Prison' (from April 4) and 'You're Still On My Mind' are rehearsal takes and could have been bettered.

Sunday 21

The Los Angeles Times publishes an interview with Roger McGuinn under the headline 'Some Of The Byrds Fly The Musical Coop'. Written by Pete Johnson, the basis of the interview (see late February) is embellished and fleshed out for a larger feature in *Hit Parader* (November 1968). Johnson writes that the group has recorded nine titles in Nashville and has been working on others in Columbia's Hollywood Studios. McGuinn says of the present-day Byrds: "I think you make your initial statement and you're either accepted or rejected, and we were accepted. Then it sort of tapers off. It's not ever as intense as when you had your first record. As far as staying power, though, I think we have it. I don't know why exactly, but it's here. I think we can stick to the Peter Paul & Mary level. As far as album sales now, we're almost in that bag. We're doing good album business."

→ Late April

💻 **US TV** [Presumably] ABC Television Center, Hollywood, CA. ABC Network *American Bandstand '68*

The group pre-records two inserts for Dick Clark's show, promoting 'You Ain't Going Nowhere' plus the old hit 'Eight Miles High'. This is one of the very rare television appearances by Parsons while with The Byrds. The show goes out on May 11 at 12:30pm and is networked throughout the US.

Tuesday 23

💻 **US TV** NBC Network Special *Where The Girls Are* 8:00–9:00pm

A musical-variety special hosted by Noel

→ An arrow denotes an estimated date.

Harrison (see entry for mid October 1967) and featuring Cher, comedian Don Adams, The Association, singer Barbara McNair, comedian Professor Irwin Corey, a nondescript pop group called Tommy Jimmy Marilyn & Mitch, and Don Peake's Big Band – plus The Byrds, who are seen in two clips recorded at the tail-end of 1967 with Gene Clark. They lip-synch 'Mr. Spaceman', which is taped at two different locations. One is in a studio with Clark, McGuinn, stand-in Jimmi Seiter, and a non-Byrd on drums; the other is shot outdoors on a freeway with Clark, McGuinn, and Michael Clarke. Clark, McGuinn, Seiter, and the mystery drummer also appear in a rendition of The Beatles' 'Good Day Sunshine' together with Harrison and McNair. Hillman is nowhere to be seen.

A stock review penned by Cynthia Lowrey of the Associated Press the following day says: "[This] was an excellent example of the current vogue in TV variety. It consisted of some interesting music, uninhibited camera work, and lots of colour and sight gags. Much of the time the musical numbers were accompanied by camera work that made them look like those soft-drink commercials aimed at the fun-loving teens."

Wednesday 24

◄)) RECORDING Columbia Recording Studios, Sunset and El Centro, Hollywood, CA. Producer Gary Usher and engineer Roy Halee.

The Byrds, with Jay Dee Maness and Clarence White, record two waltz-tempo country numbers today: 'The Christian Life' and 'Blue Canadian Rockies'. Parsons submits and sings 'The Christian Life', a spiritual tale penned by Ira and Charlie Louvin. He probably heard it on the brothers' fire-and-brimstone collection *Satan Is Real*. Hillman has brought 'Blue Canadian Rockies', a Gene Autry hit from 1950. He sings lead vocal, and Parsons probably plays the piano on the finished track as it lacks Earl P. Ball's assured drive.

Clarence White's Telecaster guitar is outfitted with a string-pulling mechanism that his close friend in Nashville West, drummer Gene Parsons, has built. It lets the player simulate the sweet cry of a pedal steel guitar. Parsons' invention consists of a spring-lever mechanism linked to the guitar strap button, which, when pressed down, raises the guitar's B-string a whole-step (tone). The contraption is encased in a hollow cap moulded like the guitar body and then screwed to the back. Today's session may well be the recording debut of the Parsons–White string bender.

Gene Parsons later recalls the origins of the prototype. "One of Clarence's innovative

guitar techniques was to chime the high E or B string and bend it up a full tone by pulling the string down above the nut. This worked great in open position, but on a particular tune he wanted to play the lick up the neck. He needed another hand to do it. We were both intrigued by the musical possibilities of having a third hand to play guitar. I knew there had to be a way for Clarence to bend the string himself. I offered to install pedals and cables like those used on pedal steel guitars, but Clarence refused because he wanted something that would fit inside his guitar case.

"After a couple of weeks of thinking about it, I came up with the idea of using the shoulder strap to actuate a string-pulling, note-bending mechanism. Not only would it fit into the guitar case, it would actually go inside the guitar! I drew up some plans that incorporated a steel guitar bridge that [pedal steel player] 'Sneaky' Pete Kleinow procured for me. After a little convincing, Clarence bravely agreed to let me install this contraption in his beloved Telecaster. He said, 'Just don't show me until it's done'."

Parsons adds: "I built the string bender for Clarence while we were still in Nashville West. In fact, Clarence got another guitar – a white Telecaster – that he played while I worked on his original guitar. Clarence did not work on the actual building of his 'bender' but was the one who created the need for it and the way to play it."

Thursday 25–Sunday 28
The Troubadour, West Hollywood, CA
The Byrds played Doug Weston's Troubadour three years ago almost to the day, and Pete Johnson reviews the opening night of their return here for *The Los Angeles Times* (Saturday 27). "They are now a quartet, consisting of two original Byrds – Roger McGuinn and Chris Hillman – and two late additions, Kevin Kelley on drums and Gram Parsons on electric piano, guitar, and vocals. McGuinn and Hillman do most of the singing, though they faded back for several original pure country numbers featuring Parsons, a fine singer and writer. The keynote of their appearance is their relaxation, which drew warm response from the audience. The earlier Byrds, though a formidable recording group, generally were sloppy and self-conscious in person. They are now in better form and are far more enjoyable than they were when they were riding a string of hits which included 'Mr. Tambourine Man', 'Eight Miles High', and 'Turn! Turn! Turn!'.

"Leading off their first set Thursday night was 'You Ain't Going Nowhere', a Bob Dylan tune done up country style, which is their current single release. This was followed by other westernish material such as 'Old John

Robertson', 'Hickory Wind', and 'Sing Me Back Home' in addition to their familiar past hits. David Crosby's departure has left their vocal blend obviously somewhat thinner on older material, but the new Byrds' ease and pleasure in performing more than makes up for the deficit. They were particularly good on the jazzy 'Tribal Gathering', a version of 'My Back Pages', which shifted into 'Baby What You Want Me To Do', and a double rendition of 'Mr. Tambourine Man', first hit-style then gentle country style."

Michael Etchinson's report in *The Los Angeles Herald-Examiner* (May 2) is lukewarm. "[The group] appear to have lost interest. Roger, formerly Jim, McGuinn played his unique sheet-of-steel Rickenbacker 12-string guitar only on 'Bells Of Rhymney'. New singer Gram Parsons' C&W contributions will never make the Grand Ol' Opry. New drummer Kevin Kelley was replaced for most of a set on opening night by drummer Michael Clarke, who may be worse than Ringo."

→ late April
The Byrds have a European tour coming up in early May, and Gram Parsons wants to bring a pedal steel guitarist along, so he calls up Lloyd Green to check if he is available. The gentle Green will remember the enquiry well 40 years later. "When Gram Parsons called me he was speaking for The Byrds. The tour they were asking me to play with them would have been the soon-aborted world tour. Music historians have subsequently dealt with all the issues about why that tour never happened and Gram's departure from the Byrds.

"Anyhow, Gram asked me very quietly if I would consider playing the tour with them. Before I could answer he added, 'Lloyd, if you agree to do this, would you have any objections to growing your hair a bit longer for the tour? If you go on stage with us with hair as short as yours, you'll be booed by our fans just like we were on the Opry.' I told him I had absolutely no objections to growing it a little longer and would do so if I were to play the tour, but there was a problem. I said I couldn't leave the studio recording scene for such a lengthy time: I was simply too busy. He understood, we had small talk for a few minutes, and the conversation was finished."

Jay Dee Maness is neither keen nor asked, preferring the security of steady gigs in the L.A. area. Instead, the group gets banjo whiz Doug Dillard along for the tour. The Dillard–Byrds connection goes way back, of course, and bringing in the banjo has an ulterior motive: where the pedal steel is synonymous with modern country, the banjo links to its bluegrass past and, particularly, Roger McGuinn's folk background.

May

Wednesday 1

🔊 **RECORDING** Columbia Recording Studios, Sunset and El Centro, Hollywood, CA. Producer Gary Usher and engineer Roy Halee.

McGuinn and Hillman may not have written anything especially for the country project, but Kelley has. Sung by the drummer, 'All I Have Are Memories' is augmented by Lloyd Green (flown to Los Angeles for the occasion) on steel and Clarence White's electric guitar. The backing track is rehearsed by a trimmed-down quartet of White, Green, Hillman, and Kelley, while an additional acoustic guitar – perhaps McGuinn's – and Kelley's lead vocal is heard on the master track.

→ Thursday 2

On the eve of the European tour, Chester Anderson interviews McGuinn for *Crawdaddy* (No. 20, January 1969). The ensuing article covers several of his favourite subjects: the Moog synthesizer; gadgetry in general; technology; science; philosophising. "It's too bad about the printed word, that's what I think," says McGuinn. "Because I'm a big fan of the unprinted word. The sound word. You lose so much that's on that tape by transcribing it into symbols. There should be a system where everyone has their own little hand recorder and they just buy the tape. Because it's obvious that the printed word is obsolete already."

Friday 3

To tie in with the imminent European visit, the latest US single 'You Ain't Going Nowhere'/ 'Artificial Energy' is released in the UK ahead of schedule. Chris Welch reviews the single in *Melody Maker* (May 18). "Yet another Bob Dylan composition, in a country and western style. The Byrds have gone through several line-up changes recently, and this was made by Roger McGuinn, Chris Hillman, Kevin Kelley, and Gram Parsons. … It's a great, happy sound, and should be a hit."

Steve Marriott of The Small Faces is the Blind Date guest in the same issue. "Nice guitar solo. No idea who it is," he says when the single is played. "I've got to look at the label. No, I wouldn't have known anyway. Dylan song. After playing my Blood Sweat & Tears album – well, you know what I mean. It's all right, and I like the guitar and harmonies, but I don't like the song. Yeah, it's 'Dylovan' all right. Not all Dylan songs are good. There seems to be a thing, 'if it's Dylan, it's good'. Well he's like everyone else. He can write, good or bad, and this is bad."

Derek Johnson in *New Musical Express* (May 18) comments: "Seems that everyone has discovered Bob Dylan all over again and is rushing to record his songs! Still, we can hardly blame The Byrds for doing so, as they've been right in there from the beginning. This, of course, is a new Dylan number – an essentially country number, typical of the influence which seems to have dominated Bob since he started writing again after his accident. A jogging beat, a nonchalant lyric, an effortless and thoroughly relaxed vocal and a hum-able tune – these are the principal ingredients."

Record Mirror (May 11) tips the song a certified hit and says: "This Dylan song must shoot the high-flying Byrds into the charts again. It's a gentle guitar-filled beat ballad with nothing as intricate as on their new LP. But nevertheless the tune is catchy and the country-filled appeal should soon be in the charts. Flip culled from their hit LP is a brass-filled drug-warning item – Hugh Masekela on trumpet and a fantastic arrangement." The single bubbles under *Record Mirror*'s Top 50 for a couple of weeks in late May and manages to crawl to Number 45 before sliding down.

The same issue of *Record Mirror* rounds up a batch of recent singles in the UK pilfered from the Bob Dylan treasure trunk of unreleased songs that has furnished The Byrds with 'You Ain't Going Nowhere' and 'Nothing Was Delivered'. Folk duo Paul McNeill & Linda Peters have also covered 'You Ain't Going Nowhere'; Earl Scruggs has chosen 'Down In The Flood'; Peter Paul & Mary let loose on 'Too Much Of Nothing' (which bears the distinction of being the first recorded cover from the Dylan tapes; it was a US Top 40 hit before Christmas); Julie Driscoll With Brian Auger & The Trinity perform 'This Wheel's On Fire' (soon a major UK hit); Marc Ellington sings 'I Shall Be Released' and so does Boz, who also puts 'Down In The Flood' on the B-side. Fuzz Face renders an instrumental version of 'Mighty Quinn', which has already provided an international smash for Manfred Mann. Mann himself produces yet another version of 'You Ain't Going Nowhere' for Unit Four + Two (released next week), the B-side of which is a self-penned tongue-in-cheek ditty called 'So You Want To Be A Blues Player'.

Sunday 5

ALSO …

Buffalo Springfield play their final performance at an 'Electric Carnival' at Long Beach Sports Arena with Country Joe & The Fish, Canned Heat, and a pair of local groups. The career of Buffalo Springfield has been a bumpy ride and even more turbulent than life in The Byrds, but this last outing sees four of the five original members together on stage: Richie Furay, Dewey Martin, Stephen Stills, and Neil Young.

→ Monday 6

The Byrds and road manager Jimmi Seiter fly out of Los Angeles, heading for Italy and Rome.

✈ **May 7–May 16, 1968:**
3RD OVERSEAS TOUR (ITALY, UK)

Tuesday 7

First International Pop Festival, Rome, Piper Club, Rome, Italy

The pompous 'First International Pop Festival' is in for a rocky start when the opening weekend (the festivities commenced on Saturday) draws small crowds to the huge Palazzo Dello Sport that has a capacity of 30,000 seats. Apparently the brainchild of American promoter D.A. Fredriksson, the event has attracted healthy publicity, moral support from Mick Jagger and British Member of Parliament Lord Harlech, and several American and British name acts.

Due to a number of factors – the biggest of which is the mysterious absence of ticket-paying fans – the festival turns into a farce. Originally set for May 4–10, this Mediterranean Monterey festival has shrunk to a four-day happening in Rome, but with the idea to move the last three days to Teatro Lirrico in Milan. When the Palazzo Dello Sport is near empty for the third day running, today's festivities are moved to the small Piper Club, and the airy idea to continue for three days in Milan is quietly dropped. The Byrds are set to play on the last day in Rome together with four British groups (Soft Machine, The Blossom Toes, Nice, and Family) and one Italian band (I Camaleonti), although the final bill is changed around as groups cancel and schedules overrun. This Tuesday night ends up with The Grapefruit, followed by Family, and finally The Byrds at around 11:00pm in front of an audience of about 800.

New Musical Express (May 18) writes: "To fill in the background, the story begins with a four-day pop festival held at a huge indoor sports stadium in Rome. The Move appeared on the third day [May 6], were involved in certain happenings, and the fourth day never came about." The Move's singer Carl Wayne tells the paper: "The festival was originally being organised by a group of San Francisco hippies who, because of lack of money, had to hand it over to Bavarian Television. They set up equipment which was really good gear and everybody was being very polite to them because they had helped to put it on."

Melody Maker (May 18) thinks it may be

"The Pop Flop of 1968" and provides another report. "According to accounts of those who were in Rome, no more than about 4,000 people attended throughout the entire festival. Many of the groups named to appear didn't turn up, but those that did included Donovan, The Move, Grapefruit, Brian Auger & Julie Driscoll, Ten Years After, The Byrds, The Association, Fairport Convention, Pink Floyd, The Nice, Family, Captain Beefheart & His Magic Band, and The Samurai." Managers Giorgio Gomelsky and Terry Ellis, who handle Brian Auger and Ten Years After respectively, are outraged. "On the first day there were about 1,200 and at one stage the organisers went out and gave away complimentary tickets," says Gomelsky. Ellis sums up: "It was an utter, complete chaotic shambles. The organisation didn't come up anywhere near the level of the idea."

Dutch music paper *Hitweek* (May 17) is also there to report. "Jim McGuinn (who calls himself Roger these days), without beard or sunglasses but with his hair trimmed short, the little blushing drummer Kevin Kelley, dark haired organist/acoustic guitarist Gram Parsons, curly haired bass player Chris Hillman, and a friend on banjo. Everybody – but this goes for the whole festival – walks around casually dressed. They play ten (10!) songs. The sound quality is not as perfect as on their records but still has its own distinctive, melancholic sound. There are moments when I almost can't keep back my tears, listening to the beautiful 'Old John Robertson', 'My Back Pages', or 'Goin' Back'. … The close harmony vocals of McGuinn and Hillman as well as their backing for Parsons' solos are extraordinary. But the capabilities of bass player Hillman and guitarist McGuinn are just as good as on their records. The stories about the Byrds' bad

reputation as a live band are totally unjust. They just kept playing. (McGuinn: 'I guess we're supposed to stop now, but we're just getting warmed up'). Unbelievable!"

📻 **EURO RADIO** The Byrds with Doug Dillard perform 'You Ain't Going Nowhere', 'Old John Robertson', 'You Don't Miss Your Water', 'Hickory Wind', 'I'll Feel A Whole Lot Better', 'Chimes Of Freedom', 'The Christian Life', 'Turn! Turn! Turn!', 'My Back Pages' (which segues into 'Baby, What You Want Me To Do'), and 'Mr. Spaceman'. The show is recorded by Italian radio KSAN-FM for a later broadcast. It is also recorded by Dutch radio VPRO, and a five-song extract of the performance plus interviews with Roger McGuinn, Gram Parsons, and Kevin Kelley is broadcast on Dutch Radio Channel Hilversum 1 on June 7 (08:00–11:00pm) as *Eerste Rome Popfesival* (plus a selection of Pink Floyd's concert). The interviews are done by radio DJ Wim Noordhoek, who also penned the review for *Hitweek*.

Gram Parsons plays acoustic guitar and sings lead on 'Hickory Wind', 'You Don't Miss Your Water', and 'The Christian Life' but otherwise mostly plays his keyboard. McGuinn plays a fair amount of six-string and an uncharacteristically fuzzy blues bending solo on the shuffle 'Baby, What You Want Me To Do'. Throughout, Hillman and Kelley make up an effective rhythm section, and Dillard rips on the banjo.

Ashley Hutchings of Britain's Fairport Convention is impressed. "I've always liked the sound of country music from back when I was a youngster listening to bluegrass and Doc Watson," Hutchings will write later in his autobiography. "And then of course The Byrds, who by far and away are my favourite group, went to country music. I was witness to the unveiling of this at the Piper Club. I was sat in the packed audience in this club and heard this fantastic mixture of country and rock coming from the stage. Gram Parsons was there, electric banjo from Doug Dillard, and interspersed with their hits 'Mr. Tambourine Man' and 'Turn! Turn! Turn!' was this amazing fresh country music.

"I spoke to Gram Parsons after the gig," says Hutchings. "We flowed out into the street … and Parsons, being fresh-faced and very enthusiastic, came out into the street as well, unlike long-in-the-tooth McGuinn, who probably hid away from the crowds until that'd subsided. I talked to Gram along with a couple of other people, and was struck by his enthusiasm, his humbleness and his excitement at being part of it all."

Parsons may also meet his future songwriting partner and friend Ric Grech today. Grech is at present the bassist and fiddle player with Family.

→ **Wednesday 8**

📺 **EURO TV** Italian/German TV A brief film segment, purportedly made by either Italian RAI-TV or a Bavarian television station, has The Byrds miming to 'Mr. Spaceman' in front of Rome's Coliseum. It is broadcast on German TV ZDF on October 16 between 10:00–10:55pm in a special on the Rome festival. Produced in colour, the intention is to exchange the programme with other member countries of the EBU (European Broadcasting Union). The video clip will be made available on the Gram Parsons DVD collection *Fallen Angel* in 2007.

→ **Thursday 9**

The group leaves Rome for a hastily arranged visit to Britain, evidently not confirmed until the end of April, although an advertisement for their London appearance on May 11 is placed in time for the edition of *Melody Maker* on newsstands on May 2.

Saturday 11

Middle Earth Club, Covent Garden, central London, UK

Third time lucky for The Byrds on their return to London, headlining at Middle Earth with Spider John Koerner, White Rabbit, and DJ Jeff Dexter. Middle Earth is London's premier underground club, situated in a cellar warehouse in Covent Garden. The club opens at 10:30pm and continues to dawn. *The Notorious Byrd Brothers* is presently at Number 15 in the UK album charts, and this time the group is well-prepared and well-received. Gram Parsons is being noticed as an influence on the group, and their flexible repertoire encompasses the expected hits, a portion of country material, and some unexpected gems from the past.

Norman Jopling reviews the show in *Record Mirror* (May 18): "[The] high flying Byrds triumph with a British audience. … The transition of The Byrds from a powerful pop group (their 'Mr. Tambourine Man' was one of the few debut discs to top both the British and US charts) to an underground unit has meant a decline in hit singles, but their new LP *The Notorious Byrd Brothers* is currently riding high here. They were here over the weekend and appeared at the Middle Earth club where they proved conclusively that their days of onstage ineffectuality were over … they were called back countless times by a mainly hippie audience, and DJ Jeff Dexter nearly ran out of nauseous hippie jargon with which to praise them.

"There were five Byrds – lead vocalist and guitarist Roger McGuinn (who had three guitars which were all used frequently), bass guitarist and supporting vocalist Chris Hillman, drummer Kevin Kelley, vocalist and acoustic guitarist Gram Parsons, and an un-named electric banjo player [Dillard]. Many of the numbers were in a plaintive country style, including 'Old John Robertson' from their hit LP and their new single 'You Ain't Going Nowhere'. Gram Parsons was the lead-ing country vocalist and he performed many poignant numbers including 'Excuse Me' [a Buck Owens number, its full title is 'Excuse Me, I Think I've Got a Heartache'], 'I Like The Christian Life', and 'Under Your Spell Again' [another Buck Owens tune].

"Their version of 'Foggy Mountain Break-down' was well received, but the numbers which brought the house down were the big single hits, for which Roger McGuinn used his famous electric 12-string guitar. They included a scintillating version of 'Eight Miles High', and others like '5D', 'I'll Feel A Whole Lot Better', 'Turn! Turn! Turn!', 'Goin' Back', 'So You Want To Be A Rock'n'Roll Star', and 'Mr. Tambourine Man'. The group's sound was very similar to their new LP, and The Byrds' first set was finished with a version of Vera Lynn's 'We'll Meet Again'. Other numbers they performed included 'Tribal Gathering', 'Baby What You Want Me To Do', and 'The Bells Of Rhymney'."

Reader Tom Mabbett of West Norwood, London, writes in *Melody Maker* (May 18): "The Byrds at Middle Earth: what a trip! I saw them both times and they were even bet-ter than their records. Something I had not expected after hearing about their 'bad stage act'. Mick Jagger and Marianne also must have thought so as they turned up to see them twice as well. Keep flying The Byrds!"

Kingsley Abbott, working for Fairport Con-vention, recalls: "I was lucky enough to get in round the back [at Middle Earth], bringing in the PA for The Byrds to use, because theirs had either disappeared or wasn't working. We had [Fairport's] PA in the van, so together with their roadie Jimmi Seiter and Fairport roadie Harvey Bramham, we carried it in and set it up. That meant I didn't get to go down in the throng. I just watched the whole thing from the side of the stage. I sat on some kind of a low bench with Roy Harper. He obviously enjoyed the gig as well.

"They played the main stage at Middle Earth, which was not that big so they were all quite close when playing. That's why Doug Dil-lard stayed at the back, partly as there really wasn't room on the front line. They were all quite stoned! There was a small room they used as a dressing room to the side, and you could get high just from the smell coming from that room.

"Gram Parsons stood out for different rea-sons, I think. Firstly, for the country music

section that he led them through, which was a revelation to many of us. I guess it took us deeper than the *Rodeo* album. They were play-ing it like they really meant it – no produc-tion gloss, just rootsy plain country songs. Secondly, Gram looked awesome in his white suit. He was tallish, slim, and cut a fine figure. He must have appealed to any women in the audience – and probably to several of the men too. He had a lot of charisma that night, and looked more positive as a performer than McGuinn, Hillman, and the rest. They were good too, but his look really stood out that night to the packed club.

"They played for a very long time that night, something like two-and-a-half hours, with a slight break. The first bit was traditional Byrds fare, and then they went into the totally dif-ferent sounding traditional American country style. Ashley Hutchings was gobsmacked. How they were presenting both the full-on electric folk rock and this wonderful roots stuff that was stripped bare of the electrics … the 12-string didn't figure. It was real back-to-basics stuff. To my mind it fits very well that [Ashley] may have seen that as a route for Fairport's direction."

Ashley Hutchings will later recall The Byrds' influence on Fairport Convention and taking Fairport toward their genre-defining *Liege And Lief* album in 1969. "When we started Fair-port in the very beginning we were highly influenced by The Byrds," Hutchings says in a conversation with Abbott. "They were my favourite group. And then Bob Dylan, and shortly after that The Band came along – and I think that Holy Trinity, at some point in the late 60s, all said that they were going to go back in time. They were going to revisit the traditional music of their country – country music, bluegrass, blues or whatever. The Band made a wonderful concoction of all these together, and it was realising that then, that [Fairport] couldn't carry on the way we were. Those guys had nailed it, so what we would do was the British equivalent of what they had done."

The Middle Earth show is widely boot-legged and, despite the murky quality, the music shines through. Here, The Byrds *rock*. The tape contains 'So You Want To Be A Rock'n'Roll Star', 'Chimes Of Freedom', 'You Ain't Going Nowhere', and 'My Back Pages' which is joined to a screaming 'Baby, What You Want Me To Do'. Parsons plays a surprisingly effective keyboard, bringing a dif-ferent dimension to the group's live act. He is featured on vocals and acoustic guitar on 'Hickory Wind', Merle Haggard's 'Sing Me Back Home', 'The Christian Life', the Buck Owens number 'Under Your Spell Again', and 'You Don't Miss Your Water'. The tape ends

with McGuinn leading the group through four phases of Byrds: the raga jazzy 'Eight Miles High', the folk-rock cornerstone 'Bells Of Rhymney', a doom-laden 'Space Odyssey' (coincidentally, Stanley Kubrick's movie *2001: A Space Odyssey* premiered in London yester-day), and the dreamy 'Tribal Gathering'.

Meanwhile, back home in the US, fans of The Byrds can see the group this afternoon on Dick Clark's *American Bandstand '68* (epi-sode No. 1832 at 12:30pm; see late April), performing 'You Ain't Going Nowhere' and 'Eight Miles High'. This is a rare television appearance of The Byrds with Gram Parsons and Kevin Kelley. Other inserts screened are with Four Jacks & A Jill (a South African group) and Tommy James & The Shondells. Besides guests and filmed clips, this week's hit parade of records is played, including Simon & Garfunkel ('Mrs. Robinson') and The Beatles ('Lady Madonna').

Sunday 12
Blaises, Kensington, London, UK

The Byrds return to Blaises, the site of their embarrassing showcase under the critical eyes of the UK's pop culturati in August 1965. After a fire completely destroyed London's prime in-club the Speakeasy on April 28, bookings have transferred to Blaises as 'The Speakeasy At Blaises'. The club stays open until the early morning hours, and The Byrds do not go on until very late.

Tony Wilson of *Melody Maker* (May 18) reviews yesterday's Middle Earth show and tonight's Blaises performance. "Whatever impression was left by The Byrds on their last visit, and it wasn't too good, was completely eradicated by two great shows … . The Byrds proved to be a highly musical group and songs such as 'Eight Miles High', 'Rock'n'Roll Star', 'Turn! Turn! Turn!' and 'Mr. Tambourine Man' drew big ovations from capacity crowds at both clubs. But the Byrds are now doing country and western-oriented material, sung in the main by Gram Parsons, and this, too, was received extremely well.

"'Sing Me Back Home', 'Hickory Wind', and 'You Don't Miss Your Water 'Till Your Well Runs Dry' were just some of the titles, and they treated them without too much of the sickly overtones so often found with performances in this genre. On the folk side the group feature, and sing excellently, the Woody Guthrie ballad, 'Pretty Boy Floyd'. With The Byrds was Doug Dillard, a brilliant banjo player and former member of The Dil-lards, playing an electric solidbody banjo built for him by Rickenbacker, but he switched to acoustic [banjo] and raised cheers with his version of Earl Scruggs's 'Foggy Mountain Breakdown'. The Byrds' sound is not far removed from that heard on their records and they come over as competent musicians and stylish singers. Welcome back, Byrds."

Wilson is engaged in a mildly heated argument with *MM* scribe Chris Welch a few months later, as they weigh the pros and cons of American visitors. Welch writes disparagingly of The Byrds' earlier London trips. Wilson writes in their defence: "The Byrds you saw weren't The Byrds I saw on their last trip earlier this year. At Middle Earth and Blaises, they played really well – I think Mick Jagger will agree with me on that. Certainly the audiences at both clubs thought so."

Indeed, Jagger, Marianne Faithfull, and Brian Jones unwind at Blaises after a busy day. Earlier in the evening, The Rolling Stones made an unannounced appearance at the 'NME Poll Winners Concert' at Wembley Stadium in northwest London – the group's first live appearance in a year, and, as it turns out, Brian Jones's last ever Stones concert. Springing 'Jumpin' Jack Flash' on an unsuspecting crowd – the single will not be released for two weeks – and then 'Satisfaction' to rapturous screams, the Stones are off as quickly as they came on.

→ Monday 13

Melody Maker interviews Roger McGuinn. "The trip wasn't planned," he explains in the paper's May 25 issue, "We went to Rome for the festival and there we were told that we were going to play in England – that was the only reason." Parsons is singled out for praise, and McGuinn comments on the country inflections: "I don't think we'll go into country music a hundred per cent. But it's pure and it hasn't really been done by pop artists. It's a fresh area, and a relief from all that psychedelic garbage." He has still not quite given up on the idea of a double album. "We have a whole country album that we are releasing – that's completed, and we'll be following that with an album of electronic music, but we haven't done that yet." The same article claims explicitly that The Byrds make two appearances at Middle Earth, at the second of which there is a petition being signed asking for the group's return as soon as possible. No documentation exists otherwise of a second show.

▮ Monday 13 Tuesday 14

Mick Jagger sends a limousine to pick up The Byrds for a ramble through the English countryside. The prehistoric monument at Stonehenge near Salisbury in southern England is the perfect location for a fabled tale of The Byrds meeting the Stones. The reminiscences of the night will become blurred by time, and perhaps dimmed by copious amounts of John-

nie Walker whisky and strong-smelling smoke, but it is certain that this is the first meeting of future blood brothers Keith Richards and Gram Parsons. A more mundane version of the story has Mick Jagger sending the Stones chauffeur out to purchase dry socks for the entire entourage.

Chris Hillman later tells music historian John Einarson: "Gram was seduced by the trappings of the business. When we went over to Europe, Mick Jagger and Keith Richards invited Roger and me to go out to Stonehenge in the middle of the night, and we took Gram with us. That was his downfall. Gram started following them around. It was embarrassing." Keith Richards will tell his biographer Barbara Charone: "Gram blew into town with The Byrds, who were playing Blaises. Gram came back to Mick's Chester Square flat with Roger McGuinn."

Plans for a return to England are already being discussed while the group is in London, and in conjunction with this, a chance pops up to do a tour of South Africa. Whereas The Byrds approach the exotic trip as a chance to experience the country firsthand, Jagger and Richards make no bones about what they think of the idea: "Their next gig was South Africa," Richards tells Barbara Charone, "and we told Gram English bands never ever went there."

Intriguingly, Jagger was asked exactly two years earlier about his views on playing South Africa, in a conversation with Jack Hutton of *Melody Maker* (May 28, 1966). "I don't see anything wrong in going to South Africa. Is it better to play to one white audience and one coloured audience or is it better not to play to either of them? Who loses out? Do the coloured people gain anything from not seeing us if they want to?" Pressing the matter, Hutton asks if the group would play only to whites. Jagger: "Oh no. But they wouldn't say that. They just say the audiences are segregated. In America it's very different. You can turn around and say, 'We won't play to segregated audiences,' and all that, which is mainly done for publicity. But if they want to segregate them, they'll segregate them no matter what you do."

▮ Wednesday 15–Thursday 16

By all accounts, The Byrds and Doug Dillard remain in London before flying straight to New York City for the weekend appearances at the Fillmore East. The Rolling Stones, meanwhile, are busy – on the Wednesday they meet the press all day to promote 'Jumpin' Jack Flash', while on the Thursday they have a business meeting before band members, girlfriends, and wives all troop off to see *2001: A Space Odyssey*.

The Byrds are one of many influences on the Stones' own approximation of Americana this year, as Jagger and Richards return to an earlier style after the dead-end experiment with *Their Satanic Majesties Request*. The Stones have taped bits and pieces for a new album during the last couple of months, and two of the first songs they try out as they return for another stretch at London's Olympic Studios, just as The Byrds fly out, are the waltz-time 'Dear Doctor' and the folk-inflected 'Factory Girl' – neither of which are terribly far from the country music that Parsons, Hillman, and McGuinn are exploring this spring.

Friday 17–Saturday 18
Fillmore East, Manhattan, New York, NY

In March this year promoter Bill Graham took over New York's Village Theatre (where The Byrds played in July 1967) in order to open an East Coast subsidiary of his Fillmore venue. The Byrds (with Doug Dillard) and Tim Buckley headline, while UK soul-pop unit The Foundations play support.

Fred Kirby gives an account in *Billboard* (June 1). "The Byrds, absent from the New York scene for some time, showed they still had complete command of the folk-rock idiom with a near-brilliant first set at Fillmore East on Saturday (18), the third of four weekend sets at the East Village theatre. … A major question the group had to answer was how their change of membership affected their familiar sound. With Jim McGuinn still on lead and [Chris] Hillman still on bass, the unit is as solid as ever. It took the large audience a while to warm up to The Byrds, however. Much of this doubtless was due to the abrupt ending of Buckley's set.

"Actually, it was a group of country numbers that grabbed the audience. Included were 'Hickory Wind' and 'You Don't Miss Your Water' with [Gram] Parsons featured, while Douglas Dillard played bluegrass banjo in 'Foggy Mountain Breakdown'. Dillard, not a regular member of the group, sat in for one weekend stand. The last three numbers of their regular program were three of The Byrds' biggest hits: 'Eight Miles High', 'Mr. Tambourine Man', and 'Turn! Turn! Turn!' These demanded and naturally got encores as the group performed 'Goin' Back' and 'Hey Joe'. In the latter, McGuinn sang just about the fastest version of the song which has received many performances around here lately.

"The program had many other features, including 'Chimes Of Freedom', 'So You Want To Be A Rock'n'Roll Star', 'Satisfied Mind', 'My Back Pages', and their latest single 'You Ain't Going Nowhere', a country tune.

McGuinn, Hillman, and Parsons on vocals were excellent throughout, while [Kelley] was first rate on drums. Many groups that have played Fillmore East recently have scored impressively with the excitement of raw power, a characteristic of much of today's music. The Byrds, however, are clearly one of the most polished acts in today's pop scene, and they, too, scored impressively."

Pete MacBeth of The Foundations tells *Melody Maker* (June 29): "We worked with The Byrds – they refused to lend us their equipment when ours was stolen. In spite of that I thought they were good on stage, as good as their records."

At the Fillmore, McGuinn is introduced to a girl who is there on behalf of her friend, Broadway director Jacques Levy. McGuinn recalls the meeting to Jud Cost of Sundazed Records many years later. "Jacques had a pretty blonde girlfriend, and he sent her backstage at the Fillmore. She said, 'My boyfriend's writing a Broadway musical and he wants you to do the score. What do you think?' And I said, 'Yeah!'" Levy is planning a musical adaptation of playwright Henrik Ibsen's *Peer Gynt*, but due to various commitments the collaboration with McGuinn does not get started for many months.

Wednesday 22

The issue of *Rolling Stone* printed today (but dated June 22) breaks the latest news on the next Byrds album. "They originally planned a variety of material for the album, but the Nashville setting and the addition of Parsons, who hails from Georgia, got them so involved in C&W that all 11 cuts will be country music."

The item indicates that a selection has already been made, saying that the songs will include Dylan's 'You Ain't Going Nowhere', their current single. The report then makes an intriguing conclusion, stating that there will also be "a number of tunes by Parsons, including 'You Don't Miss Your Water', 'I Like The Christian Life', and 'One Hundred Years From Now'." The latter is not even recorded yet – it will be taped over the weekend – and, in view of what will later happen to some of the finished vocal tracks amid accusations of artistic violation, Parsons is still very much the singer in charge on both 'You Don't Miss Your Water' and 'The Christian Life'.

Friday 24

'SRO for RFK', Los Angeles Memorial Sports Arena, Los Angeles, CA
Senator Robert F. Kennedy, John F. Kennedy's younger brother, is one of the presidential candidates for the Democrats in the 1968 election. It is a trying year for the country:

the assassination of civil rights leader Martin Luther King on April 4 has increased national tension, while opposition to the Vietnam War is widespread. President Lyndon B. Johnson's decision not to run for re-election in March improves Kennedy's chances, and with several hard-won victories in the presidential primary elections under his belt, the next obstacles are the Oregon and California Democratic primaries on May 28 and June 4 respectively.

Kennedy's liberal views strike a chord with many Hollywood celebrities, who rally round to raise money for the California election. A benefit gala is set for the enormous Memorial Sports Arena in Los Angeles tonight at 8:00pm, which expects to raise more than $500,000 for the Kennedy campaign. Loosely organised by the S.R.O. committee – presumably suggesting it will be Standing Room Only at the 16,000-seat arena – the festivity promises a cross section from Hollywood's many walks of fame: actresses (Carol Channing, Angie Dickinson), actors (Gene Barry, Gene Kelly, Teddy Neeley), athlete Roosevelt Grier, gospel singer Mahalia Jackson, comedian Jerry Lewis, composer Henry Mancini, crooner Andy Williams, and a couple of pop groups thrown in to attract the younger crowds: Sonny & Cher and The Byrds. Robert F. Kennedy will also be there himself to address his supporters.

Monday 27

◁)) **RECORDING** Columbia Recording Studios, Sunset and El Centro, Hollywood, CA. Producer Gary Usher and engineer Roy Halee.

Today marks the last session to finish the

group's next album. McGuinn has temporarily shelved the original concept of recording a musical timeline from the ancient to the modern, so Parsons is given the chance to pursue the newfound country direction with his composition 'One Hundred Years From Now'. In view of various press reports in March, this number may be the 'mystery ninth song' attempted in Nashville (see March 15).

The group has again called on the services of steel guitarist Lloyd Green, who flies in from Nashville and then back again, and Clarence White and his string-bending apparatus. For Green, the Byrds encounter has left an indelible impression. Speaking to Alastair MacKay in 2008, he will rank it "pretty close to the top, in memory and importance" – this from a session player who has appeared on more than 10,000 recording sessions during his long career.

Trusted road manager and general Byrds minder Jimmi Seiter is involved in a serious road accident on Mulholland Drive this evening. He suffers a fractured pelvis, internal injuries, and bruises and will be out of action for a couple of months. Carlos Bernal is hired to take over road management during Seiter's convalescence.

•

With a total of 15 new tracks in the can, Gary Usher and McGuinn have already picked a running order for the new album and, in the end, four songs are left off: Parsons' 'Lazy Days', the arrangement of 'Pretty Polly', Tim Hardin's 'Reputation', and Kevin Kelley's 'All I Have Are Memories'.

To Hillman's relief, the original double-album concept is laid to rest. Evaluating the project in hindsight, he will tell music historian Richie Unterberger: "With all due respect, I didn't want a bunch of 'CTA 102's or 'Moog Raga's or whatever that stuff is. It didn't work for me, and I'm glad it didn't happen. It would have made no sense at all – although there weren't that many strong parameters then. You could sort of do those kinds of projects, record-company budget willing, on that end. But no, no regrets at all. That would have been a separate deal. To put the [country and electronic] together would have been a little crazy. It would have been an interesting separate project, but … either I didn't understand what [McGuinn] was doing or I just didn't like it."

Whatever the debate over the content of the finished album, it pales in comparison to the controversy that follows McGuinn and Usher's decision to replace some of Parsons' original vocals. It is not clear at exactly which point McGuinn's vocals are dubbed, but judging by the status report in *Rolling Stone* on May 22, it must be at the end of May as the sessions

Gram Parsons at Fillmore East, New York, May 1968.

are wrapped. Parsons has already relinquished future royalties on *Safe At Home* and the name of The International Submarine Band to Lee Hazlewood, but he is still somehow, vaguely under contract to LHI Records – enough, at least, to make Columbia jump to avoid legal action if Parsons' vocals are used.

So McGuinn replaces Parsons' lead vocals on 'The Christian Life', 'You Don't Miss Your Water', and 'One Hundred Years From Now' – the latter sung harmony style with Hillman overdubbing on Parsons' original vocal. The issue with Hazlewood is resolved literally at the last minute, so Parsons' lead vocals on 'Hickory Wind', 'You're Still On My Mind', and 'Life In Prison' are retained.

Parsons will say in an interview with Dutch radio in 1972: "Columbia, for some reason, thought that if I sang on the album they would get sued because my release from Lee Hazlewood looked shaky – so a few songs they overdubbed completely and my voice was stuck way in the background and used as a guide only. … Things were really coming out well until this thing about the lawsuit, and then everything went wrong; they decided to pull out of the can … things we'd recorded purely as warm-up songs – like 'Life In Prison' and 'You're Still On My Mind' ¬– both of which could've been so much better. They were just about to scrap the last one of mine that they'd saved – 'Hickory Wind' – when the lawyer came in waving the piece of paper confirming my release."

This version of events will be persistently repeated later. For example, Hillman explains to Richard Williams in *Melody Maker* (December 19, 1970): "[Gram] did all the singing … but then we discovered that he was under contract to another label, from his old group the International Submarine Band, so we had to recut them with Roger singing lead. We could never get the same feeling into the songs, though."

Years later, Gary Usher will offer a different slant on the story when he speaks to music historian Stephen J. McParland. "During the actual sessions [in Nashville], Gram sang lead on several songs. When we came back to L.A., we took a number of Gram's leads off: not because of any contractual reasons, but because McGuinn was reluctant to have Gram sing an entire Byrds album when he was the newest member of the group. Really, the Byrds sound at that stage was McGuinn and Crosby, and with Crosby gone, McGuinn thought there might be an identity crisis. I don't ever remember anybody from Columbia's legal department sending me a memo to the effect, 'Hey, take Gram's vocals off.' Yes, there were legal problems that had to be worked out, and they were worked out."

"Whoever sang lead on the album was there because that's how we wanted it to sound. You just don't take a hit group and inject a new singer for no reason. The album had just the exact amount of Gram Parsons on it that McGuinn, Hillman, and myself wanted."

The idea that McGuinn's voice is crucial to retain a Byrds identity is, surprisingly, supported by Parsons himself. He will tell Bud Scoppa in 1970: "I didn't really appreciate, say, their third album or their fourth album – I hadn't even listened to [them]. Since then I have, and I can accept why *Sweetheart Of The Rodeo* had to be changed."

June

Saturday 1

Forest Ballroom, Dallas, TX

The group heads out on the road again, tonight opening a new club in south Dallas with a lightshow supplied by Regina Circus.

Undated June

An unconfirmed appearance in Boulder, CO – possibly at Macky Auditorium, University of Colorado – reportedly takes place this month.

Monday 3

ALSO …

The small town of Las Vegas in San Miguel County, New Mexico – and not to be confused with its bigger Nevada namesake – is the location today for a scene to be used in the new Columbia Pictures movie *Easy Rider*. The plot centres on the escapades of two bikers as they ride from Los Angeles to New Orleans. The movie features Peter Fonda as Wyatt (nicknamed Captain America because of his Stars & Stripes attire) and Dennis Hopper as Billy. It is scripted by Fonda, Hopper, and Terry Southern. Fonda is also the movie's producer, with Hopper its director. Much of it has been shot already, and today's scene calls for the stars to be arrested when driving their bikes in a small-town parade. The movie's title and overall story are already in place, but work on a music soundtrack – the one crucial element that will later make the film a classic – will not begin until the end of the year.

Tuesday 4

On May 28, Senator Robert F. Kennedy surprisingly lost the Oregon Democratic primary to Eugene McCarthy. The next showdown between the two Democratic candidates is today's California primary. A committee calling itself Hollywood For Kennedy inserts a half-page advertisement in *The Los Angeles Times* this morning, signed by more than 200 actors, actresses, movie producers, television celebrities, scriptwriters, authors, singers, songwriters, and musicians. The list is a name-dropper's delight, and although few other rock stars have signed on, The Byrds have.

Kennedy wins the California primary, but in the morning hours of June 5 he is assassinated after addressing his supporters at the Ambassador Hotel in Los Angeles. Kennedy's death scars the nation and leaves the Democratic Party floundering. The Party's Convention in Chicago in August is plagued by riots and police brutality, televised straight into people's homes. Hubert Humphrey is nominated as the Democratic candidate but narrowly loses the presidential election in November to Republican Richard Nixon.

Thursday 6

Richard Goldstein has penned an article in the *Village Voice* headed "Country Rock: Can Y'All Dig It?". The term country-rock is scarcely invented yet, but Goldstein reports on the first rumblings as country-friendly material by Moby Grape, The Stone Poneys, Buffy Saint-Marie, The International Submarine Band, and – of course – Bob Dylan is being aired on selected country music stations in the North.

Goldstein warmly recommends new LPs by John Hartford and Johnny Cash. "True, none of these albums actually represent a synthesis between rock and country; in fact, there is no key record on which to hang this movement yet. But The Byrds, who have been juicing up their golden-oldie space standards with country originals at recent concerts, are cutting an album of Nashville-plus, on the Coast. So expect to see Roger, Jim, or whatever McGuinn and company invest bluegrass with the same dignified but overwhelming calm they once brought to folk-rock.

"I don't expect The Byrds, or any of the rock musicians now taking creative refuge in country music, to give us a faithful rendition of old rockabilly riffs," says Goldstein. "The country rock of 1968 will be sophisticated, but not dishonest. I'll wager we don't get God and country and a whole lot more of Jesus from The Byrds, except in a context of nostalgic irony. I expect The Byrds to make modern, urban music, and I hope to discover the same imaginative power in their country songs that I once found in citybilly music, when it meant tearing into a bluegrass banjo riff and greasing it with big-city funk. That kind of distortion, I think, represents a legitimate kind of posh."

●

Hit Parader prepares a feature on The Byrds around this time. Compiled by Fernon Bentley, the story is devoted to a summary of the present members, and reveals that the group's next Columbia album will be called *Hickory Wind*. The feature, headed "The Byrds' Hassles End With New Members", will not be published until the magazine's December edition, and by that time the album is already in stores as *Sweetheart Of The Rodeo*.

Saturday 15

The Byrds will return to London to headline a special charity concert on July 6, according to a news bulletin in the British music press today. The show is organised by a special committee of show business and sports stars called Keystone, and their good cause is to raise money for British Boys' Clubs.

The London concert is part of a longer overseas tour that has been on the cards for some time. Following London, the group is booked for a two-week tour of South Africa and Rhodesia (later Zimbabwe) before going back to Los Angeles via Majorca for a festival on July 22. Promoter Peter Bankoff handles the trip to Africa, an opportunity the group seizes – apparently without attaching too much thought to the consequences.

South Africa in 1968 is ruled by the all-white National Party. Apartheid, the system of racial segregation, is legal. Despite international pressure and sanctions – the United Nations condemned the country's apartheid policies in 1962 and by 1968 the UN General Assembly proposes to end all cultural, educational, and sporting relations – the country still trades with many key countries such as Great Britain and the United States. The country's state-owned radio station, South African Broadcasting Corporation (SABC), adheres to strict rules. It has banned all Beatles records following Lennon's remarks on Jesus in 1966, and even The Byrds' own 'Turn! Turn! Turn!' is prohibited because its lyrical content is misconstrued as blasphemy. Remarkably, there is no television broadcasting in South Africa (it will first be introduced in the mid 1970s) as that is not in line with government policies.

McGuinn and Hillman know of the situation first-hand through Hugh Masekela and Miriam Makeba, both South African exiles. When the question of South Africa comes up, McGuinn discusses it with Makeba, whose advice, paradoxically, is the opposite of what Jagger and Richards have offered. She suggests that McGuinn goes and sees for himself. McGuinn and Hillman's one condition is that they will play for non-segregated audiences.

Whatever motives The Byrds have, they will seem later to have been naively noble. Questioned about the trip the day before the group's departure for South Africa, McGuinn explains to *Record Mirror* (August 17): "I

believe in getting through to [South African audiences] with our music. If we work there and they like us, they'll be a lot more ready to think about what we say." Hillman adds: "It all will be solved. … People will adjust because they will have to adjust, otherwise we'll all destroy ourselves." And McGuinn again: "Well, I've got great faith in humanity, and besides, good always wins in the end, just like the movies say."

Friday 21–Saturday 22
The Kaleidoscope, Hollywood, CA

The Kaleidoscope is the latest stage of the transformation of the old Moulin Rouge venue from dignified Hollywood établissement to full-blown psychedelic rock club. The Kaleidoscope held court at Ciro's Le Disc/It's Boss and then at another temporary location before taking over the lease on the Moulin Rouge when Dave Hull's Hullabaloo gave up earlier this year. For this weekend, The Byrds share the bill with The Crazy World Of Arthur Brown from England, while San Francisco group Frumious Bandersnatch is support.

Judy Sims writes in *Disc* (July 13): "The Byrds performed at the Kaleidoscope and sounded really good. There were five on stage, including the steel guitar player who isn't actually a Byrd but who plays with them most of the time." Pete Johnson in *The Los Angeles Times* (June 25): "The Byrds are The Byrds, even in their phoenix-like metamorphosis into a semi-country group, despite all the change in personnel. They are no longer as exciting as they once were, but they are good, which they once weren't, and they are now part of a tradition worth the homage they receive. They consist of: Roger McGuinn, lead guitar and vocals; Chris Hillman, bass; Kevin Kelley, drums; with the assistance of Gram Parsons, vocals, guitar and piano, and the apocryphal J.D. [Jay Dee Maness], [pedal steel] guitar."

As The Byrds head for Europe and Africa next month, Maness joins singer Norm Forrest for a steady nightclub gig in Van Nuys, CA, in addition to his studio work. Another pedal steel player, the maverick 'Sneaky' Pete Kleinow, sits in with The Byrds for a solitary California appearance around this time.

July

Monday 1
ALSO …

The Band's *Music From Big Pink* is released in the US today. Richard Goldstein reviews this epoch-making album for *The New York Times* (August 4). In part, he writes: "The Byrds, who

were pioneers in folk-rock, and among the first in pop music to use electrical distortion, have backed away from the psychedelic barrage and are preparing a country album. Like Dylan's recent work, it will probably be muted in tone and reverent in spirit. It may well rip the lid off progressive rock. Fortunately, we needn't wait for The Byrds to understand what the country-rock synthesis is all about. Already, the movement has its first major album: *Music From Big Pink* by The Band. You can tell right away that this is country music by its twang and its tenacity. But you know it's also rock, because it makes you want to move."

✈ **July 5–July 22, 1968:**
4TH OVERSEAS TOUR (UK, SOUTH AFRICA, RHODESIA)

Friday 5

The four Byrds – McGuinn, Hillman, Parsons, and Kelley – fly into London together with road manager Carlos Bernal. A concert has been added at Middle Earth, the club where the group was so well received in May, and there is also a hope that they can tape an appearance on BBC-2's weekly television show *Colour Me Pop*. This, unfortunately, does not happen. A BBC contract for them to tape the show on July 6 at Studio B at Television Centre in central London is later cancelled. The reason given in BBC paperwork is simply "not available".

Immediately following London, the group is set to fly to South Africa, but Parsons is in two minds about the whole venture, although he comes along willingly to London. McGuinn and Hillman presumably perceive his decision to join them for the first leg of the tour as an agreement to do all of it.

Saturday 6
'One-Night Summer Celebration',
Middle Earth, Roundhouse, Chalk Farm,
north-west London, UK

The Byrds are the main attraction at this special presentation, where the Middle Earth club for one night moves across town to the Roundhouse – the site of the group's 'tea party' for UK fans back in February 1967. To accommodate concertgoers, free shuttle buses are set up between Covent Garden (where Middle Earth is housed) and Chalk Farm. Jeff Dexter is MC and DJ for the night-long celebration, starting at 10:30pm and continuing through to dawn. Other acts are The Deviants, The Gun, The Iron Volcano, Izzy The Push, and The Writing On The Wall. Great British Light Show operates the accustomed mind-altering illuminations, while films are shown non-stop.

Sunday 7

'Sounds '68', Royal Albert Hall, central London, UK

The Keystone Committee in aid of the National Association of Boys Clubs has gathered a programme of mainly British artists (The Move, Grapefruit, The Alan Bown, Joe Cocker, The Bonzo Dog Doo Dah Band) plus expatriates The Easybeats from Australia, and, from America, The Byrds and Bobby Goldsboro – although Goldsboro fails to come because of illness. All participants donate their services for free. A parade of four popular BBC Radio One DJs MC the proceedings: Stuart Henry, Chris Denning, Alan Freeman, and Pete Brady. Forty LPs by The Byrds, The Move, Bobby Goldsboro, and The Easybeats will be given away to winners of a lucky-programme contest. The concert draws an audience of 4,000.

Members of The Rolling Stones and The Beatles are expected as VIP guests in the audience, and each group has reserved boxes (Beatles two; Stones one) with a total of 30 seats. Hearing this news, the organisers bring in extra police reinforcements to handle crowds. Earlier in the week, Derek Taylor – now working at Apple – tells *Disc*: "There's a very good chance that George and John will be there. I know they want to see The Byrds. I don't know about Paul or Ringo." (The Beatles are at Abbey Road recording tracks for what becomes *The White Album*.) In the end, Paul and George reputedly show up, and from the Stones camp comes Keith Richards and Bill Wyman. Mick Jagger, meanwhile, has passed The Byrds somewhere over the Atlantic on his way to Los Angeles.

"The Byrds were excellent, and vastly improved on their appearances here a few years ago," says *Melody Maker* (July 13). "Roger McGuinn, in a very sharp suit, played nice lead guitar, backed by Chris Hillman (bass), Kevin Kelley (drums), and [Gram] Parsons (organ). Outstanding was 'Eight Miles High'."

Nick Logan of *New Musical Express* (July 13) agrees, reporting how a "good section of the 4,000 audience was there to see [The Byrds] alone, and let them know it. 'Rock'n'Roll Star', which should have been a massive hit, was rock-flavoured Byrds; 'You Ain't Going Nowhere', their current release, showed the way to the country-flavoured Byrds and brought Gram Parsons to the front for two stronger country numbers, which demonstrated how the group is now thinking. Dylan's 'Chimes Of Freedom' closed an excellent set, but it wasn't enough."

According to the reviews, the performance includes 'So You Want To Be A Rock'n'Roll Star', 'Eight Miles High', 'Sing Me Back Home', and 'Chimes Of Freedom'. *Melody Maker* says The Bonzo Dog Doo Dah Band

steals the show, and high praise is also due to Joe Cocker, who is still a few months shy of his breakthrough single 'With A Little Help From My Friends'. For the Keystone Committee, the concert has been a tremendous success, and in *Melody Maker* four weeks later the Committee promises, in high spirits, to invite Elvis Presley, Frank Sinatra, Davy Jones, Bob Dylan, and Tiny Tim – all to appear free, of course – for the next bash.

The Byrds are set to leave for South Africa tomorrow, but Parsons has already voiced his strong objections about the whole trip – even though he has joined the group for the journey to London. Tony Wilson of *Melody Maker* (July 20) interviews McGuinn and Hillman in conjunction with the concert, and notes "already there were signs of a rift when … McGuinn and Chris Hillman chatted to [the paper] at the concert. They refused to be drawn on the split in the group and reckoned to get it sorted out after their South African visit".

Hillman tells Wilson: "We were kind of astonished when our album *The Notorious Byrd Brothers* was a hit in Britain. We had sort of given Britain up after 'Turn! Turn! Turn!'. I think our first tour was destructive to our British reception. But I think we've corrected that the last couple of times we've been here. … We're not like the newer San Francisco or L.A. groups. I don't think you can put us into any particular category."

McGuinn adds: "I see the group as an international entity. Wherever it lives it would be doing the same thing. We're not influenced by the West Coast sound; I think we are a group that will continue to change musical style because we don't want to be classified."

Questioned on the change of musical direction, McGuinn says: "You've got to move around. You have to keep moving or you're a sitting duck. You can notice what Bob Dylan is doing. And look at the success of artists who have gotten into a country bag – Bobby Goldsboro for example, who wasn't doing country stuff before. Buffy Saint Marie is doing country songs." In view of his great love for the idiom, it's surprising to hear Hillman add: "But country music won't last long either. It'll be more of a novelty. I have a suspicion that electronic and space music will be really big by 1970, because that's when we're supposed to have a man on the moon."

Hillman and McGuinn also speak to *Record Mirror* (August 17) at the Royal Albert Hall, and the subject of the South African trip is again debated. Apparently, it is not only Parsons who is unwilling but Kevin Kelley too. "But one problem, that of trouble between different races, seemed to bother both [Roger] and Chris," says the paper. "There

was tension in the group because they were leaving for South Africa the next morning, and two members of the group didn't want to work for segregated audiences."

The *Record Mirror* interview is more concerned with the state of the world, and McGuinn and Hillman express their eco-radical views. "[The] basic problem is that the world is too crowded," McGuinn says. "All the war babies have grown up and there's more people on earth than ever before. The older people, the establishment, can't see that we must adjust to it. Our generation is the only one who realise this adjustment must be made, because we've always grown up in a crowded world."

"Everyone with any sense is getting involved with all the things that are wrong with our society," says Hillman. "The most important thing is communication: we've lost all contact with each other. Our media of communication today is too impersonal. It reaches such a mass of people that it has no time for the individual. A mass of people in America has no real sympathetic contact with a mass of people starving in, say, Biafra. Even here, most of England has no understanding of what it's like to live in a country where you're always on the defensive with the police. Police here are great compared to our gun-totin' men in blue. I've got a natural reaction to authority – I get on the defensive. But that would be true of any American."

McGuinn: "There's a feeling of anarchy and rebellion in America today because the government has ruled with an iron fist and has led the people to where they don't want to be. It's almost like a second War Of Independence is going on. The fringe era, the people who are doing something about society, is far larger than society would like it to be. And they're powerful. Something is certainly going to happen. Air pollution and water pollution are the problems that are going to be the biggest in years to come. The survival instinct will eventually wipe out the apathy that has allowed these things to happen – not only air and water pollution, but things like people starving. America has so many natural resources that wasting them never seemed to matter before."

→ Tuesday 9

On the morning of departure for South Africa, Gram Parsons decides to remain in London. Road manager Carlos Bernal will recall the moment to Pete Frame in *Zigzag* (June 1972). "We had a South African tour, but we had a bit of trouble on the day of departure – Mr. Parsons, our boy Gram, decided he didn't want to go. It was personal and business reasons combined. [The] bags had been collected by the porters – and it came down that Gram wasn't going to go on the tour because he couldn't have things just exactly how he wanted them in the group. The things that he wanted, he could have had after a while, but he wanted them immediately – you know, he wanted a steel guitar on a lot of his tunes and things that the band wasn't prepared to jump into overnight."

McGuinn and Hillman are angry but act swiftly, installing Bernal – a strummer at best, but capable of playing a bit of guitar – in the vacant spot left by Parsons. "So Gram didn't make it to the airport, he went off somewhere and we went off to get the plane," says Bernal. "Roger asked me if I could do the guitar work on the tour, so I said sure, if you could run down some of the things for me. And we rehearsed on the plane down to Johannesburg."

•

As The Byrds fly out for the long flight to Johannesburg, including a stopover for refuelling in the Canary Islands, the missing Parsons stays put in London for a few days. Apparently he renews his friendship with Keith Richards and hangs out at Redlands, the Stone's country home in West Sussex, although there are no contemporary reports to indicate when the two actually meet. Mick Jagger is in Los Angeles to oversee mixing of the delayed *Beggars Banquet* album, awaiting both Charlie Watts and Richards who are due in a matter of days.

Despite this, Parsons seems to be back in Los Angeles by the weekend of July 12–13 at the latest – full of plans and scheming his future. He talks to *The Beat* editor W. Bonnie Golden (a pseudonym for Wina Sturgeon), who relays a report back to the *Melody Maker* office. The UK paper prints the interview in its July 20 edition. "I first heard about the South African tour two months ago," says a calm Parsons, who also refers to the London visit in May. "I knew right off when I heard about it that I didn't want to go. I stood firmly on my conviction. The Byrds are a very professional group and they thought it very unprofessional of me not to do it. I thought it was shortsighted to say it was confirmed without finding out about the South African situation first. It was just two conflicting opinions."

Golden wonders if Parsons knows anything about the South African racial policies. "I knew very little about South Africa before the tour was mentioned. I knew there was an intense problem but I didn't know what it was based on. I began to talk to people who had been born there and I found out." Golden gives *Melody Maker* readers a brief run-down of Parsons' background in Waycross, Georgia, "another place that has its race problems".

"I won't go back there except to see friends in the South," continues Parsons, "and they're not all white. I think the South in America is where you find the good, simple people concerned with the elements, the rain and the wind. In the Mountain regions, there are people who still speak in an Elizabethan accent, and it's from there that I extract some of my music. And it's where rhythm and blues come from." (The piece will be reprinted under the heading "Race Dispute Splits Byrds' Nest – Gram Parsons Refuses Gigs in South Africa" in *Rolling Stone*'s August 24 edition, printed August 1, almost verbatim.)

Parsons outlines plans for a new group, which suggests that he may have planned his defection from The Byrds for some time. "The group's already formed, although I can't say too much about it. We plan to come over in about two weeks." He sums up: "The group is basically a southern soul group playing country and gospel-oriented music, with a steel guitar," an apt description of what Parsons will later coin as 'cosmic American music'.

What Parsons is up to in the next few days is uncertain. He is in London again to meet up with Keith Richards and, according to Bill Wyman's later pedantic memoir, Parsons flies into Los Angeles in the company of Richards, Anita Pallenberg, and photographer Michael Cooper on July 20. Parsons and Richards get to know each other better, and their friendship will become closer in the years to come. "Gram showed me the mechanics of country music," Richards will recall years later in the official *According To The Rolling Stones* memoir. "He introduced me to a lot of players, and he showed me the difference between the way country would be played in Nashville and in Bakersfield – the two schools – with completely different sound and attitude. But apart from that, he was a very special guy."

Wednesday 10

The Byrds arrive at Jan Smuts International Airport in Johannesburg. Photographed on their arrival, they look bedraggled after the

long flight. The caption in *The Johannesburg Star* passes off Carlos Bernal as Gram Parsons. Although it is later implied that there is a conscious decision to have Bernal masquerade as Parsons, this is not necessarily true: Parsons' name is not known to anyone but the most die-hard fans, and as the tour progresses, Bernal is introduced as the fourth member of The Byrds under his full name.

The tour's promoter, Peter Bankoff, speaks to *The Cape Argus* (July 5) to whip up excitement. "We have been fortunate in signing up The Byrds. In America, Britain, and Europe they are the biggest crowd-pullers next to The Beatles." It turns out that an earlier enterprise by Bankoff has been stopped by the British Musicians' Union, when he tried unsuccessfully to arrange a trip to South Africa for Dave Dee Dozy Beaky Mick & Tich.

Thursday 11–Saturday 13
The City Hall, Johannesburg, South Africa

The Byrds appear as part of a package-styled pop show, playing two shows each day for three nights in the city. There are two other attractions on the tour: Lynn Holland (toted as "the Tottenham girl singer" by the local press) and The Staccatos, a group from South Africa. Adept at cover versions of US and UK hits, The Staccatos have previously recorded 'Mr. Tambourine Man' and this year have released 'My Back Pages', 'You Ain't Going Nowhere', and 'He Was A Friend Of Mine'. The group's key members are Steve Lonsdale (vocals) and Eddie Boyle (bass guitar), but the five-man line-up fluctuates. The Staccatos also back up Lynn Holland for her spot.

The tour schedule is tight, with usually two performances a day. The Byrds also promote the tour and the recent single 'You Ain't Going Nowhere' (released through the CBS-associated Gallo Africa label) with personal appearances at OK Bazaars – a chain of retail stores throughout South Africa – where, bizarrely, they mime their performance.

The local press lambasts the opening shows

The Byrds arrive in Johannesburg on July 10, 1968. From left: Roger McGuinn, Chris Hillman, Kevin Kelley, Carlos Bernal.

179

**CITY HALL
LAST 2 SHOWS!
TONIGHT
at 6 p.m. and 8.45 p.m.
THE
BYRDS**
Book at Hall from 5 p.m. onwards
25966

as The Byrds struggle to make up for Parsons' sudden defection, delivering below-par performances that waver between some country material and unstructured jams. Adding to the trauma, McGuinn is fighting a bout of flu. As with the rest of their South African appearances, The Byrds play before an all-white audience in Johannesburg – contrary to what they were promised before departure.

"We had a contract in the beginning," Bernal will tell Pete Frame in *Zigzag* (June 1972), "which stipulated that audiences would be mixed. When we arrived, we found that there had been changes in our contracts but there was nothing we could do. We were sort of trapped by the promoters. We wanted to leave but couldn't because they held the tickets and things, and then we found that we'd entered the country illegally by some way, so we were [uncertain if we would get in] trouble for being in the country illegally or whether to stick it out despite the contract changes. We decided to stick it out, mainly because we couldn't get our hands on the tickets or any of the papers you need to get out of South Africa."

The Johannesburg Star (July 12) shows some generosity in its description of the 12-song opening show. "The Byrds are a vital, imaginative, and talented group, but they were seen to be placid and wooden. Roger McGuinn has said they want to communicate with people of all ages. They will succeed through their music, but certainly not through their stage personalities."

This is nothing compared to the broadside fired off in *The Sunday Times*, which is sorry The Staccatos did not top the bill. "But the spot – unfortunately – belonged to The Byrds, who were unbelievably bad for a group which has just come from London's Albert Hall. For most of their show they half-ignored the audience. Roger McGuinn, the leader, mumbled something into the mike every now and then

to announce a new number. On occasions he laughed to himself – but he was the only one laughing. The Byrds were dressed in clothes which one wears while working in the garden. It is hard to believe this is the group which has sold over ten million records. What at one stage of the evening appeared to be the start of a number suddenly turned out to be a tuning session. The music was disjointed, sometimes out of time, and shockingly loud. Hit records of yesterday were barely recognisable."

Sunday 14

Three-hundred fans meet The Byrds when they fly in from Johannesburg to Cape Town's D.F. Malan airport. *The Cape Times* (July 15) provides a report on the group's reception. "'I Love You', 'The Byrds Are Great', and 'Welcome The Byrds' banners screamed in bright purple letters as the four young men, Carlos, Kevin Kelley, Chris Hillman, and Roger McGuinn made their way through the terminal building. The teenagers surged after them. Several carloads of fans followed The Byrds to the Green Point hotel. Autographs were signed before the group scuttled upstairs to safety."

Monday 15

**Metro Theatre, Cape Town,
South Africa**

"If there are any newspaper critics in the audience, would they please go home and blow their brains out?" That is McGuinn's opening salvo as quoted in *The Cape Times* (July 16). Terry Herbst, who reviews the first of the day's two shows, comments: "After the roasting this visiting American group got from the Sunday critics, Mr. McGuinn's 'joke' was not entirely unexpected.

"Whatever has been said about them, and while The Byrds may present a picture of untidiness and a seeming lack of concern with whether or not their audience is reacting in the way they should, it cannot be denied that these boys really know their music. So what if they look like road-menders instead of pop musicians, with their denim and suede and leather and fishermen's jerseys and cotton shirts and creased scarves? What if they did turn their backs on their audience far too often? And what if they complained about the public address system and smoked during their performance?

"All right, they looked sullen and tired, and Mr. McGuinn had a temperature of 102 and we couldn't understand a word of what he sang, although we did occasionally follow him when he spoke between numbers. Like the time he said: 'I can't sing any more. Bye.' And unplugged his guitar from the fearsome

array of amplifiers behind him and headed slowly from the stage, only to be coaxed back by a few cries of 'Where are you going?' and 'Come back, man!' The audience understood him when he said he thought it was funny that the SABC had banned one of their numbers – the words are from the Bible – when Catholic nuns in the United States used that record in classrooms. But nobody laughed so it could not have been *that* funny.

"But there is no denying that when this group gets going, musically, they are a formidable team, even if their 'fresh approach with subtle and sensitive harmonies hit a new high in musical sound' – at least, that is what the programme notes state – was launched at the audience with ear-splitting, cacophonic thunder. And it wasn't really their fault that the mild applause which greeted their final number had died before they left the stage because they were off with a speedy and unexpected 'that's all folks, goodnight' that left the audience wondering what had happened.

"Who gave a darn, anyway, that the show looked as though it had been thrown together without much thought, or that Bob James, manager of the Dave Dee Dozy Beaky Mick & Tich Pop Group (at least, that's what it says here), took over from compère John Barks of LM radio and that only those near the front of the house could hear what he said? If nothing else, The Byrds are original, looks-wise. One of them, who spent most of the time hammering a guitar, sulking with his back to the audience, had a head of luxurious black Shirley Temple curls which contrasted oddly with his droopy moustache." Herbst praises The Staccatos ("neatly-dressed, freshly-scrubbed, short-haired") and Lynn Holland, who has wisely included several songs sung in Afrikaans for her spot.

Following the first show, McGuinn collapses in the dressing room and is taken back to the hotel as The Byrds' second show is cancelled. Carlos Bernal and impresario Peter Bankoff appear on stage to explain the situation to the ticket-holders, who are offered a free screening of *Zebra In The Kitchen* as compensation.

Garner Thomson writes in *The Cape Argus* (July 16): "The collapse last night of Roger McGuinn, lead guitarist of The Byrds, was just the culmination of a night of small disasters. It could not, as they say, have happened to a nicer group." Thomson views balance Terry Herbst's harsh *Cape Times* review; he thinks little of neither The Staccatos ("uncomfortable resemblance to those guitar-heavy groups of the late 50s") nor Lynn Holland ("her voice … needs rigid control, particularly on the high notes, if irritation is to be avoided").

Of The Byrds, Thomson writes: "With all the unnerving experiences The Byrds have suffered in South Africa – of which McGuinn's collapse before the second performance last night and the terrifying bashing they received from Johannesburg critics were only two – it would be a pity to forget what this group can do when the circumstances are on their side. In London, where their appearances are still legend in pop circles, they produced professional results, well balanced and original. Their unorthodox behaviour on stage passed almost unnoticed [in London]: not so here, with an audience of young people conditioned to rigid conventions of pop music in community halls, clubs, or on stage, rather than to the fluid, causal meanderings of the television camera. Here, in spite of loud protests of the contrary, the teenyboppers of this generation are surprisingly convention-bound.

"Supporting The Byrds in a serious review is not without its hazards. One could, on one hand, be accused of banality – on the other, of intellectual bandwagoning. This must be one of the hazards of an age and a country where pop music is still not considered a music form in its own right. It seems a pity that The Byrds will almost inevitably leave South Africa on a down note – disappointing, perhaps, at the collapse of what promised to be a golden tour. Certainly, they will leave in their wake a large number of young fans who will share their disappointment. They, like me, will be dogged by the vision of what might have been."

Cape Times reader P. Burzynski also replies to Terry Herbst's review. "I, being one of the audience at The Byrds first show, would like to say that, judging by the reaction of the audience, Cape Town people do not appreciate visits by overseas artists. When our entertainers go over they get a good reception but what do we offer? Only criticism. As for the cancellation of the second show, people should remember that Roger McGuinn is also human and that being sick is not for publicity. If they want to stand with their backs to the audience, it's their way. Let us do something better in future for overseas artists. They come to entertain us and we should appreciate that."

Tuesday 16
Metro Theatre, Cape Town, South Africa

McGuinn is still in bed this morning under doctor's orders but is fit to appear for the second day of double shows in Cape Town after antibiotic treatment. Tour promoter Peter Bankoff explains to *The Cape Argus* (July 16): "We do not expect any trouble tonight. … The audience last night was very understanding, and we are extremely grateful." A spokesperson from the theatre management, meanwhile, wants to wash his hands of anything to do with The Byrds. "The Metro Theatre Cape Ltd and the management would like to make it clear that that company had no connection with The Byrds presentation, save as lessors of the theatre," says the theatre manager in the following day's *Cape Times*.

Wednesday 17
Showgrounds Hall, Port Elizabeth, South Africa

The tour proceeds to Port Elizabeth along Algoa Bay for one performance, with McGuinn still not quite well. The reviews are not too good, either. *The East Province Herald* (July 18) begins its report with a quote from McGuinn. "So this is Port Elizabeth," he says to a half empty Showgrounds Hall. "Well, it's weird, man." Apparently the audience was not very impressed with that. "But then," writes the Herald's reviewer, "the remark was a pretty general reflection of the way Mr. McGuinn has been talking since The Byrds arrived in Port Elizabeth. We were told that McGuinn's standoffishness was a result of his recent illness in Cape Town, from which he has not fully recovered yet."

The Herald will continue to cover the Byrds controversy tomorrow and speak to pop fans and press who attended the Port Elizabeth show. The paper reports how photographer Albert Daulman is met by a curt "Don't get fresh with me!" when he politely asks McGuinn to pose for a picture backstage. Another witness, music fan Derrick Adendorff, says: "What upset me is having to pay R2.50 to see a show which wasn't worth 25 cents. Our Port Elizabeth bands are better than The Byrds. They are the most disgusting group I have ever seen."

The paper has even taken the trouble to corner Graeme Pollock – South Africa's internationally renowned cricketer – for a comment. "It was ridiculous. I don't know how they got away with it. There was absolutely no contact between the band and the audience, and the music was far too loud." Local record company manager Henry Franzen attempts to balance the view. "Whenever The Byrds came into contact with the public or the press they were rude. It's a gimmick all the groups have overseas. But in South Africa, where we have a more polite folk, it just does not work." In the afternoon before the Port Elizabeth show, Franzen has been a Byrd guide. "I took them to see the beach. Happily they raced up and down King's Beach. Afterwards Roger McGuinn came to me and said: 'This is one of the most beautiful beaches I have ever seen.'"

With reference to the July 19 front page, a letter to the editor is published in the *Herald* six days later. "We sympathise with you," write three citizens of Humansdorp. "It degrades your standard. It is quite clear to us that it is not worth flying off to see these Byrds. Their puerile and uneducated statements are in keeping with what one expects of those whose star shines brightly one day and is lost in oblivion the next."

Broadcaster and music historian Richard Haslop will recall the significant visit 40 years later. "South Africa was expecting a four-piece, and a four-piece was what we got, roadie Carlos Bernal stepping somewhat shakily into the breach, and spending most of the concert I saw with his back to the audience. He clearly didn't know all the chords. He appeared in a newspaper photo of the band, identified as Gram Parsons. Those of us who bought *Melody Maker* and *New Musical Express* and knew what Parsons looked like were confused, since Bernal looked nothing like him, but only discovered later what was going on.

"McGuinn walked on stage wearing a suit and, as I recall, no shoes, Hillman was barefoot, too, I think, and spent much of the time sitting impossibly coolly on his bass amp. I was 15 years old and completely taken with the fact that my clear favourite band – only The Kinks competed – was playing in my town. If South Africa was isolated, Port Elizabeth was totally off the map. I don't remember much of the concert, though I was convinced, and remain so, that it was stunning. The reality was probably quite different. Besides the shortage of one member, McGuinn had been ill and Hillman did a fair amount of the singing. I specifically recall him singing 'The Christian Life', for example, and maybe even 'You Ain't Going Nowhere'. McGuinn's extended 'Eight Miles High' held me enthralled, and I was most impressed that Kelley hit the drums hard enough to break his sticks.

"Who knows why they came," Haslop wonders. "Only a few of us knew anything except 'Mr. Tambourine Man' and 'Turn! Turn! Turn!'. People kept yelling for these throughout the show, though 'You Ain't Going Nowhere' got a bit of radio play while they were in the country. I'm glad they did come, though. The group was hounded by negative press throughout the tour, with dark murmurings of left-wing politics and drug-taking following them around, and to say they left under a cloud is an understatement."

Trevor Martin, another Byrds fan, remembers the concert clearly. "The show was excellent. Certainly the best thing I had seen in South Africa by a million miles. All the young people who were into rock and pop music – not that many – were in the first few rows, jeans and all. The rest of the audience came because they were curious to see the 'overseas band' and were dressed conservatively. Roger McGuinn and Chris Hillman easily carried the show. The group played with real drive and verve and Kelley hit those drums hard. A musician friend of mine who was involved in supplying some of the backline commented later on how the snare-drum rim had taken a hammering. The next day a friend and I went to the airport to see the band off. We spoke briefly to McGuinn and Hillman who were sitting alone at the time. They regretted coming to South Africa and looked forward to leaving. We just told them that we loved their music and apologised for the crap scene in South Africa and Port Elizabeth in particular."

Thursday 18
City Hall, Durban, South Africa

Under the heading "Cheers, Sympathy For Byrd Roger", *The Durban Mercury* (July 19) gives The Byrds a fair review. "The leader of The Byrds … was on the verge of collapse during their second performance. Roger McGuinn … is suffering from a virus infection picked up in Johannesburg two weeks ago. During their second song in last night's final performance, Roger was unable to continue and apologised to the audience, saying he was still suffering from the influenza which caused the group to cancel one of their Cape Town shows and asked to be excused for a few minutes. The packed audience waited patiently while a doctor was called. Five minutes later, the group re-appeared amid cheers from the capacity audience and Roger McGuinn carried on. Several times during the show he apologised to the audience saying he felt dizzy, but they were in full sympathy and cheered him on. The group cut the show by about five songs, despite calls for more."

Tired and homesick, The Byrds voice their opinions on South Africa in *The Natal Mercury* (July 19). "Sick, Backward, Rude" screams the headline, and Hillman and McGuinn don't mince words. "Apartheid is all wrong and the sooner they take away the 'Whites Only' signs the better," Hillman spits. "Your country is boring and about five years behind the times. I miss television and your apartheid laws are sick." An indignant McGuinn says: "People at one of our shows were belching and making noises. Your audiences must be the worst in the world. We were told not to come here but we wanted to see the country for ourselves … we will tell everyone at home not to come here." Such views do not go unheeded, and the group receives several threatening phone calls as a result. The message is clear: get out and go home.

Lyndsay Evans offers a lone voice in defence of The Byrds when her opinions make it to print, also in the *Mercury* (July 24). "Let's face up to our inadequacies. Roger McGuinn had us taped. Talk about leading us by the nose …

I agree that they are no oil paintings, but 'uniform' among pop groups overseas is out. It's their music that is under criticism and their looks count for nothing. Another thing – who really cares about a back or two facing the audience at times? If Chris Hillman chooses to seek inspiration from the backdrop, we'll still hear the amplified sound loud and clear; just so long as he turns to the microphone during his vocals, we've got no grounds for complaint. The Byrds now return to Los Angeles with sorry tales of their South African reception. Have we helped our 'pop' cause by giving these four a tough time? Will other overseas groups take fright and give us a miss in future? Who is really to blame?"

Friday 19

Before flying out to Rhodesia, McGuinn speaks to *The Durban Mercury* about yesterday's ugly phone threats. "They were obviously from cranks, but all the same it was all very upsetting." On his condition, he adds: "I picked up flu in Johannesburg and haven't been able to shake it off. I'm really sorry if I've disappointed any of my fans."

Saturday 20
Glamis Stadium, Salisbury [Harare], Rhodesia [Zimbabwe]

The Byrds end their southern African tour with a visit to Rhodesia (later Zimbabwe), a country ruled by an all-white party under Prime Minister Ian Smith. Earlier a British colony, Rhodesia does not adhere to such systemised apartheid policies as South Africa. Still, Smith's politics result in United Nations sanctions and the country is increasingly isolated, depending on support from South Africa to the south and Portugal through its colony Mozambique to the east. "Finally, in Salisbury, Rhodesia, which is an integrated country, we were [playing to non-segregated audiences]," McGuinn says later in *Jazz & Pop* (March 1969). "And we were promised that we'd have more chances than that, which is the only reason we really went over there, but they sort of copped out."

Lynn Holland and The Staccatos are still part of the Byrds package, and tobacco company Texan sponsors the concert, MC'd by Martin Locke in the huge Glamis Stadium. There is one performance at 2:30pm. Nineteen-year-old Valerie Henshaw has free entrance as she has fixed herself a job as an usher. "International entertainment dried up," she recalls later. "I can remember seeing The Seekers, from Australia, on stage at a cinema, and, later, Matt Monro from England at the same cinema, accompanied by a piano with one leg propped up on a brick. I don't know how either act came to tour Rhodesia, but they all seemed pretty uncomfortable. So when we heard The Byrds were coming, this was huge news. We were so starved of new music. And, of course, like most students,

Bored Byrds find S.A. sick backward and rude

Herald Correspondent DURBAN.
OUTH AFRICA is a "sick" backward country with the

McGuinn, the leader of the group. "Your audiences must be the worst in the world." What upset them most were

"Your country is boring and about five years behind the times. I miss television and your apartheid laws a

we thought of ourselves as rebellious and enlightened and were thrilled to be able to see our heroes in the flesh. An open-air soccer stadium, however, was not the ideal venue sound-wise for a band. They did seem very jaded, but I don't recall this diminishing our enjoyment of the show. Afterwards, we got to mix with the band very briefly backstage."

The *Sunday Mail Reporter* (July 21) says: "The Byrds hardly caused a flutter when they flew into Salisbury yesterday morning. The American pop idols were here for an afternoon show at Glamis Stadium before flying back to California after a ten-day tour of South Africa. Almost 6,000 saw the show. Because their plane arrived early they caught fans on the hop: when the big moment for their arrival at a city record shop came, they had been and gone. At a pre-show press conference, the group leader, 26-year-old Roger McGuinn, said they were looking for a new guitarist to replace Gram Parsons."

Entertainment writer Charles Stoneman writes for *The Rhodesia Herald* (July 26). "The Byrds have flown, and are about as well-remembered in Salisbury as last month's TV shows, although this was by no means all their fault." It appears the sound system is inadequate for the vast stadium. "The Byrds, still in travel clothes, provided an intelligent, well-trained sound, ranging from psychedelic to country and western. Drummer Kevin Kelley must be among the world's best. But I saw few genuinely excited reactions among the crowd.

I left Glamis disappointed and with ears ringing … but the venue and sound amplification were a lot to blame."

•

The African tour has been a fiasco, and in their last days in South Africa the group lashes out at the country in an attempt to justify going there in the first place. Their sour comments reach the ears of entertainment journalist Fiona Chisholm at *The Cape Times*, who writes tartly on July 20: "I'm glad I'm a grimalkin and a flop with the pops. I've never been all a-twitter over the 'Birds Of A Feather', don't know who 'Who' is, and have only gleaned from the platter chatter page that 'Yummy Yummy Yummy' is 'absolutely scrummy'.

"So I saved myself an evening this week a thousand times more embarrassing than one spent listening to a warbling rendering by the vicar's wife of the ubiquitous 'I'll Walk Beside You'. I missed out on The Byrds. From all accounts – significantly from the young people who know and admire their musicianship on record – this was a night, indeed a tour, to be forgotten as quickly as possible. But feathers are still too ruffled for that.

"While still in the country on their last stop The Byrds have come out with scathing comments abut South Africa – so my man in Durban tells me. Sweet utterances like this from woolly-headed bass guitarist Chris Hillman, that we are a "sick, backward country with the rudest audiences in the worlds". Or such diplomacy from indignant group leader Roger McGuinn as that "they can't wait to get out and go home", where they intend telling everyone not to come to South Africa. As for apartheid, that, of course, is not for The Byrds.

"What upset them (besides the belches and other rude noises) were press reports that they were 'dressed like gardeners' and one critic's claim that a number sounded as if they were tuning their instruments. What hurt the audience was that the critics were right. They'd paid money to hear a group dressed like road-menders whose gimmicks were dirt, disinterest, and downright rudeness. Even played with their backs to them. No one is condemning the behaviour of the audience. And let's hope this is not the start of a new ugly pattern. But when a certain four-letter word came over loud and clear as the loudspeaker system was being tested, it was obvious this group was no Sunday boys' brigade.

"I suggest before The Byrds spread tales of their unfortunate and morale-shattering tour (as indeed it must have been) they look up the reviews and tremendous receptions given to Cliff Richard & The Shadows, Françoise Hardy, The Four Jacks & A Jill (to mention a few). Our young people are a discerning crowd. They know their pop music, plus the ins-and-outs of the different groups, as well as those anywhere, and crude behaviour aimed at selling records – apparently the more revolting you are on stage the better the discs go – just doesn't appeal to them. They know what they like and certainly react when they don't like."

Monday 22

A planned concert in Majorca on the way back from Africa is cancelled, although the group do stop over on the island on their way home to Los Angeles. 'Musica '68' is a weeklong festival in Majorca due to commence today but called off due to insufficient funds. To be held in Palma's Bullring, the concert series was planned to feature a spectacular bill today with The Byrds, The Jimi Hendrix Experience, Lulu, Eric Burdon & The Animals, Grapefruit, Los Pekenikes (a Spanish group), Sweden's Hep Stars, and BBC DJ Emperor Rosko. The rest of the week promised a mix of pop, jazz, and rock – a bill so sprawling it is ultimately crushed under its own weight. After a board meeting on June 24, the organisers say: "This was a very ambitious project which needed ambitious finance – which it didn't get."

•

The South African debacle will cast a long shadow. While the group is still there, the British Musicians' Union hails Parsons' refusal to join the tour. The union's spokesman, Harry Francis – the very same man who so strongly opposed exchange between British and American groups in 1965 – says to *Melody Maker* (July 29): "In the light of the well-known policy of the Musicians' Union, which is strongly opposed to apartheid and any other form of racial discrimination, we must applaud the action of Gram Parsons in refusing to go to South Africa with The Byrds."

Worse still, this will lead to problems when The Byrds are set to tour the UK next time. "We think that our executive committee will expect foreign musicians who are permitted to perform in Britain to conform to the Union's policy, which bans engagements in South Africa to its members, and The Byrds' decision to perform there may well lead our committee to refuse to consider future applications for foreign musicians to perform in Britain if they have recently performed there, or are likely to do so in the future." To McGuinn and Hillman's immense irritation, the controversy elevates Parsons to the hero of the story.

Judy Sims touches on the subject in her regular *Disc* column (July 20). "The Byrds are flying to South Africa for concerts. Boo. (Boo to South Africa, not boo to The Byrds.) But perhaps you English aren't so sensitive to racism and racist countries; now that it's summer in the States, we're not only sensitive but wary."

This however is as nothing compared to the blows that respected critic Nat Hentoff delivers in *Jazz & Pop* (November 1968). "Gram Parsons left The Byrds this summer because he refused to be part of its South African tour. Parsons will not play before segregated audiences. 'The Byrds,' Parsons said about the split, 'are a professional group. They thought it very unprofessional of me not to go to South Africa.' And there we are – the word 'professional'. It is considered 'professionally' correct for scientists to engage in research on chemical and biological warfare. It is consider 'professionally' correct for lawyers to work on corporate interests, no matter what social harm those interests cause. And the writers on *Time* are regarded as 'professionals' by their peers even though their copy often finally emerges in a form and with content considerably removed from its original appearance and even though *Time* is a chronic distorter of the news.

"To make the South African apartheid scene, as The Byrds did, is to be a traditional careerist. The good solider. The good professor who does his thing, and so what if his university is tied in with the Institute for Defence Analyses? I'm not saying, of course, that rock music has to be political or social to be 'valid', to be 'relevant'. What I am saying is that the people who create rock music have, like other professionals, a choice to make – between being an active, responsible part of the world or closed in on their own tight little island. A choice between old-time showbiz (a gig is there to take) and what a life is all about. It's going to be interesting to see what happens to those rock groups who have been part of the thrust for freedom – freedom of consciousness, freedom of sensuality, freedom to let go and just be. As the bread gets bigger – with all the attendant 'professionalism' required when the material stakes are higher and higher – are they going to just go along in the 'professional' manner of The Byrds?"

Reader R. Woolley from Montreal replies to Hentoff (*Jazz & Pop*, January 1969). "Nat Hentoff's criticism of The Byrds for playing to segregated audiences in South Africa was quite unjustified. Although rock musicians are, hopefully, professionals, they have one distinction which sets them apart from the professional class as a whole; they are artists. … Let's say The Byrds were all racist supporters of George Wallace. Would this detract from the beauty of 'Goin' Back'? From the precision of 'Eight Miles High'? From the impact of 'He Was A Friend Of Mine' or 'Draft

Morning'? A little perhaps, but not sufficiently enough to destroy the worth of the music, at least not for me."

Woolley continues: "Do we deny Wagner his greatness because of his nationalistic exaggerations? Or Kipling his for his condescending attitudes towards non-whites? Certainly not, however disgusted we may be with these unacceptable beliefs. I congratulate Roger McGuinn and the rest of The Byrds for having the courage to go to South Africa, knowing full well what the reaction would be. It took a strong belief in principle to risk losing the far-too-little stature they have gained."

Hentoff has his say again a couple of months later (*Jazz & Pop*, April 1969), and although he disagrees with Woolley's glorification of The Byrds, he does agree on the sentiment of an artist's independence. "That [authors] Dostoyevsky and Céline were anti-Semitic, that [classical pianist] Gieseking played under the Nazis, does not add or cannot detract from the quality of what they produced as art. I would agree with Mr Woolley that if The Byrds were devotees of George Wallace, that fact would not affect – should not affect – one's judgement of the music. … [I] do not fault The Byrds' music because they went to South Africa. I do, however, believe in the perfectibility of man, and I would hope that on reflection, The Byrds and other artists will consider the effect of their acceptance of apartheid. Because that's what it is. If you play before segregated audiences, you accept racism. There's no rationalising it. If they refuse the next tour to South Africa, they will not be better musicians thereby, but damn it, they'll have shown themselves to be much more responsive to the suffering – and the quite literal torture – that is endemic in South Africa today."

Roger McGuinn, too, gets his views across in *Jazz & Pop* (March 1969). Talking to Jay Ruby, he says: "We just did South Africa, which is a terrible place; we did 16 concerts in ten days, and I got the flu during it and still had to work, you know: like a trouper and all that. And just about worked myself right out there, and I mean, my nerves were just frayed from all of this – and I'm spoiled, in a way. I'm not used to doing all that; we were doing weekends before that. In the early days we did much more work than that and it didn't really affect me as much. But this time – I guess it also had to do with who is listening."

Ruby asks if McGuinn was playing to the same kind of audience he would play to in the US, primarily under-30s. "No," he replies, "actually everybody in the whole town would come to these concerts. It was sort of like watching the haircuts, cos there was nothing else to do. And the reviews – the press

would come to every show and review every show. The first couple of reviews were sort of OK, they didn't really say we were fantastic but they didn't really put us down. And then this old guy who likes, well, I was told he's a frustrated comic and he never really made it in show business, and he likes [tenor singer] Mario Lanza kind of people, and stuff. He knocked us for doing some things that were not kosher, to his way of thinking, in show-biz, like turning around on stage or wearing the wrong kind of clothes. He wanted us to have tuxedos, and said we were wearing scruffy clothes and we looked like gardeners; all these things that we've come to take for granted, like wearing blue jeans and funky shirts, and turning around to get feedback out of you amp, and weird little tricks that we accept here, they weren't ready for [that] down there. I'd say they were anywhere from 100 years on some levels to five or ten years behind the scene. And of course, the segregation thing is terrible, and they wouldn't let any spades in to see us."

It turns out the tour has been an economic loss, too. "In fact, they didn't even pay us all the bread, for the whole thing. They were really bad to us," laments McGuinn.

"I heard that we're banned in England because we went down there in the first place," he continues. "The English Musicians' Union is banning all the British groups who go down there, and I think that's ridiculous, man, because we did a painful, sacrificial missionary trip down there. We didn't make bread; we just sort of broke even. We went down there for more or less political reasons, to help straighten out the scene or agitate or try to change the status quo as much as we could. I thought I was going to get assassinated because of what we said in the papers. We were getting threats, and telephone calls saying get out of the country, man, or else – stuff like that. It was like Nazi Germany before the war. There was a tremendous nationalistic feeling there, sort of a self-conscious, defensive attitude that we're right, even if we're wrong. They knew they were wrong. And they knew that we knew they were wrong, and they hated us for it."

Tuesday 23
ALSO …
Skip Battin's latest venture is a group with drummer Chester McCracken called The Evergreen Blueshoes, who perform a pair of concerts with The Strawberry Alarm Clock and The Seeds. Yesterday they all played the Melodyland Theatre in Anaheim, CA, and tonight they visit the Circle Star Theatre, San Carlos, CA. The group will struggle on for another year before breaking up.

Late July
Back in Los Angeles, McGuinn and Hillman set about rebuilding the group, and with a vacancy to fill there is one obvious candidate: Clarence White. His involvement with The Byrds stretches all the way back to the group's very roots, as McGuinn will recount to Jud Cost of Sundazed Records in 2000. "[Clarence] always wanted to be in The Byrds. He felt kinda like he missed the boat, because he was doing Dylan stuff with The Kentucky Colonels before The Byrds. And he'd been working with Jim Dickson, and he thought, 'Hey, I should have been in that.' And he missed it."

As McGuinn will confirm in a 1970 interview with Vincent Flanders, White was considered a natural Byrd once McGuinn heard him. "Clarence worked on *Younger Than Yesterday* as a studio musician. And at the time when I first heard him I said, 'Wow, man, that's far out', and I wanted to hire him then, but he was busy." Hillman is keen to cement the group's country direction, and it is he who arranges the call to Clarence.

White is a rare bird in the overcrowded rock guitar field of 1968. Whereas most of his contemporaries depend on fuzz-hued blues riffs extended for minutes on end, White's greatest gift is an ability to add to a song rather than detract from it. A genuine virtuoso of acoustic bluegrass guitar, White has made the transition to electric by absorbing the mastery of studio guitarist James Burton and listening to French jazz legend Django Reinhardt.

For the past year White has kept busy with a dual career: one as a session guitarist, the other a regular sideline with The Reasons – better known under the alias Nashville West, actually the name of the club in El Monte, CA, where they have a residence. (The group does venture outside El Monte on rare occasions; on July 16, for example, they provided entertainment at the opening of the Fresno Republican Assembly's new headquarters.)

Gram Parsons also tries to entice White to join him in the project he recently described to *Beat* editor W. Bonnie Golden, but White feels his loyalty and affinity lies with The Byrds. White – like Parsons and Kelley before him – becomes an employee in the Byrds corporation, but he is in a position where he can demand a fair fee and negotiate good terms. He has yet another advantage: he knows the group's material and style well, and requires few if any rehearsals to step in at short notice.

The Byrds' new album is readied for release. McGuinn's vision of a double record straddling the musical past and future is finally laid to rest, although a companion volume devoted exclusively to electronic music will

Roger McGuinn and Chris Hillman (and to the left: Kevin Kelley with his back to the camera) at the 'First Annual Newport Pop Festival' in Costa Mesa, CA, August 4, 1968.

still be discussed a month later. Gary Usher will recall to music historian Stephen J. McParland how the album jacket came about, when the working title *Hickory Wind* is understandably rejected after Parsons goes. "The title came from Craig Butler, a graphic artist I had met through Curt [Boettcher]. I told him I was recording a country-related album with The Byrds and I wanted a different artistic approach, more tongue in cheek than serious. He brought me several concepts, one of which was a '*Sweetheart Of The Rodeo*' postcard from the 20s [actually 1933] featuring a cowgirl. I immediately fell in love with it and said 'That's it! That's the album!' I called up McGuinn and said, 'Come into the office. You're not going to believe what I've got to show you.' McGuinn came by and brought Hillman with him. I showed him the postcard, and both he and Chris loved the idea. So I just took the concept and ran with it."

August

Saturday 3
Berkeley Community Theatre, Berkeley, CA

McGuinn, Hillman, Clarence White, and Kevin Kelley make their debut as The Byrds at a concert with The Stone Poneys and Sky Blue. The 7th Ray provides sound and lights. Monkee Mike Nesmith is a surprise guest when he sits in with the group.

Looking back on his first gigs with The Byrds, White will tell *Zigzag* editor Pete Frame: "I wouldn't have felt nearly so comfortable if I'd just come in as a replacement for someone – I was able to introduce my own parts rather than copy what someone else had worked out – so I was quite happy from that point of view. … The Byrds were pretty low when I joined and I was able to take an active, creative part in the rebuilding process. We were going out for little money, doing scrappy gigs, but we knew we were going to get back up there and it was something to work for … to achieve new heights rather than maintain an existing level."

Sunday 4
'First Annual Newport Pop Festival', Orange County Fairgrounds, Costa Mesa, CA

Attempts to stage another Monterey festival this summer have been stopped by the local Monterey council and the North California police force. Stepping into the breach, L.A. DJ 'Humble Harve' Miller joins forces with Wesco Associates to put together a day-two

festival in Southern California. Calling itself the Newport Pop Festival after Newport Beach about 30 miles down from Los Angeles, the actual location is Costa Mesa, some miles inland at the fairground site. Confusingly or cleverly, the name nods to the renowned Newport festival held annually on the East Coast in Newport, RI, although that has primarily a folk and jazz programme.

Yesterday was the first day of the festival, and The Byrds perform today. The programme and running order is shifting, but the following groups appear over the two days: Alice Cooper ("a quintet of Tiny Tim-types playing avant-garde psychedelia" suggests *The Los Angeles Times*), The James Cotton Blues Band, Sonny & Cher, Steppenwolf, Gipsy Boots & Kim Fowley, Canned Heat, The Chambers Brothers, The Electric Flag, The Butterfield Blues Band, Illinois Speed Press, Tiny Tim, Things To Come, Blue Cheer, Charles Lloyd Quartet – which is interrupted by an unscheduled, unnamed, and impromptu rock group firing up their amps in the middle of the crowd – Country Joe & The Fish, Quicksilver Messenger Service, Iron Butterfly, Grateful Dead, Eric Burdon & The Animals (the weekend's only UK act), and Jefferson Airplane, who finish the festival. The Byrds are sandwiched between Country Joe and Quicksilver.

Ticket sales far outstrip that of last year's Monterey festival, so the Newport Pop Festival's claim to be the biggest rock event ever staged in California is truthful. The weather is hot and sunny and the crowds behave peacefully in spite of a few gatecrashers. But something is missing. Ann Moses reports in *New Musical Express* (August 17): "Nearly 80,000 youthful spectators jammed into the Orange Country Fairgrounds last weekend for the first (and probably the last) Newport Pop festival. Those expecting a repeat of the Monterey Pop Festival of last year were sorely disappointed." *Rolling Stone* (September 14): "The festival was regarded musically successful but on other fronts rather less than pleasing. The performers appeared on a raised stage under a striped canopy, but the young crowds were left sitting or standing in a huge, flat, dusty-dry open field under a boiling sun. Refreshment and rest room facilities were less than adequate and the sound system was not powerful enough to carry the sound to everyone present."

Digby Diehl writes in *The Los Angeles Times* (August 6): "The Byrds, replacing Gram Parsons with Clarence White, sang a series of their hits, such as 'So You Want To Be A Rock'n'Roll Star' and 'Eight Miles High', interspersed with their new country and western sound on songs such as 'The Warden' [presumably 'Sing Me

Back Home'], sung by Chris Hillman, and Bob Dylan's 'You Ain't Going Nowhere'. [It was] a mediocre performance [that] made little impression on the audience." Diehl also writes about the end of the Sunday night. "By the time Jefferson Airplane began playing, twilight had fallen and the crowd was at a pitch of tense agitation. Grace Slick managed to sing one delicate song from their new album, 'Triad', written by David Crosby, before the deluge broke." *Rolling Stone* (September 14) fills in the picture: "The second day's climax came when David Crosby started a planned pie fight with the Jefferson Airplane. In all, 250 cream pies flew back and forth … and the thousands of people present stormed the stage to join in."

Tuesday 13–Thursday 15
Avalon Ballroom, San Francisco, CA

The Byrds, Steve Miller Band, Blue Cheer, and a group called simply West appear for an unadvertised mid-week residence in San Francisco. There is some doubt as to whether these performances actually take place, as they are not part of promoter Chet Helms and his Family Dog's regular concert series. Reportedly, the occasion is the filming of a TV pilot.

Sunday 25

Roger McGuinn sits down with John Cohen and the New Lost City Ramblers' Mike Seeger for a long interview published in *Sing Out!* (Volume 18, no 5; dated December 1968–January 1969). The folk-music magazine is New York-based but the interview is apparently done in Los Angeles. (A rumoured appearance for The Byrds as part of the New York Rock Festival on August 23 does not take place.)

Although the occasion is to promote the new album *Sweetheart Of The Rodeo*, the interview winds up as a career retrospective, with a focus on McGuinn's folk background. At a time when Gram Parsons has done little to further his career beyond The Byrds except hang out with The Rolling Stones, McGuinn is generous about Gram's significance and influence. "We've always dabbled in country music on other albums, but then we ran in to [Gram] Parsons, who wants to be the world champion country singer, and he hung out with us for about three months [sic]. He was going to be in the group, but it didn't work out. While he was with us, which I consider a great thing, he led us into this direction headlong, which we would never have done. We were afraid to commit ourselves. It was a little foreign to us, being The Byrds, but as The Byrds we have always jumped around in different forms, so we dove into it."

McGuinn adds: ""If you want to get into the psychological reasoning behind it, it's sort of a backlash from the psychedelic scene, which I'm personally saturated with. I mean, we've been somewhat influential in starting that kind of stuff, with the raga-rock and jazz-rock, before it was really appreciated, and a year later these groups did it up and made a great success with it. Everyone's jumping on the bandwagon, so we wanted to get off and clear the slate for a while."

McGuinn also gives some insight into his relationship with Bob Dylan. "I'll tell you my history with Dylan: I remember him from [New York folk club] Gerde's when he was sort of scuffling. I was working and had some bread – he wasn't. He was into the in-group kind of thing and I wasn't. I was sort of on the perimeter, digging it at the time. I represented a commercial folk group – the [Chad] Mitchell thing, and that wasn't groovy. I didn't dig it either. I was doing it to get around, to get experience playing music, until it got to the point where I wasn't learning music, I was unlearning it.

"Next time I saw Dylan was in L.A. after The Byrds were working together, and we showed him our arrangement of 'Mr. Tambourine Man', and he said, wow, man, you can dance to that. He couldn't believe the transition it had gone through. In fact, we sang him some of his other stuff at Ciro's and he didn't even recognise them. And we got to be friends after a while. One time in New York I saw him, and we went to this place – some apartment where he was staying. He was on the couch and I was sitting on the floor – one of those kind of conversations. But he said he really liked what I was starting to do with my music. He thought that I had gotten my own style going and he dug it. I didn't think he would.

"He didn't start influencing me until I started singing his material. As I got into it I started to appreciate it. I started to feel what he felt when he was doing our songs – sort of a rebellious, funky attitude he had going. We had this saving grace that we were doing something with it, aside from just copying it. It wasn't a second-hand Dylan thing; it modulated to somewhere else, electrically. But then he started doing with his own music what we had done with his earlier music, so we couldn't do any more of his music because he was already doing it himself. Then recently he started writing things that he wasn't going to record. He released some underground dub tapes that he never intended to record himself, or things that were rejected from his album, I'm not sure which they were."

How do the unreleased Dylan tapes get around, the interviewer wants to know? "They go out through Columbia Records, and vari-ous people can get them," McGuinn explains. "One of the Columbia executives called me in recently and told me that we were doing great in the country thing, that they were going to put some promotion behind it. Columbia had this great idea. How would we like to do a joint album with another Columbia artist? My first choice was Bob Dylan, but I doubt if he'd consent. Well, he said, who else do you like? How about Johnny Cash? The company does take steps to get involved in what comes out in their products.

"You can't let them take care of your music. I talked to Dylan one night. I got the feeling that he was guilty about making all that bread. He said, 'I don't know, man, how you're ever going to make a million dollars. I'd like to help you somehow.' I figured he wanted someone to play with, to hang out with. He was into a talking thing. He'd vary at times between putting himself and everybody and me on, and just talking straight. We got into some beautiful philosophical things about the nature of the universe, deep stuff, then we'd go back to trivia, riffing on words, playing word games, like the 17 extensions from a word. I sort of miss him."

A discussion on the difference between trendsetters and opportunists ensues. McGuinn says: "When we started the electrification of folk music, we had no idea whether it would succeed or not. The opportunist knows he's going to win, before he does anything. Our position has been that we don't want to get locked into something that is going to be erased, something that wasn't really groovy in the first place. We don't want to be in any one bag, like folk-rock. It wasn't a long-term thing, and we didn't want to go away with it when it did. So we kept moving, and exploring. I think that's the virtue involved. If we weren't taking gambles, I would think what we are doing would be a drag. But it isn't. We're trying to avoid getting locked in that grey area between."

The interview winds up with McGuinn talking exuberantly about synthesizers, explaining the difference between manufacturers Moog and Buchla and the finer mechanics of the instrument. He exclaims: "I've got one coming! It's in the works now. We've used them on our records. Our next album is going to be all electronic music."

Friday 30

The Byrds' sixth album of new material, *Sweetheart Of The Rodeo*, is released in the US. Collecting 11 of the songs taped in Nashville and Los Angeles between March and May, it is a marked contrast to the complex and electronically fuelled *Notorious Byrd Brothers*. One of the group's trademark sounds is conspicuous

Sweetheart Of The Rodeo

A1 'You Ain't Going Nowhere' (B. DYLAN)
A2 'I Am A Pilgrim' (TRAD. ARR. R. MCGUINN/C. HILLMAN)
A3 'The Christian Life' (C. LOUVIN/I. LOUVIN)
A4 'You Don't Miss Your Water' (W. BELL)
A5 'You're Still On My Mind' (L. MCDANIEL)
A6 'Pretty Boy Floyd' (W. GUTHRIE)
B1 'Hickory Wind' (G. PARSONS/B. BUCHANAN)
B2 'One Hundred Years From Now' (G. PARSONS)
B3 'Blue Canadian Rockies' (C. WALKER)
B4 'Life In Prison' (M. HAGGARD/J. SANDERS)
B5 'Nothing Was Delivered' (B. DYLAN)

US release August 30 1968 (Mono LP CL 9670/Stereo LP CS 9670)
UK release September 27 1968 (Mono CBS 63353/Stereo CBS S 63353)
Chart high US number 77; UK none
Read more entries for March 9, 12, 13, 14, April 15, 17, 24, May 27 1968

Bonus CD tracks: 'You Got A Reputation' (T. Hardin), 'Lazy Days' (G. Parsons), 'Pretty Polly' (trad. arr. R. McGuinn/ C. Hillman), 'The Christian Life' [Rehearsal – Take #11] (C. Louvin/I. Louvin), 'Life In Prison' [Rehearsal – lake #11] (M. Haggard/J. Sanders), 'You're Still On My Mind' [Rehearsal – Take #43] (McDaniel), 'One Hundred Years From Now' [Rehearsal – Take #2] (G. Parsons), 'All I Have Are Memories' [Instrumental] (E.D. Hewitt/R. J. Ledford)

"The album itself is one of the most honest, unpretentious, and musical in the melodic sense, that I have heard in a long time ... There is a simple sincerity ... This is a great album, in spite of the fact that you may enjoy it." THE LOS ANGELES FREE PRESS, AUGUST 16, 1968

by its absence: McGuinn's electric 12-string Rickenbacker. Parsons' influence pervades the record, although some of his original solo vocals are either blended in with harmony vocals (as on 'One Hundred Years Ago') or removed or buried altogether (replaced by McGuinn's vocals on 'The Christian Life' and 'You Don't Miss Your Water'). But he is featured on his own composition 'Hickory Wind' and the country covers 'You're Still On My Mind' and 'Life In Prison'.

Chris Hillman sings lead vocals on two numbers ('I Am A Pilgrim' and 'Blue Canadian Rockies'), and McGuinn sings on the remaining tracks. Although Parsons has been out of the group for nearly two months, it is he who has written the two sole original songs on the album. *Sweetheart Of The Rodeo* is otherwise bookended by two Dylan songs and various country covers.

For the first time on a Byrds album all featured musicians are credited, although ex-International Submarine Band drummer Jon Corneal's participation is dubious – Hillman will say later in an interview with *Zigzag* (June 1972) that Kevin Kelley is the sole drummer. (An expanded version of the album – the so-called Legacy Edition – will be released in 2003 and include the four songs that did not make it to the original album, plus Parsons' original lead vocal tracks, studio rehearsals, outtakes, and a selection of tracks by The International Submarine Band.)

Sweetheart Of The Rodeo will come to be revered as a classic, but despite a lavish promotional campaign by Columbia Records ("This Country's For Byrds") and Gram Parsons' thesis that crossing over to the country audience would increase record sales, it becomes the group's poorest-selling album so far in their career, only reaching Number 77 on the *Billboard* charts. One reason for the disappointing sales may be that The Byrds' *Greatest Hits* is still selling: the group has just been awarded their first Gold Album for sales worth in excess of one million dollars.

For The Byrds, their course is changed irrevocably with *Sweetheart Of The Rodeo*. Some follow their example and record in Nashville (The Beau Brummels, for example, make Bradley's Barn there this year) while countless other rock groups – inspired by The Byrds' groundbreaking country-to-rock marriage – emphasise a stronger country influence on stage and in the studio in the years to come. Journalist Stanley Booth, commissioned to write a story on The Rolling Stones, is in London at the end of September. "[I] never even knew anything about Gram until [then]," he recalls to Jason Gross. "They had an acetate of The Byrds' record *Sweetheart Of The Rodeo*, which didn't sound like any Byrds record I

ever heard before but it sounded wonderful. They played it over and over in the [Rolling Stones] office."

The critics are divided over the album. *The New York Times* (September 1) has given the album to William Kloman to review as part of a batch of records that could be vaguely grouped together (Harper's Bizarre, and Big Brother & The Holding Company's *Cheap Thrills*, which Kloman absolutely hates – "probably the most insulting album of the year"). He writes: "From the start, The Byrds have provided unpretentious – and sometimes inspired – distillations of current trends. *The Notorious Byrd Brothers*, for example, was one of the best products of last year's psychedelic sweepstakes and is said to have saved more than one acidhead from screaming paranoia. The Byrds are nothing if not soothing.

"Their latest album is an excellently produced, urbanised version of old country and western motifs. Two Dylan songs, 'You Ain't Going Nowhere' and 'Nothing Was Delivered', are treated with characteristic and confident tastefulness. Woody Guthrie's socialist ode to 'Pretty Boy Floyd' nicely complements Gram Parsons' wistful commentary in 'One Hundred Years From Now'. People who grew up listening to Hank Williams will miss the rough edge of down-home grit in the vocals, which are more Southern Maryland roadhouse than true bluegrass, but the simplicity and honesty of the music make it the best country and western album of the recent avalanche."

Later, Robert Shelton of the *Times* adjusts Kloman's viewpoints (November 24). "The latest Byrds album [adheres] to most of the 'rules of the game' about country sound, and yet, sad to say, to this old fan of The Byrds, the album is a distinguished bore. So, purity of style is certainly not a touchstone." Time magazine (September 20) says: "Country-western purists are likely to yell 'fake' at this album. True, The Byrds don't sound exactly like Buck Owens & His Buckaroos, but they do perform the material with simplicity and in a relaxed, folky manner. Woody Guthrie's socialist hymn to Pretty Boy Floyd gets an authentic bluegrass treatment here, and 'Blue Canadian Rockies', an old Gene Autry tune, will bring back memories of the Hollywood cowboy astride his horse Champion, galloping through 'the golden poppies … round the banks of Lake Louise'. Two Bob Dylan songs, 'Nothing Was Delivered' and 'You Ain't Going Nowhere', are done with unmannered, country-elegant restraint and are improvements on the original."

Sandy Pearlman, who has written so articulately on The Byrds for *Crawdaddy*, now pens for *NY Critique* (October 10) and resorts to quoting his previous interpretations of what

he terms The Byrds' "formal mechanisms". He sums up: "Now, at last, The Byrds have produced an album sounding not all like The Byrds … as country boys, they've gotten off the magic bus."

In the Midwest, Robb Baker comments in the *Chicago Tribune* (October 6): "The Byrds showed themselves still grounded in their psychedelic background on the earlier albums, however, even in as country-flavoured a number as 'Wasn't Born To Follow'. That old influence is abandoned altogether in the [new] album, and the loss is felt. It's a completely country album (the haunting 'Space Odyssey' being paralleled with country hymns like 'I Am A Pilgrim' and 'The Christian Life'), and, sadly, has no original compositions by the members of the group."

The California press cannot agree either. *The Los Angeles Free Press* (August 16) draws a line from Dylan to the new Byrds, but acknowledges that there has always been a country & western element in the group. "The album itself is one of the most honest, unpretentious, and musical in the melodic sense, that I have heard in a long time," writes David Mark Dashew. "There is a simple sincerity about this album, and in a super-hip society it will be accused (in fact it has already been accused) of being a put on. Tragically this indictment mirrors a callous code of savoir faire whose essence sounds a death knell for all but a Dadaist aesthete. This is a great album, in spite of the fact that you may enjoy it."

Robert Hilburn in The *Los Angeles Times* (November 10) is also pleased. "This highly recommended album has some of the best country music ever achieved by a pop act. Selling well in the pop field, the 11-song effort is charged with emotion and honesty. The Byrds have drawn upon such writers as Bob Dylan, Woody Guthrie, and Merle Haggard." At the other end of the spectrum, *The Oakland Tribune* (September 29) says: "It seems as if The Byrds have gone on a western gospel kick on this LP, and the results are not very favourable. The old Byrds music is superior anyway. The only song that sounds halfway decent is 'You Ain't Going Nowhere', which is reminiscent of the better Byrds chirping. Maybe the original Byrds have flown south for the winter and these are just mocking Byrds."

Bill Yaran, music critic of the *Independent Star-News* (September 14) in Pasadena, CA, agrees. "The Byrds have finally issued their long-talked-about country and western LP, and, for me, it's a real disappointment. Just as Dylan's regression to simpler musical themes was a step backwards from the complex musical adventures embarked upon by many in the rock community (rarely successful but aesthetically commendable), The

Byrds have committed their mentor's same mistake. The best track, however, is Dylan's 'You Ain't Going Nowhere', but the worst is a horrible butchered version by Jim McGuinn of Woody Guthrie's 'Pretty Boy Floyd'. If you want good country and western music, listen to the Grand Ole Opry. If you want to hear good rock, listen to The Byrds' earlier stuff, not this."

Rolling Stone initially gives the album a fair reception in its September 14 issue, courtesy of critic Barry Gifford. "The yin-yang cycle of the musical flow continues to hold true. From straight, unamplified folk, to folk-rock, to rock, to acid-rock, to semi-C&W-rock, to affectedly-straight C&W – the next step appears all too obvious. But [the] new Byrds do not sound like Buck Owens & His Buckaroos. They aren't that good. The material they've chosen to record, or rather, the way they perform the material, is simple, relaxed, and folksy. It's not pretentious, it's pretty. The musicianship is excellent." Gifford sums up: "The Byrds have made an interesting album. It's really very uninvolved and not a difficult record to listen to. It ought to make the easy listening charts. 'Bringing it all back home' has never been an easy thing to do."

Long-time Byrds fan Jon Landau offers a second opinion in *Rolling Stone* (September 28) when he has a whole page to himself on the subject of "Country & Rock", holding up *Music From Big Pink* as an example and giving thorough reviews of Buffalo Springfield's *Last Time Around* as well as *Sweetheart Of The Rodeo*. "In the course of this program they manage to make good to brilliant use of steel guitar, country piano, fiddle, various banjo styles, acoustic flat-picked guitar, and every style of country singing. And yet the record flows with that consistency one expects from everything The Byrds do. You can hear the record turning around in circles if you listen carefully enough.

"In rock terms, the Springfield have obviously done more than The Byrds with country. For they have succeeded in translating some key country motives into rock terms. However, The Byrds, in doing country as country, show just how powerful and relevant unadorned country music is to the music of today. And they leave just enough rock in the drums to let you know that they can still play rock'n'roll. That's what I call bringing it all back home." It was rock critic Sandy Pearlman who introduced 'consistency' and 'circularity' to describe The Byrds, two key words that crop up regularly when others write now about the group.

The 'new' hip press also embraces the album: witness appraisals in *Eye Magazine* ("They play country music with grace, not grit

… 'Hickory Wind' may make you homesick for Carolina pines even if you've never been there") and *Jazz & Pop* ("I find this album to be one of the most enjoyable I've heard from some time").

September

Monday 2

Two tracks from *Sweetheart Of The Rodeo* – 'I Am A Pilgrim' and 'Pretty Boy Floyd' – are coupled for a single in the US. The stark A-side has little of the commercial potential that 'You Ain't Going Nowhere' had, and the 45 sinks without a trace.

•

Sometime at the end of August and early September, Clarence White persuades McGuinn and Hillman to hire his old friend Gene Parsons on drums. Parsons (unrelated to Gram Parsons; he was born Gene Victor Parsons in Los Angeles on September 4, 1944) has a chequered career as musician. Self-taught on guitar and banjo, he switched to bass when he joined The Castaways in the early 1960s – a country music show-band led by Floyd 'Gib' Guilbeau that plays around Colorado, Nevada, and the Pacific Northwest. When The Castaways break up, Parsons returns to his other trade, automotive engineer, a skill he learned in his father's machine shop – and which he put to good use when he constructed White's guitar string-pulling device.

Guilbeau tempts him back into the music business again, this time as a drummer. "I'd never played drums, but [Guilbeau] said any bass player could play drums," Parsons will recall in *Zigzag* (April 1974). The Guilbeau–Parsons duo work steadfastly in Gary Paxton's studio in Bakersfield from early 1967, releasing several singles as Cajun Gib & Gene on Bakersfield International. Clarence White is also a Paxton regular, and by summer 1967 a group has evolved with Guilbeau, Parsons, White, and bass player Wayne Moore. Billed mostly as The Reasons, often as Nashville West, the group breaks up when White joins The Byrds.

White lobbies for his friend to replace Kevin Kelley, as Parsons recalls in the *Zigzag* inter-view. "I was auditioned in this big warehouse in a pretty raunchy section of Hollywood. We went through a bunch of tunes and Roger and Chris concluded that they'd be happy working with me." Hillman is given the thankless task to tell his cousin, Kevin Kelley, that he is out. Kelley embarks on a sporadic career as drummer with The Train, Fever Tree, John Fahey, Phil Ochs, Jesse Wolff & Whings, and

others, but will never again receive the recognition he enjoyed so briefly with The Byrds. He dies in 2002.

•

Judy Sims is the first to interview the new foursome for a feature in *Disc* (October 5). "If anyone ever writes a manual on 'How To Survive In Rock And Roll Despite All Odds', that person should be Roger McGuinn with Chris Hillman writing the introduction. … The Byrds have been five, four, three, four, five, and four; the Byrds have been folk, rock, bluegrass, electronic, country. And it has always, somehow, 'worked out all right'. Last week I interviewed The Byrds for the first time in over a year. Roger and Chris have changed, of course, and the others were entirely new to me. The only thing that remained the same, essentially, was their presence, the 'thing' they have which has always filled me with no little awe, an intelligent and alert thing, a self-confidence that has weathered many storms and still holds steady." The interview itself is pleasant small-talk with no signs of any dissension in the group. It is McGuinn and Hillman who talk while White and Parsons sit quietly on standby.

Sunday 15

'The American Music Show', Rose Bowl, Pasadena, CA

Pinnacle Productions in conjunction with the Free Clinic (a Hollywood facility which provides free medical and psychiatric care for local residents) stage a one-day festival with an exciting and diverse bill: Joan Baez, The Everly Brothers, Big Brother & The Holding Company, The Byrds, Country Joe & The Fish, Junior Wells & Buddy Guy, The Mothers Of Invention, Buffy St. Marie, and Wilson Pickett. The Free Clinic is to receive a percentage of the profits. "But we are shying away from the word benefit," explains Sepp Donahower of Pinnacle to *The Los Angeles Times* (September 12) before the concert, "because of the strange stigma attached to the word. 'Pity us!'

'I Am A Pilgrim'

A 'I Am A Pilgrim' (TRADITIONAL, ARR. R. MCGUINN/C. HILLMAN)

B 'Pretty Boy Floyd' (W. GUTHRIE)

US release September 2 1968 (Columbia 44643)
UK release October 11 1968 (CBS 3752)
Chart high US none; UK none
Read more … March 12 and 13, 1968

It's not a benefit. Benefits have been abused." The organisers hope to fill the Rose Bowl's 70,000 capacity, but in the end no more than around 10,000 are tempted to come and the concert loses approximately $60,000.

Pete Johnson deems the music a fair success in *The Los Angeles Times* (September 16) despite the sorrowful turnout. "It would have been a good-sized audience for a routine three-act rock concert but it was far from enough to support the presentation of nine major acts in a football stadium, and the Pinnacle people lost a large sum of money. … Shortly after noon, The Byrds started the show with their electric brand of country music," writes Johnson, who goes on to describe the other acts. The show runs more or less according to plan: Wild Man Fischer is added before Frank Zappa's Mothers of Invention, while Wilson Pickett has to be dropped because of lack of time.

Following The Byrds' afternoon performance, there is a row backstage when Hillman and manager Larry Spector come to blows. A frustrated Hillman questions the way the money is handled and throws down his bass in a fit of anger, walking out. He will explain later to *Zigzag* (June 1972): "I'd got Clarence White into the group, but it wasn't really happening the way it should have been. Kevin was a good drummer, but sometimes you need to cool out and have a rest. It got a little too much for Kevin for one reason and another, and so we got Gene in because he'd been playing with Clarence for a year or two, and Clarence reckoned that he was the man for the job. I only played two gigs with The Byrds in that line-up, though, and then left. There were a lot of reasons [for leaving]. I was pretty mad at Roger and the management we had at that time. I got the feeling that they were stealing us rotten – at least, they were stealing me and Roger rotten, because the other two guys were on salary, which was fixed. We were being robbed stupid, so I said to Roger, 'I'm leaving, and you ought to do something about it too.'"

McGuinn will draw upon his recollection of these events to journalist Vincent Flanders in 1970. "Chris didn't get fired, he quit. He got uptight one time playing his bass. He didn't want to play the bass any more so he threw

THIS WEEKEND IN PASADENA

PINNACLE AND THE FREE CLINIC BRINGS YOU AN AMERICAN MUSIC SHOW AT THE ROSE BOWL SEPT. 15-1? NOON-10 PM

JOAN BAEZ
EVERLY BROTHERS
BIG BROTHER AND THE HOLDING COMPANY
THE BYRDS
COUNTRY JOE & THE FISH
JR. WELLS WITH BUDDY GUY
THE MOTHERS OF INVENTION
BUFFY ST. MARIE
WILSON PICKETT

PINNACLE

it down and quit. He was my equal partner. We were 50–50 partners by that time. It went from a five-way partnership down to a 50–50 partnership."

In another interview (*Zigzag*, March 1974), McGuinn will explain the grim economic realities. "This manager [Larry Spector], legally acting on our behalf, had renewed our contract with Columbia and the deal was renegotiated in such a way that we found ourselves effectively in the red for years. He took his commission, which was agreed at $25,000, and quit. He said, 'I'm sorry fellas … but I'm resigning, I'm giving up the management business to go and live in Big Sur.' Of course, we couldn't touch him; we'd signed contracts saying he was our legal representative and that he had power of attorney. What he'd done was sacrifice most of the other possible benefits for as large an advance as he could – and we didn't know about reading contracts; all we knew was that we trusted this guy – and he sold us down the river.

"For a start, he gave away our 100 free recording hours per album – I mean, we had managed to get that clause in our first contract back in 1964, but he gave that up in exchange for more front money. Usually when you renegotiate a contract you go for a better deal, right? Well, he went for a worse one with a bigger advance. Then he took his share and split. After this deal, Chris Hillman and I each had $50,000 in our accounts but then it dwindled to 30,000 then to 20,000, and we said, 'Hey, wait a minute, what happened to the other $60,000?'

"He told us that there were a lot of bills and expenses that had come up all of a sudden – and there was nothing we could do because he had power of attorney to do what he liked with our money. That's when Chris decided to split with what remained of his money, and he bought some land in New Mexico. I, like a dummy, left mine in, and in no time that was gone too." Despite McGuinn's serious allegations against Spector, he is retained as manager for the time being.

Newly recruited drummer Gene Parsons says later in *Zigzag* (April 1974): "Roger didn't seem too perturbed, as I recall. He reckoned that Chris was always quitting and that he always came back, but this time he didn't, and

we were in a spot because we had a gig to play in Salt Lake City later that week."

•

Hillman has served almost four years in The Byrds, and with him gone, McGuinn faces two possibilities: either lay the group to rest, or keep The Byrds airborne. Urged in part by White and Parsons and in part by a feeling of responsibility, McGuinn chooses the latter. "You know, I was so hung up on a brand-name," he will reflect many years later to Jud Cost of Sundazed Records about the period when Hillman leaves. "It was kind of sad. I had all new guys. It was like going to a new school and you had to make new friends. Well, fortunately I did, with Clarence White. He and I became very close. We were like drinking buddies and hung out together a lot and stuff. So, that was good. But at first it was a little awkward. It felt like there wasn't quite as much camaraderie on the road as there was before."

After the relative failure of *Sweetheart Of The Rodeo* and a still shaky reputation as a live attraction, The Byrds will have to work up credibility again. The finances are especially dire, and with the exception of the odd gig – Hillman reckons he plays only three to four concerts with Clarence White – the group has been off the road since the failed South African trip, which also drained the group of money. It is White and Parsons who inject the revised Byrds with aim and a purpose.

"[Roger] sure was [despondent]. There was no money in working for The Byrds," Parsons will tell *Zigzag* (March 1974). "They couldn't even pay their airline bills. The fact is, we were in debt to the airlines and we were hitting the bottom of the barrel, working some pretty bad gigs, playing down the bill to all kinds of other groups, and it was hard. For Roger, it must have been really rough, considering what a big group The Byrds had been … so he was downhearted, sure enough. But Clarence and I, on the other hand, were uphearted … we decided that The Byrds were going to become a real group again – and we started working and trying, and our optimism and effort seemed to bring up Roger's spirits again."

•

John Foley York (born in White Plains, NY, on August 3, 1946) signs on as the new Byrds bass player. Like other members before and after, he already has his connections with the group's family tree. He played with Clarence White as part of a shortlived Gene Clark Group in late summer 1967, and thus came under Larry Spector's wing. When David Crosby was ousted at the tail end of 1967, York was briefly in line as his replacement. "That is true," York will recall. "I was specifically asked, and I said no that first time."

York has crossed paths with the group on other occasions, too. As bass player with Sir Douglas Quintet he took part in the Beach Boys Summer Spectacular shows with The Byrds in summer 1966, and the barely-known group Lamp Of Childhood, with York, appeared at the Fantasy Fair & Magic Mountain Music Festival, as did The Byrds. He has gained further experience on the road with The Mamas & The Papas and with Johnny Rivers.

York plays either an old Fender Precision or an Epiphone hollowbody bass, which he runs through a couple of Fender Dual Showman amps. White also prefers Fender amplification (either a Super Reverb, a Twin Reverb, or a Dual Showman) and uses a fuzz box custom built by Red Rhodes when a grittier sound is required. With White in the group, McGuinn concentrates on the electric Rickenbacker 12-string for stage work. The special vocal blend that the original Byrds achieved has evaporated, and McGuinn in effect becomes the group's sole lead vocalist. White, Parsons, and particularly York all join for harmony vocals,

and York will be given his own vocal feature after a time.

Late September
[Possibly] University of Utah, Salt Lake City, UT
John York makes his debut with The Byrds on a weekend at the end of September, perhaps on the weekend of September 20–21. The exact date has been lost to time, but there is a possibility this is in Utah. Looking back, John York suggests: "I think it might be correct that my birst Byrds gig was in Salt Lake City. I remember that Gene Parsons brought a banjo along for the ride, which really impressed me."

Saturday 21
In the UK, The Byrds have won back lost territory with *The Notorious Byrd Brothers* (their country-rock experiment has not been released there quite yet), and readers of *Melody Maker* give the album enough votes to make it Number 8 in the category for the year's best albums – a ranking topped by Bob

Dylan's *John Wesley Harding*. The group also manages an impressive Number 5 placing in the International Group section, behind The Beatles, The Rolling Stones, Cream, and The Beach Boys – but ahead of Jimi Hendrix, The Monkees, The Union Gap, The Doors, and even The Dave Clark Five.

Tuesday 24
Barry Feinstein's movie *You Are What You Eat* premiers in the US, a lysergic cinematic mind warp ("keeps the eyeballs popping and the ear bones ringing" says *Time Magazine*) that features a short appearance by David Crosby when he was still a Byrd, as well as Carl Franzoni dancing to Frank Zappa & The Mothers Of Invention.

•

Around this time, The Byrds are commissioned to write the theme song for director Christian Marquand's adaptation of Terry Southern and Mason Hoffenberg's 1958 erotic-laden novel *Candy*, the group's second venture into Hollywood movies after 1967's *Don't Make Waves. Candy* stars an assorted cast

Not set to last: Interim Byrds with (from left) Chris Hillman, Gene Parsons, Clarence White, and Roger McGuinn – August/September 1968.

of characters, with young blonde Ewa Aulin from Sweden in the leading role alongside Hollywood stalwarts Marlon Brando and Richard Burton, while Ringo Starr (as a Mexican gardener), champion boxer Sugar Ray Robinson, crooner Charlie Aznavour, and Anita Pallenberg inhabit some of the smaller roles. The movie is already shot, mainly in Rome, much of it at the end of last year. How The Byrds land the role with this ABC production is not entirely clear, but a likely link is the group's manager Larry Spector.

Friday 27

Sweetheart Of The Rodeo is released in the UK to little fanfare. *Melody Maker* (October 12)

uses most of its review space to list all the participants before concluding: "The result is an average sort of country-flavoured set complete with various guitarists doubling banjos. Not typical Byrds music, which is rather a pity." Brian Chalker in *Record Mirror* (November 9) is equally to the point: "An item of interest to both pop and country enthusiasts is The Byrds' [new] album. All titles are tastefully rendered in the traditional country music manner – and for good measure two tracks 'Pretty Boy Floyd' and 'I Am A Pilgrim' are given the bluegrass treatment."

New Musical Express continues to use a system where one man, Allen Evans, reviews every album, necessarily resulting in shallow

pieces. "The Byrds are on a country kick," he notes on October 12, "but combining beat with it. They have augmented their instrumentation with quite a few other musicians, and harmonise the vocals with a wistful, wailing western sound. It's a bit corny at times, but doubtless it is meant to be. Good honky tonk piano on backing."

Disc (October 12) gives the album to its country & western specialist, who says, "How wise this group were to switch completely to the style of music they love and know … A stylish album." *Beat Instrumental* (November 1968) is delighted: "The Byrds seem to change direction more than the wind. They've given us folk-rock, rock'n'roll, space music, and,

Only Roger McGuinn left of the original Byrds by September 1968. From left: John York, McGuinn, Gene Parsons, and Clarence White.

with this album, country music. The now departed Gram Parsons was a big influence on the group to try these sounds, but The Byrds have always professed to have had country overtones. It's a completely successful LP, and contains the plaintive 'You Ain't Going Nowhere' and the beautiful lyrics of 'I Am A Pilgrim'. With The Byrds getting better all the time, country music seems only the beginning of their horizons." Where *The Notorious Byrd Brothers* brought The Byrds solidly back into the UK charts, *Sweetheart Of The Rodeo* never even makes the Top 50.

Saturday 28

☐ **US TV** CBS Television Studios, Hollywood, CA. CBS *Playboy After Dark*

Playboy editor and publisher Hugh M. Hefner, whose magazine is a runaway success with monthly sales in 1968 evenly around the five million mark, has begun syndicating his own television show this summer. (Actually it is his second attempt; as early as 1959 he hosted *Playboy's Penthouse* for a couple of seasons.)

CBS has built a quasi-bachelor-pad in the studio, and Hefner's weekly menu is a mix of musical guests, interviews with celebrities usually from the movie industry, and a dash of comedy thrown in. Hefner himself explains the aim to UPI Hollywood correspondent Vernon Scott: "Instead of having a formal setting with guests coming in one at a time, we want a party atmosphere so that the viewer feels he is a part of the activity. I want to give them the atmosphere of one of my clubs or my pad in Chicago. Guests will be my friends in and out of show business, comedians, musicians, good conversationalists … we hope to bring some sex and sophistication to television, which it surely needs. We've struck a responsive chord with readers. We hope to do the same with viewers."

The shows are recorded live in front of a small audience of 60s swingers, but syndication does not begin until January 1969.

Today's pre-recording features musical guests The Byrds and Marvin Gaye, comedian Pat Henry, and Lenny Bruce's mother Sally Mann, who talks about her son. The Byrds perform excellent versions of 'You Ain't Going Nowhere' (Clarence White perfectly duplicating Lloyd Green's pedal steel part with his pull-string Telecaster) and 'This Wheel's On Fire', yet another song from the batch of Bob Dylan's unreleased recordings made at his Woodstock hideaway. The show is aired in the Chicago area on February 28, 1969, and later in the Los Angeles and New York areas (May 30; July 5, 1969).

John York recalls: "We actually played live, which was rare in those days. I remember being part of a comedy sketch, too, singing

'Mary Had A Little Lamb' as a mock-chorale, vocally jamming with Marvin Gaye."

October

Saturday 5
Veteran's Memorial Coliseum, Phoenix, AZ

Iron Butterfly, Blue Cheer, The Standells, Sweetwater, and The Byrds. McGuinn and company probably undertake other concerts in Arizona on the Friday and Sunday too.

Monday 7
◁))) **RECORDING** Columbia Recording Studios, Sunset and El Centro, Hollywood, CA. Producer Bob Johnston and (presumably) engineer Tim May.

Producer Gary Usher has fallen out of favour with Columbia Records over several matters and has left the company. Bob Johnston is assigned as The Byrds' new producer, and his CV is unbeatable. He has worked with Bob Dylan (*Highway 61 Revisited, Blonde On Blonde, John Wesley Harding*), Simon & Garfunkel (including *Sounds Of Silence* and *Bookends*), and Johnny Cash's sparse and mighty *At Folsom Prison*.

As McGuinn told *Sing Out!* in August, Columbia have asked if The Byrds should be paired in the studio with another of the company's signings. McGuinn had wanted Dylan or Cash, so choosing Johnston is perhaps the closest Columbia comes to fulfilling its promise. But The Byrds–Johnston union will lack the experimentation and vigour of Gary Usher's creative period, in particular, perhaps because Johnston is used to working with headstrong artists who to a certain degree have much of their material and direction already finely worked out when they enter the studio. Where the group expects input and guidance, Johnston often chooses to lay back and let The Byrds steer the sessions themselves to some extent.

'King Apathy III' is the first McGuinn composition to be recorded in almost a year, while 'Old Blue' is a McGuinn-arranged rocked-up folk number with a longer history. He learned it from Bob Gibson & Bob (later Hamilton) Camp, who recorded it for a live album at Chicago's Gate Of Horn back in April 1961. "I was there for the whole week of gigs when [that] LP was recorded," McGuinn will tell *Mojo* magazine (June 2000). He selects *Bob Gibson & Bob Camp At The Gate Of Horn* as his Desert Island Disc in the magazine's 'Last Night A Record Changed My Life' monthly feature. "Bob Gibson was great all by himself.

He came and played banjo at my high school when my music teacher brought him to class. It was so exciting. From there I was on to Pete Seeger, Leadbelly and so many others. When Bob Camp hooked up, it was something new. His were almost Beatles harmonies, way ahead of their time."

Tuesday 8
◁))) **RECORDING** Columbia Recording Studios, Sunset and El Centro, Hollywood, CA. Producer Bob Johnston and (presumably) engineer Tim May.

'Drug Store Truck Drivin' Man', credited to McGuinn and ex-Byrd Gram Parsons, is a sarcastic jibe at DJ Ralph Emery and the worst aspects of Nashville culture. A sprightly country waltz and a minor Byrds classic, the song is boosted by Lloyd Green's pedal steel guitar, added at a later stage. McGuinn will explain how the song was conceived in an interview with *The Los Angeles Free Press* (March 6, 1969). "We were sitting in London, [Gram] Parsons and I, and there was a country song then called 'You Ain't Country'. We started in on [that song] but that sounded defensive, so we started playing around, and it's amazing sometimes how lines just come out."

McGuinn will explain the drug-store connection in *Friends* (August 1970). "[Ralph Emery] used to do commercials on the radio in between the records. … 'No matter what kind of rig you drive, step right in to your Clark Truck store and get yourself a Clark seat, it'll fix any rig, it's the most comfortable seat you can drive in the road. So get yourself a Clark seat next time you see the Clark sign on the highway. And now here … ' and he'd play a record. That kind of attitude. And I got the feeling from him, smoking his big cigar and sitting back in his Clark-like contraption in his swivel chair – but a really plush one – that it was like a Clark Truck seat. … So I got the feeling from this that he wanted to be a fucking truck driver, and I thought he's like a drugstore cowboy, a drugstore truck diving man, head of the Ku Klux Klan, for the political attitude he plugged."

According to Johnny Rogan's later discography, today the group starts recording 'This Wheel's On Fire' – the Bob Dylan tune recently pre-recorded for *Playboy After Dark* – but they will return to it on December 4.

Wednesday 9–Saturday 12
Whisky A Go Go, West Hollywood, CA

The Byrds are back at the Whisky for the first time in over a year, playing four nights in a row together with Florida group The Blues Image. The stint becomes the inspiration for a new song, as McGuinn will recount to Pete Frame in *Zigzag* (March 1974). "The Whisky

✳✳✳✳✳✳✳✳✳✳✳✳✳✳✳✳✳✳✳✳✳✳✳✳
Whisky A Go Go 9:00 pm to 2:00 am
NO AGE LIMIT
8901 Sunset Blvd.
652-4202
LAST NITE—
"STEVE MILLER BLUES BAND"
Four Days Only—October 9-10-11 & 12
"THE BYRDS"
October 17 to 20th
· LEE MICHAELS ·
Illinois Speed Press
Next
Nov. 1 & 2—
Spirit
✳✳✳✳✳✳✳✳✳✳✳✳✳✳✳✳✳✳✳✳✳✳✳✳

on Sunset Strip is a lousy place to play, and we had a bad night. I was driving Joey [Richards, a friend of McGuinn] home from a Subud meeting – he needed a ride home – and he said, 'Do you ever write melodies to lyrics?' I said, 'Sometimes,' and then later he gave me these lyrics, and we got together and knocked a song out of them. It was nothing great."

Monday 14

🔊 **RECORDING** Columbia Recording Studios, Sunset and El Centro, Hollywood, CA. Producer Bob Johnston and (presumably) engineer Tim May.

The Byrds record 'Your Gentle Way Of Loving Me', a song penned by Floyd Guilbeau and Gary Paxton and previously released as a single by Cajun Gib & Gene last year. Drummer Gene Parsons is responsible for the harmonica on the track and McGuinn is the lead vocalist.

Tuesday 15

🔊 **RECORDING** Columbia Recording Studios, Sunset and El Centro, Hollywood, CA. Producer Bob Johnston and (presumably) engineer Tim May.

The just-conceived 'Bad Night At The Whisky' is laid down, along with White's guitar instrumental 'Nashville West'. The piece, which White plays nightly on stage, is reminiscent of Buck Owens & The Buckaroos' parade number 'Buckaroo'. But they fail to capture it well today, according to Parsons.

"They wouldn't let us do this the way we wanted to," he will tell *Zigzag* (March 1974). "It didn't come out anywhere near as well as it should have. We'd recorded it before, during our Bakersfield International days, and that was much better. It had Glen D. Hardin on piano too, but the best version is on a tape that I recorded on a little bitty Sony [recorder] during a gig that Clarence, Gib, Wayne, and I did in the Nashville West club one evening."

Wednesday 16

🔊 **RECORDING** Columbia Recording Studios, Sunset and El Centro, Hollywood, CA. Producer Bob Johnston and (presumably) engineer Tim May.

McGuinn resurrects his writing partnership with Bob Hippard, who co-wrote 'C.T.A.-102', for the country number 'Stanley's Song', which is recorded today.

Friday 18

The single 'I Am A Pilgrim' coupled with 'Pretty Boy Floyd' is issued in the UK. Penny Valentine in *Disc* (October 19) says: "Stunning to hear The Byrds' new one … which spotlights their pride and joy C&W singer and doesn't sound like them at all. It's from their *Sweetheart Of The Rodeo* album, and if you've ever held The Byrds sound dear to your heart you may be as disappointed as I am by this."

Chris Welch of *Melody Maker* (October 26): "They have turn, turn, turned their backs on rock and now concentrate on country music. Violins abound, banjos plunk and the voice is suitably projected through the nose, instead of the mouth, or, as in country and eastern music, through the ears. A simple performance which reveals the yearning among groups to return to the soil and be at one with mother nature and wide open spaces. Enough of low jive cellars, the hectic pace of modern life, and the vulgar commercialism of popular music, say our exhausted beat musicians. Give us yoghurt, a horse, a banjo, a shovel and a song and we're happy. As one still up to one's neck in drugs, corruption and widescale debauchery, I must say it sounds all very tempting."

The single is performing poorly in the US and does no better in the UK, missing the charts there.

→ Sunday 20–Thursday 24

The Byrds are in Nashville for some days to record and even to perform at Grand Ole Opry as part of a Columbia Records Sales Convention. Nothing has changed in the few months that they have been away from the Music City, as bassist John York later recalls: "We played 45 seconds worth of 'Old Blue' and there was some booing from the audience."

Monday 21

🔊 **RECORDING** Columbia Studio A, 34 Music Square East, Music Row, Nashville, TN. Producer Bob Johnston and unknown engineer.

Johnston is familiar with Nashville from his many sessions with Bob Dylan, but this seems to help little as The Byrds spend fruitless days in Columbia's studio on Music Row. York again: "Recording in Nashville was a very disappointing experience. We were an embarrassment to the Good Old Boys at Columbia. Our sessions were sabotaged and we returned early to finish recording in L.A." Only a sec-

ond version of the 'Nashville West' instrumental is recorded. Not all is wasted, however, as York notes. "Roger and I wrote 'Candy' in Nashville while waiting for some dubious studio repair that never did happen."

Friday 25–Saturday 26

The Golden Bear, Huntington Beach, CA

November

Friday 1–Sunday 3

Avalon Ballroom, San Francisco, CA

The Byrds, Taj Mahal, and Genesis (a US group with guitarist Kent Henry among its ranks) play a weekend in San Francisco promoted by Family Dog. Part of the group's Saturday performance will become available as a bootleg tape and provides a peek into The Byrds' new identity. White's Telecaster twang is omnipresent, pushing the group through a set encompassing greatest hits and well-known numbers ('My Back Pages', 'Mr. Spaceman', 'So You Want To Be A Rock'n'Roll Star', 'Eight Miles High', 'He Was A Friend Of Mine', 'Goin' Back') plus a couple of songs from *Sweetheart Of The Rodeo* ('Pretty Boy Floyd' and 'You Don't Miss Your Water').

McGuinn's administration of the Byrds heritage makes for a pair of surprises in the set: Hillman's 'Time Between' (wrongly introduced as a song off *The Notorious Byrd Brothers*) and Parsons' 'Hickory Wind', which is followed by McGuinn's rambling speech on country music. "Country music sort of grows on you after awhile. … What's interesting is that the country people accepted us, which really blew my mind, you know?" Perhaps he feels a kinship with 'Hickory Wind' for a different reason. In a 1996 interview with Dan Harmon, he will remark: "Did you ever notice how much 'Hickory Wind' sounds like 'Satisfied Mind'?"

Furthermore, the Avalon tape introduces a batch of newly worked-up songs ('Old Blue', 'Drug Store Truck Driving Man', 'This Wheel's On Fire', 'Stanley's Song', 'King Apathy III', 'Bad Night At The Whisky', and 'Nashville West'). The night also leaves room for a careening take on 'Blue Suede Shoes'. McGuinn sings lead on all songs, with York mainly providing the harmonies.

Wednesday 13

Rolling Stone has a hotline to The Byrds, and the issue printed today (although dated December 7) gives a concise account of the progress of the next album, which "is shaping up as partly an extension of The Byrds' last

country LP. The material being cut has primarily a country flavour with The Byrds' ever-present touch added. … In concert, despite the change in membership, The Byrds have managed to retain a good deal of their traditional sound. This is done through the use of McGuinn's distinctive voice and 12-string guitar and the use of three-part harmonies. In their present form they made their debut at the Whisky A Go Go in Hollywood and are now performing in various locals between recording dates." The bulletin lists the eight songs laid down at this point: 'Drug Store Truck Driving Man', 'Your Gentle Way Of Loving Me', 'Nashville West', 'Stanley's Song' 'Old Blue', 'This Wheel's On Fire', 'Bad Night At The Whisky', and 'King Apathy III'.

Saturday 16

The UK music press breaks news of a planned overseas visit next year. The Byrds are to undertake a three-week tour in February under the aegis of Vic Lewis and NEMS Enter-

prises, opening with a major London concert, probably at the Royal Albert Hall. The tour never reaches fruition; indeed The Byrds will not come to England and Europe until the summer of 1970. No reason will be given as to why the 1969 dates do not materialise, but it may be that the matter of their South African visit is unresolved with the British Musicians' Union.

ALSO …

The main newsflash in *New Musical Express* is of Graham Nash leaving The Hollies. He tells *NME* in an exclusive interview: "I shall go to America and sing with some of my friends. No, not for recording, just for pleasure and experimentation. No, not Mama Cass, who, I'm sorry to hear, has throat trouble. Just some friends." Nash has been on a collision course with his band-mates for a long time, so the decision is not a sudden one. "The Hollies went through all the personality thing before Graham left them," Keith Richards will reflect

a year later in *New Musical Express* (December 6, 1969). "The problem was that Graham was the only one getting stoned, and everybody else was really straight Manchester stock. That doesn't help."

Thursday 21
Salem Armory Auditorium, Salem, OR

Friday 22
Eagles Auditorium, Seattle, WA

Saturday 23
Cordiner Hall, Whitman College, Walla Walla, WA

The Byrds are supported by a trio of Washington groups: The Sweet Roll (previously The Wailers), The Beta Band (made up of students at the college), and The Poor Man's Guardian, who play for the dance following the concert. The Byrds presumably play an (undocumented) show in Washington state tomorrow night, too.

Moustachioed Byrds: Gene Parsons, Clarence White, Roger McGuinn, John York.

ALSO ...

Over in England, Donovan opens his cosy cottage in the West Midlands to four of his friends around this weekend. By next Saturday (November 30) *New Musical Express* can tell readers: "At Donovan's Hertfordshire cottage, four group drop-outs jammed with him – John Sebastian (ex-Spoonful), David Crosby (ex-Byrds), Steve Stills (ex-Buffalo Springfield), and Graham Nash (ex-Hollies)."

Monday 25

Carver Gym, Western Washington State College, Bellingham, WA

Wednesday 27–Thursday 28

Electric Factory, Philadelphia, PA

The Byrds appear with two Philadelphia groups, The American Dream and Yum Yum.

Saturday 30

ALSO ...

Los Angeles is buzzing with musical activity this weekend. Besides concerts by Sunshine Company, Spirit, Harvey Mandel, The Jeff Beck Group, The Moody Blues, and Ten Years After, there are two newcomers who more or less make their debut in town this Saturday. One is Pogo (soon renamed Poco), a band formed by a couple of remnants of Buffalo Springfield: Richie Furay and Jim Messina, who wind up a two-week stand at the Troubadour now. The other is Gram Parsons and Chris Hillman's Flying Burrito Brothers, who open for Taj Mahal over at the Whisky A Go Go. Parsons and Hillman have put their differences aside after the South African tour and now share a pad in the San Fernando Valley, busily writing, rehearsing, and recording songs. With Sneaky Pete Kleinow on pedal steel guitar, Parsons and Hillman on guitars and vocals, plus a flexible rhythm section, the Burritos are tentatively weaving country music with a touch of rock, soul, and gospel.

December

Tuesday 3

Elvis Presley appears on an NBC television show tonight (later commonly referred to as the *68 Comeback Special*). It consists of electrifying live performances interspersed with personal stories and observations. Elvis is prodded to talk about the contemporary music scene, and is famously quoted as saying: "I think everything's improved. I like a lot of the new groups – The Beatles, The Beards ... whoever."

Wednesday 4

🔊 **RECORDING** Columbia Recording Studios, Sunset and El Centro, Hollywood, CA. Producer Bob Johnston and (presumably) engineer Tim May.

Having given up on Nashville as a suitable place to record, The Byrds make one last recording session in Los Angeles to complete the next album. They have attempted Bob Dylan's 'This Wheel's On Fire' before (see October 9) and today record two slightly different versions, the main difference being the tempo and White's wasp-like guitar buzz on the slower take – which is eventually chosen as the lead-off track on the new album.

White himself is far from pleased, as he will divulge later to *Zigzag* (April 1974). "I felt I was faking it. In bluegrass music there is a lot of gospel and blues influence and flavouring – so the blues part was in me, but there were so many people playing blues that I didn't ever feel that I could catch up with them. So I just wanted to play honest music in an honest style that I believed in and felt at ease with. ... 'This Wheel's On Fire' ... that's the most embarrassing thing I've ever done. It's horrible – I really don't know what to say, except that I wasn't ready for it. I wanted someone else to play lead on that. Oh, don't remind me of that track!"

Although the song fits The Byrds well, it has been covered successfully by The Band on *Music From Big Pink* and has already been a UK Top Five single for Julie Driscoll With Brian Auger & The Trinity.

The group also records two songs for the *Candy* movie, 'Child Of The Universe' and 'Candy'. The first is co-written by McGuinn and composer Dave Grusin, known in pop circles for his contributions to the *Graduate* soundtrack last year. Grusin writes the bulk of the *Candy* soundtrack (Steppenwolf lend a couple of previously-taped tracks to the movie), but, according to John York, The Byrds also record some instrumental background music that is only heard in the movie and is not made available on the soundtrack album. However, the song initially considered as the movie's theme song, McGuinn and York's 'Candy', is passed over and left off the soundtrack in favour of 'Child Of The Universe', although the 'Child Of The Universe' heard in the movie differs from the version that The Byrds will soon release themselves. The movie will premiere in Los Angeles at Beverley Hills Theatre on December 20.

Today's session closes with the recording of a medley of Dylan's 'My Back Pages' (which The Byrds have of course recorded earlier) and a shambling 'Baby, What You Want Me To Do', the Jimmy Reed blues that McGuinn has sung on stage countless times right from the early days at Ciro's. The two songs are linked by 18 bars of shuffling on an E chord, which is credited to all four members under the title 'B.J. Blues'. As the medley comes to a close, White kicks in 'The Break Song' (also known as 'Hold It!'), a little signature riff with McGuinn announcing in showbiz style: "I'd like to thank you very much for listening! We'll see you all later." The medley exists in two different versions, but only the take that will be originally released includes 'The Break Song'.

Saturday 7
ALSO ...

The top story in the British music press is the coming together of an ex-Hollie, an ex-Byrd, and an ex-Bufflo Springfield. Earlier in the week, journalists from the music weeklies have paid separate visits to an apartment–cum–studio on Moscow Road in central London, and Penny Valentine is agog over what she witnesses. A music revolution is taking place, she declares in today's *Disc*, "[and] it is being pioneered by Graham Nash … David Crosby … Stephen Stills, and it's the answer to all the questions about what is going to happen to pop music in the next year and all the years to come. It means the end of the group scene as we know it today.

"I spent three hours in Graham, David, and Stephen's company this week, and I came away from the flat more excited and elated by anything I've heard, seen or talked about in the music field since I first saw The Beatles. It is hard not to sound pretentious about something as big, involved, and thrilling as what these three boys are planning and are already immersed in. It is hard, because what they are doing is to finally point pop music in a strong straight direction.

"Their decision is the answer to why Eric Clapton has left the Cream, why Jeff Beck has left The Yardbirds, why Traffic, Janis Joplin, Mama Cass, Lovin' Spoonful, and the famous Paul Butterfield Blues Band all split up, and why groups in America and Britain are moving away from each other every week. … What they plan is to collect together and tie up all the loose strings of musical talent in the pop world. It is a gradual process already in motion and, finally, it may involve Clapton, Hendrix, Mama Cass and all the 'heavy' musicians in the world today."

Alan Smith concurs in next week's *New Musical Express*: "God help me from sounding pretentious, but the Nash–Crosby–Stills coming-together brings forth music to care for. They have a beautiful and utterly distinctive sound." *Melody Maker*'s Tony Wilson is not quite so convinced. "The songs were fairly simple in concept with hints of country music, folk and pop in them without being directly attributable to any of these forms".

Harmony abounds in the London apartment high above Bayswater as the privileged music journalists are given, one by one, exclusive performances of 'Lady Of The Islands', 'You Don't Have To Cry', 'Marrakesh Express', 'Guinevere', and 'Helplessly Hoping', all by the light of a gas fire. Even the fearsome David Crosby is a changed man: Valentine remembers him as "an atrociously aggressive member of The Byrds some years ago." Allan McDougall recalls in *Record Mirror* (July 11, 1970): "When Nash first invited me to 'come and have a listen' to the embryonic [trio], I was none too keen, as previous encounters with Crosby had been far from pleasant. But, round to the rented flat in Moscow Road, Bayswater, I toddled – and sure enough, David had become Nice with a capital N."

Also in London, John Sebastian talks to *Melody Maker* and *Record Mirror* (December 7), although he is back in the US when the papers are on the newsstands. "We came over about a week ago and we've just been look-ing around, taking it all in. I'll be going back in a few days; I hadn't planned to come to England. But Dave and Stephen were coming over, so I took the opportunity to take a short holiday. They're staying for a while – they're taking a flat with a recording studio in it, and they'll be working with Graham," he tells Derek Boltwood in *Record Mirror*. Asked about his involvement, he replies: "Well, I definitely won't be. I don't want to be involved in a group scene any more, and anyway I am just starting out a solo career." (Crosby, who dubs him one of The Reliability Brothers, quips in *Rolling Stone* a year-and-a-half later: "Sebastian needs a band like a stag needs a hat rack.")

Sebastian adds: "I don't know whether the others are going to form a group. I think it's unlikely that they would. … Stephen and Dave and I used to get together in California, just [to] have informal sessions with whatever musicians were around at the time. David has this great voice for harmony, he can follow a lead and really harmonise beautifully, come in right on pitch. And then suddenly Graham Nash appeared, and it was incredible. Dave has a high voice, but Graham would be about an octave and a half higher. We really get a lot of fun out of just blowing together."

Sunday 22

An unassuming note by *The New York Post*'s regular Broadway columnist Leonard Lyons – syndicated in many newspapers around the country, including today's *Cedar Rapids Gazette* – mentions that Roger McGuinn will compose the music for Ivor David Balding's *Tryout*.

Theatre producer Balding has just been in the news when he was forced to close down Broadway production *The Cuban Thing* after a tear-gas bomb put 900 spectators out on the streets. Balding is also the producer of *Scuba Duba*, a successful comedy directed by Jacques Levy that clocks up almost 700 off-Broadway performances in the years between 1967 and '69.

Even if Balding's *Tryout* project as such will never be heard of again, Levy and McGuinn will pursue the musical they so briefly discussed when they met at New York's Fillmore East back in May. The two have kept in touch, mapping out the story line, and they arrange to meet in January of the new year.

Tuesday 31
Kinetic Playground, Chicago, IL

The Byrds play a special New Year's Eve concert in Chicago – their first visit to the town since August 1967 – together with bluesman Muddy Waters and Peter Green's Fleetwood Mac.

The bill is held over into the first days of the new year.

David Crosby, Stephen Stills, Graham Nash.

In January, Roger McGuinn and director **Jacques Levy** start work on their ambitious Broadway project *Gene Tryp* ... The Byrds release *Dr. Byrds & Mr. Hyde,* and night by night slowly re-build their shattered concert reputation, concentrating on US colleges and universities besides a memorable visit to Mexico in March ... *Easy Rider* film is a major international success this year, featuring The Byrds and Roger McGuinn providing the pivotal soundtrack ... The Byrds appear on some of the summer's many pop and rock festivals: Newport, Seattle, Atlantic City, Vancouver, and New Orleans ... **Skip Battin** replaces John York as bass player in October, just as ninth album *Ballad Of Easy Rider* is released ... In the meantime, ex-Byrds Chris Hillman and Gram Parsons have founded **The Flying Burrito Brothers**, while David Crosby is escalated to superstar status as part of **Crosby Stills & Nash** and later **Young** ... The Byrds play out the year with a successful weekend at New York's Fillmore East in December.

1969

January

Friday 3–Saturday 4
Kinetic Playground, Chicago, IL

"Hopefully, 1969 won't hold many disappointments as great as this," is how Robb Baker of The *Chicago Tribune* (January 7) classifies The Byrds' Friday-night performance. The group are held over from their New Year's Eve 1968 concert for two more nights with Muddy Waters and Fleetwood Mac. Bluesman Waters is feeling unwell and leaves the stage after only one number, while Fleetwood Mac struggle with an impatient audience before winning them over with rousing rock'n'roll parodies. Topping the bill, The Byrds do not find favour with Baker. "Probably the most volatile group in the business as far as membership goes, the quartet is now composed of Roger McGuinn, Clarence White, John York, and Gene Parsons. The new bunch is very loud, even on its country-western numbers (tho' the nice thing about the country-western revival thing supposedly is its softness). They are also not very good, vocally or instrumentally."

Concert promoter Aaron Russo has converted the old Uptown Theatre into a rock venue with a hi-tech light and sound system. The venue was briefly known as the Electric Theatre before being forced to change its name after legal threats by New York's Electric Circus operation, and Russo switched the name to the Kinetic Playground. By now it has become Chicago's premier rock venue. John York recalls: "My memories of the New Year's Eve gig, well … I told the club owner [Russo] that Muddy Waters should be the headline act, not The Byrds. I felt it was a question of respect. He said no. I apologised to Muddy and he said, 'That's OK, I'm used to it.'"

Undated January

Jacques Levy flies to California to work with Roger McGuinn on Levy's ambitious adaptation of *Peer Gynt*. Since Levy and McGuinn met in New York City in May of last year at the Fillmore East shows with Tim Buckley, the project has been active. Levy has streamlined the script into a workable production and secured financial backing from Broadway producer Ivor David Balding.

Levy has based the musical on the storyline of Norwegian playwright Henrik Ibsen's witty and absurd plot, originally published in 1867, which follows the life of main character Peer Gynt against a wildly changing backdrop: the Norwegian mountain wilds; the coast of Morocco; the Sahara Desert; a madhouse in Cairo; a shipwreck on the ocean – all written in verse. The play is laden with symbolic

passages, as Peer in turn is a fortune hunter, a bridegroom, a seducer, a troll prince, an outlaw, a businessman, a prophet, a Bedouin chief, a historian, and an old man. Along the way, he encounters a colourful gallery of characters and battles with the Great Boyg, a shapeless monster that cannot be ignored or understood. Norwegian composer Edvard Grieg wrote music for the play and this became highly popular in its own right, later extracted as two suites, including the memorable 'In The Hall Of The Mountain King'.

Levy has transposed the setting to the American Wild West of the 1850s, and by cleverly rearranging the letters of *Peer Gynt* has come up with the main character (and title) *Gene Tryp*. The first time McGuinn described the project was to Jay Ruby of *Jazz & Pop* in an interview at the end of 1968 (although not published until the magazine's March 1969 edition). "It's going to be an 1840s version of *Peer Gynt*, in the Southwestern United States. … *Gene Tryp* is the lead character, he's *Peer Gynt*, and he goes through all these Siddhartha changes, finding his own self, trying to get to know himself in the end. And he goes through a thing with a chick and they're in love, and then this thing gets between them, and he has to go around, into different bags and different scenes, to get back to her. He finally gets back to her in the end, and he dies in her arms. It'll be a classic, I think. It'll be a top musical."

McGuinn reckons it'll be better than *Hair*, and he intends to involve himself in the production – a natural culmination of his interest in technology and multimedia. "We'll be using tapes and liquid projections," he enthuses. "We'll also have a 23-piece pit band in there. They'll be correlating the music. There'll be live musicians on stage doing hoedowns and stuff, and there'll be the band, and there'll be the tape. It'll all be worked out and synchronised."

During an intense period in January, McGuinn (music) and Levy (lyrics) compose much of the material needed. Following the writing session, McGuinn tells John Carpenter of *The Los Angeles Free Press* (March 6): "It has about 25 songs and we have to do the scoring of it yet. It should be mounted sometime in the fall. Casting still has to be done. It's set in the 1800s in the Southwest. It's about this Bob Dylan-type cat who steals this bride away from this marriage, goes off into the hills, drops her, and finally falls in love with this other girl and builds a little house for her. He's out chopping wood one day and this force keeps him away from the house. In the original Ibsen version, it was a bird that kept him away. He had to go all around the world because he can't go back to the house.

He becomes an Elmer Gantry-type preacher, runs for president, goes through all these different scenes. There are so many bags in it. It goes from country to bayou to hard rock. I may audition for it myself. Dylan would be good but … then Levy was considering Tim Buckley. … I'll be going to New York to work on it."

Levy and McGuinn stick to a strict working pattern. Quoted later in Bud Scoppa's Byrds book (1970), McGuinn says: "I have these six TV sets at my house, and I always have at least three of them up on the shelf in the room where I work. And I have this remote central switch that lets me operate all of them from wherever I'm sitting. So Jacques and I would sit at the table working on *Tryp* with all the TVs turned to different channels and the sound off. We'd be writing, and whenever something came on one of the stations that looked interesting, I'd just hit the volume control and we'd watch it. That's the only way we could have finished so much in such a short time."

In another 1970 interview, with Ed Ward of *Rolling Stone*, he adds: "Jacques wrote the book and he claims all the lyrics, and I claim all the music, but really it's a give-and-take thing. We collaborated [in my living room] for a month or so, working every day at night from about midnight to about five in the morning. It was really quiet and there was nobody around to bother us."

The production struggles with finance for the project in the coming months, which enforces several postponements. McGuinn will eventually alllow The Byrds to record some of the material earmarked for *Gene Tryp* over the next two or three years. It is not clear to what extent the songs are actually finished during McGuinn and Levy's workshop, but later Byrds songs known to originate from *Gene Tryp* are: 'Lover Of The Bayou', 'Chestnut Mare', 'All The Things', 'Just A Season', 'I Wanna Grow Up To Be A Politician', and 'Kathleen's Song'.

Tuesday 7

The newly recorded 'Bad Night At The Whiskey' and 'Drug Store Truck Drivin' Man' become The Byrds' 15th single in the US. It does not make the charts.

Monday 13

Students at Yale University in Connecticut are urged to bring flutes, drums, and other paraphernalia for a Peace Fest to be held tonight at Woolsey Hall, New Haven, CT, and supposedly will feature The Byrds. Besides a poster announcing the event, however, there is no news about it in the student paper and the fest is not staged.

Friday 24

FRIDAY, JANUARY 24th
THE BYRDS
THE FLOCK
THE LITTER
ARAGON
1106 W. LAWRENCE 561-8323
OPERATION SOUL

Aragon Ballroom, Chicago, IL
A concert with The Byrds and local groups
The Litter and The Flock.

Saturday 25
The Cellar, Arlington Heights, IL
The Byrds appear with support from The
Finchley Boys, a group from nearby Cham-
paign, IL.

ALSO ...
Freshly signed to A&M Records, The Flying
Burrito Brothers are introduced to the Hol-
lywood press at a specially designed barn
dance in Los Angeles. Now lining up as
Gram Parsons, Chris Hillman, Sneaky Pete,
Chris Etheridge on bass, and Jon Corneal on
drums (soon booted out in favour of Michael
Clarke), the group's debut album is to be
released in mere weeks. They plan to go to
Britain in the middle of February, and a fixed
date for the group's London arrival is set for
March 12 – the first of several failed attempts
to visit England this year.

Friday 31
**Glenn Memorial United Methodist
Church, Emory, Atlanta, GA**
Miller Francis Jr. of *The Great Speckled Bird*
(February 9–13) reviews the concert. "The
setting for such a superlative performance of
rock music could not have been more appropriate. The Electric Collage contributed a
really stunning lightshow that took wonderful
advantage of the curved structure of the walls
of the church. Even the audience was groovy.
McGuinn commented on the loud, positive
response to country elements in the concert.
One of the saddest characteristics of 'turned
on' Southern young people is the inability to
love their own music. It's not, as McGuinn
suggested, a generational problem (country
music = adults); it's primarily a social class

problem (Lawrence Welk = adults, country
music = rednecks, rock = The Beautiful, in
other words middle class, People). Hundreds
of would-be young folk and rock singers and
instrumentalists desperately rip out their
own deep country roots and at the same time
choose to become tenth-rate imitations of a
middle class Jew from Minnesota who wisely
recognised the validity of those same roots
and had to turn to them in order to find his
own musical roots."

"[The show] spotlighted the country–
Dylan polarity of Byrdsong: 'You Ain't Going
Nowhere', 'The Christian Life', 'Pretty Boy
Floyd', 'My Back Pages', 'Chimes Of Freedom', 'This Wheel's On Fire', and some
new ones including Merle Haggard's 'Sing
Me Back Home'. Prominently featured was
country musician Clarence White on lead guitar. White's brilliant solo work was the high
point of Friday night's concert. He stood
motionless, glassy-eyed, silent (he evidently
had no interest in singing), but his fingers
produced powerful vibrations that swept and
rolled through the church like a tidal wave of
electric sound.

"There were, surprisingly, two rhythm &
blues numbers – Jimmy Reed's 'Baby What You
Want Me To Do' and Chuck Berry's 'Roll Over
Beethoven'. That The Byrds could do this kind
of thing more often (and better than most) is
amply demonstrated on record by 'Captain
Soul'. ... That they choose instead to develop
the still embryonic white soul of rock is a
credit to McGuinn's good judgment and the
nonpareil musical integrity of The Byrds.

"What I had undervalued on the recordings
was Roger McGuinn's fine vocals. Their power
is of such gentle, unobtrusive nature that it
is easy to see (though not to justify) why he
has been overlooked by both fans and critics.
He has one of the most sensitive, controlled
approaches to a lyric that I've ever heard in
rock, one that somehow triumphs over the
severe limitations of his voice. He seems to
sing almost straight, without embellishments,
but there are subtleties and nuances in all the
right places that you won't hear in some other,
more flamboyant singing styles. And even his
R&B offerings steered clear of the blackface
monstrosities of white 'blues' rock vocalising
that I have begun to call The 'Spoonful' Syndrome after Jack Bruce and others of his ilk.
McGuinn's cool, understated style found its
forte in The Byrds. He is one of the unsung
heroes of rock music."

Undated January–February
🔊 **RECORDING** Columbia Recording
Studios, Studio A, Sunset and El Centro,
Hollywood, CA. Unknown producer and
engineer.

Peter Fonda, Dennis Hopper, and Terry
Southern's outlaw biker movie *Easy Rider* is
finished – most of it filmed in the spring and
summer of last year – and it is prepared for a
debut screening at the annual Cannes Film
Festival in France in May. It is a low-cost film
in line with Fonda's motives. "Dennis and I
were young men, dissatisfied and disenfran-
chised when we put *Easy Rider* together," he
will say later in his memoir *Don't Tell Dad*. "We
had lives to live that could contribute to our
country, our cause."

Now, during post-production, the soundtrack is given priority, and Fonda stumbles
on a novel approach. "Peter wanted to save
money on the soundtrack," McGuinn will
explain to Jud Cost more than 30 years later.
"So he dubbed his record collection onto the
soundtrack. Kind of a dummy-music soundtrack. He wasn't sure what he was going to
do for the score. But he got to like it after he
played it a few times. You know how you get
used to watching certain videos with certain
sounds. So he decided to leave it that way,
which was an innovative thing. Nobody had
done that yet in Hollywood. ... So Peter was
the pioneer in putting already-made music
on a soundtrack."

Fonda has already separately approached
Bob Dylan, The Band's Robbie Robertson,
and David Crosby to contribute new music
for the movie. He gives Dylan a private screening in the hope that he will allow his 'It's
Alright, Ma (I'm Only Bleeding)' to be used
in a pivotal sequence, but Dylan is unwilling
to grant Fonda permission. Fonda also hopes
to persuade Dylan to contribute a title song.
McGuinn explains the backdrop to Jud Cost.
"Peter wanted a song that was custom-written
for the movie. So he decided to try to get
Dylan to write him a song. He arranged an
appointment, flew to New York with a can of
the film, and put it in the screening room for
Dylan. And Dylan sat there, and I guess he

'Bad Night At The Whiskey'

A 'Bad Night At The Whiskey'
(R. McGUINN/J. RICHARDS)
B 'Drug Store Truck Drivin' Man'
(R. McGUINN/G. PARSONS)

US release January 7 1969 (Columbia
44746)
UK release March 7 1969 (CBS 4055)
Chart high US none; UK none
Read more ... entries for October
8 and 15 1968

Roger McGuinn on stage.

wasn't sure if he wanted to write anything for this American International-style motorcycle movie. So he wrote down some notes on a paper napkin and he said, 'Here, give this to McGuinn. He'll know what to do with it.' Peter said OK and flew back to L.A., where he gave me this little cocktail napkin. And it had the verse, 'The river flows/It flows to the sea/Wherever that river goes/That's where I want to be/Flow river flow.' And I got my guitar out and wrote the tune to it and finished off the words. I wrote another verse for it. I gave Dylan the credit for it. We called it 'Ballad Of Easy Rider'."

It is not precisely documented when the song is conceived or recorded, but The Byrds will have introduced 'Ballad Of Easy Rider' into their live set by the middle of February. The track taped for the movie is essentially a McGuinn solo-guitar/vocal performance set against Gene Parsons' lonesome harmonica. Furthermore, McGuinn and Parsons record a cover of 'It's Alright, Ma (I'm Only Bleeding)', as Dylan did not give permission to use his original in the film. Both songs are taped at Columbia's Studio A and will later be included on the original soundtrack album on ABC-Dunhill Records (DSX 50063).

February

Early February

In conjunction with the forthcoming album, Roger McGuinn does the press rounds. A feature in *Fusion* (belatedly published in April 1970) will become well known as the source of his classic quote on Gram Parsons: "[We] hired a piano player – and it turned out to be Parsons – a monster in sheep's clothing; and he exploded out of this sheep's clothing – God! It's George Jones! In a big sequin suit! And he's got his guitar and sidemen accompanying him. He took it right into the eye of the hurricane and, raaaaaooow, came out the other side. It was Japanese."

Otherwise McGuinn is in a surly mood ("your newspaper's a shuck, man!") and dismisses the four original Byrd members with "I'm glad everybody left". John York is also present, and pitches in with a few comments. "The Byrds were never in one place long enough to be categorised," he says. "They were all, as Roger said, very amateurish and were searching for a particular musical identity as individuals – so they weren't really concerned with a group identity. Mike was trying to decide: am I really a drummer? Am I a Motown drummer or a country drummer? And that went throughout all the albums. …

Nobody was afraid to experiment – thinking: maybe I'm not what I should be – maybe it's a partial shuck – but I've got the balls to go out there and keep doing it until I found out.

"One thing I'm curious about," says York, "[is that] this particular group, the way it stands now, has been together about five months, and every time we have an interview, interviewers are always concerned with the past four years." But he confirms that the new members have been accepted with open arms by loyal fans. McGuinn and York compare The Byrds to The Blue Angels, the US Navy's flight squadron, where "it doesn't matter who's driving – it's the formation".

•

McGuinn, now the sole owner of the group name, extends his control of The Byrds to cover managerial duties as he breaks ties with Larry Spector. The way he describes it to Jon Landau in *Rolling Stone* (April 5) implies that being manager is a piece of cake: "When you reach the stage The Byrds have, the only thing a manager does is answer the phone. So, now, [at] $20 a month, I have an answering service and no manager. You save a lot of money that way."

McGuinn neglects to mention Jimmi Seiter's key role, a job that encompasses most of the mundane administrative and practical chores that goes with running a group: booking; travel arrangements; accommodations; preparing recording sessions, press duties, and photo shoots; sorting out song clearances and publishing; organising TV appearances – in addition to handling equipment, lights, and sound.

Larry Spector will net a hefty profit when *Easy Rider* becomes a box office smash. As he withdraws from the music business in the mid 1970s, he will move to Big Sur and invest the cash in a successful health spa, the Ventana Inn.

•

McGuinn has already reactivated the Byrds International Fan Club, now operating out of an address on La Cienega Boulevard and run by Dorothy McGuinn – apparently Roger's mother. A monthly newsletter (*The Byrds Bulletin*) is sent to members, who are urged to build networks, place calls to local radio stations, phone regional newspapers to ask for Byrds coverage, attend concerts (a gig schedule is duly published every month), and take part in competitions. "How would you like to receive a personal phone call from The Byrds?" tempts the January edition, while the May–June bulletin says invitingly: "Be a Byrd Song Writer!" Here, fans can submit a poem, and the winner who is awarded The Best Song Poem will receive a tape of the prize-winning poem sung by The Byrds with specially written

music. No more is heard of that particular contest, after *Rolling Stone* (June 14) gently ridicules the idea and reveals the catch: that any poems entered must be accompanied by three or four newly recruited memberships.

Thursday 6–Saturday 9
Fillmore West, San Francisco, CA

The Byrds are back at Bill Graham's San Francisco venue for the first time since December 1967. In the meantime, Graham has moved from the original Fillmore Auditorium on Geary Street to the Carousel ballroom. He keeps the name, so the Carousel is known as 'Fillmore West' as of summer 1968. Also playing here this weekend are Mike Bloomfield and Pacific Gas & Electric. Bloomfield is at a loose end since the break-up of Electric Flag and has gathered an informal gang with Mark Naftalin and Nick Gravenites and others, just billed as The Jam. The Byrds play a full set on the Thursday but just a half-hour on Friday, while their performance is cut short to a mere 15 minutes on the Saturday.

Columbia Records and producer Elliot Mazer are here to oversee live recordings for a projected Bloomfield album and use the chance to record The Byrds to test equipment and sound balance. (Mazer also taped Bloomfield here last weekend, and it is those recordings that will be released as *Michael Bloomfield Live At Bill Graham's Fillmore West* in October).

The Byrds' tapes will be fished out of the vaults and cleaned up for official release in 2000. *The Byrds Live At The Fillmore February 1969* demonstrates the ability of McGuinn's new crew as a live unit, as they pick and sing their way through 16 tracks. The album covers the group's history from 'Mr. Tambourine Man' through the hits and the classics ('Chimes Of Freedom', 'Turn! Turn! Turn!', 'He Was A Friend Of Mine', 'Eight Miles High', 'So You Want To Be A Rock'n'Roll Star', 'Time Between'), right up to a selection of tracks from the just-released *Dr. Byrds & Mr. Hyde* album ('Bad Night At The Whiskey', 'Drug Store Truck Drivin' Man', 'This Wheel's On Fire', and 'King Apathy III'). The album is sprinkled with a solid dose of country material. There are three songs from *Sweetheart Of The Rodeo* ('You're Still On My Mind', 'Pretty Boy Floyd', with McGuinn on banjo, and 'The Christian Life') plus a trio of country covers: Red Simpson's 'Close Up The Honky Tonks', Buck Owens's 'Buckaroo', and Merle Haggard's 'Sing Me Back Home'. In addition, the group attempts to match its country-folk sound with Bloomfield's scorching Chicago-inspired blues with little success, as York confirms: "The jam with Mike Bloomfield was awkward musically and was never recorded."

Friday 7
ALSO …

The Turtles release 'You Showed Me' as a single in the UK (with a concurrent US release), a tune penned by Gene Clark and McGuinn back when he was Jim in 1964, and one of the songs the pre-historic Byrds rehearsed and recorded at World Pacific under Jim Dickson's tutelage. The Turtles slow the tempo down, add a catchy organ intro riff, and push the single to a US Number Six. ('You Showed Me' will have a life on its own, earning cover versions by The Lightning Seeds and Salt 'n' Peppa in the next millennium.)

Tuesday 11–Saturday 15

A string of dates at the Whisky A Go Go with The Crabs is cancelled; The Byrds are replaced by Black Pearl.

Saturday 15
Norwich University, Northfield, VT

The group plays a week of dates in the Northeast, starting in Vermont today.

Sunday 16
College Theater, Worcester State College, Worcester, MA

A dance to celebrate the end of the college's Winter Carnival. Student paper *WSC Student Voice* (February 21) conducts a quick survey among the audience. Comments range from "Too noisy, unpleasant to the ear, poor audience communication" and "Too loud – not audible," to "A great banjo!", "Great, especially Country-and-Western," and "Good material, good performers. A bit wooden in their gestures, little naturalness."

Thursday 20–Sunday 23
Boston Tea Party, Boston, MA

The Byrds and The Flying Burrito Brothers share the bill for the first of many times. "We work with [The Byrds] pretty often," Chris Hillman explains next year to *Melody Maker* (December 19, 1970). "We play an hour, they play an hour, and then we go back on stage with them and play. The people go crazy – we do a lot of the old songs, like 'Hickory Wind' and 'You Ain't Going Nowhere'. The new Byrds really have their own sound."

The Boston Tea Party is situated on the first floor of a converted Kingdom Hall on Boston's Berkeley Street. It has a capacity of 750–1,000 and has rapidly become one of the most popular rock clubs on the East Coast. The club opts for continuous shows rather than two shows a night, allowing groups to double the length of their usual performances. Club manager Don Law explains in *Rolling Stone* (April 11): "There is no question that in the short run we could be making more money by going to a two-show policy, but we would lose the spirit of the place. A good act needs to have the same audience all night to stretch out, to do things it doesn't normally do. We try to encourage that."

Offered this chance, The Byrds examine the outer limits of their repertoire, air some surprises, and introduce many of the songs they will record for their next album. During the nights in Boston, York sings a couple of songs done by The Band on *Music From Big Pink* (Dylan's 'I Shall Be Released' and the country chestnut 'Long Black Veil'). He also sings Barbara Dane's bluesy 'Way Behind The Sun' and debuts his own 'Fido'. Lee Dorsey's 'Get Out Of My Life, Woman' – recognisable to fans in-the-know as the inspiration for the rhythm and blues instrumental 'Captain Soul' – is given rough treatment, while Gene Parsons steps to the mike to sing in half-patois/half-English 'Take A City Bride', a lovely up-tempo Cajun number he earlier recorded as a single with Floyd Guilbeau. York and McGuinn share vocals on another new-found song, 'Tulsa County Blue', penned by Pam Polland of The Gentle Soul. Parsons has suggested 'Jesus Is Just Alright', a rousing gospel holler from the 1965 debut album *Tellin' It Like It Is* by The Art Reynolds Singers (a Gary Paxton production). Making use of the group's four voices, the gospel song suits The Byrds surprisingly well.

'Mr. Tambourine Man', 'My Back Pages', 'You Ain't Going Nowhere', and even 'This Wheel's On Fire' – all performed at the Tea Party – are so imbued with the electric Byrds spirit that they have become, for many, more Byrds than Bob. Here in Boston, McGuinn also blows the dust off 'It's All Over Now Baby Blue', the Dylan song the group attempted to record back in 1965. There are yet two more Dylan-connected songs debuted during these nights in late February. One is the McGuinn–Dylan collaboration 'Ballad Of Easy Rider'; the other is a brand new Dylan composition called 'Lay Lady Lay' – a song so fresh that Dylan himself recorded it in Nashville barely a week ago, on February 13 and 14. (Dylan and Bob Johnston and a gang of country players record *Nashville Skyline* between February 12 and 21 for rush-release on April 9.) York recalls the circumstances: "We learned 'Lay Lady Lay' from a recording that we heard at Roger's house [right before coming to Boston]. I guess that he got it from Bob Johnston. I believe it was the *Nashville Skyline* version."

For John York, the Boston trip will remain as a special memory for many years. "The Boston Tea Party gig with the Burritos was very special," he says later, "because we jammed together at the end, and it was magical. There was an article in *Rolling Stone* on the centre pages soon after, attesting to the power of the music that night. The Byrds set is a popular bootleg, but I don't know if anyone ever recorded the big jam at the end."

Jon Landau authors a lengthy feature in *Rolling Stone* (April 5), partly writing about *Dr. Byrds & Mr. Hyde*, but mostly devoting space to a glowing review of the Tea Party shows and an appraisal of Roger McGuinn as visionary bandleader. "On Thursday night – opening night – they started off with a medley which grabbed me at once: it included in entirety 'Turn! Turn! Turn!', 'Mr. Tambourine Man', and 'Eight Miles High'. McGuinn refers to the medley as the 'nostalgia trip' and enjoys doing it when people respond, 'even though it sometimes seems like writing the same sentence 1,000 times in a row'. What struck me is how much The Byrds, despite White's country guitar, sound like the original records. That similarity is but another confirmation of the importance McGuinn has always had in shaping the identity of the group. For it seems that he can take any three musicians who want to do it, and teach them to play 'Byrds'."

Landau recounts the story behind the session musicians on 'Mr. Tambourine Man' in 1965, then writes: "[When] it came to recording the [first] album, everyone decided they would rather do it themselves, hence the other tracks on the album were all done by the real Byrds. If one now goes back and compares the apparent 'studio musicians cuts' against the 'Byrd cuts', there are practically no discernible differences in style, which indicates how much direction McGuinn was giving to both studio musicians and Byrds. It also explains why the new Byrds are able to play the old Byrds music with such sensitivity. The Byrds are a style – primarily McGuinn's style – and each successive group of Byrds has mastered it."

"After the opening medley, The Byrds went through 11 additional songs. They don't believe in the current vogue of doing four ten-minute songs as a set. 'Too much chaff,' says McGuinn. He prefers to do his light little three-minute songs and give people as many of them as possible. His performing repertoire includes over 30 songs. … They aren't fighting with you. There is no 'wall of sound' between you and them. They play loud, but a beautiful loud – the kind of loud that draws you towards them. It all seems like an invitation to come along, like they are the original Tambourine Men."

Landau much prefers The Byrds to The Flying Burrito Brothers. "The effect of The Byrds throughout the weekend was, as it should have been, cumulative, and by Saturday even McGuinn seemed surprised at how responsive the audience was. Towards the end of the second set on Saturday night he asked Gram Parsons to sing 'Hickory Wind' with them. Eyes closed, Gram seemed to be entranced and in touch with his music in a way that he is not with the Burritos. That group is a competent, straightforward country band which lacks imagination. Each individual is an excellent musician but their collective sound is seldom satisfying. They generally lack McGuinn's ability to transcend the parochial in country without cheapening the style. But Gram Parsons with The Byrds was beautiful on *Sweetheart Of The Rodeo* and was beautiful that night. Like everyone else on the stage, he was playing for himself.

"On Sunday night the weekend culminated in an evening of perfect style. The Byrds' first set was as perfect as I have ever heard a rock band perform. They began with their lovely version of 'You Ain't Going Nowhere'. At the end McGuinn asked the audience to 'sing along',' and at this point Landau pays McGuinn the ultimate compliment. "[He has] this amazing ability to do something you couldn't accept from anyone else and make you respond; he seemed like the Pete Seeger of 1969 for a moment. From there they went through the material that was by now familiar to me but done with precision and complete effortlessness."

With both bands on stage on Sunday night, it is time for the 'Flying Byrd Brothers'. "The Burritos followed but their set never really ended," reports Landau. "After 40 minutes, Gene Parsons took over for Michael Clarke on drums and everyone else from both groups stayed on board. Everyone took turns singing the things they knew best. McGuinn did 'Pretty Boy Floyd' and 'The Christian Life'. Gram sang 'Hickory Wind' and several others. Hillman offered 'Time Between' … Clarence White and Gene Parsons sang a haunting gospel tune together. John York did a beautiful soulful 'Long Black Veil'. You get the picture, I'm sure. The best of it was 'You Don't Miss Your Water'. On the album, for some reason, McGuinn wound up singing the song even though it was Gram Parsons who had taught it to the group. Now Gram sang lead and the harmony between him and Roger was gorgeous in its flowing tranquillity."

"As is often the case in this kind of situation, things start out at a peak of spontaneity and tend to decline as the group gets farther away from its best material. Gradually the Burritos drifted off the stage, leaving things to The Byrds. And The Byrds quickly shifted the energy level back to where it had been at the start with 'Chimes Of Freedom' and 'So You Want To Be A Rock'n'Roll Star'. When they thought they had finally exhausted the audience they did their best new piece of material, 'Jesus Is Just Alright'. 'Jesus' is a song McGuinn learned from [Gene] Parsons. It will probably be their next single and has the electrifying effect on an audience that Dylan's 'Mr. Tambourine Man' used to have. The song is a spiritual, which is sung as a quartet. Parsons leads off the singing, which is a cappella except for drum accompaniment. He is gradually joined by each of the other Byrds. The instruments come in and the riff continues over a rock background. The arrangement goes back and forth between the two elements, and on Sunday night though it seemed like they did it forever, it still wasn't enough."

"After that they made a fast exit, but obviously people weren't going to let them get away. Back they came. This time McGuinn had just strummed a few chords of 'Goin' Back' … and then through a seemingly endless procession of largely obscure Byrds material [ended] with 'Mr. Spaceman' and then goodbye. The Byrds left most of the people there with a memory of the kind of thing an audience sees all too rarely. For during that weekend The Byrds were renewing their energy, spirit, and music. In a sense they were being reborn. What made it so meaningful was that it was not just The Byrds whose spirit was being renewed but also that of the audience. There were no spectators at this spectacle. Everyone was a midwife. It's so much nicer that way."

Steve Grant covers the event for *The Tech* (February 28), the student paper at Massachusetts Institute of Technology. "The Byrds took a big step Friday night towards dispelling their reputation as an awful live band. While their records still overshadow their performances in concert, their two sets at the Boston Tea Party were, for the most part, enjoyable, with plenty of excitement thrown in – a commodity seldom found on their records. The show wasn't without faults, though. … McGuinn is too infatuated with his new-found C&W style to make oldies like 'Mr. Tambourine Man' and 'Turn! Turn! Turn!' bearable. The third song in the medley, 'Eight Miles High', typified drummer … Parsons' penchant for horsing around with the oldies, but managed to conjure up some excitement, anyway. …

"But when the Byrds jump headlong into their country material, watch out. They did some material from their two latest albums, *Sweetheart Of The Rodeo* and *Dr. Byrds And Mr. Hyde*, and, for the most part, it was mean stuff. McGuinn went through a second childhood, with the swivel hips and graceful twang style, proving once again that no band can create an audience level of rapport higher than their own concern for the material. … They weren't boring, either. During 'Wheel's On Fire' – 'this wheel shall explode', it almost did happen, right there in the ballroom. 'Baby, What You Want Me To Do' rocked like mad – did you know The Byrds could pull off that sort of thing? 'Bad Night At The Whiskey' is the stuff good singles are made of. They weren't a match for The Who or The Yardbirds for sheer energy, but Julie Driscoll's 'Wheels On Fire' doesn't seem as untouchable as it once did. The Band's version can almost be forgotten.

"The Byrds have come a long way since those first albums, partly because they've changed personnel so many times and partly because McGuinn doesn't sit still for long with one style. (Surely the two are related.) The head who got McGuinn into country was one Gram Parsons. … On the bill Friday night, along with The Byrds, [the Burritos] sounded for all the world like The Everly Brothers backed up by The Byrds, what with Hillman and Parsons singing their duets and all those former Byrds doing the instrumentals. They even sang 'Wake Up, Little Susie'. Their ideas of country aren't so compelling as The Byrds', but Parsons is a fine singer whose country soul is as pure as can be.

"It was arranged to have Parsons join his old group for a family reunion on 'Hickory Wind'. For a city boy, he's done a beautiful job on this sentimental number without making it saccharine, the way The Lovin' Spoonful might have. People who have never been to South Carolina must even start to feel lonesome for the pine trees there when Parsons sings this song. … Those who thought that The Byrds couldn't do anything worthwhile after having done 'Eight Miles High' have now been proven wrong. As the least distasteful group around (have they ever done a really bad song or album?), they have given country another big push with the very down-home records they've done lately. You can watch The Beatles to see what will happen next, but The Byrds are at least as much on top of the situation."

The Byrds and The Flying Burrito Brothers go their separate ways after the Tea Party stint, and Chris Hillman and Gram Parsons embark on a strenuous cross-country tour – much of it by train – now that a trip to London is temporarily curtailed.

ALSO …

Bass player Skip Battin is struggling to keep Evergreen Blueshoes running, and he accepts the odd acting role for television to make ends meet. On Sunday at 8:30pm, Battin can be seen in a small role on NBC-TV's sitcom *The Mothers In Law*, playing opposite Deborah Walley – girlfriend of Evergreen Blueshoes drummer Chet McCracken.

Friday 28

Yale Prom, University Commons, Yale University, New Haven, CT

The Byrds are invited to play the annual Yale Prom, where Eddie Wittstein's orchestra provides the necessary pomp and circumstance before the students let loose with McGuinn's gang and then Wilson Pickett. "It was some affair!" writes *Yale Daily News* (March 2). "Everybody there agreed over and over again it was doubtless the best Prom in memory – everybody but Eddie Wittstein. Asked what he thought of The Byrds, old Eddie brusquely replied he 'didn't think much at all'. But other regulars at the dance thought the whole show was just fine. Liquor flowed freely, and Roger (Jim) McGuinn of The Byrds said he hadn't seen such heavy drinking since a Catholic high school Junior Prom in the Salinas Valley."

Also, Hugh Hefner's *Playboy After Dark* is broadcast on Channel 9 in Chicago-land at 12:50am (see September 28, 1968). The show is a tribute to Lenny Bruce, and Hefner's main guest is Lenny's mother, Sally Marr, and his manager, Marvin Worth. The musical guests are Marvin Gaye and The Byrds, while comedians Pete Barbuti and Pat Henry have segments to themselves. The improvisational theatre group The Committee also perform. The Byrds play 'You Ain't Going Nowhere'

and 'This Wheel's On Fire', taped live in front of a small audience. (This edition of *Playboy After Dark* is later screened on KTLA-5 in the Los Angeles area on May 30, and then on New York's WOR-9 on July 5.)

March

Saturday 1
ALSO ...

Nash Stills & Crosby – as their names are sequenced at this point – have been rehearsing in the quaint seaside town of Sag Harbour on Long Island, reports Britain's *New Musical Express* today in an early piece on the ex-Byrd's new venture. The trio have already recorded much of their debut album at Wally Heider's Los Angeles facility with drummer Dallas Taylor.

Sunday 2

Plans for the Broadway staging of Jacques Levy's *Gene Tryp* is made public in *The New York Times* today. The musical is set for the autumn season on Broadway, and the *Times* gives a quick outline of the project: "No, The Byrds will not be in the production, but their singing will. According to plans, the songs

they perform will be played in the theatre on recorded tapes. The logic of recruiting McGuinn lies in the fact that Tryp covers 30 years in an adventurer's life, beginning in the West in the 1850s. The musical deals with the events of the period as experienced by a robust chap named *Gene Tryp*." According to the story, rehearsals will start on July 28.

Wednesday 5

The seventh Byrds album of new material, *Dr. Byrds & Mr. Hyde*, is released in the US. It is a marked shift in the group's career; with only McGuinn left of the original five Byrds. The group is caught between the simple country style of *Sweetheart Of The Rodeo* and the multi-layered dreamscapes that culminated on *The Notorious Byrd Brothers*. The result is a confusing blend that suits the schizophrenic album title.

Some of the blame is quickly laid at the door of producer Bob Johnston. Speaking to John Carpenter of *The Los Angeles Free Press* (March 7) just as the album is released, McGuinn at first sings Johnston's praises. "He comes out into the studio and just vibrates, you know? He's beautiful. Before, about 15 or 20 girls would call or hang out, and behind the glass it was like Disneyland while we were working out there. But Bob is fantastic: comes out there, and you can tell by feel whether things are coming out all right."

By next year, the tone will change drastically. "I hate to lay a dupe, man, but Bob Johnston is an insidious dupe artist. He tells funny stories and then he cons you into his game," McGuinn tells Bud Scoppa. "He can get you because he comes out so strong, country-like. He tells little funny stories and then he cons you into his game, and you don't even know it. But they're great stories. He's almost worth it, just for that."

Gene Parsons and Clarence White agree. Parsons will tell Pete Frame of *Zigzag* (March 1974): "I don't like [the album] at all. Bob Johnston is a nice enough guy, don't get me wrong, and he's produced plenty of good records – but he wasn't a good producer for us. The album seemed to be the result of poor planning and forethought, really – it was just a bunch of tapes thrown together in one package. The sound was bad, the mixing was bad – we weren't too pleased with what he did, frankly."

White says in the same magazine: "It was Bob Johnston's baby; he's produced people like Bob Dylan and Johnny Cash, so we naturally thought that he would be great – but then we realised that those people would have their material so well-prepared that all the producer needed to do was come into the studio, put his feet up on the desk, and just

---

Dr. Byrds & Mr. Hyde

A1 'This Wheel's On Fire' (B. DYLAN/R. DANKO)
A2 'Old Blue' (ARR. & ADAP. R. MCGUINN)
A3 'Your Gentle Way Of Loving Me' (G. PAXTON/F. GUILBEAU)
A4 'Child Of The Universe' (D. GRUSIN/R. MCGUINN)
A5 'Nashville West' (G. PARSONS/C. WHITE)
B1 'Drug Store Truck Drivin' Man' (R. MCGUINN/G. PARSONS)
B2 'King Apathy III' (R. MCGUINN)
B3 'Candy' (R. MCGUINN/J. YORK)
B4 'Bad Night At The Whiskey' (R. MCGUINN/J. RICHARDS)
B5 'Medley: My Back Pages/B.J. Blues/Baby What You Want Me To Do'
      (B. DYLAN/R. MCGUINN/J. YORK/GENE PARSONS/C. WHITE/J. REED)

US release March 5 1969 (Mono LP CL 9755/Stereo LP CS 9755)
UK release April 25 1969 (Mono CBS 63545/Stereo CBS S 63545)
Chart high US number 153; UK number 15
Read more ... entries for October 7, 8, 14, 15, 16, 21, December 4 1968

Bonus CD tracks: 'Stanley's Song' (R. McGuinn/Hippard), 'Lay Lady Lay' [Alternate Version] (B. Dylan), 'This Wheel's On Fire' [Version One] (B. Dylan/R. Danko), 'Medley: My Back Pages/B.J. Blues/Baby What You Want Me To Do' [Alternate Version — Take 1] (B. Dylan/R. McGuinn/J. York/Gene Parsons/J. Reed), 'Nashville West' [Alternate Version — Nashville Recording] (Gene Parsons/C. White)

"[It] is smooth and strong like a blended whiskey. Part is kin to Sweetheart Of The Rodeo, *part the acid offspring of* Notorious Byrd Brothers. *The country tunes are tasteful sugar pops: standard country arrangements with rock overdubs for energy."* VILLAGE VOICE, MARCH 6, 1969

---

listen. So the producer's role in those sorts of cases would be reduced to making sure that there was stuff to get, or whatever, making sure the engineer has the sound right, and generally making sure that everything runs smoothly. With a group, especially one that's never recorded together before, you need someone to mediate, throw in suggestions and so on … but Bob Johnston just made sure the tape was rolling, and that was it."

The album jacket also lacks the care that went into the group's previous classics. To *Zigzag* the group is "looking like fools," to which McGuinn attempts a response. "Well, yes … we came down from outer space and became cowboys. It was partly whimsical and partly the idea that extra-terrestrials are walking among us – and might just be cowboys." Sales are pitiful, and the album just manages to make Number 153 in the *Billboard* charts.

Despite this, the record is met with generally good reviews. Jon Landau writes in *Rolling Stone* (April 5): "Before seeing the group live, I played this album several times and loved it without qualification. The various flaws became evident only after seeing the group perform and hearing how much better they do everything live. After digging six sets of them in one weekend, the album becomes a mere 'souvenir of a concert,' as McGuinn himself puts it. The Byrds are that good live."

Producer Bob Johnston is to blame, according to Landau. "[Whereas] Johnston's production on the country cuts is perfect, the sound of the rock cuts is inadequate. The instrumental tracks are too fragmented; the bass sticks out too much, the drums don't cut across the way they do live, and the rhythm is not consistent enough. The amazing power of The Byrds' vocals are reduced to the status of vocal ornaments. Also, on record, Clarence White is a somewhat hit or miss lead. He is always first rate on the country cuts but lacks consistency on rock tunes. In particular the album track of 'Wheels On Fire' suffers as a result."

"Still the captain of The Byrds, Roger McGuinn has gathered a new group of musicians under his wing," writes Johanna Schrier in the *Village Voice* (March 6). "[It] is smooth and strong like a blended whiskey. Part is kin to *Sweetheart Of The Rodeo*, part the mid [*Turn*]ing of *Notorious Byrd Brothers*. The country tunes are tasteful sugar pops: standard country arrangements with rock overdubs for energy. Especially imbued with that liquid-hoke that makes you want to laugh and cry at the same time are 'Your Gentle Way Of Loving Me' and 'Drug Store Truck Drivin' Man', a mocking lament on the Ku Klux Klan country DJ. There is also the usual

quota of space songs (one from the movie, *Candy*), UFO noises, and other electronic apparitions. … In content, *Dr. Byrds* sorely misses its moulded members. There aren't any songs with the grow-along-with-me magic that moved you on every other Byrds album. I read a lengthy review with McGuinn recently in which the entire conversation centred on machines and his mechanical toys: a robot you command with your voice, new ways to hook up special speakers, nuts and bolts. There is also a preoccupation with gadgetry and gimmicks on this new album. I can't help thinking that if Roger McGuinn got along better with people, he'd have a better band."

The Oakland Tribune (April 6): "The Byrds, after almost disappearing from recognition, have come back with a pretty good album. The four men from Los Angeles have a good arrangement of Dylan's 'This Wheel's On Fire' and 'My Back Pages'. As with their last album, [*Sweetheart*] *Of The Rodeo*, this disc has a number of songs about some type of western life."

Friday 7

The 'Bad Night At The Whiskey' / 'Drug Store Truck Drivin' Man' single is released in the UK.

James Hamilton, who every week reviews records by American artists in *Record Mirror*, writes: "Lyrics seem to be about an encounter with a Black Militant and are interspersed with and backed by beautifully mellow noises. Bitingly accurate words about a Southern bigot on the pure C&W flip. Listen to both." (Hamilton awards the single five out of five stars.) The 45 does not enter the British charts.

Sunday 9

Estadio de la Ciudad de los Deportes, Mexico City, Mexico

The group has migrated to exotic locations before (South Africa, Rhodesia [Zimbabwe], Puerto Rico), but this trip to Mexico threatens to end in disaster.

Last year's Olympic Games in Mexico City was designed to be a highpoint for the country, but the nation was troubled with political unrest in the months leading up to the 1968 Summer Games in October. Mirroring the student riots that took place across the US and in Europe that year, radicals seized the moment and put forward a list of demands as the Games led to increasing international attention. Literally a week before the Games was to open, police and military forces shot at a crowd of demonstrators in Tlatelolco (a section of Mexico City), killing and wounding many. Since then, the political situation in the country has been tense, and the government has imposed resolutions and laws to

approve use of force to quell further student demonstrations.

Today's big gathering is to represent a new start for youth culture. The show is held in a large football stadium and promoted by Los Hermanos Castro (the Castro brothers), a vocal group that has its own TV show in Mexico and has made inroads on the Las Vegas circuit. Initially, renowned jazz drummer Leo Acosta is on the bill, but the Hermanos decide to give the programme a rock'n'roll twist and hire Los Tijuana Five instead, a popular Mexican group who have recorded an album of Spanish-language versions of American and British hits such as 'California Dreamin'. Gary Puckett & The Union Gap are to headline together with The Byrds.

Eric Zolov's book *Refried Elvis: The Rise Of The Mexican Counterculture* will draw on contemporary sources and give a detailed account of the dramatic day. "The first real opportunity for the classes to come together around rock [after the Tlatelolco massacre was this] stadium concert … . It was the first truly inter-class, massive rock event in Mexico. The permit, in fact, had been in doubt until the last moment. … Profits were maximised by carving out differently priced sections from the enormous stadium. With the upper-tier priced at a mere 5 pesos (less than 50 cents), the middle-tier priced at 10 pesos (around 75 cents), and lawn chairs at 20 pesos (less than $2), the notion was to attract as broad an audience as possible. But not only was little effort made to maintain a separation between the differently ticketed sections, [also] no one was assigned to police the floor of the stadium. When the people saw that no one was watching over them, they pushed forward and invaded the lawn area without a second thought."

As a consequence, chaos reigns on the midfield and Gary Puckett & The Union Gap decides to withdraw from the concert, leaving the Castro brothers to plead for order while local Mexican groups fill time, until The Byrds – delayed at the airport – belatedly arrive. "When The Byrds finally took the stage and the first chords of 'Turn! Turn! Turn!' drifted over the inadequate sound system, sheer mayhem erupted, as the pent-up energies of waiting provoked a mad rush forward, dissolving any pretext of which seat belonged to whom." Zolov's book then quotes *El Universal* journalist Carlos Monsiváis Aceves for a description of the events. "And the seats go flying and the people scatter and the masses are the same on all sides, and the pitched battle begins, the riot, the general breakdown, the end. Seen from the summit of the stadium, the spectacle is at once formidable and convulsive."

Zolov reports: "For state authorities, the

207

concert clearly pointed to the limitations of control over mass popular culture. (The Castro Brothers were subsequently fined 50,000 Pesos [$4,000] for their negligence in organising the event.) Rock music had ceased to be the exclusive domain of the middle and upper classes. In the hands of the poor, it was even less containable."

Federico Rubli, a 15-year-old music fan, is in the middle of the field. "At the time nobody had any experience organising rock events," he recalls later, "so the concert was poorly organised. On the lawn they'd put wooden chairs, which were the best seats and the most expensive ones. So a fight started between the people sitting far away in the not-so-good seats with the 'privileged' ones who were on the lawn. The Castro brothers performed and so did Los Tijuana Five before The Byrds took the stage. At that time the fight was in full swing, and I remember Roger McGuinn playing his guitar very nervously. I remember very well the front page of the next day's *Excelsior* newspaper, showing a photo of Roger playing his guitar and close to him flying through the air the wooden leg of a chair. Anyway, they abruptly finished playing and the riot continued, and the police came in and we started to run like hell. There were 100 injured people. I think the total attendance must have been between 6,000 and 8,000 at most [official records suggest 42,000]; not too huge a crowd, but significant at the time as being one of the first massive rock events in Mexico."

In the melee more than 100 people are injured and thousands of chairs are smashed. *Zigzag* (March 1974) will quote a report from the event that says the hero of the day is hired road manager Frankie Blanco, who protects the group's equipment. "The concert in Mexico City turned into a riot," John York will remember. "It was like being in a very dangerous movie! We were trapped in Mexico for a week because almost everyone's passports had been stolen in the chaos."

→ Monday 10–Friday 14
☐ **MEXICAN TV** Unknown location, Mexico City, Mexico. [Possibly] Telesistema Mexicano [Unknown TV show]

Trapped in Mexico before new passports are produced, The Byrds make a rare TV appearance, according to John York's later recollection. "We performed on the Castro Brothers TV show. I think we did two songs, 'You Ain't Going Nowhere' and something else." No other details of the show will survive, but it may have called *La Carabina de Ambrosio*, on which the Castro Brothers appeared.

Monday 17
Melodyland Theatre, Anaheim, CA

Back in California again, The Byrds play a show with The Steve Miller Band.

Saturday 22
A news item in *Cash Box* gives an update on *Gene Tryp*.

The score is completed and financial backing to the tune of one million dollars is secured. "The show's estimated production cost makes it the first mainstream effort to be announced at such a cost initially, though several plays have reached that cost during their pre-run period. ... The musical direction of the work is along the lines of McGuinn's recent albums *Sweetheart Of The Rodeo*, *The Notorious Byrd Brothers*, and *Dr Byrds & Mr Hyde*. Tryp is to employ modern electronic equipment of recordings in the theatre for the first time, and will also make use of cinematic devices including 70mm Todd AO projection for environmental touches."

Thursday 27
◁)) **RECORDING** Columbia Recording Studios, Sunset and El Centro, Hollywood, CA. Producer Bob Johnston and unknown engineer.

The group enters the studio with Bob Johnston with the express purpose of recording a new single. Initially, they hope to record Art Reynolds's infectious 'Jesus Is Just Alright', a song that has already proved a winner at concerts, but Johnston overrules McGuinn and the others and suggests Bob Dylan's 'Lay Lady Lay' instead – another number the group has been performing live for a month. A highly commercial number, it is still an odd choice. Johnston, in his capacity as Dylan's producer, knows well that the song will be one of the tracks sure to garner the most airplay on

Dylan's forthcoming *Nashville Skyline* (set for release in two weeks' time); indeed, Columbia will release the song as a Dylan single in July. The Byrds tailor their arrangement after Dylan's Nashville version, although Johnston will sweeten the track with a female choir on April 18. (The unadorned version will later be heard on the extended CD version of *Dr. Byrds & Mr. Hyde*.)

Johnston has just been in England to produce a session for singer Georgie Fame, who combines the Dylan tracks 'Down Along The Cove' and 'I'll Be Your Baby Tonight' for a US single. Talking to *New Musical Express* (March 29) and *Melody Maker* (April 5), Johnston speaks of the virtues of the Nashville musicians; about recording Johnny Cash and Bob Dylan; and spins a record he has produced by Burl Ives. But The Byrds do not come up.

Next year, when Johnston has put a little distance between the Byrds sessions and his role in them, he will comment to Lon Goddard of *Record Mirror* (November 7, 1970): "I like Roger McGuinn, but making that Byrds album was a hassle. They started experimenting with a Moog [synthesizer] and I didn't see anything in that. I like guitars; they play a real part in bringing out the character of a performer, but a Moog? If you get it to play drums behind, it isn't real. What is there left if it plays for you?" He repeats the point to *Melody Maker* the same week, the paper reporting that the producer "dislikes the current emphasis on electronic aids in music, like the Moog and the VCS3 [portable synthesizer]. That explains why he no longer works with The Byrds." Johnston says tells Michael Watts: "I don't believe the mechanical thing can take the place of emotion. The instrument has to play the greatest part."

April

Thursday 3
Wharton Field House, Moline, IL

The Byrds swing out on the road for two extended weekends; the first in Illinois and Wisconsin, the second in Kentucky, Ohio, and Kansas.

Friday 4
Blue Village, Westmont, IL

Illinois group The Cryan' Shames is the house band at the Blue Village, a teen dive in Westmont less than 20 miles from Chicago.

Saturday 5
The Cellar, Arlington Heights, IL

The group appears with The Joe Kelley Blues Band.

Sunday 6
Premontre High School, Green Bay, WI

Monday 7
Oshkosh High School, Oshkosh, WI

Thursday 17
Henderson Community College, Henderson, KY

Friday 18
Wilson Auditorium, University of Cincinnati, Cincinnati, OH

◁ɨ) **RECORDING** [Presumably] Columbia Studio A, 34 Music Square East, Music Row, Nashville, TN. Producer Bob Johnston and unknown engineer

While The Byrds are away on the road in the Midwest, Bob Johnston takes the liberty to overdub a gospel choir on the 'Lay Lady Lay' track (see March 27). McGuinn and the other Byrds will be incensed by Johnston's violation, but there is some logic to the producer's decision. The undecorated version is close to a carbon copy of Dylan's original, and by adding the female voices, Johnston could have given the song a more personal imprint. As it stands, the choir is mixed upfront and the overall sound balance is uneven.

In an interview with Pete Frame next summer (*Zigzag No 14, August 1970*), Gene Parsons will remain annoyed. "Bob Johnston who produced it, ruined it. We'd originally recorded it with our harmonies and things and it was pretty good, but while we were on tour he took the tape to Nashville and overdubbed the ladies' voices and remixed the whole thing. It turned out to be piece of plastic crap – so it wasn't us."

Saturday 19
Gymnasium, Shawnee Mission South High School, Overland Park, KS

Concert by The Byrds with The Ides Of March. Bob Butler reviews it in *Reconstruction* (May 6), an underground newspaper located in nearby Topeka. "Ides Of March leave, Byrds come on. McGuinn looking great: leather pants, purple turtleneck, cowboy boots, thick bubble sunglasses – grew his moustache again. Start out with Dylan's 'You Ain't Going Nowhere'. Beautiful. A medley of old songs: 'Turn! Turn! Turn!', 'Eight Miles High'. Swing into 'Old Blue'. Older kids singing along. High schoolers want to know 'what's with all this country garbage?' Yell at them to shut up.

"The Byrds are halfway through their second set when the house lights go on. McGuinn is very pissed. 'Hey, who turned on the lights? Turn off the lights.' Lights still on. 'Hey, they hurt my eyes.' He looks offstage where somebody is motioning to him. 'You come out here and tell that to them.' He points at the audience. Principal of school walks onstage to vigorous booing. Black suit and tie, crew-cut. 'I'm sure we all want to thank the entertainment committee for the fine job they've done in bringing The Byrds here tonight …' – lots of booing, some kid chanting 'Bullshit bullsht bullshit bullshit' – 'but it is now 11:45pm and the concert must end in accordance with Shawnee Mission District school policy.' McGuinn looks very disgusted and starts playing one final number. 'This one's for you, Ralph.'"

Bob Butler talks to the band members in the break. Asking if Gene is related to Gram, the drummer tells him deadpan: "Yeah, man, didn't you know? All the Parsons crossed the Cumberland Gap with Daniel Boone. All at the same time. They're all related." Butler switches his attention to John York, and asks if the bass player is insecure with The Byrds always altering the personnel. "No, man, it's like a hospital, they keep changing doctors but they keep on healing."

Finally, he questions McGuinn on his interest in country & western. "Man, all those noisy groups cancelled each other out with feedback. People wanted something simple. C&W is simple. I wish things would go back to folk music."

Wednesday 23
ALSO …

Ash Grove, the folk and jazz club on Hollywood's Melrose Avenue, burns down in a bad fire during the morning hours. The club was resident home for Roger McGuinn when he first came out to Los Angeles in 1960, and Clarence White's Kentucky Colonels have played here countless times.

Friday 25

Dr. Byrds & Mr. Hyde is released in the UK and is given ample coverage in the music weeklies. Nick Logan of *New Musical Express* (May 3) writes: "Just who The Byrds are at any one time is one of the great mysteries of pop. … Nevertheless, the release of a new Byrds album ranks among the major events in a pop year and this LP shouldn't be missed. This is The Byrds pushing further into country music with a Band-like feel (the only way to feel nowadays). Might be the fact that it is produced by Bob Johnston, but Dylan, The Band, and The Byrds all seem to be moving in the same direction. There's nothing much to strain the mind on this: just easy relaxing tunes, backed by piercing country guitars and that wonderful feel. … 'This Wheel's On Fire' is tackled here and The Byrds' effective version falls between The Band and Julie Driscoll."

Record Mirror (May 3) gives the album four out of five stars. "Each Byrds LP is an event in progressive pop, or rock if you like. Their British devotees will dig this more than *Sweetheart* [but] less than *Brothers* or *Yesterday*. Their guitar work is heavier than usual on the rock sides: 'This Wheel's On Fire' would be great for the thin vocal. 'Old Blue' is beautiful mock country, while 'Drug Store Truck Drivin' Man', the story of an anti-hip DJ, is the ultimate in exaggerated cowboy music. As usual, they have a lot going on everywhere to please their travelling fans, yet it is not as together musically as *Byrd Bros*. Remnants of Gram Parsons and Chris Hillman linger on, but the heady weirdness of David Crosby's influence has almost completely vanished. Their closely-woven, softly insinuating harmonies have been replaced by outrageous country vocals, but the LP is harder and better, although not as original as *Sweetheart*. Initially, addicts may be disappointed, but after a few plays, faith in The Byrds (or Roger) will return."

Disc (May 10) has introduced a star system too for quick evaluation and rates the album four out of five stars. "The Byrds are ridiculous. They just keep on getting better but remain, always, instantly recognisable. [This is] their best album since perhaps *Younger Than Yesterday*, perfectly illustrating the two completely disparate sides of the group: far-out electronic rock and hick, twangy country. The Byrds – or at any rate Roger McGuinn, the only member of the original group left – realise this too: on the sleeve, the 'Dr Byrds' bit is in computer script, while 'My Hyde' looks as though it's been taken off a 'this man is wanted for murder and train robbery in the city of Deadwood Gulch' notice. Both their sorts of music are excellent, and work equally well, even when the two are thrown together in one song, as in 'Child Of The Universe'. Also included is the nice theme song from 'Candy' plus a beautiful medley of old hits including 'My Back Pages' and a super rocking country 'Drug Store Truck Driving Man'. An unmissable LP." (*Disc* runs a parallel review of *Nashville Skyline*, which is voted 'LP Of The Month'.) *Beat Instrumental* (July 1969) feels the juxtaposing of country material and old-style Byrds is awkward. "While it's good to have the two kinds of Byrds on one LP, the album does clash within itself at times because of this. Making it a schizoid but excellent album."

Lastly, *Melody Maker* (May 10) says: "Yes, this is a good one. The Byrds are contrasting styles with a bit of Dylan, a lot of countrified sounds and some magnificent playing. The bassline all the way through is super. It's to the credit of the group that they can switch styles and sound so musical in each [style]. Their voices are always pleasant and their harmonies excellent. The only fault with the album is the lack of notes. An explanation of the group's thinking on the album would have added immensely to the enjoyment of it." The album makes an unexpected Number 15 in the UK charts, a healthy showing after the dismal failure of last year's *Sweetheart Of The Rodeo* there.

May

Friday 2

Release date for 16th Byrds single in the US, coupling the recently recorded 'Lay Lady Lay' with 'Old Blue' from *Dr. Byrds & Mr. Hyde*. Certainly spurred on by Dylan's *Nashville Skyline*, the single creeps to Number 132 on the *Billboard* charts before falling off. Any chance of a chart comeback for The Byrds is thwarted by Columbia's decision to release

'Lay Lady Lay'

A 'Lay Lady Lay' (B. DYLAN)
B 'Old Blue' (TRADITIONAL, ARR. R. MCGUINN)

US release May 2 1969 (Columbia 44868)
UK release June 6 1969 (CBS 4284)
Chart high US number 132; UK none
Read more ... entries for October 7 1968, March 27 and April 18 1970

Dylan's original as a single in July, which makes Top Ten in the US and then Top Five in the UK, becoming one of Bob's biggest single hits ever.

ALSO ...

The 22nd Festival de Cannes, the annual two-week film festival held in the South Of France, opens today. *Easy Rider* is unveiled May 8. According to a United Press newsflash, the film is given rapturous ovations and Peter Fonda is quoted at the press reception as saying: "The wine and grass in the film were real, but not the cocaine nor the LSD." The film earns Dennis Hopper the prize as Best New Director.

Easy Rider becomes a big US box office hit after the its premiere in New York City on July 14. The accompanying soundtrack album sells strongly and will peak at *Billboard* Number 6 during September. It features Steppenwolf's 'Born To Be Wild' and 'The Pusher' – both instant biker anthems – and songs by The Holy Modal Rounders, The Fraternity Of Man, Jimi Hendrix Experience ('If Six Was Nine'), and The Electric Prunes, while a near-anonymous bunch called Smith covers 'The Weight' as The Band will not allow their version on the album, even if it is in the film.

'Wasn't Born To Follow' from *The Notorious Byrd Brothers* is The Byrds' contribution, and McGuinn has the honour of performing the title song 'Ballad Of Easy Rider' plus the cover of Dylan's 'It's Alright, Ma (I'm Only Bleeding)'. Both are sung with the accompaniment of just 12-string acoustic guitar and Gene Parsons' harmonica.

Hopper and Fonda's flamboyant characters in *Easy Rider* have real-life alter egos, as McGuinn will explain to Jud Cost in 2000. "I told Peter, 'Boy, I sure would have liked to have actually been in the movie.' And he said, 'You were.' Peter and Dennis Hopper were modelling their characters after David Crosby and me. Dennis got David down – the paranoid delusions – and Peter was like, 'I trust it'll work out all right. It'll be cool, man.' That's what he meant that I was in it. He was using me. It was a nice honour, yeah. I was really proud to have my music in it and be in it."

Speaking to Ben Fong-Torres in *Rolling Stone* (July 23, 1970) while the movie is still a hit in movie theatres, David Crosby says: "Dennis and Peter used to watch us a lot. Peter's been a good friend for years, and Dennis, too, for that matter, although I don't know him as well as I know Peter. I wouldn't say that Dennis had me down exactly. He did grow a pretty good moustache, I'll say that for him. And, as a matter of fact, although it's a really technical detail, he got the knife right, too. Pete's a sailor, too. I really dig Den-

A man went looking for America. And couldn't find it anywhere...

Cannes Film Festival WINNER 'Best Film By a New Director'

PANDO COMPANY in association with RAYBERT PRODUCTIONS presents **easy rider** starring PETER FONDA · DENNIS HOPPER · JACK NICHOLSON
Written by PETER FONDA DENNIS HOPPER TERRY SOUTHERN Directed by DENNIS HOPPER Produced by PETER FONDA Associate Producer WILLIAM HAYWARD Executive Producer BERT SCHNEIDER · COLOR Released by COLUMBIA PICTURES

nis. He's outrageous." Fong-Torres wonders if the relationship between Fonda and Hopper in the movie is comparable to that between Crosby and McGuinn. "It was frequently that. Brash extrovert that I am. Energy source. And McGuinn a laidback, highly complex, good multi-evaluating, highly trained brain."

Years later, Crosby will tell Sylvie Simmons in *Mojo* (November 2003): "Peter was just Peter, but Dennis was me, right down to the fringed jacket and the pocket-knife. He just saw that as a good image – kinda loose and crazy, laughing, fierce at times. Peter and I had been close friends since back in The Byrds – he was a big Byrds fan. They wanted [Crosby Stills & Nash] to do the music for *Easy Rider* but we were a third of the way into making the first CSN album, and we could do one or the other. Very tough – because we wanted to do it. That was an amazing movie. And the music! The way they originally had it was at the end where the guy with the shotgun drives by and *BLAM!* they blow Dennis off the bike and the bike blows up; as the shot starts to pull back there's Dylan's scratchy voice going, 'And a question in your nerves is lit and there is no answer that's fit,' and it was the most perfect juxtaposition of music and film that I've ever heard or seen in my life. It was better than the score to *Out Of Africa!* And Dylan didn't let them use it! Bob is not that smart about movies."

Saturday 3

Bowman Gymnasium, DePauw University, Greencastle, IN
The Byrds play a concert to climax the University's weeklong 'Little 500' student happening.

Meanwhile in the UK, today's *Melody Maker* reveals plans for a British visit by The Byrds in August. London's Bryan Morrison Agency has taken over UK representation of the group from NEMS Enterprises, and Steve O'Rourke says to the paper that he hopes to bring over The Byrds, Captain Beefheart, and Arthur Lee's Love at the end of the summer. In exchange for the American visitors, Tyrannosaurus Rex, Pink Floyd, Aynsley Dunbar's Retaliation, and The Pretty Things all hope to tour the US. In the end, the proposed Byrds visit does not come off.

→ Monday 5–Wednesday 7

McGuinn and The Byrds are in New York City to discuss the *Gene Tryp* production before they play some concerts in the area over the weekend.

Associated Press staff journalist Mary Campbell interviews McGuinn – probably this week – to promote 'Lay Lady Lay' and the new album and to update readers on *Gene Tryp*. He tells her: "Country albums don't sell so well. A company executive told me it's not the right direction to go in. So we tapered off country when we heard that. *Dr. Byrds & Mr. Hyde* is only partly country-oriented. We'd have done it anyway, because country was a one-time experiment." McGuinn confides to Campbell that if 'Lay Lady Lay' is a success he will consider making the next Byrds album all Dylan songs.

McGuinn's favourite subject, however, is Robert Moog's invention. "It's not bigger than an upright piano," he enthuses. "But it's a very complicated instrument, hard to get into. There are hundreds of patch-cord places on it and dials and knobs. It's like an airplane cockpit or a switchboard. I'm hoping my aptitude will give me an edge with it; my hobby is playing with electronic stuff. It's been used on classical but nobody has done it on pop yet. Mick Jagger and John Lennon have them. It's a race against time and I'd like to get there first."

The classical recording McGuinn refers to is Walter [Wendy] Carlos's revolutionary *Switched-On Bach* album that Columbia released at the very end of 1968. Demonstrating the scope of the synthesizer's musical possibilities, Carlos's album has, astonishingly, made the *Billboard* Top Ten pop charts. As McGuinn says, Jagger and The Beatles have purchased synthesizers too. Jagger got his in the spring of 1968 to compose film music but never had the diligence to work out the instrument's finer mechanics. The Byrds used synthesizers as early as November 1967 (for the *Notorious Byrd Brothers* sessions) but, as with their groundbreaking introduction to pop recording of a pedal steel guitar, their innovative use of synthesizers will be often overlooked in the years to come. McGuinn is correct when he says that nobody has made a pop record yet using synthesizers exclusively, and his aim still is to complete the electronic companion to *Sweetheart Of The Rodeo* at some point.

If there is a race, as McGuinn suggests, it is already won by George Harrison, whose *Electronic Sound* is released this month. The album is recorded entirely with a Moog synthesizer. Speaking to Vincent Flanders in 1970, McGuinn says: "I like George Harrison personally … but he released an album [of electronic music], he just got his Moog and he put it all down on tape and released it, right? Which I could have done too, but I'm not George Harrison. Like what he did with it, if I'm allowed to be a critic for a minute as a Moog synthesizer musician, was something you do the first day you get it home and you try it out, if you put the tape recorder on and let it roll. He went into a bunch of white noise riffs, a bunch of oscillator warble riffs – things that are very simple, man, and really just show off the 'novelty gadget' style. It wasn't musical."

Thursday 8
Gymnasium, State University of New York (SUNY), Stony Brook, NY

The Byrds play the Graduation Dance from 9:00pm onwards. "McGuinn has truly proven that Byrds may come and Byrds may go, but so long as he's around, The Byrds will always sound the same," says Hank Teich in *The Statesman* (May 9). "The members of the group have changed so often that it's hard to keep up with the new names. … The Byrds' new guitar man is excellent. Clarence White tunes his guitar like an old pedal steel and plays it like a regular guitar. A pedal guitar looks sort of like an organ – has two necks parallel with the ground and you play these pedals on the floor. Anyway, White's riffs are all friendly and clean, and he plays a really beautiful lead on all of the new country numbers.

"But McGuinn really takes the cake. McGuinn is The Byrds. His vocals are as sparkling and pure as ever. This may be because he appears to be out of the drug thing, which improves his performances immensely. No more little red hippie glasses; and, like The Band, 'Hey – you can see his ears now!' No longer does he take the lead [guitar] – except on the older stuff (like 'Mr. Tambourine Man'). He prefers to step aside and rhythm for White. And you know, the old stuff is almost a drag compared to that easy country sound, and I think that most of the happy gentle folk in the audience would have agreed."

Friday 9
Rhode Island University, North Kingston, RI

The Byrds and The Chambers Brothers perform as part of the University's first pop festival. A two-day affair, tomorrow features The Foundations and The Paul Reeves Revue.

Saturday 10
Trinity College, Hartford, CT

Monday 12

🎧 **SESSION** Western Recorders, Los Angeles, CA. Clarence White is one of a huge cast of musicians called in to record two backing tracks for The Monkees. White is probably there thanks to producer Chip Douglas. Andrew Sandoval's later exhaustive Monkees diary will report on the second song taped, 'Steam Engine'. "Despite the soul flavour of this driving composition, it in fact features some rather unusual non-R&B musical elements in the form of Byrds guitarist Clarence White's patented string-bender electric guitar and Red Rhodes's masterful pedal-steel playing, incorporating a fuzz effect on the breaks and solo section." Neither this song nor the other, 'Today', is released by The Monkees at this time.

→ Thursday 15

🎧 **SESSION** Unknown recording studio, Los Angeles, CA. Producer Andy Wickham.

Clarence White and Gene Parsons back The Everly Brothers for a Warner Brothers single, 'I'm On My Way Home Again' (plus its B-side 'The Cuckoo Bird). The single is released next year and gets a rave review in *Rolling Stone* (February 7, 1970). "Country music, sweet and pure as the early morning rain. Oh, mama, what a great record! … The back up is tremendous. Everybody on the session is on, together, and tight and sure. I would have bet money that there was a pedal steel on the session, but it's just old Clarence White working out on a standard electric guitar. Gene Parsons double-tracks drums and banjo, and it's a pure, fucking gas! The Everly Brothers can sing, really sing. Their close harmonies are a stone groove, especially on the 'whoo whooo's'. In fact, the whole record is a stone groove – a joyous shout to the universe. If you love country music, it's definitely worth the trouble to go out and hunt around until you find a copy."

Friday 16–Saturday 17
The Rose Palace, Pasadena, CA

Scenic Sound presents The Byrds, bluesman Albert King, and A.B. Skhy, with a lightshow by Thomas Edison. "The Byrds proved magnificent," says John Mendelsohn in *The Los*

Angeles Times (May 20). "Roger McGuinn, the last of the original Byrds, is the group's director and on-stage leader. His 12-string guitar work and mincing vocals are mainly responsible for the new Byrds ability to sound satisfying on medleys of old Byrds' hits. Bassist John York helps with soaring high harmonies reminiscent of David Crosby; Clarence White gives the group a subtle country flavour with his lead and vocal-accompanying guitar work. Ecstatically received by the audience, The Byrds' set included several Dylan tunes."

Michael Ross writes in *The Los Angeles Herald-Examiner* (May 20): "There is a misconception in pop circles that The Byrds are a good studio band but cannot play live. Perhaps this was once so. But Saturday, the band showed that the joyful spirit of the local group is undiminished. This is a tribute to Roger McGuinn, the only original Byrd left. ... Saturday, The Byrds were relaxed and flowing as they played a completely satisfying 45-minute set. Starting with Dylan's 'You Ain't Going Nowhere', blending into a medley of Byrds hits, touching both space and country and western music, the group completed the circle with a new Dylan song, 'Lay Lady Lay'. Rock shall never see their like again because the world of youthful enthusiasm they celebrated has died in pop, except in their own songs."

Ross's view is shared by Bob Barnett of *The Valley State Daily Sundial* (May 22). "The Byrds, once an assortment of egos in the way of egos, have taken for years to achieve the greatness that all their albums promised. But they finally put it all together at last weekend's Rose Palace concerts. Medleys of old hits, lots of country, and a great live version of 'My Back Pages' all provided beautiful easy listening. But their highlight was Roger McGuinn's arrangement of Dylan's 'Lay Lady Lay' off the new *Nashville Skyline* LP. McGuinn translates Dylan better than anyone in pop, putting Joan Baez's unchanging moods to shame."

"The gig at the Rose Palace in Pasadena is significant to me," John York will later recall, "because I remember that Chris Hillman was there in the audience, and I've always regretted that I did not ask him if he wanted to get up and play with the band."

ALSO ...

In Saturday's *Disc*, Judy Sims innocently reported from an accidental meeting In Los Angeles. "While walking down Sunset Boulevard the other day I spied a familiar lean figure heading into Will Wright's Ice Cream Parlour; it was none other than Neil Young, former Buffalo Springfield, and with him was none other than Steve Stills, also former Buffalo and now one-third of Crosby-Stills-Nash. We blithered happily while licking ice cream

cones, and I pumped some information. Neil will have a second album out soon backed by the same musicians who appeared with him at the Whisky [The Rockets, soon to be Crazy Horse], and Steve's group is still looking for a bass player. I trust they will find one soon, because they're booked for several concerts this summer across the country – at no less than £5,000 [about $12,000] per concert, which is somewhat incredible for a group that has never performed together."

Wednesday 21

Bob Dylan's contribution to 'Ballad Of Easy Rider' is supposed to be a secret, but the issue of *Rolling Stone* at the newsstands today (although dated June 14) can reveal that he is the wordsmith while McGuinn is the composer.

There is an epilogue, as McGuinn will recall to Jud Cost in 2000. "About a month later, when the soundtrack album was out and the credit was Bob Dylan and Roger McGuinn, I get a call from Dylan at three o'clock in the morning going, 'What is this? I don't want this credit. Take it off. I don't need the money.' He didn't want it. So I said OK. The thing generated half a million. I didn't get the money because Columbia did some clever accounting. They figured I was one-fifth of The Byrds, so they gave me a hundred thousand and they kept the other four."

Saturday 24

Hilton Washington Hotel, Washington, DC

Sunday 25

North Amherst Recreation Center, Buffalo, NY

A show promoted by radio station WKBW.

→ Monday 26

Ed Pearl, owner of the Ash Grove, has resolved to rebuild his club after it burned down on April 23. Many past performers have rallied round to offer their services for several benefit concerts, and a press conference is held today in the ash and rubble of the burned-out ruins. Roger McGuinn, blues guitarist Albert Collins, bass player Stuart A. Brotman of Kaleidoscope, and Canned Heat members Henry Vestine, Al Wilson, and Bob Hite all lend lustre to the occasion. "This is the first place I ever played as a professional entertainer back in 1960," McGuinn says in The *Los Angeles Times* (May 27). "I was very grateful to Ed for having me at $150 a week."

Friday 30

The New Place, Algonquin, IL

Saturday 31

Majestic Hills Theatre, Lake Geneva, WI

The Byrds with The Babysitters and The Geneva Convention.

June

Friday 6–Saturday 7

Pilgrimage Theatre, Hollywood, CA

The group tops the bill for the two-day benefit in aid of rebuilding the Ash Grove. Kaleidoscope, Jim Kweskin, and The Firesign Theatre are also on for both nights, while Pacific Gas & Electric is added for the Friday performance and John Hammond Jr for the Saturday.

The Pilgrimage is a small open-air amphitheatre with about 1,400 seats in the Cahuenga Pass in the Hollywood Hills, just opposite the Hollywood Bowl: the perfect surroundings for a summer-night concert. In their first L.A. appearance since October of last year, The Byrds rise to the occasion. Pete Johnson, long-time Byrds supporter, writes in *The Los Angeles Times* (June 9): "The Byrds played for more than an hour, spurred on by an enthusiastic crowd which nearly filled the outdoor theatre. ... Roger McGuinn, the sole surviving original Byrd, still does most of the singing, but the other present members of the group share the solos and contribute strong harmonies. The current membership of The Byrds also seems to be the best musical formation the group has yet had, at least from the standpoint of live performances.

"Clarence White, on second lead guitar, is a large part of their present vitality and versatility. He gives McGuinn the heavy electric support necessary on such Byrds classics as 'Eight Miles High', 'Mr. Tambourine Man', and 'Turn! Turn! Turn!', and dominates with his own bluegrass style when the group shifts into country directions." Johnson has scribbled down a partial set-list and mentions 'Give Me Oil In My Lamp' in addition to the better-known numbers. Attributed to Gene Parsons and Clarence White, it is a traditional hymn the group will record for their next album.

Underground paper *The Los Angeles Image* (June 13–26) describes scenes of hippie laxness. "Ed Pearl ... came out early Friday evening and announced that the groups would come out and set up and perform when they were ready, with the intermission in between. While on the face of things this sounds like a fairly gorky set-up, it worked extremely well, giving the concert an extremely living-room atmosphere rather than that of a pint-sized Hollywood Bowl. By the time that Kaleidoscope had finished and the second group

THE ASH GROVE FAMILY PRESENTS
An open air Concert at the Pilgrimage Theatre
with

THE BYRDS

Friday and Saturday, June 6 & 7
8:30 P.M.

Plus
Kaleidoscope,
Foreign Theatre & Jim Kweskin

PACIFIC GAS & ELECTRIC
(Fri. only)

John Hammond
(Sat. only)

All reserved seats $3.00

Don't get stuck in the "sold out" line.

TICKETS AVAILABLE NOW thru
TRS, Ticket Reservation Systems, Inc.

Dial (213) TRS 1000 for your nearest TRS outlet.

– Pacific Gas & Electric – was into their set, crowd control was entirely non-existent. The guards were busy talking to all the people around the open-air stage and never once bothered the people sitting on the walls, wandering around the equipment, and dancing behind the musicians and in the wings."

Regarding The Byrds, journalist Arthur Poe is not convinced. "Many of those present had not heard The Byrds live for several years and did not quite know what to expect. How much of the astro-pilot remained in their music? At first it seemed as if they had changed almost completely, starting off the set with a whining country thing, then going off on a rather ragged medley of old Byrds hits. OK, that was out of the way, but wasn't that a rather distinctive harmony we heard? Things were really clear, however, when the group did 'Mr. Spaceman': even with three of the four original musicians gone, the group was still in the same place. Only the channel for their music had changed. Just the same, this reviewer felt cheated. With The Byrds' early music the group was on the frontier of an entirely new thing: electric astral music. And there – on the shore of the stream, as it were – they turned back and followed the path other musicians have taken many times. No more ionosphere and drug perception. No more interpretation of this generation's lifestyle; only past history. Perhaps it was Dylan's influence." For Ash Grove owner Ed Pearl the benefit is a success, and on August 22 he will welcome patrons back to his rebuilt club.

John York will fondly recall this benefit concert. "It was outside in a big stone amphitheatre under the stars. Hippie chicks with flowers in their hair and children danced all round. It was a beautiful gig, attended by Hopi elders who were in town for a big pow-

wow. We watched Bob Dylan on the *Johnny Cash Show* on a small TV backstage before the show." (This is the premiere of the Cash show, which is recorded in Nashville and broadcast on Saturdays at 9:30pm. Dylan sings 'I Threw It All Away' and 'Livin' The Blues' backed by a full band, and then he and Cash duet on 'The Girl From The North Country'. Cash's other main guest is Joni Mitchell.)

On Friday, the 'Lay Lady Lay' single is released in the UK. The conservative Derek Johnson writes in *New Musical Express* (June 14): "A great version of one of the strongest numbers on Bob Dylan's current hit LP. OK, so the title and lyric are a trifle provocative – but aren't we supposed to be open-minded these days? The harmonic support behind the solo vocal is really outstanding – largely because The Byrds have been augmented by a girl chorus. This – plus the familiar acoustic guitars, the attractive melody and the unobtrusive beat – makes it one of the group's best discs for ages."

Chris Welch in *Melody Maker* (June 14) says: "Shining out of the slagheap this week are The Byrds with the Bob Dylan tune that invites the lady to lay on his big brass bed. Strange; of course, they are going to show magic lantern slides under the blankets. Spiffy sound and if it's not a hit I'm going on holiday. I'm going on holiday anyway, so plague rot everybody." Some of the other singles in Welch's heap include Herb Alpert ('Without Her'), Cat Stevens ('Where Are You'), and The Beach Boys ('Break Away'). *Record Mirror*'s Peter Jones observes (July 19): "The most popular track off Bobby Zimmerman's latest LP, done with powerfully deep choral bursts, jingle-jangle guitar and adequately husky lead – it's Gospel/Country&/Rock – strewth! Barn dance spirit in the flip." Jones awards the single five out of five stars.

Sunday 8

New York Times rock music critic Robert Christgau reviews four recent albums by members of the original Byrds family. David Crosby's album with "this supergroup by definition", *Crosby Stills & Nash*, is as perfect as has been expected, according to Christgau. "But it also demonstrates the dangers of perfection: the wildness that should liberate great rock is so well controlled that when it appears (as on Nash's excellent 'Pre-Road Downs') it seems to have been inserted just to prove the music is rock: the only exception is Crosby's wailing vocal on 'Long Time Gone'."

Gene Clark with Doug Dillard have set out as The Dillard & Clark Expedition with a remake of the old Presley number 'Don't Be Cruel'. In Christgau's view, "[Not] only does Presley sound better on the original,

but so does his old backup group, The Jordanaires".

He rates Roger McGuinn and *Dr. Byrds & Mr. Hyde* as "first-rate Byrds, a high recommendation. The excitement generated is no longer exquisite, I suppose, but it lasts. Its major fault has plagued the group ever since the personnel changes began two-and-a-half years ago, when Gene Clark left because he was afraid of airplanes: a lack of strong voices to harmonise behind McGuinn's studiously unpolished lead."

Noting that the album is already gone from the charts, Christgau writes that *Dr. Byrds & Mr. Hyde* seems to be "a hodgepodge when compared to the conceptual sureness of 1968's *Notorious Byrd Brothers*, a smooth-flowing post-*Pepper* studio album, and *Sweetheart Of The Rodeo*, a bittersweet tribute to country music. … Although the material is a little thinner than usual, it is not really confused: the record functions as a token of McGuinn's unfaltering love for his entire musical past – folk, rock, space, country, and live performance."

Chris Hillman and Michael Clarke are by now, of course, in The Flying Burrito Brothers with Gram Parsons, a band that Christgau terms "the real master of country-rock". To his ears, the best country-rock music so far is on the Burritos' debut album, *The Gilded Palace of Sin* (which in fact does not feature Michael Clarke, as he joined after the album was completed). Christgau says: "If this were a time for conceptual geniuses, Parsons would rank with Peter Townshend and McGuinn. He has absorbed and transmuted all the Calvinist morality, chin-up self-pity, and interpersonal warmth that grace the best country music, and found a steel guitarist (called Sneaky Pete) who adds just the right musical flavour. Among the album's masterful touches are the lyrics on 'Sin City', which sounds like four different honky-tonk songs remembered from a dream, the country renderings of two minor Dan Penn–Spooner Oldham soul classics, and 'My Uncle', a totally apropos ditty about draft dodging. A brilliant LP. And yet, for all Parsons' brilliance, you wonder whether he would have gotten it all together without working for a few months with ol' Roger McGuinn of The Byrds. If every broken group can produce as much good music as The Byrds, rock will be alive for a long time to come."

ALSO …

The Flying Burrito Brothers play the Palomino Club, North Hollywood's country-music stronghold, and reputedly Clarence White sits in on guitar.

The weekend's resident group at the Palomino is Red Rhodes & The Detours.

Thursday 12–Sunday 15

Fillmore West, San Francisco, CA

The Byrds headline with Joe Cocker & The Grease Band and Pacific Gas & Electric as support.

Tuesday 17

🔊 **RECORDING** Columbia Recording Studios, Sunset and El Centro, Hollywood, CA. Producer Terry Melcher and engineer Jerry Hochman.

Back in the studio again to start sessions for a new album, the group experiences another upheaval in the production team. Bob Johnston has failed to live up to whatever expectations The Byrds may have had, and his tampering with 'Lay Lady Lay' has not endeared him to the group. To strengthen the link to the group's glorious past, now that all the original members save McGuinn are gone, it is suggested that Terry Melcher is brought back. Since The Byrds and Melcher severed their ties four years ago – his last session with The Byrds was on November 1, 1965 – he has been involved in several projects. He has worked as producer for Paul Revere & The Raiders, The Mamas & The Papas, The Gentle Soul, and The Rising Sons, to name a few. He contributed to The Beach Boys' classic *Pet Sounds* (although in a minor role) and served as board member of the International Monterey Pop Festival in 1967. On a personal note, Melcher has worked as TV producer for his mother on *The Doris Day Show*. Melcher and girlfriend, the actress Candice Bergen, left their leased home on Cielo Drive in Benedict Canyon four months ago, and as they did so, actress Sharon Tate and husband Roman Polanski move in.

'Jesus Is Just Alright' is recorded today, a gospel rocker written by Art Reynolds. The Byrds have performed the song in concert for some months and it has quickly become a live favourite with its catchy wordless vocal intro. Terry Melcher later overdubs an unobtrusive string section.

Engineer Jerry Hochman presumably plays an important role during the sessions that stretch until the end of August because his credit on the next Byrds album will read Associate Producer.

Wednesday 18

🔊 **RECORDING** Columbia Recording Studios, Sunset and El Centro, Hollywood, CA. Producer Terry Melcher and engineer Jerry Hochman.

The group re-records McGuinn and Dylan's 'Ballad Of Easy Rider' (see entry for January–February). The *Easy Rider* theme tune is bolstered by a beautiful orchestral arrangement. McGuinn will discuss the song with Jud Cost

when it is remastered in 2000. "Here's a funny story for you. Terry [Melcher] was dating Candice Bergen at the time. I think they were living together at his mom's beach house in Malibu. I remember, before she came in, the engineers were talking about her behind her back: 'What does she do?' 'She's a debutante.' 'Well, what do debutantes do?' 'I don't know. They kind of sit around and look pretty.' So I was prepared for this girl to walk in. And she does and she's stunning. She's sitting next to me while this song is played back and I ask her, 'How'd you like it?' She gets all teary-eyed and she goes, 'It was beautiful.' Wow. That was great. So she liked the strings."

Johnny Rogan's discography will log today a first attempt at McGuinn's adaptation of the traditional British sea shanty 'Jack Tarr The Sailor'. Framed by Parsons' banjo and White's distant fuzzy guitar, McGuinn delivers a great vocal in a near-British accent. (The song will be completed on July 1.)

Thursday 19

🔊 **RECORDING** Columbia Recording Studios, Sunset and El Centro, Hollywood, CA. Producer Terry Melcher and engineer Jerry Hochman.

McGuinn sings Woody Guthrie's 'Deportee (Plane Wreck At Los Gatos)', one of the songs he arranged for Judy Collins's *Third* album back in 1963. Next up is another of the group's recently introduced concert numbers, 'Oil In My Lamp', recorded with Clarence White on lead vocals. Two variations are taped and the longest is finished for The Byrds' album-in-the-works.

Saturday 21

The Byrds are one of the early names listed for the Toronto Pop Festival at Varsity Stadium in Canada today – together with Chuck Berry, Blood Sweat & Tears, Procol Harum, Ronnie Hawkins, Dr. John, Sly & The Family Stone and others. But The Byrds pull out and do not appear.

Sunday 22

'Newport '69', Devonshire Downs, Northridge, CA

The summer of 1969 is set to be the season of rock festivals across the US. The openers were the '1969 Northern California Folk-Rock Festival' (May 23–25) and 'Detroit Rock'n'Roll Revival' (May 30–31), and now comes this Friday-to-Sunday fete in Northridge in the San Fernando Valley.

The next three months see festival fever reach Colorado ('Denver Pop Festival', June 27–29); Georgia ('Atlanta Pop Festival', July 4–5); Rhode Island (this year's 'real' Newport Festival opens its gates to rock acts on July 3–6); Maryland (Laurel Pop Festival, July 11–12, with a sister festival held in Philadelphia, PA, the same weekend); Washington ('Seattle Pop Festival', July 25–27); New Jersey (Atlantic City Pop Festival, August 1–3); Michigan ('Mount Clemens Pop Festival', August 3); Upper New York State (Woodstock, August 15–17); Washington ('2nd Sky River Rock Festival', August 30); Texas ('International Pop Festival', August 30–September 1), and Louisiana ('New Orleans Pop Festival', August 30–September 1).

Like last year's 'First Annual Newport Pop Festival' in Costa Mesa, today's organisers hijack the Newport name to surf on the goodwill of the established Newport Jazz and Folk festivals held annually on the East Coast. This year, the East Coast originals drag the West Coast impostors to court to stop the abuse of the name. Despite a court injunction, it is too late as the festival is already heavily advertised. Starting on Friday June 20 with Jimi Hendrix as the main attraction, yesterday (June 21) had Creedence Clearwater Revival and Steppenwolf as headliners, while today's programme has Booker T & The MGs, Flock, The Grass Roots, Johnny Winter, Marvin Gaye, Mother Earth, Three Dog Night, Poco, and The Byrds, with The Rascals and The Chambers Brothers topping the bill.

Already, the novelty of a rock festival is going stale. Pete Johnson writes in *The Los Angeles Times* (June 23): "The pop music festival to end all pop music festivals lured several hundred thousand hardy souls to the burlap covered expanses of Devonshire Downs in Northridge this past weekend. There they were greeted by nearly impenetrable traffic and parking snarls, helped not at all by a lack of directing signs, generally gloomy weather, a difficult viewing and listening situation, hundred-foot lines to portable toilets, and other non-festive aspects of mammoth festivals. Acoustically, the situation was impossible: an open field the size of an airport, a diffuse, slack-jawed audience and sonic competition from a constantly circling police helicopter, Air Force planes, and a dimming public address system on a neighbouring psychedelic midway. Judging by the number of bodies in attendance at Newport '69, it was a howling

Terry Melcher and Roger McGuinn at work in the studio.

success (aided by the fact that this was graduation weekend for a number of high school seniors), but the musical and sociological results of that gathering have no kinship with the word festival."

The Hollywood correspondents of the British music weeklies agree. Ann Moses explains in *New Musical Express* (July 5) how local government officials are preparing ordinances to guarantee there will never be another gathering of the rock tribes. "The crowd – many camped at nearby fields for the weekend – was in a collective daze, mostly because police raids have totally eliminated marijuana supplies in the Los Angeles area. Now every backroom chemistry lab is churning out potent versions of LSD, STP, and other speed. Kids at the concert seemed to favour something called Orange Acid. Little surprise a wild, bottle-swinging melee broke out on the last day, causing injuries to both police and attendees. … The reasons are simple: rock in this country is attracting a rowdier crowd than two years ago when long-haired, peaceful people (you had to be peaceful then to bear the insults about long hair) gathered in foggy Monterey for a weekend of fine rock. Now, however, even the infamous Hells Angels wear their hair down past their shoulders and carve peace symbols on their bikes, their jackets, and their girlfriends."

Judy Sims says in *Disc* (July 5): "I feel that the whole situation revealed the worst of both sides – the shocking disregard of the young people for property and priority …" – according to Sims, outside the grounds young people mill around, break into houses, and mess up lawns – "… and the infuriating lack of respect for personal rights on the part of the guards [a local motorcycle chapter called Street Riders] and festival promoters. The youth–authority confrontation continues with ever-increasing hostility in this country – and the Newport '69 festival only served to remind us that Monterey took place in another time when we were innocent and believed in love and flowers."

🎞 **FILMING** The performances are filmed, and unedited footage of The Byrds playing 'Sing Me Back Home', 'You Ain't Going Nowhere', and 'Old Blue' will survive. Music television historian Richard Groothuizen comments later: "The film is still in the archive, and it will probably never come out [because] the footage is too meagre: mainly one-camera shots crosscut with audience shots."

Monday 23
🔊 **RECORDING** Columbia Recording Studios, Sunset and El Centro, Hollywood, CA. Producer Terry Melcher and engineer Jerry Hochman.

More work is done on Woody Guthrie's 'Deportee (Plane Wreck At Los Gatos)'. An instrumental credited to Gene Parsons and Clarence White titled 'Build It Up' is also taped, along with John York's solo vocal 'Way Behind The Sun'. The latter will be mistitled as 'Way Beyond The Sun' when it is finally released in 1989 and credited as a traditional arrangement by Roger McGuinn rather than to its composer Barbara Dane.

Tuesday 24
🔊 **RECORDING** Columbia Recording Studios, Sunset and El Centro, Hollywood, CA. Producer Terry Melcher and engineer Jerry Hochman.

McGuinn happily invites his new crew to submit songs, and Parsons and White suggest 'There Must Be Someone (I Can Turn To)', a song by the Gosdin Brothers that in 1967 was the B-side of Bakersfield International's fifth single, 'She Still Wishes I Were You'. Parsons takes lead vocal, but according to Johnny Rogan's later discographical annotations the song is not finished today. (It will be re-recorded on July 2.) Also unfinished is McGuinn's version of the Irish folk song 'Give The Fiddler A Dram', which combines a plunking banjo with a concertina-like Moog synthesizer melody-line. The synthesis works quite well but the track will not be released until 1989.

Friday 27–Saturday 28
Fillmore East, Manhattan, New York City, NY

The group is back at the Fillmore East, this time with Raven and the UK's Procol Harum. Mike Jahn says in *The New York Times* (June 2) that The Byrds steal the thunder from the Brits. "The Byrds are as close to becoming legendary as any rock band produced in America this decade. They began with reworkings of Bob Dylan songs like 'Mr. Tambourine Man' and progressed through folk-rock to settle comfortably just to the rock side of country music. This weekend they gave what was easily one of the most moving rock performances of the year. They were taut and strong, and the sensitive, mournful vocals of Roger McGuinn were even better. They played their arrangements of folk songs like 'Old Blue' and 'Long Black Veil', Pete Seeger's 'Turn! Turn! Turn!', a spiritual 'Jesus Is Just Alright', Dylan's 'Mr. Tambourine Man', 'This Wheel's On Fire', and 'Lay Lady Lay' and their own 'Eight Miles High'. The Byrds' soaring country harmony is very suited to these airy, folk-oriented songs, and Clarence White's country-style guitar was brilliant."

Variety (July 9) writes: "One of the first groups to use many huge amplifiers and

high volume for in-person stints, the quartet has toned down to a low decibel presentation of easy-going ballads and country tunes. McGuinn has turned over his position as lead guitarist to White and now strums creatively simple electric 12-string rhythms. The quartet's mellow set comprised tunes from recent LPs such as 'Old Blue', 'Goin' Back', and the instrumental 'Nashville West'. A medley of well-known Byrds hits roused the audience."

In *Billboard* (July 19), Ed Ochs says the group is too slick. "Tasteful as an expensive suit tailored without imagination, and safe to the point of insignificance, the four Byrds glided effortlessly through 'Mr. Tambourine Man' and 'Lay Lady Lay' dressed up beautifully by Clarence White's quick, crying guitar and the baloney of the ponderous big Byrd, Roger McGuinn." To Ochs, McGuinn's stage patter is irritating. "But despite McGuinn's antics – and thanks, inevitably, to his perseverance – the Columbia group's quicksilver blend and warm, romantic truth-saying carried their fine material over a silky sea of memories as mellow and mesmerising as old camp songs from summers gone by."

ALSO …

Disc's Hollywood correspondent Judy Sims today breaks the latest news in the Crosby Stills & Nash saga. "Neil Young was supposed to open at the Troub but he was sick and it was postponed. Meanwhile, as the plot thickens, Neil Young and former Buffalo bass player Bruce Palmer have joined up with David Crosby, Steve Stills and Graham Nash (and drummer Dallas Taylor) to form Supersuper-supergroup – well, they don't have a conglomerate name yet."

Neil's co-billing with David, Stephen, and Graham is not only a shrewd business move supervised by Atlantic Records boss Ahmet Ertegun, who is genuinely motivated to have the four strong-minded men perform together. After a few false starts and cancellations (including the Newport '69 and Atlantic City festivals), Crosby Stills Nash & Young will finally debut in Chicago on August 15.

Sunday 29
Peekskill Palace, Peekskill, NY

Monday 30
📺 **US TV** [Presumably] ABC Television Studios, Manhattan, New York, NY. ABC network *Dick Cavett Show* 10:00pm

Dick Cavett is a relative newcomer to television talk shows as a host, but after his This Morning was such a success for ABC last spring, the show was quickly renamed in his honour and moved to prime time in

March this year. The Byrds perform 'Jesus Is Just Alright', presumably recorded live as the show goes out on the air. The rest of Cavett's guest-list includes Woody Allen, actress Julie Harris, and *New York Times* associate editor Tom Wicker.

July

Tuesday 1

◁)) RECORDING Columbia Recording Studios, Sunset and El Centro, Hollywood, CA. Producer Terry Melcher and engineer Jerry Hochman.

Back in the studio and Los Angeles again, The Byrds attend to two songs they've already tried out: 'Jack Tarr The Sailor' (see June 18) and 'Oil In My Lamp' (see June 19), both of which are completed today.

Wednesday 2

◁)) RECORDING Columbia Recording Studios, Sunset and El Centro, Hollywood, CA. Producer Terry Melcher and engineer Jerry Hochman.

The Gosdin Brothers' song 'There Must Be Someone (I Can Turn To)', first attempted on June 24, is finished. The stripped-down arrangement is just a trio performance by White, York, and Parsons and thus lacks any discernible trace of the trademark Byrds sound.

Friday 4

HemisFair Arena, San Antonio, TX
Steppenwolf and The Byrds perform at a show promoted by radio station KONO.

Tuesday 8

Electric Factory, Philadelphia, PA
The Byrds are headliners, while local group P.I.L.T. (an acronym for Pleasure In Little Things) take the opening slot.

Saturday 12

'Schaefer Music Festival', Wollman Skating Rink, Central Park, New York, NY
The Schaefer brewery sponsors a concert series that runs the whole summer in Central Park. With cheap tickets and top-flight acts, the festival is a popular attraction for New Yorkers. The event is a continuation of the concert series earlier sponsored by Rheingold (for whom The Byrds played here in 1967). The group will play the Schaefer festival in 1970 and 1971 as well. (Originally, The Byrds were booked to play Tippecanoe Ballroom, Lake Tippecanoe, IN, but this is cancelled to

make way for the Central Park appearance with John Lee Hooker, and instead The Ventures play that engagement.)

Catching the red-eye express back to Los Angeles after the concert, Gene Parsons pens the lyrics to a new song inspired by the couple of days spent in New York. The line "Mister rock'n'roll couldn't stay/The crowd was mad and we were had" is a reference to Chuck Berry, who declines to appear in Central Park at the last minute. Short of a rhyme, Parsons borrows the title 'Gunga Din' from a Rudyard Kipling poem.

Monday 14

The *Easy Rider* movie premiers in New York City today at the Beekman Theatre and will open in Los Angeles on August 13 at the Village Theatre. Vincent Canby reviews the movie for *The New York Times* (July 15) and points out how the soundtrack "rocks with the oddly counterpointed emotions of Steppenwolf, The Byrds, The Electric Prunes – dark and smokey cries for liberation. Periodically, like a group taking a break, the cyclists stop (and so does the music) for quiet encounters".

In a later feature for *The New York Times* in October, Vincent Canby will zoom in on the essence of Fonda and Hopper's movie. "The most exciting thing about *Easy Rider* is neither content nor style nor statement but the fact that it was made for less than $500,000 (less than the cost of one set for some super productions) by young men working outside the moviemaking establishment, and that it is apparently reaching a large audience." Also, *Easy Rider* represents Jack Nicholson's big-screen breakthrough.

Saturday 19

Roger McGuinn is in Philadelphia, PA, to meet the press. The reception is held at the city's hip Electric Factory venue. And like the rest of the nation, McGuinn is certainly following the Apollo 11 mission, launched three days ago. Neil Armstrong, 'Buzz' Aldrin, and Michael Collins man the expedition, and tomorrow evening, July 20, the lunar module Eagle lands and Neil Armstrong becomes the first human to tread on the surface of the moon.

Tuesday 22

◁)) RECORDING Columbia Recording Studios, Sunset and El Centro, Hollywood, CA. Producer Terry Melcher and engineer Jerry Hochman.

The Byrds resurrect Dylan's 'It's All Over, Baby Blue', which they initially recorded under Terry Melcher's direction four years earlier for a proposed follow-up to 'Mr. Tam-

bourine Man' (see June 28, 1965). McGuinn reintroduced the song in the group's set-list at the beginning of the year, in a slower take than the one taped in 1965, and it is a similar version that the group lays down today, with Melcher responsible for the arrangement and helping out on the harmony vocals.

Wednesday 23

◁)) RECORDING Columbia Recording Studios, Sunset and El Centro, Hollywood, CA. Producer Terry Melcher and engineer Jerry Hochman.

Pamela Polland's lilting 'Tulsa County Blue' is given two treatments, one with York as vocalist, then another and shorter version sung by McGuinn, with York relegated to harmony vocals. Polland has not released the song herself, but Anita Carter (sister of June and daughter of Maybelle) will have a fair-sized US country hit with the song in 1971, and Terry Melcher will record it as 'Take It Down To Mexico' in 1975.

Like many of the selections recorded for the new album, 'Tulsa County Blue' was featured live as early as the Boston Tea Party shows in February. Byron Berline will play fiddle to enhance the McGuinn-sung version, presumably overdubbed at a later date. Berline, an old acquaintance of Clarence White and The Dillards, is yet another musician orbiting the bluegrass scene. (When The Byrds eventually release the McGuinn–Berline version on the next Byrds album, the song's title is abbreviated to just 'Tulsa County'.)

Thursday 24

◁)) RECORDING Columbia Recording Studios, Sunset and El Centro, Hollywood, CA. Producer Terry Melcher and engineer Jerry Hochman.

Gene Parsons' song 'Gunga Din', written less than two weeks ago, is recorded today. The song is destined to become a minor Byrds classic, with its autobiographical lyric and pretty melody. Glen D. Hardin is reputed to play the organ on the track.

Friday 25

'Seattle Pop Festival', Gold Creek Park, Woodinville, Seattle, WA
The Seattle festival runs the whole weekend, and The Byrds play the Friday on a bill with Albert Collins, The Flying Burrito Brothers, Ten Years After, The Youngbloods, Bo Diddley, Santana, and It's A Beautiful Day. The festival draws a total of 70,000 over the three days, and many of the artists and groups play twice (such as Ike & Tina Turner on the Friday and Saturday) or even three times (such as The Flying Burrito Brothers, who play each day).

Rolling Stone (September 6) claims The Byrds "sleepwalked through their old numbers but woke up for the C&W tunes". The Byrds' festival repertoire in Seattle consists of 'You Ain't Going Nowhere'; 'Old Blue'; 'Long Black Veil'; [Medley:] 'Turn! Turn! Turn!' / 'Mr. Tambourine Man' / 'Eight Miles High'; Goin' Back'; 'Get Out Of My Life, Woman'; 'Jesus Is Just Alright'; 'This Wheel's On Fire', and finally 'He Was A Friend Of Mine' / 'Break Song'. The *Rolling Stone* report says Friday's highpoint came "after midnight, backstage in the artists area, where Gram Parsons honky-tonked on a piano by himself while, across the room, Byrds McGuinn and Clarence White picked through an impromptu '5D' and 'Old John Robertson' for an admiring group".

Other acts appearing at the festival are The Guess Who, Lonnie Mack, Chicago, Chuck Berry, Charles Lloyd, Spirit, Vanilla Fudge, The Doors, Led Zeppelin, and Lee Michaels. McGuinn briefly meets ex-Byrds Chris Hillman and Gram Parsons – quoted in *Rolling Stone*, Hillman calls out sociably to McGuinn: "It's good out there, almost as good as Monterey!") But when Parsons and Hillman sit down to talk with *The Seattle Helix* (Volume 9, issue 6) during the weekend, they unmercifully lash out at McGuinn. "It's very difficult to work for McGuinn on anything," says Hillman. "He's the type of guy that – it's just a job. He goes up on stage to become a musician. Offstage he's not. He doesn't buy records, he doesn't listen to the radio, he doesn't really keep up with what's happening in music. The last album that they did [*Dr. Byrds & Mr. Hyde*], it was McGuinn and the rest was a hired group."

Parsons says of McGuinn: "He's always found a way to either buy the information or gather the information that he needs to keep up with what's goin' on. He himself doesn't live that life, and he brings you down. … McGuinn wouldn't know Clarence White from – Mighty Sam, if it wasn't for Chris. As a matter of fact, he probably never heard of Mighty Sam." Hillman: "All McGuinn's doin' now is ridin' it out till it ends, just for the money. It's not a creative, productive thing any more. He pays everybody's salary every week, and he's the head Byrd." Parsons: "And everybody still writes all these comprehensive articles on him, like *Crawdaddy* and all that analytical bullshit. Singin' like Dylan, thinkin' like Dylan, sellin' like Dylan."

Hillman and Parsons' band The Flying Burrito Brothers, meanwhile, struggle with stability. The group is down to a quartet now, with Hillman back on bass. They have long since terminated ties with any regular management, but seasoned Byrds associate Jimmi Seiter has agreed to help the band out as road manager.

Saturday 26

The group misses its headlining slot at the Eugene Pop Festival held at Hayward Field, University of Oregon, OR, because they arrive too late. The day otherwise features The Doors, Alice Cooper, and several local attractions.

Monday 28

◁》 **RECORDING** Columbia Recording Studios, Sunset and El Centro, Hollywood, CA. Producer Terry Melcher and engineer Jerry Hochman.

The Byrds record 'Mae Jean Goes To Hollywood' by Jackson Browne, a singer who is trying to carve a career as a songwriter. Browne has previously recorded and performed with Nico, The Nitty Gritty Dirt Band, The Gentle Soul, and others, and has just signed a publishing contract with Criterion music. Byron Berline adds fiddle to this track, suggesting his overdub to 'Tulsa County' may also be done today (see entry for July 23). Unfortunately, the excellent 'Mae Jean Goes To Hollywood' will not make the shortlist for the new album, and it is not unearthed until a CD release in 1989.

Tuesday 29

Preflyte, an interesting album of archival recordings by The Byrds, is released today on Together Records. It collects 11 tracks from the Jim Dickson tapes recorded at World Pacific in the second half of 1964: 'You Showed Me', 'Here Without You', 'She Has A Way', 'The Reason Why', 'For Me Again', 'Boston', 'You Movin'', 'The Airport Song', 'You Won't Have To Cry', 'I Knew I'd Want You', and the demo version of 'Mr. Tambourine Man'.

Together Records is an idealistic undertaking by ex-Byrds producer Gary Usher, singer–composer Curt Boettcher, and well-heeled wheeler-dealer Mike Curb. In keeping with the spirit of '69, the new record company intends to give its artists complete control of the entire production chain – from recording sessions via artwork and promotion to the final release. The company also devises another idea, which is to release archival material by established artists, of which *Preflyte* is the first.

Gary Usher will explain to music historian Stephen McParland how Together came into possession of the early Byrds tapes. "[Together Records manager] Dick Moreland had found out about some early Byrds masters through Jim Dickson, the group's past manager. So we met with him and made arrangements to purchase them. I think we bought the entire demos for a reasonably good figure, and we released the package with a lot of public-

ity. It ended up selling a couple of hundred thousand units; a very big album." Mike Curb explains in a contemporary interview with The *Los Angeles Times* (October 5): "This isn't considered a respectable business in most places. It's capitalising on a group's later success on another label." (Together will release another archival album of interest here: *Early L.A.*, which contains the David Crosby demos 'Willie Gene' and 'Come Back Baby' recorded for Jim Dickson.)

McGuinn will mention the album to journalist Vincent Flanders next year. "I was allowed to hear it before they put it out – they needed our written permission before they could do it. I gave permission because I thought it would be an interesting historical trip. It's like a time capsule, something … like going out in the field and recording folk songs, which doesn't happen any more. If you're interested in The Byrds as an entity [and] you want to see what they started with, you can see the Beatle influences, which show up much more vividly on that than they do on our first Columbia album."

The young Lester Bangs, writing one of his first reviews for *Rolling Stone* (October 18), says the tapes sound a little rough and rather dated. "[But they] still overflow with that unique unschmaltzy beauty and lyricism that has been The Byrds' trademark. Four of the 11 songs appeared on Mr. Tambourine Man, and they sound like less-focused takes of something that later became masterful and transporting. But place this music in perspective; suppose it has been released in late 1964. Aside from the first two or three albums by The Beatles or the Stones, there was absolutely nothing out as good, as aurally visionary, as unpackaged as this. By the time The Byrds were released to the public, several other groups – The Yardbirds, The Kinks, the Spoonful – were working toward the same shift in the system, and few people realised what an innovation The Byrds were, both spiritually and musically. They took the basic lessons of The Beatles and the Stones, filtered them through Dylan and the less pretentious aspects of the folk scene, and came up with a big, new, visionary sound.

"Propelled by the ringing grandeur of McGuinn's electric 12-string and Hillman's incredibly advanced bass playing," writes Bangs, "they created a stately, transcendent sound of magnificent brilliance, lifting listeners into bold new realms of dream, turning the stoned hordes from preachy, flatulent 'folk music' to the vibrant new and old sounds of rock. And The Byrds' influence, in the years that followed, on everybody, from The Beatles to The Velvet Underground, is simply an undiminishing fact of life."

Budding guitarist, rock archivist, and free-lance writer Lenny Kaye submits his review to *Jazz & Pop* (December 1969). "'This album is eclectic.' There it was, right on the back of Turn! Turn! Turn!. It was true, of course, but to prove it you really had to dig in and separate out the roots. By that time, The Byrds sound had already been fully created; they were already a mature band and further changes (to come with 'Eight Miles High') would only be basic refinements of what had gone down previously. But *Preflyte* is earlier than that, tapes made at a time when 'Mr. Tambourine Man' featured a rougher, more military beat and The Byrds could double for the early Beatles in 'You Movin''. The influences are nearer the surface here, easier to differentiate and pick out. There are hints of The Everly Brothers, pieces of any number of early English groups, other things less definable.

"*Preflyte* features all the old Byrds," says Kaye, "dominated in those early days by the vocal and songwriting talents of Gene Clark. Clark, who became the first Byrd to leave after success, contributes seven of the 11 songs on the record and has a share in two others. … One of the more interesting things about *Preflyte* is the consistency of The Byrds' sound, especially when compared with their later post-Tambourine Man days. Even on these early recordings, they were able to create the same aura and feel that has characterised them all the way down to their present incarnation with only McGuinn remaining. Indeed, three of the songs on *Preflyte* sound nearly unchanged from their carry-over to the first album. One, 'I Knew I'd Want You', actually sounds better on this album: [here] slower and more ghostly than the final version."

Preflyte is a fair seller and makes US Number 84 – easily outstripping sales of *Dr. Byrds & Mr. Hyde*.

August

Saturday 2

**'Atlantic City Pop Festival',
Atlantic City Race Course,
Atlantic City, NJ**

Another festival, another troubled weekend. "I should have guessed by the way things started out that pop festival weekend was going to be fraught with difficulties. Any weekend that starts at 5:00am on a Friday morning has two strikes against it," writes Robb Baker in *The Chicago Tribune* (August 6). "But little did I suspect that it would end at midnight Sunday with a dead battery in a dastardly downpour,

still a hitch-hike, a two-hour nap on the concrete outside a closed bus station, and the snail's-paced trip itself away from home and bed."

The organisers have booked an impressive roster of artists, although as usual the running order is changed around as the festival progresses, with groups either pulling out, postponing their performances, or being added over the course of the three days. The original Friday bill lists Iron Butterfly, Johnny Winter (a no-show), Crosby Stills & Nash (who also fail to appear), Procol Harum, Joni Mitchell (she leaves the stage in tears after being heckled by a rude crowd), Chicago, Santana, Mother Earth, and Booker T & The MGs. Saturday offers Jefferson Airplane, Creedence Clearwater Revival, The Crazy World Of Arthur Brown (who cancel), The Butterfield Blues Band, B.B. King, Hugh Masekela, Grateful Dead (who do not perform), The Byrds, Lighthouse, and The American Dream. The Sunday is to feature Janis Joplin, The Mothers Of Invention, Canned Heat, Moody Blues (another cancellation), Three Dog Night, Joe Cocker, Dr. John, Little Richard, Sir Douglas Quintet, Buddy Miles Express, and Buddy Rich & His Big Band (who, being the odd-men-out of the festival, decide not to come). Added to the festivities are The Chambers Brothers, Tim Buckley, Lothar & The Hand People, and Aum.

The troubles start when people break down the fences around the racetrack and hundreds gatecrash the festival. *Rolling Stone* (September 6) devotes a whole page to the event but writes briefly on The Byrds: "The audience stormed the fence early Saturday while The Byrds were doing 'This Wheel's On Fire', and despite McGuinn's somewhat reluctant pleas for order (he apologised to the crowd later, saying 'they asked me to do it'), the festival was theirs from that point on." Robb Baker says in *The Chicago Tribune*: "McGuinn has to be the worst vocalist in all of rock, but one number – 'Jesus Is Just Alright' – is fantastic," before signing off with: "I heard someone say just before the battery died that last time, perhaps forever, 'On to Woodstock!' God help us all."

Tuesday 5

🔊 **RECORDING** Columbia Recording Studios, Sunset and El Centro, Hollywood, CA Producer Terry Melcher and engineer Jerry Hochman.

Sessions for the new album continue at a democratic pace. Today, John York's composition 'Fido' is recorded. Yet another number performed as early as the Boston Tea Party in February, the song is a departure from the usual Byrds fare. More rhythm & blues than

country or folk-rock, the tune even features a funky drum solo.

Saturday 9

Charleston Civic Center, Charleston, WV
A show by Brent Lewis, The Byrds, and Three Dog Night, reviewed by Ray Brack in *The Charleston Gazette* (August 16). "Either Appalachian youth are oblivious to their musical roots or, after the manner of the city hipster hiding his hick cousin, they are refusing to acknowledge their existence. The fact that the Civic Center crowd (a third of a house) responded only nominally to [the group's] country-oriented material – while old hits like 'Turn! Turn! Turn!' were enthusiastically received – didn't discernibly bother The Byrds." (Three Dog Night, meanwhile, are given such a tepid review that the Gazette is flooded by letters from irate fans.)

"Don't be down on this crowd," McGuinn says in a brief interview with the paper. "I can understand how they feel. Sure, country roots are deep here. The kids know that, and it's ironic that they reject it. But they've got to have their own thing. Their thing is rock. They don't want something their parents had. It's like my parents like Dixieland jazz. But I like progressive jazz."

McGuinn reveals the working title for the group's next long player. "Watch out for our new album, *Captain America*. It shows where we're at much better than our last album or this concert. Our mix was poor on the last album."

Captain America is a comic-book superhero created by Marvel Comics, and in the *Easy Rider* movie it is the nickname of Peter Fonda's character, Wyatt.

ALSO …

While The Byrds are visiting tranquil West Virginia, actress Sharon Tate and four others are brutally killed on the Cielo Drive property that Terry Melcher and Candice Bergen moved out of earlier in the year. It will take months before the police are able to find and raise charges against the suspects, Charles Manson and several acolytes of his pseudo-sect. These horrible murders will cast a long dark shadow over Hollywood.

Monday 11–Wednesday 13

The Boston Tea Party, Boston, MA
The group shares the stage with Colosseum, whose drummer and leader Jon Hiseman tells *Melody Maker* (September 6): "We've done extremely well in Boston. … we worked with The Byrds and the audience were digging us one minute and the next they'd be digging the other band."

Underground paper *Fusion* (issue No. 17,

September 1969) writes: "It was high-voltage energy. [McGuinn] told his first-night, first-set crowd that 'the better you like us, the better we play'. It got better all the time. Three nights of appreciative, enthusiastic crowds heard The Byrds deliver their Big Hits, a good sampling of *Dr. Byrds & Mr. Hyde* (including the brilliant 'Drug Store Truck Drivin' Man'), and some nice country-oriented stuff like 'Tulsa County', 'Jesus Is Just Alright', and 'City Bride', a bayou song. 'You Ain't Going Nowhere' and 'My Back Pages', two of their best Dylan, have never sounded better, and they did, magnificently, 'It's All Over Now, Baby Blue', hitherto untried by them. 'Get Out Of My Life Woman' and a bluesy 'Long Black Veil' were done because, said McGuinn, 'we aren't supposed to do that stuff'. It was a rock experience of the highest order (Byrd-rock, not folk-rock)."

Earl Kirmser, who writes the review, speaks with McGuinn. "Sure I still get along with David [Crosby] and Gram [Parsons], but we just couldn't get together any more," says McGuinn. "I talked to David just the other day. He said that [Graham] Nash's voice had gone." And what about Dylan? "Yeah. Saw him a couple of months ago. He still writes for us, as he does for others."

McGuinn says the next album will be called *Captain America*. "Did you see *Easy Rider*? Peter Fonda's a good friend of mine and he'll be writing the liner notes for it. Terry Melcher is our new producer, and we've already extended beyond our July 30 deadline." McGuinn revives the double-album concept, first planned during the *Sweetheart Of The Rodeo* sessions a year and a half ago. "I'd like to make it a two-album deal, but we've just got one almost done. I have a synthesizer and have been fooling around with it for some time; I'd like to do something with electronics for the second record of the album. I know [avant-garde composer Karlheinz] Stockhausen, [Turkish composer Îlhan] Mimaroglu, and all those, but I'd like to do something musical with electronics, which hasn't been done before. Right now, neither I nor Melcher can bring that off."

When McGuinn is asked how The Byrds' latest single is going, his curt reply is "nowhere." He explains: "We went to Bob Johnston, our producer with 'Jesus Is Just Alright' – he wanted us to do 'Lay Lady Lay' instead and backed us with a choir on it. Have you heard it? [It's] one of the reasons he's no longer with us."

He touches on the *Gene Tryp* project ("I understand it's down to four hours now. I've done 25 songs and I expect they'll use only 10 to 12 of them. No, we aren't performing any of them"). But McGuinn has another project

in line. "Bobby Darin wants me to play a folk-singer/junkie in his next movie. Bobby's sort of gone full circle, you know? No, really half-circle. He still goes to all the Hollywood functions, premiers and all that, but now he goes in long hair, denims, and buckskins."

The Darin project is indeed a reality. After starring in a series of successful movies, Darin wants to branch out as a director, writer, and producer and has come up with *The Vendors*. The script is about a folk-singer and his relationship with a prostitute and the music industry, but McGuinn declines to appear. Much later, he will recall to Darin biographer Michael Starr: "I agreed to do it but changed my mind. I didn't want to be portrayed as a drug dealer or a junkie. Bobby had a camera guy set up and I paid him what it cost to get out of it. He was pissed; he accepted my resignation but didn't like it because he went out of his way to set it up. I gave him my word and changed my mind. I felt badly about it." Darin gives the role to unknown Gary Wood, and although the film is completed it is never shown.

In parting, Kirmser wants to know if The Byrds are heading to Woodstock at the weekend, already the most talked-about festival this summer. "The guy wanted us to do it for free," McGuinn discloses. "I said, man, it costs us at least $2,700 to get out and back to California. He said, well, Dylan's playing for free. I said yeah, but he lives just down the road."

Friday 15–Saturday 16
Aragon Ballroom, Chicago, IL

While The Byrds play Chicago (with Tim Buckley and Linda Ronstadt) almost half-a-million people gather at Max Yasgur's farm in Woodstock, upstate New York, to enjoy three days of peace and music. The event transcends even the great hopes and dreams of the festival's organisers and participants, and will come forever to symbolise the positive energy generated by the American counterculture. The Byrds were offered the opportunity to perform at the festival but declined. Still, they are there in spirit, as late on Friday night Joan Baez and guitar player Jeffrey Shurtleff dedicate their take on 'Drug Store Truck Drivin' Man' to the Governor of California – "Ronald Rayguns". (The performance will become available on the 2004 DVD *Woodstock Diaries*.)

ALSO ...

While The Byrds play a second night at the Aragon on Saturday, across town, at Chicago's Auditorium Theatre, Crosby Stills Nash & Young finally make their stage debut. The group plays a half-acoustic/half-electric show before flying straight on to Woodstock for

their second ever appearance in the early-morning hours of Monday August 18.

Monday 18
'Manhattan College Scholarship Concert Series', Gaelic Park, The Bronx, NY

The Byrds end an eight-part summer concert series arranged in conjunction with radio station WOR-FM. Teasingly, they are billed alongside 'Mystery Group', but what or who hides behind the name, or if it is in fact a group in its own right, is not entirely clear.

Friday 22
'Vancouver Pop Festival', Paradise Valley Resort, Squamish, British Columbia, Canada

As in the US, several big rock festivals are held in Canada this summer. The Byrds missed out on the Toronto Pop Festival in June but appear today in attractive Paradise Valley. "The gig in British Columbia was in a really beautiful natural environment," John York will recall, "some of the most beautiful country I have ever seen. It was breathtaking."

Candi Promotions has rounded up an impressive selection of performers but cannot decide until the last minute whether the festival should go ahead. Finally they agree to proceed, so it's a race to promote the event and attract festival-goers. "Festival's Definitely On!" screams a whole-page ad in *The Georgia Straight* (August 21–27), which lists a jumble of names: Chicago Transit Authority, Grateful Dead, The Flying Burrito Brothers, The Byrds, Rotary Connection, Merrilee Rush, Canned Heat, Guess Who, Chrome Cyrcus, Poco, Little Richard, The Chambers Brothers, Strawberry Alarm Clock, Love, Alice Cooper, and The Grassroots. A late news item in *The Vancouver Sun* (August 20) also promises Jeff Beck, Smith, The Rascals, Mary Weather, Taj Mahal, Tarantula, Sonny Terry & Granny Magee [sic], and Lee Michaels, although some of these – such as Jeff Beck – get lost in the shuffle. Thanks to countless volunteers and great efforts by Seattle promoter Boyd Grafmyre, the festival miraculously goes ahead.

The Byrds appear on the festival's first day, together with Chrome Crycus, The Collectors, The Flying Burrito Brothers, Tarantula, Canned Heat, and Little Richard. To relieve the wait between equipment break-downs and set-ups, Mickey Mouse and Donald Duck cartoons are screened as night falls. On the Monday following the festival, Eileen Johnson of *The Vancouver Sun* sums up her impressions of the weekend. "The Hasty Pop Festival: An Attempt at an Impossible Task" runs the headline, and she declares that everything – the music, the sound system, the weather, the lightshow – was excellent and that no one suffered from overcrowding – because the festival is so poorly attended. Bert Gartner and his Candi Promotions have attempted to put the festival together in record time, and with around 15,000 people milling about for a festival that will break even with 30,000 paying guests, the organisers lose an estimated $75,000 Canadian.

Jimmi Seiter, now working for The Flying Burrito Brothers, tells the paper: "There will be no more pop festivals in Canada. When the word gets out, as it will Monday morning, no agent in the US will book a group into a Canadian pop festival. Maybe if Boyd Grafmyre has something to do with it they will: it was only because of him that we came. But this is too much of a fiasco and this cat running it doesn't care or even know how to care. Many of the groups haven't been paid, but we all have valid signed contracts and we will be paid or we will file suit."

The Squamish Times (September 3) poses the question: "Are Rock Festivals necessary?" in an editorial, and wonders why local workmen hired by the festival barely have their modest bills covered, while the performers are guaranteed huge fees (topped by The Rascals, who receive $15,000). "Many of the young people who attended the festival were dismayed and shocked at some of the activities which accompanied it," notes the *Times*. "Some have said they have no desire to attend another one. This is good, and perhaps the best way for the young people to discover a sense of values."

So what of the music? *The Squamish Times* correspondent arrives too late on the Friday to catch The Byrds, but the *Vancouver Sun* writes that "the new Byrds and the old Byrds, now The Flying Burrito Brothers, each put on fine country and folk-rock shows, then performed together in a grand reunion that lasted more than an hour, to the crowd's delight".

Tuesday 26
◁)) **RECORDING** Columbia Recording Studios, Sunset and El Centro, Hollywood, CA.

'Wasn't Born To Follow' (UK)

A 'Wasn't Born To Follow' (C. KING/ G. GOFFIN)
B 'Child Of The Universe' (G. CLARK)

UK release 26 1969 (CBS 4572)
Chart high US none
Read more ... entries for November 30 1967 and December 4 1968

Producer Terry Melcher and engineer Jerry Hochman.

Today's session – a day in the studio with just McGuinn and producer Melcher – will be the last for some time. The two are paying tribute to the Apollo 11 expedition, with 'Armstrong, Aldrin, And Collins'. The number is a throwaway, consisting of a voice calling out a 20-to-1 countdown, then the sound of a space ship lifting off, followed by a short folksy ditty. How the song has ended up with McGuinn is unclear; it is copyrighted by Zeke Manners (with Scott Seely), a 60-year-old radio host and composer of innumerable songs.

Friday 29–Saturday 30
Kinetic Playground, Chicago, IL
The Byrds are back in Chicago after just two weeks, this time to play a special end-of-summer weekend with Taj Mahal and Cat Mother & The All Night Newsboys. "That gig in Chicago with Taj Mahal brings back memories," John York will recall. "I wanted to hear the combination of Clarence White and [Mahal's guitarist] Jesse Edwin Davis, so we asked if Taj cared to jam with us. I was very disappointed when the offer was refused."

Sunday 31
'New Orleans Pop Festival', Baton Rouge International Speedway, Prairieville, LA
The festival summer season draws to a close with a gathering at a racetrack near Baton Rouge in Louisiana. As it is Labour Day Weekend, the Monday is a federal holiday, and the two-day festival attracts a 50,000 crowd. The Byrds presumably play on the Sunday following yesterday's concert in Illinois, and the other performers are Axis, Canned Heat, Cat Mother & The All Night Newsboys, Chicago Transit Authority, Country Joe & The Fish, Deacon John & The Electric Soul Train, Grateful Dead, Lee Michaels, Iron Butterfly, It's A Beautiful Day, Jefferson Airplane, Janis Joplin, Oliver, Pot Liquor, Santana, Snowrabbit, Spiral Staircase, Sweetwater, Tyrannosaurus Rex, White Fox, Whizbang, and The Youngbloods, while Glenn McKay's Headlights provide a lightshow.

September

Sunday 7
'Aquarian Age', Folsom Stadium, University of Colorado, Bolder, CO
The Byrds are a late addition to this Colorado University show with Country Joe & The Fish, The Steve Miller Band, Tim Hardin, Buddy

Guy, The Sons Of Champlin, and local group Conal Implosion. Student paper *Chinook* (September 11) briefly notes that it "was very definitely good", perhaps due to the "receptive, stoned audience". The reporter continues: "Of course, the show was a little long, and a lot of people got cold, and for some reason the johns were hard to find, and in some instances, locked up; those were minor things, though, compared to the impact of the show as a whole."

Friday 19
Gymnasium, Valparaiso University, Valparaiso, IN
The group appears with The Ides Of March.

Saturday 20
Cardinal Hayes Auditorium, College of Mount Saint Vincent, Riverdale, NY

Friday 26
Carnegie Hall, New York City, NY
The Byrds have the honour to open the doors of New York's esteemed Carnegie Hall to rock concerts after a period where the venue has barred pop stars from performing. Riots in 1964, first with The Beatles (on February 12) and then The Rolling Stones (on June 20), convinced the hall's management that rock concerts should be banned forever. It is promoter Howard Stein who persuades the management to reverse the ban, although today's two shows – 8:30pm and midnight, with The Byrds, The Flying Burrito Brothers, and The Holy Modal Rounders – probably do not attract the rowdiest clientele anyway.

Ed Ochs from *Billboard* (October 11) dismisses The Flying Burrito Brothers because he cannot stand Gram Parsons. "[The] screaming pretensions and garish self-delusions reduced the potentially excellent band to a group ego trip. Parsons' voice is matronly and his sickly Elvis fantasies are unpleasant to watch." So compared to this, The Byrds are a relief. "Their priceless collection of Dylan readings are, of course, great to hear again, but the new Byrds are good enough to get by without them, working their patented synthesis of pop and country, which they have perfected well enough to pass in either market. Though still drawing pictures of his lyrics in the air like a daffy painter without a canvas, Roger McGuinn has still whipped The Byrds into semi-sacred status in rock circles, and it is McGuinn's quality voice that has put them there. Clarence White's underrated guitar effort has glued together the ever-feathering Byrds, and with the force of McGuinn's ego, pushed them higher."

Record World (October 11) notes: "Both [Burritos and Byrds] have a strange attitude toward the audience. Although they were cheered after almost every number, they seemed bored with the adulation. Their music was impeccable and the diverse gathering had nothing but praise, but their unemotional performance made them Andy Warhols of pop music."

The two groups combine for a jam at the end. *Record World* describes it as perfunctory, but it is toted as the highpoint of the night in *The East Village Other* (September 1969), whose reviewer watches the second show far into the night. "There were five guitars, three drummers, and one tambourine–vocalist (Gram Parsons of the Burritos). And the sound was tremendous. They did a too-short 20 minutes climaxed by a stunning version of 'Eight Miles High'."

Over in Britain, an unusual UK-only single is released, coupling two film-related Byrds tracks: 'Wasn't Born To Follow' from the *Easy Rider* soundtrack on the A-side backed with 'Child Of The Universe' from Candy. *Easy Rider* premiered in London at the beginning of September to full houses, but that does not translate to sales of this rather unnecessary Byrds single. It is generally passed over by the music weeklies, but Ric Grech of supergroup Blind Faith (at least, until that group is officially announced as disbanded in a matter of weeks) is played the track in *Melody Maker*'s Blind Date (October 4). "This is a track from *The Notorious Byrd Brothers* album and it's great," says Grech. "I remember hearing this about two years ago. I don't see why they are releasing it as a single now except that it will get some publicity from the film *Easy Rider*. [In the movie] they play this and other records in the background. The Byrds have always been one of my favourite groups."

James Hamilton, who reviews singles by US artists in *Record Mirror* (October 25), notes: "One of the songs featured in *Easy Rider* is this Byrds *Notorious* LP track, a full-sounding country-tinged gentle stomper, uneventful but for the good freaky phasing. Duller and slower flip, from their *Dr & Mr* LP." Hamilton gives it four out of five stars.

October

Wednesday 1

'Ballad Of Easy Rider' is released as the 17th Byrds single in the US and goes some way toward recapturing old glories. Cruising along on the publicity generated by the movie, the single sails up to a respectable Number 65 in *Billboard* – the best chart showing since 'My Back Pages' two years ago. It will also be the

group's last ever single that can be termed, however modestly, a hit. (Slightly less impressive in *Cash Box*, however, where it stalls at Number 87.)

Saturday 4
Civic Auditorium, Albuquerque, NM
Concert with Three Dog Night, Blue Cheer, and The Byrds.

Sunday 5
Sam Houston Coliseum, Houston, TX
The Byrds, Jefferson Airplane, Grateful Dead, and Poco star in a 'rock jubilee' promoted by Sonic Productions. The show begins at 1:00pm as promised but as delays increase during the afternoon, the schedule lags behind the advertised 6:00pm closing. Finally, at 10:00pm, the plug is pulled on Jefferson Airplane.

John York is ready for a change. "The gig in Houston was disappointing to me because the audience waited several hours for the show to begin, and then we gave them a very short 40-minute show," he recounts later. "I thought they deserved more because they had waited so long for us to play. That's when I talked about leaving the band to Gene and Clarence, which led to a phone call soon after, telling me I was out of the band."

•

It turns out Parsons and White already have York's replacement, Skip Battin, ready and waiting in the wings. Speaking to author John Einarson, York adds: "I was going to give it another six months, [and] save some money, because it wasn't working for me. I imagine I would have felt better about it the next day, but in the meantime they went to Roger and said, 'John's going to quit. We've got this friend of ours who'd be perfect.' And that's how it went down. Skip came in and was a force to be reckoned with. The Byrds have always been like a pond that reflected whatever was in the sky above it: you get a real honest representation of what was going on with the members of the band."

Clyde 'Skip' Battin has a long musical career that stretches back to 1954 – rock'n'roll's Year Zero, the year Elvis Presley recorded 'That's Alright Mama'. Older than many of his rock contemporaries, Battin started out with Earl Mock & The Mockingbirds and The Pledges in Arizona in the mid 1950s before enjoying success in 1958–60 as one half of Skip & Flip with Gary Paxton. They racked up a couple of national minor hits ('Cherry Pie', 'Fancy Nancy', and 'It Was I') and toured around the US. In the early 60s Battin moved to California, where he enrolled at University College of Los Angeles, worked as a part-time actor, and kept a sideline as recording artist and musician. He crossed paths with future song-

writing partner Kim Fowley; took advantage of his old career by forming Skip & The Flips; and appeared as a solo artist on local L.A. television to promote the single 'Searchin'. 1965 is the watershed moment.

"I remember the first night I saw The Byrds at Ciro's," Battin will tell Barry Ballard in the fanzine *Omaha Rainbow* (December 1976), "which was really the clincher. We got out of our suits, out of our slicked-down hair, out of doing jukebox songs and started doing original material. We had the idea that we wanted to do electric bluegrass, 'bluegrass rock', after seeing The Byrds doing electric folk. I'd always liked bluegrass from my country days."

Battin performed under various guises (often spelling his name with a 'y', as in 'Battyn'), and joined The Evergreen Blueshoes, with whom he recorded an album in 1968. Blueshoes guitarist Al Rosenberg introduced Battin to Clarence White, and – independently of this – Battin played on a recording session with Gene Parsons, probably through their mutual acquaintance Gary Paxton. Another session he participated in was for the Gene Vincent album I'm Back And I'm Proud (a Kim Fowley production), possibly recorded just this summer.

With John York out of The Byrds, the way in is open for Battin. "When Gene asked me whether I was interested in playing bass for The Byrds I jumped at the chance," he tells Barry Ballard. "The Byrds had been in my head all the time and it was a case of wanting something real bad over a long period of time."

Looking back on his career, Battin will recall his initiation to Hans Hanegraaff in a 1985 conversation. "It was pretty hard to know what they were talking about before they hired me. They needed a bass player. I met Clarence during my Evergreen period.

'Ballad Of Easy Rider' (US)

A 'Ballad Of Easy Rider' (B. DYLAN/ R. McGUINN)

B1 'Wasn't Born To Follow' (C. KING/ G. GOFFIN)

B2 'Oil In My Lamp' (G. PARSONS/ C. WHITE)

US release October 1 1969 (Columbia 44990)
Chart high US number 65
Read more … entries for November 30 1967 (B1), June 19, July 1 (B2), June 18, 1969 (B1)

... We played together in living rooms. So we knew each other casually, because he was very busy at the time; he was a Byrd.

"One day I was called to do a demo session for Bob Rafkin. ... The session had Gene Parsons on drums as well. So we had a good time. A week or ten days later I got a call from him, if I was interested in joining The Byrds? I said I was and he asked me to come over for rehearsals and a try-out. I said give me a week to think about it – and I spent a week studying all the Byrds songs. I got the idea I was going to make it, that my life was changing in a positive way. So, I met Roger the first time at the rehearsal and played one Byrds song after another on stage in an empty hall, and it came through real well."

White and Parsons may know Battin, but to McGuinn he is a new acquaintance. "I'd never met Skip before," McGuinn confirms to Jud Cost in 2000. "I don't remember how that happened, either. I think somebody brought him around and he was good. So that was it. It was very loose. We almost took the first person who came in the door. Things just fell together. It wasn't like a real tight ship. We were just kinda flying by the seat of our pants. And it came out great. I was real happy about it."

Friday 10
'Gansett Tribal-Rock Festival', Rhode Island Auditorium, Providence, RI

Sponsored by Gansett (an abbreviation of Narragansett Beer), this little festival is planned to star Crosby Stills Nash & Young, plus Country Funk, before CNSY cancel their entire East Coast tour because of the death of David Crosby's girlfriend Christine Hinton – killed in a senseless car accident on September 30. Sly & The Family Stone and The Byrds are booked as replacements, but possibly The Byrds may drop out at the last minute, even if the show goes ahead with Sly.

Saturday 11
Fieldhouse, St Joseph's College, Philadelphia, PA

The group appears with Lothar & The Hand People and The American Dream. By all accounts this is John York's last night with The Byrds. However, the group may play a third concert this weekend, as York will recall: "I have a feeling that one of the last gigs I played with the band was in Florida. The concert was on a stage overlooking a huge swimming pool at a university."

Byrds fan Ken Young recalls of the Philadelphis gig: "I remember them looking a lot hairier than the *Dr. Byrds & Mr. Hyde* version of the band. When The Byrds came on I was sitting on the side of the fieldhouse in front of Clarence, several rows back. It was the first time I had seen his Telecaster close up and I remember noting how thick it was. I couldn't figure out how he was getting those steel-like tones out of the Tele. Anyhow, he was amazing. I at first felt ambiguous about Clarence, because I fell in love with The Byrds when 'Mr. Tambourine Man' first came out, so McGuinn's Rickenbacker was a big part of my interest in the group. Clarence's addition put the Rick a bit more in the background and, to me at least, adding the country-style Tele to some of the old Byrds hits didn't necessarily improve them. But that doesn't take away from what a spectacular player Clarence was and the new dimension he added to the group."

Friday 17
Carl Edward King Memorial Gymnasium, Morris Harvey University, Charleston, WV

Skip Battin debuts with The Byrds as their new bass player. "The first gig was in Charleston," he will recall in 1985.

"A gym isn't dandy for a rock concert," writers Ray Brack of *The Charleston Gazette* (October 25), who favourably reviewed the group's last visit to West Virginia on August 9. "Morris Harvey students and alumni at the school's homecoming concert last week could hear The Byrds' lead singer Roger McGuinn only when he called for more PA volume. Most of the time they heard a badly-distorted parody of The Byrds' concise country rock, as the sound bounced around jai alai-like off the concrete-block gymnasium walls.

"Many students were bothered more by the new Byrds country-canted repertoire unveiled live to West Virginia just a few weeks ago at the Civic Center. The MH crowd seemed to prefer the Byrds proper rock stuff like 'Mr. Spaceman' and 'Ballad Of Easy Rider' to such country material as 'Old Blue', 'Nashville West', and 'Send Me Back Home'. Still, it appears from here that the big Byrds comeback is going to be built on their skills in selecting and performing songs in the country idiom, many of which are distinctly hillbilly. Look for some rockabilly song, performed perchance by The Byrds, to hit the top of the charts during the next 12 months." Even if Brack's bold prediction will not come true, The Byrds have sown the seeds of a new California country rock sound that others will harvest in just a few years time.

Saturday 18
Atwood Hall, Clark University, Worcester, MA

The group appears with Tim Hardin, who – according to the student paper review (October 24) – is in a rush to get off the stage as quickly as possible. The Byrds, on the other hand, turn in a smooth performance. "[They] love their music and will work to make sure that it sounds the way it should. In comparison to Hardin the difference was like night and day. There's also something sentimental about listening to The Byrds – they seemed to have been around as long as one can remember rock. However, The Byrds are by no means dated. ... Saturday's performance indicated that a lot of people owe a great deal to The Byrds. Their guitar playing is more than just competent; in fact, the lead guitarist, Clarence White, gave rise to speculation that he had six fingers."

Friday 24–Saturday 25
Electric Factory, Philadelphia, PA
Support by The Litter.

Tuesday 28
Jerry Hopkins interviews a content Roger McGuinn. He has become the father of a second son three days earlier at his Los Angeles home. The interview is printed in *Rolling Stone* (dated November 29; published November 5) and serves to update readers on McGuinn's busy calendar. Also, Skip Battin is officially introduced as the new Byrd.

"We're putt-putting along OK these days and if everything happens as we think it will, The Byrds might really begin to happen again," says McGuinn. The new album is now called *Easy Rider* (the earlier working title *Captain America* is not mentioned again), and he thinks it has "more meat, it's more together. I thought *Sweetheart Of The Rodeo* was a good album, but it was rather specialised. This one has more variety. Rock. Gospel. Songs by Woody Guthrie, Dylan, Pam Polland, even Zeke Manners. There's some country, of course, but really country music was just a trip for me – something Gram Parsons and Chris Hillman got me into."

Concurrently, McGuinn's pursues two main projects outside The Byrds: One is *Gene Tryp*, the other is the Moog synthesizer. Jacques Levy is preoccupied with directing the West Coast ensemble of *Oh! Calcutta!*, an erotic revue that has already caused havoc in New York and is set to open at San Mateo's On Broadway Theatre in October. But he intends to get back to *Gene Tryp* as soon as possible. "It isn't likely anyone will hear many of the songs before we open on Broadway anywhere from winter to next fall," McGuinn explains to Hopkins. "Certainly we didn't use any of them on our new album, nor do we plan to record them in the near future. Perhaps in performance we'll do one every now and then, but if

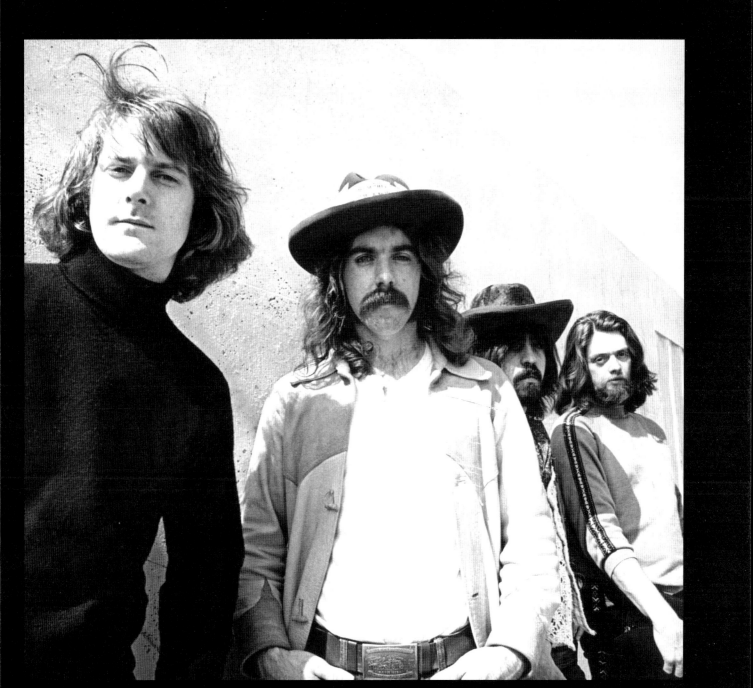

we recorded them, the material would be old by the time we reached the stage; then people would say we were using old album material in the musical."

McGuinn constantly explores the synthesizer, but is unsure where to apply it. "I think I'm making real progress with the thing," he alleges. "I have most of the technical patching down, but what I should be doing is spending two or three hours a day with it, like I did when I was learning how to play the guitar." McGuinn has perhaps taken the words of the instrument's inventor, Robert Moog, to heart. "There are maybe 25 people in the world who have the necessary competence in both physics and music," Moog says in *The Los Angeles Times* (August 24).

Although McGuinn has blended the instrument subtly on many Byrds recordings with splendid results, he still envisions something grander and more significant. The latest opportunity is to write the score for a science-fiction film directed and co-produced by Englishman Tony Foutz and producer Douglas Trumbull, the man who provided special effects for *2001: A Space Odyssey*. The cast of characters features the unlikely team of Gram Parsons and Michelle [Gilliam] Phillips, and

much of the film has already been shot at a flying-saucer convention in the Joshua Tree National Park, some 100 miles west of Los Angeles. The *Rolling Stone* interviewer, Jerry Hopkins, outlines the brief plot in his article – "Parsons and Miss Gilliam portray two 'intergalactic flower children' who travel in a flying mobile home – and according to later accounts that's about the extent of the story.

There is a postscript to the movie before it is finally shelved. Interviewed by a Seattle underground rag in April of next year – the film by then even given a title, *GR69* – McGuinn will say he is about to compose the score. Then, when quoted in *Friends* (August 7, 1970), the story goes that McGuinn has completed the music. Despite an updated title – *Ecology 70* – this will be the last anyone hears of the project, although it may inspire co-producer Douglas Trumbull and his next project, the ecological science-fiction epic *Silent Running*.

Friday 31
National Guard Armory, St. Louis, MO
Umberto Orsini presents a Halloween Trippers Treat (8:00pm–1:00am) starring The Byrds.

Ballad Of Easy Rider

A1 'Ballad Of Easy Rider' (B. DYLAN /R. MCGUINN)
A2 'Fido' (J. YORK)
A3 'Oil In My Lamp' (G. PARSONS/C. WHITE)
A4 'Tulsa County' (P. POLLAND)
A5 'Jack Tarr The Sailor' (TRAD. ARR. R. MCGUINN)
B1 'Jesus Is Just Alright' (A. REYNOLDS)
B2 'It's All Over Now, Baby Blue' (B. DYLAN)
B3 'There Must Be Someone (I Can Turn To)' (V. GOSDIN/C. GOSDIN/R. GOSDIN)
B4 'Gunga Din' (G. PARSONS)
B5 'Deportee (Plane Wreck At Los Gatos)' (W. GUTHRIE/M. HOFFMAN)
B6 'Armstrong, Aldrin And Collins' (Z. MANNERS/S. SEELY)

US release November 10 1969 (Stereo LP CS 9942/CK 9942)
UK release January 16 1970 (Stereo CBS S 63795)
Chart high US number 36; UK number 41
Read more ... entries for June 17, 18, 19, 23, 24, July 1, 2, 22, 23, 24, August 15, 26 1969

Bonus CD tracks: 'Way Beyond The Sun' (trad. arr. McGuinn), 'Mae Jean Goes To Hollywood' (J. Browne), 'Oil In My Lamp' [Alternate Version] (G. Parsons/C. White), 'Tulsa County' [Alternate Version] (P. Polland), 'Fiddler A Dram (Moog Experiment)' (trad. arr. McGuinn), 'Ballad Of Easy Rider' [Long Version] (B. Dylan/R. McGuinn), 'Build It Up ' [Instrumental] (C. White/G. Parsons)

"It is not entirely appropriate to use any Byrds album as a benchmark for the current Byrds though, as McGuinn and the group have gone through some changes, musical and personnel, since the album you might be thinking about. A stylistic integrity returns with this release, however, and although the music is sincere, it is generally unmoving." JAZZ & POP, JUNE 1970

November

Monday 10
The association with the *Easy Rider* movie has given The Byrds renewed recognition, so the group's ninth album of original material is wisely named *Ballad Of Easy Rider*. To further emphasise the connection, Peter Fonda has agreed to write the liner notes. Paraphrasing 'It's All Over Now, Baby Blue', Fonda weaves in two encounters with The Byrds: the Fourth Of July party at sister Jane's Malibu home in 1965; and spiraling to Pensacola in John Lear's small jet aircraft in 1966. Fonda says in *The Los Angeles Times* (February 15, 1970): "That's where it started for me, on the beach with The Byrds."

The album follows the course staked out by *Dr. Byrds & Mr. Hyde*, but the contributions are more democratically spread this time. On the last album, McGuinn sang every song; this time John York and Clarence White have one lead vocal each, while Gene Parsons has two. McGuinn, who has been saving original songs for *Gene Tryp*, has the title track as his sole songwriting credit on the album. The varied input might suggest a sprawling collection of songs, but *Ballad Of Easy Rider* is a more even and cohesive album than its predecessor. The sound of the old Byrds, however, is irretrievably gone. This is best demonstrated by comparing the version of Bob Dylan's 'It's All Over Now, Baby Blue' here with the one that the group and Terry Melcher recorded four years earlier as a proposed follow-up to 'Mr. Tambourine Man'. The 1965 version is fast-paced and vigorous, with McGuinn's Dylan-like nasal vocal and ringing 12-string guitar at the centre of the action; the 1969 interpretation is languid and lazy with an emphasis on clean harmony vocals and White's soothing string-bends.

Ed Leimbacher reviews the album for *Rolling Stone* (December 27) in tandem with the Steve Miller Band's *Your Saving Grace*. "The Byrds, of course – under the aegis of McGuinn the Survivor – are renowned for a rich, thickly-textured instrumental sound and equally distinctive vocal harmony. Every new Byrds album seems a continuation of the last; few surprises occur – instead, it's just like a visit with old friends. ... But musicians like to confound critics. Everyone who's written about The Byrds has detected, in retrospect at least, their all-along C&W soul; now McGuinn is denying that as mostly mythical, as having been merely the influence of Parsons and Hillman on the group. His claim won't wash for *Dr. Byrds* (cut after their departure), but it just might for *Ballad Of Easy Rider* – because this album exhibits several cuts with a whole

The Byrds. "Easy Rider." America has been waiting for them both.

When Peter Fonda asked Roger McGuinn, lead Byrd, to write the score and sing the title song for his film, it was no accident. "Easy Rider" is about a new direction in America. The Byrds are a new direction in American music.

Their new single, **"Wasn't Born to Follow"**, is also from the movie. And it's already number 1 on KXOA in Sacramento, and number 16 on KFRC in San Francisco — "Easy Rider" country — and spreading fast.

They've also got a new album that's causing a lot of excitement. The Byrds. Bigger than ever. And ever setting the trends.

On Columbia Records®

THE BYRDS
BALLAD OF
EASY RIDER
INCLUDING:
BALLAD OF EASY RIDER / OIL IN MY LAMP
ARMSTRONG, ALDRIN AND COLLINS
IT'S ALL OVER NOW, BABY BLUE
JESUS IS JUST ALRIGHT

'new' sound. Unfortunately, it's also only intermittently successful.

"The title cut, for example, adds strings (!); but it flows gently, sweet Dylan, brief and to the point, and McGuinn's voice truly makes you feel free. 'Fido' comes next – 'Bird Dog' revisited – with cowbells and conga rhythms and a definitely non-Byrds harmony (evidently McGuinn's no longer requiring the other voices to complement his). Followed then by old-time Byrds-gospel, 'Oil In My Lamp'. Jaunty guitar interplay, but a paltry song. McGuinn's feeling vocal and Clarence White's hick picking bring it all back home with 'Tulsa County Blue': 'I don't know just where I'll go …'. A bizarre rendition of 'Jack Tarr The Sailor' closes out the top side.

"The bottom side's equally confused – strong and sure for 'Jesus Is Just Alright' and a slow-as-molasses-or-Fudge 'It's All Over Now, Baby Blue'. For the latter, McGuinn contributes a much more inventive vocal than he did for *Easy Rider* (the film) and White's guitar spices and spruces everything up. But the rest's a long dying fall – nice enough, but from The Byrds you expect more and better. … The Byrds are still on the wing, but seem a little woozy and wobbly."

Todd Selbert writes in *Jazz & Pop* (June 1970): "Pretty good Byrds – their best effort since the stunning *The Notorious Byrd Brothers*. It is not entirely appropriate to use any Byrds album as a benchmark for the current Byrds though, as McGuinn and the group have gone through some changes, musical and personnel, since the album you might be thinking

about. A stylistic integrity returns with this release, however, and although the music is sincere, it is generally unmoving. The majority of the cuts are in a country-and-south-western vein. 'Jesus' is two minutes of hard-driving Gospel According To The Byrds, 'Baby Blue' is just fine Dylaniana and 'Someone' is a believable lament, but the rest are listenable but forgettable. Alas, The Byrds of *Fifth Dimension*, *Younger Than Yesterday*, and *The Notorious Byrd Brothers* appear to have flown. Those albums were their zenith and the apogee of lyrical popular music native to the United States in the past decade.

The Oakland Tribune (March 15 1970) says: "Probably the best album this veteran folk rock group has done in recent years. Roger [McGuinn's] smooth vocals on the superb title tune, which he wrote and recorded differently for the film, contrasts nicely with his crusty singing on 'Jack Tarr The Sailor'. Bob Dylan's 'It's All Over Now, Baby Blue' and an old Woody Guthrie tune should satisfy those many old Byrds fans. However, new tunes such as 'Jesus Is Just Alright' and 'Fido' are the best of the Byrds at present."

Ballad Of Easy Rider is the group's first Top 40 album (it makes US Number 36) since *Younger Than Yesterday*.

Friday 14
Dillon Gymnasium, Princeton University, Princeton, NJ

The Byrds play one concert at 8:00pm at Princeton, but many come to shout abuse or boycott the concert – not because of The Byrds, but because many students feel it is inappropriate to stage a rock concert on the weekend of the Moratorium Day march on Washington, DC. "Despite the sponsors' claim that the concert was a 'time for peace', some felt that it was a Fascist, capitalist, etc, enterprise," writes assistant editor Andrew Wilson of *The Princetonian* (November 17). Despite the chaos surrounding the concert, The Byrds give a strong performance. "They did nearly every kind of song imaginable, Cajun, country, Chuck Berry, space music, their old hits. … The Byrds magic has been transferred safely through dozens of changes: they have become more a tradition than a group of musicians. Their virtuosity, their calm, the sense of effortless soaring that infuses their music – all these make the Byrds mystique. From a purely rational point of view it's absurd to talk about mystique and magic, but when talking about man and music, it's absurd to talk about pure rationality. So I trust that The Byrds will soar on."

Saturday 15
Loyola College, Baltimore, MD

The Byrds may be playing to empty seats in Baltimore because many of Loyola's students attend the massive Moratorium Day march 30 miles away in Washington, DC, to protest against the US involvement in the Vietnam War. The march attracts a remarkable half-a-million demonstrators. Loyola students plan to read the names of the war dead during an all-night vigil.

Sunday 23–Wednesday 26

Thelma, Los Angeles, California, USA

The group plays the second opening of a new Sunset Strip club – Elvin Bishop premiered the club the previous week – and share the stage with Colorado group Zephyr. "I was able to hear The Byrds at Thelma, the 'new club in town'," reports Judy Sims in *Disc* (December 6). "It's a very small place with black walls, vaguely reminiscent of the 50s and beatnik coffee houses; the stage is small, but the sound is good, and The Byrds sounded very fine indeed. Sneaky Pete, steel guitarist for The Flying Burrito Brothers, was sitting in with The Byrds, and the bass payer was also temporary – Skip Battin, and he's much too good to remain temporary. Clarence White on guitar, Gene Parsons on drums, and the venerable Roger McGuinn – actually animated, dancing, gesturing, joking, having a good time, looking younger than he did four years ago. The audience didn't react (except to applaud appreciatively after each number), which was disappointing because I thought his newfound fun should be encouraged. Aside from McGuinn's antics, The Byrds musicianship was impeccable."

John Mendelsohn reviews the Sunday night for *The Los Angeles Times* (November 25). "Say what you will about them, The Byrds are the best local group winging to spend a winter Sunday night with, as the Roger McGuinn-owned and operated foursome made clear with a uniformly delightful opening set at intimate new Thelma's two evenings ago. Once the laughing-stock of the rock cosmos for their inestimably awful stage act, The Byrds in their present incarnation are as solid a live act as is to be found, both instrumentally and vocally. Former Kentucky Colonel Clarence White, a stocky little bearded man, plays a thickly country-flavoured full guitar and sings parts without ever displaying the most negligible emotion or moving his lips. Mr Skip, the new Byrd, plays bass and wears a perpetual distant smirk. Gene Parsons simultaneously drums up a small storm and high-harmonises himself red in the face. And McGuinn, who does nearly all of the group's lead-singing, alternately minces around his microphone and swings and sways while playing second guitar."

Mendelsohn lists many of the songs performed ('Old Blue', 'He Was A Friend Of Mine', 'Drug Store Truck Drivin' Man', 'Close Up The Honky Tonks', 'Take A City Bride', 'Jesus Is Just Alright', 'This Wheel's On Fire', 'Ballad Of Easy Rider') to exemplify the group's multi-rooted diversity, and picks two highlights: "[The] first when McGuinn tipped his proverbial hat to Byrds history by donning weird sunglasses to sing 'Mr. Spaceman'; the second when Clarence got to cut loose in an instrumental called 'Nashville West'."

Friday 28

Florida Presbyterian College, St. Petersburg, FL

With The Flying Burrito Brothers presently on hold, Jimmi Seiter is working as road manager for The Byrds again.

The rarely performed '5D' is played tonight, according to the review in *The St. Petersburg Times* (November 29).

Friday 28–Sunday 30

'First Annual Palm Beach Music And Art Festival', Palm Beach International Raceway, West Palm Beach, FL

The Rolling Stones are winding up their wildly successful North American tour in Florida on the last day of the Palm Beach festival. The Stones have not toured the States since the summer of 1966 but have comfortably made the transition from a pop group punching out 30-minute shows to cocky entertainers who go on stage each night after justifiably being introduced as The Greatest Rock'n'Roll Band In The World.

The Byrds, who play on the Saturday, are among the names appearing on posters for the festival together with The Chambers Brothers, Country Joe & The Fish, Grand Funk Railroad, Janis Joplin & The Full Tilt Boogie Band, Jefferson Airplane, Johnny Winter, King Crimson, Pacific Gas & Electric, Rotary Connection, Sly & The Family Stone, Spirit, Steppenwolf, Sweetwater, and The Rugbys, while Iron Butterfly and Vanilla Fudge are late additions. The festival draws a crowd of 40,000 over the weekend, and the three-day event stretches to four days when the Stones do not appear until 4:30 Monday morning. The conditions are not perfect, with heavy rains through Friday night and with temperatures dropping to the cool mid 30s.

An incident reported by United Press Inc chillingly recalls life in a police state. Florida Governor and Republican Claude R. Kirk Jr visits the festival on Friday and demands that a youth be arrested, with a warning that he won't tolerate Florida becoming a playground for hippies. "The Republican governor ordered the boy's arrest following a brief conversation in which he asked the longhaired youngster how he felt," reports *The Panama City News* (November 29). "The teenager responded 'pretty good' but refused to tell Kirk where he was from. 'Take him,' said Kirk, gesturing to [Palm Beach County] Sheriff William Heidtman. Two deputies grabbed the boy, dragged him struggling to a squad car, and drove him away as an angry group of more than 200 youths shouted profanities at the governor. The deputies refused to say what charges would be lodged against the boy, who looked about 15 years old.

"'These kids think they can play in Florida,' Kirk told newsmen. 'Well, they are wrong. You can't play anywhere in this state or in Palm Beach County.' … A youth who … described himself as an underground newspaper editor told Kirk, 'If you start arresting people for not doing anything, then these kids are going to get violent and someone's going to get hurt.' 'Good,' snapped Kirk, who turned and left the Palm Beach Speedway." *Rolling Stone*

(December 27) reports how Sheriff Heidtman dispatches narcotics agents – dressed in hippy garb with bell-bottom trousers and beads – to circulate among the audience. Despite the disguise, they are easily spotted as they stick out with their crew-cut hairstyles and military sunglasses.

December

Friday 5

**THE BYRDS
in Concert
LEBANON VALLEY COLLEGE
Friday, December 5   9:00 P.M.**

Reserved Seats $4 and $3
Tickets available at Marty's Music Store
Lebanon Music Store — or at the door

Lynch Memorial Gym, Lebanon Valley College, Annville, PA

Saturday 6

Upsala College, East Orange, NJ

Joe Cocker teams up with The Byrds for one concert at 8:00pm. Pat Long of student paper *The Stag* (December 17) chats with an upbeat Roger McGuinn backstage after the show. "Did you see the reaction that we got tonight?" he asks. "Three standing ovations and three encores – have you ever seen The Byrds perform like that before? I consider it going uphill, slowly but surely; the whole thing is happening more than ever before. We have a better, tighter, more responsible, more professional, more musical, more dynamic, more interesting, more delightful group than ever before. Forget who The Byrds were ever before, erase it!" Looking ahead to next weekend's New York concerts, he adds jokingly: "My sights are set beyond the Fillmore East; my sights are set on Mars and Pluto and Venus and indeed other galaxies."

Asked if he considers going solo, McGuinn says: "I had thought about it – and forget it. It isn't where it's at. The Byrds is a brand name, like Whirlpool, General Electric, Cadillac. It's actually more like a Lear Jet, you know? And why should we stop and call ourselves the Falcon when we call ourselves Lear Jet instead. It doesn't make it. A rose is a rose whether you call it a babushka or not, as Shakespeare would say."

ALSO …

To celebrate their just-completed North American tour, The Rolling Stones have decided to add a free thank-you concert. Having unsuccessfully tried to get permission to use the Golden Gate Park, the group settles for a racetrack in the small town of Altamont, just east of San Francisco. Remarkably, some 300,000 people turn up today (the concert location was announced less than 24 hours earlier), but the circumstances work against the Stones: an inadequate sound system; a foot-high makeshift stage; poor sanitary conditions; jammed traffic; an unruly crowd; and a security team of Hells Angels swinging lead-filled billiard cues – all conspire to turn the day into a nightmare. Crosby Stills Nash & Young and The Flying Burrito Brothers, who debut new recruit Bernie Leadon on guitar, are reduced to sideshows in the chaos leading up to the late-afternoon performance by the Stones.

Sunday 7

Baldwin Senior High School Gymnasium, Baldwin, NY

Writer–editor and guitar player Chip Lovitt will fondly recall today almost 40 years later. "My best friend and fellow Fillmore East concert-mate, Matt Cooper, was president of the school's General Organisation, at Baldwin High School, a typical Long Island, NY, suburban high school. As a lark, Matt called up Premier Talent in New York to see if they might have a concert act for us. They suggested The Byrds, who were touring a lot in the NY area. The price was $800 for support act NRBQ [New Rhythm & Blues Quartet] and $2,000 for The Byrds. Since it was a Sunday night, we got 'em for a reduced fee.

"While The Byrds' equipment was there – I remember tall Fender Dual Showman amps and other Fender equipment – the band was late. When my friend nervously said to their road manager that he was concerned, he half-smiled, half-sneered, and said, 'Kid, they've been doing this since you were in short pants.' The Byrds showed up soon after and did a set that was about an hour and 20 minutes long.

"Clarence White's style was unique. He had taken his bluegrass roots, electrified them, and added some Buck Owens and Don Rich-influenced Bakersfield twang. Then he combined those elements with a unique behind-the-beat syncopated style. Listening to him play that night, I thought he sounded like no other guitar player I'd ever heard. Many of us 17-year-olds were guitar players who were totally awed by the band, especially

IN CONCERT

**JOE COCKER
THE BYRDS**

UPSALA COLLEGE

VIKING HALL
EAST ORANGE, N.J.

Sat., Dec. 6, 8 P.M.

All Seats $4.50

ADVANCE TICKET SALES

By Mail: To Ticket Dept., Upsala
Bamberger's: All Stores
Montclair State College (Student
Activities Office)
Madison Photo Shop — Madison
Saturn Boutique — Millburn
Viking Hall — Mon., Fri., 9-5 Upsala

For Information
CALL   **266-7000**

Clarence's amazing licks. We had never heard anyone play like that, and what he was doing remained a mystery until years later when I learned he was playing a B-bender-equipped Tele. Of course, Clarence could do all those bends, double-stops, and double-string-bends without the Bender, but this was the height of his string-bending powers. The Byrds rocked the auditorium with hits like 'Mr. Tambourine Man', 'Turn! Turn! Turn!', 'Eight Miles High', and more.

"Anyway, before the show, Clarence was backstage standing there, his usual quiet self. The beard made him look a little aloof, even though I would later learn he was a funny, friendly man to his friends, family, and those he knew. But all of The Byrds, being rock stars, didn't really seem too accessible. That concert made a huge impression on me and most of us music fans that night. It might just have been the coolest day of my high school life, to stand in the wings at my high school auditorium as this legendary band played ten feet away."

Monday 15

Two tracks from *Ballad Of Easy Rider*, 'Jesus Is Just Alright' and 'It's All Over Now Baby Blue', are coupled for The Byrds' new US single, and it will just about sneak into the *Billboard* Hot Hundred at Number 97.

Friday 19–Saturday 20

Fillmore East, Manhattan, New York City, NY

Four strands of 60s rock come together at Bill Graham's Fillmore East: The Byrds with Californian country-folk-rock; The Nice from the UK with Keith Emerson's fiery Hammond organ-wielding classical music and pop; cleverly arranged horn-driven rock by The Sons of Champlin; and Dion, recently reinvented as a singer-songwriter but with a career stretching back to pre-60s doo-wop quartet Dion & The Belmonts.

The Friday show is reviewed in *Hartford's Other Voice* (January 7, 1970), one of many underground papers flourishing at the end of the 1960s. "[Not] especially an example of Byrd magic, it was a remembrance of what it can be and what it has been and what it shall be also, McGuinn's voice coming though everything, and the smile, and the hands making a four-dimensional story to go with the music. The Byrds are one group which has this amazing communication quality, as though everyone on the stage is aware of the others who

are also human beings becoming something new, on that stage. And they like it, that the audience is there and can go someplace with them – or at least someplace else thanks to the music, which is such a nice fuel propellant for anybody."

Saturday 27–Monday 29

A local Los Angeles organisation of promoters calling itself Mid-Winter Pop Festivals Inc books several acts for a three-day festival, 'The Indian Creek Celebration And Music Appreciation Seminar', to be held in a wooded area of rolling hills just north-east of San Luis Obispo, CA, a couple of days before New Year's Eve. The promoters reputedly shell out $300,000 to reserve 13 name acts, including The Byrds, Iron Butterfly, The Chambers Brothers, Johnny Winter, and Country Joe & The Fish, and expect attendance in the region of 200,000–300,000. By the weekend of December 20–21, people arrive at Indian Creek with tents and sleeping bags.

The Altamont disaster has left local California authorities unwilling to give permission for any gathering of large crowds, and lawmen practically see red when a gathering equals a rock festival. Despite clever attempts to draw attention away from the bad image that festivals have gained (such as the rock festival in Florida this weekend that features an out-of-place evangelist, the Reverend Billy Graham) or hide the festivities under a different guise (the Indian Creek festival, for example, is a 'seminar'), the San Luis Obispo project is doomed. The local sheriff, the governor's office, the state disaster office, and nearby city and county authorities join forces to stop the organisers. On December 18, County Supervisors unanimously adopt an ordinance forbidding assemblies of more than 5,000 persons for a period of three months – and that's the end of the seminar.

'Jesus Is Just Alright'

A 'Jesus Is Just Alright'
(A. REYNOLDS)
B 'It's All Over Now, Baby Blue'
(B. DYLAN)

US release December 15 1969
(Columbia 45071)
UK release February 20 19670 (CBS 4753)
Chart high US number 97;
UK none
Read more ... entries for June 17 and July 22 1969

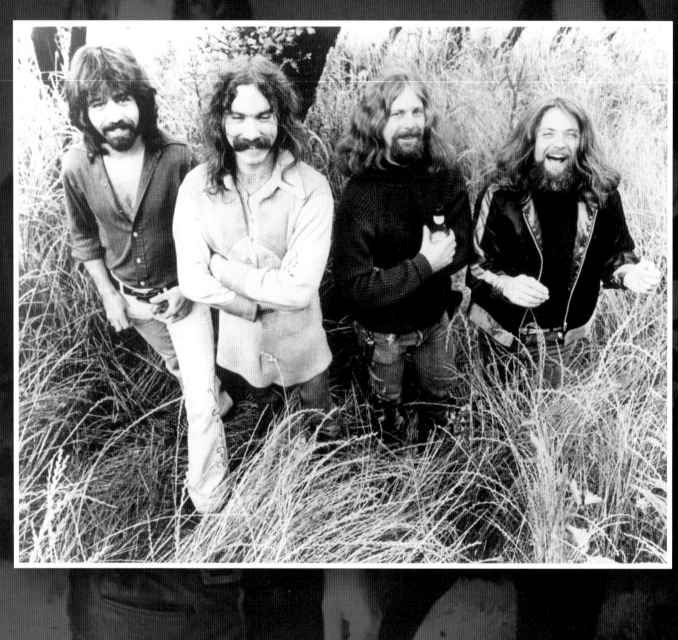
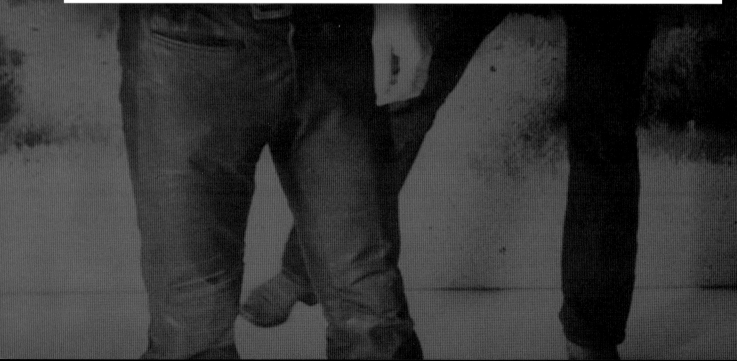

The Byrds record tracks for a live album in March, proving their worth as a first-rate concert attraction ... A planned recording collaboration with **Bob Dylan** unfortunately falls through, but the group records an album's worth of fresh studio material during May and June ... The sessions see the group reunited with former producer Terry Melcher and original manager and mentor Jim Dickson ... The rejuvenated Byrds play **summer festivals** in England and West Germany and several concerts in the Netherlands

1970

to great critical acclaim ... The annual exotic trip takes the group for a visit to The Bahamas in July, this time to promote upcoming half-live/half-studio double album *(Untitled)* ... One-off single 'Chestnut Mare' fails in the US, but is a **surprise UK hit** early next year ... Roger McGuinn is featured in the *Rolling Stone* Interview in October ... The Byrds keep playing steadily around the US to consistently fine reviews.

January

Friday 2–Sunday 4
Fillmore West, San Francisco, CA

The Byrds ring in the new year and the new decade in San Francisco with Fleetwood Mac and blues singer John Hammond Jr. A couple of the performances will later be widely bootlegged and become further proof of The Byrds' eclectic and flexible repertoire.

Roger McGuinn still has the nerve to add further songs from the Bob Dylan catalogue, and 'Positively 4th Street' will remain a staple in the live act for some time. Gene Clark's 'I'll Feel A Whole Lot Better' makes a brief comeback in the set-list, while the group's new bass player, Skip Battin, is featured singing a rather shaky lead vocal on 'You All Look Alike'. The song is the first of many Battin–Kim Fowley collaborations that will be generously featured on the next three Byrds albums. Throughout the weekend, McGuinn is the featured lead vocalist, except on that Battin song and 'Take A City Bride', sung by drummer Gene Parsons. McGuinn introduces the 'Close Up The Honky Tonks'/'You're Still On My Mind'/'Sing Me Back Home' medley with a long ramble on the merits of country and western music. "Country is a weird subject," he intones. "We dig the music! We're not preaching politically."

Much of the time, guitarist Clarence White is the centre of the musical action, nimbly embellishing songs or spinning out fluid solos. The balance between White and McGuinn has shifted to star White as the group's main lead guitarist. Looking back on their partnership, McGuinn will explain many years later to Jud Cost: "Clarence had impeccable timing, beautiful syncopation. For the first year Clarence was in the band, we did a lot of duets on guitar. But after a while – he was such a monster – I just listened."

The exception is 'Eight Miles High', which has always been McGuinn's chance to stretch out and create jagged 12-stringed sheets of sounds. In concert, the song is all that remains of the inventive raga-rock era and by now is the group's only concession to out-and-out jamming – complete with a bass-guitar solo – a trend that otherwise The Byrds thankfully avoid.

(Right now as The Byrds add elasticity to their raga-rock classic, Dutch group Golden Earring make the song the centrepiece of their live act. Earring's album *Eight Miles High* – containing a 19-minute version of the title track – is distributed in the US by Atlantic Records, and the group toured the US with moderate success for the first time in late 1969.)

Monday 5
'Benefit show for the Alcatraz Indians', Aquarius Theatre, Hollywood, CA

The Aquarius Theatre is the latest guise of a venue that The Byrds have visited before; once the Moulin Rouge, the theatre switched names to the Hullabaloo Club, and then the Kaleidoscope, before becoming the Aquarius Theatre when the musical *Hair* opened there at the end of September 1968. *Hair* is still running, but Mondays are a day off, so tonight's slot at 8:30pm is set aside for a benefit concert in support of the Indian occupation of Alcatraz. The Byrds, Eric Burdon & War, and Delaney & Bonnie & Friends have all offered their services for free. Alcatraz Island in the San Francisco Bay closed down as a federal prison in 1963, but in November last year a tribe of Indians claimed the island as unused federal land, arguing that it logically should revert to Indian ownership under terms of an old treaty with the Sioux nation. (The US Government will forcibly end the occupation in June 1971.)

Tuesday 6
ALSO ...

Crosby Stills Nash & Young make their much-anticipated UK debut at the Royal Albert Hall in London, and David Crosby is still smarting from his earlier encounters with the British music press. "I know when I read this in the British pop press," he says in *Record Mirror* (January 17), "it will be 'the fabulous, wonderful, out of this world, wonderful, incredible Youngsby, Nills, Crash and Stungs, et cetera.' [I'm] embarrassed by the pop press in this country, man. ... The press here just won't give the readers anything but prefabricated publicity stories."

Wednesday 7
🖃 **US RADIO** McGuinn does a phone interview with radio station KLWW to promote Saturday's concert in Oklahoma.

Saturday 10
Civic Center Music Hall, Oklahoma City, OK

Concerts West presents The Byrds, Country Joe & The Fish, and The Youngbloods, who unfortunately get on the wrong airplane and step off in Dallas, TX, and thus miss the first show. Dave Dryden writes in The Oklahomian (January 11): "The Byrds carried the burden at a three-band rock concert Saturday night ... while another winged object carried their scheduled co-stars in Dallas. ... The Byrds exhibited a degree of stage polish rare among rock groups, and the balance of their instruments and voices made the listener feel as if he were in a recording studio instead of

an airport. They performed for almost an hour and apparently left most of the several hundred young people who half-filled the auditorium with the feeling they had gotten their money's worth. Before one number, singer Roger McGuinn warned, 'We played this one in Dallas. Nobody liked it. But we're going to play it anyway.' The song, 'He Was A Friend Of Mine', based on the assassination of President Kennedy, drew by far the loudest applause of the evening. The crowd cheered again when The Byrds played a medley of their early recordings, a feature many teens complain are too often omitted by rock groups. Included were 'Turn! Turn! Turn!' and 'Mr. Tambourine Man'."

Sunday 11
Veterans Memorial Coliseum, Grand Rapids, MI

Ortaggus Productions presents the group with Brown Sugar, The Travel Agency US, and the Crystal Ball Light Show, for one show at 3:00pm.

Friday 16
Mid-South Coliseum, Memphis, TN

Golden Star Productions presents The Byrds and local Memphis group Country Funk plus headliner Steppenwolf in a show that draws 8,000 fans. The show is reviewed in *Billboard* (February 7). "Roger McGuinn, leader of The Byrds, who were making their first Memphis appearance, played to the delight of the audience while singing most of the songs from their new Columbia album, *Ballad Of Easy Rider*, including 'Jack Tarr The Sailor', 'Tulsa County Blue', 'Jesus Is Just Alright', 'It's All Over Now, Baby Blue', and numerous others during their 55-minute stay on the stage. The heavy 12-string country guitar that McGuinn played was one of the favourites for the evening."

🖃 **US TV** [Presumably] WHBQ Television Studios, Memphis, TN. WHBQ-TV (Channel 13) *Talent Party*

The Byrds appear on television while in Memphis, miming to 'Jesus Is Just Alright' and 'Mr. Tambourine Man'. The show's format allows no luxury, as Parsons takes his place behind the drums – nothing more than a prop – with the initials "TP" (for *Talent Party*) on the bass-drum head. The backing tracks are just the recorded versions, which in the case of 'Mr. Tambourine Man' bizarrely means that the four on camera mime to a hit single from 1965 that only McGuinn actually appeared on. George Klein, a school buddy of Elvis Presley and a member of the singer's informal 'Memphis Mafia' entourage, is the show's host. *Talent Party* is broadcast tomorrow locally on Channel 13 at 5:00pm.

This Friday also marks the UK release date of the *Ballad Of Easy Rider* album, launched with the catchphrase "The Byrds – Always Beyond Today" but otherwise with little fanfare. For some reason, complimentary copies are apparently not sent to the music weeklies as none of the four big ones (*Melody Maker*, *New Musical Express*, *Disc*, and *Record Mirror*) carries a review.

The album is a minor hit, and makes it Number 41 in the UK album charts.

Saturday 17
Hill Auditorium, University of Michigan Campus, Ann Arbor, MI

A show presented by Canterbury House with support by Commander Cody & His Lost Planet Airmen, a hillbilly-rock combo that will be paired with The Byrds on many occasions. Cody's men, with their irresistible blend of showmanship and musical expertise, are a hit with the crowd, according to Bert Stratton in *The Michigan Daily* (January 18). "Out walk three guitarists and a drummer – The Byrds, and an immediate downer, like where's your fiddle, steel guitar, piano, or anything else? Well, The Byrds got around the problem: they played impeccable guitar, and they harmonised when they sang. That was plenty. Lead Byrd, Roger [McGuinn], led the transition from the raucous Cody mood to the feminine toughness that exudes from his personality. Watching [McGuinn] take over on the country-rock song 'You Ain't Going Nowhere' or the early hit 'Mr. Spaceman' is just as interesting as listening to [Cody]. Small motions that the people up front caught, like the brush of his hand though his long hair, or a gentle smile … and he's different when the music starts. His feelings are out front. Behind the stage, just as he was going to open the door and walk out for the second set, he told his bassist how tired he was, but then quickly added, 'But when I open this door (to the stage), I'm a different person.' Music does that to him. So much so that the other men, even the very talented guitarist Clarence White, are almost unnoticed. They, understandably, call McGuinn 'chief synthesizer' on his latest record."

Sunday 18
Anaheim Convention Center, Anaheim, CA

KRLA Radio presents Three Dog Night, McGuinn's old friend Hoyt Axton, and The Byrds billed as 'Special Guest Stars' for one show at 7:30pm. Judy Sims writes in *Disc* (January 31): "The one and only event of the week [and] a sell-out concert … . [Axton] stood alone with an acoustic guitar in front of 15,000 very young people who were most anx-

KRLA PRESENTS

THREE DOG NIGHT
HOYT AXTON
AND SPECIAL GUEST STARS THE **BYRDS**
ANAHEIM CONVENTION CENTER
SUN., JAN. 18 7:30 PM
All seats reserved at $5.50, 4.50, 3.50
Available at all Computicket and Ticketron Outlets.
Available at Anaheim Convention Center Box Office,
Mutual Agencies, All Wallich's Music Stores, and
United Calif. Banks in Orange County. Mail Orders Accepted.
For information call (714) 635-5000
Produced by CONCERT ASSOCIATES

ious to drool over Three Dog Night and, to a lesser degree, The Byrds; Hoyt carried it off … The Byrds were 'just all right' – that is, they were quite good, well-paced, and definitely together. There was a full-throated cheer when they walked on – tangible evidence of one of rock's longest lasting fan–group relationships. The Byrds' people are loyal and nearly fanatical and have been there in front for five years. McGuinn looked great, and there was noticeably less country music, ending with a vintage Byrds medley – 'Turn! Turn! Turn!', 'Mr Tambourine Man', and 'Eight Miles High'."

Jeff Sherwood writes of the gig in *The Van Nuys Valley News* (January 22). "When this structure was built, it may not have been conceived it would be used for musical events, or at least not ones requiring audiences to sit in back of the performers, or so far in front of them they need binoculars," he complains of the Convention Center. "The Byrds [have] gone through countless changes in personnel, which their sound testifies to. To please the large audience, they ran through a medley of old hits which weren't much. … Roger McGuinn, the only Byrd never to have flown the coop, sings lead in most of the numbers. He has a distinctive voice, but the rest of the group seems to lack musicianship. In the new style, The Byrds have a country sound like The Flying Burrito Brothers."

Sherwood, writing again in the same paper a few days later (January 30), offers a second opinion. "The new Byrds have a strong country influence, similar to The Flying Burrito Brothers and The Band, which is a good improvement. Although the group has new members, its new material is good. If the members would stay away from the old

songs, they could be one of the top groups musically."

Thursday 22–Saturday 24
Boston Tea Party, Boston, MA

The group returns to the Tea Party for three concerts with Cajun fiddler and singer Doug Kershaw, who comes away with top honours according to Peter Schifrin's review in *Broadside/Free Press* (February 11–24), although the headliners also impress.

"The Byrds began their first set with 'You Ain't Going Nowhere' and did a lot of other Dylan songs as well, though some, such as 'It's All Right, Ma' seemed dated. Playing with them was Skip Battin, who replaced bass man John York about three months ago, just after The Byrds cut *Easy Rider*. Battin performed his own 'You All Look Alike', a solid country blues that resembled 'The Weight' as done by The Band. Most of the show was songs The Byrds have already recorded, some of the best being 'You Don't Miss Your Water' and '[Old] Blue'. Their old Top-40 hits, such as 'Mr. Spaceman' and 'Rock'n'Roll Star', done next to selections from their last two albums, demonstrated how much they have improved since moving away from rock into country.

JANUARY 22, 23, 24
THE BYRDS
DOUG KERSHAW
THE BOSTON TEA PARTY 15 LANSDOWNE ST. 536-0915
tickets - Truc - Headquarters East - New Directions - George's Folly - Kansas-Sebastian

Their old folk-rock songs are clever but their country and western is beautiful. Lead singer Roger McGuinn's voice and style are at their best in electric country rock, as he proved in the second show with a country medley that included "an empty bottle and a broken heart and you're still on my mind". He seems to enjoy country music and certainly lets himself go more in that medium."

Monday 26
'Queen's Snowball '70', Grant Hall, Queen's University, Kingston, Ontario, Canada

From Boston, the group moves across the border to Canada for a show in Ontario together with Lighthouse, a popular Canadian rock group fronted by drummer Skip Prokop. Alan Broadbent jots down his impressions in the student paper *Queen's Journal* (January 29). "The Byrds played for about 50 people in Grant Hall on Monday night. Actually, there was closer to 1,100 people at the second set, but the crowd had been stunned by the volume and spectacle of the Toronto group, Lighthouse, and wasn't prepared to put out any effort to appreciate the Byrds. ... When The Byrds came on stage, the crowd was still in a mood of shock from the barrage of the Lighthouse. As a result, they were not prepared to make an effort to grasp the musicianship and complexities of The Byrds.

"This is a new flock of Byrds.... At Queen's on Monday night, The Byrds had changed in one way. Most of the personnel was different. But McGuinn was still there. And he is a superb musician, and is highly respected in the popular music field. He has always been the moving force in The Byrds, as he is now. With this new group, he has selected three musicians whose primary area of expertise is in the country field. His lead guitarist is an extremely quick finger-style picker. The drummer is not flashy, but he is knowledgeable and very seldom does something foolish. The bass player was the only theatrical Byrd, and his bass solo in 'Eight Miles High' was truly obscene.

"And so at Queen's on Monday night, The Byrds displayed their virtuosity in the entire spectrum of pop music of this decade. And the audience did not react. The response was just a shade removed from indifference. ... Appreciation of art is not a matter of whether or not you like it. It is, in the first instance, if you understand it. Art is not, nor should it be, a shower bath. To understand, you do not sit back and make it come to you. You pursue, you search, and you work until you understand. The response to The Byrds on Monday night was a matter of too few people willing to work, to reach out to some of the finest music available in the popular field. It was a matter of too many people in want of a shower."

Friday 30
Binder Physical Education Building, Hartwick College, Oneonta, NY

The Byrds and comedian David Frye play before 1,700 students at the culmination of Hartwick College's Winter Weekend, where students have raised $5,500 for Biafra relief aid.

February

Sunday 1
Massey Hall, Toronto, Canada

The group headlines with support by stand-up comedienne Maury Hayden and the drums–organ duo Teagarden & Van Winkle in what local reviews describe as an altogether disappointing show. Melinda McCracken says in *The Globe & Mail* (February 2): "The concert was sold out, as most rock concerts are these days, but the show itself was far below the audience's expectations. It was one of those nights when the house lights go on and off at the wrong moments, equipment men seem to take an eternity plugging things in, and things generally seem to be unbalanced and going in the wrong direction. Maury Hayden was fortunate to have remained on stage for as long as she did; Teagarden and Van Winkle stayed on almost too long. And following them, just when the audience was ready to take a break and go out for a smoke, the house lights stayed off and everybody milled around in the dark. Maury Hayden made the mistake of asking for the house lights to be turned on – and they stayed on for the rest of her performance.

"When the Byrds finally did arrive – after 20 minutes of darkness – the volume of their mikes and amplifiers was set so high that by the fourth song it was getting hard to take. The fourth song was The Byrd's latest single, 'Jesus Is Just Alright'. Roger McGuinn is the only original member left. ... The Byrds now don't seem to still have what a group has that has grown together and stuck together."

RPM Weekly (February 14), the premier Canadian music trade paper, reports: "Finally, before the midnight hour, The Byrds made their appearance. After 15 minutes of plugging in and rearranging equipment, which had previously taken the stage crew half-an-hour to prepare, they began the set. On the opening number it became apparent that the sound system was worthy of a barn in Northern Ontario and not much else. Many of the paying customers covered their ears to prevent further damage as the ear-splitting din continued. Small parts of the number were vaguely distinguishable but the distortion and volume made it impossible to appreciate in any way the artistry of The Byrds. Before the second song began, members of the audience screamed over the feedback to turn the volume down; the sound man responded by cutting gain on the instruments but leaving the mikes at their hopelessly distorted level, with the exception of the lead guitarist's which, as far as anyone knows, was never plugged into the board.

"Even going against such a situation, The Byrds gave what was expected of them: a fairly tight run through their past hits and some of their newer material, including their present chart item 'Jesus Is Just Alright'. The group, who when coming out on stage had asked for an introduction and in response a member of the audience had yelled out, 'Ladies And Gentlemen – The Byrds!', reached the climax of their act with a true pop milestone, 'Eight Miles High', which unfortunately became a screaming, roaring blast of distorted sound – at which point this reviewer, and many other members of the audience, walked out."

An uncredited review is printed in Britain's *New Musical Express* (February 14). "It's a shame The Byrds have gone so country. When they played to a capacity crowd of 2,500 in Toronto recently, their repertoire was integrated with C&W numbers, which made for very dull listening. This was probably because their long string of hits are folk-rock or country-rock orientated, and with the inclusion of pure country there was no contrast. However, they did play for over an hour, and everyone enjoyed tracks from their new album *Ballad of Easy Rider* and their old hits, including 'Mr Tambourine Man', 'Mr Spaceman', 'So You Want To Be A Rock'n'Roll Star', 'All I Really Want To Do', and 'Turn! Turn! Turn!'. 'Eight Miles High' was the clincher of the evening. Of special interest was their current Columbia single, 'Jesus Is Just Alright', which has a very commercial sound but, predictably, has received little or no airplay." ('All I Really Want To Do' is most unlikely to be a part of the set now and must be a misinterpretation; the group has not performed it live since 1965/66.) According to the *New Musical Express* story, Skip Battin and Kim Fowley's 'You All Look Alike' is to be the next Byrds single.

Friday 6–Sunday 8
Ash Grove, Hollywood, CA

The Byrds were one of several acts who performed for free last summer to help raise funds for the burned-out Ash Grove, and this weekend they make their debut proper at the rebuilt club. McGuinn has played here in his pre-Byrds days but it is Clarence White who knows the place best from countless appearances with The Kentucky Colonels in the early 60s.

Tyler Lanton is at the Ash Grove on behalf of *The Los Angeles Free Press*. "The Byrds have grown considerably and their [L.A.] gig brought a lot of sophistication to light. Their choice of material is impeccable and they have really learned to handle their audiences. They charitably handed out old favourites, beginning with 'You Ain't Going Nowhere' and [ran] through popular singles. … During their Ash Grove engagement, several yet unrecorded songs came up, one of which was 'Lover Of The Bayou'. This song encompassed the individuality of both Roger McGuinn and Clarence White, with Roger's familiar 12-string licks laced with beautiful country-style picking by Clarence. … Probably the most enjoyable part of each set was the segment in which Clarence, Roger, and drummer Gene Parsons picked up acoustic guitars and, accompanied by bassist Skip Battin, offered such tunes as 'Amazing Grace' and 'You All Look Alike'. The highlight of the night was Clarence White's brilliant execution of 'Black Mountain Rag', an old fiddle tune which he flatpicked with such accuracy and taste that he brought down the house."

Bluegrass duo Vern & Ray round out the program, and they are joined by a succession of friends such as Doug Kershaw, Bill Keith (banjo), Herb Steiner (mandolin), Byron Berline, Roger Bush, and, of course, Clarence White. Intriguingly, Lanton notes that there are discussions to put together a joint Doug Kershaw & The Byrds album, which makes sense as they perform a few concerts together this year. Regrettably, the plan does not come off.

Meanwhile, plans for The Byrds to visit the UK in the fall are announced in Saturday's *Record Mirror*, provisionally together with Jefferson Airplane and The Four Seasons. Vice president Danny O'Donovan of the American Program Bureau sets up the tour, but in fact The Byrds will be flown over earlier, making a fall trip unnecessary.

(The proposed ban by the British Musicians' Union following their journey to South Africa in 1968 will be lifted when the group submits South African newspaper clippings proving they spoke out vociferously against apartheid.)

Sunday 8

☐ **US TV** [Presumably] KHJ studios, North Hollywood, CA. KHJ-TV Channel 9 *Groovy Show* 6:00pm

The Byrds, Little Richard, and The Dells appear on *Groovy Show*, now hosted by KHJ DJ Robert W. Morgan. It is the latest incarnation of the *Groovy!* television show that Michael Blodgett at the end of 1967 left to Sam Riddle, who transformed it into *The Groovy Game,* before Morgan took over the reins in early 1969 as *Groovy Show*. The group presumably appears live on the programme, as it goes out on the air, before returning to the Ash Grove in the evening. Unfortunately no record will survive of what they perform on the TV show.

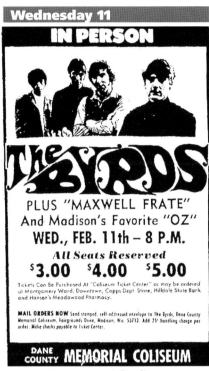

Wednesday 11

IN PERSON

The BYRDS

PLUS "MAXWELL FRATE"
And Madison's Favorite "OZ"
WED., FEB. 11th – 8 P.M.

All Seats Reserved
$3.00 $4.00 $5.00

Tickets Can Be Purchased At "Coliseum Ticket Center" or may be ordered at Montgomery Ward, Downtown, Capps Dept. Store, Hilldale State Bank and Hansen's Meadowood Pharmacy.

MAIL ORDERS NOW Send stamped, self-addressed envelope to The Byrds, Dane County Memorial Coliseum, Fairgrounds Drive, Madison, Wis 53713. Add 25¢ handling charge per order. Make checks payable to Ticket Center.

DANE COUNTY MEMORIAL COLISEUM

Dane County Memorial Coliseum, Madison, WI

The group perform here with support by folk singer Maxwell Frate and local group The Oz. David Wagner, who reviewed The Byrds' performance in Appleton, WI, back in March 1966, is on hand to cover tonight's concert for *The Capital Times* (February 12). "The Byrds hopped on to the Coliseum stage last night with all the enthusiasm of four tired swallows who couldn't find [San Juan] Capistrano. It might have had something to do with the 45-minute stretch of silence in the huge dome before they came on. Those in the audience of 1,500 who weren't restless or jockeying for better seats were left gasping with impatience.

"When they did play, the group kept pretty much to its studio orientation. The songs would have made appropriate singles, as many of them have, or individual cuts for a new side. There just wasn't any of that relax-'em, lay-back-and-listen sound, where one song goes on for half-an-hour and every member of the group has a chance to get his chops in (the style California concerts have developed). And when they did try some of the climactic 'fireworks' stuff (as they called it) for jeans city, they barely had time to light the fuse before it was all over. 'Nashville West', one of their finale specialities, lasted about six minutes.

"There was a fine spot at the end of their last medley of hits, though, when Clarence White was given room to move on his down-

home style guitar. The man is unmatched at those Nashville country sides and changes. And Roger McGuinn on the 12-string proved to be almost as interesting when he was given time to work out the capricious, nearly anti-rhythmical skating he is known for. It sounded superb against White's steady Tennessee earth. The rest of the one-hour appearance by The Byrds was the smooth and gentle country-rock they originated for their album *Sweetheart Of The Rodeo*. The only unexpected moment was a four-part harmony on 'Amazing Grace', which they sang a cappella.

"It should be added that The Byrds had to clear another obstacle to get rid of the late-wait-blues in the crowd. John Little, one of WISM's top-40 jockeys who keeps an active hand in the local rock'n'roll business, attempted to loosen up the audience with his finest MC style after Maxwell Frate finished singing. It involved four new Byrds albums which he was prepared to give away to the best 'impressionists'. The first impression was to be of Tiny Tim. Someone came to the stage and got an album for it. The next voice to be imitated was John Wayne's. There were groans, but no takers. Finally, Little settled on a belching contest. 'This'll be a gas,' he said to the helpless listeners. Incredible."

Another articulate review comes from Lynne C. Rasmussen in *The Wisconsin State Journal* (February 12). "The audience was sitting on the ice for The Byrds' concert at the Dane County Memorial Coliseum Wednesday night, and it was painfully obvious. Only once did the small crowd break into spontaneous applause and The Byrds had already left the stage before enough belated enthusiasm could be generated to bring them back for a well-deserved encore. The four singers, who play three guitars and drums with unusual competence, seemed to be having a good time, despite their listeners' unresponsiveness, as they moved from country western to Simon & Garfunkel to neo-bubble gum and back again.

"Besides the inevitable medley of 'our greatest hits' – in this case, 'Turn! Turn! Turn!', 'Mr. Tambourine Man', and 'Eight Miles High' – The Byrds sang 'Monster Named Blue' [sic!], 'You All Look Alike', 'Nashville West', and their newest release, 'Jesus Is Just Alright'. They succeeded with the harmony of 'Amazing Grace', a song that really requires an intricate sound studio or somebody's quiet back porch. They also tried a sing-along (unsuccessful) on 'Drug Store Truck Drivin' Man'."

The a cappella rendition of the traditional hymn 'Amazing Grace', sung in four-part harmony, is a recent introduction to the group's encores.

Friday 13
Indianapolis Coliseum, Indianapolis, IN

The Byrds and Steppenwolf. In conjunction with the Indianapolis visit, writer Vincent Flanders interviews McGuinn. "That's been part of our fun," he reflects while taking about the group's contradictory constant-yet-evolving nature. "We knew about getting locked into a bag like so many groups did. [Others] had success for a while and they were locked into their bag and their bag just fell down and they fell down with it. Like we would do a Houdini from every bag that we got locked into with handcuffs on. We'd pick the locks and jump out of the bag. Tah dah! Here we are in the country field; here we are in the rock field; here we are in the jazz field."

Among the many topics discussed are McGuinn's ideas for a guitar synthesizer. "My only hang-up [with the regular synthesizer] is the keyboard. I'm not a keyboard cat. I'm waiting for a guitar neck to come out or otherwise I have to make one myself, and I'm not in town long enough to really get involved in the project – it'd take six months to get a working guitar neck. Paul Beaver, the West Coast franchise for Moog, is allegedly trying to make one. I don't know if he will or not or how he'll work it. It's a difficult proposition because of the mechanics involved. You'd have to have switches that are small enough to put six across per fret – on the guitar neck – which is very small. In fact, they don't make switches that small yet. They make little buttons that small, but the switch itself is about an inch long so logistically it can't be done that way."

"I had a solution in my head that I haven't proposed to anyone in the electronics field," McGuinn reveals. "My solution was to make a converter that would take the actual tone of the guitar through a preamp and then convert it into a voltage that would control the oscillators. It sounds good, but it would be hard to do." (Roughly expressed, that is what instrument manufacturers Roland (in Japan) and ARP (in the US) will do when the first commercial guitar synthesizers are introduced in 1977. The Roland GR-500 will depend upon a heavily modified guitar, while the ARP Avatar will let the player use a regular guitar outfitted with an extra pickup to gain access to synthesizer sounds.)

Saturday 14
Concordia College, Moorhead, MI

Sunday 15
Labor Temple, Minneapolis, MN

A provisional booking at Husson College, Bangor, ME, is cancelled in favour of a Minneapolis show with Teagarden & Van Winkle

and singer-guitarist Ken Schaffer. There are two shows (at 6:30 and 9:30pm) and Thomas Utne attends both for *The Minnesota Daily*. "The Byrds is just all right with me, yeah (do-doodo-do-do-doodo-diddoo). So relaxed, so relaxing. So clean, so cleansing. So fresh, so refreshing. Such happy songs, such a happy me. No encore, no customary Labour Temple standing ovation for The Byrds' second show, despite its biggest crowd yet. Such a happy crowd. Too relaxed, too off-edge (too stoned?), and too peaceful to blow it with a lot of screaming."

Utne gives a thorough description of the pros and cons of McGuinn's new men. He concludes: "I have to acknowledge my avoidance of a direct comparison of the Old and New Byrds. As much as I'm wild about today's Byrds, despite their critics' charges that they just don't have the balls, whatever that means (a vogue expression), I must admit my true preference: hands down, the Early Byrds' got the worm, baby."

Friday 20
'Winter Carnival', Chapin Hall, Williams College, Williamstown, MA

"Yes, that was McGuinn. Roger McGuinn. But there was no frizzled hair or notorious granny glasses," writes Bo Bovaird in the student paper *Williams Record* following the show. "Just some blond guy who needed a shave and said, 'We're not really The Byrds.' And they weren't, until he sang the Dylan words in the Jim McGuinn voice and ripped us all back to high school. Well, that was him – he'd changed his name and the others weren't the same. But Byrd music – about a tambourine man, a spaceman, a rock'n'roll star, a president – burst through all barriers, knowing no season and surviving all the changes under heaven.

"We were ripped from high school to Dallas, to some Cloud Nine Nashville at least eight miles higher than we started, McGuinn made explosions with his mouth, and Captain America smoulders still in a roadside grave. Their music and words trained us well."

The Byrds play two sets at Williamstown, with no support act, and after the intermission the temperature raises a couple of notches, according to Bovaird. "As they sang 'Jesus Is Just Alright' our hippy dippy selves were transformed into a Southern Baptist Revival, our necks flushing red in tripping, ripping fervour. The Byrds were in control. They were doing what they liked and did best. Exciting a crowd of 1,200 with their music. Though most of the crowd left after the last song, the excitement stayed packaged within the walls of Chapin." A picture of Battin in big fur hat framing his beard and long hair accompa-

nies the review. With an unspecified object dangling in a chain around his neck, Battin resembles Rasputin with a bass guitar.

Meanwhile, the recent American single 'Jesus Is Just Alright' is issued in the UK today with the same flip side as the US issue, 'It's All Over Now Baby Blue'. "What's this – The Byrds going gospel?" Derek Johnson asks quizically in *New Musical Express* (February 21). "Well, not really! Because, although this song is written in the repetitive gospel style, the boys' treatment is more in the country-rock idiom. Highlights are the group's ear-catching vocal harmonies – which at one point give way to jazz-slanted scat – and the fiery percussion which drives the routine along relentlessly."

The guest in *Melody Maker*'s regular Blind Date (February 21) is Scottish football player Peter Marinello, now playing for Arsenal. A keen pop fan, obviously, he readily recognises most of the records he is played. "They're all going in for this religious bit now! Who is it? Oh, The Byrds. They've made a lot of good records, but they haven't had a big one for a long time, and I don't think this is going to do it for them. But it'll probably do very well in the States."

Saturday 21
St Anselm College, Manchester, NH

Sunday 22
University of Maine, Orono, ME

Undated February

McGuinn receives a phone call suggesting a tempting collaboration, as later revealed in *Rolling Stone*. "Well, I'm more on the inside of it than most people because we were supposed to work with Dylan at the time," McGuinn explains later to writer Ed Ward. "I got a call from Clive Davis, president of Columbia, saying, 'How would you like to work with Dylan?' We'd previously discussed doing albums with other Columbia artists." McGuinn did indeed speak about collaborating with "other Columbia artists" when he was interviewed for Sing Out! in August 1968.

"So I said, 'Sure thing, let's get together. Just tell me when and where.' So I called Dylan and he wasn't there, but he returned the call and said, 'Did Clive Davis call you about doing an album?' and I said, 'Yeah, but I don't know what we'd do. Do you have any ideas?' and he said, 'No, I haven't thought about it myself. Maybe if you come in with some of the old stuff and I do too that'll be all right.' I think he meant some of his old stuff, so it would be all his publishing.

"So I said, 'Well, the only thing we could do is go into the studio and see what happens, right?' And I asked him if he had any material to spare, and he said no, that he was kind of hard up, that he hadn't been writing as much as he used to, and I mentioned that we all get fat and lazy and he laughed. And we wound up the conversation by saying that we'd be in touch with each other, nothing definite." The Dylan–Byrds session is soon a reality, and a studio date is set for March 2 in New York, but due to an unfortunate misunderstanding it does not happen.

Friday 27

GRAND

FUNK

RAILROAD

and

THE

BYRDS

FRIDAY, FEB. 27

Tully Gym   8 PM

Tally

$2.50 single

$4.00 double

Tickets on sale at Union Ticket Office

Tully Gymnasium, Florida State University, Tallahassee, FL
The group supports Grand Funk Railroad. To Robert Mann in *Amazing Grace* (February 1970) there is little doubt which of the two groups he prefers. Grand Funk Railroad "moved me from high to nausea in less than three songs," he writes, although he finds The Byrds not up to the par of previous performances. He observes: "To myself, 'Jesus Is Just Alright' is a revolutionary lyric; much more radical than when the lead guitar player of G. Funk complained of his inability to remove his clothes because of 'the man' (whoever he is)."

The reviewer meets four tired Byrds backstage ("I'm strung out, man") before they head back for the encore. "During their encore they told us right where they were at when they laid down 'sell your soul to the company'. They played the concert, but why? Did they really feel up to playing, or were they just like the Greenwich to New York commuter? 'What'd you pay for your riches and fame, it's all a strange fame, you're a little insane.' And with this song, they set the stage for [Grand Funk Railroad]."

Saturday 28

Colden Center Auditorium, Queens College of City University of New York, Flushing, New York, NY
LIVE RECORDING After years of touring with a volatile line-up, McGuinn has now reintroduced the values of professionalism that were once instilled in him when he toured with The Limeliters, Chad Mitchell, and Bobby Darin. With Clarence White, Gene Parsons, and now Skip Battin, he has built The Byrds into a first-rate and dependable concert attraction. Parallel to this, The Byrds have deftly managed the uneasy transition from the 60s to the 70s. Rock concerts have become events, attracting larger crowds than ever before, with ticket-buyers expecting full-out entertainment. The Rolling Stones tour at the end of 1969 raised the ante, presenting high-energy shows that could last up to two hours. Mick Jagger and Keith Richard introduced an acoustic segment – even if only a couple of songs to break the pace, but still a novel idea. Crosby Stills Nash & Young, the biggest concert draw in the US right now, start out acoustically before ending up their shows with a head-on electric blast.

The Byrds' elastic repertoire is frequently updated and moulded as songs are added or numbers discarded. They decide to record a pair of performances – the one tonight and tomorrow's New York concert – for a projected release. Live albums have a history in rock'n'roll as the quick cash cow: easy to produce and a simple marketing ploy to fill the gap between new studio recordings. As rock groups embrace the extended improvisation that has until now been exclusively a jazzman's domain, the rock live album becomes an artistic statement rather than a greatest hits collection performed in front of an audience. Eric Clapton and Cream's haughty *Wheels Of Fire* from 1968 kicked off the trend, and 1969 saw groundbreaking live recordings by Jefferson Airplane (*Bless Its Pointed Little Head*), Mike Bloomfield & Al Kooper (*The Live Adventures Of …*); MC5 (*Kick Out The Jams*); Quicksilver Messenger Service (their part-studio/part-live *Happy Trails*), and, at the end of the year, Grateful Dead's seminal *Live/Dead*.

With *Gene Tryp* on hold for the time being, McGuinn decides to use some of the best material he has earmarked for the musical. He sings the boasting tale of a country outlaw, 'Lover Of The Bayou', in a hoarse voice oddly resembling one of the vocal guises that Bob Dylan will adopt a few years later. The song is so strong that, briefly, it will be considered as singles material.

The Byrds also introduce an acoustic set that will be expanded later, but for the moment it consists of 'Willin'' – sung by

Gene – and 'Soldier's Joy'/'Black Mountain Rag'. The first is written by Lowell George, a guitarist–singer who has been part of Frank Zappa's ever-fluctuating Mothers Of Invention, the second a medley of two fiddle tunes transferred to Clarence White's lightning-quick fingers. Some of the material recorded tonight is saved for the group's next album, while four selections – 'You All Look Alike', 'Nashville West', 'Willin'', and 'Black Mountain Rag' – will be released much later on the CD boxed set *There Is A Season* in 2007. (Appearing with The Byrds at Colden for the one show at 8:30pm are David Cohen & The Stoned Gas.)

March

Sunday 1

Felt Forum, Madison Square Garden Center, New York, NY
LIVE RECORDING The Felt Forum is a 5,600-seat theatre within New York's Madison Square Garden complex, and The Byrds play the last of a three-night benefit in aid of Ad Venture, a non-profit advertising agency to promote black and Puerto Rican-owned businesses. The group shares the bill with The Association, retro rockers Sha Na Na, and The Frost. As with yesterday's date, the Byrds concert is recorded for a proposed live album.

In 2000, a batch of songs from tonight's show will be released: 'You Ain't Going Nowhere', 'Old Blue', 'My Back Pages', and the two songs that climax the *Easy Rider* movie: Dylan's 'It's All Right Ma (I'm Only Bleeding)' and 'Ballad Of Easy Rider', broken only by McGuinn reciting the chilling line spoken by the redneck truck driver in the film's very last sequence: "Hey hippie, get a haircut! You want me to blow your brains out?"

Billboard (March 14) reviews the three Ad Venture concerts (none of them a sell-out), and Fred Kirby notes of Sunday's headliner: "Columbia Records' Byrds followed and were as good as ever. Although Roger McGuinn is the only member left from the original Byrds, his distinctive voice is enough to give the country-rock quartet its unique sound. Ad Venture's acts were strong in entertainment values. Unfortunately, New York area youth proved too limited in their tastes to attend in sufficient numbers."

James Stoller covers the Byrds' two New York concerts in *The Village Voice* (March 26) and argues that the group is the ultimate American 'auteur' band – an extension of the influential auteur theory in film criticism, which suggests that a movie reflects its director's personal vision. "From the beginning," writes Stoller, "led by their admiral, singer–guitarist Roger McGuinn, The Byrds applied their secret formula, involving equilibrium and regularity, to everything they did. Sometimes, by perfecting a chord or adding harmony in a Dylan or folk song, they would irradiate it with otherness.

"Although a recording studio has generally been an important element in their excellence, The Byrds were in town … recording a 'live' album. Appropriately, three exceptional musicians now accompany McGuinn. Clarence White's thoughtful technological-country lead guitar adds meticulous flavouring and helps break down and revitalise Byrds oldies. Gene Parsons, a warm and steady drummer and singer, provides the reliable bedrock support that was one of bassist Chris Hillman's contributions to the original group. The newest Byrd, swinging bassist Skip Battin, brings the live act a useful funkiness. And McGuinn's sculptured singing had the focused, mainlining power of a laser (reportedly, by the way, one of his playthings): his caustic, and compassionate folksinger's voice is one of rock's unique, most soul-satisfying instruments.

"After five years, The Byrds' music has cooled: they no longer have a sound to blow your mind (if those were ever the words for it), only to nourish it. … McGuinn, understanding his musical ideas as a vessel for personality, its salvage, chose not to go unbounded. To the extent that the audience looks to the rock hero not just for the music, but – more deeply – for a way to live, McGuinn now seems all the more exemplary. Against the seductive fashion which cast rock groups as on-stage therapy-groups, he chose responsibility for the product of his band, even at the risk of its apparent dissolution.

"Unlike the teasing Beatles ('you can talk to me') or Stones ('you can come all over me'), he never kindled or fed an audience's fantasies, nor did he project his own. Instead, he was able to succeed without crossing the old, but still operating, boundaries: respecting his audience and honouring his often traditional material, he gave The Byrds an intelligent classic perspective like practically nothing else in rock. In a medium marked by melodrama, he held to the tactful pursuit of craft.

"At Queens College and the Felt Forum, the touring Byrds played, as is their custom, to audiences somewhat less than devoted and sometimes more than rude. Particularly in the hard light of Queens Colden Auditorium, without benefit of Fillmore East patchouli pretensions, teenagers and their society don't seem to have changed substantially in recent decades.

"In two selections introduced in their concerts, The Byrds acknowledged and purified some recent trends. 'Lover Of The Bayou' sets swamp-rock lyrics to hard-driving music something like the Stones' 'Sympathy For The Devil' and 'Shelter', but very patterned and formal. McGuinn sings it with new bite. Even better is 'Willin', an unpatronising song about a trucker – another side of the coin from 'Jesus Is Just Alright', which the live Byrds now deliver as a chilling warning from the heartland. With all four Byrds strumming unamplified instruments as they harmonise, 'Willin' recalls work by Crosby Stills & Nash and The Band. But for flutter (Crosby et al) it substitutes form; for the pathos (The Band), poise. Painstaking and exquisite, it signals a new direction for The Byrds, should they choose to pursue it. Alertly adapting this secret formula, both these songs are derivative and both, in estimable ways, improve upon their models."

Monday 2

The Byrds have set the day aside for a Bob Dylan recording session, which is cancelled due to regrettable circumstances. McGuinn picks up the story in *Rolling Stone* (October 29). "So we got to New York and did a couple of gigs – Felt Forum and Queens College – and that took care of the weekend. By Monday we were still in town, but waiting for some kind of word. Finally the guys took a 12:00 plane back to the Coast. And at 1:00 I got a call from Billie Wallington, a friend of mine at Columbia, and she said that the session was in [Columbia Records' New York] Studio B at 2:30. Well, I explained to her what the situation was, and she called Dylan, and he was pissed off that we didn't have the courtesy to sit around and wait for his phone call.

"Well, the crux of it all was that Clive [Davis] was supposed to come down to the show the night before but he didn't show up, and we could have settled it all right there. The other thing was a political thing with Bob Johnston. We'd fired him as our producer, right, and Bob Johnston, as producer, is responsible for notifying the musicians of the time of the session within 12 hours. It's a union regulation. He knew where we were, but he didn't call us and Clive didn't call us. Like I say, it was political."

In the end, no session takes place today, but by tomorrow, March 3, Dylan is at Columbia and putting down his first studio recordings since those in Nashville ten months ago. He and Bob Johnston spend Tuesday, Wednesday, and Thursday at Columbia's New York facility. With The Byrds flown, various musicians are hastily brought in to assist Dylan – Al Kooper, guitarist David Bromberg, and others. Many of the songs taped during these three days are then taken to Nashville for cleaning and overdubbing (Dylan himself is apparently not present for that operation) under the supervision of Bob Johnston and released in June as the double album *Self Portrait*.

Self Portrait will contain mostly versions of other writers' material, with some live recordings from last year's Isle of Wight festival tagged on, and is met with almost universally poor reviews. The New York sessions do, however, feature a couple of new Dylan compositions – 'Went To See The Gypsy' and 'Time Passes Slowly' – that will be held over for his next album, the acclaimed *New Morning*.

The *Rolling Stone* interview will be conducted after *Self Portrait* is issued, and so McGuinn is able to speculate about what kind of role The Byrds could have played in such a setting. "What I think it would have amounted to is that we would have been backup musicians for Dylan, like The Band, on a couple of cuts on his new album, which he never mentioned to us. He said it could be a separate album, The Byrds and Dylan, and I asked him what kind of billing we'd get on it, and he said well, he didn't know, but Clive assured me that we'd be getting at least 33 per cent billing on it. I would have liked to have done it, if it had worked out at all.

"In view of the circumstances," McGuinn continues, "I'm just as glad that we didn't get on this particular album that came out, because it was poorly prepared – that's my opinion. [Dylan] came into the studio prepared to use a lot of outtakes from *Nashville Skyline* and a lot of the Isle of Wight stuff, which is just a … live recording rather than anything musically good. The New York stuff, 'Wigwam' and a lot of those, are pretty good. So I understand the album thoroughly. I understand why there are repeats to fill time because he didn't have enough new material to do it, why he used a lot of old folk songs that everybody's known for 10 or 12 years. … He's probably taking publishing on them as re-arrangements of public domain material. It's a standard trick. I've done it myself. But I usually make a few changes. 'Old Blue': that's one."

Friday 6
Panther Hall, Fort Worth, TX
The group performs with support by Space Opera for two shows; 8:00pm and 10:00pm.

Saturday 7
T.C. Williams High School Auditorium, Alexandria, VA
The Byrds headline with Tractor playing the opening slot. William C Woods writes a glowing review in *The Washington Post* (March 9). "The Byrds are a group to make one regret the wasting of superlatives on smaller talents.

It's true that rock does yield its strongest liquor to restless enthusiasm, and I'm sure that, in the past, I've made my own immodest nominations for 'best group', 'best lead guitar', 'best lead vocal' and so on. But now the time has come to reassign some of these labels to the places where they really belong.

"From the opening tune to the final encore, the group moved with swift grace and passion through most of its repertoire – a song bag that spans the entire history of the rock revolution. It's not easy to pick one highlight out of a show that was an unbroken series of them. But, perhaps, the finest moment came when lead singer Roger McGuinn … unplugged his electric guitar and went into an acoustic truck-driver classic ['Willin''] followed by a fast fiddle tune transposed for guitar. Lead guitarist Clarence White held the audience on the edge of his frets while he rang the changes on this one. … This is a group that makes a critic helplessly reveal his prejudices; it seems to me impossible to praise them highly enough, though I suspect that may be for extra-musical reasons.

"By the end of the show, the most beautiful thing going was Roger McGuinn's face. He had just done two full concerts, ending this one with five encores to an incessant standing ovation, and he must have been exhausted – all of them must have been. But they played on and on and on, and nobody could stand for it to stop. McGuinn was beaming down on the crowd at his feet with the serene joy of an artist who had done his work well and has been properly rewarded with more than money. This time, for The Byrds and for their audience, everything was delivered."

Undated March

🎧 **SESSION** There seems to be a two-week lull in The Byrds' touring activities in the middle of March, and possibly this is the opportunity that Clarence White needs to briefly dip back into the session world again. He is still an in-demand guitarist, and this year he contributes guitar to several albums.

For example, the *Suite Steel* album is a symposium showcasing pedal steel guitar players crossing over to the rock medium, featuring stellar instrumentalists Buddy Emmons, Sneaky Pete, Rusty Young, J.D. Maness, and Red Rhodes. Recorded at L.A.'s Elektra Sound Recorders, White makes up the rhythm section but has scant solo space. It will be released in the summer.

White contributes to more recordings released during 1970. He reconnects with Paul Revere & The Raiders guitarist Freddy Weller for *Listen To The Young Folks* and is heard to good effect on country singer Johnny Darrell's *California Stop-Over*, an album that contains versions of both 'Mae Jean Goes To Hollywood' and 'Willin''.

White joins an all-star cast to back ex-Beau Brummels singer Sal Valentino for the single 'Silkie'/'A Song For Rochelle', together with Leon Russell (piano), Chris Etheridge (bass), Ry Cooder (guitar), and Milt Holland (drums). Despite a thumbs-up in *Rolling Stone* (October 1), the single sinks without a ripple.

•

🎧 **SESSION** Gene Parsons is also lending out his talents, and he guests on an eponymous album by folk singer and songwriter Malvina Reynolds released in June. Besides Parsons, the album features members of The Sunshine Company and producer Alex Hassilev, one of the original Limeliters. Interviewed by *The Los Angeles Times* (June 8), the 70-year-old Reynolds says: "They didn't have to do my album, but they like my songs."

Another session credited to Parsons is the soundtrack to *Performance*. The movie will premier in New York City in August – with the soundtrack album following right behind – and attracts immediate attention because of Mick Jagger's acting debut in the role of a washed-up rock singer. Parsons overdubs bits and pieces on some of the original tracks, presumably on the recommendation of producer Russ Titelman.

Undated March/April

Roger McGuinn has been asked to take part in a novel idea in music teaching. The Music Educators National Conference has joined forces with Youth Education Incorporated of New York City to develop a first-of-its-kind teaching package on the musical characteristics of rock. The compendium is planned for distribution in the fall of 1970, and Coca-Cola USA has offered financing. Possibly the project is never completed, but McGuinn retains some fond memories.

"It was a filmed interview with [Music Director of the Los Angeles Philharmonic Orchestra] Zubin Mehta for distribution to junior high schools, sponsored by Coca-Cola," he tells Ed Ward in *Rolling Stone*. "It was gonna be an interview with Mehta, but he kind of dominated the proceedings. At one point, though, he really blew it, and I said, 'Mr Mehta has just admitted that he's just capitalising on rock'n'roll to appeal to a younger audience because his older audience is dying off.' He did say that, in almost so many words, and I just sort of encapsulated that whole thing. And he was doing one of the loud numbers where rock'n'roll musicians don't really know what's going on in classical music these days." (Mehta has flirted with rock earlier in the year on the music television special *The Switched-on*

Symphony, an uncomfortable mix of Santana, Jethro Tull, The Nice and others with a symphony orchestra.)

Saturday 28

Staging a rock festival has become a very risky business in the wake of the bad press generated by Altamont. The three-day Easter Holiday 'Southwest '70 Peace Festival' has lined up an impressive list of performers: The Byrds, Delaney & Bonnie & Friends, Barry McGuire, Sundance, The Flock, Johnny Winter, Zephyr, Canned Heat, Muddy Waters, Truth, Freddie King, Bloodrock, Joe Kelly Blues Band, Bangor Flying Circus, Blue Mountain Eagle, Sweetwater, Beast, and The Frantics.

Trouble starts as news reaches local residents in Dickens (population 315), TX, the festival's intended location. "We're not vigilantes," barks local spokesman Moyne Kelly to *The Abilene Reporter News* (March 20), "but we're going to protect our homes." Dickens resident Charles McArthur says to another local Texas newspaper that townspeople are "afraid they were going to be raped, plundered and burned out". The conflict heightens when the farmer who offered to lease land to the organisers claims he has misunderstood the verbal agreement and seeks a temporary restraining order. In the end, the protests by the townspeople of Dickens win through and the festival is moved to a property nearby Lubbock.

The weather is unkind, with blustering winds, blowing dirt, heavy rain, and even a tornado alert. *The Lubbock Avalanche Journal* reports on Good Friday (March 27) that turnout is small (estimated at 2,300, whereas 20,000–30,000 was the promoter's prediction) and the festival is plagued by all manner of problems. In the end, the Thursday opening is postponed until the following day – extending the festivities until Sunday instead of the planned end on Saturday.

On Friday, the music finally strikes up with Barry McGuire, Bloodrock, and some local groups. Saturday brings a bit of sunshine and a peak attendance with a 3,500-strong crowd there to hear Bangor Flying Circus, Truth, and The Byrds – who in fact cancel their performance due to inclement weather. Even if attendance is disappointing, the law is here in full force, with 350 state police, uniformed patrolmen, Texas Rangers, and plain-clothes officers.

Mass arrests ensue and festival-goers pack Lubbock County Jail to the rafters as they are brought in on a wide array of offences. On Sunday, the rains return and bring the festival to a limp finish. According to the *Avalanche Journal* (March 30), the musical highpoint comes when a local band fires up 'Jesus Is

239

Just Alright' in honour of Easter Sunday and as a tribute to the no-show Byrds.

Sunday 29
Fountain Street Church, Grand Rapids, MI

Odd as it may sound, the venue is a regular Baptist church but has hosted concerts by rock groups before – Grateful Dead, for example, visited here in 1968. The Byrds play supported by Phlegethon.

April

Friday 3
University of Calgary, Calgary, Alberta, Canada

Saturday 4
Eagles Auditorium, Seattle, WA

The group is a special guest at a show presented by Seattle promoter Boyd Grafmyre. The Paul Butterfield Band and Blue Mountain Eagle supplement the bill, and these two acts are held over for a Sunday show tomorrow. Janine Gressel says in *The Seattle Times* (April 6): "The Byrds [drew] three encores from the first audience and two from the second. The fact that their second show ended at about 2:00am may have been why there were only two encores that time around. The Byrds stole the show, however, with their lively country beat and happy music.

"The group successfully bridged the gap from old to new material by updating their past hits in the new style. Thus they were able to slip in their old songs without the concert sounding like a 'greatest hits' session. In addition to their use of electric guitars, they also performed several numbers using acoustics. One, an instrumental, was a showcase for the nimble fingers of the lead guitarist. The songs ranged from 'Mr. Tambourine Man', one of their first hits, to 'Ballad Of Easy Rider' and 'Jesus Is Just Alright', more recent recordings. They ended the concert with a medley which traced their musical styles from folk-rock through psychedelia and hard-rock to blues and now country-rock."

"Their first encore was [an] a cappella rendering of the hymn 'Amazing Grace'. The Byrds have spanned many style changes in rock since their early days. The reason for their enduring success was evident at the concert – technical proficiency, a sense of innovation, and the ability to inject warmth and charm into their music, no matter what style."

McGuinn is interviewed by local music paper *Ye Olde Musicke Columne* prior to the show and is asked who he likes in the contemporary music scene. "I like Creedence Clearwater Revival. The Band. I like some of *Déjà Vu*, a couple of cuts off that – not the whole album. I like 'Helpless' and the beginning and the end of the song 'Déjà Vu', but I don't like the middle. I think that's a cop-out – it's going back to 'Everybody's Been Burned'. … Yeah, Crosby's copping out there. But the [vocal] thing that he does in the beginning is very nice, and the Beatles refrain is very nice – and the bass solo a la John Coltrane is all right, too."

When asked to name Byrds favourites, he replies: "I like 'Renaissance Fair', I like 'Jesus Is Just Alright', the album cut, not the single. They sped the single up too much. I like 'Mr. Tambourine Man', the single. Let's see, what else? Oh, I like 'Tribal Gathering'. I like that. … And lately, let's see, I like 'Baby Blue', except I think it should have gone somewhere else. It should have done something more than it did. It should have gone up instead of stopping. It sort of petered out."

Sunday 5
[Unknown venue/location], WA

The Byrds remain in the Washington area for another performance, which will become available as an unofficial tape, revealing the group in good shape. (It is possible that the tape is a recording of yesterday's show, as a planned second night for The Byrds at Eagles Auditorium is later dropped.)

→ Wednesday 8

The Flying Burrito Brothers are at the start of a weeklong residence (Tuesday 7–Sunday 12) at The Troubadour in West Hollywood, when Roger McGuinn, Gene Parsons, and Clarence White step on stage to join in the fun.

The Burritos have stuck to a steady line-up for some time, with Gram Parsons, Chris Hillman, Sneaky Pete, Bernie Leadon, and Michael Clarke. (Leadon is probably eyeing support act Longbranch Pennywhistle with interest – a duo of which one half is his future partner, guitarist and singer Glenn Frey.)

Burrito DeLuxe, the second Burritos album is out this month – produced by Jim Dickson on Hillman's recommendation – and the group has a round trip to London lined up to headline the Camden Rock Festival on May 1. Then fate intervenes, as Judy Sims can report in *Disc* (April 25): "Shortly after the Burritos finished their gig at the Troub, Gram Parsons was involved in a motorcycle accident which left him in the hospital with serious face injuries." Parsons will stay in hospital for a couple of weeks before he is able to perform again.

Thursday 9
Stetson University, Orlando, FL

Friday 10
Harvey Hubble Gymnasium, University of Bridgeport, Bridgeport, CT

One show at 8:00pm, with Ambergris opening for the group.

ALSO …

Over in Britain, the front page of *The Daily Mail* reads "Paul Is Quitting The Beatles" in bold type, officially pronouncing the end of the band after months of internal strife and bickering.

Saturday 11
McHugh Hockey Rink, Boston College, Chestnut Hill, MA

The Byrds in one show at 8:30pm with Spider John Koerner and Little Willie Murphy. "The Byrds, pioneers of electric rock, once again proved their talent," says Peter Schifrin of *Broadside/Free Press*. "[The] show resembled The Byrds' January appearance at the Tea Party but included about five new songs, some exceptionally good instrumentals, especially by lead guitarist Clarence White, and, sadly, not very much of their solid country material.

"Beginning with a voodoo rock 'Lover Of The Bayou' (which lead singer Roger McGuinn once wrote for a Broadway musical), The Byrds showed their competence with such Dylan songs as 'Wheels On Fire' and 'It's All Right Ma'. Other top selections were their mournful adaptation of 'He Was A Friend Of Mine' to John Kennedy, the country-rock 'Old Blue', and a medley of their hits that culminated in a rousing 'Mr. Spaceman'. The audience reacted most enthusiastically, though, to a bit of country-style guitar picking by White. The show closed with an a cappella 'Amazing Grace' in typical perfect Byrds harmony."

Sunday 12
Worcester State College, Worcester, MA

Wednesday 15
Loyola College, Baltimore, MD

Skip Battin's new composition 'Well Come Back Home' is added to the group's set.

→ Thursday 16
Cornell University, Ithaca, NY

The Byrds visit Ithaca during one of their East Coast forays this spring, although the exact date is not known.

Friday 17
Dickinson College, Carlisle, PA

Saturday 18
Leonard Gymnasium, American University, Washington DC

"I've never seen so many stoned Christians in my whole life," McGuinn cheerfully addresses the boisterous crowd before Gene Parsons kicks off 'Nashville West' at breakneck speed. McGuinn's comment will be preserved on a well-circulated bootleg tape, which shows The Byrds in rare form as they rip through two electric halves divided by a short acoustic segment. A long 'Eight Miles High' is particularly ominous as Battin's bass roars and Parsons' drums rattle.

Earlier in the evening, Tim Hardin entertained the riotous audience. After the intermission, a member of the audience has the bright idea to clear the floor of the reserved seating. "Reserved seats are for pigs! Let's tear them down!" is the battle cry, leading to chaos in the hall.

"As The Byrds started to set up their equipment, the liberated masses in the front rows stood up to get a better view, which, of course, obstructed everyone else's view," writes Steve Goldberg in *The Eagle* (April 24). "This precipitated shouting matches between the front and back halves of the audience. Finally, The Byrds came on, and the shouting between the front and the back increased about who should sit down. But enough of the Animal Farm analogies: the vibes were very bad at first but The Byrds gradually changed everyone's mood, and when Roger McGuinn responded to angry shouts from the back by saying that he would sit down, everyone laughed."

Friday 24
Muhlenberg College, Allentown, PA

Saturday 25
Walsh Auditorium, Seton Hall University, South Orange, NJ

Sunday 26
Genesee Community College, State University of New York, Batavia, NY

May

Friday 1
Aragon Ballroom, Chicago, IL

The Byrds visit Chicago for the first time since August of last year, in a show with Al Kooper, Bangor Flying Circus, Second City Cast, and One Man's Family. It is the first venture in Chicago promoted by American Tribal Productions Inc, a subsidiary of the company behind the *Hair* musical. The Aragon is an old theatre building that dates back to the Roaring 20s and can hold a crowd of 8,000. In 1967, it housed the Cheetah Club (where The Byrds played) before it reclaimed the Aragon name and was rented out to various promoters.

American Tribal Productions Inc signals a new era – "monster rock concerts as a total cultural experience" – and has booked the ballroom for every weekend right through the summer. At present, the venue reigns alone as the city's premier rock place – the Kinetic Playground closed after a fire in November of last year and will not reopen for another couple of months. The inauguration of the new concert series draws 3,700 people, but the promoters lose money as almost 1,200 make it in for free, bursting through the wooden front doors after bending open a couple of huge, steel fire-doors.

Lynn Van Matre in *The Chicago Tribune* (May 3) sums up The Byrds' portion of the show briefly: "[They] started the whole trend toward country-rock [and] gave a noteworthy set of country and folk-rock with their versions of the traditional 'Old Blue' and some Dylan songs."

Saturday 2
'The Woods Of Dartmouth', Cedar Dell Pond, Southeastern Massachusetts University, Dartmouth, MA

Yet another festival runs into trouble as the town of Dartmouth refuses to grant the organisers permission to hold the proposed event. Unfortunately, the students promoted the festival, booked groups, and attracted the national media before finding out at the last minute that they would need permission.

To bypass the decision, the organisers resort to an option suggested by a quick-thinking lawyer: Bring on the bands, but drop any entrance fees – technically making it a free event and thus sidestepping the necessary paperwork – and instead ask for donations to cover the estimated $60,000 overhead. Initially, profits generated from the festival were to be earmarked for a scholarship fund but now the organisers face a loss.

According to contemporary reports, attendance is in the region of 30,000 over the weekend, and while students pass the hat for donations in lieu of an admission fee, the crowds lie in the sun on Saturday listening to The Byrds, Orpheus, The Guess Who, Rhinoceros, Manfred Mann, The J. Geils Band, plus lesser known groups such as Eastern Sound, Pig Iron, and Tombstone Blues.

Thursday 7
Armory Auditorium, Jonesboro, AR

Friday 8
Field House, University Of Toledo, Toledo, OH

The Byrds play Ohio, which just four days earlier – on May 4 – was rocked by shootings at Kent State University outside Akron, OH. It all began last weekend when the mayor of Kent asked the Ohio Governor for assistance from the National Guard to help quell brimming student riots. The demonstrations come in the wake of President Richard Nixon's announcement to the nation on April 30 about America's invasion of Cambodia, which spells an extension of the Vietnam War, despite his election promise to end warfare. On the afternoon of May 4 things go terribly wrong at Kent State University when the National Guard kills four students. The shootings lead to worldwide media outrage and to student strikes on college campuses across the United States. Protest actions at the University of Toledo are fairly peaceful.

Saturday 9
'Montreal Pop Festival', The Forum, Montreal, Quebec, Canada

A 12-hour pop festival in Montreal's cavernous Forum draws around 10,000 fans to hear The Byrds, Grand Funk Railroad, Al Nichols & Friends, Robert Charlebois, The Amboy Dukes, Russell Thornberry, The Collectors, Frijid Pink, Pops Merrily, La Nouvelle Frontiere, and Mashmakhan.

The Montreal Gazette (May 11) notes: "Underground favourite was definitely [Roger] McGuinn and his still-flying Byrds. Unlike The Beatles, who are ever-present, The Byrds are a group with a past: it was good to see that there still is a McGuinn and that his new group still plays those high, sweet notes. With two lead guitars (one country pickin', the other hard rockin') and a beautiful bass player, they had no trouble justifying the pre-show excitement. The Byrds went from country to hard rock to mainstream, but really soothed everyone's heads playing 'Mr. Tambourine Man' and 'Turn! Turn! Turn!'."

The Montreal Star (May 11) comments: "Almost everybody had a good time. But the oppressive physical circumstances suggest not only covetous concessionaires but somewhat insensitive organisers. Official reason: stubs could be swapped outside. A security problem which surely might have had a better solution than restricting so many for so long to the stale murky arena. It's irrelevant to say the vibes were beautiful in there; there should have been the option to come and go. You can even leave Mass when you need to.

"The music was very heavy. Extremely heavy, you might say, after eight or nine hours. Fortresses of amps and speakers, hordes of equipment managers dragging them around, lights, pretty girls, action – things looked promising at 1:00pm. With the notable exception of The Byrds and Charlebois, the most offensively ill-made music was played at unrelenting volume for hours and hours. The Hanley Sound System (a big improvement) reproduced the sound with merciless accuracy. … Rock music should be loud and dirty but it shouldn't be boring.

"There was some [magic] provided by The Byrds, who took a while warming up but, once there, displayed the most diversified and coherent set of the day. 'Wheel's On Fire', 'Old Blue', 'You All Look Alike', and 'Jesus Is Just Alright' were memorable. Diminutive Clarence White played super acoustic and electric guitar, by far the best heard all day. The Byrds have sounded better before, but their sound has never been more welcome."

The day-long event passes uneventfully; the only distraction is a new ritual among concertgoers, a phenomenon that is about to spread wide and become de rigueur as the 1970s progress. "A tribute, started when The Doors appeared here and later expanded when Led Zeppelin performed, caused most of the worry," writes the *Gazette*. "[This was a] tribute involving lighting a match and holding it high – a tribute to peace by Beatle John Lennon – which turned the darkened Forum into a fairyland. But Saturday the thing escalated into lightning newspapers, whole books of matches, and even starting small bonfires. When the situation seemed dangerous the house lights were turned on."

(Lennon and Yoko Ono staged a 'bed-in' in Montreal in May last year, and Canada's Prime Minister Pierre Trudeau was the first world leader to grant the couple a visit in December '69.)

Sunday 10
Veteran's Memorial Hall, Columbus, OH

Friday 15
Baseball Stadium, Ohio University, Athens, OH
An odd billing pairs The Byrds with interplanetary voyager and jazz eccentric Sun Ra and his Intergalactic Solar Arkestra & Troupe.

Saturday 16
Purdue University, Lafayette, IN

Sunday 17
Memorial Stadium, Indiana University, Bloomington, IN
Jefferson Airplane is the main draw, while The Byrds and B.B. King offer support.

Monday 18
Minneapolis Auditorium, Minneapolis, MN
Originally set for Labour Temple in Minneapolis, then moved to the Auditorium.

Tuesday 19
High School, Minneapolis, MN
Fan-club sheet *The Byrds Bulletin* lists this dance date at an unspecified high school in the Minneapolis area.

Friday 22–Saturday 23
The Warehouse, New Orleans, LA

Sunday 24
'Piper Rock Festival', Newton Falls, OH
The organisers of the this festival have been chased from site to site. The original location in Peace Park north of Akron proved unsuitable and so the festival is scheduled for Ascot Park, a horseracing track near Akron, but a restraining order stops the festival not only in the park but the whole county. Nelson Ledges – a racetrack in a neighbouring county – is next in line, before the festival finally lands on a farm in Newton Falls. Ignoring a court injunction prohibiting the festival, the organisers go ahead anyway but have to battle with rains and a thunderstorm.

About 5,000 show up to hear Kenny Rogers & The First Edition, Cold Blood, Smith (the group from the *Easy Rider* soundtrack), and latecomers Alice Cooper. Canned Heat sort of appear, as band members Bob 'The Bear' Hite and Alan 'Blind Owl' Wilson sit in with Pig Iron, yet another of the day's performers. The Rascals are billed to appear but apparently do not show up, while The Byrds show up but refuse to go on in the face of possible electrocution in the pouring rain.

Monday 25
RECORDING Columbia Recording Studios, Sunset and El Centro, Hollywood, CA. Producer Terry Melcher and engineer Chris Hinshaw.

Sessions for the next Byrds album begin. Roger McGuinn, Clarence White, Gene Parsons, and Skip Battin have stockpiled a lot of fresh material, particularly as McGuinn has decided to let his *Gene Tryp* songs become regular Byrds songs. It seems that the group has not been in the studio since August of last year, so today probably marks Battin's recording debut as a Byrd.

Two of McGuinn and Jacques Levy's *Gene Tryp* songs, 'All The Things' and 'Lover Of The Bayou', are recorded but not completed; neither is the excellent 'Yesterday's Train', co-written by Parsons and Battin.

Tuesday 26–Thursday 28
RECORDING Columbia Recording Studios, Sunset and El Centro, Hollywood, CA. Producer Terry Melcher and engineer Chris Hinshaw.

The session files that will be collected during the later Columbia CD reissue programme and in Johnny Rogan's exhaustive discography are not as complete as for the rest of The Byrds' back catalogue. During this mid-week period a further four contributions to the group's next album are initiated if not completed. Three of these originate from the pen of Battin: 'Well Come Back Home', 'You All Look Alike' (co-written with Kim Fowley but sung by McGuinn), and 'Hungry Planet' (where Fowley and McGuinn each get a co-credit).

Clocking in at nearly eight minutes, the solemn 'Well Come Back Home' will have the distinction of becoming the longest studio track by The Byrds as Battin wails a Buddhist mantra over and over again during the fadeout. The lyrical theme of 'Hungry Planet' is ecology, a subject that will ring more loudly as the years pass: "Oh the people kept chopping down/All my finest trees/Poisoning my oxygen/Digging into my skin." It is also the only track on the coming album to feature a touch of synthesizer. The fourth song begun at these sessions is Lowell George's 'Willin', which will be finished on May 31.

Sunday 31
RECORDING Columbia Recording Studios, Sunset and El Centro, Hollywood, CA. Producer Terry Melcher and engineer Chris Hinshaw.
'Willin' (see May 26–28) is a song The Byrds have performed live for some time and that both Parsons and White are acquainted with, albeit from different directions. Parsons has come to the song through Russ Titelman, while White has played guitar for the version that country singer Johnny Darrell has cut. Lowell George himself has just assembled his band, Little Feat, who will record their version of 'Willin' in a couple of months.

•

In a sensible business move, McGuinn gathers around him the back-office team that so successfully nurtured the original Byrds back in 1965: Terry Melcher is retained as producer after his efforts on *Ballad Of Easy Rider*, and publicist Billy James is brought back into the fold. James is sparkling with enthusiasm, as he confides to *Rolling Stone*. "Roger is my only brush with genius. The man's incredible."

Even the old Byrds management team of Eddie Tickner and Jim Dickson is reinstated. Tickner's role is strictly administrative and thus represents a huge relief to McGuinn, who since Larry Spector's firing in early '69 has doubled as bandleader and manager. Parsons explains to Pete Frame in July: "Roger had to work his heart out and just didn't have time to take care of every little thing that had to be taken care of – we couldn't help him too much because we didn't know enough about it. Eddie Tickner has been taking care of business transactions for Clarence and me for a while and he agreed to take The Byrds back."

The temporary return of Dickson is surprising, as his parting from The Byrds in 1967 was far from smooth. However, his knowledge, strong input, and good taste were never in doubt, and Dickson's relationship with McGuinn was never as rocky as that with the tempestuous David Crosby. Melcher allows Dickson back in but makes sure he retains power. "Getting Dickson was a magnanimous gesture on my part, almost a revenge," Melcher will later tell Byrds historian Johnny Rogan.

In a Byrd frame of mind, Dickson tries to reignite Gene Clark's sagging career by booking some sessions at the Record Plant, a studio facility in Los Angeles, at the turn of May–June. Since leaving The Byrds in 1966, Clark's commercial fortunes have been in steady decline, and his expedition with Doug Dillard has run its course after two poor-selling (albeit critically acclaimed) albums. For the Record Plant sessions, Dickson orchestrates a virtual reunion of the original five Byrds, as they all appear on two new Clark compositions 'She's The Kind Of Girl' and 'One In A Hundred'. (Dickson has recently reconnected with Chris Hillman and Michael Clarke too in his capacity as producer of the Flying Burrito Brothers album *Burrito DeLuxe*.)

"All five original Byrds are on [the two tracks]," Dickson says to Bud Scoppa in early June. "David [Crosby] did some beautiful harmony on [them] – and Roger went back and improved his guitar after David did the harmony, it was so good. Roger had to go back and put some more stuff on it."

However, not all wounds are healed after the acrimonious break-up of the original five, as Dickson will recall to author John Einarson years later. "Not everybody was prepared to be in the same room as Gene [Clark]. But they weren't against him. So I got them one at a time, though I think Michael [Clarke] and Chris [Hillman] did the basic track with Gene, and I brought in McGuinn to overdub guitar and David to overdub harmony."

Further embellishments are done to the songs in July, and then in February and April 1971, with Bernie Leadon (guitar), Milt Holland (drums), and Bud Shank (flute) adding parts along the way. Despite all efforts put into these two tracks, which should have been considered as a strong challenge to the singles charts, they will remain unreleased until Gene Clark's *Roadmaster* album in late 1972.

June

Monday 1–Friday 5

◁) **RECORDING** Columbia Recording Studios, Sunset and El Centro, Hollywood, CA. Producers Terry Melcher and Jim Dickinson and engineer Chris Hinshaw.

The Byrds, Terry Melcher, and Jim Dickson spend a week in the studio to complete the bulk of the next album. The daily routine begins at 6:00pm with the group recording well into the night. Two songs attempted on May 26, 'All The Things' and 'Yesterday's Train', are re-recorded in slightly shorter versions, with Terry Melcher adding piano to 'All The Things'.

Perhaps the best two of McGuinn and Jacques Levy's collaborations from *Gene Tryp* – 'Just A Season' (taped June 2) and 'Chestnut Mare' (taped June 3) – reflect the newfound Byrds unity: here with splendid vocals against a rich blend of acoustic and electric instruments, and with acoustic guitars taking the upper hand. The lyric of 'Chestnut Mare' is Levy's Westernization of Peer Gynt's 'buck-ride', the opening dialogue in Henrik Ibsen's original play. Where Gynt rides a reindeer, *Tryp* battles with a mare. McGuinn composed his chord sequence for the song way back in the spring of 1962 when he visited the Dominican Republic with The Chad Mitchell Trio.

The Wednesday session also yields a 15-minute jam pushed by White's lead guitar, of which two sections will later be extracted and released as 'White's Lightning' on the Byrds Box Set in 2000 – highlighted by an all-too-rare example of White playing bottleneck – and *There Is A Season* in 2006 as 'White's Lightning Pt 2'.

'Truck Stop Girl', written by Lowell George and sung by White, features Melcher on piano. White also gets to sing and play mandolin on 'Take A Whiff On Me', Leadbelly's ode to cocaine.

Interviewed by Andy Childs for *Zigzag* (March 1975), Lowell George will have this to say about the two songs of his that The Byrds recorded. "Russ Titelman was starting a publishing company and he asked me if I wanted to co-publish ['Willin''] with him and see what he could do with it. … Somehow a demo of the tape got out and it was the rage of the Troubadour. People like Linda Ronstadt heard it and The Sunshine Company. All these people heard the tune and cut it. Then we did 'Truck Stop Girl' at some sessions, and Clarence White covered that, and I thought he did a fantastic job. And so from some of those demos, [Little Feat] got signed to Warner Brothers and went and did the first album."

During the week, the live tracks from the two New York concerts on February 28 and March 1 are edited and mixed, a task that is left in the hands of Dickson. Melcher will later tell Johnny Rogan: "I didn't co-produce the album with Dickson. What I did was allow him to edit the live tapes while I was cutting the studio part of the album. On the live side, we came back with five hours of live music, and I gave Dickson those tapes. We got on well because he didn't have any power. One thing about Dickson, though: he's got taste."

Out of the five live hours, Dickson picks 'Lover Of The Bayou' (making the studio recording from May 25 redundant), Bob Dylan's 'Positively Fourth Street' (previously unrecorded by The Byrds), 'Nashville West', 'So You Want To Be A Rock'n'Roll Star', 'Mr. Tambourine Man', 'Mr. Spaceman', and a 16-minute version of 'Eight Miles High', which despite its duration is still edited down a little from its full length.

Friday 5

The old Beefeaters' single 'Please Let Me Love You'/'Don't Be Long' is reissued in the UK today and is among the batch of 45s reviewed by Chris Welch in tomorrow's *Melody Maker*, although it is not clear if he is aware these are Beefeaters in Byrds clothing. "They are good, damn them. It will probably be a hit – blast their teeth." Next week, *Record Mirror* (June 13) says: "From the 1964 forerunner of the original Byrds group, a blatant copy of The Beatles as they were then ('Liverpool Sound')."

Tuesday 9

◁) **RECORDING** Columbia Recording Studios, Sunset and El Centro, Hollywood, CA. Producers Terry Melcher and Jim Dickinson and engineer Chris Hinshaw.

Yet another leftover from *Gene Tryp*, McGuinn and Levy's 'Kathleen's Song' is recorded today but ultimately left off the new album at the 11th hour. It will be re-recorded in its entirety for a later Byrds album (see January 26, 1971).

During the June sessions, the group brings in some friends to bolster three tracks. Sneaky Pete Kleinow overdubs a pedal steel part on 'Yesterday's Train', while Byron Berline plays fiddle on 'You All Look Alike'. Gram Parsons, who is back in shape after his recent motorcycle accident at the end of April, adds a ghostly harmony line to McGuinn's lead vocal on 'All The Things', possibly overdubbed today.

The day after the session, Gram Parsons is interviewed by Jacoba Atlas (published *Melody Maker*, July 25). "It was a good night," he says of the Byrds recording date. "I'm not a studio musician like a lot of people; I can't change the way I play as easily as they can. But I still like to get around and try out new things." Looking back on his time with the group, he muses: "Being with The Byrds confused me a little. I couldn't find my place. I didn't have enough say-so; I really wasn't one of The Byrds. I was originally hired because they wanted a keyboard player. But I had experience being a frontman and that came out immediately. And [McGuinn] being a very perceptive fellow saw that it would help the act, and he started sticking me out front."

Thursday 11

◁ **RECORDING** Columbia Recording Studios, Sunset and El Centro, Hollywood, CA. Producer Jim Dickinson and engineer Chris Hinshaw.

One last day is spent wrapping up the group's next album, primarily fine-tuning selected tracks. Melcher has called in sick, so Dickson calls the shots. As usual, the session does not begin until the evening and runs well into the night. McGuinn adds a 12-string guitar part to 'All The Things'. Next, White overdubs an acoustic guitar to 'You All Look Alike' and then an extra electric guitar to 'Hungry Planet'.

Publicist Billy James is present and so is journalist Bud Scoppa, who is here to gather material for his forthcoming Byrds biography, a small portion of which will be published in *Circus* (September 1970). Scoppa asks Dickson what he considers his role in the project. "I'm doing, ah – I'm not quite sure yet," he admits. "I was asked to stay by a group of people." James interjects: "Terry and Jim had a conversation and they both felt they could learn something from each other."

The group has commissioned artist Eve Babitz to produce the jacket art for the new album, and she drops by the studio during the evening with photos she intends to use – shot recently by Nancy Chester at Griffith Observatory in Hollywood's Griffith Park.

As dawn approaches, McGunn, White, Battin, and Parsons gather around a microphone to sing 'Amazing Grace' a cappella, the hymn they usually perform this way to end the encore section of concerts. It is intended as the final track on the new album but will eventually be left off and not released before 2000 – and then as a 'hidden' track on a CD reissue.

Friday 12
Freedom Hall, Louisville, KY

Saturday 13
[Unknown venue], Nashville, TN

→ Saturday 13–Sunday 14
▢ **US TV** Doug Underwood Ranch, Nashville, TN. WNET Channel 13 *Fanfare: Earl Scruggs, His Family And Friends*

Banjo master Earl Scruggs has recently dissolved his more-than-20-year-long partnership with acoustic guitarist Lester Flatt and is launching a new career. Scruggs' two sons – Gary (the eldest, a bass player) and Randy (a guitarist) – join their father in The Earl Scruggs Revue along with Jody Maphis (son of country couple Rose Lee and Joe Maphis). Whereas Lester Flatt continues in the strict bluegrass tradition, The Earl Scruggs Revue updates its sound with a timid rock edge.

Scruggs is signed for an hour-long special on National Education Television, according to a news item in a local Kentucky newspaper on May 14, where Scruggs' wife and manager Louise says the hour-long feature will "depict several facets of the life of the performer and his family".

The Byrds are guests and may possibly record their segment at this time. The location is a ranch in Nashville and the two-song segment features McGuinn, White, Parsons, and Battin with Earl Scruggs (banjo), Gary Scruggs (bass and vocals), and Randy Scruggs (acoustic guitar) playing Dylan's 'You Ain't Going Nowhere' and a traditional number, 'Nothin' To It'. The TV show will be broadcast on January 10, 1971, and the two numbers are also heard on *Earl Scruggs: His Family & Friends* (Columbia Records) in November 1971.

✈ June 17–July 8, 1970: 5TH OVERSEAS TOUR (WEST GERMANY, HOLLAND, UK)

→ Wednesday 17
The Byrds fly out from Los Angeles to London as the starting point of a three-week tour of Europe. Trusted road manager Jimmi Seiter accompanies the group for the trip, which concentrates on the summer festival circuit, with four major events lined up in Sweden (ultimately cancelled), West Germany, Holland, and England, plus a few selected single dates added as the tour progresses.

As soon as the entourage arrives in London, Jimmi Seiter hires Stuart 'Dinky' Dawson to help out as soundman on the European dates. Once a DJ in Sheffield, Dawson has gained invaluable experience as road manager and soundman for Fleetwood Mac during the last two years, visiting the smallest dives and the

largest concert halls as Peter Green's group rose from club attraction and outmanoeuvred The Beatles and The Rolling Stones in the singles charts during 1969. Dawson is an expert soundman and will make sure the live Byrds sound is as good as circumstances allow. With The Byrds' equipment loaded into a rental truck, Seiter and Dawson head off for West Germany by ferry from London via Ghent in Belgium.

Thursday 18
A projected appearance on the *Piknik* television show in the Netherlands, to be filmed today for VPRO-TV, is cancelled as the organisers of Kralingen Pop – the festival where The Byrds will perform next weekend – object to the group's appearance, presumably on the grounds that they want exclusive rights. Frank Zappa stands in for The Byrds, and a disgruntled McGuinn says to the Dutch music paper *Aloha* (July 10): "It should have been a perfect way to promote the Kralingen gig."

Friday 19–Saturday 20
The group is billed to appear at the 'Festival Of The Midnight Sun' to be held at a racetrack in Mantorp, Linköping, Sweden, but fails to appear. As the festival promises many international rock names, *Melody Maker* and *New Musical Express* dispatch correspondents to Sweden.

Roy Carr writes laconically in *New Musical Express* (June 27): "The sheer desolation and bleakness of the location coupled with the sparse bedraggled revellers evoked reminiscences of Zabriskie Point." Poor turnout hampers the event, and only 5,000 out of an expected 100,000-strong throng show up to appreciate Juicy Lucy, P.J. Proby, Kim Fowley, Chuck Berry, Blue Mink, Elton John, Alexis Korner, The Move, and others.

Saturday 20
'Open Air Rock Circus', Radstadion, Frankfurt, West-Germany

A two-day festival in Frankfurt features The Byrds as headline act on the first day (Saturday) and Deep Purple tomorrow (Sunday). Other attractions over the weekend are Steamhammer, Family, Jackie Lomax, Chuck Berry, Orange Peel (a German group that fills time during changeovers), Black Sabbath, and others.

Werner Kühn-Koditek, a young Byrds fan, recalls later: "A really good performance, but it took three songs before they hit their stride. I remember the band started with 'Ballad Of Easy Rider' as Roger imitated the bike crash with his voice at the beginning. It was amazing to see Gene Parsons playing bass-drum, hi-hat, banjo, and harp all at once in one song! In

→ An arrow denotes an estimated date.

the middle of 'Eight Miles High' the audience freaked out."

→ Monday 22

The Byrds fly from Frankfurt to Amsterdam's Schiphol airport and arrive at noon, booking into the Museum Hotel. A press conference is held at 3:00pm. McGuinn is a direct descendent on his mother's side from the family of Dutch naval officer and national hero Piet Pieterszoon Hein, who lived in the 15th century. Naval officer Hein led the attack on the Spanish fleet in 1628 and captured a large booty in gold and silver, which was turned over to the Dutch government. (His mother, Dorothy Hein, visited the Netherlands in the mid 50s to do research on the family's roots.)

Wednesday 24

Fantasio II, Amsterdam, The Netherlands

The Byrds sneak in a combined rehearsal and concert.

Thursday 25

The Byrds entourage travels from Amsterdam to the Skyway Hotel near Rotterdam, where they arrive at 3:00pm. The Rotterdam Tourist Board charters a bus to take them to Delfshaven so that McGuinn can see the Piet Hein statue (see Monday 22). *The Byrds Bulletin*'s fall edition writes: "[McGuinn's ancestry] prompted civil leaders in Rotterdam to give a dinner in The Byrds' honour and take them on a tour of Piet Hein's statue and birthplace."

Saturday 27

Holland Pop Festival '70, Kralingse Bos, Kralingen, Rotterdam, The Netherlands

The organisers of the Kralingen pop festival and Fred Bannister at UK's Bath festival have joined forces in an exchange programme to cut costs and make it feasible for many US artists to make the trip across the Atlantic. Besides The Byrds – who play on Saturday night – the Dutch festival features Santana, The Flock, Canned Heat, Chicago Art Ensemble, Country Joe McDonald, Dr John, Jefferson Airplane and offshoot Hot Tuna, plus a long list of British performers: Al Stewart, Caravan, East Of Eden, Family, Fairport Convention, Fotheringay, John Surman, Mungo Jerry, Pink Floyd, Quintessence, Renaissance, Soft Machine, Third Ear Band, and Tyrannosaurus Rex. Added to that are an equally long list of Dutch groups, most relegated to a smaller stage with the exception of jazz man Han Bennink and folk-blues group CCC Inc.

The Byrds appear for a reputed fee of $6,000 and are one of the big hits of the festival. After three encores, one of the promoters,

Berry Visser, steps on stage and pleads: "We can't go on with more encores; the schedule will overrun! However, if you are interested, The Byrds will do an extra concert next Saturday in De Doelen at 8 o'clock."

The Byrds dig deep into their songbook and perform 'You Ain't Going Nowhere', 'Old Blue', 'My Back Pages'/'Baby, What Do You Want Me To Do', 'Black Mountain Rag'/'Soldier's Joy', 'It's Alright, Ma (I'm Only Bleeding)', 'He Was A Friend Of Mine', 'Chimes Of Freedom', 'You All Look Alike', 'Jesus Is Just Alright', 'All The Things', 'Buckaroo', 'Nashville West', 'Just A Season', 'Turn! Turn! Turn!', 'Mr. Tambourine Man', 'Eight Miles High', 'So You Want To Be A Rock'n'Roll Star', 'Mr. Spaceman', 'Ballad Of Easy Rider', and finally 'Amazing Grace'.

Equipped with a sound system imported from London, the music rings loud if not always clear to a crowd variously estimated at somewhere between 40,000 and 100,000 for the weekend. The festival is given fair coverage in the British music press and even picks up a review in *Rolling Stone* (August 6). "The festival was held at … a public facility five minutes from the centre of town. Some of the musical offerings wouldn't have drawn a crowd in Boise, Idaho, and the sound system was no better. The crowd, egged on by the local press, thought it was another Woodstock, and in truth the two festivals did have something in common: rain. … [The] reserves, in the approximate words of Mississippi Fred McDowell, 'did not play no rock'n'roll'. A few,

like Sandy Denny's new group, Fotheringay, were fine, but people who had shelled out 40 guilders ($11.25) had to endure endless folky-hokey bullshit, one group that played something like Bavarian violin music, and long waits between sets.

"Strangely enough, no one seemed to feel ripped off. It was Holland's first big … festival and the closest thing to an all-star line-up that ever played there. Besides, everybody's favourite group was there. To the Dutch music-lover, that would be The Byrds. They did half-a-dozen encores, climaxing with an a cappella chorus of 'Amazing Grace'. It capped off a perfectly execrable set. The group sounded as if it had been assembled that afternoon. During a medley of 'Turn! Turn! Turn!' and 'Mr. Tambourine Man', the musicians were so far off on individual trips that Roger McGuinn, who should know those tunes by now, was off-key. The audience went into a frenzy of applause and stomping anyway." Despite the disparaging stance held by *Rolling Stone*, the weekend passes into festival folklore as a peaceful gathering without police intrusion or any public disturbances.

DJ Carl Mitchell of Radio North Sea International covers the festival for *Record Mirror* (July 4). "Saturday: Whereas rain would have washed out many an event, especially in Holland, the organisers plodded on. Couples disappeared under sheets of polythene while others removed their clothes. … The Byrds gave us the second performance of the day of 'It's All Right Ma, I'm Only Bleeding', Al

The festival crowd in Kralingen, June 27, 1970.

Stewart [who Mitchell terms a 'second rate Dylan'] had offered the same song earlier in the afternoon, and they were a great success. Three encores as well for 'Eight Miles High' and 'Mr Tambourine Man'."

Nick Logan writes in *New Musical Express* (July 11): "The crowd was around the 50,000 mark, held in on one side by a huge lake, on the arc-lit waters of which a pair of ducks were gently bobbing around, quite probably stoned by the downbreeze over the crowd. The Byrds were completing an excellent set when we arrived, and were to do three encores. Fotheringay, not appearing until the third and final night, had come along specifically to see the legendary American band."

The Dutch press also welcomes the group, and *Aloha* (July 10) is confident this is the best Byrds line-up ever. "It was magnificent. I can't say otherwise. What a band, what an impish, ingenious guitar player Clarence White is, what a moving voice Roger McGuinn has, and, last but not least, what a powerful bassist Skip Battin is. Although I never saw the band before this line-up, I believe, like McGuinn says, this is the best version when it comes to live concerts."

The UK's *Record Mirror* will later publish some statistics from the event. A survey conducted by sociological students at the festival shows that almost 30,000 males and 5,000 females (out of the estimated 100,000 crowd) had drugs in their possession; about 20,000 carried contraceptives; and 83 per cent of the audience was Dutch. By September, the financial figures for the festival are presented, showing a shocking deficit of $150,000. The loss is explained by the many who cut holes in the fencing surrounding the area and got in for free. It turns out only 27,000 festival-goers had paid the full entrance fee.

▣ **FILMING** The weekend is filmed, and edited material will be premiered as *Stamping Ground* next year, featuring The Byrds rocking out on a loose 'Old Blue'.

The group's performance of 'Jesus Is Just Alright' is screened on *Polygoon*, the weekly Dutch cinema news bulletin, seen in the run from Thursday July 2 until the following Wednesday.

Sunday 28
Bath Festival Of Blues & Progressive Music '70, Bath & West Showground, Shepton Mallet, Somerset, UK

This two-day festival takes place about 12 miles south of Bath and is promoted by Fred Bannister, gathering an impressive line-up of American and British artists. Although the weather shifts between heavy rain and bright sunshine, the organisers are rewarded with a remarkable crowd of 150,000 fans from all

over Britain, far beyond Bannister's estimate of 60,000. The weekend even manages to turn a profit for the industrious promoter, a rare feat in the hazardous festival business.

Artists appearing (in alphabetical order) are The Byrds, Canned Heat, Colosseum, Country Joe McDonald, Donovan, Dr. John, Fairport Convention, Flock, Frank Zappa, Hawkwind, Hot Tuna, It's A Beautiful Day, Jefferson Airplane, Joe Jammer, John Mayall, Johnny Winter, Keef Hartley, Led Zeppelin, Maynard Ferguson, The Moody Blues, The Pink Fairies, Pink Floyd, Santana, and Steppenwolf.

The Sunday programme falls well behind schedule, and Led Zeppelin's monumental show earlier at sunset drains the audience of energy. As the last strains of Zeppelin's fifth and last encore die away, thousands file out as nightfall descends. Following Zeppelin, Grace Slick decides to ease Jefferson Airplane down after a short set to make way for Hot Tuna and Country Joe, before McGuinn's company takes to the air in the early morning hours of Monday.

The damp Sunday night has brought another hazard: heavy gusts of wind combined with rain play havoc with the equipment, and, of course, touching live microphones and electric guitars can be highly dangerous. In the face of this, The Byrds pull out their secret weapons: acoustic guitars, miked drums, a banjo, and a rubber mat for Battin – whose bass is the only amplified instrument on stage.

The Byrds switch to unplugged mode and juggle the set accordingly without batting an eye, taking the wet and cold crowd on a journey though Byrds history past and present: 'It's All Right Ma (I'm Only Bleeding)', 'Ballad Of Easy Rider', 'Willin'', 'Soldier's Joy', 'Goin' Back', 'Baby, What You Want Me To Do', 'Drug Store Truck Drivin' Man', 'You Don't Miss Your Water', 'Jesus Is Just Alright', 'Turn! Turn! Turn!'/'Mr. Tam-

bourine Man'/'Eight Miles High', 'Oh Mary, Don't You Weep', 'Black Mountain Rag', 'Just A Season', 'Amazing Grace', 'So You Want To Be A Rock'n'Roll Star', 'You Ain't Going Nowhere', 'Old Blue', 'Wasn't Born To Follow', 'Glory, Glory' (making its one-off debut tonight), and finally 'Take A Whiff On Me'.

By the time The Byrds come on stage in the early morning hours of Monday, the crowd has dwindled to 15,000 and some reviewers, such as Roy Carr in *New Musical Express*, have left the area and have to rely on second-hand reports. Some brave journalists stick it out, and Roy Shipton of *Disc* (July 4) is one. "[Those who went early] missed The Byrds, whose acoustic set must earn them a bonus glass of cider."

"Roger McGuinn led The Byrds through an incredibly peaceful acoustic sunrise service," writes Chris Hodenfield in *Rolling Stone* (August 6), but perhaps exaggerates when he claims that "maybe eight, maybe 16 encores, were called for". Chris Charlesworth reports in *Melody Maker* (July 4): "The Byrds saved the day by abandoning their electric gear and using an acoustic line-up running through familiar old Byrds tunes … . They had the audience singing along with them as dawn broke. They played two-and-a-half hours." At 5:00am in the morning, The Byrds leave the stage to Dr. John, who – bereft of electric instruments – "clutched a shepherd's crook and mumbled Afro-Cajun jive accompanied by throbbing bongos" according to Charlesworth.

Reader John Gillard writes in to *Disc* (July 18): "After hearing everyone rave about the grossly overrated and tuneless Led Zeppelin, I would like to pay tribute to The Byrds' fantastic set at the Bath festival. It was refreshing to hear such beautiful harmonies and actually make out the words – unfortunately not the case with most other groups there. Owing to a power failure, The Byrds played their

The Byrds at Bath.

entire set acoustic yet still produced some of the most together and competent music of the festival."

ALSO ...

The Flying Burrito Brothers play their last gig with Gram Parsons at the Jam Factory in San Antonio, TX. By now, Parsons has lost interest in the group, and his lackadaisical stage behaviour more or less forces Chris Hillman to fire him.

July

→ Wednesday 1–Friday 3

The Byrds have extended their European visit to include a return to the Netherlands from July 4 to 8 and meanwhile hang out in London. With spare time on their hands, group and wives do the sightseeing rounds and speak to the press. Mike Ledgerwood quotes an unnamed Byrd for a feature in *Disc* (July 16). "For the most part festivals are very disorganised. And a lot of time they're set up by people who don't know music. We played a gig in Germany where the stage was about 80 feet high and the people looked like ants. Bath was very well organised as far as festivals go and was pretty well together as far as facilities went, we thought. But we had played in Rotterdam the night before and our roadies almost killed themselves to get the equipment in on time. Then we found we didn't go on till three or four in the morning because there were so many groups going on in front of us."

Skip Battin speaks to *Melody Maker* (July 11). "Bath was tremendous, a fantastic experience. The whole thing was beautiful. At first we did not think we would be able to go on. We were told we could not use our electric gear due to the rain. Then we decided to do it acoustically. I was stood on a rubber mat at the back of the stage in the dry part. But I felt very alien there, so, getting braver and braver, I gradually moved to the front. I don't think I would have played the electric bass if I had known [of the electrical danger]. I'm not that brave. … This is my first trip to London and I am very impressed. London is very much like New York – but man, so much more friendly."

The musicians magazine *Beat Instrumental* (September 1970) speaks to Clarence White and Skip Battin. "In the States, we would have [left the festival]," White says of their Bath appearance, "but a lot of people came to see us, and we think that the English have always been into good music. Playing at that time was better than walking away."

Battin interjects: "Bath was a unique experience. We did an unusual set, an experimental one – this was not by design but by accident. We'd been hanging around since seven that evening, and when we finally got on we had to use acoustic instruments, but we played better than we'd ever done. It was very satisfying. We normally do an acoustic interlude in our act, but we can do anything acoustic – we didn't know that when we started our act at Bath."

White tells Beat that the Parsons–White String Bender (the copyrighted name now in place) is to be marketed soon. "In the end we sat down with Leo Fender and agreed that Fender was to market it. We can trust him."

Roy Carr interviews Gene Parsons for *New Musical Express* (August 8). "Around the time Clarence White and I joined, The Byrds almost died in the States. We weren't getting much bread, and there just didn't seem to be very much enthusiasm in the band. But then when Skip Battin joined, somehow things got a bit better. Internally, we all became like brothers. Suddenly things started to improve. Things are getting so good now that it seems as though we can do no wrong. The public's acceptance, particularly on the East Coast and in the South, is really fantastic."

Parsons talks about the success of the *Easy Rider* soundtrack, but adds: "Personally, I feel that more so it has been our live performances that has helped us to regain our popularity. We are just influenced by [country and bluegrass]. Therefore, we are not accepted in Nashville. Lots of straight Nashville musicians actually put down Earl Scruggs, simply because he recently worked with us on a television documentary. I think they are afraid of the change. In the same way that they were afraid of loosening the slaves. Actually, the Nashville roots came from the black people, though the country folk may not like to admit it. Leadbelly was country, and so were many others."

Of the upcoming album, Parsons says: "I think that people will also like the studio tracks. It has a country feel with some numbers being played entirely acoustic, with Clarence on mandolin. Other songs are in the almost traditional Byrds style but a whole lot funkier. When we played the tapes to members of the old Byrds, they really dug it."

Gene Parsons also talks to Pete Frame for a feature in *Zigzag* (No 14, August 1970). The article covers a lot of ground, from his pre-Byrds days to the rejuvenated Byrds, from Bob Johnston to the failed Bob Dylan session, from *Easy Rider* to Gram Parsons.

"We were going to do that album with Dylan," explains Parsons. "They set up the studio time and asked us to do it, but we were really upset because they hadn't given

us enough warning and we were booked up too heavily – there was no way we could have done it, and Columbia are mad at us now."

Why don't The Byrds produce themselves? "Well, we're not allowed to," says Parsons. "I wish we could, but Columbia stipulates that their groups must have producers. However, Terry Melcher gave us plenty of freedom, but in fact some of the tunes on our next album will be produced by us. But Terry is very much with us, and when it comes to mixing he's got a very good ear. Soon as we get back to L.A., he's going to have the album ready for us to listen to. He's pretty good – even played piano on a couple of tunes."

So, what about the new record? "Well, I think the new double album is probably a hundred per cent improvement on *Ballad Of Easy Rider* – it's much more together as a result of Skip's arrival. There was a conflict with John York, who was our bass player, all through that album and I'm surprised that it came out as well as it did."

Phil Hardy, from the English underground paper *Friends* (August 7), speaks to McGuinn, Parsons, and Battin for a discussion on Byrds past and present. McGuinn explains the lyrics of 'CTA-102' and 'Drug Store Truck Drivin' Man'; Battin talks about the switch to country music; Parsons speaks warmly of the recent Earl Scruggs session.

Having democratically shared out press duties to his band mates, McGuinn does the 'Blind Date' spot in *Melody Maker* (July 11) alone, passing comment on an admittedly bland stack of singles – by Matthews Southern Comfort, Redbone, the Ian Anderson Country Blues Band, The Edgar Broughton Band, The *Fifth Dimension*, and Judith Durham. "We were right next door to them in the studio in L.A. when they were cutting their album," says McGuinn upon hearing the Redbone track. "I know the guys. I met them. They are American Indians. Some of them just came off the reservation. It's like soul – a good solid beat, but I didn't particularly dig the words."

Penny Valentine, one of the British music journalists who championed The Byrds from day one, scores an exclusive interview with the Byrd leader ("I dig being captain!") for *Disc* (July 11). Regarding popularity, McGuinn relays a great little story. "Joe Cocker once said the most honest and fine thing about success: that it was great as long as you knew your way home. I like to think I do know my way home." McGuinn's passion for film and acting is debated, and he talks about the projects The Byrds have been involved with so far: *Candy, Don't Make Waves* ("awful, but good experience"), *Gene Tryp*, and of course *Easy Rider*.

"I was really pleased with [*Easy Rider*]. I

know a lot of people have this idea that the film was about The Byrds. Fonda was a friend of mine and once said that his character was based on me, and Hopper's on Dave Crosby. I don't know – certainly Fonda didn't pump us for the script. That was already written. But I did identify strongly with the film once it was completed. I was shattered at the end [of it]."

McGuinn says he has aspirations as a director, but to do that convincingly he "should either be an ex-actor or a technical genius". He also discloses that he is working on the score for Tony Foutz and Douglas Trumbull's science fiction movie that began filming last year. Mentioning the project to Phil Hardy in the *Friends* (August 7) interview, McGuinn gives the title as *Ecology 70*, while in *Disc* it is taken down as *Rudibaker 70*. In the end it does not matter, as neither his musical score nor the actual movie will ever be completed.

Meanwhile, Dinky Dawson has won approval from The Byrds for his work on the live sound and is hired full time. The group has noticed the quality of the British PA system manufactured by WEM (Watkins Electric Music), and Dawson is given the job to purchase a suitable system and streamline it for use in the States.

•

⌨ **UK RADIO** [Unknown location] London BBC Radio 1 *Scene And Heard*

BBC Radio One interviews Gene Parsons for *Scene And Heard*, a weekly show with the latest news from the pop world. The show is broadcast on July 5, and for his troubles Parsons is paid the princely sum of £6 (about $15).

Saturday 4
De Doelen, Rotterdam, The Netherlands

As promised at the Kralingen festival a week ago, The Byrds return to Rotterdam for another concert, for which they are paid 10,000 Dutch guilders (about $2,800). The show does not commence until midnight and runs well into the morning hours of the Sunday, with 2,000 Byrds fans shouting for more.

De Rotterdamse Courant (July 6) writes: "Roger, Gene, Clarence, and Skip were prepared to give it all to repeat the success of the week before. This worked: at 4 o'clock in the morning the sunlight arrived and everybody went home extremely happy. Promoter Berry James Visser and The Byrds were very satisfied after the successful show and they gave the audience what they wanted: country music with a relaxed feeling. McGuinn was predominant on vocals along with his typical guitar sound with the other Byrds in the back-

ground. During this three-hour show (minus a long break) we got Kralingen without the misfortunes of that gig (the rain and a defective sound system) in perfect sound quality, the showmanship of McGuinn, the virtuosity of Clarence, and the satisfactory drumming of Parsons.

"The set before the break was hardly interesting and not up to the high level of Kralingen; it was all rusty, loud, and hardly representative of the polished sound you would have expected. Battin's pumping bass drowned McGuinn's strained voice. After the break, the sound balance was restored, Clarence's classic playing style returned, and McGuinn guided his band through the songs, much to the delight of the audience." The crowd refuses to let The Byrds go until they have played four encores (another review claims they do ten), and when they finally straggle back for the a cappella 'Amazing Grace', the promoter begs the audience to leave the band alone and let them go.

Sunday 5

BBC Radio One broadcasts *Scene And Heard* (3:00–4:00pm) including an interview with Gene Parsons (see July 1–3).

Tuesday 7
Concertgebouw, Amsterdam, The Netherlands

⌨ **EURO RADIO** Following a photo session in the afternoon at Leidseplein in central Amsterdam, the group takes the stage at one of the foremost concert halls in the world. The two shows (at 7:00 and 10:30pm) are recorded in their entirety by Dutch radio VPRO, and apparently it is the second show that is used for a later radio broadcast.

The broadcast features: 'You Ain't Going Nowhere', 'Lover Of The Bayou', 'Old Blue', 'Well Come Back Home', 'My Back Pages'/'Baby, What You Want Me To Do', 'He Was A Friend Of Mine', 'Willin'', 'Black Mountain Rag'/'Soldier's Joy', 'Take A Whiff On Me', 'This Wheel's On Fire', 'It's All Right Ma I'm Only Bleeding', 'Ballad Of Easy Rider', 'Jesus Is Just Alright', 'All The Things', 'Buckaroo'/'Nashville West', 'Turn! Turn! Turn!'/'Mr. Tambourine Man'/'Eight Miles High'/'Hold It', 'So You Want To Be A Rock'n'Roll Star', 'Positively Fourth Street', 'Mr. Spaceman', 'You Don't Miss Your Water', 'Chestnut Mare', 'Chimes Of Freedom', and 'Amazing Grace'.

Peter Schroder of *De Volkskrant* (July 8) writes about the first show. "The performance was even more inspired than in Rotterdam; the four-part harmonies were unbelievably spot-on, and musically the back-up had an even better foundation (perhaps fuelled by

the enthusiasm of the audience). The rich diversity in music varied from rocking Jimmy Reed blues to country & western; from the loud 'This Wheel's On Fire' to the subtle and personal 'He Was A Friend Of Mine'. It all sounded more articulate – even the bizarre bastard-jazz and teenybopper send-up by Skip Battin during 'Eight Miles High'. This line-up is well-oiled and probably the best and most inventive pop group playing today."

Schroeder praises each member (describing White as a "a rather misanthropic whiz-kid guitar player") before concluding: "If it wasn't for the next concert waiting to begin at 10:30pm, this performance could have gone on until the middle of the night."

Wednesday 8
De Doelen, Rotterdam, The Netherlands

An extra concert in Rotterdam is added by public demand.

Thursday 9

It is probably today that The Byrds return home to Los Angeles.

ALSO …

Crosby Stills Nash & Young wind down a US tour at Metropolitan Sports Center, Minneapolis, MN. Cruising in the wake of their *Billboard* Number One album *Déjà Vu*, they are now the highest-paid American rock group touring. Despite tempting offers to continue, the four men have decided to pursue various solo projects. Over the coming months, David Crosby potters about and completes his first solo album, *If I Could Only Remember My Name*, for release in February 1971.

Early

The group is back in Los Angeles again, and Terry Melcher plays them the finished mixes for the next album, completed in their absence. Apparently, there is an unresolved copyright problem on some songs demanding that they be re-recorded, according to a news item in *Melody Maker* (August 1). Keith Howell at CBS in London is the source, but the situation is apparently worked out and there is no documentation of further recording sessions at this time.

Monday 20
'Schaefer Music Festival', Central Park, NY

The Byrds take part in the Schaefer Music Festival, as they did last year. They appear with Van Morrison for two shows (7:00pm and 9:30pm), the first of which is slightly marred by light rain. Mike Jahn catches the first show for *The New York Times* (July 22). "Hearing The Byrds is always a pleasure. [They were also] one of the first folk-rock bands, playing what essentially was folk music with electric instruments. The music is amazingly unchanged today, considering the group's excursions into country and electronic-distortion music; but the concert here showed another trend.

"The Byrds always were known for tight, short songs. Playing in Central Park Monday, they showed an inclination toward longer, semi-improvisational numbers. Clarence White, guitarist, worked some interesting jazz runs into a long, complex, and unfolky prelude to one of the group's better-known songs, 'Eight Miles High'. For some time they have been playing their more familiar songs, such as 'Eight Miles High', 'Turn! Turn! Turn!', and 'Mr. Tambourine Man' as a medley, but this touch of jazz and the long instrumental was unexpected and welcome."

Journalist Bud Scoppa sees the second show and collects impressions for his Byrds biography. "By the time the second set at Central Park started, the threat of rain had passed, [and] The Byrds pranced out to great swells of cheering from the overflow crowd. After tuning carefully, they roared into 'Lover Of The Bayou', a new song. It has the energy-flow of 'Jesus Is Just Alright' but it's darker, more sinister. White turned up his volume knob and held his notes for long moments as he played. His guitar literally howled. Parsons whacked his drums unmercifully, and Battin thumped at the thick strings of his long-neck bass."

"The three-hit medley included a driving 20-minute jam on 'Eight Miles High'. During the song, McGuinn and White gradually stopped playing and walked behind the speakers, leaving the rhythm section to build on the song's skeleton. People below were dancing and looking up at Skip, who was so far forward that his feet came over the edge of the 10-foot-high stage. He was as mesmerised by the dancers as they were by his music. He started dancing himself, unstrapping his bass and twirling it in the air as if it were his partner. The other two came back, waited for the right moment, and crashed back into the song with their searing guitars. Finally, they sang the verse, releasing all the tension that the jam had built up.

"Then the break song: McGuinn said a quick goodnight to the audience, knowing full well he'd be back in a moment for an encore. The Byrds leaped back on the stage, played a rather sloppy but rapturous 'Rock'n'Roll Star', with McGuinn doing a parody of his own guitar style. Then, waving and smiling, he said, 'We have to stop – they won't let us play any more,' referring to the midnight closing of the park. 'You've been great. Goodnight, everybody.' As he walked off the stage, McGuinn seemed to be floating.

He knew as well as anyone else in the place that The Byrds had done the perfect show: not that they had played perfectly, but that they'd beautifully meshed their music – and through it, themselves – with the mood of the people who'd come to see and hear them.

"There were massive shouts for more. No one was moving from his seat or his spot in the aisle, even when the house lights went on and the spotlights were turned off. The concert was over, but no one was willing to accept the fact. McGuinn knew that this special audience needed some special touch to fulfil it. He had it. Cheers went up. McGuinn walked back on to the stage. He tried a microphone – it had been turned off. So he leaned forward, cupped his hands and shouted, 'Whether we're allowed to or not – mikes or no mikes – we're gonna do one more song for you.' The audience clamour was so resounding that the producer had no choice but to tell his soundman to turn the mikes back on.

"Without instruments, White, Parsons, Battin, and McGuinn stood behind their mikes. In a slightly hoarse but still rich four-part harmony, they sang 'Amazing Grace' to the initially bewildered audience. By the time they were halfway though the hymn, everybody knew that they weren't joking – but McGuinn's smile still gave the cynics an out. As the four Byrds reached the last line of the hymn, the warmth that had been welling up in everyone throughout the evening burst forth in a tremendous swooping sound – not a cheer, more like a gargantuan murmur – that enveloped everything. As The Byrds turned and left the stage this last time, the people knew instinctively they could not yell for more. There was nothing left for either The Byrds or the audience to give; they'd all reached a deeper level than anyone had expected. Everybody knew they'd be back again."

📺 **US TV** [Unknown studio and location], WNET *Oscar Brand: The Show*

The group appears on *The Show*, hosted by Canadian folk singer and songwriter Oscar Brand. Records will not survive to show what the group performs or when the programme is broadcast, but possibly it is as soon as tomorrow – Wednesday is the weekday on which *The Show* regularly airs. The Byrds are presumably .... appearance is not announced in this week's TV guides.

Playhouse In The Park, Philadelphia, PA
While the group plays in Philadelphia supported by Wax (two shows; at 7:30 and 10:00pm), a news story in today's *New Musical Express* presents plans for a European tour for

the two last weeks of November, to include a major London venue. In the event, the project will be ditched.

'Summerthing', Ringer Playground, Allston, Boston, MA

'Summerthing', Jamaica Pond, Boston, MA
Mayor Kevin White has instigated a summer concert series for the people of Boston, held in different parks around the city. Sponsored by the Office of Cultural Affairs, concerts are held between June 22 and August 17, many of them at Harvard Stadium.

The Byrds play two consecutive days at two different locations: on the Monday with Bo Diddley and Chris Smithers, and the Tuesday reputedly with Chuck Berry. This is Dinky Dawson's first dates as soundman for The Byrds in the US following his three festival jobs in Europe last month and the first time the group tests out the specially-assembled British sound gear. Thanks to a faulty stereo splitter, the sound is badly distorted, almost costing Dawson his job, as he will recount in his memoir, *Life On The Road* (1998).

"At the [second show,] after a few audience members walked up and complained to me, I finally marched over to the speaker columns on the other side of the stage to discover the distortion. Testing everything I could without yanking the band's sound all together, I finally tried bypassing the stereo box and putting the

PA system in mono. Now everything sounded fine – even louder and clearer, in fact. So the problem centred in that stereo box, which, fortunately, I'd have time to repair and reattach to the system before the next gig.

"Was that the end of the problem? Definitely not! Roger McGuinn tarred and feathered me in his hotel room the next day. His wife had called him from Los Angeles, saying that one of her friends had reported that the sound at the show absolutely sucked! 'Why have you spent so much of my money on something that doesn't work?' he screamed at me. After listening to the tapes of the two shows and my account of how I'd finally isolated the problem, he finally accepted my explanation about the defective stereo box. … His face twisted from a scowl into a smile as he told me simply, 'Well then, get on with it.' After that situation passed, it would be a while before I had any more trouble getting along with Roger McGuinn."

Over 8,000 people attend the Monday show, and Ben Edmonds comments in the *Phoenix* (August 8): "Looseness has always been a Byrds trademark, but the looseness they displayed on Monday night bears no relationship to their imbalance and untogetherness of the past two years. They now possess a relaxed awareness of themselves as a unit, this attitude being best expressed in the performance of Clarence White. Previously super-nervous and uptight on stage, he now seems much more at ease with himself and the rest of the band. His playing was fluid and always appropriate. The most pressing musical problem for The Byrds has always been to find a drummer who could keep time, and Gene Parsons has remedied nicely. With all four members of the band singing, those beautifully characteristic Byrd harmonies have finally been brought home again."

A long 'Eight Miles High' triggers a mass dance explosion in the crowd, and Edmonds is pleased to report how "the thing that most distinguished this Byrds performance from so many past Byrds performances was the obvious enthusiasm displayed by the band. They were making music again and having fun at it, and the crowd loved every last minute of it".

Wednesday 29

The Byrds, Jimmi Seiter, and Dinky Dawson fly out to The Bahamas to attend a four-day Columbia Records Convention. Columbia has placed a lot of faith in the group's next album, named *(Untitled)* after rejecting Billy James's half-joking suggestion to call it *The First Byrds Album* in honour of the group's newfound strength. Two other working titles bandied about are *Phoenix* and *McGuinn White Parsons & Battin*.

A misunderstanding results in the cryptic title they settle upon, although the story will vary a little. Preparing the final song-list for post-production and artwork, Terry Melcher – as he later tells Johnny Rogan – simply types "Untitled" for the album name when filling out the paperwork. In an ad campaign for the album ("Byrdman raps"), McGuinn says it is James who receives a phone call from Columbia Records and tells the record company "as yet untitled" when asked for the title. Anyway, the name sticks, and a press package is prepared for the sales corps attending the convention. Promotional copies of the album wrongly print 'Kathleen's Song' as one of the numbers on the studio album.

According to Dinky Dawson's riveting life-on-the-road memoir, the trip to The Bahamas is an extraordinary experience. Someone has the bright idea to spike the wine served to the sales representatives with LSD. "By the time the resort staff brought the dessert," writes Dawson, "the room was buzzing like a rowdy truck-stop as everyone spoke very loudly, including the head table of Clive Davis, all of the VIPs, and various top brass. The speeches began, some of which meandered absently into drivel or dissolved into outright laughter, but the label reps didn't really notice, since their minds were occupied by the beautiful patterns their fingers could make or games to be played with objects on the table."

Much hilarity centres on 'Rubber Ducky', a Columbia single taken from the children's TV show *Sesame Street*. The promotional kit comes complete with a quacking yellow plastic duck. "The rubber ducks received a rigorous workout, and one speaker could barely be heard above all the quacks and laughter as he floundered about in a rambling speech about the *Sesame Street* single's upcoming ad campaign."

Thursday 30

Columbia Records Convention, [Unknown resort], Freeport, The Bahamas

The Byrds perform for just one night at the convention, but as Dawson has the job to mix the sound for the other artists performing (Donovan tomorrow and Miles Davis on Saturday August 1), the group stays put in The Bahamas.

August

Sunday 2

The group and entourage fly from Freeport to Miami en route to Los Angeles.

Wednesday 5

The Kentucky Colonels reunite for a show at Ash Grove as part of the club's ten-day 'Country Jamboree' festival. The idea is to promote up-and-coming country and bluegrass artists, with some well-known guests thrown in to attract the larger public. Roland White is not able to attend the reunion, so the Colonels are reduced to a trio of Clarence White, Roger Bush (double bass and guitar), and Billy Ray (banjo). Not counting a brief reunion at the Ash Grove in April 1967, this is the first public outing for The Kentucky Colonels since the end of 1965. "Highlighting their performance were numerous brilliant guitar solos by White, Ray's consistently inventive banjo-picking, and the group's amazingly tight three-part vocal harmonising," writes Michael Sherman in *The Los Angeles Times* (August 7).

Sunday 9

Despite a nationwide tendency now against rock festivals, many brave souls still attempt the impossible. Some Oklahoma promoters work with Tom Carr Productions out of Memphis to bring in artists for the two-day 'Turner Falls International Pop Festival' in Davis, Oklahoma, for the Labour Day weekend. Local residents try to stop the festival, citing hazardous health risks, but the promoters get unexpected help from District Attorney Burke Mordy, who says there are no legal grounds to refuse permissions.

As usual, many of the booked artists are tentative (Steve Miller Band, Eric Burdon & War, Crabby Appleton, and The Chambers Brothers are early contenders), so the final posters for the festival range from the unknowns (Aphro-city, Courtship, Heavy Sugar, Soul Purpose, Sugarloaf), the better-knowns (Bloodrock, Mason Proffit, Zephyr), to the well-knowns (Flying Burrito Brothers, Pacific Gas & Electric, The Byrds). The original site in Lawton, Oklahoma, is eventually surrendered after further local protests, but a suitable location is found in the picturesque Arbuckle Mountains. This site also runs into opposition, from the Oklahoma Governor, and the festival is halted after all, despite the fact that The Byrds have already made the trip from Los Angeles.

There is a postlude, as *Time* magazine mentions the festival in passing in a long article on what it describes as the 'new class warfare', in other words the strain between the young and the old. The magazine writes (issue dated August 17): "In Oklahoma, hundreds tried to attend a banned rock festival in Turner Falls Park. Worried about 'drugs, nudity, free love, and lawlessness', Governor Dewey Bartlett blocked the kids with 300 National Guardsmen."

The Byrds 1970: Clarence White, Gene Parsons, Roger McGuinn, and Skip Battin.

The observation drives local Oklahoma paper *Ada Evening News* (August 17) to fume: "Speaking of loose journalistic practices, did you see the short paragraph in *Time Magazine* about the Turner Falls festival ban? Time blithely sipped over the facts and declared [that] Gov Bartlett halted the festival which 'hundreds of young people were poised to attend' by the use of 300 National Guard troops. Now, it's true, Guardsmen were nearby, north of Ardmore. But, as we all know, they were not used by the Governor. Only 100 or so Highway Patrol troopers blocked the Falls entrance. It makes one wonder about the credibility of the magazine and, indeed, its integrity."

Thursday 13–Sunday 16
**Fillmore West,
San Francisco, CA**

The Byrds play what turns out to be their last engagement for Bill Graham on the West Coast, in a four-day run with Commander Cody & His Lost Planet Airmen and Big Brother & The Holding Company, who stand in for Poco. Music journalist Ed Ward of *Rolling Stone* attends the show, but is not very impressed (October 29). "By the time The Byrds came on, Big Brother's wretched excesses had made me tired of rock'n'roll, and somehow The Byrds came off as boring. Leaving, I reflected that their last two albums had come off that way too, and wondered why. They were just slipping into 'Mr. Tambourine Man' as I hit the street."

British author and journalist Charlie Gillett sees the Sunday show but is another non-fan, and huffs in his *Record Mirror* report (August 29): "The Byrds came on sometime after midnight, and I hadn't really slept for about three days, and anyway I never really did dig The Byrds. I fell asleep. But I do remember that for the first time I got a sense of who McGuinn was. '[You] Ain't Goin' Nowhere' is a nice lullaby."

Gillett is tired; Commander Cody is dismissed as "OK playing straight copies of country & western, but they're just ham when they try 'Stranded In The Jungle' and 'Riot In Cell Block Number 9'." Big Brother do not impress him either until guest singer Nick Gravenites comes on stage to enliven the act. Gillett writes of the following night: "The Grateful Dead again, at the Fillmore West. If the Byrds have usually left me cold, the Dead have been an irritation."

Mid-August

Roger McGuinn is the subject of The *Rolling Stone Interview*, the magazine's expansive and probing monthly feature on various rock notabilities. (In years to come, the feature will also encompass movie stars, cultural personalities, and political leaders.) The interview is conducted at McGuinn's home in Sherman Oaks and runs in *Rolling Stone* No. 69, dated October 29.

"You know, I told you I wanted to get back at David Crosby," says McGuinn to journalist Ed Ward, referring to the ex-Byrd's cover story in *Rolling Stone* on July 23. "But you'll never guess where I was yesterday. Over at his house, man. And I had a real mellow time. We were talking about the sea, and, man, David's sure mellowed some."

In fact, the Crosby *Rolling Stone* interview from July gave McGuinn his due. "[He's] certainly one of the farthest-out musicians on the scene. Before, then, now," said Crosby of his former colleague, although the singer is not keen on the recent Byrds. "Yeah. I've also listened to their records. I think they should care more about what they're doing. If they're going to use that name I think they should care more about what they're doing."

The McGuinn *Rolling Stone* interview is a thorough and well-written trawl through his career, from his enrolment at the Old Town School of Music in Chicago, through his time with The Limeliters, The Chad Mitchell Trio, Bobby Darin, and into his Byrds career.

Of the fateful South African trip, McGuinn says: "I was curious. I was hip to it, knew it was a fascist country, and Miriam Makeba – I'd worked with her in the Mitchell Trio and the whole Belafonte Enterprises trip – she told me the whole thing, how the Nazi storm-troopers work down there, shooting people in the head in the middle of the street and just leaving them there. … I was curious to find out where the people were at to allow things like that to go on. And in spite of all the bad press we got for it at the time, I thought it was a valuable experience. … I was extremely paranoid, because it was just after Bobby Kennedy had been shot, and I was afraid, but Miriam Makeba had said I should see it first hand, and you weigh that against Mick Jagger telling me not to go – I mean, it might not be hip, but it sure was interesting and valuable."

Gene Tryp is in limbo at the moment, as McGuinn explains. "Jacques Levy: every time I approach him, he says it's gonna be together, and it's his department, really, to see that it gets together. He's got all the people." After giving Ward a brief synopsis of the story, he adds: "It's got a lot of topical things in it; a lot of sex and violence, all the essentials for a good play. But they cut the budget from $750,000 to $300,000, so that's gonna kill a lot of the special effects. They were gonna have a river running on stage in one scene that'd have to run in and out on wheels, and all kinds of expensive props that'd kill you if you ever tried to take the show on the road.

"They told me to go see [theatrical producer and Tony Award winner] David Merrick about it, and he's a very practical businessman, having been a millionaire and lost it and gotten it all back, so he's very practical about it. He asked me who was gonna be in it and I believe that Jacques had told him that he might get [star of *Midnight Cowboy*] Jon Voight to play the lead part, because he sings and plays guitar, and Merrick said it'd last six months or a year and then it'd drop off like a rocket. He was very practical about it – just rejected it flat out. But we've got Don Kirshner interested in it. I've known him since the Bobby Darin days, and he's sort of committed to doing something with it. Columbia came up on their bid from $50,000 to $150,000. So I think that with some help from other sources, it might get finances by sometime in '71. But it might not."

•

In fact, it will take more than 20 years for *Gene Tryp* to reach the stage, and then in a condensed form. In 1992, Levy will be a teacher at Colgate University's theatre programme in Hamilton, NY, when he directs *Just A Season* for four nights (November 19–22, 1992) at the university theatre – his final *Gene Tryp* revision. The show will feature McGuinn as both musician and in an acting role, while the cast and orchestra are made up of students.

Friday 21–Sunday 23
Ash Grove, Hollywood, CA

The Byrds are added for a weekend at the Ash Grove, where bluesman Freddie King holds down a long residence together with singer–guitarist Robbie Basho. For the Sunday performance, Linda Ronstadt and John Hammond Jr join The Byrds for a song each. Ronstadt, who has just finished a six-day run at the Greek Theatre with Tommy Roe, sings John D. Loudermilk's 'Break My Mind', while Hammond rocks through the Hank Snow number 'I'm Moving On'.

The Los Angeles Times review (August 25) covers King's jaw-dropping performance in detail and spends hardly any ink on The Byrds "who offered little to get excited about save for the guitar wizardry of Clarence White". *The Long Beach Free Press* shares the same sentiments; according to its correspondent, King "melted the plastic around my press card" while The Byrds "sounded like garage band musicians, and a somewhat disinterested garage band at that."

A three-day festival to be held this weekend in Anza, CA, has promised The Byrds among a multitude of names, but again it is a case of promoters going ahead before the necessary arrangements have been cleared. Dubbed

'Fiesta De Vida' – the Festival of Life – the event's entrance ticket would give you Buffy St Marie, big-band jazz drummer Louie Bellson, hallowed California DJ Wolfman Jack, a selection by the cast of Hair, authentic Indian tribal entertainment, Johnny 'Guitar' Watson, and Redbone – just to name a few of the billed attractions. By Thursday August 13 the local undersheriff confirms no permits have been issued, despite promoter Ernie 'Chief' Salgado's many advertisements in *The Los Angeles Free Press*. In the days leading up to the festival, workers busily prepare the Cahuilla Indian Reservation for the events – while Riverside County officials issue temporary restraining orders. In the end, Salgado is arrested for violating court orders forbidding festival preparations, and the 'Fiesta De Vida' dies.

•

Jimmi Seiter and Dinky Dawson share a place in Sherman Oaks, CA, which is soon christened Byrdhouse as the group adopts it as their rehearsal space and party central. "It was madness, a non-stop lovefest," Dawson will say in his autobiography, where he relates tales of girlfriends, management, business associates, band members, and hangers-on as they play, booze, and party away. (The group rehires Carlos Bernal around this time, the roadie who briefly worked with The Byrds while Seiter was recuperating in the summer of '68.)

Friday 28
[Unknown venue], Peoria, IL

The group's itinerary says they visit Peoria for a festival, but there are no advertisements locally so it is perhaps cancelled.

September

Friday 11–Saturday 12
Fillmore East, Manhattan, New York, NY

Dinky Dawson gives an accurate picture of the lightshows that are commonly part of live shows and which are refined to a fine art in Bill Graham's Fillmore theatres. "The guys operating the lightshow behind the group latched on to the energy and the mood," he writes in his later book, "perfectly synchronising their swirling colour patterns with the song's frenzied tempo. At one point, Roger and Clarence turned around and actually seemed to be drawn into the lightshow, playing along with the pulsating white colour." As McGuinn breaks into the *Easy Rider* medley "the lightshow operators locked into a fantastic thematic groove, flashing shots of Peter

Fonda and Dennis Hopper from the movie mixed with photos of The Byrds and swirling liquid colour patterns".

Delaney & Bonnie & Friends are special guests at the Fillmore, while Great Jones fills the opening slot, and there are two shows each night. The Byrds introduce a new McGuinn song during the New York weekend, 'I Trust', which is targeted as the group's next single.

Variety (September 23) says: "Although Roger McGuinn is the lone original Byrd, the quartet has retained the distinct Byrd sound while expanding upon its early roots. Combo's tight set covered a wide range from McGuinn's acoustic 'Mr. Tambourine Man' to a hard rock instrumental introduction to 'Eight Miles High'. In addition to performing a number of new tunes, The Byrds dipped into their back pages and came up with some of their past standards. Clarence White's guitar work excelled, from a crisp electric guitar that captured the sound of a pedal steel to a bluegrass fiddle-style on acoustic."

→ Sunday 13

After the Fillmore concerts, Elizabeth Walker interviews McGuinn for a feature in *Rock* (November 16). The chat touches many areas, including religion. "No, I'm not a Buddhist, nor am I any other form of organised religion, really. I'm sort of a free spirit. Nichiren Shôshû [the religion Skip Battin subscribes to] is a very loose organisation, not very strict. [Battin] chants – it embarrasses me how much he chants every day. He chants for hours at a time. The thing about his thing that I can't understand is that he does it asking the spiritual forces for toys – whatever you want, you know? – goodies, car, colour TV – and he gets it. But you've got to pay for it too."

Monday 14

(Untitled) is the first Byrds album of the new decade and their tenth so far, released in the US today. Excluding later greatest-hits packages, it will also turn out to be the group's only double album, combining a live record with a studio record – and specially priced to compete with single albums and give fans value for their money. The striking jacket photos show the four Byrds on one of the stone staircases leading up to Los Angeles' Griffith Observatory. When it is opened wide, the photos are mirrored symmetrically, resembling the graphic works of M.C. Escher.

Even if McGuinn remains the only original Byrd, *(Untitled)* connects with the group's past glories in a way that none of the other post-1967 albums manages. Terry Melcher and Jim Dickson are credited as co-producers of a lucid collection of songs, while Derek Taylor is called upon to write half the liner

notes. (Jim Bickhart, another old friend of the group, contributes the other half.)

Taylor writes with his usual eloquence – just as he did for the *Turn! Turn! Turn!* album in 1965. "This is not one of those big deal ambition-striving 'concept' albums," he says. "McGuinn once said Byrds albums are electronic magazines. This one is too, but it contains more pictures than any of the others. And the pictures move."

Sales for the album are strong, with more than 100,000 advance orders, and it makes a fair US Number 40 in the *Billboard* charts. Lester Bangs writes in *Rolling Stone* (November 26): "This double set is probably the most perplexing album The Byrds have ever made. Some of it is fantastic and some is very poor or seemingly indifferent (which is worse), and between the stuff that will rank with their best and the born outakes lies a lot of rather watery music, which is hard to find much fault with but still harder for even a diehard Byrds freak to work up any enthusiasm about.

"The current Byrds pinnacle is reached in the rushing jam, which whirls out of 'Eight Miles High' to wend and soar through 16 minutes of solid, texturally mature, and consistently inspired improvisation. After the theme's brief statement, McGuinn gradually rechannels its abstractions into a tight series of iconic C&W variations, followed by an intense Skip Battin outing, which must be the first recorded live rock bass solo that hasn't bored me to scowling fidgets. Now halfway through the side, the song completes it with a fine series of taut dervish interplays between all guitars, and drummer Gene Parsons propels them all the way with a tireless swirl of complex patterns. Much more work like this and they might even begin to re-establish their 65–68 position in the influential forefront of the rock vanguard.

"The studio album is something else again, simultaneously failing to deliver an alternative to dead-end nostalgias and adding almost nothing to the evidence of healthy renaissance given in 'Eight Miles High'. Experimentation of the kind that made the key-spanning leads of 'Miles' a one-of-a-kind guitar statement are simply and totally absent, but so are any pristine little masterpieces in classic Byrds style like 'Gunga Din'. Rather, initial listenings suggest a kind of comfortable blandness to leave no memories of striking songs to haunt you through your day like past Byrds ditties, and the ultimate impression left by the new batch is of a lack of energy or true vitality nearly as consistent as their studio polish. (I almost wish The Byrds would get some grease on their glossy panels.) Not one of them bids fair to join the landmarks of the past.

"'Chestnut Mare' is probably the best – it

has nice changes, and an airy, pleasant sound that somehow fails to exhilarate, even though everything is framed as clear as a View Master slide of Big Sur pine cliffs on a crisp spring morning. 'Chestnut Mare' is probably the studio disc's standout," Bangs summarises, before giving readers an account of the merits of the other studio tracks.

"What the Byrd perplex seems to come down to is this: J. Roger McGuinn and all Cos. have been plowing pastures in the same admittedly verdant American valley for just a season too long now. Their old riffs have run dry, leaving them and us casting around for something to rejuvenate a beloved but declining institution. But The Byrds have through all shifting crews remained a great rock'n'roll band, with innovative and experimental abilities aplenty. Standing after this album at almost schizophrenic crossroads, The Byrds within the coming months should either break from limbo

with a magnificently exploratory resurgence along the lines of 'Eight Miles High' or sink through even drearier morasses than those in the second half of this album, conceivably even grounding finally as something akin to the Gary Puckett & The Union Gap of Hip-Country. Either way, they've given us a longer ride and more moments of cleansing joy than we could ever have hoped for."

Given his stature as Byrds biographer, Bud Scoppa's lengthy review in *Rock* (November 16) is naturally brimming with praise. Of the opening 'Lover Of The Bayou' he writes: "[It's] the rawest, most explosive item on the whole double album. McGuinn's vocal sounds like he's deliberately avoiding clearing his throat for 48 hours – it's just perfect. White's guitar sweeps through the song in blazing arcs, with McGuinn's calm, stately 12-string, Parsons' uncompromising drumming, and Battin's bottom-heavy bass playing moving in

counterpoint." Closing down, Scoppa terms the album "easily their best recorded performances so far – in its own class as much as the records of the old Byrds were – and I think one of the best half-dozen albums of 1970. Watch out for the next one".

Ben Edmonds's case study in *Fusion* (No 46, December 11) focuses on the group's return to form. "I must admit that they had me scared for a minute there, though. Dissension had always been an integral part of Byrds history, an ever-present footnote to their musical changes. But for the past couple of years, things had been going just a little bit out of hand. Group members came and went like Volkswagen parts, leaving old Roger McGuinn the sole surviving member of the original band. Faceless names like Kevin Kelley and John York went through the motions of being The Byrds, but it just wasn't the same. A mirror reflection of dissension within the band, their live shows were little more than a skeleton exercise in nostalgia. On record during this period, their material tended to be thin and somewhat undefined. They lacked artistic substance, and only the presence of McGuinn gave any clues as to the identity of the band.

"This situation came to a recorded head with the release of their [*Ballad Of*] *Easy Rider* album. Clearly, it was the only blatantly mediocre album The Byrds have ever released, one which I called 'transitional' largely out of respect for their past. It was at times like these that The Byrds found out who their real friends were, for only the staunchest of fans could have weathered those lean days. And there were times when even the staunchest must have been tempted to give them up for dead.

"Let the word be spread, however, that The Byrds are alive and doing just fine. They have been together in their present incarnation for over a year now, and all signs seem to say that The Byrds are once again a band. … All of which brings us to The Byrds latest (and first double) release: *(Untitled)*. After the disappointment of [*Ballad Of*] *Easy Rider*, it is a pure joy to see that The Byrds are flying as high as ever. *(Untitled)* is a joyous re-affirmation of life; it is the story of a band reborn. It is especially gratifying to those of us who maintained, in the face of adversity, that The Byrds were everything we had initially taken them for. The welcoming home of old friends is always cause for celebration."

Like other critics, Edmonds singles out 'Chestnut Mare' as "an instant Byrds classic", and he concludes his lengthy four-column review: "Their wings finally healed, The Byrds have conclusively justified the faith held in them by so many for so long. Those who aban-

---

(Untitled)

A1 **'Lover Of The Bayou'** (R. MCGUINN/J. LEVY)
A2 **'Positively 4th Street'** (B. DYLAN)
A3 **'Nashville West'** (G. PARSONS/C. WHITE)
A4 **'So You Want To Be A Rock 'n' Roll Star'** (R. MCGUINN/C. HILLMAN)
A5 **'Mr. Tambourine Man'** (B. DYLAN)
A6 **'Mr. Spaceman'** (R. MCGUINN)
B1 **'Eight Miles High'** (G. CLARK/R. MCGUINN/D. CROSBY)
C1 **'Chestnut Mare'** (R. MCGUINN/J. LEVY)
C2 **'Truck Stop Girl'** (L. GEORGE/B. PAYNE)
C3 **'All The Things'** (R. MCGUINN/J. LEVY)
C4 **'Yesterday's Train'** (G. PARSONS/S. BATTIN)
C5 **'Hungry Planet'** (S. BATTIN/K. FOWLEY/R. MCGUINN)
D1 **'Just A Season'** (R. MCGUINN/J. LEVY)
D2 **'Take A Whiff On Me'** (H. LEDBETTER/J. LOMAX/A. LOMAX)
D3 **'You All Look Alike'** (S. BATTIN/K. FOWLEY)
D4 **'Well Come Back Home'** (S. BATTIN)

US release September 14 1970 (Columbia G-30127)
UK release November 13 1970 (CBS S 64095)
Chart high US number 40; UK number 11
Read more … entries for February 28, March 1, May 25, 26–28, 31, June 1–5, 9, 11 1970

Bonus CD tracks: (*Unissued*): 'All The Things (R. McGuinn/J. Levy) [alternate version], 'Yesterday's Train' (G. Parsons/S. Battin) [alternate version], 'Lover Of The Bayou' (R. McGuinn/J. Levy) [studio version], 'Kathleen's Song' (R. McGuinn/J. Levy) [alternate version], 'White's Lightning Pt.2' (R. McGuinn/C. White) [studio outtake], 'Willin'' (L. George) [studio version], 'You Ain't Going Nowhere' (B. Dylan) [live version], 'Old Blue' (Trad. Arr. R. McGuinn) [live version], 'It's Alright Ma (I'm Only Bleeding) (B. Dylan) [live version], 'Ballad Of Easy Rider' (B. Dylan/R. McGuinn) [live version], 'My Back Pages' (B. Dylan) [live version], 'Take A Whiff (On Me)' (H. Ledbetter/J. Lomax/A. Lomax) [live version], 'Jesus Is Just Alright' (A. Reynolds) [live version], 'This Wheel's On Fire' (B. Dylan) [live version]

"The current Byrds pinnacle is reached in the rushing jam, which whirls out of 'Eight Miles High' to wend and soar through 16 minutes of solid, texturally mature, and consistently inspired improvisation … Much more work like this and they might even begin to re-establish their 65–68 position in the influential forefront of the rock vanguard."
ROLLING STONE, NOVEMBER 26, 1970

doned ship during the past three years on the presumption that it was sinking have been proven guilty of hasty judgment. The Byrds continue to grow musically and lead stylistically, but they do so with an unfailing sense of their past. Each step in their growth process has left its distinct impression on their sound, and on the lives of all those who've grown up with them as well. History will no doubt bear out the significance of The Byrds' contribution to American popular music, but, for the time being, such speculations are worthless because *(Untitled)* says that The Byrds will be making their distinctive contributions for quite some time to come."

Jazz & Pop (January 1971) says: "The great Byrds resurgence carries with it one unfortunate note. One is motivated to ask all these legions of new, devoted Byrd fans where they were when 'Eight Miles High' was banned from radio stations around the country back in '65 [sic], and where they were when The Byrds led movements in psychedelic-raga-folk-Bach-rock? Were they all too busy listening to The Rolling Stones? Were they all on sabbaticals to Australia? Who knows?" quizzes Bruce Harris rhetorically.

"In any case, The Byrds are finally getting the recognition they no longer deserve. Or, that is to say, no longer deserved till *(Untitled)*. After their super classic masterwork LP, *The Notorious Byrd Brothers*, a brilliant Sergeant Pepper sort of thing, The Byrds went country on the best country-rock album by anybody to date, *Sweetheart Of The Rodeo*. But their next two albums, as they suffered through more odd permutations in their endless personnel changes, were disappointing. … *(Untitled)*, for all its flaws, brings The Byrds back as the super cosmic-cowboys of all time, and is without question their greatest achievement since *Notorious*."

What Harris terms as flaws is primarily the live half ("Every double album forces an artist to stick out his neck twice when he should only have to face the critical blade once"), whereas the studio half is given top marks. 'Chestnut Mare' is "the best track on the album and a milestone for The Byrds, right up there along with the original 'Eight Miles High', 'Everybody's Been Burned', and 'Change Is Now'". Harris is also fond of 'Yesterday's Train', saying it carries The Byrds "further into the realm of ... the country music. The essential Byrds philosophy-cum-paradox – having your heads in the clouds while your feet are still on the ground … could nowhere be better expressed than in a simple country-like tune about reincarnation." In short, he says that *(Untitled)* "is the new Byrds at their best. If for a while it seemed their flight was finished, perhaps it was only because they had finally arrived".

Don Heckman rounds up recent albums by Elton John, Santana, and The Voices Of East Harlem along with *(Untitled)* in *The New York Times* (November 29). "Most noticeably, the folk-music emphasis has lessened, replaced by a sometimes quite impressive jazz feeling. The Byrds do not make the mistake of placing themselves in direct competition with more adept jazz groups, but, obviously influenced by the musical tastes of Roger McGuinn, they seem to be chartering an improvisational style not unlike that employed by Jefferson Airplane and The Grateful Dead in their jams."

However, Hekman admits "that devoting the entire side of one disk to a concert performance of 'Eight Miles High' extends my listening patience pretty close to the breaking point". To conclude, he writes: "There aren't too many groups I can think of who can match the sheer survival power of The Byrds. In an age of instant faddism, their long-term musical excellence should be congratulated."

•

Vice President Spiro Agnew is on the campaign trail to gather Republican votes for President Richard Nixon in the November midterm election. On Monday September 14 he visits Las Vegas and attends a dinner party for Nevada Republicans. In a speech to the assembled $100-a-couple guests, Agnew claims the United States has been permeated by blatant drug-culture propaganda. He sweepingly attacks entertainers, parents, broadcasters, and the press, who all allegedly spread the culture. Moreover, it is being tolerated because "all the while that this brainwashing has been going on, most of us have regarded it as good, clean, noisy fun". Agnew places blame on the older generation, with its use of alcohol, sleeping pills, and pep pills, who have helped set the stage for the drug-culture phenomenon. He admits popular music is "complex and exciting" and deserves attention, but the "cumulative impact of some of their work advances the wrong cause". While he is having a go at general moral decay, he urges voters to elect a "Congress which will stop the waves of pornography and moral pollution and assure it will never be the wave of the future".

To back up his case, Agnew cites the Beatles lyric "I get high with a little help from my friends" – explaining helpfully to his audience that 'friends' in this case equals 'drugs' – and also quotes Steppenwolf's 'Don't Step On The Grass, Sam' and Jefferson Airplane's 'White Rabbit'. The Byrds are not spared either, as Agnew singles out 'Eight Miles High' as an example of a convoluted drug message.

Ed Tickner, who seldom acts as spokesman for The Byrds, is prodded to comment: "A lot of hullaballo was raised over that song, but if you listen to the lyrics, you'll see the

song is about the group's first trip to England as rock'n'roll stars. There isn't even any subtlety in that song advocating the use of drugs. Eight miles high refers to how high the airplane flies. Does 'Smoke Gets In Your Eyes' advocate the use of tobacco? That's how silly it could get."

Agnew's speech is picked up by dozens of newspapers across the country, and so is Tickner's reply. In 1966, the controversy over 'Eight Miles High' probably hindered its commercial chances, but by now Agnew's condemnation only serves to help ensure the song's immortality.

Thursday 17–Saturday 19
Whisky a Go Go, Hollywood, CA

The Byrds and The Flying Burrito Brothers play six shows over three nights at the Whisky A Go Go, marking McGuinn and company's first return here since October 1968. The Burritos debut new man Rick Roberts now, while the rest of their line-up remains: Chris Hillman, Michael Clarke, Sneaky Pete, and Bernie Leadon.

Robert Hilburn combined article/review in *The Los Angeles Times* (September 22) has the headline "Byrds Regaining Balance In Flight". He writes: "The Byrds showed why the momentum is starting to build up once again. Things began rather slowly in the opening set: McGuinn was a little reserved; the audience response was modest. But Clarence White's vocal and guitar work on 'Truck Stop Girl' breathed some life into both The Byrds and the audience. Apparently reacting to the increased audience interest, McGuinn seemed to begin putting more force into his own vocals. The instrumentation throughout was solid, tight (slightly country-tinged) rock. Very smooth and very nice. The Byrds are back. And they may be better than ever."

Hilburn obviously misses the final show on Saturday, when the two groups combine for a long and wild Notorious Burrito Brothers show, as is their habit whenever they share the bill.

Sunday 20
University of the Pacific, Stockton, CA

Concert with The Byrds, It's A Beautiful Day, Lamb, Stuart Little Band (from Stockton), and A Brother, My Cousin & I.

Wednesday 23
Fillmore East, Manhattan, New York, NY

☐ **US TV** NET *Fanfare: Welcome To Fillmore East*

The Byrds fly back to New York City again to appear on a special television show filmed by NET (National Educational Television, the precursor to the later PBS) as part of its Fanfare programmes. Graham has gathered a star line-up for one night, starring The Byrds (with Jimmi Seiter lending a hand on percussion), Albert King, The Elvin Bishop Group, Sha Na Na, Van Morrison, and The Allman Brothers Band, plus Joe's Lights. The participants keep their sets short to allow everyone to be featured. On October 11, the hour-long show is syndicated for the first time across the US. The show is produced by Tom Slevin and Kip Cohen under the direction of David Acomba.

Besides the two songs 'Jesus Is Just Alright' and 'Eight Miles High' featured in the broadcast (see October 11), four songs will later be officially released as bonus tracks when The Byrds catalogue is repackaged on CD: 'Take A Whiff On Me' and 'Jesus Is Just Alright' (on *(Untitled)*/*(Unissued)*), and 'Baby What You Want Me To Do' and 'I Trust' (on the boxed set *There Is A Season*).

Thursday 24

Gymnasium, University of Nebraska, Lincoln, NB

The group meets up with The Flying Burrito Brothers again.

Friday 25

Meehan Auditorium, Brown University, Providence, RI

Tim Hardin is the opening act for the group tonight. The review in *The Brown Daily Herald* (September 28) accuses The Byrds of being almost too perfect, too close to their recorded show. Things begin to loosen up as the four members lead into the second electric half and particularly the closing 'Eight Miles High'. "What people didn't expect was the very effective drum and bass solo sandwiched in the middle of their last song. It was effective because instead of coming off like someone who'd listened to too many Ginger Baker records, their drummer played some exciting, original music with the bass just helping him along. McGuinn rejoined them to do some very uninhibited and vigorous guitar work. Their performance peaked just when it should have."

Saturday 26

Virginia Military Institute, Lexington, VA

Dinky Dawson describes this as a contender for the weirdest Byrds gig ever, as he will recount in his book. "Precisely 15 minutes before show time, all the cadets filed into the gym decked out in their finest uniforms, with dates on their arms. The entire company stood to attention while the school's officers entered last and sat down; then everyone else

took their seats. When Jimmi [Seiter] ran on stage to introduce the band you could have heard a pin drop – no one clapped or reacted. After the first song, the assembly continued to sit in silence, and I felt embarrassed for poor Roger and the boys. After several long seconds of utter stillness, the commandant began to clap his hands, then everyone else joined in. The whole show went that way, each song ending in absolute quiet until the leader showed his appreciation, signalling permission for the rest to follow." By the second half, the school officials have left the building and normality returns as the cadets shed jackets and loosen ties for a rocking and rowdy late night.

October

Friday 2

Calvin College, Grand Rapids, MI

Saturday 3

Iowa State University, Ames, IA

A show with Iron Butterfly.

Sunday 4

Ellis Auditorium, Memphis, TN

The Byrds and The Flying Burrito Brothers combine for a disappointing show in Memphis with a poor turnout, according to the trade magazine *Amusement Business*. According to a Dutch interview that Battin will do next year, the local sheriff stops the show when the crowd gets uppity during the Byrds–Burritos encore.

Tuesday 6

🔊 **RECORDING** Columbia Recording Studios, Sunset and El Centro, Hollywood, CA. Producer Terry Melcher and engineer Chris Hinshaw.

The Byrds, Terry Melcher, and Chris Hinshaw are back at Columbia to record McGuinn's 'I Trust'. (The song is also known by its full title 'I Trust (Everything Is Gonna Work Out Alright)'.) This is a one-off, as the group will wait until January of next year before further working in the studio again, although a session in New York is reputedly booked for October 19. For the uplifting lyric of today's song, McGuinn has transposed his old adage "But somehow I know/That everything's gonna work out all right" into a song.

Surprisingly, the group also attempts a run-through of Gene Clark's 'Think I'm Gonna Feel Better', a song from the *Gene Clark With The Gosdin Brothers* album from 1967. It is sung by White, who also played guitar on Clark's

original recording. Jimmi Seiter, the group's right-hand man for so many years, is heard rattling a tambourine on the track. Seiter often slips into an unassuming position to the left of Parsons at concerts now and joins the group as unofficial fifth member on congas and assorted percussion.

Wednesday 7

The McGuinn interview by Ed Ward conducted earlier in the summer (see mid August) is printed today in *Rolling Stone* (issue No 69, dated October 29). Six pages long, the feature would certainly warrant McGuinn a front cover was it not for the recent death of Janis Joplin, on October 4, which dictates a last-minute switch.

Saturday 10

'Threshold '70 Involvement', Coliseum, West Virginia University, Morgantown, WV

The Byrds' primary touring circuit is American colleges and universities, and the group proves a popular attraction at these venues, where the pay is good and they are treated well. Colleges and universities are usually off the trodden path, so attendance is strong, and the group can sustain popularity in these places even if it is not a Top Ten act any more.

This week is West Virginia University's Homecoming. Attractions include a homecoming parade; crowning of the homecoming queen; a football game; and concerts by Doc Severinsen and The Trinidad Tripoli Steel Band; while The Chambers Brothers and The Byrds headline Saturday night's rock show.

Sunday 11

Gymnasium, State University of New York, Plattsburgh, NY

NET debuts its new concert series *Fanfare*, a programme that emphasises music culture in every shade from opera to rock. Tonight's show features selections filmed recently at Bill Graham's Fillmore East (see September 23) as *Fanfare: Welcome To Fillmore East*. The show is broadcast on WNDT Channel 13 in the New York area (with a simultaneous FM broadcast on WNEW-FM), on KCET Channel 28 in Los Angeles, and across the US on a series of NET-affiliated stations.

The complete running order is The Byrds ('Jesus Is Just Alright' and 'Eight Miles High'), Elvin Bishop Group ('Crazy About You'), Albert King ('Oh Pretty Woman' and 'Blues Power'), Sha Na Na ('Walk Don't Run' and 'Teen Angel'), and Van Morrison ('These Dreams Of You' and 'Cypress Avenue'), interspersed with interviews with Bill Graham and Joe's Lights. (The Allman Brothers Band, who also were filmed, are ultimately cut from the programme.)

Writing in *The Los Angeles Times* (October 12) following the premiere, Robert Hilburn notes: "The unevenness of the *Welcome To Fillmore* segment centred chiefly on the same trap that televised rock always seems to fall into: an attitude that some 'backstage colour' is essential to a successful rock programme. Because of its desire to get 'colour', there were such unrelated, somewhat distracting scenes of such off-stage activities as Fillmore East owner Bill Graham telling his feelings about performers, members of Sha Na Na mugging for the camera, and workmen putting up marquee letters.

"It seems that rock must certainly have a large enough and sophisticated enough audience these days for television crews to present a straight concert and leave all the side trimming in the can. In addition, the segment was guilty of trying to stuff too many artists into a single programme, thus preventing the acts from establishing any real musical identity. Limiting the acts to three would have made for a more realistic experience." Hilburn notes 'Eight Miles High' as a highlight of the broadcast.

Monday 12

Bill Graham and Mike Ahern hold a 'Rock Relics Auction' at the Fillmore East in New York tonight, perhaps the first ever rock memorabilia sale. Through ads in the city press, the auction has urged New Yorkers to 'buy peace' to help raise funds for a group supporting anti-war election candidates.

Tom Zito in *The Washington Post* explains how the idea came about. "Several months ago Mike Ahern, the Fillmore's stage manager, was trying to clean up the basement of the auditorium. One of his assistants collected a large assortment of items that had been left by various rock bands. He asked Ahern what they could do with the stuff." To which Ahern replies: "Let's have an auction!"

A long list of items go under the hammer, while Elvin Bishop, Mungo Jerry, Sha Na Na, and Edgar Winter offer music for free. Among the items sold are one of Pete Townshend's smashed guitars; Keith Moon's cigarette lighter; a vial of rose petals thrown by Mick Jagger at Madison Square Garden in '69; Joni Mitchell's spiral notebook containing the handwritten draft of all the songs of her first album, *Song To A Seagull*; Roger Daltrey's fringed, tie-dyed suede jacket worn at this year's Isle of Wight festival; B.B. King's orange plush-lined guitar case; Fats Domino's gold lamé tie; Ginger Baker's drumstick; B.J. Wilson's broken bass drum head (which goes for $32.50); Carlos Santana's switchblade knife;

and a Swiss army knife that once belonged to Roger McGuinn. The auction is visited by a crowd of about a thousand and raises around $15,000 for the good cause.

Mid-October

Back at his Sherman Oaks home, Roger McGuinn is interviewed by Michael Ross for a story in *Creem* (November 1970). Ross allows his readers a peek into McGuinn's study. "We're in his den, crammed with a crying baby; five television sets; a row of guitars; a letter from Pete Seeger thanking The Byrds for their recording of 'Turn! Turn! Turn!'; a photograph of Albert Einstein; a well-thumbed paperback edition of Robert Heinlein's *Stranger In A Strange Land;* a sturdy mahogany table holding a synthesizer manufactured by R.A. Moog & Co of Trumansburg, NY; a dozing manager; innumerable electronic toys; gadgets; and souvenirs.

"Time passes, but it isn't clock time. I don't know exactly: Byrd-time, maybe. We talk haphazardly – about sinister British journalists; about the difficulty of working within a monolithic recording organisation; about laughter as a way of alleviating the true fucking true pain of living; about his aspirations to act ('but not in any folk-rock-doc'); about clairvoyance; about motivational research; about *Tryp*, his off-and-on Broadway collaboration with Jacques Levy; about Van Dyke Parks; about his theory that artists are either underestimated or overestimated in their time ('I prefer to be overestimated'); and about the heartache of yourself overestimating your audience." The latter observation leads to a long ramble by McGuinn on Einstein, the failed '5D' single, and spirituality.

Ross reports that McGuinn is involved in not one but three recording projects. One is the next Byrds album; another is a solo McGuinn synthesizer recording; and the third is a collaboration between The Byrds and The Flying Burrito Brothers. The proposed Byrds–Burrito union would be a natural extension of the many gigs that McGuinn and Hillman's crews have shared recently. Unfortunately the exciting idea never gets beyond this brief mention.

Thursday 15–Saturday 17

Boston Tea Party, Boston, MA

The Byrds are visited backstage by Dinky Dawson's old boss, Peter Green of Fleetwood Mac, who is in the Northeast visiting friends and spending time at Goddard College in Plainfield, VT. Green left Fleetwood Mac in the spring, a disillusioned and very changed man, and Dawson is brought down by the sorry sight. (Myron LeFevre appears with The Byrds for the Boston Tea Party weekend gigs.)

Friday 16

Sargent Gymnasium, Boston University, Boston, MA

According to an advertisement in *The Boston Phoenix*, The Byrds are booked to play here while in Boston – possibly at an afternoon concert before going back to the Tea Party tonight.

Sunday 18

University of Connecticut, Storrs-Mansfield, CT

Friday 23

'Brooklyn Rock', 46th Street Palace, Brooklyn, NY

'Brooklyn Rock' promotes a series of concerts in October and November, starting tonight with The Byrds, Great Jones, and Cactus. The rest of the month and November looks like this: Iron Butterfly (October 30); Big Brother & The Holding Company, The Youngbloods, and Country Joe (November 6); Grateful Dead/Hot Tuna (November 11–14).

The Byrds concert collides with Derek & The Dominoes' debut at the Fillmore East, hampering attendance in the 2,500-seat theatre. The first show pulls about a quarter of the hall's capacity, although the second show is better visited. John Koegel in *The Hofstra Chronicle* (October 29) notes how 'Take A Whiff On Me' is now dedicated to Spiro Agnew, a spin McGuinn has introduced after the Vice President's recent broadside against drugs in popular culture (see September 14). "Take a whiff, take a whiff, take a whiff on me/ Oh, Spiro, take a whiff on me," he sings.

Koegel's review starts: "No one should go through life without seeing The Byrds in concert at least one time," before he urgently concludes: "Don't miss The Byrds next time they play New York: their live show is outstanding."

The Byrds' latest US single is released, extracting two superior tracks from *(Untitled)*:

'Chestnut Mare'

A 'Chestnut Mare' (R. MCGUINN/J. LEVY)
B 'Just a Season' (R. MCGUINN/J. LEVY)

US release October 23 1970 (Columbia 45259)
UK release January 1 1971 (CBS 5322)
Chart high US number 121; UK number 19
Read more ... entries for June 1–5 1970

'Chestnut Mare' – in a condensed form to fit the radio format – with 'Just A Season' as a B-side. It is a rather unnecessary exercise, as most fans already have the album, and the single never goes higher than Number 121 in the *Billboard* charts.

Saturday 24
Bloomfield College, Bloomfield, NJ

A good quality tape from the show will go into circulation, and it offers a couple of surprises. 'Lover Of The Bayou', the standard set-opener this year, leads into a tough take on 'Johnny B. Goode'. The second surprise is 'Home Sweet Home' (also labelled 'In The Morning I'll Be Gone' on some tapes), a number The Byrds perform for some time this fall (inserted after the 'My Back Pages'/'Baby What You Want Me Do' medley) before it slips quietly out of the repertoire. (With a week off, the group returns to California after finishing up here in New Jersey.)

Friday 30–Saturday 31
Pirates World, Dania, FL

The Byrds fly into Miami on a morning flight, bumping into Jim Morrison and his attorney Max Fink, who are on the way to Florida to hear the jury's verdict in the so-called 'Miami Trial'. The trial follows a Doors concert in Miami the year before, when on March 1 Morrison allegedly exposed himself on stage.

The trial has cast the future of The Doors in serious doubt, but this does not put a damper on the party atmosphere aboard the plane as Clarence White and the Doors singer engage in a friendly knife-throwing game in the upstairs lounge of the large Boeing 747 plane while downing copious amounts of brandy. Arriving in Miami, Morrison is sentenced to a maximum penalty of eight months for indecent exposure and profanity. An appeal is filed, but Morrison will never live to see the case back in court.

The Byrds, meanwhile, perform at an amusement park in Dania, near Miami–Fort Lauderdale. Promoted by San Francisco Opera House Inc, the two nights also feature The James Gang and The Flying Burrito Brothers. The open-air venue has a 'stage' that is little more than a simple steel construction under the stars. When the stage lights are turned on, trouble begins. "At that moment," Dinky Dawson will relate in his biography, "every flying bug within 20 miles took wing for the open hangar, launching an insect plague of biblical proportions on our gig. Clarence gathered bugs in his mouth every time he sang, Roger used his arms like windmills to fend off the swarms, and everyone collected a multitude of bites and rashes as the show continued."

November

Friday 6
Curry College & Joan D'Arc Academy, Milton, MA

The Byrds enter an active two-month period of touring, although they will mostly adhere to their usual regime of weekend concerts with weekdays off back home in Los Angeles. Even if Jim Dickson's alliance with The Byrds the past summer has proved shortlived, Ed Tickner elects to remain as manager. He flies to London this month to arrange a concert tour of the UK and Europe next year.

Saturday 7
Clark Memorial Gymnasium, Rochester Institute of Technology, Rochester, NY

Sunday 8
Clarkson College, Potsdam, NY

Wednesday 11
Suffolk County Community College, Selden, NY

The Byrds appear with The Flying Burrito Brothers. Local student publication *The Compass* (November 18) does not review the performance but publishes brief snippets from a backstage conversation with the four Byrds. Battin prefers to play colleges, as he explains: "There's no violence at colleges. At the Fillmore we encounter a lot of drunks and freaks. That's a drag." White thinks The Byrds are a hard group to classify, and Battin interjects: "We don't plan what we do, it happens, that's all. Tonight we're The Freak Barons. Tomorrow we might be cowboys, or maybe spacemen."

McGuinn dismisses the notion that The Byrds should record an album with The Flying Burrito Brothers, as so recently implied in Michael Ross's *Creem* article. "No good would ever come of it," he says matter-of-factly. He also distances himself from comparisons

Three of four Byrds: McGuinn, Battin, Parsons.

with The New Riders Of The Purple Sage (or simply NRPS), a country-rock gang that has sprung out of Grateful Dead. Although the NRPS will not release their debut album for almost another year, they have opened steadily for Grateful Dead since July 1969, with Jerry Garcia flexing his talents on pedal steel guitar.

Friday 13

University Of Maryland (UMBC), Catonsville, MD

(Untitled) is released in the UK today. Following their summer appearances at Bath and in the Netherlands, interest in The Byrds reaches new heights in Europe. Welcomed by excellent reviews, (Untitled) climbs to Number 11 in the UK album charts. Not since their initial LPs, Mr. Tambourine Man and Turn! Turn! Turn!, has the group scored so well in Britain.

Disc (November 7) grants the album a top rating of four stars. "[This] is probably the most intelligent collection of songs ever assembled on a double LP. For just under £3 [about $7] you can get a complete picture [of the group] as they are today. First record features the group live, playing their hits like 'Mr. Tambourine Man' and 'Rock And Roll Star' and demonstrating what a really tight funky sound they can produce. The vocals are deeper and more aggressive than on the original versions, and the bass–drum section is especially addictive.

"Highlight, though, is 'Eight Miles High', taking up an entire side and playing 15 minutes instrumentally before exploding into the vocal piece. In the studio, The Byrds show they retain all their imagination yet at the same time retain their unique sound – the country-rock, often verging on bluegrass with fiddles and harp. 'Truck Stop Girl' and 'Take A Whiff' are our favourite tracks here – and it's really encouraging to find a group that doesn't feel obliged to pander to the alleged 'heavy' wave."

The heading in New Musical Express (November 28) is "Byrds Pick-Me-Up". Roy Carr writes: "In retrospect, not only were The Byrds the original catalysts for the mid-60s West-Coast rock explosion but also Uncle Sam's first good-music band. Off-hand, I can't recall any other completely unknown group making such an auspicious debut and then sustaining the overall quality of their productivity. Even The Beatles, Stones, Beach Boys, Buffalo Springfield and Lovin' Spoonful had to expose their progress over a period of consecutive album releases. Five years and ten albums later, The Byrds still retain an artistry and freshness unmatched by most others in their genius. Even changes of key personnel

and direction haven't dulled their appeal or magical charms. I've always found a Byrds album to be the perfect pick-me-up when staring a new day. Indeed, on warm, summer mornings they can be guaranteed to give one a spirit of wellbeing.

"'Eight Miles High' proves to be an absorbing instrumental tour-de-force, which takes up the whole of one [side]; never does it bore or become tedious. Of the studio cuts which are contained on the second album, 'Chestnut Mare' with its spoken narrative will I'm sure prove to be a much requested item in years to come. In complete contrast, the traditional 'Take A Whiff On Me' is an almost pure skiffle rave-up. Like good wine, The Byrds have matured into a good vintage, benefiting from the presence of Skip Battin on bass and Gene Parsons, a peer amongst drummers. The much respected Clarence White complements the line-up, taking the lead vocal on a couple of tracks."

Richard Williams writes in Melody Maker (November 7): "There are few bands whose music has the power to evoke nostalgia for an era rather than for an isolated moment of time. There are even fewer who can do it at the same time as making music which is completely representative of the present, too. The Byrds have this, and (Untitled), apart from being simply their most satisfying work to date, is full of these complex memory-folds.

"Take the live version of 'Mr. Tambourine Man', for instance. … It starts exactly like the single, sticking your head firmly in 1965, but mid-way through the verse, Clarence White storms in with twisting guitar licks which completely alters the time-scale. … 'Eight Miles High', taking up one side, is an intuitive Dead-style jam packed with goodies, while 'So You Want To Be A Rock'n'Roll Star' and 'Lover Of The Bayou' are outstanding. Yet the studio sides contain one song, 'Chestnut Mare', which is arguably the most complete Byrds song yet. McGuinn sings about chasing and catching a wild horse, and in doing so captures a perfect relationship with nature which extends to the dense but mellow guitar work. The rest of the studio tracks are gentle and melodic with 'Well Come Back Home' spreading into a raga-rock essay. Simply a great album, and 'Chestnut Mare' … whew!" The album is picked as one of Melody Maker's 'Month's Choice' records for November, along with recent LPs by Emerson Lake & Palmer, Family, Curved Air, Aretha Franklin, and others.

Saturday 14

Baldwin Gym, Drew University, Madison, NJ

Yet another Byrds-plus-Flying Burrito Brothers

show, and once again they all get together for a grand finale. The Byrds have brought along Terry Melcher on keyboards for this show, and he will perform with the group on selected concerts until Christmas. With Jimmi Seiter also on percussion, The Byrds expand to six players.

For the second show at 11:00pm, Melcher and White sit in with the Burritos. The Byrds play a short half-hour set before 'Mr. Tambourine Man' signals the entrance of every Burrito in attendance. Soon the stage is filled with two drummers (Gene Parsons and Michael Clarke), Sneaky Pete's pedal steel, Melcher on organ, two rhythm guitarists (McGuinn and Rick Roberts), two lead guitarists (White and Bernie Leadon), Chris Hillman and Skip Battin both on bass guitars, and Seiter handling assorted percussion. The show ends with a 20-minute 'Eight Miles High' where Battin and Hillman and Parsons and Clarke go toe-to-toe in a long drums-and-bass interlude.

Neil Shapiro of The Metropolitan (November 18) reviews the first show ("Fabulous! Fantastic! Great! Supreme!") before a 3,500-strong audience, while the student paper Drew Acorn (November 20) covers the second show with the same fervour. "The Byrds and The Flying Burrito Brothers were made for each other. That is because it was a jam which included both groups that branded an already successful show a sensational concert last Saturday in the gym." There is a comic moment when McGuinn unexpectedly puts his foot through a chair he uses as a prop as he sings 'Mr. Tambourine Man'. "The crowd couldn't hold back a laugh – and neither could McGuinn."

Friday 20
Gymnasium, Catholic University, Washington, DC

Crank and Parker Case are the support acts.

Saturday 21
Duke Indoor Stadium, Duke University, Durham, NC

Terry Melcher (organ) and Jimmi Seiter (percussion) strengthen the four-piece Byrds on several selections tonight, but according to Bobby Nowell's review in *The North Carolina Anvil* (November 28) the night belongs to opening act Poco. Regarding The Byrds, Nowell cannot quite make up his mind. 'Mr. Tambourine Man' supposedly bores the crowd, while 'Eight Miles High' has "become somewhat ridiculous, drawn out to nearly a half-hour with Battin soloing on bass for nearly five minutes". On the other hand, the McGuinn–White interplay on 'This Wheel's On Fire' is "simply unbelievable". The 5,000 in the stadium obviously find it to their liking, calling the group back for three encores.

Sunday 22
Gymnasium, Old Dominion University, Norfolk, VA

With UK group May Blitz.

Tuesday 24
Ohio Theatre, Columbus, OH

Friday 25–Tuesday 29
A planned swing through four Southern states is cancelled. The tentative dates are in Albuquerque, NM; El Paso and Fort Worth, TX; Shreveport and Monroe, LA; and Little Rock, AR.

Thursday 26
Music Hall, Cleveland, OH

The band has Thanksgiving Dinner at the home of Skip Battin's parents before playing Cleveland's Music Hall with Elton John as support. A short review is printed in the *Chronicle-Telegram* (December 1). "Although The Byrds did a comfortable show, including a free-moving 'Eight Miles High', it was Elton John who surprised everyone, especially with a song called 'H.T.W.', which turned out to be a piano-thumping version of 'Honky Tonk Women'."

Undated November
Billboard's Elliot Tiegel conducts an interview with McGuinn in Los Angeles, which is published concurrently in UK's *Record Mirror*

(December 19). McGuinn admits he is frustrated with the group's country-bent direction, a sore point that he will bring up from time to time over the next two years. "I'm fed up to the gills with country music. I don't care if I never sing another country song in my life. Gene Parsons and Clarence White wouldn't like it, but Skip Battin wouldn't mind.

"It's not my style, really. I can do a shot but I don't feel at home with it, because I'm a city boy from Chicago. I have more of a love for old-time folk and jazz. I was sort of pressured into country music. Some of our personnel changes were toward a country orientation, but it's gotten out of hand. … We're into more of [Dylan's] old stuff like 'Positively Fourth Street'. It fits the attitude for our audience – Dylan accounts for 15 per cent of our material."

Regarding the Byrds repertoire, Tiegel notes that about a quarter of the set is acoustic. McGuinn: "With acoustic guitars, your vocals become dominant. There is no drums, no bluegrass things. Acoustical instruments are coming back. It's fun to play when you're jamming around in someone's living room, and it offers a different taste to our shows. It's like coming down to earth again. We're trying to keep our sound levels down, as opposed to five years ago when we were oblivious to that and we didn't realise that kids can get their ears hurt. When we turn down our levels we find that it allows for a better voice balance in the public address system. Everything is miked off the guitar amplifiers."

Undated November
Roger McGuinn is but one of ten rock stars who prepare a short 'speed kills' public service announcement, broadcast on radio stations nationwide. The other nine are Grace Slick, John Sebastian, Bob Hite, Peter Tork, Frank Zappa, Stephen Stills, John Mayall, Chad Stewart, and Eric Burdon. The anti-amphetamine campaign is planned by the Do It Now Foundation, a California-based non-profit organization.

"Hi, this is Roger McGuinn of The Byrds. There are many ways to get high, but speed is not the one to use. If you really wanna burn out your body, ruin your heart, lungs, or kidneys, speed'll do that for ya. If you wanna die in about five years, speed'll do that for you too. Put speed down now, won't you? Do it now."

To go with the radio spots, the foundation has assembled an album called *First Vibration*, which is sold exclusively through the mail and with the help of radio stations. It took 18 months to get clearance from the various record companies, but the album boasts an unmatched list of stars: The Beatles (who have

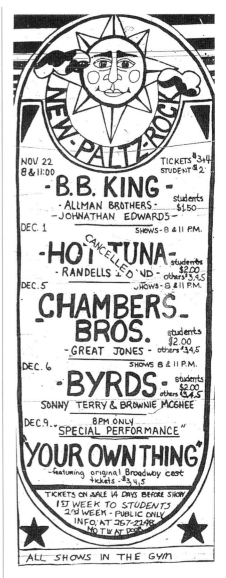

donated 'Nowhere Man'), Donovan, Jefferson Airplane, Canned Heat (naturally with 'Amphetamine Annie'), Jimi Hendrix, Buffalo Springfield, and others, while The Byrds' contribution is 'Artificial Energy'. The album comes with a booklet of anti-drug messages from Donovan and poet Allan Ginsberg.

December

Thursday 3
Bridges Auditorium, Pomona College, Pomona, CA

A college concert together with Norman Greenbaum, the man behind 'Spirit In The Sky'.

Friday 4
Pennsylvania Military College, Chester, PA

Saturday 5
Newark State College, Union, NJ

Sunday 6
State University of New York (SUNY), New Paltz, NY

Blues duo Sonny Terry & Brownie McGhee is the opening act. A soundboard recording from The Byrds' performance will survive, showcasing a rare Clarence White vocal on 'Home Sweet Home'.

ALSO ...
The Flying Burrito Brothers – Chris Hillman, Michael Clarke, Bernie Leadon, Sneaky Pete Kleinow, and Rick Roberts – finally make their long-awaited British debut, at London's Lyceum. The Burritos have tried to set up a visit to Britain ever since Gram Parsons and Chris Hillman started the band back in the fall of 1968. Roy Carr reviews the concert for *New Musical Express* (December 12), and glows: "The high Flying Burrito Brothers dispelled any preconceived doubts and re-created the marvellous sounds which first endeared them to our ears."

Speaking in *Melody Maker* (December 19) following their London debut, Chris Hillman says of the new Byrds album: "It's really good, isn't it? Roger's rebuilt the whole band, and it's excellent – more power to him for sticking it out when everybody is splitting up and doing this and that. I don't really care too much for the long jam on 'Eight Miles High'; I like the song very much, but the idea of jamming on an A chord doesn't appeal to me at all. ... Mind you, Clarence is an incredible guitarist, and he and Gene Parsons work very well together."

Saturday 12
Assembly Hall, University of Illinois, Champaign, IL

A crowd of 4,000 show up to hear The Byrds supported by Head East for one show at 8:00pm. "Band put on amazing performance," says *The Daily Illini* (December 15), picking 'Mr. Tambourine Man', 'Eight Miles High', 'Chestnut Mare', and 'Truck Stop Girl' as the evening's favourites.

Monday 14
Jesse Auditorium, University of Missouri, Columbia, MO

Friday 18
Oberlin College, Oberlin, OH

Concert sponsored by Loran County Community College, featuring The Byrds and Streetmasse.

Sunday 27

KRLA PRESENTS
THE BYRDS
RY COODER
ALSO SPECIAL GUEST STAR
REDEYE
SUN. DEC. 27 • 8 P.M.
Santa Monica Civic
All seats reserved at $5.50, $4.50, $3.50
Available at all Ticketron outlets, Wallich's Music City Stores,
Mutual Agencies and S.M. Civic Box Office (191-9961)
Produced by CONCERT ASSOCIATES (A Filmways Company)

Santa Monica Civic Auditorium, Santa Monica, CA

The Byrds again expand their line-up to feature Terry Melcher on piano and Jimmi Seiter on percussion for this headlining appearance in Santa Monica, their first concert appearance (as opposed to college and club dates) in the Los Angeles area for a long time. Support acts are Ry Cooder and Redeye, a group that has grown out of The Sunshine Company.

"If one accepts the fact that The Byrds are a truly fine rock group," Robert Hilburn notes with slight frustration in *The Los Angeles Times* (December 29), "then [one] is almost compelled to explore why the group is not (a) a bigger force on the current music scene and (b) more exciting than it is in concert."

McGuinn puts it down to The Byrds being a local group and hence being taken for granted. But Hilburn says: "Maybe McGuinn is right, but the group's latest album is an excellent two-record set, and it is only making mild impact on the nation's list of Top 50 sellers. If The Byrds were receiving the reception, East or West, their music deserves, the album would be higher on the charts and the audience Sunday at Santa Monica would have been more involved." Hilburn has a suggestion. "Perhaps putting more spotlight on Clarence White, an excellent guitarist and distinctive vocalist, would help recapture some of the excitement that seems regrettably missing now."

Jerry Dunn Jr writes scathingly in *The Los Angeles Herald Examiner* (December 29): "It is sometimes fun to attend a bad concert, and The Byrds were gracious enough to provide one Sunday night. ... It needs a sense of humour to watch pop stars acting like pop stars. You either laugh or you yawn. Founder and sole surviving member of the original Byrds, Roger McGuinn is stylish,

self-impressed, and blissfully arrogant. He's more important than you or I could hope to be. Most of his time was spent making asides to friends in the first row and making withering comments to those in the other hundred rows. 'So ...,' he sneered, 'this is Santa Monica.' In addition there was a running ego battle being waged against lead guitarist Clarence White."

Dunn's main criticism is what he describes as a total lack of communication on stage, but all is not dark. "The nicer music which managed to sneak around all these self-imposed obstacles included 'Truck Stop Girl' and 'Chestnut Mare' from a new album."

Elliot Tiegel in *Billboard* (January 9, 1971) finds little fault with the show. "The Byrds offered a musical greeting card for local fans, and this gesture was totally received. For the group, the ... concert was of prime importance because local youngsters have taken the band for granted and the concert thus had a missionary underpinning.

"McGuinn was vocally dominant on eight of the songs. Clarence White, the second guitarist, lent a softer vocal sound to his own offerings, 'Truck Stop Girl' and 'Home Sweet Home'. When McGuinn and White switched to acoustic guitars for four numbers, the audience really responded, especially on the fast country tune 'Black Mountain Rag'. Drummer Gene Parsons played some funky harmonica on 'Take A Whiff' (with its cocaine reference), which the audience dug." After a long 'Eight Miles High', the group is called back for an encore medley of 'So You Want To Be A Rock 'n' Roll Star' and 'Mr. Spaceman'.

Tuesday 29
Gymnasium, Porterville College, Porterville, CA

Thursday 31
'Mod World Expo 1971', The Coliseum, Chicago, IL

The 'Mod World Expo 1971' has combined with a pop festival ('The 1971 Chicago Indoor Pop Festival') to attract the maximum number of teenagers to a four-day trade show running into the new year. Promoted by A.M.S. Productions, more than 200 booths are represented at the fair, displaying everything from camping equipment to motorcycles and anything else in between. The show is held in the International Amphitheatre every day between 11:00am and 8:00pm, while the New Year's Eve 8:00pm concert with The Byrds is moved to the nearby Coliseum. (The January 1–3 '71 concerts take place in the International Amphitheatre, with The Byrds held over for a second appearance on the first day of the new year.)

Clarence White and Roger McGuinn, Britain, May 1971.

The month of **January** is spent **recording a new album** in Hollywood, but the sense of direction that has previously driven the band seems to be missing ... Over the next months, the tracks are bolstered by lavish orchestrations, much to the group's disappointment ... In May, The Byrds **return to Europe** for eight appearances in England and a further eleven appearances plus TV shows on the Continent ... Critics are unanimous in their praise of the concerts, but the impression is marred by the poor reception

1971

the group's eleventh album, *Byrdmaniax*, receives ... To redeem matters, The Byrds **fly to London to record** a self-produced album during a week in July ... Columbia Records match The Byrds with jazz and heavy metal groups for selected showcase dates in November and December, in between performances around the US ... Novelty single, **'America's Great National Pastime'** is released in the US in November and becomes a radio hit in California but fails to chart nationally.

January

Friday 1

'Mod World Expo 1971', Donovan Hall, International Amphitheatre, Chicago, IL
The Byrds remain in Chicago following their New Year's Eve show at the Coliseum, and today they play twice at the International Amphitheatre as part of the ongoing 'Mod World Expo 1971'. The programme starts at 11:30am with Gypsy, Illusion, Sugarloaf, and Lee Michaels before The Byrds come on at 4:00pm. Then the order is reshuffled: Sugarloaf, Illusion, and Lee Michaels, before The Byrds play again at 9:15pm. (Tomorrow and Sunday's dates feature McKendree Spring, Mason Proffit, Canned Heat, Buddy Miles, and others.)

The previously released 'Chestnut Mare'/ 'Just A Season' US single is released in the UK today. "Fast Moving 'Mare' Could Be Byrds New Hit," writes Derek Johnson in next week's *New Musical Express* (January 9). "It's been quite a while since we were last treated to a Byrds single, and this is very welcome, even though it's taken from their *(Untitled)* album as, in my estimation, it's one of their best-ever tracks. The story of a man trying to catch a wild horse, it admirably conjures up the illusion of the great outdoors and evokes an atmosphere of exuberance and stimulation. A fast-moving folk-beaty item, laden with all the familiar Byrds trademarks – with 12-string electric guitar and rattling tambourine dominant. This group's been a bit out of favour lately, but it's in with a chance here." Into the charts it goes, rising to UK Number 19 in Record Retailer, week ending February 27,

while doing even better in the list compiled by *New Musical Express*, where it hits Number 15 for a single week in March.

Sunday 3

The Byrds are back in Los Angeles and have set aside the next three weeks for rehearsals and recording sessions for their next album.

Saturday 9

◁)) **RECORDING** Columbia Recording Studios, Sunset and El Centro, Hollywood, CA. Producers Terry Melcher and co-engineer/producer Chris Hinshaw with engineers Eric Prestidge and Glen Kolotkin.

Although the group recorded a solitary session in the autumn of last year (see October 6) that produced a couple of songs, further studio work on a follow-up to *(Untitled)* has been put aside until now. Today's return to Columbia with Terry Melcher will be symptomatic of the position for the coming weeks: no clear direction is staked out and little new material is prepared by Roger McGuinn, leaving opportunities open for Skip Battin, Clarence White, and Gene Parsons to contribute as they see fit.

Starting with a clean slate, first on the agenda is a bland cover version of Helen Carter's 'Is This My Destiny?' (the title will be changed to 'This Is My Destiny', then to plain 'My Destiny'), a country number that Clarence White sings. Uncharacteristically, the song features a piano well to the fore – played by Terry Melcher – at the expense of Byrds trademark 12-string guitars. (Sneaky Pete Kleinow plays pedal steel guitar on the finished track; his contribution is probably overdubbed at a later date.)

As the sessions unfold during January, engineer Chris Hinshaw is promoted to co-producer along with Melcher. Jim Dickson, however, is not here following his temporary comeback on the *(Untitled)* album. Insider Dinky Dawson will recollect in his biography a tense time as all four members experience marital problems. "Because of the emotional warfare raging outside the studio doors, there couldn't have been a worse time to record a new Byrds album. The atmosphere within the studio also became distracting when the band had to be stuffed into the complex's tiniest recording space. Barbara Streisand and her full orchestra needed the largest room and Sly Stone had booked the final medium-sized space, so we'd just have to squeeze around each other and be patient."

Terry Melcher is elevated to the status of Byrds manager at this time, although with what mandate and in what capacity is not entirely clear. Ed Tickner is still around as accounting manager.

Sunday 10

Public Broadcasting Service (the new name adopted by NET, the National Educational Television) screens *Earl Scruggs: His Family & Friends*, another installment in its *Fanfare* series. The show is broadcast on Channel 13 at 10:00pm in the New York area and at the same hour on Channel 20 in San Francisco, and on a series of PBS affiliates around the country. The hour-long programme features Earl Scruggs & His Revue (primarily his two sons Gary and Randy) recorded at various informal locations – a back porch, in a living room, or a backyard at a ranch – with a long list of friends: Bob Dylan ('Nashville Skyline Rag'), Doc Watson, The Morris Brothers, Joan Baez, Bill Monroe, and The Byrds. Recorded in Nashville last spring (see June 12–14, 1970), Scruggs and sons plus The Byrds perform 'You Ain't Going Nowhere' and 'Nothin' To It'.

Monday 11

◁)) **RECORDING** Columbia Recording Studios, Sunset and El Centro, Hollywood, CA. Producers Terry Melcher and co-engineer/producer Chris Hinshaw with engineers Eric Prestidge and Glen Kolotkin.

Today is set aside exclusively for three new Skip Battin/Kim Fowley collaborations: 'Tunnel Of Love', 'Citizen Kane', and 'Absolute Happiness'. With Battin as lead vocalist and composer, the three tracks stray away from the musical unity that marked last year's album *(Untitled)*. At a later date, the backing tracks will be fleshed out with keyboards and orchestral arrangements (see entry for mid-March to early April), leaving little resemblance to the typical Byrds sound. Jimmi Seiter plays tambourine and percussion while studio stalwart Larry Knechtel – the very same guy who provided the swooping bass line on 'Mr. Tambourine Man' – adds piano and organ.

Wednesday 13–Sunday 17

Ash Grove owner Ed Pearl has persuaded Clarence White and his brothers Roland and Eric to reunite for a residence at his club. Joined by banjo player Pat McCloud and fiddler George 'Smoke' Dawson, and finding time for just eight hours of rehearsal (held on Tuesday January 12), The White Brothers still turn in a blistering performance. Michael Sherman of *The Los Angeles Times* (January 15) is exultant. "Tearing into a mixed bag of country and bluegrass standards (including 'Roll In My Sweet Baby's Arms', 'In The Pines', 'Blue Moon Of Kentucky', and 'Dixie Breakdown') with style and grace, the group sounded (and felt) as if they had been together for years. Clarence White, whose guitar playing cannot be over-praised (he truly is a musician's musician), was almost matched in terms of sheer virtuosity by brother Roland's superb mandolin stylings, while Eric played a mean country bass."

Friday 15
ALSO ...

Prosecutor Vincent J. Bugliosi delivers the closing statement in the Charles Manson case. The grisly details surrounding the Manson murders have held the nation spellbound for months. Summarizing the 30-week trial a few days later, *The Long Beach Independent* (January 26) writes: "Bugliosi told the jury during the lengthy trial that Manson wanted to expedite the black-white race war, which he labelled Helter Skelter, and therefore slaughtered rich white people, hoping black people would be blamed. Although this was the primary motive, the prosecutor claimed, a secondary motive – and especially the reason for the onslaught on the Tate home – was Manson's rejection by the former occupant of the home, record producer Terry Melcher. Melcher, son of actress Doris Day, had refused to record Manson's music."

Bugliosi's statement puts Melcher under severe stress, and he has to testify in court on August 23.

Fearing for his life, Melcher hires a bodyguard to follow him around.

Sunday 17

◁) RECORDING Columbia Recording Studios, Sunset and El Centro, Hollywood, CA. Producers Terry Melcher and co-engineer/producer Chris Hinshaw with engineers Eric Prestidge and Glen Kolotkin.

Session logs list four songs recorded today, although they are certainly not all completed on this occasion. One is 'Glory Glory Hallelujah', another number from the Art Reynolds psalm book (originally sung by Thelma Houston), but it lacks the immediacy of 'Jesus Is Just Alright', despite Larry Knechtel's strident piano. The song was given a one-off airing at last year's Bath festival but has apparently not been part of the group's regular live set since then.

Short of new material, McGuinn pulls out another of his *Gene Tryp* collaborations with Jacques Levy, the lightweight 'I Wanna Grow Up To Be A Politician'. The track is finished two days later.

The third song recorded today – Jackson Browne's stately 'Jamaica Say You Will' – makes its debut here, before Browne includes the song as the opening track on his self-titled debut album next year. Browne's own version will feature Clarence White on guitar – fittingly, as he sings the lead vocal on The Byrds' interpretation.

Browne himself is here today to teach the group how the song goes. A take with Browne on piano is taped, but his contribution is unfortunately not used. Battin will tell Barry Ballard of *Omaha Rainbow* (December 1976): "We had done a dynamite cut of 'Jamaica Say You Will', which Jackson Browne had played piano on, and it was not even used. He had come in and taught us the song and Gene, Clarence, Jackson, and I laid down this beautiful track, which was really hot and very tasty, but for some reason it was considered the demo."

Finally, the group records a great version of Bob Dylan's 'Just Like A Woman' with Jackson Browne guesting on piano. The song is later adorned with an organ overdub but does not make the final cut for the new album.

Tuesday 19

◁) RECORDING Columbia Recording Studios, Sunset and El Centro, Hollywood, CA. Producers Terry Melcher and co-engineer/producer Chris Hinshaw with engineers Eric Prestidge and Glen Kolotkin.

'I Wanna Grow Up To Be A Politician' (see January 17) is completed.

Friday 22

◁) RECORDING Columbia Recording Studios, Sunset and El Centro, Hollywood, CA. Producers Terry Melcher and co-engineer/producer Chris Hinshaw with engineers Eric Prestidge and Glen Kolotkin.

At last, a new song from the pen of McGuinn. 'Pale Blue', co-written with Gene Parsons, is a ballad that will later be bolstered by a string arrangement. The basic track is finished on January 26.

Sunday 24

◁) RECORDING Columbia Recording Studios, Sunset and El Centro, Hollywood, CA. Producers Terry Melcher and co-engineer/producer Chris Hinshaw with engineers Eric Prestidge and Glen Kolotkin.

The Byrds return to bluegrass territory with the throwaway 'Green Apple Quick Step'. Cooked up by White and Parsons, the instrumental features White on acoustic guitar, Parsons on banjo, and Battin on bass, while White's dad Eric plays harmonica. A lovely outtake will survive with Parsons and White explaining the tune's structure to White senior. Melcher later calls in Byron Berline to overdub fiddle on the finished track (see entry for mid-March to early April).

Tuesday 26

◁) RECORDING Columbia Recording Studios, Sunset and El Centro, Hollywood, CA. Producers Terry Melcher and co-engineer/

producer Chris Hinshaw with engineers Eric Prestidge and Glen Kolotkin.

As indicated by Johnny Rogan's later Byrds discography, the group attends to 'Pale Blue' (see January 22) today, while McGuinn also re-records 'Kathleen's Song', which was originally earmarked for *(Untitled)* (see June 9, 1970), here recorded in a sparse arrangement framed by acoustic guitars. This, too, will be treated to extensive overdubs at a later date (see entry for mid-March to early April). 'Kathleen's Song' is McGuinn and Levy's song to the heroine in *Gene Tryp*, to the lady who waits faithfully for the return of the wandering *Tryp*.

McGuinn has relayed a status report to *Melody Maker* (published in the paper's January 30 edition) in which he speaks of as many as 18 songs being recorded and describes the results as heavier and earthier than the group's last albums. "We're trying to move away from country music," McGuinn says, "but there will still be some of it there; it overlaps." He mentions 'I Wanna Grow Up To Be A Politician' and 'Citizen Kane', while a third number is a tale of a person returning to find that people and things have changed. "It's kinda sad," McGuinn remarks. He says the album is devoid of synthesizers. "I'm trying to find new electronic sounds; it's very easy to get stock riffs using things like oscillators."

Rob Partridge of *Record Mirror* (February 20) also speaks to McGuinn by phone during the January sessions. Again there is talk of an abundance of material and a change of direction. "I don't want to overdo any one style. We've done country rock music for such a long time that it's perhaps right that we should move somewhere else for the next album. One track will probably be a country number, but so far we've recorded about 16 numbers – there's a possibility that this could be a double album, even, though at the moment obviously I don't really know how it's gong to appear – I don't even know when it's likely to be released.

"But the album will be much more solid than before – there will be gospel-influenced numbers and love songs on it. At the moment we've recorded so many numbers we'll now have to go through them, eliminating the songs we don't want. That, of course, involves basic judgements – finding out how many songs duplicate each other in their basic message." Partridge inquires about the group's country direction. "Country music was like going to a sanatorium for a rest. It was so peaceful after all the noise.

"I make the analogy that we're basically like an electronic magazine," McGuinn continues. "The country music was a special issue and *Sweetheart* an exploration into new fields of music. But The Byrds problem seems to be that they are always ahead of things. It's hard to recall when we actually started with country music, though. Gram Parsons, of course, was a country musician before he joined The Byrds, and the music seemed to be that way too – we'd been going that way for a long time but we'd never gone into it fully."

According to surviving studio documentation, today is the last session for the group's coming album. Eleven songs are accounted for in the session files, but if one is to believe McGuinn's statements in the music press, half a dozen more are recorded but not accounted for. (The 11 are: 'My Destiny', 'Tunnel Of Love', 'Citizen Kane', 'Absolute Happiness', 'Glory Glory', 'I Wanna Grow Up To Be A Politician', 'Jamaica Say You Will', 'Just Like A Woman', 'Pale Blue', 'Green Apple Quick Step', and 'Kathleen's Song'.) One specific number mentioned in the spring edition of fan-sheet *The Byrds Bulletin* is 'Blue Grease'. Credited to White and Parsons, it sounds like an instrumental in the 'Green Apple Quick Step' vein, but the song is never heard of again.

Friday 29
Berkeley Community Theatre, Berkeley, CA

The group heads back on the road for the first time in four weeks, beginning a fairly intense schedule of crisscrossing the United States before going to Europe in May.

Today's one show at 8:00pm is with John Hartford, the multi-instrumentalist who helped out on the group's Nashville sessions for *Sweetheart Of The Rodeo* in March 1968.

Some of the recently recorded songs are woven into the set ('Jamaica Say You Will' and 'I Wanna Grow Up To Be A Politician'), while the acoustic segment is extended to allow a return of 'Pretty Boy Floyd' with Parsons on banjo. The shows are usually bookended by 'Lover Of The Bayou' and the expansive 'Eight Miles High', while the encores include a further batch of old hits such as 'Mr. Spaceman' and 'So You Want To Be A Rock'n'Roll Star'.

Jimmi Seiter joins them on stage as percussionist whenever it is convenient. The group sticks to a fairly rigid repertoire for the next five or six months. Despite McGuinn's increasing democracy in the studio, on stage it is a different matter: here he dominates as the lead vocalist on nearly every song. The exceptions are a couple of White vocals ('Truck Stop Girl' and 'Jamaica Say You Will'), but neither Battin nor Parsons have any solo showcases any more, although they of course contribute plenty of harmonies and backing vocals. White makes a rare concession to showman-

ship when he takes to wearing a large royal-blue velvet cape over his pure white suit this winter.

•

🎧 **SESSION** White is involved in a pair of sessions for other artists during the first months of the year. One is Paul Siebel's *Jack-Knife Gypsy*, which is released on Elektra in May in the UK and probably at the same time in the US. Another key session features White's unmistakable riffs on the title cut of *L.A. Getaway*, a sort-of supergroup consisting of Joel Scott-Hill, ex-Burrito bass player Chris Etheridge, and ex-Turtles drummer Johnny Barbata. The album is released over the summer and is given a splendid review in *Rolling Stone* (December 23).

•

🎧 **SESSION** Jim Dickson is assigned the producer's chair for Bob Gibson's first album in eight years. Dickson calls on a large cast of notables to back the folksinger–guitarist on his *Bob Gibson* album on Capitol, including David Crosby, Chris Hillman, and Roger McGuinn. Precise documentation does not survive to indicate when the tracks are recorded, but safe to say they are cut in Los Angeles. The album is released in the US in May.

February

Saturday 6
'College Ski Festival', Nick Rajkovich Physical Education Center, Northwestern Michigan College, Traverse City, MI

Traverse City is invaded by hundreds of skiers for the college's eighth annual ski festival, and The Byrds plus Touchstone provide the musical entertainment.

Tuesday 9
Finch Field House, Central Michigan University, Mount Pleasant, MI

While the group is in Michigan, an earthquake shakes their hometown, killing several and causing millions of dollars in damage. The epicentre is some miles north of the city of Los Angeles, but none of the group's families are hurt, although McGuinn's house in Sherman Oaks is damaged.

Friday 12
Le Moyne Athletic Center, Le Moyne College, Syracuse, NY

Saturday 13
Morrell Gymnasium, Bowdoin College, Brunswick, ME

The Byrds are preceded on stage by Tony Williams' Lifetime, a pionerrinng jazz-rock group featuring John McLaughlin and Jack Bruce.

Sunday 14
'All-Tech Weekend', Costello Gymnasium, Lowell Technological Institute, Lowell, MA

The Byrds and Paul Butterfield climax the 'All-Tech Weekend', which saw Sha-Na-Na and Jonathan Edwards playing last night. The concert draws a near capacity crowd according to the local review in *The Lowell Sun* (February 16). "The famous Byrds who 'play what we feel inside' opened up their set with joyful moonshine country tunes. During the first half of the set they played several acoustical pieces with folk guitars. High points of the act were 'Black Mountain Rag', a real country-inspired and fast-paced number, and the well-known 'Mr. Tambourine Man'. Bob Dylan's influence on the group was readily seen in this number.

"Gene Parsons, the drummer, did a few numbers on his banjo, which were very well received. 'Pretty Boy Floyd', another country song, was also typical of the sound. 'Jamaica Say You Will', soft and pretty, showed off the group's excellent harmony and interesting acoustical effects with muffled drums and folk guitars. 'Take A Whiff On Me' ended up the country set, and Gene Parsons contributed some harmonica background to the number.

"After they switched back to electrical guitars, the music took a turn to harder rock. It had a harsher style in which the group excels. High points of the rock set were 'Jesus Is Just Alright', a modern, heavy number which one bystander said 'the kids really like to groove on'. 'Eight Miles High' ended the act. The Byrds came back two more times and played three numbers in their encores including 'So You Want To Be A Rock'n'Roll Star' and 'Mr. Spaceman'. Both the group and the audience got together during the performance. The Byrds left the stage to a standing crowd shouting for more."

The reviewer, Christine Black, sits down with McGuinn backstage for a brief chat. "I think the music has gone up in stage performance but down in recording," the Byrd leader says, promising readers that he will do something about it.

Monday 15
Bank Street Armory, Fall River, MA

Originally set for the town's Durfee Theatre.

Wednesday 17
Carnegie Hall, New York, NY

The group visits New York's premier concert hall for one show at 8:00pm, with Redeye. By now, the group's acoustic interlude consists of 'Black Mountain Rag'/'Soldier's Joy', 'Pretty Boy Floyd', 'Mr. Tambourine Man', and 'Take A Whiff On Me', before the second fully-electric set takes off with 'Chestnut Mare', 'Jesus Is Just Alright', and 'Eight Miles High'.

The show receives good notices in *Record World* and *Billboard* (both February 27). Bob Moore Merlis in *Record World* takes exception to 'Eight Miles High' "which has unfortunately become an 'In-A-Gadda-Da-Vida'-like signature number for them" but is otherwise very impressed by the group's wide-reaching repertoire and high-quality musicianship. They are called back for three encores.

"Their Carnegie Hall concert was a capsule history of the group," Nancy Erlich suggests in *Billboard*. "With perfect ease and continuity, they passed from country music to hard rock to Dylan songs and back. It was mostly familiar material from their Columbia albums, but The Byrds in concert do not quote their records. They create their songs all over again."

Thursday 18
CW Post Campus, Long Island University, Brookville, NY

Today is Battin's birthday – he turns 37 – and the 3,000 in the hall celebrate this by joining in a rousing 'Happy Birthday To You'. Campus paper *The Pioneer* (February 25) notes: "When listening to The Byrds in concert, it is apparent that they have been around for a while. Though there have been minor changes in personnel, the collective sound of The Byrds remains polished and very professional. The concert at Post certainly showed this professionalism. Each member of The Byrds knows plenty about performing, an art that too many rock musicians could care less about. With professionals like The Byrds on stage, it was no wonder that the Post audience called for almost half a dozen encores." *The Delphian* (March 10) terms the performance dynamite: "A quarter of the way through, the people in the aisles were up and shaking about, halfway-through standing ovations were the norm, and by the last quarter the entire audience were on chairs, unable to keep their bodies still."

□ **UK TV** London, England BBC-1. *Top Of The Pops* (episode No. 373 at 7:00pm)

BBC's perennial *Top Of The Pops* is in its seventh year and in many ways still Britain's premier pop show, broadcasting a compilation of the week's hit singles every Thursday. It is not a strict 'Top Ten' format but allows other chart action to be featured too. Today's edition, introduced by DJ Tony Blackburn, screens inserts by Hot Chocolate, Martha Reeves & The Vandellas, Chairmen Of The Board, Neil Diamond, Judy Collins ('Amazing Grace'), Smokey Robinson & The Miracles, Mungo Jerry, George Harrison (whose 'My Sweet Lord' is at Number One), Marvin Welch & Farrar (featured in the 'LP spot'), and The Byrds. 'Chestnut Mare' has just entered the UK Top 30 this week and, as there is no specifically recorded insert for the occasion, the BBC presumably comes up with its standard solution: using available clips and stills to make a suitable montage or primitive video while the single plays in the background.

Friday 19
Palace Theater, Albany, NY

The Byrds, Cactus, and Redeye appear in a National Student Productions (NSP) promotion. The NSP has initiated a concert series throughout February and March with many top-line acts. However, the arrangers are forced to curtail the programme after tonight's show because of poor attendance. Tonight's triple bill only manages to fill one-third of the 2,200-seat theatre.

The reporter from *The Albany Student Press* (February 26) is relieved when The Byrds finally take the stage for the second show. "Down came the monster systems Cactus used and up went some compact, neatly shining amps and speakers. The equipment, which was set up within ten minutes (that must be the all-time record), would have looked more at home at a folk concert. Down came the platform between orchestra pit and stage, and on came The Byrds, 3:00am in the morning, and, finally, music!

"They opened with an acoustic number, Clarence White singing in his mournful way. Nice. And then, Byrdsrock. 'My Back Pages', 'Lover Of The Bayou', an awesomely powerful song – McGuinn, a rock'n'roll angel in a black preacher's suit, Clarence White … blue-caped, unleashing their electric guitars, flexing their musical muscles. Every note clearly heard (their sound system, so small in appearance, is a gem), every word easily understood. Roger's voice has roughened just the slightest from his choirboy days, just enough to give it the bite and power he needs. The country excursion mellowed and rounded The Byrds without detracting from their power; they may play softly and gently, but they can still unleash that flood of power and rush of blood that is what rock'n'roll is basically about. More acoustic music: 'Mr. Tambourine Man', the stanzas they didn't use on their smash single of so long ago. Electric 'Tambourine Man'; by whipsawing from acoustic to electric numbers they give you that surge of power in your head without blasting your ears."

While the reporter works himself up, the crowd is tired at this time of the morning. "They try to get the audience to clap a beat. It won't; the audience is dead. Having gladly submitted to rape by Cactus the beast lies back, prostrate, organs too roughly misused to respond. All too soon comes the monster jam – 'Eight Miles High'. They try, oh, how they try, to take the audience there, but the beast lies slouched on the floor, unheeding, uncaring." Despite the group's heroic efforts they fail to wake the audience, and after a 40-minute performance, McGuinn waves goodbye with: "We're tired, you're tired, goodnight. God bless you!"

The university publication from nearby Plattsburgh, *Cardinal Points* (March 2), also covers the second show. Alan Lebowitz says the group "were incredibly together", this despite the fact that he claims that McGuinn is "obviously drunk". *Albany Student Press* (February 22) publishes a brief interview with the Byrd leader. Conducted in the intermission at the Palace Theatre, a visibly laidback McGuinn is asked if there's a new album on the way. "Yeah, we got one finished. No title yet. It could be a few months before Columbia gets around to releasing it."

Saturday 20
Gymnasium, Monmouth College, West Long Branch, NJ

Redeye support The Byrds tonight, too, for a sell-out show at the Monmouth college gymnasium. There is an incident with a stolen microphone, delaying the group's performance for a short while before the missing equipment is sorted out. This does not put a damper on the show, which the Monmouth student paper (March 5) claims is the best the school has seen in the past two years. After a lengthy ovation, the group comes back for two encore segments: first 'Mr. Spaceman' and 'So You Want To Be A Rock'n'Roll Star', then 'Jesus Is Just Alright' and finally 'Amazing Grace'.

Sunday 21
State University of New York (SUNY), Buffalo, NY

The Byrds appear with Poco.

Friday 26
Viking Hall, Upsala College, Orange, NJ

Two shows with Canned Heat and Factory pull a 3,000 capacity crowd, according to trade magazine *Amusement Business* (March 6).

Saturday 27
Field House, United States Naval Academy, Annapolis, MD

Another contrasting concert, as described in the underground rag *Harry* (March 12). "The

Byrds at the Naval Academy? Far out! Even if someone was putting us on, it was still worth looking into. As we pulled into the Naval Academy Saturday night, things didn't look too good. Billions of sailors in white gloves and academy threads all over the place, and as we approached the auditorium, our tension was steadily mounting. But then the freaks started coming and, by the time the concert started, several hundreds of them made their way into the Field House, and the combination of the two cultures was too much.

"The sailors were really digging it, but it's too bad the Naval Academy has rules for everything. The sailors had to have special permission to take off their jackets when things got hot, and smoking and drinking in any form would be considered outrageous. Even one of the Directors of the Academy was overheard as saying, 'Isn't it a shame half of these hippies are high on pot.'"

The show is a high-flying success, according to the review. "The Byrds are still warm and sincere people who just dig entertaining people, whether they be sailors or freaks, and have definitely proved that Air Power has supremacy over Naval Power."

Sunday 28
Men's Gymnasium, State University of New York (SUNY), Binghamton, NY

March

→ Monday 1–Saturday 6
🔊 **RECORDING** Columbia Recording Studios, Sunset and El Centro, Hollywood, CA. Producers Terry Melcher and co-engineer/producer Chris Hinshaw.

Back in Los Angeles, The Byrds reputedly make some minor studio adjustments to the material already recorded. Documents do not survive to detail what is being done, and it is not clear if Melcher's refinement of the tracks has already begun (see entry for mid-March to early April), but judging from McGuinn's non-committal words to the press this week, this is probably not the case.

•

During the week's break from touring, McGuinn is interviewed by Ritchie Yorke, whose story runs in *New Musical Express* (March 20), *Winnipeg Free Press* (May 29), and *Jazz & Pop* (May 1971) with slight variations. In *New Musical Express*, McGuinn updates readers on the coming album. "The majority of things … are out of left field. It goes more into country than the last album, but it also goes way out of that scene, too.

"We run sort of a funky image," he continues. "Country fans won't accept us because of our long hair, whiskers, and the hip image. It's so much easier to get acceptance as a country artist going cityward than a city artist going country, and that prompted us to get out of it. They didn't exactly love us to death, those true-blue country fans. We're a staple item on FM [radio]. It keeps us alive. You can live off FM now. It only used to cater to a minority of album freaks, but now it seems that the FM audience have become the majority."

McGuinn admits to Yorke that he is a bit out of touch with the current album scene. "I dig some bits of Joe Cocker and the Crosby Stills & Nash output but I didn't like the Leon Russell album until I had seen him perform. Then it was like a programme from his concert." He has not heard the new (eponymous) *Stephen Stills* LP. "He didn't come over to the house like David did and play the disc and jump up and down and shout: 'I'm a star, I'm a star.' But fooling aside, I really do love David. He is a star."

Of the next Byrds album, McGuinn says obliquely in *Jazz & Pop*: "[It] will probably come out in about two months, [and] has things that are reminiscent of earlier albums, to make the transition less abrupt. But the majority of things are out of left field. It goes more into country than the last album, but also goes way out of that scene."

Thursday 4
Artist Mary Leonard makes facemasks of the four Byrds in Los Angeles. "They make a plaster mask of your face," McGuinn explains to writer Ritchie Yorke, "and then come up with a chromium mask from it. It's pretty far out." The masks will eventually grace the jacket of the new Byrds album.

Sunday 7
Hec Edmonson Pavilion, University of Washington, Seattle, WA
The group makes a swing northwestwards for three concerts before crossing over to the West Coast again. Tonight, The Joy Of Cooking and Delaney & Bonnie & Friends share the stage. The crowd totals 9,300.

Stephen Chensvold writes in *The Seattle Post Intelligencer*: "Whether doing a fast boogie formed around the sure bass work of Skip Battin and the 'make it look easy' licks of White, or when playing the distinctive Byrd sound of heavy 12-string and country harmony, The Byrds emit a professionalism of an extraordinary degree. In each number, the group displayed a strong sense of dynamics, even if it meant covering the drums with a blanket to gain the desired effect. Vocally, their four-part harmony is deliberate, controlled, and in

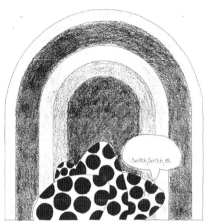

time. Close to midnight, the spotlight focuses stage right while the Pavilion explodes for a fourth time. They come back again. A quiet hymn. It's over."

Over at *The Seattle Times*, Janine Gressel glows. "Unlike many bands which discard old hits as new material is developed, The Byrds continue to include their old favourites in their concerts. But as they have evolved as a group, they have rearranged the oldies to suit their new musical stylings. Thus, 'My Back Pages' had a more upbeat, Western sound and 'Tambourine Man' became a quiet, almost acoustical-sounding ballad with some tricky new rhythms to keep the song fresh."

Tuesday 9
Pamplan Sports Center, Lewis & Clark College, Portland, OR
The brief review in Oregon underground paper *Willamette Bridge* (March 11–17) is more enamored with The Joy Of Cooking, a Bay Area two-girl-three-boy group that opens the show. "We left feeling high/low – still loving The Byrds because we had always loved them, but wishing that the audience would have danced more and harder, and the band would have been less on their own head trips and more with the people."

Wednesday 10
Kennedy Pavilion, Gonzaga University, Spokane, WA
As with yesterday's date, The Joy Of Cooking is the opening act.

Friday 12
Memorial Gymnasium, Juniata College, Huntingdon, PA

→ An arrow denotes an estimated date.

The Flying Burrito Brothers are booked to open for The Byrds but cancel for unknown reasons; they are replaced by Manhattan Transfer.

The show gets off to a late start because the truck with The Byrds' equipment is delayed and ticket holders are barred from entering the gymnasium. As the rain pours outside, many simply turn away and leave. An indignant letter to *The Daily News* (March 20) complains: "Expecting a large crowd, myself and two others … arrived a little before 7:00pm. At 8:15pm we left the area outside the gymnasium where hundreds of young people were still standing in the pouring rain waiting to be admitted into the building. … These youths deserve an official apology!"

Saturday 13
Eastman Theater, University of Rochester, Rochester, NY

→ mid-March–early April
OVERDUBS While The Byrds are out on the road, Terry Melcher ropes in arranger Paul F. Polena to score strings and horns and sweeten most of the tracks that The Byrds have completed in January. The strings will be prominently heard on 'Pale Blue', 'Kathleen's Song' (which features a full orchestral arrangement with horns), and 'Jamaica Say You Will'.

A conspicuous saxophone and a full horn section are tacked on to 'Tunnel Of Love', while 'Citizen Kane' is dressed up in quasi-vaudeville style with muted trumpets, and 'I Wanna Grow Up To Be A Politician' is converted into a blaring marching band at the half-way mark. In addition, a female choir is overdubbed on 'Glory, Glory' (with Merry Clayton wailing away), 'I Trust', and 'Tunnel Of Love'. Sneaky Pete adds pedal steel on 'I Trust' and 'My Destiny', while Byron Berline records three separate fiddle parts for 'Green Apple Quick Step'. Larry Knechtel, who may have been present for some of the initial January sessions, is heard on 'Glory, Glory' (piano), 'Tunnel Of Love' (organ and piano), 'Citizen Kane' (piano), 'Absolute Happiness' (organ), 'I Wanna Grow Up To Be A Politician' (piano), and 'My Destiny' (piano).

Much of the overdub material distracts from the music rather than adding to it, and 'Tunnel Of Love' and 'Citizen Kane' end up sounding like two of the least Byrds-like numbers in the group's entire catalogue.

No studio documentation will survive in accessible form to detail the overdubs and when they are done, but publicist Billy James – quoted in UK's *Disc* (May 8) – indicates that these sessions may stretch well into April. What is certain is that the overdubbing is done without White, Battin, or Parsons being present. McGuinn, however, may be involved to some extent. Byrds historian Johnny Rogan will take producer Terry Melcher to task many years later, but the producer will defend the orchestrations (reportedly done at a cost of $100,000) and confirm he dealt with only McGuinn and thus, indirectly, has his approval.

Friday 19
Gymnasium, Trenton State College, Trenton, NJ

Saturday 20
Mahopac High School Auditorium, Mahopac, NY

Sunday 21
Colden Center Auditorium, Queens College of City University of New York, Flushing, New York, NY

Bonnie Raitt supports The Byrds, at the same venue where a year ago the group taped portions of the live half of *(Untitled)*. The March programme at Colden Hall is otherwise Byrd-bent: jazz guitarist Charlie Byrd is billed for March 13, while the week before the Student Association screens the 1938 movie *Gunga Din* starring Cary Grant.

The Colden Hall patrons have a reputation for rowdiness, and the organisers have called in extra security men, who carry guns. The reporter in *Knightbeat–Newsbeat* (March 30) is aghast to the point where the musical content becomes secondary in his review. "The first sight that greeted me at the concert was the rear view of one of our 'enforcement' officers carrying a gun. Yes, it was a gun all right, but it defied my imagination as to what possible use there was for a gun at a concert; a Campus Concert no less. Furthermore, I was always under the impression that our security squad was unauthorised to carry guns. I am either mistaken, or something very wrong has happened. Assuming that I am wrong, I still am very much opposed to anybody carrying a weapon of any sort."

Phil Mintz of *The Phoenix* (March 29) observes that the group is on a trip into nostalgia. "Which brings us to the subject of whether The Byrds that played at Colden on Sunday night were the real Byrds or not, the ones that gave us all those experiences to measure our lives with. In one respect you could claim that Roger (Jim) McGuinn is The Byrds anyway, so there they were. But, to paraphrase Andrew Loog Oldham, The Byrds aren't just a group, they are more of a way of life. It really doesn't matter who is The Byrds now, who was, and who wasn't. They are a way of life, and when someone quipped that McGuinn was going to join CSNY, and call them The Byrds, it was perhaps only half a joke.

"The concert on Sunday night was itself an expedition into nostalgia. Just over a year ago, The Byrds played what was probably the last great concert at Colden, the last one with a sense of community in that place. And The Byrds did it all by themselves. They took an unruly and fairly disrespectful audience and had them standing together and singing 'Oh Mary, Don't You Weep' while Louis Palmieri was shutting off the microphones to get them off the stage."

The unruly elements are evidently still here a year later, as Mintz pours out his frustration. "Too bad some of that nostalgia didn't rub off on the idiots. The idiots are the Colden institution that ruins concerts for other people by being generally obnoxious – smoking dope, making noise, rushing to the front, and destroying things. Sunday night, The Byrds worked no magic on the idiots, though they played better than ever. The concert had to be curtailed due to danger to The Byrds' equipment, but of what there was, there was incredible beauty. And that can't be forgotten because of some idiots."

Thursday 25
The Byrds are advertised to play a concert at Boston's Music Hall but the event is seemingly is cancelled.

Friday 26–Saturday 27
The Capitol Theatre, Port Chester, NY

Concert with Mother Earth and folk singer Eric Andersen, who replaces Great Jones. There are two shows each night, and the four shows gross a total of $29,596. *Billboard* (April 10) notes: "The Byrds did one of their finer sets spiced with instrumentals on both acoustic and electric guitars. 'Eight Miles High' and 'Have A Whiff On Me', an old Leadbelly tune which many groups seem to be doing lately, represented The Byrds' ability to adapt to either electric or acoustic instruments. The Columbia artists also did their single 'Chestnut Mare'."

Sunday 28
University of Delaware, Newark, DE

Late March
The new Byrds album is completed and announced in fan-sheet *The Byrds Bulletin* (Spring 1971) under the title *Expensive*. Twelve tracks are listed: 'I Wanna Grow Up To Be A Politician', 'Absolute Happiness', 'Blue Grease', 'Green Apple, Quick Step', 'Citizen Kane', 'My Destiny', 'Tunnel Of Love', 'I Trust', 'Kathleen', 'Pale Blue', 'Glory, Glory', and 'Jamaica'. Perhaps this is

considered the correct running order for now, but it will later be changed. Some of the song titles will be subtly adjusted: 'Kathleen', for example, becomes 'Kathleen's Song', while Jackson Browne's 'Jamaica Say You Will' will get its full title.

Seemingly, producer Terry Melcher is not yet finished doctoring the tapes, and some further overdubs are possibly done even after this initial announcement. 'Blue Grease', credited to Parsons and White, is eventually dropped and no documentation will survive to explain its fate. Wisely, in view of the album's critical reception, the *Expensive* title will prove shortlived.

April

Friday 9

McGaw Memorial Hall, Evanston, IL

The Byrds perform one show at 8:00pm sponsored by the Orgy Of The Arts. An earlier booking at O'Shaughnessy Auditorium, St Paul, MI, for today is cancelled in favour of this appearance.

Saturday 10

Marietta College, Marietta, OR

The group appears with The Flying Burrito Brothers in their first joint concert in many months. The Burritos have a third, self-titled, album waiting to be released, but founding member Sneaky Pete is about to leave and be replaced by Al Perkins.

●

Coming back to Los Angeles again, The Byrds enjoy a two-week break. According to Dinky Dawson's later book, every time the group returns to L.A., Terry Melcher has added further overdubs to the recordings for the new album, in their absence and without their consent. Melcher's fiddling with the tracks does not go down well with The Byrds, but the producer will later claim – perhaps rightfully – that the material is already weak and the overdubs are done in an effort to improve the results. The group is appalled at Melcher's manhandling of the tracks, but little if nothing is done to stop the results being mixed and readied for release. By the time the group visits England next month, Parsons and McGuinn in particular will voice their displeasure with the production – three months before the album is released in the UK.

McGuinn tells veteran English journalist Keith Altham in May: "You're talking about Terry Melcher's little surprises. I walked into the studio in L.A. and discovered a 30-piece orchestra – and walked out again, thinking it

was the wrong studios. I asked a guard which studio we were in and got directed right back to the same studio where the orchestra was striking up one of our songs. We weren't very happy with the mixes on the album, but we sent the lot up to San Francisco and had them remixed. We fired Terry as manager, because he wasn't managing and quit as producer."

Gene Parsons, talking to the *State Beacon* (October 26) – a student paper in New Jersey – gives an example of Melcher's offences. "On one song, 'Jamaica [Say You Will]', they took the bad take, Clarence sang his rear off, he really did, and they didn't like it. On one take, it was a little too fast, but we really cooked, and we had a thing we wanted to do with it. So, they took the bad take and put strings and French horns and chicks and harps and fried potatoes and everything else on it."

White adds: "The more they stack up orchestration, like they bring in 50 people and put on all the strings and cellos and that crap on it, the track tends to tune sharp through the earphones. That's cool if you can go back in and sing to that track after they put all that stuff on, but if your vocal is on there and Terry, the producer, likes it, then it's gonna stay. Naturally, if they're sharp the voice is going to sound like I'm singing flat. So I am: I'm singing flat through the whole song."

●

The next official news bulletin on the album comes later in April, when Billy James gives *Disc*'s Hollywood correspondent Judy Sims a test pressing with a running order seemingly identical to the one recently reported in *The Byrds Bulletin*. At least the final title is in place. "Just heard an acetate of The Byrds' next album, *Byrdmaniax*, to be released in May or June," Sims writes in the paper's May 8 edition. "And it's wonderful. There's no information on it except titles. So I don't really know who plays what or sings what, but I do know that several songs are written by Skip Battin and Kim Fowley (yes, the same Kim Fowley we all know and love). … It opens with 'I Wanna Grow Up To Be A Politician', a funny spoof on the way America runs things, written several years ago (by McGuinn and Jacques Levy) as part of the Broadway musical which was never produced.

"Billy James, long-time friend and now publicist for The Byrds, reports that the production/recording of this album – which took place in January and part of February – was 'insane'. Terry Melcher, back again as producer (he produced their very first recordings), is still mixing and remixing. One of the original titles for this album was *Byrdmania*, which was rejected. Then McGuinn suggested *Expensive*. Rejected. So between personal crises

and exhaustion and a nigh-unbelievable touring schedule, The Byrds made a fine album anyway. 'Green Apple Quick Step' is an instrumental, bluegrassy and fun, with good banjo. There are nice ballads like 'Kathleen's Song'." McGuinn's vocal obviously catches Sims off guard, as she concludes: "I can't positively identify the voice, but I assume it's Skip. It certainly doesn't sound like McGuinn (whose voice is familiar and fine on 'Politician')."

Friday 23

A proposed booking at Pratt Institute, Brooklyn, New York, NY, is cancelled.

Saturday 24

St. John's University, Jamaica, Queens, NY

The group appears at a show with comedian Steve Martin, folk singer Eric Andersen, and The Nitty Gritty Dirt Band. With roots reaching back to 1966, the Dirt Band have led a life in the shade of their better-known L.A. contemporaries The Byrds. They have pursued a folk-country direction with emphasis on acoustic instruments and a good-time jug band/bluegrass feel. Following in the footsteps of The Byrds, they too will soon make the journey to Nashville to record the old-timey *Will The Circle Be Unbroken* with many guest artists. Recorded in August this year, the triple-album succeeds in bridging the gap between the young brigade of carefree California and the old guard of traditional Nashville.

The Byrds are slightly rusty after their two-week layoff, and White says to *The Torch* (April 30) that he feels a little uncomfortable on stage. All the same, the paper votes White "by far one of the greatest guitarists in rock music today" based on his St John's performance.

Tuesday 27

State University of New York (SUNY), Fredonia, NY

●

At the end of April, Terry Melcher is out of the Byrds camp for good. White will tell the student paper *State Beacon* (October 26): "[Melcher] just flipped out on *Byrdmaniax* and he let loose and put anything he wanted on it. We really got burned and tried to do everything we could: we got mad and we just said we had to get rid of him. So, nobody would say the three words to him: 'You are fired.' So I thought … I'll try it, and I fired him. That was good for about three days, cos I'm not signed with Columbia anyway, so it didn't make any difference.

"He came back, and he went along with me and said I'm ready to work, and finally Roger said those three words, 'You are fired.' That's

when he split. He was also our manager which was, ah, really horrible. Well, he didn't hurt us, but he couldn't do anything to help us either. You know, we could just do it ourselves. If you have the right road managers and get the right mind to keep away from crazy managers that are after your money, well then you're fine, you could do it yourself. You need a good agent." In the same interview, White manages to speak respectfully of Melcher, calling him an "incredible producer".

The departure of Melcher happens around the same time as Eddie Tickner again withdraws from The Byrds' business (he continues to work for The Flying Burrito Brothers though). This brings the burden of management back to Roger McGuinn again, who will shoulder the responsibility from now on.

✈ **April 28–May 30, 1971: 6TH OVERSEAS TOUR (UK, HOLLAND, BELGIUM)**

Wednesday 28

The Byrds fly out from New York after yesterday's concert in Fredonia. Jimmi Seiter, Carlos Bernal, Dinky Dawson, and McGuinn's girlfriend Linda Gilbert join the entourage for the trip across the Atlantic. Upon arrival in London they go straight to a press conference.

The month-long European visit will be a highpoint in the group's career and firmly places The Byrds back in the rock mainstream. Although the group played selected live dates in England in 1967, 1968, and 1970, this is their first full-scale UK tour since 1965. Reviews are consistently good, and on stage the four men project an unfettered unity.

'Chestnut Mare' has proved a surprising latter-day hit single and (Untitled) is still selling. The Byrds fit right into the flowering UK rock scene, where disparate trends such as progressive rock, folk music, heavy rock, and the first inklings of glam blossom side by side. A glance at the charts for week ending May 1 sees albums by The Groundhogs, Jethro Tull (Aqualung), Jimi Hendrix (Cry Of Love), and Yes (The Yes Album) orbiting the Top Ten (admittedly below more conservative choices such as Andy Williams, but also there are Simon & Garfunkel's evergreen Bridge Over Troubled Water and Leonard Cohen's Songs Of Love And Hate). The rest of the Top 50 is populated by a further mix of UK and US artists, including David Crosby, Led Zeppelin, Elton John, Leonard Cohen, Neil Young, T. Rex, and Steeleye Span, to name a few.

The Byrds spend their first evening in London at the Roundhouse watching Deep Purple as part of a week-long Camden Arts Festival.

May

Saturday 1

The Byrds enjoy themselves at London's Speakeasy – the club where they played in March 1967 – in the company of PR man Allan McDougall.

●

Spending a few off days in London before the tour starts, McGuinn, White, and Parsons all speak to various members of the music press. New Musical Express (May 8) corners Parsons in a "?-Time With The Byrds" conducted by Richard Green, who says he has heard that the new album is rumoured to be almost a Bridge Over Troubled Water production. "There are a lot of the same musicians who were on Bridge Over Troubled Water, and a lot of it isn't particularly to my taste," Parsons says. "There are a few tunes that are funky and crude, but basically it has been well orchestrated. I'm a little sad about that because it's not the way to go."

Green wonders why they do not have more control of the final result. "Because of the time element, and we're working so much on the road." The NME journalist, still not satisfied, asks if it really has become what he calls the producer's idea of how it should sound. Parsons needs a thoughtful pause before he answers. "Yeah. I shouldn't say that, because it's not good for promotion, but that's right. I'm looking forward to the next one." Parsons is so uninterested in the new album he is not even aware of its title. "Roger!" he calls across the room. "Have we got a definite title yet?" McGuinn informs Parsons and the NME man: "It's Byrdmaniax – with an X at the end."

Melody Maker devotes a two-page spread on May 8 to The Byrds and combines interviews with White (by Richard Williams) and McGuinn (by Roy Hollingworth) with a review from the opening show of the tour. The Clarence White feature delves into his illustrious past, tracing his career right up to The Byrds. For White, his Byrds connections are deeply rooted. "[The Kentucky Colonels] broke up in '66, and that's when I started to do what I've been wanting to do since '64 – I wanted to electrify folk music. I'd suggested it in '64, but none of the other guys [in the Colonels] thought it was a good idea. Vanguard and Elektra had been bidding for me to do a guitar album for them, and I'd started getting material.

"The first demo I got was of 'Mr. Tambourine Man', sung by Dylan and Ramblin' Jack Elliott. I've still got it – I guess it must be worth a lot now, right? Anyway, I thought that's folk music, let's do it – but I guess some people are always a little ahead of their time. Then

when I heard The Byrds' version a year later … ! So in '66 I bought a Telecaster and started playing country music, getting more power and using bigger and bigger amps … just like rock'n'roll. It was like learning a completely different instrument, and I began to do a lot of studio work on the Coast.

"Some of the first sessions I did were with The Byrds, because I used to know Chris Hillman – he was a bluegrass musician, and we'd played together a lot at jams and parties. He got me to do their sessions, and I've been on all their albums from [Younger Than Yesterday] onwards. I could actually respect what they were doing, because the time was right for it. Then Chris asked me to join the band. I was into studio work, making about $60,000 a year, but it didn't take me long to realise that ever since the age of six I'd been used to entertaining people by playing music and that what makes me most happy is the response from an audience. So I just couldn't do sessions any more, and I was real glad to join The Byrds. Honoured, too."

White mentions guitarist James Burton, describing him as incredible. "He started playing before they had light strings, so he'd use banjo strings as the top three, and he could really bend 'em. He was the first to do that country thing, and he's a great blues guitarist – I've never met anyone else who knew [how to do] that."

White lists his guitars for the benefit of Melody Maker's readers. His main one is a Fender Telecaster ("because he gets the best sound out of it") but he also has a couple of Les Pauls: a 1952 model, that he's going to modify with the string bender, and another that he confides he does not "even take out of the closet – it's still got its original case, even". White uses a fuzz box, but only sparingly to give his beefed-up amps that little extra kick.

He has plans for a solo album, which he describes as a mixture of bluegrass and what he terms as "real nice tunes". He says he wants to use some songs by Jackson Browne and makes a reference to The Orange County Three – an obscure label stuck on singer-songwriters Browne, Steve Noonan, and Tim Buckley years ago by a California paper. "I stopped singing after The Kentucky Colonels," White admits, "and I never wanted to do it again until I heard [Browne's] material. I think that his stuff will influence me into writing – he's so good, and he'll be successful."

Meanwhile, Melody Maker journalist Roy Hollingworth writes reverently of his first meeting with the head Byrd. "Maybe it's wrong to prejudge, but I always thought Roger McGuinn, high-flying Byrd, would be the coolest human I'd ever wish to meet. Well, as the song goes, that ain't necessarily so. A cup of fine tea for this man in blue suit, cowboy boots, and flying wings, and he sips and smiles. No, this wasn't an interview, more like a conversation, in which one guy did most of the talking – slow, drawling rather, in a voice that never raised itself above that 'I'll whisper you a secret' level. It sort of slips out from beneath the now-full beard. His lazy eyes have a habit of meeting yours, and staying there. An optical arrest, and it's good being prisoner."

McGuinn confesses: "As far as writing is concerned, well, I've not been doing all that much. 'Chestnut Mare' was the last one I wrote, and I'm proud of that one – and I've never said anything like that about a song before. I like the lyrics, the storyline, and melody. It's interesting and exciting. You wanna know what it's about? Right, I'll tell you. It's an adaptation of Peer Gynt's chase of the reindeer or whatever it was, you know … Well, we changed that into a chestnut mare instead of a deer, cos you tend to find chestnut mares in America. The narrative became American, sort of old-time cowboy."

'Mr. Tambourine Man' retains a special place in McGuinn's heart, and in his mind the song is elevated to the level of a hymn. "At the beginning it's me speaking to God. Saying 'Hey Mr. Tambourine Man play a song for me, I've got nothing else to do, I've got nothing else to do,' that sort of thing. Then 'on that jingle jangle morning', well, I want to be following Him. It's like a spiritual testimonial. 'Take me for a trip on your magic swirling ship', well, that's relating to a spiritual experience. I got this overwhelming sensation of electricity with it. Like 'my hands couldn't feel to grip.' It was such an experience that I couldn't do anything except submit. I'd go anywhere with Him, and I sort of made a vow of allegiance. 'I'll follow you anywhere.' I don't know what Dylan meant by it. But, frankly speaking, if I hadn't meant what I meant with it, it wouldn't have been a hit.

"I dig the success of Harrison with 'My Sweet Lord'," says McGuinn, "a sort of sugarcoated spiritual thing rather than Billy Graham's used-car approach. The word God is unimportant to me, the word is. Call it the world, call it the life force."

What does McGuinn think of Bob Dylan? "Yes, I'm concerned about him. I'm concerned as a friend. I've got to think of this, you see. Does a performer have an obligation to the public? If so, he has shaken that obligation. I find it disappointing to see someone who was so brilliant come down to such a mediocre show. After *Self Portrait*, I though that was sufficient to pull him together. I thought the next [*New Morning*] was going

to be great. Yes, like you, I regarded him as a brother, I wanted to protect him from criticism. But somehow that feeling has gone, I can't protect him anymore."

Does McGuinn owe anything to Dylan? "No, I don't think we owe anything. He owes me something. Somehow he doesn't appreciate what we did for him. He may appreciate, but he hasn't shown it. 'Mr. Tambourine Man' was a big asset for him, and when we continued recording his stuff, it gave him a real boost. He's told me that. He's told me he wants to make me a millionaire. He's said to me, 'Look I'm a millionaire, and I want you to get to the same place, and you're not going to do it singing with The Byrds.' He told me that I'd do it writing songs. Writing 12 songs and throwing 11 away, every day. He was right, but I haven't found time to do that. I don't want to make a million, anyway."

Disc (May 15) sets aside a spread on The Byrds, with a detailed discography, an appraisal by Derek Taylor, a Hollywood report from Judy Sims, and a brand new Roger McGuinn interview by Caroline Boucher. "[He] challenges you with a steely glare to contradict, question, or generally doubt his infallibility," the woman from *Disc* notes of McGuinn's imposing appearance. "He's still living true to his reputation of being a rather scary gentleman, despite shorter hair and fatter gut. … He talks aggravatingly quietly. If you ask him to speak up he bellows. He stutters a bit."

McGuinn tells Boucher that he hopes to meet George Harrison during his UK stay as he loves the ex-Beatle's worldwide smash hit 'My Sweet Lord'. "It's a kind of sneaky prayer, rather like 'Turn! Turn! Turn!'. And I like that, because I'm religious in my own way. I believe everything is alive. I'm the opposite to agnostic."

Sims looks back on her many encounters with The Byrds since 1965 and draws a picture of her pivotal meeting with the feared five. "The first time I saw The Byrds was at a small TV Press conference in Los Angeles where they were taping a *Shindig* segment. … Afterwards, Derek Taylor, already their press officer, sat down and talked to me as if I were a real person – he always did – in a period of my life when I frequently felt less than human. I was then and still am helpless in the face of cryptic, cutting remarks, a verbal play at which The Byrds excelled. Their fearless iconoclasm, their dismissal of the rudimentary quotient of 'manners', frightened me then, but it appealed to me enormously. They were getting away with it. For the first time in my life it occurred to me that even I could question some of the things I'd been told were 'right'. Still, I felt that Crosby or McGuinn,

those quick tongues, would find me stupid, so I approached them nervously."

Sims says here real interview with The Byrds was in Taylor's office, "high over the Sunset Strip, … an hour of unrelieved tension. And when it went smoothly, when they didn't attack me (they being Crosby and McGuinn again, as the others had overslept), I felt I'd won a Pyrrhic victory."

For Taylor, The Byrds always were and always would be very special. When in *Disc* he once again puts pen to paper to write about his favourite group bar The Beatles, the affection shines through. "Me, I thought The Byrds were heaven, just heaven. All of the time, good times and bad, I loved them like sons. Still do. The Beatles I loved, too, like they were Thor and Wotan from Wallasey, and that, and I was always a bit frightened of them. But The Byrds, oh, The Byrds, they were just brilliant naughty kids.

"The bottom line of it all is the conception, the idea of The Byrds. It is really old-fashioned – the conception of the bandleader with His Own Thing, and a fine band of interpretive musicians who understand what the Thing is. The only thing is that the bandleader must lead the band and His Own Thing must be right. Roger McGuinn is the bandleader … Quiet please – cue David Crosby. David was The Byrds, too, vital, I mean, vital, in the early years. So were Chris Hillman (plug: Burritos) and childlike, lovable Mike Clark (drumming Burrito) and Sir Richard Rabelais himself, Gene Clark – all great Byrds, and today's Byrds are great Byrds all.

"You know, I know of people who actually Ascend Into Better Realms, who fly with Angels when The Byrds do 'Chimes Of Freedom'. These people came upon The Byrds when it began. They were the children of the Love Generation, the very first, when it all happened right there in California when The Byrds began and the Spoonful joined.

"Me? They pulled me from misery and despair as a new floundering immigrant in Hollywood, asked me to fly with them, and gave me two-and-a-half per cent of gross and always paid. … What is all of this about? Well, it is about a positive energy and McGuinn, the Master Harnesser and his Men, and the direction they take on their magic swirling ship and the dancing spell they cast our disappearing way, and it is about the feeling that when The Byrds are wailing, we can truly trust that everything will work out all right."

Monday 3
Colston Hall, Bristol, Gloucestershire/ Avon

The Byrds tour bus leaves London and drives to Bristol in the West Country for a concert at

Colston Hall. The group's set sticks fairly close to the one they've played in the US lately. Two-thirds of the set is electric while one-third is an unplugged middle-section consisting of 'Black Mountain Rag'/'Soldier's Joy', 'Mr. Tambourine Man', 'Pretty Boy Floyd', and 'Take A Whiff On Me'.

Rita Coolidge & The Dixie Flyers (with extra guitarist Marc Benno) is the opening act for the whole European tour. Coolidge is out to promote her self-named debut album, which features large doses of Clarence White's guitar.

Gavin Pietre writes in *Disc* (May 8): "The big fight on Monday was Byrds, Rita Coolidge and Dixie Flyers versus the Bristol Colston Hall acoustics. The Byrds happily triumphed. Rita Coolidge, making her debut, and the Dixie Flyers were KO'd in the first round. The Byrds opened with 'Lover Of The Bayou' from the CBS sampler album *Together!*, then slipped into *Younger Than Yesterday*, and really sorted themselves out with a minor electric jam session. They receive my accolade, especially, for switching from electric to acoustic to electric, with minimum fuss and maximum professionalism.

"The acoustic set began with a short, nimble-fingered ragtime tune which caused an uproar loud enough to be heard by the Hillbillies in Tennessee, who have been churning that out for years. Ironically, 'Mr. Tambourine Man' came in for the wooden treatment; ironic, because the Byrds made their name electrifying Dylan and were now playing their version of Dylan in Dylan style. They delved straight back to the roots with Woody Guthrie and Huddy Ledbetter before switching back to electric with the single hit, 'Chestnut Mare'.

"The Byrds took three encores, which was interesting in that it really bared them musically. After their first encore, 'So You Want To Be A Rock'n'Roll Star', the best and most exciting of all white rock songs, with that incredible bassline, they shed their harmonies and polish. They searched their communal brain for material and became a raw rock'n'roll band, then delved further back until, instead of doing Byrd versions of Woody Guthrie songs, they sounded just like Woody Guthrie. For a Byrd freak like me, it was a bit upsetting to hear The Byrds miss out on harmonies from time to time and go askew with guitar solos, but the fact that they care for the audience came over and made up for everything."

Ric James writes about the show for *New Musical Express* (May 8). "It is to be reported that they are a very good rock'n'roll band – and a terrific country and western band too. Starting electrically with 'Bayou', McGuinn's

big 12-string led them into 'You Ain't Going Nowhere', proving that Roger is the best Dylan interpreter there ever has been. 'Truck Stop Girl' by Clarence suffered a little from a faulty PA system but was otherwise excellent. On stage, Clarence is a very commanding figure in his white cloak, and later proved to be an incredible guitar-picker when he and McGuinn race acoustically through 'Black Mountain Rag' before they launched into a new and very pretty version of the perennial 'Mr. Tambourine Man'. Then Roger and Clarence took us on a little historical trip through their musical routes with Woody Guthrie's 'Pretty Boy Floyd' (featuring drummer Gene Parsons on the banjo) and a rousing version of Leadbelly's 'Take A Whiff On Me'. The Byrds' biggest ovation, naturally, was for their recent hit 'Chestnut Mare' – a smacking good song."

Melody Maker's Roy Hollingworth has joined the bus trip from London. "Bristol not only saw one Byrds performance," he writes in the paper on May 8, "but an encore that stretched way over half-an-hour. The serenity of the sunny day had fed The Byrds. They couldn't stop playing. The splendidly warm audience didn't want them to stop, and, darn it, this group didn't want to stop either. And this was the first gig in a country that in the past has proved rather unfortunate for this cowboy unit.

"So what makes a group so beautiful? A good concert? Well, yes, but it wasn't perfect. There were a few sound hassles, which at times drowned McGuinn's tight-lipped vocals. There was an abundance of embarrassing feedback. 'I've never had anything so horrible happen to me. I walked up to the mic and it just squealed,' said Clarence White, a magnetic, complex guitarist. Yet forget these things, because there was something that counteracted these bugs. It was a sense of warmth, honesty, a sort of homeliness. Something close to an audience. No matter how many changes have been stitched into the group's tapestry, the original picture remains the same – and if you want an assessment, they are better than they've ever been before.

"Rita Coolidge and the Dixie Flyers are already rolling and reeling on stage. The Byrds take a quick eyeful and casually walk backstage. There's no heaviness, just coolness as the door is shut and half-a-dozen guitars and a banjo are tuned to perfection. Rita finishes. There's no gap; quickly mouthed instructions as ideas and thoughts pass among the group. There's a slow handclapping starting to grow outside. A nod, eyebrows are raised, and The Byrds take the stage.

"Their interpretation of the Dylan songbook reaches the roots with a 'yee-har' acous-

tic trip, with Parsons figuring and fingering a furious banjo. Then 'Eight Miles High' runs long, building on a complex riff with high-pitched guitar harmonies. McGuinn introduces those gorgeous space-bound guitar notes that makes The Byrds. Then there's jingle jangle guitar work between White and McGuinn. 'Mr. Spaceman', 'So You Want To Be A Rock'n'Roll Star', and it goes on. It's not a case of slinging out the old stuff. It's just fun for everybody. McGuinn really gets into it, stands back and delivers a screaming rock'n'roll intro, and the group bop into 'Roll Over Beethoven', and the whole place rocks and rolls – and what a beautiful rock'n'roll band this is."

Wednesday 5

☐ **UK TV** [Presumably] BBC Television Centre, London, London. BBC-1. The Byrds film a video appearance of their next single 'I Trust' to be broadcast tomorrow (May 6) on *Top Of The Pops* at 7:00pm.

The group is apparently a last-minute addition to the show, as their appearance is not mentioned in the weekly TOTP pre-show blurb in *Disc* (May 8).

☐ **UK TV** CBS Studios, 164 New Bond Street, central London. BBC-2. It is probably today that The Byrds video-record an insert for BBC-2's *Disco-2*, broadcast on May 27. Documentation of the recording will not survive, but the group pre-records 'Truck Stop Girl' and 'Jesus Is Just Alright' at CBS's London studio. The group finds the facility to their liking and intends to return here soon to record.

•

☐ **US RADIO** Radio station WGN, Chicago, IL. *Happy 30th Bob Dylan* 10:00am–noon Meanwhile in the US, DJ and radio personality Roy Leonard presents a two-hour tribute to Dylan with specific pre-recorded contributions by The Byrds and others. The extent of The Byrds' participation is not known.

Thursday 6
Fairfield Halls, Croydon, Greater London

Before they go on stage at the Fairfield Halls, the same location the group visited back in August 1965, The Byrds can be seen on BBC TV's *Top Of The Pops* (episode No. 384, at 7:00pm) performing their soon-to-be-released single 'I Trust' (see entry for yesterday). Others appearing on today's programme are Freda Payne, The Rolling Stones (Jagger in pink strutting to 'Brown Sugar'), East Of Eden, The Peddlers, French singer Severine, Sakkarin (one of Jonathan King's many guises), Perry Como, Dawn, and Dave & Ansell Collins, while Shirley Bassey is in the 'LP Spot'.

The Fairfield concert begins at 7:45pm, with ticket costs ranging from a cheap 65p to the top price at £1.25 (about $1.50 to $3). Chris Charlesworth of *Melody Maker* (May 15) writes: "The Byrds are like an institution. They seem to have been around as long as the Houses of Parliament with their own particular style of rock. The faces may have changed but the institution carries on. Perhaps what's why the concerts on their current British tour were sold out weeks in advance. Opportunities to see The Byrds are few and far between, but the magic is still there. Hearing them play and recognising the many songs on their albums is an uplifting experience.

"The passing of time seems to have altered the style slightly. At Fairfield Halls, Croydon, on Thursday – and presumably, everywhere else – 'Mr. Tambourine Man' takes on a Dylanish look, 'Eight Miles High' is almost an instrumental jam and 'Jesus Is Just Alright' is a wild rocker. Roger McGuinn conjures up an almost unique guitar tone, sharing the lead guitar with Clarence White, whose voice alone must have earned him a place in the band. White demonstrated his fingerpicking abilities on some acoustic bluegrass reels before settling down to the heavy stuff. A couple of classics from The Byrds' song book, ['Mr. Spaceman'] and 'So You Want To Be A Rock'n'Roll Star', brought the act to a close."

Friday 7
City Hall, Newcastle upon Tyne, Northumberland/Tyne & Wear
Today is also the official release date of a single exclusively for the European market, combining McGuinn's 'I Trust (Everything Is Gonna Work Out Alright)' with 'This Is My Destiny' as a taster from *Byrdmaniax*. Possibly the release may be postponed a week or two as the single is not reviewed until the end of the month. Derek Johnson, regular singles reviewer in *New Musical Express* (May 22), is not wild about the track. "Ever since the days of 'Mr. Tambourine Man', The Byrds have evolved a distinctive sound of their own, even though they are no longer confined solely to folk-oriented music. And the sound of this philosophic beaty ballad is rich and pungent – with colourful harmonies supporting the soloists, organ, walloping drums and the inevitable tambourine. Yet, although I played it three times on the trot, I wasn't particularly impressed by the song itself."

James Hamilton, who reviews singles by American artists for *Record Mirror* (May 29), is also not fond of the 45. "Unfortunately, everything didn't work out better than average. Nice steel and lazy slowness, but nothing truly memorable." *Disc* (May 22) too joins the disappointed ones. "Slide guitar opens a

very countrified piece which … wafts over and around you but never quite sticks. … This has none of the appeal of 'Chestnut Mare', which should have marked their big chart return. It might sell to a few converted by the concert tour, but to me [it] is just another unoriginal country ditty." Sales-wise, The Byrds need not have bothered. Despite the appearance on *Top Of The Pops* and the ongoing tour, the single does not chart.

Saturday 8
Liverpool University, Liverpool, Lancashire/Merseyside
One show at 7:30pm, with all tickets going for 85p.

Sunday 9
City Hall, Sheffield, Yorkshire/South Yorkshire
Today is originally set for a trip north of the border to Edinburgh's Usher Hall in Scotland, but the gig is replaced by this Sheffield date. Back in his hometown, Dinky Dawson has the tour bus swing by his mother's place for a meal, before the group plays to a full house in the City Hall. Joe Cocker, also a Sheffield lad, jumps on stage during Rita Coolidge's set to sing four numbers.

Monday 10
Town Hall, Birmingham, Warwickshire/West Midlands

Tuesday 11
Free Trade Hall, Manchester, Lancashire/Greater Manchester

Wednesday 12
As the British leg of the European tour is nearing its end, the group does some last-minute press interviews in London. McGuinn listens to the pick of recent releases in *Melody Maker*'s weekly Blind Date (May 22), a column he has visited before, in 1965 and '70. The stack of records includes newies by The Band, Dee Dee Warwick, Cowboy, Mick Abrahams, Marc Benno, Ashton Gardner & Dyke, Laura Nyro, and Mylon [LeFevre]. McGuinn is played a bootleg recording of 'This Wheel's On Fire', which he recognises right away. "Sounds like The Band live. That was obviously a live recording, unless it was in the studio with people and recorded through a tin can. It sounds like The Band and Robbie (Robertson) did a long guitar break. I was looking around the room and no one seemed really knocked out with it, no one's foot was really tapping. I've heard this is Dylan's favourite version of the song, but having done the song ourselves it's hard for me to judge."

Battin has asked specifically for his inter-

view with *Record Mirror* to be held in the paper's office, just so he could hail a cab and say "Seven Carnaby Street, please!" Speaking to Lon Goddard for the paper's May 22 issue, Battin discusses the group's longevity, its audience, and the differences between the US and Europe. "England has a lot of qualities missing back home. For a start, the people on the street aren't in such a neurotic state as those in America. Here, they are willing to help you, give directions; they seem to want to communicate with you, and they're pleasanter on every level. They even seem to dress more alike among the age groups – seems to be less of a gap. The number of people that want to communicate with you here just blows my mind – it's great. I can go into a bar for a pleasant drink, where in the States you either go in for a fight or sexual stimulation."

McGuinn does a separate interview for *Record Mirror* today (published in the paper on June 19), conducted by Keith Altham – the seasoned PR man and journalist who was among the throng of British newspapermen who tried to shoo The Byrds away when they descended on London in 1965. Altham has regarded McGuinn as the only interesting member of the original Byrds ("never could make it with David Crosspatch," he huffs) and says: "It is good to be able to report, as Roger suspected all along, that everything will turn out all right in the end! … And has."

McGuinn gives a lesson in history. "At that time The Beatles had just bailed the British economy out of a mess and The Byrds coming was something of a threat both politically and economically. We were just four [sic] very scared kids. We played at Ciro's in L.A. and we were magical – no one scrutinised, no one criticised, everyone was too busy having a good time and getting smashed out of their heads. In England we arrived under the electron microscope – it was very difficult. We were not conditioned to interviews

'I Trust (Everything Is Gonna Work Out Alright)' (UK)

A 'I Trust (Everything Is Gonna Work Out Alright)' (R. MCGUINN)
B '(Is This) My Destiny' (H. CARTER)

UK release May 7 1971 (CBS 7253)
Chart high UK none
Read more … entries for October 6 1970 and January 9 1971

or the kind of reception we got. We were a sandwich between The Beatles and Dylan [and] more often than not I couldn't tell if we were good or not, because there was a kind of mass hypnosis which made us seem good even though we were not. It has taken time to arrive where we are."

He adds: "To me, the 'Tambourine Man' was Allah. The eternal life force – it was almost an Islamic concept. '5D' was a very intellectual, a metaphysical trip based upon Epstein's theory of the eternal mesh in the universe. I was aware of the ambiguity which some people might read into it about drugs, but that was not my intent, nor was it my intention with '5D' or 'Mr. Spaceman'."

Bringing readers up to date, McGuinn gives his evaluation of *(Untitled)*. "'Chestnut Mare' was the most satisfying track on [the album] for me, but it could have been better – I ran out of breath on the final note, for example. 'Take A Whiff On Me' was nice but went on a just a little to long, and I cannot understand why 'Eight Miles High' is banned and this is not. I like the synthesizer on 'Hungry Planet' but the number fell a little short of our expectations. I was not happy with 'You All Look Alike', because there was another vocal which I would have preferred they had used."

McGuinn is not too keen on *Byrdmaniax* and refers to the record's lavish orchestrations as Terry Melcher's "little surprises". Melcher has been fired, he explains to Altham, and the tapes sent for a remix up in San Francisco. But when *Byrdmaniax* is finally released, it will not be clear if the remixes are used or not, and no other documentation of the salvage operation will survive.

(Altham wrongly repeats the persistent myth that only McGuinn played on the *Mr. Tambourine Man* album, which prompts reader John Dowler to write to *Record Mirror* (July 10) and clear up the misconception.)

✉ **UK RADIO** [Unknown location] London, BBC Radio 1 *Scene And Heard*

Keith Altham also interviews McGuinn for Radio One's regular pop report *Scene And Heard*. The segment lasts 4:38 and is transmitted on May 22. Regulated by BBC's standard fees, McGuinn receives £6 (about $15) for the interview.

•

Pete Frame, editor and leading light of the respected UK music magazine *Zigzag*, interviews McGuinn, White, and even Carlos Bernal, assembling quotes for a series on The Byrds that runs in *Zigzag* issues Number 27 to 33 between December 1972 and June 1973, plus a last instalment in *Zigzag* Number 41 (March 1974).

White tells Frame of the struggle when he joined in August 1968. "We weren't in a position to pick and choose. In those days, if a group broke up, the DJs would throw their records aside and the papers would forget them. Nowadays, it's good publicity to split up – look at CSNY and people like that. But in 1968 it was bad news. … Our reputation was off the bottom of the page. The Byrds were known for showing up late, not showing up at all, doing five songs and walking off – we had to start from scratch. Colleges, particularly, had a bad taste in their mouth about The Byrds, and we had to prove that we were serious.

"Since then, we've never been late for a show, we do a longer set than the contract demands because we enjoy playing, we go out there straight and do it right – well, as straight as we should be. And we slowly worked back up and got our good reputation back. In fact, the colleges in the States have this pamphlet which has details of campus attractions and groups to book and all that sort of stuff, and each act is given a grading in respect of value for money, punctuality, ability to entertain, audience attraction, and things like that. And we got a perfect grading on every category. … That really freaked us. But, like I say, three years ago, when I'd just joined, it was a different story – uphill all the way, and steep too!"

Thursday 13
Royal Albert Hall, London, central London

The group's visit to London's esteemed Albert Hall is recorded live, and *Record Mirror* (May 29) even speculates that it should be added to make *Byrdmaniax* a double album. Eventually, in 2008, the album will be officially packaged as *Live At Royal Albert Hall 1971*, featuring the drum and twang of a complete Byrds concert: 'Lover Of The Bayou', 'You Ain't Going Nowhere', 'Truck Stop Girl', 'My Back Pages'/'Baby, What You Want Me to Do', 'Jamaica Say You Will', 'Black Mountain Rag'/'Soldier's Joy', 'Mr. Tambourine Man', 'Pretty Boy Floyd', 'Take A Whiff (On Me)', 'Chestnut Mare', 'Jesus Is Just Alright', 'Eight Miles High', 'So You Want To Be a Rock'n'Roll Star', 'Mr. Spaceman', 'I Trust', 'Nashville West', and lastly 'Roll Over Beethoven'.

The night is captured in print by *Record Mirror*'s Miles Maxillian (May 22). "The Byrds at the Albert Hall last Thursday were so good you could taste them. … To begin with, most of the audience was on its feet the moment The Byrds walked on to the stage. The static electricity of anticipation was already in the air. In their first few numbers [the group], ably augmented by Jimmi Seiter on percussion, demonstrated the instrumental and harmonic interaction and perfection for which they are justly famous. The progression moved from bluegrass licks to the acoustic 'Mr. Tambourine Man' and on into 'My Back Pages' and the most recent single 'Chestnut Mare'.

"The first peak of the performance came with 'Jesus Is Just Alright', which moved smoothly into a Skip Battin bass guitar solo, then an extended group improvisation which subtly hinted at and ultimately led into 'Eight Miles High'. The song hasn't stood still, as those who have heard it recorded live on the Byrds' most recent album [will know]. … It was a fitting close to the organised set, but the concert was far from over.

"The first called-for encore was met with performances of 'So You Want To Be A Rock'n'Roll Star' and 'Mr. Spaceman'. The Byrds' response to a second encore call was three more songs, ending with Chuck Berry's 'Roll Over Beethoven'. By this time the audience was in a fever of delirium, its thirst for more still unquenchable. As if by then The Byrds had not given enough, had not really said it all, they returned to the stage a third time to put the last period on the last statement … an a cappella four-part-harmony treatment of 'Amazing Grace' that was almost sacred. This concert was an event."

Maxillian evidently is a pseudonym for Brian Blevins, who polishes his review a bit for a second opinion in *Cream* (June 1971). "From the start they flashed that instrumental interaction and colouring, the perfection of vocal harmonies, for which they are justly famous. … The Albert Hall concert – [the] end of the road in The Byrds' first serious British tour – progressed from bluegrass licks by McGuinn and White through to an acoustic 'Mr. Tambourine Man' and on into more Dylan with 'My Back Pages'. Then the new single 'Chestnut Mare', [and] the group plugged in again.

"But the first peak of the concert came with 'Jesus Is Just Alright', which, after a brief run-through of the song's formal structure, melted into an amazing bass guitar solo from Battin, eventually picked up by the others in an improvisation which surged on and on, always building, vaguely hinting harmonically at what was to come, and then, like an ejaculation, 'Eight Miles High'. The very song that introduced McGuinn's utterly distinctive 12-string sound – that huge overlay of jangling sonority that is the identity of The Byrds just as surely as Miles Davis spells his name with his trumpet tone. The song hasn't stood still: as The Byrds have changed – they have and they haven't, actually – so has the song.

"It was a fitting close to the organised set, but the concert was far from over. The first call for an encore was met with equally transfixing performances of 'So You Want To Be

A Rock'n'Roll Star' and 'Mr. Spaceman'. Off the stage and then back again – for three numbers ending with Chuck Berry's 'Roll Over Beethoven' (a little rock'n'roll for the folks). The audience, its thirst even now unquenched, deliriously [screamed] for more. As if by then The Byrds had not done it all, they returned to the stage a third time for a magic coda – an a cappella four-voice harmony of 'Amazing Grace'. The Albert Hall became a church."

Friday 14
De Doelen, Rotterdam, The Netherlands

☐ **EURO TV** The pirate station Radio Veronica has broadcast spots for the group's two-week Dutch tour for several days, and an expectant press corps meets The Byrds as their KLM plane touches down at Zestienhoven Airport. A reception is held at the nearby Skyway Hotel, and the day's highlights are broadcast on *Midweek*, Nederland 2, VARA, on May 26 between 7:05–7:55pm. One of the group portraits taken today will later adorn the sleeve for the Dutch issue of 'I Trust (Everything Is Gonna Work Out Alright)'.

Interviews with all four are taped. Battin and Parsons are asked about *Byrdmaniax*, and where Battin remains diplomatic ("I haven't heard the final mixes yet. … It is possibile it could be terrible, and it's also a possibility it could be great"), Parsons speaks his mind. "I'm not completely satisfied with that at all, because it was overproduced. We were on the road an awful lot and our producers took the basic tracks we'd laid down and put horns, strings, and so forth on there. So we didn't have the time to write the parts for the horns and strings. So there are a lot of things on there that don't have anything to do with our group."

At midnight, The Byrds play a rapturously received concert at De Doelen, and the promoter decides to stage a return to the club two days later. Like all of the dates on the Dutch tour, promoter Mojo presents the concert in cooperation with Radio Veronica (hence the diligent radio advertising) and pop newspaper *Muziekkrant Oor*.

Saturday 15
Concertgebouw, Grote Zaal, Amsterdam, The Netherlands

The Byrds hold a special place in the hearts of Dutch music fans, as Willem Jan Martin points out in his review in *Trouw* (May 17). "When it comes to acknowledging the qualities of The Byrds, our country has always taken the leading position. Most of their singles have reached our charts. Americans are barely able to enthuse about The Byrds at the moment,

even though the group exists in its strongest musical combination ever. Well, so be it: the Americans don't know what they're missing. It didn't stop The Byrds from embarking on a 14-day Dutch tour. Thank you Mojo concerts!"

That said, the reviewer complains of bad sound for the first couple of numbers and an uncoordinated group. Things pick up when they reach 'Truck Stop Girl' and 'Jamaica Say You Will' and peak with the acoustic intermezzo, where Parsons' banjo playing on 'Pretty Boy Floyd' brings the house down. 'Eight Miles High' is too long and boring, but the audience calls the group back for a number of encores, with "sounds that defy all scepticism, but this we already knew from last year. The repertoire wasn't too different but the band has become even better". A second show at 11:00pm is added when the 7:00pm concert sells out.

Sunday 16
De Doelen, Rotterdam, The Netherlands

The Byrds return for an extra Rotterdam concert, as promised on Friday. Booked at short notice, the attendance is thin for the afternoon concert at 3:00pm.

Tuesday 18
Vorst Nationaal, Brussels, Belgium

☐ **EURO TV** RTBF TV *Pop Shop: That's For The Byrds*

The group makes its first and only visit to Belgium. Tonight's show is filmed by Belgian TV, for which a portion is broadcast on October 28 as a special edition of *Pop Shop* devoted to The Byrds. Featuring highlights from their stage act, the television special contains 'Lover Of The Bayou', 'You Ain't Going Nowhere', 'Truck Stop Girl', 'Baby, What You Want Me To Do', 'Soldier's Joy'/'Black Mountain Rag', 'Pretty Boy Floyd', 'Take A Whiff On Me', 'Jesus Is Just Alright', 'Mr. Spaceman', and 'BJ Blues'.

Wednesday 19
☐ **EURO TV** Radio Bremen Television Studios, Bremen, West Germany ARD–1 *Beat Club*

Recorded live, The Byrds (with Jimmi Seiter on percussion) tape several selections for *Beat Club*, perhaps the premier rock TV show on mainland Europe. The cameras capture The Byrds performing 'Soldier's Joy'/'Black Mountain Rag', 'Chestnut Mare', 'Mr. Tambourine Man', 'So You Want To Be A Rock'n'Roll Star', and 'Eight Miles High'. With the exception of 'Mr. Tambourine Man' and 'So You Want To Be A Rock 'n' Roll Star', the other three selections are transmitted this coming Saturday, even if the 23-minute version of 'Eight Miles High' is abbreviated. 'So You Want To Be A

Rock'n'Roll Star' is held over for a screening on October 28, 1972, while 'Mr. Tambourine Man' will remain unseen in Radio Bremen's vaults.

Thursday 20
De Prins Willem-Alexanderhal, Emmeloord, The Netherlands

Following the detour to Belgium and West Germany, The Byrds are back in the Netherlands for further concerts.

Friday 21
Diekmanhal, Enschede, The Netherlands

Saturday 22
Het Turfschip, Breda, The Netherlands

There is an incident during the soundcheck when Jimmi Seiter discovers a tape machine discreetly placed off stage, hooked up to three high-quality microphones on stage, and ready to roll. Despite protests from the tape operator with assurances of approval from The Byrds' management, Seiter unceremoniously expels him from the theatre.

Beat Club (episode Number 67) is aired in West Germany from 2:30–3:30pm. Besides The Byrds (see May 19) performing 'Chestnut Mare', 'Black Mountain Rag', and an edited 'Eight Miles High', this afternoon's show features inserts by Kraftwerk and Rory Gallagher.

Across the channel, Keith Altham's interview with McGuinn is broadcast on BBC Radio One's *Scene And Heard* 2:00–3:00pm (see May 12).

Sunday 23
Musis Sacrum, Arnhem, The Netherlands

It is a very hot day, and as there is no air conditioning in this 2,000-seat theatre, The Byrds are forced to drop their final encore, 'Amazing Grace', for the first time on the tour. Musis Sacrum is a venerable theatre building and, fearing trouble, the manager has removed all seating, so the audience has to sit on the floor.

Another sell-out, so a second show at 11:00pm is added.

Wednesday 26
Highlights from The Byrds' arrival and press reception in Rotterdam (see May 14) are broadcast on VARA-TV's *Midweek* between 7:05–7:55pm.

Thursday 27
The group is one of the featured attractions on BBC-2's *Disco-2* (see May 5), performing 'Truck Stop Girl' and 'Jesus Is Just Alright'.

277

Friday 28
De Martinihal, Groningen, The Netherlands

Saturday 29
De Stadsschouwburg, Eindhoven, The Netherlands

Sunday 30
De Vliegermolen, Voorburg, The Netherlands

Originally today's concert is set for Utrecht but is later replaced by this date in Voorburg, some 30 miles away. The group will remain in the Netherlands for a couple more days, but as it turns out this will be the last concert of the group's 1971 visit to Europe.

Monday 31
□ **EURO TV** NOS Studio complex, Hilversum, the Netherlands VARA TV *Midweek*

As with their Belgian visit two weeks ago, a complete Byrds performance is filmed – which is quite a rarity – this time by Dutch television. Following an afternoon soundcheck (performing 'Jesus Is Just Alright'), the group mingles with the press and photographers. Interview snippets with the four members are conducted for inclusion in the final programme. The show is first broadcast on June 23 and then again in an abbreviated edition on September 17.

The complete performance runs: 'Lover Of The Bayou', 'You Ain't Going Nowhere', 'Truck Stop Girl', 'My Back Pages'/'BJ Blues'/'Baby What You Want Me To Do', 'Jamaica Say You Will', 'Chestnut Mare', 'Jesus Is Just Alright', 'Eight Miles High', 'Black Mountain Rag', 'Mr. Tambourine Man', 'Pretty Boy Floyd', 'Take A Whiff', 'So You Wanna Be A Rock'n'Roll Star', 'Mr. Spaceman', and 'Roll Over Beethoven'.

When edited and broadcast at the end of June, several numbers are omitted ('Lover Of The Bayou', 'Jesus Is Just Alright' [the soundcheck take is used instead], 'Chestnut Mare', 'Black Mountain Rag', 'Pretty Boy Floyd', 'Take A Whiff On Me', 'So You Want To Be A Rock'n'Roll Star', and 'Roll Over Beethoven'), while the extended 'Eight Miles High' is cut to avoid it dominating the valuable screen time.

June

Friday 4–Sunday 6
Back in January when the European tour was booked and laid out, it concluded with three gigs in Scandinavia: in Copenhagen,

Denmark on June 4, to be followed by a trip to Sweden on Saturday (Gothenburg) and Sunday (Stockholm). At the last minute, the northern dates are cancelled and the group decides to fly back to the US. The reasons for the cancellations are not entirely clear; Dinky Dawson's book will suggest that McGuinn calls off the dates almost on a whim. Reportedly, McGuinn insists the group should fly back to try to rescue *Byrdmaniax* – a futile operation as the album is already completed.

Saturday 5
The group is booked to tape an appearance on BBC-2's television programme *In Concert*. The show is in its third season, and The Byrds were among the attractions contracted for the spring and summer serial along with Gordon Lightfoot, Gilbert O'Sullivan, Neil Diamond, Jimmy Webb, David Gates, Carole King, James Taylor, and – if the Musicians' Union will allow – The Band.

However, a last-minute decision enforces a change in Byrdplans, as *New Musical Express* reports next month (July 10). Quoting the show's producer Stanley Dorfman, *NME* says: "[The BBC] had planned to film a show of The Byrds in concert while they were in this country. But after the necessary work permits had been arranged, the news of the closing of the Fillmore concert halls in America was announced, and the group flew back home to appear at these venues. However, The Byrds are still anxious to appear in the *In Concert* series when they are next in the country."

Whatever their intentions, The Byrds never get a second chance on *In Concert*, and the show is not on their list of engagements when the group returns to Britain in January 1972.

Wednesday 9
Fillmore East, Manhattan, New York, NY

Bill Graham has decided to close down his Fillmore venues East and West and explains his motives in a long interview published in *Melody Maker* (May 8). "Ever since the creation of the Fillmores, it was my intention to do nothing more, nor less, than present the finest contemporary artists in this country, on the best stages and in the most pleasant halls. The scene has changed and, in the long run, we are all to one degree or another at fault. All that I know is that what exists now is not what we started with, and what I see around me now does not seem to be a logical extension of that beginning. Therefore I am taking this opportunity to announce the closing of the Fillmores and my eventual withdrawal from producing concerts."

The Byrds are given the honour to appear

for one night in the last month's run at Graham's New York establishment – together with McKendree Spring and Eric Anderson – although the final concert here will not be until June 27. Over on the West Coast, Graham shut the lights at Fillmore West on Independence Day 1971 after a show by Santana and Creedence Clearwater Revival. (Despite the promoter's grand claim that he will abdicate from concert productions, he will continue to work in this capacity right up until his tragic death in a helicopter crash in 1991.)

Tonight, a special guest is introduced as Reggie & The Frank N. Steins, but when a jumpsuited figure walks on stage it turns out to be Elton John, who is in New York City a day early for his Carnegie Hall show tomorrow. Well on his way to megastardom, Elton has just released the live album *11–17–70* (*17–11–70* to UK record buyers), which makes the US Top Five this summer.

Jan Flato notes in an undated review in *Billboard*: "[The Byrds] are one of the only groups around today who can still successfully perform their mid-60s songs without rearranging them." (A tape that will come into circulation from a radio show on New York's WNEW-FM may be from this Fillmore East show; it features 'Glory Glory' and surprise returns of 'Ballad Of Easy Rider', 'Wasn't Born To Follow', and 'Positively Fourth Street' among the standard fare of hits and classics.)

"You've got to be pretty much of a pervert to think that playing good is selling out," comments *Circus* (September 1971) in a rather flippant two-page piece on The Byrds, as a preview of their coming *Byrdmaniax* album. "Which is exactly what they did last time they played the now-defunct Fillmore East – play good, that is." Following this lone New York concert, The Byrds fly home for a couple of weeks rest.

Wednesday 23
Midweek, the TV show taped during the Dutch tour before the summer (see May 31), is broadcast on Nederland 2 VARA at 08:20–09:15pm tonight. The programme is unique in that it devotes 55 minutes to The Byrds only, starting with several selections from the TV studio concert: 'You Ain't Going Nowhere', 'Truck Stop Girl', 'My Back Pages'/'BJ Blues'/'Baby, What You Want Me To Do', 'Jamaica Say You Will', 'Jesus Is Just Alright', 'Eight Miles High' (edited down to TV-friendly length), and 'Mr. Tambourine Man'.

The performance is followed by interviews with McGuinn (talking about the 1970 visit to the Netherlands) and Parsons (sending regards to 'Louis Chevrolet', an in-joke referring to his troubles with a '38 two-door Chevy Sedan he has recently sold). The interview section is broken by 'Jesus Is Just Alright' (taken from the soundcheck), after which there are inserts with White and Battin before the television show is rounded off with 'Mr. Spaceman'.

Also today, the Byrds' 11th album – *Byrdmaniax* – is released in the US. It is packaged in a fold-out jacket, the front and back of which depicts the sculpted facemasks of McGuinn, White, Parsons, and Battin created by artist Mary Leonard. Jimmi Seiter is promoted to fifth member of the group, credited with "tambourine, percussion, road manager, tour guide, babysitter, body guard, Mummy and Daddy".

The album contains 11 tracks of uneven quality, and marks an odd situation where the group members have unanimously distanced themselves from the finished product. The few who bother to review the album will, in the main, confirm these feelings. All the same, the album does fair business chart-wise, racking up a Number 46 position in *Billboard*.

Richard Meltzer's long review in *Rolling Stone* (August 19) is particularly vicious. "What a boring dead group. But then again aren't they all? Right, that puts it all in a different perspective. Increments of pus. Anything unfestering is a bonus. Two halfway decent cuts make an album a winner, maybe even one. The cover features death masks of the Byrds. But the eyes are closed and lots of stiffs have the eyes open. When you're alive and having your face cast you have to watch out for your eyes. So it looks like things have returned to the pre-fanatical days before the plaster casting of cocks, Claes Oldenburg is a big cheese again, and mere faces are worthy of consideration.

"Jeez, you'd think it was 1964 again and this was a Billy J. Kramer album with an exceptional cover. But it's only another Byrds bummer, and the Byrds have never picked any bones about bummer covers; it's never been an abrupt descent, and they've always just kind of accepted one after another. What a great bunch of mock stoics they are and always have been."

Going through the album track-by-track, Meltzer finds little to mollify his sharp words. Oddly enough, he thinks 'Tunnel Of Love' and 'Absolute Happiness' are passable – two Battin/Fowley creations later rejected by most Byrds fans – while 'Kathleen's Song' and 'Jamaica Say You Will' ("by Jackson Browne, so there's no way it could be bad") also narrowly find favour with the writer.

San Diego Community Concourse, San Diego, CA
Back in action for the first time in almost

three weeks, the group visits a venue they have played twice before: first as support to The Rolling Stones in May 1965 and then with Gram Parsons in March 1968. Tonight's concert is with Hedge & Donna, Jerry McCann, and Show of Hands.

Following the San Diego concert, The Byrds return to Los Angeles to prepare material for a new album. Shaking off the disappointing experience with *Byrdmaniax*, the group decides to do the opposite of Melcher's elaborate and costly methods: they plan to leave Los Angeles and instead spend a week in London to record an album's worth of songs with no outside help. What's more, the four Byrds decide that they will produce the sessions themselves. Having recently worked at CBS's London studio on a BBC assignment, the group has enjoyed the relaxed British approach, as opposed to the rigid rules that reign in American studios.

Although the recent European tour has been an unqualified success, back home on California soil the group sinks into a state of idleness. The dynamic balance that worked so well on *(Untitled)* and brought out the best in every member is strained after the *Byrdmaniax* debacle. Paradoxically, McGuinn's democracy leads to a lack of direction. While

White, Battin, and Parsons are encouraged to compile material for recording, quality-control suffers as McGuinn enters a dry spell as a songwriter.

July

US TV [Presumably] Little Theatre, West 44th Street, Manhattan, New York, NY. Channel 11 *The David Frost Show*

David Frost is a British television personality who juggles two talk shows on different continents; he has his own weekly show at home on London Weekend Television but commutes between London and New York City every week to present his own syndicated talk show in the States. By the summer of 1971, the show has been going for two years and is now in its third season. Backed by good viewer ratings, Frost's programme is a light mix of names from the news, some celebrities, and musical inserts.

With *The David Frost Show*, The Byrds make their first US television appearance this year, broadcast on July 22. Their segment starts with performances of 'So You Want To Be A

Byrdmaniax

A1 'Glory, Glory' (A. REYNOLDS)
A2 'Pale Blue' (R. MCGUINN/G. PARSONS)
A3 'I Trust' (R. MCGUINN)
A4 'Tunnel of Love' (S. BATTIN/K. FOWLEY)
A5 'Citizen Kane' (S. BATTIN/K. FOWLEY)
B1 'I Wanna Grow Up To Be A Politician' (R. MCGUINN/J. LEVY)
B2 'Absolute Happiness' (S. BATTIN/K. FOWLEY)
B3 'Green Apple Quick Step' (GENE PARSONS/C. WHITE)
B4 'My Destiny' (H. CARTER)
B5 'Kathleen's Song' (R. MCGUINN/J. LEVY)
B6 'Jamaica Say You Will' (J. BROWNE)

US release June 23 1971 (Columbia KC 30640)
UK release August 6 1971 (CBS S 64389)
Chart high US number 46; UK none
Read more ... entries for January 9, 11, 17, 19, 24, 26, March 1–6, undated April 1971

Bonus CD tracks: 'Just Like A Woman' (B. Dylan), 'Pale Blue' (R. McGuinn/G. Parsons), 'Think I'm Gonna Feel Better' (G. Clark), [hidden track] 'Green Apple Quick Step' (G. Parsons/C. White)

"What a boring dead group. But then again aren't they all? Right, that puts it all in a different perspective. Increments of pus. Anything unfestering is a bonus. Two halfway decent cuts make an album a winner, maybe even one. The cover features death masks of the Byrds. But the eyes are closed and lots of stiffs have the eyes open."
ROLLING STONE, AUGUST 19, 1970

Rock'n'Roll Star' and 'Mr. Spaceman', followed by a commercial break. Next, McGuinn introduces the group and gives a brief career bio. Then it is into 'Black Mountain Rag' and 'Mr. Tambourine Man' before another commercial break.

The insert ends with McGuinn interviewed by Frost and the group playing two songs from the new album, 'I Wanna Grow Up To Be A Politician' and 'Citizen Kane'. Frost and McGuinn engage in a discussion on gadgets: McGuinn shows off his Sinclair wristwatch/pocket television and records and plays back a snippet of their conversation on a mini tape recorder.

Saturday 17
'Schaefer Music Festival', Wollman Skating Rink, Central Park, New York, NY
The Byrds make their annual trip to this festival, which they visited in 1969 and '70. The skating rink has a capacity of 5,000, and *Amusement Business* reports that both shows (7:00 and 9:30pm) sell out. J.F. Murphy & Salt are the opening act.

Sunday 18
'Garden State Folk Festival', Wall Stadium, Belmar, NJ
This is a folk festival with Richie Havens and The Byrds as the main drawing cards, while Bert Summer, Dave Van Ronk, David Ray, Nick Holmes, and Carolyn Hester bring up the rear. A young Bruce Springsteen reportedly makes the arduous 250-or-so mile journey from Richmond, Virginia, in time for The Byrds' performance. Springsteen has played a daytime show in Richmond with a shortlived ten-piece band that he leads.

✈ July 19–July 29, 1979:
7TH OVERSEAS TOUR (UK)

→ Monday 19
The Byrds fly to London for a week of recording sessions, and along the way they have been booked for an appearance at a folk festival in Lincolnshire.

Thursday 22
🔊 **RECORDING** CBS Studios, 164 New Bond Street, central London. Producers The Byrds with engineer Mike Ross.

The group settles in at Columbia Records' London facility, together with experienced house engineer Mike Ross, who has overseen countless sessions over the years, including many for soundman Dinky Dawson's previous bosses in Fleetwood Mac.

Despite the group's optimism and we'll-show-'em attitude, there has been scant time between touring commitments to prepare enough new material so soon after the *Byrdmaniax* failure.

The first day in the studio is devoted to three songs rehearsed before they came to London. Larry Murray's 'Bugler' is the poignant childhood story of a boy and his dog, borrowed from Murray's debut album *Sweet Country Suite*. Sung by White, the song will be finished back home in Los Angeles at a later date. (See entry for mid August.) 'Lazy Waters' is another cover, written by singer-songwriter Bob Rafkin, whose sole claim to fame will be The Byrds' version of this song. It is sung by Battin, who also plays piano on the tune.

Lastly, the group records a co-operative effort, 'Antique Sandy', where even Jimmi Seiter receives one-fifth of the credit. The lady in question is Seiter's old girlfriend Sandy, whom he and The Byrds met in Virginia Beach way back in July 1966. Like the other songs taped today, the song is built around acoustic instruments and vocals.

In the US, *The David Frost Show* (Episode No 599) with the group's performances is syndicated on television around the country (see July 15); some stations broadcast the it in the afternoon while other areas such as Los Angeles (KTTV) and New York (Channel 11) air the programme at 8:30pm. Frost's other guests are golf champion Jack Nicklaus and comic actor Chuck McCann.

Saturday 24
'A Concert Of Contemporary International Folk Music', Tupholme Abbey, near Lincoln, Lincolnshire
Perhaps inspired by their storming appearance at the Bath festival last year, McGuinn's men are billed as 'Acoustical Byrds' at Lincoln, although in fact they sneak in their electric guitars without anyone's objections.

The day starts with reinvented 60s pop singer Dion and continues with Sonny Terry & Brownie McGhee, Steeleye Span, Tim Hardin, Pentangle, The Incredible String Band, Fotheringay (with Sandy Denny), Tom Paxton, The Byrds, and finally James Taylor. Ralph McTell is billed but fails to appear.

Nick Logan in *New Musical Express* (July 31) writes about "the awesome thrust and musicianship of The Byrds" and describes them as simply tremendous. "Though billed as 'acoustic' Byrds there was a case for the Trades Descriptions Act, as against the most beautiful ocean blue sky, the sun setting in the opposite line of sight, they rampaged breathtakingly first into 'So You Want To Be A Rock'n'Roll Star' and with scarcely a pause into 'Mr. Spaceman'. Such was their driving force, even with the switch to acoustic on 'Bugler', vocals by Clarence White, that the time taken between numbers to set up seemed non-existent.

"Much of the time there were the four of them shoulder to shoulder in a line – three guitars and Gene Parsons' banjo – four immovable bodies against the sky, four guitar necks aimed skywards at almost identical angles, four right hands skilfully at work, 16 fingers picking and flicking in furious formation. 'Mr. Tambourine Man', Woody Guthrie's 'Pretty Boy Floyd', then back to electric line-up for 'You Ain't Going Nowhere', 'My Back Pages' 'Jesus Is Just Alright', an encore of 'Chestnut Mare', and a bonus in the gospel 'Glory Glory'. It was sheer joy to just rock back on your heels and let it all swamp over."

Melody Maker (July 31) says: "On paper the most interesting act of the day must have been the inclusion of The Byrds, billed to do 'an acoustic' set – something I know they are well capable of, but it nevertheless looked as though it could [become] something totally different. I felt a bit rotten when I mouthed 'wow' at the sight of Jim McGuinn's 12-string Rickenbacker on stage, plus the presence of Clarence White's electrical set-up. But then, as the crowd took on a completely new look, I realised I wasn't the only cat around panting with hot breath for a little rock'n'roll. Yes, it was a remarkable change in audience reaction. With the quietness and serenity of the whole day, one wondered if there were any freaks present at all. My God, there were. There was a sudden bustling, and excited chattering in the thick black air. A few campfires belching flimsy exhaust from inadequate fuel wrought havoc in the night, and there was a great cheer as McGuinn, White, Battin, and Parsons took the stage.

"No messing, they launched straight into 'So You Want To Be A Rock'n'Roll Star', and there it was, the first real electricity of the day, and it was so incredible. 'We're really scheduled to do an acoustic set, so we'll try a little,' said McGuinn. The audience were barking for 'Eight Miles High', so there was some element of frustration amidst the invisible squatters. Parsons adopted banjo, and McGuinn and White acoustic guitars. We had a lazy, down-home 'Mr. Tambourine Man', and then the reeling country of Woody Guthrie's 'Pretty Boy Floyd'. They were perfect, faultless, and rapidly turning into the best bag of the day – for me anyway.

"A hoedown instrumental, featuring some hectic flat-picking from White, got everyone up and clapping. McGuinn cooled it all down by introducing a new song, 'Antique Sandy' – a set of gentle, drifting chords that are so much the prime quality of The Byrds. Next, an acoustic 'Chestnut Mare', and then more

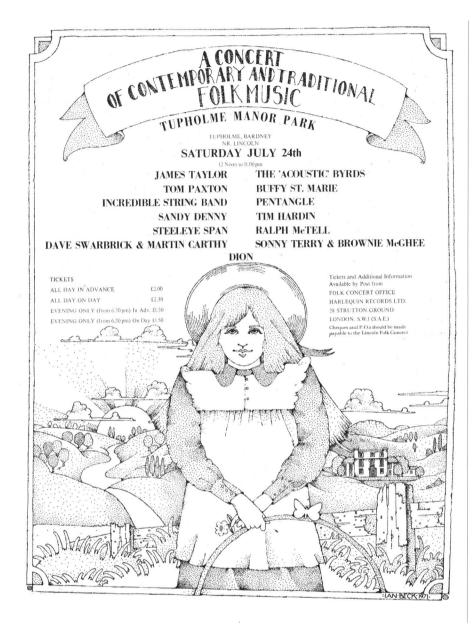

earlier covered by Chris Hillman and Gram Parsons on The Flying Burrito Brothers' album *Burrito DeLuxe*.

McGuinn's 'Tiffany Queen' lifts rhythm and melody from any number of Chuck Berry tunes, substituting Berry's classic guitar intro with a tepid Keith Richards variation. The track sounds peculiarly like an English boogie band, and that feeling is retained for 'B.B. Class Road'. A joint Parsons/Dinky Dawson number, the simple lyric is dedicated to "all road managers who are worth a dang anywhere in the world – we'd like you to know that we think of you".

On the morning following the session, Parsons is woken by *Disc* for an interview (August 7). He speaks reverently of 'Tiffany Queen' and 'Farther Along'. "I believe there must be some sort of thing guiding us along because there's a lot of luck involved. Roger got up, wrote a song, wrote the words, we arranged it, did it, and got it finished. It was like magic; it just fell into place. Then we did another track, a gospel one ['Farther Along'], and that came out so beautiful, so meaningful, we just sat around a cried a little."

Parsons suggests the new album should be called *Home Made* "because there's not one musician on it [besides] us. And it's magical the way it's recording – straight away, first or second takes." He still gripes about *Byrdmaniax*. "We went out on the road when we'd finished making [it] and when we came back we found that they'd dubbed on flugelhorn, fiddle, strings, and a chick choir. And they said it was too late to take it off because they'd spent $100,000 on the overdubbing and it was all pressed up. It'll probably be a monster, but we hate it."

Tuesday 27

🔊 **RECORDING** CBS Studios, 164 New Bond Street, central London. Producers The Byrds with engineer Mike Ross.

The songwriting team of Skip Battin and Kim Fowley supplies 'America's Great National Pastime'. The tune is a continuation of their previous novelty songs 'Citizen Kane' and 'Tunnel Of Love', which have become a sub-genre in the Byrds songbook. 'Bristol Steam Convention Blues', also recorded, is a pleasant and inconsequential bluegrass number by Parsons and White with banjo, mandolin, and acoustic guitar.

Wednesday 28

🔊 **RECORDING** CBS Studios, 164 New Bond Street, central London. Producers The Byrds with engineer Mike Ross.

In record time, the group wraps up album sessions in London. A couple of original compositions (Gene Parsons' 'Get Down Your

shouts for 'Eight Miles High'. 'We were a little worried about doing electric, but we really dig acoustic. That's what they said we've gotta do,' said McGuinn. But then it was 'You Ain't Going Nowhere' and then some space-boogies. The encore produced another new number, 'Glory, Glory', and such fine applause. I don't think even James Taylor's excellent set had the glorious, flying quality of those super-Byrds."

The group's repertoire offers a couple of surprises (the return of 'Willin'") and two new songs ('Antique Sandy' and 'Bugler'). In full it runs as follows: 'So You Want To Be A Rock'n'Roll Star', 'Mr. Spaceman', 'I Wanna Grow Up To Be A Politician', 'Bugler', 'Black Mountain Rag', 'Mr. Tambourine Man',

'Pretty Boy Floyd', 'Antique Sandy', 'Willin', 'You Ain't Going Nowhere', 'My Back Pages' / 'Baby What You Want Me To Do', 'Jesus Is Just Alright', 'Chestnut Mare', and 'Glory, Glory'.

On their drive back to London, late at night, the group is observed playing table-soccer in a roadside café.

Sunday 25–Monday 26

🔊 **RECORDING** CBS Studios, 164 New Bond Street, central London. Producers The Byrds with engineer Mike Ross.

There are three songs on today's agenda, one of them White's arrangement of the traditional gospel song 'Farther Along'. Well-known in bluegrass circles, the song was

Line' and another Battin/Fowley creation, 'Precious Kate') plus a perfunctory cover of The Fiestas' 1959 hit 'So Fine' make up the last three selections for the album. Although some refinements will be made in Los Angeles upon their return – primarily on 'Bugler' – The Byrds have fulfilled their objective to record a whole album cheaply and quickly.

Thursday 29

The Byrds fly out of London, heading for Canada.

Friday 30

'Man And His World (M&HW)', Place Des Nations, Montreal, Quebec, Canada

The Byrds and April Wine (a group from Canada) are among the many attractions vying for attention at M&HW. The Place Des Nations is a large outdoor venue that was erected as part of Montreal's Expo '67 when a series of international pavilions were built for the 1967 World's Fair. The fair closed at the end of that year but the pavilions continue to present exhibitions, music, art shows, and movies at the various venues under the collective name 'Man And His World'.

Saturday 31

Lenox Arts Center, Lenox, MA

The Art Center in the Berkshire Hills of western Massachusetts near Tanglewood opened on July 1 with a summer programme of weekly workshops, musical plays, concerts, and poetry readings. The Byrds with opening act Chris Smithers draw 3,800 for tonight's concert. The stage is set at the bottom of a sloping field of grass, and the serene surroundings are perfect for rock'n'roll on a summer's day.

Too perfect, as it turns out. The Byrds are suddenly interrupted at the end of their performance by the formidable presence of Police Chief William F. Obanhein (already notorious because of his portrayal of 'Officer Obie' in the Alice's Restaurant movie, in which he plays himself) and a patrolman.

The Berkshire Eagle (August 2) writes: "The problem came to a head about 9:15pm Saturday, when the tones of The Byrds … reportedly were quite audible during Prokofiev's 'Piano Concerto No 3' being played in the Tanglewood Shed a mile to the northwest." After complaints and a deluge of phone calls, Obanhein and his fellow patrolman travel over to the Arts Center in an effort to have the volume lowered. "Both were waving their hands downwards. Indicating they wanted the sound lowered," the report continues. "Obanheim scuffled briefly with Jim Seiter, one of the Byrds, and a second, unidentified man. Then the two officers parted, and the

group completed its song within five minutes. It was the last amplified instrumentation of the evening."

The front-page news is accompanied by a long scholarly review by Nick King in the same paper. He says: "But the rock-vintage first number was only a mild prelude to the almost overwhelming build and beat The Byrds are capable of. The faster-moving 'Mr. Spaceman' reached out expressively to the audience and brought many to their feet. Percussionist Jim Seiter supplied the swing beat by eighth-note strikes on the tambourine; McGuinn and Battin combined voices in western-influenced harmony; and McGuinn and second guitarist Clarence White furnished the staccato-like up-and-down resonance typical of the group.

"They moved right into 'Chestnut Mare' – a six-minute talking number with a rich, mounting refrain – without a break. This sensual ballad was probably most pleasing to the males in the audience while causing fem-libbers to blush in indignation. The sexual implications and theme of masculine dominance are more than undertones but, in the best tradition of reversal, he 'loses hold and she gets away'. McGuinn's soft, almost nasal drawl is at its best here.

"Particularly fantastic was The Byrds' 17-minute grand finale – the building, driving 'Eight Miles High'. Bass guitarist Battin had a five-minute field day as he manipulated his Fender bass, showing his talent that is essential to The Byrds' sound. Parsons and Seiter traded off some fine patterns on the drums and congas before McGuinn reappeared and added the final ingredient, a shimmering bank of music which mounted for minutes while the entire audience danced in anticipation."

It is at this point that the police chief makes his entrance amid boos from the crowd and The Byrds round off the show. After a five-minute standing ovation, they return for an encore with a disarming gesture: "Strategically, they presented a spiritual-like barbershop quartet without instrumentation. The hyped-up crowd just melted with the mellow sound and, when it ended, everyone departed peacefully."

A reader's letter a few days later in the *Eagle* (August 6) gives a report from the turf. "[When] the world-famous Byrds had played only one hour, the jubilant crowd – clapping, shouting, and rocking – suddenly buzzed with talk. 'What's going on?' During the performance of a Byrds song, two police officers had walked right up on the stage. When Jim Seiter, the percussionist–road manager Byrd, went over to see what was the matter, he was literally pushed aside by one of the policemen.

That, understandably, brought shouts of disapproval. But Jim just went back to playing. Then, one of the Byrds stagehands, obviously trying to avert catastrophe, walked over to the policeman; in a matter of seconds, he, too, was shoved aside. He, likewise, just walked away." In early August, the manager of the Arts Center is given a formal ultimatum that any further incidents will spell the revocation of all licences.

August

Sunday 1

Oakdale Music Theatre, Wallingford, CT

Randy Burns & The Sky Dog Band precede The Byrds. Playing to a capacity house (2,400), The Byrds "haven't lost their basic virtues of harmonic beauty and technical brilliance". So says the review in *The Hartford Times* (August 2) under the headline "Byrds Make Beautiful Music". Ron Georgeff writes: "McGuinn, the only original Byrd, sets the group's mien – detached, ironic, but given to occasional lashes of visible, demonic absorption in their music, like when bassist Skip Battin leaps and shakes his long hair. The Byrds have usually managed to stay pretty much on the crest of rock music, shifting to catch the right winds."

Tuesday 3

Armory, Indianapolis, IN

Friday 6

Byrdmaniax is released in the UK and meets a kinder critical response than in the US. It appears that the group's badmouthing of the album has lowered expectations to the point where reviewers are surprised that it has any redeeming qualities at all.

Roy Hollingworth, who a few weeks ago gave The Byrds a blinding review of their concert at the Lincoln festival, says in *Melody Maker* (August 14): "From what I'd already been told, and how I'd regarded the new Byrds album, I was beginning to believe this was going to be a bummer. And – excuse the poetry – nothing would have upset summer more than a Byrds bummer. So I was more than a little worried by the time needle hit the wax. Moral: never take any notice of nasty rumours; they can paint horribly distorted pictures. This is in fact one sweet length of bursting Byrds sunshine so perfect in quality and quantity you'd feel an absolute heel to ask for more.

"For a start there's the best treatment of a song since the gentleman upstairs knows when in 'Glory, Glory' (not the [Liverpool Football Club's] Kop version but one culled from a certain A. Reynolds). It's such a glorious fusion of chiming 12-string, McGuinn's dry lyrics, and a handful of chanting ladies into the bargain. Certainly a lion of an opening track, and one wonders how on earth they can follow it, but it all cools for 'Pale Blue', one of these range-riding laments with howling whiskey-harp, for that wishing-we-were-home effect – another gem from McGuinn's romantic pen. 'I Trust' follows this languid Byrds mood, but picks up a boppier backbeat to foil the heavy use of female chorale effects.

"I just couldn't believe the Skip Battin/Kim Fowley composition 'Tunnel Of Love' – ceaseless eights on the old piano and Lazy-K basslines give it all the qualities of a syrupy '58 single, and it's just a gas." Hollingworth continues in the same vein, finding 'Citizen Kane', 'I Wanna Grow Up To Be A Politician', 'Green Apple Quick Step', 'My Destiny', 'Kathleen's Song' ("smooth, curling webs of honey with a softly picked acoustic fronting massive orchestration"), and 'Jamaica Say You Will' all to his liking. He sums up: "Ridiculously varied, and true to everything I expect from the best rock'n'roll band this side of 1984."

"Another fine album by The Byrds," notes *Record Mirror* (August 21). "The line-up which scored so successfully with *(Untitled)* has extended itself even further here. It's musically more ambitious than that double-album but the lyrics are generally lighter." The only fault the unnamed reviewer can find is a few blurry vocals; otherwise "it's a near-perfect bit of Byrds".

The dissident is Richard Green of *New Musical Express* (August 14). "Gene Parsons did quite a good anti-selling job on this album a few months ago. His main complaint was that the producers – Terry Melcher and Chris Hinshaw – had made their idea of a Byrds album and not the group's idea. How right he is. Orchestration is all very well for some bands, but not, on this showing, for The Byrds. When the true history of rock comes to be written, The Byrds will get a deserved place of honour on the strength of tunes like 'Mr. Tambourine Man', 'Eight Miles High', and 'So You Want To Be A Rock'n'Roll Star'. Hopefully the writer will not have listened to *Byrdmaniax* or he may drastically alter his opinion.

"The first two tracks are so untypical Byrds as to be forgettable (the orchestration makes 'Pale Blue' abominable) and 'Absolute Happiness' is the sort of thing you expect The Sweet to turn up, while 'Citizen Kane' is pure Temperance Seven. 'Tunnel Of Love' gets close to The Byrds' own sound, as does 'I Wanna

Grow Up To Be A Politician', but the best two tracks have been saved till last. 'Kathleen's Song' shows the band's acoustic leaning in a good light and, despite the intrusion of the over-orchestration once again, 'Jamaica Say You Will' is well worth a listen."

Despite the charitable reviews, the album does not make a dent in the UK charts. *Byrdmaniax* will soon pale and among fans it become perhaps the least-liked album in the Byrds catalogue.

Undated August

🔊 **RECORDING** Columbia Recording Studios, Sunset and El Centro, Hollywood, CA. Producers The Byrds with engineer Eric Prestidge.

The new album is "99 per cent finished", in the words of Dinky Dawson, but some post-production is attended to now in Los Angeles. Primarily this involves overdubs and a new vocal track on 'Bugler' (see July 22), a song White says he messed up on purpose in London to allow him time to sing a satisfactory vocal.

He tells Pete Frame of *Zigzag* (July 1973): "When we got back to L.A., I took the tape into the studio and did the vocal again and dubbed on a bit of mandolin too. Then we – just me and the engineer – spent a long time mixing it. I really love that song; I think it's the best thing I ever did with The Byrds." (The song features a pedal steel guitar solo played by drummer Parsons, another facet of his many talents.)

Wednesday 11

The Evening Independent (August 7) out of Massillon, OH, claims The Byrds will sing 'Turn! Turn! Turn!' at a Good News Forum at the local St John's United Church of Christ tonight. Despite the trumpeting, there is no record of such an appearance in soundman Dinky Dawson's annals.

Friday 20

Staples High School Auditorium, Westport, CT

The Byrds' 20th single in the US, 'Glory Glory' coupled with 'Citizen Kane', is released and makes Number 110 in the *Billboard* charts and 65 in *Cash Box*.

Saturday 21

Hofstra University, Hempstead, NY

Sunday 22

Melody Fair Theatre, North Tonawanda, NY

Originally this was booked for Saturday 21st. Dinky Dawson describes the North Tonawanda

WESTPORT'S SUMMER FESTIVAL

THE BYRDS
In Concert
FRIDAY
AUGUST 20
STAPLES AUDITORIUM
WESTPORT, CONN.
7:00 & 10:00
TICKETS $5.00

YAC

TICKET OUTLETS – WESTPORT: KLEINS, RECORD HUNTER, BUFFALO CLOTHIERS–NORWALK: SUNSHINE RECORDS, CROSSROADS–FAIRFIELD: IDEA–STAMFORD:THROUGH THE LOOKING GLASS–DARIEN:MUSIC BOX

concert, near Buffalo, as a poorly attended, dismal affair with everyone in a dark mood.

Jimmi Seiter, the group's long-standing road manager, trusted minder, and lately on-stage percussionist, decides to leave the group here and now, this weekend. He has served The Byrds since 1966 but is fed up by deteriorating relationships between group members. The man who has so expertly handled the roles of "tour guide, babysitter, bodyguard, Mummy and Daddy" (as his roll-call of honours reads on *Byrdmaniax*) will continue in the music business, working with Gram Parsons and Alice Cooper among others.

•

Skip Battin moves to northern California this month, while Gene Parsons has already upped his L.A. roots and settled in the small town of Caspar, CA, a little north of San Francisco.

'Glory, Glory'

A 'Glory, Glory' (A. REYNOLDS)
B 'Citizen Kane'
(S. BATTIN/K. FOWLEY)

US release August 20 1971 (Columbia 45440)
UK release October 1 1971 (CBS 7501)
Chart high US number 110; UK none
Read more ... entries for January 11 and 17 1971

September

Saturday 4
Convention Hall, Asbury Park, NJ

Sunday 5
South Shore Music Circus, Cohasset, MA

Wednesday 8
Manhattan Center Ballroom, Manhattan, New York, NY
A concert with Bonnie Raitt.

Saturday 11
Gymnasium, Fairleigh Dickinson University, Rutherford, NJ

Sunday 12
Woods Brown Amphitheatre, American University, Washington, DC
US RADIO American University has a licence on it own public radio station, WAMU-FM 88.5, which tapes and later broadcasts the group's performance here. The set is a slight development of the spring repertoire, but apparently several songs have been cut from the transmission. The broadcast features: 'Lover Of The Bayou', 'So You Want To Be A Rock'n'Roll Star', 'Mr. Spaceman', 'I Wanna Grow Up To Be A Politician', 'Soldier's Joy'/'Black Mountain Rag', 'Mr. Tambourine Man', 'Pretty Boy Floyd', 'Nashville West', 'Citizen Kane', 'Tiffany Queen', 'Chestnut Mare', 'Jesus Is Just Alright', 'Eight Miles High', 'Hold It (Break Song)', and 'Roll Over Beethoven'.

Friday 17
Dutch television re-broadcasts parts of *Midweek*, the TV show taped during the European tour (see May 31 and June 23). Adding eight previously-screened songs by The Flying Burrito Brothers, the hour-long *Het Byrdssyndicaat* (Nederland 1 VARA at 7:05–7:55pm) features The Byrds playing 'You Ain't Going Nowhere', 'My Back Pages'/'BJ Blues'/'Baby What You Want Me To Do', 'Chestnut Mare', 'Jesus Is Just Alright', 'Take A Whiff', 'So You Want To Be A Rock'n'Roll Star', and 'Baby What You Want Me To Do' (reprise).

Wednesday 22
The Music Hall, Boston, MA
The review in *The Mass Media* (October 4) gives a graphic description of the ups and downs of a Byrds performance careening from the powerful to the pathetic. Michael McDonough writes: "Rock music, by its very nature, should be a real interaction between the audience and the band, and Wednesday night at the Music Hall, The Byrds came on, delivered their product to the consumers, and left. McGuinn and company are a nice mediocre rock band from the 60s that has made its mark, created an audience, and is now satisfied to rest on its past accomplishments.

"It's too bad, because when the band first came on stage, for those first few moments when they took control and launched into their demonic 'Lover Of The Bayou', McGuinn in his leather pants and shoulder length blond fair, Clarence White looking an evil country gentleman, ripping off nasty little leads, and the drums and bass providing a good heavy bottom, for these first few moments they were great. Really great. The formula was working, their emotional detachment was perfect, it fit the tune well. As they progressed into their set, however, they faltered. What had been a proud, sneering aloofness quickly became a general disinterest, and what had been a real live rock band soon degenerated into something as stiff and mechanical as a jukebox."

Things perk up briefly when the group straps on acoustic guitars. "[The group] once again started out superbly. They went through several tunes, showing off Clarence White's guitar picking and generally playing damn good country music. They even did an acoustic version of 'Mr Tambourine Man', one of the best I've ever heard. The audience received each number with prolonged applause and kept calling for more ('Get it on!'). The problem was that as anxious as the audience was to hear more, The Byrds were just as anxious to get it over with, which they did shortly."

Back to electricity, and the man from *Mass Media* complains of a jump in volume with each song played, until 'Eight Miles High', which is "generally boring and lacked direction and had one of the blandest bass solos I've ever heard". The audience does not seem to mind, as people dance in the aisles and the group is called back for two encores, 'Roll Over Beethoven' and 'Old Blue'. (Earlier in the evening, J.F. Murphy & Salt provided the opening slot.)

Friday 24
Wesleyan Arena, Wesleyan University, Middletown, CT
A proposed two-night stand at the Capitol Theatre, Port Chester, NY, this Friday and Saturday is called off.

ALSO …
Bob Dylan records with folk guitarist Happy Traum in New York City, putting on tape four songs earmarked as extra cuts for the double album *Bob Dylan's Greatest Hits Volume II* for November release. Dylan is scarcely in a recording studio this year, much less recording any genuinely new material. Three of the songs cut today are re-recordings of the already infamous basement reels from Dylan's Woodstock hibernation 1966–67: 'I Shall Be Released', 'Crash On The Levee', and 'You Ain't Going Nowhere', while the fourth song – 'Only A Hobo' – will remain unreleased for another 20 years.

Roger McGuinn's take on 'You Ain't Going Nowhere' on *Sweetheart Of The Rodeo* contained a slip of the tongue, as he mistakenly twisted the original Dylan lyric "Pick up your money/pack up your tent" as "Pack up your money/pick up your tent". For the version Dylan records today, he rewrites the introductory verse, keeps McGuinn's mistake, and pays double homage to The Byrds: "Cloud so swift the rain fallin' in/Gonna see a movie called 'Gunga Din'/Pack up your money, pull up your tent, McGuinn!"

Saturday 25
Carmichael Auditorium, University of North Carolina, Chapel Hill, NC
An enterprising person tapes tonight's concert, which will later circulate among Byrds collectors. The tape documents the Byrds repertoire this fall. 'Lover Of The Bayou' remains the opening number, and the expected mix of hits and Dylan songs are of course here. 'So You Want To Be A Rock'n'Roll Star' and 'Mr. Spaceman' have moved up from the encore slot to take their natural position at the beginning of the set.

The acoustic break has become a mid-show ritual, now expanded to include the rousing bluegrass number 'Roll In My Sweet Baby's Arms'. White sings two lead vocals ('Bugler' and 'Truck Stop Girl'), but Battin is stripped of his solo vocal showcase ('Citizen Kane' was part of the set in the summer) although he is the cheerleader on 'Roll In My Sweet Baby's Arms'. Just one song – 'I Wanna Grow Up To Be A Politician' (with McGuinn on banjo) – has survived the transition from *Byrdmaniax* to the live act, while only 'Tiffany Queen' and White's 'Bugler' are considered worthy stage material from the summer's London sessions. 'Eight Miles High' remains a cornerstone, while a couple of minor Byrds classic ('Drug Store Truck Drivin' Man' and 'Old Blue') are dusted off and brought back as encores on this occasion.

The complete tape contains: [Electric] 'Lover Of The Bayou', 'So You Want To Be A Rock'n'Roll Star', 'Mr. Spaceman', 'Bugler', 'I Wanna Grow Up To Be A Politician', 'My Back Pages'; [Acoustic] 'Black Mountain Rag', 'Mr. Tambourine Man', 'Pretty Boy Floyd', 'Roll In

285

My Sweet Baby's Arms'; [Electric] 'You Ain't Going Nowhere', 'Nashville West', 'Tiffany Queen', 'Truck Stop Girl', 'Chestnut Mare', 'Jesus Is Just Alright', 'Eight Miles High', 'Drug Store Truck Driving Man', 'Old Blue', and 'Roll Over Beethoven'.

Sunday 26
Gymnasium, Middlesex County College, Edison, NJ

The Middlesex's student publication *Quo Vadis* gives the group a good review (October 7). Following a performance by local New Jersey group Heavy Trucking, The Byrds delight the crowd with two electric sets and one acoustic spot. Called back for three encores, the group also tips its hat to the past with a rendition of Gene Clark's 'I'll Feel A Whole Lot Better'. Despite a near capacity crowd, the student committee suffers a loss after expenses are paid. The Byrds' fee is $7,500.

October

Friday 1

The 'Glory Glory'/'Citizen Kane' single, already out in the States, is released in the UK. David Hughes of *Disc* (October 9) comments: "There's something of a mythical aura surrounding the Byrds. I tend to think of their fans liking everything they do, whether it's good, indifferent or plain awful – and they've had songs in all of those categories. Still, myth aside, this is from the *Byrdmaniax* album and was exceptionally well received during their set at the Lincoln festival, probably because it is such a good live sound. One of those join-in-and-sing gospelly things with tambourine, fast paddy drums, Leon Russell-style piano and a good rolling chorus. McGuinn sings the main vocal with the others in unison but well in the background. Sadly, much of the live atmosphere is lost in the studio and it sticks at the same volume and tempo throughout, suffering from lack of light and shade." He terms the single quite correctly a 'no hit'.

Melody Maker does not review it but gives it to Keith Emerson to spin in his Blind Date guest spot (October 9). "I still can't quite suss out the singer. I'd say it was The Byrds. B-i-n-g! Their last album I bought was *The Notorious Byrd Brothers*. The piano intro was like the intro to a Joe Cocker tune. But I like the piano steaming along. The guitar solo didn't happen. They seem to be on a Jesus trip – laying their burden down. ... Because of the record player you are using, there is a lot of sibilance on the voice. When is the *MM* going to get a good stereo?"

Friday 8
Auditorium Theatre, Chicago, IL

The Byrds return to McGuinn's hometown for a disappointing half-filled house with singer Bonnie Koloc in support. The city's major

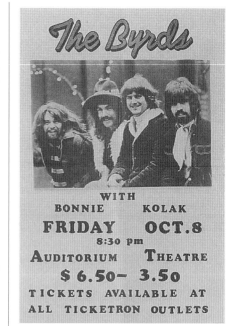

papers cover the show, and Lynn Van Matre notes in *The Chicago Tribune* (October 11): "Having gone through at least ten personnel changes (conservatively speaking) since those first folk-rock days – with lead guitarist and vocalist Roger McGuinn the only constant in the now four-man group – The Byrds are neither who or quite what they were then. As times and trends change, it often happens that the innovators get left behind, and this seems to have been the case with The Byrds – today at any rate. But they are still solid."

Jack Hafferkamp says in *The Chicago Daily News* (October 11): "Today's Byrds ... are probably better than any of the previous configurations. Yet in spite of all their combined abilities, it's overwhelmingly true that when you're hot, you're hot, and when you're not, you're etc. Right now The Byrds are not hot. McGuinn himself said so when I talked to him last week. The idea of this concert, he said, was to rekindle an interest in the group and its new recording, *Byrdmaniax*. ... But if McGuinn was disappointed by the small audience Friday night, it didn't show. The Byrds played a fine, long set. In addition to their regular electric material, they also did several songs acoustically. At least that's how the objective side of me would report it. My other half often had a hard time paying attention. I kept thinking that I had heard it all before. Sort of the 'who wants yesterday's news' concept."

ALSO ...

Stephen Stills has just settled in at Miami's Criteria Studios to start work on a new project. Drummers Dallas Taylor and Joe Lala are

---

Greatest Hits Vol. II (UK)

A1 'Ballad Of Easy Rider' (R. MCGUINN)
A2 'Jesus Is Just Alright' (A. REYNOLDS)
A3 'Chestnut Mare' (R. MCGUINN/J. LEVY)
A4 'You Ain't Going Nowhere' (B. DYLAN)
A5 'I Am A Pilgrim' (TRAD. ARR. R. MCGUINN/C. HILLMAN)
A6 'Goin' Back' (C. KING/G. GOFFIN)
B1 'I Trust' (R. MCGUINN)
B2 'Lay Lady Lay' (B. DYLAN)
B3 'Drug Store Truck Drivin' Man' (R. MCGUINN/G. PARSONS)
B4 'Wasn't Born To Follow' (C. KING/G. GOFFIN)
B5 'The Times They Are A-Changin'' (B. DYLAN)
B6 'Get To You' (R. MCGUINN/C. HILLMAN)

UK release October 29 1971 (CBS S 64650)
Chart high UK none
Read more ... entry for October 29

"As the sleeve notes points out, The Byrds ... were always at the vanguard of intelligent music, and this second volume of their best-known tracks ably demonstrates their skill as interpreters and writers. There's something of an indefinable spirit, an infectiousness, about everything they touch." NEW MUSICAL EXPRESS, OCTOBER 30, 1971

there with him, and he has three Burrito Brothers, Chris Hillman, Al Perkins, and Rick Roberts, flown down to Florida. Also here this weekend in Miami is Bill Wyman, who drops by to co-write and record 'Love Gangster' with Stills today.

The Flying Burrito Brothers are in a state of flux at the moment after Bernie Leadon left in the summer to form The Eagles, but have evolved into a seven-man self-contained revue capable of playing the purest bluegrass, some rocking rhythm & blues, and hard country.

Saturday 9
Kent State University, Kent, OH

Thursday 14
The film from last year's Kralingen festival in the Netherlands (see June 27, 1970) premiers in West Germany. Called *Love And Music* (sometimes known as *Rock Fieber*), the title is later changed to *Stamping Ground* for next year's US distribution. The film features The Byrds performing 'Old Blue', plus Al Stewart; Dr. John The Night Tripper; Family; Tyrannosaurus Rex; Canned Heat; Jefferson Airplane; Flock; It's A Beautiful Day; Country Joe; Santana; and Pink Floyd.

Friday 15
Agriculture and Technology College, State University of New York (SUNY), Morrisville, NY

Saturday 16
Heiges Field House, Shippensburg State College, Shippensburg, PA

The Byrds are originally booked for Shady Grove, Gaithersburg, MD, tonight, but the date is later replaced with this Pennsylvania show, together with someone who calls himself just plain Fred.

Sunday 17
Shea Auditorium, William Patterson College, Wayne, NJ

John Byrne of the Patterson student paper sits down with White and Parsons for an interesting chat, published in *The State Beacon* (October 26 and November 17). Three topics of particular merit are discussed. One regards the process leading up to the new album; another is White's relationship to Parsons; and the last centres on the first inklings of a reunion of the original Byrds – news that eventually will lead to the downfall of the present Byrds.

After Parsons dismisses *Byrdmaniax* as "a piece of shit", he talks about the London sessions. "That new album, we did it in five days in England. I mean, the whole thing, except for one or two tracks we had to remix in L.A.

But all the cutting was done within five days: we worked from 12 midnight to 2 in the morning, every night, for five nights, so that no one would come and bother us. And it's real natural and real live sounding. You know it's just us, no one else but us, on the album."

The parting with Terry Melcher may have been painful, but White gives the producer his due. "Terry is an incredible producer, no matter what anybody says. He started out really good; he got us back into the market. Let's face it, he did The Byrds' first album, Mr. Tambourine Man, the second album, and then The Byrds fired him. … When we got him back, it was for [Ballad Of] Easy Rider, and that brought us right back into the market. But with each album, he got a little too far out for The Byrds."

White recalls Chris Hillman's attempts to get him into the original Flying Burrito Brothers back in 1968. "[But when] he mentioned Gram Parsons, I said no, because I can't work with scatterbrain people. He would've drove me completely crazy!"

White does not think too highly of David Crosby, either. "Now, David has some rotten things to say about the new Byrds, and he doesn't know any one of us, so he doesn't have the right to say it. Crosby has always been talking about how the original Byrds are much better than the new group is now. He has to be some sort of idiot to believe what's he's saying. I agree: he was an idiot and he's paying karma for it.

"[Now] he's trying to talk Roger into doing …" White breaks off and explains that what he's about to say has never been revealed apart from in his discussions with McGuinn. "David Crosby approached Roger to get the old Byrds together and do an album. So, in other words, he's not doing so good."

The student reporter wonders what White's reaction was to this idea. "Well, [McGuinn] was looking for opinions, and I said I think he'd be stooping low to do it with [Crosby] because he never had anything good to say about the new group. He never gave the new group a chance, he said you were hard to work with. Why should you stoop down at that level: you're not running to him and asking him to do an album. He's running to you. And I said [to McGuinn] do you need him? He said, 'No I don't really need him; I've got everything I want here.' So, tell him you're too busy. There's always a time when people screw you around like that but always pay for it later. That's the reason you just forget about him. You don't worry about what they say."

Crosby's comment to Ben Fong-Torres in *Rolling Stone* in July of last year still rankles with White. There, Crosby said: "If they're going to use that name [The Byrds], I think

they should care more about what they're doing." Crosby dismissed McGuinn's crew, "the other cats", as "sidemen".

In all fairness, Crosby motives for reforming the original Byrds are, on the whole, born out of sincerity. And despite White's piece of advice, McGuinn will indeed go with Crosby and hatch a plan to put back together the five original Byrds.

Thursday 28
Belgian television broadcasts *Pop Shop: That's For The Byrds*, filmed at Vorst Nationaal in Brussels (see May 18) on RTBF at 6:25–6:55pm.

Friday 29
Shady Grove Music Fair, Gaithersburg, MD

Perhaps fearing that *Byrdmaniax* is not what the European fans want, Columbia compiles a second greatest-hits volume for the British market. Plainly titled *The Byrds Greatest Hits Volume 2* and released today, this collection gathers many but not all of the UK singles released since the first greatest hits album in October 1967 (an obvious omission is 'Lady Friend') plus some stray tracks that might loosely be filed as favourites ('Drug Store Truck Drivin' Man', 'Wasn't Born To Follow', 'The Times They Are A-Changin'', and 'Get To You'). The title is a deliberate misinterpretation: only 'Chestnut Mare' has been a genuine hit.

New Musical Express writes (October 30): "The 'greatest hits' tag is a bit of a misnomer but this 'best of' set is an indispensable acquisition for any student of the cream of American rock, particularly of the roots and influences. As the sleeve notes points out, The Byrds through a mesmerising series of personnel changes were always at the vanguard of intelligent music, and this second volume of their best-known tracks ably demonstrates their skill as interpreters and writers. There's something of an indefinable spirit, an infectiousness, about everything they touch."

Saturday 30
Painter's Mill Music Fair, Owings Mills, MD

Sunday 31
Gymnasium, Wilkes College, Wilkes-Barre, PA

November

Monday 1
New Commons Cafeteria, Fairleigh Dickinson University Gym, Teaneck, NJ

In September, the group visited the Fairleigh Dickinson's other campus in nearby Rutherford, NJ, and tonight they play FD's cafeteria in Teaneck with The Matchmakers. Wayne Riker from the university's newspaper (November 4) complains of McGuinn's on-stage behaviour ("marred by his egocentricity, puerility, and poor attitude") and concludes: "You can make a lot of money doing a dull routine performance at any rinky dink college, as The Byrds did on Monday night." Despite this, the reporter admits that they are "a very good group". He is taken with their "unique vocals (especially McGuinn's sensitive voice), and the imaginative bass filling by Battin combined precisely with Parsons's fast, accurate foot. Most impressive was Clarence White's almost perfect feel on guitar as his leads were tasteful, expressive, and creative; he is a master of note phrasing." The songs the group performs are also to Riker's liking, with the exception of 'Eight Miles High'. "A shame [that] a lyrical and musical giant of the 60s had to be included in a jam with a token verse at the end; it's like Simon & Garfunkel jamming on 'Old Friends'."

Friday 5
Memorial Gymnasium, Vanderbilt University, Nashville, TN

Saturday 6
University of Virginia, Charlottesville, VA

Surprisingly, The Beach Boys open for The Byrds in Charlottesville. Although commercial fortunes have been changing for The Beach Boys since their 60s heyday, they are still a hotter property than McGuinn's group. They are touring in support of the well-received *Surf's Up* (which makes the US Top 30) with a large ensemble of auxiliary musicians.

Thursday 11
'The New Rock & Roll Circus', Springer's Ballroom, Portland, OR

The Byrds fly up for a trio of dates in the Northwest, where the group is paired with singer-songwriter Bill Withers ('Ain't No Sunshine'). For this trip and in the future, the ground crew is expanded as new man Al Hersh joins as road manager to take Jimmi Seiter's place.

Friday 12
Paramount Northwest, Seattle, WA

Seattleite Neal Skok attends the concert and notes down the set list, revealing a fairly standard Byrds show but with a rare performance of the 'Bristol Steam Convention Blues' instrumental. The group performs 'Lover Of The Bayou', 'So You Want To Be A Rock'n'Roll Star', 'My Back Pages', 'Nashville West', 'Bugler', 'Jesus Is Just Alright', and then 'Baby What You Want Me To Do' crossing into a slightly elongated acoustic set: 'Black Mountain Rag', 'Mr. Tambourine Man', 'Pretty Boy Floyd', 'Bristol Steam Convention Blues', 'Roll In My Sweet Baby's Arms', and 'I Wanna Grow Up To Be A Politician'. The second electric set consists of 'Tiffany Queen', 'Truck Stop Girl', 'Chestnut Mare', and 'Eight Miles High/Tag/Break Song'. The encores are 'Roll Over Beethoven', 'Mr. Spaceman', and 'I'll Feel A Whole Lot Better'.

Saturday 13
RFK Pavilion, Gonzaga University, Spokane, WA

Wednesday 17
Farther Along is officially released in the US, although the in-the-store date seems to be several weeks later. Put out less than five months after *Byrdmaniax*, the group's 11th album of new material is the result of the quickest studio sessions in their entire career. Intended as a confidence-booster after the disappointing *Byrdmaniax*, the new album does not reclaim former glories. It is an improvement over its predecessor, but the stripped-down approach reveals The Byrds as handy craftsmen rather than innovative artists. The delayed damage caused by *Byrdmaniax* translates into poor sales – *Farther Along* stalls at US Number 152.

Music critic James Brown in *The Los Angeles Times* (February 13, 1972) cuts right to the core. "For those who cheered The Byrds in the mid 60s for their efforts in creating a happy medium between rock and folk music, *Farther Along* must serve as a definite low point. If not for the phenomenal success of 'Great National Pastime' (a novelty song if there ever was one) there would be absolutely nothing to recommend. The Byrds have seemingly traded in their originality to play the role of the country bumpkin desperately trying to think of new ways to say 'I

SATURDAY, NOVEMBER 20

BYRDS

"Their music is time-less—besides they've always been ahead of their time."
—Bud Scoppa, THE BYRDS

BLUE OYSTER CULT

"This is no Led Zeppelin, it's no helium zeppelin, it's hydrogen zeppelin, the real thing, the one and only."
—The New York Herald

MAHAVISHNU ORCHESTRA

featuring

JOHN McLAUGHLIN

"John McLaughlin, he's the one, that's the killer."
—Miles Davis, Zygote

TICKETS $3.00

S.U.N.Y. Cortland

Lusk Fieldhouse
ONE COSMIC SHOW
at 9

TICKETS AVAILABLE AT

Midtown Records Ithaca
Eggbert Union, Ithaca
Corey Union, Cortland
McNeil's, Cortland
Hi-Fi Records, Johnson City
Record Runner, Syracuse

love my baby'. As if hackneyed lyrics were not enough, The Byrds complement these with practically the same melody line for each song, in an effort, I presume, to get it right. The 'new' Byrds' answer to the old Byrds is a weak one indeed."

Rolling Stone (March 16, 1972) finds it OK. Ben Gerson says: "Clarence White continues to sing his tight-lipped white-gospel laments; Gene Parsons his love-lorn ballads. McGuinn and Skip Battin both do novelty songs, though in their more serious moments Battin's songs tend to have a spiritual cast, while Roger's tend to be pastel tributes to women." Going through the album song by song, Gerson notes of White's contribution: "'Bugler' perpetuates the tradition of Byrds animal songs like 'Old Blue' and 'Chestnut Mare', and like the other two is a childhood idyll. Clarence intones, 'Bugler, bugler, bless your hide/Jesus gonna take you for a chariot ride ...'." He notes dryly that "today, the occasional Byrds breakdown is more likely to be bluegrass than nervous," before observing that "[in] case you haven't already noticed, the key to all of this is that McGuinn (not to mention his 12-string and the traditional harmonies) no longer, in effect, dominates the group. If you believe, as I do, that The Byrds, with some exceptions, have been supremely good only insofar as Roger has been in control, this fact can be the source of some chagrin. All of the other band members (their exceptional virtuosity aside) possess strong personalities and don't hesitate to express them, but they are also severely limited in their range.

"There is a programmatic certainty to their music at this point, which at first glance happily signifies that a first-generation band has successfully remade itself, but after repeated exposure disappoints one with its inflexibility. And McGuinn, as just one member out of four, seems rather as predictable as the rest. This is not an outstanding album, either by Byrds or contemporary standards, though, for at least a Byrds fan, it contains several seductive tunes and some exemplary musicianship. But beneath the old Byrds sound, and this new, quartered approach, there is a more fundamental commitment, and that is to survival.

"The Byrds, I think, are entertaining in the old-fashioned sense. They release albums at amazingly regular intervals; they continue to be one of America's best performing bands, and wind up each performance with the kind of break bar-bands use to designate the end of a set. McGuinn, like the elder Muddy Waters or T-Bone Walker, lays back; after years of scuffling along, he, like those older bluesmen, is happy to let the rest of the band do the majority of the work. Digging in for the long haul entails a slowed pace of growth, a curtailment of artistic ferment. Yet in an age of meteoric rises and falls, sheer longevity is unfashionably reassuring."

Andy Mellen in *The Winnipeg Free Press* (February 19, 1972) represents the many who, considering it all, are relieved that The Byrds have come back after the creative dip of their previous albums. He notes: "[While] not being anywhere the equal of *Younger Than Yesterday* or even *Dr. Byrds and Mr. Hyde*, [it] is an encouraging LP, offering some assurance that Roger McGuinn and friends still have their fingers on the pulse of what's happening musically in 1972.

"*Farther Along* is a happy surprise, a gloriously shining ray of light after that brief but unfortunate dark spell. If you had given up hope for The Byrds, give them one more chance and I'm sure you'll be convinced that the good times are here again. Yeah. Jesus Is Just Alright with me; so are The Byrds."

A view seconded by an upbeat Fred Sternlicht in the Stony Brook student paper *Statesman* (December 10), who writes: "The new disc ... demonstrates McGuinn mastery of the three minute song. Although all four Byrds contribute songs, McGuinn's dominance is present as the master of economy in idea. Nothing on this album is superfluous to the songs contained thereon. Most of the rest of the album is [a] tour de force or the various techniques for which The Byrds have become known ... The album is, in short, typically superb. Every song is a potential favourite of mine, so I won't even try to pick one."

Thursday 18
University of New Hampshire, Durham, NH
Columbia Records help bankroll a two-part, seven-date promotional tour by three of the company's groups. On paper, it is a disparate threesome sandwiching The Byrds between the heavy metal thunder of Blue Öyster Cult and the high voltage jazz jolt of John McLaughlin's Mahavishnu Orchestra.

Saturday 20
Lusk Field House, State University of New York (SUNY), Cortland, NY
Second show with Blue Öyster Cult and McLaughlin's Mahavishnu Orchestra. The three groups come together again for five concerts in December.

Wednesday 24
Hollywood Palladium, Los Angeles, CA
The Byrds, Delaney & Bonnie & Friends, and Mason Proffit are not a strong enough bill to sell more than half of the Palladium's 5,000 capacity. Trade paper *Amusement Business* notes that new promoter Chris Fritz simply disappears after the show.

The Los Angeles Times (November 27) says: "Once upon a time, in the innocent pre-funk days of 1965, good folk shook their heads and the little girls freaked over the antics of Jim McGuinn and his bee-you-tee-ful Byrds. They were strictly West Hollywood product, a sprawling, vital, enormously sensuous band. Since then, incalculable rock bands have passed through town, but the various Byrd-bands have remained, if not quite a joy forever, then at least a most reliable indication of pop's various directions, declines, and falls. Besides, they kept their magic beat. The Byrds brought that magic beat back to the Strip Thanksgiving Eve, and were greeted by a goodly audience of their admirers at a positively wholesome Palladium dance-concert.

"When The Byrds are good, they are very very good; when they're bad, they're atrocious. From almost any point of view, The Byrds were very very good. As nostalgia, rock, roll – it hardly matters which. They played their hits, the spiritual ones like 'Mr. Tambourine Man', the tongue-in-cheek ones like 'So You Want To Be A Rock'n'Roll Star', the ones that the crowd called out for. And also weaved in some of their new tunes." The review goes on to list the members of the present incarnation, saying that The Byrds without McGuinn would be "like The Great Gatsby without Gatsby".

Friday 26
PNE Gardens, Vancouver, British Columbia, Canada
A weekend north of the border in Canada for the group, starting with a Friday concert with Chief Dan George & Fireweed. The turn-out is insufficient, but The Byrds rise to the occasion anyway, according to Brian McLeod in *The Vancouver Sun* (November 27). "I think

Farther Along

A1 'Tiffany Queen' (R. MCGUINN)
A2 'Get Down Your Line' (GENE PARSONS)
A3 'Farther Along' (TRAD. ARR. C. WHITE)
A4 'B.B. Class Road' (GENE PARSONS/S. DAWSON)
A5 'Bugler' (L. MURRAY)
B1 'America's Great National Pastime' (S. BATTIN/K. FOWLEY)
B2 'Antique Sandy' (R. MCGUINN/S. BATTIN/GENE PARSONS/C. WHITE/J. SEITER)
B3 'Precious Kate' (S. BATTIN/K. FOWLEY)
B4 'So Fine' (J. OTIS)
B5 'Lazy Waters' (B. RAFKIN)
B6 'Bristol Steam Convention Blues' (GENE PARSONS/C. WHITE)

US release November 17 1971 (Columbia KC 30150)
UK release January 21 1972 (CBS S 64676)
Chart high US number 152; UK none
Read more ... entries for July 22, 25–26, 27, 28, undated August 1971

Bonus CD tracks: 'Lost My Drivin' Wheel' (D. Wiffen), 'Born To Rock 'n' Roll' (R. McGuinn), 'Bag Full Of Money' (R. McGuinn/J. Levy)

"For those who cheered The Byrds in the mid 60s for their efforts in creating a happy medium between rock and folk music, Farther Along *must serve as a definite low point ...The Byrds have seemingly traded in their originality to play the role of the country bumpkin desperately trying to think of new ways to say 'I love my baby'."*
THE LOS ANGELES TIMES, FEBRUARY 13, 1972

289

there's a correlation between small numbers and good music. It seems that when a concert turns turtle at the turnstiles, it provides that perfect breathing space for the musicians to stretch out, like a bevy of cats on a not-too-warm afternoon. When that happens, the music takes on that peculiar magical quality that goes far beyond mere patterns of notes and chords. There was just such a performance Friday night at the PNE Gardens. And the basic reason behind the whole gathering was the L.A.-based musical museum known as The Byrds.

Moose Valley Farms presents

FRIDAY NOV. 26 **THE BYRDS** (with fireweed) 8:30 – GARDENS
TICKETS AT GASTOWN TICKET CENTER AND OUTLETS. PH 687-2537

"The Byrds have a unique kind of power, the kind that you get from flying eight miles high for more than six years. When they play, the audience is very much their audience, a group that remembers all of the old milestones like 'Eight Miles High', and 'Mr. Tambourine Man'.

"The Byrds, under the ever watchful eye of Roger McGuinn, are only too pleased to gratify the audience's desires; but on Byrd terms, which roughly translated means that the song may be the same, with the rhythm and guitar licks changed to protect the innocent ghosts of such former flyers as David Crosby and Chris Hillman.

"There's no doubt about it: McGuinn has his fingers on the pulse of time in the today

'America's Great National Pastime'

A 'America's Great National Pastime' (S. BATTIN/K. FOWLEY)
B 'Farther Along' (TRAD. ARR. C. WHITE)

US release November 29 1971 (Columbia 45514)
UK release January 1972 (CBS 7712) [possibly withdrawn]
Chart high US none; UK none
Read more ... entries for July 25–26, 27 1971

sense, and it shows in the subtle little ways in which he modifies the music his boys make with each passing year. A busier bass here and a meaner guitar lick there, and presto, The Byrds leap into the space age like any other 70s heavy. One little touch I couldn't help but smile over was the unique bluegrass acoustic means with which the Byrds translated 'Mr. Tambourine Man'. Considering the Dylan acoustic origins of the song, it was an interesting exercise in full cycles. And the audience lapped it up like an animated barn looking for a dance."

Saturday 27
The Corral, Calgary Stampede, Calgary, Alberta, Canada
Fireweed, Northwest Company, and the Seeds Of Time play support to The Byrds. Seeing the large contingent of cowboy hats in the audience, McGuinn shuffles the set a bit to emphasise the group's country sounds. The performance is welcomed by Ellen Nygaard of *The Calgary Herald* (November 29). "The Byrds plugged their well-worn guitars into $90,000 worth of equipment and put the other groups to shame in every respect. To give the previous bands credit, there are very few musicians as professional as The Byrds. With only one man remaining from the original (circa 1965) Byrds, Roger McGuinn, they have managed to preserve their unique sound and tight arrangements. For over an hour, they moved almost non-stop from 'So You Want To Be A Rock'n'Roll Star', through 'Nashville West', an instrumental, to a final encore of 'Roll Over Beethoven'.

"At this point in the evening, my usually surly critic's disposition disappeared completely. From here on, I shall be forced to rhapsodise. The incredible versatility of all four members of the band ... was evident in the range of their repertoire. They performed their favourite country-bluegrass style, early rock'n'roll, and hard rock with equal expertise. In an unrecorded version of 'Mr. Tambourine Man', McGuinn and White used acoustic guitars, with excellent back-up from Parsons on harmonica and Battin on bass, to produce a country-blues arrangement as good as and possibly better than the original. They switched abruptly to rock about as hard as anyone could want it, with a 20-minute version of 'Eight Miles High'. Battin, probably one of the best bass players in the business, undertook a lengthy solo with unbelievable poise and accuracy.

"One member of the crowd was moved to comment that he suspected at first the sound was being dubbed. 'But they were playing it,' he gasped. Probably the most pleasant aspect of the performance, excluding the superb

musicianship, was the professional stage presentation. While the other bands had treated us to several minutes of nonsensical chatter, including a brief argument between the lighting technician and the first band, The Byrds played two numbers before saying a word. They moved smoothly from song to song, not bothering to inflict their stage chatter on the 2,000 in attendance."

Sunday 28
Kinsmen Fieldhouse, Edmonton, Alberta, Canada
After the positive reviews for the Friday and Saturday concerts, Jon Faulds in *The Edmonton Journal* (November 29) sums up the Canadian mini-tour on a down note. "Ooooh, groan ... not another rock show, the disgruntled teenager mumbled amid general rumblings of discontent. Yes, my son, tonight it is thy duty to attend The Byrds at the Kinsmen Fieldhouse on pain of betraying thy youthful principles, the six shows you have seen in the past two weeks notwithstanding. I exaggerate of course, but it seemed to me that the majority of the rather small crowd at the Kinsmen Fieldhouse last night was there as much out of habit as anything else.

"Responding perhaps to this unexciting attitude, The Byrds put on an unexciting performance that sparkled just occasionally enough to reassure us of their professional status. As was expected, they performed a number of selections for which they are justly famous: 'Mr. Tambourine Man', 'My Back Pages' to name two. Regrettably, the band last night bore little resemblance to that which originally made these songs renowned. The two having only guitarist Roger McGuinn in common. They could not perform them in the spirit in which they were conceived and, after the initial pleased recognition, the songs had little appeal."

The acoustic set is the night's only bright moment according to Faulds. "[The] Byrds settled back into a style a little closer to their collective hearts at the moment: traditional folk and bluegrass tunes for acoustic guitars.

Here, guitarist Clarence White was in his element. Reared on old-time fiddle tunes and Canadian jigs, and having toured in a band with his brothers who called themselves The Kentucky Colonels, he picked his way through the traditional 'clichés' with a dexterity that highlighted his taste rather than overshadowing it. The enthusiasm with which his intricate running accompaniment was received peaked during his excursions on the mandolin, on which he was joined by the drummer doubling on banjo, McGuinn backing on 12-string guitar, and the bassist. Together they presented a rather incongruous sight, two parts back-to-the-land longhairs, one part Mexican desperado, one part mod sophisticate, connected only because they happened to be playing that airy confection, traditional folk music, with obvious skill and not so obvious pleasure."

As soon as this is over and electricity returns, The Byrds "managed to lose all the identity they had managed to build up with the traditional by wasting their time with a few undistinguished rock boogies. Following those were a couple of country items in which White's frenetic guitar clashed with the songs' otherwise easy flow. A bass solo sparked a moment's absorbed attention with an involved passage of difficult slurs, executed excellently, that nonetheless did not quite justify the solo's length. The Byrds displayed little satisfaction with their performance and appeared only too happy to leave the stage after it was over, to the traditional standing applause. A standing ovation in Edmonton has lost all meaning completely." (As with yesterday's date, The Seeds Of Time are second on the bill tonight.)

Monday 29
Skip Battin and Kim Fowley's 'America's Great National Pastime' coupled with 'Farther Along' is the new Byrds single in the US. A novelty track off *Farther Along* with no discernable Byrd-sound at all, the single receives strong airplay on the West Coast but fails to chart.

December

Friday 3
**University of Maine,
Bangor, ME**
Following the two dates on the Columbia promo jaunt in the middle of November, The Byrds, Blue Öyster Cult, and John McLaughlin's Mahavishnu Orchestra head out on the road again for a further five dates on the East Coast.

Saturday 4
**Keaney Gymnasium,
University of Rhode Island, Kingston,
South Kingstown, RI**
An undated review from tonight's Rhode Island show, authored by Mike Lynn, says of The Byrds: "They seemed about as excited about performing in Rhode Island as I was about having my hand stepped on by a confused young lady. And the audience was not much better. They seemed to be in a [hypnotist] Kreskin-like trance."

Then something happens. "Toward the end of the performance an atmosphere of subtle warmth began to build. The Byrds went off quietly after their final number, and then out of nowhere came this immense standing ovation. The people woke up! The Byrds came back, and all of a sudden the evening took a drastic turn for the better. People stood up and danced, the performers began to move around. They even smiled. The kind of thing you see at a good concert. Off they went after two encores, and back they came after another standing ovation. And now The Byrds were really hot. The music came out sweet and the lyrics were sung with some feeling. Smiles appeared on the no-longer sleepy faces. Everyone was standing up clapping, having a gay old time. Then it ended, just as it was starting."

📷 **FILMING** The whole concert is filmed professionally, but it appears that no footage of either The Byrds, Blue Öyster Cult, or The Mahavishnu Orchestra will survive. "I am still confused as to why Columbia sent all those men and spent all that money to film a concert in a run-down, half-filled gym," writes Lynn. "I imagine someone at Columbia is wondering the same thing."

Thursday 9
**Clarkson College of Technology,
Potsdam, NY**
The Byrds, Blue Öyster Cult, and The Mahavishnu Orchestra.

Friday 10
**Patrick Gymnasium, University of
Vermont, Burlington, VT**
The Byrds, Blue Öyster Cult, and The Mahavishnu Orchestra.

Saturday 11
**Pritchard Gymnasium, State University
of New York (SUNY), Stony Brook, NY**
The review in *The Statesman* (December 17) pinpoints the trouble with matching three such arbitrary acts on a single bill. Tonight there are two houses, and, with changeovers, this results in an over-long night. "I would like to know who puts together these hopeless three-part shows. ... Here I would like to gripe that there was absolutely no reason for a third group in the late show. John McLaughlin is fine, probably one of the best guitarists in his field. ... Together The Mahavishnu Orchestra plays some haunting tunes with a fine jazz oriented backing. But what about Blue Öyster Cult? I refuse to waste the space.

"But, ah, The Byrds, actually you couldn't really ask for a finer bunch of musicians. Roger McGuinn, formerly Jim, finally got it together after all those rocky years that included the

departures of David Crosby (who?), Chris Hillman, Mike Clarke, and Gene Clark, the Byrd who wouldn't fly. That was in the old days, circa 1965. ... Since then all of McGuinn's Byrds have either left for stardom or gone to The Flying Burrito Brothers.

"At one point in the concert Saturday night The Byrds put down their electric rock'n'roll symbols and picked up acoustic instruments. Even the drummer helped with a little banjo and harp. They got it together to play some really fine down-home country and bluegrass music. It seems as if The Byrds really know what it is to make fine music as well as treat a crowd to some old-time big hits. One of their best tributes was the fact that when they left at a quarter to five [in the morning] almost everybody was still there to give them a well deserved standing ovation. I think that the majority of people who were at the concert would agree that The Byrds were a good thing for Stony Brook."

Sunday 12
Richmond Arena, Richmond, VA
This appearance in Richmond is tagged on after the Columbia promo tour, and will be the last Byrds concert until the new year. Coming back to Los Angeles, the group spends Christmas at home. As life off the road temporarily returns to normality, McGuinn uses the opportunity to marry Linda Gilbert, while Dinky Dawson contemplates the future. "I began to wonder what the point was in touring if everyone had to be so miserable to each other," the group's soundman will later confess in his autobiography. "But since every other gig or so was still utterly brilliant, everyone simply accepted the negatives now, because the few moments of triumph on that stage seemed worth it – at least for the moment."

Roger McGuinn at Stony Brook, December 11, 1971.

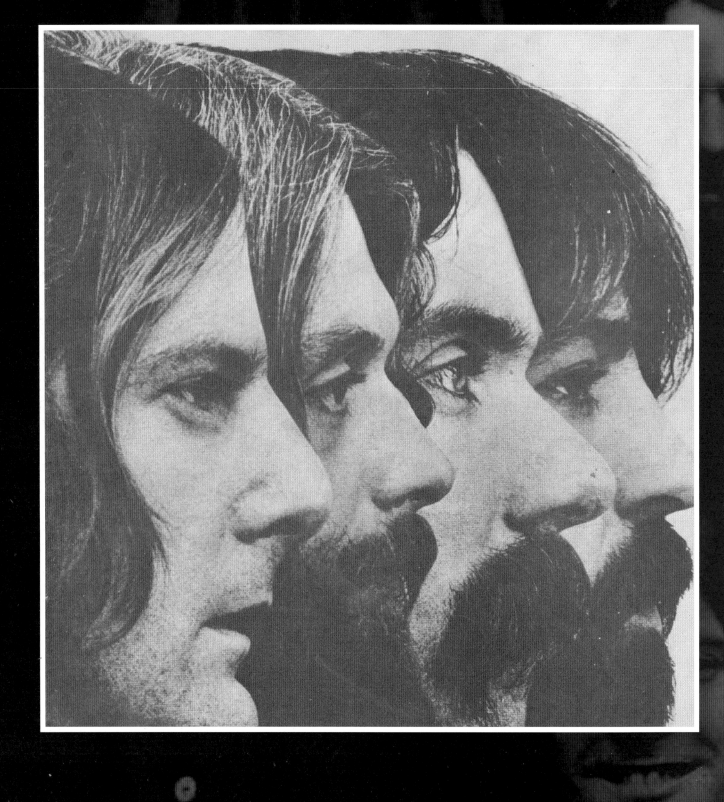

From left: Roger McGuinn, Skip Battin, Gene Parsons, Clarence White.

A hastily arranged overseas tour in January finds The Byrds making a **French debut** besides playing concerts in London, just as their twelfth album *Farther Along* is released in Europe ... **January newsflash** in England says **the original five Byrds will reunite** for recording and touring purposes ... The news takes time to break in the US, but by early spring a record

1972

deal is worked out, opening the way for a reunion to take place ... Meanwhile, the touring Byrds wind down at the end of May as Gene Parsons is fired ... New replacement is **studio ace John Guerin**, who makes his stage debut with the group in September ... A few scattered recording session by the touring Byrds are finally halted as **Gene Clark, Michael Clarke, David Crosby, Chris Hillman, and Roger McGuinn** record an album's worth of material under Crosby's guidance ... While the original Byrds rekindle old flames, the touring Byrds continue to undertake selected concerts.

January

Friday 7

The latest US Byrds single, 'America's Great National Pastime' coupled with 'Farther Along', is released in Europe in preparation for the group's overseas tour later in the month.

For reasons unknown, the single seems to be withdrawn in the UK, and none of the music weeklies carries a review. However, it is available in West Germany and the Netherlands.

Judy Sims reports in *Disc* this month (January 29) how the song is a big radio hit in California, although airplay in this case does not push the record into the US charts.

Wednesday 12

RECORDING Columbia Recording Studios, Sunset and El Centro, Hollywood, CA. Producers The Byrds.

The group – Roger McGuinn, Clarence White, Gene Parsons, and Skip Battin –gets together after a four-week layoff to record the rollicking 'Lost My Drivin' Wheel'. Written by David Wiffen and earlier covered by Tom Rush, the song may possibily be considered as a potential single with its elaborate guitar textures, smooth bass line and radio-friendly chorus. But the recording will not be heard until it is issued on a remastered version of *Farther Along* in 2000. It never becomes part of the group's stage repertoire, but McGuinn will re-record the song for his 1973 solo album in a less impressive version.

As it turns out, today's session will be one of the rare excursions to the studio this year by the Clarence White-era Byrds.

•

SESSION Hollywood correspondent Judy Sims, always a source to trust on the California music scene, reports in *Disc* (January 22) how Terry Melcher has just finished his first solo album. She informs readers that all original Byrds members except David Crosby appear on the finished product. "Terry does a couple of ex-Byrd Gene Clark's songs," Sims explains further.

Terry Melcher, as the album is called, will await release until the spring of 1974. By then, the announced Gene Clark songs are nowhere in sight, but there are other ties to The Byrds: Clarence White, Michael Clarke, and Chris Hillman are all credited as players on the album, and among the songs Melcher covers are McGuinn/Levy's *Gene Tryp* number 'Just A Season' and the traditional bluegrass number 'Roll In My Sweet Baby's Arms' that The Byrds have been performing in concert lately.

January 14–January 23, 1972: 8TH OVERSEAS TOUR (UK, FRANCE)

Friday 14

The Byrds arrive in Britain for a brief European tour. Soul singer Isaac Hayes has unexpectedly cancelled his European visit due to recording commitments in America, and The Byrds are asked to replace him at the annual MIDEM show in the south of France. The group have been vacationing and, as they have no bookings lined up until February, they eagerly pick up the option. The trips to Europe in 1970 and 1971 have infused The Byrds with renewed team spirit, but this visit will prove to be their last overseas journey. To fill up a blank itinerary besides the MIDEM appearance, a couple of London concerts and a show in Paris are booked on the fly.

Saturday 15

A hastily arranged press conference is staged in London.

Sunday 16

The Rainbow Theatre, Finsbury Park, north London

The Rainbow used to be the Finsbury Park Astoria, a venue The Byrds played during their first visit to the UK in August 1965. Then, the British music press panned them; now they are welcomed with open arms. The concert (with Tranquillity in support) is booked at such short notice that there is no time to run advertisements in the music press. Almost by word of mouth, the Sunday appearance sells out, and a second show is added the following day. The first night is not without hitches: the PA system wreaks havoc on the sound, but the lightshow with special effects for 'Eight Miles High' works smoothly.

Lon Goddard reports in *Record Mirror* (January 22): "The Rainbow is a great testing ground for upcoming acts, but sometimes it can be a real test for a pro as well. Full marks to Roger McGuinn and the other Byrds for not going berserk under the worst possible equipment difficulties. Loud crackles and an endless buzz remained throughout their long set, despite the attempts of anxious engineers to locate the problem. On numbers like 'Chestnut Mare', 'My Back Pages', 'Chimes Of Freedom', a strung-out version of 'Eight Miles High' and more, the volume drowned out the amp drone, but on acoustic numbers like 'Mr. Tambourine Man', it was occasionally noticeable. Between songs, it was very apparent. McGuinn's euphoric nature and sheer professionalism enabled him to plough through it where other lesser musicians would have walked off or put a boot through the

speakers. "Despite the problems, The Byrds played with grand flair, magnificent ability and unmistakable character. Each was brilliant: Clarence White and his blinding guitar work, Gene Parsons for terrific taste in drumming, Skip Battin for speedy, effortless and superb bass, and Roger for a great individual voice, fine guitar, good nature and trousers three inches too low."

Brian Southall of *Disc* (January 22) gives the concert top marks, even if he confuses Battin's name with that of UK rock group Skip Bifferty. "It's always nice to see a really professional band, and at the Rainbow theatre on Sunday night The Byrds proved that they are sheer professionals. Bugged throughout by really bad hums and buzzes from their equipment, they persevered and won over an audience only too willing to be won over with country-rock'n'roll. The interference got so bad that at times the four of them stood for minutes on end while technicians skilfully looked for the fault by kicking and punching the amps. Roger McGuinn summed up their frustration, 'In the old days we used to play without all this junk.'

"But despite it all, The Byrds proved that they rate amongst the world's greats with, in the conditions, tremendous versions of 'I Wanna Be A Politician', Skip Bifferty's 'Rollin' In My Lovin' Baby's Arms', and McGuinn excelling on 'Chestnut Mare'. There was Gene Parsons' expert banjo picking and, throughout, the fine lead guitar work of Clarence White. 'Mr. Tambourine Man' suffered at the hands of the hum and one or two wrong notes but there was still a certain magic about it.

"When they finally launched into an extended 'Eight Miles High' then they showed what a decade or more in the business does for you. It was brilliant, with Parsons and Bifferty combining in a most effective drum-bass duet, while McGuinn and White sent their guitars, if not quite eight miles high, certainly as high as they could get them. Two encores rounded the night off and a rip-roaring 'Roll Over Beethoven'."

Music World (January 22), a short-lived British rock weekly, points out that there "really isn't that much to say about The Byrds any more. Their legendary recordings of Dylan songs put them at the top of the tree in the mid 60s and, give or take a branch or two, they've stayed there." For writer Paul Phillips, the unplugged part is the most satisfying. "Lead guitarist Clarence White and drummer Gene Parsons come on like a hippie Flatt & Scruggs while McGuinn, visibly more at ease than with the electric music, sings up a real hoedown storm. Bassist Skip Battin smiled for the first time during his rendition of 'Roll In My Sweet Baby's Arms', and the whole acoustic set was something of an eye-opener. Why is it that a group like The Byrds can draw whoops and hollers from an audience that probably wouldn't be seen dead near the Wembley Country Music Festival?"

Monday 17
The Rainbow Theatre, Finsbury Park, north London

The Byrds and Tranquillity play a second show at London's Rainbow. An unofficial recording from the show reveals a near-identical repertoire to the group's sets from the end of 1971. A minor surprise is the reintroduction of Dylan's 'Chimes Of Freedom', which has been in and out of favour with the group since 1965.

The first electric set contains 'Lover Of The Bayou', 'So You Want To Be A Rock'n'Roll Star', 'Mr. Spaceman', 'Bugler', 'I Wanna Grow Up To Be A Politician', and 'My Back Pages'/'Baby What You Want Me To Do', before the group breaks for an acoustic interlude with 'Black Mountain Rag', 'Mr. Tambourine Man', 'Pretty Boy Floyd', and lastly 'Roll In My Sweet Baby's Arms', the singalong cheered on by Battin. The second electric set features 'Tiffany Queen', 'Chestnut Mare', 'Jesus Is Just Alright', 'Chimes Of Freedom', and 'Eight Miles High'/'Break Song'. Called back for an encore, The Byrds perform 'Nashville West', 'I'll Feel A Whole Lot Better', and 'Roll Over Beethoven'.

→ Tuesday 18

After a very late night at London's Speakeasy – where McGuinn falls asleep at his table – the group meets the music press for interviews today. Talking to Michael Watts of *Melody Maker* (January 29), McGuinn discusses the sound gremlins at the Rainbow performance. "First off, there was a power failure, so that had to be taken care of. And then the power came back on and it just melted the equipment. But the grounding [earth] wasn't right in any case. And after [that] I broke a string. It was the Rainbow's equipment as well as our own, and we were trying to coordinate the two and it didn't work, though we'd checked it out in rehearsals and it was OK."

On the subject of the previous album ("I hated *Byrdmaniax* … [it] was just an awful thing, and I think it hurt us"), McGuinn describes the dismissal of the group's ex-producer as a conflict of loyalty. "Maybe the times had just changed and it wasn't right for him or us. Terry [Melcher] had some problems with two of the guys in the group, Gene and Skip. He didn't get on with them, and that's part of the producer's job. I'd sooner work with him on my own than as part of the group, I think."

Noting McGuinn's pioneering use of the Moog synthesizer, Watts asks why he does not bring it out on the road. "Because those instruments get out-dated so quickly," McGuinn replies, "and they're too finicky, subject as they are to temperature and voltage changes." (Another player who shares McGuinn's passion is Pete Townshend. In a survey on the future of rock guitar in the same January issue of *Melody Maker* in which the McGuinn interview is printed, the Who guitarist says: "As a guitar player I am very interested in developments where a guitar can control a synthesizer. Roger McGuinn is trying the same thing because, like me, his piano playing is very limited. I see a future for the guitar, but probably only because I'm a guitar player myself. I am investing in a future for it by adding peripheral equipment to it.")

New Musical Express (January 22) publishes an interview with White and Parsons. Reporter Danny Holloway is an old fan – he first saw The Byrds at Long Beach in May 1965 supporting The Rolling Stones – and is keen to hear what constitutes Byrds music. White: "We wouldn't be honest if we played straight rock'n'roll music, because that's not what we feel. We have a lot of country influence and jazz and folk and rock, et cetera. If you're just natural and honest and just play what you feel, it's gonna represent everyone's influence on the group's music. I hope that it comes out a nice blend. I sorta like it."

Parsons, who so adamantly disliked *Byrdmaniax*, is happy with *Farther Along*. "That's a fairly pure album and it's a pretty fair representation of where we were at eight months ago. There's quite a cross-section of music – gospel, and rock'n'roll, boogies, there's even polkas on there and a bit of bluegrass. It's one of the best we've put out, I think."

Battin also gets in a word when interviewed by *Disc* (January 29). "Being a Byrd includes everything in my life," he tells Caroline Boucher. "It's a part of my life and I'm a part of its life – a very big part both ways." He talks about the new Byrds record. "It's a diversified album. It's clean, and we limited the things we did to ourselves without any augmentation – we produced it ourselves too, and learned a lot from that. Producing means getting the very best out of the performance, and by the best I mean capturing the emotion that the artist means to convey. The more perfectly you can convey the emotion to the ear of the listener, the better the production, and that involves getting the correct sound mechanically. And I think with this album we got down mostly first takes, or within the first four anyway.

"The areas on the album which are country are deep in country music, otherwise it varies

from bluegrass with Clarence on mandolin and Gene on banjo to electrified 12-string Chuck Berry-ish rock things, like 'Tiffany Queen'." Battin's aim? "I want to see The Byrds be a great influence musically."

Battin is given a whole-page feature in *Record Mirror* (February 5) and takes readers back to the beginnings of rock'n'roll. "It was '51 or '52 when the electric bass came in and pulled us right out of an era and into rock. With the upright bass, it just wouldn't have happened. I was playing country rhythm guitar as a profession when this rock'n'roll thing came out of rockabilly music. I met a guitarist who was playing this new type of music – after [Bill] Haley – and it was much louder. The drums didn't seem to be necessary to it. When I saw an electric bass, I was amazed. I switched over to it and went right to work. I had a couple of hits with The Pledges and some, including 'Cherry Pie', with Skip & Flip in 1959."

Battin goes through his various groups right up to the time he joins The Byrds. "[The Byrds] will last as long as they're relevant, creative, innovative, and appealing," he declares. "We try to keep those qualities. Every time we play, it's almost spontaneous – like the first time. Everyone has complete freedom – sometimes I throw the bass up in the air or just stroll around the stage during numbers. The first step is knowing the material very well. Then you can abuse it – but you have to know it correctly. We can play 'Mr. Spaceman' in our sleep, we've done it so many times, but it's a good song that gives you freedom to stretch out on. Even more so than 'Eight Miles High'. I get off vocally too – rapping with people off stage and so on. I don't say much on stage, because it just isn't me to be glib. The highest form of communication is just looking at people."

•

While The Byrds are in London, Chris Hillman stays at Stephen Stills's estate down in Surrey where they rehearse when they are not up in London to record. As yet unnamed, their new group includes five more highly experienced members: Al Perkins, Joe Lala, Dallas Taylor, Paul Harris, and Calvin 'Fuzzy' Samuels.

Meanwhile, The Flying Burrito Brothers come into London later in January – but with no original members left and their Byrds connections just a dim memory. Led by Rick Roberts, the rest of the group are Byron Berline, Kenny Wertz, Roger Bush, Don Beck, Eric Dolton, and Allan Munde.

→ Wednesday 19

The Byrds fly to Cannes for their first-ever concert appearances in France.

→ An arrow denotes an estimated date.

Thursday 20

MIDEM Conference, Cannes, France

Shorthand for 'Marché International du Disque et de l'Edition Musicale', MIDEM has become Europe's leading music-industry trade fair and marketplace. The conference, which celebrates its fifth anniversary this year, focuses mainly on the business side of music but also presents concerts, with a bewildering array of different artists and groups appearing each year.

The 1972 festival features Billy Preston, Curtis Mayfield, Shawn Phillips, Buffy St Marie, the Afro-Caribbean band Osibisa, Australian songstress Helen Reddy, France's Nicoletta and Danyel Gérard, soul singer Al Green, Norwegian rock quintet Titanic, a trio of French rock groups – Zoo, Triangle, and Martin Circus – and a Russian artist with an unpronounceable name. The MIDEM conference is considered hopelessly unhip by the rock press, a view reinforced this year when the organisers write to Led Zeppelin's fierce manager Peter Grant and invite "Mr. Zeppelin and his musicians" to appear.

Into this circus fly The Byrds. Ray Coleman writes in *Melody Maker* (January 29): "Poco and The Byrds starred at MIDEM's first attempt to reach young people: an all-night marquee at the sea's edge holding 6,000. Poco played the sort of slick, precise set you'd expect after a half-hour delay caused by equipment trouble. The French compère didn't attempt to play records to bridge the gap, but despite this the crowd bore the primitive conditions quite well.

"The Byrds were as fine as The Byrds can be. Gendarmes attended the concert, which also featured Stray, Cat Mother [& The All Night Newsboys], and Germany's Birth Control. But there was no trouble, to the evident astonishment of bored policeman. The event was MIDEM's most positive move ever in providing relevant music to the right audience."

New Musical Express (January 29) also has a correspondent in Cannes. "On the Thursday night the innovation of having a circus tent, with its side flaps open to allow even more youngsters to stand around outside it, to house a rock show was a great success. In this way some got a free show, headed by The Byrds and Poco from America (and both very excellent and much appreciated)."

Friday 21

To tie in with last week's UK visit, *Farther Along* is released in Great Britain. *Melody Maker* (January 29) starts with a summary of the disastrous *Byrdmaniax* before going through *Farther Along* track-by-track. "[It] opens with 'Tiffany Queen', and it is immediately clear that the Byrds are getting back to boogie and rock. The wonderfully familiar Dylan-like vocals highlight McGuinn's composition about a lady who goes around with 'a Tiffany lamp over her head'. There's more boogie choruses and solos after the slow opening of Gene Parsons' 'Get Down Your Line' and it's followed by Clarence White's arrangement of the title track. A mellower feel to it than, say, The Flying Burrito Brothers favoured on their *Deluxe* album. 'B.B. Class Road' is a Byrds tribute to roadies.

"The last track on side one, 'Bugler', is a beauty. A mandolin intro very reminiscent of Rod Stewart's 'Maggie May' presages the tale of a hound and 'a redneck child'. It's another man's-best-friend story, akin to 'Chestnut Mare' but substituting the canine for the equine. Sad to tell, however, 'Bugler' gets run down by a truck. Just know how they feel – our cat met the same fate. It's a beautiful track anyway.

"Side two opens with the Skip Battin/Kim Fowley tune 'America's Great National Pastime', and some real good hobbies they've got too. … Two love songs come next – 'Antique Sandy' and 'Precious Kate'. Sandy is a real nice country girl who'd 'take down the washing for her man to wear and she'd try not to get eaten by the bear'. While it's Kate's fate to 'be inside the centre of the California earthquake'. Nice girls all the same. Further evidence of the return to laidback rock'n'roll is their version of 'So Fine', the Johnny Otis track done a la Byrds harmony.

"Another beautiful cut is 'Lazy Waters', a song of longing for a return to the country. It features some nice, yearning harmonica, and no way is it corny. The closer is a mad, steaming banjo-picking track, and a good note to end on, for throughout the album their instrumental work is, as usual, exemplary. Written by Gene Parsons and Clarence White, 'Bristol Steam Convention Blues' has some great banjo–mandolin duet passes. Good to hear the Byrds stretching their wings again. There can be little doubt that the settled personnel the band have enjoyed for an unprecedented length of time has done their music and understanding the power of good. *Byrdmaniax* was the bad news – now for the good news."

Caroline Boucher rates it three out of four stars – in other words 'good' – in *Disc* (January 29). "After *Byrdmaniax*, The Byrds vowed that the next album should be unsullied by anybody from outside the group, and this album is the result – very ethnic Byrds. It's a varied album – starting off with a raging rock number, 'Tiffany Queen', and rambling through country things to the bluegrass 'Bristol Steam Convention Blues' with lovely banjo and mandolin. There are some splendid send-up type numbers – like the rock 'BB Class Road' to 'America's Great National Pastime'. 'Lazy Waters' is a good example of old Byrds harmonies (why don't they do more harmonies now?) and is a wistful, reflective little song. They still haven't written anything as exhilarating as 'Eight Miles High' or come up with an album as brilliant, but it's as good as *Turn! Turn! Turn!*"

Lon Goddard comments in *Record Mirror* (February 5): "The Byrds are slowly drifting away from the more apparent country influences that came to the fore with *Sweetheart Of The Rodeo* and combining into a hybrid that features more of the approach utilised on their earlier albums. McGuinn's voice is still inimitable and attractive in its pleading manner – especially on 'Lazy Waters'. Clarence White's tasteful guitar is a major victory too; their sound and Gene Parsons' banjo is as effective as his excellent drumming. The Byrds are an undying natural resource, unified by Roger's expert guidance."

Despite all the kind words, sales are depressingly low and the album does not make the UK album charts.

Saturday 22

L'Olympia, Paris, France

☐ **EURO TV** RTF/ORTF 2 (French TV Channel 2) *Les Byrds A L'Olympia*

The Byrds make their Paris debut at the stately Olympia theatre, where a wildly enthusiastic 3,500-strong audience threatens to tear the building apart after the group plays the allotted time. Arranged on short notice, the hour-long concert is set to run between 7:00 and 8:00pm so as not to disturb other bookings at the theatre. Faced with a rowdy crowd, the management pleads with the group to go back for a couple of encores to pacify the crowd. In the end, The Byrds perform for another 15 minutes.

French TV films the show, and 25 minutes are broadcast on February 5. The television programme consists of: 'Lover Of The Bayou', 'So You Want To Be A Rock'n'Roll Star', 'Mr. Spaceman', 'Roll In My Sweet Baby's Arms', 'My Back Pages'/'BJ Blues'/'Baby What You Want Me To Do', 'Eight Miles High', 'Amazing Grace', and 'Roll Over Beethoven'.

→ Sunday 23

The tour over, White, Battin, and Parsons fly back home to the US, while McGuinn spends a week in London resting. According to *Melody Maker*'s news pages (January 29), The Byrds plan to return to Britain in April for concerts and recording sessions.

Saturday 29

A newsflash in *Disc* trumpets "BACK TO THE NEST FOR THE BYRDS?", relaying the first official report on the reformation of the original five Byrds. The item continues: "America's original Byrds are expected to reform for a unique one-album-only deal. ... The album will be on the US Asylum label, which now also has Joni Mitchell, and will be distributed in Britain by EMI, *Disc* understands. McGuinn, with the current Byrds line-up, is understood to have special permission from CBS Records to make the album. This could mark the end of an alleged McGuinn–Crosby dispute which has kept them apart for some years now."

The events leading up to *Disc*'s top story will not be revealed until the end of the year when *Rolling Stone* interviews McGuinn and Crosby (published in the edition dated January 4, 1973). Judy Sims will write about how one day producer Terry Melcher – presumably right before Christmas last year – invited McGuinn down to Marina del Rey one day. "David Geffen just happened to be sitting in a restaurant with us," McGuinn recalls to Sims. "It was the first time I'd met Geffen – I didn't know who he was or what he was into. Geffen and Melcher were in cahoots. The people invited on the cruise were Gene Clark, Michael [Clarke], myself, Chris [Hillman] – David [Crosby] was out of town. A lot of people had the idea at the same time ... but Geffen put it in the papers to make it happen."

Crosby remembers it differently. "Melcher was never involved, no way. You know what it was? Terry got Gene [Clark] down here to work on [Melcher's] album, then he asked Chris and Michael and Roger to work on it and said, 'Gee, fellas, everybody's here except David. How about that?' But at no time did we ever plan to do [a reunion album] with any producer except ourselves."

It will take months before the idea of a union becomes a reality. Indeed, Crosby has not been party to the latest development, even if it was he who approached McGuinn in the first place about the idea – independent of any involvement by Geffen, Melcher, or others. For the moment it sounds too good to be true, and the news does not break in the US quite yet. But McGuinn, Clark, Crosby, Hillman, and Clarke will get together at the end of the year, to the delight of the group's many fans.

February

Friday 4
Ritz Theatre, Port Richmond, Staten Island, NY
McGuinn, White, Battin, and Parsons reunite for their first US concert in almost two months. The excitement of the European expedition

soon wears off as The Byrds fall into their regular pattern of touring around the States, concentrated on weekends, with the weekdays off. Their concert repertoire continues much in the same vein as established over the last five to six months, although a couple more songs from *Farther Along* are eventually added. Plans are laid to venture overseas again, but the enthusiasm and sense of purpose that drove The Byrds in 1970 and '71 disappear slowly as the months pass.

Saturday 5
Capitol Theatre, Passaic, NJ
Singer-songwriter duo Brewer & Shipley open for The Byrds, as they will do on many other occasions this year. There are two shows (8:00 and 11:30pm), both sold out. Under the aegis of promoters Al Hayward and John Scher, rock concerts at the 3,200-seat Capitol Theatre have managed to create a Fillmore East for New Jerseyites. Going for nothing less than an all-round experience at a time when promoters are cutting down on expenses, Hayward and Scher have hired Pig Light to run a lightshow and screen Flash Gordon movies in the break between groups. "If all you get is sound, you could go home and hear it on your stereo," Scher reasons in *The New York Times* (March 5).

Concerts at the Passaic venue are important enough to drag the New York press across the Hudson River. Ira Mayer is here tonight for *The Village Voice* (February 10). "Saturday night at the Capitol Theatre ... Roger McGuinn and friends went through about an hour of their standards at a sound level that might well be termed obscene. Thanks to the guy sitting next to me, I at least got a piece of paper towel to put in my ears in order to cushion the noise. When members of the audience started yelling between numbers that it was too loud, McGuinn just chuckled and ignored it. And when he later asked for more volume on the stage monitors, someone loudly suggested he come out into the audience.

"The Byrds have been together a long time, playing essentially the same material (of the three or four times I've heard them, there's never been a set without 'So You Want To be A Rock'n'Roll Star', 'Mr. Spaceman', and 'Eight Miles High'), and maybe they're tired of doing it. But there is enough talent there – they are fine musicians with more than adequate voices for this kind of music – to try a few new things instead of trying to blast their audience into an uncaring stupor. And if it wasn't their idea to have it loud, why the hell didn't they respond to the shouts to turn down the volume? (Nor was it just too loud up front. As I walked to the back of the large theatre ... it didn't seem any less painful.)"

Friday 11
Kenyon College, Gambier, OH
A member of tonight's audience will later recall that The Byrds have somehow been separated from their instruments, so they resourcefully put out a call to see if any students can help. In the end, McGuinn borrows a Hagstrom 12-string, Battin ends up with a Fender bass adorned with a Grateful Dead sticker on it, and White has to play a standard guitar without his string-bending device. Reportedly, this does not stop the group from playing a fabulous show.

Saturday 12
Memorial Hall, Mount Union College, Alliance, OH
One show at 8:00pm.

Friday 18
Davis Gymnasium, Bucknell University, Lewisburg, PA

Saturday 19
Gymnasium, Hamilton College, Clinton, NY

Sunday 20
Robert F. Kennedy Hall, Queensborough Community College, Bayside, New York, NY

Friday 25
Reid Gymnasium, Western Carolina University, Cullowhee, SC

Saturday 26
Winston-Salem Coliseum, Wake Forest University, Winston-Salem, NC
While The Byrds continue their uneventful weekend outings this month, today's *New Musical Express* breaks news of a planned UK visit during the latter half of May. No contracts are signed yet, but it is hoped the group will headline a major rock festival. In the end, the visit is cancelled. The same paper also relays the month-old news of the planned reunion of the original Byrds.

Sunday 27
Gymnasium, Elon College, Burlington, NC

March

Thursday 2
Draught House, Thornton, CO
A busy spring schedule takes The Byrds back to Colorado for the first time 1969.

297

Friday 3

Gunter Hall, University Of Northern Colorado, Greeley, CO

Saturday 4

Payne Gymnasium, Westminster College, Salt Lake City, UT

Prior to the concert, David Proctor from *The Salt Lake Tribune* (March 3) interviews McGuinn. "Trends are funny things," the Byrd leader suggests. "Individuals get credit for doing certain things, but really [a trend] is a group of people and a group of ideas that just seem to emerge some place. The trends are out there; you just have to find them. As far as I'm concerned I guess it would be nice to do another big thing, but right now the music scene as a whole is rather stagnant. There are small things here and there but nothing like The Beatles."

Asked by the reporter if he foresees any new trends, McGuinn replies: "Well, this is my own personal observation, but I think there is a trend that might be establishing itself. Remember after the Korean War, there was a musical reaction to peace? There was a period of balmy, Calypso-type music. I think it might be happening again now. What with the end of the Vietnam War in sight and all. The music is reflecting the people's hope for peace in the world. After all, there seems to be less wild, frenzied music than a few years ago. That's just what I feel; I don't know how true it will be."

He gives a rundown of what concert-goers can expect. "Let's see, we start with 'Lover Of The Bayou', 'The Bugler', 'America's Great National Pastime', 'Chimes Of Freedom', 'I Wanna Grow Up To Be A Politician', and 'My Back Pages'. Then we do some acoustic things like 'Mr. Tambourine Man' the way Dylan did it. We go back to electric and do 'Rock'n'Roll Star', 'Mr. Spaceman', 'Chestnut Mare', and 'Eight Miles High'. If we do encores, they'll be 'Jesus Is Just Alright', 'Roll Over Beethoven', and 'I'll Feel A Whole Lot Better'. It depends a lot on the audience, how many we do. We don't jam or mess around much; we'll keep it tight. That's our 60-minute show."

In parting, McGuinn is asked about a solo album. "Sure, there are a lot of things I'd like to do that I can't do with this group. There is nothing committed right now, but I'll do one. I'd also like to get into television acting, but I haven't gotten any offers yet."

Reviewing the second Saturday show (with opening act Holden Caulfield) in the *Tribune* (March 6), Proctor cannot help but detect a feeling of stagnation. "The Byrds present a rather depressing dichotomy in their live shows. On one hand they seem to get off on the music as much as the audience does, picking and playing and all. On the other hand, as soon as the music stops, so do The Byrds. Their thank-yous to the people are very perfunctory, and one is overwhelmed with the thought that this is just another in a long line of gigs. You do the same show for perhaps the hundredth time, right down to the last solo line, you say 'thank you', you leave and get called back for an encore, and you leave again. Not that this is any different than 99 per cent of the other bands' situations; it was just that Saturday night it was brought out rather forcibly. The whole concert seemed to roll along, but it didn't really take off until the acoustic portion. Clarence White's work on 'Black Mountain Rag' was super, as was his picking on the electric mandolin earlier."

ALSO …

Stephen Stills has named his new group Manassas, officially unveiled to the public via the British music press next weekend. A truly eclectic ensemble, the seven-man Manassas has found its own path out of the remnants of Crosby Stills Nash & Young. Stills has today invited the press down to his house near Guildford, south of London, and Bernie Leadon – in Britain to record the debut album by The Eagles – joins in the fun as *Melody Maker* (published March 11) snaps a picture of him, Stills, and Chris Hillman playing away.

Sunday 5

Lumberjack Gym, Northern Arizona State University, Flagstaff, AZ

Support by Holden Caulfield.

Thursday 9

US TV [Unknown studio] Nashville, TN. *Country Suite*

On their way to the East Coast again, The Byrds stop by Nashville to tape a television show with host Billy Edd Wheeler. Playing wholly unplugged (apart from a discreet electric bass), the group rips through 'Roll In My Sweet Baby's Arms' – McGuinn with 12-string Martin guitar, Parsons on banjo, White nimbly switching between acoustic six-string and mandolin, and Battin thumping an eight-bar bass solo. Following an introduction by Wheeler and a commercial break, White and the group play 'Black Mountain Rag' / 'Soldier's Joy' and McGuinn introduces 'Mr. Tambourine Man' as "our favourite Bob Dylan song", with Parsons on harmonica. Except for overlong hair, the four play and look like any traditional top-notch bluegrass combo. The insert ends with a quick interview with the host. (The broadcast date is unclear, but it is possible that the show goes out live.)

Friday 10

Academy of Music, Manhattan, New York, NY

Two shows (8:00 and 11:30pm) and a triple bill with The Byrds, Dave Mason, and J.F. Murphy & Salt in downtown Manhattan.

Music Editor Mel Friedman of *Newsbeat* (March 14) experiences the live Byrds for the first time.

"I must admit that I expected to hear one perpetual open D-chord," he says, but is pleasantly surprised. (Another note in the same paper says the group plays a final encore of the usual 'Roll Over Beethoven' followed by a rare rendition of the rockabilly classic 'Blue Suede Shoes'.)

University student newspaper *The Villanovan* (March 15) detects a lack of enthusiasm at the start. "The turning point of the set came about three-quarters of the way through with a fairly new song, ['Chestnut Mare'], which was partially in a 'Leader Of The Pack' style and done superbly. The analogy between the horse and a girl/love was pretty evident, and it seemed to strongly affect the audience and the group."

The music trade papers *Variety* and *Billboard* (March 15) are split on their views. *Variety* says The Byrds' brand of country rock "still ranks first" and praises McGuinn's vocals and White's guitar mastery. Sam Sutherland of *Billboard*, on the other hand, sees a group in decline.

"When the most recent configuration of The Byrds began touring three years ago, their act was tight and very polished," writes Sutherland. "The band would walk onstage briskly, already tuned and ready to plug in and sweeten the air with the first clean bars of 'You Ain't Goin' Nowhere'. Sadly, [this] performance suggested that The Byrds aren't really going anywhere. What had been a highly evolved and very personal style of music, highlighted by Clarence White's economical and always lyrical guitar and McGuinn's classic vocals, was survived by a grim parody of itself that was no longer fresh or precise. Perhaps this act, one of Columbia Records' most venerable bands, was simply tired. Perhaps the chronic PA problems blunted their fire. Or, and this seems to be more likely, the performance's ennui was evidence of creative menopause within one of the most distinctive and certainly influential bands of the last decade."

Saturday 11

Sunshine Inn, Asbury Park, NJ

The group appears with special guest MC Allison Steele, the 'Nite Bird' of New York's WNEW-FM radio.

CONCERT HALL PRESENTS
SATURDAY MARCH 11

THE BYRDS
2 SHOWS 8 & 10 P.M.
Special Guest M.C.
WNEW F. M. Radio's Nite Bird
ALLISON STEELE

Sunday 12
Central Connecticut State University, Bristol, CT

Wednesday 15
Virginia Beach Dome, Virginia Beach, VA

Two shows at 7:00 and 10:00pm with The Byrds supported by Tranquillity.

Thursday 16
Capitol Theatre, Port Chester, NJ

One show at 8:00pm presented by Fantasia Productions, with special guest stars J. F. Murphy & Salt.

Saturday 18
State University of New York (SUNY), Alfred, NY

Sunday 19
Palestra, University of Pennsylvania, Philadelphia, PA

Wednesday 22
ALSO ...
Stephen Stills and Chris Hillman debut the mighty Manassas at the Concertgebouw in Amsterdam, the Netherlands. Robert Ellis covers the concert for *New Musical Express* (April 1) and says the music "and the vibes were enough, and they were beautiful", a precise yet pale summary of the group's fabulous debut performance. Traversing American music history though their multitude of roots, Manassas tip their hats to The Byrds with performances of 'Bound To Fall' (a song attempted at the *Notorious Byrd Brothers* sessions). McGuinn's serenade 'He Was A Friend Of Mine', and the country number 'You're Still On My Mind' from *Sweetheart Of The Rodeo*.

Friday 31
Fort Homer W. Hesterly Armory, Tampa, FL

The Byrds fly to Florida for the weekend at the start of a jaunt through the South. Commander Cody & His Lost Planet Airmen are the opening act here.

April

Saturday 1
Sportatorium, Miami, FL

McKendree Spring is added to the bill, which also features Commander Cody & His Lost Planet Airmen. Jane Ross of *The Miami Herald* (April 3) finds McKendree Spring far better than the headliners, and she ignores Cody's Airmen. "It can't be pleasant for a group to be greeted by an audience screaming for their oldie-goldies, not knowing or caring about material from their last three album efforts. Yet The Byrds gave them what they wanted, including 'Mr. Tambourine Man', although the power failed mid-tune. Clarence White, Gene Parsons, Skip Battin, and McGuinn did some fine things on their instruments, although the latter's vocals were weak and muddy. The songs that went over best were the older ones, written by others, witness to the group's creative limbo."

Wednesday 5
Blackham Coliseum, University of Southwest Louisiana, Lafayette, LA

Someone in the audience makes a cassette tape of The Byrds' performance, which serves up a surprise version of Gene Parsons' 'B.B. Class Road' halfway through the otherwise standard Byrds repertoire this spring. With Battin taking a vocal solo on 'America's Great National Pastime' and directing the singalong 'Roll In My Sweet Baby's Arms', McGuinn has eased up his onstage vocal monopoly. White, of course, always had a vocal showcase (at present it is 'Bugler') in addition to his role as featured instrumentalist.

The full set runs as follows: 'Lover Of The Bayou', 'Bugler', 'America's Great National Pastime', 'Chimes Of Freedom', 'I Wanna Grow Up To Be A Politician', 'My Back Pages', 'Black Mountain Rag', 'Mr. Tambourine Man', 'Roll In My Sweet Baby's Arms', 'B.B. Class Road', 'So You Want To Be A Rock'n'Roll Star', 'Mr. Spaceman', 'Tiffany Queen', 'Chestnut Mare', and 'Nashville West', 'Eight Miles High'/'Break Song', plus the two encores 'Turn! Turn! Turn!' and 'I'll Feel A Whole Lot Better'.

Friday 7
Symphony Hall, Memorial Arts Center, Atlanta, GA

Cultures collide as The Byrds invade Atlanta's Symphony Hall, a highbrow venue usually reserved for classical performances. "Perhaps the strongest negative factor associated with this concert was the poor attendance and associated ills," writes Joe Roman in the underground newspaper *Great Speckled Bird* (April 17).

"By associated ills, I am referring to the weird vibes. No one seemed very comfortable. Famous Artists, the agency that promoted the show, normally deals with people like Engelbert Humperdinck, Dionne Warwick, and others in that vein. The ushers, many of whom seemed to be making their first verbal contact with the Woodstock generation, seemed very ill at ease. Prohibition of foods and drinks and the smallness of the hall … had an unsettling effect on some of the crowd."

And what of the concert itself? White plays with customary excellence, sounding "like no other as he plays steel guitar licks and with an ease and proficiency that most guitar players are able to achieve on only the simplest, most clichéd riffs". Roman singles out Parsons' drumming as the main flaw. "I had an image once during the show of three well-tuned athletes running effortlessly around a track, being followed by a slightly overweight kid with his shirt tail hanging out and his shoe untied.

"A hallmark of The Byrds has always been their versatility. If you had stepped out of the hall for a moment in the middle of the show, you would have been surprised to return and see a bluegrass band on the stage. … Now, how many bands can do that?" (Mick Greenwood opens for The Byrds on this occasion.)

Sunday 9
Carolina Coliseum, University of South Carolina, Columbia, SC

Saturday 15
Wade Stadium, Duke University, Raleigh, NC

Show with Mark Almond and Seatrain as support acts.

Tuesday 18
RECORDING Columbia Recording Studios, Sunset and El Centro, Hollywood, CA. Producers The Byrds.

In a spring full of distractions and a lack of focus, is seems to be out of the question to gather the touring Byrds together for a new album. Recording a new single, however, is within grasp, and the group returns to the studio today to tape McGuinn's 'Born To Rock And Roll'. The song is much better than the trite title suggests; it is a pleasant rocker with the Byrds sound updated with a female choir, a piano, and what sounds like a soprano saxophone.

But the idea of a single is dropped, and the song will remain unreleased until it finally appears on the remastered *Farther Along* in 2000. The song will be re-recorded at the end of the year when the original Byrds reform (see mid October). Not content with this, McGuinn will then record it once again for his third solo album. The later attempts pale compared to today's spirited version. (It might well be that the overdubs to today's version are done later in the year when McGuinn begins work on his own solo album and re-records the track, as both versions feature the female backing-vocals and the piano.)

Wednesday 19
ALSO …
Gene Clark begins a series of recording sessions that stretch well into June. With Chris Hinshaw as producer (the man who co-produced *Byrdmaniax*), Clark calls on the services of Clarence White among others. At another of the sessions, McGuinn puts harmony vocals on to Clark's rendition of the Lester Flatt and Earl Scruggs number 'Rough And Rocky'.

The results will be collected on the Dutch-only album *Roadmaster* at the end of the year, an album that also contains three songs produced by Jim Dickinson in 1970 at a session that constituted a Byrds reunion of sorts (see entry for May 31, 1970).

Wednesday 26
Jersey City State College, Jersey City, NJ

Thursday 27
Ritz Theatre, Elizabeth, NJ

Friday 28
Campus Center, Allegheny College, Meadville, PA
The film from the Dutch Kralingen festival (see June 27, 1970) premiers at movie theatres in the Los Angeles area. Previously on general distribution in Europe as *Love And Music* (see October 14, 1971), the title is changed to *Stamping Ground* in the US. Robert Hilburn in *The Los Angeles Times* (April 29) gives it a lukewarm reception, comparing it unfavourably with the Woodstock movie and complaining of the Byrds insert being limited to one number ('Old Blue').

Saturday 29
Butler University, Indianapolis, IN

Sunday 30
Fieldhouse, Carthage College, Racine, WI
Madera open for The Byrds.

•

The group's dealings with money and wages have become an issue, and Parsons questions the profit-sharing system that McGuinn has devised. Looking back on the last lap that the group is running in this spring of '72, McGuinn sighs to Robert Bowman in *Cheap Thrills* (December 1976): "It was a dying spiritual thing there. It wasn't happening. The group was falling apart from within, the same way other groups had before. From ego problems, from old ladies saying, 'I think my old man ought to get more out of this.' Some of those things … I hate that, but it happens. It got down to where certain parties in the group thought they were getting cheated on the payroll, which wasn't the truth, and I had to fire them because they were jerks."

Bowman asks McGuinn to clarify if he owns the Byrds name and the others are on a set salary. "That was the way towards the end, yeah. But we also had profit sharing. It was very fair. Certain members got more than others according to their worth. Like Clarence White always got more. He, at times, got twice as much as anybody else."

May

Monday 1
Clarence gets back to work on the Gene Clark sessions today and on Wednesday May 3 (see April 19). After a break for a few weeks, work will pick up again on May 30 and continues into June.

Thursday 4
City College, New York, NY

Friday 5
Smith Opera House, Geneva, NY

Sunday 7
Erie Community College, Williamsville, NY

Monday 8
State University of New York (SUNY), New Paltz, NY

Saturday 13
Indiana University of Pennsylvania, Indiana, PA
Tired of life in The Byrds, soundman and road manager Dinky Dawson is at the end of his tether when McGuinn decides to go onstage with an unsolved grounding (earth) problem, despite explicit warnings to the contrary. Dawson smashes a door in pure frustration (scaring singer Tom Rush, who has just finished his opening spot) and makes up his mind to leave the entourage at the end of the month.

Over in Britain, *New Musical Express* publishes a grand survey of The Decade's Top Hundred, the 100 top-selling singles in the UK from 1962 to '71. The survey includes only records that reached the top of the hit parade, so some which sold steadily without making Number One are not shown, even though they may have outsold bona fide chart-toppers. The chart is topped by The Beatles ('She Loves You'), while 'I Want To Hold Your Hand', Ken Dodd's 'Tears', 'Can't Buy Me Love', and 'I Feel Fine' make up the rest of the Top Five. The Byrds are at Number 80 with 'Mr. Tambourine Man'.

Sunday 14
Michigan State University, East Lansing, MI

Friday 19
Memorial Auditorium, Dallas, TX
The group strikes out for three nights in Texas, all with Edgar Winter & White Trash, while for this Dallas show Buzzy Linhart is added to the bill.

Saturday 20
AstroHall, Houston, TX

Sunday 21
HemisFair Arena, San Antonio, TX
One show at 8:00pm.

Friday 26
Ritz Theatre, Port Richmond, Staten Island, New York, NY
Eric Anderson opens for The Byrds.

Saturday 27
Palace Theatre, Waterbury, CT

Sunday 28
Convention Center, Ocean City, MD
As the month of May comes to an end, McGuinn and The Byrds in effect take two months off. Dinky Dawson uses the opening to resign as road manager.

Although there have been lapses of inactivity since The Byrds started touring way back in 1965, this break is different. McGuinn feels trapped within the country-folk-rock format and wants to adjust the group's direction. He promises radical changes. Parallel to this, the re-formation of the original five Byrds is (unhurriedly) coming together, but right from the start this is considered a recording project rather than a touring unit – which gives the present Byrds no purpose beyond going on the road to churn out a well-tried repertoire and pick up easy money.

June

Thursday 1

Gene Clark continues recording sessions in Los Angeles (see April 19 and May 1) with Clarence White as his right-hand man. Further work is done on June 5, 6, 12, and 13. The results are not earmarked for a definite project and will be collected on *Roadmaster*. During the sessions, Clark revisits his past with a re-recording of the old Byrds single 'She Don't Care About Time'.

Early June

Writer Eric Rudolph speaks to McGuinn for a feature that is eventually published in *Crawdaddy* (October 1972). The undated interview with an unusually frank McGuinn is conducted in a New York City hotel, and may possibly take place when The Byrds play Staten Island at the very end of May.

For his story, Rudolph uses material from two occasions: a second interview is done next month (see late July). McGuinn challenges the notion that today's Byrds can keep flying and denounces the contributions made by the present band members. Although he blames himself for the situation, he is equally clear that there will be changes.

McGuinn surveys the past history of The Byrds. "We've made some mistakes, or I have," he tells Rudolph matter-of-factly. "I've made a lot of mistakes. Like hiring Kevin Kelley or John York. I'm afraid the same thing is true of Gene Parsons. ... Well, his work has been going downhill. He had a shot at being very versatile and very adaptable, and I really like the guy, but he didn't grow, he just sort of stagnated. In fact, he dropped a little bit in proficiency. He messes up on songs he doesn't like, which is a symptom of his stubbornness. It's all psychosomatic: he's a good drummer, but he's been fucking up lately, and I think it's because he feels a sense of alienation.

"But the fact is, we can get better effects. He's a hell of a good country drummer, but I wanna get out of country music. See, the thing is, I've changed my mind about what I want to play, which is my prerogative and also my track record. I've always gone through a lot of different bags of music, mostly because I don't want to be classified. I guess I'll always be an experimental folk musician of some sort. I'm not saying that my versatility is up to that of the jazz cats, but that's the sort of concept we're going to: versatility."

McGuinn outlines the new direction more specifically. "Well, more rock'n'roll, man, and synthesizer, like, well, back to where we left off at *Notorious Byrd Brothers*. That's what I want to get into. I know I'm capable of it, it's just

I feel that I've been loaded down by people who weren't sympathetic or tolerant of that in me. [They would] veto it – jump on me, gang up on me, make it just really impossible, really a drag. They destroy my creativity, they come around and hassle me. If I pull out the synthesizer at the session, they say, 'Look, this is our session too, and we don't want you wasting your time on that thing.'"

By now, McGuinn has worked himself up. "It's my band, man, my session, and they're beating me up. I mean bullying me into what they wanted to do, and they did it and it was a bomb, and I'm glad. Mostly Skip and Gene. Skip is good, but some of his lyrics are schlock. I mean some of mine are too. I don't like some of his songs. They just don't express the same attitude that The Byrds had back in [the earlier days]. They're a little cheap, they're a little cheaper than I want to get. So I'm gonna make sure they don't get on the albums.

"I'm happy with Skip, he's a good bass player, but like he sort of monopolised the last album for material and it wasn't that good. Gene and Skip were sort of a coalition, they said, 'Look, we're the new Byrds, and we feel insecure about it, we want a chance to express our musical abilities.' And I said OK, democratic, or something. I don't want to be the tyrant that everybody said I was. If it had been a huge success I woulda been happy. It was an experiment and it failed: back to the drawing board. That's what I'm doing."

On a lighter note, the reunion of the original Byrds is discussed. "I'm excited about the idea," McGuinn tells Rudolph. "I can't imagine – it will be real high, for one thing: high energy level going on, a lot of internal excitement from all the guys involved, sort of a happy reunion. ... I have sort of an innate feeling that it will come out fucking great, I really do. I think some original things will get together, maybe some revamping on old things for kicks. Sounds like fun, like going to a circus or something, a carnival. It's got a certain life or death ... like a tightrope walker, if he falls he's dead. These are people who know how to do the tightrope-walking act pretty well. I have faith in them."

Saturday 24

ALSO ...

The Los Angeles Times carries an interview with Gram Parsons, who is ready to make his first solo album with Merle Haggard at the board. After he quit The Flying Burrito Brothers in the summer of 1970, Parsons has spent time roaming around Europe with The Rolling Stones but has done precious little to further his own career, until Eddie Tickner takes charge and secures him a contract with Warner Brothers.

"We're going to do the album in Bakersfield where [Haggard] records. Actually, Bakersfield is just the place for me," Parsons tells Robert Hilburn. "It's the sound I wanted to get all along – that bright, crisp, Bakersfield sound. I think I came the closest to that sound on the *Safe At Home* album, and it was what I was after in the *Sweetheart Of The Rodeo* album but everything got changed around. That's why I left The Byrds." (Eventually, the Merle Haggard deal falls through and Bakersfield is dropped. Slightly delayed, sessions will get underway in September at the Wally Heider studio in Los Angeles.)

July

Sunday 9

The Barn, Peoria, IL

The Byrds are booked for a lone concert appearance in Illinois, care of local promoters Love Inc. This may be cancelled, however, as no other dates for the group are lined up at this time.

•

With time on his hands, Skip Battin signs a contract with Signpost Records and tapes most of his debut solo album this month. In the interview that Battin later does for *Omaha Rainbow* (December 1976), he describes the circumstances around the sessions. "We took that summer [of 1972] off and I secured this record contract. ... 'America's Great National Pastime' had created an interest in Kim [Fowley] and I as a writing team, so we took our best songs and put them together as a demo tape. Signpost, who had already shown an interest, said OK, let's do it. I called [drummer] Billy Mundi back from New York to do the tracks and Jimmi Seiter, Clarence, and Roger were all involved. Gene was gone at the time. Most of the songs were already written, but we did write some especially for that album. 'Captain Video' is, of course, directed at McGuinn, but he liked it and laughed." Mundi is not able to make all the sessions, so Battin and Fowley call on studio expert John Guerin to finish the album.

Saturday 15

The news of a reunion of the original Byrds, first revealed in the British music paper *Disc* half a year ago (see January 29) and then picked up by *New Musical Express* (February 26), takes until the summer to fully break in the US. Although The Byrds' popularity may be on the wane there, David Crosby is a fully-fledged superstar, and anything he touches is newsworthy. It is not that the reunion is a

301

whim, either; January's *Disc* item explained in plain terms the necessary business mechanisms that have to be ironed out to make the reunion a reality.

It is *Rolling Stone* (dated March 2, printed February 8) that relays the sensational news in the US, admittedly tucked away in the paper's 'Random Notes' column. The item says: "20/20 News: Roger McGuinn, in Europe with The Byrds, is talking about getting all the original Byrds back together for one album." The paper predicts the chances are good if it was not for company trouble. "The label would be David Geffen's Asylum, and that's where it gets sticky. The Byrds are on Columbia, and Geffen and Clive Davis are not of a feather." Covering the Byrds reunion for *Rolling Stone*, Judy Sims later confirms the Davis–Geffen feud is so heated they had to have McGuinn as an intermediary.

Since that first newsflash in January, a crucial meeting has taken place. "The idea started to jell around April," McGuinn recounts later to Chuck Thegze of *The Los Angeles Times*. "I broke the ice with David and Chris. None of us knew that the other one wanted it."

By this summer of 1972, everyone involved has agreed to the union and the last kinks in the deal are ironed out. Today, the news is filtered to the UK via *Melody Maker*'s US correspondent, who writes: "Believe it or not, the original Byrds are coming back together for at least one album. It's all been arranged by David Geffen of Asylum Records, and it's Asylum Records that will be releasing the product. The re-formed Byrds will be Roger McGuinn, David Crosby, Gene Clark, and Chris Hillman." Michael Clarke's name is conspicuous by its absence, but that is probably just a typesetter's error. But tracking down Clarke has been a problem. Since he left The Flying Burrito Brothers last year, Clarke has lived carefree days in Hawaii.

The *MM* news item continues: "A spokesman for McGuinn said the group should be recording this autumn with a tentative release date set at the end of the year. McGuinn got special permission from Clive Davis of Columbia Records to record for the 'rival' label. There are no plans for a tour." In fact, the deal is a bit more complicated. In return for McGuinn's participation on an Asylum release, he and Crosby are down to make a duo recording on Columbia Records in the future.

Billboard prints the reunion story in its July 29 issue, and its British sister publication *Record Mirror* writes the same day: "The original Byrds are to re-form to cut an album. Roger McGuinn, Dave Crosby, Chris Hillman, Gene Clark, and Michael Clarke go to the L.A. Record Plant in California next month to cut the album for Asylum, who will release it in

the States in October." On August 23, *Variety* too publishes the story.

Managers David Geffen and Elliot Roberts guide the careers of Crosby Stills Nash & Young and others, and founded their own record company last year, because – in Geffen's words – "we couldn't get some of the new artists we believed in [to be] signed by existing labels" (*New York Times*, September 3). With few artists in its stable, Asylum is able to fully concentrate on promoting records and nursing talent. This spring and summer have seen debut releases by Judee Sill, Jackson Browne, Jo Jo Gunne, and The Eagles. Where Jo Jo Gunne will have a respectable Top 40 hit single and then gradually slide out of view, The Eagles will soar to dizzying heights in the years to come with their near-perfect extension of the Byrds sound. A quartet of experienced musicians who have paid their dues in various country, rock, folk, and bluegrass groups, The Eagles have chosen their name as a reverent nod to The Byrds.

Critics hail the eponymous *Eagles* debut album, but Rob Brinton in Britain's *Disc* (August 12) is a lone dissident. His rant hits right at the heart of what many will later find wrong with The Eagles. "[This] end-of-the-line country muzak … probably began with Dylan's *John Wesley Harding* album, stoked up with The Byrds' *Sweetheart Of The Rodeo* and resulted in Chris Hillman forming The Flying Burrito Brothers to turn out the great *Gilded Palace Of Sin*. … Somehow this is just too plush and lifeless; nice yes, a little bit like treacle. … They take us through ten brilliantly engineered songs, so lacking in depth you feel you're drowning in a puddle. Honestly, it's no wonder America soaks up our talent if this is they best they've got to offer. The titles sum up the backbone of what amounts to armchair and fireside listening. … The ultra chic way they've taken Gene Clark's 'Train Leaves Here This Morning' and smoothed away the feeling is painful. In short, hear it all done properly on [The Flying Burrito Brothers' album] *Gilded Palace Of Sin*."

→ mid-July

Eric Rudolph, who spoke to McGuinn several weeks ago (see entry for June), picks up the thread with the Byrd leader for a second chat. Added to the previous interview, the two discussions are edited for a six-page feature in *Crawdaddy* (October 1972) with the title 'McGuinn Back To The Drawing Board'.

In the previous interview, McGuinn expressed dissatisfaction with Parsons and Batton. Now he informs Rudolph that Parsons is no longer a member of The Byrds. "For once, it wasn't a personality conflict," McGuinn explains. "He was tired, and it showed in his work. There are no hard feelings."

Where the previous encounter with Rudolph found McGuinn rather despondent, he now sees possibilities for The Byrds. A priority is to get out of country music as soon as possible and back into the rock mainstream. "Because we sort of pioneered [country-rock] along with Dylan and a couple of other people. I don't know who was first and I don't really care. It's been three years, and that's a long time to be in one bag. I feel like I'm stifled in this place. I wanna get a breath of fresh air somewhere.

"And so I think good solid hard rock'n'roll. Not psychedelia, just some good old-fashioned solid rock'n'roll with a nice solid beat, maybe funny words, or innocuous words, or intellectual words, or whatever we decide to put on it. Or no words at all. Maybe a riff on those sex records with the breathing. I like heavy music, it turns me on. I want to be able to do it. It's frustrating to me not to have a band that can really sound like pooooh!!! I've got the material but I don't have the band to implement it. My musical head is going one place and my band is staying the same, so I have to make an adjustment."

Clarence White is not a victim of the purge, although McGuinn is unsure of his function in a new set-up. "I haven't thought specifically what Clarence's role would be in this, but I know that he's versatile enough to do it. I think he got into a rut, too, as good as he is. He's an excellent musician, but I think he's in a rut musically. I think he could break out of that, cos he's playing the same licks he's been playing for three years. I guess I am too, but I thought he had more, could stretch out a little more. Like he digs Django Reinhardt, things like that. He gets further out if you just ever ask him to, or suggest to him one day that maybe he could get a little farther out in his playing – the next day he'll do it, without saying a word. Even afterward he won't come up to you and say, 'Hey, did you hear what I did?' He's a real deadpan. I like him: real poker face, and a good friend. I really dig Clarence.

"Clarence and I haven't really been able to balance out properly. We're great friends and I respect his work. There's nothing he can do about it either, cos he's even tried. But the thing is, frankly, he intimidates me! He's so fucking good I just don't know what to do! Granted, he's specialised; but as far as potential, we pretty well balance out.

"In a way, I did let Clarence take over, but I plan to overcome that. Little by little, cos I have a lot of ego, man. But I'm subtle about it, I'm sort of insidious, I creep up on things. I also procrastinate and bullshit a lot. … I think I'm going to get a six-string and play double six-string lines with Clarence. Cooperate with him a little more, get a little more elaborate without instrumentation."

McGuinn's creativity has woken up again ("I've just written four songs in the last two months!") and he is keen to have The Byrds back in the charts. "Like, I'm waiting for a hit record. I know I've got one. The ones that didn't make it are just par for the course. There was something wrong or they would have been. A hit single: right!" Which song Roger has in mind, the article does not say, but elsewhere Rudolph says that '[I Was] Born To Rock And Roll' is the new 45, which it is not. McGuinn may suggest to him that it should be, but it is neither officially announced as such nor given a catalogue number.

McGuinn updates *Crawdaddy* on the progress of the Byrds reunion. Apparently, the five old Byrds have not actually sat down together yet, but obviously Crosby and McGuinn have begun the groundwork. Crosby is assigned the producer's role, and they will all be doing original material as well as songs by Jackson Browne, Joni Mitchell, and Neil Young. Rudolph writes: "To do the album, much manoeuvring was necessary. Atlantic insisted that it be on one of their labels, because of David Crosby's appearance. But Columbia didn't like the idea of a Byrds album on any other label: so McGuinn and Crosby are going to do an album for Columbia." He adds, incredulously: "A McGuinn and Crosby album? Sounds about as likely as a Lennon and McCartney."

Thursday 20

Stephen Stills, Chris Hillman, and Manassas tour the United States and tonight play the Memorial Auditorium in Sacramento, CA, where Roger McGuinn joins them onstage for a couple of songs.

Friday 21–Sunday 22

Manassas play three nights at the Community Theatre, Berkeley, CA, where Stills & co keep a door open for old friends. The Saturday is the big night, where singer-guitarist Steven Fromholz, Roger McGuinn, and even Graham Nash and Neil Young appear at various points during the evening. McGuinn performs with Manassas for 'Bells Of Rhymney' and 'So You Want To Be A Rock'n'Roll Star' and then comes back later in the set for 'He Was A Friend Of Mine'. Surely in actuality the event could theoretically turn into a brief McGuinn Stills Nash & Young performance, but the closest they get is the finale following 'Carry On' (with Nash and Young) when everyone gathers on stage to sing 'Find The Cost Of Freedom' accompanied only by Stills' guitar.

For many, the Manassas shows are simply too eclectic while at the same time dominated by

Stills. As Staff writer Doris G. Worsham of *The Oakland Tribune* (July 26) says: "Stills concerts usually come in three parts – good, better, and better still." She goes on: "Among the other highlights of the show was Stills, Hillman, and McGuinn presenting McGuinn's melodious tune 'He Was A Friend Of Mine'. The audience joined in the joyous songfest. Hand clapping and singing filled the auditorium." For Todd Tolces of *Melody Maker* (August 5), the highpoint is "when McGuinn came out to do 'So You Want To Be A Rock'n'Roll Star' [and] things sounded much better. Unfortunately he left after a second number and Stills went back to doing some acoustic".

The low point is Stills' quasi-blues pandering. "Unintelligible," says Doris G. Worsham, suggesting it should be deleted from future shows. "If he wants to improve his dialect, he should take lessons – though it would hardly improve his presentation." Earlier in the tour, Lynn Van Mattre chides in *The Chicago Tribune* (May 1): "His 'Delta Blues' – strongly reminiscent of a Caucasian version of Cheech & Chong's Blind Lemon Chitlin – are almost embarrassing."

Sunday 30

The Byrds cancel a performance at Arie Crown Theatre, Chicago, IL, where they were due to appear tonight with The New Riders Of The Purple Sage.

August

Wednesday 2

Between drummers at the moment, The Byrds presumably cancel an announced appearance at Atlanta Sports Arena, Atlanta, GA (with Eric Anderson and, again, The New Riders of the Purple Sage).

Early August

Searching for inspiration, McGuinn invites Jacques Levy to his home to see if the two can recreate the creative partnership that yielded *Gene Tryp*. (By now, McGuinn has left Sherman Oaks and moved house to Malibu on the Pacific coast.) McGuinn explains in *New Musical Express* (November 4) that the two write about 14 songs in eight days; many will end up on his first solo album.

Their collaborations include 'I'm So Restless', 'My New Woman', 'Draggin'', 'Bag Full Of Money', 'Hanoi Hannah', 'M'Linda', and 'Sweet Mary', and this inspirational burst may also lead to some of the songs that McGuinn does on his second solo album, *Peace On You* (1974), which contains a further six

McGuinn/Levy compositions. Shedding light on their relationship, McGuinn will explain in a 1976 interview how the writing process that he and Levy use has developed methodically over the years. He tells Robert Bowman in *Cheap Thrills* (February 1977): "We kick around the idea and then start to sculpt it into a form of some kind or other. I always come up with a melody and he invariably will do the mathematics on getting all the verses to fit into place and everything; he's very good at that. I do lyrics too; I don't just sit around and watch him. But I don't do the majority of the words. It's like we have a basic concept and he might be having trouble with a line and I'll stick in words here and there. We sit around with a [Sony] TC-55 recorder and a guitar, pencil and paper, a thesaurus, a rhyming dictionary, and a regular dictionary. That's our system."

Friday 11

The Byrds presumably cancel a planned return-booking today to Fort Homer W. Hesterly Armory, Tampa, FL, where they last performed in late March.

Friday 18

For the fourth year running, The Byrds have been booked to play the Schaefer Music Festival in Central Park, New York City, but this year they have to cancel because McGuinn has fired Parsons and they are without a drummer. Comedian George Carlin stands in for the group on a bill with singer-songwriter Jim Dawson.

Undated August

RECORDING Wally Heider's Studio, Cahuenga & Selma, Hollywood, CA. Producer Roger McGuinn.

McGuinn, White, and Battin return to the studio in Byrds guise for what will be the last time. In reality, the event can just as well be viewed as the first session for Roger McGuinn's solo album, and significantly the recording takes place at Wally Heider's studio facility in downtown Hollywood rather than at Columbia Studios.

Three of the songs from Jacques Levy and McGuinn's recent writing workshop are laid down: 'Bag Full Of Money', 'Draggin'', and 'I'm So Restless'. Drummer John Guerin fills the vacancy left by Parsons. The lilting waltz-time 'Bag Full Of Money' will later be given an overhaul with an unidentified pedal steel guitar, possibly by Buddy Emmons. 'Bag Full Of Money' will see the light of day on a CD reissue of *Farther Along* in 2000; 'Draggin'' and 'I'm So Restless' will remain unreleased. A while later, McGuinn re-records all three songs for his first solo album.

'Bag Full Of Money' goes a long way to fulfil McGuinn's brash declaration of intent to *Crawdaddy*'s Eric Rudolph. "We're going to get into studio gimmicks like phasing, using a synthesizer in strategic places, nice harmonies. Get back into some nice, free intricate harmonies, and getting the fuck out of country music."

John Guerin (born in Hawaii on October 31, 1939) is a fairly new member of L.A.'s studio community but comes with a versatility that enables him to play straight jazz or TV shows and anything in between. Over the last ten years, he has played or recorded with notables such as Buddy De Franco and Thelonious Monk, and has come to prominence in the rock field due to his work with Frank Zappa on *Lumpy Gravy*, *Hot Rats*, and *Chunga's Revenge*. Soon, Guerin will join the touring Byrds between his studio commitments as, in effect, the official replacement for Gene Parsons.

→ mid-to-late August

So far, the reunion of the original Byrds has just been a drawing-board exercise, and the true test comes when all five get together at Roger McGuinn's Malibu home, for what journalist Roy Carr calls "a memorable soiree". Chris Hillman is the busiest of the five, but he has just come off a month-long North American tour with Manassas.

McGuinn will later recall this first rehearsal to Roy Carr in *New Musical Express* (March 17, 1973). "It was really quite remarkable. The voices immediately gelled together, and to me it sounded like we'd never been apart. Naturally, everyone was a little nervous. There was this feeling of apprehension among us all – some more than others. This was something David and I were acutely aware of but, underneath the superficial nervousness that we all shared, both Gene [Clark] and I felt positive that it would really work all over again.

"Everyone had come along to the rehearsal with material and proceeded to show each other what they had to contribute. We listened to everything and afterwards passed judgement as to whether they were suitable or not. Of course, there was always the possibility that we might do something far worse than anything we'd ever done in the past, and that it would prove to be tremendously embarrassing to all concerned. Funnily enough, we didn't play any of the old songs that evening. Thankfully, any doubts we had of the outcome had vanished by the end of that first rehearsal. One thing is very certain. If, in the initial stages, things hadn't worked out to our mutual satisfaction, then we would have scrapped the entire project and said no more about it."

McGuinn expands on his recollections to Cameron Crowe in *Creem* (June 1973). "Uh, tense. Everybody was a little nervous about things. It was very business-like. David and I had been playing songs to each other for a couple of days beforehand, so David started off by saying, 'Roger why don't you show them one of your songs?' We all went around the room and everybody showed his material. Then we all exchanged opinions about what was good and what wasn't. Very businesslike. We got into a groove after that, when we finally started recording."

Gene Clark recounts his impressions of that first day to Chuck Thegze of *The Los Angeles Times* (February 4, 1973). "We all sat down with our guitars," he remembers, "and started playing Roger's song, 'Sweet Mary'. And then we moved into David's rocker 'The King Is Dead [Long Live The King]'. We all were silent and we could feel it working. We were singing but we didn't talk, and then David just stopped and paused with his hand above the neck of his guitar. He started laughing and said simply, 'Hot nuts!' And the magic started happening."

It's possible that Michael Clarke does not attend this first meeting. McGuinn indicates that much when he speaks to a student paper following a St Louis performance in early September. Clarke is in Hawaii: "He does it all the time," the Byrd leader says. "I'm sure he'll make it back in time to record. It's just the kind of person he is."

Friday 25

Unexpected news of the present Byrds comes from an unlikely source when *The Salt Lake Tribune* writes: "Clarence White and Gene Parsons have flown the coop on McGuinn. They are replaced by ex-Burrito Chris Etheridge and ex-Beach Boy Bruce Johnston, but so far for recording purposes only." Even if Parsons has left and White has not, the information is credible enough – McGuinn is presently recording his debut solo album in Los Angeles, where both Etheridge and Johnston contribute to various tracks.

McGuinn's solo sessions will continue on and off for some months yet, and he uses the opportunity to re-record several songs already taped (but not released) by The Byrds: 'Lost My Drivin' Wheel', 'Draggin'', 'Bag Full Of Money', and 'I'm So Restless'. In its new guise, the latter is just a duo recording featuring McGuinn and Bob Dylan. (McGuinn later confesses that Dylan only did the harp in the middle of the song after a bit of gentle arm-twisting and that the harmonica heard elsewhere on the track is his own.)

Editor Barry Ballard of *The Byrds Bulletin* (Fall–Winter 1972) asks Byrds fans to watch out for the "Skyjacker ballad", an oblique reference to McGuinn and Levy's 'Bag Full Of Money' lyric about the true story of an unidentified man who hijacked a Boeing 727 in November 1971 and escaped on a parachute with the ransom, somewhere over the Pacific Northwest – never to be found again. Meanwhile, McGuinn, shorn of beard and his hair by now slightly trimmed, has his photo taken for the album jacket around this time.

September

Early

The Byrds break in new drummer John Guerin with a couple of rehearsals before they embark on their first field trip in almost three months. Lack of time unfortunately restricts McGuinn, White, and Battin simply to teaching Guerin the existing set rather than use the opportunity to update and extend the repertoire. The only oddity is 'Mr. Tambourine Man', which the group will perform twice: first as part of the acoustic interval, and then in an electric version when they plug in for the final third of the show.

Ever since the visit to Britain in January, McGuinn has preached how jazz is the key to redress the balance in the lopsided, countrified Byrds. In the short run, his solution is to encourage White's Django interest and add a jazzy drummer to the mix. But to the public at large, the sound does not change.

→ Thursday 7 or Friday 8
[Unknown venue/location]

John Guerin debuts as a drumming Byrd at an unknown location. (A couple of unconfirmed gigs in the autumn of 1972 are Southern Connecticut State University, CT and State Theater, Waterbury CT.) The group fall back into their irregular touring schedule with weekdays – sometimes weeks – off, and gigs on the weekend. This suits Guerin's calendar very well as he maintains a hectic session schedule in Los Angeles. Al Hersh is now head of the road-management team and travels with The Byrds wherever they go. Instead of carrying a sound system and a permanent soundman, the group now chooses to hire a PA system.

Friday 8–Sunday 10

The group is one of the main drawing cards at a weekend festival in Mount York, nearby Poynette, WI, but the event is cancelled at the very last minute. It is reminiscent of the problems that plagued the many small happenings that popped up around the US in the summers of 1970 and '71, when festival organisers clashed with locals and lawmen. Legal obstacles effectively stop this festival, while another Wisconsin festival is halted two weeks later because the promoters fail to obtain – of all things – a Cabaret Licence, under a recently adopted ordinance.

Saturday 9
Quadrangle, Washington University, St. Louis, MO

Richie Havens, John Sebastian, and The Byrds pull in an audience of 7,000. Spokesman McGuinn talks to *Student Life* (September 12). "This is only our second day out on this tour. Our drummer has only been playing with the group on two gigs, and he's doing real good for such a short time. We'll get better as a band, hopefully. There are good nights and bad. For every good thing there's a throwback – positive force and negative. The only things that get to me are the same songs: I've been playing with this band for seven years – sometimes it does get repetitive. But that's the business."

McGuinn has three recording projects on his plate at the moment, but none of these involves the present Byrds. The first is the reunion album; the second is a new Byrds' Greatest Hits collection; and the third is his own solo album. When asked about the difference between a Byrds album and a solo album, he replies: "Actually, no difference. Just politics, business; another phase."

Friday 15
McAlister Auditorium, Tulane University, New Orleans, LA

"We've been playing colleges and theatres primarily along the East Coast," McGuinn says in a phone interview a couple of days later for Philadelphia's underground newspaper *Different Drummer* (November 2). "We just did a gig at Tulane, and the response was great. There's nothing like the gratification you get from a good audience. And I still like to play."

He takes the opportunity to give a brief situation report on the reunion project. "That's supposed to come together as soon as Hillman gets off the road with Stills," says McGuinn, confirming that studio time has been booked until November 15. "I have a couple of songs for it, Crosby has a couple, and Hillman seems to. Gene Clark probably has about 80 or so. ... We've decided to do two songs from each of the four writing members and four songs from outside people – maybe Jackson Browne or Joni Mitchell; maybe we can find a good new Neil Young song to do, which would be nice."

McGuinn is in the middle of recording his solo album, too, and says that Crosby is helping him out. The man whom he fired for obnoxiousness five years ago is back and

is having a significant impact on McGuinn's musical outlook. "The thing is that David had been a considerable jazz influence when he left – I fired him because he was unmanageable at the time. He even admits that now, and anyway, we've become friends again."

Saturday 23
County College of Morris, Randolph, NJ

Ken Fecteau from nearby Patterson University pens a critical review of The Byrds' performance in *The State Beacon* (October 17). "Despite Guerin's questionable talent as a drummer, all The Byrds' individual talent cannot make up for the fact that the group is not together yet because it has only performed three times before an audience and twice in rehearsals. The second glaring problem is the group is still doing old arrangements suited for Parsons' slam-bang style, while John Guerin's forte seems to be jazz influenced, flowing and free. Only time and new material can remedy The Byrds' present ills. They are highly adaptable musicians, and nearly any musical endeavour they attempt will meet with success. The Byrds seem to always be on the verge of spawning a new musical renaissance. They have the talent and the creativity to pull it off, but living in the past is not the answer. Periods of transition are nothing new to The Byrds, and with a concentrated effort on everyone's part, 'somehow I know it will work out all right'."

Thursday 28
The Dome, C.W. Post College, Greenvale, NY

The Byrds are still able to pull off excellent performances if the reviews are accurate in college paper *The Delphian* (October 11) and *The Hofstra Chronicle* (October 20). Today's 2,800-seat auditorium is sold out, and the Greenvale student paper comments: "McGuinn is a showy, kind of cocky performer who always pleases and entertains his audiences. Whenever he takes to the stage, he transmits a certain charismatic magic that draws a crowd to him."

The highlight is the second half, from 'Baby, What You Want Me To Do' to the 'Eight Miles High' jam, which brings the house down during Battin's bass solo. Guerin's drum spot is a low point ("nothing but mediocre") but culminates in a five-minute standing ovation all the same. Four encores are called for, as the group soars through 'I'll Feel A Whole Lot Better', 'Roll Over Beethoven', 'Bells Of Rhymney', and, finally, 'Mr. Tambourine Man'.

The Hofstra paper reports that McGuinn is in good form, White is "superb on lead guitar, turning out some blistering riffs on his stubby guitar", and Battin is enjoying himself

while the group demonstrates its ability to jam effectively.

Friday 29
[Possibly Suffolk Community College], Suffolk, NY

Saturday 30
John J. Long Student Center, University of Scranton, Scranton, PA

Today's concert features The Byrds, John Hartford (songwriter and banjo master who contributed to *Sweetheart Of The Rodeo*), and The Earl Scruggs Revue.

As unlikely as it may sound, *New Musical Express* reports today that Terry Melcher has produced Roger McGuinn's first solo LP, which is just completed. McGuinn may not have been the strongest critic of Melcher's work on *Byrdmaniax*, but he did fire him last year. It is a lesson unlearned, as McGuinn later admits to Robert Bowman of *Cheap Thrills* (December 1976). "Unfortunately, Terry Melcher, who was the producer on the first attempt at the *Roger McGuinn* album, did a whole wrong production, in my opinion, and we had to do it again.

"He put on all kinds of tape delay on my voice and wired effects that mudded it up and made it sound very plastic and stupid," McGuinn explains. "It was all chromium and plastic, nothing like I wanted. I sort of bent over backwards in turn and made it more folkie than it should have been. I wanted to be a little more hard-sell than it came out. It came out real soft."

Word goes around that Melcher should receive credit for his work on the album, which McGuinn brushes aside. "He deserved no credit whatsoever. It was a big setback. He deserves to pay me $50,000 for studio time. The album ended up being done in bits and pieces."

October

Sunday 1
DAR Constitution Hall, Washington DC

Thursday 5

A performance at the Tower Theatre, Upper Darby, PA, with Henry Gross and Commander Cody & His Lost Planet Airmen is postponed due to a death in McGuinn's family. The concert is rescheduled for December 15.

Friday 6
Academy of Music, New York City, NY

Originally booked for Saturday, the show is

pushed back a day. As The Byrds and Commander Cody & His Lost Planet Airmen have the same agent, they once again share the stage, while ex-Sha Na Na singer Henry Gross is also billed. The two shows gross a total of $27,000 of a potential $34,500. The group flies in from California in the morning and returns home tomorrow.

John Guerin is not able to make this round-trip due to other commitments, so drummer Jim Scherz (also known as Jim Moon) sits in for a single night. Although Scherz will later drum with Spanky & Our Gang and Kim Fowley, he is an unknown quantity in 1972. He can thank his friend and neighbour Skip Battin for a brief moment in the Byrds spotlight.

The New York Times (October 8) observes curtly: "The current edition of The Byrds was less appealing [than Cody]. Processing one of the fine old names in rock, the group, with Roger McGuinn its leading light at the moment, did little more than rehash old favourites like 'Eight Miles High' and 'Mr. Tambourine Man'."

Fred Kirby in *Variety* is a little more helpful. "The headliners ran through old faves plus some newer tunes with tight instrumentation and vocal work," he writes, complimenting every member of the group – even the newcomer on drums, who acquits himself well and "fits in perfectly with his solo".

Julie Webb of *New Musical Express* today (November 4) corners McGuinn backstage for an interview and meets an assertive Byrd admiral. "I'm the leader and that's it. I control things like who is in the group, although I let them play what they want. Musically I carry a lot of weight, and vocally, and I do the introductions – nobody else talks to any great extent – in fact, at all."

McGuinn assures Webb he is not leaving The Byrds and speaks enthusiastically about going overseas again. "I don't like long tours because I go crazy. But even so we're hoping to come to Britain in January. An extended tour, that is – not just weekends. I love England – the last time we came over it was great – we had a good time. I think that, to the British, we are from California [and that] makes us very exotic or something. ... We're getting away from country music towards the highest jazz. Like these [he gestures to the other band members] are jazz fellas, who could help us gravitate to that. I like jazz very much and really want to play it in some form or another."

Friday 13

Marwick-Boyd Auditorium, Clarion State College, Clarion, PA

The Byrds replace The Temptations for the homecoming weekend concert in Clarion.

John Guerin is probably back on drums. Local Boston group Orphan precedes The Byrds for the 7:30pm show (and if the sale of tickets goes as expected, a second show will be arranged for 9:45pm).

→ Saturday 14

Painters Mill Music Fair, Owings Mill, MD

Amusement Business says the group is booked here for two shows on Friday 13 October, opening the fall season, but they may play today instead. The shows have a potential $27,800 gross.

→ Sunday 15

Southern Connecticut State College, New Haven, CT

Another homecoming concert headlined by The Byrds, although the exact date in October remains unconfirmed.

→ Monday 16–Friday 27

🔊 **RECORDING** Wally Heider's Studio 4, Calhuenga & Selma, Hollywood, CA. Producer David Crosby and engineer Doc Storch (Sandy Fisher) and Raghu Markus.

Roger McGuinn, Gene Clark, David Crosby, Chris Hillman, and Michael Clarke finally get together at Wally Heider's studio in Los Angeles. It has been a long time coming. Last time the five recorded together was on February 21, 1966.

Hillman has just wound up a European tour with Manassas, and before flying out from London he speaks of his expectations for the reunion. "I'm really looking forward to doing it. We'll be recording during the week and I'll be going out on gigs with Manassas on the weekends," he tells Michelle O'Driscoll of *Disc* (October 21). "I can't help feeling I'd like CSN to do another album, or even The Beatles. I don't like all the bitching and, as long as people's fond memories aren't shattered, I think it's valid."

No conclusive documentation of the Wally Heider sessions will survive, but The Byrds have block-booked the studio between October 15 and November 15. Because McGuinn and Hillman have gigs lined up in this period, the recordings over the next four weeks tend to be done piecemeal. Intent on making the project a success, the five reach out to each other more like strangers than close friends. Where their relationships in the years from 1964 to '66 were full of tension and drama, now, seven years down the road, their politeness will at times rob the recordings of emotion.

The group approaches the sessions in a democratic fashion. Each member except Michael Clarke contributes a pair of songs

each. Three cover songs are also recorded – reinforcing the feeling that the individual members may be keeping their best material for other projects. In hindsight, Hillman suggests as much. "I'll be honest," he will tell author John Einarson. "I contributed my worst material, because I was getting ready to do a solo album. ... I was saving all my good stuff and contributed this throwaway stuff that was awful."

Clark supplies 'Changing Heart' plus 'Full Circle', a superb song he taped earlier in the summer with Clarence White on guitar. Thematically, 'Full Circle' could well be written for the Byrds homecoming, and it is briefly the working title for the project. McGuinn brings in 'Sweet Mary', a sorrowful song in the great British ballad tradition. It is one of the songs he and Jacques Levy have recently concocted (see early August). For his second contribution, McGuinn takes the easy route and teaches the group 'Born To Rock And Roll', which he has already attempted with The Byrds (see April 18).

Crosby has written 'Long Live The King' especially for the reunion, and he too resorts to dig up a previously released song – 'Laughing' from his solo album *If I Could Only Remember My Name* – for his second required contribution.

Throughout, McGuinn's electric 12-string drone is conspicuous by its absence. Overall, the songs have an acoustic foundation with unobtrusive bass and drums and prudent use of electric guitars. Instead, Hillman's pretty mandolin or Gene Clark's plain harmonica takes centre stage, while Crosby's influence is obvious in the way the vocal harmonies are charted: it is closer to the high-sounding CSNY blend than the wall of voices that The Byrds of old raised.

The sessions have barely begun before Hillman is off on the weekend of October 20–22, playing with Manassas in Oklahoma and the Midwest. Presumably he is back in Los Angeles on Monday October 23 to rejoin the others in the studio.

Hillman submits 'Things Will Be Better' and 'Borrowed Time', the former co-written with Manassas drummer Dallas Taylor, the latter with Manassas percussionist Joe Lala. Taylor is in fact involved in the sessions, as he confirms in *New Musical Express* (April 7, 1973). "I've done a bit of songwriting," he tells Steve Clarke. "There's a song I wrote with Chris on The Byrds' album – called 'Things'll Get Better' [sic] or something like that. Don't know the title, I didn't bother with the title. I let them handle that. I play congas and tambourine on The Byrds' album – which they didn't give me credit for because it's supposed to be the original Byrds."

Thursday 19

R. Jack Bauer Productions out of Milwaukee has booked The Byrds for a four-day 'Singing Hills Shantifest' (October 12–15) at a ski resort in Preston, MI. Bauer was behind the Mount York festival that came to nothing (see September 8–10) and now hopes to attract 15,000 to a "rock festival with religious overtones". To that end, he hires Himalayan yogi mystic Swami Rama – and supposedly The Byrds, who stick out like a sore thumb on a programme that can only tempt with obscure groups such as Junction, and Ethyl Methyl & The Keystones.

As heavy rain falls and thick fog and a steady mist descend on the ski slope, *The Winona Daily News* dispatches a reporter to find 20 freezing souls huddled around campfires on Saturday morning. One mystery is cleared up: "One of the groups expected to appear was The Byrds, but not the internationally known group some of the spectators had come to see." Investigating the matter, the paper writes: "The tickets Bauer issued for this festival were the same he sold for an unsuccessful festival in Mount York, Wisconsin. ... According to the ticket disclaimer, no refunds were made: 'Absolutely no refunds or exchanges or allowances under any circumstances whatsoever' the backs of those tickets read."

Even if fears of trouble prove totally unfounded – hardly surprising as the handful of attendees is about half of the police force of 40 on duty for the weekend – the Village Council quickly passes an ordinance to stop similar undertakings in the future. Bauer, for his part, is undaunted and ready to try again. "The facilities here are excellent," he tells the *Daily News* (October 23). "It's a perfect natural amphitheatre with the stage at the bottom of the hill."

Saturday 28

State Theatre, Kalamazoo, IL
McGuinn breaks from the studio sessions to tour with the 'other' Byrds, as he, White, Battin, and Guerin leave for a weekend in the Midwest. Tonight, the group makes up one third of a bill with Leon Russell and Edgar Winter. Russell, who once played on records by The Byrds and a multitude of others, is suddenly a rock star in his own right with a hit single ('Tightrope') and a smash album (*Carney*).

▢ **EURO TV** Radio Bremen, West Germany ARD–1 *Beat Club* 03:15pm (Episode No 81, Season Eight)

Those in Europe who receive transmissions from West Germany's Radio Bremen can tune in to see a previously unscreened clip of The Byrds (with Jimmi Seiter on percussion) singing 'So You Want To Be A Rock'n'Roll Star', filmed last year (see May 19, 1971). Manassas also appears, performing 'Rock & Roll Crazies'/'Cuban Bluegrass' and 'Jet Set (Sigh)'. The rest of the show is made up *Beat Club*'s usual indiscriminating jumble of artists: Mick Abrahams Band; The Grease Band; Heads Hands & Feet; James Taylor; Three Dog Night; Ike & Tina Turner; and Carole King.

Sunday 29

Pieri Gymnasium, Dean Junior College, Franklin, MA
The Byrds are supported by Skip Prokop's big-band Lighthouse. An unofficial tape, mislabelled as recorded on September 12, presumably comes from tonight's show and finds the four-man Byrds plunging into a list of songs identical to their spring repertoire.

→ Monday 30–Tuesday 31

◁》 **RECORDING** Wally Heider's Studio 4, Calhuenga & Selma, Hollywood, CA. Producer David Crosby and engineer Doc Storch (Sandy Fisher) and Raghu Markus.

The Byrds occupy Heider's for further sessions before McGuinn returns to the road on November 1. Sessions may well continue without him, but Hillman is also commuting between Los Angeles and the Manassas touring party.

November

Wednesday 1

Curtis Hixon Hall, Tampa, FL
The Byrds and Eric Anderson appear for one show at 8:00pm, presented by the University of Tampa.

Friday 3

Sunshine Inn, Asbury Park, NJ
Two shows with The Byrds.

Saturday 4

Statistics department: *New Musical Express* publishes a giant 'Chart Of The Charts 1952–1972'. It is based on the UK singles charts published weekly in the *NME*, with 30 points awarded for a Number 1 position, 29 points for the Number 2 position, and so on down to one point for Number 30. The Byrds are ranked at a modest Number 269 with 413 Points, while Elvis is enthroned at the top (13,762 points), followed by Cliff Richard (9,555 points), and The Beatles at Number 3 (6,555 points).

→ Saturday 4–Wednesday 8

◁》 **RECORDING** Wally Heider's Studio 4, Calhuenga & Selma, Hollywood, CA. Producer David Crosby and engineer Doc Storch (Sandy Fisher) and Raghu Markus.

McGuinn is presumably home in Los Angeles between tour dates to resume work on the reunion album. In the months leading up to the studio gatherings, McGuinn discussed some cover songs that the group were keen to try. Jackson Browne's name has been bandied about, but none of his songs get recorded. In the end, the reformed Byrds record three songs by other writers. David Crosby selects and sings Joni Mitchell's beautiful 'For Free' (from her *Ladies Of The Canyon*), while Gene Clark takes the lead vocals on two Neil Young numbers. One is 'Cowgirl In The Sand', which is taken from Young's 1969 album *Everybody Knows This Is Nowhere*. The other is a gem that Young has yet to release himself, '(See The Sky) About To Rain', but which he has performed live since 1970. The Byrds teach themselves the song from a bootleg recording.

Best Of The Byrds: Greatest Hits Vol. II (US)

A1 'Ballad Of Easy Rider' (R. MCGUINN)
A2 'Wasn't Born To Follow' (C. KING/G. GOFFIN)
A3 'Jesus Is Just Alright' (A. REYNOLDS)
A4 'He Was A Friend Of Mine' (R. MCGUINN)
A5 'Chestnut Mare' (R. MCGUINN/J. LEVY)
B1 'Tiffany Queen' (R. MCGUINN)
B2 'Drug Store Truck Drivin' Man' (R. MCGUINN/GRAM PARSONS)
B3 'You Ain't Going Nowhere' (B. DYLAN)
B4 'Citizen Kane' (S. BATTIN/K. FOWLEY)
B5 'I Wanna Grow Up To Be A Politician' (S. BATTIN/K. FOWLEY)
B6 'America's Great National Pastime' (S. BATTIN/K. FOWLEY)

US release November 10 1972 (Columbia KC 31795)
Chart high US number 114
Read more ... entry for November 10

(The song will eventually appears on Young's *On The Beach* album in 1974.)

Johnny Barbata, the drummer on Crosby Stills Nash & Young's gold album *Four Way Street* from last year, will recall in his biography: "[The Byrds] were going to release 'Cowgirl In The Sand', a song that Neil Young wrote. David didn't like the track, so he had Wilton Felder – the famous tenor sax player of The Jazz Crusaders – play bass. David had me play drums. The song came out great, and Wilton was a monster on bass [but] of course he never got credit on the album, until now! I am sure Crosby wanted to keep the Byrds mystique intact."

The intrusion of Barbata and Felder may be a case of Crosby overstepping the line as producer, a criticism that will be raised – perhaps unfairly – in hindsight by both McGuinn and Hillman. Four years later, McGuinn will give one version to Robert Bowman in *Cheap Thrills* (December 1976), by which time his views are well soured. "It was because Crosby had all the power on that, because of the [Asylum] people. Then he was producer and trying to prove a point. He wanted to make sure that it was fair that I was the leader of The Byrds all these years and he wanted to see if he couldn't do it himself, and obviously he couldn't, so that's good. It was a David Crosby ego trip, actually."

Despite his rough characterisation of Crosby, McGuinn also says: "I finally made friends with Crosby and it's great. … I mean, he really likes me." When Bowman confronts McGuinn with the accepted view that members are holding material back for their own projects, he innocently replies: "Yeah, although I don't think I was guilty of that. I gave them my best stuff at the time."

As McGuinn will recall many years later to author John Einarson, there is a particular element that has always been present, but now even more so. "It was too much of a party. David had this incredibly strong pot. Half a joint and you couldn't do anything. We were stoned out of our minds the whole time. I don't remember much recording. I remember just sitting around getting high."

Thursday 9

Tower Theatre, Upper Darby, PA

The Byrds head back for a weekend of concerts on the East Coast, starting with an appearance in the Philadelphia area that was earlier postponed (see October 5). Folk singer-songwriter Jonathan Edwards and Peter Kaukonen's Black Kangaroo complete the bill.

Friday 10

Pace College, New York City, NY

Two shows with support by musical comedy troupe Travis Shook & The Club Wow.

Saturday 11

Physical Fitness Center, Hofstra University, Hempstead, NY

The group headlines for one concert at 8:00pm on Long Island. Special guest attraction Paul Butterfield Blues Band have to cancel, so in comes Seatrain and Speedway Johnny as replacements.

Sunday 12

The Byrds cancel an appearance at the Civic Center Auditorium, Atlanta, GA, where they should have headlined in a concert with The New Riders Of The Purple Sage.

→ Monday 13–Wednesday 15

🔊 **RECORDING** Wally Heider's Studio 4, Calhuenga & Selma, Hollywood, CA. Producer David Crosby and engineer Doc Storch (Sandy Fisher) and Raghu Markus.

Coming off the road again, McGuinn is certainly back at Heider's as sessions for The Byrds reunion album are nearing the end, although work may well continue beyond November 15. Under Crosby's supervision, 11 tracks are completed and readied for the group's second coming. No known outtakes or alternative versions will come to light in later years, but one more tune possibly stems from the October 15–November 15 sessions: McGuinn's 'My New Woman'. A churning 5/4 pulse breathes life into the song, bringing memories of *The Notorious Byrd Brothers*. Charles Lloyd tracks a saxophone during the final mix.

•

As soon as 'The Asylum Byrds' have wrapped up sessions, Judy Sims is given exclusive interviews for an article in *Rolling Stone* (published December 12, and on newsstands until January 4, 1973). Despite the old members' outward impression of renewed brotherhood, Sims is unable to gather them all in the same place at one time. Instead, she conducts separate interviews with McGuinn, with Crosby (in his manager's office), and with Hillman (at the Chateau Marmont), while Gene is just quoted briefly.

"It was so much fun I'm sure we'll want to make more records," Crosby tells her. "No schedule, maybe one a year, but certainly I want to do it again. We made a really fine record. To me it's a fulfilment of what we could have been; it's what I was hoping for. We're all much better at it." Hillman agrees. "It turned into a good record. Three or four weeks ago I had my doubts, but all of a sudden I started to hear an album. I've been on the road a lot lately, and everybody's been asking me about the Byrds album; I think the average kid in the street thinks it will be like what The Byrds sounded like five years ago. There's a little of that flavour, but it's different." McGuinn, for his part,

found himself "grinning from ear to ear listening to the playback. It's good rock'n'roll with good words and good vocals".

A recurring theme is how the years apart have done them all good, as Crosby aptly describes to Sims. "The impression I was left with more than anything else was how much everyone, particularly Gene and Chris, had grown. I had a wonderful time doing it, working with all of them. Stress that. I dug it a lot. I didn't have to do it – I did it because I like those guys in spite of what's gone down. I'm enormously pleased with the album.

"Michael played incredibly well," Crosby continues. "He *cooked*. He played things I didn't even know he knew how to play. Gene is so much stronger. Chris has grown amazingly; he plays a lot of lead guitar on this record. We all play lead, and Roger does some amazing stuff."

Hillman elaborates: "David was really a joy. … It was a little shaky at first: David and I started fighting on the phone first thing. He felt maybe Manassas would sabotage the Byrds thing, he thought I'd go off on tour and not show up. Funny, you're really tight five, six years ago, you go away, but you have that image of that person when you last saw them. David isn't like what he used to be. But then, we were all very young."

The future of the union is open at the moment. McGuinn talks again of the plans for a joint album with Crosby and his own solo project, and he also says he will disband the White/Battin Byrds. What then are the chances of the old Byrds going out on the road? "There's too much reason to do it and not enough not to," McGuinn says. "Besides, we always played rotten before, and I'm curious to see if we can pull it together."

•

The reunited Byrds stage a fake concert at The Troubadour for the benefit of photographer Henry Diltz. Two shots will be used for promotional purposes and the jacket of their album, and the one with the five lined up at the Troubadour's bar will be first published in Judy Sims' *Rolling Stone* feature.

Monday 20

Columbia Records releases *The Best Of The Byrds: Greatest Hits, Volume II* in America. Five years after the initial Byrds compilation, this second volume is constructed as a companion to the first. However, as The Byrds have charted few bona fide hit singles since 1967, the collection is padded out with various album tracks.

The striking jacket photo shows the four visages of Messrs McGuinn, Battin, Parsons, and White from the side, the photo will prove durable enough to be used on yet another compilation, the double *History Of The Byrds*, in 1973. *The Best of The Byrds: Greatest Hits, Volume II* climbs to US Number 114 before trailing off. If nothing else, promotion of the album sustains the life of the touring Byrds for another few months.

Selecting tracks for compilations is usually the record company's domain, but as McGuinn has mentioned in interviews he is involved to some extent. Critics such as Bud Scoppa question the logic of the selections. He writes in *Rolling Stone* (April 12, 1973): "If you were asked to put together an anthology album of one of the longest-lived, most productive rock groups ever, and you had the total output of the group to choose from, I'll bet you wouldn't come up with anything remotely resembling this album. It's not that the obvious selections aren't included, it's that so little else is. With some imagination and commitment, *The Best of The Byrds* might have been the equal of the group's first anthology, *The Byrds' Greatest Hits*, surely one of the most satisfying collections ever put together. That first album made itself, of course; at the time it was put together (late 1967) there were only four albums to pick from, and to leave off any of that album's 11 selections would have been an obvious and unthinkable goof.

"This time there was some room to stretch out; when this project was planned, there were a dozen albums, and all but the early hits – like 'Mr. Tambourine Man', 'Turn! Turn! Turn!', 'Eight Miles High', and 'So You Want to Be A Rock'n'Roll Star' – were ripe for the picking. With this wealth of material to choose from, you'd think it would have been difficult to hold this collection down to a double or even a triple LP set. But the selectors evidently had to strain to come up with 11 songs to fill this rather short single LP. If it hadn't been for the best-selling *Easy Rider* soundtrack album featuring The Byrds, they might not have managed that many."

The inclusion of 'He Was A Friend Of Mine' from 1965 merits an exploration of the group's back catalogue, reasons Scoppa, but he wonders why no other album tracks from the 1965–67 period are included. He wants to know why Gram Parsons is non-existent and – the biggest sin – where are the singles-only tracks such as 'She Don't Care About Time' and 'Lady Friend'?

He sums up: "If side one is random but listenable, then the second side, which ends with the three cuts from the last two mediocre albums, runs like a convincing synopsis of the group's decline. If this album was all you had to go by, you might think that McGuinn and Battin shared the leadership of the group (and Battin was the only Byrd, past or present, who never managed to work

his own style in with the overall style of the group); that the Byrds' interest in country music has been purely satiric … ; that White and Gene Parsons have been no more than anonymous back-up musicians; and that The Byrds eventually developed into a dime-store American version of The Bonzo Dog Band. I hope not too many unwary listeners draw any of these conclusions from *The Best of The Byrds*. Believe me, this isn't it."

Music critic James Brown in *The Los Angeles Times* (December 17) sees no problems with the collection, because The Byrds are the rare exception "who are able to come up with a second volume of material to equal the first [greatest-hits album]. … The Byrds prevailed. Their style has been allowed to evolve naturally through personnel changes and public opinion. We're quite sure there will be a *Volume 3.*"

Saturday 25

California correspondent Jacoba Atlas says in *Melody Maker* that Gene Parsons has signed a recording contract with Warner Brothers. Parsons is already busy at work on a solo album with producer Russ Titelman, and among his allies are Gib Guilbeau and Clarence White. The album, *Kindling*, will be released next summer.

December

Saturday 2

Plans are laid to bring the CBS Byrds back to Britain once again, and, according to today's *Melody Maker*, a London student council is pegging dates for a 15-gig tour at colleges and universities throughout the UK. Possible venues listed are London City Polytechnic, Trent Polytechnic, and universities at Brunel (London), Sussex, Hull, Reading, Liverpool, Leeds, Bristol, Newcastle, and Sheffield. In the end, the tour is shelved.

Friday 8
Aragon Ballroom, Chicago, IL

"Personnel come and go – today Roger McGuinn is the only bona fide original Byrd – but the songs stay pretty much the same with the group that once launched so many trends," writes Lynn Van Matre in *The Chicago Tribune* (December 11). "Lest you forget, the repertoire should have brought back memories: 'Eight Miles High' was one of the first space-drug rockers. Friday they did 'Mr. Tambourine Man' twice, the second time as their second encore (and the last time around they got all the words right). It's quite true The Byrds keep doing the same things. It's also a fact that they

still manage to make them worth listening to." With The Byrds in Chicago today are Commander Cody & His Lost Planet Airmen and Peter Kaukonen's Black Kangaroo.

Saturday 9
University Of Iowa, Iowa City, IA

A concert starring The Byrds along with Commander Cody & His Lost Planet Airmen and The Earl Scruggs Revue (father Earl with sons Gary and Randy plus Josh Graves on dobro). The news of the Byrds reunion may lead fans to believe McGuinn, Clark, Crosby, Hillman, and Clarke have started playing concerts too, as the review in *Sun Rise* (January 1973) implies. "Those expecting the original Byrds were somewhat disappointed as Roger McGuinn and company took the stage. It appeared that the last known Byrds had taken stages on tour together one last time for promotional purposes for *Greatest Hits, Vol. II*, just released. Inasmuch as publicising yourself is a lot like work, The Byrds didn't appear to be into playing very much, and only half-heartedly played oldies. They summed up an era (the first era) of country-rock in a rock'n'roll format, ironically, since McGuinn has decided on that direction for his new (unnamed) group. Although The Byrds were a bit of a disappointment, it was something to hear McGuinn's voice flying through the mic – the same voice that's been flowing out of speaker cabinets for almost a decade, and hear his familiar 12-string riffs. Mighty tasty."

Friday 15
Tower Theatre, Upper Darby, PA

The Paul Butterfield Blues Band are special guests, while Commander Cody & His Lost Planet Airmen traipse along for The Byrds' second appearance here this autumn.

Saturday 16
[Texas A&M University], Kingsville, TX

Monday 18
Municipal Auditorium, Austin, TX

Dave Inman presents The Byrds and Dr. John & The Meters for one show at 8:00pm.

Saturday 23
Westbury Music Fair, Westbury, NY

The Byrds are lined up for one last pre-Christmas booking. The music industry paper *Amusement Business* (December 16) suggests an expected $15,000 gross for one show. With this concert, Roger McGuinn and The Byrds bid farewell to a year of contradictions. As old Byrds come back to reclaim former glories, current Byrds peddle the same repertoire with diminishing interest.

David Crosby and Roger McGuinn.

Two kind of Byrds exist briefly side by side in the first months of the year: The **touring kind** and the **original kind** … The touring Byrds limp to the finish line as Roger McGuinn decides to discharge Skip Battin … A last weekend of concerts on the East Coast finds Chris Hillman and percussionist Joe Lala temporarily drafted at the end of February, but further hoped-for appearances with an enlarged Byrds withers…Meanwhile, the original Byrds come **full circle** when the self-titled *Byrds* album is released in March, the group's thirteenth album … The album's lukewarm reception spells the end of any further plans … Tragedy hits twice this year as the most influential ex-Byrds outside the original five meet **untimely deaths**: first **Clarence White** in July, then **Gram Parsons** in September … As Roger McGuinn embarks on a solo career, **The Byrds are laid to rest.**

1973

January

Thursday 4

Rolling Stone issue number 125 (dated today, although it was printed on December 12 last year) publishes Judy Sims' feature, titled 'Reunion Of Old Byrds: A Time For Peace'. For fans of The Byrds, it can be read as a new year's resolution. For the present Byrds, the media hoopla surrounding the reunion of the old Byrds makes it hard to tour, as many concertgoers expect the original five to appear on stage. For Clarence White and Skip Battin, it spells the end of their years as Byrds. But they do not come unprepared: Battin has just released a solo album, while the dependable White has many options open as an in-demand session player, well-trusted backup musician, and bluegrass virtuoso.

Saturday 20

'Earl Scruggs, His Family & Friends', Ahern Field House, Kansas State University, Manhattan, KS
Roger McGuinn, Clarence White, Skip Battin, and John Guerin dress up as The Byrds again as they join Joan Baez, The Nitty Gritty Dirt Band, Tracy Nelson & Mother Earth, David Bromberg, and Ramblin' Jack Elliot in a tribute concert to Earl Scruggs.

Diligently promoted by the KSU Union Program Council, the event attracts a sell-out crowd of 7,600 to the small town of Manhattan in south-eastern Kansas. Kicking off at 8:30pm, the show winds up at 8 on Sunday morning with the sound of The Earl Scruggs Revue racing through bluegrass anthem 'Foggy Mountain Breakdown'. Many have hopes for an unscheduled appearance by Bob Dylan, but he does not show up.

▣ **FILMING** Richard G. Abramson and Michael C. Varhol, two ex-army men, have taken it upon themselves to film the concert for a full-length movie. It will take two-and-a-half years for the footage to reach the screen, but their labour of love is finally premiered at the Eisenhower Theatre in Washington DC, on November 16, 1975, under the title *Banjoman*. A special sound system is installed to maximise the aural experience.

Associated Press film critic Donald Sanders writes cautiously: "Perhaps [there is] too little of Scruggs' playing and too much from his admirers. ... Six cameras were used in the film, and while individual shots are impressive, there is a monotony that turns out to be cloying. There isn't, after all, much drama in endless shots of fingers picking guitars or singers nuzzling microphones and emoting and suffering into them. Fortunately, there are between-scenes shots of Scruggs talking

about his poverty-stricken boyhood in North Carolina and his start in music. He comes through as a shy, hesitant man who loves his profession."

The Byrds are seen and heard performing 'Mr. Tambourine Man' and 'Roll Over Beethoven'. Both tracks will make their way to the soundtrack album, and they will also be found on the retrospective Byrds CD boxed set *There Is A Season* in 2007. As it stands, 'Roll Over Beethoven' will be the only commercially available example of John Guerin drumming with The Byrds.

Sunday 21

Cowtown Palace, Kansas City, MO
The Byrds drive the 100-or-so miles from Manhattan for a concert in Kansas City, supported by British rock group Pete Banks & Flash. On this occasion, The Byrds seem to pull their act together, suggests a glowing review in *Westport Trucker* (February 1973). "A couple of hours prior to the concert I was informed that everyone who had ever been in The Byrds would converge upon Cowtown Ballroom later that evening. Well, that isn't exactly what occurred – but it was close enough to satisfy me. Ace songwriter–vocalist Roger McGuinn was the commander of the four-man entourage of talent that appeared. The blondish boyish superstar jaunted onto stage and, after directing two or three efforts from the *Farther Along* LP, took the band (as well as the crowd) into that fantasyland that few people can even imagine – much less enter.

"Doing almost entirely their super hits from the past – from 'I'll Feel A Whole Lot Better' to 'So You Want To Be A Rock'n'Roll Star' to 'Chestnut Mare' to the best jam of the evening, 'Eight Miles High' – I've never heard The Byrds tighter. They did everything at this gig that The Grateful Dead is supposed to do, only better. To steal a quick quip from that TV cigarette commercial of the 50s – 'it's what's up front that counts'. That certainly applied to this concert because what's up front was McGuinn, Clarence White, and Skip Battin, the swashbuckling bassist who splits vocal duties with McGuinn.

"After a while I just laid back against the dressing room door, closed my eyes, and melted into utopic oblivion. Those guitar riffs could have lasted three seconds or three weeks. I can't be sure. One thing for certain – they were awfully fucking good ... ohhhh those guitars! White and McGuinn glided up and down the necks with utter glee. Add Battin's bottom and the most harmonious of vocals and you've got one helluva jam. If you were there you know what I mean; if you weren't you should start crying right about now. And nobody even missed David Crosby."

A 60-minute cassette tape of the concert will reveal some exciting titles in an otherwise staid set. The rarely performed 'Wasn't Born To Follow' is brought back, presumably because it featured on last year's *The Best Of The Byrds: Greatest Volume II*. There is a surprising resurrection of 'It Won't Be Wrong' – a song they cannot have been performed since '65/66 – and 'The Water Is Wide' from McGuinn's forthcoming album is premiered.

It is usually accepted that John Guerin is the drummer this weekend, but a comment in the review may throw this into doubt. "Due to hospitalisation, a studio drummer had to sit in, but nobody really cared." As bookings dwindle to a trickle, so does Guerin's interest. Last fall, McGuinn was forced to call on the services of the inexperienced Jim Scherz (Jim Moon). With Guerin out of the picture, McGuinn now turns to Dennis Dragon.

Another musician on the periphery of the Los Angeles scene, Dragon has played drums for years in various groups, besides working as a sound engineer. He and his brother Daryl have also toured and recorded with The Beach Boys, which is probably how he is known to The Byrds. These are busy years for Dragon, as he later recalls. "You know, I was doing so much drumming around that time that I honestly don't recall the exact gigs."

February

Friday 2 [Saturday 3]

☐ **US TV** Presumably] NBC Television Studios, Burbank, CA. NBC network. *Midnight Special* 1:00am–2:30am

The *Midnight Special* is an experiment in television programming, devised by producer Burt Sugarman. The NBC show premiers tonight at one hour after midnight, so technically it is Saturday 3rd. A further 12 episodes are lined up, and a pilot was aired on August 6 last year.

Sugarman explained to the Associated Press how the idea came about. "NBC in New York puts on a movie after the *Johnny Carson Show* [but] NBC in Los Angeles and most other cities go black. NBC research has discovered that there is a potential audience at that hour of 3.4 million homes. Our aim was to reach for the 18–33 age bracket, the young married and daters who attend concerts and movies but don't watch much television. They are a very desirable market for advertisers, but there aren't enough of them to warrant a show in prime time."

The debut show is introduced by Helen Reddy and features the hostess herself (singing 'I Am Woman', 'Peaceful', and 'Come On John'), The Ike & Tina Turner Revue, comedian George Carlin, Curtis Mayfield, Don McLean, Rare Earth, Kenny Rankin, The Impressions, and The Byrds. The show closes with Reddy and Mayfield with The Impressions singing 'Amen'. The studio is described as "an arena in reverse" where the 500 spectators sit in the middle while the performers are arranged around the rim.

The show has been pre-taped at some point in January, and The Byrds perform an acoustic 'Mr. Tambourine Man' and an electric 'So You Want To Be A Rock'n'Roll Star' with John Guerin on drums. In some areas, the show is broadcast simultaneously on radio, for example on WMAQ-FM in Chicago. (Reportedly, a video recording of 'Turn! Turn! Turn!' exists that is held over for planned screening on April 6, 1973, but it is apparently dropped. 'So You Want To Be A Rock'n'Roll Star', however, will be re-run on the show's second anniversary on January 31, 1975, with a new introduction by McGuinn, and then again on April 11, 1980.)

The Chicago Tribune's Jack E. Anderson interviews producer Sugarman on the eve of the premiere. Asked about the poll conducted for the pilot, Sugarman comments: "What completely surprised us is that the survey found that the average viewer of the concert was an adult of 28 with wife and two kids, well educated, and in the upper-middle income bracket. We had expected a much younger audience. We'll be getting a flow [of viewers] from the Carson show just preceding it." Sugarman, asked about the future of the show, is close to the mark. "An interesting aspect of this show is that it might be the start of 24-hour network programming. Not necessarily in rock music, but all kinds of programming."

Staff writer James Brown of *The Los Angeles Times* (February 3) singles out Curtis Mayfield for praise in his review of the show's premiere but writes rather offhandedly of The Byrds. He says they are "reduced to one original member and sounding like a band trying to imitate The Byrds".

Concurrently with NBC-TV's *Midnight Special* endeavour, ABC-TV screens the bi-weekly *In Concert*. Contrary to rumours, The Byrds do not appear on that show – which is recorded at 46th Street Theatre in New York, a venue also known as Bananafish Gardens – although a solo McGuinn is a guest there on March 7, 1975.

Saturday 3

Chuck Thegze has interviewed Gene Clark about the Byrds reunion in today's *Los Angeles Times*. "We've filled in on the high and low registers," Clark says, "and there is a lot more acoustic guitar work. We are simply better Byrds than before." Thegze notes that the group has chosen Neil Young and Joni Mitchell songs over Bob Dylan covers this time around. "We all discussed doing a Dylan song, but we couldn't find one. It's incredible and a shame, but we couldn't find one. Dylan has changed. And we were choosing songs, as we have always done, for their lyrical value; and that to us right away meant Neil Young."

Friday 9
McDonough Arena, Georgetown University, Georgetown, Washington DC
John Guerin played with the group on the recent *Midnight Special* TV taping, but that did not require much effort as it took place in nearby Burbank. However, he is unable to make the weekend trip to the East Coast, and it is presumably Dennis Dragon who takes over the sticks at short notice. Brewer & Shipley open for The Byrds.

Saturday 10
Willard Straight Hall, Cornell University, Ithaca, NY
The Byrds, Seatrain, and Orphan play one show at 8:30pm. Considering that the group is on its last legs, the four play with surprising vigour. An audience tape reveals a repertoire that has barely changed over the last 12 months, but there is a sense of fun from the moment 'Lover Of The Bayou' kicks in and the encores end with yet another blast through 'Roll Over Beethoven'.

Wednesday 14
Clarence White joins a side project founded by fiddler Richard Greene assembled to back Bill Monroe for an appearance on KCET-TV in Hollywood. Greene plays with Seatrain, the group that provided support for The Byrds in Ithaca four days earlier. Calling themselves Muleskinner, this bluegrass supergroup of sorts is made up of Bill Keith (banjo), Dave Grisman (mandolin), and Peter Rowan (guitar, vocals) in addition to White and Greene. In the end, Monroe is not able to make the taping today so Muleskinner play the show alone. Intended as a one-off diversion, Muleskinner soon gets serious: they record an album during April and the same month play six nights at the Ash Grove (April 17–22).

Undated February
🎧 **SESSION** McGuinn is involved in recording sessions for Bob Dylan's soundtrack to Sam Peckinpah's movie *Pat Garrett & Billy The Kid*. Dylan has an acting role in the film (in true Dylan fashion, his character is named 'Alias') and has been invited to compose the soundtrack. After a largely unsuccessful visit to Columbia's Mexico City studio in January with mainly local musicians, Dylan moves his sessions to a soundstage in Burbank, CA. The exact extent of McGuinn's involvement is not known, but he plays guitar and banjo and adds backing vocals on many tracks, including the classic 'Knockin' On Heaven's Door'.

McGuinn mentions the session when he speaks to *Rolling Stone* around April–May. "My relationship with Dylan is, like, he calls up and says, 'Can you come over and play?' and I say yes or no. I might do some more [soundtrack] sessions with him. Maybe."

As reported in *Rolling Stone* (June 7), director Peckinpah is in attendance as the musicians record while the film appears on a screen in the studio. McGuinn and Bruce Langhorne play guitars, Byron Berline is on fiddle, and Russ Kunkel taps a tambourine. "It was nice," McGuinn allows. "Very creative music, a lot different from what you imagine a film score. Very exciting."

Friday 16
Rockland Community College, Suffern, NY
The Byrds return to the East Coast for another roundtrip, taking in two college dates. Presumably Dennis Dragon is again behind the drums.

Saturday 17
Williams College, Williamstown, MA
The Byrds have a booking tomorrow (February 18) in Passaic but it is postponed until February 24.

•

The Byrds have a third East Coast weekend coming up, when McGuinn decides to fire Skip Battin. The bass player, who has served loyally since October 1969, is suddenly found to be ineffective, but the action seems more a result of McGuinn's carelessness than true desperation. The Road Byrds stand in the way of The Reunion Byrds, and McGuinn has already told reporters that he will wind the group down as soon as contractual obligations are fulfilled.

McGuinn persuades Chris Hillman to come back, but that is necessarily not a long-term solution: Hillman's band with Stephen Stills, Manassas, is touring heavily and has its second album ready to ship, so Hillman just accepts the invitation as there is clearly an emergency. As the Byrds rhythm section has lately consisted of drummers-for-rent, Hillman brings in Joe Lala, the percussionist in Manassas.

Battin will give his version to Barry Ballard in *Omaha Rainbow* (December 1976). "David Geffen from Asylum was wanting to put together the original Byrds and there was a lot of pressure on Roger to do so. He went with it, and I left the group at his request, because he was going to replace me with Hillman, and Mike [Clarke] was going to come back on drums. When I left The Byrds there was only one tour left to do, and that was just a two or three-day tour of the East Coast. Clarence called me after the first gig and said, 'Oh man, it's over.' And it was. He was quite upset and thought that Roger had made a big mistake, and evidently he did."

Actually, McGuinn toys briefly with a grander scheme, a sort of Byrds Revue, to fulfil the engagements booked for early March and to promote the Asylum album. According to a pre-show blurb for a Connecticut concert on March 9, the group is referred to as "the Original Byrds", consisting of White, Hillman, and Lala, plus Battin and Gene Clark, and "there is a possibility that other former members of the band will appear also".

•

Roy Carr of *New Musical Express* has been sent to California to interview McGuinn. "This week, Roger McGuinn disbanded The Byrds to reform The Byrds," he heads the article that is published in the paper's March 17 edition. McGuinn announces: "It's a forward step backwards, and not a hype. Neither is it something that was scraped out of the bottom of a can. It's a brand new product and one which I'm certain will make a lot of people happy.

"In future, any other band that I put together – and that includes one I'm fixing up with Clarence White and Chris Hillman – won't be called The Byrds. It'll be called something else. From here on in, the only group of musicians who will be known as The Byrds, and who will record and tour under that name, will be the original five. What I do on my own will be entirely different."

Why, asks Carr? "You see, the only thing that the original band didn't accomplish was, simply, staying together," says McGuinn, "or at the very least, being open to each other and really attempting to work together. Personally, I always enjoyed the high moments with the original Byrds line-up, and this time around it feels like we're most definitely getting back to that.

"The years have helped a lot. Sure, there are still some tensions between David and I, but we're much older now and can handle these things so much better than before. Tensions like the ones that existed between us used to be intolerable within the tolerance level of the old band. ... In some ways, Crosby and I are very much like each other, in that we both need to bounce our creative ideas [off] of other people, and because of that alone I particularly enjoy working with him. On our

own, we do all right. But together we've got that chemistry to create things we just can't do alone. I suppose it was inevitable that one day Crosby and I would get around to making an album together, and very shortly we'll both get into the studio and do that."

To Roy Carr, the 12-string chime represents the Byrds sound more than anything else. "This is not entirely true," McGuinn protests. "I only have the capacity to be a portion of what you consider to be the sound of The Byrds. If, as in the past, I get other people to do things like the original members created, then I suppose it sounds somewhat like The Byrds. However, I never claimed to carry the sound, and this new album will substantiate that fact."

Winding up, McGuinn voices a cautious hope for the future of The Byrds. "It's a casual relationship which is not as uptight as it was before. That's what cracked it, things being too intense. Look, when you're tied to people, it drives you crazy and eventually leads up to crises, which is not conducive to creativity. This is something that won't happen a second time, for, you see, we now have this tentative situation whereby we'll contact each other, perhaps once a year, to cut an album and maybe undertake a tour. In this way, we won't crack the group."

•

While in California, Roy Carr also sits down to talk to Gram Parsons at the singer's Coldwater Canyon home. The interview is printed in *New Musical Express* on May 12. Parsons has just released his first solo album, *GP*, which marks the debut appearance of singer Emmylou Harris on a major label. The Fallen Angels, Parsons' new group, is built around Harris's pure voice. "She's so very important to this band. You see, there aren't so many country tenor singers around except for those straight session Nashville cats.

"When I first joined The Byrds," says Parsons, "I was quite pleased with the results, simply because it had been so damn hard for me to get a real country thing going. But the more I played with The Byrds, the more I wished I could get them to do real country songs like [George Jones's] 'That's All It Took', instead of some of their more familiar songs, which I felt were a waste of time. At this point, we were working to really big audiences but weren't getting the response we could have gotten had we pursued the direction of the Rodeo album."

Carr describes Parsons as very laidback, although he becomes heated when the infamous South African tour is mentioned. "I was raised in the South by some wonderful black people, and what common sense I have I owe to them. Listen, man, I couldn't play before

segregated audiences. That's something no person should ever do. I think the South African government are nothing but a bunch of skunks and really behind the rest of the civilised world."

For a long time, it was hoped that Keith Richards would produce Parsons' album. He explains the circumstances to Roy Carr. "Unfortunately, for a number of reasons, including Keith's prior commitments and the lack of suitable musicians in Britain, all I did was sing and pick with the Stones and sing on 'Lovin' Cup' and 'Sweet Virginia'."

A couple of months later, Nick Kent brings up the question during the Stones' European tour (*New Musical Express*, September 29). Mick Jagger grins: "It's always in the air, innit, Keith?" The Stones guitarist says: "I hadn't seen Gram for some time. He had a band together and made an album with Glen Hardin and James Burton. He was into a very purist country trip – stuff like 'Streets Of Baltimore'."

•

Cameron Crowe speaks to Roger McGuinn for a feature in *Creem* (June 1973). Most of the interview is conducted now, while some snippets are added in a later conversation. Talk centres on the reunited Byrds, and McGuinn reveals that they have been offered a hefty $100,000 for one concert in London next summer – an offer they will never get around to picking up.

Friday 23
Memorial Auditorium, Burlington, VT

Back on the East Coast for the third weekend in a row, The Byrds who take the stage tonight are Roger McGuinn, Clarence White, Chris Hillman (bass, vocals), and Joe Lala (drums). The group appears with Jonathan Edwards and Orphan at an event sponsored by the St. Michael's Student Association of St Michael's College.

Rehearsals have been nonexistent, so Hillman and Lala are forced to play it by ear as McGuinn more or less keeps to the standard Byrds set. It shows, too, according to John Hanrahan's review in student paper *Michaelman* (February 1972). "They had replaced their bass player, Skip Battin, with Chris Hillman, who is or was a member of Manassas, a backup group for Steve Stills. He was not altogether with the group. His bass work was satisfactory, but he was very poor on vocals, forgetting words. Gene Parsons is the drummer for The Byrds and I don't really know if that was him on stage – it if was, he's gotten his hair cut and forgotten how to play the drums. He found himself more than once out of time with the music. The only definite

The original five back again: Gene Clark, Chris Hillman, Michael Clarke, David Crosby and Roger McGuinn.

remnants of The Byrds were Roger McGuinn and Clarence White. Roger McGuinn was the only one who tried to make something out of the concert, [and although] Clarence White played well, he did not seem to care too much or know too much where he was."

On the other hand, Doug Collette of another student newspaper, the University of Vermont's *Cynic* (March 1), thinks it the "most satisfying rock'n'roll show" he's seen "this entire school year". Support acts Orphan and Jonathan Edwards are excellent, he says, and he writes of The Byrds: "They had some problems Friday night: Chris Hillman, the original Byrds bassist, and an unknown drummer had just gotten into the group with Roger McGuinn and Clarence White, and the two newcomers were obviously not fully integrated into The Byrds' stage act. Yet The Byrds I saw last week were, despite their apparent aloofness, enthusiastic, seeming to really enjoy the music they were playing and the audience that was enjoying it.

"Most of their set was vintage, definitely vintage, including classics like 'Chimes Of Freedom', 'So You Want To Be A Rock'n'Roll Star', plus some infectious bluegrass and a touch of Chuck Berry. Hillman's spectacular bass guided the new drummer and provided a steady bottom for McGuinn's jet-engine 12-string and White's outer-space-country leads. … The new Byrds have the potential to be a force as inspiring in the 70s as were their predecessors in the 60s. At least that was the thought I had when they left the auditorium stage for the last time, and that's the most cheerful, optimistic feeling I've had in a long time."

Skip Battin discusses the end of his time with the group in an interview conducted in Europe in 1985. "At the end, we'd hit a plateau," the ex-Byrd will tell Hans Hanegraaff. "We weren't growing any more. Things got a little tired. Maybe some personal conflicts developed as they do – and they will over a five-year period – and maybe Roger felt it was time for a change. … I think when we broke up The Byrds there was a lot of pressure from the experts, the original Byrds, to do a reunion, and that's what they did. Gene Parsons was the first one to go, replaced by John Guerin and other drummers. Roger himself said: Gene, it's time for you to go. And then it was time for me to go. So there was only Roger and Clarence left, only for one weekend. They only played for one weekend without me. That was the end. After that there was no more Byrds."

Saturday 24
Capitol Theatre,
Passaic, NJ

A milestone in the Byrds calendar. Clarence White's loyalty is stretched to the limit after tonight's aimless performance (with Brewer & Shipley in the support slot), plagued by lack of rehearsals and poor playing. Despite the short notice, the programme for the concert features photos of both Chris Hillman and Joe Lala. Indeed, the group has several appearances lined up right through May, but now McGuinn decides to cancel all upcoming bookings and set the travelling Byrds on the ground.

Johnny Rogan's later Byrds biography, *Timeless Flight Revisited*, will quote a review in *The Free Aquarian*, a local Hackensack paper. "It was Hillman who messed things up for the band," writes the reviewer. "He is viewing the spring tour as a part-time job or a favour to Roger, but he isn't thinking in terms of the music. He even admitted that he doesn't enjoy playing bass any more, but that fact didn't stop him from playing so loudly that he drowned out Clarence's guitar throughout most of the late show. Clarence asked him several times on stage to turn it down, but Chris merely threw his head back, smiled, and kept on playing. Hillman had also refused to rehearse with the band, and it was evident that he doesn't know most of the songs."

As Rogan's biography details, there is plenty of underlying tension, because Hillman and Lala have been paid exceedingly well for the weekend. "I must admit we didn't play $2,000 worth of music," Hillman excuses himself to Rogan. "I wish I could have rehearsed with him, but I just didn't know songs like 'Chestnut Mare' and 'Lover Of The Bayou' – I flew out there to rehearse, but there was no time to. We only did a weekend. We flew out on Friday morning from Colorado. We had a soundcheck for half an hour, and that was the time [in which] we were supposed to learn these songs. We tried our damnedest. If we'd only had six hours to rehearse, it would have been better."

March

Wednesday 7

Asylum Records releases the Byrds reunion album in the US. It is simply titled *Byrds* after the prophetic (and arguably better) *Full Circle* is dropped. The album is sometimes erroneously referred to as *Gene Clark, Chris Hillman, David Crosby, Roger McGuinn, Michael Clarke*, as their names are printed at the top of the album jacket.

The album consists of 11 songs recorded mainly during a four-week period between October and November of last year and reflects five musicians who did not let the past rest in peace and instead have consciously developed their sound. Anticipation runs high among critics and fans, but many disapprove of the lack of an instantly identifiable Byrds sound.

Released on a label other than Columbia, the album stands alone in the Byrds canon. But in hindsight it will seem a commendable project and a dignified end to a remarkable eight years. Even here, at the very end of their career, The Byrds are pioneers. In the decades to come, reunions and comebacks by 60s groups will fill up stadiums or travel around on cheesy pop package-tours. The pretext for the quick money will invariably be nostalgia.

Of course, the Byrds reunion is a sound business decision, but McGuinn, Clark, Crosby, Hillman, and Clarke are first and foremost motivated by a genuine desire to create new music together. The album is a big seller, making US Number 20 on the *Billboard* charts and thus becoming the highest charting Byrds album since the golden era of Mr. Tambourine Man and Turn! Turn! Turn! (not counting the Top Ten greatest hits album in 1967).

The critical response in the US is lukewarm at best, best summed up by Jon Landau's crushing headline in *Rolling Stone* (April 12): "The Byrds: Not Only Not Their Best, It's Barely The Byrds."

"To tell you the truth, I would rather write about some of the fine new albums released since the first of this year," he begins, and lists records by Dr John, Todd Rundgren (*A Wizard/A True Star*), Dusty Springfield (*Cameo*), Judee Sill, Jimmy Cliff's soundtrack to *The Harder They Come*, and Bob Seger's *Back In '72*.

"But at the moment, I am obliged to comment on the most disappointing and one of the dullest albums of the year, Byrds. At their best, they were once my favourite white American rock'n'roll band, but not only isn't this their best – it is barely them. … The Byrds were the most stylistically unified of American rock bands, but, paradoxically, this is an album without a style. It has little to do with the original band except that it is performed by its nominal members."

Unfortunately, Landau perpetuates an old myth. "I say nominal because everyone knows that only Roger McGuinn performed instrumentally on most of *Mr. Tambourine Man*, the most auspicious debut American album in pop 60s rock, outdone internationally only by the Stones' *England's Newest Hitmakers*. The rest of the music was supplied by Joe Osborne, Hal Blaine, and, if memory serves, Leon Russell. It was music that combined contemporary material with high-pitched, almost whiney harmony and the full-bodied ring of McGuinn's Rickenbacker 12-string guitar. … When the group decided to play its own music on *Turn! Turn! Turn!* they were forced to equal, if not copy, the style that had been handed them by the L.A. studio musicians [and] they simply weren't up to it."

As a footnote to this, it should be mentioned that Landau is not just misinformed – he contradicts what he wrote earlier. When he covered The Byrds' appearance at the Boston Tea Party in February 1969 (*Rolling Stone*, April 5 1969), he painstakingly made the point that the original Byrds demanded to play on their debut album.

Landau briefly goes through the various Byrds albums from that time and onward, and he likes everything right up until "the much underrated" *Ballad Of Easy Rider* and 'Chestnut Mare'. "Despite the fact that he was one of the lesser songwriters in the band, McGuinn always made the greatest contribution to its stylistic supremacy.

"The depressing thing about this album is not the absence of the old form, but the absence of any form at all. Byrds is 11 songs, some good, some bad, sung in rotation by different, dislocated members of a non-existing band. It was undoubtedly made in a friendlier environment than the old records … but the new environment seems to have made for a slick, undirected piece of jelly instead of a firm, rooted, moving album."

Landau longs for the time when The Byrds could sound "like some exotic mixture of velvet and nails". Gene Clark provides the best material ("he transcends the mediocrity of the arrangements with relative ease"), while McGuinn's numbers are to Landau's ears "distressingly ordinary".

Hillman has two lightweight, enjoyable pieces of fluff, even if 'Things Will Be Better' actually sounds like a Byrds song to Landau. "Crosby's ponderousness on 'Long Live The King' and 'Laughing' bear some vague relationship to the superb 'What's Happening!?!?' of *Fifth Dimension* but wind up as empty shells of songs, closer to the absurd paranoia of 'Almost Cut My Hair' than his great Byrds number."

Robert Hilburn of *The Los Angeles Times* (March 27) shares many of the same sentiments as Landau. "The first thing you have to say about the Byrds album is that it reflects the professionalism you'd expect from five guys who have been associated with as many successful records as the original Byrds. But the next thing you have to say is that it is decidedly dispensable, a modest collection that hardly serves as the cause for celebration. Not only does the album lack the creative spark

of The Byrds' early folk-rock fusion, but it fails to match the best moments of the post-Clark/Crosby Byrds – such songs as 'Ballad Of Easy Rider', 'Chestnut Mare', 'America's Great National Pastime', 'Jesus Is Just Alright', and 'You Ain't Goin' Nowhere'."

To Hilburn, the cover songs are the best, although he would still prefer to hear the original versions. 'Full Circle' and 'Born To Rock And Roll' are OK, but "they are merely appealing [rather] than vital". Hilburn writes in closing: "The remaining songs, two each by Hillman and Crosby, range from modest to less. That doesn't add up enough to build much momentum."

In August, McGuinn will refer to the album as just a vague memory. "At the time we did the Byrds reunion album we were very pleased with it," he says to *The Daily Review* (August 24) of Hayward, CA. "Then when it came out the press tore it up. Looking back on it, the album isn't as good as it could have been, but if I remember right we were very pleased with it at the time."

He repeats that view to *Crawdaddy* (October 1973). "Musically it wasn't terrible. It could have been a lot worse, right?" But a few years later, his criticism has moved to outright damning. "I think it was not a miserable disaster. It was worse than that. It was mediocre," he tells the Canadian rock paper *Cheap Thrills* (December 1977).

In conjunction with the album's release, Chris Hillman does a phone interview from his Colorado home for *The Los Angeles Times* (March 25). "It was very pleasant working together in the studio," he tells Lorraine Alterman. "Everybody was a little more grown-up. We had a good time and that's why I think we'll probably do another album later on."

He observes: "I don't think we were responsible for doing as much as people might say. It's just at the time – '64, '65 – all kinds of things were going on, not only in music but in everything else. That's when those troubles were going down in colleges and there were riots. Music was a part of it, as were films and whatever else was being created at the time. I imagine The Byrds, as well as other groups, had a lot to do with some part of it, but it wasn't only in music. It was a turbulent time, but very creative for everybody."

Friday 9

A pre-show blurb for an appearance at the University Gym in Fairfield, CT, claims this will be one of the last appearances of The Original Byrds, and tempts with a show featuring Roger McGuinn, Chris Hillman, Clarence White, Joe Lala – the four who careered through the lacklustre weekend in Vermont and New Jersey two weeks ago – plus Gene Clark and Skip Battin. In the end, the appearance is cancelled.

Byrds

A1 'Full Circle' (G. CLARK)
A2 'Sweet Mary' (R. MCGUINN/J. LEVY)
A3 'Changing Heart' (G. CLARK)
A4 'For Free' (J. MITCHELL)
A5 'Born To Rock 'n' Roll' (R. MCGUINN)
B1 'Things Will Be Better' (C. HILLMAN/D. TAYLOR)
B2 'Cowgirl In The Sand' (N. YOUNG)
B3 'Long Live The King' (D. CROSBY)
B4 'Borrowing Time' (C. HILLMAN/J. LALA)
B5 'Laughing' (D. CROSBY)
B6 '(See the Sky) About To Rain' (N. YOUNG)

US release March 7 1973 (Asylum SD5058)
UK release March 24 1973 (Asylum SYLA 8754)
Chart high US number 20; UK number 31
Read more … entries between October 16–November 15 1972

"What's important is that The Byrds have overcome the novelty of reforming and really do cut it here. The band's direction is no-nonsense, straight-ahead music. There's not any cultural preaching or sloppy outtakes as intros … I'm glad to report that The Byrds make it on the strength of the music alone." NEW MUSICAL EXPRESS, MARCH 31, 1973

Friday 16

The Byrds have been booked for a weekend in the South with Paul Butterfield's Better Days, starting tonight with a show at the Civic Auditorium in Albuquerque, NM. A blurb in *The Albuquerque Journal* on the day before the concert says The Byrds consist of McGuinn, Clarence White, Skip Battin, and Joe Lala – confirming that McGuinn has a last-minute hope to honour these concerts.

In the event, Eric Weissberg & Deliverance have to stand in for The Byrds. According to the *Journal* (March 26), "The Byrds were unable to appear because their lead guitarist broke his wrist in a car accident," which is of course a made-up excuse.

Weissberg has just narrowly missed *Billboard*'s Number One position with 'Duelling Banjos', the theme song from John Boorman's acclaimed thriller *Deliverance*. While he hurriedly forms a group to take on the road, Warner Brothers is equally quick to put out the purported soundtrack album from the movie. In reality, it is just the hit single packaged with a re-release of *New Dimensions In Banjo And Bluegrass*, a ten-year-old Elektra album featuring Weissberg and others, including Clarence White on guitar.

Saturday 17

Today's Byrds concert at the Coliseum in El Paso, TX, is also cancelled, even if pre-show blurbs in *The El Paso Herald-Post* promise an appearance by "Chris Hillman and Roger McGuinn". In effect, The Byrds are no more.

Byrds bookings for the rest of March and April are cancelled, affecting the following announced appearances: Valley Forge Music Fair, Valley Forge, PA (March 23); Case Auditorium, Boston, MA (24); University of Maryland, College Park, MD (25), plus a stray date in Mount Holyoke College, South Hadley, MA (29).

'Full Circle'

A 'Full Circle' (G. CLARK)
B 'Long Live The King' (D. CROSBY)

US release April 11 1973 (Asylum 11016)
UK release June 22 1973 (Asylum AYM 517)
Chart high US number 109; UK none
Read more ... entries between October 16–November 15 1972

Friday 23

The *Byrds* album is released in the UK, and is received more kindly than in the US. Danny Holloway writes in *New Musical Express* (March 31): "We've learned to have reservations about these things, haven't we? A group dies a slow and painful death and decides to re-assemble after eight years. Motivation? Most people will say money, but I'd have to disagree with that lame answer. More than likely, they're yearning for that magical rush that Byrds' music gave them.

"David Crosby's production was the first thing that really impressed me about this album; the sound is rich and full and the many acoustic instruments are recorded exceptionally well. Crosby has emphasised The Byrds' highs: the cross-picking of guitars and their impressive harmonies. But Chris Hillman's bass-playing isn't as melodic or as distinctive as on early recordings (on which many people have alleged he didn't play) and Michael Clarke's drumming is mixed pretty far back on most cuts.

"What's important is that The Byrds have overcome the novelty of reforming and really do cut it here. The band's direction is no-nonsense, straight-ahead music. There's not any cultural preaching or sloppy outtakes as intros; they've chosen to present their songs as well-played and produced as possible – and, without the in-vogue gimmicks, it's difficult for any band to make it. I'm glad to report that The Byrds make it on the strength of the music alone."

Holloway's favourite is 'For Free', which he finds perplexing. "I've always hated Joni Mitchell's music as much as anybody could. I'd feel uneasy, then queasy, and then threaten to vomit if anyone dared to play her stuff in my presence."

He also prefers Clark and Hillman's stuff over McGuinn's and Crosby's. "An obvious single would be Hillman's 'Things Will Be Bet-

---

'Things Will Be Better' (UK)

A 'Things Will Be Better'
  (C. HILLMAN/D. TAYLOR)
B 'For Free' (J. MITCHELL)

UK release April 24 1973 (Asylum AYM 516)
Chart high US none; UK none
Read more ... entries between October 16–November 15 1972

---

ter', which bops with fervour, and McGuinn's Rickenbacker plays some tasty lines. ... After all is said and done, all five of the original Byrds can look back on this one with a lot of pride. And all the old Byrds fans who'll buy it out of duty will be glad to know that they're not being taken for a ride. It's nice to see somebody return with a lot of care. It would've have been so easy to have blown it." The album makes UK Number 31.

April

Wednesday 11

Two tracks are lifted from the *Byrds* album for an obligatory single in the US, pairing 'Full Circle' with 'Long Live The King'. It makes a paltry US Number 109 in *Billboard*'s chart (87 in *Cash Box*). In June, Asylum attempts to push 'Cowgirl In The Sand' as a topside (coupled with 'Long Live The King' again) but with even poorer sales.

Monday 23
ALSO ...

The second album by Manassas (featuring Chris Hillman), *Down The Road*, is released. It will be viewed as anti-climatic after the impressive debut album, and soon after the group breaks up amidst rumours of a reunion of Crosby Stills Nash & Young.

Friday 27

In the UK, Asylum's distributor EMI picks Chris Hillman's 'Things Will Be Better' as the single off the reunion album and puts Joni Mitchell's 'For Free' on the B-side. Charles Shaar Murray comments wearily in *New Musical Express* (April 28): "The Great Byrds reunion seems to have been a trifle disappointing, and this single is appropriately lacklustre. Written by Chris Hillman and Dallas Taylor, only McGuinn's characteristic 12-string makes it sound like The Byrds at all. Ah well – if EMI thinks it's gonna be a hit, then who am I to ... ."

May

Wednesday 2
ALSO ...

Clarence White, now an ex-Byrd, gathers The Kentucky Colonels together for a short low-key British tour of colleges and universities, starting at the Bishop Lonsdale College in Derby.

Chris Hillman, David Crosby, Gene Clark.

Interviewed by *New Musical Express* (June 9) during the tour, White says of the Byrds break-up: "I'm sad in a way because [The Byrds were] a good group – at times. But I found that latest album, the one where the old Byrds got together, a little disappointing, like any other person would – I expected to hear that old jingle-jangle sound and it wasn't quite there."

Saturday 5

New Musical Express publishes a lengthy interview with McGuinn.

Titled 'Tales Of An Early Byrd' and conducted by West Coast PR man Patrick William Salvo, the interesting question–answer feature traces McGuinn's story back to 1964 and ends with David Crosby's ousting in late 1967.

"Stupid decision," McGuinn says of that act. "It was a thick, hot-headed thing to do. An ego trip. It helped, though, because now everybody is friendly. And it's cool."

Saturday 12

McGuinn inaugurates his solo career with a performance at the Bristol Bay Club in Long Beach, CA. It is a momentous occasion, not only for the fact that this is his solo first concert in almost ten years, but also because he chooses to do it completely acoustic – a tradition he will return to in the 90s.

Rolling Stone writes up a brief note in its June 21 issue. "Full circle: Roger McGuinn performed solo, just him and his guitar. ... For nearly two-and-a-half hours, he played some 25 songs, Byrd tunes, songs off his solo album, including a skyjacker ballad called 'Bag Full Of Money'. He told the audience how the bridge of another new tune, 'M'Linda', features a Moog creating the sound of steel drums playing the tunes from the 7-Ups and Tidy Toilet Bowl cleaner ads – 'to give it commercial appeal'. And, introducing 'My Sweet Woman', a liberation lullaby, he explained that he wasn't against the Woman's Movement as long as he was left alone. 'I mean, I'm a rock'n'roll star,' he said, 'but I'll still take out the trash.'"

The Long Beach performance is unique, however, as McGuinn has already formed a group for touring purposes and to promote his eponymous solo album. In that band, McGuinn plays electric guitars, with John Guerin (drums), Mike Wofford (keyboards), and David Vaught (bass guitar) making up the rest of his quartet. Their debut is set for New York City on May 18, but McGuinn still entertains plans of a tour by the old Byrds. "I have to talk to Crosby about getting the availability of time for rehearsal and performances," he tells *Rolling Stone* (June 7). "The last meeting I had with Geffen [and] Crosby, it was definitely positive in that direction; we just don't have the specifics on it. The tour might be from mid-June to mid-July. If I say it, it might happen."

Friday 18

McGuinn and band make their debut at the Academy of Music, New York, NY, in a show with Commander Cody & His Lost Planet Airmen and J.F. Murphy & Salt.

Billed as The Roger McGuinn Band in capital letters with a reassuringly 'Formerly Of The Byrds' in smaller type below, McGuinn's new venture does not exactly bring the house down.

John Rockwell in *The New York Times* (May 21) is already bemoaning the fact that The Byrds have come apart. "The Byrds were on of the great rock group of the sixties and their potential, had they not broken up, was even greater than their accomplishment. For a while this spring, it looked as if they might get together again. But after an album had been produced, their plans collapsed, and then the Roger McGuinn Band that finally showed up at the Academy of Music this weekend consisted of McGuinn and three non-Byrd backup musicians. McGuinn still sings with a sweet folk tenor, plays guitar agilely, and looks as seraphically pretty as ever. But the performance at Friday's late show hardly broke new ground or suggested more than a functional fulfilment of previously booked dates."

Meanwhile, yet another Byrds compilation is released on CBS in the UK. *The History Of The Byrds* is a well-balanced selection of the group's best songs spread over four sides of vinyl, starting with 'Mr. Tambourine Man' and ending with 'America's Great National Pastime' 28 songs later, although no tracks from the reunion album on Asylum are featured. When folded out, the inside jacket is adorned with Pete Frame's elaborate Byrds family tree, tracing the group's roots through their many capers over the years.

History Of The Byrds (UK)

A1 'Mr. Tambourine Man' (B. DYLAN)
A2 'Turn! Turn! Turn!' (ECCLESIASTES/P. SEEGER)
A3 'She Don't Care About Time' (G. CLARK)
A4 'Wild Mountain Thyme' (R. MCGUINN/C. HILLMAN/M. CLARKE/D. CROSBY)
A5 'Eight Miles High' (G. CLARK/R. MCGUINN/D. CROSBY)
A6 'Mr. Spaceman' (R. MCGUINN)
A7 '5D (Fifth Dimension)' (R. MCGUINN)
B1 'So You Wanna Be A Rock 'n' Roll Star' (R. MCGUINN/C. HILLMAN)
B2 'Time Between' (C. HILLMAN)
B3 'My Back Pages' (B. DYLAN)
B4 'Lady Friend' (D. CROSBY)
B5 'Goin' Back' (C. KING/G. GOFFIN)
B6 'Old John Robertson' (C. HILLMAN/R. MCGUINN)
B7 'Wasn't Born To Follow' (C. KING/G. GOFFIN)
C1 'You Ain't Goin' Nowhere' (B. DYLAN)
C2 'Hickory Wind' (GENE PARSONS/B. BUCHANAN)
C3 'Nashville West' (GENE PARSONS/C. WHITE)
C4 'Drug Store Truck Drivin' Man' (R. MCGUINN/GRAM PARSONS)
C5 'Gunga Din' (GENE PARSONS)
C6 'Jesus Is Just Alright' (A. REYNOLDS)
C7 'Ballad Of Easy Rider' (B. DYLAN /R. MCGUINN)
D1 'Chestnut Mare' (R. MCGUINN/J. LEVY)
D2 'Yesterday's Train' (GENE PARSONS/S. BATTIN)
D3 'Just A Season' (R. MCGUINN/J. LEVY)
D4 'Citizen Kane' (S. BATTIN/K. FOWLEY)
D5 'Jamaica Say You Will' (J. BROWNE)
D6 'Tiffany Queen' (R. MCGUINN)
D7 'America's Great National Pastime' (S. BATTIN/K. FOWLEY)

UK release May 18 1973 (CBS 68242)
Chart high UK none
Read more ... entry for May 18

June

Tuesday 12–Sunday 17

McGuinn and his three-piece band play two shows a night for a week at The Troubadour in Los Angeles. Gene Clark, Bruce Johnston, and Elaine 'Spanky' McFarlane sit in during the residence. *Los Angeles Times* critic Robert Hilburn covers the Wednesday appearance, and writes (June 16): "Even though Roger McGuinn has officially disbanded The Byrds and begun a solo career, he was obviously still in the shadow of his old group. … There was conversation about The Byrds around the club before he went on stage and the inevitable comparisons after he left. To make The Byrds' shadow even more obvious, there was an ex-Byrd (Gene Clark) on stage with him and another ex-Byrd (Gram Parsons) in the audience. And: McGuinn finished this 45-minute set with three Byrds tunes: 'Chestnut Mare', 'Mr. Spaceman', and 'So You Want To Be A Rock'n'Roll Star'.

"Predictably, the three songs drew more audience response than the new songs McGuinn previewed from his upcoming solo album. The shadow of The Byrds is something that is going to help McGuinn and hurt him, but it may well end up hurting more than helping. The problem he now faces is the same one that plagued The Byrds in recent years – the need to re-establish momentum. … There is variety to his new material (the songs range from a piece based on 'Little Deuce Coupe', the tale of two 747s drag racing across the country, to a piece of reggae fluff) but little impact. His vocals lacked conviction and his four-piece rhythm section lacked punch. McGuinn seems reduced to a modest collection of songs, most of them reflecting a degree of accessibility and pleasantness, but less than is necessary to make you start spreading the word. Hard road ahead."

Nat Freedland of *Billboard* (June 30) is more upbeat. "If Roger McGuinn's forthcoming Columbia solo album catches [anywhere] near the energy and exciting musicianship of his in-person act, all those years of effort to keep The Byrds' name alive with consistently shifting personnel will seem an ironic exercise in futility. … Some of his most effective first-hearing songs had a darkly satiric quality which may point to the best direction for him to concentrate on. There was a chilling ballad of a disgruntled ex-paratrooper who got away with a skyjacking ransom. Then Bruce Johnston showed up for a Beach Boys' parody about two 747 jets 'Draggin' Cross The USA'. Also sitting in were Spanky (& Our Gang) McFarland and another original Byrd, Gene Clark."

•

Some time following the Troubadour residence, the grandiosely named Patrick Snyder-Scumpy interviews McGuinn at his Malibu home for *Crawdaddy* (November 1973). The possibilities of a tour by the original Byrds is dimmer now. "We hung The Byrds up," Roger announces. "I own the copyright on the name but now there's no group, performing or recording, using it. The possibility of a tour with the original members depends on whether Crosby Stills Nash & Young can get it together. If they can't and David's looking for something to do, then we'll do it."

Of the Asylum album, McGuinn thinks aloud: "Crosby, in retrospect, tells me he didn't have enough slack on the Byrds album. If I had done one more tune or sung lead on one of the tunes already on there, it would have been better. He also said he shouldn't have done 'Laughing' a second time. When you're involved in the studio, it's really difficult to see the forest from the trees, to use a cliché. You get so wrapped up in it. The enthusiasm and morale were really great, so we all felt really good. Unfortunately, we forgot that we could never possibly be as good as when we had been together on the road for six months and then come in to do an album. We would have had to spend at least six months living together to get it on that really high level again."

McGuinn adds with a smile: "And I'm glad my album came out looking better, because that made me look good. I didn't plan it that way, but it just came out nice."

Monday 18
ALSO …

While McGuinn and Clark share the stage for seven days on the West Coast, several second-generation Byrds rally for the anniversary celebration Midnight Sun Company, the Philadelphia promoters. Clarence White and Gene Parsons plus Chris Etheridge, Sneaky

Pete, and Roger Bush join Gram Parsons' Fallen Angels for the concert at the Tower Theatre in Upper Darby, PA. (The entourage visited Baltimore, MD, on Saturday 16 and Annapolis, MD, on Sunday 17.) It is a day to remember: as events turn out, this will be the last public performance by Gram Parsons.

Afterward, White returns to Los Angeles to rejoin his brothers for a residence at Ash Grove (which stretches well into July) while also starting recording sessions for his first solo album.

July

Friday 6

Following the failure of the previous UK single 'Things Will Be Better', Asylum releases 'Full Circle' (but still slaps 'Things Will Be Better' on the B-side) in the hope that it will sell better. Tony Tyler's silly review in *New Musical Express* (July 7) is symptomatic of a jaded target group. "Totally daft profundities rhymed on a Moon/June basis and backed by inoffensive jangling guitar and offensive, annoying mandolin. Gene Clark wrote this cosmic cowpoke jangalong tripe. So much for your commitments, ole buddy. Someone has just told me that The Byrds are a Big Group. I can't dismiss this single just like that. I need at least another ten words. Eight. Another six should do it. That's it."

Sunday 15

Tragedy strikes when a reckless car-driver kills Clarence White. The accident happens as White unloads gear after a gig at the small BJ Tavern club on Sierra Highway in Palmdale. The driver, a young woman, is booked on suspicion of drunken driving and manslaughter.

'Cowgirl In The Sand' (US)

A 'Cowgirl In The Sand' (N. YOUNG)
B 'Long Live The King' (D. CROSBY)

US release June 1973 (Asylum 11019)
Chart high US none
Read more … entries between October 16–November 15 1972

'Full Circle' (UK)

A 'Full Circle' (G. CLARK)
B 'Things Will Be Better' (C. HILLMAN/D. TAYLOR)

UK release August 8 1975 (Asylum AYM 545)
Chart high UK none
Read more … entries between October 16–November 15 1972

His years with The Byrds brought great recognition, but the 29-year-old musician had not tapped his full potential at the time of his death. "He will be missed," Robert Hilburn concludes in a brief eulogy in *The Los Angeles Times* (July 28), four words that barely describe Clarence White's senseless death yet aptly summarise the undiminished regard in which he is held forever after.

The funeral is held on July 19 at a Catholic church in Palmdale attended by more than 100 musician friends, among them many fellow Byrds young and old: Roger McGuinn, Gram Parsons, Chris Hillman, and Gene Parsons. When the service finishes, Gram Parsons steps forward to sing 'Farther Along' – and soon the whole congregation joins in.

Sunday 22

The brand new solo album *Roger McGuinn* is featured in a rather non-committal way in *The Los Angeles Times*. "The only impressive tracks are 'I'm So Restless', a look at the musical and sociological messages of Dylan, Lennon, and Jagger, and 'Bag Full Of Money'." Long-time Byrds fan Bud Scoppa is not able to muster great enthusiasm either. His long review in *Rolling Stone* (August 16) closes with: "[It] is not a great album – just a very good one, with several notable successes and a few failures easily ignored."

In Britain, there is a different story when the album is released at the beginning of August. Jerry Gilbert in *Sounds* thinks his readers are "going to love this variety show for McGuinn, who at last seems to have put all this talents up on a veritable pedestal."

Michael Oldfield in *Melody Maker* (August 18) pens a panegyric paean that is used wholesale as an advertisement. Having first washed his hands of a new Alice Cooper album, Nick Kent in *New Musical Express* (also August 18) reports with relief: "Now this is a little more like it. Of course, it would be ludicrous to expect a sudden reconciliation with the original classic Byrds feel and quality coming from this, Roger McGuinn's first solo album, but all in all it's a surprisingly pleasant creation and one that will at least soothe out the incredible depression that followed after that abysmal Asylum Byrds reunion album."

September

Saturday 1

New Musical Express publishes an 'NME Consumer's Guide' to The Byrds, rating their albums one by one. It is compiled and written by Roy Carr, Charles Shaar Murray, and

BLAZING COFFIN FOUND IN DESERT
Rock Singer's Body Stolen and Set Afire

A coffin containing the body of a k-rock singer was found ablaze in ~~ Tree Nat~~ Monument

its mind and wanted the body flown from Van Nuys Airport.
The body was turned over ~

An autopsy was performed on the body of Parsons after he died at Hi Desert Memorial Hospital in Yuc Valley at 12:~ W~

Joe Stevens (now a renowned photographer; he was the chauffeur on the group's first American cross-country tour in the summer of 1965). Together with Pete Frame's comprehensive serial in *Zigzag* (issues 27 to 33 between December 1972 and July 1973), this is the first real appraisal of The Byrds' recording catalogue.

Wednesday 19

Barely two months after Clarence White's death comes another mindless tragedy. Gram Parsons is found unconscious by the manager of the Joshua Tree Inn in California and rushed to hospital where he dies upon arrival. At the time of his death, Parsons had planned a tour of Britain with an extended Country Gazette to encompass Skip Battin, Sneaky Pete, and Gene Parsons.

Parsons' family has arranged for the coffin to be flown to New Orleans for the funeral, but on Thursday June 20 it is stolen by two men who take it back to the Joshua Tree National Monument. Some hours later, the coffin with Parsons' body is found ablaze along a desolate trail in the national park. Newspapers describe it as a "ritual ceremony", and Chief Park Ranger Don Colville is quoted in a UPI newsflash saying that it reminded him of a "Viking funeral, the kind the Norsemen got when they died at sea". (A few days later, Phil Kaufman, Parsons' road manager, and Michael Martin are charged and plead guilty of the theft and are fined $300 each.)

Thus ends the life of perhaps the biggest influence on The Byrds' career outside the Original Five. The highly talented Gram Parsons managed to re-direct the group's sound and helped to define the country-rock idiom. His legend will grow into cult status in the years to come, but at the time of death he is just – to quote the obituary in *New Musical Express* (October 6) – "the superstar who didn't quite make it".

Two years later, journalist Ron Tepper will ask Roger McGuinn if the deaths of Clarence White and Gram Parsons had any emotional impact. "Are you kidding?" Roger retorts. "It tore me up. Especially Clarence. Gram, well, he was my friend. But Clarence, he was my buddy. He's the closest friend I have ever had. I think about him all the time; still do."

October–December

McGuinn christens his four-man group The Adventures Of Roger McGuinn and tours steadily through the months of October, November, and into December, adhering to the Byrds pattern with gigs clustered around weekends and weekdays off.

Interviewed by Nat Kirsch in *Billboard* (November 17), McGuinn speaks about the creation of a TV show for the Topanga Canyon cable network. "[I will] be producing the show myself. It's a two-man deal, the cameraman and me. I'm working on a format similar to the old Pete Seeger PBS shows, with just me and my guests talking and playing some music."

Perhaps McGuinn foresees the changes in the decades to come better than most. He signs off: "I think the combination of audio and video is going to be an important part of the future of music, and while I'm not into special effects, I do want to be a part of that future."

Roger McGuinn with early proto-type mobile phone.

The Byrds After 1973

Despite the many hopes for a repeat of a Byrds reunion following the album the original five released in the spring of 1973, this will not happen until many years later – and then just for a single night. Before that, the closest they will come is the staging of an ambitious concert to be held in Los Angeles to combine The Byrds, Buffalo Springfield, and Crosby Stills Nash & Young on July 6, 1974 – a family gathering that collapses under its own weight when it is obvious that there are too many egos involved. (Crosby Stills Nash & Young, however, do get back together to make a sell-out appearance at London's Wembley Stadium on September 14, 1974; evidence of their immense drawing power.)

Free of each other again following the comeback album, Gene Clark, Michael Clarke, David Crosby, Chris Hillman, and Roger McGuinn all take different roads into the coming decades, although they will have a habit of crossing each other's paths. Following a pair of solo albums (*Peace On You* and *Roger McGuinn & Band*), McGuinn joins the Rolling Thunder Revue. He is personally invited by Bob Dylan to join the large and flexible entourage of the famous and the not-so-famous and shares the stage with Dylan, Joan Baez, and Ramblin' Jack Elliot to serenade 'Chestnut Mare' and other songs from his comprehensive song book. In the wake of the Rolling Thunder express, McGuinn records *Cardiff Rose* (1976) with producer Mick Ronson, one of his fellow Rolling Thunder travellers. In 1977 he makes *Thunderbyrd*, which contains Tom Petty's 'American Girl' – a song McGuinn reputedly thought was one of his own compositions the first time he heard it.

In those years, David Crosby sees CSNY fall apart again but reinforces his partnership with Graham Nash for two bestselling albums (*Wind On The Water* in 1975 and *Whistling Down The Wire* in 1976), although Crosby's legendary drug abuse will strain relations with his old comrade. Chris Hillman, on the other hand, partakes in a drawing-board exercise, The Souther Hillman Furay Band, with John David Souther and ex-Buffalo singer–songwriter Richie Furay. It is not a great success either artistically or commercially, and after two albums, Hillman resorts to a solo career with the albums *Slippin' Away* and *Clear Sailin'*.

Gene Clark releases his masterpiece *No Other* in 1974, but few are listening, even if the critics hail the album as a rightful classic, and

in the spring of 1977 someone has the bright idea to combine McGuinn, Clark, and Hillman for a tour of Britain. According to contemporary reports, the shows waver between the splendid and the horrendous, and as the tour nears its end, Hillman suddenly defects, citing unreasonable economic arrangements. Despite this, the three form a more stable line-up and when they play concerts in San Francisco and Los Angeles in December 1977, David Crosby joins them on stage for a few songs. It is to be no more than an informal Byrds hootenanny, as Crosby is not invited for the trio's two albums, *McGuinn Hillman & Clarke* (1979) and *City* (1980), the latter credited to "McGuinn & Hillman, featuring Gene Clark". This is a sign of the sensitive relationship between the three ex-Byrds, as by next year McGuinn and Hillman alone record an album without Clark.

Hillman and McGuinn take up solo careers again, and McGuinn briefly reunites with two members of the extended Byrds family – Gene Parsons and Skip Battin – as The Peacemakers for a tour of Britain in 1994. In the mid 1980s, McGuinn begins a new regime: Married for the fourth time and a New Born Christian, he comes full circle as a troubadour in the true sense, travelling around with his wife Camilla McGuinn as manager and minder, playing solo in smaller halls and clubs. He does not leave the regular music business totally behind; in 1991 he puts out the well-received *Back From Rio*, which produced a minor radio hit with 'King Of The Hill'. McGuinn is a natural guest at Bob Dylan's *30th Anniversary Concert Celebration* in October 1992, where he comes on near the end to deliver a striking version

of 'Mr. Tambourine Man' before sharing the mike with Dylan, Eric Clapton, Neil Young, Tom Petty, and George Harrison for a rendition of 'My Back Pages'. As the 1990s unfold, McGuinn will also embrace new technology eagerly, making his music available online for downloading on his website.

Besides David Crosby, it is surprisingly Michael Clarke who will have the greatest commercial success in the decade following the second break-up of the original Byrds. Playing drums with the fairly successful Firefall (a country-rock group formed by ex-Flying Burrito Brothers singer and guitarist Rick Roberts), he finds himself playing for large audiences again and sees singles and albums by Firefall makes US Top Thirty.

Unfortunately, Clarke is motivated to form a kind of pseduo-Byrds that will cause much anger and frustration among his former band-mates. First, he treads water with Gene Clark for *Firebyrd*, an eponymous album in 1984, before he puts together several incarnations of new Byrds from 1988 onward. It is correctly billed as A Tribute To The Byrds, but promoters will have a tendency to highlight just the 'Byrds' part of the name. To authenticate the name, Clarke draws on the extended Byrds family. At one point, this congregation consists of Clarke, Skip Battin, John York, and even Carlos Bernal. The matter ends up in the court, where Clarke and his former band-mates battle over the rights to the name 'Byrds' through a complex judicial process. That is perhaps only to be expected, but what is surprising is the fact that Clarke wins the court case in May 1989 and gains full legal ownership of the name 'The Byrds'.

Four-fifths of The Byrds back together in December 1977: Gene Clark, David Crosby, Roger McGuinn, and Chris Hillman.

(An unintended outcome of Clarke's actions is that Crosby, McGuinn, and Hillman decide to join forces and reclaim the Byrds name for three shows in January 1989. Even if the shows delight fans, the three do not follow up with more performances, although they record some brand new tracks for an upcoming archival project.)

Throughout the 1970s and the 80s interest in The Byrds is always there, and their influence is readily acknowledged. Even in the storm of the punk years of 1975–77, a UK group called Starry Eyed & Laughing tip their hat to the Byrds sound with ringing Rickenbackers and high harmonies. Home in the US, Tom Petty & The Heartbreakers and R.E.M. are just two of many groups who use the building blocks of The Byrds to construct their sound.

In 1987, the specialist label Murray Hill releases *Never Before*, an album that collects several previously unreleased gems on one album. With the advent of the CD age, the group's albums are subject to an elaborate reissue program by Columbia Records. It begins with the archival CD box set *The Byrds*, at the end of 1990, which straddles the group's career from the earliest days right up to a couple of new recordings made by Crosby, McGuinn,

and Hillman in 1989. Expanded versions of *Mr. Tambourine Man, Turn! Turn! Turn!, Fifth Dimension*, and *Younger Than Yesterday* in 1996 mark the start of the reissue series.

In the 1990s, any reunion of The Byrds seems out of the question. Both McGuinn and Hillman have found their own niches – Hillman making good business with The Desert Rose Band – while Crosby plunges further into deep drug abuse. However, there is one event that will bring all five back together – their induction into the Rock'n'Roll Hall Of Fame. On January 16, 1991, the five original Byrds get back on a stage to briefly perform 'Mr. Tambourine Man', 'Turn! Turn! Turn!', and 'I'll Feel A Whole Lot Better'. It is in the nick of time: Gene Clark's health is deteriorates, and on May 24, 1991 he is found dead in his California home. Two years later, on December 19, 1993, Michael Clarke dies from liver failure.

The enlarged Byrds family also suffers causalities: Skip Battin, suffering from Alzheimer's disease, dies at his home in 2003, while Kevin Kelley succumbs in 2001. John Guerin, the drummer who never really was a proper Byrd, dies in 2004. (As of this writing in 2008, both Gene Parsons and John York are performing and recording various projects.)

More than 40 years after The Byrds fused folk and rock to record 'Mr. Tambourine Man', Roger McGuinn, David Crosby, and Chris Hillman are still very active. Crosby has miraculously overcome his drug addiction, after a spell in prison, while Hillman keeps performing and touring. Sadly, the door on another Byrds reunion seems to be closed. According to recent interviews, Crosby and Hillman would not mind, but McGuinn is adamant. "Absolutely not," he replies to music writer John Nork when asked in 1997 if he had any plans for more work with The Byrds. "No, I don't want to do that. I just want to be a solo artist. The Byrds are well documented. I don't think we need any more from the Byrds."

In 2007 came another box set, *There Is A Season*, which also contained a DVD of ten clips from old and rare television appearances. Doing promotion for the album, McGuinn summed up for *Mojo* (October 2006): "I'd have to say that 'Mr. Tambourine Man' has a big place in my heart. Terry Melcher at Studio A rolled out those big speakers and played it to us and we went: 'Wow, did we do that?' It sounded so great and it sounded like a hit. And it was in mono. Terry didn't believe in stereo. He said it was a passing fad."

The Byrds are inducted in the 'Rock'n'Roll Hall Of Fame', January 1992: David Crosby, Roger McGuinn, Gene Clark, and Chris Hillman.

Concert location index 1965–1973

THE BAHAMAS
Freeport, Columbia Records Convention, [Unknown resort], July 30 1970

BELGIUM
Brussels, Vorst Naational, May 18 1971

CANADA
Calgary (Alberta), University of Calgary, April 3 1970; Calgary Stampede, Nov 27 1971
Edmonton (Alberta), Kinsmen Fieldhouse, Edmonton, Nov 28 1971
Kingston (Ontario) Grant Hall, Queen's University, Kingston, Jan 26 1970
Kitchener (Ontario) Bingeman Park Arena, June 20 1966
London (Ontario) London Gardens, London, June 21 1966
Montreal (Quebec) The Forum, Montreal, May 9 1970; Place Des Nations, Montreal, July 30 1971
Squamish (BC) 'Vancouver Pop Festival', Paradise Valley Resort, Aug 22 1969
Toronto (Ontario) Varsity Arena, June 22 1966; 'Toronto Pop Festival', Varsity Stadium, June 21 1969 [CANC]; Massey Hall, Feb 1 1970
Vancouver (BC) PNE Gardens, Vancouver, Nov 26 1971
Winnipeg (Manitoba) Manitoba Auditorium, Winnipeg, June 23 1966

ENGLAND
Basingstoke (Hampshire), St Joseph's Hall, Aug 18 1965
Bath (Somerset), Bath Pavilion, Aug 16 1965; 'Bath Festival Of Blues & Progressive Music '70', Bath & West Showground, Shepton Mallet, June 28 1970
Birmingham (Warwickshire/West Midlands), Town Hall, May 10 1971
Bournemouth (Hampshire), Gaumont Theatre, Aug 15 1965
Bristol (Gloucestershire/Avon), Corn Exchange, Aug 11 1965; Colston Hall, May 3 1971
Coventry (Warwickshire), Coventry Theatre, Aug 8 1965
Croydon (Greater London), Fairfield Halls, Aug 5 1965; Fairfield Halls, May 6 1971
East Grinstead (Sussex), White Hall, Aug 10 1965
Harlesden (Middlesex), 32 Club, Aug 6 1965
Hove (Sussex), Town Hall, Aug 12 1965
Ipswich (Suffolk), Gaumont Theatre, Aug 13 1965
Lincoln (Lincolnshire), 'A Concert Of Contemporary International Folk Music', Tupholme Abbey, July 24 1971
Liverpool (Lancashire/Merseyside), Liverpool University, May 8 1971
London, Flamingo Allnighter, Aug 6 1965; Pontiac, Putney, Aug 7 1965; Finsbury Park Astoria, Finsbury park, Aug 14 1965; Speakeasy Club, March 14 1967; Middle Earth Club, Covent Garden; March 11 1968; Blaises Club, March 12 1968; 'One-Night Summer Celebration', Middle Earth, Roundhouse, Chalk Farm, July 6 1968; 'Sounds '68', Royal Albert Hall, July 7 1968; Royal Albert Hall, May 13 1971; Rainbow Theatre, Jan 16–17 1972
Manchester (Lancashire/Greater Manchester), Free Trade Hall, May 11 1971
Morecambe (Lancashire); Starlight Ballroom, Aug 4 1965
Nelson (Lancashire), Imperial Ballroom, Aug 3 1965
Newbury (Berkshire), Corn Exchange, Aug 18 1965
Newcastle upon Tyne (Northumberland/Tyne & Wear), City Hall, May 7 1971
Portsmouth (Hampshire), Guildhall, Aug 17 1965 [CANC]
Sheffield (Yorkshire/South Yorkshire), City Hall, May 9 1971
Slough (Buckinghamshire), Adelphi, Aug 7 1965
Wembley (Greater London), Starlight Ballroom, Aug 14 1965
Worthing (Sussex) Assembly Hall, Worthing, Aug 12 1965

FRANCE
Cannes, MIDEM Conference, Jan 20 1972
Paris, L'Olympia, Jan 22 1972

ITALY
Rome, 'First International Pop Festival, Rome', Piper Club, May 7 1968

MEXICO
Mexico City, Estadio de la Ciudad de los Deportes, March 9 1969

THE NETHERLANDS
Amsterdam, Fantasio II, June 24 1970; Concertgebouw, July 7 1970; Concertgebouw, Grote Zaal, May 15 1971
Arnhem, Musis Sacrum, May 23 1971
Breda, Het Turfschip, May 22 1971
Eindhoven, De Stadsschouwburg, May 29 1971
Emmeloord, De Prins Willem-Alexanderhal, May 20 1971
Enschede, Diekmanhal, May 21 1971
Groningen, De Martinihal, May 28 1971
Rotterdam, 'Holland Pop Festival '70', Kralingse Bos, Kralingen, June 27 1970; De Doelen, July 4 1970; De Doelen, July 8 1970; De Doelen, May 14 1971, De Doelen, May 16 1971
Voorburg, De Vliegermolen, May 30 1971

PUERTO RICO
San Juan, Estadio Hiram Bithorn, April 30 1967

RHODESIA [ZIMBABWE]
Salisbury [Harare], Glamis Stadium, July 20 1968

SOUTH AFRICA
Johannesburg, The City Hall, July 11–13 1968
Cape Town, Metro Theatre, July 15–16 1968
Port Elizabeth, Showgrounds Hall, July 17 1968
Durban,City Hall, July 18 1968

UNITED STATES OF AMERICA
ALABAMA, *Birmingham*, Temple Theatre, Dec 10 1966; *Huntsville*, Madison County Coliseum, Nov 17 1965; *Florence,* [Unknown venue], Nov 10 1965 [CANC?]
ARKANSAS, *Jonesboro*, Armory Auditorium, April 7 1970; *Little Rock*, Barton Coliseum, March 19 1966
ARIZONA, *Flagstaff*, Northern Arizona State University, Lumberjack Gym, March 5 1972; *Phoenix*, Veterans Memorial Coliseum, Dec 17 1965; VIP Club, Feb 17–18 1967; Veteran's Memorial Coliseum, Oct 5 1968; *Tucson*, [Sunset Rollarena], Dec 18 1965; *[Unknown city],* [Unknown location], Dec 19 1965
CALIFORNIA, *Anaheim*, Anaheim Convention Center, Dec 22 1967; Melodyland Theatre, March 17 1969; Anaheim Convention Center, Jan 18 1970; *Bakersfield*, Bakersfield Civic Auditorium, March 30 1966; *Berkeley*, Berkeley Community Theater, Feb 25 1966; Berkeley Community Theater, Aug 3 1968; Berkeley Community Theatre, Jan 29 1971; *Camarillo*, Adolfo Camarillo High School Gym, May 7 1966; *Costa Mesa*, 'First Annual Newport Pop Festival', Orange County Fairgrounds, Aug 4 1968; *Covina*, Covina High School Colt Gym, March 23 1966; *Daly City*, Cow Palace, Oct 2 1965 [CANC?]; 'The Beach Boys Summer Spectacular', Cow Palace, June 24 1966; *Eagle Rock*, Occidental College Hillside Theatre, May 7 1966; *Fresno*, Convention Hall, Ratcliffe Stadium, May 22 1965; Wonderland Bowl, April 22 1967; *Hollywood*, Ciro's Le Disc, March 21–27 1965; Ciro's Le Disc, April 2–10 1965; Ciro's Le Disc, April 16–211965; Ciro's Le Disc, April 23–25 1965; The Troubadour, April 26–28 1965; Ciro's Le Disc, May 31 1965 + June 1–3 1965; Ciro's Le Disc, June 7–12 1965; Ciro's Le Disc, June 15–16 1965; Ciro's Le Disc, June 28–30 1965; Ciro's Le Disc, July 1–2 1965; Palladium, Aug 26 1965; The Trip, Oct 2 1965; The Trip, Oct 4–17 1965; The Broadway Shopping Mall, Oct 18 1965; The Trip, Jan 10–16 1966; Los Felix Jewish Community Center, Hollywood High School Auditorium, Jan 30 1966; The Trip, March 4–10 1966; 'Beach Boys Summer Spectacular', Hollywood Bowl, June 25 1966; Whisky A Go Go, Sept 2–11 1966; Whisky A Go Go, May 16–24 1967; Whisky A Go Go, Aug 31 1967 + Sept 1–3 1967; Ciro's Le Disc, March 28 1968; The Troubadour, April 25–28 1968; The Kaleidoscope, June 21–22 1968; Whisky A Go Go, Oct 9–12 1968; Pilgrimage Theatre, June 6–7 1969; Aquarius Theater, Jan 5 1970; Ash Grove, Feb 6–8 1970; Ash Grove, Aug 21–23 1970; Whisky a Go Go, Sept 17–19 1970; *Huntingdon Beach*, Golden Bear, Nov 16–19 1967; Golden Bear, Dec 16–17 1967; The Golden Bear, July 18–20 1967; The Golden Bear, Oct 25–26 1968; *Long Beach*, Civic Auditorium, May 16 1965; *Los Angeles*, Ingalls Auditorium, East Los Angeles College, March 4 1965; 'Stop The War', Church, [guess] March 20 1965; Hollywood Bowl, July 3 1965; Fairfax High School, Bonus Auditorium, Oct 14 1965; Hamilton High School Old Gym, April 1 1966; Los Angeles Memorial Sports Arena, May 24 1968; Thelma, Nov 23–26 1969; Hollywood Palladium, Nov 24 1971; *Monterey*, 'Monterey International Pop Music Festival', Monterey County Fairgrounds, June 17 1967; *Northridge*, 'Newport Pop Festival', Devonshire Downs, June 22 1969; *Palos Verdes Estates*, Palos Verdes High School, Oct 29 1965; *Pasadena*, La Salle High School Auditorium, Jan 29 1966; Rose Bowl, Sept 15 1968; The Rose Palace, May 16 1969; The Rose Palace, May 17 1969; *Pomona*, Pomona College, Bridges Auditorium, Dec 3 1970; *Porterville*, Porterville College, Gymnasium, Dec 29 1970; *Sacramento*, Municipal Auditorium, May 12 1965; Sacramento County Fair, May 28–30 1965; *San Bernardino*, Swing Auditorium, May 15 1965; Swing Auditorium Orange County Fairgrounds, March 15 1966; Swing Auditorium, Nov 25 1967; *San Diego*, Community Concourse, Convention Hall, May 17 1965; International Sports Arena, Jan 13 1968; Community Concourse, March 22 1968; San Diego Community Concourse, June 25 1971; *San Francisco*, Jack Tar Hotel, [possibly] March 6 1965; Peppermint Tree, April 30 1965 + May 1–4 1965 and May 7–10 1965; Peppermint Tree, May 12–13 1965; New Civic Auditorium, May 14 1965; Fillmore Auditorium, Sept 16–17 1966; Winterland, March 31 1967; Winterland, April 1 1967; Fillmore Auditorium, April 2 1967; 'The Magic Mountain Music Festival on Mt. Tamalpais', Mill Valley, June 10 1967; Fillmore Auditorium, Sept 7–9 1967; Fillmore Auditorium, Dec 7 1967; Winterland, Dec 8–9 1967; Avalon Ballroom, Aug 13–15 1968; Family Dog, Nov 1–3 1968; Fillmore West, Feb 6–8 1969; Fillmore West, June 12–15 1969; Fillmore West, Jan 2–4 1970; Fillmore West, Aug 13–16 1970; *San Jose*, Civic Auditorium, May 21 1965; Civic Auditorium, April 7 1967; *San Leandro*, Rollarena, Oct 21 1966; *San Luis Obispo*, 'Indian Creek Celebration and Music Appreciation Seminar', Dec 27–29 1969 [CANC]; *San Mateo*, College of San Mateo Gym, March 16 1966; *Santa Barbara*, Santa Barbara High School Auditorium, Feb 19 1966; La Playa Stadium, June 11 1967; *Santa Monica*, The Cheetah, April 16 1967; Santa Monica Civic Auditorium, Dec 27 1970; *Stockton*, Stockton Civic Auditorium, June 13 1965; University of the Pacific, Sept 20 1970; *Venice*, 'KRLA Radio Promo Show', Cheetah, Jan 26 1968; *West Covina*, Carousel Theater, Feb 9–10 1968; *Wilmington*,

NEW MEXICO; *Albuqueque*, Civic Auditorium, Oct 4 1969; Civic Auditorium, March 16 1973 [CANC]

NEW YORK, *Albany*, Palace Theater, Feb 19 1971; *Alfred*, State University of New York (SUNY), March 18 1972; *Baldwin*, Baldwin Senior High School Gymnasium, Dec 7 1969; *Batavia*, State University of New York, Genesee Community College, April 26 1970; *Bayside*, Queensborough Community College, Robert F. Kennedy Hall, Feb 20 1972; *Binghamton*, State University of New York (SUNY), Men's Gymnasium, Feb 28 1971; *The Bronx*, 'Sound Blast 66', Yankee Stadium, June 10 1966; Fordham University, April 29 1967; 'Manhattan College Scholarship Concert Series', Gaelic Park, Aug 18 1969; *Brooklyn*, 46th Street Palace, 'Brooklyn Rock', Oct 23 1970; *Brookville*, Long Island University, C.W. Post Campus, Feb 18 1971; *Buffalo*, North Amherst Recreation Center, May 25 1969; State University of New York (SUNY), Feb 21 1971; Melody Fair Theatre, Aug 22 1971; *Clinton*, Hamilton College, Gymnasium, Feb 19 1972; *Cortland*, State University of New York (SUNY), Lusk Field House, Nov 20 1971; *Flushing*, Queens College of City University of New York, Colden Center Auditorium, Feb 28 1970; Queens College of City University of New York, Colden Center Auditorium, March 21 1971; *Fredonia*, State University of New York (SUNY), April 27 1971; *Geneva*, Smith Opera House, May 5 1972; *Greenvale*, C.W. Post College, The Dome, Sept 28 1972; *Hempstead*, Hofstra University, Aug 21 1971; Hofstra University, Physical Fitness Center, Nov 11 1972; *Island Park*, Action House, June 3–4 1966; *Ithaca*, Cornell University, April 16 1970; Cornell University, Willard Straight Hall, Feb 10 1973; *Long Island*, Lido Beach, Malibu Beach Club, July 8 1966; Lido Beach, Malibu Shore Club, July 21 1967; *Mahopac*, Mahopac High School Auditorium, March 20 1971; *Morrisville*, State University of New York (SUNY), Agriculture and Technology College, Oct 15 1971; *New Paltz*, State University of New York (SUNY), Dec 6 1970; [Venue missing], May 8 1972; **NEW YORK**, The Village Gate, Oct 5–9 1966; The Village Gate, Oct 11–16 1966; Village Theater, Manhattan, July 22 1967; 'The Rheingold Music Festival', Central Park, July 28 1967; Columbia University, McMillan Theater, Feb 18 1968; Fillmore East, May 17–18 1968; Central Park, June 24 1969; Fillmore East, June 27–28 1969; 'Schaefer Music Festival', Central Park, July 12 1969; Carnegie Hall, Sept 26 1969; Fillmore East, Dec 19–20 1969; Madison Square Garden Center, Felt Forum, March 1 1970; 'Schaefer Music Festival', Central Park, July 20 1970; Fillmore East, Sept 11–12 1970; Fillmore East, Sept 23 1970; Carnegie Hall, Feb 17 1971; Brooklyn, Pratt Institute, April 23 1971; Fillmore East, June 9 1971; 'Schaefer Music Festival', Central Park, July 17 1971; Manhattan Center Ballroom, Sept 8 1971; Academy of Music, March 10 1972; City College, May 4 1972; Central Park, Wollman Rink, Aug 18 1972 [CANC]; Academy of Music, Oct 6 1972; Pace College, Nov 10 1972; *Odessa*, The Fontainebleu Inn, July 12 1966; *Oneonta*, Hartwick College, Slade Auditorium, Jan 30 1970; *Peekskill*, Peekskill Palace, June 29 1969; *Plattsburgh*, State University of New York, Gymnasium, Oct 11 1970; *Port Chester*, The Capitol Theatre, March 26–27 1971; Capitol Theatre, March 16 1972; *Potsdam*, Clarkson College, Nov 8 1970; Clarkson College of Technology, Dec 9 1971; *Queens*, Jamaica, St. John's University, April 24 1971; *Riverdale*, College of Mount Saint Vincent, Cardinal Hayes Auditorium, Sept 20 1969; *Rochester*, Rochester Institute of Technology, Clark Memorial Gymnasium, Nov 7 1970; University of Rochester, Eastman Theater, March 13 1971; *Selden*, Suffolk County Community College, Nov 11 1970; *South Fallsburg*, The Raleigh Hotel, July 13 1966; *Staten Island*, Ritz Theatre, Port Richmond, Feb 4 1972; Ritz Theatre, Port Richmond, May 26 1972; *Stony Brook*, Stony Brook University, Oct 1 1966; State University of New York, Gymnasium, May 8 1969; Pritchard Gymnasium, SUNY, Dec 11 1971; *Suffern*, Rockland Community College, Feb 16 1973; *Suffolk*, [Possibly Suffolk Community College], Sept 29 1972; *Syracuse*, LeMoyne College, LeMoyne Athletic Center, Feb 12 1971; *West Hempstead*, Island Garden, March 25 1966; *Westbury*, Westbury Music Fair, Dec 23 1972; *White Plains*, Westchester County Center, Nov 28 1965; Westchester County Center, March 26 1966; *Williamsville*, Erie Community College, May 7 1972

NORTH CAROLINA, *Burlington*, Elon College, Gymnasium, Feb 27 1972; *Chapel Hill*, University of North Carolina, Carmichael Auditorium, Sept 25 1971; *Cullowhee*, Western Carolina University, Reid Gymnasium, Feb 25 1972; *Durham*, Duke University, Duke Indoor Stadium, Nov 21 1970; *Raleigh*, Memorial Auditorium, Nov 22 1965; Duke University, Wade Stadium, April 15 1972; *Winston-Salem*, Winston-Salem Coliseum, Feb 26 1972

OHIO, *Alliance*, Mount Union College, Memorial Hall, Feb 12 1972; *Athens*, Grover Center, Nov 20 1965; Ohio University, Baseball Stadium, April 15 1970; *Bexley*, Holiday Swim Club, [possibly] Aug 21 1966 *Cincinnati*, University of Cincinnati, Wilson Auditorium, April 18 1969; *Cleveland*, Public Hall, Nov 26 1970; *Columbus*, Veteran's Memorial Hall, April 10 1970; Ohio Theatre, Nov 24 1970; *Gambier*, Kenyon College, Feb 11 1972; *Kent*, Kent State University, Oct 9 1971; *Monroe*, LeSourdesville Lake Amusement park, Stardust Garden Ballroom, July 19 1965; *Nelson Falls*, 'Piper Rock Festival', April 24 1970 [CANC]; *Oberlin*, Oberlin College, Dec 18 1970; *Oxford*, Miami University, Withrow Court, Feb 17 1968; *Painesville*, Lake Theatre, Dec 10 1965; *Sandusky*, Cedar Point Ballroom, July 21 1965; *Toledo*, University of Toledo, Field House, April 8 1970; *Youngstown*, Idora Park, Idora Park Ballroom, July 18 1965; Stambaugh Auditorium, Nov 19 1965; [Possibly] Powers Auditorium, [Possibly] Aug 20 1966

OKLAHOMA, *Davis*, 'Turner Falls International Pop Festival', Turner Falls, Arbuckle Mountains, Aug 9 1970 [CANC]; *Oklahoma City*, Convention Center, Jan 10 1970

OREGON, *Eugene*, 'Eugene Pop Festival', University of Oregon, Hayward Field, July 26 1969 [CANC]; *Marietta*, Marietta College, April 10 1971; *Portland*, Portland Memorial Coliseum, May 28 1967; Lewis & Clark College, Pamplan Sports Center, March 9 1971; *Salem*, Salem Armory Auditorium, Nov 21 1968

PENNSYLVANIA, [*unknown city*], [Unknown venue], Dec 11 1965; *Allentown*, Muhlenberg College, April 24 1970; *Annville*, Lebanon Valley College, Lynch Memorial Gym, Dec 5 1969; *Carlisle*, Dickinson College, April 17 1970; *Chester*, Pennsylvania Military College, Dec 4 1970; *Clarion*, Clarion State College, Marwick-Boyd Auditorium, Oct 13 1972; *Huntingdon*, Juniata College, Memorial Gymnasium, March 12 1971; *Indiana*, Indiana University of Pennsylvania, May 13 1972; *Johnstown*, Cambria County War Memorial Arena, Nov 23 1965; *Lewisburg*, Bucknell University, Davis Gymnasium, Feb 18 1972; *Meadville*, Allegheny College, Campus Center, April 28 1972; *Philadelphia* Electric Factory, Nov 27–28 1968; Electric Factory, July 8 1969; St. Joseph's College, Fieldhouse, Oct 11 1969; Electric Factory, Oct 24–25 1969; Playhouse In The Park, July 25 1970; University of Pennsylvania, Palestra, March 19 1972; *Pittsburgh*, 'KQV Thanksgiving Shower of Stars', Civic Arena, Nov 24 1965; *Scranton*, University of Scranton, John J. Long Student Center, Sept 30 1972; *Shippensburg*, Shippensburg State College, Heiges Field House, Oct 16 1971; *Upper Darby*, Tower Theater, Nov 9 1972; Tower Theatre, Dec 15 1972; *Wilkes-Barre*, Wilkes College, Gymnasium, Oct 31 1971

RHODE ISLAND, *North Kingston*, Rhode Island University, May 9 1969; *Providence*, Veterans War Memorial Auditorium, July 14 1966; Brown University, Meehan Auditorium, Sept 25 1970; Rhode Island Auditorium, Oct 10 1969; *South Kingstown*, University of Rhode Island, Kingston, Keaney Gymnasium, Dec 4 1971

SOUTH CAROLINA, *Columbia*, University of South Carolina, Carolina Coliseum, April 9 1972; *Greenville*, Municipal Auditorium, Nov 12 1965

SOUTH DAKOTA, *Sioux Falls*, Annex, July 6 1965

TENNESSEE, *Clarksville*, National Guard Armory, Nov 14 1965; *Martin*, University of Tennessee, Nov 15 1965; *Memphis*, Mid-South Coliseum, Jan 16 1970; Ellis Auditorium, Oct 4 1970; *Murfreesboro*, Middle Tennessee State University, Memorial Gymnasium, Nov 9 1965; *Nashville*, Municipal Auditorium, Nov 7 1965; Columbia Records Sales Convention, Grand Ole Opry, Oct ? 1968; [Unknown venue], June 13 1970; Vanderbilt University, Memorial Gymnasium, Nov 5 1971

TEXAS, *Austin*, Municipal Auditorium, Dec 18 1972; *Corpus Christi*, Memorial Coliseum, May 9 1966; *Dallas*, Market Hall, March 12 1966; Forest Ballroom, June 1 1968; Memorial Auditorium, May 19 1972; *El Paso*, Coliseum, March 17 1973 [CANC]; *Fort Worth*, Will Rogers Coliseum, May 13 1966; Panther Hall, March 6 1970; *Houston*, [Unknown venue], May 8 1966; 'Houston Pop Festival', Sam Houston Coliseum, Oct 5 1969; AstroHall, May 20 1972; *Kingsville*, [Texas A&M University], Dec 16 1972; *Lubbock*, 'Southwest '70 Peace Festival', March 28 1970 [CANC]; *San Antonio*, HemisFair Arena, July 4 1969; HemisFair Arena, May 21 1972

UTAH, *Salt Lake City*, Terrace Ballroom, April 9 1968; [Possibly] University of Utah, [Circa] Sept 20 1968; Westminster College, Payne Gymnasium, March 4 1972

VERMONT, *Burlington*, University of Vermont, Patrick Gymnasium, Dec 10 1971; St Michael's College, Feb 23 1973; *Northfield*, Norwich University, Feb 15 1969

VIRGINIA, *Alexandria*, T.C. Williams High School Auditorium, March 7 1970; *Charlottesville*, University of Virginia, March 16 1968; University of Virginia, Nov 6 1971; *Lexington*, Virginia Military Institute, Sept 26 1970; *Norfolk*, Old Dominion University, Gymnasium, Nov 22 1970; *Richmond*, Richmond Arena, Dec 12 1971; *Virginia Beach*, Alan B. Shepard Civic Center, July 17 1966; Virginia Beach Dome, March 15 1972; *Williamsburg*, College of William & Mary, William & Mary Hall, Dec 3 1965

WASHINGTON, *Bellingham*, Western Washington State College, Carver Gym, Nov 25 1968; *Federal Way* North Lake Ballroom, May 26 1967; *Olympia*, [unknown venue], ? April 1968; *Portland*, The New Rock & Roll Circus, Nov 11 1971; *Seattle*, Opera House, Nov 25 1965; 'Trips Festival', Seattle Center Arena, May 30 1967; Eagles Auditorium, April 12 1968; Eagles Auditorium, Nov 22 1968; 'Seattle Pop Festival', Gold Creek Park, Woodinville, July 25 1969; Eagles Auditorium, April 4(–5?) 1970; Paramount Northwest, Nov 12 1971; University of Washington, Hec Edmonson Pavilion, March 7 1971; *Spokane*, Gonzaga University, R. F. K. Pavilion, March 10 1971; Gonzaga University, R. F. K. Pavillion, Nov 13 1971; *Tacoma*, University of Pugent Sound, Fieldhouse, April 11 1968; *Walla Walla*, Whitman College, Cordiner Hall, Nov 23 1968; *Westport*, Pat O'Day's Dunes, May 27 1967

WEST VIRGINIA, *Charleston*, Charleston Civic Center, Aug 9 1969; Morris Harvey University, Carl Edward King Memorial Gymnasium, Oct 17 1969; *Morgantown*, Coliseum, West Virginia Unviersity, Oct 10 1970

WISCONSIN, *Appleton*, Lawrence University Chapel, March 7 1966; *Green Bay*, [Riverside Ballroom], July 19 1966; Premontre High School, April 6 1969; *Lake Geneva*, Majestic Hills Theatre, May 31 1969; *Madison*, Orpheum Theatre, March 4 1966; Dane County Memorial Coliseum, Feb 11 1970; *Oshkosh*, Oshkosh High School, April 7 1969; *Poynette*, York Farm, Sept 8 1972 [CANC]; *Racine*, Carthage College, Fieldhouse, April 30 1972; *Sturgeon Bay*, [Unknown venue], July 18 1966

WEST GERMANY

Frankfurt, 'Open Air Rock Circus', Radstadion, June 20 1970

Recording session index 1964–1973

Key to entries

Artist / recording date / recording studio or location / songs / miscellaneous

1964

Circa July–August 1964 / World Pacific Studios, Los Angeles, CA / 'The Only Girl I Adore' / performed by The Jet Set

Undated late summer 1964 / World Pacific Studios, Los Angeles, CA / 'Don't Be Long', 'Please Let Me Love You' / performed by The Jet Set, Ray Pohlman (bass) and Earl Palmer (drums)

[Possibly] September 1964 / World Pacific Studios, Los Angeles, CA / 'Tomorrow Is a Long Ways Away', 'You Showed Me', 'I Knew I'd Want You', 'You Won't Have to Cry', 'Mr. Tambourine Man' / performed by The Jet Set Mark I: Jim McGuinn, Gene Clark, David Crosby, Michael Clarke

Undated November 1964–February 1965 / World Pacific Studios, Los Angeles, CA or Columbia Recording Studios, Los Angeles, CA / 'The Reason Why' (version I–II), 'You Won't Have to Cry' (electric version), 'She Has a Way', (versions I–IV), 'You Showed Me' (instrumental track + electric version), 'Here Without You' (version I–III), 'I Knew I'd Want You' (electric version I–II), 'Boston' (instrumental track instrumental + versions I–II), 'Tomorrow Is a Long Ways Away' (electric version), 'For Me Again' (versions I–II), 'It's No Use' (version I–III), 'You Movin'' (version I–IV), 'The Airport Song', 'Mr. Tambourine Man' / performed by The Jet Set Mark II–The Byrds: Jim McGuinn, Gene Clark, David Crosby, Chris Hillman, Michael Clarke

1965

January 20 1965 / Columbia Recording Studios, Studio A, Hollywood, CA / 'Mr. Tambourine Man', 'I'd Knew I'd Want You' / performed by McGuinn, Clark, and Crosby plus Bill Pittman and Jerry Cole (guitars), Larry Knechtel (bass guitar), and Hal Blaine (drums). Leon Russell (electric piano) listed on session logs but his parts are seemingly mixed out.

March 8 1965 / Columbia Recording Studios, Studio A, Hollywood, CA / 'All I Really Want To Do', 'She Has A Way', 'It's No Use'

April 14 1965 / Columbia Recording Studios, Studio A, Hollywood, CA / 'Spanish Harlem Incident', 'The Bells Of Rhymney', 'We'll Meet Again', 'You Won't Have To Cry', 'It's No Use', 'I'll Feel A Whole Lot Better', 'I Love The Life I Live (And I Live The Life I Love)', 'Words And Pictures'

April 22 1965 / Columbia Recording Studios, Studio A, Hollywood, CA / 'Here Without You', 'Don't Doubt Yourself Babe' / The Byrds reportedly back Jackie DeShannon for 'Splendour In The Grass'

June 28 1965 / Columbia Recording Studios, Studio A, Hollywood, CA / 'The Times They Are A-Changin'', 'It's All Over Now, Baby Blue', 'She Don't Care About Time', 'The Flower Bomb Song'

[Presumably] August 25 1965 / Columbia Recording Studios, Studio A, Hollywood, CA / 'The Times They Are A-Changin'' (discarded)

August 28 1965 / Columbia Recording Studios, Studio A, Hollywood, CA / 'She Don't Care About Time', 'The World Turns All Around Her'

September 1 1965 / Columbia Recording Studios, Studio A, Hollywood, CA / 'The Times They Are A-Changin'' – possibly two versions, including instrumental backing track for Hullabaloo appearance on September 22–23 1965

September 10 1965 / Columbia Recording Studios, Studio A, Hollywood, CA / 'Turn! Turn! Turn! (To Everything There Is A Season)'

September 14 1965 / Columbia Recording Studios, Studio A, Hollywood, CA / 'The Day Walk'

September 16 1965 / Columbia Recording Studios, Studio A, Hollywood, CA / 'Set You Free This Time',

September 17 1965 / Columbia Recording Studios, Studio A, Hollywood, CA / 'Satisfied Mind'

September 18 1965 / Columbia Recording Studios, Studio A, Hollywood, CA / 'It Won't Be Wrong', 'Stranger In A Strange Land', 'I Don't Ever Want To Spoil The Party'

October 1 1965 / Columbia Recording Studios, Studio A, Hollywood, CA / 'Wait And See'

October 4 1965 / Columbia Recording Studios, Studio A, Hollywood, CA / 'Oh! Susannah'

October 20 1965 / Columbia Recording Studios, Studio A, Hollywood, CA / 'If You're Gone'

October 22 1965 / Columbia Recording Studios, Studio A, Hollywood, CA / 'Lay Down Your Weary Tune'

October 26–27 1965 / Columbia Recording Studios, Studio A, Hollywood, CA / 'The Times They Are A-Changin'', 'Satisfied Mind', 'Circle Of Minds'

November 1 1965 / Columbia Recording Studios, Studio A, Hollywood, CA / 'He Was A Friend Of Mine'

December 22 1965 / RCA Recording Studio, Sunset Boulevard, Hollywood, CA / 'Eight Miles High' (version I), 'Why' (version I)

January 24 1966 / Columbia Recording Studios, Studio A, Hollywood, CA / 'Why' (version II)

1966

January 25–26 1966 / Columbia Recording Studios, Studio A, Hollywood, CA / 'Eight Miles High' (version II)

February 11 1966 / Columbia Recording Studios, Studio A, Hollywood, CA / 'Why' (version III)

February 24 1966 / Columbia Recording Studios, Studio A, Hollywood, CA / [no documentation; possibly cancelled]

April 28–29 1966 / Columbia Recording Studios, Studio A, Hollywood, CA / 'Mr. Spaceman', 'What's Happening?!?!'

May 3 1966 / Columbia Recording Studios, Studio A, Hollywood, CA / '2-4-2 Fox Trot (The Lear Jet Song)'

May 4 1966 / Columbia Recording Studios, Studio A, Hollywood, CA / 'John Riley'

May 6 1966 / Columbia Recording Studios, Studio A, Hollywood, CA / 'Instrumental' aka 'Blues?' or 'Thirty Minute Break' (see May 18)

May 16 1966 / Columbia Recording Studios, Studio A, Hollywood, CA / 'I Come And Stand At Every Door'

May 17 1966 / Columbia Recording Studios, Studio A, Hollywood, CA / 'Hey Joe (Where You Gonna Go)'

May 18 1966 / Columbia Recording Studios, Studio A, Hollywood, CA / 'Captain Soul' (The tape box identifies the recording date as May 6 and not May 18)

May 19 1966 / Columbia Recording Studios, Studio A, Hollywood, CA / 'I See You'

May 23–24 1966 / Columbia Recording Studios, Studio A, Hollywood, CA / '5D', 'John Riley', 'Wild Mountain Thyme'

May 25 1966 / Columbia Recording Studios, Studio A, Hollywood, CA / Overdub session for '5D', 'Wild Mountain Thyme', 'John Riley'

July 28–29 1966 / Columbia Recording Studios, Studio A, Hollywood, CA / 'I Know My Rider', 'Psychodrama City'

November 28 1966 / Columbia Recording Studios, Studio A, Hollywood, CA / 'So You Want To Be A Rock'n'Roll Star'

November 29 1966 / Columbia Recording Studios, Studio A, Hollywood, CA / 'Have You Seen Her Face'

November 30 1966 / Columbia Recording Studios, Studio A, Hollywood, CA / 'Time Between', 'Mind Gardens'

December 1 1966 / Columbia Recording Studios, Studio A, Hollywood, CA / 'CTA 102'

[Possibly] December 3 1966 / Columbia Recording Studios, Studio A, Hollywood, CA / [Possibly] 'Milestones'

December 5 1966 / Columbia Recording Studios, Studio A, Hollywood, CA / 'My Back Pages'

December 6 1966 / Columbia Recording Studios, Studio A, Hollywood, CA / 'Thoughts And Words', 'Renaissance Fair'

December 7 1966 / Columbia Recording Studios, Studio A, Hollywood, CA / 'Everybody's Been Burned'

December 8 1966 / Columbia Recording Studios, Studio A, Hollywood, CA / 'The Girl With No Name', 'It Happens Each Day'

1967

February 3 1967 / Columbia Recording Studios, Studio A, Hollywood, CA / 'My Back Pages' overdub

April 26 1967 / Columbia Recording Studios, Studio A, Hollywood, CA / 'Don't Make Waves', 'Lady Friend'

May 4, 10, 23 1967 / Columbia Recording Studios, Studio A, Hollywood, CA / Overdub sessions for 'Lady Friend'

June 5, 14 1967 / Columbia Recording Studios, Studio A, Hollywood, CA / Overdub sessions for 'Lady Friend'

June 14 1967 / Columbia Recording Studios, Studio A, Hollywood, CA / 'Old John Robertson'

June 21 1967 / Columbia Recording Studios, Studio A, Hollywood, CA / 'Old John Robertson'

July 31 1967 / Columbia Recording Studios, Studio A, Hollywood, CA / 'Universal Mind Decoder', 'Draft Morning'

August 1 1967 / Columbia Recording Studios, Studio A, Hollywood, CA / 'Universal Mind Decoder', 'Draft Morning'

August 2–3 1967 / Columbia Recording Studios, Studio A, Hollywood, CA / 'Universal Mind Decoder', 'Draft Morning'

August 14 1967 / Columbia Recording Studios, Studio A, Hollywood, CA / 'Universal Mind Decoder', 'Dolphin's Smile'

August 15 1967 / Columbia Recording Studios, Studio A, Hollywood, CA / 'Dolphin's Smile'

August 16 1967 / Columbia Recording Studios, Studio A, Hollywood, CA / 'Dolphin's Smile', 'Tribal Gathering'

August 17 1967 / Columbia Recording Studios, Studio A, Hollywood, CA / 'Triad', plus possibly 'Bound To Fall'

August 29–30 1967 / Columbia Recording Studios, Studio A, Hollywood, CA / 'Change Is Now' (aka 'Universal Mind Decoder'), 'Tribal Gathering'

September 5–6 1967 / Columbia Recording Studios, Studio A, Hollywood, CA / 'Goin' Back'

October 9, 11, 16 1967 / Columbia Recording Studios, Studio A, Hollywood, CA / 'Goin' Back'

October 23, 30 1967 / Columbia Recording Studios, Studio A, Hollywood, CA / 'Space Odyssey'

November 1 1967 / Columbia Recording Studios, Studio A, Hollywood, CA / 'Space Odyssey', 'Moog Raga'

November 13 1967 / Columbia Recording Studios, Studio A, Hollywood, CA / 'Get To You', 'Song #2' (aka 'Flight 713')

November 29 1967 / Columbia Recording Studios, Studio A, Hollywood, CA / 'Natural Harmony'

November 30 1967 / Columbia Recording Studios, Studio A, Hollywood, CA / 'Wasn't Born To Follow', plus overdubs for 'Tribal Gathering'

December 5 1967 / Columbia Recording Studios, Studio A, Hollywood, CA / overdubs for 'Tribal Gathering'

December 6 1967 / Columbia Recording Studios, Studio A, Hollywood, CA / 'Artificial Energy'

1968

March 9 1968 / Columbia Studio A, 34 Music Square East, Music Row, Nashville, TN / 'You Ain't Going Nowhere', 'Hickory Wind'

March 11 1968 / Columbia Studio A, 34 Music Square East, Music Row, Nashville, TN / 'Lazy Days'

March 12 1968 / Columbia Studio A, 34 Music Square East, Music Row, Nashville, TN / 'Pretty Boy Floyd'

March 13 1968 / Columbia Studio A, 34 Music Square East, Music Row, Nashville, TN / 'I Am A Pilgrim'
'Pretty Polly'

March 14 1968 / Columbia Studio A, 34 Music Square East, Music Row, Nashville, TN / 'Reputation'

March 15 1968 / Columbia Studio A, 34 Music Square East, Music Row, Nashville, TN / 'Nothing Was Delivered' (plus possibly 'One Hundred Years From Now' demoed in Nashville this week)

April 4 1968 / Columbia Recording Studios, Studio A, Hollywood, CA / 'Life In Prison'

April 15 1968 / Columbia Recording Studios, Studio A, Hollywood, CA / 'You Don't Miss Your Water (Till Your Well Runs Dry)'

April 17 1968 / Columbia Recording Studios, Studio A, Hollywood, CA / 'You're Still On My Mind'

April 24 1968 / Columbia Recording Studios, Studio A, Hollywood, CA / 'The Christian Life', 'Blue Canadian Rockies'

May 1 1968 / Columbia Recording Studios, Studio A, Hollywood, CA / 'All I Have Are Memories'

May 27 1968 / Columbia Recording Studios, Studio A, Hollywood, CA / 'One Hundred Years From Now'

October 7 1968 / Columbia Recording Studios, Studio A, Hollywood, CA / 'King Apathy III', 'Old Blue'

October 8 1968 / Columbia Recording Studios, Studio A, Hollywood, CA / 'Drug Store Truck Drivin' Man', 'This Wheel's On Fire'

October 14 1968 / Columbia Recording Studios, Studio A, Hollywood, CA / 'Your Gentle Way Of Loving Me'

October 15 1968 / Columbia Recording Studios, Studio A, Hollywood, CA / 'Bad Night At The Whisky', 'Nashville West' (version I)

October 16 1968 / Columbia Recording Studios, Studio A, Hollywood, CA / 'Stanley's Song'

October 21 1968 / Columbia Studio A, 34 Music Square East, Music Row, Nashville, TN / 'Nashville West' (version II)

December 4 1968 / Columbia Recording Studios, Studio A, Hollywood, CA / 'This Wheel's On Fire', 'Child Of The Universe', 'Candy', Medley: 'My Back Pages'–'Baby, What You Want Me To Do'–'The Break Song' (aka 'Hold It!'). The Byrds also record incidental instrumental music for Candy soundtrack

1969

Undated January–February 1969 / Columbia Recording Studios, Studio A, Hollywood, CA / 'Ballad Of Easy Rider', 'It's Alright, Ma (I'm Only Bleeding)' / Performed by Roger McGuinn and Gene Parsons for Easy Rider soundtrack

March 27 1969 / Columbia Recording Studios, Studio A, Hollywood, CA / 'Lay Lady Lay'

April 18 1969 / Columbia Studio A, 34 Music Square East, Music Row, Nashville, TN / 'Lay Lady Lay' overdub session (no Byrds are present)

June 17 1969 / Columbia Recording Studios, Studio A, Hollywood, CA / 'Jesus Is Just Alright'

June 18 1969 / Columbia Recording Studios, Studio A, Hollywood, CA / 'Ballad Of Easy Rider', 'Jack Tarr The Sailor'

June 19 1969 / Columbia Recording Studios, Studio A, Hollywood, CA / 'Deportee (Plane Wreck At Los Gatos)', 'Oil In My Lamp'

June 23 1969 / Columbia Recording Studios, Studio A, Hollywood, CA / 'Deportee (Plane Wreck At Los Gatos)', 'Build It Up', 'Way Behind The Sun'

June 24 1969 / Columbia Recording Studios, Studio A, Hollywood, CA / 'There Must Be Someone (I Can Turn To)', 'Give The Fiddler A Dram'

July 1 1969 / Columbia Recording Studios, Studio A, Hollywood, CA / 'Jack Tarr The Sailor', 'Oil In My Lamp'

July 2 1969 / Columbia Recording Studios, Studio A, Hollywood, CA / 'There Must Be Someone (I Can Turn To)'

July 22 1969 / Columbia Recording Studios, Studio A, Hollywood, CA / 'It's All Over Now, Baby Blue'

July 23 1969 / Columbia Recording Studios, Studio A, Hollywood, CA / 'Tulsa County Blue'

July 24 1969 / Columbia Recording Studios, Studio A, Hollywood, CA / 'Gunga Din'

July 28 1969 / Columbia Recording Studios, Studio A, Hollywood, CA / 'Mae Jean Goes To Hollywood', possible fiddle overdub for 'Tulsa County Blue'

August 5 1969 / Columbia Recording Studios, Studio A, Hollywood, CA / 'Fido'

August 26 1969 / Columbia Recording Studios, Studio A, Hollywood, CA / 'Armstrong, Aldrin, And Collins'

1970

February 28–March 1 1970 / Colden Auditorium and Felt Forum, New York, NY / 'Lover Of The Bayou', 'Positively Fourth street', 'Nashville West', 'So You Want To Be A Rock'n'Roll Star', 'Mr. Tambourine Man', 'Mr. Spaceman', 'Turn! Turn! Turn!', 'Eight Miles High', 'You Ain't Going Nowhere', 'Old Blue', 'My Back Pages', 'It's All Right Ma (I'm Only Bleeding)', 'Ballad Of Easy Rider' / Live recordings

May 25 1970 / Columbia Recording Studios, Studio A, Hollywood, CA / 'All The Things', 'Lover Of The Bayou', 'Yesterday's Train'

May 26-28 1970 / Columbia Recording Studios, Studio A, Hollywood, CA / 'Well Come Back Home', 'You All Look Alike', 'Hungry Planet', 'Willin''

May 31 1970 / Columbia Recording Studios, Studio A, Hollywood, CA / 'Willin''

June 1–5 1970 / Columbia Recording Studios, Studio A, Hollywood, CA / 'All The Things', 'Yesterday's Train', 'Truck Stop Girl', 'Take A Whiff On Me'

June 2 1970 / Columbia Recording Studios, Studio A, Hollywood, CA / 'Just A Season'

June 3 1970 / Columbia Recording Studios, Studio A, Hollywood, CA / 'Chestnut Mare', 'White's Lightning', 'White's Lightning Pt 2'

June 9 1970 / Columbia Recording Studios, Studio A, Hollywood, CA / 'Kathleen's Song' (version I – later recut)

/ Gram Parsons overdubs harmony vocals on 'All The Things'

June 11 1970 / Columbia Recording Studios, Studio A, Hollywood, CA / Overdub session for 'All The Things', 'You All Look Alike', 'Hungry Planet', 'Amazing Grace'

October 6 1970 / Columbia Recording Studios, Studio A, Hollywood, CA / 'I Trust' (aka 'I Trust (Everything Is Gonna Work Out Alright)'), 'Think I'm Gonna Feel Better'

1971

January 9 1971 / Columbia Recording Studios, Studio A, Hollywood, CA / 'Is This My Destiny?'

January 11 1971 / Columbia Recording Studios, Studio A, Hollywood, CA / 'Tunnel Of Love', 'Citizen Kane', 'Absolute Happiness'

January 17 1971 / Columbia Recording Studios, Studio A, Hollywood, CA / 'Glory Glory', 'I Wanna Grow Up To Be A Politician', 'Jamaica Say You Will', 'Just Like A Woman'

January 19 1971 / Columbia Recording Studios, Studio A, Hollywood, CA / 'I Wanna Grow Up To Be A Politician'

January 22 1971 / Columbia Recording Studios, Studio A, Hollywood, CA / 'Pale Blue'

January 24 1971 / Columbia Recording Studios, Studio A, Hollywood, CA / 'Green Apple Quick Step

January 26 1971 / Columbia Recording Studios, Studio A, Hollywood, CA / 'Pale Blue', 'Kathleen's Song' (version II) / Other songs recorded during January 1971 include 'Blue Grease'

[Circa] March 1–6 1971 / Columbia Recording Studios, Studio A, Hollywood, CA / Overdub sessions, unspecified songs

[Circa] mid-March–early April 1971 / Columbia Recording Studios, Studio A, Hollywood, CA / Horns, strings and vocals overdubs on 'Pale Blue', 'Kathleen's Song', 'Jamaica Say You Will', 'Tunnel Of Love', 'Citizen Kane', 'I Wanna Grow Up To Be A Politician', 'Glory, Glory', 'I Trust', 'My Destiny', 'Green Apple Quick Step'

July 22 1971 / CBS Studios, 164 New Bond Street, central London / 'Bugler', 'Lazy Waters', 'Antique Sandy'

July 25–26 1971 / CBS Studios, 164 New Bond Street, central London / 'Farther Along', 'Tiffany Queen', 'B.B. Class Road'

July 27 1971 / CBS Studios, 164 New Bond Street, central London / 'America's Great National Pastime'

July 28 1971 / CBS Studios, 164 New Bond Street, central London / 'Get Down Your Line', 'Precious Kate', 'So Fine'

[Undated] August 1971 / Columbia Recording Studios, Studio A, Hollywood, CA / Overdub session 'Bugler'

1972

January 12 1972 / Columbia Recording Studios, Studio A, Hollywood, CA / 'Lost My Drivin' Wheel'

April 18 1972 / Columbia Recording Studios, Studio A, Hollywood, CA / 'Born To Rock And Roll'

[Undated] August 1972 / Wally Heider's Studio, Calhuenga & Selma, Hollywood, CA / 'Bag Full Of Money', 'Draggin'', 'I'm So Restless'

October 16–27 1972, 30–31, November 4–8, 13–15 [booked for October 15–November 15] Wally Heider's Studio, Calhuenga & Selma, Hollywood, CA / 'Changing Heart', 'Full Circle', 'Sweet Mary', 'Born To Rock And Roll', 'Long Live The King', 'Laughing', 'Things Will Be Better', 'Borrowed Time', 'For Free', 'Cowgirl In The Sand', '(See The Sky) About To Rain' / Possibly also 'My New Woman' / other musicians appearing on the sessions include Joe Lala, Johnny Barbata, Wilton Felder

Radio and TV appearances 1965–1973

Key to entries

Broadcast date / Recording date (one date only = broadcast date) / show name / channel [TV] station / Location / Songs / Miscellaneous

(Repeats and later syndicated broadcasts in other regions are usually not noted.)

Television 1965–1973

April 26 1965 / [same] / *The Lloyd Thaxton Show* / KCOP Channel 13 / KCOP Television Studios / Los Angeles, CA / 'Mr. Tambourine Man' [+ possible others]

May 8 1965 / Late April 1965 / *Shivaree* / KABC Channel 7 / Hollywood, CA / KABC Studios / 'Mr. Tambourine Man', 'I Knew I'd Want You'

May 8 1965 / Undated May 1965 / *Shivaree* / KABC Channel 7 / Hollywood, CA / KABC Studios / 'Mr. Tambourine Man', 'I Knew I'd Want You'

May 11 1965 / May 5–6 1965 / *Hullabaloo* / NBC network / NBC Television Studios / Manhattan, New York, NY / 'Mr. Tambourine Man', 'I'll Feel A Whole Lot Better'

May 27 1965 / [same] / *The Lloyd Thaxton Show* / KCOP Channel 13 / KCOP Studios / Los Angeles, CA / 'I'll Feel A Whole Lot Better', 'Mr. Tambourine Man', 'Chimes Of Freedom'. The two latter songs are held over for a later undated transmission.

June 23 1965 / June 10 1965 / *Shindig* / ABC network / ABC Television Center / Hollywood, CA / 'Not Fade Away', 'Mr. Tambourine Man' / Jim McGuinn and David Crosby appear in the opening medley, singing 'Long Tall Sally'

July 1 1965 / [same] / *Top Of The Pops* / BBC-1 / (no performance, just playback plus visual backdrop) / 'Mr. Tambourine Man'

July 7 1965 / [Possibly] late June 1965 / *Where The Action Is* / ABC network / Pickwick Gardens / Hollywood, CA / 'Mr. Tambourine Man' and 'I'll Feel A Whole Lot Better'

July 15 1965 / [same] / *Top Of The Pops* / BBC-1 / (no performance, just playback plus visual backdrop) / 'Mr. Tambourine Man' (possible repeat of July 1 1965 clip)

July 17 1965 / [Possibly] late June 1965 / *Hollywood A Go Go* / KHJ-TV / KHJ Studios / Sunset Boulevard, Hollywood, CA / 'Mr. Tambourine Man', 'I'll Feel A Whole Lot Better', 'All I Really Want To Do' / Show is later syndicated nationally

July 22 1965 / [same] / *Top Of The Pops* / BBC-1 / (no performance, just playback plus visual backdrop) / 'Mr. Tambourine Man' (possible repeat of July 1 1965 clip)

[Undated] July 1965 / [Presumably between] July 27–31 1965 / *Teen Town* / [Unknown TV station] / [Unknown TV studio] / [Unknown songs performed]

August 5 1965 / [Possibly] late June 1965 / *Where The Action Is* / ABC network / Pickwick Gardens / Hollywood, CA / 'The Bells Of Rhymney'

August 7 1965 / August 3 1965 / *Ready Steady Go!* / Redifusion-TV / Wembley Studio 1 / north-west London, UK / 'Mr. Tambourine Man', 'All I Really Want To Do'

August 4 1965 / [same] / *Scene At 6.30* / Granada TV / Manchester, UK / 'Mr. Tambourine Man', 'All I Really Want To Do'

August 9 1965 / [same] / *Gadzooks!* / BBC-2 / Television Theatre / central London, UK / [Probably] 'All I Really Want To Do'

August 12 1965 / August 10 1965 / *Top Of The Pops* / BBC-1 / Television Centre Studio 2 / central London, UK / 'All I Really Want To Do'

August 19 1965 / August 10 1965 / *Top Of The Pops* / BBC-1 / Television Centre Studio 2 / central London, UK / 'All I Really Want To Do'

August 11 1965 / [same] / *Discs A Go-Go* / TWW (Television Wales and the West) / TWW Television Centre / Bristol, UK / [Probably] 'All I Really Want To Do'

August 21 1965 / August 19 1965 / *Thank Your Lucky Stars* / ABC-TV / Alpha Television Studios, Aston / Birmingham, UK / 'All I Really Want To Do'

August 26 1965 / August 10 1965 / *Top Of The Pops* / BBC-1 / Television Centre Studio 2 / central London, UK / 'All I Really Want To Do'

September 8 1965 / [Possibly] July 22 1965 / *The Mike Douglas Show* / KYW-TV / KYW-TV Studios, Cleveland / 'I'll Feel A Whole Lot Better' plus another unknown recording (presumably 'Mr. Tambourine Man')

September 16 1965 / [Probably] early September / *Shindig* / ABC network / ABC Television Center / Hollywood, CA / 'I'll Feel A Whole Lot Better', 'The Bells Of Rhymney' / The group appears in the opening medley, performing 'California Sun'

October 16 1965 / October 10 1965 / *Shivaree* / KABC Channel 7 / Hollywood, CA / KABC Studios / 'Turn! Turn! Turn!', 'I'll Feel A Whole Lot Better'

October 23 1965 / October 7 1965 / *Shindig* / ABC network / ABC Television Center / Hollywood, CA / 'I'll Feel A Whole Lot Better', 'The Bells Of Rhymney' / Jim McGuinn and Gene Clark appear in the opening medley, singing 'I'm A Loser'

November 3 1965 / [Presumably] late October 1965 / *The Lloyd Thaxton Show* / KCOP Channel 13 / KCOP Studios / Los Angeles, CA / 'Turn! Turn! Turn!'

November 6 1965 / [Presumably] early November 1965 / *Hollywood A Go Go* / KHJ-TV / KHJ Studios / Sunset Boulevard, Hollywood, CA / 'Turn! Turn! Turn!' / Show is later syndicated nationally

November 19 1965 / [Presumably] late October 1965 / *The Lloyd Thaxton Show* / KCOP Channel 13 / KCOP Studios / Los Angeles, CA / 'The Times They Are A-Changin''

November 29 1965 / September 22–23 1965 / *Hullabaloo* / NBC network / NBC Television Studios / Manhattan, New York, NY / 'The Times They Are A-Changin'' / Original broadcast date before postponement is October 4

December 12 1965 / [Presumably same] / *The Ed Sullivan Show* / CBS network / CBS Studio 50 / Manhattan, New York, NY / 'Turn! Turn! Turn!' / 'Turn! Turn! Turn!' [live] and 'Mr. Tambourine Man' [lip-synch]

December 25 1965 / [same] / *Top Of The Pops* / BBC-1 / (no performance, just playback plus visual backdrop) / 'Mr. Tambourine Man' (possible repeat of July 1 1965 clip)

January 21 1965 / [same] / *9th Street West* / KHJ Channel 9 / [Presumably] KHJ Studios / Sunset Boulevard, Hollywood, CA / Jim McGuinn appears as speaking guest

February 5 1966 / [Presumably] late January 1966 / *Hollywood A Go Go* / KHJ-TV / KHJ Studios / Sunset Boulevard, Hollywood, CA / 'Mr. Tambourine Man', 'It Won't Be Wrong', 'Turn! Turn! Turn!'.

February 15 1966 / [Possibly same] / *The Lloyd Thaxton Show* / KCOP Channel 13 / KCOP Studios / Los Angeles, CA / 'Mr. Tambourine Man', 'Set You Free This Time'

February 19 1966 / February 14 1966 / *Shivaree* / KABC Channel 7 / Hollywood, CA / KABC Studios / 'Set You Free This Time', 'It Won't Be Wrong'

February 21 1966 / [Possibly] mid-February 1966 / *Where The Action Is* / ABC network / Unknown outdoor location / 'Set You Free This Time'

February 22 1966 / [same] / *Murray The K's All-Star Special* /

WNEW-TV / Manhattan, NY / [Unknown songs] / Show repeated on March 26 1966

March 24 1966/ [Possibly] mid-February 1966 / *Where The Action Is* / ABC network / Unknown outside location / 'Set You Free This Time', presumably repeat of February 21 1966 transmission

March 24 1966/ [Possibly] mid-February 1966 / *Where The Action Is* / ABC network / Unknown outside location / 'It Won't Be Wrong'. Also 'Set You Free This Time', presumably repeat of February 21 1966 transmission.

April 9 1966 / [Presumably same] / *New American Bandstand* / ABC Network / ABC Television Center / Hollywood, CA / Chris Hillman appears as speaking guest in the show's 'hot line'

June 17 1966 / [Presumably] late May / *Arlene Dahl Beauty Spot* / KABC-TV / [Probably] ABC Television Center / Hollywood, CA / Jim McGuinn and David Crosby appears as speaking guests

July 16 1966 / [Presumably same] / *Summertime On The Pier* / KYW-TV / Steel Pier / Atlantic City, NJ / [Unknown songs]

September 17 1966 / [Presumably] September 11 1966 / *Boss City* / KHJ-TV / [Presumably] KHJ Television Studios / Hollywood, CA / [Unknown songs]

October 15 1966 / October 10 1966 / *Clay Cole Diskotek* / WPIX Channel 11 / [Unknown studio] / New York, NY / [Unknown songs]

February 24 1967 / [Possibly] December 3 1966 / *The Songmakers* / ABC Network / Columbia Recording Studios / Sunset and El Centro, Hollywood, CA / 'Milestones'

March 5 1967 / [Presumably] March 4 1967 / *Drop In* / STV-1 / Svensk Radio / Stockholm, Sweden / 'So You Want To Be A Rock'n'Roll Star', 'Mr. Tambourine Man', 'Eight Miles High'

March 16 1967 / March 15 1967 / *Top Of The Pops* / BBC-1 / Lime Grove Studios, central London / central London, UK / 'So You Want To Be A Rock'n'Roll Star'

March 30 1967 / March 15 1967 / *Top Of The Pops* / BBC-1 / Lime Grove Studios, central London / central London, UK / 'So You Want To Be A Rock'n'Roll Star' repeat performance

April 3 1967 / March 5–8 1967 / *Diamoci Del Tu* / Radiotelevisione Italiana (RAI) / Studio 3, Corso Sempione / Milan, Italy / 'Mr. Spaceman'

April 15 1967 / [Presumably same] / *Boss City* / KHJ-TV / [Presumably] KHJ Television Studios / Hollywood, CA / [Unknown songs]

April 25 1967 / [Possibly] November–December 1966 / *Inside Pop: The Rock Revolution* / CBS Network / [Possibly] Columbia Recording Studios / Sunset and El Centro, Hollywood, CA / 'Captain Soul' plus Jim McGuinn interview

July 25 1967 / [same] / *The Tonight Show* / NBC network / [Presumably] NBC Television Studios / Manhattan, New York, NY / 'Renaissance Fair', 'Lady Friend', 'Have You See Her Face'

July 27 1967 / [Presumably] mid-July 1967 / *American Bandstand '67* / ABC Network / ABC Television Center / Hollywood, CA / 'Lady Friend', 'Eight Miles High'

October 22 1967 / October 13 1967 / *The Smothers Brothers Comedy Hour* / CBS Network / CBS Television Center / Hollywood, CA / 'Mr. Spaceman', 'Goin' Back'

November 2 1967 / [same] / *The Joey Bishop Show* / ABC Network / Joey Bishop Productions Office / Hollywood, CA / [Unknown songs]

November 4 1967 / [Presumably same] / *Boss City* / KHJ-TV / [Presumably] KHJ Television Studios / Hollywood, CA / 'Goin' Back'

November 14 1967 / November 4–5 1967 / *Groovy!* / KHJ-TV Channel 9 / Valley Plaza Park and Recreation Center / Hollywood, CA / 'Goin' Back'

April 23 1968 / [Presumably] mid-October 1967 / *Where The Girls Are* / NBC Network / [Unknown location] / Hollywood, CA / 'Mr. Spaceman'. Gene Clark and Jim McGuinn also appear with Noel Harrison and Barbara McNair to sing 'Good Day Sunshine'

May 11 1968 / [Presumably] late April 1968 / *American Bandstand '68* / ABC Network / ABC Television Center / Hollywood, CA / 'You Ain't Going Nowhere', 'Eight Miles High'

October 16 1968 / [Presumably] May 8 1968 / [*Unknown show*] / German TV ZDF / Piper Club / Rome, Italy / 'Mr. Spaceman' (show recorded by either Italian RAI-TV or a Bavarian television station)

February 28 1969 / September 28 1968 / *Playboy After Dark* / CBS / CBS Television Studios / Hollywood, CA / 'You Ain't Going Nowhere', 'This Wheel's On Fire' (Syndicated in other areas later)

[Possibly] March 1969 / [Between] March 10–14 1969 / [*Unknown TV show*] / [Possibly] Telesistema Mexicano / [Unknown location] / Mexico City, Mexico / 'You Ain't Going Nowhere', possibly others

June 30 1969 / [same] / *Dick Cavett Show* / ABC network / [Presumably] ABC Television Studios / Manhattan, New York, NY / 'Jesus Is Just Alright'

January 17 1970 / January 16 1970 / *Talent Party* / WHBQ-TV (Channel 13) / [Presumably] WHBQ Television Studios / Memphis, TN / 'Jesus Is Just Alright', 'Mr. Tambourine Man'

February 8 1970 / [same] / *Groovy Show* / KHJ-TV Channel 9 / [Presumably] KHJ studios / North Hollywood, CA / [Unknown songs]

[Possibly] July 22 1970 / July 21 1970 / *Oscar Brand: The Show* / WNET Channel / [Unknown studio and location] / [Unknown songs]

October 11 1970 / September 23 1970 / *Fanfare: Welcome To Fillmore East* / WNET Channel / Fillmore East / Manhattan, New York, NY / 'Jesus Is Just Alright', 'Eight Miles High'

January 10 1971 / [Possibly] June 13–14 1970 / *Fanfare: Earl Scruggs, His Family And Friends* / WNET Channel / Doug Underwood Ranch / Nashville, TN / 'You Ain't Going Nowhere', 'Nothin' To It'

February 18 1971 / [same] / *Top Of The Pops* / BBC-1 / (no performance, just playback plus visual backdrop) / 'Chestnut Mare'

May 6 1971 / May 5 1971 / *Top Of The Pops* / BBC-1 / [Presumably] BBC Television Centre / central London, UK / 'I Trust'

May 22 1971 / May 19 1971 / *Beat Club* / ARD–1 / Radio Bremen Television Studios / Bremen, West Germany / 'Soldier's Joy'/'Black Mountain Rag', 'Chestnut Mare', 'Eight Miles High'. (A version of 'Mr. Tambourine Man' is recorded but never broadcast)

May 26 1971 / May 14 1971 / *Midweek* / Nederland 2, VARA / Skyway Hotel / Rotterdam, The Netherlands / From press reception

May 27 1971 / [Possibly] May 5 1971 / *Disco-2* / BBC-2 / CBS Studio / New Bond Street, central London, UK / 'Truck Stop Girl', 'Jesus Is Just Alright'

June 23 1971 / May 31 1971 / *Midweek* / Nederland 2, VARA / NOS Studio complex / Hilversum, the Netherlands / 'You Ain't Going Nowhere', 'Truck Stop Girl', 'My Back Pages'/'BJ Blues'/'Baby, What You Want Me To Do', 'Jamaica Say You Will', 'Jesus Is Just Alright', 'Eight Miles High' (abridged version), 'Mr. Tambourine Man'. Interviews with Roger McGuinn and Gene Parsons.

September 17 1971 / May 31 1971 / *Het Byrdssyndikaat* / Nederland 2, VARA / NOS Studio complex / Hilversum, the Netherlands / Abbreviated edition of the show that was transmitted on June 23 1971, featuring 'You Ain't Going Nowhere', 'My Back Pages'/'BJ Blues'/'Baby What You

Want Me To Do', 'Chestnut Mare', 'Jesus Is Just Alright', 'Take A Whiff', 'So You Want To Be A Rock'n'Roll Star', 'Baby What You Want Me To Do'

July 22 1971 / July 15 1971 / *The David Frost Show* / Channel 11 / [Presumably] Little Theatre / West 44th Street, Manhattan, New York, NY / 'So You Want To Be A Rock'n'Roll Star', 'Mr. Spaceman', 'Black Mountain Rag', 'Mr. Tambourine Man', 'I Wanna Grow Up To Be A Politician', 'Citizen Kane'

October 28 1971 / May 18 1971 / *Pop Shop: That's For The Byrds* / RTBF TV / Vorst Nationaal / Brussels, Belgium / 'Lover Of The Bayou', 'You Ain't Going Nowhere', 'Truck Stop Girl', 'Baby, What You Want Me To Do', 'Soldier's Joy'/'Black Mountain Rag', 'Pretty Boy Floyd', 'Take A Whiff On Me', 'Jesus Is Just Alright', 'Mr. Spaceman', 'BJ Blues'

February 5 1972 / January 22 1972 / *Les Byrds A L'Olympia* / RTF–ORTF 2 (French TV Channel 2) / L'Olympia / Paris, France / 'Lover Of The Bayou', 'So You Want To Be A Rock'n'Roll Star', 'Mr. Spaceman', 'Roll In My Sweet Baby's Arms', 'My Back Pages'/'BJ Blues'/'Baby What You Want Me To Do', 'Eight Miles High', 'Amazing Grace', 'Roll Over Beethoven'

March 9 1972 / [same] / *Country Suite* / [Unknown channel] / [Unknown studio] / Nashville, TN / 'Roll In My Sweet Baby's Arms', 'Black Mountain Rag'/'Soldier's Joy', 'Mr. Tambourine Man'

October 28 1972 / May 19 1971 / *Beat Club* / ARD–1 / Radio Bremen Television Studios / Bremen, West Germany / 'So You Want To Be A Rock 'n' Roll Star'

February 2 1973 / [Presumably] January–February 1973 / *Midnight Special* / NBC network / NBC Television Studios / Burbank, CA / 'Mr. Tambourine Man', 'So You Want To Be A Rock'n'Roll Star' (possibly also 'Turn! Turn!')

Radio 1965–1973

August 4 1966 / [Presumably same] / *Almanac* / Radio WFMT / [Presumably] WMFT studio / Chicago, IL / Jim McGuinn appears as speaking guest

October 22 1966 / [Presumably same] / *Café Feenjon* / Radio WKCR-FM / Cafe Feenjon / New York, NY / [Unknown songs]

[Undated] November 1966 / [Presumably same] / *The Young Set* / Radio KNX-Hollywood / [Unknown studio] / Los Angeles, CA / Jim McGuinn and David Crosby appear as speaking guest

March 11 1967 / [same] / *Where It's At* / BBC Light Programme / Studio B6, Broadcasting House / central London, UK / David Crosby appears as speaking guest

March 14 1967 / [same] / *Pop Inn* / BBC Light Programme / Paris Theatre / central London, UK / The Byrds appear as speaking guest

March 29 1967 / February 28 1967 / *Tonårskväll: The Byrds I Sverige* ['Teenage Night: The Byrds In Sweden'] / Radio Sweden / Studio 4, Stockholm / Stockholm, Sweden / 'Hey Joe', 'My Back Pages', 'Mr. Tambourine Man', 'He Was A Friend Of Mine', 'So You Want To Be A Rock 'n' Roll Star', 'Bells Of Rhymney', 'Roll Over Beethoven', 'We'll Meet Again' / Show length: 20 minutes

June 27 1967 / February 28 1967 / *Popgäster i Stockholm – The Byrds* ['Pop Guests In Stockholm – The Byrds'] / Radio Sweden / Studio 4, Stockholm / Stockholm, Sweden / 'Hey Joe', 'My Back Pages', 'Mr. Tambourine Man', 'He Was A Friend Of Mine', 'So You Want To Be A Rock 'n' Roll Star', 'Bells Of Rhymney', 'Roll Over Beethoven', 'We'll Meet Again' / Show length: 29 minutes, extension of February 28 1967 recording

December 2 1967 / [Presumably same] / *The Jim Stagg Show* / Radio WCFL Action Line / [Presumably] WCFL studio / Chicago, IL / The Byrds appear as speaking guest

March 13 1968 / [same] / [*Dick Emery's Show*] / Radio WSM / WSM studio / Nashville, TN / The Byrds appear as speaking guest

March 15 1968 / [same] / *The Grand Ole Opry* / Radio WSM / Grand Ole Opry / Nashville, TN / 'Sing Me Back Home', 'Hickory Wind', 'You Ain't Going Nowhere'.

March 15 1968 / [same] / [*Unknown*] / Radio WRVU / Vanderbilt University / Nashville, TN / The Byrds appear as speaking guest

June 7 1968 / May 8 1968 / *Eerste Rome Popfesival* ['First Rome Pop Festival'] / Dutch Radio Channel Hilversum 1 / Piper Club / Rome, Italy / Five songs are extracted from complete performance: 'You Ain't Going Nowhere', 'Old John Robertson', 'You Don't Miss Your Water', 'Hickory Wind', 'I'll Feel A Whole Lot Better', 'Chimes Of Freedom', 'The Christian Life', 'Turn! Turn! Turn!', 'My Back Pages'–'Baby, What You Want Me To Do', 'Mr. Spaceman'. Complete performance is recorded by Italian radio KSAN-FM for a later undated broadcast

January 7 1970 / [same] / [*Unknown*] / Radio KLWW / Oklahoma City, OK / Jim McGuinn appears as speaking guest

July 5 1970 / [Between] July 1–3 / *Scene And Heard* / BBC Radio 1 / [Unknown studio] / central London, UK / Gene Parsons appears as speaking guest

[Undated] July–August 1970 / July 7 1970 / [*Untitled show*] / radio VPRO / Concertgebouw / Amsterdam, The Netherlands / 'You Ain't Going Nowhere', 'Lover Of The Bayou', 'Old Blue', 'Well Come Back Home', 'My Back Pages'/'Baby, What You Want Me To Do', 'He Was A Friend Of Mine', 'Willin'', 'Black Mountain Rag'/'Soldier's Joy', 'Take A Whiff On Me', 'This Wheel's On Fire', 'It's All Right Ma I'm Only Bleeding', 'Ballad Of Easy Rider', 'Jesus Is Just Alright', 'All The Things', 'Buckaroo'/'Nashville West', 'Turn! Turn! Turn!'/'Mr. Tambourine Man'/'Eight Miles High'/'Hold It', 'So You Want To Be A Rock'n'Roll Star', 'Positively Fourth Street', 'Mr. Spaceman', 'You Don't Miss Your Water', 'Chestnut Mare', 'Chimes Of Freedom', 'Amazing Grace'.

May 5 1971 / [Unknown] / *Happy 30th Bob Dylan* / Radio WGN / [Unknown location] / Chicago, IL / Probably The Byrds as speaking guests

May 22 1971 / May 12 1971 / *Scene And Heard* / BBC Radio 1 / [Unknown studio] / central London, UK / Roger McGuinn appears as speaking guest

[Possibly] June 9 1971 / [same] / [*Unknown show*] / WNEW-FM / [Possibly] Fillmore East / New York, NY / 'Lover Of The Bayou', 'Chimes Of Freedom', 'Chestnut Mare', 'Positively 4th Street', 'Eight Miles High', 'Turn! Turn! Turn!', 'Ballad Of Easy Rider', 'Wasn't Born To Follow', 'You Ain't Going Nowhere', 'So You Want To Be A Rock'n'Roll Star', 'Mr. Tambourine Man', 'Glory Glory', 'Mr. Spaceman'

September 12 1971 / [same] / [*Unknown show*] / WAMU-FM 88.5 / American University / Washington, DC / 'Lover Of The Bayou', 'So You Want To Be A Rock'n'Roll Star', 'Mr. Spaceman', 'I Wanna Grow Up To Be A Politician', 'Soldier's Joy'/'Black Mountain Rag', 'Mr. Tambourine Man', 'Pretty Boy Floyd', 'Nashville West', 'Citizen Kane', 'Tiffany Queen', 'Chestnut Mare', 'Jesus Is Just Alright', 'Eight Miles High', 'Hold It (Break Song)', 'Roll Over Beethoven'.

Bibliography & sources

BOOKS CONSULTED

Badman, Keith: *The Beach Boys* (Backbeat Books 2004)

Barbata, Johnny: *The Legendary Life Of A Rock Star Drummer* (Published privately)

Blaine, Hal and Mr. Bonzai: *Hal Blaine And The Wrecking Crew* (Rebeats Publications, 2003)

Booth, Stanley: *The True Adventures Of The Rolling Stones* (Acapella, 1984)

Cott, Jonathan: *Dylan On Dylan – The Essential Interviews* (Hodder, 2006)

Crosby, David and Gottlieb, Carl: *Long Time Gone* (Doubleday, 1988)

Crosby, David and Gottlieb, Carl: *Since Then – How I Survived Everything And Lived To Tell About It* (Penguin Group, 2006)

Dawson, Dinky and Alan, Carter: *Life On The Road* (Billboard 1998)

Densmore, John: *Riders On The Storm – My Life With Jim Morrison And The Doors* (Bloomsbury, 1991)

Des Barres, Pamela: *I'm With The Band – Confessions Of A Groupie* (Chicago Review Press, 1987)

Drummond, Paul: *Eye Mind – The Saga Of Roky Erickson And The 13th Floor Elevators, The Pioneers Of Psychedelic Sound* (Process, 2007)

Einarson, John and (with) Furay, Richie: *There's Something Happening Here – The Story of Buffalo Springfield* (Quarry Press, Inc., 1997)

Einarson, John: *Desperados – The Roots of Country Rock* (Cooper Square Press, 2001)

Einarson, John: *Mr. Tambourine Man – The Life And Legacy Of The Byrds' Gene Clark* (Backbeat Books, 2005)

Fein, Art: *The L.A. Musical History Tour – A Guide To The Rock And Roll Landmarks Of Los Angeles* (Faber And Faber, 1990)

Fonda, Peter: *Don't Tell Dad* (Hyperion Books 1998)

Fong-Torres, Ben: *Hickory Wind – The Life And Times Of Gram Parsons* (Pocket Books, 1991)

Frame, Pete: *More Rock Family Trees* (Omnibus 1998)

Frame, Pete: *The Complete Rock Family Trees* (Omnibus 1980)

Griffin, Sid: *Million Dollar Bash – Bob Dylan, The Band, And The Basement Tapes* (A Jawbone Book, 2007)

Grushkin, Paul D.: *The Art Of Rock* (Artabras, 1987)

Heylin, Clinton: *Bob Dylan – The Recording Sessions, 1960–1994* (St. Martin's Griffin 1997)

Hinton, Brian and Wall, Geoff: *Ashley Hutchings – The Guv'nor & The Rise Of Folkrock* (Helter Skelter Publishing, 2002)

Lewisohn, Mark: *The Complete Beatles Chronicle* (Pyramid Books 1992)

Lewisohn, Mark: *The Complete Beatles Recoding Sessions* (Hamlyn 1998)

Lifson, Hal: *Hal Lifsons's 1996! – A Personal View Of The Coolest Year In Pop Culture History* (Bonus Books, 2002)

Loewenstein, Dora and Dodd, Philip: *According To The Rolling Stones* (Phoenix, 2003)

Marcus, Greil: *Like A Rolling Stone – Bob Dylan At The Crossroads* (Public Affairs, 2005)

McParland, Stephen J.: *The California Sound – An Insider's Story* (Music Books, 2000)

Menck, Ric: *The Notorious Byrd Brothers* (Continuum, 2007)

Meyer, David N.: *Twenty Thousand Roads – The Ballad Of Gram Parsons And His Cosmic American Music* (Villard, 2007)

Miles, Barry: *The Beatles – A Diary* (Omnibus Press 1998)

Neill, Andy and Kent, Matt: *Anyway Anyhow Anywhere: The Complete Chronicle of The Who 1962–1982* (Friedman/Fairfax 2002)

Palao, Alec – Clarence White liner notes

Priore, Domenic: *Riot On Sunset Strip – Rock 'n' Roll's Last Stand In Hollywood* (A Jawbone Book, 2007)

Rawlings, Terry; Badman, Keith and Neill, Andrew: *Good Times Bad Times. The Definitive Diary Of The Rolling Stones 1960–1969* (Complete Music Publications Limited 1997)

Rogan, Johnny: *Crosby, Stills, Nash & Young – The Visual Documentary* (Omnibus Press, 1996)

Rogan, Johnny: *Timeless Flight Revisited – The Sequel* (Rogan House 1993)

Sandoval, Andrew: *'The Monkees: The Day-By-Day Story of the 60s TV Pop Sensation'* (Backbeat 2005)

Scoppa, Bud: *The Byrds* (Scholastic Book Services, 1971)

Shaw, Greg: *The Doors On The Road* (Omnibus Press 1997)

Skues, Keith: *Pop Went the Pirates: History of Offshore Radio Station* (Lambs' Meadow Publications 1994)

Starr, Michael: *Bobby Darin – A Life* (Taylor Trade Publishing 2004)

Tashian, Barry: *Ticket To Ride – The Extraordinary Diary Of The Beatles' Last Tour* (Dowling Press, Inc., 1997)

Taylor, Derek: *As Times Goes By* (Straight Arrow Books, 1973)

Unknown Author: *The Byrds – Back Pages – A Collection Of Cuttings* (Unknown Publisher, 1989)

Unterberger, Richie: *Eight Miles High – Folk-rock's Flight From Haight-Ashbury To Woodstock* (Backbeat Books, 2003)

Unterberger, Richie: *Turn! Turn! Turn! – The '60s Folkrock Revolution* (Backbeat Books, 2002)

Verbeke, Henri; Lucarelli, Francesco; Frollano, Stefano and van Diggelen, Lucien: *Crosby, Stills, Nash & Sometimes Young – Vol. 1, 2, 3* (Gopher Publishers, 2002)

Walker, Michael: *Laurel Canyon – The Inside Story Of Rock And Roll's Legendary Neighborhood* (Faber And Faber, Inc., 2006)

Wyman, Bill: *Rolling With The Stones* (Dorling Kindersley 2002)

Zimmer, Dave: *Crosby, Stills & Nash – The Authorized Biography* (Omnibus Press, 1984)

Zolov, Eric: *Refried Elvis: The Rise of the Mexican Counterculture* (University of California Press 1999)

MAGAZINES AND NOTABLE ON-LINE INTERVIEWS

Anderson, Chester: *'The Afternoon We Interviewed ...'* (Crawdaddy No 20, January 1969)

Anon.: *'An American Dream'* (Hit Parader july 1966)

Anon.: *'Roger McGuinn – Questions and Answers'* (Fusion April 1970)

Anon: *'McGuinn Spills Beans'* (Different Drummer November 2 1972)

Ballard, Barry: *Omaha Rainbow No. 11 – Skip Battin interview* (December 1976)

Bowman, Robert: *Three-part interview with Roger McGuinn* (Cheap Thrills November, December 1976, February 1977)

Byrne, John: *'Rap Session With The Byrds'* (State Beacon October 21 1971)

Carpenter, John: *Roger McGuinn interview* (L.A. Free Press march 7 1969)

Carr, Brian: *'A Non-Interview With Gene Clark and the Byrds'* (Los Angeles Free Press September 1966)

Cohen, Herman: *Interview With Roger (Jim) McGuinn Of The Byrds* (Sing Out! August 25 1968)

Cost, Jud: *Roger McGuinn interview available at www.sundazed.com*

Crowe, Cameron: *'Roger McGuinn On Past, Present and Future Byrds'* (June 1973)

Doyle, Tom: *Chris Hillman interview available www.eventguide.ie*

Ellis, Andy: *Roger McGuinn interview* (Guitar Player October 2004)

Emery, John: *Jim McGuinn interview* (Beat Instrumental, September 1965)

Feigel, Bob: *'Real Teen Revolt-Byrds'* (KRLA Beat November December 1965)

Fong-Torres, Ben: *David Crosby Interview* (Rolling Stone July 23 1970)

Frame, Pete (editor): *Zigzag Nos 14, 27– 33, 41*

Granny: *'Gene Flies Away'* (Hit Parader November 1966)

Gross, Jason: *Stanley Booth Interview available at www.furious.com*

Hanegraaf, Hans: *Skip Battin interview available at www.americanmusicbelgium.com*

Hardy, Phil: *'Byrds Droppings'* (Friends August 7 1970)

Harmon, Dan: *From Folk To Flyte – Roger McGuinn interview available at www.ibiblio.org*

Harris, John: *David Crosby Interview* (Mojo March 2007)

Johnson, Pete: *'Some Of The Byrds Fly The Musical Coop'* (April 21 1968)

Johnson, Pete: *The Problems of Being Roger McGuinn Byrd Survivor* (Hit Parader September 1968)

Kelly, Chris: *Chris Hillman interview available at Crested Butte Weekly, www.cbweekly.com*

Landers, Rick: *Roger McGuinn interview* (Modern Guitars February 15, 2006)

Mackay, Alastair: *Lloyd Green interview* (Uncut March 2008)

Nolan, Tom: *The Frenzied Frontier of Pop Music* (Los Angeles Times November 27 1966)

Nork, John: *Interviews with Chris Hillman, Roger McGuinn, David Crosby, and Roy Halee for The TrackingAngle* (Volume 2, February 1997)

Perlman, Arlene: *'The Byrds At Home* (Flip Magazine march 1966)

Proctor, David: *'This Byrd's Still Soaring High'* (Salt Lake Tribune March 3 1972)

Reed, Leslie: *'Things You Don't Know About the Byrds'* (Hit Parader June 1966)

Ross, Michael: *'Roger McGuinn Is The Byrds'* (Creem December 1970)

Ruby, Jay: *An interview with Roger McGuinn* (Jazz & Pop March 1969)

Rudolph, Eric: *McGuinn Back to the Drawing Board* (Crawdaddy October 1972)

Salvo, Patrick William: *'Tales Of An Early Byrd'* (New Musical Express May 5 1973)

Snyder-Scrumpy, Patrick: *'Roger McGuinn: Older Than Tomorrow'* (October 1973)

Straubing, Michelle: *'Byrds Report On British Scene; Say English Dug Dylan First'* (The Beat October 15 1965)

Tepper, Ron: *Roger McGuinn interview* (Vermont Cynic 11/20/75)

Turchick, Efram: *Carl Franzoni interview available at www.sundazed.com*

Turchick, Efram: *Interview with Carl Franzoni* (online)

Tyler, Kieron: *Bobby Darin – And This Is Me* (Mojo March 2005)

Unterberger, Richie: *Interviews with Sean Bonniwell, Chris Hillman, Barry McGuire available at www.richieunterberger.com*

Various: *The Byrds cover feature* (Uncut August 2003)

Vincent Flanders: *Roger McGuinn interviews from 1969 and 1970 available at www.vincentflanders.com*

Walker, Elizabeth: *Roger McGuinn interview* (Rock November 16 1970)

Ward, Ed: *Roger McGuinn Interview* (Rolling Stone October 29 1970)

Williams, Richard: *From Byrd To Burrito – interview with Chris Hillman* (Melody Maker December 19 1970)

Yorke, Ritchie: *'The Byrds Still Aloft'* (Jazz & Pop may 1971)

Young, Joe: *Interviews with Chris Hillman, Roger McGuinn, David Crosby for Musician* (May 1991)

WEB

Two recommended Byrds websites:

Byrdwatcher – A Field Guide To The Byrds of Los Angeles http://ebni.com/byrds/. Despite not being updated since 1999, this is an excellent and recommended site.

ByrdsFlyght at http://users.skynet.be/

Index

Acknowledgements

AUTHOR'S THANKS

I wish to thank those whose significant contributions made this book possible.

A sincere thank you goes to Joe McMichael, who got the ball rolling in the first place and gave me the challenge, for which I am very grateful.

A special thanks to my fellow researchers and kindred spirits who so generously have shared their time, input, and expertise: Clark Besch, Greg Shaw, Jerry Fuentes, Marc Skobac, Neal Skok, Nick Warburton, Richard Groothuizen, and Richie Unterberger. Last but not least my good friend Doug Hinman, whose sharp mind, kind assistance and cheerleading enthusiasm has been invaluable to the project.

I wish to thank the many who experienced The Byrds firsthand, and who kindly shared stories, anecdotes, allowed me to use their quotes, and thus give the book a sense of the spirit of the times. In order of appearance: Trina Robbins; Rod McLean Barken; Lloyd Thaxton; Janey Milstead; Bob McVittie and Denny Flannigan of The Moonrakers; David Stine; Gary Rowles; Aron Kay; Richard Schulman; Jerry Burgan of We Five; Stan Enderby; Rick Hinman; Bob Cianci (noted music journalist and musician and author of *Great Rock Drummers Of The Sixties*); Roger Ballou; Jon Keliehor of The Daily Flash; Tony Martin; Richard Lewis; Penny A. Einmo (for the Puerto Rico memories); John Nork; Kingsley Abbott; Richard Haslop; Trevor Martin; Brian Lonsdale, Valerie Henshaw (for the Zimbabwe memories); Federico Rubli (for the Mexico memories); Richard Groothuizen; Ken Young; Chip Lovitt; Werner Kühn-Koditek; Neal Skok.

For those who have worked with The Byrds – either on stage or behind the scenes – and generously contributed to this project, I would like to thank: Carl Franzoni (dancer extraordinaire); Jimmi Seiter (for valuable input); John York (for the memories); Lloyd Green (a true gentleman); Jay Dee Maness; Gene Parsons (including information on the Parsons–White Stringbender); Dinky Dawson (for a peek at the files); Dennis Dragon.

For assistance in the research and documentation of live performances and radio and TV appearances, I would like to thank: Anders Svenus; Andy Finney (for the Elektra connection); Andy Neill (*BBC* and *Colindale* research); Anne Goddard (again, for kinship, kindness, and the Canadian newspaper copies); Annette Carson; Art Sides; Bill Small; Bob Grilli; Børge Skilbrigt (always a pleasure); Bruno Bartra; Chris Bishop (at www.garagehangover.com); Chris LeDrew (for the steel guitar connection); Chris Prior; Claus Rasmussen (for his repeatedly valiant assistance in tracking down information from American newspapers); Craig The Airplane Man; David Dann (for the Mike Bloomfield quote); David Stringfellow (at Vanderbilt University, Nashville, TN); Eric Zolov (for the Mexican connections); Gary Hall; Gerard Davelaar; Gert Eggens (*Hitweek* transcription); Hans Nyman; Helga Hjort (for not throwing the old pop papers away); Jan Tonnesen (for the Byrds picture); Jason Brabazon; Jeanne Andersen (at *St. Louis Park Historical Society*); Jim McVeety; Joe Hedio; Johann Heidenbauer; John Delgatto (at Sierra Records); John Einarson; John Madsen; John Trubee; Johnny Rogan; Jon 'Mojo' Mills (for diligent assistance with the photos); Jon Moore (at *San Diego Rock Archive*); Jonee Miller; Joop Spiering; Kevin Becketti; Knut Skyberg (for The Hollies stuff); Knut-Anders Løken; Lennart Wrigholm; Les Peterson; Lou Newman; Mark Ritucci; Mike Crowder; Olle Lundin (for the last-minute Swedish articles); Penny Andrea Einmo (for the Puerto Rico information); Per Sannes Heger

(Elvis lives!); Peter Feldman; Pete Shout; Petrie le Roux (at the *National Library of South Africa* in Cape Town); Piers Hemmingsen; Raffele Galli (for everything Italian); Richard Greenberg; Rick Hinman; Ron Thums (at *Radio Rumpus Room*, KFAI, Minneapolis/St. Paul); Ross Hannan; Stephen J. McParland; Steven Roby; Stuart Rosenberg; *The Herb Caen Magazines & Newspapers Center's Staff;* Thomas Aubrunner (for the Clarence White and Gene Parsons information); Tom McQuown (for the copies), and Werner Kühn-Koditek (for *The Byrds Bulletins*).

On the home front: Anders for the scanning and the typing; Jakob for the bibliography; Eivind for being Eivind; and last but not least, the one and only Gro for patience, understanding, and appendix expertise.

I am indebted to my editor Tony Bacon for steering the project my way.

PUBLISHER'S THANKS

The publisher, Jawbone Press in London, would like to thank Doug Hinman.

JACKET DESIGN

Adam Yeldham.

PICTURE CREDITS

The photographs reproduced came from the following sources, listed here by page number followed by photographer and/or agency or collection. We are grateful for the help of all these individuals and organisations.

Jacket: Getty Images. **4** The Byrds, Redfern's; McGuinn, Corbis. **5** The Byrds, Getty Images; Reunion Byrds, Henry Diltz/Corbis. **6** Getty Images. **18** Bob Dylan, Wikipedia. **22** Getty Images. **16** *Cosmopolitan.* **29** *Disc.* **32** © Lloyd Thaxton. **34** www.wastedspace.com. **36** Jan Tonnesen. **41** Getty Images. **43** Facsimile from *The Way We Lived Back Then.* **45** Getty Images. **47** *Disc.* **51** Chris Walter. **55** Redferns. **56** Chris Walter. **58** Facsimile from *Bristol Evening Post.* **59** Facsimile from *Western Daily Press.* **60** Facsimile from *Croydon Advertiser.* **61** Chris Walter. **65** Getty Images. **72** Clark Besch collection. **76** Redferns. **81** Redferns. **82** *Hollywood High Yearbook 1966.* **88** Marc Skobac collection. **89** Getty Images. **94** Clark Besch collection. **96** Clark Besch collection. **97** Getty Images. **98** Corbis. **99** Clark Besch collection. **105** Getty Images. **110** *Hullabaloo* magazine. **113** Clark Besch collection. **116** Rex Features. **120** Trina Robbins/*Crawdaddy.* **123** Rex Features. **125** Redfern's. **129** Penny A. Einmo collection. **132** Neal Skok. **133** Corbis. **134** Corbis. **135** Rex Features. **136** Getty Images. **141** Rex Features. **146** Richard Lewis. **147** Getty Images. **148** Getty Images. **154** Getty Images. **159** Getty Images. **160** *Miami University Yearbook 1968.* **163** Getty Images. **164** Getty Images. **171** Raffele Galli. **175** Getty Images. **179** Facsimile from *The Johannesburg Star.* **185** Getty Images. **191** Getty Images. **192** Getty Images. **195** Getty Images. **196** Werner Kühn-Koditek collection. **197** Corbis. **198** Redfern's. **202** Redfern's. **208** Federico Rubli collection. **214** Clark Besch collection. **217** Redfern's. **220** Redfern's. **225** Getty Images. **227** Clark Besch collection. **230** Getty Images. **246** New Musical Express. **251** Getty Images. **258** Werner Kühn-Koditek collection. **262** *Cream.* **271** Redfern's. **284** Getty Images. **291** *The Statesman.* **292** Columbia Records. **310** Corbis. **315** Corbis. **319** Corbis. **322** *Crawdaddy.* **323** Getty Images. **324** Redfern's.

All **ads, newspaper cuttings etc** are from Christopher Hjort's collection.

US RELEASE DATES

Release dates for original Byrds US singles and US albums cited in the book adhere to previously published discographies, but it should be noted that these in several instances do not match contemporary review dates in neither *Billboard* nor *Cash Box*. Discrepancies are noted under the respective entries for the various releases.

CHART POSITIONS

Chart positions are taken from the published charts in *Record Mirror/Record Retailer* (UK) and *Billboard* (USA) if not otherwise noted.

STOP PRESS

The Byrds appeared on *Drop-In* (Swedish TV) on March 5, 1967. Other artists appearing on the show were The Beatles, Cream, and Jimi Hendrix.

The Byrds performed at Lyman Auditorium, Southern Connecticut State University, New Haven, CT, on September 22, 1972.

UPDATES

If you have any additions or corrections to the material in this book, the author would be pleased to hear from you. He may be contacted by email: hjort@gazette.no or you can write to him: Christopher Hjort, Hjørungveien 5, 0375 Oslo, Norway.

TYPOGRAPHY & EQUIPMENT

The book is set in ITC New Baskerville 8.5/10 point, a typeface named after the English master typefounder John Baskerville (1706–1775), while headers, subtitles, and appendixes are set in Frutiger, a sans serif typeface by the Swiss type designer Adrian Frutiger (b 1928).

The book was written, researched, and designed on a Macintosh PowerBook G4 using Adobe and Microsoft software.

"We try to avoid boxes and labels and categories as much as we can. We're musicians; we play music. If we were going to use a label, it would have to be folk, bossa nova, jazz, Afro."

David Crosby, 1966